WIMBLEDON

FROM SOUTHERN LEAGUE TO PREMIERSHIP

– *A Complete Record* –

BOOKS BY CLIVE LEATHERDALE

Football

WIMBLEDON: FROM SOUTHERN LEAGUE TO PREMIERSHIP – A COMPLETE RECORD
ENGLAND: THE QUEST FOR THE WORLD CUP – A COMPLETE RECORD
SCOTLAND: THE QUEST FOR THE WORLD CUP – A COMPLETE RECORD
IRELAND: THE QUEST FOR THE WORLD CUP – A COMPLETE RECORD
THE ABERDEEN FOOTBALL COMPANION
ABERDEEN: THE EUROPEAN ERA – A COMPLETE RECORD (*in preparation*)
SOUTHEND UNITED: 101 GREAT GAMES (*in preparation*)

Dracula and Vampirism

DRACULA: THE NOVEL & THE LEGEND
  A STUDY OF BRAM STOKER'S GOTHIC MASTERPIECE
THE ORIGINS OF DRACULA
  THE BACKGROUND TO BRAM STOKER'S GOTHIC MASTERPIECE
CALMET'S TREATISE ON VAMPIRES AND REVENANTS (*as editor*)
THE JEWEL OF SEVEN STARS (*as editor*)

International Relations

BRITAIN AND SAUDI ARABIA 1925-1939: THE IMPERIAL OASIS

Far Eastern Travel

THE VIRGIN WHORE AND OTHER CHINESE CHARACTERS
  TIANANMEN, TRAVELS AND TRAUMAS
TO DREAM OF PIGS: TRAVELS IN SOUTH AND NORTH KOREA

Education

SO YOU WANT TO TEACH ENGLISH TO FOREIGNERS

WIMBLEDON

FROM SOUTHERN LEAGUE TO PREMIERSHIP

– *A Complete Record* –

CLIVE LEATHERDALE

Desert Island Books

First Published
in 1995 by
DESERT ISLAND BOOKS
34 Hamlet Court Road, Westcliff-on-Sea, Essex SS0 7LX
United Kingdom

British Library Cataloguing-in-Publication Data
A catalogue record for this book is available from the British Library

ISBN 1-874287-09-0

Printed in Great Britain
by
Biddles Ltd., Guildford

PHOTOGRAPH CREDITS

Surrey Comet – pages 19, 21, 24, 28, 33, 63
The Morning Star – page 29
Wimbledon News – page 50
South London Press – page 62
Daily Mirror – page 105
Kicksports Foto – page 130
Allsports – page 148
Phil Smith – pages 36, 61, 69, 89, 95, 101, 104, 111, 114, 115, 126, 129, 134, 135, 141, 145, 156
Paul Willatts – pages 76, 77, 82, 83, 85, 93
Colin Green – page 47

Contents

Preface

One evening in the weeks leading up to the millennium, television will no doubt screen a riveting 'Sports Review of the Century'. Football, of course, will feature prominently and include nostalgic footage of the game's greatest players, teams and triumphs.

George Best is a certainty, so are the Busby Babes and probably, our World Cup heroes of '66 – although, who knows, England may yet win again before the year 2000. There will also be a series of awards, with the nominations for the Club of the Century headed inevitably by Arsenal, Manchester United, and Liverpool.

But if justice is to be done on that memorable night then those worthy but so obvious contenders will be swept aside – by Wimbledon.

Yes, the Crazy Gang for Club of the Century, and before anyone has convulsions I commend them to study this book. The author presents the club's case for the award in meticulous detail and his preference for clear-cut statistics over emotional rhetoric only adds to its impact.

The facts cannot be disputed and setting aside club loyalties and judged dispassionately, Wimbledon's rise from amateur and non-league obscurity to Premier League stardom, has to be the soccer success story of the century.

Whether television companies include a 'Club of the Century' category in any sporting awards to mark the millennium remains to be seen. But at least this book is a worthy recognition of all we have achieved and for that we are honoured and grateful.

Joe Kinnear

Author's Note

Memories fade with time. In the case of Wimbledon FC, the researcher is also bedevilled by other handicaps. During the 1960s and for much of the '70s the Dons were a part-time club with part-time facilities. Match programmes and handbooks from these years are sketchy and often inaccurate. Press reports likewise. Clusters of matches over Bank Holidays were reported scantily, or ignored altogether. At other times journalists were on strike, leaving the sports pages empty. Besides, there exist no videos to check what really happened against what was scribbled down at the time, often in haste, and without the benefit of slow-motion replays to verify what was written.

No criticism is intended in these comments. Indeed, it is a wonder that the record of the Dons in their Southern League era is as complete as it is. Independent ferreting, here and there, has filled in almost all the gaps, though the reader should be alert to sections of this book where accuracy cannot be vouchsafed.

From the late 1960s team formations switched from the traditional WW to 4-2-4, 4-3-3, and other variations. This meant that teams were no longer laid out from 1 to 11 in the time-honoured way. The left-back, for example, still wore No 3, but his name usually appeared fifth, following that of the goalkeeper, right-back, and two centre-backs. Little confidence should therefore be placed in the shirt numbers given for any particular player in Wimbledon's latter seasons in the Southern League.

The statistical pages of this book seek to provide the names of all 22 players (plus substitutes) to grace each Wimbledon match. In the Southern League era this was no easy task. It was a matter of whim whether or not the local press spelled out Wimbledon's opponents. I am grateful to historians of clubs from Nuneaton to Gloucester, Corby to Cambridge, and many others, for digging out dusty team-sheets from bygone times and conveying them to me.

Despite their assistance, opposition line-ups remain incomplete. Some clubs are defunct; others have merged or been taken over, their records lost. Still others did not reply to my requests for information. When unable to detail opponents, I resort to the match programme – denoted by a 'P' in the right-hand column. Clearly, this is not necessarily the team that took the field.

Substitutes present another problem. In the early years their names were sometimes listed irrespective of whether or not they actually came on.

This book records full details of every league game Wimbledon have played since 1964, plus those of all major cup competitions. Minor tournaments – such as the Midweek Floodlight League, the Group Cup, the Leyland-Daf Cup – have been omitted. Partly, this is because details are hard to come by; partly it is to prevent a big book growing yet bigger.

This is, of course, not the first book to follow the fortunes of Wimbledon FC. I am happy to acknowledge the material provided in *Mission Impossible* (by Leigh Edwards and Andy Watson), the 'Wimbledon Centenary Book' (Michael Lidbury), and Gillian Hawtin's little study of her uncle Ernest and the Dons' origins in 'An Old Centrals' Man'.

My thanks to Reg Davis, Ron Balch, Terry May, Andy Watson, Leigh Edwards and Donal Cullen for their assistance at various stages of this project.

CLIVE LEATHERDALE

Genesis

Wimbledon, grown in the present century from a secluded village to a prosperous corner of south-west London, is a name famous in three sports. All the world venerates the tennis, that bastion of upper-crust Englishness, the strawberries and cream, the insistence on playing in white, and on grass.

Not so long ago Wimbledon Speedway enjoyed comparable acclaim. National champions, riding in an elegant stadium in an atmosphere of 2-stroke, the Dons were once the bees knees of the cinder track. Now they are sadly extinct.

Of an evening the whiff of fuel shrouded the unprepossessing soccer ground just up the road. For it was there, in a stadium with no name, and known by the street that ran by – Plough Lane – that an upstart amateur football team took on ideas above its station and soared into football's stratosphere.

Born in 1889; amateurs until 1964; semi-pros until 1977. By 1986 Wimbledon had climbed aboard Division 1. They snatched the FA Cup two years later, and ever since have thumbed their noses at the big-wigs who whinged and whined about their rightful place; who pontificated with scant evidence on the pitch that ashes to ashes, dust to dust, Wimbledon FC would soon return whence they came.

The British love the underdog. Or so they say. Certainly they cheer when some gutsy unknown pulls the rug from under a seed on the centre court. But on the soccer pitch it does not work that way. Wimbledon, as every supporter knows, are more reviled than revered.

This is in part a vestige of the English class system. Glamour clubs like Manchester United and Arsenal are spoken of in terms of sporting aristocracy. Lesser lights, no matter the talent at their disposal, find themselves disparaged as workmanlike, or some other proletarian put-down. Playing at Plough Lane, a name redolent of back-breaking manual labour, encapsulates Wimbledon's bucolic image.

That image was also built on the style of play preached by Dave 'Harry' Bassett during his long association with the club. Detractors dismiss it as the big hoof, belting the ball upfield as speedily as possible. Tactics appropriate to red-necks.

'Give a man the reputation of an early riser,' someone once said, 'and he may sleep till noon.' Even today, Wimbledon struggle to shrug off accusations of hard, direct football, even though their style has softened to the point where it earns grudging admiration from less blinkered onlookers.

DID YOU KNOW?

Several Old Centrals were active in the temperance movement. Alcohol was a major social problem, and beer much stronger than it is today.

Tall oak trees come from small acorns. In Wimbledon's case the tree blossomed late and quickly. But success is all the sweeter for that. Our story begins in 1889, the year after Jack the Ripper had plagued the capital. Wimbledon at the time was not yet a suburb of London. It was a detached village, with signs of settlement dating back to the time of William the Conqueror and beyond.

Wimbledon Common was the cradle of Wimbledon FC. Former pupils of the Old Central School in Camp Road formed a team called Wimbledon Old Centrals. They laid claim to a 'pitch' on the common, by Robin Hood Road, adopted a strip of navy and white, and borrowed the Fox and Grapes Inn to act as changing rooms.

Matches were what we might call friendlies, apart from those dignified as local cup tournaments. Another pitch soon had to be found, for the ball terrorised gentle folk out for a stroll, or bounced off passing carriages. Some of the Old Centrals' early opponents make curious reading – Tooting Church Institute, Peckham Adults, Rabbits & Sons and, intriguingly, Wimbledon Gentlemen.

By 1905 the club had renamed itself Wimbledon FC. Registering with the Surrey FA entitled it to compete for the Amateur Cup and, shortly, the FA Cup. But continual changes of committees, of pitches and of club colours undermined any sense of continuity. Concern was expressed that big clubs across the Thames – Chelsea and Fulham – were poaching Wimbledon's potential supporters and threatening the club's future. In 1910 even the local press ignored the team, which briefly stopped playing, existing in name only.

The Dons' rebirth was kick-started by a council-supported rival team that played at the speedway and greyhound stadium off Plough Lane. One or two Wimbledon players switched over, so that out of the ashes of one club sprouted the shoots of another. By 1912-13 the metamorphosis was complete. The new club was backed by the local authority, stuck with the name 'Wimbledon', and moved down the road to a reclaimed patch of swamp that would be home for the next 79 years.

Organised soccer was mothballed by the Great War. Most players were of military age and went off to fight the Kaiser. In the meantime Plough Lane was refurbished, so it might accommodate 500 seated spectators under cover. With shirts sporting a large 'W' – which for some reason offended the FA – the Dons were in 1919 admitted to the Athenian League, and 9,000 spectators attended a

WHAT I HEAR

'Hawtin [the Dons' half-back] was great while he lasted, but on explaining in French the offside rule to the Referee, he was ordered off. He did not improve matters with his parting shots.'

local derby with Tooting in the Amateur Cup. Among the Dons heroes of the time was Billy Cotton, the future band-leader.

In 1921 Wimbledon entered the expanded Isthmian League, amateur football's elite corps, where they would remain for 43 years. The team enjoyed little early success, other than in various local tournaments for small-fry – the South London Charity Cup, for example, and the Surrey Charity Shield.

The Dons began to leave their mark in the early 1930s. In 1929-30 they reached the 1st Round of the FA Cup and the semi-finals of the Amateur Cup, where they lost 0-2 to Bournemouth Gas Works at Portsmouth's Fratton Park. Wimbledon raced to the Isthmian championship in 1931 and 1932 – on the first occasion creating a new points record, and picking up *five* cups on the way. Coincidentally, the revamped Plough Lane had become a stadium fit for champions, being officially opened on 29th August 1931 by Sir Frederick Wall, Secretary of the Football Association. These triumphs were well-timed. The depression was squeezing football hard, and the Dons had to negotiate an overdraft to keep afloat.

In 1934-35 Wimbledon made the 2nd Round of the FA Cup, losing 1-5 to Southend United at Plough Lane. Drawn at home to the sailors of HMS Victory in Round 3 of the Amateur Cup, a mighty crowd of 18,080 inspired the Dons to a 3-0 win. They reached the Final, meeting five-times winners Bishop Auckland at Middlesbrough's Ayresome Park. A goalless draw necessitated a replay at Stamford Bridge. 32,000 spectators saw Doc Dowden put Wimbledon ahead, but the lead was overturned.

The blow was softened as Wimbledon won their third Isthmian title, and retained it in 1936 for their fourth championship in six years. The Dons even merited their very own cigarette card.

During World War II Plough Lane was requisitioned by the Army and the National Fire Service, and even survived a German bomb.

The late 1940s were heady times for football, and Wimbledon's reassembled team was soon making an impact. In 1947, with Doc Dowden now coach, the Dons were given a second shot at the Amateur Cup. This time their opponents in the Final were Leytonstone; the venue, Highbury. The gate was 47,000, and millions more tuned in to commentary on nationwide radio. Sadly, the outcome was the same – a 1-2 defeat, having scored first.

In October 1951, 16-year-old Johnny Haynes, already an England schoolboy international, made his debut for the Dons, and scored to boot. Unfortunately, Haynes was on Fulham's books, and they hastily resummoned him. Another future 'name' was Mickey Stewart – the Surrey cricketer – who scored the goal that won for Wimbledon the London Intermediate Cup in 1952.

In 1955 Les Henley – once of Arsenal and Reading – took charge. It was he who introduced the new strip – blue shirts and white shorts – and who signed 6ft 3in Ulsterman Eddie Reynolds from Tooting and Mitcham. Reynolds' goals in 1958-59 helped secure the Dons' first Isthmian title since 1936, establishing yet another points record in the process and going the season unbeaten at home.

Third for the next two seasons, they were champions again in 1962, and a year later rewrote the record books. In the FA Cup they saw off 3rd Division Colchester, 2-1 – the Dons' first competitive triumph over a Football League team. In Round 2 they lost 1-2 at Bristol City.

In the Amateur Cup Wimbledon swept all before them and were rewarded with their third Final and their first at Wembley. On 4th May 1963, in front of a 45,000-strong crowd, Sutton United felt the force of Eddie Reynolds' forehead. Four goals, all headed, a feat achieved neither before nor since. Wimbledon won the Cup 4-2.

Another header, this time against Walthamstow in the league, kept the Isthmian trophy at Plough Lane. Reynolds was the talk of amateur football.

In 1963-64, though Malcolm Allison's Bath City proved too strong in the FA Cup, and Enfield dumped the Dons from the Amateur Cup, Wimbledon were in no mood to surrender their league crown. They were initially stretched by Hendon, who would break the Isthmian scoring record with 124 goals. But the north London side fell away, leaving the Dons to celebrate a hat-trick of titles.

Off-field tensions precipitated the upheavals that were to follow. Accusations of illegal payments to amateur players provoked an FA investigation, the outcome of which was to oblige all amateur clubs to declare their adherence to certain principles. Wimbledon refused to do so. They were the first club to take this stand, though not the only one.

With the ball still in the air, Clacton Town announced their resignation from the Southern League. Wimbledon leapt at the chance of turning professional. Chairman Sydney Black informed a packed meeting of supporters that he and the management committee would stand down if the proposed switch was blocked. Protest withered away, and at the Southern League's annual meeting Wimbledon were duly voted on board.

BRIDESMAIDS 1964-71

SOUTHERN LEAGUE DIVISION 1 1964-65

1st Division	Runners-Up (Promoted)
Southern League Cup	3rd Round
FA Cup	4th Qualifying Round

Election to the Southern League threw Wimbledon FC to the winds of financial (mis)fortune. They might make money, or they might lose it. For one thing, their horizons were wider. No longer were their opponents clustered around the metropolis. Excursions would be required as far west as Merthyr Tydfil in Wales and Burton Albion in the north midlands. Such journeys in the 1960s were neither cheap nor quick. Nor were part-time footballers always sure to be released by their various employers. As for supporters, how many had the time and funds to cheer their team in distant parts? A planned supporters' coach for the first away match, at Gloucester, had to be cancelled when less than half the seats were sold.

The term 'Premier League', indicating a division above the 'first', is a novelty only for the highest echelons of English football. The concept had been introduced in 1975 to designate the professional elite in Scotland, and was already in place in the Southern League. In order to reach the Premier, the Dons had to win promotion from the 1st Division, to which they had been elected.

Those least affected by the change in status were the players and manager. Les Henley was still in charge, approaching his 10th anniversary with the club. Of the players, with few exceptions, those who slayed Sutton at Wembley were still on board – Kelly in goal, Law at the back, Reynolds up front, all ably supported by Les Brown, Dave Willis, Bobby Ardrey, Ted Murphy, John and Brian Martin. Two new signings would prove vital. Winger Paul Hodges from Wycombe Wanderers, and Scottish Amateur International Gerry O'Rourke would weigh in with plenty of goals.

Whatever the lingering misgivings of the Wimbledon public at the shift to pro football, 3,432 turned out to see the Dons take on their inaugural Southern League visitors, Poole Town, and their crop of former internationals. Wimbledon failed to score, but that would stand as a rare blot on an astonishing season. An Irishman (Reynolds), a Scotsman (O'Rourke), and an Englishmen (Hodges) got drunk on goals. Wimbledon blasted 108 in league matches alone, a total they have never subsequently matched.

With four clubs promoted, Wimbledon were always up with the hunt. The major cups did not detain them long. Premier League Romford, after a replay, ended their interest in the FA Cup, and Premier League leaders Chelmsford extinguished Wimbledon's aspirations in the Southern League Cup.

In the league, from January 1965 the Dons seemed permanently lodged in second place, too far behind Hereford to entertain serious thoughts of catching them, but with breathing space between themselves and the cut-off line beneath them. As amateurs, they traditionally finished strongly. They now stayed true to themselves, winning all seven games in April to finish the season at a gallop.

Reynolds' own goal-tally was a prodigious 57 in all competitions. Some doubted he had the necessary resources to succeed at this level. He could score with his head all right, but what about with feet? The doubters included his manager, Les Henley. Reynolds had started the season slowly. An injury in October absented him from the side, but by the time he was fit Henley had brought in Johnny Cartwright, a deep-playing forward from Premier League Bath City. Cartwright was never intended as a simple replacement, though many at Plough Lane saw it as such and were not pleased. Reynolds was a Plough Lane folk-hero; Cartwright's style far too subtle to stand comparison.

A spell of one win in six at the end of the year made the natives restless. The clamour for Henley to reinstate Reynolds grew ever louder. The manager finally brought him back, not in place of Cartwright, but alongside him. Big Eddie promptly smashed three of the seven goals that sank Ashford, scored one in his next game, two more in his third, and ensured that for the rest of the season no one else stole his No 9 shirt.

DID YOU KNOW?

Canterbury officials were so flummoxed when two players were sent off in their match with Wimbledon that they sweetened the players' tea with salt.

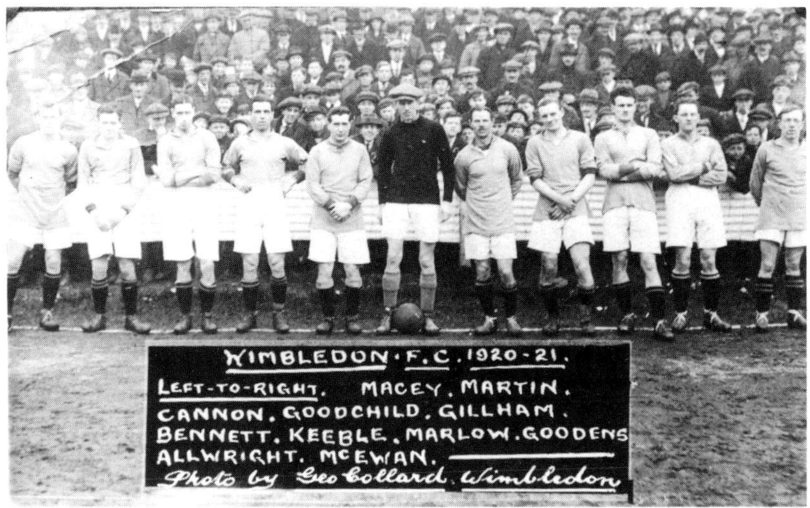

The Athenian League Dons team about to entertain Cardiff Corinthians in the Amateur Cup (12th February 1921). Wimbledon won 1-0.

The figures are staggering. Reynolds bagged another hat-trick in February, two more hat-tricks in March, yet – as if with a point to prove – delayed his final salvo. Three matches remained. Reynolds scored three apiece at Gravesend and Hillingdon, then, before his adoring fans, scored all four in the demolition of Merthyr Tydfil.

The record books went up in smoke. Those 10 took his league tally to 40 from just 34 games. With three more in the Southern League Cup, Reynolds overtook the totals of every other player in Premier and 1st Division alike. He had bagged *nine* league hat-tricks in one season, and two thirds of his goals came from his boots, not his head. Reynolds had averaged more than a goal a game in amateur football; to do so against semi-pro defenders was something else. Small wonder 1st Division defences were glad to see the back of him.

To say that Reynolds hogged the limelight, unfairly detracts from other vital contributions. Only four other players in either division outscored Gerry O'Rourke. Mike Kelly in goal drew admiring comment from all who saw him, while skipper Roy Law threw down the gauntlet to anyone who suggested a better centre-half existed in the Southern League.

The team's achievements (they also won the Eastern Professional Floodlight League) clearly went to a few heads. The Dons applied to join the Football League. Just one, derisory, vote was received.

It would be many years before they got more.

DID YOU KNOW?

In Wimbledon's final 12 matches of 1964-65 Eddie Reynolds smashed 21 goals and claimed SIX hat-tricks!

Match of the Season

Burton Albion 4 Wimbledon 4

1st Division, 9th January 1965

This was a season rich in memorable matches. Some were too one-sided to win the ultimate vote – the 7-1 and 6-2 demolitions of Ashford and Burton at Plough Lane, for example. The 2-1 win at champions-in-waiting Hereford was undoubtedly the best *result*, if not the best *match*. The 4-3 victory at Hillingdon was achieved after promotion had been secured, so that fixture lacked a cutting edge. Two matches ended 4-4 – at home to Gloucester and away to Burton Albion. That match at Eton Park was as thrilling as any, and is still fondly remembered by Burton fans as one of the finest spectacles to have graced the stadium.

The match was played in early January. Wimbledon were already out of both the Southern League Cup and the FA Cup and had their minds focused on promotion. Les Henley's first professional signing, Tom McCready, made his debut.

Southern League Cup-winners in 1964, Burton were two points behind the Dons, but owed their high standing to their daunting home record. Played 10; won 10. Albion's front line included Round and Barker, two of the division's leading scorers.

The pitch was treacly, the entertainment bountiful. Twice Burton went in front, twice the Dons pegged them back. In the second half, goals in quick succession by Eddie Reynolds and Paul Hodges looked set to shatter that proud home record, but back came Burton with late strikes from Jackson and Moore to divide the spoils and earn all 22 players a euphoric reception as they trooped muddily off. Not the least surprising feature of the game was that eight different players scored. Burton's winning run had ended, and they had failed to close the points gap.

With hindsight, the result deflated Burton and inflated Wimbledon. It carried the Dons to second place, a position they never relinquished. But Burton's bubble had burst. Three weeks later they were crushed 2-6 at Plough Lane, and they ended the season mid-table.

SOUTHERN LEAGUE PREMIER 1965-66

Premier Division	5th
Southern League Cup	2nd Round
FA Cup	2nd Round

Not content with confronting a host of new teams in a new league, Wimbledon now had to tear up that itinerary for another.

If the club fretted over how it would cope with the Martian strangeness of professional football, imagine now, 12 months later, as the players prepared to step out among the giants of non-league football. Surveyed from Wimbledon's place in the FA Carling Premiership, these doubts seem quaint. Even so, players and supporters must have gulped when the fixture list sent the Dons to Weymouth, to face the defending champions, in their very first Premier match. It was much like being asked to open up at Old Trafford or Anfield today. Supposing the Dons were walloped; would they ever recover?

Les Henley had added two new faces. Full-back Barry Cordjohn arrived from Portsmouth (for whom he had played 14 matches in the English 2nd Division), and Dave Peters pulled on the No 7 shirt, which had seen so many wearers the previous season.

The Dons did lose at Weymouth, but only by the narrowest margin. They acquitted themselves well and avoided red faces. The visit of Guildford a week later was to shape the season ahead. Guildford's Mick Lill had been a team-mate of Cordjohn at Pompey, and put City ahead after just six minutes. Peters hit back before half-time, and after the break the visitors crumbled under a torrent of Wimbledon attacks that brought four more goals.

So, the Dons went nap in their first Premier home match. Such feats do not ordinarily betoken a side headed for relegation, but it was to prove a false dawn so far as Wimbledon were concerned. By early October the team were in the doldrums. They had won just two of their first nine and been trounced at home by Bedford. Worse, Eddie Reynolds had gone off the boil. He was still the club's top goal-getter, with five, but goals were often Reynolds' only contribution to a match. To many readers, that sounds trite. What else is a striker supposed to do? But Henley reckoned young Ian Cooke could find the net almost as often, and offer more besides.

Cooke's impact was stunning. Two goals at Worcester, one at home to Cambridge United, two more at Nuneaton, his first hat-trick in December against Tonbridge. 14 goals in 13 games was Reynolds' class, and fans were quick to acknowledge the pearl in

Q What do Sittingbourne, Hinckley, Canterbury, Deal, Barry, Trowbridge, and Tunbridge Wells have in common?
A They all played league football against Wimbledon in Season 1964-65. Never before and never since.

their midst. But still they badgered Henley to bring back the Ulsterman. Not in place of Cooke, but the hapless Johnny Cartwright, whose intelligent scheming could not compensate for a measly season's goal-haul of three. Plough Lane supporters are no different from others when it comes to baiting players they think don't come up to scratch, and Cartwright bore the brunt of their disaffection.

All this time, Wimbledon were leaping up the table. This was just as well, for they had been k.o.'d from the cups in frustrating fashion. The 10 goals they belted past Sittingbourne in the 1st Round of the Southern League Cup were undone in Round 3 by one strike from Hastings' Bobby Smith (he of Tottenham, England, and ample girth). In the FA Cup a 7,000 crowd saw goalkeeper Frank Smith punch into his own net against Folkestone.

Smith had signed in November in curious circumstances. In Mike Kelly Wimbledon already possessed a fine keeper. The dilemma was whether to hang on or cash in. When Kelly broke his jaw Smith was snapped up from QPR, for whom he had played 60-odd games in Division 3. But what about Kelly, once his jaw mended? As often happens, the incumbent triumphed. Smith played his part in the Dons' good form and Kelly demanded to go.

Ironically, he went to QPR, where he spent four seasons before moving on to Birmingham City. Kelly was destined for Division 1. In the debate over Kelly v Smith, few doubted Wimbledon had lost the better keeper; but, equally, few believed the club could have kept him.

Kelly's departure, in March 1966, preceded by a few weeks that of Eddie Reynolds. He signed for Ashford Town before moving back to Northern Ireland, to play for Derry City. Without Kelly and Reynolds, the head and toe of Wimbledon's Amateur Cup-winning side had been severed. A clutch of other stalwarts were also served notice to quit. Les Brown, Brian Keats, Ted Murphy and Brian Rudge all sampled life in the Southern League, but for one reason or another were not retained.

DID YOU KNOW?

The final match of Mike Kelly's professional career was at Portman Road in April 1975. Bobby Robson's Ipswich beat Kelly's Birmingham City 3-2.

SOUTHERN LEAGUE TEAM
Back Row (left to right). Dave Willis, Joe Wallis, Roy Law, Tommy McCready, Stuart Davies, Mike Kelly. **Front Row.** Brian Keats, Brian Martin, Eddie Reynolds, Johnny Cartwright, Paul Hodges. **Inset.** Gerry O'Rourke.

The team that shattered goalscoring records in gaining promotion from Division 1.

On the field, Wimbledon's momentum carried them to the top. A fairy tale looked set to become real. Could Wimbledon be crowned champions at the first attempt? There were some who dreaded the prospect. If it materialised, what then? If the Southern League bed proved too small, where else could the club go? The Football League was a bridge too far. All things come to those that wait, says the proverb, but expectant Dons fans were in no mood for waiting. Season upon season they had known nothing but titles, cups, and promotions.

Wise heads say it was for the long-term good of the club that the Premier title eluded them. It was lost away from home. The run-in brought six away defeats, the goals dried up, and – alarmingly – leads were sacrificed. Too often Wimbledon went in front, then lost, a sign of a soft touch. Easter, in particular, betrayed Wimbledon's hopes, setting a trend that would persist for some seasons.

The Dons finished 5th, disappointing only in that they had slipped from 1st. The club won nothing for the first time in recent memory. Worryingly, average gates, in a season that saw just one home defeat, were down on that which had brought promotion.

Undaunted, the club again applied to join the Football League. This time they failed to get anyone to back them. 'Nul points,' as the Eurovision Song Contest would have it.

FOLKESTONE TOWN'S THEME SONG (after beating the Dons in the FA Cup)
(sung to the tune of 'Sons of the Sea')

'We are Folkestone Town, Dover couldn't get us down,
Nor Canterbury, nor Margate, we beat Bexley, too,
Gillingham and Wimbledon, now we're playing Crewe.
Folkestone on the shore, they really know the score,
They drink Wilf's vintage water from Drellingore Pump 4.'

FA Cup Round 3 Result: Folkestone 1 Crewe 5.

Match of the Season

Worcester City 1 Wimbledon 4

Premier Division, 23rd October 1965

Wimbledon bagged 100 goals in league, FA and Southern League Cups. While down on what had gone before, that number would dwarf what was to come.

Best home performances were against Guildford (5-1) and Tonbridge (6-1). Away, the 5-4 win at Rugby demands celebration, but, sadly, details are lacking. Wimbledon managed five at Romford, too, on a ground that would become a graveyard for the next decade.

The circumstances of Wimbledon's 4-1 victory at Worcester are worth exploring. It was, for one thing, the first match in which Ian Cooke was preferred to Eddie Reynolds. Cooke had stood in for the concussed Irishman back in September, but immediately stood down again once Reynolds was *compos mentis.*

Henley prudently chose an away match to axe Reynolds, far from an irate Plough Lane. Henley was taking a gamble, but, with Wimbledon in the wrong half of the league, one that he felt he could postpone no longer.

The Southern League has traditionally been a happy hunting ground for former 1st Division footballers – internationals even – playing out their days with greying temples and thickening waistlines. The crowds flock to see them, out of a sense of nostalgia, mostly, and younger players benefit from tips handed down and lessons learned.

Worcester City were unusual only to the extent of having three internationals in their side, an Englishman, a Welshman and an Irishman. The Englishman was Norman Deeley, a raiding right-winger in his Wolverhampton days, who was called up by Walter Winterbottom for England's 1959 tour of South and North America.

Brian Martin tangles with Poole's Peter Rutley. (5th March 1966)

Deeley was capped in the Maracana against Brazil (0-2) and in Lima against Peru (1-4).

Dai Ward, an inside-forward, had won two caps for Wales against England, in a career that took him from Bristol Rovers to Brentford.

Peter McParland, the Irishman, will forever be remembered as the Aston Villa winger whose thunderous challenge on Manchester United's Ray Wood in the 1957 FA Cup Final left the ball in the net and the goalkeeper with a fractured cheek-bone. McParland won 34 caps for Northern Ireland.

All three players were still in their early 30s, all young enough to be a nuisance. Worcester were handily placed in the league, and without Reynolds' aerial threat this had the makings of a home banker.

Ian Cooke had other ideas. It took him 12 minutes to score his first league goal. Though Norman Deeley levelled, goals by Hodges and Cooke gave the Dons a 3-1 interval lead. Hodges scored a fourth immediately after the turnaround to inflict upon Worcester their heaviest defeat for six seasons.

SOUTHERN LEAGUE PREMIER 1966-67

Premier Division	4th
Southern League Cup	Semi-Final
FA Cup	1st Round

Football in 1966-67 attracted huge attention, for England had won the World Cup in the summer. The people's game caught the popular imagination in a way not seen since the post-World War II heyday. Attendances soared the length of the land. Even Plough Lane's crowds were up. Coincidentally, the Dons sported a new strip, blue shorts instead of white, to give an 'all blue' look.

Another novelty was the introduction of substitutes. Old habits died hard, however, and the idea took time to catch hold. Few managers thought of introducing a 12th man for tactical reasons, only for injury – and a bad one at that. Not till the end of October did Henley field his first sub; he used only eight all season.

Two new faces lined up for the league opener away at Corby – David Hyde and Terry McDonald. Goals by Tom McCready and Ian Cooke gave Wimbledon a welcome winning start.

It was just the tonic, for whereas in 1964-65 they had had to haul themselves up by the bootstraps, this time they were out of the trap like greyhounds. Win followed win, so that by late October the team were unbeaten and six points clear at the top of the league.

Second-placed Hereford were next in line at Plough Lane. Roy Law tamed the once great John Charles and with a minute to go the game was goalless. But then Hereford broke away to take both points from a free-kick. King's Lynn's late equaliser at Plough Lane deprived the Dons of a further point, whereupon they travelled to Chelmsford and lost 0-3.

Henley's team were wobbling. Two further away losses deposed them from the top. Midland League Grantham then expelled them from the FA Cup with barely a whimper. Many fans opted for Christmas shopping rather than turn out for the visit of Folkestone, whose win in the FA Cup a year earlier still rankled. But those preferring Woolworth's to the Wombles missed a goal feast. The Dons led 3-2 at half-time, but then came the avalanche. Cooke hit five of Wimbledon's nine-goal total, and for good measure added four more a week later in the 6-1 demolition of Corby. Nine goals in successive league games. Not even Eddie Reynolds could boast feats like that.

That explosion of goals, plus the Bank Holiday, enticed the season's biggest crowd to see Barnet on Boxing Day. Cooke was

HOOLIGANS!

Against Cheltenham at Plough Lane, fans behind the goal bombarded visiting keeper Meeson with polo-mints. He pleaded with the referee for protection.

out, injured, but the team won comfortably, and again the next day in the return at Underhill.

By this time Wimbledon's *élan* had recaptured the leadership. The goals continued to fly in; four against Poole, five against Worcester. By early February it seemed all they had to do was keep a steady nerve and the title was theirs.

It had been the same story a year earlier. But again February proved to be a month as dismal as its reputation. Two thirds of the season was behind them, but the finishing line remained over the horizon. Beginning with the 0-1 loss at Wellington, Wimbledon went 10 games with only one win. In mid-slump Barnet put paid to their hopes in the Southern League Cup, winning 3-1 at Underhill in the semi-final before five coachloads of miserable Dons supporters. Dreams of a league and cup double were shattered.

Easter, too, was depressing. Three games; three defeats. Away from home, Wimbledon were losing to anyone and everyone.

The malaise reflected a collapse of nerve as much as of goalscoring – though Ian Cooke never quite recovered from that mid-season injury. Twice against Romford the Dons took an early lead; twice they ended up thrashed 1-4. Clearly, the defence was not as it was, or as it should be.

For all Wimbledon's spring failings, the inability of rivals to string together a winning run meant that the pack jostled to the very end. Somehow or other the Dons retained top spot into April, as dog ate dog all around them. Even on half-power Wimbledon might have limped over the line ahead of the pack, but Chelmsford, Guildford, and then Nuneaton each snatched draws with cruelly late goals. Two wins from the last two fixtures would still have landed Wimbledon the crown.

Even that proved beyond them. Looking back, it seemed easier to win the championship than lose it. It was as if the players harboured a death wish; a failure of inner belief. Romford won the title with a miserly 52 points. In no other season during Wimbledon's tenure would it be won with less than 57.

Bridesmaids were the Dons, and, did we know it, bridesmaids they would remain. Their ritual application to join the Football League was rewarded by one vote.

Wimbledon celebrate winning the 1975-76 Southern League Cup. Dickie Guy holds the trophy; Roger Connell the base.(v Yeovil, 10th April 1976)

Match of the Season

Wimbledon 1 Nuneaton 1

Premier Division, 9th May 1967

A short-list of two, really, in this season that promised so much but ended up with so little. True, other matches enthralled or frustrated supporters. At home, almost every match up to the New Year had something to commend it, whether for high scoring or some other drama, and the thrashing of Poole, Worcester, and Bath early in 1967 confirms that this was a fruitful season for Plough Lane-goers. Never again in the Southern League would they see their side come close to 62 home goals – a mite under three goals per game.

There was little to cheer on the travel front after Christmas, which makes the defeat at Barnet in the Southern League Cup sad but not wholly unexpected. Yet that semi-final yields to the one match that might have brought the championship to Plough Lane.

The visit of Nuneaton Boro in May could hardly have been better engineered. Both clubs had 48 points. Two more points would reel in leaders Barnet, Romford, and Weymouth, and hand the winners pole position for their one outstanding match. A draw for either side was likely to be as useless as a spent cartridge.

DRESSING ROOM UNREST?

'Too often there were rumblings of discontent in the dressing room, talk of incentives and unprecedented friction between players and management. I have seen little in the professionals to suggest they have the club's interests really at heart. Desire for individual glory and gain, certainly. But for the club, regrettably no.'
Peter Miller, writing in the club handbook.

If past results were anything to go by, Nuneaton would not have fancied their chances. They had lost 0-3 and 0-4 in 1965-66, and only a late equaliser at Manor Park two weeks before this crunch match had denied Wimbledon a third straight win over Boro.

The 4,000 fans who rolled up hoping against hope could rarely have seen such a sight as greeted them on the half-hour. The game was goalless when Paul Cutler received the ball in the centre-circle. The youngster had signed for Nuneaton from Crystal Palace, and will probably never know why he decided to try his luck from 50 yards. Perhaps he saw Frank Smith off his line; perhaps it was an intended pass that went astray.

Either way, the ball flew over the transfixed goalkeeper and into the net. The turf refused to open up and devour Smith, although that must have been his dearest wish. Wimbledon now had to score twice to extract anything meaningful from the match. They managed one goal, and that was coloured by controversy. Roy Law later admitted that he had kicked the ball out of keeper Fred Crump's hands. Commendably honest, perhaps, but silence would have been the nobler virtue. Especially as his goal would ultimately deprive Nuneaton of the title.

In the event, the draw did not scupper Wimbledon's prospects. With one match outstanding, one point separated four sides, and a favourable combination of results could still have dredged the big prize. Wimbledon played at Bath. And lost.

SOUTHERN LEAGUE PREMIER 1967-68

Premier Division	Runners Up
Southern League Cup	1st Round
FA Cup	2nd Round

If 1966-67 was frustrating, season 1967-68 was traumatic. For the third season in a row the Dons headed the table for long stretches, but ended up panting breathlessly in the slipstream of others.

May's despondency hung over into August. The gate for the first match, at home to Dover, barely topped 2,000. Two players made their debuts. Peter Hobbs would not remain long with the club, but Jimmy Collins would become a mainstay, inheriting the captaincy in due course.

The first month suggested Wimbledon would struggle to repeat their championship challenges of the past. Their first six games brought two wins, two draws, and two defeats – one of these a 1-4 thumping at Nuneaton. The Dons were short on firepower and appeared handicapped by the absence of the injured Ian Cooke. To compound matters, Wimbledon tumbled at the first hurdle of the Southern League Cup, put out by the holders, Guildford City.

With attendances yet to improve, the directors contemplated switching to Friday night soccer. Happily, coinciding with Cooke's return, the team picked up the breeze. Basement-club Poole came to SW19 and were buffeted by an eight-goal whirlwind, in which Cooke helped himself to four goals. The 4-0 defeat of strugglers Burton in November set in train a six-game winning sequence. The team spurted from 10th to 1st, to go into the Christmas programme top of the league for the third year running.

By then they had a new No 9. Johnny Cartwright had never been taken to supporters' hearts. To beef up the attack Henley splashed out £1,500 on Worcester City's Eddie Bailham. The manager had taken heed of Bailham's showing in Worcester's previous visit. Doomed City had lost 5-3, but Bailham had scored all three of his team's goals. If he could strike so well for a losing side, what might he do for a winning one?

Bailham was also a full, as opposed to an amateur, international. That the country was the Republic of Ireland (then among the no-hopers of world football), and that he won only one cap (while on the books of Shamrock Rovers) was immaterial. His cap had been won against England in Dublin in 1964. Despite the inclusion of Noel Cantwell and Johnny Giles, Ireland lost 1-3 to an England team fielding four of the side that would later win the World Cup.

The moment that would haunt Bailham arrived after half-time. Ireland were on the attack, 1-2 down. A chance fell to him, but he hit the post. An inch or two denied Bailham the boast of being an international goalscorer.

Not always as fit as he might be, given to putting on weight, Bailham was blessed with a natural talent that depending on whim either destroyed opponents or obliterated him from view. Bailham's career at Plough Lane would be punctuated with highs and lows. He scored in his first two matches, then suffered five barren games, then smashed a hat-trick. It was ever thus with Eddie Bailham.

That threesome, against Nuneaton in January, was opportune. The Dons had had a miserable Christmas. Margate had beaten them twice, and Bailham's anonymous performances had the crowd on his back. He had only been with the club a month; but his invisibility was highly visible.

He was at least excused blame for the 0-4 hiding by Bristol Rovers in the 3rd Round of the FA Cup. Bailham was cup-tied.

Freed from distraction, Wimbledon resumed their quest for the title. January to mid-March harvested 17 points from 9 games and provided a handy cushion at the top of the league. Only Cambridge United seemed to be within striking distance. Then disaster. A rat-a-tat-tat of three quick defeats, and suddenly the gap was gone.

It was at this low point that the Dons' chairman and benefactor for much of his lifetime, Sydney Black, passed away. Unwell for many years, he surely hoped to live long enough to see his cherished club crowned champions for the first time. The visit of new leaders Cambridge United now assumed extra poignancy. Both teams stood for a minute's silence and played in black armbands.

At the back of players' minds was the knowledge that no Dons team had lost four Southern League matches in a row. O'Rourke's screamer near the end averted that fate, but left time for Ian Hutchinson (soon to project his legendary long throws for Chelsea) to equalise and steal the Dons' thunder.

The Easter programme was still to come. It was not so bad as some. Wimbledon shared the six points available, but were indebted to Bailham's injury-time equaliser at Stevenage, against a club which had recently gone into liquidation and whose team played on a pitch of sand.

That match marked the debut of an admired young goalkeeper, Dickie Guy. Guy had shown such promise that he had already represented the Isthmian League and England's Amateur Youth team. He missed the opening matches of the season as a result of a rugby crossbar collapsing upon him in training, but was now given his chance by Frank Smith's damaged ankle. It was not an

Jeff Bryant and Ricky Marlowe celebrate their goals against Leatherhead. (14th December 1976)

auspicious baptism. Two of Stevenage's three goals might have been prevented. Smith was quickly reinstated.

Three wins from four games returned Wimbledon to the top, and with two home games to round off the season they looked set fair for the title. Once again they blew it.

Wimbledon's application to the Football League earned one vote.

Match of the Season (1)

Wimbledon 1 Chelmsford 2

Premier Division, 4th May 1968

No one likes finishing second, and the pain is worse when the cup is dashed from the lips. That was how it was in the fag end of 1967-68. Wimbledon had three matches to play, all at home. First up were Hastings, bottom. Wimbledon hit five. The fifth goal took them to No 1, above Chelmsford on goal-average.

Chelmsford? They had done a Shergar in the Derby and come from nowhere. Beginning in February they had embarked on a run of 11 wins, beating Wimbledon at New Writtle St, and then, crucially, Cambridge United twice over Easter.

Alf Biggs scores Bristol Rovers' first goal in the FA Cup 2nd Round tie at Plough Lane.(6th January 1968)

Chelmsford City have fallen on hard times, but in the 1960s and 70s they were the cream of non-league football, boasting a neat stadium and entertaining hopes of joining the Football League. With central Essex not represented among the '92', this was no vain hope. All they needed, or so it seemed, was a championship team.

Up front Chelmsford boasted the unlikeliest-sounding double act in football. Tony BUTCHer and Billy CASSIDY may have sounded like something out of Hollywood, but they put fear into Southern League defences. Like the characters played by Paul Newman and Robert Redford, the one depended upon the other. But when in tandem they were deadly, set for 100 goals this season between them. Nobble Butcher and Cassidy, and you nobbled Chelmsford.

Not that that was in the minds of Roy Law and Co. Wimbledon had two games to play; Chelmsford three, all away. The goal-average was too close to call. The Dons had to win. If they did, the odds would be stacked against Chelmsford.

The crowd of 5,028 was the largest to watch Wimbledon in the Southern League. City committed a foul a minute for the first quarter of an hour, but could not stop Bailham running 40 yards to score. At New Writtle St the Dons had taken the lead too, but had succumbed 2-3. Surely Chelmsford couldn't come back twice.

They could. Block scored from the edge of the box. Worse, a hand controlled the ball in the course of Chelmsford's second goal.

The dream had died. It mattered little that the Dons beat Barnet 5-0 in their last match. The bridesmaids tag was etched in stone.

Match of the Season (2)

Wimbledon 0 Bristol Rovers 4

FA Cup, 2nd Round, 6th January 1968

In the minds of many in non-league football it is giant-killing in cups that matters. Championships may come and go; but toppling the full-time boys offers a richer psychological prize.

The Dons' latest opportunity was reward for beating Romford in Round 1. Bristol Rovers were a big enough name themselves; they were also the gateway to Round 3, which was uncharted territory for Wimbledon.

Bristol Rovers belonged to that indeterminate level, forever migrating between the old 2nd and 3rd divisions, without ever tasting the sweet waters of the 1st or the brine of the 4th. They were at the time a nondescript 3rd Division side, who would slide down the table and miss relegation by just two points.

They had no big names to speak of. They did, however, have two forwards – Alfie Biggs and Harold Jarman – who each played over 400 games for the club. Theirs was a symbiotic relationship, the winger – Jarman – making goals for the No 9. Biggs held the record as the most prolific goalscorer in Bristol Rovers' history.

It was necessary to go back to Wimbledon's Wembley season, 1962-63, for their last FA Cup clashes against league sides. That dream had ended against Bristol City. Roy Law, Bobby Ardrey, and Brian Martin survived for this second bite at a Bristol cherry.

Rovers forfeited their blue and white quarters for red and white stripes, taking the field before a crowd of 9,356, Plough Lane's largest since the club turned professional. Referee George McCabe had been a linesman during the 1966 World Cup.

David and Goliath cup matches have a predictable outcome. David plays out of his skin, and loses. That was also the way against Bristol Rovers. The Dons had most of the ball, most of the play, and – if such excuses are sought – most of the ill-fortune. Ian Cooke hit the bar at one end, but every time Rovers reached the other – which was not very often – they scored.

The result, 0-4, with two more goals to Alfie Biggs, left the Dons scratching their heads and pondering the injustice of it all.

DID YOU KNOW?

**Plough Lane matches were usually marshalled by 18 policemen.
For the visit of Bristol Rovers in the FA Cup that number was raised to 36.
Their hire cost Wimbledon £3 per bobby.**

SOUTHERN LEAGUE PREMIER 1968-69

Premier Division	3rd
Southern League Cup	1st Round
FA Cup	4th Qualifying Round

Some clubs never recover from missing the big prize by a whisker. Especially doing so twice. Would Wimbledon fall away completely? Or would they come back for yet another crack at the title? Financial pressures had squeezed the number of professionals on the staff down to 16. Clearly, it would be harder than ever for the Dons to be champions come May.

Their poor start did not help. By the end of August they had played five league games, winning one; they had lost 0-3 to Weymouth at Plough Lane, and they had been dumped from the Southern League Cup by those demons from Chelmsford.

The way things were going, Wimbledon would struggle to finish in the top half. One problem confronting Les Henley was what to do about Ian Cooke. The player had gifts, but where best to employ them? The arrival of Eddie Bailham and, now, the gangling giant from Margate, John O'Mara – as a plausible reincarnation of Eddie Reynolds – gave Henley skill and muscle in attack. But that meant pushing Gerry O'Rourke out wide and Cooke, as often as not, deeper into midfield.

The consequence was a goal famine. Cooke and O'Rourke had scored 66 times between them in 1967-68. Removed from the enemy nerve-centre, they would manage just 21 in 1968-69. This shortfall needed to be made up, but Bailham blew hot and cold all season and O'Mara would play only 15 games. For the first time, no Wimbledon name was up there with the Southern League's leading goal-poachers.

With the team dithering they crashed to their worst embarrassment since turning professional, losing at home 0-2 to the amateurs of Woking in the FA Cup. 'Words fail me,' wrote Peter Miller of the *Wimbledon News*, at the ineptitude of it all.

The wonder is that Wimbledon regrouped to mount a championship challenge. But mount it they did. A run of autumn draws put the losing habit behind them, and before you knew it the draws had turned into wins. The points tally accelerated upwards. This was less a consequence of the front line sharpening its aim, as the back line adding steel. All things being relative, this was a defensively minded Henley team. How else could the shortcomings in attack be overcome?

GRIM OMENS

'A few weeks ago the rope of the flagpole snapped, and as the flag we have is in very tatty condition we will probably not replace it until next season.'
Note in the club programme, January 1969

Wimbledon had lost just once in 13 games when, in January, they set off on an eight-game winning streak that by early March had opened up a gap of six points. The run would have been nine, and started one game earlier, but Poole had recovered from 0-3 at half-time to square the match. Nevertheless, Wimbledon had gone half a season with just the one reverse. 'The title is as good as theirs,' whooped the *Wimbledon News*.

But three obstacles remained. First, Wimbledon had travelled this road before. Every season since winning promotion they had topped the table at some stage, and in the past had failed to stay the distance. Second, Easter was still to come. Third, and this was a new hazard, the Dons faced a congested backlog of away fixtures. Of their final 14 games, four were at home and 10 away.

The winning run came to a rude halt, 0-3 at Hereford. Three points out of six over Easter were enough to keep the Dons top as the finishing tape came into sight. Just four games remained, at home to struggling Burton, then three tough away trips.

Wimbledon's dreams exploded at Plough Lane in the shape of an outrageous downfield punt by Albion goalkeeper Fred Potter. The wind, the hard ground, and Dickie Guy's poor positioning contributed to a freak goal, the ball sailing on and bouncing once, twice, and over Guy's head into goal. Burton's shock win would rescue them from relegation and leave Wimbledon fans shaking their heads, wondering if their team were cursed.

The Dons failed to win another match. The damage, of course, had been inflicted in key home fixtures. First Nuneaton, then Chelmsford, now Burton – for the third season in a row Plough Lane was the scene of championship nightmares. Each time the title had been in the Dons' own hands, but their hold was weak.

SOUTHERN LEAGUE STARLETS; FOOTBALL LEAGUE STARS

1 Kelly (Wimbledon & QPR)

2 Book (Bath & Manchester C)	**3 Carroll (Cambridge C & Ipswich)**
4 Bailey (Bedford & Gillingham)	**5 Collins (Chelmsford & Spurs)**
6 Gulliver (Weymouth & Bournemouth)	**7 French (Wellington & Luton)**
8 Cave (Weymouth & Torquay)	**9 Ritchie (Kettering & Sheffield W)**
10 Curran (Corby & Wolves)	**11 Hutchinson (Cambridge U & Chelsea)**

WIMBLEDON F.C., 1968-69

(L. to R.): Back Row: D. Willis, B. Martin, F. Smith, R. Law, R. Guy, T. McCready, R. Ardrey, J. Collins. Front Row: E. Bailham, R. Colfar, G. O'Rourke, P. Hodges, I. Cooke, D. Malley, J. O'Mara, S. Davies.

Looking back over 1968-69, the imbalance of home and away fixtures had to some extent put Wimbledon in a false position, which only became apparent once the season had evened out. To finish 3rd was praiseworthy, though it signalled the first retrograde step. The sequence of 5th, 4th, 2nd, 3rd, highlighted the sad fact that each of the top positions had been occupied except the one that mattered.

Moreover, on two counts there was cause more for pessimism than optimism. Few regulars at Plough Lane enthused over the standard of football on offer. This was not a vintage Wimbledon side; wins had been carved out of stone rather than fashioned with the rapier. The change in style was reflected in the number of paying customers, the average dipping below 2,000 for the first time, and not once topping 3,000. A decision had already been taken to scrap the reserve team to cut costs. For a year or two, until its restoration, either you played for the first team or you didn't play at all.

So, another anticlimactic season was over. On a sour note, too. A testimonial match against Chelsea attracted a crowd of 5,250, of whom a few visiting fans seemed set on trouble. Admission gates were wrecked, railings uprooted, and a crossbar snapped.

Match of the Season

Wimbledon 3 Dover 1

Premier Division, 7th April 1969

Wimbledon never scored more than three goals a game, so no goal-pageants catch our eye. In fact, there are precious few contenders, perhaps one reason why the crowds stayed away in droves. The 3-3 home draw with future champions Cambridge United looks good on paper, but was marked by much negative football, mainly from the visitors, and was played in the wake of the FA Cup debacle against Woking.

Brighter spirits were generated by the visit of Dover over Easter. A holiday crowd of 2,890, the biggest of the season, came to see if the table-topping Dons had what it took to stay there. The visitors had nothing to play for, being marooned in mid-table. Their side was noteworthy mainly for the inclusion of two future Dons. Centre-half Chris Hurley would arrive in 1972 – and then be out of the door in double-quick time. Dover's skipper, full-back John Martin, would not just be a future Don; he was also a past Don, a member of the Amateur Cup-winning side. He had played in Wimbledon's first four Southern League matches in 1964, but injury and adequate defensive cover saw him transferred in 1967. He would soon be re-signed by the Dons and back in harness.

At the back of every Wimbledon supporter's mind was the question, did the Dons have the bottle and the luck necessary to win the title. The question of bottle would be deferred. Against Dover the question of luck was answered in the affirmative. On a surface so bone-hard that John O'Mara trotted out in baseball boots, the ball took to bouncing so high and so unevenly that constructive play was out of the question. Half an hour of ping-pong football had been consumed when the ball reared up in the Dover penalty box and glanced off Clewlow's hand. Few considered the offence intentional. Most referees would have taken heed of the conditions. This one did not, and Eddie Bailham duly calmed the nerves by scoring from the penalty spot. Dover players were so incensed that several patted the referee on the back in mock congratulation. They were lucky not to be sent off.

The break was all Wimbledon needed. They ran out 3-1 winners. The fans trooped away thinking the corner had been turned.

SOUTHERN LEAGUE PREMIER 1969-70

Premier Division	5th
Southern League Cup	Winners
FA Cup	1st Round
FA Challenge Trophy	1st Round

Like a giant boulder hauled by a score of men to the top of a mountain, the weight of expectation was proving too much for Wimbledon FC. There was, within and without the club, that sick feeling that they had blown it; that the side was getting older and weaker, and that having failed to secure first prize when at its peak they would now never do so. With no reserve team, and with a professional squad down to the knuckle, the talk was less of titles than of financial survival.

The team to play at Kettering in the opening match showed two new faces – Peter Shreeve, midfielder, signed from Chelmsford, and learning the ropes for future management; and right-back John Martin, a former Don, returned from Dover. The retirement of his namesake, Brian, was good news for statisticians. Just one 'Martin' appeared on the team-sheet.

Wimbledon's form in August and September gave cause for optimism. One defeat in 10 games saw the Dons tucked into second place, with the bonus of having advanced to the 2nd Round of the Southern League Cup for the first time in three years.

In fact, cup competition sapped much of the team's energies for the rest of 1969 and beyond. Wimbledon needed three attempts to get past Crawley in the FA Cup, though they would crush them 9-0 in the league. In the 1st Round proper, in November, the Dons fell to league leaders Hillingdon. Two days later Plough Lane played host to the Final of the London Challenge Cup.

The London Challenge Cup (later the London Senior Cup) was sanctioned as one of the Dons' manifold first team competitions. With its narrow geographical intake, and its mix of fired-up amateur sides and frustrated reserves from the rich and mighty, it had an unsatisfactory complexion. It pulled in the crowds whenever a big name was drawn, purely in the hope of seeing famous faces.

Wimbledon's recent record in the tournament was abysmal. They hadn't won a match for five years; now they were in the Final, and their opponents were Arsenal. The gate of 4,494 was double that of anything in the league, and treble that for the coming Southern League Cup Final, which says much about the standing of the London Challenge Cup among football's rank and file.

An away day on British Rail. From left to right: Glen Aitken (in the patched jeans), Dave Lucas, Dickie Guy, Bob Stockley (in the leather).

It was an unwritten rule of thumb for big-wigs that they did not pack their side with too many first-teamers. Much though supporters would love to see them, this was for Football League entrants a reserve-team tournament.

Arsenal tried to please everyone. Their team read: Johnson, Rice, Nelson, Roberts, Carmichael, Kelly, George, McLintock, Gould, Kennedy, Davies. Try telling Bobby Gould that this Cup was a doddle and that he need only go through the motions. It was he who sank Wimbledon, scoring in the 11th and 87th minutes, to cancel out Hugh McLeish's 77th minute volley. Gould's late winner denied the Dons a replay on the hallowed pitch at Highbury.

In the league, Wimbledon for a while had to do without Dickie Guy. Part-time sport enables all-rounders to participate in more than one. Several county cricketers played Southern League soccer. The Dons had such a specimen, Graham Roope, Surrey and – later – England batsman. Roope had been signed as understudy to Guy and when the latter was injured stood in for half a dozen games.

The goalkeeping position was the least of Henley's worries. Apart from the nine-goal blitz of Crawley, which came and went with the suddenness of a tropical storm, the Dons failed to exceed three goals a match in the league. Notwithstanding that nine-goal bonus, the final haul would be the lowest the team had yet posted, and ensured that any success on the pitch would be indebted to defensive fortitude.

A run of narrow New Year victories carried Wimbledon to 1st position. This was the fifth successive season that they had enjoyed such an elevated view and once again hard-nosed fans began to ask the unthinkable. Could the team do it this time?

The signs were hopeful. In a top-of-the-table tussle with Hillingdon the visitors ran up a two-goal lead with 20 minutes to play. O'Rourke's reply looked to be merely a token as the game entered its seventh minute of injury time. It was then that Cooke took a corner, Law headed down, and O'Mara fired the equaliser. On such moments are championships won and lost. Wimbledon had enjoyed precious few 'moments' in previous seasons.

At the time Wimbledon were on course for two prizes. They had not dallied long in the FA Challenge Trophy, a new competition for non-leaguers, which dangled the carrot of a Wembley final. Dartford had put the Dons out in Round 1. But in the Southern League Cup, encouraged by successive home draws, Wimbledon marched onwards. Victory in February over league and cup holders Cambridge United earned a place in the semi-finals.

Sadly, disillusionment had gripped supporters to such an extent that they stayed away *en masse*. Hillingdon's league visit had enticed just 2,163 from the comfort of their fire-sides, the season's best, a figure that barely exceeded the *worst* not so long ago. But the semi-final with Cambridge drew a paltry audience of 1,452.

The club could not long survive on such gates. Henley was asked to take a pay cut, and only the hope that the directors might hold out for more prevented John O'Mara being sold to Poole for the princely sum of £500. Mutterings in the press and among supporters questioned the wisdom of the club turning professional. The romance and gallantry of top-flight amateur football captured hearts far more than did the mean-spirited defensiveness and swingeing cost-cutting that was part and parcel of the Southern League.

In the title-race it was a case of not being able to teach an old dog new tricks. Hillingdon won the second 'four-pointer', and Easter proved as depressing as usual. The Dons lost two out of three, including a 1-5 mauling at Margate – the first time Wimbledon had shipped five goals since turning professional.

At home the team won regularly enough, but on their travels they lost five of the last six and slid miserably down the table. The Dons finished 5th, eight points behind Cambridge United, whose second successive championship was enough to see them voted into the Football League, at the expense of Bradford Park Avenue.

This time a ray of sunshine peeped into Wimbledon's darkness.

Match of the Season

Wimbledon 3 Romford 0

Southern League Cup Final, 1st Leg, 2nd April 1970

The Southern League Cup Final was played over two legs, though the outcome of this one was effectively settled in the first. The Dons had reached the semi-final in 1967, and now went one stage further.

A neutral venue – perhaps a 1st Division ground – might have generated greater interest. But coming hard on the heels of the 1-5 league thrashing at Margate, just 1,505 could be bothered to attend. That was fewer than at most league games, and was swelled by a noisy contingent of Romford supporters.

Wimbledon's record against their opponents was dreadful. Romford and Chelmsford at the time seemed capable of beating the Dons irrespective of form or circumstance. Wimbledon's 3-0 league win in March was their first over Romford in eight attempts, and was immediately succeeded by a 0-2 defeat at Brooklands.

Romford were another of the Southern League's ambitious clubs who have since floundered. They were having an indifferent season in the league, so, unlike Wimbledon, had all their eggs in the Cup. Harry Clarke's side was able to call upon the services of Bobby King and Colin Flatt, who had seen league action with nearby Southend United, and the experienced Harry Obeney, now in his fifth season with the club, who had learned his trade at West Ham, Millwall, and elsewhere.

Two-leg soccer was a rarity in those days. Other than in the 1st round of the Southern League Cup, clubs had little experience of it. Nowadays, different teams and tactics would be employed for home and away legs, and one-goal deficits from the latter treated as 'good results'. No tortuous tactics attended such matches in earlier times. Obviously, a better result was expected at home than away, but the two teams would invariably be unchanged from one to the other, with little thought given to playing an extra defender here, an extra winger there.

As so it was that with three minutes on the clock Obeney's foot intercepted Bobby Ardrey's cross (or was it an attempt on goal?). Goalkeeper Andy Smith stood no chance with the deflection. Romford had barely restarted the game when John Martin crossed from the right and an off-balance O'Mara somehow managed to head a second goal. Game and set to the Dons, and the match, too, when O'Mara set up Stuart Davies for a third before half-time.

In the second leg Romford needed a quick goal. Flatt obliged, but Bobby King's error enabled O'Mara to restore the margin.

SOUTHERN LEAGUE PREMIER 1970-71

Premier Division	8th
Southern League Cup	Semi-Final
FA Cup	1st Round
FA Trophy	3rd Round

Two new players kicked off the new season. Alan Burton and Keith Sanderson were signed less with the championship in mind than to check the creeping malaise.

Burton had seen action with the Dons in their Isthmian days, prior to spending nine years with Aldershot. Now he was free-transferred back to lend his know-how to the front line. Sanderson also had a wealth of league experience. He had known Wembley glory when 3rd Division QPR, complete with Rodney Marsh, came from behind to overhaul West Brom in the 1967 League Cup Final.

The Dons sprang out of the traps with rapid wins over Nuneaton and Romford. But before hopes were raised they lost four of their next five – the last of which by four goals to Telford, who had gone into the match bottom and pointless. The Dons were adrift in the bottom half of the league and crippled by injury. Burton broke his collar-bone and was out for months, Bailham had to play despite being unfit, and Bobby Ardrey – now a permit player – was summoned out of semi-retirement.

The next matches were critical. Fortunately, five of the next six were at home. Dickie Guy kept six clean-sheets, leading to yet more covetous glances. The Dons won 1-0 at Plough Lane three times in a row, more *catenaccio* than cavalier, but then – just to show that the Dons retained some semblance of flair – Bedford went for five and Ashford for four. O'Rourke and Cooke bagged hat-tricks and somehow Henley's alchemy lifted the team to 3rd.

Though Wimbledon failed to assert themselves at Peterborough in the FA Cup, they had little time for despondency, having an appointment with Tottenham at White Hart Lane in the Final of the London Challenge Cup.

It was a moot point whether it was preferable to play Spurs home or away. The vast acres of White Hart Lane echoed to the lament of 2,829 die-hards. Though Spurs fielded seven players with first-team experience, they hadn't the caché of the Arsenal XI. Never mind, the outcome was the same. A greasy pitch and a greasy ball proved Wimbledon's undoing. Guy failed to cling on to Woolacott's header, and, despite building sustained pressure late in the game, the Dons lost 0-1.

Q	**Which Dons game exploded with two Bassetts, and neither Bassett was Harry?**
A	**Referee F Bassett sent off Roy Law for throwing a punch at Worcester City's George Bassett on 29th August 1970.**

Five straight wins carried Wimbledon into the New Year on the crest of a wave. They were two minutes from a sixth, when Bath broke the spell with a late leveller.

Touch wood, this Dons side had gumption. They recovered from 1-3 to draw with Margate, then came from behind to topple Bedford. These are the hallmarks of potential champions. But – as any supporter of the time knew – winter was Wimbledon's buddy; spring their curse. For the umpteenth time they mounted a mid-season challenge; the umpteenth time – maybe because they were an ageing team – they tailed away. This season was the first during which they never at any stage claimed top spot. Second was the best they managed, but once the heat was on, they wilted.

On their own pitch they remained formidable. In seven seasons of Southern League soccer they lost at home just 14 times. Plough Lane was a fortress, the Anfield of non-league stadia. No wonder visiting teams suffered that sinking feeling as they boarded their coach to SW19. Few of them knew the thrill of winning there. The walls of the visitors dressing room were stained with tears.

Wimbledon's away column was their undoing. They would not win away again, signing off with two draws and seven defeats. Those draws were against sides set for relegation, and a very late equaliser at Kettering prevented an eighth loss. Of the few goals scored in those sad weeks two were self-inflicted by opponents.

This, in any language, was relegation form. The season could not end quickly enough. The Dons' final league position – 8th – and their points total – 48 – were the worst they had known.

The club was in crisis. Money lay at the root of it. Home gates had dipped below 1,500, a drop of 50% in five years. Of course, dwindling attendances were football's problem, not Wimbledon's alone. The post-1966 World Cup euphoria had proved short-lived. England were no longer world champions and gates were down.

It must be said that Wimbledon's support was drying up quicker than most. This was the first time Plough Lane's average gates were lower than for the league as a whole. And to account for this we have to look to problems specific to Wimbledon. It was not for want of results that supporters had become disillusioned. It was for want of romance, a nostalgia for amateur soccer, and for want of a championship or two. Old hornets resurfaced: was there, or was there not, room in London for another professional club?

Les Henley had ruled for 16 years and the directors feared the club had become becalmed. The squad lacked the spirit of youth; so too did the manager. A fresh breeze was needed, and that needed a fresh man. This was a harsh verdict on Henley, whose record was exemplary, but it was reasoned that without a sea-change the club's predicament could only worsen.

Pressure mounted. Henley could hardly be sacked while the team were winning, but defeats by Hereford and Barnet, followed by a goalless home draw with Dover, were enough to convict him. Outsiders were bemused. Wimbledon had sacked their first ever manager, yet his team were 3rd and chasing two cups.

Local newspapers were inundated with letters arguing back and forth. Here was a good manager, with a proven track record. Who was to say that any replacement would fare any better? Stick with the man you know; or bring in the devil you don't?

Henley's contract ran till the summer, and he agreed to stay on until his successor was ready to take over. The players, wedded to Henley's ways and uncertain of their futures, were understandably distracted. This was no time to lose sight of the cups. Notice was served on Henley five days before an FA Trophy tie with champions-elect Yeovil. Over 3,000 turned out, a disproportionately big crowd, lured less by the prospect of reaching Round 4 for the first time than to pay homage to Henley and to speculate upon the future. Younger supporters had never known life without Henley. An era was coming to an end, and Dons folk of every description congregated to share the moment.

The match ended 1-1. In the replay, Wimbledon were swept aside, 0-4. One week later Henley sent out a patched up side at Weymouth in the semi-finals of the Southern League Cup.

A second cup triumph would have served as a fitting epitaph for the man who, at that time, had masterminded Wimbledon FC through its finest hours. Sadly, his injury-stricken team proved inferior on the day, and Dickie Guy's error – dropping the ball from a cross – sowed the seeds of another defeat. Seven days later Dover banged five more goals past Guy, and with John O'Mara hastily sold to Brentford for £750 before the transfer deadline, the vista of a terrifying post-Henley future began to crystallise.

Though Marvin Hinton, formerly of Chelsea, was one of several high profile candidates, the lucky man was appointed some time before he actually took charge. The players endured a limbo period where their old manager was laying down the law, while the new one was watching from the stand. Mike Everitt formally took over for the final three matches, winning one, losing two.

Match of the Season

Peterborough 3 Wimbledon 1

FA Cup, 1st Round, 21st November 1970

Leatherhead from the Athenian League stood between the Dons and the FA Cup 1st Round in 1970-71, and for much of a frantic encounter at Fetcham Grove the amateurs held a one-goal advantage – courtesy of a rare mistake by Roy Law. It took two out of the ordinary strikes by the much maligned Eddie Bailham to turn the tables on the home team and send Wimbledon through to face Peterborough.

DID YOU KNOW?

Les Henley's Dons never won the Southern League championship, but their six Premier seasons under him showed they were consistently the best team.

Points won 1965-6 – 1970-71	Pts			
1 WIMBLEDON	306		4 Yeovil	290
2 Chelmsford	298		5 Romford	289
3 Weymouth	290		6 Hereford	275
			7 Cambridge U	260

For the Dons this was not viewed as a plum tie. The distance was too far, takings likely to be too small and the opposition too strong.

Peterborough 'Posh' United were famed giant-killers in their own right. Admitted to the Football League in 1960, in place of Gateshead, they had won promotion at the first attempt on the back of a record 134 goals. They knocked Portsmouth out of the FA Cup and forced a 4th Round replay with Aston Villa. The following year it was Newcastle's turn to perish. In 1965 Posh captured the nation's hearts, famously beating mighty Arsenal in Round 4, overcoming Swansea in Round 5, before falling to Chelsea in the quarter-final. In 1967 they were at it again, reaching the 4th Round yet again, whereupon Sunderland smacked them 7-1.

The following season disaster struck. The football authorities got wind of illegal payments to players and came down on the club with unprecedented severity. To serve as a warning to others, Peterborough were demoted back to Division 4, despite finishing 9th in Division 3.

Three years on, the club were still coming to terms with the trauma. Struggling to keep their best players, they barely avoided having to apply for re-election in 1969, and had yet to find the formula for rebuilding a winning side.

Player-manager Jim Iley had known good times as a wing-half with Newcastle United. Defensive king-pin John Wile was under constant surveillance by the big clubs, and would soon be on his way to WBA. In attack, young Colin Garwood would make a career out of hopping from one club to another, scoring handsomely, and being sold on. As for Jim Hall, Peterborough dare not let him go. An England Youth player, he would spend seven years with the club, rewarding them with 122 league goals.

On paper, toppling a modest 4th Division side like Peterborough should not be beyond a club with Football League aspirations. But tactics went out of the window 21 seconds after the start, by which time Keith Sanderson had inexplicably rolled the ball into the path of Garwood, who duly scored. Those who were present insist that Sanderson momentarily forgot Wimbledon were playing in red, and thought he was passing to a team-mate.

Whatever the case, a difficult tie now looked insuperable. It was effectively decided late in the first half. Bobby Moss put Posh two up – Sanderson again at fault. Ian Cooke pulled one back, but was shortly stretchered off with a severely gashed knee – Stuart Davies deputising. With Wimbledon bereft of the necessary firepower, Roy Law was pushed up as makeshift forward. The only addition to the scoring came when Jim Hall hammered in the final nail 10 minutes from time.

THE LOCUST YEARS 1971-74

SOUTHERN LEAGUE PREMIER 1971-72

Premier Division	10th
Southern League Cup	1st Round
FA Cup	4th Qualifying Round
FA Trophy	1st Round

The replacement of Les Henley by Mike Everitt meant substituting amateur values by professional ones, and meant hauling the club, kicking and screaming, into the modern age.

For all his virtues, Henley was an amateur man whose greatest managerial triumphs had come in the amateur age. But the game had moved on. The late 60s and 70s were times of stifling, boring football, a product of Italian defensive techniques and Alf Ramsey's 1966 wingless wonders. To read Southern League match reports of that era is to wonder why anyone bothered to watch at all. Games were brutal, guileless, and lop-sided. The visiting side packed eight men in front of their goal and belted the ball into touch to waste time. There was little joy in the 'people's game'.

Wimbledon's directors argued that to succeed in this cut-throat environment it was necessary to do as the Romans do, and appoint an exponent of this new brand of no-nonsense football.

Mike Everitt, the directors' choice, epitomised everything that was wretched about the game. Like Henley, he had begun life at Arsenal. He spent the lion's share of his playing career helping Northampton climb from the 4th Division to the 1st, then like Humpty Dumpty, fall all the way back again. In mid-descent Everitt was transferred to Plymouth. He had dropped out of the Football League by the time the vacancy at Plough Lane arose. Still only 30, he was young enough to play for a few more seasons. In signing a manager, the club signed a defender as well. Two for the price of one.

Everitt laid his cards on the table. He was a fitness fanatic who believed passionately in the work ethic. His players must run until they dropped, and to beef them up he introduced a military regime of cross-country runs and endless weight-training. Not all the players were prepared to accept the changes demanded. Winger Paul Hodges, for one, who had been with the club throughout its Southern League years, failed to see eye to eye and in the heat of the moment stormed out. Hodges would return to see out the season. The same could not be said of John Martin, Dave Willis, Stuart Davies, and Keith Sanderson. These were the first crop of players axed by the new manager.

As for Everitt's tactics, keeping goals out assumed greater importance than knocking them in. Especially on opponents' grounds. Before the curtain raiser at Hereford Everitt announced: 'We want 0-0 draws away from home.' One could almost hear the sighs of those who believed football to be about entertainment. Wimbledon FC entered the years that the locust would consume.

New managers often prefer to step into an ailing club, where they have nothing to live up to and where matters can only improve. This was hardly the case with Wimbledon. With one exception, the Dons had never finished lower than 5th. Everitt was not brought in to match that record, but to improve upon it. With no previous managerial experience to call upon, that was likely to prove a tall order. In sweeping away much of the old guard Everitt had to recruit from near and far. By the close of his first full season he had introduced no fewer than 11 new faces – tantamount to a whole team. He signed his quota of young bucks to cover every blade of grass, but at the expense of continuity and team-work. Wimbledon's reserve team was restored to accommodate most of the new intake.

In transitional circumstances it would have been unreasonable to expect too much too soon. Six points from the first six games suggested the team would tread water in the months ahead. Everitt's new centre-forward from Fulham, Alan Morton, settled in quickly and shared the early season goals with Ian Cooke. Another of his signings, midfield tearaway Selwyn Rice, would prove valuable to Everitt's successors. But Rice was one of the few.

Whatever the chemistry of the side, it inexplicably gelled into an explosive cocktail. Seven wins off the cuff in September and early October launched the team to the top. This was the sixth season out of seven that Wimbledon had peered down upon the rest, an astonishing record, matched only by their inability to stay there.

WAS IT WORTH IT?

Margate's reward for beating Wimbledon in the FA Cup in 1971-72 was a tie at Bournemouth. The good news: the gate was 12,000. The bad news: Margate lost 0-11, and Ted McDougall scored nine of them.

It was the nature of the wins, as much as anything, that raised eyebrows. Not a 1-0 to be seen; rather a monsoon of 19 goals.

The bigger they come; the harder they fall. By the end of January the dream was dead, the team was in tatters, and supporters were baying for Mike Everitt's blood. In each of the cups Wimbledon were floored at the first hurdle – including numbing home and away defeats by the minnows of Waterlooville in the Southern League Cup. League form disintegrated, too. Four wins in 15 games saw the pretenders to the throne rudely displaced.

Matters came to a head after Everitt's request for funds to buy yet more players had been brusquely refused. Before their very eyes Dons supporters saw their team ripped apart – 1-5 by Yeovil in the FA Trophy. A week later Wimbledon lost 1-4 at Weymouth, and the following week Plough Lane witnessed yet another mauling, 1-4 by Chelmsford. Never under Les Henley had Plough Lane known such disenchantment.

These were the worst trio of results in memory, and Everitt made certain players take the can. He and Eddie Bailham were chalk and cheese, and Bailham was swiftly despatched on a free-transfer to Cambridge City (where he predictably started bulging the net).

Supporters vent their spleen on players as well as manager, especially those signed by Everitt. Chris Hurley, a centre-half from Dover, had no sooner arrived than he was pressed into service as a makeshift striker. The fans didn't fancy him, either in defence or attack. Rarely can a new player have been barracked so swiftly as Hurley, who lasted less than a dozen games in Wimbledon colours.

The club finished 10th, their worst ever position. The irony of it all was that, for whatever reason, Everitt's preferred strategy was scattered to the winds. He had wanted 0-0s, but didn't get any. On the contrary, the Dons' 75 league goals was the fourth highest in the league. It was their highest total since 1967-68 and would never be topped, not even by Allen Batsford's title-winning teams.

WHY DID KING CHARLES I TREAT WIMBLEDON FC AS ROUNDHEADS?

Because in 1628 he issued a statute which decreed that no other market may be established within seven miles of Kingston's. Wimbledon had hoped to site a market in Plough Lane to raise revenue. The High Court forbade it.

Ian Cooke equalises for the Dons at Bath City.(25th September 1971)

It was the defence, supposedly Everitt's forté, that was the team's undoing. It was to that area of operations that the manager turned his attention in the close season. First he needed a clear-out. Roy Law announced his retirement. Others of the old guard – Hodges, Shreeve, and Collins – were pensioned off. Out they went, along with three of Everitt's own signings – Morton, Hurley, and Malcolm Stanley.

Match of the Season

Wimbledon 2 Hereford 1

Premier Division, 2nd October 1971

Cambridge United's elevation to the Football League in 1971 buoyed up the hopes of those seeking to follow. United's credentials had been impeccable – back-to-back titles, with a Southern League Cup for good measure. Now Hereford, too, were set to move into the big time.

But Hereford's record was flimsier. They failed to claim the championship once, never mind twice. They would finish 1971-72 runners-up to the equally hopeful and more deserving Chelmsford City. Hereford had been 4th the season before, and nowhere before that. Two goodish seasons would be all they needed to satisfy the powers that be.

DOYEN OF THE SOUTHERN LEAGUE.

When Roy Law retired he had played for the Dons for 14 years. Other players showing similar club loyalties included – John Tredwell (15 years with Folkestone), Dicky Moore (12 years with Hillingdon), Bob McEwan (11 years with Worcester), and Tony Hobson (11 years with Weymouth).

But in Hereford's case it was not league form that counted. It was their exploits in the FA Cup. Goals by Radford and George, replayed *ad nauseam* on television ever since, would see off Newcastle United in a celebrated 3rd Round replay. Whereupon Hereford took West Ham to a replay in the next round too. Wimbledon had never yet reached Round 3, never mind Round 4, so Hereford's achievement was something special.

These dramas lay months in the future when Hereford came a-calling in the league. The match was critical to Wimbledon, for they had won their last six and were poised to go top for the first time. Hereford were also jostling for the leadership. The gate topped 2,000 for the first time in many months. Perhaps soothsayers among them got wind that David Icke – future TV sports commentator, Green activist, and self-declared Godhead – would be in goal for Hereford. If so, they were to be disappointed. Fred Potter deputised between the sticks.

In Wimbledon's early Southern League days Hereford regularly emerged victorious at Plough Lane, but results had since been reversed. Should Hereford lose it would be for the fifth time in as many years.

They did lose, but a trifle controversially. Jimmy Collins opened the scoring. Alan Morton's goal, which put the Dons two up, looked offside to everyone in the ground. Except to the man in black. Tyler's riposte was incidental. Wimbledon had won the battle; but Hereford would win the war.

SOUTHERN LEAGUE PREMIER 1972-73

Premier Division	12th
Southern League Cup	2nd Round
FA Cup	3rd Qualifying Round
FA Trophy	3rd Round

Most Wimbledon supporters welcomed the idea of new players – but only if they were better than the old ones. 'Different' did not necessarily mean 'better'. For all Mike Everitt's wheeling and dealing, the fact remained that with the exception of David Armstrong every player he signed was a free transfer. Clubs rarely toss away gold with the brass, and the general feeling at Plough Lane was that the playing input was not a patch on the exodus. The latest crop of imports, however, included two capable full-backs – Bob Stockley, who would come of age with the arrival of Allen Batsford, and John Loughlan, destined to become Wimbledon skipper.

This time Everitt meant business when he pledged Wimbledon to all-out defence. An eight-game unbeaten start was a Dons record, but closer inspection revealed those eight to contain six draws. Two 0-0s and four 1-1s were unlikely to set pulses racing, even if they did leave the manager purring with satisfaction.

Any suggestion that 1972-73 would be an improvement on its predecessor was destroyed in five disastrous days in October. First, Stevenage from the lower reaches of the Division 1 came to Plough Lane in the Southern League Cup and won 3-1. It was a shock, the more so considering that the result was the reverse of that recorded just 10 days earlier when the two teams clashed in the FA Cup.

What stuck most in fans' throats was the fact that Stevenage had become a retirement home for pensioned-off Dons. It was galling to see Paul Hodges and Jimmy Collins (Peter Shreeve was dropped by Stevenage) roll back the years and strut around Plough Lane's pastures in the manner of old. The match took on a symbolic air, Henley's old brigade versus Everitt's new. And Henley won.

As if that wasn't bad enough, Sutton United, Wimbledon's most famous amateur victims, despatched the Dons from the FA Cup. Once again, it was a case of old triumphing over new, for Sutton were coached by Roy Law, as true a Don as ever lived. The sight of Law leaping for joy on the touchline was a sharp reminder of better times. Once again the air was thick with dissent over having left the amateur world – where Wimbledon were giants – and joining the professionals, where time and again they were also-rans.

Dave Bassett and Roger Connell torment Chorley's Barrow after Wimbledon's equaliser in the FA Trophy Round 3, 1976-77.

A sign of how far the Dons had sunk in popular esteem came with Everitt's attempts to sign a striker. One name after another was canvassed, but all preferred to stay where they were or move elsewhere.

There was little else to report from the rest of the season. An encouraging win at Nuneaton in the FA Trophy, where Andy Marchant scored the Dons' only hat-trick of this low-scoring campaign, pitted Wimbledon against Bedford in Round 3. With the Dons having beaten their opponents twice in the league, they had every hope of reaching the quarter-finals. In the event, they lost 1-3.

In the league, mediocrity was writ large, even to the extent of finishing the season with a perfectly symmetrical record: P42, W14, D14, L14, F50, A50, Pts42. By occupying 12th position, Wimbledon finished below half-way for the first time. Lack of goals – 50 being the Dons' lowest in the Southern League – hardly encouraged more bodies through the turnstiles. So few came through in any case that it was a wonder the machinery was not all rusted up. Gerry O'Rourke was the latest old-boy to depart, signed by title-chasing Chelmsford a week after playing against them in April.

Mike Everitt had been brought in to invigorate the club in all aspects. He had had his year of grace, and despite statements from the board that his position was secure – indeed, he was even said to be signing an extension to his contract – he was clearly a manager under pressure. And then, in the blink of an eye, he quit.

DID YOU KNOW?

In 1972-73, to boost their application to join the Football League, Yeovil held a local song contest. It was won by a ditty with the catchy title 'Elect Yeovil'. It had innumerable verses and was sung to the tune of Smokey Blue. Presumably they are still singing it in Somerset.

Match of the Season

Wimbledon 2 Telford 1

Premier Division, 27th January 1973

So few grapes to select from in a season of drought. What recommends the match with Telford is that it came at a time of relative optimism. The Dons were still alive in the FA Trophy, and by winning five out of six in the league had dragged themselves up to the dizzy heights of 8th place. So excited were fans by the prospect that over 1,000 of them turned out for the match, a rarity in these troubled times.

Telford were old adversaries. They were previously known as Wellington FC. When the club reinvented itself as Telford, in 1969, they put the Indian sign on Wimbledon, who lost 0-4 twice in succession on their Shropshire travels. Now, in January 1973, Telford were riding high in the league, though they would tail away in the spring.

Telford enjoyed the services of an international goalkeeper. Bobby Irvine had picked up eight Northern Ireland caps in the early 1960s, playing alongside Danny Blanchflower, Billy Bingham, and Derek Dougan. Spearheading Telford's attack were Jack Bentley and Micky Fudge. The evergreen Bentley had been tormenting Southern League defences for nine seasons, topping Telford's scoring lists on each occasion. His team-mate, Fudge, would never live down his sensational debut for WBA, for whom he scored a hat-trick against Tottenham. Sadly, for him, he would only add two more goals in a dozen games for the Baggies.

Most of the drama in a match played in murky conditions came in the closing minutes. Wimbledon were hanging on to Ian Cooke's goal. Fudge levelled, but a comedy of errors in injury time cost Telford the points. Stewart Ross almost put through his own goal; Irvine somehow kept the ball out; but it fell to the predatory Cooke. The final whistle blew and the Dons were smiling. Briefly.

SOUTHERN LEAGUE PREMIER 1973-74

Premier Division	12th
Southern League Cup	3rd Round
FA Cup	1st Round
FA Trophy	1st Round

One would not think that Mike Everitt, with his questionable record, would be in much demand. Whatever the circumstances, the facts state he presided over the worst Dons side in memory.

As such he was thought unlikely to brush aside the claims of 35 other candidates for the managership of Brentford, newly relegated to Division 4. But he landed the job.

The new season was just days away. The subsequent upheaval at Plough Lane eventually saw a new chairman, Jack Beavan, installed as well as a new manager. Gossip insisted that Les Henley was to make a second coming, but the new man, when announced, was Dick Graham, former boss of Colchester United.

Like another of Colchester's managers – Mike Walker – Dick Graham was a goalkeeper in his playing days, guarding Crystal Palace's net in the years following World War II. As a manager, Graham was famous for one thing – Colchester's 3-2 defeat of Leeds in the FA Cup in 1971. When recruited by Wimbledon, he had been out of football for a year, but he had experience, contacts, and a hard-man reputation. Just the job, thought the directors.

He also had a supermarket business to attend to, which delayed his arrival until the season was a couple of games old. The embers of Mike Everitts's reign had registered one victory and one defeat when Graham supervised the players for the home fixture with Weymouth. The score – 5-2 – was the stuff of dreams. Two more quick wins at home elevated the team to 3rd. Was this the Messiah?

Among the new faces, Stan Brown and Joe Gadston had been signed by Everitt (Brown appointed captain). Malcolm Crosby, on loan from Aldershot, and Phil Bloss were added by Graham.

A home defeat by Chelmsford and a 3-3 draw with Guildford – a thriller in which versatile full-back Andy Marchant broke a leg and never really recovered – suggested the winter might be harder than the autumn. In fact, four months were to separate one home league win from the next. The Dons were expelled from the FA Cup by King's Lynn, a 1st Division side, in a match marred by mutinous behaviour by home 'supporters', and endured a marathon four match sequence with Wealdstone before squeezing through to Round 2 of the Southern League Cup.

FROM CHIEF SUPERINTENDENT CALVERT, NORFOLK JOINT POLICE

'It would be remiss of me to close without paying tribute to the attitude and conduct of the spectator supporters of your [Wimbledon] club. In my view their behaviour throughout was above criticism.'
After King's Lynn fans caused trouble during their 1-0 win in the FA Cup.

When Wealdstone exacted revenge in the FA Trophy, winning by the only goal at Plough Lane, Wimbledon's season was in shreds. Attendances fell through the floor. From an average of 2,894 in 1966-67, they were now down to three figures. A miners' strike and an unbowed Tory Government had reduced the country to a three-day working week. A ban on flood-lit evening matches encouraged many clubs to experiment with Sunday football for the first time. In Wimbledon's case, this did not mean a game on Sunday *instead* of Saturday, but as well as. The Dons returned from a goalless draw at Nuneaton to lose 0-2 to Grantham in a Southern League Cup replay before another sub-1,000 crowd.

The month of March would stand, not just as the nadir of 1974-75, but of Wimbledon's Southern League career. Maidstone began by winning 3-0 at Plough Lane. A week later Hillingdon, rooted to the foot of the league, came, saw, and conquered by the same score. An historic low of just 554 supporters watched the match.

These defeats stretched the patience of manager and directors to breaking point. Graham quit amid a flurry of allegations and counter-allegations. He had found the shift from full-time to part-time football more difficult than he had anticipated. He had also relinquished his supermarket business in order to take up full-time terms, only for these to be retracted a matter of days later.

New skipper John Loughlan and trainer Danny Keenan picked the team for the rest of the season, but enjoyed little early success. Struggling Hillingdon's first home win provided Boro with a priceless double. Against Grantham at Plough Lane, a penalty by winger Mick Mahon – Graham's Christmas present to the Dons – gave Wimbledon a first-minute lead. Grantham pulled back to win 3-1. The following week Ian Cooke put the Dons in front at title-chasing Kettering. But Kettering won 2-1. The run of defeats now stretched to five, the team could not win even when scoring first, and – worst of all – they were now just one point above the trap-door. Mid-table anonymity gave way to relegation panic.

Victory over Atherstone in the next match sparked a defiant sequence of one defeat in nine games, and the storm clouds passed. Wimbledon would live to fight another season in the Premier Division.

WIMBLEDON'S DARKEST HOUR

With 10 games to play, the Dons are one point above the relegation places.

		P	W	D	L	F	A	Pts
16	Folkestone	33	8	11	14	44	50	27
17	WIMBLEDON	32	9	9	14	37	45	27
18	Hillingdon	33	8	11	14	34	52	27
19	Tonbridge	33	7	12	14	29	42	26
20	Bedford	31	7	11	13	33	35	25
21	Margate	30	9	6	15	38	49	24
22	Worcester	29	6	9	14	37	51	21

Nevertheless, the Dons had for the first time lost more than they won. Worryingly, the final points tally had dropped for *seven* seasons in succession. What distinguished 1973-74 from previous campaigns was that, in the past, no matter how badly Wimbledon played away, they came up trumps at Plough Lane. Through good seasons and bad, Wimbledon's home record was daunting.

Until now. In 13 years of Southern League football, the Dons never lost more than four home matches a season. Everitt's teams, for all their deficiencies, lost just five times at Plough Lane in two years. In 1973-74, under Dick Graham, supporters endured eight home losses in the league, added to those inflicted by Grantham and Wealdstone in various cups. The goals-against column was a colossal 35. From October, just one visiting team failed to score. Wimbledon had never known dark days like these.

Here was a club in desperate straits, on and off the pitch. Player of the year Steve Langford emigrated to Australia, leaving behind just seven players under contract. The bank was banging on the door, demanding that the overdraft be cleared or the club folded.

DID YOU KNOW?

Squad numbers were not the invention of the FA Carling Premiership. Maidstone introduced them for their players in 1973.

Match of the Season

Wimbledon 3 Atherstone 2

Premier Division, 6th April 1974

Wimbledon did not score many goals in 1973-74, and those they did were clustered into a handful of matches. The 5-2 bonanza with Weymouth, in Graham's inaugural match, takes some beating. The

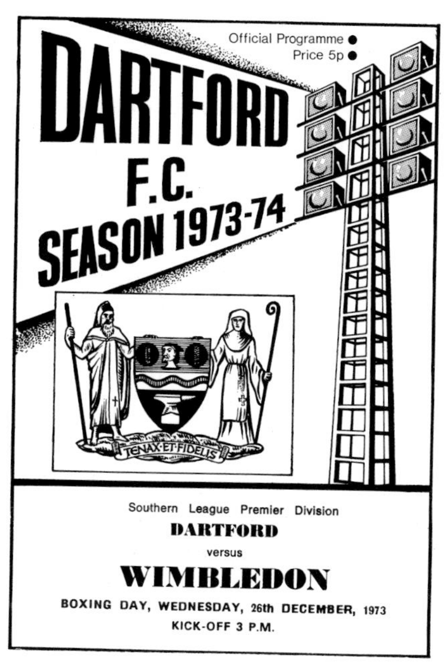

Dartford are heading for the championship, but they are held 1-1 by the Dons in this Christmas fixture.

2-2 home draw with Romford, the six goals shared with Guildford, these too offered rare thrills for Dons fans starved of excitement. A crowd of 2,385, Plough Lane's biggest for two and a half years, saw the Dons reach the FA Cup Round 1 with a 1-0 win over Maidstone.

But the match that weighed above all others was the home fixture with Atherstone. Five defeats on the trot had cost the Dons their manager, their confidence, and in all probability their inner belief that they could avoid the drop.

Atherstone Town, or the Adders, to give them their delightful nickname, were probably the least welcome side to have to play at that stage. Not because they were particularly good – they were anonymous in mid-table – but because they were new. They had only been admitted to the Southern League 1st Division North a year earlier, and had clinched promotion at the first attempt. Shades of Wimbledon *circa* 1964-65.

Atherstone thereby became the smallest town to be represented in the Premier Division – the Burnley of the Southern League. The Adders were performing well enough, playing with the careless abandon that disconcerts backs-to-the-wall opponents whose fingernails are down to the quick. Atherstone's matches had already surpassed a ton of goals, the most in the league, and goalkeepers at both ends were usually the busiest players on the pitch.

After a goalless first half at Plough Lane it took Atherstone just seconds after the interval to score, and send Wimbledon hearts diving into their stomachs. With each minute that ticked away the likelihood of a sixth successive Dons defeat increased. But then two new boys took a hand.

Jeff Bryant was still a babe, though he would stick around frustrating visiting forwards well into the Football League era. He had signed from Fulham and been pitched into Mile Everitt's final matches of the previous season.

In the summer it came to light that while on Fulham's books he had registered a false age when hoping to be selected for the England Youth Team. The authorities took a dim view and slapped a five-month ban on the player. Wimbledon felt hard done by: it was the club that was made to suffer. In this respect the ban would anticipate that later imposed on Vinnie Jones in the 'video scandal'. The Dons were punished, even though the 'offence' was committed when Jones was on Chelsea's books.

In any case, the length of the ban seemed inordinately harsh on a young player who had earned a first-team place on merit. He had returned to the side in January and would remain ever-present throughout the season. Now he sought to atone for past indiscretions, heading the equaliser. It was Bryant's first league goal at Plough Lane.

Atherstone returned the ball to the centre circle, kicked off and foolishly presented it to Mick Mahon. Mahon had been signed from Colchester in December. A veteran of the U's cup win over Leeds, he was formerly an England amateur international who now combined his wing-play for Wimbledon with teaching at a school near Colchester.

Mahon's greatest moment in a Wimbledon shirt would be delayed a season, but he was already something of a talisman for the Dons. He now uncorked a daisy-trimmer from 25 yards, and in the space of a minute Wimbledon went from 0-1 down to 2-1 up.

Had it ended there and then the match would have merited the tag match of the season. But Atherstone were not inclined to lay down their arms. A few minutes later they were back on terms. Wimbledon could not afford to drop even one point, and Mahon made sure they did not. He treated Plough Lane, and goalkeeper Johnson to an action replay of his first goal. Another long-range shot, another roar from the crowd, and Wimbledon had won 3-2.

The tide had turned, and when Mahon scored a hat-trick against high-flying Kettering, he pencilled in his name in the Wimbledon hall of fame.

BATSFORD'S BOYS 1974-77

SOUTHERN LEAGUE PREMIER 1974-75

Premier Division	Champions
Southern League Cup	Semi-Final
FA Cup	4th Round
FA Trophy	Quarter-Final

Dick Graham's removal in March allowed the directors the whole summer, if need be, to find a replacement. It is arguable that, but for the ill-starred experiments with Everitt and Graham, El Dorado may never have come to Plough Lane. These managers played an important part in the unfolding history of Wimbledon FC.

Graham's Achilles heel was his unfamiliarity with the part-time game. The board would not go down that road again. The curtain had barely fallen on 1973-74 when they announced that the new boss was to be Allen Batsford.

Batsford would be the first Wimbledon manager in modern times not to have plied his playing skills in the Football League. As a manager, too, he flourished in the twilight world of non-league soccer. He had made his mark as manager of Isthmian League Walton & Hersham – first, by masterminding victory in the 1973 FA Amateur Cup Final; second, outwitting Brian Clough's Brighton to the tune of 4-0 at the Goldstone Ground in an FA Cup replay.

Like Konrad Lorenz with his ducklings, Batsford blazed a trail wherein all and sundry followed. In his footsteps to Plough Lane marched half his Walton & Hersham cup-winners. Dave Bassett, Dave Donaldson, and Billy Edwards took the same direct route as the manager. Front-men Keiron Somers and Roger Connell had in the interim signed for Hendon. They, too, needed no second invitation to join forces again. The first match of the new season saw all five of them ensconced. Each would play a pivotal role in the triumphs to come.

Wimbledon fans at Nuneaton to support their team in that first match saw little to cheer. Dickie Guy gave away a penalty, Selwyn Rice was ordered off, and the assortment of Batsford's imports and Graham's left-overs seldom played with one mind. Not for nine years had the Dons lost their opening Southern League fixture.

With hindsight, Nuneaton were grateful to play the Dons when they did. It began against Yeovil on 20th August and ended at Cambridge City on 3rd December. 'It' being the longest run of successive victories Wimbledon had ever known and, let us be honest, are ever likely to know. In various competitions 22 scalps were taken, half of them in the Southern League.

One might think that with 22 points from 12 games the Dons would have a clear lead over the rest. In fact, they were not even top. Or second. With the team proving just as irresistible in the cups – which took precedence in the fixture list – numerous league engagements had to be postponed. And when a free Saturday did present itself, Romford took fright and called the match off. More than a month was lost in the autumn between one league game and the next. Once Wimbledon's cup-bubbles burst, lost ground could be made up. But of course, those bubbles never did burst, leading to the most jam-packed finalé the club would ever know.

Press speculation about George Best buying the club was almost forgotten in the mounting excitement that attended the team's FA Cup progress. The Dons had no pedigree in the competition, had never gone beyond Round 2, and therefore never been paired with top rank opposition. In those days, moreover, the Dons had to embark on four qualifying rounds, just to reach the 1st Round proper. And when in some Berkshire field a player called Adams put Bracknell ahead, four minutes into the first of those qualifying ties, Round 1 looked a long, long way off.

But the Dons survived. Guy kept his net intact thereafter, and – once Kettering had been seen off in Round 2, before the largest assembly at Plough Lane in 11 years – the promised land beckoned.

The adventures with Burnley and Leeds were fun. But they threatened to prove costly. The fixture backlog meant the Dons had to play 11 games in March and 12 in April – and even more if they reached the finals of the various cups still open to them.

In the space of three days Wimbledon were dumped from the FA Trophy (by Scarborough in the quarter-final) and from the Southern League Cup (by Kettering in the semis). All that was left was the London Senior Cup – from which they had earlier sought to pull out, to ease fixture congestion – and, of course, the championship.

Q	**Two former Dons have the same surname and the same initial. They played in the same position (central defence), and came from the same club, in the same season (1974-75). Who were they?**
A	**Gary Smith signed, and Graham Smith re-signed on loan, from Brentford.**

They claimed the London Senior Cup by beating Leatherhead 2-0, though the championship looked beyond them.

History is littered with fine teams forced to play too often, too soon, and falling by the wayside. Three Easter defeats (how often have the Dons lamented that festival in these pages?) – two of them at home – were followed by two away draws. Five games without a win, four in a row without a goal, and just eight games left.

Had any of the front-runners – Nuneaton, Yeovil, or Kettering – held their nerve, the pressure might have proved insurmountable. But each was prey to end of season jitters. The league table was in any case meaningless: at one stage the Dons had 10 games in hand. Supporters did not need reminding that Wimbledon were famous for falling on their faces in the spring, and had little reason to suppose Batsford could succeed where others had failed.

Nuneaton finished their programme before everyone else, setting a target of 54 points. In an extraordinary climax the Dons lost just one more game. The title was secured in the penultimate match, on 1st May, with a 1-1 draw at home to Telford.

The Dons had scaled peaks unimaginable when viewed from the trough of the previous summer. Strikers Connell and Somers – the bearded wonders, whom Kettering manager Geoff Vowden scathingly dismissed for not pulling their weight – netted more than their share, and helped rejuvenate Ian Cooke in the process. All three scored more than 20 goals, but it was Cooke, one of the old guard, the last survivor of Wimbledon's entry into the Southern League, who was voted player of the year.

Several opponents exceeded Wimbledon's tally of 63 league goals. Indeed, so had each of Les Henley's teams. The key to Batsford's success – other than the luxury of an injury-free season that enabled him to pick his favoured 11 from one match to the next – was encapsulated in the seven-game FA Cup run that saw not one goal conceded. Defence was paramount. The Dons yielded a miserly 33 goals in 42 league matches, the lowest in the division, and by a wide margin the lowest in Wimbledon's Southern League history.

The club had a shock in store when applying for membership of the Football League. They polled just four; Kettering, who finished fourth, polled 20 – confirmation that location counted for more than ability.

Match of the Season (1)

Burnley 0 Wimbledon 1

FA Cup, 3th Round, 4th January 1975

Although every small club dreams of catching a big fish in Round 3, there were only 22 top division teams, against 41 other names waiting to come out of the hat. Only a one-in-three chance.

Strange to say, the name 'Burnley' did not draw whoops of joy. They were too good to offer realistic chances of victory and too unglamorous for the tie to hog the limelight. The attendance was unlikely to make Wimbledon millionaires, and Lancashire was too far away for the Borough of Merton to migrate north for the day.

The passage of time distorts the relative standing of clubs. The 1980s and 90s have been hard on Burnley; the club would find themselves in Division 4 when Wimbledon were in Division 1. But in January 1975 Burnley were a handsome outfit, much admired within the game, shrewdly nursing young and selling ripe. In this respect, they were the Wimbledon of their time.

Jimmy Adamson's team were riding 7th, following a run of one defeat in nine games. Two months later they would climb to 2nd and challenge for the most open championship in years. Brian Flynn (only 19) and Leighton James (21) would earn innumerable caps for Wales. Ray Hankin (18) and Paul Fletcher (23) were strikers of no great height but plenty of promise. Full-back Keith Newton had played for England in the 1970 World Cup.

This, then, was the measure of Wimbledon's task as players and supporters clogged the motorways heading north. The records showed that not since Darlington in the 1920s had a non-league side beaten a 1st Division team away from home in the FA Cup.

Batsford was aware of the hazard presented by Leighton James on the wing, so he assigned Dave Bassett to, shall we say, quieten him, and also made sure James was confronted by two defenders whenever he had the ball. Half-time arrived with the game goalless. Four minutes after the interval Burnley keeper Alan Stevenson parried Ian Cooke's shot and Mick Mahon drove in the loose ball.

Adamson sent on a second winger to stretch the Dons' defence, but Dickie Guy saved expertly from Hankin and Fletcher and Wimbledon hung on to record a win that sent shock-waves around the country. Within an hour of the final whistle the draw was made for Round 4. There were 16 ties, but Dons players and supporters did not have long to fret. Team No 7 was 'Leeds United'. Gasps of 'yes, yes,' filled the seconds until the next words were read out – 'will play ... Wimbledon.'

The wives get in on the act during the Dons' super cup run: Back: Keenan, Somers, Guy, Edwards, Donaldson, Hall. Front: Batsford, Lucas, Cooke, Stockley, Aitken.

Match of the Season (2)

Leeds 0 Wimbledon 0

FA Cup, 4th Round, 25th January 1975

Leeds sounds a tougher obstacle than Burnley. It was not. In fact, this was the most vulnerable Leeds side in years. Though defending champions, they had lost manager Don Revie to the England job, recruited and sacked Brian Clough in the space of 44 days, and now asked new boss Jimmy Armfield to stabilise a wobbly ship that was top-heavy with ageing ballast. Harvey, Bremner, McQueen, Eddie Gray, Lorimer (Scotland), Reaney, Madeley, Clarke (England), Giles (Ireland) were the pick of Leeds' international crop.

Back in November Leeds stood 19th in the league and suffered a 0-3 defeat by 4th Division Chester in the League Cup. Armfield had begun to pull things round, but by January they were barely in the top half. With the league title, realistically, beyond recall, the FA Cup and European Cup were all Leeds had to play for.

Wimbledon's appeal for Yorkshire folk can be measured in the gate – 46,230 was Elland Road's largest of the season so far. This number included two train-loads of Dons fans. The multitude witnessed a cup-tie that is still talked about and argued over.

The Wombles greet Ian Cooke and Dickie Guy as they take the field at Elland Road for the FA Cup 4th Round tie with Leeds United.

As at Turf Moor, Wimbledon trotted out for the second half with the game still goalless. Though the ball was in Leeds' possession for long stretches, chances were few and the Dons looked secure.

Wimbledon were eight minutes from a sensational draw when Bassett clattered Eddie Gray and Leeds had a penalty. Lorimer aimed low to Guy's right, the keeper was down in a flash, and the ball flew back into play. The Dons had been reprieved. News of the 0-0 draw created bigger waves than did the win at Burnley, and film clips of the penalty were networked around the country. The Dons would later reflect on having equalled the record of seven consecutive FA Cup-ties without conceding a goal.

The replay was scheduled for Plough Lane on the Tuesday. Tickets were gobbled up within 90 minutes of going on sale, and touts created anger and confusion by distributing forgeries. Fear of the consequences, together with a rain-sodden pitch, invited a late cancellation.

'Mr Bob Lord, a member of the Football League Management Committee, is visiting the ground on Tuesday. The Club is anxious that he should receive the right impression. Volunteers are required to sweep the stands, terraces, etc. PLEASE BRING YOUR OWN BROOMS.'
Note from the match programme with Dagenham, 15th March 1975.

The FA Cup replay at Selhurst Park. Leeds' keeper David Harvey is pressured in his goalmouth. (10th February 1975)

The tie was switched to Selhurst Park, and attracted an enormous crowd in excess of 45,000, by far the largest ever to have attended a 'home' Wimbledon fixture. Lady Luck deserted the Dons. Johnny Giles' harmless shot was going nowhere until it struck Bassett and wrong-footed Guy.

There was praise galore for the mighty Dons, but some criticism too. Batsford appeared to have little thought to attack Leeds, and sent out a side instructed to defend in depth. Other than for the first few minutes, Wimbledon seldom crossed the halfway line in any numbers. It was a predictable moan with a predictable answer – Batsford had players equipped to defend but not to score.

Leeds would be eliminated in the quarter-finals, after three replays, by Ipswich Town, but would progress to the Final of the European Cup, where their hopes were cruelly dashed by Bayern Munich.

'What can I possibly say about Wimbledon? They must surely be the best advertisement non-league football has ever had . . . To play four tough Southern League matches per week and keep picking up enough points must be the finest performance of all.'
Atherstone v Wimbledon match programme, 2nd May 1975.

SOUTHERN LEAGUE PREMIER 1975-76

Premier Division	Champions
Southern League Cup	Winners
FA Cup	2nd Round
FA Trophy	2nd Round

They say it is harder to keep your crown than to win it in the first place. Batsford strengthened his squad with the signings of full-back Henry Falconer and striker Billy Holmes.

The first months of 1975-76 were a replica of the previous season. The Dons reeled off win after win. By early October this run had stretched to eight in the league, plus home and away victories over Hillingdon in the Southern League Cup. They had also beaten Kettering (1-0) in the annual fixture between the champions and the cup-winners – a sort of Charity Shield for the Southern League. The one reverse (0-1) had come at Wigan in the first leg of the challenge between the Southern and Northern Premier League champions. Come November, the Dons won 2-1 on aggregate after extra-time.

The Dons enjoyed one crucial advantage this season. Spared the first three FA Cup qualifying rounds, they did not fall foul of league postponements. Consequently, they led the table from the start.

One key member of the side had departed. Although full-back Bob Stockley had earned rave reviews, Batsford was unconvinced. As Stockley had a suspension carried over, and was ineligible for the first game, Batsford had gone for a permanent replacement rather than a stand-in. Unwilling to rot in the reserves, Stockley signed for Atherstone, the Dons' next opponents.

Stockley had a useful debut, snuffing out Mick Mahon, scoring – but having the effort disallowed – and contributing greatly to the Dons' 1-2 reverse. They lost their next match, too, against Bath, who arrived at Plough Lane winless and bottom of the table.

It was not long before Batsford lost two more key players, this time to injury. Keiron Somers' partnership with Roger Connell had been a corner-stone of the team's success. But the duo were not to everyone's taste. Connell, in any case, had been sidelined with hepatitis. Batsford widened his options by signing Billy Holmes from Barnet, preferring to play all three forwards when possible.

'Half an hour before the match (v Kettering on 20th September 1975) Micky Mahon was quietly sitting in the dressing room reading his favourite literature – science fiction.'
Match programme with Telford, 27th September 1975.

The formula succeeded until Somers suffered cartilage trouble. He was out for months and returned for just the occasional match, mostly as substitute. By March, Mick Mahon's troubled knee could stand the strain no longer, and another icon of the Batsford miracle was consigned to wondrous memory. In Mahon's case an able replacement was at hand. John Leslie filled his boots, his position, and acquired a reputation to match. Leslie would score the season's only hat-trick, a foursome in fact, in the 6-0 win at Stourbridge.

Inevitably, Wimbledon fancied themselves in the FA Cup. A 6-1 mauling of Kingstonian set up an appetising 1st Round tie at Nuneaton, who once again had emerged as the Dons' principal title challengers. Coincidentally, Nuneaton had established a club record of 18 unbeaten games, and held a party, of sorts, before kick-off to celebrate. This was asking for trouble, and Wimbledon ran out 1-0 winners. The result pitted them against 4th Division Brentford in Round 2. The Dons lost 0-2, and 10 days later Isthmian Leaguers Enfield despatched them from the London Senior Cup after a replay.

A January hiccup dropped Wimbledon down to 5th in the league. Their last serious cup reverse came early in February, when Dagenham, at the second attempt, proved too strong in the FA Trophy. It was a humiliating loss, but was overshadowed by the glare of victories elsewhere.

Wimbledon were still in contention for the league and the Southern League Cup double, and this time they were not to be denied. Yeovil were beaten 2-1 in the two-leg Final, following which the Dons stormed to the title, crossing the finishing line with two matches to spare. The first of these, against Wealdstone at Plough Lane, saw six players expelled. Just think, Wimbledon were celebrating the championship. Goodness knows what might have happened had they needed points to secure it.

Batsford's recipe second-time round showed a modified formula. Goals were up by spreading the responsibility. No player managed 20 overall, and Ian Cooke failed to make double figures in the league for the first time in his Wimbledon career. 13 Dons chipped in with goals, the hallmark of a successful side. No team beat the Dons twice, and never did Wimbledon lose once they were ahead.

DID YOU KNOW?

Wimbledon set one unenviable record in 1975-76. Their match with Wealdstone in April resulted in SIX players being sent off – a Southern League record; three of whom were Dons – a club record. The players were dismissed two by two at regular intervals, like Come Dancing.

With the defence even meaner, and with five more points earned than in 1974-75, the team were improving still. These were powerful arguments to put before the Football League. When Cambridge United posted successive championships, plus a Southern League Cup, they had been voted on board. Wimbledon now matched Cambridge's achievement, but did not fare so well. The voting figures for the fourth and final vacancy read: Workington 21 votes, Yeovil 18, Kettering 14, Wimbledon 3. The Dons were one vote down on the previous year. But these figures carried a message. Yeovil were within three votes of supplanting Workington. Had Yeovil acquired them, Workington would have been out and could not offer themselves as sacrificial victims 12 months hence. But for Yeovil's failure, Wimbledon might still be in the Southern League.

Match of the Season (1)

Wimbledon 0 Brentford 2

FA Cup, 2nd Round, 13th December 1975

The Wealdstone match would qualify for any black-list. The 3-3 draw at Kettering on New Year's Day, against player-manager Derek Dougan's ambitious team, had enough incident – of the right kind – to demand nomination. The FA Cup win at Manor Park, wrecking Nuneaton's record-breaking celebrations, leaves a smile.

We shall focus first on Brentford in the FA Cup. The ties between the clubs were extensive, on the playing side and the managerial. In 1971 John O'Mara had gone to Griffin Park, and been sold on to Blackburn Rovers for a fat profit. Batsford had brought Gary and Graham Smith from Griffin Park, and goalkeeper Paul Priddy, too, as understudy to Dickie Guy. Priddy had since returned to the Bees and would play against the Dons. Manager Mike Everitt however, had moved on. The club had not revived under his stewardship, and John Docherty was now at the helm.

Brentford were in the nether reaches of Division 4. Their leading scorers were Roger Cross, who at one time or other would play for half the teams in London, and Terry Johnson, a lively winger signed from Southend, but who had just been sent off at Rochdale. Brentford had failed to score only twice all season, but away from home they looked vulnerable, having lost their last seven.

The Dons weren't in the best nick themselves. They hadn't won in the league for five weeks. Notwithstanding, it would be no great upset if Brentford were sent packing. In the light of the previous year's heroics, Wimbledon were expected to dispose of their neighbours without ado.

Such is the price of high expectations. Plough Lane's biggest gate for eight years – 8,395 – saw Brentford turn the form-book upside down. After a quarter of an hour Guy was heard to call 'leave it'. But the ball eluded him and Johnson punished the mistake.

Worse was to follow. Aitken fouled Sweetzer in the box, and, though Guy got a finger-tip to the penalty, Brentford led 2-0.

Wimbledon piled men forward in the second half. Mahon hit a post, Priddy stood firm, and Allen Batsford got so worked up he was cautioned by referee Nippard. But the damage had been done.

Match of the Season (2)

Wimbledon 2 Yeovil 1

Southern League Cup Final, 2nd Leg, 10th April 1976

Wimbledon's march to their second Southern League Cup extended over six months and required 11 matches – a quarter of a season.

Yeovil have long been among the leading lights of non-league football, famous for their then sloping pitch and for their periodic giant-killing exploits in the FA Cup – the one no doubt contributing to the other.

There was a natural edge to matches between Wimbledon and Yeovil, partly because they were often competing for the same prizes, partly because each considered the other among the more physical and ungracious of opponents. Admiration was mutual and grudging. Having at one stage led the 1974-75 title challenge, Yeovil had gone off the boil in 1975-76, though a late sally would carry them into second place. The Final, then, was fought by the best two sides in the league. Yeovil were going for a record fifth Southern League Cup triumph.

As the first leg had ended all square, the second was transformed into a one-off Final which disadvantaged Yeovil only theoretically. Manager Stan Harland crowed about his side's fine away record, especially against the leading sides, and which included a goalless draw at Plough Lane in January. In forward Dick Plumb, now in his second spell with the club, Yeovil had just the man to 'nick one' and steal the Cup.

An own-goal, however, undid all Yeovil's calculations. Frank McMahon's header went astray, and when Ian Cooke added a second goal on the hour the destiny of the cup looked settled. In a frantic climax Ken Brown twice missed horribly for Yeovil. Had either of his chances gone in, Plumb's last minute goal would have been more than mere consolation.

SOUTHERN LEAGUE PREMIER 1976-77

Premier Division	Champions
Southern League Cup	2nd Round
FA Cup	3rd Round
FA Trophy	3rd Round

On the pitch, all was glory; off it, all was pain. The club was broke. Before 1976-77 got under way an outsider was brought in to do the sums. Ron Noades, former chairman of Southall, set himself two objectives: to prune the playing staff (four players departed, including Keiron Somers to Slough); and to galvanise efforts to gain entry to the Football League. These efforts were hindered by the departure of Brian Hall – team coach and Batsford's right-hand man – also to Slough. Hall's had been a keen contribution to two titles.

Whether or not by coincidence, Batsford's players started poorly, failing to score in their three opening Southern League fixtures. A season's best win– 5-1 over Wealdstone – set up five victories that lifted the team into more familiar regions. But they won just one of their next five and were dragged back into mid-table.

It was now late November, and unless checked this inconsistency would wreck hopes of a third title. Barnet had already dashed the Dons' hopes of retaining the Southern League Cup, and Northern Premier champions Runcorn had earned a 1-0 first-leg advantage in the annual challenge. Both these defeats had been at Plough Lane.

Indiscipline was another factor. Suspensions carried over from the previous season meant *six* players were barred from starting the new one, at Romford, where *five* Dons made their competitive debuts. But old habits die hard. Billy Holmes was sent off with the Romford game barely underway. Then, at Maidstone, Dave Bassett and Selwyn Rice were both dismissed. Sure, other teams rolled up their sleeves when facing the mighty Dons, but Batsford's boys were not shrinking violets either.

Happier times soon returned. The deficit against Runcorn was overturned in the away leg, allowing Wimbledon to retain the non-league champions' cup. In the FA Cup the Dons were exempt from all qualifying rounds. In Round 1, against Woking, Dickie Guy celebrated his 500th first-team appearance with a clean sheet. The winners of the 2nd Round match with Leatherhead looked forward to a home tie with Jack Charlton's Middlesbrough. The Dons won the local skirmish, then took Boro to a replay.

More importantly, the Dons had rediscovered their touch in the league. Ricky Marlowe had signed on a free transfer from Brighton,

Wimbledon celebrate a hat-trick of Southern League championships.

and his critical goals, such as the injury-time winner against Gravesend, helped lift the team inexorably upwards.

The last two thirds of the season enticed record-breaking form, the one serious setback being against Chorley in the FA Trophy. Wimbledon fell in the second replay, but Chorley's Steve Galliers impressed so much that he would soon be on his way to Plough Lane.

In the league, Wimbledon were irresistible, losing just once in 25 games, at Dartford. That aside, the Dons stayed unbeaten from 27th November till season's end. They hit top spot on 26th March, whereupon home wins over chief rivals Kettering and Minehead ensured they could not be caught. Wimbledon were Southern League champions for the third season in a row, equalling Merthyr Tydfil's record set in the 1950s. For good measure the Dons also won back the London Senior Cup.

Wimbledon accumulated 63 points, which number not only exceeded the total of the two previous seasons, but was also the most of any champions since the Dons joined the Southern League.

DID YOU KNOW?

Dave Bassett's first appointment as captain provoked angry letters to the press, protesting about promoting Wimbledon's 'worst disciplined player'.

DID YOU KNOW?

A poll to determine which Southern League club had the best match programme voted as follows: 1st Dartford, 2nd Kettering, 3rd Burton Albion.

The goals-against column – 22 – was the meanest the Southern League had known in that period, and was the lowest total ever registered by any champion team.

These were redoubtable figures. Guy, of course, was a fixture in goal, as were the back four protecting him. The defence was also buttressed by Dave Bassett and skipper Glen Aitken in midfield. This was just as well, for at times the goalscoring department spluttered. Keiron Somers and Mick Mahon had already gone. Ian Cooke played rarely and scored yet more rarely, Billy Holmes was productive more for his energy than for his goals, while John Leslie – like Cooke – missed much of the season through injury. All this increased the burden on Roger Connell, the only Don to reach double figures in the league, and topping the scoring charts for the third season in succession.

It says something about the sense of priorities at Plough Lane that the player of the year award went to Billy Edwards. This was the sixth year the poll had operated, and all but once a defender had won it. Midfielder Ian Cooke was the only exception, and no forward had so far topped the voting.

They say that good teams are built from the back, and to that extent Wimbledon were proving to be very good indeed. This did not mean they could be called exciting. Functional was the more appropriate adjective, especially away from home, while at Plough Lane it often took limitless patience to break down the defensive barricades of visiting sides. Entertainment, as widely understood, ranked low in the minds of managers and coaches, at Wimbledon and elsewhere. But, then again, what could be more entertaining than winning?

Besides, all the indicators suggested that the Dons had not yet peaked. All of a sudden the Southern League environment seemed constricting; the urge to burst up into the Football League was stronger than ever.

DID YOU KNOW?

England World Cup heroes Jimmy Greaves (Chelmsford) and Geoff Hurst (Telford) played against the Dons in consecutive games in April 1977. In Telford's return match in May Hurst scored – the only World Cup winner ever to score against Wimbledon.

DID YOU KNOW?

The Dons played a total of five FA Cup-ties against Division 1 opposition, and conceded just two goals - and own-goal and a penalty.

Match of the Season (1)

Wimbledon 0 Middlesbrough 0

FA Cup, 3rd Round, 8th January 1977

The tie with Middlesbrough provided another opportunity to convince the powers that be that Wimbledon were good enough. On the pitch they did so; off it, they shot themselves in the foot. For an aspiring League club, the attendance was wretchedly small. Wimbledon blamed apathy on Teesside; Middlesbrough blamed high ticket prices, while neutrals blamed the stultifying football preached by Jack Charlton.

Boro were treading water in Division 1. Like all sides managed by Big Jack, direct tactics was the strategy, keeping goals out the aim. Boro saw nothing amiss with passing back to the goalkeeper from the halfway line, and would employ this tactic to advantage at Plough Lane. Graeme Souness, soon on his way to Liverpool, brought steel to a Boro side already well-endowed with that commodity. One winced at the prospect of he and Bassett in ballistic collision.

The portents were for a scrappy game. It was no less grim in actuality, not helped by an unnatural 2 pm kick-off (Boro refusing to play under Plough Lane's floodlights) or by a dreadful pitch that had frozen in muddy lumps and only just thawed. Charlton, half-serious, reckoned it had been doctored.

The less said about the 90 minutes the better. This was match of the season only on paper, though the result looks mighty impressive for the Dons.

The pitch was white with snow for the Ayresome Park replay, which nevertheless enticed a crowd of nearly 23,000. After buffeting the Dons for 50 minutes, the home side won the tie with a penalty, earned and taken by David Armstrong, after he was tumbled by full-back Kevin Tilley. This time Dickie Guy had no answer.

Match of the Season (2)

Wimbledon 2 Kettering 0

Premier Division, 25th April 1977

In their early seasons in the Southern League Wimbledon were several times favoured with title-winning opportunities late in the season at Plough Lane. They blew them all. Now came another.

Kettering manager Derek Dougan was a larger-than-life figure, articulate, and a polished centre-forward with Northern Ireland and Wolves, the club with whom he is inextricably associated, even though he did not move to Molyneux until he was 29 years old.

Dougan had moved to Kettering initially as player-manager, figuring prominently in a titanic 3-3 duel with the Dons in 1975-76. With his high profile, Dougan was seen as just the man to take hugely ambitious Kettering into the Football League. To achieve their goal they had threatened to break ranks with the Southern League, who judged that multiple applications spread the votes too thinly, and that chances were improved if focused on the champions alone. So fearful were Kettering that they might miss the boat that there was ill-judged talk that – should they be denied the championship – they were prepared to withdraw from the Southern League to further their ends. This never happened, but it illustrates the weight of destiny that hung over this crucial match.

Coincidentally, England cricket captain Tony Greig had recently joined the Wimbledon board of directors. Kettering were two points behind the Dons, both teams having seven games to play. A defeat for Kettering would leave them little time to claw back the points.

Matches against the Poppies greatly favoured the home side. Wimbledon had never won at Kettering in nine attempts, but had won seven out of eight at Plough Lane. Though Dougan was not playing, he could call upon expensive signing Roy Clayton to score goals, and youthful midfielder Billy Kellock to provide them. Kellock already had Football League experience, and would see much more with the likes of Peterborough and Southend.

The import of the match was not lost on Dons fans – the crowd was the largest in the league for eight years. Kettering were under the cosh from the first whistle. When John Leslie headed Wimbledon in front shortly before half-time he raced over to gesture to Kettering supporters. The most charitable explanation was that he soothsayed the final score – 2-0, though on-field acts interpreted as provocative have subsequently been outlawed.

Jeff Bryant's late goal sealed Kettering's demise, if it did not yet secure Wimbledon's crown.

THE YO-YO YEARS 1977-1982

LEAGUE DIVISION 4 1977-78

Division 4	13th
League Cup	2nd Round
FA Cup	1st Round

Tension in the summer reached fever pitch for all concerned with Wimbledon FC. In previous election campaigns London clubs found fewer allies than the likes of Kettering, Hereford, and Cambridge United. Football was about demography, it seemed, not about footballers. Civil liberties groups and other anti-discrimination campaigners might have had something to say about that had they lent an ear. In Wimbledon's case, the playing field did not appear to be level. Nor was it in Yeovil's, of course, but here we are talking about a different kind of playing field.

But this time Wimbledon held several aces. The first stemmed from a change of policy on the part of the Southern League, which now stipulated that the champions alone be put forward, provided their stadium facilities were up to scratch.

The advantage to the Dons was obvious. No longer did they have to compete with Yeovil and Kettering, against whom in the past they had been overshadowed. Wimbledon would compete directly against Division 4's dribs and drabs.

Or so they thought. For a while it seemed that Wimbledon would carry the torch of non-league football. But late in the day the Northern Premier champions, Altrincham, threw their hat into the ring. Their ground was thought to be deficient, but the prospect of having the field laid bare of Kettering and Yeovil – and with only Wimbledon's customary flimsy challenge to overcome – proved too tempting for the Cheshire club to pass up.

This was not necessarily bad news. The threat posed by an extra challenger was offset by the probability that Altrincham would split the Northern vote. Each vote for Altrincham would mean one vote less for Southport and Workington.

The second ace was Ron Noades, who mounted a vast publicity campaign that reached the eyes and ears of everyone who mattered.

The third ace was the players themselves. The team's sheer strength, their high profile following their FA Cup exploits, could no longer be dismissed on the grounds of their London postmark.

Recent seasons had been kind to Division 4 newcomers. Cambridge United and Hereford had won early promotion to higher divisions. They had been assisted in their entry qualifications by the endemic weakness of half a dozen poorly attended, poorly equipped league clubs, all in the north of England. Bradford Park Avenue and Barrow had already lost the battle for Football League survival, and others were sure to follow.

But this raised another point. With two southern clubs replacing two northern ones, was it proper that the exercise be pursued a third time? To do so meant a further erosion of northern soccer. Many doubted whether it was in the wider interests of the game that this should happen. In short, demographic factors brought a smile to Altrincham while hindering Wimbledon at every turn – first, by being from London, second, by being from the south. Thatcherite considerations would have swept these objections aside; the principle of the survival of the fittest would have overridden all others. But these were Labour times, when props and subsidies to deprived regions was political orthodoxy.

Those seeking re-election were Halifax, Hartlepool, Southport, and Workington. All were regular visitors to the re-election committee. The plight of Workington, in particular, seemed desperate. Bottom in 1977, they had been bottom in 1976, too, and next to bottom in the two seasons before that. They struggled to survive on a wing and a prayer. Wimbledon trained their guns on the broken and chipped terracing of Workington's Borough Park.

London's Café Royal is associated more with the likes of Oscar Wilde and the capital's literati than with the rough and tumble of football. Yet it was in these bohemian surroundings that on 17th June, 1977 the delegates assembled. They numbered 48, one from each 1st and 2nd division club, plus four to represent the 3rd and 4th divisions. Each delegate had four votes.

Lord Westwood announced the figures: 'Altrincham 12 votes' (not nearly enough for Altrincham, but which clubs had lost those votes?); 'Halifax 44, Hartlepool 43, Southport 37' (all three were safe, as expected). Now it was down to the last two. 'Workington

21'. A stifled groan from the Wimbledon contingent; Workington had received 21 the previous year and survived. 'Wimbledon 27!'

The Dons had done it. But had they been admitted on their merits or Workington's liabilities? The fact that Southport, who finished 23rd in 1976 and 1977 got 37 votes, 10 more than the Dons, points to the latter. If nothing else, Wimbledon got their timing right, pouncing when Workington were stripped of credibility.

What of the thoughts of players and supporters as they geared themselves for the challenges ahead? Pessimists thought the team would be lucky to survive a season or two; others insisted the team could dip their toes into a higher division, as Cambridge United and Hereford had done. A few scatter-brains, heads in the clouds, doubtless dreamed of Wembley, or facing Arsenal, Liverpool, and Manchester United in Division 1.

Wimbledon were the first part-time club to be admitted to the Football League. Batsford's immediate task was to strengthen the side within these constraints. With training still restricted to afternoons and evenings, Batsford was able to retain the services of most of his players – the only significant departures being Ricky Marlowe, Leo Markham, and on the eve of the new season, long-serving Ian Cooke. The rest were happy to try their luck, along with whoever Batsford brought in. Steve Galliers arrived from Chorley for £1,500, and hung around long enough to sample life in Division 1 nine years later. Dave Galvin came from Gillingham, Geoff Davies was formerly with San José Earthquakes, and Willie Smith with Leatherhead. All were free transfers. More names would be added in the months ahead.

First opponents in the League Cup were 3rd Division Gillingham, whose three-pronged attack of Ken Price, Danny Westwood, and Republic of Ireland international Damien Richardson had between them bagged over 150 goals for the club. Westwood gave the Gills a half-time lead at Priestfield Stadium, but a late header from Billy Holmes squared the tie, and in the second leg the Gills were swept away. Wimbledon had come through their first test.

Now for Halifax in the league. The Shaymen had spent recent seasons in the 3rd Division and only slipped back down in 1976. Nevertheless, the fixture computer was kind. Halifax had just staved off re-election, and Wimbledon could wish for no better opportunity to claim their first victims.

DID YOU KNOW?

Wimbledon were so hard up when they entered the Football League that they begged supporters to collect and donate halfpennies.

Phil Summerill scores at Reading in the 2-2 draw. (1st October 1977)

A gate of 4,616, fuelled by curiosity and a sense of occasion, witnessed six goals, five of them in a helter-skelter second half that saw Wimbledon take the lead with four minutes to play, then squander it seconds later. An early contender for match of the season, surely. Not according to the managers. 'Disgraceful,' raged Batsford of his team's performance. 'They won't set Division 4 alight,' scoffed Halifax's manager, Alan Ball Senior.

Had we known, Halifax were simply warming up. They were destined to become treble-chance champions that season, drawing 21 times.

Fears that rough waters lay in store intensified at Brentford, where the Dons were sunk 1-4. Seven goals conceded in the space of 48 hours was seven too many for Allen Batsford, who dropped three players. One was Dickie Guy, probably the one player whose public profile was larger than that of his club. He was now in his 10th season, and had not missed a league game since 1968.

In the minds of many supporters he was a scapegoat. Richard Teale, signed as cover from Fulham a few days earlier, was thrown into goal, knowing that to supporters he was usurping the place of their hero. This was no way to build his confidence or theirs. Teale's tenure lasted 16 games in league and cup, by which time he had plucked the ball out of his net 28 times. He was in the side that

Roger Connell opens the scoring against Bournemouth. (11th March 1978)

claimed a belated first victory, against Northampton, but endured more bad games than good. Something had to give. Batsford restored Guy, and Richard Teale never played league football again.

The Dons' poor form was puzzling, for they were basically the same unit that had swept all before them in the Southern League. Some fans questioned the wisdom of joining Division 4. Better a big fish in a small pond than a minnow in the ocean. Much the same anguish had attended the first seasons in the Southern League, when the nostalgic harped back to the glory days of old.

Guy returned to a team languishing in the bottom four. Paul Denny and Phil Summerill were also introduced, but results did not pick up. Humiliated in the 1st Round of the FA Cup by Isthmian Leaguers Enfield, Wimbledon entered the New Year with a 0-3 mauling at Swansea, who became the fifth team in a row to score three against the Dons. Confidence drained away as through an open tap. Allen Batsford resigned.

DID YOU KNOW?

Allen Batsford was not the only casualty of the defeat at Swansea. On the way to the match the players' coach stopped at a service station. When it departed it left Dave Galvin behind. He missed the match.

A personality clash with chairman Ron Noades was held to blame. Managerial disputes with football club chairmen take predictable lines – the one demanding instant success, the other demanding time, money, and non-interference from above. The present case was no different, whatever the minutiae.

Into Batsford's shoes stepped his assistant, Dario Gradi, once booted out by Chelsea, but who in the close season had been recruited from his number two position at Derby County. Gradi shared with his predecessor the coincidence of never having played League football. He, in turn, named the club's combative 33-year-old skipper, Dave Bassett, as his deputy. Bassett, too, except for the past few months, had no practical experience of League soccer.

Gradi took stock. One thing was obvious. His part-time players were not fit enough, and unless something radical was done the club would endure the red faces of seeking to retain the League place so painstakingly won. The fitness question had been partially addressed in the autumn, when Allen Batsford had gone full-time himself. Gradi now shook off the last vestiges of part-timerism.

The new boss also needed to impose his authority on disgruntled players unaccustomed to losing. When Dickie Guy – who had kept just one clean sheet in 11 matches since his recall – arrived late for the home fixture with Scunthorpe, Gradi turned a deaf ear to the goalkeeper's excuses and pitched in Ray Goddard, a £4,500 signing from London rivals Millwall. Goddard had been around a long time. He had played almost 300 league matches for Leyton Orient and 80 for the Lions, but had lost his place at the Den to young Nicky Johns, later to spend many seasons with Charlton.

But Goddard was not the only surprise Gradi was to spring. He had that same month introduced Alan Cork, who had failed to impress at Derby County. Cork was only 18, but Phil Summerill had not scored in 12 games, and apart from a handful of appearances the following season his Plough Lane days were over.

It is almost anticlimactic to report that the Scunthorpe match was a bore-draw. But the clean sheet did wonders for morale. Goddard would be beaten just once in his first five games, and against all expectations Dickie Guy was consigned to memory.

It mattered not that young Corkie failed to find the net until his sixth outing. Gradi had simultaneously restored the No 9 shirt to transfer-listed Roger Connell, top scorer in each of Wimbledon's Southern League championship seasons. Connell responded by banging in 11 goals in 18 matches to top the scoring charts yet again. His goals compensated for Cork finding his feet alongside, and with Goddard doing his stuff at the other end, and newcomer Les Briley (signed for a club record £16,000 fee from Hereford) buzzing in midfield, Wimbledon steadily pulled clear of danger. Five goals were smashed past Rochdale (at home) and Southport (away), and only defeat at Barnsley in their last match robbed the Dons of an improbable place in the top half of the table. Gradi had made his mark.

So had Dave Donaldson. At 35, Donaldson was the oldest player to make his debut in the Football League. 'Mr Cool' did not disappoint, being the clear choice of supporters' player of the year.

DID YOU KNOW?

Only three Dons who opened 1977-78 against Halifax concluded it against Barnsley. These were Dave Galvin, Roger Connell, and John Leslie.

Match of the Season

Tottenham 4 Wimbledon 0

League Cup, 2nd Round, 31st August 1977

Mighty Tottenham were in the not-so-mighty 2nd Division when they entertained Wimbledon in this all-London cup-tie. Manager Keith Burkenshaw was destined to take Spurs back up at the first attempt, helped by a core of fine players on his books. Steve Perryman, plus England internationals Glenn Hoddle and Peter Taylor, all took the field against Wimbledon, as did stalwarts John Pratt, Terry Naylor, Neil McNab, and John Duncan. It was not till the following season that the Argentine duo, Osvaldo Ardiles and Ricardo Villa, descended on north London.

More's the pity, for their inclusion would surely have swelled the 23,000 attendance.

Wimbledon, in late August, were down in the dumps, still seeking their first league win and their first clean sheet. Dickie Guy had just lost his place in goal to Richard Teale. What wouldn't the bearded crusader have given for the chance to defy Spurs as he had once defied Burnley, Leeds, and Middlesbrough?

The result was to be no fairy tale. Two headers by Spurs' free-scoring Scottish centre-forward, John Duncan, midway through the first half, gave the home side a margin Wimbledon seldom looked like closing. Had the result stayed as it was they might have trooped off at the end with heads held high. But two more goals within a minute near the end soured the mood. Duncan completed his hat-trick with yet another header, whereupon centre-half Keith Osgood fired in from the penalty spot.

LEAGUE DIVISION 4 1978-79

Division 4	3rd (Promoted)
League Cup	2nd Round
FA Cup	3rd Round

So much for Wimbledon's probationary season. 'Fair,' would read any headmaster's end-of-year report. 'Could do better.' This time round, no excuses would be found in novelty. Results were all.

Gradi's team had latterly shown promotion form, and no major signings were made in the summer. The only change was to the kit: Wimbledon now turned out in yellow shirts and blue shorts. Apart from a drastic setback at Everton in the League Cup, the team swept through the early months without the smell of defeat. Subsequent losses at Huddersfield and Barnsley only briefly dislodged the Dons from the No 1 spot.

The first major test came on Boxing Day with the visit of once-proud Portsmouth. A combination of Bank Holiday and prestigious opposition pulled in nearly 8,000 spectators. Sadly, a 2-1 interval lead was overturned by three Pompey goals. The next fixture was an FA Cup 3rd Round tie with Southampton. The Dons lost 0-2. Arctic weather delayed resumption of league commitments for a month. The next four games harvested maximum points and goals in abundance. In front of their own despairing fans Torquay were hit for six (four goals to Cork), a total never subsequently exceeded by any Dons side in a league match.

Then, without warning, the goals evaporated. Having plundered 14 in four matches, Cork and Co failed to find any in the next four. Defeat at bottom-placed Halifax marked Wimbledon's fifth loss in seven, and the team slipped out of the promotion frame.

Rather than bolster an ailing attack, Gradi sought to shore up his defence. It was time to buy. With the transfer deadline looming Gradi paid £45,000 for QPR's Tommy Cunningham. Still in his early 20s, Cunningham was rich in 1st Division experience, but the arrival at Loftus Road of the hugely promising Glenn Roeder from Leyton Orient shut the door on his prospects. Gradi's partnership of Cunningham alongside Paul Bowgett – snapped up from Spurs' reserves – proved to be a Gradi masterstroke. The ship settled and Cork and Leslie rediscovered their scoring touch. Bournemouth went for four, Torquay for five (to add to the six at Plainmoor). Promotion to Division 3 was all but guaranteed at York, with Cork's hooked winner. He ended his first full season with 25 goals in all competitions. The spies were out in force.

PEARLS OF WISDOM

'So, supporters, no derisory remarks. Remember, if the lads were any better than they are, they would be with First Division sides.'
Ken Chaplin, writing in the club handbook 1978-79

The Dons' total of 78 league goals outdid those of London rivals and was rewarded by celebratory bubbly from the *Evening News*.

Other than at Everton, there were few black marks against this wonderful season. Gradi had placed the emphasis on youth, the average age of his team being just 23. The introduction of the new and the weeding out of the old meant the day of reckoning had arrived for Dave Donaldson, Jeff Bryant, and Roger Connell. All three had lived through the fires of Goodison Park, but none could hold down a first-team place come May. Donaldson and Bryant were granted free transfers in recognition of services rendered, while Connell quit the game and settled in Ireland.

Equally unfortunate was Les Briley, who had set the team ablaze the previous year. Injury wrecked his season. Steve 'little tiger' Galliers was handed Briley's all-action role, and performed with such energy that he won the player of the year award hands down.

Match of the Season

Everton 8 Wimbledon 0

League Cup, 2nd Round, 29th August 1978

It seems perverse to select this ultimate humiliation as Wimbledon's match of the season, especially in a promotion-winning campaign. The Dons played their part in several memorable contests – notably Southampton in the FA Cup; a cracker at Grimsby; two top-of-the table clashes with Portsmouth; and another late in the season at Reading. But Wimbledon failed to win any of these. The only contender they won was the extra-time nail-biter at Bournemouth in the FA Cup.

The League Cup-tie at Goodison was watched by 23,000 spectators, the largest crowd by far to view Wimbledon in action. As the result stands in the record books as the most devastating in the Dons' history, it is only fitting that the match be revisited.

DID YOU KNOW?

In February 1979 Dario Gradi predicted Wimbledon would be in Division 1 'within 10 years'. He was wrong. They reached Division 1 within 7 years.

Ray Knowles scores against Portsmouth, but the Dons lose 2-4. (26th December 1978)

Having fared badly at 2nd Division Spurs 12 months previously, some supporters quailed at the thought of what damage Everton might inflict. Gordon Lee's team had finished 3rd the previous season, and had opened the new term with three wins out of three. Several players were full internationals, among them bustling striker Bob Latchford, who had recently forced his way into the England team. Latchford's record at Goodison was 83 goals in 156 league games, impressive for a 'sniffer', remarkable for a target man.

Midfielder Martin Dobson had won five England caps at one time. Scottish goalkeeper George Wood had been overlooked by Ally MacLeod for the World Cup fiasco of Argentina '78, but would be capped by the season's end.

The Dons were also undefeated, and with Alan Cork fresh from a hat-trick, he for one relished the challenge. Bryant, Donaldson, Galliers and Connell were the only survivors of White Hart Lane.

DID YOU KNOW?

To win by five clear goals away from home is rare; to do so in successive seasons even rarer. Wimbledon's feat in winning 5-0 at Southport, followed by 6-1 at Torquay was last matched by Liverpool.
In 1989-90 the Reds won 6-1 at Coventry, and in 1990-91 by 7-1 at Derby.

John Leslie cracks in a shot against Huddersfield. (3rd March 1979)

DID YOU KNOW?

Wimbledon's 6-1 and 5-0 victories over Torquay in 1978-79 are not unique. The last team to beat another by five clear goals TWICE in one season was Southend United (5-0, 5-0) versus Aldershot in 1989-90.

'At all costs avoid an early goal,' warned Gradi. Yet it took Latchford just eight minutes to break through. He'd claimed a hat-trick just after the hour, and two more goals in the closing minutes took him to five. Only a select few players – George Best, Bobby Tambling, Andy Cole, among them – have ever bagged five goals in a competitive match against League opposition. Latchford took the gloss from Martin Dobson's hat-trick, the first and last of his career.

The Dons slunk away at the end. Gradi had some spirits to lift before Friday night's visit to Stockport. 'We want eight!' jeered County fans. Cork's goal silenced them and sent Wimbledon top of the league.

DID YOU KNOW?

Few teams beat another THREE times in one season. In 1978-79 the Dons beat Bournemouth twice in the league, having already knocked them out of the FA Cup (in a replay, after extra-time).

LEAGUE DIVISION 3 1979-80

Division 3	24th (Relegated)
League Cup	4th Round
FA Cup	2nd Round

Promotion for newcomers was hardly unprecedented. Cambridge United and Hereford had done the same within a season or two of admission. Cambridge had come straight down. Getting up was the easy part: staying up was another matter.

Other than signing full-back Steve Jones from Walsall, Gradi's team was unchanged. The Dons sank Aldershot with six goals in two League Cup-ties, but the Shots were still in Division 4 and offered little hint of what life might be like in the higher sphere.

A home defeat in the first match often betokens troubled times. And so it proved when Chester scored twice in a minute to leave Wimbledon gasping. The Dons never recovered. They were bottom by September, when former Chelsea favourite Ray Lewington finally teamed up. He had been playing across the Atlantic, and his arrival was delayed by red tape.

Lewington's performances paid early dividends. Not until his sixth game did he sample defeat, a run that carried the team to the relative heights of 16th. But old habits returned. The defence started haemorrhaging again, and by Christmas Wimbledon were bottom once more.

But they were still alive in the FA Cup and had contributed to some stirring matches in the League Cup. These produced two extra-time marathons and one penalty shoot-out – with Orient – settled by Ray Goddard! Plymouth were dismissed at the second attempt, in extra-time, to project Wimbledon into the 4th Round for the first time. They hoped to meet a giant; instead they got Swindon Town, whom they had beaten recently in the league. This time a late goal by Chic Bates won the day.

More extra-time excitement awaited Wimbledon in the FA Cup, where Portsmouth from Division 4 put paid to Wimbledon's dreams after a second replay. All told, 12 cup-ties were contested in this otherwise depressing season.

DID YOU KNOW?

1979-80 brought two special humiliations to Wimbledon FC.

1. **They conceded 6 goals at home (to Grimsby) for the one and only time.**
2. **They finished bottom of their league for the one and only time.**

Alan Cork makes it 2-0 with this header against Swindon Town. (13th October 1979)

Three consecutive league wins in February instilled hope, but failed to propel the team clear of the bottom four. When the spiral of defeats returned – among them a critical loss at home to bottom-club Bury – Gradi took drastic steps. Lewington and the club had become mutually disillusioned. He moved to Fulham, and his No 11 shirt passed to Paul Denny. Next out was free-kick specialist Steve Parsons. He went to Orient (for £43,000) and dynamo Les Briley to Aldershot.

The club's financial difficulties were so intractable that no player was considered too precious to be sold. All were all up for grabs. In this soul destroying atmosphere Gradi was expected to motivate his demoralised troops to stave off the drop.

It proved beyond him and them. Though Alan Cork and John Leslie rattled in 23 goals between them, the defence could not compensate and was breached 82 times. One of the few players who could hold up his head was Steve Galliers, who retained his player of the year award.

DID YOU KNOW?

Three times en route to relegation Wimbledon scored three goals but failed to win – 3-4 v Sheffield Wednesday, 3-3 v Colchester, 3-6 v Grimsby.

Match of the Season

Wimbledon 3 Sheffield Wednesday 4

Division 3, 27th October 1979

This was not the Dons' heaviest scoring match – that came later with a 3-6 mauling by Grimsby. Nor was it the most nerve-tingling. That accolade probably went to the League Cup replay with Orient, eventually decided on penalties. But for big-name opposition and goals in abundance, the visit of Sheffield Wednesday gets the vote. The match lured to Plough Lane the season's only league crowd in excess of 6,000. It also produced a goal in a thousand.

The idea of Wimbledon playing in the same division as Sheffield Wednesday was enough to make hearts a-flutter. These northern giants, with a stadium to drool over, had fallen on lean times. They were managed by Jack Charlton, who had brought Middlesbrough to Plough Lane in the Cup three years previously. Dave Bassett worshipped at the same altar as Big Jack, but he was not yet in charge.

By late October the Owls had climbed to fourth, but were so inconsistent that they had yet to forge two consecutive victories. They arrived in SW19 fresh from beating Grimsby, so would create some small record if they won again. Wednesday's attack was indebted to the heavy scoring of much-travelled Terry Curran, but handicapped by the absence of his usual side-kick, Andy McCullough. Ian Porterfield – who scored an FA Cup winner for Sunderland – patrolled the midfield in this, his last season.

Wimbledon had lost just once in seven. But that defeat had been in their last match: the 0-4 drubbing at Colchester constituted their heaviest league defeat.

Against Wednesday the goals flew in like clockwork. It was 1-1 by the quarter-hour; 2-2 on the hour. But it was Wimbledon's first goal, by John Leslie, that lingered in the mind. His volley was spectacular enough, but it was preceded by 15 passes without an Owl getting a sniff of the ball.

At 2-2 Ray Goddard brought down Jeff King. Defender Mark Smith converted (he would score nine goals that season, all from the spot). Curran added a fourth and all looked lost. But Alan Cork popped up again to set up a rousing climax to a rousing match. The Owls had at last won twice in a row. Promotion awaited them.

LEAGUE DIVISION 4 1980-81

Division 4	4th (Promoted)
League Cup	2nd Round
FA Cup	4th Round

Promotion, relegation, and now promotion again. Players and supporters were becoming giddy.

Little happened before December to suggest 1980-81 might turn out better than expected. The 11 players who kicked off the new season with a 2-2 home draw with Bradford City had each contributed to dumping the club back into Division 4 in May. Top scorer John Leslie had looked set to sign for Halifax, reputed to have put in an improbable bid of £50,000. Improbable, not in the sense of inflating Leslie's worth, but in the knowledge that the Yorkshire club had never paid out that kind of money for anyone.

Leslie stayed put. He and Cork would share a third season in tandem, and each blossomed in the presence of the other. Dave Beasant (signed from Edgware for £100!) took over in goal.

The season began slowly, the Dons overcoming Aldershot for the second year running in the 1st Round of the League Cup, before bowing out to Sheffield Wednesday in the 2nd. High point of the first three months was poking seven goals past Windsor & Eton in the FA Cup. New signing Dave Hubbick took a blow on the head, but helped himself to a hat-trick that he had trouble remembering afterwards. Defeat at Bury in the league left the Dons with more defeats than wins to their name.

The turnaround was as mysterious as it was dramatic. Gradi had not introduced fresh players; those already on the books suddenly started to believe in themselves. Torquay and Bournemouth were brushed aside in the league, Swindon and Oldham (after a replay) in the Cup. Wrexham in Round 4 might even lead to Wembley.

It was an ill-kept secret that chairman Ron Noades had his mind elsewhere than on Wembley. The pitifully small crowds Wimbledon attracted in their previous promotion year suggested the club was destined to dwell in the backwaters. Noades planned to buy out Crystal Palace and haul Wimbledon FC along to Selhurst Park in his wake. Not so much ground sharing as a complete merger. In those days the feasibility of mergers was aired in many football circles, but no clubs had yet gone ahead, other than on a temporary basis.

In this context, Wimbledon's 1-2 defeat in north Wales amounted to little. Bigger fish were frying. No sooner had the team coach returned down the M1 than Noades was off across south London.

His bright young manager went with him, leaving Wimbledon managerless and, seemingly, with little option but to shack up too.

Wimbledon's outraged fans took up their placards, the board took up their pencils, and plumped for the status quo. Plough Lane would continue to be home to the Dons.

A new manager was found by promoting the incumbent assistant, Dave Bassett – installing Alan Gillett as his deputy.

Nowadays, everyone with a passing interest in English football knows the name of Dave 'Harry' Bassett. In 1981 he was a thirty-something nobody of no great achievement. One season in League Division 4 was all he had achieved in a playing career almost wholly played out at amateur or semi-professional level. But for being on the books of Wimbledon, he would surely never have sampled League football at all.

Bassett had hung up his boots in 1978, following his appointment as Gradi's number two. Bassett was a hard man as a player, and remains a hard man as a manager. He is the quintessential man's man, a player's man, someone who thinks nothing of attending press conferences in his birthday suit, of calling a spade a bloody spade, and whose transparent honesty endears him to his players as much as to his employers.

If Bassett possessed any tactical acumen – and there were those who doubted it – this was dwarfed by his ability to communicate, on TV as well as in the dressing room. Bassett had charm, a roguish, boyish smile, an eloquence that belied the bluntness of his message. New fangled methods get short shrift with Dave Bassett. 'Get the ball up there, and get bodies up there after it,' sums up his team talks, but none could deny the fighting spirit he instilled into those bodies. Bassett was tailor-made for Wimbledon, and the club for him. The Crazy Gang were on the march.

Bassett inherited a team knocked out of both cups, in mid-table, and without a bean to spend on new players. Somehow, he not only consolidated the improvement shown under Gradi, but turned his rag-bag team into winners. A 3-2 success at Port Vale on 31st January set them on their way. By mid-March, an eight-match unbeaten run had carried the Dons to 6th. Then came Bassett's first setback, a 1-4 thrashing at Darlington that saw two of his over-zealous players expelled from the pitch. One of these was the irrepressible Steve Galliers, whose punishment – for the sending off and for collecting too many disciplinary black marks – saw him banned for five matches. How did manager and players react? By dropping just two points from the next seven games.

Three matches now remained. Bassett was fortunate in that he timed his late surge in a division plagued with mediocre teams.

Back: Goddard, Downes, Smith, Cunningham, Beasant, Jones, Cork, Denny, Hodges.
Front: Joseph, Brown, Ketteridge, Armstrong, Galliers, Leslie, Hubbick, Belfield.

Southend and Lincoln were already over the horizon, but even at this late stage two places remained to be contested by Doncaster, Peterborough, Wimbledon, and any other late-comers. Wigan were out of the running, but they beat the Dons 2-1. Two to go, both at home. Only one was needed, as Rochdale were swept away to leave Bassett cherishing the first of many promotions. Player of the year was goalkeeper Dave Beasant, in his first season with the club.

Match of the Season

Wrexham 2 Wimbledon 1

FA Cup, 4th Round, 24th January 1981

The odd thing about this fine season was that the whole was greater than the parts. Few individual games stand out. Only once did Wimbledon put more than three goals past opponents. Most significant results ended in tight-fisted 1-0 triumphs, such as that over rivals Doncaster Rovers in early April. Nor did the cup campaigns produce glorious victories or heroic defeats. Smashing seven goals in one FA cup-tie was the stuff of headlines, but the victims were amateurs. Winning at 2nd Division Oldham was probably the best result; it also carried the Dons into the 4th Round

DID YOU KNOW?

Wimbledon finished 4th in 1980-81 with just 55 points. This is the lowest total ever to secure promotion from Division 4 after a full, 46-match programme.

for only the second time. The tie was given added spice by Wrexham's feat in putting out cup-holders West Ham in the 3rd Round after two replays.

Wrexham spring to mind as an impoverished Welsh club, almost within commuter distance of Merseyside, with a capacious stadium and a team that perennially inhabits the lower reaches of the Football League. It was not always so. In 1980-81 they were at their peak, enjoying their third season in Division 2. They would alert statisticians by finishing with 38 points for the third season in a row. Relegation was a constant worry, and would be realised in 1983.

What gave the Dons special hope was that the Welshmen seemed blighted at home. They had not tasted success at the Racecourse Ground since October, and would muster just five home wins all season.

The names of two Wrexham players caught the eye. Much-capped full-back Joey Jones had returned to the principality after a period at Anfield. In attack, Wrexham looked to Dixie McNeill, scorer of some 200 league goals for Exeter, Northampton, Lincoln, Hereford, and now Wrexham. His record while at Edgar Street of 85 strikes from 128 league matches speaks for itself. He was still dangerous, but he had just turned 34, and as a feared striker was clearly on borrowed time.

This, then, was the measure of Wimbledon's task. They hadn't lost in league or cup for nearly two months, and entertained realistic hopes of making the 5th Round for the first time.

In the event, the Dons failed to grasp the mettle until the game was almost beyond them. Steve Fox did not score many goals for Wrexham, but it was his effort that separated the sides at half-time. Dixie McNeill then eluded Smith and Cunningham to direct a second-half header past Beasant. Wimbledon then woke up. Denny quickly halved the arrears to set up a tense finish. On the evidence of the final 25 minutes Wimbledon deserved a replay; on the evidence of the 90 they did not.

Out of the cup, and within hours without a manager, when Gradi skipped over to join Ron Noades at Crystal Palace.

LEAGUE DIVISION 3 1981-82

Division 3	21st (Relegated)
League Cup	1st Round
FA Cup	2nd Round

Wimbledon FC have been fortunate with their benefactors. In earlier times the enthusiasm and financial backing of Sydney Black had for many years kept creditors from the door. In 1982 the name of Sam Hammam first surfaced in connection with the club, as its major shareholder. Over the years his involvement would become even deeper. Hammam's financial acumen and boundless commitment would guide the club through the 1980s and 90s.

But on the pitch? Oh dear! It was up, down, up, and down again for bouncy Wimbledon.

Once again the summer saw no major comings and goings. The crew that came up must stay up without reinforcements. Another of those silly tournaments – the Group Cup – was crammed into the start of an already congested season.

August and September set the tone: being remembered as among the most depressing months in Wimbledon's league history. A 1-4 thumping at Swindon in the first match provided a taste of things to come. The Dons lost their first *five* games at Plough Lane, four in the league and once in the League Cup – to 4th Division Aldershot, a team they had beaten in Round 1 in the previous two seasons. When Wimbledon were scorched 1-5 at Lincoln on 10th October, they could show just two points from nine games, and were seemingly in a spiral of doom. With three points now rewarded for each victory, the Dons were cast adrift at the bottom.

They had also lost key players. Alan Cork had broken a leg at Walsall. His predatory talents would be sorely missed. Skipper Tommy Cunningham had been sold to Orient for £34,000, and a few weeks later Galliers was sold for twice as much to Palace.

Wimbledon's belated first victory, over Chester, attracted a puny crowd of just 1,659. A last-minute winner against Plymouth by on-loan Terry Boyle three days later fleetingly suggested better things. But injuries and departures wrecked Wimbledon's chances of sustaining the improvement. Worst of all, the amateurs of Enfield came from behind in the FA Cup to plunder four second-half goals. 'Men against boys,' thundered Bassett. 'They had the men.'

The Dons enjoyed a productive spell after Christmas, taking 10 points from four games. But they had left themselves too much to do. After losing 1-6 at Gillingham in February – the worst league

DID YOU KNOW?

The Dons' Dave Hubbick was once All England Schoolboys boxing champion.

defeat, at that time – there was nowhere to hide. The Dons' fate was effectively sealed by a winless eight-game sequence in March and April. It was small consolation to reach the final of the meddlesome Group Cup, losing 2-3 to Grimsby from Division 2. And Plough Lane was rocked when unhappy Dave Clement took his own life. Clement, a one-time England international with QPR, had been recruited to plug the breaches in defence. He had broken a leg in January, an injury so serious that it threatened his career.

Bassett had two pressing worries. First, how to shore up a defence that was failing to defend. Second, how best to channel the excessive zeal his players exhibited on the pitch. Like it or not, Wimbledon were underlining their reputation as one of the most physical, some would say dirty, sides in the league, a tag they struggle to shrug off today. Whatever the rights and wrongs, the Dons' disciplinary record was lamentable, and long suspensions further handicapped the side's battle against relegation.

In the circumstances it was a marvel that they rallied to the extent that they did. A home defeat by Oxford on 20th April appeared to extinguish all hope. Eight matches remained, yet these harvested 19 points. The Dons were three points behind Walsall going into their final fixture, but needed to win by double figures to overhaul them. Needless to say, that proved beyond them.

Francis Joseph ended the campaign as makeshift centre-forward, top-scoring with 13 goals, and meriting the player of the year title.

Match of the Season

Brentford 2 Wimbledon 3

Division 3, 26th April 1982

Little doubt about this one. In a season that saw the Dons slide miserably from both major cups, and plummet through the Division 3 trap-door for the second time, this victory had the ingredients of melodrama. Brentford enjoyed the best away record in the division;

DID YOU KNOW?

Wimbledon were relegated in 1981-82 on 53 points. This was the highest number of points for any relegated team until 1988-89, when Southend United went down with 54 points.

Physio Owen Harris carries out running repairs to Dave Beasant's back.

their promotion hopes, however, were sabotaged at Griffin Park, where defeats outnumbered victories. The Bees were enlivened by ex-England 'bad boy' Stan Bowles and future Glasgow Ranger Terry Hurlock, but they had no proven goalscorer. No Brentford player would manage more than eight league goals all season.

Wimbledon looked beyond salvation. The game was 11 minutes old when they trailed to a wicked Bowles free-kick. Gary Johnson then doubled the lead with a magical strike. It was then that Francis Joseph made his presence felt. Joseph was the first black player to play League football for Wimbledon. He was no centre-forward, but the loss of Cork forced Bassett to improvise. In March, Joseph swapped the No 11 shirt for the No 8 and was sparked into goalscoring life. His two strikes against Brentford took the tally of the 'black pearl' to seven in 12 outings. The result destroyed Brentford's season and momentarily breathed life into Wimbledon's.

DID YOU KNOW?

Wimbledon were relegated in 1981-82 despite scoring three or more goals in a match NINE times. The most recent team to equal this unusual distinction was Crewe Alexandra in 1990-1991.

SCALING EVEREST 1982-1986

LEAGUE DIVISION 4 1982-83

Division 4	Champions (Promoted)
Milk Cup	1st Round
FA Cup	1st Round

The pre-season loss of Francis Joseph to rivals Brentford dented confidence among the squad, even as it boosted the club's bank balance. Less than a year after departing for Crystal Palace, Steve Galliers was back, for a knock-down £15,000.

Three other newcomers were in from the start – Chris Dibble and Tony Tagg, free transfers from Millwall, and Gary Peters from Fulham, who also cost nothing but who was made captain.

The Football League Trophy, which replaced the Group Cup as an irksome pre-season warm-up, gave little hint of what was to come. Wimbledon were quickly eliminated – as they were by Brentford in the newly named Milk Cup. In the league, too, they hardly set the division alight, drawing four of their first five fixtures.

It was then that Wimbledon found their form. Six wins and 20 goals carried them clear of all pursuit and gave notice that this was a forward-line to be reckoned with. On 23rd October, at Bristol City, the Dons surrendered the last unbeaten record in the country. This isolated setback did not prevent Bassett being awarded his first Bells' manager of the month award.

'Who have won more away games than Liverpool, scored twice as many goals as Arsenal, but still have only as many supporters as Rochdale?'
(Wimbledon, of course.)
Lament by the Wimbledon News.

Bristol City's Shaw saves from Evans, with Ketteridge watching. (23rd October 1982)

It proved to be the kiss of death. The Dons lost all three matches in November, the last of which was at home to Halifax Town, a team that had forgotten the art of winning. Wimbledon tumbled out of the promotion places and Bassett contemplated drastic surgery. Elimination by Northampton in the 1st Round of the FA Cup was the last straw. In all his long career Bassett never acted so decisively as now, in Plough Lane's Night of the Long Knives.

With promotion slipping away, Bassett reshuffled his tactics and his team. Gone was the sweeper and man-for-man marking, so instrumental in those early victories. Bassett axed not just one or two players, but six, more than half the team. Shirt numbers 3, 4, 5, 6, 7, and 8 were handed to others – among them on-loan debutants, Steve Hatter and Phil Ferns. This was a high-risk strategy, and Bassett knew it. His team of strangers might fall to pieces.

The next game, at Darlington, assumed ominous proportions. Inside the first minute Ferns' cross was headed in by John Leslie, and thereafter the team looked in little danger. Victory at Rochdale a week later confirmed that they were back on the rails.

The Dons carried on winning into the New Year, until a last minute sickener by Billy Whitehurst gave table-topping Hull the points in a Plough Lane thriller. But Wimbledon would not lose again that season, which still had 22 games to run.

DID YOU KNOW?

Steve Hatter was purchased with donations from supporters who threw coins into a blanket carried around the pitch.

Those 22 games harvested 51 goals; in only six of them did Wimbledon fail to score at least twice. Chief predator was John Leslie, nobly assisted by gangling Stewart Evans. But 16 goals were also contributed by promising youngsters Glyn Hodges and Steve Ketteridge in midfield, and by April even Alan Cork was back in the side, a year and a half after that dreadful leg fracture at Walsall. He weighed in with five goals in seven games before flying out to play summer football in Sweden.

With such diverse sources of firepower, Wimbledon had all the answers to the questions 4th Division defences could throw at them. They proudly picked up Capital Radio's £25,000 prize for being the first London club to reach 80 league goals.

But the championship was reward for team effort. Ever-present skipper Gary Peters stabilised the rearguard. Wally Downes and Kevin Gage did their jobs well, and in Glyn Hodges Wimbledon possessed a player admired from all quarters.

Despite their net-bulging exploits, the team stayed locked in 4th place till late February, then climbed to 3rd. By early March they were 2nd, and victory over a Hartlepool side fielding the Linighan brothers – Andy and David – carried them back to the top for the first time since October.

Promotion was clinched over Easter at Crewe. The Dons had done it with four games to spare. All they could lose now was the championship. That was hardly in doubt, and the TV cameras were in place to witness the coronation at Gigg Lane. Bury would have gone up, too, had they drawn, but Beasant pulled off a thrilling save from the penalty spot to deny them.

Wimbledon nearly pulled off an unprecedented double ton, having to settle for 98 league points and 96 league goals.

The pity, as the Dons piled win upon win, was that crowds remained tiny. Only once did they peep above 4,000, and that was for the confrontation with rivals Port Vale in April. The idea was mooted of scrapping the reserve side and loaning out players who were not first-team regulars. Better financial news came with the announcement that the club had paid off Merton council, and now owned the Plough Lane stadium outright.

For his massive contribution of 23 league goals, John Leslie was voted player of the year. For keeping 16 clean-sheets, Dave Beasant was voted runner-up.

DID YOU KNOW?

Between 1978-79 and 1982-83, the Dons went – UP – DOWN – UP – DOWN – UP. No other club has changed divisions over five successive seasons.

Match of the Season

Wimbledon 1 Port Vale 0

Division 4, 23rd April 1983

So many candidates in this – in statistical terms – Wimbledon's finest ever League season. How about that home thriller with Hull, the six-goal feast against Aldershot, the seven-goal tightrope with York, or the pageant at Bury? All these have some claim to be match of the season, but for sheer nail-biting tension, no-prisoners asked or taken, the highly charged home fixture with Port Vale took some beating. It also enticed Plough Lane's biggest gate.

Vale and Wimbledon were locked together. The Valiants had won 1-0 at Burslem earlier in the season and were seeking a precious double. With just half a dozen matches to play, this was the classic six-pointer. Promotion was all but guaranteed to the winners, and with Chelsea in desperate trouble at the tail end of Division 2 mischievous Dons fans indulged in wistful dreams of excursions to Stamford Bridge.

Wimbledon had beaten Vale twice in securing promotion two years previously: the 3-2 win at Vale Park had been Dave Bassett's first game in charge of the Dons.

Port Vale's current side included Barry Siddall, an 'England Youth' goalkeeper. Young Mark Bright was also on their books, though he would not play. Neither would Ernie Moss (who scored at Vale Park) nor Jimmy Greenhoff.

The Valiants sported an ominously strong away record, and arrived with three recent wins under their belts. Leading scorer Bob Newton was enjoying a rich vein of form and had scored in all three.

Vale set about combating Wimbledon's irresistible force with their own immovable object. They had come for a point, and although Wimbledon clocked up 17 corners it looked increasingly as though the visitors would leave with their reward. Five minutes remained when Steve Ketteridge forced a path through two challenges to beat Siddall for the vital goal. The crowd may have been small, but they made a mighty din.

The reverse was brushed off by Vale, who also went up – 3rd.

CANON LEAGUE DIVISION 3 1983-84

Division 3	Runners Up (Promoted)
Milk Cup	4th Round
FA Cup	2nd Round

Sponsorship threatened to sweep away all that was traditional in soccer. A year earlier the League Cup had been transformed into some oddity called the Milk Cup. Now the Football League itself had found sponsors, and renamed itself the Canon League.

Even the Dons were at it, signing a deal with Mileta that brought with it a new strip – paler blue with shadow-stripes.

Not that that mattered to the players, who had a familiar problem to resolve. This was their third sojourn in Division 3. The previous two had ended in tears and instant relegation.

Bassett was not helped by the loss of his chief predator. John Leslie severed the last remaining link with the Southern League era when opting to team up with the then unknown Steve Bruce and Tony Cascarino at Gillingham.

Little was expected of the one import. Nigel Winterburn arrived on loan from Oxford to fill the full-back vacancy left by Brian Sparrow's recall by Arsenal. The rest of the team had earned their spurs the previous season. Dave 'Lurch' Beasant was constantly being spied upon, by Liverpool and other luminaries.

The league opener was away to relegated Bolton. With Leslie gone and Cork not yet back from summer football in Sweden, this was a testing baptism. Powder-puff finishing cost the Dons the points, and they also failed to score at Southend in the Milk Cup. Two defeats made the visit of Newport assume unwanted pressure.

In two previous seasons in Division 3 Wimbledon had never scored more than three goals a match. With Cork now harnessed alongside Evans, that record was swept away. Cork helped himself to a hat-trick – to follow that against Chester in his farewell match in the spring – as Wimbledon hit the Welsh team for six.

It was early days, but teams capable of beating others by six goals are rarely contenders for relegation, and the confidence that spread through the manager and players was palpable. Three days later Wimbledon ran in three goals against Bournemouth. Next up at Plough Lane were Southend in the Milk Cup second leg. Six more goals for Wimbledon, this time in a 10-goal extravaganza that went to extra-time, and was rewarded by a date with Nottingham Forest.

By the time Brian Clough's all-stars journeyed south for the first leg, the Dons were hovering just outside the promotion places.

Forest lost 0-2 and set off back up the M1 bruised in mind and body. When they could do no better than draw the return leg, Brian Clough was man enough to personally congratulate the Dons in their dressing room. The results against Forest answered one question. This Wimbledon team was too good to go down!

But Bassett had a problem. His gung-ho forwards were smashing them in as merrily as they had in Division 4. This was just as well, for the defence was breached so often that – but for the gluttony of 'Champagne' Cork, 'Good' Evans, and Hodges – relegation might not have been an idle threat. Before the turn of the year the Dons lost 0-4 at Walsall, 1-5 at Scunthorpe, 1-4 at home to Burnley. They also beat Brentford and Millwall, both by 4-3. By season's end only four teams in the division had conceded more goals. All in all, these figures highlight the massive entertainment Wimbledon provided in this ultimately famous season.

Wimbledon's involvement in the Milk Cup extended to late November. Having seen off Oldham in the 3rd Round, they fell at Rotherham in the 4th. This was galling; they would beat the Merry Millers twice in the league, and were left to rue Hodges' late chip which rebounded off a post into the goalkeeper's arms.

Nor did the FA Cup detain the Dons beyond Round 2, where they came off worse – 2-3 – at Brentford.

Match for match it is difficult to contest the claim that this was Wimbledon's most memorable league campaign. The Dons won 6-2 at Orient, and when later in February Dave Beasant repulsed a last-minute Rotherham penalty, the three points carried the Dons top.

Four successive draws spelled eight dropped points and toppled them from their perch. Hull's unanswerable superiority in their 4-1 win at Plough Lane in early April took some digesting. Perhaps the Dons had had a bad day; perhaps they were in a false position all along.

A run of 2-1 wins, followed by a quick double over FA Cup semi-finalists Plymouth Argyle, set up a climactic clash at Bramall Lane with Sheffield United.

Another 2-1 win, and now just three points were needed from two games to make sure. More than 6,000 fans 'packed' Plough Lane for the visit of John Leslie's Gillingham, and when Kevin Gage opened the scoring after ten seconds the promotion bubbly was set to uncork.

But on an evening of tortuously fluctuating emotions, Gillingham struck three times in the second half to leave Wimbledon players and supporters clutching their heads. Then news filtered through that Sheffield United had lost at Bolton. Sensationally, unbelievably, Wimbledon were in Division 2.

DID YOU KNOW?

In 1983-84 Wimbledon were promoted despite conceding 76 goals. No other team has ever won promotion from any division after conceding so many.

Amid the euphoria, other contributory achievements were dwarfed or overlooked. The Dons attack, for example, scored 97 league goals, one more than the record set the previous season. Once again Capital Radio's prize for London's leading goal-getters was headed for Plough Lane, despite a stiff challenge from Chelsea.

Managers do not like to single out players when a team does well, preferring collective praise. But some individual performances in 1983-84 demand recognition. Alan Cork's 29 league goals was a club record, all the more welcome in that he had previously failed twice to make his mark in the 3rd Division

Dave Beasant had not missed a match for three seasons, but could hardly have been happy at picking the ball out of the net 76 times. Nor could newcomer Nigel Winterburn, yet such was his work-rate, his timely tackling, the panache of his sorties down the left, that he won the hearts of supporters from the outset and claimed the player of the year award in his first season.

Other heroes included powerhouse Glyn Hodges, who added to his nine goals last season with 15 this, a healthy number for a non-striker.

Not all football-lovers gave the Dons the credit they deserved. Once again referees took exception to the team's robustness. The players accumulated so many disciplinary points that it appeared that a warning about their future conduct from Lancaster Gate the previous year had gone unheeded.

The other downside was the size of the crowds. Here was, demonstrably, the best team in the club's history, yet only once was a gate of 6,000 exceeded, and that was for the celebratory final match.

The season almost ended in shock and tears. Dave Bassett, a blue blooded Don if ever there was one, was lured by Ron Noades to succeed Dario Gradi at Crystal Palace. The crisis lasted four days, at the end of which Bassett returned to Plough Lane, where his heart and allegiance lay, and declared himself ready to face the challenge of Division 2.

DID YOU KNOW?

In 1983-84 Wimbledon scored 97 goals and conceded 76. No other team has subsequently overtaken this aggregate total of 173 goals in a season.

Policemen chat as Mark Morris heads goal No 3 against Port Vale. (17th September 1983)

Match of the Season

Sheffield United 1 Wimbledon 2

Division 3, 5th May 1984

Spoiled for choice in this exhilarating campaign. Three games in the Milk Cup stake large claims to the match of matches – the 10-goal bonanza with Southend, which set up two momentous matches with Cloughie's Forest. Half a dozen league games, in any other season, would have proudly commanded attention. But for impact, timing, attendance, and result, the promotion-decider at Bramall Lane brooks little argument.

The fact that Dave Bassett in later years spent many enjoyable years with the Blades adds retrospective piquancy to the encounter.

United, at the time, were managed by Ian Porterfield, scorer of the winning goal for Sunderland in the 1973 FA Cup Final. These were resurgent days for football in the steel city, with Wednesday already promoted back to Division 1, and United not daring to fall by the wayside. A double-promotion would boost the city no end.

Sheffield United had won their last four. Their home form was awesome, beaten just once, and almost outscoring Wimbledon on their own patch. The bulk of these goals were claimed by Keith

Edwards, not very tall, not very fast, but so sharp in front of goal that he would later sign for Scottish giants Aberdeen. Edwards had already mustered 31 in this prolific season, more than Cork, and that says something. With much-admired winger Colin Morris – who had hurt the Dons in the past in his Southend days – contributing another 19, Wimbledon's leaky defence would surely be put to the test.

The importance of this match to the Yorkshire side can be gauged by the size of the crowd, nearly 23,000. Not only was this Bramall Lane's biggest of the season, it was – apart from the local derby with Rotherham – 5,000 greater than for any other home fixture. It was also, come to that, the largest crowd at that time ever to have watched the Dons in league action.

With Hull City going well, defeat for either side might prove fatal. All in all, the match had some claim not merely to be the Dons' match of the season, but their most vital since they entered the Football League.

And how resourcefully they played, and how succulent was the moment four minutes before half-time for Stewart Evans. Twice he had hoped to sign for the Blades; twice Ian Porterfield had intimated that he was not good enough. How that rejection must have stuck in Porterfield's gullet as the beanpole striker put the Dons in front. Midway through the second-half, Cork nabbed a goal of his own, to take him closer to Keith Edwards' tally. Even though Colin Morris halved the arrears, Wimbledon hung on for a famous and merited win.

It was a pity that some of Sheffield United's fired-up fans did not take defeat quite as graciously as their players. During the match a bottle was tossed on the pitch in the direction of Dave Beasant, and afterwards hundreds of aggrieved fans turned their spleen on Wimbledon supporters.

United might have lost the battle, but they won the war. When, in their last game, Hull failed to beat Burnley by enough goals, the Blades went up in third place, having the same points as Hull, the same goal-difference, but having outscored their rivals.

CANON LEAGUE DIVISION 2 1984-85

Division 2	12th
Milk Cup	1st Round
FA Cup	5th Round

Dave Bassett had achieved two successive promotions. This feat is not, as it happens, uncommon. A team's winning habits have a tendency to persist in the higher sphere. Three successive promotions is another matter. No one has yet managed that, and Bassett did not need to examine the history books to realise that consolidation was his realistic aim.

No current Wimbledon player had any 2nd Division experience, so strengthening the squad was Bassett's priority. To this end he relinquished the services of Dean Thomas, and more surprisingly, those of his captain, Gary Peters. Into his place came John Kay, a £25,000 buy from Arsenal. Kay had made a dozen or so first team appearances for the Gunners before losing his No 2 shirt to Colin Hill. Combative midfielder Dave Martin cost £35,000 when moving across London from Millwall. Other stop-gap arrivals included Phil Handford and Paul O'Berg from Gillingham and Scunthorpe.

When the fixture computer pulled out the name of Manchester City as Wimbledon's inaugural 2nd Division opponents, supporters were apt to rub their eyes. Here was confirmation that the Dons had arrived: the gate too – 8,365 – was a league record at Plough Lane. City manager Billy McNeill brought with him a cosmopolitan side, most of whom had earned international honours of one kind or another.

Teams like Manchester City consider it an insult against nature if they are not playing at the highest level. Having narrowly failed to win promotion in the spring, they would provide the most testing of opponents.

City played their part in a stirring match that both sides insisted they should have won. Wimbledon led 2-0 after 14 minutes and might have been four or five ahead by the time City woke up and snatched a goal shortly before half time. McNeill's furious dressing-room words had their effect, for the visitors were shortly back on terms, and by the end the Dons were being run ragged.

DID YOU KNOW?

In 1983-84 Wimbledon won 4-3 twice in a row. In 1984-85 they won 5-0 twice in a row. Repeating unusual scores in this way is extremely rare.

Glyn Hodges scores v Manchester City in the first match in Division 2. (25th August 1984)

The match finished 2-2, with Wimbledon alternating between the scintillating and the lamentable. Looking back, that was how it seemed to be all season, with the Dons climbing the highs – back-to-back 5-0 thrashings of Crystal Palace and Sheffield United – and plunging the depths – hit by 10 goals in consecutive games at Oxford and Carlisle. The darkest days were the earliest: one point to show from their first three matches, and dumped from the Milk Cup by Portsmouth. But recovery was swift. Stuck in 13th position week after week, the Dons finally finished 12th.

Bassett would have settled for that in August. It was necessary to go back six years to find the last occasion the Dons were neither promoted nor relegated. How odd, how boring, to be becalmed.

This was the season Bassett introduced Lawrie Sanchez, signed from Reading. Sanchez made his debut in the defeat at Birmingham before Christmas, but in 20 games netted five precious goals. Other prominent arrivals were Andy Thorn and Brian Gayle. They – like Andy Sayer and Paul Fishenden – came through the Dons nursery, the end-product of a fruitful youth policy.

Q	**What was Dave Bassett wearing at the press conference after the home match with Grimsby on 11th November 1984?**
A	**Just a smile.**

Goalmouth anguish in the FA Cup-tie with West Ham. (4th March 1985)

It would have been remarkable had the Dons managed 90-plus goals for a third successive season, let alone in the 2nd Division. They managed 71 – from four fewer fixtures – a disappointing figure only in the light of what had gone before. The team were the third highest scorers in Division 2, outscoring two of the three promotion sides. Cork managed 11 from an injury-hit campaign, but Stewart Evans climbed new heights with his tally of 14, and Paul Fishenden weighed in with a further 10.

Why then, with such a bristling forward line, did Bassett's troops not make more of an impact? The answer – once again – was that he was bedevilled by defensive frailty. The 75-goal debit column was only one fewer than in the previous season. Only the two basement clubs out-leaked Wimbledon's defence. Such miserable figures could have done little for the confidence of Beasant and Winterburn – knowing that top clubs were still eyeing them. Winterburn, indeed, retained his player of the year trophy.

An attack worthy of Division 1, a defence suited to Division 3. That was Wimbledon's season in a nutshell. It made for spectacle, but managers are not fond of spectacle. By early April, Bassett had had enough of this extravagance. He rang the changes, brought in Andy Thorn as an extra defender, to play sweeper, and the flood of goals at both ends dried up like a puddle in a drought.

DID YOU KNOW?

Wimbledon's fixtures in 1984-85 produced 146 league goals at either end, an average of 3½ per match, the highest in Division 2. This followed their total of 173 the previous season, averaging 3¾, the highest in Division 3.

All this is significant, because one year later, when Wimbledon made that ultimate leap to Division 1, the goals figures would be miserly. Bassett's team would have learned new tricks.

It is no coincidence that league honours and cup runs seldom go hand in hand. During their most recent promotion seasons Wimbledon had departed the knock-out tournaments at the earliest opportunity. Now, safely tucked up in mid-table they felt emboldened to seek Wembley. They did not get there, but they certainly left their mark. They were helped, of course, by automatic entry into Round 3, where they hosted Burnley, of fond FA Cup memory.

A 3-1 win was followed by a further appointment with Brian Clough. Having disposed of Forest over two legs in the Milk Cup in 1983-84, there were many who reasoned that Forest would not get caught out again. They were wrong.

Wimbledon were now in Round 5 for the first time, though true to expectations in this topsy-turvy season, West Ham brought them down to earth with a bump, 1-5 in an Upton Park replay.

Match of the Season

Wimbledon 1 Nottingham Forest 0

FA Cup, 4th Round Replay, 30th January 1985

Two cracking Sunday clashes with Crystal Palace were worthy contenders for match of the season, not to mention the opener with Manchester City, or the 3-3 draws with Wolves and Barnsley. But the sense of occasion demands that this time we do not overlook Nottingham Forest.

This was not a vintage Forest outfit. Memories of league and European championships were fading, and the current team were resigned to challenging for cup success. The season had opened badly, falling to Bruges in the UEFA Cup at the first hurdle. When relegation-bound Sunderland expelled Forest from the Milk Cup, Brian Clough's side were pegged in mid-table with only the FA Cup for solace.

No longer was Clough able to field a team brimming with internationals. A year later Steve Hodge (by that time with Aston Villa) would represent England in the Mexico World Cup. Forwards

Gary Birtles and Peter Davenport promised so much that both, at one time or other, ended up as Old Trafford misfits. Birtles had been out injured for almost a year, and now made his long-awaited comeback. All three Forest players had lined up against the Dons in the Milk Cup 15 months previously.

Having sold Peter Shilton, Clough preferred to pluck his goalkeepers from Holland. Van Breukelin came first; now Hans Segers arrived from PSV Eindhoven. Segers cost just £50,000, and joined forces with yet another Dutchman, midfielder Johnny Metgod.

The FA Cup was, and would remain, the only domestic trophy to elude Brian Clough. With Forest's season otherwise dissolved into nothingness, this was their one chance of glory. To prepare, Clough flew his players to Tenerife to get their minds in tune.

In view of Wimbledon's extravagance in both goalmouths, it surprised everyone that the tie ended goalless – the Dons' first barren match in almost two years. Forest had done everything but score. They had hit the post, had two shots whacked off the line, and kept Dave Beasant on his toes throughout. But they hadn't beaten him, and so it was back to Plough Lane for a replay.

Both teams were unchanged. The No 11 shirts were again filled by Hodge and Hodges, to the confusion of commentators.

A crowd in excess of 10,000 – surpassed only by the visit of West Ham in the next round – witnessed a match different in style to that in the Milk Cup, but similar in outcome. In the Milk Cup, Forest had been virtually overrun. In the FA Cup, Wimbledon likewise endeavoured to frustrate Forest's elegant passing by means of hard-running harassment, but this time Forest had done their home-work. They were far from second fiddle this time, which made for an even more intriguing contest. But Paul Fishenden's early goal gave the Dons an advantage they held till the end.

The one regrettable moment came when a Steve Galliers challenge on Hodge provoked Brian Clough to leap from his dugout in rage. But Clough was gracious in defeat, hiding his shame.

CANON LEAGUE DIVISION 2 1985-86

Division 2	3rd (Promoted)
Milk Cup	3rd Round
FA Cup	3rd Round

In the summer of 1985 Dave Bassett sat down to do some hard thinking. Football had been shaken to the core by the tragedies of Heysel and Bradford City. Reassessment of life's priorities engaged everyone connected with the sport. Bassett had come a long way. So had his players. Many, inside and outside the club, thought it had come as far as it could, and that taking a mortgage in Division 2 should mark the summit of its ambitions.

Bassett was not made to stand still. He would strive to get the last ounce from himself and his players. But the kamikaze attacking – and defending – of the past couple of years had to stop. If Wimbledon were ever to grace the promised land, they would have to lock up their goalmouth. This meant teaching old dogs new tricks, for Bassett hadn't the money to bring in new ones. Ian Holloway (£35,000 from Bristol Rovers), was the only close-season addition to the squad, though John Fashanu and Dennis Wise would arrive before season's end.

Having gone a decade and a half without an opening-day win, Wimbledon viewed the visit of Middlesbrough with hope and trepidation. Boro had barely survived relegation at the end of the previous season, so this was, on paper, as good a chance as any for the Dons to make a winning start. Stewart Evans headed a quick goal, Gage and Sanchez added two more, and Boro seldom extended Wimbledon's five-man defence. The mould had been broken.

A four-goal hiding at Sheffield United suggested briefly that Wimbledon were back to square one. But that reverse paved the way for a sequence of grim 1-0 victories that carried Wimbledon into the top three. Bassett stayed true to his new, no-nonsense philosophy. '1-0 to the Arsenal' may be the Highbury refrain of the 1990s. In the mid-80s it might have been adapted to the Dons, too. Always hard, they were now mean as well.

Enjoying a bye in the 1st Round of the Milk Cup, Wimbledon swept five goals past Blackburn in the 2nd to set up a keenly awaited tie with Tottenham. Riots in the Broadwater Farm estate necessitated several postponements. The match provided a major test for the Dons who, by beating Carlisle 4-1 on the preceding Sunday, had climbed to 2nd. Sceptics insisted the bubble would

DID YOU KNOW?

Dave Bassett had been at Plough Lane for 12 years, but never enjoyed an opening day victory prior to Middlesbrough in 1985-86. Not since beating Nuneaton 2-0 in 1970-71 had the Dons triumphed in the first league fixture.

burst, but, either way, the performance at White Hart Lane would be held up to scrutiny.

Peter Shreeve's Tottenham were mid-table in Division 1, despite being armed with the talents of Clemence, Perryman, Hoddle and Waddle. Steve Galliers was the lone Don with active memories of the 0-4 crushing eight years previously. There was little likelihood of a repeat scoreline, but second-half goals by Gary Mabbutt and David Leworthy did not flatter the home side. The Dons had failed an important test. They won just one of the next six in the league and slipped to 7th. The sceptics seemed to have been proved right.

But then the sun reappeared. A second successive 5-0 tanning of Sheffield United – with Dennis Wise making his debut – set up three wins over Christmas.

It was now that Wimbledon played a key fixture. Considering their promotion push, elimination at the hands of Millwall in the 3rd Round of the FA Cup did not hurt unduly. But the manner of defeat did. Millwall welcomed back John Fashanu after suspension, and his performance that day was pivotal in the demolition of the Dons. Millwall might have had six. Dave Bassett took note. Fashanu was a player tailor-made for Wimbledon's style. Bassett had seen it at first hand, and it was not long before the phones started ringing.

These were worrying times for Wimbledon. The loss at Millwall was preceded by defeat by Portsmouth – in front of Plough Lane's largest league crowd – and succeeded by another at Oldham. Bassett stirred the pot again. 16 games remained, and Wimbledon streaked to the finishing post unbeaten. They leaked just nine more goals, a far cry from the up-and-at-'em approach of yesteryear.

As for the forward line, by late March Wimbledon could count on John Fashanu to lend his head and – to some – his elbows in good cause. He had cost £125,000, a blockbuster of a fee for Wimbledon, and three times as much as they had ever paid for anyone else. Looking back, never was money more wisely spent.

DID YOU KNOW?

It took Wimbledon 404 league games and 649 goals since joining Division 4 to reach Division 1. In 7 of their first 9 seasons in the Football League the Dons were either promoted or relegated.

DID YOU KNOW?

Of the12 Dons who clinched promotion to Division 1 at Huddersfield, eight had been in the side that two years earlier had won promotion from Division 3. The exceptions were Thorn, Fairweather, Sanchez, and Fashanu.

As for Nigel Winterburn, he was called-up by Dave Sexton for the England Under-21s to play Italy in Pisa. Winterburn thereby became the first Don in their professional era to win international honours for England. Glyn Hodges had done so for Wales, but he had suddenly found himself out in the cold at Plough Lane. He was recalled for the visit of Sunderland, and a second-half hat-trick ensured that Hodges kept his place.

As the promotion candidates jockeyed for position, it became clear that – with Norwich out of sight – three clubs were chasing two places. Of these, Portsmouth looked the most vulnerable. They had led the table till December, but were now showing signs of cracking. One win in six in April meant they looked increasingly likely to miss out. Were Pompey to stay the distance, the Dons' forthcoming visit to rivals Charlton Athletic would not be for the faint-hearted.

Although Wimbledon had the luxury of games in hand, their final three fixtures were away from home. Three points from the first of these, at Huddersfield, would secure promotion and defuse the tension surrounding the trip to the Valley. Lawrie Sanchez got the crucial goal at Leeds Road. This allowed the Dons to party with Charlton instead of waging war.

Wimbledon's success was a triumph for DIY. Other than Fashanu and Sanchez, the team was logged with players who had come through the youth side, or been picked up for free, or for peanuts from other clubs. Dave Beasant and Nigel Winterburn, to name but two, could command plenty of noughts in any transfer fee. Winterburn had been at Plough Lane three seasons, and now picked up the player of the year award for the third time. Dave Beasant, yet again, was pushed into second place.

Just for the record: in 1985-86 nobody beat Wimbledon twice, no London club beat them at all (in the league), and Wimbledon were the only side to do the double over champions Norwich.

DID YOU KNOW?

Wimbledon scored just 58 goals in winning promotion to Division 1. Only once in their nine-year league career had they scored fewer. But they conceded just 37 goals, easily their best defensive record.

Right team, wrong sport. Back: Evans, Morris, Thorn, Beasant, Cork, Gage, Downes.
Front: Sayer, Hodges, Galliers, Smith, Fishenden.

Match of the Season

Huddersfield 0 Wimbledon 1

Division 2, 3rd May 1986

It was the occasion that elevates this game to match of the season. Pride of place should, perhaps, go to the Boxing Day 'boxing' of Crystal Palace, or the home win over leaders Norwich in March. A visit, albeit a winning one, to a struggling northern club would not otherwise have detained us in our search for stirring fixtures in this – yet another – breathtaking season.

The best that could be said of Huddersfield Town on the morning of Saturday, 3rd May was that they would not be relegated. Four late wins had staved off that threat. Just the one game remained, and for Huddersfield, if not for the Dons, it was meaningless, a chance to spoil the fun for others, but nothing more. Even for Wimbledon, it was not the last throw of the dice.

That Town had pulled clear of the drop was due largely to the recent purchase of Duncan Shearer from Chelsea. Shearer scored a hat-trick in his first full game, followed that with a pair in his next, and welcomed the Dons to Leeds Road by posting seven goals in his first six games. Clearly, he presented a threat to Wimbledon. In

Q Why did No 8 – Cork – look so miserable when the final whistle went at Huddersfield?
A The Terriers' No 8 was also a Cork – David Cork.

time, Shearer would be signed by Aberdeen, and in 1994-95 would win the first of several caps for Scotland.

Shearer was a star in the making. Joey Jones was a star of the past. The former Liverpool defender stood in the record books as Wales' most capped player of all time.

Aside from these two, it was hard to find other evidence of Yorkshire threat, other than that posed by history. Town had done the double over the Dons the previous season, and drawn 2-2, after leading 2-0, at Plough Lane in November.

The match was played in thunder, lightning, and driving rain. Hundreds of hopeful Dons supporters had travelled north to be present at the making of history. What they saw was hardly classic; the conditions alone ruled that out. Huddersfield were determined to be party-poopers, and in the closing minutes paid the price by having Terry Curran and Paul Raynor sent off. By that time Sanchez had claimed one of several priceless goals that would illuminate his long career with Wimbledon, taking a short free-kick from Kevin Gage and firing past Brian Cox.

The match was a personal triumph for Mark 'Guppy' Morris. Farmed out to Aldershot on loan earlier in the season, he was recalled by Bassett when Brian Gayle and Andy Thorn fell victim to cartilage trouble. Morris looked rejuvenated, and now coped as well as anyone with Duncan Shearer. Bassett paid Morris the highest compliment when insisting that he would have been the manager's choice of player of the year.

Referee George Courtney's final whistle provoked celebratory scenes unequalled by anything in Wimbledon's short league career. Champagne corks exploded. Shirts were tossed to the fans, and in Beasant's case his shorts too. Only one man seemed numbed by the experience, unable to take it in. And that was Dave Bassett.

SHE SAID IT

'I am not surprised by these achievements. After all, if we can sell Newcastle Brown to Japan, Bob Geldof can have us running around Hyde Park, and if Wimbledon can make it to the First Division, there is surely no achievement beyond our reach.'
Rt Hon Margaret Thatcher, Prime Minister.

LIFE AT THE TOP 1986-1991

TODAY LEAGUE DIVISION 1 1986-87

Division 1	6th
Littlewoods Cup	2nd Round
FA Cup	Quarter-Final

Wimbledon's elevation to the highest league in the land ranks among the incredible feats of club football. Isthmian League amateurs in 1963; Division 1 professionals in 1986. No other club has started so low and climbed so high. Had Wimbledon at that point tumbled back into the lower divisions, their accomplishments could never be erased. We know now, of course, that Wimbledon did not tumble back; they stayed there. And more.

Strange to say, even as the Dons prepared for life in football's Big Top, little effort was made to reinforce the squad. It is a soccer cliché to say 'they got us here; they deserve a chance.' But in Wimbledon's case it was true. Besides, there was no money to buy. Other than Dennis Wise – a giveaway by Southampton – the players who kicked-off in August had won promotion in May.

Fate now played a little trick. Having asked the Dons to sample life in Division 2 by opening against Manchester City, it was ditto in Division 1. The match marked a milestone in the career of Dave Beasant. He had last missed a game in May 1981 and had been ever-present for five seasons. With Liverpool's Bruce Grobbelaar now injured, Beasant held the record for the longest uninterrupted run of league appearances.

Otherwise, he took few good memories from the match. Andy Thorn's free-kick put Wimbledon in front, but 10 minutes later the Dons trailed 1-3 and fell apart. Should they have lost their second game, at home to Aston Villa, confidence might have drained away.

The Lawrie Sanchez café. Fashanu comes cheap at 50p.

Happily the Dons triumphed in a match featuring a sending off, a penalty, and two goals in the final three minutes. It was an early contender for match of the season, but the fact that Plough Lane could entice no more than 6,366 paying customers for the visit of the former European Champions cast a shadow over the win. Further confirmation that, come what may, the Dons would remain a small-time club.

In any case, Wimbledon's first win was promptly followed by their second; their third; their fourth. Each was by 1-0, underlining that Bassett's earlier helter-skelter textbook was consigned to the bin. Never mind, last-gasp goals at Charlton and Watford saw Wimbledon proudly perched on top of Division 1. That was another first, something never yet repeated.

With hindsight, Wimbledon had enjoyed a gentle introduction to the stresses and strains of high society. They were not to know that their first four opponents would fill the bottom four places, come the end of the season. Besides, beating anyone was triumph enough. But once the big boys started turning up the Dons faltered. They lost five of the next six, and, but for a last-minute Fashanu equaliser against Southampton, would have lost the lot.

All told, the Dons won twice in 13 games – a run that included a damning exit from the Littlewoods Cup at the hands of 4th Division

Luton's Mick Harford hides behind Les Sealey as Brian Gayle takes off. (17th October 1987)

Cambridge. By this time alarm bells were shrill. By the end of November the Dons had sunk from 1st to 14th, with the visit of Manchester United to come.

A 1-0 win was just the tonic. The Dons promptly bashed Chelsea 4-0 at Stamford Bridge – their best win of the season – and before the New Year had seen off Sheffield Wednesday (3-0) and West Ham (3-2). The win at Upton Park was another testament to the Dons' fighting spirit. Twice behind, they twice hit back quickly, and Carlton Fairweather snatched a second-half winner.

It cannot be said that Bassett's tactics endeared Wimbledon to the toffs. 'A pygmy club that played like apes.' That summed up the disparaging view expressed from many quarters. Yet again, referees were busy cautioning Wimbledon players by the score. Bassett appeared not to give a hoot, provided the team kept winning, for results proved just how successful his direct style was. The namby-pamby stuff could be left to others.

Defeat at Highbury on New Year's Day ignited another surge upwards. Indeed, the first 90 days of 1987 would prove to be the most productive of the season – just one league defeat in 10 outings, and a cascading run in the FA Cup that took the Dons to the quarter-finals for the first time. Wimbledon were drawn at home at every stage. When 2nd Division Sunderland led 1-0 with three

DID YOU KNOW?

Alan Cork's goal against Leicester on 30th August 1986 elevated him to membership of an exclusive club – players who have scored in all four divisions. Other members include Ted McDougall and Frank Worthington.

minutes to play, another cup campaign seemed to have come to a premature and inglorious end. But Wimbledon pulled rabbits out of hats, and then disposed of Portsmouth in Round 4 to set up a mouth-watering 5th Round tie with Everton. Howard Kendall's team included three players – Gary Stevens, Trevor Steven, and Peter Reid – who had seen action in the 1986 World Cup finals.

Everton had overhauled Arsenal and would soon be champions. They had ditched Wimbledon twice in the league, the 0-3 defeat at Goodison standing as the Dons' worst of this baptismal season.

This, then, was the measure of the task confronting Dave Bassett and his players before a nationwide live BBC audience. The Dons recovered from losing a quick goal to overpower their opponents, helped by a towering contribution from John Fashanu.

Into the last eight, and the twin towers of Wembley were in sight. Out of the hat came Spurs at home, and this time it was ITV's turn to cover the match. Wimbledon had won 2-1 at White Hart Lane earlier in the season. Sadly, very late goals by Chris Waddle and Glenn Hoddle settled the outcome. It would be Wimbledon's last defeat in that competition for two years.

The season had enough life in it for Wimbledon to throw a few more shocks, none bigger than when winning 2-1 at Anfield, against a Liverpool side that had briefly wrestled top spot from Everton. By now the Dons had insinuated themselves in the top half of the table, and another burst of late scoring, which brought maximum points from their final four matches, lifted them to 6th. No one in their wildest dreams believed Wimbledon could finish so high. But for the tragedy of Heysel and the resulting ban on English clubs, Wimbledon would have qualified for the UEFA Cup. They have never done so since.

Match of the Season

Wimbledon 1 Manchester United 0

Division 1, 29th November 1986

So many thrillers, most of them on opponents' pitches. The best *result* of the season was surely the league win at top-of-the-table Liverpool. Three wins on London grounds were also praiseworthy:

DID YOU KNOW?

When Wimbledon entertained Oxford United on Boxing Day 1986 the teams had met in 3rd, 2nd, and 1st Divisions. The Dons have played no one in all four divisions, and have never played Wrexham and WBA at all (in the league).

at West Ham; at Tottenham, where Lawrie Sanchez and Graham Roberts were sent off; and at Chelsea.

The most tumultuous victory at Plough Lane was doubtless that over Everton in the FA Cup. But the match which meant so much to both sides, and which in the long term proved so valuable to Wimbledon, was that with Manchester United in November.

The previous season it had looked as if Ron Atkinson would lead United to their first championship since 1967. But they had slumped in the spring, and continued in the new season where they had left off. They were not short on star quality. Paul McGrath, Kevin Moran, and Frank Stapleton would play many times for Jack Charlton's Republic of Ireland. Danes John Sivebaek and Jesper Olsen had seen action in the Mexico World Cup. But the midfield was missing the injured Gordon Strachan and Bryan Robson.

With no end in sight to their dismal form, and with United billeted in the bottom three, Ron Atkinson was handed his cards. Alex Ferguson was recruited from Aberdeen in his place. The match at Plough Lane was Ferguson's third in charge, and he needed results – quickly.

Wimbledon were no less desperate. They had lost their last three, won two of the last 13, and unless the fall was arrested appeared to be plunging back where they had come from. This was, in short, a match between losers.

It threw up an unlikely winner, someone who would go on to make a happy habit of winning. Vince – as he was then known – Jones had signed from non-league Wealdstone and made his Wimbledon debut the previous Saturday, at Nottingham Forest. His punch (not an opponent, the ball) had given away the penalty that cost the Dons the match. Now he repaid his debt by heading in Glyn Hodges' corner-kick for the only goal of the game. Jones' exuberant celebration – rushing to salute rows of his family and friends in the stand – will live in the minds of all who witnessed it.

Those three points turned Wimbledon's season around. To cap it, they went on to win at Old Trafford, too, thanks to Dennis Wise in the last minute. A famous double in a famous season.

BARCLAYS LEAGUE DIVISION 1 1987-88

Division 1	7th
Littlewoods Cup	4th Round
FA Cup	Winners

For the first time since Wimbledon joined the Football League they kicked off the new season without the manager with whom they had concluded the old, and without three key players.

When Dave Bassett took over in January 1981 Wimbledon were in Division 4 and going nowhere. Six and a half years later he had built one of the best teams in the country. He must have wondered what was left to achieve for a club which was, according to many, living beyond its means. Bassett was much in demand, and so were his players. Nigel Winterburn picked up his fourth player of the year award in as many seasons, and became the first of many Dons to be sold for a sack of gold. Arsenal paid £400,000 for him. Glyn Hodges later signed for Newcastle, for a further £200,000.

As for Bassett, he now made one of the few bad decisions in an otherwise exemplary managerial career. He accepted an offer from Watford to step into the shoes of Graham Taylor, who likewise had lifted an unfashionable club from the depths to the heights. By taking his assistant, Alan Gillett, and other backroom staff – not to mention centre-half Mark Morris – Bassett ensured that Wimbledon would kick off the following season with a fresh managerial crew and a team shorn of three heroes.

The club were richer financially but poorer communally. Togetherness had got the Dons where they were. That togetherness was now shredded. How could they replace Bassett? Who could possibly fill the boots of Winterburn and Hodges?

The choice of managerial successor was crucial. One has only to peer across to Vicarage Road to see the dangers. Bassett chanced his arm at a club moulded in the image of another. Watford would be immediately relegated. Nor have they ever looked likely to return.

Such a scenario would haunt Sam Hammam if he chose wrongly. He could not appoint from within, for Bassett had taken his lieutenants with him. Hammam therefore had to look elsewhere for the kind of man who would continue Wimbledon's traditions and not tinker with them.

Bobby Gould was long enough in the game to know what he was doing, wise enough to leave well alone, and brave enough as a player to know the value of physical courage. Backing him up was Don Howe, an ex-England international and long-time England coach. Howe's chief difficulty, away from his beloved Arsenal, was to avoid calling his new club *the* Wimbledon.

Gould had to go shopping. He had no back four; he had lost Vince Jones to the surgeon's knife; and almost had no goalkeeper – but Gould vetoed Beasant's proposed transfer. The new manager snapped up four defenders – John Scales (£70,000) from Bristol Rovers, Terry Phelan (£100,000) from Swansea, Eric Young (£70,000) from Brighton, and Clive Goodyear (£50,000) from Plymouth. First opponents, would you believe, were Watford.

John Barnes had left for Anfield, and that was one jewel Watford could not afford to lose. They were headed through the trap-door, but not before Luther Blissett had given them a winning start. Two substitutions were now permitted in league games, and when Paul Miller followed Vaughan Ryan off the bench he raised the number of Dons debutants in one match to four.

The Football League had voted to reduce Division 1 from 22 clubs to 20. This season there were 21, an odd number in more senses than one, for each week one team found itself without a game. The computer, however, had again been generous, arranging fixtures in the opening weeks against almost all the future strugglers. Oxford would finish bottom, but it took a last-minute Cork goal to snatch a draw. Aided by modest opposition, Wimbledon's new boys were given time to gel, and as late summer turned to autumn the team were once again nudging into the top half of the table. Highlight was the 3-0 whipping of Tottenham at White Hart Lane.

Wimbledon were doing nicely in the Littlewoods Cup, overcoming Rochdale (squeakily) and Newcastle to face a 4th Round trip to Oxford. Later, in the league, the Dons would win 5-2 at the Manor Ground, but now the Oxford jinx struck again. Brian Gayle made the mistakes, and Saunders and Phillips punished them.

In the league, Wimbledon went from strength to strength. Going nap at Oxford was their fifth win in a row. They had lost once in 13 games and stood 5th. The players were cock-a-hoop and in the right frame of mind to launch an assault on Wembley.

By spring the line-up had changed considerably from that which Bassett had bequeathed. Gould had boys doing the job of men. Vaughan Ryan had forced his way into the first team. Vince Jones was back, and Dennis Wise's never-say-die performances in the No 11 shirt so intoxicated fans that he would be their player of the year.

Gould had reached for Sam Hammam's cheque-book, signing pint-sized Terry Gibson from Manchester United for £200,000, a fee that eclipsed the previous record paid out for Fashanu. Gibson had never settled at Old Trafford and took his time doing so at Plough Lane. For the time being he had injury to contend with as well.

DID YOU KNOW?

The last time the Dons had beaten anyone THREE times in one season was in 1978-79, when Bournemouth were the victims. In 1987-88 the Dons beat Newcastle THREE times, including in both the Littlewoods and FA Cups.

And so to the FA Cup. First to chance their arm were Ron Atkinson's West Brom, who would miss relegation to Division 3 by one point. They should not have ruffled feathers, and, once their initial flurry was spent, they did not.

Next up were Mansfield. The Stags would miss the drop by two points, in their case into Division 4. On their own ground they could prove a nuisance, and would have done so but for Beasant's penalty save when Wimbledon led 2-1.

Most of the small fry were now out of the way, so Round 5 was always likely to throw up a big 'un. Newcastle at St James's Park had the makings of a tough tie. But the Dons had a curse on the Geordies, winning 2-1 at Newcastle earlier in the season, and by the same score in the Littlewoods Cup at Plough Lane.

A combination of sour grapes and disapproval of Wimbledon's up-and-at-'em style invited Tynesiders to boo the Dons onto the pitch. Perhaps their venom was aimed at Vince Jones, who during the recent goalless draw at Plough Lane had been memorably snapped abusing Gascoigne's manhood. Terry Gibson had returned to the side for that match, and only six minutes had elapsed in the cup-tie when he headed in Wise's free-kick.

Newcastle's principal threat was thought to lie in the boots of 20-year-old Gascoigne and those of Brazilian star Mirandhina – one of several Latin white elephants. When Brian Gayle doubled the Dons' lead, that should have settled it, but Neil McDonald hit back at once, and it took a late Fashanu goal to assure Wimbledon of their place in the quarter-finals for the second year running.

Up popped Watford, without a league win since they completed the double over the Dons in January. This was no longer Dave Bassett's Watford: manager and club had seen the error of their ways and parted company, Bassett taking up a post at Sheffield United. Glyn Hodges and Mick Morris were still at Vicarage Road. Dean Holdsworth was set to break into Watford's first team, though he took no part in this match.

At half-time the Dons trailed 0-1 in goals and 10-11 in players, Brian Gayle having taken a dislike to Watford goalscorer Malcolm Allen. But goals from substitute Eric Young and John Fashanu saw Wimbledon into the semis and extinguished the last ray of hope from Watford's season.

DID YOU KNOW?

Wimbledon beat the sharks but lost to the tadpoles. They defeated champions Liverpool in the FA Cup, but won 1 of 8 matches against four relegated teams.

Now all that separated Wimbledon from Wembley was Luton Town. This was another lucky break. There are those who insist in front of the TV cameras that they don't mind who they get. That is nonsense. In truth Wimbledon were thrilled to avoid Liverpool and Nottingham Forest, first and third respectively in the league. These two giants were left to wage their own semi-final, depriving the public at large of a Final to drool over.

Ray Harford's Luton were also-rans in the league, but created merry havoc in every cup they entered. They were bidding to reach Wembley for the *third* time in a matter of weeks. They had lost the Simod Cup Final, 1-4 to Reading, and already booked their place in the Final of the Littlewoods Cup – to be played two weeks hence – when they would defeat Arsenal 3-2.

In the meantime, dreams of the twin towers had bewitched the Dons. It was fortunate they had no relegation dog-fight on their hands, when the dual focus might have proved too distracting to sustain. Once they had seen off Spurs 3-0 at Plough Lane, they went eight league games without a win. Strangely, their league position did not suffer. They would end the season in 7th place.

League results with Luton were all square. The semi-final was staged at White Hart Lane, with the Dons arriving in cars and a mini-bus, rather than a posh coach, to prevent grandiose ideas.

Luton's Mick Harford, like his managerial namesake, would one day lend his favours to the Dons. But not today. Harford's 48th minute goal seemed to set up another Luton appointment with Wembley. Happily, a Fashanu penalty, followed by Wise sliding through the mud to convert Cork's cross, rewrote the script. Luton would have to settle for two finals; Wimbledon would settle for one!

Match of the Season

Liverpool 0 Wimbledon 1

FA Cup Final, 14th May 1988

Win or lose, Wimbledon's accomplishment in reaching Wembley took some digesting. It was just five years since the club was in Division 4. Dave Beasant and Alan Cork were the only players with memories of those basement years, and they would cherish the Final all the more because of those humble beginnings.

DID YOU KNOW?

Just two of the 1988 FA Cup-winners were still playing for the Dons in 1995-96. Vinnie Jones and Andy Thorn both left and then rejoined.

There could be no tougher opponents than Liverpool, who in 1988 were at the peak of their immense powers. They had just been crowned league champions for the sixth time in nine seasons. Their team bristled with internationals from England (Beardsley, Barnes, McMahon), Scotland (Nicol), the Republic of Ireland (Whelan, Houghton, Aldridge), Denmark (Molby), and even Zimbabwe (Grobbelaar). There were no Welsh caps for the simple reason that Ian Rush was playing for Juventus.

Managed by Kenny Dalglish, Liverpool were as overwhelming favourites as it was possible to be. They had last lifted the FA Cup in 1986 and the pastures of Wembley held no more terrors than did their training ground.

Wimbledon would have it no other way. Their reputation was built on solid foundations of underdogs and giant-killers. Rather Liverpool than, say, Watford.

The match may be summed up by Don Howe's tactical acumen, and a handful of incidents that turned the outcome Wimbledon's way. The tactics concerned how to cope with John Barnes, who had blossomed at Anfield into a mesmerising wide-player whose threat no 1st Division defence had yet successfully neutered. Barnes had romped away with both the players' and the football writers' player of the year prizes for 1988.

Howe's solution was to glue Dennis Wise to him, breaking up the supply lines between Barnes, Beardsley, and Houghton. The tactic worked a treat. Barnes was seldom seen.

But Liverpool were no one-man team. If Barnes' magic was curtailed, there were nine other outfield players to turn to. There was also the referee. Brian Hill did not have the best of games, but at least his questionable decisions were equally divided. He favoured the Dons in the first half when Beardsley netted, only to find that Hill had blown against Andy Thorn's earlier foul. Had the referee played the advantage, Liverpool would have been ahead.

When Hill intervened in the second half, it was to award Liverpool a penalty that was surely unmerited. Clive Goodyear's tackle on John Aldridge looked legitimate. Cup Finals were no time to miss penalties: in fact, no one had ever done so at Wembley. But Aldridge had been below par and at that very moment was about to be substituted by Craig Johnston. Beasant had studied Aldridge's penalty technique and noticed that, although he was equally adept

Back row (left to right): Lawrie Sanchez, Peter Cawley, Eric Young, Dave Beasant, Andy Thorn, Brian Gayle, Alan Cork.
Middle row (left to right): Carlton Fairweather, John Scales, Paul Miller, Simon Tracey, John Fashanu, Vinny Jones, Clive Goodyear.
Bottom row (left to right): Andy Clement, Ian Hazel, Terry Gibson, Terry Phelan, Dennis Wise, Vaughan Ryan, Laurie Cunningham, John Gannon.

at sending them to left or right, if the keeper stood his ground Aldridge preferred to shoot right – to the goalkeeper's left.

His research proved priceless. Beasant stayed upright as long as he dared, then flung himself to pull off a thrilling save. Aldridge's number was up, in more senses than one, and off he trudged, having missed from the spot for the first time for Liverpool. The Reds rarely threatened after that, losing the Cup to Lawrie Sanchez's deft glancing header from Dennis Wise's free-kick in the first half. Beasant lifted the trophy – the first goalkeeper-captain to do so; the first keeper to save a penalty in the Final – wearing a smile that said it all.

The crowds next day lining the streets to Wimbledon Town Hall were estimated at 25,000, vastly more than turned up week after week to watch the team in action.

25 years after Wimbledon lifted the Amateur Cup at Wembley, they had returned to lift the FA Cup. Nothing in English football can trump that.

BARCLAYS LEAGUE DIVISION 1 1988-89

Division 1	12th
Littlewoods Cup	4th Round
FA Cup	Quarter-Final

The last pretence at being party-poopers, gate-crashers, minnows, had been shredded. By finishing 6th, then 7th, plus winning the FA Cup, Wimbledon were among the undisputed giants of the land. Were it not for Heysel they would have taken their proud place among the contestants for the Cup-Winners' Cup. The roll-call in 1988-89 included Barcelona and Sampdoria, who would meet in the Final. One closes one's eyes and sighs at the lost prospect of Wimbledon trooping out at Barcelona's Nou Camp in their quest for a European prize.

Still, Wimbledon were not alone in suffering. Each successful English side was similarly excluded for five long years. Denied the incentive of Europe, Wimbledon could console themselves with the stocking-filler of the Simod Cup.

One consequence of the Dons' new status was quickly apparent. The players – inhabiting the shadows one minute, basking in the bright lights the next – were not keen to commit their futures to Plough Lane. Brian Gayle was snapped up by Manchester City for £350,000, small beer compared with the fees commanded by Dave Beasant and Andy Thorn. Each was signed by Newcastle United for around £850,000. The Magpies' interest was understandable: they had lost three times to the Dons in one season. They followed the well-worn maxim: whom you cannot imitate, buy!

The departure of star names fuels the disquiet of those beneath them in the pecking order, as they contemplate the dismantling of a winning team and sniff the temptation of mammon. Rumbles and grumbles disrupted the Dons throughout August and September. Fielding a new goalkeeper and two new defenders they lost 1-2 to a rejuvenated Liverpool at Wembley in the Charity Shield, were swamped 1-5 at home by Arsenal, and with just one point from five matches found themselves by early October peering up at everyone. Of the 13 players who took part in Wimbledon's second Wembley adventure, only seven would be central to Gould's plans come May.

By the time of their overdue first win, over Everton on 1st October, the Dons were trying out their third goalkeeper. He, Hans Segers, purchased from Forest for £125,000, would hang around long enough to threaten Dave Beasant's total appearances.

DID YOU KNOW?

Dave Beasant was ever-present for Wimbledon for 7 seasons. His run began in August 1981 and continued with Newcastle and Chelsea until he broke a finger in October 1990.
By that time he had played 394 consecutive league games, just 7 short of the record held by Tranmere Rovers' centre-half Harold Bell, established in the first nine seasons after World War II.

Segers was short for a goalkeeper, yet enjoyed a penchant for booming downfield clearances that added to Wimbledon's battery. Segers was the most high-profile of the new intake, which included Keith Curle (a record £500,000 signing from Reading in October) and several 'unknowns' – Paul Miller, who came through the ranks, and 'Detzi' Kruszynski. This infusion of new blood, plus the return to midfield of Vinnie Jones, galvanised the club. From early December into early April Wimbledon were unstoppable, winning 14 matches in league and cups and losing five. Of these five, just three were in the league. The Dons were up to 8th.

Highlights of this burst were twin victories apiece over Millwall and Nottingham Forest, and hitting Luton and Derby for four. Victory at Villa Park in the 4th Round of the FA Cup was followed by overhauling Grimsby in the 5th.

Spring was therefore immeasurably more exciting than autumn. John Scales, 12th man in the FA Cup Final, was playing with such command that he would land the player of the year award. Segers had also settled instantly, Wise caused big clubs to take notice, and John Fashanu's special brand of elbow grease even found favour with England manager Bobby Robson. Fashanu would pick up caps against Chile and Scotland in May, becoming the first Wimbledon player to earn full England honours. Dennis Wise had been called up too, though in his case he would have to wait awhile longer – until after moving to Chelsea – to pull on an England shirt.

The bubble burst – and the season effectively died – with an FA Cup quarter-final at Goodison Park. At the time, the tie had seemed a routine stepping stone on the path to another date with Wembley.

It was not to be. Wimbledon went down with a surprising lack of splash. They would win just one of their final nine in the league, ending the season as miserably as they had begun it, and finishing 12th. They would have settled for that in October: it was bitterly disappointing in the light of the expectations of March.

The Dons saved their final bullet for their final match – at Highbury. This was the season of the Hillsborough nightmare. Despite Merseyside's anguish, Liverpool set off in pursuit of George

Robbie Turner is sandwiched by Manchester Utd's Robson and Bruce. (22nd October 1988)

Graham's team, and were heartened by news of Wimbledon's fight-back – drawing 2-2. Paul McGee's second-half equaliser denied the Gunners maximum points, and set up that Anfield climax.

Match of the Season

QPR 4 Wimbledon 3

Division 1, 8th April 1989

Most of the scores that stand out in 1988-89 were unfavourable – the Charity Shield, the drubbing by Arsenal, elimination from the FA Cup at Everton – and this match at Loftus Road, the highest-scoring feast in which Wimbledon participated. At the time, the Dons were merrily cutting everyone down to size. Three defeats in 19 league games meant that, on form, Wimbledon had little to fear from anyone, other than Arsenal and Liverpool. And certainly nothing from QPR.

QPR had done away with their artificial pitch, but Trevor Francis's first venture into football management had cloudy beginnings. As Wimbledon bounced up the table, Rangers were sliding down. They failed to beat anybody in January and February, but had picked up a bit in March.

DID YOU KNOW?

Wimbledon enjoyed two own-goals in 1988-89. Both were against Liverpool in the league. Despite this assistance, the Dons won neither match.

David Seaman and Paul Parker staunchly protected Rangers' goalmouth. QPR's problems lay in midfield and attack. Ossie Ardiles and Trevor Francis had been lost to the side since January. The arrival of Nigel Spackman and Peter Reid in the spring fortified that area of operations, plus the added goal-power provided by Colin Clarke, who took some of the responsibility off Mark Falco's shoulders.

QPR had already put paid to Wimbledon in the Littlewoods Cup, winning by a Falco goal after three hours' graceless endeavour. The league fixture at Plough Lane had also ended 0-1. With no team having scored more than one past Segers in a dozen matches, few punters were prepared to bet on a goal bonanza at Loftus Road.

Wimbledon took four minutes to take the lead, with their first goal against QPR in four matches. Northern Ireland international Alan McDonald had pulled down Fashanu, who picked himself up to score from the spot after a retake.

For the next hour Wimbledon tossed to the wind all the lessons they had learned over four hard months. Rangers players took turns to thump the ball past Segers. The Dons found themselves trailing 1-4, and in Rangers' current mood a record defeat could not be ruled out. But goals from Sanchez and Fashanu cut the deficit to one, and with another 10 minutes who knows what might have been.

Defeat is defeat, and one followed another as Wimbledon limped across the finishing line. For QPR a win was a win. Four more followed in its wake, the effect of which was to see Rangers overtake the Dons and finish 8th.

BARCLAYS LEAGUE DIVISION 1 1989-90

Division 1	8th
Littlewoods Cup	4th Round
FA Cup	3rd Round

The exodus at the close of 1988-89 was not as painful as it might have been, or as it would become in future years. The manager stayed *in situ*, though he lost his right-hand man, Don Howe, whose eminence by this time made him something of a guru in the affairs of English football.

One senior player did depart. Vinnie Jones was the essence of Wimbledon, the epitome of the club's spirit. Leeds fancied a helping of that spirit and lured him north for a £650,000 fee.

His loss initially proved incalculable. Yet again the team were tortoises at the start. Yet again they opened the season by losing at home to London rivals – Chelsea, this time. Fashanu failed to score for five games, and goals would remain at a premium all season.

It fell to young Vaughan Ryan to fill Vinnie's boots. Few players have the requisite commitment and rapport with the crowd, and Ryan found his ears assaulted by a few spectators who could not adjust to their loss.

When, in October, the Dons lost successive home games to Liverpool and Nottingham Forest it seemed certain that a long, hard winter awaited them. They were next to bottom and faced a stack of daunting away fixtures – at Hillsborough, White Hart Lane and Goodison Park.

But Gould somehow turned things round. Before a team starts winning it must stop losing. Three clean sheets lightened the burden on those up front, and suddenly the losses became draws and the draws became victories. Of the remaining 28 games the Dons would lose five. That 'keep on till the end' spirit was never more manifest than at the turn of the year, when last-minute goals in three successive matches retrieved points that appeared to have been squandered. No amount of good results seemed able to hoist the Dons above halfway in the table, and it took a last-minute winner at QPR in the final match to drag them up to 8th.

Just nine league defeats, all told. That was bettered only by champions Liverpool. Never before or since have Wimbledon lost so few matches in the top division, or conceded so few goals. To that extent it was surprising that they did not sustain their league assault. But those pluses were cancelled by two whopping minuses. The Dons were damp squibs in front of goal. They could not score;

Eric Young scores in the last match with Liverpool before the Cup Final. (26th March 1988)

neither could they win at home. On both counts this was the most fragile season they would know since turning professional in 1964.

Loss of form, injury, and age contributed to the meagre returns of Fashanu, Gibson and Cork, who played barely 50 matches between them. Dennis Wise weighed in with nine precious goals, and without these the picture might have been dark. For Fashanu, it was a season of contrasts. With just one league goal to his name by February, he must have wondered where his next was coming from. He was left out of the team for long spells, and when he did return responded in the best possible way, claiming 10 goals in the final 13 matches.

Wimbledon's defence earned nothing but plaudits. Eric Young, John Scales, and skipper Keith Curle had erected an impenetrable wall in front of Hans Segers, whose shot-stopping, drop-kicking, and all-round reliability won him the player of the year award.

DID YOU KNOW?

In 1989-90 Wimbledon picked up more points away than at home. Only the bottom two teams- Charlton and Millwall – had worse home records. Only champions Liverpool earned more points away. And no one lost fewer games on their travels than the Dons.

John Fashanu is about to be pulled down for a penalty at Villa Park. (24th February 1990)

Match of the Season

Chelsea 2 Wimbledon 5

Division 1, 2nd December 1989

Chelsea and Wimbledon stand at opposite extremes of the soccer spectrum. While the Dons are ridiculed for their lowly upbringing, Chelsea have indulged in a public swagger ever since the days of Tommy Docherty and Peter Osgood in the swinging 60s.

Matches between the teams are invariably tight, as commentators are wont to say of local derbies where neither team gives an inch. Bobby Campbell's newly promoted Chelsea won 1-0 at Plough Lane on the opening day of the season, and stayed in the top half-dozen more or less all season.

Like the Dons, though, Chelsea found home points less easy to accumulate than away ones. By the time of Wimbledon's visit, Chelsea were unbeaten in six games, and their home record read – won 3, drawn 5, lost 0. Every chance of one point; precious little of three.

Protecting Chelsea's goal was Dave Beasant, still enjoying the longest uninterrupted run of appearances in modern times. His transfer to Newcastle had exposed a hitherto concealed fragility,

EVENING STANDARD'S COCKNEY CHAMPIONSHIP
(Based on results of London derbies + Luton, 1989-90)

	P	W	D	L	Pts
1 Chelsea	16	9	3	4	30
2 Spurs	16	9	1	6	28
3 DONS	16	7	5	4	26
4 Arsenal	16	7	5	4	26
5 Palace	16	7	3	6	24
6 QPR	16	6	5	5	23
7 Luton	16	5	6	5	21
8 Charlton	16	4	2	10	14
9 Millwall	16	0	6	10	6

and after just 20 appearances he had returned to the capital. It was nevertheless weird, seeing Lurch standing guard at the wrong end of the pitch after all those years with the Dons. Chelsea's ace striker Kerry Dixon had been picked for England (as substitute) in the 1986 World Cup. Dixon's scoring record over the years showed one goal for every two games. Year in, year out, he was among the most feared predators in the English game.

The Dons were beginning to assert themselves after their dismal start, though defeat at home to Aston Villa had not helped their league position or their confidence. With Fashanu experiencing the worst drought of his career, Gould's patience finally ran out. He dropped the big man, brought back Terry Gibson, and instructed Gibson and Wise to raid Beasant's goal by the terrestrial rather than the airborne route.

Dixon put Chelsea ahead in the first minute. Gibson equalised in the second. It was that kind of match. But Gould had pulled off a tactical masterstroke. By the close the Dons had scored five, mostly shared among Gould's midget strike-force.

The score was so unexpected that journalists assembled in the press lounge were deafened by raucous celebrations issuing from the Dons' dressing room. The one player to experience mixed emotions was the axed John Fashanu. As the goals rained in, Fash felt joy for his team-mates, coupled with understandable dismay. How on earth was he going to win back his place?

BARCLAYS LEAGUE DIVISION 1 1990-91

Division 1	7th
Rumbelows Cup	2nd Round
FA Cup	4th Round

This time it was not just star players wanting away from Plough Lane, but star managers, too. Bobby Gould had enjoyed three years in charge and had masterminded the FA Cup win, but once he made clear that he did not wish to extend his contract beyond its expiry in December 1990, it was mutually agreed that he and the club should part company in the close season.

Gould was replaced – initially on a caretaker basis – by his deputy, Ray Harford. This was a shrewd choice, for Harford had extracted the best from another 'unfashionable' club – Luton Town. He had guided the Hatters to the Littlewoods Cup in the same season that Gould's Wimbledon claimed the FA Cup.

Harford's name lends itself to functional, unromantic football. By and large this approach had served Luton well, but when the team coughed and spluttered the manager's preferred style was held accountable. Harford was elbowed out in January 1990.

This did not mean he was held in low regard by the football hierarchy. Far from it. He would shortly be invited to combine his Wimbledon duties with managing the England Under-21s.

Having sold Winterburn and Hodges in 1987, Beasant and Thorn in 1988, and Vinnie Jones in 1989, Plough Lane in the summertime once again resembled Christie's and Sotheby's. Hardly a week passed without a nought or two being added to Dennis Wise's putative transfer value, and Chelsea's offer to pay £1,600,000 to take him to Stamford Bridge was too good to turn down.

With the new season about to start Crystal Palace swooped for Eric Young – the fee £850,000. Young teamed up with past-and-future Don Andy Thorn. Their centre-back combination would help carry Palace to 3rd place in the league and the FA Cup Final.

Young was expendable because Harford enjoyed a surfeit of dependable stoppers. Gould had had to perm any two from Young, Curle, and Scales, with one of them usually playing out of position.

DID YOU KNOW?

Before a ball had been kicked, promoted Swindon were relegated for financial misdemeanours. The legal battle over who should replace them delayed publication of the fixture list almost until the new season began.

With Young departed, the promising Dean Blackwell came into the picture, forcing Harford for the most part to play Scales in midfield.

But Wimbledon were not just seeking to sell. Warren Barton had made such a splash in his one season with Maidstone – teaming up with Steve Galliers to drive the Stones to the 4th Division play-offs – that Wimbledon paid £300,000 to bring him on board.

The fair-haired Barton was exclusively a full-back at Maidstone, but Harford was quick to perceive the player's versatility. Roger Joseph was playing too well to be budged from right-back. Barton wore No 4, was pushed into midfield in place of Vaughan Ryan, missed only one game, and won over supporters to such an extent that he would be voted player of the year.

This, then, was the extent of Harford's personnel changes in what was Wimbledon's centenary season. It would also be their last at Plough Lane. Come next August they would ground-share with Crystal Palace.

When the Dons were trounced by three second-half Arsenal goals it was the fifth season in a row that they had got off to a losing start. A Fashanu winner at QPR in the next match, followed by a spate of September draws left the team suspended below halfway but clear of imminent danger.

Wimbledon fared badly in the Rumbelows Cup (aka the League, Milk, and Littlewoods Cup), where Plymouth from Division 2 disposed of the Dons home and away to extend their miserable sequence of recent cup flops.

By late October the Dons were impatient for their first home win, yet compensated by remaining unbeaten on their league travels. Victory at Sheffield United squeezed them into the top half, but then came a 3-4 thriller at resurgent Palace, where two goals from Paul McGee – taking Wise's role and playing it manfully – could not stave off defeat.

Warning bells sounded when four more goals were surrendered at Tottenham, but that defeat was a prelude to four straight wins – among them the first at home – plus handsome triumphs over Norwich and QPR. The 12-point bonanza elevated the team to 6th and set up an appetising fixture at unbeaten leaders Arsenal. The result – 2-2 – helped mask the shame of losing to 2nd Division Ipswich in the Zenith-Data Cup for the second successive season. Another run of defeats left the manager shaking his head, scratching his chin, and musing upon the baffling inconsistency of his team.

Another upturn followed. The apex of this fine spell was the 5-1 demolition of Tottenham – Spurs' worst and Wimbledon's best result of the season.

Hans Segers finds a sponsor and a nice fat cheque.

When the Dons overturned a first-minute deficit against Nottingham Forest they were back up to 6th and set on their highest ever position. Among the scorers that day was Andy Clarke, newly signed from non-league Barnet, whose adhesive ball-skills – adroit and gauche in equal measure – delighted and baffled opponents and team-mates alike.

The low-point of the otherwise heady first months of 1991 came at inappropriately named Gay Meadow in the FA Cup. Wimbledon had earned their place in Round 4 with a last gasp, extra-time victory over Aston Villa, thanks to a goal that flew in off a Villa defender's knee. Those with a mind for such things reckoned the Dons' name was on the Cup. One main rival was out of the way and only Shrewsbury blocked their path to Round 5. Shrewsbury were three off the bottom in Division 3, had not won a league game at Gay Meadow for three months, and had just been beaten 2-6 at home by Torquay in the Leyland-Daf Cup.

All Shrewsbury had going for them was the novelty of a new chief. John Bond had managed Norwich and Manchester City in his time, but few moments in football gave him as much pleasure as Gary Shaw's goal, which dumped Wimbledon on their backsides.

Wimbledon drew a veil over that result and concentrated on climbing the league. This was made difficult by a backlog of away

John Scales clears from Chelsea's Gordon Durie in a 2-1 win. (17th November 1990)

fixtures, but the Dons made light of the burden, winning three in a row. It might have been four but for the Sunderland crossbar that kept out Barton's fierce strike.

The Dons had to settle for 7th, finishing in the top eight for the fifth time in six seasons. With English clubs readmitted to European competition, Wimbledon would ordinarily have been chasing a UEFA Cup place. Sadly, rules and regulations reduced the number of places available.

Once again the Dons' home form blunted their progress. To that extent 1990-91 was a near replica of the previous campaign. One point more, one place higher. Timid at home; fearless away. In 1990-91 just four teams posted worse home records; only the top three garnered more away points.

The chief difference with the previous season was that this time Fashanu had no Dennis Wise to take the goalscoring weight off his shoulders. Fash responded magnificently. His 20 goals – all in the league – put him up with the best.

Success may be measured in many ways. Ray Harford was not the only one summoned to the England cause. Keith Curle, Dean Blackwell, and Roger Joseph – significantly, all defenders – earned representative international honours at 'B' or Under-21 level. Joe Kinnear, overseeing the reserves, was voted Clubman of the Year.

Match of the Season

Arsenal 2 Wimbledon 2

Division 1, 15th December 1990

Yet again Wimbledon saved their best for their travelling support. The 2-1 win at Villa in April stirred the emotions, as did the 3-4 loss at Crystal Palace. The 4-0 win at Norwich was nominated Barclays Performance of the Week.

But the 2-2 draw at Highbury spoke volumes for Wimbledon's character. That particular Arsenal side laid claim to be the among the strongest ever. What else can one say of a team that goes through a season with just one league defeat? Arsenal's record showed an almost unbroken string of 'W's – one of which had been earned at Plough Lane on the opening day of the season.

Manchester United were the only blot on the Arsenal landscape. An on-pitch brawl at Old Trafford had resulted in points deductions for both sides. With Liverpool also having made a superlative start, Arsenal felt aggrieved that the destiny of the championship should be decided by committee. When Manchester United called in on Highbury in the Rumbelows Cup they won by a freakish margin – 6-2. Arsenal responded in style, inflicting a crushing first defeat on Liverpool. The chase was on.

The only blemish on Arsenal's 100% home league record was a goalless draw with Spurs. Most visitors not only lost, but lost badly – Chelsea (1-4), Southampton (0-4), Liverpool (0-3). Ian Wright was still at Crystal Palace, otherwise one shudders to think how prolific the attack might have been. Alan Smith did the bulk of Arsenal's scoring in those days.

Wimbledon had the confidence of four league wins behind them, but that counted for little as Arsenal swept into a two-goal lead. The quick feet of Anders Limpar and the quick brain of Paul Merson created first-half goals for Merson and skipper Tony Adams. At that point bets were off. But with the referee checking his watch at the end of the first half Detzi Kruszynski pulled one back.

Messrs Seaman, Adams, Bould, Dixon, and Winterburn have taken long-term residence in Arsenal's defence, which was well equipped to protect narrow advantages. With 90 minutes elapsed they looked to have done so again. But then Wimbledon were awarded a free-kick near the halfway line. Keith Curle took it, Adams and Bould set themselves to clear, but Fashanu launched himself in front of Seaman and the ball went in. Arsenal were indignant. Fash was that kind of player, scoring that kind of goal.

SELHURST PARK 1991-96

BARCLAYS LEAGUE DIVISION 1 1991-92

Division 1	13th
Rumbelows Cup	2nd Round
FA Cup	3rd Round

For 79 years Plough Lane had been home to Wimbledon FC. When the ground first opened trams were running and young men itched to fight in the Great War. But no amount of enhancement in the 1990s could make the stadium fit for top class soccer. This was not for want of trying, but stuck on an urban crossroads it simply did not allow space for expansion or improvement. The conflicting interests of local authorities frustrate the ambitions of many forward-thinking clubs, Wimbledon among them.

If the Dons could not expand, they had to move. The only practical option was Crystal Palace, whose Selhurst Park stadium offered the necessary facilities and whose capacity was unlikely to be frequently tested. Wimbledon FC would not be put in the position, say, of Bristol Rovers and Chester, who lodged in inferior accommodation in distant towns. The Dons were more like partners with their landlords, enjoying separate offices and a distinct identity. But there were drawbacks. There was no tube link with SW19, and rail and buses were awkward, obliging many fans to travel by private transport. Such was the price to be paid for giving the team the stadium they deserved.

That said, an empty Selhurst was worse than a half-full Plough Lane, and it took time for Dons fans to make the adjustment. For the first season or two attendances were embarrassingly small. This compounded the team's difficulties. Playing in an empty, new stadium initially stripped them of 'home' advantage.

DID YOU KNOW?

In three seasons – 1989-90, 1990-91, and 1991-92 – Wimbledon were knocked out of NINE consecutive cup competitions by teams from lower divisions.

Ever since Wimbledon joined the elite they had sacrificed at least one player each summer. In 1991 it was the turn of skipper Keith Curle, sold to Manchester City for an astronomical £2,500,000. Not that 'Sooty' wasn't worth it, but City chairman Peter Swales had always been one to pay over the odds. Young Scott Fitzgerald took his chance, seizing the No 5 shirt and jealously fending off challenges to it for most of the season.

The other newcomer would make an even greater impact. Robbie Earle had been a one-club man with Port Vale, illuminating their midfield and surging forward whenever possible to score 90 goals at an average of one every four games. Many strikers would be proud of such a strike-rate. Clearly, any club buying him would get two players for the price of one, and Earle would not come cheap. In fact, the £775,000 transfer fee was a then Wimbledon record. Earle repaid his investment in his first season, missing just two games, and scoring 15 goals (14 in the league plus one in the Zenith-Data Cup), which was the quota Harford had demanded of him. Earle shared the goalscoring duties with the ever-reliable Fashanu, and it was for the good of the team that he did. No other player added more than five. Small wonder Earle ran away with the tribute of player of the year.

The fixture computer invited the Dons to open against Chelsea. It was now five years since anybody other than Chelsea or Arsenal kicked off the new season. This time the Dons did not lose; in fact, they were just four minutes from winning.

Two other London derbies followed – against West Ham and Crystal Palace. The Palace match was the first between landlords and tenants, and the attendance of nearly 17,000 brought home to the Dons what they were missing. Gates of 3,000 would not be uncommon in the months ahead.

On the pitch, the loss through injury of Lawrie Sanchez, pre-season, and Carlton Fairweather, shortly after, hurt the team badly. The Dons blew hot and cold, losing four in a row in September – including a home defeat by Peterborough in the Rumbelows Cup – followed by back-to-back victories to take them up to 7th.

Events off the pitch now shook Wimbledon to the core. The club had not lost a manager mid-season since Dave Bassett replaced Dario Gradi in 1981. But the combination of Jack Walker's mint and Kenny Dalglish's renown convinced Ray Harford that his future lay

DID YOU KNOW?

Wimbledon's Player of the Year award is frequently given to newcomers. Dons to have won it after one full season are: Francis Joseph, Nigel Winterburn, Warren Barton, and Robbie Earle.
Old favourites like Alan Cork, Lawrie Sanchez and John Fashanu never won it!

with Blackburn Rovers. Harford turned his back on a team 7th in Division 1 to become deputy at a team nowhere in Division 2.

Still, chairmen know there is little point trying to hang on to managers determined to go. The worst of it was that Don Howe had recently rejoined the club. Having two England coaches on board had added immensely to Wimbledon's kudos, but amid the behind-the-scenes politicking Howe departed too.

Rather than promote from within, Sam Hammam offered the manager's job to Peter Withe, assistant coach at Huddersfield, with Mick Buxton brought in as Withe's back-up. In his playing days Withe functioned as a typical English target-man, brave and brawny, whose most famous goal – a miscue from two yards – won the European Cup for Aston Villa in 1982. Withe's battering-ram approach had impressed Bobby Robson sufficiently to earn him 11 England caps, from which he managed one goal (against Hungary).

Withe had never known control of a football club. The loneliness of command can prove a terrible burden. Some first-time managers learn from their mistakes; others never get a second chance. The best that can be said of Withe's time with the Dons was that man and club were patently not suited. Withe was a fitness fanatic who sought to rule with an iron fist, and who immediately alienated all around him. He was only days into the job before Wimbledon's senior players began to voice their disquiet.

Ideally, Withe would not have chosen Peterborough as his first opponents. Harford's team had lost the first leg of the Rumbelows Cup-tie, and Withe had to repair the damage at London Road in the second. The 2-2 draw was not enough. Any fair-minded person could see the tie had been lost at Selhurst, but Withe was tagged as a loser from the start.

The three months that followed were as dark as any Wimbledon had known. By mid-January Withe had overseen 17 games and enjoyed one win, and even that required Oldham missing penalties and hitting both goalposts. Withe would deny that his tactics were ultra defensive, but the facts show his players scored a grand total of just eight goals. The team slumped to 17th, relegation loomed, and the players were on the brink of mutiny. A home defeat by 2nd Division Bristol City in the FA Cup proved the last straw.

MANAGERIAL RECORDS 1991-92 – LEAGUE ONLY

	P	W	D	L	F	A	Pts
Ray Harford	12	5	2	5	21	19	17
Peter Withe	13	1	7	5	8	14	10
Joe Kinnear	17	7	5	5	24	20	26

What fuelled the crisis was the fact that this was the final season before the Premier League came to fruition. Tittle-tattle and self-centred gossip had been echoing around club boardrooms for years. The fat cats wanted to get yet fatter, demanded a greater share of television rights, and were now poised to be administered directly by the Football Association rather than by the Football League. Either that or they threatened to break away and go it alone. Clubs feared financial disaster if excluded from the new elite. Relegation from Division 1 was bad enough even at the best of times; in 1991-92 it smacked of finality and death. Wimbledon had to stay up or – faced with threatened legislation introduced to cover such matters as stadium ownership and minimum gates – they might never get back.

These considerations forced Hammam's hand. Withe was denied the time he demanded and he and Buxton were dismissed following a home defeat by Chelsea. This time Hammam did not look beyond the confines of the club. Harford's assistant, Joe Kinnear, became Wimbledon's third manager in four months, with youth-team boss Terry Burton promoted as his right-hand man.

Kinnear had been an international footballer in his own right. A classy full-back with Tottenham in the late 60s and early 70s – picking up League Cup, FA Cup, and UEFA Cup winners' medals – he had also earned 26 caps with the Republic of Ireland. Sadly, for him, the Ireland national team at the time were cannon fodder, denying him opportunities to make an international name for himself in European Championships and World Cups. The ladder to Premier League management had taken him to Malaysia, Doncaster Rovers, and Wimbledon reserves.

Spouting a 'back to basics' philosophy, Kinnear swept through the club like a messiah. In the space of seven unbeaten games the Dons picked up 15 points and more or less banished fears of the drop. Kinnear's reception by the fans was such that Hammam once sent him back onto the pitch to milk their acclaim. The players, too, sensed the new mood. Under Withe, John Fashanu had demanded a move; under Kinnear he signed a new contract, effectively pledging himself to the cause of Wimbledon FC for the rest of his time at the top.

John Fashanu scores, then gets sent off against West Ham. (24th August 1991)

So, season 1991-92 ended more optimistically than could have been imagined. True, 13th was Wimbledon's lowest ever position in Division 1 (Fashanu's late penalty miss in the final match cost the team 12th place) and three first-hurdle cup exits at the hands of lower division sides was little less than shameful. But this was a time to count blessings, not to carp. Stability and self-belief had returned.

An era had also passed. Alan Cork, the last surviving link with Division 4, was released to join Dave Bassett at Sheffield United. No longer would Dons fans sing to their hero: 'he's got no hair but we don't care'. The odd thing about Corky is he never cost anyone a penny. He came on a free transfer and he left on one.

ALAN CORK'S WIMBLEDON RECORDS IN THE FOOTBALL LEAGUE

1	Most Wimbledon goals	160
2	Most Wimbledon appearances	425
3	Most goals in a match	4 v Torquay, 1979
4	Most goals in one season (including cups)	33 in 1983-84
5	The only Wimbledon player to score in all four divisions.	

Match of the Season

Liverpool 2 Wimbledon 3

Division 1, 8th April 1992

A tough one to call. The other obvious candidate is the 3-5 defeat by Tottenham, in which Gary Lineker, in his final season, became the first Spurs player for 14 years to score four goals in a match.

We will stick with Liverpool at Anfield, partly because the match typified the Dons' rejuvenation under Joe Kinnear, partly because they twice came from behind to win. Of all the worrying aspects of 1991-92, one of the most disturbing was the way opponents clawed their way back to victory. Five times Wimbledon led, then lost.

Graeme Souness's Liverpool teams were more vulnerable than most. This was his first full season in charge, and Souness was not one to live in the shadow of Shankly, Paisley, Fagan, and Dalglish. In some respects he was making the same mistakes as Peter Withe, doing too much, too soon, too confrontationally.

Souness had axed several prominent players – Hysen, Molby, Beardsley, Staunton. Few of his replacements would pass muster.

In early April Liverpool lay just outside the medal positions. They had lost at home just twice. Manchester United and Leeds were too far ahead to be caught, but an unintimidating crop of opponents in the FA Cup had helped Liverpool march to the semi-finals, where they had been held by Portsmouth after extra-time. Wimbledon's visit came three days later. Leg-weary players and an impending replay invited Souness to chop and change his line-up.

Or, rather, it fell to Ronnie Moran to chop and change. Informed that his arteries were clogged, Souness was rushed off for heart by-pass surgery. The tabloids ran the story for days on end.

As for Wimbledon, Kinnear, had already achieved his immediate ambitions – to see the Dons safely into the Premier League. The match at Anfield presented the opportunity to claim a big scalp, and there had not been many of those this season.

It took Michael Thomas just six minutes to put the Reds in front. Goals by Sanchez, Ronnie Rosenthal, and Andy Clarke made it 2-2 midway through the second half. Then Fashanu took a hand. Full-back Rob Jones tackled – fairly, he thought – and Fashanu went down. Referee Key endorsed Fashanu and pointed to the spot. Anfield erupted. The referee had been conned, Jones insisted. The protest was to no avail. They never are, and Fashanu himself scored past Grobbelaar.

Liverpool went on to win the FA Cup.

FA PREMIER LEAGUE 1992-93

Premiership	12th
Coca-Cola Cup	3rd Round
FA Cup	5th Round

A new era, or so the football authorities hoped. Apart from greatly increased TV money, few punters doubted that at heart the Premier League was a hollow exercise in public relations. Referees in green was one novelty, though as an attempt to improve standards Premier matches would have the pick of officials.

While Sam Hammam searched hither and thither for a purpose-built stadium within Merton Borough, Joe Kinnear sought to strengthen his squad. He acquired one key player but lost another. Brentford's top scorer, Dean Holdsworth, was seen as the perfect foil to John Fashanu's artillery. With Mickey Bennett and Detzi Kruszynki moving in the opposite direction, as make-weights, Holdsworth's value on paper took him above the £1 million mark. To balance the books Terry Phelan departed for Maine Road, where he joined forces with Keith Curle for a hefty £2,500,000.

Kinnear's emotional rescue act backfired in the first few weeks. Expectations were too high, perhaps. Sam Hammam's offer of free season-tickets, should the club lift the inaugural Premier title, looked a safe bet. Six games played, two points earned, Fashanu injured, and home defeats recorded by Ipswich, Coventry, and Manchester City – hardly *la crème de la crème* of the Premier League.

With fixtures against Arsenal, Liverpool, and Manchester United looming, what price Wimbledon's winless sequence extending into the winter frosts? But nothing typified the spirit of the Crazy Gang so much as the way they came from behind to beat Arsenal and Liverpool in turn, then – on 31st October – grabbed a late winner at champions-to-be Manchester United.

Kinnear was not blind to the fact that his side needed bite in midfield. Who better to supply it than Vinnie Jones, who had served a season apiece at Leeds, Sheffield United, and Chelsea. Hammam swooped to bring him back. Jones returned to a hero's welcome, then was sent off in his second game, against Blackburn.

Oddly, the three famous scalps did not spark an upturn in form. The Dons were still in the bottom three by the time they notched their first victory over mere mortals – Oldham in December. Dean Holdsworth would remember that 5-2 victory fondly. He had managed just three goals hitherto, one more than the hamstrung

Fashanu, who missed the start of the season and never got into his goal-scoring stride. Much depended on Holdsworth filling the vacuum, and his double strike against Oldham did him the power of good.

Everton hung over Wimbledon's season like a shroud. Howard Kendall's team cropped up in the Coca-Cola Cup (the Dons losing a Selhurst replay); again in the FA Cup (Wimbledon triumphing in a Goodison replay), and, of course, twice in the league. The matches were undistinguished and short on goals, apart from the sixth and final meeting, in the league at Selhurst, which the Dons lost 1-3. That result, in front of the smallest crowd Premier League football has known, consolidated the Dons' desperate league position. The signs were that Wimbledon's membership of the super-elite would be brief.

Kinnear hadn't the money to buy salvation. It had to be achieved by his existing crew, minus the injured Sanchez. The Dons had required 25 matches to earn 24 points. It took them just four games to accumulate another 12. Among the distinguished victims were champions Leeds, plus Arsenal for the second time. Liverpool had already been beaten twice in this craziest of seasons. Defeat at White Hart Lane in the FA Cup was fair exchange for 12 life-giving league points.

By late March the Dons were in mid-table and seemingly safe. But this was to be no ordinary season. Fear of relegation to the anonymity of the Endsleigh League acted like an adrenalin shot to the Premier's strugglers – who kept on winning. One of them, Oldham, buried six goals past Segers in April.

The curtain on 1992-93 came down with the visit of Manchester United. The game was switched to Sunday in the hope of a block-busting title-decider. But Aston Villa had already thrown in the towel, turning the match into a party to celebrate United's first championship since 1967. Had Wimbledon won handsomely they would have finished 9th. They lost 1-2 and finished 12th.

Crystal Palace were relegated on 49 points, losing just four matches more than they had won. Wimbledon were too close for comfort. Their mid-table position was a charade, for their safety margin was a meagre five points. This had been the Dons' closest flirtation with relegation.

DID YOU KNOW?

The crowd for the visit of Manchester United in May 1993 was 30,115. This remains Wimbledon's largest home league gate. It raised the average home attendance for 1992-93 by over 1,000.

Kinnear and Dons' former manager Harford get chummy before the game with Blackburn.

Match of the Season

Wimbledon 3 Arsenal 2

Premier Division, 5th September 1992

A season that sees the champions-to-be defeated on their own patch, and Liverpool and Arsenal beaten home and away, is not short on joyous memories. The home victory over the Gunners gets the nod because of circumstance. Wimbledon had lost all three matches at Selhurst Park, and had a habit of losing to Arsenal at the best of times. Bolstered by the lethal Ian Wright, Arsenal had a one-man match winner.

Wright put Arsenal in front, converting Campbell's cross at the far post. Sanchez fired in low from eight yards, and the score was 1-1 as the game entered the final 10 minutes. Then Earle's clever chip pierced Arsenal's offside trap, leaving Fashanu in splendid isolation. Fash took his time, too long really. David Seaman half-saved, but could not deny Fashanu his first goal of the season.

This time it was Arsenal who hit back quickly, as Segers spilled Winterburn's cross. The Dons looked resigned to one point, at best, until Fashanu and Adams collapsed in a heap and Earle rifled in the loose ball.

FA CARLING PREMIERSHIP 1993-94

Premiership	6th
Coca-Cola Cup	Quarter-Final
FA Cup	5th Round

After one season the Premier League was handed to commercial sponsors. The brewery – Carling – promptly introduced the concept of squad numbers. Each player would retain his personal number throughout the season, with his name emblazoned above it. This enabled players to be more easily recognised on the pitch, boosted merchandising by encouraging sales of replica shirts, but caused statisticians no end of trouble keeping track.

Wimbledon introduced a kit change of their own, switching to navy shirts, shorts and socks. As for the team, for the first time since embracing the elite in 1986 the summer passed without any stars waving goodbye. The Dons defence was bolstered by the signing of Alan Kimble, a full-back with 300 appearances for Cambridge United. Kimble's squad number was 35.

Bearing in mind Wimbledon's chronic first-match failings, it was cause for jubilation when newly promoted West Ham were sunk by two second-half goals at Upton Park. Now, at last, the Dons were not left behind at the gun. The change in fortunes persisted into October, by which time Wimbledon had won four and drawn four of their first nine games.

Leeds put a dampener on things, handing out a 4-0 smack at Elland Road. Newcastle dished out the same treatment, the Dons lost to Ipswich and West Ham at home, and with Christmas approaching early season optimism was replaced by mid-season gloom. The team were down to 15th, with an appointment at handily-placed Aston Villa unlikely to bring reward.

Dean Holdsworth's winning goal at Villa Park appears with hindsight to have been the golden egg. Three days later Liverpool were sent packing after a sensational Coca-Cola Cup replay, to send the Dons into the quarter-finals with a home tie against Sheffield Wednesday. Never had the Dons gone so far in this competition.

Wembley must have seemed tantalisingly close. Manchester United and other big-name opponents had been avoided, and Wednesday had started the season so badly that Premier survival was an obvious priority. Unfortunately, the Owls had run into irresistible form. One defeat in their last 21 games told its own story, and Mark Bright's swivel and shot from long range decided the outcome. It would be little consolation when the fixture was

DID YOU KNOW?

When the Dons won at West Ham in the first match of 1993-94 it was their first opening-day success since joining the top division in 1986. It was only their second first-match triumph in 23 seasons. Since 1971-72 that record now showed 2 wins, 10 draws, 11 defeats.

immediately replayed in the league. This time the scores were reversed.

Selhurst Park's next cup visitors were Manchester United. Unbeaten in 32 games, Alex Ferguson's champions were seeking an unprecedented domestic treble. This tie would determine who would reach the last eight of the FA Cup. The match was played on Sunday before a vast TV audience, United taking the opportunity to shine and to treat the nation to wonder goals that Wimbledon could only applaud. Manchester's punishment, like Wednesday's, was held over till their next visit. United would lose at Selhurst in the league.

In the Premiership Wimbledon hit the accelerator. With the transfer-deadline looming, Kinnear unveiled his latest Brentford acquisition. Marcus Gayle had supplied many of the crosses that enabled Dean Holdsworth and Gary Blissett to smash 41 goals in winning the 3rd Division title in 1992. Now all three were with Wimbledon. Though Blissett stayed on the margins, Gayle worked instant magic. His first nine games saw seven wins and two draws. That purple patch hoisted Wimbledon into contention for UEFA Cup places. Among their prized scalps were Leeds, Spurs and both title contenders, Manchester United and Blackburn Rovers.

Such was Wimbledon's capacity to inflict lasting damage that Everton dreaded their visit to Goodison for the final match. Everton were in crisis. Howard Kendall, their svengali, had stepped down and Mike Walker, his successor, supervised a relentless stream of defeats. He led the Toffees into the last game knowing that a draw would condemn them to relegation for the first time in the club's history. It was win or bust, and even a win might not be enough.

For Wimbledon, their exhilarating run began a match or two too late. They could finish 5th, if they won and Leeds lost at doomed Swindon. But not even 5th place would present a passport to Europe.

DID YOU KNOW?

Since World War II only six Gayles have played league football in England. Three of them have played for Wimbledon – Brian, John, and Marcus.

Not No 4, Vinnie. Supporters voted you No 2 in the Wimbledon popularity stakes.

After 20 minutes Wimbledon led 2-0, Goodison was hushed, Everton's fate sealed. Then the referee intervened, awarding the home side a phantom penalty. Then Hans Segers – hitherto a model of consistency – failed to get a hand on Horne's scuffed shot. With Goodison ablaze, Stuart drove in the winner. The Dons trooped off looking sheepish, unleashing a tide of dark questions.

So the Dons finished 6th, equalling their best placing. For Joe Kinnear, season 1993-94 was to prove especially rewarding. Three times he was named Carling Manager of the Month. To cap it all, he was voted Manager's Manager of the Year.

Q Prior to Everton in May 1994, when was the last time Wimbledon lost a match in which they had led by two goals?
A Never. Not since turning professional in 1964.

Match of the Season (1)

Wimbledon 2 Liverpool 2 (aet)
Coca-Cola Cup, 4th Round Replay, 14th December 1993

Season 1993-94 threw up any number of matches to savour. But two stand out, and in their different ways are impossible to separate. A tense Coca-Cola Cup win over Kevin Keegan's resurgent Newcastle set up an away tie at Liverpool. The Dons were moral victors, but needed a late Robbie Earle equaliser to salvage a replay and bring Graeme Souness's Reds back to Selhurst Park. There, in biting wind and driving sleet, which encouraged John Barnes to wear gloves throughout, both teams treated the crowd to over two hours of nerve-jangling excitement. Advantage swung this way and that, denying victory to either side until the last kick of the extended match.

Holdsworth drew first blood for Wimbledon, the chance carved out by Vinnie Jones' sweeping pass out to Peter Fear. When Fashanu streaked away, one on one with Grobbelaar, it looked curtains for Liverpool, but Fash dallied and Ruddock got back to block. Souness immediately pulled off Jan Molby and Mark Wright, and when Scott Fitzgerald fouled McManaman from behind, marauding defender Neil Ruddock fired in from Barnes' short free-kick to level the scores. Liverpool's offside trap never looked secure, and Jones' long ball caught them napping. Again Fashanu was clear, again he made a hash of it, but this time the ball ricocheted off Grobbelaar along the goal-line to where Robbie Earle was waiting.

After 93 minutes, with the referee ignoring piercing whistles to blow for time, Liverpool launched one last attack. Steve Nicol crossed, two Dons defenders inadvertently flicked on, and under a challenge from McManaman Hans Segers incredibly punched the ball into his own net.

Liverpool had the bit between their teeth. In extra-time Fashanu, who could do nothing right, felled substitute Mark Walters on the edge of the box, but Segers redeemed himself with an expert save from John Barnes' penalty.

No more goals, so yet more penalties, five apiece, until one side or the other cracked. Joy for Wimbledon, Jamie Redknapp's effort was stopped by Segers' legs. Despair, Grobbelaar palmed Vinnie Jones' attempt up in the air. Ecstasy, as Mark Walters' feeble effort bobbled against Segers' shins. Relief, as Brian McAllister – who had never scored a goal in his life – fired into the top corner off Grobbelaar's fingertips. Frustration, as young Robbie Fowler makes it 3-3.

Now all eyes flew to the young Don striding forward. Neal Ardley was a trainee midfielder of much promise but little experience. Would his nerve hold? Shame on the doubters: the roar told its own story. Squadrons of Dons winged their way to all corners of the stadium.

DID YOU KNOW?

In 1993-94 Dean Holdsworth became the first Don to be top scorer and ever-present in one season. He was also runner-up as Player of the Year. He claimed Wimbledon's first hat-trick since 1989, and the first brace of hat-tricks in one season since Alan Cork in 1978-79.

Match of the Season (2)

Wimbledon 4 Blackburn Rovers 1

Premiership, 29th March 1994

Victory over Liverpool in the Coca-Cola Cup ended with anti-climax against Sheffield Wednesday. But then the Dons got their second wind and, unable to be kings themselves, wielded the knife as king-makers.

First to be slain were Blackburn. This was King Kenny's second season in the top division with Rovers. They had finished 4th in 1993 and were now breathing hard down Manchester United's neck. They had been defeated once in four months in the league, but crucially had lost Scottish international defender Colin Hendry to injury. The veteran Republic of Ireland stopper, Kevin Moran, filled his position.

Hendry's absence was little noticed in a first half that saw Jason Wilcox ease past Warren Barton to put Rovers in front. Short of putting stimulants in his players' half-time orange juice, it was hard to see how Joe Kinnear could turn the tables. Wimbledon had lost 0-3 at Ewood Park six weeks earlier, and a repeat score could not be ruled out.

What a tonic, then, as the Dons emerged for the second period to put Rovers to the sword. It took five minutes for Earle to latch upon Segers' punt and slalom into the box. Fashanu took the ball off his toe to equalise. With a quarter of an hour left the score was still 1-1. But then Henning Berg turned Jones' projectile into his own goal. Rovers now had to attack, but the gaps they left played into Wimbledon's hands. Peter Fear's sweeping right-wing move enabled Holdsworth to head against Flowers' body and tap in the rebound, whereupon Earle capped a memorable night by volleying the fourth. The result was cheered in Manchester no less than in south London.

FA CARLING PREMIERSHIP 1994-95

Premiership	9th
Coca-Cola Cup	3rd Round
FA Cup	5th Round

With the curtain set to rise on the new season John Fashanu suddenly went. He and Lawrie Sanchez had been the last links with the original Crazy Gang. Sanchez had left the fold in March, bound for Swindon Town.

Fashanu's symbolic loss was incalculable. The crude, muscular target man had honed his skills to become England class. He had the caps to prove it. But his looks and his eloquence in front of the camera also made him a catch for the media, for whom he was devoting more and more of his time and energy. He was, in fact if not in name, already a part-time Wimbledon player. His quota of goals in recent seasons had dipped as Dean Holdsworth took over his mantle. All things considered, it was easier to replace Fashanu than Holdsworth. But what price a 30-something 'almost-has-been' with an eye to the big screen?

The answer was £1.3 million. Aston Villa were happy to pay it and Kinnear more than happy to accept. A good bit of business, he winked, and he was right, especially as Fashanu was soon lost to the game through injury, and his replacement – the even more grizzly Mick Harford – cost just £50,000 from Coventry.

But trouble was brewing. Matters were not helped by another wretched start. Two points from four matches left the Dons staring upwards, as was customary in August and September. By then they had waved goodbye to John Scales, who had matured from a shy lad signed from Bristol Rovers into a highly accomplished central defender. As Sam Hammam rightly said, Scales had given his best years to the Dons and it was no longer right to stand in his way. Several northern clubs were determined to get him, but it was Liverpool who paid £4 million to acquire his signature. Before the season was out Scales would win his first full England cap. His place in the Wimbledon side was taken by Alan Reeves, a £200,000 purchase from Rochdale in the bad-lands of Division 3. Vinnie Jones assumed the captaincy, and it was not long before he heard Welsh choirs in his head and was capped by Wales.

Hitherto it had been policy to sell players in the summer, not with the season under way, as happened with Scales. The worry was that, shorn of two big names, others would demand to leave. Clubs with ambition hang on to their jewels; they don't sell them –

DID YOU KNOW?

Liverpool's win in October 1994 was their first over Wimbledon in 10 attempts. The last match under Kenny Dalglish was drawn, whereupon Graeme Souness's Liverpool failed to beat the Dons EIGHT times in league and cup.

though that maxim could never apply to a club like Wimbledon. Nevertheless, noises emanating from the dressing room suggested that Warren Barton and Dean Holdsworth wanted away. Unless nipped in the bud, protest could fester.

Failure to beat Leicester in match No 5 might have turned a drama into a crisis. But Mick Harford scored the first of several timely goals, which – accompanied by an own-goal – deprived Leicester of any reward. Sadly, four defeats on the run in October confirmed that this was likely to be a season of injury, struggle, and torment. Last of the four was at Anfield, where a Liverpool side with John Scales in their ranks won as they pleased.

Kinnear had no choice but to splash out. First to arrive, or rather return, was Andy Thorn. Six years earlier Thorn had been sold to Newcastle for £850,000. Still only 28, he now re-signed from Crystal Palace on a free transfer. Next in was Norwich's speedy Nigerian forward Efan Ekoku, who first hit the headlines by scoring four goals at Everton. Ekoku's signing (he cost £920,000, a club record) was followed by that of Oyvind Leonhardsen from Rosenborg (for £700,000) and the Millwall duo, Kenny Cunningham and Jon Goodman – whose combined fee was £1.3 million. Wimbledon had never previously paid out that kind of money.

Added to Reeves, the intake amounted to half a team. Such an infusion of new blood might backfire if the newcomers' enthusiasm was offset by playing among a team of strangers.

The season was effectively saved in the space of 10 whirlwind days in November. Aston Villa and Newcastle were defeated in games awash with goals. Both times the Dons squeezed through by the narrowest of margins. Light could be seen at the end of the tunnel.

The team blew hot and cold for the rest of the season. Injuries hit the club hard, especially those to Holdsworth and Robbie Earle, whose combined goal-potential was irreplaceable. In their absence two winning streaks were followed inexorably by two losing ones.

DID YOU KNOW?

Arsenal were the last club never to have finished lower in the league than the Dons. Wimbledon rectified this in 1994-95.

December and January brought eight unbeaten games, including a first ever win at Southampton. The backlash was one win in the next seven. Losing 1-7 at Aston Villa was the biggest caning the Dons had ever taken. 'Never again,' vowed Kinnear.

Four wins in the spring were rewarded by a place in the top eight, but these merely precipitated a winless sequence which lasted to the season's end. Seven games, the middle five without a goal. Three successive goalless draws – against Everton, Liverpool, and Arsenal – was another Wimbledon 'first'. Goalkeeper Neil Sullivan broke his leg against Nottingham Forest in the final match. Sullivan had been given an overdue run in the side as a result of Segers losing his sharpness and confidence.

All things considered, to finish 9th in a season of trauma was worthy of a medal.

Match of the Season

Wimbledon 4 Aston Villa 3

Premiership, 9th November 1994

Nothing runs this momentous match close in the match-of-the-season stakes. It was to prove as critical in the affairs of Aston Villa as those of Wimbledon.

As a manager, Ron Atkinson had nothing left to prove. He had lived life at the top – at the Hawthorns, Old Trafford, Hillsborough – not to mention Atletico Madrid – and in the main fostered fancy football and winning teams. In March his Villa side had won the Coca-Cola Cup, beating the overwhelming favourites Manchester United.

But inexplicably Villa were in the doldrums. Unbeaten in their first five games of the season, they had collapsed to take just one point from the next eight. No one could put their finger on what had gone wrong – other than that many of his players were getting long in the tooth – and even that could not account for the sudden switch in fortunes. Never the most patient of men, Villa chairman Doug Ellis was getting edgy.

Wimbledon were no healthier. Kinnear's team had lost six of their last seven. In short, here were the two most out of form sides in the league. Whoever lost was asking for trouble.

DID YOU KNOW?

Top scorer in 1994-95 was Efan Ekoku with 9. This is the first occasion that the Dons' leading marksman has failed to reach double figures.

DID YOU KNOW?

Nigel Spink played in goal for Chelmsford City at Plough Lane in the Southern League in April 1976. His next visit was 13 years later, with Aston Villa in Division 1. In 1982 he had helped Villa win the European Cup.

The Dons did not relish facing John Fashanu, but he was injured. Villa brought back Mark Bosnich in goal in place of the veteran Nigel Spink.

Kinnear threw midfielder Leonhardsen into the fray. 'Leo' was a veteran Norwegian international with 40 caps. His goal in Oslo had smashed England's World Cup hopes, and by taking part in USA '94 he became the first Don to have graced the World Cup finals.

The fact that neither team could defend made this a pulsating match for spectators, whose numbers were reduced by a wet and miserable evening. Wimbledon struck first. Ekoku was felled in shooting stride by Ehiogu and Warren Barton smote home the penalty. Yet five minutes after half-time Villa led 3-1. And it might have been worse: Houghton had shot wide of an empty goal with Villa still trailing. But Gary Parker banged in Dwight Yorke's low cross from two yards, and Parker was instrumental in Villa taking the lead. His powerful angled shot was parried by Segers but fell to Dean Saunders.

Villa shrugged off the expulsion of skipper Andy Townsend to extend their lead after half-time. Saunders beat the offside trap to walk the ball round Segers. The season had barely begun, but this was the sixth time the Dons had conceded three goals in a match.

They must have been close to despair, but they rose up to twist the lion's tail. Gary Elkins' cross from the by-line was headed in by Neal Ardley. A man short, and with a precious lead to protect, Villa manned the pumps. Jones let rip from 35 yards, only to see the ball ping back off the angle. With seven minutes remaining he tried again. This time the ball flew low, clipped a defender and wrong-footed Bosnich. Into the last minute, and intricate footwork by Barton and Earle set up Leonhardsen to crack the ball inside the near post.

Ron Atkinson paid the ultimate price for Villa's defeat. He was sacked next morning. Wimbledon also got their come-uppance. When the teams next met, at Villa Park in February, Brian Little's team exacted revenge to the tune of 7-1.

FA CARLING PREMIERSHIP 1995-96

This time it was Warren Barton's turn to go. His departure to Newcastle for more than £4 million broke the Dons' transfer record but left statisticians in a quandary. He had won his first England cap in the ill-fated international in Dublin, abandoned because of yobs. He was sold before he could win another cap. Was he, or was he not, a member of Wimbledon's international brigade?

The other change to the side was in goal. With Neil Sullivan recuperating from his broken leg, and Hans Segers out of favour, the one position that seemed secure was up for grabs. Kinnear went to Leyton Orient to tempt Paul Heald to sign.

The summer had seen the shenanigans of the Inter-Toto Cup, an unwelcome circus dangling the carrot of extra UEFA Cup places. With some reluctance Wimbledon took their place among England's representatives, played their 'home' matches at Brighton, fielded teams of unknowns, and sank without trace.

And what a Jekyll and Hyde start to the season. One defeat in the first five games raised eyebrows. The team were up with the early pace-setters. It soon became clear that this Dons side was breaking new ground. Wimbledon teams habitually score few but concede fewer. Such notions had to be revised in the wake of implausible results. Who could believe Wimbledon would share *nine* goals in a Coca-Cola Cup-tie with Charlton, and *six* more in the second leg. Losing 1-6 at Newcastle bode ill for the months ahead. Though Wimbledon are used to adversity, with a quarter of the season gone, they had posted just two clean sheets. One was against Liverpool – a result achieved in surreal circumstances.

TEAM OF ALL-STARS SOLD BY WIMBLEDON

	1 D Beasant £850,000		
2 N Winterburn £400,000	5 A Thorn £850,000	6 K Curle £2,500,000	3 T Phelan £2,500,000
4 W Barton £4,000,000	7 V Jones £650,000	8 J Scales £4,000,000	11 G Hodges £200,000
	9 J Fashanu £1,300,000	10 D Wise £1,600,000	

Substitutes: E Young (£850,000), B Gayle (£350,000)

Total value of the All-Stars: £20,050,000

One for the scrapbook. Wimbledon's most popular player, Alan Cork, scores his penultimate goal for the club – against Coventry. (31st August 1991)

Match of the Season

Wimbledon 2 Leeds 4

Premiership, 23rd September 1995

Match of the Autumn rather than Match of the Season. Selhurst Park was not short on spice in the first months of 1995-96. The win over Liverpool required just one goal, self-inflicted at that, but it was scored within seconds of Vinnie Jones' umpteenth dismissal (which the referee subsequently had the good sense to annul). Wimbledon's 10 men barely escaped from their penalty area after that. For an hour Liverpool's strikers played pinball with Heald and the woodwork, but could not break through.

Games with Howard Wilkinson's Leeds followed an unfortunate pattern. The Dons got stuffed up there, and participated in goal-droughts at home. This particular match broke the mould, and all because of a muscular Ghanaian striker called Tony Yeboah. Signed from Eintracht Frankfurt, Yeboah specialised in ballistic shooting from near and far.

The second of Yeboah's three goals against the Dons invited disbelief, as he controlled the ball on his thigh, dinked his way inside one challenge, and detonated a shot from 22 yards in off the crossbar. Wimbledon contributed mightily to a memorable match, but their two headed replies were too little, too late.

WIMBLEDON'S COMPLETE SOUTHERN LEAGUE RECORD

		Home					Away					Total					
	P	W	D	L	F	A	W	D	L	F	A	W	D	L	F	A	Pts
Margate	22	8	2	1	21	11	6	1	4	21	18	14	3	5	42	29	31
Telford*	24	7	5	0	23	10	4	3	5	11	16	11	8	5	34	26	30
Weymouth	24	8	3	1	22	9	4	2	6	14	21	12	5	7	36	30	29
Yeovil	24	8	2	2	15	6	3	5	4	9	15	11	7	6	24	21	29
Nuneaton B	24	9	3	0	28	6	2	4	6	11	15	11	7	6	39	21	29
Burton Alb	18	8	0	1	27	6	5	2	2	15	11	13	2	3	42	17	28
Bedford	18	7	1	1	23	5	6	1	2	11	6	13	2	3	34	11	28
Dover	22	8	2	1	19	7	2	4	5	11	19	10	6	6	30	26	26
Hillingdon B	22	5	5	1	24	13	4	1	6	14	16	9	6	7	38	29	24
Barnet	18	6	1	2	22	9	4	2	3	13	10	10	3	5	35	19	23
Cambridge C	18	5	4	0	15	9	2	4	3	10	10	7	8	3	25	19	22
Kettering	18	8	0	1	16	5	0	5	4	12	18	8	5	5	28	23	21
Poole	18	6	3	0	23	7	2	2	5	10	14	8	5	5	33	21	21
Chelmsford	24	4	4	4	15	15	3	3	6	9	19	7	7	10	24	34	21
Hereford	16	5	1	2	14	7	4	1	3	11	12	9	2	5	25	19	20
Worcester	16	3	4	1	11	8	3	3	2	14	11	6	7	3	25	19	19
Guildford*	16	4	3	1	22	12	3	1	4	14	11	7	4	5	36	23	18
Romford	20	5	3	2	17	11	2	1	7	13	19	7	4	9	30	30	18
King's Lynn	12	5	1	0	14	6	2	1	3	5	5	7	2	3	19	11	16
Corby	8	4	0	0	16	4	3	0	1	6	3	7	0	1	22	7	14
Tonbridge*	8	4	0	0	15	3	3	0	1	6	4	7	0	1	21	7	14
Bath	14	3	0	4	15	13	3	2	2	7	6	6	2	6	22	19	14
Gravesend	8	4	0	0	11	3	2	1	1	7	3	6	1	1	18	6	13
Folkestone	10	4	0	1	18	6	2	1	2	8	7	6	1	3	26	13	13
Dartford	14	3	2	2	8	7	1	1	5	5	13	4	3	7	13	20	11
Atherstone	8	2	1	1	7	5	3	0	1	6	2	5	1	2	13	7	11
Cambridge U	10	2	3	0	9	6	1	0	4	5	10	3	3	4	14	16	9
Maidstone	8	2	1	1	5	6	2	0	2	6	6	4	1	3	11	12	9
Grantham	8	3	0	1	7	6	1	1	2	1	4	4	1	3	8	10	9
Merthyr Tydfil	4	2	0	0	10	0	1	1	0	2	0	3	1	0	12	0	7
Wealdstone	6	2	0	1	10	4	1	1	1	2	1	3	1	2	12	5	7
Ashford	4	2	0	0	11	1	1	1	0	4	2	3	1	0	15	3	7
Rugby	4	1	1	0	4	2	1	1	0	5	4	2	2	0	9	6	6
Stourbridge	4	2	0	0	6	0	1	0	1	7	2	3	0	1	13	2	6
Gloucester	6	1	2	0	8	7	0	1	2	3	7	1	3	2	11	14	5
Stevenage	4	1	1	0	3	0	0	2	0	4	4	1	3	0	7	4	5
Crawley	4	2	0	0	10	0	0	1	1	1	3	2	1	1	11	3	5
Sittingbourne	2	1	0	0	5	2	1	0	0	2	1	2	0	0	7	3	4
Hinckley	2	1	0	0	5	1	1	0	0	2	0	2	0	0	7	1	4
Barry	2	1	0	0	3	1	1	0	0	3	1	2	0	0	6	2	4
Trowbridge	2	1	0	0	4	2	1	0	0	4	2	2	0	0	8	4	4
Hastings	2	1	0	0	5	0	1	0	0	1	0	2	0	0	6	0	4
Brentwood	2	1	0	0	2	1	1	0	0	2	0	2	0	0	4	1	4
Redditch	2	1	0	0	3	0	1	0	0	3	0	2	0	0	6	0	4
Minehead	2	1	0	0	1	0	1	0	0	1	0	2	0	0	2	0	4
Ramsgate	4	1	1	0	3	1	0	0	2	2	5	1	1	2	5	6	3
Deal	2	0	1	0	2	2	1	0	0	7	0	1	1	0	9	2	3
Tunbridge W	2	0	1	0	1	1	1	0	0	4	1	1	1	0	5	2	3
AP Leamington	2	0	1	0	0	0	1	0	0	3	0	1	1	0	3	0	3
Canterbury	2	0	1	0	0	0	0	1	0	1	1	0	2	0	1	1	2
Waterlooville	2	0	1	0	1	1	0	1	0	1	1	0	2	0	2	2	2
Dunstable	2	1	0	0	3	0	0	0	1	0	1	1	0	1	3	1	2
52 Opponents	546	174	66	33	585	250	100	63	110	354	364	274	129	143	939	614	677

** reconstituted clubs*

WIMBLEDON'S COMPLETE FOOTBALL LEAGUE / PREMIER RECORD – TO 1994-95

		Home					Away					Total					
	P	W	D	L	F	A	W	D	L	F	A	W	D	L	F	A	Pts*
NORWICH	20	7	2	1	16	6	6	2	2	13	6	13	4	3	29	12	43
SHEFFIELD UTD	16	6	2	0	22	3	2	2	4	8	15	8	4	4	30	18	28
TOTTENHAM	18	4	2	3	19	14	4	2	3	16	14	8	4	6	35	28	28
ASTON VILLA	16	4	2	2	14	12	4	1	3	9	11	8	3	5	23	23	27
SHEFFIELD WED	18	4	3	2	14	10	3	3	3	9	10	7	6	5	23	20	27
NOTTINGHAM F	16	5	2	1	17	9	2	2	4	9	13	7	4	5	26	22	25
BOURNEMOUTH	8	4	0	0	12	3	4	0	0	8	4	8	0	0	20	7	24
CHARLTON	12	4	1	1	14	7	3	2	1	5	3	7	3	2	19	10	24
COVENTRY	18	3	2	4	9	9	3	3	3	11	10	6	5	7	20	19	23
EVERTON	18	4	3	2	13	11	1	5	3	8	13	5	8	5	21	24	23
MANCHESTER C	16	4	3	1	9	5	1	4	3	5	11	5	7	4	14	16	22
QP RANGERS	18	2	3	4	8	10	4	1	4	12	12	6	4	8	20	22	22
YORK	8	4	0	0	11	5	3	1	0	10	3	7	1	0	21	8	22
SOUTHAMPTON	18	3	3	3	12	12	1	6	2	12	13	4	9	5	24	25	21
CHELSEA	16	2	4	2	9	9	2	4	2	15	12	4	8	4	24	21	20
OLDHAM	10	4	1	0	11	3	2	1	2	6	9	6	2	2	17	12	20
WEST HAM	12	2	1	3	5	5	4	1	1	10	8	6	2	4	15	13	20
LIVERPOOL	18	1	4	4	8	11	3	3	3	13	15	4	7	7	21	26	19
MANCHESTER U	18	3	2	4	10	12	2	2	5	5	11	5	4	9	15	23	19
TORQUAY	8	3	0	1	10	2	3	1	0	11	4	6	1	1	21	6	19
ARSENAL	18	3	0	6	11	22	1	6	2	8	12	4	6	8	19	34	18
CREWE	8	2	2	0	6	3	3	1	0	7	1	5	3	0	13	4	18
CRYSTAL PALACE	14	3	2	2	11	8	2	1	4	13	12	5	3	6	24	20	18
LUTON	12	4	0	2	12	3	1	3	2	5	7	5	3	4	17	10	18
MILLWALL	12	2	3	1	11	11	2	3	1	6	5	4	6	2	17	16	18
STOCKPORT	8	3	0	1	7	3	2	2	0	6	3	5	2	1	13	6	17
HARTLEPOOL	8	4	0	0	13	1	1	1	2	4	6	5	1	2	17	7	16
NEWCASTLE	10	4	1	0	14	5	1	0	4	4	10	5	1	4	18	15	16
NORTHAMPTON	8	3	1	0	8	2	1	3	0	7	4	4	4	0	15	6	16
ROCHDALE	8	4	0	0	15	4	1	1	2	2	5	5	1	2	17	9	16
DERBY	8	3	1	0	10	3	1	2	1	4	6	4	3	1	14	9	15
NEWPORT	8	2	1	1	11	3	2	2	0	5	2	4	3	1	16	5	15
PORT VALE	8	4	0	0	7	2	1	0	3	3	6	5	0	3	10	8	15
BRENTFORD	8	1	2	1	4	4	3	0	1	9	9	4	2	2	13	13	14
CARLISLE	8	3	1	0	10	2	1	1	2	6	11	4	2	2	16	13	14
HALIFAX	8	2	1	1	10	8	2	1	1	5	4	4	2	2	15	12	14
HUDDERSFIELD	10	3	1	1	8	4	1	1	3	3	9	4	2	4	11	13	14
SWINDON	8	2	2	0	6	1	2	0	2	7	8	4	2	2	13	9	14
DONCASTER	8	2	1	1	7	6	2	0	2	6	4	4	1	3	13	10	13
DARLINGTON	8	2	2	0	7	3	1	1	2	5	8	3	3	2	12	11	12
HEREFORD	6	2	1	0	3	0	1	2	0	5	2	3	3	0	8	2	12
PLYMOUTH	6	3	0	0	6	2	1	0	2	2	6	4	0	2	8	8	12
ALDERSHOT	8	3	0	1	14	4	0	2	2	3	7	3	2	3	17	11	11
BRADFORD C	8	3	1	0	9	4	0	1	3	3	9	3	2	3	12	13	11
EXETER	6	1	2	0	5	4	2	0	1	6	2	3	2	1	11	6	11
MIDDLESBROUGH	8	2	2	0	7	2	1	0	3	4	6	3	2	3	11	8	11
OXFORD	12	1	2	3	9	12	2	0	4	10	15	3	2	7	19	27	11
SCUNTHORPE	10	1	4	0	8	6	1	1	3	3	11	2	5	3	11	17	11
BARNSLEY	10	1	3	1	6	6	1	1	3	4	10	2	4	4	10	16	10
BLACKBURN	12	2	3	1	8	7	0	1	5	1	12	2	4	6	9	19	10
CHESTER	6	2	0	1	7	3	1	1	1	4	5	3	1	2	11	8	10
LEEDS	14	2	3	2	4	6	0	1	6	5	22	2	4	8	9	28	10
NOTTS CO	4	2	0	0	5	2	1	1	0	4	3	3	1	0	9	5	10
PETERBOROUGH	4	2	0	0	4	2	1	1	0	4	1	3	1	0	8	3	10

	P	Home W	Home D	Home L	Home F	Home A	Away W	Away D	Away L	Away F	Away A	Total W	Total D	Total L	Total F	Total A	Pts*
SHREWSBURY	4	2	0	0	6	2	1	1	0	3	2	3	1	0	9	4	10
SOUTHEND	10	2	0	3	7	7	1	1	3	4	6	3	1	6	11	13	10
WIGAN	6	2	1	0	5	3	1	0	2	4	5	3	1	2	9	8	10
BURY	6	1	0	2	4	6	2	0	1	5	3	3	0	3	9	9	9
GRIMSBY	10	1	2	2	9	10	1	1	3	5	8	2	3	5	14	18	9
HULL	8	2	0	2	8	9	0	3	1	3	4	2	3	3	11	13	9
LEICESTER	4	2	0	0	3	1	1	0	1	5	6	3	0	1	8	7	9
MANSFIELD	6	2	1	0	6	4	0	2	1	3	4	2	3	1	9	8	9
PORTSMOUTH	10	2	1	2	11	13	0	2	3	2	5	2	3	5	13	18	9
TRANMERE	4	2	0	0	6	1	1	0	1	2	3	3	0	1	8	4	9
LINCOLN	6	1	1	1	4	3	1	1	1	3	6	2	2	2	7	9	8
BRISTOL CITY	4	1	1	0	2	1	1	0	1	5	5	2	1	1	7	6	7
FULHAM	6	1	1	1	3	4	1	0	2	4	7	2	1	3	7	11	7
PRESTON	4	1	1	0	5	4	1	0	1	5	5	2	1	1	10	9	7
READING	8	1	3	0	3	2	0	1	3	3	8	1	4	3	6	10	7
ROTHERHAM	4	1	0	1	3	2	1	1	0	2	1	2	1	1	5	3	7
BRISTOL ROV	4	1	1	0	2	1	0	2	0	3	3	1	3	0	5	4	6
CARDIFF	2	1	0	0	2	1	1	0	0	3	1	2	0	0	5	2	6
GILLINGHAM	6	1	0	2	2	5	1	0	2	2	7	2	0	4	4	12	6
WALSALL	4	2	0	0	4	0	0	0	2	0	5	2	0	2	4	5	6
WATFORD	6	1	0	2	4	6	1	0	2	1	3	2	0	4	5	9	6
BURNLEY	4	0	1	1	1	4	1	1	0	4	2	1	2	1	5	6	5
CHESTERFIELD	4	1	1	0	4	2	0	1	1	0	2	1	2	1	4	4	5
SUNDERLAND	4	1	1	0	5	2	0	1	1	1	2	1	2	1	6	4	5
BLACKPOOL	4	1	0	1	6	2	0	1	1	1	4	1	1	2	7	6	4
BRIGHTON	4	1	1	0	1	0	0	0	2	1	4	1	1	2	2	4	4
COLCHESTER	4	1	1	0	5	4	0	0	2	0	7	1	1	2	5	11	4
LEYTON ORIENT	2	0	1	0	2	2	1	0	0	6	2	1	1	0	8	4	4
SOUTHPORT	2	0	1	0	2	2	1	0	0	5	0	1	1	0	7	2	4
STOKE	2	1	0	0	1	0	0	1	0	0	0	1	1	0	1	0	4
BOLTON	2	1	0	0	4	0	0	0	1	0	2	1	0	1	4	2	3
IPSWICH	6	0	1	2	1	4	0	2	1	3	4	0	3	3	4	8	3
WOLVES	2	0	1	0	1	1	0	1	0	3	3	0	2	0	4	4	2
SWANSEA	2	0	1	0	1	1	0	0	1	0	3	0	1	1	1	4	1
BIRMINGHAM	2	0	0	1	1	2	0	0	1	2	4	0	0	2	3	6	0
89 OPPONENTS	770	193	105	87	660	427	119	110	156	461	576	312	215	243	1121	1003	1151

** 3 points given for a win throughout*

WIMBLEDON'S SEASONAL RECORDS

	Div			Home					Away					Total					
		Pos	P	W	D	L	F	A	W	D	L	F	A	W	D	L	F	A	Pts
64-65	SL1	2	42	14	6	1	61	23	10	7	4	47	29	24	13	5	108	52	61
65-66	SLP	5	42	12	8	1	49	14	8	2	11	31	33	20	10	12	80	47	50
66-67	SLP	4	42	12	7	2	62	27	7	4	10	26	33	19	11	12	88	60	49
67-68	SLP	2	42	14	4	3	53	18	10	3	8	32	29	24	7	11	85	47	55
68-69	SLP	3	42	14	4	3	38	22	7	8	6	28	26	21	12	9	66	48	54
69-70	SLP	5	42	15	4	2	43	16	4	8	9	21	36	19	12	11	64	52	50
70-71	SLP	8	42	15	4	2	47	19	5	4	12	25	35	20	8	14	72	54	48
71-72	SLP	10	42	14	4	3	50	24	5	3	13	25	40	19	7	16	75	64	45
72-73	SLP	12	42	10	9	2	32	17	4	5	12	18	33	14	14	14	50	50	42
73-74	SLP	12	42	9	4	8	32	35	6	7	8	18	21	15	11	16	50	56	41
74-75	SLP	1	42	14	3	4	36	15	11	4	6	27	18	25	7	10	63	33	57
75-76	SLP	1	42	14	6	1	44	10	12	4	5	30	19	26	10	6	74	29	62
76-77	SLP	1	42	17	3	1	38	10	11	4	6	26	12	28	7	7	64	22	63
			546	174	66	33	585	250	100	63	110	354	364	274	129	143	939	614	677

		Pos	P	W	D	L	F	A	W	D	L	F	A	W	D	L	F	A	Pts
77-78	4	13	46	8	11	4	39	26	6	5	12	27	41	14	16	16	66	67	44
78-79	4	3	46	18	3	2	50	20	7	8	8	28	26	25	11	10	78	46	61
79-80	3	24	46	6	8	9	34	38	4	6	13	18	43	10	14	22	52	81	34
80-81	4	4	46	15	4	4	42	17	8	5	10	22	29	23	9	14	64	46	55
81-82	3	21	46	10	6	7	33	27	4	5	14	28	48	14	11	21	61	75	53
82-83	4	1	46	17	4	2	57	23	12	7	4	39	22	29	11	6	96	45	98
83-84	3	2	46	15	5	3	58	35	11	4	8	39	41	26	9	11	97	76	87
84-85	2	12	42	9	8	4	40	29	7	2	12	31	46	16	10	16	71	75	58
85-86	2	3	42	13	6	2	38	16	8	7	6	20	21	21	13	8	58	37	76
86-87	1	6	42	11	5	5	32	22	8	4	9	25	28	19	9	14	57	50	66
87-88	1	7	40	8	9	3	32	20	6	6	8	26	27	14	15	11	58	47	57
88-89	1	12	38	10	3	6	30	19	4	6	9	20	27	14	9	15	50	46	51
89-90	1	8	38	5	8	6	22	23	8	8	3	25	17	13	16	9	47	40	55
90-91	1	7	38	8	6	5	28	22	6	8	5	25	24	14	14	10	53	46	56
91-92	1	13	42	10	5	6	32	20	3	9	9	21	33	13	14	15	53	53	53
92-93	Prem	12	42	9	4	8	32	23	5	8	8	24	32	14	12	16	56	55	54
93-94	Prem	6	42	12	5	4	35	21	6	6	9	21	32	18	11	13	56	53	65
94-95	Prem	9	42	9	5	7	26	26	6	6	9	22	39	15	11	16	48	65	56
			770	193	105	87	660	427	119	110	156	461	576	312	215	243	1121	1003	

GUIDE TO SEASONAL SUMMARIES

Col 1: Match number (for league fixtures); Round (for cup-ties).
e.g. 2:1 means 'Second round; first leg.'
e.g. 4QR means 'Fourth qualifying round, replay.'

Col 2: Date of the fixture and whether Home (H) or Away (A).

Col 3: Opposition.

Col 4: Attendances. Home gates appear in Roman; Away gates in *Italics*.
Figures in **Bold** indicate the largest and smallest gates, at home and away.
Average home and away attendances appear after the final league match.

Col 5: Respective league positions of Wimbledon and their opponents.
Wimbledon's position appears on the top line in Roman.
Their opponents' position appears on the second line in *Italics*.
Where possible, these positions relate to the conclusion of the match.
Occasionally they relate to the commencement of the match.

For Cup-ties, the division and position of opponents is provided.
e.g. 3:19 means the opponents are 19th in Division 3.
From 1984-85 these positions relate to the commencement of the match.
Beforehand they relate to positions at the end of the season.

Col 6: The top line shows the result: (W)in, (D)raw, or (L)ose.
The second line shows Wimbledon's cumulative points total.

Col 7: The match score, Wimbledon's given first.
Scores in **Bold** indicate Wimbledon's biggest win and heaviest defeat.

Col 8: The half-time score, Wimbledon's given first.

Col 9: The top lines shows Wimbledon's scorers and times of goals in Roman.
The second line shows opponents' scorers and times of goals in *Italics*.
A 'p' after the time of a goal denotes a penalty; '(og)' an own-goal.
The third line gives the name of the match referee.

Team line-ups: Wimbledon teams appear on the top line, irrespective of whether they are home or away. Opposition teams appear on the second line in *Italics*.
A 'P' in the right-hand column denotes the team shown in the match programme, which is not necessarily the team that played.
Players of either side who are sent off are marked !
Wimbledon players making their league debuts are displayed in **Bold**.

Substitutes: Names of substitutes appear only if they actually took the field.
A player substituted is marked *
A second player substituted is marked ^
A third player substituted is marked "
These marks do not indicate the sequence of substitutions.

N.B. For clarity, all information appearing in *Italics* relates to opposing teams.

No	Date	Att	Pos	Pts	F-A	H-T	Scorers, Times, and Referees	1	2	3	4	5	6	7	8	9	10	11	
1	H POOLE				D 0-0	0-0		**Kelly**	**Martin J**	**Willis**	**Ardrey**	**Law**	**Murphy**	**Brown**	**O'Rourke**	**Reynolds**	**Moore**	**Hodges**	
	22/8	3,432		1				*Chandler*	*Millward*	*Starkes*	*Osmond*	*Brown*	*Goldie*	*Swallow*	*Henderson*	*France*	*Mason*	*Davock*	
							Ref: B Homewood	Dons waste a hatful of chances against a team packed with star names. Dover's player manager, Doug Millward, won a championship medal with Ipswich in 1961-62. Jackie Henderson won seven Scottish caps. Bobby Mason is formerly of Wolves and Ray Swallow of Arsenal.											
2	A GLOUCESTER				D 2-2	1-0	O'Rourke 5, Wallis 80	Kelly	Martin J	Willis	**Wallis**	Law	Murphy	Brown	O'Rourke	Reynolds	Moore	Hodges	
	27/8	*3,000*		2			*Coldray, Willis (og)*	*McClusky*	*Ashall*	*Palmer*	*Prosser*	*Cox*	*Casey*	*Livingstone*	*Coldray*	*Wells*	*Jacques*	*Durrant*	
								Gloucester City's spanking new stadium is the scene for Wimbledon's first Southern League goal, scored by new Scottish signing Gerry O'Rourke. Wallis outjumps taller defenders for the Dons' second goal. A goalpost snapped, holding up play while it was replaced.											
3	A ASHFORD		8		W 2-0	1-0	Reynolds 31, O'Rourke 75	Kelly	Martin J	Willis	Ardrey	Law	Murphy	Brown	O'Rourke	Reynolds	Moore	Hodges!	
	29/8	*1,196*	*10*	4				*Sanders*	*Hamblin*	*Hunt*	*Smith*	*Sage*	*Griffiths*	*Collins*	*Garden*	*Nicholas*	*Baker*	*Rees*	
							Ref: A Davis	Stocky winger Paul Hodges is sent off for the first time in his career, after clashing with Ashford full-back Hamblin. 25 minutes are left to play, but Wimbledon are so incensed they go in search of a second, killer goal, assisted by kicking down Ashford's sloping pitch.											
4	A RAMSGATE		8		L 1-2	1-1	O'Rourke 30	Kelly	Martin J	**Rudge**	Ardrey	Law	Murphy	Brown	O'Rourke	Reynolds	Moore	Hodges	
	12/9	*1,353*	*5*	4			*Younger 25, Robertson 80p*	*Bickerstaff*	*Winfield*	*Pardey*	*Turner*	*Priestly*	*McDonald*	*McGlinchey*	*Roche*	*Richardson*	*Robertson*	*Younger*	*P*
							Ref: S Goldstone	Wimbledon's first Southern League defeat comes about after John Martin hobbles off, leaving the side a man short for more than an hour. When Brian Rudge's hand interrupts a raging shot a penalty is awarded against him. Ramsgate's nimble forwards threatened further goals.											
5	H GLOUCESTER		8		D 4-4	2-2	O'Rourke 3, 52, Hodges 9, Brown 46	Kelly	**Coote**	Rudge	Ardrey	Law	Murphy	Brown	O'Rourke	Reynolds	Moore	Hodges	
	15/9	3,000	*19*	5			*Prosser 30, Hawkins 32, Jacques 60,*	*McClusky*	*Ashall*	*Palmer*	*Prosser*	*Cox*	*Casey*	*Livingstone*	*Wells*	*Jacques*	*Williams*	*Hawkins*	
							Ref: P Alcock *[Williams 80]*	Wimbledon twice led by two goals, but in the end are content to share the spoils against a team which hit the woodwork three times in addition to their four goals. Kelly in goal has a nightmare match, gifting Gloucester two free headers. The Dons were in tatters by the end.											
6	H SITTINGBOURNE		11		W 5-2	1-1	Moore 39, Reynolds 47, 63, 80,	Kelly	Coote	Willis	Ardrey	Law	Murphy	Brown	O'Rourke	Reynolds	Moore	Hodges	
	19/9	2,700	*21*	7			*Davis 27, 60* [O'Rourke 72]	*McDermott*	*Griffiths*	*Lusted*	*Wigham*	*Greenwood*	*Pearce*	*Crayford*	*Whyte*	*MacKinnon*	*Raynor*	*Davis*	*P*
							Ref: R Pearce	Sittingbourne are bottom without a point to their name. Wimbledon's first home Southern League win is emphatic enough. Eddie Reynolds' hat-trick includes no headers, a rarity. His season's tally stands at nine. The low gate was blamed on the local amateur teams playing at home.											
7	A MERTHYR TYDFIL				D 0-0	0-0		Kelly	Rudge	Willis	Wallis	Law	Murphy	Brown	O'Rourke	Reynolds	Moore	Hodges	
	22/9	*5,000*		8				*Vearncombe*	*Griffiths*	*Lawson*	*Wood*	*Williams*	*Jenkins D*	*Fry*	*Davies*	*Cadwallander*	*Jenkins B*	*Tucker*	
								Merthyr went into this match with five league wins out of five. Their side includes three full Welsh internationals, among them the former Newcastle star Reg Davies. It is he who comes nearest to scoring with a sizzling shot that flies over the crossbar. This is a fine point to secure.											
8	A HINCKLEY				W 2-0	1-0	Hodges 33, 55p	Kelly	Coote	Willis	Ardrey	Law	Murphy	Brown	O'Rourke	Reynolds	Moore	Hodges	
	26/9	*766*		10				*Brownsword*	*Goodyer*	*Golder*	*Nicholas*	*Haines*	*Shepherd*	*Elliott*	*Rhodes*	*Mellor*	*Joyce!*	*Mansell*	*P*
							Ref: R White	No match for softies, and settled by two controversial goals. Hinckley were awarded a free-kick in their goalmouth. The keeper 'passed' the ball for the full-back to take it, but Hodges intercepted and scored. The ref said the kick had been taken. Joyce was expelled for fouling Law.											
9	A HEREFORD		6		W 2-1	1-1	Reynolds 16, Moore 57	Kelly	Rudge	Willis	Wallis	Law	Murphy	Brown	O'Rourke	Reynolds	Moore	Hodges	
	30/9	***5,123***	*1*	12			*Rudge 13 (og)*	*Wallace*	*Thomas*	*Timms*	*Griffiths*	*Daniel*	*Tyrer*	*Collins*	*Rodgerson*	*Punter*	*Derrick*	*Burbeck*	
							Ref: J Marsh	In retrospect, this will stand as Wimbledon's finest result of the season. Unbeaten Hereford are already way out in front, and this will stand as their only home defeat. Trowbridge were the last team to play here, losing 0-7. The Dons shrug off Rudge's own-goal to win from behind.											
10	H CORBY		6		W 5-2	3-1	Brown 20, O'Rourke 25, 44, 53, 70	Kelly	Coote	Willis	Ardrey	Law	Murphy	Brown	O'Rourke	Reynolds	Moore	Hodges	
	3/10	3,235	*8*	14			*Crawford 40, Stanley 64*	*Read*	*Whittaker*	*Walker*	*Rennie*	*Parsons*	*Wright*	*Stenhouse*	*Stanley*	*Crawford*	*Curran*	*Jagger*	
							Ref: R Challis	O'Rourke was so deadly that Corby eventually paid him the compliment of putting three men on him. But by then the damage had been done. In addition to his quartet, the Scottish forward had a fifth 'goal' disallowed, and near the end raised the roof by dribbling past four opponents.											

11		H	KETTERING		2	W	2-1	1-0	Hodges 5p, 78p	Kelly	Coote	Willis	Ardrey	Law	Murphy	Brown	O'Rourke	Cartwright	Moore	Hodges	
	10/10			3,214	*4*	16			*White 85*	*Smethurst*	*Norton*	*Ramshaw*	*Dodge*	*White*	*Evans*	*Salmon*	*Kerry*	*Bleanch*	*Wyld*	*Blount*	*P*
									Ref: A Dimond	Les Henley signs Bath City's deep-lying centre-forward Johnnie Cartwright before kick-off. No one at Plough Lane appears to have heard of him. There is talk that this marks the end for Eddie Reynolds, 261 goals in six seasons. The second half of this match is played in a hailstorm.											
12		H	GRAVESEND		2	W	3-1	1-0	O'Rourke 15, 80, Moore 60	Kelly	Coote	Willis	Ardrey	Law	Murphy	Brown	O'Rourke	Cartwright	Moore	Hodges	
	24/10			3,000	*19*	18			*Corthine 61*	*Sinclair*	*Jest*	*Bellett*	*Howells*	*Newcombe*	*Finnison*	*Corthine*	*Roche*	*Easles*	*Lloyd*	*Myer*	*P*
									Ref: P Lancaster	No matter the result, this was a lifeless display by a Wimbledon side playing its fourth game in seven days. George Coote is the only amateur still in the team. Gerry O'Rourke's double means he is now the division's leading scorer. Gravesend & Northfleet put up little resistance.											
13		A	CANTERBURY			D	1-1	1-0	Cartwright 43	Kelly	Coote	Willis	Ardrey	Law	Murphy	Brown!	O'Rourke	Cartwright	Moore	Hodges	
	31/10			*1,284*		19			*Tomkys 84p*	*Cox*	*Bichard*	*Buscall*	*Hodgkins*	*Carragher!*	*Bailey*	*Tomkys*	*Dick*	*Grovers*	*Horne*	*Heard*	
									Ref: W Mann	What a tale. Two men sent off, another carried off. The Kent side's Vic Groves played regularly for Arsenal's first team last season, and he takes the eye. Canterbury had missed their previous six penalties, but not this one. The tea in the dressing rooms was 'sweetened' with salt!											
14		H	DEAL		2	D	2-2	1-0	Hodges 40, 50p	Kelly	Coote	Willis	**Davies**	Law	Murphy	Brown	O'Rourke	Cartwright	Moore	Hodges	
	7/11			3,500	*9*	20			*Holder 61, Green 82*	*Long*	*Cavell*	*Woodison*	*Baxter*	*Manning*	*Dunn*	*Hinchelwood*	*Green*	*Prior*	*Holder*	*Russell*	*P*
									Ref: B Jakeman	Stuart Davies makes his league debut, thanks to Ardrey going down with flu. The star of the match was a solitary Deal supporter, an enormous individual who kept up a one-man raucous commentary from the touchline. It was afterwards suggested that he once played for Wimbledon.											
15		A	STEVENAGE		2	D	1-1	0-1	Cartwright 89	Kelly	Coote	Willis	Ardrey	Law	Davies	Brown	O'Rourke	Cartwright	Moore	Hodges	
	14/11				*14*	21			*England 3*	*Peacock*	*Standing*	*Oakley*	*Freely*	*Mills*	*Hiner*	*Watson*	*Walker*	*Ince*	*Brooks*	*England*	
									Ref: J Jackson	Gerry O'Rourke is going through a barren patch, and if it continues he might be dropped. Star of this match was Stevenage's former England international, Johnnie Brooks. Just one minute remained when Mills deflected O'Rourke's hopeful cross straight into the path of Cartwright.											
16		A	CRAWLEY		5	L	0-2	0-0		Kelly	Coote	Willis	Ardrey	Law!	Davies	Brown	O'Rourke	Cartwright	Moore	Hodges	
	28/11			*2,000*	*3*	21			*Healer 60, Jennings 89p*	*Lowe*	*Jones*	*Puddephatt*	*Cockell*	*Jennings*	*Finch*	*Robertson*	*Healer*	*Kent*	*Davidson*	*Buckley*	
									Ref: O Venning	This top-of-the-table cracker, played on a cabbage patch pitch, was regularly interrupted by invasions by three dogs. Crawley were branded the dirtiest side in the league. The dropped Eddie Reynolds scores four for the reserves, and the clamour to bring him back gathers momentum.											
17		H	BARRY		4	W	3-1	0-1	O'Rourke 84, 87, Cartwright 90	Kelly	Coote	Willis	Ardrey	Law	Davies	Brown	O'Rourke	Cartwright	Moore	Hodges	
	5/12			**1,500**	*22*	23			*Gully 11*	*Twigg*	*Short*	*Bright*	*Elias*	*O'Carroll*	*McLaughlin*	*Clark*	*McCaubey*	*Seatter*	*Gully*	*Sellick*	
									Ref: G Keeble	Barry prop up the league. They have already conceded 60 league goals before Christmas, and arrive at Plough Lane having lost 2-7 at Deal the previous evening. Barry's lowly standing, and murky drizzle, account for the poor crowd. But for 80 minutes unthinkable defeat beckons.											
18		A	POOLE		5	L	**1-3**	0-3	Davies 89	Kelly	Coote	Willis	Ardrey	Law	Davies	**Brookes**	O'Rourke	Cartwright	Moore	Hodges	
	12/12			*1,155*	*3*	23			*Donovan 8, Henderson 14, McGhee 16*	*Chandler*	*McGhee*	*Osmond*	*Goldie*	*Brown*	*Bellett*	*Donovan*	*Henderson*	*France*	*Pring*	*Davock*	
										Reliable skipper Roy Law blames himself for two goals. After a quarter of an hour the game is over. In the second half Poole lose Bellett, injured, and Davies lobs a consolation goal near the end. The Dons have no one in the class of Poole's inside-forward Jackie Henderson.											
19		H	ASHFORD		5	W	**7-1**	4-0	Hodges 13, Reynolds 22, 23, 80, Cart' 40,	Kelly	Coote	Willis	**Dobson**	Law	Davies	**Keats**	O'Rourke	Reynolds	Cartwright	Hodges	
	19/12			2,200	*18*	25			*Garden 47* [Keats 70, O'Rourke 72]	*Sanders*	*McIntyre*	*Hamblin*	*Griffiths*	*Smith*	*Stone*	*Nicholas*	*Garden*	*Robertson*	*Baker*	*Rees*	
									Ref: W Mann	Eddie Reynolds is at last recalled, and how does he respond? With a hat-trick. In addition to the seven-goal total, two more are disallowed, and Paul Hodges misses from the penalty spot – blazing over – for the first time ever. Brian Keats scores on his debut, in the Dons' biggest win.											
20		H	TUNBRIDGE W		4	D	1-1	0-1	Reynolds 60	Kelly	Coote	Willis	Dobson	Law	Davies	Brown	O'Rourke	Reynolds	Cartwright	Hodges	
	26/12			2,700	*17*	26			*Griffiths 41*	*Marshall*	*Stevens*	*Noakes*	*Gordon D*	*Sibley*	*McNichol*	*Gordon M*	*Wedge*	*Robinson*	*Dougan*	*Griffiths*	
									Ref: R Wood	This freezing Boxing Day fixture enables Tunbridge Wells to belie their lowly position with some neat, creative soccer. Their player-manager, John McNichol, once graced Chelsea and Crystal Palace. Eddie Reynolds' header rescued a point for the Dons that looked to be slipping away.											
21		A	TUNBRIDGE W		3	W	4-1	4-0	Hodges 20p, Reynolds 23, 28, Brown 39	Kelly	Coote	Willis	Dobson	Law	Davies	Brown	O'Rourke	Reynolds	Cartwright	Hodges	
	28/12				*18*	28			*Griffiths 75*	*Marshall*	*Stevens*	*Noakes*	*Gordon D*	*Sibley*	*McNichol*	*Gordon M*	*Grant*	*Robinson*	*Douglas*	*Griffiths*	
										Wimbledon wear all-white on a snow-covered pitch, and their invisible presence evidently befuddles the Kent side. Les Brown has to hobble off before the end with knee-ligament damage. Reynolds keeps up his record of scoring in each match since his recall.											

No	Date		Att	Pos	Pts		F-A	H-T	Scorers, Times, and Referees	1	2	3	4	5	6	7	8	9	10	11	
22	A	DOVER		3		D	1-1	1-0	Keats12	Kelly	Coote	Willis	Ardrey	Law	Davies	Keats	O'Rourke	Reynolds	Cartwright	Hodges	
	2/1		*1,215*	*14*	29				*Imlach 88*	*Price*	*Little J*	*Langley*	*Kirkup*	*Swain*	*Little R*	*Imlach*	*Easton*	*Forster*	*Obeney*	*Griffiths*	
									Ref: W Mann	Dover were so outclassed it was almost a travesty that they should snatch a late equaliser. Wimbledon's high percentge of drawn games is undermining their promotion push. Dover's former Scottish international Stuart Imlach was signed in a railway carriage en route to the game.											
23	A	BURTON ALB		2		D	4-4	2-2	O'Rrk 15, Keats 33, Reyn 65, Hodges 70	Kelly	**McCready**	Willis	Ardrey	Law	Davies	Keats	O'Rourke	Reynolds	Cartwright	Hodges	
	9/1		*1,100*	*5*	30				*Barker 11, Round 27p, Jackson 80,*	*Lines*	*Tye*	*Reeves*	*Walters*	*Aston*	*Bate*	*Jackson B*	*Barker*	*Round*	*Jackson A*	*Moore*	*P*
									Ref: R White *[Moore 85]*	Burton are defending a 100% home record, and this swashbuckling match on a treacly pitch brings it to an end. This is Wimbledon's second 4-4 draw of the season, both of which stood at 2-2 at half-time, and in both of which the Dons led 4-2 with time running out.											
24	H	RAMSGATE		2		W	2-0	1-0	Reynolds 37, O'Rourke 80	Kelly	McCready	Willis	Ardrey	Law	Davies	Keats	O'Rourke	Reynolds	Cartwright	Hodges	
	16/1		2,417	*8*	32					*Linton*	*Winfield*	*Pardey*	*Turner*	*Priestly*	*McDonald*	*Corthine*	*Roche*	*Muir*	*Richardson*	*McGlinchey*	*P*
									Ref: D Grounds	Thick mud and driving wind and rain turn this match into a farce. Reynolds is suffering from a festering carbuncle on his thigh, but he is desperate to play, knowing that otherwise he might not get back in the side. He scores with a diving header. Ramsgate hit the woodwork twice.											
25	A	TROWBRIDGE		2		W	4-2	3-1	Keats 7, Hodges 21, O'Rourke 35, 70	Kelly	McCready	Willis	Ardrey	Law	Davies	Keats	O'Rourke	Reynolds	Cartwright	Hodges	
	23/1		*1,200*	*16*	34				*Meacock 40, Morris 85p*	*Ford*	*Brown*	*Cook*	*Akers*	*Morris*	*Head*	*Johnson*	*Meehan*	*Holmes*	*Noake*	*Meacock*	*P*
										Wimbledon's quickest goal of the season, after seven minutes, enables them to seal the points before half-time. Law was a passenger on the wing for much of the second half. Kelly touched Morris's late penalty, but couldn't keep it out. He has never yet saved from the spot.											
26	H	BURTON ALB		2		W	6-2	3-1	O'Rourke 3, 10, 74, Reynolds 36	Kelly	Rudge	Willis	Ardrey	McCready	Davies	Keats	O'Rourke	Reynolds	Cartwright	Hodges	
	30/1		2,990	*6*	36				*Jackson 37, Round 88* [Hodges 55, 58]	*Lines*	*Tye*	*Reeves*	*Walters*	*Aston*	*Bate*	*Jackson D*	*Jackson A*	*Round*	*Barker*	*Barcumshaw*	
									Ref: R Moore	Promotion rivals Burton are stunned by this devastating score, which was preceded by one minute's silence for the death of Sir Winston Churchill. Injured skipper Law was hardly missed. Gerry O'Rourke turns on the skills before a disappointingly small crowd.											
27	H	HINCKLEY		2		W	5-1	5-0	Keats 7, Reynolds 13, 30, 40, O'Rourke 23	Kelly	McCready	Willis	Ardrey	Law	Davies	Keats	O'Rourke	Reynolds	Cartwright	Hodges	
	6/2		2,679	*16*	38				*Haines 50*	*Catlin*	*Reading*	*Shepherd*	*Nicholas*	*Haines*	*Appleton*	*Toon*	*Rhodes*	*Heal*	*Golder*	*Puddy*	
									Ref: R Pearce	It is now 15 goals from three games, and 26 in their last seven for rampant Wimbledon. Hinckley keeper Catlin was at fault for at least two goals, and no easier hat-trick will come Reynolds' way. The team are unbeaten in 11 games since his return. The second half is one big yawn.											
28	A	CORBY				L	0-1	0-1		Kelly	McCready	Willis	Ardrey	Law	Davies	Keats	O'Rourke	Reynolds	Cartwright	Hodges	
	13/2		*1,020*		38				*Goodall 39*	*Alexander*	*Whittaker*	*Pollard*	*Wright*	*Parsons*	*Armour*	*Stenhouse*	*Rennie*	*Goodall*	*Crawley*	*Jagger*	
										Corby have not lost at home since the opening day of the season. Kelly's mistake – lobbed after straying from his line – does not cost the Dons the game. The missed chances up front do that. Reynolds' carbuncle on his thigh is so painful that he has to stand on the coach journey.											
29	A	KETTERING				D	2-2	0-1	Cartwright 64, Reynolds 75	Kelly	McCready	Willis	Ardrey	Law	Davies	Keats	O'Rourke	Reynolds	Cartwright	Hodges	
	20/2		*1,455*		39				*Billings 27, Salmon 80*	*Smethurst*	*Harding*	*Norton*	*Dodge*	*White*	*Ramshaw*	*Hooper*	*Turner*	*Billings*	*Salmon*	*Taylor*	
										Wimbledon were second fiddle for much of this match. Cartwright scored against the run of play. After Reynolds made it 2-1 the Dons fell back to protect their lead, and were hanging on desperately after Salmon had somehow climbed above everyone to equalise.											
30	H	HEREFORD		2		L	1-2	0-0	Reynolds 78	Kelly	McCready	Willis	Wallis	Law	Davies	Brown	O'Rourke	Reynolds	Cartwright	Hodges	
	27/2		**4,385**	*1*	39				*Derrick 60, Attwood 70*	*Wallace*	*Vale*	*Timms*	*Griffiths*	*Daniel*	*McIntosh*	*Burbeck*	*Rodgerson*	*Punter*	*Derrick*	*Attwood*	*P*
									Ref: L Holland	The runaway leaders extend their lead to 11 points, by inflicting Wimbledon's first home defeat and avenging their own by the Dons earlier in the season. Despite the occasion, this was largely a defensive stalemate, effectively settled by Attwood's back header. That made it 0-2.											
31	H	TROWBRIDGE		2		W	4-2	4-2	Reynolds 1, 3, 37, O'Rourke 32	Kelly	McCready	Willis	Wallis	Law	Davies	Brown	O'Rourke	Reynolds	Cartwright	Hodges	
	2/3		1,577	*15*	41				*Johnson 27, Head 45*	*Ford*	*Brown*	*Cook*	*Akers*	*Morris*	*Head*	*Johnson*	*Meehan*	*Holmes*	*Noake*	*Weaver*	
									Ref: H Puley	Reynolds beats Trowbridge on his own, volleying past Ford in the first minute, and seeing the keeper fumble his header two minutes later. By the quarter hour he might have had five. The Dons sealed their first Southern League win in a month by half-time. Then they went to sleep.											

No	Venue	Opponent	Att	Pos	Res	F-A	H-T	Scorers, Times, Referees	1	2	3	4	5	6	7	8	9	10	11	
32	A	BARRY		2	W	3-1	0-0	Reynolds 55, 56, 85	Kelly	McCready	Willis	Wallis	Law	Davies	Brown	O'Rourke	Reynolds	Cartwright	Hodges	
6/3			*542*	*22*	43			*Gully 70p*	*Osborne*	*Pratt*	*Thomas*	*Knight*	*O'Carroll*	*McLaughlin*	*Ashley*	*Svensson*	*Whitlock*	*Gully*	*Clark*	
									The players flew to this match. In two planes! 542 is Barry's biggest home gate of the season. Though they are bottom of the league, they field Swedish 'B' international Ingvar Svensson. He is felled for the penalty. Reynolds' second successive hat-trick makes him the Dons' top scorer.											
33	H	CANTERBURY		2	D	0-0	0-0		Kelly	McCready	Willis	Wallis	Law	Davies	Brown	O'Rourke	Reynolds	Cartwright	Hodges	
8/3			2,457	*14*	44				*Tennant*	*Bichard*	*Buscall*	*Clugston*	*Garragher*	*Hodgkins*	*Tomkys*	*Ray*	*Wells*	*Dann*	*Heard*	
								Ref: P Lancaster	This best-forgotten match was ruined largely by the stifling, negative tactics of the Kent team. Kelly did not even touch the ball for the first 15 minutes. The crowd booed the players, and then turned on the referee – Mr Lancaster – for his seemingly erratic decisions.											
34	A	DEAL			W	7-0	3-0	Hodges 4, Davies 8, O'Rourke 30, [Cartwright, Reynolds 77, 80, 87]	Kelly	McCready	Willis	Wallis	Law	Davies	**Martin B**	O'Rourke	Reynolds	Cartwright	Hodges	
20/3			***352***		46				*Long*	*Cavell*	*Woodison*	*Baxter*	*Manning*	*Dunn*	*Hinchelwood*	*Green*	*Prior*	*Holder*	*Russell*	*P*
									Wimbledon's biggest win of the season, achieved on a quagmire pitch that required hoofing tactics, was a personal reward for Eddie Reynolds, who scored all three of his goals in the final minutes. He also hit a post. O'Rourke missed a penalty and Brian Martin shot wide from six feet.											
35	H	STEVENAGE		2	D	0-0	0-0		Kelly	Willis	McCready	Wallis	Law	Davies	Martin B	O'Rourke!	Reynolds	Cartwright	Hodges	
27/3			2,061	*4*	47				*Peacock*	*Standing*	*McAllister*	*Hirer*	*Mills*	*Freeman*	*Watson*	*Walker*	*Ince*	*Brookes*	*England*	*P*
								Ref: P Saubergue	Two successive goalless matches at Plough Lane. This had far more drama than the first. Five minutes from time O'Rourke was sent off by referee Saubergue for belting an opponent. He faces suspension. Reynolds hit the bar at the death, and at the end was booked in his frustration.											
36	A	SITTINGBOURNE		2	W	2-1	0-1	Reynolds 55, Hodges 65p	Kelly	Willis	McCready	Wallis	Law	Davies	Keats	Martin B	Reynolds	Cartwright	Hodges	
3/4			*675*	*22*	49			*Raynor 41*	*McDermott*	*Griffiths*	*Lusted*	*Wigham*	*Greenwood*	*Pearce*	*Crayford*	*Whyte*	*MacKinnon*	*Raynor*	*Davis*	*P*
									Wimbledon enjoy some jam when Cartwright takes a swallow-dive in the box and somehow wins a penalty against the bottom team. O'Rourke is out injured, and on this sloping pitch Kelly's defiance earns Wimbledon two precious points they hardly deserve.											
37	H	DOVER		2	W	3-0	2-0	Hodges 10p, Reynolds 18, Willis 80	Kelly	Rudge	Willis	Wallis	Law	Davies	Martin B	O'Rourke	Reynolds	Cartwright	Hodges	
6/4			2,680	*14*	51				*Price*	*Little J*	*Langley*	*Carey*	*Swain*	*Little R*	*McQuade*	*Clewlow*	*Obeney*	*Easton*	*Griffiths*	
								Ref: L Fish	Dover's Roy Little played in the 1956 FA Cup Final for Manchestser City. It is he who handles Reynolds' header for the penalty. Another Dover celebrity is Harry Obeney, once of West Ham. Centre-half Swain, biggest player on the pitch, made a nuisance of himself at corners.											
38	H	CRAWLEY		2	W	1-0	1-0	O'Rourke 42	Kelly	Willis	McCready	Wallis	Law	Davies	Martin B	O'Rourke	Reynolds	Cartwright	Hodges	
10/4			3,242	*10*	53				*Low*	*Skinner*	*Puddephatt*	*Cockell*	*Jones*	*Finch*	*Robertson*	*Carter*	*Jennings*	*Burton*	*Buckley*	
								Ref: J Griffiths	Crawley have four games in hand on the Dons, so this is a critical result, secured when the unmarked O'Rourke heads in Hodges' cross. No prisoners are taken on either side in a match played in torrential rain. Crawley's ex-Chelsea John Burton 'scored', but was given offside.											
39	H	HILLINGDON B		2	W	3-1	2-0	O'Rourke 10, Cartwright 25, 57	Kelly	Willis	McCready	Wallis	Law	Davies	Martin B	O'Rourke	Reynolds	Cartwright	Hodges	
16/4			4,182	*7*	55			*Huxford 60p*	*Coats*	*Huxford*	*Moore*	*Batt*	*Newcombe*	*Watson*	*Woodhouse*	*Townend*	*Hayes*	*Parsons*	*Hills*	*P*
								Ref: R Evans	Three games in four days can secure promotion. Hillingdon need to win all three Easter fixtures, two of them against Wimbledon, to stay in the hunt. This vital win is credited to Johnnie Cartwright, who scores twice in one game for the first time since his arrival from Bath City.											
40	A	GRAVESEND			W	4-1	1-0	Keats 31, Reynolds 55, 70, 75	Kelly	Willis	McCready	Wallis	Law	Davies	Martin B	O'Rourke	Reynolds	Cartwright	Keats	
17/4			*826*		57			*Ritchie 80*	*Sinclair*	*Jest*	*Bellett*	*Howells*	*Newcombe*	*Finnison*	*Corthine*	*Roche*	*Easles*	*Lloyd*	*Ritchie*	*P*
									The players' coach broke down en route to this crucial fixture, which secures promotion at the first attempt. Keats misses with a twice-taken penalty, but a second-half hat-trick by Reynolds in a howling wind launches the celebrations. Kelly drops the ball for Ritchie's late consolation.											
41	A	HILLINGDON B		2	W	4-3	2-2	Reynolds 35, 37, 88, Keats 60	Kelly	Willis	McCready	Wallis	Law	Davies	Keats	Martin B	Reynolds	Cartwright	Hodges	
19/4			*2,100*	*5*	59			*Batt 5, Watson 40, Heron 70*	*Coats*	*Huxford*	*Bisset*	*Batt*	*Newcombe*	*Watson*	*Woodhouse*	*Townend*	*Hayes*	*Lang*	*Heron*	*P*
								Ref: H Stennett	O'Rourke is out, suspended. He sits out a thriller, capped by yet another hat-trick from Reynolds, and won at the death by his majestic late header. The aim now is to finish as high as possible. Hereford are already champions, but runners-up spot beckons the Dons.											
42	H	MERTHYR TYDFIL		2	W	4-0	1-0	Reynolds 13, 68, 85, 87	Kelly	Willis	McCready	Wallis	Law	Davies	Keats	Martin B	Reynolds	Cartwright	Hodges	
24/4			3,275	*7*	61				*Vearncombe*	*Owen*	*Lawson*	*Griffiths*	*Williams*	*Harris*	*Tucker*	*Davies R*	*Jenkins*	*Davies P*	*Fry*	*P*
		Home	*Away*					Ref: A Dimond	Merthyr have faded after the brightest of starts. Reynolds is running out of superlatives. Four more today means 10 goals in three games. His season's tally is 57, a club and personal record. He also missed 10 games. Biggest cheer of the match came when he kicked the ref by mistake.											
Average		2,877	*1,651*																	

SOUTHERN LEAGUE DIV 1 (CUP-TIES)

Manager: Les Henley

SEASON 1964-65

Southern League Cup	F-A	H-T	Scorers, Times, and Referees	1	2	3	4	5	6	7	8	9	10	11
1:1 A DOVER 8 W	1-0	1-0	Reynolds 20	Kelly	Martin J	Willis	Wallis	Law	Murphy	Brown	O'Rourke	Reynolds	Moore	Hodges
2/9 *22*				*Price*	*Little J*	*Langley*	*Larey*	*Swain*	*Little R*	*Griffiths*	*Kirkup*	*Forster*	*Vaesson*	*Easton* P
				Wimbledon will draw here later in the league, so this is a good result against their first opponents in this new competition. Dover will lose at home in the league just four times, and they have it all to do in the second leg. This is only Eddie Reynolds' second goal of the season.										
1:2 H DOVER 8 W	4-2	2-2	Hodges 35, 36p, Reynolds 60, 80	Kelly	Martin J	Willis	Ardrey	Law	Murphy	Brown	O'Rourke	Reynolds	Moore	Hodges
8/9 4,103 *22*			*Forster 8, 40p*	*Price*	*Little J*	*Langley*	*Larey*	*Swain*	*Little R*	*Griffiths*	*Kirkup*	*Forster*	*Vaesson*	*Easton*
			(Dons win 5-2 on aggregate)	Mickey Moore steps out of legendary Bobby Hamm's shadow and is indisputably man-of-the-match. Two Hodges goals inside a minute ignite the match. Eddie Reynolds was denied a hat-trick by a linesman's flag in the second half. Now for Tonbridge in Round 2.										
2 A TONBRIDGE W	2-0	0-0	O'Rourke 65, 80	Kelly	Coote	Willis	Ardrey	Law	Murphy	Brown	O'Rourke	Cartwright	Moore	Hodges
12/10 *P:13*				*Crump*	*Cardan*	*Lovell*	*Bowman*	*Kilford*	*Truett*	*Kemp*	*Taylor*	*Simmonds*	*O'Donnell*	*Wright*
			Ref: G Keeble	Premier Division Tonbridge sneer down upon Wimbledon. John Cartwright's deep-lying style confuses his team-mates as much as his opponents. The Dons hang on through the first half, despite being outplayed, but get stronger once they go in front.										
3 A CHELMSFORD L	1-2	0-1	O'Rourke 74	Kelly	McCready	Willis	Ardrey	Law	Davies	Cooke	Cartwright	Reynolds	Moore	O'Rourke
7/12 *P:1*			*Nicholas 10, Salt 90*	*Collier*	*Ling*	*Gillett*	*Salt*	*Eades*	*Smith*	*Bosling*	*Bowstead*	*Butcher*	*Thurgood*	*Nicholas*
			Ref: G Reed	Chelmsford top the Premier Division table, and in the 60s were one of the most progressive clubs outside the Football League. The Wimbledon coach arrives just 10 minutes before kick-off. The recalled Reynolds does nothing. Seconds from time Kelly punches a free-kick out to Salt.										

FA Cup	F-A	H-T	Scorers, Times, and Referees	1	2	3	4	5	6	7	8	9	10	11
4Q H ROMFORD 2 D	1-1	0-1	Hodges 90p	Kelly	Coote	Willis	Ardrey	Law	Murphy	Brown	O'Rourke	Reynolds	Moore	Hodges
17/10 5,195 *P:9*			*Coates 10*	*Dunbar*	*Read*	*Tapping*	*Elias*	*Rutter*	*Reed*	*Sanders*	*Coates*	*Brown*	*McLeod*	*Barnett*
			Ref: Weller	This match detonates in injury time, when the Premier League team are comfortably holding on to a first-half lead. Referee Weller then gives a penalty against Romford centre-half Keith Rutter. Pandemonium ensues, and the ref threatens to abandon the game. Hodges nets from the spot.										
4Q A ROMFORD 2 L	1-2	1-0	Reynolds 38	Kelly	Coote	Willis	Ardrey	Law	Murphy	Brown	O'Rourke	Reynolds	Moore	Hodges
R 19/10 *5,000 P:9*			*Coates 53, 80*	*Dunbar*	*Read*	*Tapping*	*Elias*	*Rutter*	*Reed*	*Sanders*	*Coates*	*Brown*	*McLeod*	*Barnett*
				This defeat, secured ten minutes from time, means Wimbledon will miss out on the fun and frolics of the 1st Round proper, and sends their conquerors on to meet old rivals Enfield. In the closing minutes Paul Hodges is bought down twice without winning a penalty.										

	P	W	D	L	F	A	W	D	L	F	A	Pts
		Home					Away					
1 Hereford	42	19	1	1	76	14	15	3	3	48	25	72
2 WIMBLEDON	42	14	6	1	61	23	10	7	4	47	29	61
3 Poole	42	16	2	3	54	21	10	4	7	38	35	58
4 Corby	42	16	3	2	53	15	8	4	9	35	40	55
5 Stevenage	42	14	5	2	63	15	5	8	8	20	28	51
6 Hillingdon B	42	13	4	4	64	31	8	3	10	41	32	49
7 Crawley	42	13	2	6	47	22	9	3	9	36	30	49
8 Merthyr Tyd	42	12	6	3	45	15	8	3	10	30	44	49
9 Gloucester	42	13	5	3	42	21	6	5	10	26	44	48
10 Burton Alb	42	15	3	3	56	22	5	4	12	27	53	47
11 Canterbury	42	10	8	3	47	21	3	8	10	26	32	42
12 Kettering	42	8	9	4	36	21	6	4	11	38	43	41
13 Ramsgate	42	13	2	6	37	23	3	6	12	14	36	40
14 Dover	42	12	5	4	35	19	2	5	14	19	40	38
15 Hinckley	42	10	3	8	33	31	2	6	13	22	50	33
16 Trowbridge	42	7	3	11	40	51	7	2	12	28	53	33
17 Ashford	42	7	6	8	37	33	4	2	15	23	65	30
18 Barry	42	8	5	8	31	44	3	2	16	16	59	29
19 Deal	42	7	6	8	42	50	0	7	14	19	77	27
20 Tunbridge W	42	9	3	9	29	40	1	3	17	22	67	26
21 Gravesend	42	7	3	11	36	41	2	4	15	21	60	25
22 Sittingbourne	42	6	4	11	39	42	2	1	18	19	61	21
	924	249	94	119	1003	615	119	94	249	615	1003	924

Odds & ends

Double wins: (7) Ashford, Sittingbourne, Hinckley, Gravesend, Barry, Trowbridge, Hillingdon.
Double losses: (0).

Won from behind: (5) Sittingbourne (h & a), Barry (h), Hereford (a), Hillingdon (a).
Lost from in front: (0).

High spots: Winning the last 7 games and unbeaten in the last 12.

Low spots: 1 win in the first 5 games; 1 win in 6 games up to 19th Dec.

3 players score 16 or more league goals.
Eddie Reynolds smashes personal and club scoring records.

Ever-presents: (1): Mike Kelly.
Hat-tricks: Eddie Reynolds (9), Gerry O'Rourke (2).
Leading Scorer: Eddie Reynolds (44).

	Appearances			Goals			
	Lge	SLC	FAC	Lge	SLC	FAC	Total
Ardrey, Bobby	**22**	3	2				
Brookes, Rodney	**1**						
Brown, Les	**23**	3	2	**3**			**3**
Cartwright, John	**32**	2		**8**			**8**
Cooke, Ian		1					
Coote, Geoff	**16**	1	2				
Davies, Stuart	**29**	1		**2**			**2**
Dobson, R	**3**						
Hodges, Paul	**41**	3	2	**16**	2	1	**19**
Keats, Brian	**13**			**7**			**7**
Kelly, Mike	**42**	4	2				
Law, Roy	**41**	4	2				
McCready, Tom	**19**	1					
Martin, Brian	**9**						
Martin, John	**4**	2					
Moore, Mickey	**18**	4	2	**3**			**3**
Murphy, Ted	**14**	3	2				
O'Rourke, Gerry	**39**	4	2	**27**	3		**30**
Reynolds, Eddie	**34**	3	2	**40**	3	1	**44**
Rudge, Brian	**6**						
Wallis, Joe	**16**	1		**1**			**1**
Willis, Dave	**40**	4	2	**1**			**1**
22 players used	**462**	**44**	**22**	**108**	**8**	**2**	**118**

No		Date		Att	Pos	Pts	F-A	H-T	Scorers, Times, and Referees	1	2	3	4	5	6	7	8	9	10	11
1	A		WEYMOUTH			L	0-1	0-0		Kelly	**Cordjohn**	Willis	Martin B	McCready	Davies	**Peters**	O'Rourke	Reynolds	Cartwright	Hodges
		21/8		*3,100*		-			*Tizard 65*	*Clarke*	*Sheppard*	*Charlton*	*Barry*	*Hobson*	*Gough*	*Hannigan*	*Dowsett*	*Jackson*	*May*	*Tizard* P
									Ref: E Edworthy	Weymouth provide tough opposition, as expected of defending Premier champions, even though they now fielded just three of their championship side. The Dons were under pressure, but looking firm, when Tizard volleyed just inside a post.										
2	H		GUILDFORD			W	5-1	1-1	Peters 23,89, Davies 55,85,O'Rourke 60	Kelly	Cordjohn	Willis	Martin	McCready	Davies	Peters	O'Rourke	Reynolds	Cartwright	Hodges
		28/8		3,144		2			*Lill 6*	*Vasper*	*Watts*	*Nicholas*	*Massey*	*French*	*Porter*	*Lill*	*Cliss*	*Stevens*	*Colfar*	*Vafiadis*
									Ref: P Jefferies	Mick Lill has just joined Guildford from Portsmouth, and his early strike gives Wimbledon the jitters, and winger Vafiadis is a constant thorn. But the visitors have no answer to the tidal wave of second-half attacks. The only oddity is that Eddie Reynolds somehow failed to score.										
3	A		CHELMSFORD		13	D	0-0	0-0		Kelly	Cordjohn	McCready	Martin	Law	Davies	Peters	O'Rourke	Reynolds	Cartwright	Keats
		4/9		*3,401*	*3*	3				*Medlock*	*Costello*	*Gillott*	*Docherty*	*Hopkins*	*Smith*	*Duncan*	*Butcher*	*Houghton*	*Smillie*	*Imlach*
										Rough, tough stalemate, with sporadic outbreaks of soccer savagery. The Dons have had to open against three of last season's top four Premier sides, yet have acquitted themselves well. Eddie Reynolds looks slow and lost, while Tom McCready is booed for his tough tackling.										
4	H		CHELMSFORD		12	D	2-2	2-2	Peters 7, Reynolds 19	Kelly	Cordjohn	McCready	Martin	Law	Davies	Peters	O'Rourke	Reynolds	Cartwright	Keats
		11/9		3,125	*3*	4			*Houghton 9, Butcher 31*	*Medlock*	*Costello*	*Gillott*	*Docherty*	*Eades*	*Smith*	*Brennan*	*Butcher*	*Houghton*	*Smillie*	*Imlach*
									Ref: P Saubergue	Eddie Reynolds bags his first Premier goal, a header, inevitably, and having restored his team's advantage, they look likely to hold it. But second-half injuries to Keats (who stayed on as a passenger) and Cartwright (who was carried off nursing his ankle) left the Dons hanging on.										
5	A		CAMBRIDGE U			L	2-3	1-2	Cordjohn 43p, Reynolds 80	Kelly	Cordjohn	McCready	Martin	Law	Davies	Peters	O'Rourke	Reynolds	**Cochrane**	Murphy
		13/9		*4,003*		4			*Boggis 12, Amato 22, Barrett 46*	*Smith*	*Boggis*	*Tedds*	*Scurr*	*Finch*	*Graham*	*Hobbs*	*Amato*	*Turley*	*Barrett*	*Bennett*
									Ref: F Webb	Injuries to Keats and Cartwright mean unexpected call ups for Cochrane and Murphy. But the Dons' left flank is vulnerable throughout the match. The turning point was David Barrett scoring through a ruck of players just after the break. Wimbledon had just scored just before it.										
6	H		BEDFORD		17	L	**1-3**	0-1	O'Rourke 87	Kelly	Cordjohn	McCready	Ardrey	Law	Davies	Peters	O'Rourke	Reynolds	Moore	Hodges
		18/9		2,920	*1*	4			*Paton 45, Bailey 51, Brown 54*	*Collier*	*Morgan*	*Aviss*	*Bailey*	*Collins*	*Skinn*	*Benning*	*Hall*	*Brown*	*Paton*	*Sturrock*
									Ref: R Pearce	Bedford are top of the league, and this defeat leaves Wimbledon sixth from bottom. Bedford cram in their goals either side of half-time, but are greatly superior. Near the end Moore missed the ball with his head, it fell through Reynolds' legs, and O'Rourke hoofed it out of the ground.										
7	A		CHELTENHAM		17	W	2-1	1-1	Reynolds 3, 62	Kelly	Cordjohn	McCready	Martin	Law	Davies	Brown	Moore	Reynolds	O'Rourke	Hodges
		25/9		*1,367*	*7*	6			*Hurford 27*	*Nicholls*	*Thorndale*	*Claypole*	*Carson*	*Holder*	*Etheridge*	*Hurford*	*Ferns*	*Horlick*	*McCool*	*Green* P
									Ref: W Johns	Cheltenham forfeit their unbeaten home record to the angry Dons, courtesy of a brace by Eddie Reynolds. He is concussed in the second half following a clash of heads with the home keeper, and played out time in a daze. At times Cheltenham played eight men in defence.										
8	A		MARGATE			L	**1-3**	1-1	O'Rourke 40	Kelly	Cordjohn	McCready	Ardrey	Law	Davies	Martin	Moore	**Cooke**	O'Rourke	Hodges
		27/9		*2,155*		6			*Jarman 30, Ballagher 55, Thomson 69*	*Hughes B*	*Bracewell*	*Hopkinson*	*Blackley*	*Harrop*	*Waldock*	*Jarman*	*Holder*	*Ballagher*	*Thomson*	*Hughes C*
										'Ian Cooke is no Eddie Reynolds,' pronounced the *Wimbledon News* after this match. The young debutant had come in for the injured target man. With two regular wingers also out injured, Wimbledon, and Cooke, struggled to find that vital punch. Yet they rallied in the last minutes.										
9	H		HEREFORD		16	D	1-1	1-0	Reynolds 9	Kelly	Cordjohn	McCready	Ardrey	Law	Davies	Peters	O'Rourke	Reynolds	Moore	Hodges
		2/10		2,805	*3*	7			*Fogg 54*	*Isaac*	*Vale*	*Timms*	*McCall*	*Daniel*	*McIntosh*	*Punter*	*Rogerson*	*Fogg*	*Derrick*	*Jones*
									Ref: H Stennett	Wimbledon reject an offer by Millwall for their star goalkeeper, Mike Kelly. Reynolds returns after his head injury and nods in Hodges' corner-kick. This match, between two promoted sides, is a corker, but the Dons feel hard done by. Davies' scoring free-kick was ruled indirect.										
10	A		KING'S LYNN			W	1-0	1-0	O'Rourke 60	Kelly	Cordjohn	McCready	Ardrey	Law	Davies	Brown	O'Rourke	Reynolds	Moore	Hodges
		9/10		*1,793*		9				*Walls*	*Haskins*	*Sharp*	*Brooks*	*Baker*	*Wright*	*Bacon*	*Bowstead*	*Laverick*	*Havenhand*	*Partridge*
										It isn't Gerry O'Rourke's goal that settles the points for Wimbledon; it is Mike Kelly's saves. No wonder league clubs are looking at him. Saves from Laverick and Partridge had the home side clutching their heads. O'Rourke scored after beating three defenders out near the corner flag.										

No	Venue	Opponents	Pos	Res	F-A	H-T	Scorers, Times, Referees	1	2	3	4	5	6	7	8	9	10	11	
11	A	WORCESTER	11	W	4-1	3-1	Cooke 12, 27, Hodges 24, 47	Kelly	Cordjohn	McCready	Ardrey	Law	Davies	Brown	Cooke	O'Rourke	Cartwright	Hodges	
	23/10	*3,100*	*8*	11			*Deeley 18*	*Tennant*	*Brack*	*Peck*	*McEwan*	*Madley*	*Palin*	*McParland*	*Deeley*	*Crawley*	*Ward*	*Cutler*	
								Worcester's heaviest defeat for six seasons, comes about despite fielding three full internationals – Norman Deeley (England), Dai Ward (Wales), and Peter McParland (Northern Ireland). The big talking point is that Reynolds has been dropped for Cooke, despite being top scorer.											
12	H	CAMBRIDGE U	12	W	2-0	1-0	Brown 42, Cooke 48	Kelly	Cordjohn	McCready	Ardrey	Law	Davies	Brown	Cooke	O'Rourke	Cartwright	Hodges	
	26/10	2,856	*9*	13				*Slack*	*Tedds*	*Finch*	*Graham*	*Baker*	*Scurr*	*Hobbs*	*Barrett*	*Turley*	*Day*	*Maughan*	
							Ref: J Tree	Wimbledon have won four in a row away from home, and return to Plough Lane full of confidence. In fact, they need two defensive blunders to claim the points. Les Brown scores his first goal of the season. Young Ian Cooke was booed before the end. This win lifts the Dons to 4th.											
13	H	CAMBRIDGE C	5	D	1-1	0-0	Brown 65	Kelly	Cordjohn	McCready	Ardrey	Law	Davies	Brown	Cooke	O'Rourke	Cartwright	Hodges	
	30/10	3,060	*7*	14			*Gregory 60*	*Caine*	*Carroll*	*Poole*	*Moyse*	*McGugan*	*McNally*	*Spears*	*Ward*	*Bailham*	*Gregory*	*Wall*	
							Ref: C Brownlow	City do not offer the stiffest of challenges, but Wimbledon do not wake up to their task until they are a goal down and reduced to 10 men, following McGugan's crippling foul on Paul Hodges just before half-time. Gregory's lob was cancelled out by Brown in a goalmouth melee.											
14	A	NUNEATON B	5	W	3-0	2-0	Murphy 15, Cooke 40, 46	Kelly	Cordjohn	Willis	Ardrey	Law	Davies	Brown	Cooke	O'Rourke	Cartwright	Murphy	
	6/11	*2,454*	*19*	16				*Wilson*	*Thompson*	*Bettany*	*Hopkin*	*Watts*	*Allen*	*Ashe*	*Arnold*	*Atkinson*	*Bell*	*Murray*	
								Dreadful Borough hand Wimbledon all three goals on a plate, one for old-timer Ted Murphy, and a pair for Ian Cooke, who has mustered six goals in his first six outings. At the other end, Mike Kelly did not have a single direct shot to save. Dave Willis was also recalled to the side.											
15	A	CORBY	6	W	1-0	0-0	O'Rourke 77	**Smith**	Cordjohn	Willis	Ardrey	Martin	Davies	Brown	Cooke	O'Rourke	Cartwright	Murphy	
	20/11	*1,152*	*3*	18				*Alexander*	*McBain*	*Pollard*	*Riley*	*Needham*	*Armour*	*Haazs*	*Stenhouse*	*Goodall*	*Garden*	*Jagger*	
							Ref: J Jackson	Kelly has broken his jaw, so the day before the match Wimbledon splash out £1,500 on QPR keeper Frank Smith. He plays an absolute blinder against a team which scored 13 goals in their previous two games. His defiance and O'Rourke's goal ensure Corby's first home defeat.											
16	H	WELLINGTON	1	W	3-0	3-0	Cooke 14, Brown 21, Davies 40	Smith	Cordjohn	Willis	Ardrey	Martin	Davies	Brown	Cooke	O'Rourke	Cartwright	Murphy	
	23/11	**1,836**	*2*	20				*Richards*	*Whitehouse*	*Fuller*	*Salt*	*Clarke*	*Goodall*	*Boner*	*Birch*	*Bentley*	*Blackman*	*Campbell*	*P*
							Ref: G Reed	A day to remember, though not for the appalling weather. Eight unbeaten leagues games – including this, against the table-toppers – takes the Dons to the top of the table for the first time. Pick of the goals was Davies', the Dons' third. Driving the ball forward he struck it from 30 yards.											
17	H	YEOVIL	1	D	0-0	0-0		Smith	Cordjohn	Willis	Ardrey	Martin	Davies	Brown	Cooke	O'Rourke	Cartwright	Murphy	
	27/11	2,897	*9*	21				*Shilvers*	*Herrity*	*Harris*	*Albury*	*Lambden*	*Reed*	*Pounder*	*Harding*	*Hurst*	*Taylor*	*Ashe*	
							Ref: R Challis	This was bread and butter stuff from the new leaders, who cling on to top spot despite dropping a home point. Maybe the players had their minds on the FA Cup-tie next week. Biggest talking point was a brief second-half floodlight failure, and Frank Smith's third straight shut-out.											
18	H	TONBRIDGE	1	W	**6-1**	3-0	O'Rourke 12, 61, Cooke 15, 45, 70,	Smith	Cordjohn	Willis	Ardrey	Law	Davies	Brown	Cooke	O'Rourke	Cartwright	Hodges	
	11/12	2,468	*14*	23			*Jones 84* [Brown 65]	*Crump*	*Carolan*	*Lovell*	*Truett*	*Kilford*	*Anderson*	*Saunderes*	*Kemp*	*Jones*	*Taylor*	*Archer*	*P*
							Ref: R Evans	What a difference a week makes. Having lost in the FA Cup, they swamp the Tonbridge net. O'Rourke's corner-kick flies straight into the goal, and Wimbledon are on their way. Tonbridge saw as much of the ball, but had no answer to Hodges' wing-play. The new floodlights are used.											
19	A	FOLKESTONE		L	**1-3**	1-1	Cooke 1	Smith	Cordjohn	Willis	Ardrey	Law	Davies	Peters	Cooke	O'Rourke	Cartwright	Hodges	
	27/12	*2,697*		23			*Tredwell 45, 55, Churms 77*	*Cochran*	*Russell*	*Bell*	*Campbell*	*Patrick*	*Catleugh*	*Ireland*	*Churms*	*Biggs*	*Tredwell*	*Legate*	*P*
							Ref: T Knell	Not content with putting Wimbledon out of the FA Cup, Folkestone now inflict their first league defeat in three months. This, despite Ian Cooke's first minute header. Seconds before the break Frank Smith strays too far from his goal-line and is lobbed. Where is Eddie Reynolds?											
20	H	KING'S LYNN	2	W	3-0	0-0	O'Rourke 82, Cartwright 83,	Smith	Cordjohn	Martin	Ardrey	Law	Davies	Peters	Cooke	O'Rourke	Cartwright	Hodges	
	1/1	2,708	*13*	25			[Cordjohn 87p]	*Walls*	*Haskins*	*Sharp*	*Bowstead*	*Wright*	*Brooks*	*Bacon*	*Davies*	*Lindsay*	*Laverick*	*McNamee*	*P*
							Ref: A Tilley	For all but the final eight minutes of this match Wimbledon were dreadful, and their fans, still suffering from Folkestone-itis, were not slow to let them know it. The 'Bring back Reynolds' campaign mounts, but then Peters slips the ball through to O'Rourke and the floodgates open.											
21	A	CAMBRIDGE C	3	L	1-2	1-1	Dennis 13 (og)	Smith	Cordjohn	Martin	Ardrey	Law	Davies	Peters	Cooke	O'Rourke	Cartwright	Hodges	
	8/1	*3,497*	*8*	25			*Bailham 30, 52p*	*Heath*	*Carroll*	*Dennis*	*Moyse*	*McGugan*	*McNally*	*Spears*	*Ward*	*Bailham*	*McVittie*	*Wall*	
							Ref: B Setchell	Wimbledon slip to third, and learn that Mike Kelly, unable to reclaim his place, wants a move. For the second away match running, the Dons lose despite taking the lead. This time they are sunk by two goals from former Eire international Eddie Bailham, whose penalty wins the day.											

No	Date	Att	Pos	Pts	F-A	H-T	Scorers, Times, and Referees	1	2	3	4	5	6	7	8	9	10	11
22	H WORCESTER		3	W	2-0	1-0	Peters 43, Reynolds 51	Smith	Cordjohn	Martin	Ardrey	Law	Davies	Peters	O'Rourke	Reynolds	Cartwright	Hodges
	15/1	2,040	*9*	27				*Black*	*Brack*	*Peck*	*Mullen*	*Madley*	*Bassett*	*McParland*	*Deeley*	*Crawley*	*Ward*	*Cutler*
							Ref: C Brownlow	Cooke is down with flu, so Les Henley brings back Eddie Reynolds, who, surprise surprise, duly scores. The scorer was so excited he hurt his damaged hand by crashing it down on the top of the crossbar. FA secretary Dennis Follows took in this match, played on a frosty pitch.										
23	A ROMFORD		2	W	5-1	2-1	Davies 38, Peters 43, 52, Cordjohn 67p	Smith	Cordjohn	Martin	Ardrey	Law	Davies	Peters	Cooke	O'Rourke	Cartwright	Hodges
	22/1	*2,954*	*8*	29			*Aggio 18* [Cooke 71]	*Earle*	*Read*	*Harris*	*Reed*	*White*	*Gibbs*	*Sanders*	*Aggio*	*Kelly*	*Tapping*	*Barnett*
								Romford had gone nine games without defeat, take the lead, but troop away from Brooklands shell-shocked. Aggio had put them in front from close range while Smith was still guarding a post. But a hopeful swipe from Davies puts the Dons level. Cooke is fit, and displaces Reynolds.										
24	H WEYMOUTH		2	D	1-1	1-1	Cartwright 13	Smith	Cordjohn	Martin	Ardrey	Law	Davies	Peters	Cooke	O'Rourke	Cartwright	Hodges
	29/1	**4,200**	*1*	30			*Barry 7*	*Donnelly*	*Gulliver*	*Stocker*	*Barry*	*Hobson*	*Hall*	*Camp*	*Gough*	*Jackson*	*Forrest*	*Horobin*
							Ref: K Gates	Plough Lane welcomes its first 4,000 league crowd of the season in expectation of seeing the two points that will see the Dons leap-frog over Weymouth and back to the top. But the tough tackling visitors, who committed 25 fouls, are happy to fall back and trade space in midfield.										
25	A GUILDFORD		1	W	1-0	1-0	O'Rourke 17	Smith	Cordjohn	Martin	Ardrey	Law	Davies	Peters	Cooke	O'Rourke	Cartwright	Hodges
	5/2	*2,721*	*22*	32				*Gill*	*Hunt*	*Nicholas*	*Porter*	*French*	*Watts*	*Colfar*	*Cliss*	*Stevens*	*Harley*	*Vafiadis*
								There were those who claimed Wimbledon had the luck of the devil in this match. They reclaim top spot after somehow surviving a barrage from bottom-placed Guildford. The home team hit a post, saw another shot hooked off the line, and kept up frantic pressure until the end.										
26	A POOLE		3	L	0-2	0-1		Smith	Cordjohn	Martin	Ardrey	Law	Davies	Peters	Cooke	O'Rourke	Cartwright	Hodges
	12/2	*1,053*	*21*	32			*McGhee 30, Bellett 55*	*Chandler*	*McGhee*	*Balsom*	*Bellett*	*Brown*	*Osmond*	*Pring*	*Rutley*	*France*	*Henderson*	*Mason*
								Having been outclassed by the bottom club last week, the Dons are no better against the club next to bottom. Wimbledon rarely look like scoring, and fall behind after Smith handles outside his box. McGhee rifles in the free-kick. Reynolds, in reserve, overslept and missed the bus.										
27	H MARGATE		3	W	4-0	1-0	O'Rourke 7, 76, 82, Cordjohn 79	Smith	Cordjohn	Martin	Ardrey	Law	Davies	Peters	Cooke	O'Rourke	Cartwright	Hodges
	19/2	2,825	*17*	34				*Hughes B*	*Bracewell*	*Clifton*	*Blackley*	*Harrop*	*Marshall*	*Scott*	*Holder*	*Randall*	*Thomson*	*Hopkins*
							Ref: R Bartley	Superman Gerry O'Rourke enjoys a storming game, not just for his three fine goals, his first Premier hat-trick. Miserable Margate deserved nothing, but a shot that flashed across Smith's goal 15 minutes from time injected some urgency into the Dons.										
28	H POOLE		2	W	2-0	0-0	Peters 78, Hodges 83	Smith	Cordjohn	Willis	Ardrey	Law	Davies	Peters	Martin	O'Rourke	Cartwright	Hodges
	5/3	2,860	*22*	36				*Higgins*	*McGhee*	*Balsom*	*Bellett*	*Brown*	*Osmond*	*Mason*	*Rutley*	*Henderson*	*Pring*	*Davock* *P*
							Ref: R Wood	When O'Rourke waltzed round four defenders to shoot laughably wide, it looked like being one of those days. Indeed just 12 minutes remained when – to a backdrop of barracking fans – Peters shot into the net, courtesy of a defender's deflection. Poole never threatened a second victory.										
29	A BEDFORD		6	L	0-2	0-0		Smith	Cordjohn	Willis	Ardrey	Law	Davies	Peters	Cooke	O'Rourke	Cartwright	Hodges
	12/3	***4,108***	*2*	36			*Sturrock 48, Benning 60*	*Collier*	*Morgan*	*Skinn*	*Wright*	*Collins*	*Bailey*	*Benning*	*Paton*	*Hall*	*Sturrock*	*Lovell* *P*
							Ref: M Walker	It is tight at the top, but this win carries Bedford to 2nd and drops the Dons to 6th. Bedford reached the FA Cup 4th Round, losing to Everton. This is their biggest gate in two years. A thrilling match finally slips away from Wimbledon when Smith carries Benning's cross over his line.										
30	H CHELTENHAM		7	D	1-1	0-0	O'Rourke 75	Smith	Willis	Martin	Ardrey	Law	Davies	Peters	Cooke	O'Rourke	Cartwright	Hodges
	19/3	2,257	*15*	37			*Claypole 85p*	*Nicholls*	*Thorndale*	*Claypole*	*Green*	*Etheridge*	*Carson*	*Hurford*	*Corbett*	*Horlick*	*Ferns*	*McGlinchey* *P*
							Ref: F Burling	No sob story this, as Roy Law brings down Horlock for a late penalty. One point was the least Cheltenham deserved for their efforts. Their offside trap frustrated O'Rourke time and again. His goal entered the net via a post and keeper Nicholls, who keeps wicket for Gloucestershire.										
31	A RUGBY			W	5-4	4-4	Cartwright, Cooke, Hodges, Davies, [Ardrey]	Smith	Willis	Martin	Ardrey	Law	Davies	Peters	Cooke	O'Rourke	Cartwright	Hodges
	23/3	***740***		39				*Smethurst*	*Bramwell*	*Lawton*	*Walker*	*Scott*	*Radford*	*Morrow*	*Sweenie*	*Walsh*	*Denial*	*Senior* *P*
							Ref: J Griffiths	A pulsating thriller that produces a score never repeated by any professional Wimbledon team. It is equally unsusual in that five different Dons score all the goals. Inevitably, teams that concede five at home are struggling, and Rugby will be relegated. The Dons also hit five at Romford.										

No. / Date	H/A	Opponent / Att			F-A	H-T	Scorers, Times, Referees	1	2	3	4	5	6	7	8	9	10	11	
32	A	HEREFORD	6	L	0-2	0-1		Smith	Willis	Martin	Ardrey	Law	Davies	Peters	Cooke	O'Rourke	Cartwright	Hodges	
26/3		*2,850*	*7*	39			*Rodgerson 6, Fogg 89*	*Issac*	*Vale*	*Timms*	*McCall*	*Daniel*	*McIntosh*	*Punter*	*Rodgerson*	*Fogg*	*Derrick*	*Jones*	
							Ref: J Marsh	Just two points separate the top seven, so this defeat is not critical for Wimbledon, who won at Edgar Road last season. Hereford deserved the points, secured by Rodgerson's early floater over Smith's head, and Fogg's late tap in after a shot was cleared off the line.											
33	H	NUNEATON B	5	W	4-0	2-0	Cooke 23, 74, 88, O'Rourke 30,	Smith	Cordjohn	Martin	Ardrey	Law	Davies	Peters	Cooke	O'Rourke	Cartwright	Hodges	
2/4		2,265	*13*	41				*Potts*	*Thomson*	*Bettany*	*Watts*	*Brewerton*	*Allen*	*Ashe*	*Hopkin*	*Fowkes*	*Lovett*	*Carter*	
							Ref: R Moore	Les Henley runs the gauntlet of irate Dons fans for not recalling Reynolds, and not even the scoreline satisfies them, nor Ian Cooke's third hat-trick of the season. Boro arrived at Plough Lane on a winning run, but were left fuming by Cooke's opener, which looked offside.											
34	H	DARTFORD	6	W	3-0	2-0	Peters 6, Cooke 39, Hodges 52	Smith	Cordjohn	Martin	Ardrey	Law	Davies	Peters	Cooke	O'Rourke	Cartwright	Hodges	
8/4		3,005	*15*	43				*Bourne*	*Sitford*	*Maybe*	*Pike*	*Burns*	*Stevens*	*Dennis*	*Ripley*	*Gill*	*Ackerman*	*Wheeler*	*P*
							Ref: J Clarke	Wimbledon aim for three Easter wins to boost their title challenge, and make it one out of one despite the resistance shown by Dartford's young keeper Bourne. The Kent team enjoyed body-checking their opponents, and were three down before they started to play a bit.											
35	A	TONBRIDGE		L	1-2	1-1	O'Rourke 20	Smith	Cordjohn	Willis	Ardrey	Law	Davies	Peters	Cooke	O'Rourke	Cartwright	Hodges	
9/4		*1,149*		43			*Crush 22, Phelps 57*	*Crump*	*Carolan*	*Akers*	*Truett*	*Kilford*	*Lovell*	*Saunders*	*Taylor*	*Kemp*	*Phelps*	*Crush*	*P*
							Ref: K Gates	A heavy pitch saps the Dons, after they had gone in front through O'Rourke's gem. The Scot set off from the centre-circle and skirted three defenders and the goalkeepr to score. But ex-Palace Geoff Truett keeps Tonbridge moving, and almost immediately sets up the equaliser.											
36	A	DARTFORD	6	L	2-3	0-1	O'Rourke 52, Cordjohn 54p	Smith	Cordjohn	McCready	Wallis	Law	Davies	Cooke	Martin	O'Rourke	Cartwright	Hodges	
11/4		*1,780*	*15*	43			*Ripley 16, Dennis 73, Stevens 85*	*Bourne*	*Sitford*	*Mabey*	*Pyke*	*Burns*	*Stevens*	*Dennis*	*Ripley*	*Gill*	*Ackerman*	*Wheeler*	*P*
							Ref: C Brownlow	Injuries and loss of form necessitate this team shake-up. It looks like being Wimbledon's day when they move 2-1 in front from the penalty spot after Davies had been toppled. Smith then saved from the spot at the other end. But Dennis's back-header set up Dartford's final fling.											
37	H	CORBY	5	W	4-1	2-1	Cooke 11, 49, 70, Martin 43	Smith	Cordjohn	McCready	Ardrey	Law	Davies	Cooke	Martin	O'Rourke	Cartwright	Hodges	
16/4		2,116	*12*	45			*Riley 36*	*Alexander*	*McBain*	*Pollard*	*Riley*	*Needham*	*Armour*	*McQuade*	*Stenhouse*	*Goodall*	*Garden*	*Jagger*	
							Ref: A Mason	Eddie Reynolds has gone! After nine years with the Dons he has signed for Ashford Town. His departure coincides with Wimbledon losing twice over Easter. His young replacement, Ian Cooke, replies with another hat-trick of his own. Brian Martin nets his second of the season.											
38	A	YEOVIL	6	L	0-2	0-1		Smith	Cordjohn	McCready	Ardrey	Law	Davies	Cooke	Martin	O'Rourke	Cartwright	Hodges	
23/4		*2,134*	*10*	45			*Harding 13, Muir 52*	*Jones*	*Herrity*	*Harris*	*Albury*	*Burfield*	*Read*	*Pounder*	*Taylor*	*Harding*	*Muir*	*Ashe*	
								Wimbledon have blown their title chances with this, their fifth away defeat in six games. They've become easy touches on opponents' grounds. Apart from a Martin header that grazed a post, nearly all the chances were occurring at the other end. A day's golf now, then on to Wellington.											
39	A	WELLINGTON	6	D	1-1	1-0	Cooke 25	Smith	Cordjohn	Martin	Ardrey	McCready	Wallis	Peters	Cooke	O'Rourke	Cartwright	Hodges	
25/4		*1,409*	*14*	46			*Campbell 70*	*Knight*	*Whitehouse*	*Clarke*	*Salt*	*Hair*	*Goodall*	*Matthews*	*Birch*	*Bentley*	*Campbell*	*Williams*	
							Ref: B Watkins	Wimbledon's three-day away excursion came to a fruitless end when Barry Cordjohn missed a crucial penalty. The Dons were 1-0 up at the time. Peters had been fouled, but the full-back shot over from the spot. Wimbledon are five points off the top and running out of fixtures.											
40	H	RUGBY	6	D	2-2	1-0	Martin 23, O'Rourke 63	Smith	Cordjohn	McCready	Ardrey	Law	Davies	Cooke	Martin	O'Rourke	Cartwright	Hodges	
30/4		2,008	*20*	47			*Senior 59, Walsh 72*	*Smethurst*	*Bramwell*	*Lawton*	*Wright*	*Walker*	*Bennett*	*Morrow*	*Walsh*	*Denial*	*Sweenie*	*Senior*	
							Ref: L Holland	Relegation-threatened Rugby cannot believe their luck at finding Wimbledon's defence so generous. A bright sunny day seemed to bring out all that was sloppy in the home team. Too many players – Gerry O'Rourke excepted – seemed to be just going through the motions.											
41	H	FOLKESTONE	6	W	2-0	0-0	Cooke 58, O'Rourke 70	Smith	Cordjohn	McCready	Ardrey	Law	Davies	Peters	Cooke	O'Rourke	Cartwright	Hodges	
3/5		2,002	*19*	49				*Cochran*	*Russell*	*Bell*	*Campbell*	*Patrick*	*Catleugh*	*Ireland*	*Churms*	*Biggs*	*Gallagher*	*Legate*	
							Ref: B Homewood	Folkestone have inflicted more misery on the Dons than any other team this season. Before Cooke opened the scoring Wimbledon had hit the woodwork three times, twice in one attack, but had come desperately close to going behind. Catleugh's scoring volley was ruled offside.											
42	H	ROMFORD	5	D	0-0	0-0		Smith	Cordjohn	McCready	Ardrey	Law	Davies	Peters	Cooke	O'Rourke	Cartwright	Hodges	
7/5		2,200	*7*	50				*Smith J*	*Read*	*Cann*	*Reed*	*White*	*Gibbs*	*Sanders*	*Aggio*	*Obeney*	*Tapping*	*Barnett*	
	Home	*Away*					Ref: C Brownlow	This was an apology of a football match. How different from that magical January day when the Dons won 5-1 at then league-leaders Romford. The visiting fans drowned the whimperings of the home supporters, and put them to shame. Nothing else was worth remembering.											
Average	2,646	*2,362*																	

Southern League Cup	F-A	H-T	Scorers, Times, and Referees	1	2	3	4	5	6	7	8	9	10	11	
1:1 A SITTINGBOURNE	W 3-1	1-1	Cartwright 27, O'Rourke 53, Davies 65	Kelly	Cordjohn	McCready	Martin	Law	Davies	Peters	O'Rourke	Reynolds	Cartwright	Keats	
31/8 *570*			*Raynor 40*	*Jarman*	*Parry*	*Lusted*	*John*	*Greenwood*	*Brockington*	*Hollingworth*	*Curran*	*Raynor*	*Davis*	*Smith*	*P*
				Skipper Law returns to the side after suspension, to face the team that propped up Division 1 last season. The quaintly-named Bull ground is illuminated by feeble floodlights. Eddie Reynolds still hasn't scored this season, but at least he hit the post in this match.											
1:2 H SITTINGBOURNE	W 10-0	4-0	O'Rourke 17, 70, 75, Reynolds 25, 43,	Kelly	Cordjohn	Willis	Martin	Law	Ardrey	Peters	O'Rourke	Reynolds	Cartwright	Keats	
7/9 2,649			Cordjohn 35p Cartwright 54, John 60 (og),	*Jarman*	*Parry*	*Lusted*	*John*	*Greenwood*	*Brockington*	*Hollingworth*	*Curran*	*Raynor*	*Davis*	*Smith*	
			Ref: G Keeble [Keats 85, 90] (Dons win 13-1 on aggregate)	Poor Sittingbourne are swept away in this torrent. Even the out-of-touch Reynolds manages two unstoppable headers. One sympathised with Arthur Raynor, the Sittingbourne No 9, who did his best to hit back. Ardrey returns to the first team, and enjoys the romp.											
2 **Bye**															
3 A HASTINGS	L 0-1	0-1		Kelly	Cordjohn	McCready	Ardrey	Law	Davies	Brown	Cooke	O'Rourke	Cartwright	Murphy	
3/11 *2,921*			*Smith 37*	*Agate*	*Coney*	*Cockburn*	*Stone*	*Bishop*	*Goundrey*	*Back*	*Olah*	*Smith*	*Sawyer*	*Burden*	
			Ref: C Homewood	In his day, Bobby Smith was a swashbuckling centre-forward with Tottenham and England. He scored 176 league goals in the white shirt of Spurs. Last season he scored 18 goals from 31 matches for Brighton. He sidefoots Buck's drive into the net. Offside rules out two Dons' goals.											

FA Cup	F-A	H-T	Scorers, Times, and Referees	1	2	3	4	5	6	7	8	9	10	11	
4Q A FAREHAM	W 3-0	1-0	Cooke 26, O'Rourke 67, 78	Kelly	Cordjohn	McCready	Ardrey	Law	Davies	Brown	Cooke	O'Rourke	Moore	Hodges	
16/10 *2,479*				*Houghton*	*Wilson*	*Pearce*	*Thomas*	*Wilson*	*Weston*	*Marchant*	*Watts*	*Metherall*	*Fitzjohn*	*Cook*	
			Ref: R Mitchener	O'Rourke, then with Hendon, lost to Fareham three years previously in the Amateur Cup. Fareham won the Hampshire League last season, and pull in a record crowd that spills almost onto the touchline. The Dons were in no mood to be soft touches, but Fareham deserved a goal.											
1 H GRAVESEND 5	W 4-1	2-0	Cooke 25, 31, 68, O'Rourke 80	Kelly	Cordjohn	Willis	Ardrey	Law	Davies	Brown!	Cooke	O'Rourke	Cartwright	Hodges	
13/11 5,089 *1:10*			*Chamberlain 67*	*Brooman*	*Winfield*	*Brady!*	*Hatsell*	*Chamberlain*	*Jones*	*Palethorpe*	*Waites*	*Bleanch*	*Towers*	*D'Arcy*	*P*
			Ref: J Osborne	A sensational cup-tie, not only for Cooke's first competitive hat-trick for the Dons, but for the ugly scenes that attended the expulsion of Gravesend full-back Brady in the first half, and Wimbledon's Les Brown in the second. The tannoy instructed supporters to stay off the pitch.											
2 H FOLKESTONE 1	L 0-1	0-0		Smith	Cordjohn	Willis	Ardrey	Law	Davies	Brown	Cooke	O'Rourke	Cartwright	Murphy	
4/12 7,027 *14*			*Smith 69 (og)*	*Cochran*	*Russell*	*Bell*	*Campbell*	*Patrick*	*Catleugh*	*Ireland*	*Churms*	*Biggs*	*Tredwell*	*Legate*	*P*
			Ref: D Wells	This is the round that determines who will face the big boys in Round 3, a feat Wimbledon have never performed. It is a massive match for players and supporters alike. Folkestone have just put out Gillingham. Dons lose to a crazy own-goal, during which Smith dislocates his jaw.											

	P	W	D	L	F	A	W	D	L	F	A	Pts
		Home					Away					
1 Weymouth	42	16	3	2	38	8	6	10	5	32	27	57
2 Chelmsford	42	12	8	1	46	19	9	4	8	28	31	54
3 Hereford	42	16	3	2	55	14	5	7	9	26	35	52
4 Bedford	42	16	2	3	52	19	7	4	10	28	38	52
5 WIMBLEDON	42	12	8	1	49	14	8	2	11	31	33	50
6 Cambridge C	42	15	5	1	43	13	4	6	11	24	39	49
7 Romford	42	13	2	6	47	31	8	5	8	40	41	49
8 Worcester	42	16	1	4	50	23	4	7	10	19	31	48
9 Yeovil	42	13	5	3	54	23	4	6	11	37	47	45
10 Cambridge U	42	15	4	2	51	25	3	5	13	21	39	45
11 King's Lynn	42	12	4	5	39	23	6	3	12	36	49	43
12 Corby	42	12	5	4	37	24	4	4	13	29	49	41
13 Wellington	42	10	8	3	47	29	3	5	13	18	41	39
14 Nuneaton B	42	11	4	6	38	25	4	4	13	22	49	38
15 Folkestone	42	11	6	4	37	24	3	3	15	16	51	37
16 Guildford	42	12	3	6	52	35	2	5	14	18	49	36
17 Poole	42	12	2	7	40	33	2	5	14	21	42	35
18 Cheltenham	42	10	4	7	38	35	3	5	13	31	64	35
19 Dartford	42	11	5	5	43	24	2	2	17	19	45	33
20 Rugby	42	9	6	6	41	38	2	4	15	26	57	32
21 Tonbridge	42	9	5	7	39	36	2	1	18	24	65	28
22 Margate	42	8	7	6	49	48	0	3	18	17	63	26
	924	271	100	91	985	563	91	100	271	563	985	924

Odd & ends

Double wins: (5) Guildford, King's Lynn, Worcester, Nuneaton, Corby.
Double losses: (1) Bedford.

Won from behind: (2) Guildford (h), Romford (a).
Lost from in front: (4) Folkestone (a), Cambridge C (a), Tonbridge (a), Dartford (a).

High spots: 10-game unbeaten run (7 wins and 3 draws) from Oct to Dec, lifting the team from 16th to 1st.

Low spots: Winning just 2 of the first 9, and 2 of the last 8 games.
Crashing out of the Southern League Cup to Hastings.

Ever-presents: (1) Gerry O'Rourke.
Hat-tricks: Ian Cooke (4), Gerry O'Rourke (2).
Leading Scorer: Ian Cooke & Gerry O'Rourke (25 each).

	Appearances			Goals			
	Lge	SLC	FAC	**Lge**	SLC	FAC	**Total**
Ardrey, Bobby	**35**	2	3	**1**			**1**
Brown, Les	**10**	1	3	**4**			**4**
Cartwright, Johnnie	**36**	3	2	**3**	2		**5**
Cochrane, Hugh	**1**						
Cooke, Ian	**31**	1	3	**21**		4	**25**
Cordjohn, Barry	**39**	3	3	**5**	1		**6**
Davies, Stuart	**41**	2	3	**5**	1		**6**
Hodges, Paul	**35**		2	**5**			**5**
Keats, Brian	**2**	2			2		**2**
Kelly, Mike	**14**	3	2				
Law, Roy	**36**	3	3				
McCready, Tom	**20**	2	1				
Martin, Brian	**29**	2		**2**			**2**
Moore, Mickey	**5**		1				
Murphy, Ted	**5**	1	1	**1**			**1**
O'Rourke, Gerry	**42**	3	3	**18**	4	3	**25**
Peters, Dave	**27**	2		**8**			**8**
Reynolds, Eddie	**10**	2		**6**	2		**8**
Smith, Frank	**28**		1				
Wallis, Joe	**2**						
Willis, Dave	**14**	1	2				
(own-goals)				**1**	1		**2**
21 players used	**462**	**33**	**33**	**80**	**13**	**7**	**100**

No	Date		Att	Pos	Pts		F-A	H-T	Scorers, Times, and Referees	1	2	3	4	5	6	7	8	9	10	11	12 sub used
1	A	CORBY				W	2-0	1-0	McCready 37, Cooke 50	Smith	Martin	McCready	Ardrey	Law	Davies	**Hyde**	Cooke	O'Rourke	Cartwright	**McDonald**	
	20/8		*1,300*		2					*Alexander*	*McBain*	*Pollard*	*Rennie*	*Knox*	*Barratt*	*Walker*	*Gadston*	*Goodall*	*Garden*	*Harber*	
									Ref: F Harrison	Sizzling weather; sizzling performance by Wimbledon. David Hyde impressed on his debut with some power-shooting. The Corby team appeared to have been entirely rebuilt during the summer. The turning point came at 0-0, when Roy Law appeared to handle. No penalty!											
2	H	YEOVIL				W	2-0	1-0	Cooke 39, O'Rourke 56	Smith	Martin	McCready	Ardrey	Law	Davies	Hyde	Cooke	O'Rourke	Cartwright	McDonald	
	27/8		3,026		4					*Jones*	*Read*	*Harris*	*Albury*	*Lambden*	*Muir*	*Harding*	*Foley*	*Riding*	*Taylor*	*Reece*	
									Ref: E Edmunds	Only two teams have won their first two games, and Wimbledon are one of them. Yet this was not a good match or an enjoyable one. Yeovil were intent on not losing. Only in the final half-hour did Yeovil come out of their shell, and then they pressed the Dons too close for comfort.											
3	H	HILLINGDON B		1		W	3-0	0-0	Cooke 58, 74, Hyde 86	Smith	Martin	McCready	**Adams**	Law	Davies	Hyde	Cooke	O'Rourke	Cartwright	McDonald	
	10/9		2,719	*21*	6					*Cakebread*	*Huxford*	*Goodall*	*McNeice*	*Newcombe*	*Moore*	*Whitehouse*	*Watson*	*Hayes*	*Townend*	*Hills*	
									Ref: R Challis	Newly promoted Hillingdon hold their own for the first 45 minutes. The match turns on Hyde's injury just after the turnaround. Rather than introduce a substitute, Henley perseveres with Hyde, who responds by setting up the first goal for Cooke, and banged in the third himself.											
4	A	POOLE		1		D	1-1	1-1	Cooke 7	Smith	Martin	McCready	Adams	Law	Davies	Hodges	Cooke	O'Rourke	Cartwright	McDonald	
	13/9		*1,359*	*11*	7				*Henderson 44*	*Wakeham*	*McGhee*	*Balsom*	*Brewster*	*Brown*	*Davock*	*Pring*	*Rutley*	*France*	*Henderson*	*Coxon*	
									Ref: R Peter	Wimbledon concede their first league goal and drop their first point in front of Poole's biggest gate for months. Ex-Scotland Jackie Henderson had bothered the Dons in previous seasons, and he keeps up this unfortunate habit by blasting home from 30 yards on half-time.											
5	H	WEYMOUTH		1		W	3-1	1-0	Hodges 23, 62, Davies 63	Smith	Martin	McCready	Adams	Law	Davies	Hodges	Cooke	O'Rourke	Cartwright	McDonald	
	17/9		3,305	*11*	9				*Cave 50*	*Clarke*	*Keith*	*Stocker*	*Dowsett*	*Hobson*	*Barry*	*Hannigan*	*Cave*	*Jackson*	*Gough*	*Camp*	
									Ref: L Holland	How can Wimbledon really be top of the league when they are playing such lifeless soccer? That is what fans are demanding to know, after yet another indifferent performance that won both points. Weymouth keeper Johnnie Clarke hands the first and last goals on a plate.											
6	H	CAMBRIDGE C		1		D	4-4	2-2	O'Rourke 7, McDonald 22, 60, Adams 51	Smith	Martin	McCready	Adams	Law	Davies	Hodges	Cooke	O'Rourke	Cartwright	McDonald	
	20/9		2,824	*20*	10				*Bailham 36, Aitchison 37, Fusedale 50,*	*Caine*	*Moyse*	*Lye*	*Ward*	*McGugan*	*McNally*	*Aitchison*	*Fusedale*	*Bailham*	*Stevens*	*Wall*	
									Ref: H Puley *[Stevens 73]*	Wimbledon led 2-0 and 4-3 in this topsy-turvy match that twice featured two goals inside a minute. Lowly Cambridge jolt the league leaders to the core, and in the closing minutes Fuesdale strikes a post and Bailham shoots against a defender. Naughty, complacent Dons!											
7	A	WORCESTER		1		W	3-1	3-1	Hodges 2, Davies 22, O'Rourke 27	Smith	Martin	McCready	Adams	Law	Davies	Hodges	Cooke	O'Rourke	Cartwright	McDonald	
	24/9		*2,103*	*21*	12				*Hodgkinson 30*	*Collins*	*Wood*	*Peck*	*Muller*	*Madley*	*Bassett*	*MaCready*	*Deeley*	*Carter*	*Hodgkinson*	*Hooper*	
										Next to bottom Worcester have lost all but one match this season. After just seven games the Dons have opened up a four-point gap at the top. Worcester's half-back George Bassett blunders for Wimbledon's second goal, heading into the path of Stuart Davies.											
8	H	WELLINGTON		1		W	2-1	0-0	Cooke 55p, 65	Smith	Martin	McCready	Ardrey	Law	Davies	Hyde	Cooke	O'Rourke	Cartwright	McDonald	
	1/10		2,412	*9*	14				*Martin 56 (og)*	*Knight*	*Whitehouse*	*Humble*	*Salt*	*Hair*	*Goodall*	*Matthews*	*Hart*	*Bentley*	*Blackburn*	*Jagger*	
									Ref: F Bassett	The Dons extend their unbeaten run, thanks to an eventful second half that sees Ian Cooke's penalty quickly cancelled out by Brian Martin's own-goal. Cooke pops up later to steal the winner. These are important points, for Wellington are challenging on the heels of the leaders.											
9	A	CAMBRIDGE U		1		W	1-0	1-0	Cooke 30	Smith	Martin	McCready	Ardrey	Law	Davies	Hyde	Cooke	O'Rourke	Cartwright	Hodges	
	8/10		*3,385*	*14*	16					*Slack*	*Toon*	*Poole*	*Scurr*	*Baker*	*Finch*	*Fairchild*	*Barrett*	*Fahy*	*Turley*	*O'Neill*	
										This gripping match enables Wimbledon to pull six points clear. United keeper Slack cannot hold Hodges' low shot, and Cooke is quickest to the loose ball. The goal came against the run of play, and Finch responded with four long-range shots to threaten Frank Smith.											
10	A	CHELTENHAM		1		D	0-0	0-0		Smith	Martin	McCready	Ardrey	Law	Davies*	Hodges	Cooke	O'Rourke	Cartwright	McDonald	Cordjohn
	22/10		*1,834*	*22*	17					*Meeson*	*Thorndale*	*Radford*	*Carson*	*Etheridge*	*Green*	*Hudd*	*Hereford*	*Horlick*	*Murray*	*Thorne*	
									Ref: J Price	This is top versus bottom. Cheltenham have only scored four league goals this season, yet surprisingly the Dons fail to score for the first time. When Barry Cordjohn replaced Stuart Davies after half-time he became Wimbledon's first ever substitute player.											

No	Venue	Opponent / Date	Att	Pos	Pts	Res	F-A	H-T	Scorers, Times, and Referees	1	2	3	4	5	6	7	8	9	10	11	12
11	H	HEREFORD		1		L	0-1	0-0		Smith	Martin	McCready	Ardrey	Law	Adams	Hodges	Cooke	O'Rourke	Cartwright	McDonald	
		25/10	4,221	*2*	17				*McIntosh 89*	*Wallace*	*Vale*	*Timms*	*Griffiths*	*Daniel*	*McIntosh*	*Jones*	*Rodgerson*	*Charles*	*Derrick*	*Holliday*	
									Ref: R Evans	Hereford are second to the Dons, though they now close the gap to four points. They entice Plough Lane's biggest gate of the season so far. The great John Charles has signed for Hereford from Cardiff. He already has 13 goals, the best in the league, but Law allows him little space.											
12	H	KING'S LYNN		1		D	3-3	1-1	Hodges 1, Cooke 71, Wright 85 (og)	Smith	Martin	McCready	Ardrey	Law	Adams	Hodges	Cooke	O'Rourke	Cartwright	McDonald	
		29/10	2,830	*8*	18				*Lindsay 6, 70, Banson 87*	*Coe*	*Chilleystone*	*Sharpe*	*Brooks*	*Porter*	*Wright*	*Bacon*	*Davies*	*Lindsay*	*Laverick*	*Banson*	
									Ref: F Burling	Paul Hodges volleys Wimbledon's quickest goal of the season. Skipper Roy Law blunders badly for the goal that puts King's Lynn 2-1 in front. The visiting left-half puts through his own goal to give the Dons a late lead, but they can't hold on to that. The Dons don't look like champions.											
13	A	CHELMSFORD		1		L	0-3	0-1		Smith	Martin	McCready	Ardrey	Law	Davies	Hodges	Cooke	O'Rourke	Cartwright	McDonald	
		5/11	*2,538*	*4*	18				*Butcher 30, Leggett 53, Houghton 85*	*Medlock*	*Costello*	*Jones*	*Shreeve*	*Eades*	*Docherty*	*Leggett*	*Butcher*	*Houghton*	*Bren*	*Thurgood*	
										Chelmsford fans reckon this the match of the season. It is played in torrential rain, and allows future-Don Peter Shreeve to dictate the game. O'Rourke never got past Eades. Ardrey switched flanks to cover danger-man Butcher, who promptly scores to put Chelmsford one up.											
14	H	BEDFORD		1		W	5-0	3-0	Cartwright 2, Cooke 30, 50, 76 [McDonald 43]	Smith	Martin	McCready	Ardrey	Law	Davies	Hodges	Cooke	O'Rourke	Cartwright	McDonald	
		12/11	3,010	*15*	20					*Robinson*	*Morgan*	*Skinn*	*Willis*	*Collins*	*Cooley*	*Benning*	*Riley*	*Fogg*	*Paton*	*Sturrock*	
									Ref: F Lane	Wimbledon's first hat-trick of the season falls to Ian Cooke. He would have had four had he not blasted a penalty over the bar. The kick-off had to be delayed while two late Bedford players got changed. They need not have bothered. Bedford didn't manage one serious shot.											
15	A	GUILDFORD		2		L	1-2	0-1	Cooke 75	Smith	Martin	McCready	Ardrey	Law	Davies	Hodges	Cooke	O'Rourke	Cartwright	McDonald	
		19/11	*2,902*	*9*	20				*Vafiadis 25, McCready 84 (og)*	*Vasper*	*Gunter*	*Anthony*	*More*	*Bishop*	*Watts*	*Knight*	*Burge*	*Brown*	*Gregory*	*Vafiadis*	
									Ref: L Holland	Hereford leap above the Dons as a result of this surprise home defeat. Ex-Don Les Brown leads the Guildford attack, and here and in seasons to come enjoys memorable duels with his close friend Roy Law. Tom McCready smashes a back-pass beyond the absent Smith for the winner.											
16	A	WEYMOUTH		2		L	0-3	0-3		Smith	Cordjohn	Willis	Ardrey	McCready	Davies	Hyde	Cooke	O'Rourke	Cartwright	Hodges	
		3/12	*1,525*	*3*	20				*Hall 15p, Gough 30, Jackson 44*	*Clarke*	*McDonald*	*Stocker*	*Barry*	*Hobson*	*Hall*	*Cave*	*Dowset*	*Jackson*	*Gough*	*Camp*	
										The Dons try to fight their way back to form and several are booked. Cooke headed against the bar at 0-0. Then Ardrey floors Dowsett for the penalty. Gerry O'Rouke has only scored in two league games so far, and might soon be dropped. Weymouth have games in hand on the Dons.											
17	H	FOLKESTONE		2		W	**9-2**	3-2	Cooke 2, 30, 55, 81, 87, Hyde 7, Davies 84, [O'Rourke 70, 80]	Smith	Cordjohn	McCready	Ardrey	Law	Davies	Hyde	Cooke	O'Rourke	Cartwright	Hodges	
		10/12	**2,070**	*21*	22				*Biggs 3, Churms 38*	*Cochran*	*Russell*	*Bell*	*Campbell*	*Patrick*	*Carleugh*	*Ireland*	*Churms*	*Biggs*	*Ballagher*	*Legate*	
									Ref: R Pearce	This extraordinary result comes out of nowhere. Folkestone won at Plough Lane in FA Cup last season, but get their come-uppance in the mud. Cooke manages five goals, but it is only in the last 10 minutes that the visitors collapse. This was the Dons biggest Southern League win.											
18	H	CORBY		1		W	6-1	1-1	Cooke 38, 60, 68, 75, Hyde 72, [Cartwright 74]	Smith	Cordjohn	Willis	Ardrey	Law	Davies	Hyde	Cooke	O'Rourke*	Cartwright	Hodges	**Piper**
		17/12	2,200	*16*	24				*Goodall 45*	*Alexander*	*McBain*	*Pollard*	*Rennie*	*Needham*	*Claypole*	*Stenhouse*	*Barratt*	*Knox*	*Kelcher*	*Goodall*	
									Ref: J Tree	Victory over Stevenage in the Southern League Cup, and now another goal-bonanza. Cooke snaps up another four goals, having shot over from the penalty spot before he was off the mark. Corby were grateful it wasn't 10. This win takes the Dons back above Hereford at the top.											
19	H	BARNET				W	3-0	2-0	Hyde 11, 33, Hodges 87	Smith	Cordjohn	McCready	Ardrey	Law	Davies	Hyde	Cartwright	O'Rourke	Piper	Hodges	
		26/12	**4,304**		26					*Smith*	*Voyce*	*Jenkins*	*Picking*	*Roach*	*King*	*Whyte*	*Eason*	*Figg*	*Oxley*	*Turley*	
									Ref: G Keeble	Nine goals in two Saturdays for Cooke, but he is injured and missed the visit of Barnet. During the second half Frank Smith decides to change his boots, and is nearly booked for time-wasting. Hyde scores his first with a fierce free-kick; his second with a clever goal built from deep.											
20	A	BARNET				W	2-0	1-0	O'Rourke 30, 48	Smith	Cordjohn	McCready	Ardrey	Law	Davies	Hyde	Piper	O'Rourke	Cartwright	Martin	
		27/12	*3,156*		28					*Smith*	*Quinton*	*Jenkins*	*Picking*	*Roach*	*King*	*Turley*	*Ratty*	*Whyte*	*Oxley*	*Finch*	
									Ref: F Bassett	A double over Barnet. Wimbledon are the only championship hopefuls to take full points over Christmas. Hyde makes both goals for O'Rourke. Fog shrouds the pitch by the end, and it is touch and go whether the referee will allow the match to complete its course.											
21	A	YEOVIL		1		L	0-3	0-2		Smith	Cordjohn	McCready	Ardrey	Law	Davies	Hyde	Cartwright	O'Rourke	Piper	Hodges	
		31/12	*2,776*	*4*	28				*Taylor 8, 25, 70*	*Chilvers*	*Herrety*	*Read*	*Albury*	*Lambden*	*Muir*	*Harding*	*Harris*	*Foley*	*Taylor*	*Rees*	
										Barry Cordjohn misses Wimbledon's third recent penalty, as their four-game winning run comes to an abrupt end. Yeovil's veteran David Taylor steals the show with a hat-trick, though all eyes are turned to keeper Frank Smith. Taylor's first two goals are down to him.											

SOUTHERN LEAGUE PREMIER DIVISION   Manager: Les Henley   SEASON 1966-67

No	Date		Att	Pos	Pts	F-A	H-T	Scorers, Times, and Referees	1	2	3	4	5	6	7	8	9	10	11	12 sub used
22	H	POOLE		1	W	4-0	2-0	McCready 8, Hyde 27, O'Rourke 54, 78	Smith	Cordjohn	McCready	Ardrey	Law	Davies	Hyde	Cartwright*	O'Rourke	Piper	Hodges	McDonald
	7/1		2,256	*14*	30				*Wakeham*	*McGhee*	*Balsom*	*Osmond*	*Brown*	*Davock*	*Saunders*	*Rutley*	*Bellett*	*Pring*	*Henderson*	
								Ref: J Griffiths	Yet another penalty miss. A fourth in recent games – this time from David Hyde, after he had been grassed by Brown. This result takes the Dons four points clear at the top. But this is also FA Cup 1st Round day. Wimbledon are aggrieved they are not still in the FA Cup.											
23	A	HILLINGDON B		1	L	3-4	1-4	Davies 14, Cooke 52, Newcombe 65 (og)	Smith	Cordjohn	McCready	Ardrey	Law	Davies	Hyde	Cooke	O'Rourke	Cartwright	Hodges	
	14/1		*1,635*		30			*Woodhouse 21, Hills 24, Townend 25*	*Cakebread*	*McNeice*	*Moore*	*Batt*	*Newcombe*	*Adams*	*Woodhouse*	*Watson*	*Townend*	*Sawyer*	*Hills*	
								Ref: F Bassett *[Sawyer 31]*	Boro are haunted by relegation, but recover from a goal down to score four in 10 minutes. Ian Cooke returns after injury and hits a post just on half time. At 2-4 Cartwright also hits a post, but this time Newcombe swipes the rebound into his own net to set up a grandstand finish.											
24	A	CAMBRIDGE C		1	D	1-1	1-0	Hodges 20	Smith	Cordjohn	McCready	Ardrey	Law	Davies	Hyde	Cooke	O'Rourke	Cartwright	Hodges	
	21/1		*3,157*	*16*	31			*McVittie 90*	*Bevis*	*Moyse*	*Lye*	*Ward*	*McGugan*	*McNally*	*Spears*	*McVittie*	*Bailham*	*Stevens*	*Wall*	
								Ref: J Clarke	Brentford's cash crisis means they might have to pull out of the Football League. If they do, Wimbledon are determined to apply for their place. On the pitch, Hodges scores against the run of play. No one can begrudge Matt McVittie side-footing City's late, late equaliser.											
25	H	BURTON ALB		1	W	1-0	0-0	O'Rourke 68	Smith	Cordjohn	McCready	Ardrey	Law	Davies	Hyde	Cooke	O'Rourke	Cartwright	Hodges	
	28/1		3,097	*13*	33				*Potter*	*Finey*	*Shepherd*	*Fitchett*	*Haines*	*Carver*	*Edwards P*	*Keating*	*Jackson*	*Barker*	*Edwards B*	
								Ref: R Wood	The lead is now six points, but Nuneaton have five games in hand. Burton keeper Potter has a fine game, but O'Rourke pounces upon his one mistake, the ball skidding into the net after a corner had been half-cleared. Bobby Ardrey had hit the crossbar in the first half.											
26	H	WORCESTER		1	W	5-3	2-1	Cooke 28, O'Rourke 44, Ardrey 65, Hodges 88,	Smith	Cordjohn	McCready	Ardrey	Law	Davies	Hyde	Cooke	O'Rourke	Cartwright*	Hodges	Martin
	4/2		2,955	*21*	35			*Bailham 43, 50, 55* [Lovatt 80 (og)]	*Black*	*Brack*	*Peck*	*McEwan*	*Madley**	*Mullen*	*MacCready*	*Lovett*	*Bailham*	*Gould*	*Hopper*	
								Ref: K Ridden	Conceding three goals to the 21st placed team sounds like bad defending. But Smith had to go off for a while with a damaged ankle, and deputy keeper Hyde conceded a goal immediately. Goal of the match was surely Lovatt's thunderbolt own-goal for the Dons.											
27	A	WELLINGTON		1	L	0-1	0-1		Smith	Cordjohn	McCready	Ardrey	Law	Davies	Hyde	Cooke	O'Rourke	Cartwright	Hodges	
	11/2		*2,945*	*7*	35			*Blackburn 31*	*Irvine*	*Whitehouse*	*Humble*	*Salt*	*Hair*	*Goodall*	*Matthews*	*Hart*	*Bentley*	*Blackburn*	*Jagger*	
									This is Wellington's sixth straight win, and the score does little to reflect their superiority on their Bucks Head ground. Alan Blackburn scores the decisive goal from a flick-on by Jack Bentley, the league's leading scorer. Cooke forces a thrilling save from Bobby Irvine.											
28	A	BURTON ALB		1	L	0-2	0-0		Smith	Cordjohn	McCready	Ardrey	Law	Davies	Hyde	Cooke	O'Rourke	Cartwright	Hodges	
	18/2		*1,841*	*13*	35			*Round 80, 87*	*Potter*	*Finney*	*Shepherd*	*Bate*	*Haines*	*Keating*	*Round*	*Carver*	*Tait*	*Barker*	*Edwards*	
								Ref: G Keil	The Dons still cling to top spot despite this, their seventh away defeat in nine games. Wimbledon's best player is goalkeeper Frank Smith, who prevented a heavier defeat, despite the Dons' pressure. Stan Round's first goal came when he swept a corner through a defensive shield.											
29	H	CAMBRIDGE U		1	D	1-1	0-1	Ardrey 53	Smith	Cordjohn	McCready	Ardrey	Law	Davies	Hyde	Cooke	O'Rourke	Piper	Hodges	
	25/2		2,763	*5*	36			*Barrett 4*	*Haggis*	*Toon*	*Tedds*	*Scurr*	*Baker*	*Bennett*	*Dickinson*	*Barratt*	*Ward*	*O'Neill*	*Turley!*	
								Ref: A Hart	Wimbledon had won their previous seven at home. United are unbeaten in 1967, but played most of the second half with 10 men after John Turley was dismissed for kicking Cooke. Cooke also missed a late sitter, but he is distracted by his impending wedding, his mind elsewhere.											
30	A	HEREFORD		1	W	2-1	1-0	Cartwright 10, Hyde 70	Smith	Cordjohn	McCready	Ardrey	Law	Davies	Hyde	Martin	O'Rourke	Cartwright	Hodges	
	4/3		***4,342***	*4*	38			*McCall 87*	*Appleby*	*Vale*	*Timms*	*McCall*	*Neville*	*McIntosh*	*Griffiths*	*Rodgerson*	*Charles*	*Derrick*	*Page-Jones*	
								Ref: W Johns	Cooke is officially absent, at the altar. Even so, the Dons secure revenge for their one home defeat this season. Roy Law has the beating of John Charles both in the air and on the ground. The turning point came when Griffiths struck Smith's post when the Dons led 1-0.											
31	H	BATH		1	W	6-2	3-0	O'Rourke 2, 15, Carson 12 (og), Hyde 55	Smith	Cordjohn	McCready	Ardrey	Law	Davies	Hyde	Martin	O'Rourke	Cartwright	Hodges	
	11/3		2,790	*19*	40			*Horton 75, Carson 85* [Hodges 65, Martin 90]	*Parker*	*Swift*	*Ward*	*Carter B*	*Carter W*	*Gough*	*Lofty*	*Horton*	*Denton*	*Walker*	*Carson*	
								Ref: G Reed	Bath have not won in 1967 and turn up at Plough Lane six minutes late. Referee George Reed slips down steps to the dressing room at half-time and hurts his back. Linesman Harrington takes over, and a spectator – John Fell – runs the line in plimsolls and trousers tucked in socks.											

No	Venue	Opponent	Att	Pos	Pts	Res	F-A	H-T	Scorers, Times, and Referees	1	2	3	4	5	6	7	8	9	10	11	12
32	H	CHELTENHAM		1		D	0-0	0-0		Smith	Cordjohn	McCready	Ardrey	Law	Davies	Hyde	Cooke	O'Rourke	Cartwright	Hodges	
18/3			2,244	*16*	41					*Meeson*	*Thorndale*	*Radford*	*Carson*	*Etheridge*	*Ferns*	*Green*	*Hudd*	*Horlick*	*Gadstone*	*Thorne*	P
									Ref: B Homewood	Cheltenham's offside trap kills the game. The crowd behind one goal are so incensed that they throw pennies and polo mints at the visiting goalkeeper, who pleads with the refereee for protection. Cheltenham player-manager Bob Etheridge is booked for bad-mouthing.											
33	A	ROMFORD		1		L	**1-4**	1-3	White 12 (og)	Smith	Cordjohn	McCready	Ardrey	Law	Davies	Hyde	Martin	O'Rourke	Cartwright	Hodges	
24/3			*4,300*	*8*	41				*King 20, Barnett 30, 32, Obeney 80*	*Smith*	*Taylor*	*King*	*Reed*	*White*	*Sorrell*	*Sanders*	*Aggio*	*Obeney*	*Tapping*	*Barnett*	P
									Ref: J Jackson	The Brooklands pitch is so hard that every time the ball bounces it creates a mini duststorm. Ian Cooke is dropped by Les Henley. The Dons got a break when David Hyde's free-kick is deflected into goal, but Romford swamp the Dons for the rest of the first half.											
34	A	KING'S LYNN				L	1-2	0-0	Hodges 89	Smith	Martin	McCready	Cartwright	Law	Davies	Hyde	Cooke*	O'Rourke	Piper	Hodges	Wallis
25/3			*1,961*		41				*Scott 53, McGuigan 60*	*Coe*	*Chilleystone*	*Sharp*	*Brooks*	*Porter*	*Wright*	*Bacon*	*Davies*	*Lindsay*	*Scott*	*McGuigan*	P
										In an attempt to stop the rot Henley recalls Cooke and switches all the players around. King's Lynn go ahead with a goal from Dick Scott, who has just signed from Lincoln City. McGuigan's fabulous shot makes it two, before Hodges pulls one back direct from a corner.											
35	H	ROMFORD		1		L	**1-4**	1-1	Hyde 8	Smith	Martin	McCready	Ardrey	Law	Davies	Hyde	Cartwright	O'Rourke	Piper	Hodges	
27/3			2,500	*8*	41				*Sorrell 26, Obeney 57, 81, Barnett 80*	*Smith*	*Taylor*	*King*	*Reed*	*White*	*Sorrell*	*Sanders*	*Aggio*	*Obeney*	*Tapping*	*Barnett*	P
									Ref: J Craigie	The dreadful Easter has brought the Dons three defeats in four days, in which time Romford twice hit them for four. As in the first match, Hyde's free-kick puts the Dons ahead, but by the end Romford fans are chanting 'easy, easy'. When did Plough Lane last suffer that taunt?											
36	H	CHELMSFORD		2		D	1-1	1-0	Davies 21	Smith	McCready	Willis	Ardrey	Law	Davies	Hyde	Martin	O'Rourke	Cartwright	Hodges*	McDonald
1/4			2,110	*9*	42				*Law 88 (og)*	*King*	*Smith*	*Jones*	*Shreeve*	*Eades*	*Docherty*	*Mason*	*Smith B*	*Houghton*	*Thurgood*	*Leggett*	P
									Ref: R Challis	Wimbledon know the title has slipped away, and this lifeless match is the consequence. Stuart Davies responds to cries of 'hit it', when shooting from long range, but his strike is cancelled out by an astonishing own-goal from Law, who swipes at a loose ball with nobody near.											
37	A	BEDFORD		2		W	1-0	1-0	Hyde 4	Smith	McCready	Willis	Ardrey	Law	Davies	McDonald	Hyde	O'Rourke	Cartwright	Hodges	
8/4			*2,247*	*21*	44					*Collier*	*Morgan*	*Skinn*	*Newman*	*Collins*	*Cooley*	*Benning*	*Cleary*	*Fahy*	*Paton*	*Denton*	
									Ref: D Hutchinson	Yet again it is David Hyde's prowess from free-kicks that gives the Dons an advantage. Thereafter they owe everything to Frank Smith, though even he is helpless when Denton's 82nd minute shot comes back off the bar. The Dons are just two points behind leaders Weymouth.											
38	H	GUILDFORD		2		D	2-2	0-0	Ardrey 57, Hyde 73	Smith	McCready	Willis	Ardrey	Law	Davies	Hodges	Hyde	O'Rourke	Cartwright	McDonald	
15/4			3,143	*10*	45				*Colfar 80, Burge 82*	*Vasper*	*Gunter*	*Anthony*	*Massey*	*Bishop*	*More*	*Burge*	*Colfar*	*Brown*	*Gregory*	*Vafiadis*	P
									Ref: W Woods	Had they won, Wimbledon would have gone back to the top. Guildford have won the Southern League Cup, and stage a late recovery to wreck the Dons' hopes. Burge appeared to handle the ball before equalising, and the outraged Smith chases the referee to the centre-circle.											
39	A	NUNEATON B		2		D	3-3	2-2	Hodges 5p, Martin 45, 47	Smith	McCready	Willis	Ardrey	Law	Davies	Hyde	Martin	O'Rourke	Cartwright	Hodges	
22/4			*3,826*	*5*	46				*Cutler 1, Richards 9, Ashe 87*	*Crump*	*Thompson*	*Wilson*	*Watts*	*Ball*	*Allen*	*Ashe*	*Richards*	*Crawley*	*Cutler*	*Senior*	
									Ref: Stangroom	When Smith fumbles Ashe's effort in the closing minutes another precious point has been snatched away. Boro had only been beaten at home once this season. The Dons were awarded a penalty, but no one wants to take it. Up stepped Paul Hodges, scoring through the keeper's legs.											
40	A	FOLKESTONE		3		W	4-1	3-1	Hodges 12, 43, Hyde 44, O'Rourke 80	Smith	McCready	Willis	Ardrey*	Law	Davies	Hyde	Cooke	O'Rourke	Cartrwright	Hodges	Martin
6/5			***870***	*22*	48				*Ballagher 30*	*Cochran*	*Russell*	*Bell*	*Campbell*	*Patrick*	*Carleugh*	*Ireland*	*Churms*	*Biggs*	*Ballagher*	*Legate*	P
										Folkestone are bottom of the league, and their resistance is entirely physical. Willis breaks his nose, Ardrey has to be substituted, and Cartwright is a virtual passenger. Les Henley has managed the club for 12 years and now signs a new three-year contract.											
41	H	NUNEATON B		4		D	1-1	0-1	Law 75	Smith	McCready	Willis	Martin	Law	Davies	Hyde	Cooke	O'Rourke	Cartwright	Hodges	
9/5			4,000	*5*	49				*Cutler 30*	*Crump*	*Thompson*	*Wilson*	*Allen*	*Ball*	*Watts*	*Ashe*	*Crawley*	*Richards*	*Hales*	*Cutler*	
									Ref: B Homewood	Paul Cutler's goal will never be forgotten, by Frank Smith or any of those who saw it. Cutler was in the centre-circle when he speculatively let fly. Smith stood transfixed as the ball flew over his head. Law admits that for his equaliser he kicked the ball out of keeper Crump's hands.											
42	A	BATH		4		L	0-1	0-0		Smith	McCready	Willis	Martin	Law	Davies	Hyde	Cooke*	O'Rourke	Cartwright	Hodges	Wallis
13/5			*1,506*		49				*Horton 65*	*McAuley*	*Swift*	*Thresher*	*Carter W*	*Whitehouse*	*Gough*	*Ashe*	*Hooper*	*Clare*	*Horton*	*Walker*	P
		Home	*Away*						Ref: B Marchant	A blanket finish. At start of play Weymouth and Romford have 50 points, Wimbledon and Nuneaton 49. This bitter, spiteful match provoked Dons fans to invade the pitch and chase the referee, who ruled out two Dons penalties and a 'good' goal. A win would have left the Dons third.											
Average		2,894	*2,453*																		

Southern League Cup	F-A	H-T	Scorers, Times, and Referees	1	2	3	4	5	6	7	8	9	10	11	12 sub used
1:1 H DARTFORD	W 3-1	1-1	Hyde 4, Cooke 53, Cartwright 85	Smith	Martin	McCready	Ardrey	Law	Davies	Hyde	Cooke	O'Rourke	Cartwright	McDonald	
30/8 1,382			*Davies 17 (og)* Ref: B Homewood	*Balderstone*	*Sitford*	*Mabey*	*Carter*	*Burns*	*Lilles*	*Barrdouth*	*Stevens*	*Nicholas*	*Ripley*	*Wheeler*	
Stuart Davies brings about the first goal scored against the Dons this season, back-heading under pressure past Smith. Up front, the Dons player to catch the eye was David Hyde. His thunderous free-kick after just four minutes was just one of several thunderbolts he unleashed.															
1:2 A DARTFORD	D 2-2	0-1	Cooke 60, O'Rourke 75	Smith	Martin	McCready	Adams	Law	Davies	Hyde	Cooke	O'Rourke	Cartwright	McDonald	
7/9 *1,362 1:14*			*Nicholas 5, Carter 85* Ref: P Lancaster (Dons win 5-3 on aggregate)	*Balderstone*	*Sitford*	*Mabey*	*Stevens*	*Burns*	*Lillis*	*Wheeler*	*Carter*	*Nicholas*	*Ripley*	*Dennis*	
Dartford needed a quick goal to make a fight of it, and they achieved it. Not until Cooke and O'Rourke punctured their defence in the second half was the tie made safe for Wimbledon. Dons fans kept up a cacophany of support, so unlike their usual somnolent state at Plough Lane.															
2 A STEVENAGE	W 3-1	2-0	O'Rourke 10, McDonald 40, Cooke 85	Smith	Cordjohn	McCready	Cartwright	Law	Davies	Hyde	Cooke	O'Rourke	Piper	McDonald	
12/12 *1,022 1:8*			*Brooks 51* Ref: O Venning	*Peacock*	*Standing*	*Robinson*	*Pratt*	*Stevens*	*Hiner*	*Chandler*	*Walker*	*Cutler*	*Brooks*	*England*	
Just 48 hours earlier the Dons had hit nine past Folkestone. Neither Ardrey nor Hodges was given time off work from their employers. Stevenage are chasing promotion in Division 1, but are sunk by transfer-listed Terry McDonald's crucial goal before half-time.															
QF A MARGATE	W 4-0	4-0	O'Rourke 10, 35, 44, Hodges 39	Smith	Cordjohn	McCready	Ardrey	Law	Davies	Hyde	Cooke	O'Rourke	Piper	Hodges	
6/2 *1,153 1:1*				*Pye*	*Warner*	*Gillott*	*Clifton*	*Harrop*	*Marshall*	*Jarman*	*Amato*	*Randall*	*Kydd*	*Burden*	
Fog shrouds the pitch like a grey blanket, but cannot prevent O'Rourke's first hat-trick of the season. The contest is over by half-time. The nearest Margate come to making a fist of it in the second half is when Amato fires a penalty at Frank Smith, after McCready impeded Jarman.															
SF A BARNET	L 1-3	1-2	O'Rourke 40	Smith	Cordjohn	McCready	Ardrey	Law	Davies	Hyde	Cooke	O'Rourke	Cartwright	Hodges	
14/3 *4,005*			*Eason 5, 30, Picking 47* Ref: G Keeble	*Goymer*	*Voyce*	*Jenkins*	*Picking*	*Roach*	*King*	*Whyte*	*Eason*	*Figg*	*Smith K*	*Turley*	
Wimbledon won 2-0 at Underhill in the league over Christmas, but that counts for nothing. They have never yet been drawn at home in this competition. Another missed penalty does not help the Dons' cause. They are 1-3 down when Hodges takes it, but Goymer punches it out.															

FA Cup	F-A	H-T	Scorers, Times, and Referees	1	2	3	4	5	6	7	8	9	10	11	12 sub used
4Q A DARTFORD	D 2-2	0-1	Hodges 46, Cooke 51	Smith	Martin	McCready	Ardrey	Law	Davies	Hyde	Cooke	O'Rourke	Cartwright	Hodges	
15/10 *3,800 1:18*			*Moss 9, Crooke 71* Ref: R Pearce	*Jones*	*Sitford*	*Mabey*	*Lillis*	*Burns*	*Stevens*	*Wheeler*	*Vickers*	*Carter*	*Moss*	*Simmons*	*Crooke*
Dartford have the reputation, deserved or otherwise, of being among the most 'rugged' teams in the league, even though they are struggling near the foot of Division 1. Dartford concede 18 first-half fouls. When Crooke makes it 2-2 he becomes the first sub to score against the Dons.															
4Q H DARTFORD	W 3-0	2-0	Hyde 17, Hodges 21, Cooke 65	Smith	Martin	McCready	Ardrey	Law	Davies	Hyde	Cooke	O'Rourke	Cartwright	Hodges	
R 18/10 3,849				*Jones*	*Sitford*	*Mabey*	*Burns*	*Lillis*	*Stevens*	*Wheeler*	*Moss*	*Carter*	*Vickers*	*Simmons*	
Dartford blew their chances when not winning at the first attempt. It is not long before they realise that a place in the 1st Round proper is beyond them. When Paul Hodges puts them two goals down with less than a quarter of the match played, they have little to offer but muscle.															
1 A GRANTHAM	L 1-2	0-1	Cooke 53	Smith	Martin*	McCready	Davies	Law	Ardrey	Hyde	Cooke	O'Rourke	Cartwright	McDonald	Cordjohn
26/11 *3,845 ML:5*			*Martin 39 (og), South 56* Ref: R Harper	*Crawford*	*Jowett*	*Akers*	*Harrison*	*Farmer*	*Brown*	*South*	*Bly*	*Alexander*	*Wood*	*Butters*	
Grantham lie fourth in the Midland League, with a 100% home record so far. Their player-manager is Terry Bly, once a dangerous striker with Norwich and Peterborough. Brian Martin had a nightmare match, heading an own goal on a heavy pitch, with a cricket square adjoining.															

		Home					Away					
		W	D	L	F	A	W	D	L	F	A	Pts
1 Romford	42	14	5	2	44	18	8	3	10	36	42	52
2 Nuneaton B	42	16	4	1	59	21	5	5	11	24	34	51
3 Weymouth	42	12	6	3	42	17	6	8	7	22	23	50
4 WIMBLEDON	42	12	7	2	62	27	7	4	10	26	33	49
5 Barnet	42	12	6	3	46	27	6	7	8	40	39	49
6 Guildford	42	13	6	2	46	19	6	4	11	19	32	48
7 Wellington	42	12	5	4	39	23	8	2	11	31	44	47
8 Cambridge U	42	9	6	6	38	25	7	7	7	37	42	45
9 Chelmsford	42	10	7	4	41	24	5	8	8	25	35	45
10 Hereford	42	11	5	5	51	26	5	7	9	28	35	44
11 King's Lynn	42	13	7	1	55	21	2	7	12	23	51	44
12 Cambridge C	42	10	6	5	41	31	5	7	9	25	39	43
13 Cheltenham	42	10	4	7	32	31	6	7	8	28	40	43
14 Yeovil	42	11	7	3	44	22	3	7	11	22	50	42
15 Burton Alb	42	12	4	5	41	25	5	1	15	22	46	39
16 Corby	42	9	6	6	30	26	6	3	12	30	49	39
16 Poole	42	9	7	5	30	20	5	4	12	22	45	39
18 Hillingdon B	42	7	6	8	33	34	4	7	10	16	36	35
19 Bath	42	10	6	5	36	29	1	6	14	15	45	34
20 Worcester	42	6	4	11	30	33	5	4	12	29	46	30
21 Bedford	42	8	5	8	37	23	0	8	13	17	49	29
22 Folkestone	42	4	6	11	25	34	2	9	10	19	47	27
	924	230	125	107	902	556	107	125	230	556	902	924

Odds & ends

Double wins: (5) Corby, Worcester, Bedford, Folkestone, Barnet.
Double losses: (1) Romford.

Won from behind: (1) Worcester.
Lost from in front: (3) Romford (h & a), Hillingdon (a).

High spots: Starting the season with unbeaten 10 games.
62 home goals is Wimbledon's highest in the Southern League.

Low spots: 7 games with just 1 win, up to 3 Dec, dropping to 2nd place.
Finishing the season with 2 wins in the last 11, dropping to 5th place.
Before this season Wimbledon had never lost by more than 2 goals. This season they lose by 3 goals five times.

Plough Lane's smallest crowd sees the biggest win – 9-2 v Folkestone.
5 own-goals is the most Wimbledon will enjoy in the Southern League.
Dons players concede 7 own-goals in all competitions.

Wimbledon are the league's top scorers, and so is Ian Cooke.

Ever-presents: (2) Frank Smith, Gerry O'Rourke.
Hat-tricks: Ian Cooke (3), Gerry O'Rourke (1).
Leading Scorer: Ian Cooke (30).

	Appearances						Goals			
	Lge	Sub	SLC	Sub	FAC	Sub	**Lge**	SLC	FAC	**Total**
Adams, Brian	**7**		1				**1**			**1**
Ardrey, Bobby	**34**		3		3		**3**			**3**
Cartwright, John	**41**		4		3		**3**	1		**4**
Cooke, Ian	**30**		5		3		**24**	3	3	**30**
Cordjohn, Barry	**18**	(1)	3			(1)				
Davies, Stuart	**40**		5		3		**5**			**5**
Hodges, Paul	**37**		2		2		**12**	1	2	**15**
Hyde, David	**32**		5		3		**12**	1	1	**14**
Law, Roy	**41**		5		3		**1**			**1**
McCready, Tom	**41**		5		3		**2**			**2**
McDonald, Terry	**16**	(2)	3		1		**3**	1		**4**
Martin, Brian	**25**	(2)	2		3		**3**			**3**
O'Rourke, Gerry	**42**		5		3		**14**	6		**20**
Piper, Ron	**7**	(1)	2							
Smith, Frank	**42**		5		3					
Wallis, Joe		(2)								
Willis, Dave	**9**									
(own-goals)							**5**			**5**
17 players used	**462**	**(8)**	**55**		**33**	**(1)**	**88**	**13**	**6**	**107**

SOUTHERN LEAGUE PREMIER DIVISION Manager: Les Henley SEASON 1967-68

No	Date	Att	Pos	Pts	F-A	H-T	Scorers, Times, and Referees	1	2	3	4	5	6	7	8	9	10	11	12 sub used
1	H DOVER			W	2-1	1-0	Cartwright 20, O'Rourke 74	Smith	McCready	Willis	Wallis	Law	**Collins**	Hyde	**Hobbs**	O'Rourke	Cartwright*	Hodges	Cooke
	19/8	**2,036**		2			*Ryan 51*	*Price*	*Martin*	*Dennis*	*Stepney*	*Swain*	*Morgan*	*Stack*	*Ray*	*Ryan*	*Kelly*	*Peters*	
							Ref: G Keeble	Wimbledon have signed three new players – Jimmy Collins from Brighton, Peter Hobbs from Cambridge United, and Dickie Guy from Tooting. The first two make their debuts against Dover, who play in zebra-hooped shirts. Smith fumbles Kelly's shot and Jim Ryan pounces.											
2	A WELLINGTON		7	D	0-0	0-0		Smith	McCready	Willis	Ardrey	Law	Collins	Hyde	Hobbs	O'Rourke	Cartwright	Hodges	
	26/8	*2,145*	*4*	3				*Irvine*	*Whitehouse*	*Newton*	*Salt*	*Clarke*	*Ray*	*Matthews*	*Hart*	*Bentley*	*Blackburn*	*Jagger*	
							Ref: G Trout	Frank Smith now atones with a blinder in goal for the Dons, making a flying save from Matthews in the opening minutes, and always the master of his goal. Roy Law provides him with sterling support. Wimbledon carve out almost nothing by way of scoring chances.											
3	A HASTINGS			W	1-0	0-0	O'Rourke 85	Smith	Martin	McCready	Ardrey	Law	Collins	Hyde	Hobbs	O'Rourke	Cartwright	Hodges	
	2/9	*1,497*		5				*Cullen*	*Sargent*	*Nash*	*Strachan*	*Brady*	*Smith*	*Knight*	*Harmer*	*Gregory*	*Norman*	*George*	
							Ref: C Kirk	Hastings' stadium, Pilot Field, has little to enjoy from this match. Newly promoted Hastings have now lost their first four, and were just five minutes from celebrating their first point when Gerry O'Rourke pops in the winner. Hastings field ex-Chelsea star Tommy Harmer.											
4	H HILLINGDON B		5	D	0-0	0-0		Smith	Martin	McCready	Ardrey	Law	Collins	Hyde	Hobbs	O'Rourke	Cartwright	Hodges	
	9/9	2,164	*13*	6				*Lowe*	*McNeice*	*Moore*	*Goodare*	*Newcombe*	*White*	*Herd*	*Fairchild*	*Doherty*	*Carter*	*Hills*	
							Ref: L Holland	Boro are second best in everything but goals, which appear to have dried up completely for the normally free-scoring Dons attack. The first half saw them win 15 corners. After the break Hillingdon livened up. Fairchild missed a sitter and Law's challenge on Hills looked illegal.											
5	A CHELTENHAM			L	0-2			Smith	Martin	McCready	Wallis	Law	Davies	Hyde	Hobbs	O'Rourke	Collins	Hodges	
	13/9	*1,837*		6			*Gadston (2)*	*Meeson*	*Thorndale*	*Radford*	*Carson*	*Jefferies*	*Green*	*Ferns*	*Hudd*	*Gerrard*	*Gadston*	*Thorne*	
							Ref: G James	After weathering an early storm by the Cheltenham forwards, the Dons' rearguard appeared to have taken their measure. The referee had also disallowed a goal by Hodges. A far-post header gave Cheltenham the lead, and when the Dons poured forward they were hit on the break.											
6	A NUNEATON B		8	L	**1-4**	0-2	Cooke 85	Smith	Martin	McCready*	Ardrey	Law	Davies	Hyde	Hobbs	O'Rourke	Collins	Hodges	Cooke
	16/9	*4,202*	*12*	6			*Ashe 37, Richards 40, Wright 75, 80*	*Crump*	*Jones*	*Wilson*	*Watts*	*Ball*	*Allen*	*Ashe*	*Wright*	*Richards*	*Cutler*	*Smith*	
							Ref: F Burling	Frank Smith prevents a complete rout. Seldom have Wimbledon been under the cosh as much as they were in the first half, when they did not manage a single shot on target. Ian Cooke's late goal was the first by a Dons' sub. He had come on for McCready as a half-time substitute.											
7	H HEREFORD		12	W	2-0	1-0	Hodges 20, Davies 57	Smith	Martin	Willis	Collins	Law	Davies	Hodges	Hyde	Cartwright	Ardrey	O'Rourke	
	23/9	2,200	*3*	8				*Appleby*	*Griffiths*	*Timms*	*McIntosh*	*Lambden*	*Jones*	*Punter*	*Rodgerson*	*Charles*	*Derrick*	*Holliday*	
							Ref: K Ridden	Having been pitifully beaten by Enfield in the London Professional Cup, Les Henley opts for a complete team reshuffle against the early pace-setters. Hereford were one of two sides to win at Plough Lane last season. Both goals are down to keeper Appleby, who goes off injured.											
8	H GUILDFORD		11	D	1-1	0-0	Cartwright 60	Smith	Martin	Willis	Collins	Law	Davies	Cooke	Hyde	Cartwright	Collins	O'Rourke	
	7/10	2,416	*14*	9			*Brown 82*	*Vasper*	*Gunter*	*Anthony*	*Massey*	*Bishop*	*More*	*Burge*	*Watts**	*Brown*	*Colfar*	*Vafiadis*	*Gregory*
							Ref: R Challis	Another lifeless performance. The out-of-sorts Cooke plays his first full game, but accomplishes little. In the 8th minute Martin 'fouled' Vafiadis for a harsh penalty, which Gunter drove over Smith's crossbar. Ex-Don Les Brown won his personal duel with Roy Law, for once.											
9	A YEOVIL		11	W	2-1	0-0	Hyde 82, 83	Smith	Martin	Willis	Collins	Law	Hobbs	Cooke	Hyde	Cartwright	Ardrey	O'Rourke	
	14/10	*2,763*	*2*	11			*Allen 87*	*Jones*	*Herrity*	*Smith*	*Harris*	*Burfield*	*Muir*	*Vowles*	*Thompson*	*Allen*	*Taylor*	*Weller*	
							Ref: I Kennard	A late double burst by David Hyde inflicts upon Yeovil their first defeat of the season, and marks Wimbledon's first win at the Huish. Hyde rammed in Cooke's low cross to break the deadlock. Smith infringes the new four-pace rule for goalkeepers, but saves the ensuing free-kick.											
10	H POOLE		4	W	**8-1**	4-0	Cooke 30, 33, 37, 75, Cartwright 45, 80	Smith	Martin	Willis	Collins	Law	Davies	Cooke	Hyde	Cartwright	Ardrey	O'Rourke	
	21/10	2,245	*22*	13			*Taylor 67* [O'Rourke 65, 85]	*Chilvers*	*Hibberd*	*Balsom*	*Brewster*	*Brown*	*Taylor*	*Harding*	*Pring*	*France*	*Rutley*	*Pitman*	
							Ref: G Reed	Nothing that Wimbledon have achieved this season prepares them for this onslaught. Ian Cooke can't hit a barn door of late, but now he bags a hat-trick in seven minutes. Three of his four goals are diving headers, all from left-wing crosses. Cooke also fluffs a penalty kick.											

No	Venue	Opponent	Pos	Res	F-A	H-T	Scorers, Times, Referees	1	2	3	4	5	6	7	8	9	10	11	sub
11	H	ROMFORD	4	D	1-1	0-0	Hyde 77	Smith	Martin	Willis	Collins!	McCready	Davies	Cooke	Hyde	Cartwright	Hobbs	O'Rourke	
	4/11	2,862	*8*	14			*Tapping 85*	*Smith*	*Read*	*King*	*Sorrell*	*Gibbs*	*Reed*	*Sanders*	*Flatt*	*Obeney*	*Tapping*	*Barnett*	
							Ref: F Bassett	These two sides are due to meet soon in the FA Cup, and serve up an ale-house clash on a rain-swept pitch. Romford are defending champions. Cooke missed his second penalty in consecutive games. Midway in the second half Collins was sent off for trying to strangle an opponent.											
12	A	CAMBRIDGE U	10	L	1-3	1-2	Cartwright 26	Smith	Martin	Willis	Ardrey	McCready	Davies	Cooke	Hobbs	Cartwright	Collins	O'Rourke	
	11/11	*2,938*	*9*	14			*Houghton 6, O'Neill 45p, Ward 90*	*Slack*	*Lindsey*	*Grant*	*Scurr*	*Baker*	*Hardy*	*Barrett*	*O'Neill*	*Houghton*	*Ward*	*Hall*	
								Hyde will miss several games with cartilege trouble. The Dons point the finger at the referee for ending their unbeaten run. The penalty they insist was 'offside'; the third goal was scored after five minutes injury time – yet there were no injuries. Wimbledon now drop to 10th.											
13	H	BURTON ALB	10	W	4-0	0-0	O'Rourke 73, 90, Cooke 76, 89	Smith	Martin	Willis	Collins	McCready	Davies	Hodges	Cooke	Cartwright	Ardrey	O'Rourke	
	18/11	2,117	*21*	16				*Potter*	*Finney*	*Shepherd*	*Carver*	*Young*	*Goodall*	*McClelland*	*Garden*	*Hutchinson*	*Metcalfe*	*Hills*	
							Ref: R Evans	For over an hour this was an entirely forgettable game. The Dons were enduring jeers and slow-handclaps when Hodges' cross came back off the crossbar for O'Rourke to head in the rebound. Lowly Burton, who had looked the better side in the first half, promply fell apart.											
14	A	CORBY	7	W	3-2	1-1	Davies 5, Bailham 46, O'Rourke 70	Smith	Martin	Willis	Collins	McCready	Davies	Hodges	Cooke	**Bailham**	Ardrey	O'Rourke	
	25/11	***542***	*19*	18			*Aldread 3, Sturrock 90p*	*Alexander*	*McBain*	*Pollard*	*Addy*	*Knox*	*McNeil*	*Lofty*	*Burns*	*Sturrock*	*Aldread*	*Campbell*	
							Ref: J Simms	Henley has splashed out £1,500 on Eddie Bailham, Worcester City's 26-year old centre-forward. When on the books of Shamrock Rovers, Bailham won a full Eire cap v England. Bailham takes the place of Cartwright, dropped for the first time. He never plays for the Dons again.											
15	A	CAMBRIDGE C	1	W	3-0	1-0	O'Rourke 9, 64, Bailham 47	Smith	Martin	Willis	**Malley**	McCready	Davies	Hodges	Cooke	Bailham	Ardrey	O'Rourke	
	28/11	*2,302*	*16*	20				*Bevis*	*Scott*	*McNally*	*Graham*	*McGugan*	*Brennan*	*Spears*	*McGeorge*	*Stevens*	*Foley*	*Banson*	*McVittie*
							Ref: K Ridden	Another debut, this time for Dennis Malley – in for the suspended Collins – as Wimbledon go top of the league for the first time this season. For the second successive match Bailham scores at the start of the second half, and later thumps the crossbar. The Dons look revitalised.											
16	H	KING'S LYNN	1	W	1-0	1-0	Cooke 6	Smith	Martin	McCready	Malley	Law	Davies	Hodges	Cooke	Bailham	Ardrey	O'Rourke	
	2/12	2,764	*19*	22				*Coe*	*Haskins*	*Sharp*	*Way*	*Porter*	*Wright*	*Davies*	*Tough*	*Lindsay*	*Jenkins*	*Clarke*	*P*
							Ref: M Taylor	Wimbledon were top at this time in the last two seasons, but blew it over Easter. Bailham has a quiet home debut, but Law returns after a six-week absence. The goal-rush never materialised, though keeper Norman Coe saved his team on numerous occasions.											
17	A	DOVER	1	W	2-1	0-1	Hobbs 60, O'Rourke 75	Smith	Martin	Willis	Hobbs	McCready	Davies	Hodges	Cooke	Bailham	Ardrey	O'Rourke	
	16/12	*1,727*	*14*	24			*Gregory 15*	*Price*	*Martin*	*Dennis*	*Kelly*	*Swain*	*Morgan*	*Griffiths*	*Ray*	*Ryan*	*Gregory*	*Clewlow*	
							Ref: C Cuthbert	The Dons did not deserve both points, and only got them because of Frank Smith's heroics. Dover field former Don John Martin at right-back. The goal that put Wimbledon level was a faint-hearted effort by Peter Hobbs that somehow found the back of the net.											
18	H	WELLINGTON	1	W	4-2	1-1	O'Rourke 27, 60, Cooke 86, 87	Smith	Martin	Willis	Collins	Law	Davies	Hodges	Cooke	Bailham	Ardrey	O'Rourke	
	21/12	2,229	*10*	26			*Jagger 31, Matthews 50*	*Irvine*	*Harris*	*Newton*	*Salt*	*McKinney*	*Ray*	*Matthews*	*Hart*	*Bentley*	*Dunmore*	*Jagger*	
							Ref: J Craigie	Wimbledon's FA Cup opponents, Bristol Rovers, are up in the stand, running the eye over the Dons and their iffy floodlights. They pronounce themselves impressed on both counts. This is the Dons' sixth straight league win, and the first time they have conceded two goals at home.											
19	H	MARGATE	1	L	1-3	1-1	Cooke 36	Smith	McCready	Willis	Collins	Law	Davies	Hodges	Cooke	Bailham	Ardrey	O'Rourke	
	26/12	3,057	*15*	26			*Amato 18, Fahy 63, Burden 68*	*Hughes*	*Clifton*	*Marshall*	*Grace*	*Harrop*	*Kydd*	*Jarman*	*Amato*	*Fahy*	*O'Mara*	*Burden*	
							Ref: C Kirk	Margate play like crude heavyweights, but succeed in shattering Wimbledon's unbeaten home record. Bailham has a bad game, and so does Law, who is given the runaround by the lanky Fahy – who volleys Margate into the lead. The Dons showed no will to win in the later stages.											
20	A	MARGATE	1	L	0-3	0-2		Smith	Martin	McCready	Malley	Law	Davies	Hodges	Hobbs	Bailham	Collins	O'Rourke	
	30/12	*2,086*	*15*	26			*Burden 2, Fahy 4, O'Mara 46*	*Hughes*	*Clifton*	*Marshall*	*Snowden*	*Harrop*	*Grace*	*Jarman*	*O'Mara*	*Fahy*	*Kydd*	*Burden*	
							Ref: R Challis	A five-day double over the Dons for Margate. Ardrey and Willis miss the game with flu. Law deflects Burden's shot in the second minute, and Frank Smith is blamed for Margate's second and third goals. This is not the build-up Wimbledon wanted for their cup-tie with Bristol Rovers.											
21	H	NUNEATON B	3	W	5-2	3-1	Bailham 3, 12, 90, O'Rourke 35, [Hodges 83]	Smith	Martin	McCready	Collins	Law	Davies	Hodges	Cooke	Bailham	Ardrey	O'Rourke	
	20/1	2,389	*11*	28			*Wright 8, 73*	*Crump*	*Jones*	*Hill*	*Watts*	*Aston*	*Allen*	*Wright*	*Keeley**	*Richards*	*Cutler*	*Smith*	*Hope*
							Ref: F Lane	With three crushing defeats behind them, this is a vital game for Wimbledon. Bailham's hat-trick silences his growing band of critics. But this win was not as convincing as the score suggests. Boro fought hard throughout. It takes two late Dons goals to secure both points.											

SOUTHERN LEAGUE PREMIER DIVISION　Manager: Les Henley　SEASON 1967-68

No	Date	Att	Pos	Pts	F-A	H-T	Scorers, Times, and Referees	1	2	3	4	5	6	7	8	9	10	11	12 sub used
22	H WEYMOUTH		2	W	2-1	2-0	Cooke 6, Hodges 31	Smith	Martin	McCready	Collins	Law	Davies	Hodges	Cooke	Bailham	Ardrey*	O'Rourke	Malley
	27/1	2,377	*12*	30			*Camp 64*	*Clarke*	*Dowsett*	*Canavan*	*Buckingham*	*Hobson*	*Gough*	*Hannighan*	*Camp*	*Cave*	*Jackson*	*Bennett*	
							Ref: R Evans	Bailham's only visible contribution to this lamentable match was to take occasional throw-ins. Smith's accomplishments were to take a goal-kick, and send the ball over his own goal-line, and dribble up to the halfway line and be dispossessed. Mickey Cave gives Law a hard time.											
23	A HEREFORD		1	W	3-1	3-1	O'Rourke 20, Cooke 26, 34	Smith	Martin	McCready	Collins	Law	Davies	Hodges	Cooke	Bailham	Malley	O'Rourke	
	3/2	*2,730*	*8*	32			*Dodson 22*	*Isaac*	*Griffiths*	*Page-Jones*	*Summerhayes*	*Lambden*	*Jones*	*Rodgerson*	*McIntosh*	*Charles*	*Derrick*	*Dodson*	
								This result sends the Dons back to the top on goal-average ahead of Barnet, helped on their way by O'Rourke's deflected shot. Dave Dodson's solo goal quickly levels the score. Ian Cooke's 'double' means Hereford have conceded three at home for the first time in many months.											
24	H CAMBRIDGE C		1	W	2-1	1-0	Davies 13, 90	Smith	McCready	Willis	Collins	Law	Davies	Hodges	Cooke	Bailham	Malley	O'Rourke	
	10/2	2,411	*21*	34			*Cartwright 84*	*Bevis*	*Moyse*	*Lye*	*Brennan*	*Collins*	*McNally*	*Stevens*	*Cartwright*	*Foley*	*McVittie*	*Denton*	
							Ref: A Hart	John Cartwright, ousted by the arrival of Eddie Bailham, has signed for struggling Cambridge City. Wimbledon were scant value for their win, secured in injury time by a 25-yarder from Stuart Davies, after Cartwright had settled scores against his old team.											
25	A WEYMOUTH		1	W	3-1	2-1	Cooke 5, O'Rourke 20, Malley 85	Smith	Martin	McCready	Collins	Law	Davies	Hodges	Cooke	Bailham	Malley	O'Rourke	
	17/2	*1,901*	*10*	36			*Parks 42*	*Clarke*	*Canavan*	*Stocker*	*Barry*	*Hobson*	*Buckingham*	*Camp*	*Parks*	*Cave*	*Gough*	*Bennett*	
							Ref: G James	No quibbles about this win, against the club that have been champions twice in the past three seasons. Dennis Malley's shot on the run clinches the points after Mickey Cave and Eddie Bailham had missed glorious chances at either end.											
26	A GUILDFORD		1	D	1-1	1-1	O'Rourke 20	Smith	Martin	Willis	McCready	Law	Davies	Hodges*	Cooke	Bailham	Malley	O'Rourke	Wallis
	24/2	*2,015*	*11*	37			*Burge 25*	*Spratley*	*Gunter*	*Anthony*	*Massey*	*Bishop*	*Merry*	*Davies*	*Gregory*	*Burge*	*Hudson*	*Vafiadis*	
							Ref: G Reed	Four clubs – Romford, Chelmsford, Cambridge United, and Wimbledon – are all chasing league status should Port Vale's financial irregularites see them demoted from the Football League. This was a brutal match, the fourth between the sides this season. Davies hit the bar near the end.											
27	H YEOVIL		1	W	3-0	2-0	Davies 14, 40, O'Rourke 85	Smith	Martin	McCready	Collins	Law	Davies	Hyde	Cooke	Bailham	Malley	O'Rourke	
	2/3	2,635	*12*	39				*Jones*	*Herrity*	*Smith*	*Thompson*	*Harris*	*Muir*	*Myers*	*Vowles*	*Bramley*	*Mitten*	*Weller*	
							Ref: B Chapman	Even the most ardent Dons fan is asking how his team can be top, and enjoying so many breaks. David Hyde returns after his cartilege operations. Yeovil centre-forward Bramley angers Wimbledon with his persistent fouling. The second half is one continuous yawn.											
28	A BARNET		1	W	2-0	1-0	Malley 39, Bailham 88	Smith	Martin	McCready	Collins	Law	Davies	Hyde	Cooke	Bailham	Malley	O'Rourke	
	9/3	*2,608*	*3*	41				*Goymer*	*Thompson*	*Jenkins*	*Ward*	*Roach*	*King*	*Anderson*	*Eason*	*Figg*	*Searle*	*Turley*	
							Ref: G Keeble	Barnet, the one-team leaders, have gone off the boil. It is 1-0 when Hyde's free-kick is headed back across the box by O'Rourke to Malley. It is 2-0 when Goymer fails to hold Stuart Davies' cross from the goal-line and Eddie Bailham is first to the loose ball.											
29	A POOLE		1	W	3-0	1-0	Bailham 42p, Cooke 73, 78	Smith	Martin*	McCready	Collins	Law	Davies	Hyde	Cooke	Bailham	Malley	O'Rourke	Willis
	16/3	*1,098*	*20*	43				*Whiting*	*Hibberd*	*Balsom*	*Brewster*	*Brown*	*Rutley*	*Down*	*Taylor*	*Allen*	*Pring*	*Evans*	
							Ref: G Griffiths	Wimbledon's surge has now earned them 17 points from nine games. Only Cambridge United appear to be within striking distance. Poole had been trounced 8-1 in October, but had recently been pulling clear of the drop. A needless handball gave Bailham his chance from the spot.											
30	H CHELTENHAM		1	L	1-2	1-0	Bailham 9	Smith	McCready	Willis	Collins	Law	Davies	Hyde	Cooke	Bailham	Malley	O'Rourke*	Hobbs
	23/3		*6*	43			*Horlick 55, 74*	*Meeson*	*Thorndale*	*Green*	*Carson*	*Jefferies*	*Etheridge*	*Hudd*	*Radford*	*Horlick*	*Gadstone*	*Thorne*	
							Ref: W Dance	Cheltenham's only tactic in this ill-tempered, windswept match is the offside trap. This does not prevent Bailham scoring through Meeson's legs. Cooke then hits the bar and watches the rebound fly into Meeson's arms. Smith's fragile handling is blamed for both Cheltenham goals.											
31	A CHELMSFORD		1	L	2-3	1-3	O'Rourke 7, Davies 60	Smith	McCready	Willis	Collins	Law	Davies	Hodges	Cooke	Bailham	Malley	O'Rourke	
	25/3	***5,055***	*3*	43			*Shreeve 18p, Butcher 21, 33*	*Medlock*	*Costello*	*Smith*	*Shreeve*	*Eades*	*Docherty*	*Leggett*	*Butcher*	*Cassidy*	*Gordon*	*Pulley*	
							Ref: D Bullard	Chelmsford are pushing hard for election to the Football League. Butcher and Cassidy (not to mention the Sundance Kid) are the division's top scorers. O'Rourke's flying header gets the Dons off to a great start in this thriller, but Davies then upends Leggett for a penalty.											

No	Ven	Opponent	Att	Pos	Pts	Res	F-A	H-T	Scorers, Times, Referees	1	2	3	4	5	6	7	8	9	10	11	12
32	A	ROMFORD		3		L	0-1	0-1		Smith	Martin	McCready	Collins	Law	Davies	Hodges	Cooke	Bailham	Malley	O'Rourke	
	30/3		*2,457*	*7*	43				*Obeney 22*	*Smith*	*Read*	*King*	*Sorrell*	*Gibbs*	*Obeney*	*Sanders*	*Aggio*	*Flatt*	*Tapping*	*Barrett*	
									Ref: J Craigie	Three straight defeats drop the Dons to third. They are comprehensively outplayed by Romford, and without indomitable resistance by Smith and Law they would surely have been put to the sword. Obeney plays a one-two with Aggio before scoring the only goal.											
33	H	CAMBRIDGE U		3		D	1-1	0-0	O'Rourke 82	Smith	Martin	McCready	Collins	Law	Davies	Hodges	Hyde	Bailham	Ardrey	O'Rourke	
	6/4		3,843	*1*	44				*Hutchinson 87*	*Barker*	*Lindsey*	*Grant*	*Scurr*	*Baker*	*Hardy*	*Wall*	*Chambers*	*Hutchinson*	*Payne*	*Barrett*	
									Ref: J Griffiths	Wimbledon have never lost four Southern League games in a row, so this is a major test for them, against the new leaders. Gerry O'Rourke's sensational strike from the corner of the penalty box deserved to earn victory. Before kick-off the crowd stood in memory of Sydney Black.											
34	H	STEVENAGE		3		W	3-0	1-0	Cooke 14, Bailham 70, Hodges 89	Smith	Martin	McCready	Collins	Law	Davies	Hodges	Cooke	Bailham	Malley	O'Rourke	
	12/4		2,900	*17*	46					*Peacock*	*Gitsham*	*Keenan*	*Stevens*	*Mills*	*Walker*	*Powell*	*Smith*	*Bannister*	*McLeish*	*Chandler*	
									Ref: S Lover	Stevenage are headed for liquidation. Wimbledon's first win in five games is set in train by Cooke's angled drive, after the ball had been deflected to him by a defender. A bone-hard pitch makes life difficult for both teams. Mills was happy to credit his own-goal to Paul Hodges.											
35	A	BURTON ALB		3		L	1-2	1-2	Davies 16	Smith	Martin	McCready	Collins	Law	Davies	Hodges	Cooke	Bailham	Malley	O'Rourke	
	13/4		*2,117*	*18*	46				*Notley 27, Goodall 40*	*Potter*	*Finney*	*Shepherd*	*Carver*	*King*	*Goodall*	*Metcalfe*	*Gordon*	*Parker*	*Notley*	*Tait*	
									Ref: D Hutchinson	Keeper Smith injures an ankle after five minutes. O'Rourke deputises for a while, then gives way, as Smith returns to limp through the rest of the match. Davies' goal gives the Dons hope, but a semi-fit Smith cannot keep out Albion. The Dons apply frantic second-half pressure.											
36	A	STEVENAGE				D	3-3	1-3	O'Rourke 42, 54, Bailham 90	**Guy**	Martin	McCready	Collins	Law*	Davies	Hodges	Cooke	Bailham	Malley	O'Rourke	Willis
	15/4		*1,700*		47				*England 17, 20, Powell 37*	*Peacock*	*Gitsham*	*Keenan*	*Stevens*	*Mills*	*Walker*	*Powell*	*Smith*	*Bannister*	*Brooks**	*England*	*Long*
										Stevenage have only another month in existence. Dons players and supporters cannot believe their eyes when they arrive, for the pitch is made not of grass but sand. Flints lie all over the surface, and wags demand buckets and spades. Dickie Guy makes two bloomers on his debut.											
37	H	CORBY		3		W	1-0	1-0	O'Rourke 27	Smith	Martin	McCready	Collins	Law	Davies	Hodges	Cooke	Bailham	Malley	O'Rourke	
	20/4		2,371	*21*	49					*Alexander*	*McBain*	*Caldow*	*Addy*	*McGugan*	*Barratt*	*Aldread*	*Goodall*	*Zelos*	*McNeil*	*Burns*	
									Ref: K Ridden	Corby are headed for the drop and should have been hit for six. They miss their absent player-manager, Eric Caldow, the former Glasgow Ranger and Scottish full-back. O'Rourke handed off a defender before scoring. Thereafter the Dons are jeered for a string of amazing misses.											
38	A	HILLINGDON B		2		W	1-0	0-0	Langley 80 (og)	Smith	Martin	McCready	Collins	Law	Davies	Hodges	Cooke	Bailham	Malley	O'Rourke	
	22/4		*1,572*	*4*	51					*Lowe*	*McNeice*	*Langley*	*Batt*	*Newcombe*	*Adams*	*Fairchild*	*Parker*	*Townend*	*Carter*	*Watson*	
									Ref: J Clarke	Wimbledon were on the rack for 80 minutes, with Smith's goal leading a charmed life. Hillingdon, who include ex-Don Brian Adams, chalk up some bizarre misses. Carter hits the post while standing on the goal-line. Player-manager Jim Langley then bundles the ball into his own net.											
39	A	KING'S LYNN				L	0-1	0-0		Smith	Martin	McCready	Collins!	Law	Davies	Hodges	Cooke	Bailham	Malley	O'Rourke	
	27/4		*1,517*		51				*Lindsay 60*	*Coe*	*Haskins*	*Sharp*	*Way*	*Porter*	*Wright*	*Savino*	*Davies*	*Lindsay*	*Jenkins*	*Tough*	
									Ref: J Jackson	Shortly after King's Lynn score their controversial goal, Jimmy Collins is sent off for the second time this season. He had taken a dislike to Peter Tough. The goal came when Smith appeared to be impeded at a corner-kick, enabling Malcolm Lindsay to score for the Linnets.											
40	H	HASTINGS		1		W	5-0	2-0	Martin 15, Cooke 41, 63, Bailham 50, [Hodges 80]	Smith	Martin	Willis	Collins	Law	Davies	Hodges	Cooke	Bailham	McCready	O'Rourke	
	30/4		1,824	*22*	53					*Cowan*	*Barry*	*Nash*	*Leck*	*Rutter*	*Smith*	*Duncan*	*Cowey*	*Meadows*	*Strachan*	*George*	
									Ref: L Constable	Only if Wimbledon won by five or more goals would they overtake Chelmsford on goal-average. Bottom-placed Hastings can't manage a single worthwhile shot. Brian Martin volleyed his first goal of the season to set up the rout. Dennis Malley was dropped.											
41	H	CHELMSFORD		1		L	1-2	1-1	Bailham 37	Smith	Martin	Willis	Collins	Law	Davies	Hodges	Cooke	Bailham	McCready	O'Rourke	
	4/5		**5,028**	*2*	53				*Block 40, Butcher 65*	*Medlock*	*Costello*	*Smith*	*Shreeve*	*Eades*	*Dochetry*	*Leggett*	*Butcher*	*Cassidy*	*Gordon*	*Block*	
									Ref:F Lane	The most critical Southern League match in Wimbledon's history. Chelmsford have a game in hand, so the Dons must win. Instead, City inflict a cruel double, after the Dons had gone in front again. Block equalises off the bar, and the winner has a touch of handball about it.											
42	H	BARNET		2		W	5-0	2-0	Cooke 9, Hodges 13, 89, Bailham 69, [Malley 77]	Smith	McCready	Willis	Collins	Law	Davies	Hodges	Cooke	Bailham	Malley	O'Rourke	
	11/5		2,800	*7*	55					*Barr*	*Thompson*	*Jenkins*	*Ward*	*Roach*	*King*	*Anderson*	*Eason*	*Figg*	*Searle*	*Ratty*	
		Home	*Away*						Ref: J Marshall	Wimbledon had to win and hope that Chelmsford lost. The first happened, but not the second. There could be few complaints at the destination of the championship, considering Chelmsford defeated the Dons twice. Just one draw would have given Wimbledon the crown.											
Average		2,676	*2,255*																		

Southern League Cup	F-A	H-T	Scorers, Times, and Referees	1	2	3	4	5	6	7	8	9	10	11	12 sub used
1:1 A GUILDFORD	D 2-2	1-1	Hobbs 5, O'Rourke 52	Smith	McCready	Willis*	Ardrey	Law	Collins	Hyde	Hobbs	O'Rourke	Cartwright	Hodges	Wallis
29/8 2,414			*Watts 35, Brown 80*	*Vasper*	*Gunter*	*Anthony*	*Massey*	*Bishop*	*More*	*Watts*	*Burge*	*Brown*	*Colfar*	*Vafiadis*	
			Ref: R Evans	Guildford are defending the Southern League Cup, and play their part in a thrill-a-minute cup-tie. O'Rourke's deflected goal from 20 yards seemed to have set up the Dons nicely for the second leg, but, in addition to their equaliser, Guildford hit the post twice in the dying minutes.											
1:2 H GUILDFORD 7	L 1-2	1-1	Hodges 26	Smith	Martin	McCready	Ardrey	Law	Collins	Hyde	Hobbs	O'Rourke	Cartwright	Hodges	
5/9 2,911 *12*			*Colfar 44, 80*	*Vasper*	*Gunter*	*Anthony*	*Watts*	*Bishop*	*More*	*Burge*	*Colfar*	*Brown*	*Gregory*	*Vafiadis*	*P*
			Ref: R Pearce (Dons lose 3-4 on aggregate)	Early in the second half, first Hyde hit a post, then O'Rourke followed suit. It was that sort of match for Wimbledon. Roy Law slipped to allow Colfar – shortly to sign for Wimbledon – to score the decisive goal. O'Rourke ballooned the ball over the crossbar during the final assault.											

FA Cup	F-A	H-T	Scorers, Times, and Referees	1	2	3	4	5	6	7	8	9	10	11	12 sub used
4Q H ASHFORD 4	W 3-0	2-0	Cooke 25, Hyde 28, O'Rourke 63	Smith	Martin	Willis	Collins	Law*	Davies	Cooke	Hyde	Cartwright	Ardrey	O'Rourke	Hobbs
28/10 2,462 *1:17*				*Taylor*	*Sillett*	*Hunt*	*Dodge*	*French*	*Parnell*	*Gillingwater*	*Cochrane*	*Angel*	*Crush*	*March*	
			Ref: G Palmer	This match was played in atrocious conditions. Ardrey played on despite being dazed from a head collision. Law had to be substituted as a result of his knee injury. The decisive factor of the match was Ashford's young keeper, Taylor, who looked sadly out of his depth.											
1 H ROMFORD	W 3-0	1-0	Hodges 35p, 88, Hobbs 76	Smith	Martin	Willis	Malley	McCready	Davies	Hodges	Cooke	Hobbs	Ardrey	O'Rourke	
9/12 4,995				*Smith*	*Read*	*King*	*Sorrell*	*Gibbs*	*Taylor*	*Sanders*	*Aggio*	*Obeney*	*Tapping*	*Barnett*	*P*
			Ref: B Homewood	A thunderous match played on a snowbound pitch during a blizzard. Both sides wanted it postponed. After an hour the referee consulted a linesman about continuing, but by then Wimbledon were ahead and wanted the job done. Tossing up beforehand, the coin was lost in the snow.											
2 H BRISTOL ROV	L 0-4	0-2		Smith	Martin	McCready	Collins	Law	Davies	Hodges	Cooke	Hobbs	Ardrey	O'Rourke	
6/1 9,356			*Biggs 23, 43, W Jones 64, Ronaldson 80*	*Taylor L*	*Hillard*	*Munro*	*Williams*	*Taylor S*	*Stone*	*Mabbutt*	*Ronaldson*	*Biggs*	*Jones W*	*Jones R*	
			Ref: G McCabe	3rd Division Bristol Rovers stand between Wimbledon and the 3rd Round of the FA Cup. The Dons have their chances, but it is Rovers who take theirs. Alf Biggs is their all-time leading scorer, and he capitalises on Martin's mistake. The gate is the biggest since the Dons turned pro.											

		Home					Away					
	P	W	D	L	F	A	W	D	L	F	A	Pts
1 Chelmsford	42	16	2	3	55	20	9	5	7	30	30	57
2 WIMBLEDON	42	14	4	3	53	18	10	3	8	32	29	55
3 Cambridge U	42	13	6	2	45	17	7	7	7	28	25	53
4 Cheltenham	42	17	2	2	62	23	6	5	10	35	44	53
5 Guildford	42	12	4	5	34	16	6	9	6	22	27	49
6 Romford	42	13	4	4	41	24	7	4	10	31	36	48
7 Barnet	42	13	5	3	56	30	7	3	11	25	41	48
8 Margate	42	16	4	1	52	14	3	4	14	28	57	46
9 Wellington	42	8	8	5	40	30	8	5	8	30	36	45
10 Hillingdon B	42	14	3	4	36	15	4	6	11	17	39	45
11 King's Lynn	42	15	2	4	39	18	3	6	12	27	39	44
12 Yeovil	42	13	6	2	35	12	3	6	12	10	31	44
13 Weymouth	42	12	5	4	40	24	5	3	13	25	38	42
14 Hereford	42	11	6	4	35	24	6	1	14	23	38	41
15 Nuneaton B	42	10	6	5	36	26	3	8	10	26	38	40
16 Dover	42	13	5	3	34	14	4	1	16	20	42	40
17 Poole	42	10	3	8	29	26	3	7	11	26	48	36
18 Stevenage *	42	10	5	6	36	23	3	4	14	21	52	35
19 Burton Alb	42	11	4	6	35	25	3	2	16	16	48	34
20 Corby	42	6	8	7	27	34	1	5	15	13	43	27
21 Cambridge C	42	7	3	11	33	39	3	3	15	18	42	26
22 Hastings	42	2	5	14	20	44	2	3	16	13	50	16
* *liquidated*	924	256	100	106	873	516	106	100	256	516	873	924

Odds & ends

Double wins: (9) Dover, Hastings, Hereford, Yeovil, Poole, Corby, Cambridge C, Weymouth, Barnet.
Double losses: (3) Margate, Cheltenham, Chelmsford.

Won from behind: (3) Wellington (h), Corby (a), Dover (a).
Lost from in front: (4) Cheltenham (h), Burton (a), Chelmsford (h & a).

High spots: 6 straight wins in Nov and Dec lift the Dons from 10th to 1st.
17 points from 9 games from January to March.

Low spots: 3 successive defeats over Easter.
Losing at home to Chelmsford in effective title decider.

Ever-presents: (1) Gerry O'Rourke.
Hat-tricks: Ian Cooke (1), Eddie Bailham (1).
Leading Scorer: Gerry O'Rourke (24).

	Appearances						Goals			
	Lge	Sub	SLC	Sub	FAC	Sub	**Lge**	SLC	FAC	**Total**
Ardrey, Bobby	**18**		2		3					
Bailham, Eddie	**29**						**13**			**13**
Cartwright, Johnnie	**11**		2		1		**5**			**5**
Collins, Jimmy	**38**		2		2					
Cooke, Ian	**33**	(2)			3		**21**		1	**22**
Davies, Stuart	**37**				3		**8**			**8**
Guy, Dickie	**1**									
Hobbs, Peter	**11**	(1)	2		2	(1)	**1**	1	1	**3**
Hodges, Paul	**33**		2		2		**7**	1	2	**10**
Hyde, David	**16**		2		1		**3**		1	**4**
Law, Roy	**36**		2		2					
McCready, Tom	**37**		2		2					
Malley, Dennis	**21**	(1)			1		**3**			**3**
Martin, Brian	**35**		1		3		**1**			**1**
O'Rourke, Gerry	**42**		2		3		**22**	1	1	**24**
Smith, Frank	**41**		2		3					
Wallis, Joe	**2**	(1)		(1)						
Willis, Dave	**21**	(2)	1		2					
(own-goals)							**1**			**1**
18 players used	**462**	**(7)**	**22**	**(1)**	**33**	**(1)**	**85**	**3**	**6**	**94**

No	Date	Att	Pos	Pts	F-A	H-T	Scorers, Times, and Referees	1	2	3	4	5	6	7	8	9	10	11	12 sub used
1	H HEREFORD			W	3-1	1-0	Bailham 39, 46, Bird 56 (og)	Smith	Martin	Willis	Malley	Law	Davies	Hodges	Cooke	Bailham	McCready	O'Rourke	
	10/8	2,315		2			*Charles 89*	*Davis*	*Evans*	*Bird*	*Summerhayes*	*Purcell*	*Jones*	*Scarrott*	*White*	*Charles*	*Derrick*	*Lewis*	
							Ref: F Burling	Les Henley has signed Ray Colfar from Guildford and towering John O'Mara from Margate, though both wait for their debuts. Bailham looks to have shed a stone in weight. Hereford include five internationals, including John Charles, who scores against the Dons for the first time.											
2	A HILLINGDON B			D	2-2	2-0	Cooke 8, 19	Smith	Martin	Willis	Malley	Law	Davies	Hodges	Cooke	Bailham	McCready	O'Rourke	
	12/8	*1,961*		3			*Watson 87, 89*	*Lowe*	*McNeice*	*Langley*	*Watson*	*Newcombe*	*Moore*	*Salmon*	*Cozens*	*Townend*	*Carter*	*Vafiadis*	
							Ref: P Hunter	A freak goal puts the Dons in front. Keeper Lowe punches the ball into Ian Cooke's face, and it flies into the net. Two goals give Hillingdon a point they deserve. Cozens had hit a post at 0-2. Watson beats Frank Smith in the air to pull one back, then runs 50 yards to equalise.											
3	A RUGBY			D	0-0	0-0		Smith	Martin	Willis	McCready	Law	Davies	Hodges	Cooke	Bailham	McCready	O'Rourke	
	17/8	*1,298*		4				*Richards*	*Hinde*	*Harrald*	*Walker*	*Clarke*	*Hopkin*	*Whittle*	*Brady*	*Whitehead*	*Senior*	*Denton*	
							Ref: M Walker	Wimbledon might have had 10, but end up with nought. They hit the post twice, and have other efforts disallowed or cleared off the line. Mark Richards in goal also does newly promoted Rugby proud.											
4	H WEYMOUTH			L	**0-3**	0-2		Smith	Martin	Willis	Malley*	Law	Davies	Cooke	**O'Mara**	Bailham	McCready	Hodges	**Colfar**
	24/8	1,983		4			*Glover 3p, Parks 43, Etheridge 79*	*Clarke*	*Glover*	*Rounsevell*	*Barry*	*Hobson*	*Hall*	*Bennet*	*Etheridge*	*Parks*	*Jackson*	*Edwardson*	
							Ref: G Simpson	Having just lost 0-3 to Chelmsford in the Southern League Cup, Wimbledon suffer a similar score in the league. More blunders by Frank Smith mean that Dickie Guy's introduction cannot be long delayed. Both O'Mara and Colfar make their long-awaited league debuts.											
5	A NUNEATON B		13	L	2-3	1-1	O'Mara 21, 70	Smith	**Noble**	Willis	Cooke	Law	Davies	Hodges	O'Mara	Bailham	McCready	O'Rourke	
	31/8	***5,345***	*4*	4			*Jacques 10, 83, Jackson 75*	*Crump*	*Jones*	*Smith*	*Drake*	*Aston*	*Boot*	*Wright*	*Jackson*	*Jacques*	*Cutler*	*Allen*	
							Ref: J Smith	Is John O'Mara the new Eddie Reynolds, Dons fans ask, as he powers in two goals. Wimbledon enjoyed territorial advantage throughout, but Nuneaton's new signing, Jacques, rewards his team with two goals of his own. Boro's equaliser and winner are both long-range efforts.											
6	H HILLINGDON B		13	W	2-1	2-0	Bailham 13p, O'Mara 32	Smith	McCready	Willis	Collins	Law	Davies	Hodges	Cooke	Bailham	O'Mara	O'Rourke	
	3/9		*2*	6			*Cozens 85*	*Lowe*	*McNeice*	*Langley*	*Watson*	*Newcombe*	*Moore*	*Fairchild*	*Cozens*	*Townend*	*Carter*	*Vafiadis*	
							Ref: J Marshall	This is the Dons' first win in seven in league and cup, since the first day of the season. Football League scouts are out in force, but it isn't a Wimbledon player they are spying upon, but Hillingdon's John Cozens, who scores courtesy of Smith's error. Bailham nearly fluffs his penalty.											
7	A CHELTENHAM		14	W	3-1	2-0	O'Mara 23, Davies 27, Hodges 57	Smith	McCready	Willis	Collins	Law	Davies	Hodges	Cooke	Bailham	O'Mara	O'Rourke	
	7/9	*2,005*	*11*	8			*Thorne 78*	*Meeson*	*Thorndale*	*Radford*	*Carson*	*Jefferies*	*Booth*	*Hurford*	*Hudd*	*Horlick*	*Lloyd*	*Thorne*	
							Ref: B Watkins	Cheltenham had not lost at home for 10 months. At 0-2 Cheltenham's Clive Lloyd misses from the penalty spot, a third consecutive miss. This terrific Wimbledon performance was set up by John O'Mara's fifth goal in five games.											
8	H KING'S LYNN		12	W	3-1	1-0	Bailham 43p, Hodges 47, 88	Smith	McCready	Willis	Collins	Law	Davies	Hodges	Cooke	Bailham*	O'Mara	O'Rourke	Colfar
	10/9	2,119	*10*	10			*Davies 65*	*Coe*	*Haskins*	*Sharpe*	*Brooks*	*Mullett*	*Wright*	*Savino*	*Hawksby*	*Lindsay*	*Jenkins*	*Clarke*	*Davies*
							Ref: P Saubergue	Paul Hodges is the architect of this win, scoring two and being fouled by Haskins for the penalty. Hodges' second goal is candidate for goal-of-the-season. He outstrips three defenders and shoots on the run. Ian Cooke is trying to adapt to life playing in midfield.											
9	H ROMFORD		9	L	0-2	0-0		Smith	McCready	Willis	Collins	Law	Davies	Hodges	Cooke	O'Mara	O'Rourke	Colfar	
	14/9	2,019	*5*	10			*Flatt 66, Barnett 85*	*Smith*	*Moyse*	*King*	*Andrew*	*Gibbs*	*Obeney*	*Barnett*	*Read*	*Flatt*	*Aggio*	*Fry*	
							Ref: B Chapman	Bailham is out, injured, and without him the Dons flounder. Flatt robs Law out by the touch-line and floats the ball over Frank Smith. O'Mara was booked for a clash with the Romford keeper, who later went to hospital with chest injuries. The crowd drained away before the end.											
10	H YEOVIL		11	W	1-0	0-0	Bailham 49	Smith	Martin	Willis	Collins	Law	McCready	Hodges	Cooke	Bailham	O'Mara	O'Rourke	
	28/9	1,732	*6*	12				*Jones*	*Herrity*	*Smith*	*Slee*	*Harris*	*Muir*	*Elliott*	*Thompson*	*Mitten*	*Taylor*	*Myers*	
							Ref: R Evans	Yeovil enjoy an unfortunate reputation for thuggery and bad sportsmanship. They resort to the offside trap in this match, which attracts Plough Lane's smallest crowd so far. Once Wimbledon had scored tempers became so frayed that the referee had to stop play and lecture both captains.											

No	Venue	Opponent	Pos	Res	F-A	H-T	Scorers, Times, and Referees	1	2	3	4	5	6	7	8	9	10	11	12
11	A	CAMBRIDGE U	11	L	0-2	0-2		Smith	Martin	Willis	Collins	Law	McCready	Hodges*	Cooke	Bailham	O'Mara	O'Rourke	Colfar
	5/10	2,917	*14*	12			*Nicholas 13, Saunders 45*	*Slack*	*Lindsey*	*Grant**	*Scurr*	*Baker*	*Hardy*	*Saunders*	*Chambers*	*Nicholas*	*Walker*	*Horrey*	*Ward*
							Ref: J Jackson	Wimbledon have never won at the Abbey Stadium. Bailham was blotted out by Jackie Scurr. The Dons were 0-2 down when Henley sent on Ray Colfar for Paul Hodges. This livened up the team, who had chances to score, but Bailham and O'Rourke squandered them.											
12	H	WELLINGTON	10	D	1-1	0-0	Cooke 60	Smith	Martin	Willis	Collins	Law	Davies	Colfar	Cooke	Bailham	McCready	O'Rourke	Hodges
	12/10	1,674	*22*	13			*Fudge 72p*	*Irvine*	*Harris*	*McKinney*	*Hart*	*Ball*	*Rey*	*Matthews*	*Fudge*	*Bentley*	*Houghton*	*Jagger*	*Croft*
							Ref: J Griffiths	This abject showing against the rock-bottom team takes some believing. Both Hodges and O'Mara were dropped. Keeper Irvine won eight caps for Northern Ireland when with Linfield and Stoke, and he takes the honours now. Law and McCready bring down Houghton for the penalty.											
13	A	BURTON ALB	6	W	**3-0**	1-0	O'Rourke 35, 87, Cooke 71	Smith	Martin	Willis	McCready	Law	Davies	Hodges	Cooke	Bailham	Collins	O'Rourke	
	19/10	*936*	*20*	15				*Surman*	*Finney*	*Walton*	*Bailey*	*King*	*Goodall*	*Metcalfe*	*Cleevely*	*Vincent*	*Brown*	*Scattergood*	
							Ref: J Chappell	Before this match Gerry O'Rourke had scored just once in 16 games. He trebles that tally with two goals. The match turned at 1-0, when Brown found himself with only Frank Smith to beat, but lofted his shot over. The Dons are looking forward to their FA Cup-tie with Woking.											
14	H	WORCESTER	6	D	1-1	0-0	Hodges 60	Smith	Martin	Willis	Collins	Law	Davies	Hodges	Cooke*	O'Mara	McCready	O'Rourke	Malley
	26/10	2,071	*19*	16			*Middleton 50*	*MacLaren*	*Griffiths*	*Bassett*	*Stuart*	*Madley*	*Huxford*	*Middleton*	*Gould*	*Reynolds*	*Allchurch*	*Ward*	
							Ref: A Myers	Referee Myers found himself threatened with physical assault by players of both sides. No one has any idea why he gave a second-half penalty to Wimbledon. Dave McLaren saved it, and then was awarded a goal-kick! Welsh maestro Ivor Allchurch misses a great chance for Worcester.											
15	H	CAMBRIDGE U	7	D	3-3	2-1	Bailham 7, 78, Davies 33	Smith	McCready	Willis	Collins	Law	Davies	Colfar	O'Rourke	Bailham	Malley	Hodges	
	9/11	1,658	*6*	17			*Cassidy 31, 52, Baker 65*	*Slack*	*Lindsey*	*Brown*	*Scurr*	*Baker*	*Hardy*	*Horrey*	*Gregson*	*Cassidy*	*Nicholas!*	*Saunders*	
							Ref: G Keeble	Oh dear! After Woking, this! Wimbledon's lowest crowd so far watches in agony as Smith concedes two more soft goals. Once in front United time-wasted at throw-ins by throwing the ball out of play as far away as they could. Tony Nicholas was sent off near the end.											
16	A	WORCESTER	6	D	1-1	1-0	Colfar 44	Guy	Martin	Willis	Collins	Law	Davies	Colfar	Cooke	Bailham	McCready	O'Rourke	
	16/11	*1,349*	*19*	18			*Reynolds 87*	*Knight*	*Griffiths*	*Bassett*	*Stuart*	*Madley*	*McEwan*	*Round*	*Gould*	*Reynolds*	*Allchurch*	*Middleton*	
							Ref: J Smith	At last Frank Smith is dropped. He has played his last game for Wimbledon. Dickie Guy's first game of the season is matched by Ray Colfar's first goal. Guy saves impressively from Ivor Allchurch, and when he is beaten Dave Willis clears off the line.											
17	H	KETTERING	6	W	1-0	0-0	Bailham 64p	Guy	Martin	Willis	Collins	McCready	Davies	Colfar	Cooke	Bailham	O'Rourke	Hodges	
	23/11	1,517	*17*	20				*Harvey*	*Ashby*	*Needham*	*Gammon*	*Reed*	*Peck*	*Daldy*	*Evans*	*Gully*	*Goodall*	*Walden*	
							Ref: M Taylor	Newly promoted Kettering have their minds on an exciting FA Cup run. The all-important goal comes when Tony Needham pulls down Paul Hodges and Eddie Bailham scores from the penalty spot.											
18	A	MARGATE	3	W	2-0	0-0	Bailham 62, Colfar 83	Guy	Martin	Willis	Collins	Law	Davies	Colfar	Cooke	Bailham	McCready	O'Rourke	
	30/11	*1,529*	*21*	22				*Ede*	*Yorath*	*Campbell*	*Clifton*	*Harrop*	*Houston*	*Amato*	*Grace*	*Jest*	*Moffatt*	*Jenkins*	*Jarman*
								Wimbledon are now up to third, just one point behind Yeovil. Clifton struck the bar early on, with Guy beaten, but Bailham is the difference between the sides. He scores one and makes the other for Colfar.											
19	H	CHELMSFORD	3	W	1-0	1-0	Cooke 14	Guy	Martin	Willis	Collins	Law	Davies	Colfar	Cooke	Bailham	McCready	O'Rourke	
	7/12	1,658	*5*	24				*Leiper*	*Smith*	*West*	*Shreeve*	*Eades*	*Costello**	*Leggett*	*McLeish*	*Moy*	*Gordon*	*Block*	
							Ref: J Tree	Never, until now, have Wimbledon beaten Chelmsford in five seasons of Southern League football. But Chelmsford have lost their deadly duo, Butcher and Cassidy, and look powder-puff without them. Ian Cooke, in oceans of space, heads the only goal from Eddie Bailham's cross.											
20	A	CHELMSFORD	3	L	0-2	0-2		Guy	Martin	Willis	Collins	Law	Davies	Colfar	Cooke	Bailham	McCready	O'Rourke	
	14/12	*1,874*	*5*	24			*Moffatt 28, McLeish 43*	*Leiper*	*Smith*	*West*	*Gordon*	*Eades*	*Shreeve*	*Shires*	*McLeish*	*May*	*Moffatt*	*Block*	
							Ref: E Reynolds	Revenge is swift for Chelmsford, as the Dons barely mustered a single shot on goal. On a frost-covered pitch, the trousered Guy makes his first serious mistake since his introduction. He fails to hold McLeish's volley and Tony Moffatt – a midweek signing from Margate – pounces.											
21	H	GUILDFORD	3	W	3-1	2-0	Cooke 31, Bailham 39, Law 65	Guy	Martin	Willis	Cooke	Law	Collins	Colfar	Bailham	O'Rourke	McCready	Hodges	
	21/12	1,884	*19*	26			*Burns 69*	*Brooks*	*Shaw*	*Anthony*	*More*	*Bishop*	*Watts*	*Burge*	*Idle*	*Burns*	*Lamble*	*Dodson*	
							Ref: S Lover	A curate's egg performance, blowing hot and cold. Lowly Guildford have just sacked manager Albert Tennant. Roy Law is so excited by scoring his first goal of the season that he immediately blunders in defence to present Les Burns with a simple reply.											

SOUTHERN LEAGUE PREMIER DIVISION — Manager: Les Henley — SEASON 1968-69

No	Date	Att	Pos Pts	F-A	H-T	Scorers, Times, and Referees	1	2	3	4	5	6	7	8	9	10	11	12 sub used
22	H BARNET		3 W	2-1	1-0	Colfar 41, 65	Guy	McCready	Willis	Cooke	Law	Collins	Colfar	Bailham	O'Rourke	O'Mara	Hodges	
	26/12	2,313	*12* 28			*Eason 58*	*Barr*	*Lye*	*Jenkins*	*Ward*	*Ferry*	*King*	*Powell*	*Meagher*	*Embery*	*Eason*	*Meadows*	
						Ref: R Wood	This result flattered the Dons. Barnet miss the injured Roy Figg. John O'Mara – big, brave, and clumsy – is already the target of the Plough Lane barrack-boys. Colfar strikes out of the blue from Guy's clearance to put the Dons one up. At 2-1, Meagher hooks against the crossbar.											
23	A BARNET		2 D	1-1	1-1	King 2 (og)	Guy	McCready	Willis	Collins	Law	Davies	Hodges	Cooke	Bailham	O'Mara	O'Rourke	
	28/12	*1,370*	*13* 29			*Meadows 20*	*Barr*	*Lye*	*Jenkins*	*Ward*	*Ferry*	*King*	*Powell*	*George*	*Embery*	*Eason*	*Meadows*	
						Ref: F Lane	Ray Colfar – two goals on Boxing Day – is injured and misses this snowy, return match with Barnet. Early on, Barnet's Powell 'scored' off a post, but Stuart Davies' scoops the ball out and the referee waves play on. The Dons enjoyed an own-goal, too, so this was a lucky day.											
24	H POOLE		2 D	3-3	3-0	Davies 15, Hodges 36, Cooke 39	Guy	Martin	Willis	Collins	Law	Davies	Hodges	Cooke	Bailham	McCready	O'Rourke	
	4/1	**1,429**	*15* 30			*Down 50, Murphy 55, Allen 86*	*Whiting*	*Brewster*	*Balsom*	*Eyden*	*Brown*	*Shergold*	*Down*	*Taylor*	*Allen*	*Pring*	*Murphy*	
						Ref: E Reynolds	An unbelievable score, given that Wimbledon were coasting, three goals up, at half-time, and should have led by six. Brian Martin has a nightmare second half, contributing to Poole's first two goals. At 3-2 the Dons panic, but cannot hold out. Cooke's effort at 3-3 is disallowed.											
25	A POOLE		2 W	3-1	1-0	O'Rourke 41, 56, Bailham 63	Guy	Martin	Willis	Collins	Law	Davies	Colfar	Bailham	O'Rourke	McCready	Hodges	
	11/1	*1,429*	*16* 32			*Down 54*	*Rafferty*	*Brewster*	*Balsom*	*Rutley*	*Eyden*	*Shergold*	*Down*	*Taylor*	*Allen*	*Pring*	*Murphy*	
						Ref: B Facey	Poole are put in their place this time. Only goal-average keeps the Dons off the top now. Henley tries out a 4-3-3 formation but that has no part to play in the Dons' second and third goals, which are down to Poole's debutant keeper Rafferty. He rushes out for No 3 but misses the ball.											
26	H NUNEATON B		2 W	2-0	0-0	Martin 71, O'Mara 75	Guy	Martin	McCready	Collins	Law	Davies	Hodges	Cooke	Bailham	O'Mara	O'Rourke	
	25/1	2,000	*11* 34				*Crump*	*Jones*	*Smith*	*Drake*	*Aston*	*Allen*	*Jackson*	*Boot*	*Jacques*	*Cutler*	*Richards*	
						Ref: K Ridden	Two blistering second-half goals keep Wimbledon second in the table, after the spectators endured a wretched first half. Brian Martin's screamer is his first goal of the season, and John O'Mara's towering header from Hodges' cross was no less appreciated by the crowd.											
27	H MARGATE		2 W	2-1	1-1	Bailham 26, Hodges 80	Guy	Martin	Willis	Collins	Law	Davies	Hodges	Cooke	Bailham	McCready	O'Rourke	
	1/2	1,843	*20* 36			*Amato 1*	*Thomas*	*Yorath*	*Houston*	*Clifton*	*Harrop*	*Marshall*	*Amato*	*Jest*	*Smith*	*Flannigan*	*Burden*	
						Ref: C MacKnight	Margate have by far the worst defensive record in the league. They beat the Dons twice last season, and there is little to choose between the sides this time. Margate are helped by Amato's goal after just 30 seconds, when Guy and McCready left a through-ball to each other.											
28	H CHELTENHAM		2 W	1-0	0-0	O'Rourke 73	Guy	Martin	Willis	Collins	Law	Davies	Colfar	Cooke	Bailham*	McCready	O'Rourke	Hodges
	15/2	1,515	*17* 38				*Meeson*	*Thorndale*	*Conboy*	*Carson*	*Jefferies*	*Radford*	*Hurford*	*Hudd*	*Houghton*	*Horlick*	*Lloyd*	
						Ref: F Bassett	Wimbledon have a game in hand over leaders Cambridge United, whom they trail on goal-average. O'Rourke enjoys his first home goal of the season, playing centre-forward once Bailham was substituted. By the end, O'Rourke's shirt was in shreds, courtesy of desperate defenders.											
29	A GUILDFORD		2 W	3-2	3-1	Massey 7 (og), O'Rourke 15, 40	Guy	Martin	Willis	Collins	Law	Davies	Colfar	Cooke	O'Rourke	McCready	Hodges	
	22/2	*1,624*	*21* 40			*Moore 2, Davies 80*	*Palmer*	*Burns*	*Anthony*	*Massey*	*Bishop*	*Moore*	*Davies*	*Idle*	*Burge*	*Williams*	*Lamble*	
						Ref: G Keeble	Wimbledon have stacks of away fixtures piling up. Guy fumbles Moore's early shot, but Bob Massey compensates with a spectacular own-goal from Hodges' cross. Colfar torments his old club by projecting a stream of crosses throughout, one of which is converted by O'Rourke.											
30	A BEDFORD		1 W	1-0	1-0	O'Rourke 26	Guy	Martin	Willis	Collins	Law	Davies	Hodges	Cooke	O'Rourke	McCready	Colfar	
	1/3	*1,661*	*18* 42				*Collier*	*Harris*	*Ryder*	*Skinn*	*Stevens*	*Hodgkinson*	*Sealey*	*Paton*	*Cooley*	*Cleary*	*Adams*	
						Ref: L Holland	Newly promoted Bedford are in a relegation dogfight. O'Rourke's 26th minute header sends the Dons two points clear at the top with a game in hand. Bailham, now fit again, cannot get back in the side. Bedford's only productive spell came early in the second half.											
31	A WELLINGTON		1 W	2-0	0-0	Hodges 60p, Cooke 72	Guy	Martin	Willis	Collins	Law	Davies	Hodges	Cooke	O'Rourke	McCready	Colfar	
	3/3	*1,596*	*13* 44				*Irvine*	*Whitehouse*	*Harris G*	*Croft*	*Coton*	*Ray*	*Matthews*	*Hart*	*Bentley*	*Fudge*	*Jagger*	
						Ref: R Marshall	This Monday evening match produces Wimbledon's third away win on the trot, but Wellington made the Dons sweat for the points. Jack Bentley is chasing his 200th goal for the club, but he is short-changed by Roy Law. The keeper uproots Cooke to concede the penalty-kick.											

No	Venue	Opponent / Date	Att	Pos	Pts	Res	F-A	H-T	Scorers, Times, Referees	1	2	3	4	5	6	7	8	9	10	11	12
32	H	RUGBY		1		W	2-0	1-0	Cooke 31, McLeish 73	Guy	McCready	Willis	Collins	Law	Davies	Colfar*	Cooke	O'Rourke	**McLeish**	Hodges	Bailham
		8/3	2,100	*21*	46					*Cortlett*	*Cholerton*	*Burckitt*	*Austin*	*Walker*	*Hopkin*	*Docker*	*Harrold*	*Notley*	*Whithead*	*Senior*	
									Ref: W Bundy	Wimbledon have signed 20-year-old Hugh McLeish on a free-transfer from Chelmsford, where he had been ever-present this season. Rugby field their own new man, Barry Notley from Burton. The Dons are six points clear. 'The title is as good as theirs,' says the *Wimbledon News*.											
33	A	HEREFORD		1		L	**0-3**	0-2		Guy	Martin	Willis*	McCready	Law	Davies	Bailham	McLeish	O'Rourke	Cooke	Hodges	Malley
		15/3	*2,372*	*11*	46				*Derrick 26, Charles 31, Timms 46*	*Davies*	*Bird*	*Timms*	*Summerhayes*	*Mullen*	*Punter*	*Scarrott*	*White*	*Charles*	*Derrick*	*Lewis*	
									Ref: F Bassett	Whoops-a-daisy. Wimbledon's first defeat of 1969, after eight league wins, comes at a ground where they have won three times in four visits. Flu ruled out Collins and Colfar. Alan Scarrott crosses for the first two goals. John Charles' effort brings his 31st strike of the season.											
34	H	BEDFORD		1		W	**3-0**	1-0	O'Rourke 6, 51, McLeish 61	Guy	Martin	McCready	Collins	Law	Davies	Colfar	Bailham	O'Rourke	McLeish	Hodges	
		22/3	1,833	*17*	48					*Collier*	*Skinn*	*Burridge*	*Fogg*	*Roach*	*Hodgkinson*	*Churchill*	*Sealey*	*Cooley*	*Cleary*	*Adams*	
									Ref: M Thorpe	Hillingdon are catching up fast, and have home games in hand. Strange to say, but this 3-0 result is Wimbledon's best at home this season, which says much for this goal-shy team. Under their new manager, Bedford had won their last three. Ian Cooke misses the match with flu.											
35	A	KING'S LYNN		1		D	0-0	0-0		Guy	Martin	Willis	Collins	Law	Davies	Bailham	McLeish	O'Rourke*	McCready	Hodges	Colfar
		29/3	*1,494*	*6*	49					*Coe*	*Haskins*	*Sharp*	*Brooks*	*Porter*	*Mullett*	*Lindsay*	*Rudd*	*Jenkins*	*Wright*	*Tough*	
									Ref: K Ridden	Under normal circumstances, a draw King's Lynn – unbeaten at home – would be a welcome result. But all the chasing clubs won, to narrow Wimbledon's lead. Both teams play cautious football, and the game dies before the end. Hodges might have had a penalty when hacked down.											
36	A	DOVER		1		L	0-1	0-1		Guy	Martin	Willis	Collins	Law*	Davies	Hodges	McLeish	Bailham	McCready	O'Rourke	O'Mara
		4/4	*1,874*	*9*	49				*Chandler 16*	*Price*	*Martin*	*Dennis*	*Clewlow*	*Swain*	*Huxley*	*Chandler*	*Horton*	*Kelly*	*Searle*	*Gregory*	
									Ref: M Thorpe	That Easter bogey has struck the Dons again. Dover had not won in four games, and the match is so scrappy that the Dons are booed off the pitch. Once behind, Wimbledon seemed to fall apart. Their best chance fell to Paul Hodges, but he shot wide when clean through.											
37	A	ROMFORD		1		D	2-2	0-0	Bailham 52, O'Mara 80	Guy	Martin	Willis	Collins	McCready	Cooke	Hodges	Bailham	O'Mara	McLeish	O'Rourke	
		5/4	*2,626*	*4*	50				*Fowler 58, Sanders 65*	*Smith*	*Read*	*King*	*Freeman*	*Taylor*	*Andrew*	*Sanders*	*Topping*	*Flatt*	*Fry*	*Aggio*	*Fowler*
									Ref: D Drewitt	Romford are one of Wimbledon's bogey sides. They lie fourth and are chasing the Dons hard. Romford substitute Fowler scores with his first touch. Wimbledon salvage a point when John O'Mara heads in Eddie Bailham's cross.											
38	H	DOVER		1		W	3-1	1-0	Bailham 33p, Cooke 60, Hodges 85	Guy	Martin	Willis	Collins	McCready	McLeish	Hodges	Bailham	O'Mara	Cooke	O'Rourke	
		7/4	**2,890**	*9*	52				*Ray 65*	*Price*	*Martin*	*Clewlow*	*Hurley*	*Swain*	*Kelly*	*Buckley*	*Horton*	*Ray*	*Chandler*	*Gregory*	
									Ref: W Dance	Championship fever is in the air, for this is Wimbledon's biggest league crowd so far. The pitch is so hard that O'Mara plays in basketball boots. The Dons win a penalty when an awkwardly bouncing ball glances off Clewlow's hand. Dover are so upset that they clap the referee.											
39	H	BURTON ALB		2		L	1-2	0-1	Hodges 90	Guy	Martin	Willis	Collins	McCready	Davies*	Hodges	Cooke	Bailham	McLeish	O'Rourke	O'Mara
		12/4	1,903	*20*	52				*Potter 24, Bostock 84*	*Potter*	*Bailey*	*Watton*	*Cleevely*	*King*	*Goodall*	*Metcalfe*	*Price*	*Notley*	*Brown*	*Bostock*	
									Ref: D Chainey	Catastrophe! Guy's blunder of blunders sinks the Dons. Burton keeper Fred Potter's downfield punt catches the wind and bounces, once, twice over poor Guy, who, blinded by the sun, falls into the net with the ball. Wimbledon never recover. It is as if they are under a curse.											
40	A	KETTERING		3		L	1-3	1-1	Bailham 4	Guy	Martin	Willis	Collins	McCready	Cooke	Colfar	Bailham	O'Mara	McLeish	O'Rourke	
		19/4	*1,664*	*9*	52				*B Daldy 13, Lawman 70, Ashby 74p*	*Harvey*	*Daldy J*	*Ashby*	*Gammon*	*Peck*	*Evans*	*Walden*	*Daldy B*	*Webster*	*Goodall*	*Lawman*	
									Ref: C MacKnight	Wimbledon get the start they want, but cannot hold on to Eddie Bailham's early goal. The longer the game went on, the more the Dons realised that the victory they desperately needed was going to elude them. The game petered out in the final minutes.											
41	A	WEYMOUTH		3		D	2-2	0-1	Davies 60, Hodges 80	Guy	Martin	Willis	Collins	Law	Davies	Bailham	Cooke	O'Rourke	McCready	Hodges	
		23/4	*1,207*	*6*	53				*Bennett 35, 85*	*Clarke*	*Glover*	*Rounsevell*	*Barry*	*Hobson*	*Hall*	*Adams*	*Etheridge*	*Jackson*	*Muir*	*Bennett*	
									Ref: J Smith	Even though Wimbledon have missed out on the championship, come what may, they serve up spirited entertainment. With hindsight, their glut of away fixtures late in the season meant that, earlier on, they enjoyed a false position at the top of the table.											
42	A	YEOVIL		3		D	0-0	0-0		Guy	Martin	Willis	Collins	Law	Davies	Bailham	Cooke	O'Rourke	McCready	Hodges	
		3/5	***890***	*8*	54					*Jones*	*Herrity*	*Smith*	*Slee*	*Harris*	*Thompson*	*Elliott*	*Plumb*	*Mitten*	*Myers*	*Weler*	
		Home / *Away*							Ref: R Peters	The smallest crowd in Yeovil's history watch this bore-draw. That is partly due to this being Yeovil's fifth match in six days. Wimbledon will finish third whether they win, lose, or draw. The game marks the final appearance for Brian Martin, retiring after 16 years with the club.											
Average		1,923 / *1,858*																			

Southern League Cup		F-A	H-T	Scorers, Times, and Referees	1	2	3	4	5	6	7	8	9	10	11	12 sub used
1:1 H CHELMSFORD		L 0-3	0-2		Smith	Martin	Willis	Malley	Law	Davies	Hodges	Cooke	Bailham	McCready	O'Rourke	
20/8	2,430			*Moy 8, Gordon 9, Butcher 53*	*Leiper*	*West*	*Smith*	*Shreeve*	*Eades*	*Costello*	*Leggett*	*Butcher*	*Moy*	*Gordon*	*Block*	
				Ref: P Hunter	Three mistakes by Frank Smith result in three goals for Chelmsford. He is stranded out of his goal, for the first, when Moy lobs him from 25 yards. The third goal is an overhead kick by Butcher. Wimbledon's forwards continually fall victim to Chemsford's offside trap.											
1:2 A CHELMSFORD		D 3-3	3-2	O'Rourke 42, O'Mara 44, Hodges 45	Smith	Noble	Willis	Cooke	Law	Davies	Hodges	O'Mara	Bailham	McCready	O'Rourke	
26/8	*3,674*			*Moy 38, 43, Coughlin 71*	*Wilkie*	*West*	*Smith*	*Shreeve*	*Eades*	*Coughlin*	*Leggett*	*Butcher*	*Moy*	*Gordon*	*Block*	
				Ref: J Marshall (Dons lose 3-6 on aggregate)	Chelmsford are still unbeaten this season. Wimbledon recover their self-respect by contributing to this cracking cup-tie, which produces five goals in seven minutes at the close of the first half. The Dons miss the injured Bobby Ardrey and the suspended Jimmy Collins.											

FA Cup																
4Q H WOKING		L 0-2	0-1		Smith	Martin	Willis	Collins	Law	Davies	Colfar	O'Mara	Bailham	McCready	O'Rourke	
2/11	2,346			*Tindall 32, Waughman 46*	*Farris*	*Hill*	*Elton*	*Goodwin*	*Povey*	*Sexton*	*Finn*	*Carver*	*Waughman*	*Tindall*	*Malcolmson*	
				Ref: G Palmer	This is Wimbledon's greatest humiliation since turning professional. They had never lost to the amateurs of Woking in their last six seasons in the Isthmian League. Smith fumbles Law's back-pass for the first goal. 'Words fail me,' wrote Peter Miller in the *Wimbledon News*.											

		Home					Away					
		W	D	L	F	A	W	D	L	F	A	Pts
1 Cambridge U	42	17	2	2	42	12	10	3	8	30	27	59
2 Hillingdon B	42	15	6	0	41	18	9	4	8	27	29	58
3 WIMBLEDON	42	14	4	3	38	22	7	8	6	28	26	54
4 King's Lynn	42	15	6	0	46	17	5	3	13	22	43	49
5 Worcester	42	14	4	3	37	15	5	7	9	16	32	49
6 Romford	42	13	4	4	38	20	5	8	8	20	32	48
7 Weymouth	42	12	6	3	31	16	4	9	8	21	25	47
8 Yeovil	42	12	7	2	33	17	4	6	11	19	33	45
9 Kettering	42	12	5	4	33	18	6	3	12	18	37	44
10 Dover	42	11	5	5	39	21	6	4	11	27	40	43
11 Nuneaton B	42	12	3	6	44	20	5	4	12	30	38	41
12 Barnet	42	11	6	4	49	26	4	4	13	23	40	40
13 Chelmsford	42	12	5	4	43	23	5	1	15	13	35	40
14 Hereford	42	12	4	5	46	25	3	5	13	20	37	39
15 Wellington	42	10	5	6	40	23	4	5	12	22	38	38
16 Poole	42	12	4	5	43	23	4	2	15	32	53	38
17 Burton Alb	42	11	3	7	35	28	5	2	14	20	43	37
18 Margate	42	12	3	6	50	32	2	4	15	29	58	35
19 Cheltenham	42	14	3	4	43	18	1	2	18	12	46	35
20 Bedford	42	10	4	7	32	25	1	8	12	14	38	34
21 Rugby	42	9	4	8	25	26	1	2	18	13	57	26
22 Guildford	42	4	6	11	22	30	3	5	13	19	43	25
	924	264	99	99	850	475	99	99	264	475	850	924

Odds & ends

Double wins: (4) Cheltenham, Margate, Guildford, Bedford.
Double losses: (0).

Won from behind: (2) Margate (h), Guildford (a).
Lost from in front: (2) Nuneaton (a), Kettering (a).

High spots: Wonderful mid-season run of 1 defeat in 21 games. The Dons won the last 7 of these. This run lifted Wimbledon from 10th to 1st.

Low spots: Poor start, 1 win in the first 5 games.
Terrible finish, 1 win in the last 8 games.
The humiliation of losing to Woking in the FA Cup.

Ever-presents: (1) Tom McCready.
Hat-tricks: (0).
Leading Scorer: Eddie Bailham (15).

	Appearances						Goals			
	Lge	Sub	SLC	Sub	FAC	Sub	Lge	SLC	FAC	Total
Bailham, Eddie	**36**	(1)	2		1		**15**			**15**
Colfar, Ray	**18**	(4)			1		**4**			**4**
Collins, Jimmy	**36**				1					
Cooke, Ian	**37**		2				**10**			**10**
Davies, Stuart	**35**		2		1		**4**			**4**
Guy, Dickie	**27**									
Hodges, Paul	**35**	(2)	2				**10**	1		**11**
Law, Roy	**37**		2		1		**1**			**1**
McCready, Tom	**43**		2		1					
McLeish, Hugh	**9**						**2**			**2**
Malley, Dennis	**4**	(2)	1							
Martin, Brian	**33**		1		1		**1**			**1**
Noble, Barry	**1**		1							
O'Mara, John	**15**	(2)	1		1		**6**	1		**7**
O'Rourke, Gerry	**41**		2		1		**10**	1		**11**
Smith, Frank	**15**		2		1					
Willis, Dave	**40**		2		1					
(own-goals)							**3**			**3**
17 players used	**462**	**(11)**	**22**		**11**		**66**	**3**		**69**

SOUTHERN LEAGUE PREMIER DIVISION   Manager: Les Henley   SEASON 1969-70

No Date		Att	Pos	Pts	F-A	H-T	Scorers, Times, and Referees	1	2	3	4	5	6	7	8	9	10	11	12 sub used
1	A KETTERING			D	2-2	2-1	Cooke 16, Bailham 18	Guy	Martin J	Willis	Davies	Law	**Shreeve**	Hodges	Bailham	O'Mara	McCready	Cooke	
	9/8	*895*		1			*Gully 17, Lawman 51*	*Fallon*	*Daldy J*	*Ashby*	*Gammon*	*Reed*	*Webster*	*Daldy R*	*Gully*	*Goodall Maur*	*Goodall Mick*	*Lawman*	
							Ref: F Burling	Wimbledon's reserve team has been cut to save money, and the club faces financial ruin. Only 15 professionals are left on the payroll. These include Peter Shreeve, signed from Chelmsford. Henley abandons 4-2-4 in favour of 4-3-3. Lawman's shot squeezes through Guy's fingers.											
2	H DOVER			W	2-1	1-1	Cooke 3, Bailham 75p	Guy	Martin	Willis	Davies	Law	Shreeve	Hodges	Bailham	O'Mara	McCready	Cooke	
	12/8	1,710		3			*Clewlow 36*	*Price*	*Cartwright*	*Hall*	*Morgan*	*Arnott*	*Hurley*	*McNally*	*Clewlow*	*Chandler*	*Foster*	*Fursden*	
							Ref: R Evans	Ian Cooke heads in Paul Hodges' corner. Clewlow's volley squares things. Then John O'Mara's shot appears to strike Hall on the chest. The Dons make no appeal, but the referee points to the penalty spot. Eddie Bailham is more concerned with accuracy than with justice.											
3	H NUNEATON B		3	W	2-1	1-1	Bailham 13, O'Mara 86	Guy	Martin	Willis	Collins	Law	Shreeve	Hodges*	Bailham	O'Rourke	McCready	Cooke	O'Mara
	16/8	1,802	*19*	5			*Keeley 43*	*Crump*	*Jones*	*Thompson*	*Allen*	*Aston*	*Graham*	*Keeley*	*Jackson*	*Metcalfe*	*Jacques*	*Aggio*	
							Ref: D Stone	Gangling John O'Mara comes on with 15 minutes to play. He keeps falling over and earns the derision of the crowd. The ref is also knocked off his feet. Then O'Rourke hits the bar and O'Mara smashes the ball in. Earlier, Bailham's shot had trickled through goalkeeper Crump's legs.											
4	A POOLE		3	L	1-3	0-2	Hodges 60	Guy	Martin	Willis	Collins	Law	Davies	Hodges	Bailham	O'Rourke	McCready	Cooke	
	23/8	*755*	*17*	5			*Down 5, Hodgson 15, Murphy 75*	*Rafferty*	*Brewster*	*Balsom*	*Shergold*	*Brown I*	*Eyden*	*Down*	*Pring*	*Hodgson*	*Brown M*	*Murphy*	
							Ref: I Kennard	Dickie Guy gives away a soft goal after five minutes and Wimbledon never recover. Second-half Dons pressure was rewarded when Hodges scores from Bailham's centre, but Poole break away again and Murphy scores during a goalmouth melee.											
5	H YEOVIL		8	W	2-1	1-0	Cooke 18, Hodges 75	Guy	Martin	Willis	Collins	Law	Shreeve	Hodges	Bailham	O'Rourke	McCready	Cooke	
	30/8	1,802	*17*	7			*Housley 86*	*Jones*	*Herrity*	*Lowrie*	*Mitten*	*Harris*	*Smith*	*Housley*	*Lumb*	*Myers*	*Weller*	*Williams*	
							Ref: W Bundy	The Dons were coasting, took their foot off the pedal and almost paid the penalty. Cooke had scored from Hodges' corner, and a fluffed back-pass had enabled Hodges to double the lead. But Housley's fine header pressed panic buttons in the Dons defence for the closing minutes.											
6	A DOVER		8	D	1-1	0-0	Cooke 60	Guy	Martin	Willis	Collins	Law	Shreeve	O'Mara!	Cooke	Bailham	McCready	O'Rourke	
	1/9	*2,618*	*3*	8			*Chandler 50*	*Price*	*Cartwright*	*Arnott*	*Hurley*	*Hall*	*Morgan*	*Clewlow*	*Foster*	*McNally*	*Chandler*	*Fursdon*	
							Ref: P Hunter	Dover have a 100% home record and pull in their biggest crowd for three years. Robin Chandler ran 50 yards to put the home team in front, at whch point O'Mara – already booked – flattened Cartwright and was sent off. The Dons are up against it, but they pull pack and then hang on.											
7	A NUNEATON B		5	D	0-0	0-0		Guy	Martin	Willis	Collins	Law	Shreeve	Bailham	O'Mara	O'Rourke	McCready	Cooke	
	6/9	*2,709*	*21*	9				*Richards*	*Jones*	*Aston*	*Goodall*	*Thompson*	*Allen*	*Boot*	*Jackson*	*Keeley*	*Aggio*	*Gedney*	
							Ref: J Rees	O'Mara and O'Rourke had the best chances for the Dons – the former hitting a post and the latter's header hooked off the line. The Dons were winning on points as the game entered injury time, whereupon Dickie Guy excelled by pulling off the save of the match.											
8	H WEYMOUTH		7	D	0-0	0-0		Guy	Martin	Willis	Collins	Law	Shreeve	Bailham	O'Mara	O'Rourke	McCready	Cooke	
	9/9	2,110	*10*	10				*Clarke*	*Glover*	*Rounsevell*	*Barry*	*Hobson*	*Hall*	*Adams*	*Muir*	*Allen*	*Kearns*	*Bennet*	*P*
							Ref: J Craigie	Wimbledon lose their 100% home record, though the game was more entertaining than the goalless scoreline might suggest. Weymouth pulled all 11 players behind the ball in the second half, but might have lost when O'Rourke's shot on the run crashes off the bar into the keeper's arms.											
9	H HEREFORD		2	W	3-1	2-0	Hodges 23, 24, O'Rourke 80	Guy	Martin	Willis	Collins	Law	Shreeve	Hodges	O'Mara	O'Rourke	McCready	Cooke	
	13/9	2,198	*8*	12			*Mullen 67*	*Whitbread*	*Rosser*	*Bird*	*Summerhayes*	*Brown*	*Jones*	*Scarrott*	*Lloyd*	*Charles**	*Tyler*	*Punter*	*Mullen*
							Ref: G Keeble	This brutal encounter warranted 10 minutes stoppage time. The match produced two bookings, one penalty and 50 fouls. Hodges scored twice in a minute against long-haired keeper Whitbread. At 2-1 Hodges' spot-kick was saved. Whitbread claims to have saved 14 out of 18 penalties.											
10	A CHELMSFORD		2	D	1-1	1-0	Hodges 14	Guy	Martin	Willis	Collins	Law	Shreeve	Hodges*	Bailham	O'Rourke	McCready	Cooke	O'Mara
	20/9	*2,254*	*9*	13			*Aitken 53*	*Wilkie*	*West*	*Honeywood*	*Andrews*	*Harrity*	*Smith*	*Aitken*	*Moffatt*	*Fogg*	*Price*	*Thornley*	*P*
								A good point overall, but Wimbledon will look to the moment when a second point slipped away. Just two minutes remained when Jimmy Collins let fly, only to see his shot strike a defender and smash against a goal-post. The Dons still haven't won away from home all season.											

No	H/A	Opponent	Pos	Res	F/T	H/T	Scorers, Attendances, Referees	1	2	3	4	5	6	7	8	9	10	11	12	
11	H	CHELMSFORD	3	L	0-1	0-1		Guy	Martin	Willis	Cooke	Law	Davies	Bailham	McLeish	O'Rourke	McCready	Hodges		
27/9		2,401	*4*	13			*Amato 35*	*Wilkie*	*Costello*	*Honeywood*	*Andrews*	*Harrity*	*Smith*	*Aitken*	*Moffatt*	*Fogg*	*Price*	*Amato*		P
							Ref: D Drewitt	Wimbledon's first home defeat of the campaign denied them the chance to overhaul Hillingdon at the top of the league. Plough Lane's biggest crowd turned out in anticipation, but all they saw was Chelmsford City control the match from start to finish.												
12	A	YEOVIL	5	L	1-3	1-3	Bailham 27p	Guy	Martin	Willis	Collins*	Law	Shreeve	Hodges	Bailham	O'Rourke	McCready	Cooke	Colfar	
4/10		*2,117*	*16*	13			*Plumb 11, Housley 24, Myers 45*	*Jones*	*Herrity*	*Smith*	*Harris*	*Dixon*	*Hughes*	*Housley*	*Plumb*	*Myers*	*Thompson*	*Davies*		
							Ref: I kennard	The only wonder is that nobody was sent off. Guy was so enraged by Yeovil's third goal, when Myers bundled both keeper and ball into the net that he had to be restrained by team-mates. Bailham had scored off the post with a penalty, but was later booked for lashing out at Dixon.												
13	H	KETTERING	7	W	3-1	1-0	Bailham 30, 89, O'Rourke 78	Guy	Martin	Willis	Cooke	McCready	Shreeve	Colfar	Bailham	O'Rourke	Collins	Hodges		
11/10		2,078	*18*	15			*Guy 74 (og)*	*Harvey*	*Daldy J*	*Ashby*	*Gammon*	*Reed*	*Peck*	*Walden*	*Daldy B*	*Webster*	*Evans*	*Lawman*		P
							Ref: F Lane	A shirt-sleeved crowd were starting to jeer but stayed to cheer. The Dons went ahead when keeper Harvey came for a high ball and missed it altogether. Then it was Guy's turn, fumbling a corner into his own net. Gerry O'Rourke replied with his first league goal of the season.												
14	A	BRENTWOOD	5	W	2-0	1-0	O'Rourke 5, Cooke 80	Guy	Martin	Willis	Cooke	McCready	Shreeve	Colfar	Bailham	O'Rourke	Collins	Hodges		
18/10		*1,275*	*2*	17				*Dunbar*	*Maynard*	*Jones*	*Pyatt*	*Snowdon*	*Loughton*	*Dilsworth*	*Moy*	*Diggins*	*O'Connell*	*Halliday*		
							Ref: R Wood	Newly promoted Brentwood are joint leaders and Barry Diggins is the league's leading scorer. O'Rourke's early scoring header was the signal for Wimbledon to fall back and defend in depth. Five teams are now on 17 points, with the Dons placed 5th on goal-average.												
15	H	BATH	4	L	1-2	0-2	Cooke 62	Guy	Martin	Willis	Cooke	Law	Collins	Colfar*	Bailham	O'Rourke	McCready	Hodges	O'Mara	
25/10		2,089	*11*	17			*Gough 28, Owen 43*	*McAuley*	*Burt*	*Taylor*	*Carter*	*Lambden*	*Gough*	*Parker*	*Allen*	*Owen*	*Taylor*	*Clark*		
							Ref: J Griffin	This shock home defeat is all the more shocking as it is Bath's first away victory. The visitors used the long ball sensibly in the rain-sodden conditions. The Dons' moment of hope came when Roy Law chipped in a free-kick and Ian Cooke darted through to halve the deficit.												
16	H	POOLE	4	W	1-0	0-0	O'Rourke 63	Guy	Martin	Willis	Collins	Law	Shreeve	Hodges	Bailham	O'Rourke*	McCready	Cooke	O'Mara	
8/11		1,923	*12*	19				*Rafferty*	*Brewster*	*Balsom*	*Eyden*	*Brown I*	*Ferns*	*Down*	*Taylor*	*Peterson*	*Hodgson*	*Murphy*		
							Ref: R Wood	One defensive error settled this dour, unappetising match. Poole had been on top in the first half, though Rafferty had to touch Law's diving header onto the crossbar. But after the hour Balsom was caught in possession by Bailham, who set up O'Rourke for the winner.												
17	A	WORCESTER	4	D	1-1	0-0	McLeish 71	Guy	Martin	Willis	Collins	Law	Davies	Colfar	McLeish	O'Rourke	McCready	Cooke		
22/11		*2,028*	*17*	20			*Clements 75*	*Knight*	*Griffiths*	*Bassett*	*Carson*	*Madley*	*McEwan*	*Clements*	*Hudd*	*Hitchens*	*Gould*	*Robinson*		
							Ref: J Rees	Worcester have just signed Gerry Hitchens, the former England international who had returned from many years playing in Italy. A goalless draw was averted by McLeish's header which bounces down, up, and in off the bar. Hudd blew his chance to level, but then set up Clements.												
18	A	KING'S LYNN	4	L	1-2	1-0	O'Rourke 27	Guy	Martin	Willis	Collins	Law	Davies	Colfar	McLeish	O'Rourke	McCready	Cooke		
26/11		*895*	*19*	20			*Lindsay 50, Coughlin 55*	*Coe*	*Kerr*	*Sharp*	*Brooks*	*Porter*	*Wright*	*Savino*	*Coughlin*	*Lindsay*	*Jenkins*	*Clarke*		P
								Two points would have taken Wimbledon top, though Hillingdon have six games in hand. Hodges, Shreeve, and Bailham are all out injured. Gerry O'Rourke went through on his own to put the Dons ahead, but they returned yet again to losing after they had their noses in front.												
19	A	BURTON ALB	4	W	3-2	1-0	Hodges 40, Cooke 60, O'Mara 73	**Roope**	McCready	Willis	Collins	Law	Davies	Hodges	Cooke	O'Mara	Shreeve	O'Rourke		
6/12		*553*	*22*	22			*Cleevely 80p, Thomas 83*	*Potter*	*Norman*	*Watton*	*Cleevely*	*King*	*Bailey*	*Thomas*	*Marshall*	*Brown*	*Bostock*	*Scattergood*		P
							Ref: G Keil	Graham Roope heard he was playing only in the morning, Guy having gone down with flu. Roope plays cricket for Surrey and is looking forward to touring with the MCC. He is not to blame for Burton's goals. O'Mara has rejected a move to Poole and is involved in all three goals.												
20	H	CRAWLEY	3	W	**9-0**	4-0	O'Mara 4, 40, 85, Cooke 13, 42, 89, [Davies 50, Hodges 55, O'Rourke 87]	Roope	McCready	Willis	Davies	Law	Shreeve	Hodges	Cooke	O'Mara	Collins	O'Rourke		
13/12		1,622	*20*	24				*Patrick*	*McMullen*	*Wheeler*	*Jennings**	*Leedham*	*Haining*	*Tomkys*	*Livesey*	*Goodgame*	*Bragg*	*Basey*	*Houghton*	
							Ref: Walton	After scoring six against Hastings in the Southern League Cup, the Dons register their biggest ever Premier League win. Yet it had taken them three attempts to get past these same opponents in the FA Cup. Crawley had five players axed after conceding 11 in their two previous games.												
21	A	WEYMOUTH	5	D	1-1	0-0	Hodges 54p	Roope	**Kelsall**	McCready	Davies	Law	Shreeve	Hodges	Cooke	O'Mara	Collins	O'Rourke		
20/12		*1,176*	*1*	25			*Kearns 67*	*Clarke*	*Rounsevell*	*Stocker*	*Barry*	*Hobson*	*Hall*	*Bennett*	*Jackson*	*Ryder*	*Kearns*	*Allen*		
								The pitch was so muddy that no lines were visible. Henley gives a debut to amateur Alan Kelsall at full-back, through the debutant is later booked. The Dons' penalty came when Rounsevell handled Davies' header. Neither Roope nor Kelsall were at fault for Kearns' header.												

SOUTHERN LEAGUE PREMIER DIVISION Manager: Les Henley SEASON 1969-70

No	Date		Att	Pos	Pts	F-A	H-T	Scorers, Times, and Referees	1	2	3	4	5	6	7	8	9	10	11	12 sub used
22	H	BARNET		2	W	2-1	1-1	Cooke 8, Hodges 57p	Roope	McCready	Willis	Davies	Law	Shreeve	Hodges*	Cooke	O'Mara	Collins	Colfar	McLeish
	26/12		1,677	*11*	27			*Eason 13*	*McClelland*	*Lye*	*Jenkins*	*Lawler*	*Embery*	*King*	*Powell*	*George*	*Meadows*	*Eason*	*Thorne*	
								Ref: L Burden	Barnet keeper Jack McClelland once played for Arsenal and Northern Ireland, while striker Eason is currently, along with Ian Cooke, the league's top scorer. The decisive penalty came when Cooke was knocked over. In the last minute Law deflected a goal-bound shot over his bar.											
23	A	BARNET		2	D	1-1	1-1	O'Mara 7	Roope	McCready	Willis	Davies	Law	Shreeve	McLeish*	Cooke	O'Mara	Collins	Colfar	Bailham
	27/12		*1,801*	*15*	28			*George 31*	*McClelland*	*Lye*	*Jenkins*	*Lawler*	*Embery*	*King*	*Powell*	*George*	*Meadows*	*Eason*	*Thorne*	
								Ref: F Burling	Wimbledon maintain their record of never having lost to Barnet in the Southern League. O'Mara headed in easily at the far post to put the Dons in front. Though Barnet levelled, Cooke could have won it for Wimbledon in the last minute, but he missed from two yards.											
24	H	CAMBRIDGE U		2	W	2-1	0-1	Cooke 48, Shreeve 73	Roope	McCready	Willis	Davies	Law	Shreeve	Colfar	Cooke	O'Mara	Collins	O'Rourke	
	3/1		1,810	*5*	30			*Roope 40 (og)*	*Slack*	*Thompson*	*Grant*	*Hardy*	*Eades*	*Meldrum*	*Gregson*	*Walker**	*Cassidy*	*Harris*	*McKinven*	*Slack*
								Ref: D Burlingham	United are the defending champions. They take the lead with a laughable own-goal, as Roope gathers the ball, then chests it into his own net. George Harris has scored 14 goals in his last nine games, but is kept quiet, as Cambridge tumble to their first away defeat since August.											
25	A	CAMBRIDGE U		2	L	1-2	1-2	Hodges 25	Guy	Martin	Willis	Davies	McCready	Shreeve	Hodges	Cooke	O'Rourke	Collins	Colfar	
	17/1		***3,088***	*5*	30			*Hardy 15, Gilchrist 39*	*Barker*	*Thompson*	*Grant*	*Hardy*	*Eades*	*Meldrum*	*Horrey*	*Walker*	*Gilchrist*	*Harris*	*McKinven*	
								Ref: G MacKnight	The Dons tumble from the Football Challenge Trophy before their return match with Cambridge. United employ the offside trap even in home matches. Henley drops Roope and O'Mara, and must do without the injured Law. In the second half United came closest, Hardy hitting a post.											
26	H	KING'S LYNN		1	W	2-1	2-0	Cooke 8, Bailham 19	Guy	Collins	Willis	Davies	Law	Shreeve	Hodges	Cooke	Bailham	McCready	O'Rourke	
	24/1		1,735	*15*	32			*Lindsay 73*	*Coe*	*Radcliffe*	*Sharp*	*Brooks*	*Porter*	*Mullet**	*Lindsay*	*Coughlin*	*Jenkins*	*Wright*	*Clarke*	*Savino*
								Ref: B Chapman	This win takes the Dons to the top for the first time. Bailham returns to the side after a bad injury sustained against Arsenal in the London Challenge Cup. King's Lynn's substitute Savino causes all the damage, and Wimbledon are hanging on grimly by the end.											
27	A	CRAWLEY		1	D	1-1	0-0	Bailham 70	Guy	McCready	Willis	Davies	Law	Shreeve	Hodges	O'Mara	Bailham	Collins	Colfar	
	31/1		*973*	*21*	33			*Haining 46*	*Maggs*	*Cockell*	*Tharme*	*Leck*	*Leedham*	*Bragg*	*Standing*	*Griffiths*	*Haining*	*Livesey*	*Blaber*	
								Ref: A Hart	The last time these teams met Wimbledon hit nine. But Cooke is out with cracked ribs and O'Rourke is attending the birth of his child. In their absence Bailham misses a sackful. The one he did get needed two attempts: his first hit the goalkeeper; his second went in off the goal-post.											
28	H	TELFORD		1	W	2-0	1-0	Collins 37, Hodges 89	Guy	Martin	Willis	Collins	Law	Shreeve	Hodges	Bailham	O'Rourke	McCready	Colfar	
	3/2		1,598	*14*	35				*Irvine*	*Whitehouse*	*Croft*	*Ball*	*Flowers*	*Ray*	*Fudge*	*Harris*	*Bentley*	*Murray*	*Jagger*	
								Ref: C Watts	Before this season Telford used to be known as Wellington. They have recruited former-England stalwart Ron Flowers as player-manager. The Dons' first goal is a free-kick by Jimmy Collins that curls round the wall; the clincher – at the death – followed a boob by goalkeeper Irvine.											
29	H	GLOUCESTER		1	D	1-1	0-0	Hodges 65	Guy	Martin	Willis	Collins	Law	Shreeve	Hodges	Bailham	O'Rourke	McCready	Colfar	
	7/2		1,798	*19*	36			*Law 87 (og)*	*Jones*	*Vale*	*Page-Jones*	*Anderson*	*McQuarrie*	*McCool*	*Rice*	*Rodgerson*	*Stevens*	*Fraser*	*Hurford*	
								Ref: K Chapman	A game of two howlers. Wimbledon took advantage when McQuarrie tried to pass back to his goalkeeper, but directed the ball into the path of Hodges. Then, with time running out, Roy Law's lunging interception carries Rodgerson's volley wide of the stranded Guy.											
30	H	HILLINGDON B		2	D	2-2	0-0	O'Rourke 82, O'Mara 90	Guy	Collins	Willis	Davies	Law	Shreeve	Bailham	Cooke	O'Mara	McCready	O'Rourke	
	28/2		**2,163**	*3*	37			*Bishop 51, Carter 71*	*Lowe*	*Batt*	*Langley*	*Moore*	*Newcombe*	*Watson*	*Fairchild*	*Carter*	*Terry*	*Bishop*	*Vafiadis*	
								Ref: G Keeble	This top-of-the-table thriller appears to be heading Hillingdon's way – they also put the Dons out of the FA Cup. Guy handed them their first goal on a plate, with a misplaced throw-out. The game has seen seven minutes injury time when Law heads down Cooke's corner to O'Mara.											
31	A	BATH			W	1-0	1-0	Collins 45p	Guy	Ardrey	Willis	Davies	McCready	Shreeve	Cooke	**Harney**	O'Mara	Collins	O'Rourke	
	14/3		*1,576*		39				*McAuley*	*Burt*	*Taylor*	*Carter*	*Lambden*	*Gough*	*Parker*	*Allen*	*Owen*	*Taylor*	*Clark*	*P*
									Paul Harney's debut match ends Bath's four-game winning sequence at home. Bobby Ardrey also plays his first league match in two years. The decisive goal is hotly contested. Seconds before the interval the ball rears up wickedly and strikes the unsuspecting Lambden on the arm.											

No	Date	Venue	Opponent	Att	Pos	Pts	Res	F-A	H-T	Scorers, Times, and Referees	1	2	3	4	5	6	7	8	9	10	11	12
	17/3			1,666	*15*	41					*Smith*	*Morris*	*King*	*Sorrell*	*White*	*Andrew*	*Sanders*	*Cutler*	*Barnett*	*Obeney*	*Tapping*	
										Ref: A Hart	This dress-rehearsal for the Southern League Cup Final goes firmly Wimbledon's way. Shortly after the first goal Colfar replaced promising newcomer Harney. Davies' goal went in off Bill White. With this win the Dons are still in the hunt for a league and cup double.											
33		A	HILLINGDON B		2		L	0-1	0-0		Guy	Ardrey	Willis	Davies	McCready	Shreeve	Hodges	Cooke	O'Mara	Collins	O'Rourke	
	21/3			*1,368*	*4*	41				*Bishop 57*	*Lowe*	*Batt*	*Langley*	*Watson*	*Newcombe*	*More*	*Reeve*	*Terry*	*Bishop*	*Fairchild*	*Knox*	
										Ref: D Drewitt	This is a critical defeat for Wimbledon. Despite the importance of the match for both sides, neither rises above the ordinary. The goal is reward for John Bishop, who ran 20 yards before shooting past Guy. Wimbledon never seemed to raise themselves for a final furious onslaught.											
34		A	ROMFORD		2		L	0-2	0-0		Guy	Ardrey	Willis	Davies	McCready	Shreeve	Hodges	Cooke	O'Mara	Collins	O'Rourke	
	28/3			*1,576*	*17*	41				*Williams 52, Barnett 80*	*Smith*	*Read*	*Tapping*	*Obeney*	*King*	*Andrew*	*Sanders*	*Fowler*	*Williams*	*Flatt*	*Barnett*	
										Ref: J Clarke	Apart from the injured Law, Henley has a full-strength squad from which to choose, whereas Romford are compelled to plug their side with reserves. It is these who overrun the midfield to set up Williams for the first goal. The second is a 25-yard lob from Barnett.											
35		H	MARGATE		2		W	2-1	1-0	Collins 35, Cooke 78	Guy	Ardrey	Willis	Davies	Law	Shreeve	Hodges	Cooke	O'Mara	Collins	O'Rourke	
	30/3			1,562	*11*	43				*Smith 83*	*Steel*	*Yorath*	*Dennis*	*Rutley*	*Swain*	*Houston*	*Clifton*	*Robinson*	*Ray*	*Smith*	*Harland*	
										Ref: W Dance	This match was disrupted by wind, by rain, and by smoke from a fire started by vandals. Roy Law returns to the side, which gets back to winning ways thanks to a second goal scored by Ian Cooke. O'Mara engineered the chance. Smith's riposte set up an exciting finale.											
36		A	MARGATE		2		L	**1-5**	0-1	Cooke 56 *[Harland 85]*	Guy	Martin	Willis	Davies	Collins	Shreeve	Cooke	Harney	O'Mara	Bailham	O'Rourke	
	31/3			*971*	*11*	43				*Ray 10, 75, Yorath 70p, Smith 80,*	*Steel*	*Yorath*	*Dennis*	*Rutley*	*Swain*	*Houston*	*Clifton*	*Robinson*	*Ray*	*Smith*	*Harland*	
										Ref: M Taylor	Once again Easter proves to be a graveyard for the Dons' championship aspirations. The score is deceptive, for it stood at 1-1 with just 20 minutes to play. Margate's second goal arose from a dubious penalty, when Cooke 'fouled' Smith. Ray then 'threw' their third into the net.											
37		A	HEREFORD		3		W	2-1	0-0	Hodges 55, O'Mara 65	Guy	Martin	Willis*	Davies	McCready	Shreeve	Hodges	Cooke	O'Mara	Collins	O'Rourke	Harney
	4/4			*1,693*	*8*	45				*Tyler 87*	*Davies*	*Bird*	*Timms*	*Jones*	*Brown*	*Mullen*	*Summerhayes*	*Tyler*	*Charles*	*Round*	*Punter*	*P*
										Ref: G Keil	Strange to say, this is Wimbledon's first league double of the season. Hereford were unbeaten at home since November, but wasted chances at 0-0. Jones missed an open goal and Bird hit Guy's crossbar. Jones misjudged the back-pass from which Paul Hodges put the Dons ahead.											
38		H	BURTON ALB		3		W	2-0	1-0	Cooke 20, 65	Guy	Martin	Shreeve	Davies*	McCready	Cooke	Hodges	Harney	O'Mara	Collins	O'Rourke	Colfar
	7/4			**1,277**	*22*	47					*Potter*	*Norman*	*Watton*	*Cleevely*	*Hickton*	*Makay**	*Marshall*	*Bostock*	*Waller*	*Sweenie*	*Scattergood*	*Woodburn*
										Ref: B Chapman	The Dons frittered away chances galore against the basement team. They hit a post twice and had two goals disallowed, against a side still seeking its first win in 1970. Ian Cooke's goals keep him ahead of the pack in the division's goal-scoring stakes.											
39		A	TELFORD				L	0-4	0-1	*[Jagger 85]*	Guy	Martin	Willis	Davies	McCready	Cooke	Hodges	Colfar	O'Mara	Collins	O'Rourke	
	15/4			*1,821*		47				*Bentley 4, Owen 48, Fudge 55,*	*Richards*	*Whitehouse*	*Croft*	*Flowers**	*Ray*	*Fudge*	*Harris*	*Bentley*	*Murray*	*Jagger*	*Hart*	*Owen* *P*
											Wimbledon were comprehensively outplayed at Bucks Head. The opening goal was set up by Brian Hart, who broke away and delivered the cross from which the towering Bentley climbed higher than the Dons' defence. Sub Owen replaced Flowers, and made one and scored one.											
40		H	BRENTWOOD		3		W	2-1	1-1	Cooke 28, 54	Guy	Martin	Willis*	Davies	McCready	Shreeve	Hodges	Cooke	O'Mara	Collins	Colfar	Harney
	18/4			1,606	*13*	49				*Halliday 16*	*Dunbar*	*Jones*	*Butterfield*	*Maynard!*	*Loughton*	*O'Connell*	*Dilsworth*	*Stevenson*	*Diggins*	*Moy*	*Halliday*	
										Ref: P Saubergue	A sprightly match, played in constant drizzle, which saw the division's newcomers fall to the Dons for the second time. With half-time approaching, and the score at 1-1, Brentwood's Chick Maynard abused a linesman and was sent off. Brentwood faded once they fell behind.											
41		A	GLOUCESTER				L	0-3	0-1		Guy	Martin	Willis	Davies	McCready	Shreeve	Hodges	Cooke	O'Mara	Collins	O'Rourke	
	23/4			***514***		49				*Ferns 8, McQuarrie 47, Stevens 52*	*Jones*	*Vale*	*Page-Jones*	*Anderson*	*Biggart*	*Ferns*	*Hurford*	*Steven*	*McQuarrie*	*McCool*	*Fraser*	
											Gloucester have lost five of their previous six at home, yet Wimbledon succumb without a fight. Dave Willis makes the first costly mistake, mistiming a back-pass which was seized upon by Willie Ferns. The game was just eight minutes old, and the Dons never recovered.											
42		H	WORCESTER				D	0-0	0-0		Guy	Martin	Willis	Davies	McCready	Shreeve	Hodges	Harney	O'Mara*	Collins	O'Rourke	Bailham
	25/4			1,681		50					*Knight*	*Griffiths*	*Bassett*	*Carson*	*Madley*	*McEwan*	*Clements*	*Hudd*	*Hitchens*	*Gould*	*Robinson*	*P*
		Home		*Away*						Ref: C Watts	Nothing is at stake in this tedious game. Young David Harney looked Wimbledon's best player, while Tommy McCready easily blotted out Gerry Hitchens. Champions Cambridge United will now be elected to the Football League.											
Average		1,824		*1,581*																		

Southern League Cup	F-A	H-T	Scorers, Times, and Referees	1	2	3	4	5	6	7	8	9	10	11	12 sub used
1:1 A DUNSTABLE	W 3-1		O'Rourke + 2 own goals	Guy	Martin	Willis	Collins	Law	Davies	Hodges	Bailham	O'Rourke	McCready	Cooke	
21/8 272			*Finch*	*Williams*	*Davis*	*Noble*	*Collins*	*McGlasson*	*McNally*	*Mapp*	*Finch*	*Dixon*	*McGonagle*	*Benning*	
			Ref: W Woods	Dunstable's team is almost entirely amateur. That may explain their extraordinary generosity, for they gift Wimbledon not just one goal, but two. The Dons' recent results in knock-out competition make them grateful for all the assistance they can get. They should get through now.											
1:2 H DUNSTABLE	W 2-0	0-0	O'Rourke 82, Bailham 87	Guy	Martin	Willis	Collins	O'Mara	Shreeve	Hodges	Bailham	O'Rourke	McLeish	Cooke	
26/8 1,262				*Swinburn*	*Davis*	*Noble*	*Collins*	*McGlasson*	*McNally*	*Mapp*	*Huntley*	*Finch*	*Walker*	*Benning*	
			Ref: K Ridden (Dons win 5-1 on aggregate)	This win marks Wimbledon's first cup success, of any kind, for two years. With central defenders Law and McCready both out injured, John O'Mara sports the No 5 shirt, and Hugh McLeish plays his first game of the season. The Dons hit the goal-frame twice before scoring.											
2 H DOVER 7	W 2-0	0-0	Bailham 57, 80p	Guy	Martin	Willis	Cooke	McCready	Shreeve	Colfar	Bailham	O'Mara*	Collins	O'Rourke	McLeish
7/10 2,117 *5*				*Price*	*Cartwright*	*Thursdon*	*Horton*	*Arnott*	*Hurley*	*Chandler*	*Clewlow*	*Hall*	*Foster*	*Marley*	*McNally*
			Ref: W Dance	A poor match, which, without the occasional spark of magic by Eddie Bailham, would surely have ended goalless. He breaks the deadlock by rounding two Dover players, drawing the goalkeeper, and firing home. He later added a second from the penalty spot after a handling offence.											
3 H HASTINGS	W 6-2	3-0	O'Rourke 21, 24, Hodges 22p, O'Mara 49,	Roope	McCready	Willis	Collins	Law	Davies	Hodges	Cooke	O'Mara	Shreeve	O'Rourke	
9/12 1,066			*Coates 54, Jeans 73* [Cooke 60, 80]	*Cowen*	*Warner*	*Nash*	*More*	*Drake*	*Anderson*	*Price*	*Jeans*	*Barry*	*Coates*	*Turner*	
			Ref: J Craigie	Wimbledon's smallest crowd of the season witnesses this handsome win. Three goals in four thrilling minutes settle the argument, with O'Rourke and O'Mara setting up chances for each other throughout the match. Hodges added a penalty, following a handling offence.											
QF H CAMBRIDGE U	W 1-0	1-0	Hodges 30	Guy	Martin	Willis	Davies	McCready	Shreeve	Hodges	Bailham	O'Mara	Collins	O'Rourke	
9/2 1,452				*Barker*	*Thompson*	*Grant*	*Hardy*	*Meldrum*	*Slack*	*Horrey*	*Walker*	*Gilchrist*	*Harris*	*McKinven*	
			Ref: S Lover	United are defending the league and cup double, but lose their grip on one prize after this thriller, in which Dickie Guy was the undoubted hero. United had hit eight past Crawley 48 hours earlier. Following Hodges' screamer, Les Henley pulled O'Mara back to play as sweeper.											
SF H BEDFORD 2	W 1-0	0-0	O'Mara 79	Guy	Ardrey	Willis	Davies	McCready	Shreeve	Cooke	Bailham*	O'Mara	Collins	O'Rourke	Hodges
10/3 1,483 *14*				*Barron*	*Skinn*	*Coolley*	*Scurr*	*Roach*	*Wright*	*Davies*	*Cleary*	*Brown*	*Fry*	*Adams*	
			Ref: F Bassett	Wimbledon cannot complain about the luck of the draw. This is their fourth home tie on the trot. They are, however, without Law, and Bobby Ardrey plays his first game in two years. On a quagmire pitch, substitute Hodges delivers the corner from which O'Mara powers the winner.											
F:1 H ROMFORD 3	W 3-0	3-0	Obeney 3 (og), O'Mara 6, Davies 36	Guy	Martin	Ardrey	Davies	McCready	Shreeve	Colfar	Cooke	O'Mara	Collins	O'Rourke	
2/4 1,505 *11*				*Smith*	*Read*	*Tapping*	*Sorrell*	*King*	*Andrew*	*Sanders*	*Cutler*	*Flatt*	*Obeney*	*Barnett*	
				With their title hopes dashed yet again, the Southern League Cup offers Wimbledon their only chance of a trophy. A wretchedly small crowd sees bogey-team Romford swept away in the first leg. Ardrey's header goes in off Obeney, and O'Mara is off balance heading a quick second.											
F:2 A ROMFORD 3	D 1-1	1-1	O'Mara 39	Guy	Martin	Willis	Davies	McCready	Shreeve	Hodges	Cooke	O'Mara	Collins	O'Rourke	
10/4 *1,786* *11*			*Flatt 12*	*Smith*	*Read*	*Tapping*	*Sorrell*	*King*	*Andrew*	*Sanders*	*Cutler*	*Flatt*	*Obeney*	*Barnett*	
			Ref: J Griffiths (Dons win Cup 4-1 on aggregate)	Romford needed a quick goal, and Colin Flatt's header provided it. A mistake by King enables O'Mara to race away and slide the ball past Smith, and that effectively presents Wimbledon with their first prize since turning professional.											

FA Cup	F-A	H-T	Scorers, Times, and Referees	1	2	3	4	5	6	7	8	9	10	11	12 sub used
4Q H CRAWLEY 4	D 0-0	0-0		Guy	Martin	Willis	Collins	Law	Shreeve	Hodges	Bailham	O'Rourke	McCready	Cooke	
1/11 2,530 *18*				*Maggs*	*Cockell*	*Tharme*	*Leck*	*Leedham*	*Bragg*	*Basey*	*Haining*	*Goodgame*	*Livesey*	*Standing*	
			Ref: P Saubergue	Crawley's red shirts are massed in defence. Wimbledon's only obvious tactic is to pump high balls forward. It is actually Crawley who come closest to scoring, when after 70 minutes Basey glances a header against the post, but Guy gets down to recover.											
4Q A CRAWLEY 4	D 0-0	0-0		Guy	Martin	Willis	Collins	Law	Shreeve	Hodges	Bailham	O'Rourke	McCready	Cooke	
R 4/11 *3,256* *18*	*aet*			*Maggs*	*Cockell*	*Tharme*	*Leck*	*Leedham*	*Bragg*	*Haining*	*Basey*	*Goodgame*	*Livesey*	*Blaber*	
			Ref: P Saubergue	A nerve-racking replay. Crawley's fanatical support get behind their team from the start. When Guy dropped a shot from Basey, Goodgame somehow hooked the loose ball out of the net. In the second half Basey headed against the crossbar. Lucky Wimbledon live to fight again.											

4	N CRAWLEY		4 W	2-0	0-0	Bailham 66p, 85	Guy	Martin	Willis	Collins	Law	Shreeve	Hodges	Bailham	O'Rourke	McCready	Cooke
2R 10/11		1,983	18				*Maggs*	*Cockell*	*Tharme*	*Leck*	*Leedham*	*Bragg*	*Standing*	*Basey*	*Goodgame*	*Livesey*	*Haining*
	(at Guildford)					Ref: P Sauberge											

Played at neutral Guildford, this tie is finally settled after 278 minutes of goalless action. Charlie Livesey hit a post for Crawley, the third time they had done so in three ties. When Cockell whipped away Cooke's legs, the referee awarded Wimbledon a hotly disputed penalty.

1	A HILLINGDON B		4 L	0-2	0-0		Guy	Martin	Willis	Cooke	Law	Shreeve	Colfar	Bailham	O'Mara	McCready	O'Rourke
15/11		3,856	1			*Carter 63, Vafiadis 80*	*Lowe*	*Barr*	*Langley*	*Reeve*	*Newcombe*	*Moore*	*Fairchild*	*Cozens*	*Terry*	*Carter*	*Vafiadis*
						Ref: B Daniels											

Just five days after overcoming Crawley, Wimbledon fall to pace-setters Hillingdon, beaten just once this season. Pat Terry's aerial command is the decisive factor, though Wimbledon squander four good chances before falling behind. A monsoon swept the ground at 1-0.

FA Challenge Trophy

1	A DARTFORD		L	2-3	2-1	O'Mara 30. Cooke 42	Roope	McCready	Willis	Davies	Law	Shreeve	Hodges	Cooke	O'Mara	Collins	O'Rourke
10/1		1,377				*Grace 20, Burns 60, Nicholas 75*	*Morton*	*Stevens*	*Richardson*	*Pyke**	*Burns*	*Morgan*	*Osborn*	*Webb*	*Nicholas*	*Grace*	*Cheesewright Waters*
						Ref: B Merchant											

This new competition pits the Dons against Dartford, chasing promotion from Division 1. Wimbledon's first defeat in 10 games brooks no argument, as shots rained upon poor Roope from all angles. He takes the blame for two goals, compensating for two gifts at the other end.

		Home						Away					
	P	W	D	L	F	A	W	D	L	F	A	Pts
1 Cambridge U*	42	14	3	4	49	20	12	3	6	35	30	58
2 Yeovil	42	15	2	4	48	22	10	5	6	30	26	57
3 Chelmsford	42	13	4	4	42	19	7	7	7	34	39	51
4 Weymouth	42	8	11	2	34	12	10	3	8	25	25	50
5 WIMBLEDON	42	15	4	2	43	16	4	8	9	21	36	50
6 Hillingdon B	42	13	5	3	35	19	6	7	8	21	31	50
7 Barnet	42	12	8	1	41	14	4	7	10	30	40	47
8 Telford	42	11	6	4	39	25	7	4	10	22	37	46
9 Brentwood†	42	12	6	3	39	13	4	7	10	22	25	45
10 Hereford	42	14	4	3	46	18	4	5	12	28	47	45
11 Bath	42	14	4	3	40	17	4	4	13	23	38	44
12 King's Lynn	42	14	3	4	51	27	2	8	11	21	41	43
13 Margate	42	12	4	5	48	24	5	4	12	22	40	42
14 Dover	42	10	6	5	30	17	5	4	12	21	33	40
15 Kettering	42	11	3	7	41	31	7	0	14	23	44	39
16 Worcester	42	9	7	5	24	13	5	3	13	11	31	38
17 Romford	42	13	3	5	39	25	0	8	13	11	37	37
18 Poole	42	5	12	4	29	25	3	7	11	19	32	35
19 Gloucester	42	9	4	8	34	33	3	5	13	19	40	33
20 Nuneaton B	42	11	6	4	37	20	0	4	17	15	54	32
21 Crawley	42	6	7	8	30	37	0	8	13	23	64	27
22 Burton Alb	42	3	4	14	18	35	0	5	16	6	47	15
* *Football Lge*	924	244	116	102	837	482	102	116	244	482	837	924
† *withdrew*												

Odds & ends

Double wins: (3) Hereford, Brentwood, Burton.
Double losses: (0).

Won from behind: (2) Cambridge U (h), Brentwood (h).
Lost from in front: (1) King's Lynn (a).

High spots: Winning the Southern League Cup.
1 defeat in 14 games, December to mid-March. Dons top in January.
Beating Crawley 9-0.

Low spots: Losing 1-5 at Margate, the first time the Dons have conceded 5.
Winning away from home only 4 times.

Ever-presents: (0).
Hat-tricks: Ian Cooke (1), John O'Mara (1).
Leading scorer: Ian Cooke (24).

	Appearances					Goals				
	Lge	Sub	SLC	FAC	FAT	Lge	SLC	FAC	FAT	Total
Ardrey, Bobby	**5**		2							
Bailham, Eddie	**21**	(2)	5	4		**8**	3	2		**13**
Colfar, Ray	**14**	(3)	2	1						
Collins, Jimmy	**39**		8	3	1	**3**				**3**
Cooke, Ian	**38**		7	4	1	**21**	2		1	**24**
Davies, Stuart	**28**		6		1	**2**	1			**3**
Guy, Dickie	**36**		7	4						
Harney, David	**5**	(2)								
Hodges, Paul	**31**		5/1	3	1	**13**	2			**15**
Kelsall, Alan	**1**									
Law, Roy	**28**		2	4	1					
McCready, Tom	**40**		7	4	1					
McLeish, Hugh	**4**	(1)	1/1			**1**				**1**
Martin, John	**28**		6	4						
O'Mara, John	**26**	(4)	7	1	1	**8**	4		1	**13**
O'Rourke, Gerry	**36**		8	4	1	**7**	4			**11**
Roope, Graham	**6**		1		1					
Shreeve, Peter	**36**		7	4	1	**1**				**1**
Willis, Dave	**40**		7	4	1					
(own-goals)							3			**3**
19 players used	**462**	**(12)**	**88/2**	**44**	**11**	**64**	**19**	**2**	**2**	**87**

/ denotes substitutes

SOUTHERN LEAGUE PREMIER DIVISION   Manager: Les Henley / Mike Everitt   SEASON 1970-71

No	Date	Att	Pos	Pts	F-A	H-T	Scorers, Times, and Referees	1	2	3	4	5	6	7	8	9	10	11	12 sub used
1	A NUNEATON B			W	2-0	0-0	Burton 53, Cooke 57	Guy	Law	Martin	**Sanderson**	McCready	Shreeve	**Burton**	Cooke	O'Rourke	Collins	Hodges	
	15/8	*3,152*		2				*Crump*	*Jones*	*Aston*	*Wilkinson*	*Burkitt*	*Boot*	*Allen*	*Cutler*	*Punter*	*Jacques*	*Smith*	
							Ref: G Keil	Hugh McLeish and Ray Colfar have been released, and newcomers Keith Sanderson and Alan Burton step straight into the side. Sanderson won a League Cup medal with QPR in 1967. Nuneaton stayed up last season because Cambridge U went into Division 4. Law plays full-back.											
2	H ROMFORD			W	2-1	1-0	Cooke 38, Hodges 48	Guy	Martin	Law	Sanderson	McCready	Shreeve	Burton	Cooke	O'Rourke	Collins	Hodges	
	18/8	1,600		4			*Flatt 82*	*Smith*	*Howe*	*Nicholas*	*Andrew*	*King*	*Sorrell*	*Tapping*	*Freeman*	*Chandler*	*Flatt*	*Nixon*	
							Ref: W Dance	Romford always seem to be losing to the Dons these days, and keeper Andy Smith saves them from a hiding in this rain-spoiled match. Cooke scored the first, shooting home from out wide after a neat build-up. Colin Flatt's late strike for Romford flattered his team.											
3	H YEOVIL			L	2-3	1-2	Cooke 44, Collins 90	Guy	Martin	Law	Collins	McCready	Shreeve*	Burton	Cooke	O'Rourke	Sanderson	Hodges	O'Mara
	22/8	1,545		4			*Plumb 29, Myers 32, Dixon 60*	*Clark*	*Hughes*	*Smith*	*Myers*	*Dixon*	*Harris*	*Howley*	*Grey*	*Plumb*	*Thompson*	*Clancy*	
							Ref: G Keeble	Wimbledon have played worse and won. Plumb's header, in off the bar, puts Yeovil in front. The Dons wasted chances a plenty by the time centre-half Dixon ran 25 yards and shot from the same distance to give them a mountain to climb.											
4	A WORCESTER		7	L	1-2	1-1	Cooke 4	Guy	Law!	Martin	Sanderson	McCready	Shreeve	Burton	Cooke	O'Mara	Collins	O'Rourke	
	29/8	*1,571*	*20*	4			*Howell 43, Hitchens 75*	*Knight*	*Wood*	*Bassett*	*McEwan*	*Kyle*	*McQuarrie*	*Aggio*	*Inglis*	*Hitchens*	*Barton*	*Howell*	
							Ref: F Bassett	Roy Law is sent off for the second time in his career, this time by referee F Bassett for punching another Bassett – George – in the face after 53 minutes. The score was 1-1 at the time, and Law's expulsion helps Worcester achieve their first ever win over Wimbledon.											
5	H NUNEATON B		10	W	4-0	3-0	Burton 10, Cooke 25, 87, McCready 36	Guy	Law	Martin	Sanderson*	McCready	Shreeve	Burton	Cooke	O'Rourke	Collins	Hodges	O'Mara
	5/9	1,400	*14*	6				*Crump*	*Jones*	*Burkett*	*Smith*	*Aston*	*Goodall*	*Billington*	*Cutler*	*Jacques*	*Boot*	*Punter*	
							Ref: K Ridden	This win secures a quick early-season double for the Dons. Just before their first goal Keith Sanderson limped off with a torn hamstring, and on came John O'Mara. Within seconds Burton's rising drive put them in front. Cooke's chip and McCready's strong header sealed the win.											
6	A ROMFORD		6	L	0-1	0-0		Guy	Law	Martin	Collins	McCready	Shreeve	Burton	Cooke	O'Rourke	O'Mara	Hodges	
	9/9	*1,272*	*13*	6			*Obeney 60p*	*Smith*	*Obeney*	*Howe*	*Sorrell*	*King*	*Andrew*	*Sanders*	*Flatt*	*Chandler*	*Tough*	*Tapping*	P
							Ref: P Saubergue	A very strong wind at Romford spoilt this game, but Wimbledon had their chances, especially in the first half. On the hour Romford were awarded a penalty, which they converted. At the end of 90 minutes the Dons were grateful not to have conceded more goals.											
7	A TELFORD		13	L	0-4	0-2		Guy	Law	Martin	Davies	McCready	Shreeve	Burton*	Cooke	O'Rourke	Collins	Hodges	Bailham
	12/9	*1,700*	*21*	6			*Flowers 13, Owen 40, 74, Bentley 50*	*Irvine*	*Grice*	*Croft*	*Flowers*	*Coton*	*Ray*	*Fudge*	*Roberts*	*Bentley*	*Murray**	*Owen*	*Hart* P
							Ref: R Baldwin	Alan Burton collides with keeper Irvine on the hour, and his broken collar bone will keep him out of action for months. But there are no excuses for this thrashing by the bottom club, who went into this match with no points and only two goals.											
8	H KETTERING			W	1-0	1-0	Bailham 39	Guy	Law	Martin*	Davies	McCready	Shreeve	Bailham	Cooke	O'Rourke	Collins	Hodges	O'Mara
	19/9	1,464		8				*Clamp*	*Logan*	*Ashby*	*Peck*	*Reed*	*Addy*	*Walden*	*Bradbury*	*Gully*	*Goodall*	*Lawman*	P
							Ref: R Wood	Injuries are straining Wimbledon's playing resources. Eddie Bailham would not have played otherwise, yet he uncorks the volley that settles this match. The score-line does not tell the extent of Wimbledon's superiority. John Martin is now added to the injury list.											
9	H WEYMOUTH		13	W	1-0	0-0	O'Rourke 80	Guy	Ardrey	Willis	Davies	McCready	Shreeve	Bailham	Cooke	O'Mara*	Collins	O'Rourke	Hodges
	22/9	1,400	*18*	10				*Rose*	*Rounsevell*	*Glover*	*Barry*	*Hobson*	*Handrick*	*McCarthy*	*Kearns*	*Allen*	*Bumstead*	*Burnett*	
							Ref: F Webb	It is a wonder the Dons can field 11 players. Bobby Ardrey, now a permit player, was hastily told to come along and get changed. Cooke had to play in midfield. When O'Mara missed two sitters he was replaced by Hodges. Barry's inattentive back-pass produced the goal.											
10	A YEOVIL		6	D	0-0	0-0		Guy	Ardrey*	Willis	Sanderson	McCready	Shreeve	Bailham	Cooke	O'Mara	Collins	O'Rourke	Davies
	26/9	*2,341*	*4*	11				*Clark*	*Herrity*	*Dixon*	*Myers*	*Harris*	*Smith*	*Housley*	*Grey*	*Gilchrist*	*Thompson*	*Clancy*	
							Ref: T Jones	Law has been suspended for four weeks for his sending off. Three days before this match Yeovil sold top striker Dick Plumb to Charlton for £7,000, and they have no one to replace him. The best chances fell to Wimbledon's Bailham and Collins, but their shots were saved.											

No	H/A	Opponent / Date	Att	Pos	Res	FT	HT	Scorers, Times, Referees	1	2	3	4	5	6	7	8	9	10	11	12	13
11	H	WORCESTER		5	W	1-0	1-0	Cooke 13	Guy	Martin	Willis	Sanderson	McCready	Shreeve	Bailham	Cooke	O'Mara	Collins	O'Rourke		
		3/10	1,365	*13*	13				*Knight*	*Wood A*	*Wood L*	*McEwan*	*Kyle*	*McQuarrie*	*Aggio*	*Barton*	*Derrick*	*Howell*	*Inglis*		
								Ref: J Marshall	Three successive 1-0 home wins. Glaring misses by Bailham, O'Rourke and O'Mara keep the score down. Sanderson springs the offside trap in the build-up to the goal, Cooke finishing well from a pass by O'Rourke. Worcester's new signing, Albert Derrick, enjoys a fine debut.												
12	H	BEDFORD		5	W	**5-0**	2-0	O'Rourke 11, 35, 65, Bailham 87, [Cooke 90]	Guy	Martin	Willis	Sanderson	McCready	Shreeve	Bailham	Cooke	O'Rourke	Collins	Hodges		
		17/10	**1,865**	*14*	15				*Heyes*	*Skinn*	*Harris*	*Scurr*	*Roach*	*Lawson*	*Fry*	*Cleary*	*Figg*	*Coughlin*	*Hawksby*		
								Ref: F Lane	Before kick-off O'Rourke was dropped for the first time, but when O'Mara called off, the Scot was reinstated. O'Rourke had managed just one goal all season; now he responds with a hat-trick, rounded off with a super header. Bedford had just been k.o.'d by amateurs in the FA Cup.												
13	H	ASHFORD		3	W	4-0	2-0	Bailham 22, Cooke 45, 50, 84	Guy	Law	Martin	Sanderson	McCready	Shreeve	Bailham	Cooke	O'Mara	Collins	O'Rourke		
		24/10	1,581	*17*	17				*Gambrill*	*Sillett*	*Hunt*	*Weston*	*Harrop*	*Street*	*Ware*	*Gillingwater*	*Crush*	*Horton*	*Back**	*Bielkus*	
								Ref: C MacKnight	Brighton and other clubs are said to be eyeing Guy, who keeps his sixth home clean-sheet in a row. Bailham danced round former Chelsea defender Peter Sillett to score the first; goalkeeper Gambrill drops O'Rourke's corner for the lurking Cooke to score the second goal.												
14	A	DARTFORD		3	L	1-2	0-2	McCready 48	Guy	Law	Martin	Sanderson	McCready	Shreeve	Bailham	Cooke	O'Mara	Collins	O'Rourke		
		31/10	*1,413*	*20*	17			*Halliday 5, Guy 30 (og)*	*Hawke*	*Morgan*	*Stevens*	*Judges*	*Burns*	*Richardson*	*Ripley*	*Payne*	*Mitchell*	*Halliday*	*Cheesewright*		
								Ref: J Hazell	Dickie Guy's bubble bursts when punching a corner-kick into his own net. Wimbledon have never won at Dartford, and their rutted pitch does no one any favours. Alan Ball lookalike Ken Halliday volleyed the first goal. A late screamer by John O'Mara whistled over the crossbar.												
15	A	KING'S LYNN		4	W	2-0	1-0	Cooke 38, O'Rourke 86	Guy	Law	Martin	Sanderson	McCready	Davies	Bailham	Cooke	O'Rourke	Collins	Hodges		
		14/11	*1,134*	*21*	19				*Steel*	*Ricketts*	*Kerr*	*Davies*	*Robinson*	*Wright*	*Oliver*	*Hale*	*Rudd*	*Jones**	*Clarke*	*Brooks*	*P*
								Ref: J Hazell	Wimbledon's first away win since the opening day of the season is achieved aganst a side fielding ex-Spurs and Wales winger Cliff Jones, who did not last 90 minutes. The Dons pressed continually with three men up. The first goal came from Hodges' corner, headed back by O'Rourke.												
16	A	CAMBRIDGE C		5	L	1-2	1-1	O'Mara 40	Guy	Martin	Willis	Collins	McCready	Shreeve	Bailham	O'Rourke	O'Mara	Law	Hodges		
		24/11	*1,916*	*15*	19			*Marshall 27, Keenan 65*	*Peacock*	*Way*	*Keenan*	*Elliott*	*Baker*	*Smith*	*Bannister*	*Griffin*	*Marshall*	*Hunter*	*Hyde*		
								Ref: K Ridden	More blunders by the much-hyped Dickie Guy. The Dons are still downcast at being knocked out of the FA Cup, and endure further misery when ex-Don David Hyde hits a free-kick which Guy gathers before allowing the ball to spill. The Dons are without Cooke and Sanderson.												
17	H	CAMBRIDGE C		5	W	3-2	0-1	O'Mara 60, Bailham 78p, O'Rourke 87	Guy	Law	Martin	Davies	McCready	Shreeve	Bailham	O'Rourke	O'Mara	Collins	Hodges		
		28/11	1,659	*15*	21			*Marshall 10, 89*	*Peacock*	*Way*	*Keenan*	*Elliott*	*Baker*	*Smith*	*Bannister*	*Griffin*	*Marshall*	*Hunter*	*Hyde*		
								Ref: P Saubergue	Once again Guy lets his side down. He should have saved Marshall's effort, but is beaten at home for the first time since August. A volley by O'Mara temporarily silences the big man's own critics. When Way fists out O'Rourke's shot the linesman, not the referee, gives the penalty.												
18	A	CHELMSFORD		3	W	1-0	1-0	McCready 39	Guy	Law	Martin*	Davies	McCready	Shreeve	Sanderson	Hodges	O'Mara	Collins	O'Rourke	Willis	
		5/12	*2,774*	*2*	23				*Dunbar*	*Maynard*	*Smith*	*Loughton*	*Snowdon*	*Delea*	*Coakley*	*Dilsworth*	*Moy*	*Butcher*	*Price*		
								Ref: J Gibson	Title rivals Chelmsford are beaten by Tom McCready's header, which lifts the Dons to 3rd. Peter Shreeve excels against his former club, who have gone six games without a win. Wimbledon were under the cosh throughout the second half.												
19	H	DARTFORD		2	W	1-0	1-0	O'Rourke 40	Guy	Willis	Shreeve	Davies	McCready	Sanderson	Hodges	Cooke	O'Mara	Collins	O'Rourke		
		12/12	1,611	*11*	25				*Hawke*	*Morgan*	*Richardson*	*Payne*	*Burns*	*Judges*	*Mitchell*	*Ripley*	*Nicholas*	*Halliday*	*Cheesewright*		*P*
								Ref: F Burling	The Dons climb to 2nd place with this win over their future opponents in the FA Trophy. No prisoners were taken in this clash, which saw the Dons take the field without both regular full-backs. Dartford's combative Barry Judges was booed every time he touched the ball.												
20	H	KING'S LYNN		3	W	2-1	0-0	Law 52, Cooke 63	Guy	Martin	Shreeve	Davies	Law	Sanderson	Hodges	Cooke	O'Mara	Collins	O'Rourke		
		2/1	1,300	*19*	27			*Oliver 51*	*Steel*	*Ricketts*	*Radcliffe*	*Books*	*Porter*	*Robinson*	*Jones*	*Oliver*	*Young*	*Wright*	*Clarke*		
								Ref: W Woods	Wimbledon boast the best home record in the league, nine wins out of 10. King's Lynn have not won away at all, so this result was tighter than expected. Tom McCready missed the match through a family bereavement. Roy Law, up for Hodges' corner, bags his first of the season.												
21	A	MARGATE			W	4-0	3-0	Hodges 13, O'Mara 23, 35, Davies 75	Guy	Law	Martin	Sanderson	McCready	Davies	Hodges	Cooke	O'Mara	Collins	O'Rourke		
		9/1	*1,317*		29				*Dalrymple*	*Yorath*	*Lloyd*	*Clayton*	*Stevens*	*Houston*	*Baber*	*Cochrane*	*Summers*	*Ray**	*Jarman*	*Smith*	
									This is the Dons biggest away win since beating Romford 5-1 in 1966. John O'Mara enjoyed his return to Hartsdown Road, and scored twice. Paul Hodges opened the way with a 30-yard lob that Dalrymple misjudged. O'Mara soared above Stevens to score the second.												

No	Date		Att	Pos		Pts	F-A	H-T	Scorers, Times, and Referees	1	2	3	4	5	6	7	8	9	10	11	12 sub used
22	A	BATH			D		2-2	2-0	Hodges 5, O'Rourke 33	Guy	Law	Martin	Sanderson	McCready	Shreeve	Hodges	Cooke	O'Mara	Collins	O'Rourke	
	11/1		*1,126*			30			*Taylor 78, Savage 88*	*McAuley*	*Burt*	*Taylor T*	*Petts*	*Swift*	*Laycock*	*Parker**	*Savage*	*Leutch*	*Taylor D*	*Allen*	*Faulkes*
										The Dons were just two minutes away from their sixth straight win. Bath were playing their fifth match in 10 days. Their fight-back was launched by an amateur, 19-year-old Dick Savage, who first crossed for Dick Taylor, then got on the end of Faulkes' cross.											
23	H	MARGATE		2	D		3-3	0-2	Cooke 48, O'Mara 72, O'Rourke 78	Guy	Law	Martin	Davies	McCready	Shreeve	Hodges	Cooke	O'Mara	Collins	O'Rourke	
	23/1		1,602	*16*		31			*Baber 24, 70, Houston 35*	*Dalrymple*	*Yorath*	*Lloyd*	*Wickens B*	*Paton*	*Stevens!*	*Baber*	*Cochrane*	*Summers*	*Houston*	*Wickens J*	*Brown*
									Ref: A Gorham	Margate belie their lowly status, though the Dons hit the woodwork twice and have a goal disallowed. At 0-2 Hodges fires a penalty straight at the keeper. John Baber scores two fine goals for Margate, and makes a third. In injury time Stevens was sent off following a clash with Cooke.											
24	A	BEDFORD			W		3-1	2-1	O'Mara 16, Shreeve 40, O'Rourke 68	Guy	Law	Martin	Davies	McCready	Shreeve*	Hodges	Cooke	O'Mara	Collins	O'Rourke	Bailham
	1/2		*1,574*			33			*Jones 10*	*Barron*	*Skinn*	*Harris*	*Scurr*	*Roach*	*Lawson*	*Fry*	*Cleary*	*Figg*	*Coughlin*	*Jones*	
										Wimbledon's third double of the season is their reward for this entertaining fixture. Before the match Bedford signed Cliff Jones, who faced the Dons earlier in the season with King's Lynn. He gets off the mark with an early header. O'Mara has his finest game in Dons' colours.											
25	A	HEREFORD		3	L		1-2	0-0	Bailham 59	Guy	Martin	Willis	Davies	McCready	Shreeve	Burton	Bailham	O'Mara	Collins	O'Rourke	
	13/2		***5,093***	*2*		33			*McLaughlin 68, Jones 72*	*Potter*	*Griffiths*	*Bird*	*Jones*	*Tucker*	*Charles*	*McLaughlin*	*Tyler*	*Meadows*	*Owen*	*Walker*	
									Ref: G Trout	This climactic battle of the top two swung on a raised linesman's flag. With two minutes left Bailham shot through Potter's legs, but was given offside. The linesman had stood in at the last moment, and came from Hereford. John Charles and John O'Mara enjoyed a memorable duel.											
26	H	BARNET		3	L		0-2	0-2		Guy	Martin	Willis	Davies	McCready	Shreeve	Burton	Bailham	O'Mara	Collins	O'Rourke	
	16/2		1,572	*11*		33			*Eason 22, Powell 40*	*McClelland*	*Lye*	*Jenkins**	*King*	*Embery*	*Ward*	*Powell*	*Ferry*	*Adams*	*Eason*	*Woodhouse*	*Gregory*
									Ref: R Burville	This is the Dons' first league defeat by Barnet, who had always lost at Plough Lane. The nearest Wimbledon came to a goal was when Embery deflected the ball past his own post. No excuses were offered for the result. Wimbledon were simply outplayed.											
27	H	DOVER		3	D		0-0	0-0		Guy	Martin	Shreeve	Davies	McCready	Sanderson	Cooke	O'Rourke	O'Mara	Collins	Hodges*	Bailham
	20/2		1,789	*10*		34				*White*	*Clewlow*	*Hall*	*Hurley*	*Carragher*	*O'Connell*	*Armstrong*	*Marley*	*Moy*	*Gould*	*Harrison*	*Fursdon*
									Ref: K Ridden	It is down to 3rd now, as another home point slips away, this time to mid-table Dover. Cooke returns to the side, in place of Bailham. With only six points from their last seven matches, Wimbledon are well off the championship pace. The Dons hit the crossbar three times.											
28	A	BARNET			L		1-2	1-0	Ferry 23 (og)	Guy	Martin	Shreeve	Davies	McCready	Sanderson	Bailham	Cooke*	O'Mara	Collins	O'Rourke	Willis
	23/2		*1,662*			34			*Ward 69p, Eason 73*	*McClelland*	*Lye*	*Jenkins*	*Ward*	*Embery*	*King*	*Powell*	*Ferry*	*Woodhouse*	*Eason*	*Adams*	
									Ref: A Harrington	Incidents off the pitch affected this match as much as incidents on it. Ferry slices O'Rourke's lob into his own goal. Powell goes down under Shreeve's challenge for the penalty. Before it was taken Guy was hit by an object thrown from the crowd. Play is held up for four minutes.											
29	H	BATH		3	W		5-2	4-2	O'Mara 3, Hodges 9, Cooke 11, O'Rourke 33,	Guy	Martin	Willis	Davies	McCready	Law	Hodges	Cooke*	O'Mara	Collins	O'Rourke	**Toal**
	6/3		**849**	*12*		36			*Petts 13, Peters 40* [Davies 85]	*McAuley*	*Royston*	*Faulkes*	*Burt*	*Swift*	*Laycock*	*Parker*	*Allen*	*Taylor*	*Petts*	*Peters*	
									Ref: P Hunter	In part because of a snowstorm, in part because of Henley's sacking, in part because of the FA Trophy humilation by Yeovil, this is the Dons' lowest ever attendance. Five different Wimbledon players scored the goals. Among the applicants for manager is Marvin Hinton, ex-Chelsea.											
30	A	DOVER		8	L		**1-5**	0-2	Clewlow 89 (og) *[Marley 51, Moy 77]*	Guy	Law	Martin	Davies	McCready	Sanderson	Hodges	Cooke	O'Rourke	Collins	Toal	
	20/3		*750*	*13*		36			*Harrison 8, Clewlow 35, Hurley 48,*	*White*	*Clewlow*	*Hurley*	*Arnott*	*Carragher*	*Fursdon*	*Armstrong*	*Gould*	*Moy*	*Marley*	*Harrison*	*Cartwright*
									Ref: C Cuthbert	On a morass of a pitch, Wimbledon foolishly play a short-passing game, and are torn apart. Having said that, all the key decisions go against them.Three of Dover's goals have question marks against them, and Guy looks fragile in goal. O'Mara has been sold to Brentford for £750.											
31	H	HEREFORD		8	W		2-0	1-0	Bailham 36, Cooke 70	Guy	Martin	Law	Davies	McCready	Sanderson	Bailham	Cooke	O'Rourke	Collins	Hodges	
	23/3		1,240	*5*		38				*Potter*	*Bird*	*McLaughlin*	*Jones*	*Tucker*	*Charles*	*Tyler*	*Owen*	*Meadows*	*Smee*	*Walker*	
									Ref: W Dance	Despite sliding down the table, Wimbledon are still the league's leading goal-scorers. They have won just once in their last nine games, in all competitions, as they take on Hereford, who have two games in hand on leaders Cambridge City. Yet the Dons look effortlessly superior.											

No / Date		Opponent	Att	Pos	Res	Pts	F-A	H-T	Scorers, Times, Referees	1	2	3	4	5	6	7	8	9	10	11	12
32	A	KETTERING		8	D		2-2	0-0	Bailham 49, Davies 90	Guy	Willis	Shreeve	Sanderson	McCready	Davies	Bailham	Cooke	Law	Collins	Hodges	
27/3			676	20		39			Gully 85, Reid 87	Clamp	Peck	Ashby	Goodall	Reed	Addy	Walden	Howells	Webster	Gully	Newball	
									Ref: J Griffiths	It is all-change as Roy Law leads Wimbledon's attack. Those who left early missed a pulsating climax. On 85 minutes Ken Gully's diving header levels the scores. Then Mick Reid outjumps the Dons' defence to head Kettering in front. Davies' volley restores parity at the death.											
33	A	ASHFORD		5	D		2-2	1-2	Law 18, Bailham 47	Guy	Willis*	Shreeve	Sanderson	McCready	Davies	Bailham	Cooke	Law	Collins	Hodges	Toal
29/3			710	21		40			Ware 3, Day 40	Gambrill	Weston	Hunt	Day	Harrop	Dodge	Ware	Gillingwater	Crush	Horton	Back*	Nash
									Ref: F Lane	Ashford lie 21st and adopt a policy of all-out attack in an effort to stave off relegation. In the second half Roy Law retreats from centre-forward to full-back in place of the injured Willis. Substitute Colin Toal missed chances to sew up a win for Wimbledon.											
34	H	CHELMSFORD		6	D		1-1	1-0	Bailham 3	Guy	Law	Shreeve	Davies	McCready	Sanderson	Bailham	Cooke	Collins	O'Rourke	Hodges	
3/4			1,460	5		41			Stevenson 78	Dunbar	Smith	Butterfield	Loughton	Snowdon	Delea	Price	Stevenson	Petersen	Ferry	Dilsworth	
									Ref: K Chapman	The referee's inexplicable decisions ruin the match for everyone. When Stevenson's rocket free-kick flies back off the stanchion, the referee gives a goal-kick, but is persuaded by irate City players to check the mud-stain on the rails and consult a linesman. The goal is rightly given.											
35	H	TELFORD		6	D		2-2	2-1	Cooke 13, Burton 38	Guy	Law	Shreeve	Davies	McCready	Sanderson	Cooke	Burton	Bailham	O'Rourke	Hodges*	Harney
6/4			1,211	18		42			Hart 22, Fudge 54	Irvine	Weir	Harris	Flowers	Coton	Ray	Fudge	Hart	Bentley	Murray	Jagger	
									Ref: C MacKnight	Dull, dreary and dismal, sums up this match, despite the four goals. High balls are the only tactics on display. Telford are without ex-England Ron Flowers, and have their eyes fixed firmly on their looming FA Trophy Final. Ian Cooke opens the scoring with a mis-hit shot.											
36	H	HILLINGDON B		6	W		4-0	1-0	Cooke 32, 50, 70, Burton 80	Guy	Law	Shreeve*	Sanderson	McCready	Davies	Bailham	Cooke	Collins	O'Rourke	Hodges	Burton
9/4			1,578	12		44				Lowe	Batt	Bishton	Watson	Newcombe	Maynard	Fairchild	Bishop	Reeve	Carter	Vafiadis	
									Ref: D Drewitt	Another soft match for the Dons, for Hillingdon, too, have a date at Wembley for the FA Trophy, where they will lose 2-3 to Telford. The best goal of the match was the first, Ian Cooke sprinting to connect with Keith Sanderson's low cross – the first of Cooke's hat-trick.											
37	A	POOLE		6	L		0-2	0-1		Guy	Law	Willis	Sanderson	McCready	Davies	Burton	Cooke	O'Rourke	Collins	Hodges	
10/4			534	17		44			Keeley 21p, Arrowsmith 88	Robinson	Brewster	Thornhill	Pegram	Brown I	Ferns	Down	Keeley	Brown J	Taylor	Arrowsmith	
									Ref: I Kennard	Unlike Telford and Hillingdon, Poole are fighting for their Premier lives. Jimmy Collins has switched to playing sweeper for Wimbledon. The vital first goal was given away by Tom McCready, who hauled down John Brown after the Poole forward had evaded three defenders.											
38	A	HILLINGDON B		6	L		0-2	0-0		Guy	Martin	Law	Sanderson	McCready	Davies	Bailham	Cooke	O'Rourke	Collins	Burton	
12/4			1,459	13		44			Bishop 60, Reeve 77	Lowe	Batt	Bishton	Higginson	Newcombe	Maynard	Fairchild	Bishop	Reeve	Carter	Vafiadis	
									Ref: J Craigie	The result turned on a missed penalty by Eddie Bailham while the game was still goalless. Newcombe had handled in the box, but Bailham's spot-kick was too close to Lowe. Bishop's header claimed the first goal; Reeve's shot, which flew in off Guy's shoulder, claimed the second.											
39	H	GLOUCESTER			W		3-2	2-0	McCready 37, Burton 41, Cooke 80	Guy	Martin	Law	Sanderson	McCready	Davies	Burton	Cooke	O'Rourke	Collins	Hodges	
17/4			1,250			46			Holder 50, Ferns 65	Goodman	Vale	Layton	Anderson	Biggart	Rice	Hurford	Holder	Andrews	Fraser*	Ferns	Hudd
									Ref: F Lane	Les Henley takes charge for the last time, before handing over to Mike Everitt, appointed some time earlier. The Football League rejects plans for a 5th Division, which is bad news for Southern League aspirants. Collins misses a penalty after Goodman throws the ball in Cooke's face.											
40	H	POOLE			W		1-0	1-0	Cooke 15	Guy	Martin	Shreeve	Law	McCready	Collins	Bailham	Toal*	O'Rourke	Cooke	Hodges	Burton
20/4			1,341			48				Buck	Brewster	Thornhill	Pegram	Brown I	Ferns	Down	Taylor	Brown J	Keeley	Arrowsmith	
									Ref: S Lover	This was a more or less convincing win for the new manager. Cooke's header from Hodges' corner was worth the two points, though Poole had the audacity to hit Guy's woodwork twice in the last ten minutes. Player-manager Mike Everitt will play next season, but not this.											
41	A	GLOUCESTER			L		1-2	1-1	Toal 34	Guy	Martin	Shreeve	Law	McCready	Collins	Burton	Toal	O'Rourke	Cooke	Bailham	
24/4			372			48			Holder 4, Andrews 78	Goodman	Vale	Layton	Anderson	Biggart	Rice	Hurford	Holder	Andrews	Fraser*	Ferns	Hudd
										This retained list has no place for Willis, Martin, Davies, Harney, and Sanderson. All are defenders, so Everitt will have to do some shopping in the summer. Gloucester are already relegated, having lost their last seven games, so this goes down as an unexpected defeat.											
42	A	WEYMOUTH		6	L		0-2	0-2		Guy	Martin	Shreeve	Davies	Willis	Collins	Burton	Toal	O'Rourke	Cooke	Hodges	
30/4			1,037	10		48			Davies 5 (og), McCarthy 45	Clarke	Flay	Glover	Miller	Hobson	Rounsevell	McCarthy	Adams	Allen	Hill	Ames	
		Home	Away						Ref: D Chainey	Not so long ago both these teams were challenging for honours. Now they are nowhere. This is, in fact, Weymouth's first win in nine, helped by the discarded Davies, running the ball into his own goal after just five minutes. Wimbledon finish 8th, their lowest ever position.											
Average		1,486	1,644																		

Southern League Cup					F-A	H-T	Scorers, Times, and Referees	1	2	3	4	5	6	7	8	9	10	11	12 sub used
1:1	H	BURTON ALB		W	4-1	2-1	Butler 1 (og), Cooke 35, 71, Hodges 81	Guy	Law	Martin	Sanderson	McCready	Shreeve	Burton	Cooke	Collins	Hodges	O'Rourke	O'Mara
25/8		1,368					*Butler 22*	*Allsop*	*Finney*	*Goodwin*	*Bostock*	*Nickton*	*Tucker*	*Wright*	*Masefield*	*Cowlishaw*	*Smith*	*Butler*	
							Ref: L Burden	The Dons are defending their trophy. Apart from their four goals, they hit the woodwork four times against newly relegated Burton. The Dons got off to the perfect start, Butler turning the ball past his keeper after just 50 seconds. But his was the satisfaction of an equaliser.											
1:2	A	BURTON ALB		L	0-1	0-1		Guy	Law	Martin	Sanderson	McCready	Shreeve	Burton	Cooke	O'Mara	Collins	O'Rourke	
1/9		*1,003*					*Cowlishaw 20*	*Alsop*	*Finney*	*Goodwin*	*Bostock*	*Nickton*	*Tucker*	*Wright*	*Masefield*	*Cowlishaw*	*Smith*	*Riley*	
							(Dons win 4-2 on aggregate)	Burton won; Burton lost; Burton v Burton. Just some of the riddles conjured up by this match. Alan Burton took on Burton Albion, who won the leg but lost the tie. The only goal came when an Albion corner was only partially cleared, and the ball was driven back in.											
2		Bye																	
3	H	BEDFORD	3	W	2-1	1-0	Scurr 42 (og), Hodges 60p	Guy	Law	Martin	Davies	McCready	Shreeve	Hodges	Cooke	O'Mara	Collins	O'Rourke	
21/12		746	*8*				*Lowe 87*	*Barron*	*Skinn*	*Cooley*	*Scurr*	*Lawson*	*Roach*	*Cleary*	*Fry*	*Figg*	*Lowe*	*Davies*	
							Ref: J Griffiths	Wimbledon beat these opponents 5-0 in the league, but this is a much harder assignment. In the first minute Guy throws the ball to the feet of Figg, who is so astonished he miskicks. Scurr heads Davies' cross into his own net, and O'Rourke is toppled for the penalty.											
QF	H	CHELMSFORD	3	W	4-3	1-1	McCready 30, 49, Bailham 51, 65	Guy	Martin	Willis	Davies	McCready	Shreeve	Hodges	Bailham	O'Mara	Collins	O'Rourke	
11/2		1,495	*6*				*Price 23, 82, Coakley 80*	*Dunbar*	*Smith*	*Butterfield*	*Loughton*	*Snowdon*	*Harrity*	*Dilsworth*	*Coakley*	*Ferry*	*Price*	*Thornley*	
							Ref: G Keeble	Chelmsford score first, then trail 1-4, and finally score twice in the last 10 minutes in this entertaining, topsy-turvy match. It proves to be a personal triumph for centre-half Tom McCready, who bags the two goals – one with head, one with foot – that overturn that early upset.											
SF	A	WEYMOUTH		L	0-2	0-0		Guy	Martin	Willis	Davies	McCready	Law	Hodges	Sanderson	O'Mara	Collins	O'Rourke	
10/3		*2,000*					*Adams 75, Allen 86*	*Clarke*	*Flay*	*Glover*	*Miller*	*Hobson*	*Rounsevell*	*McCarthy*	*Adams*	*Allen*	*Hill*	*Ames*	
								The Dons are one step away from their second successive Southern League Cup Final. They are handicapped by injuries, and by Dickie Guy dropping the ball under an aerial challenge with Trevor Allen. Adams pounced. The Dons went two down when failing to clear a free-kick.											

FA Cup								1	2	3	4	5	6	7	8	9	10	11	12
4Q	A	LEATHERHEAD	4	W	2-1	0-1	Bailham 72, 85	Guy	Law	Martin	Sanderson	McCready	Shreeve*	Bailham	Cooke	O'Mara	Collins	Hodges	O'Rourke
7/11		*1,350*	*A:5*				*Mills 20*	*Cuthbert*	*Davies*	*Brazier*	*Hill*	*Reid*	*Adam*	*Slade*	*Mills**	*Skinner*	*Lavers*	*Webb*	
							Ref: B Robinson	Fetcham Grove is the venue for this potentially hazardous tie. Wimbledon were within 20 minutes of a humilating exit from the FA Cup. Law's badly directed header had let in Mills for a goal the Athenean Leaguers well deserved. It took two exquisite Bailham goals to rescue the Dons.											
1	A	PETERBOROUGH	5	L	1-3	1-2	Cooke 34	Guy	Law	Martin	Sanderson	McCready	Shreeve	Bailham	Cooke*	O'Rourke	Collins	Hodges	Davies
21/11		*5,919*	*4:8*				*Garwood 1, Moss 32, Hall 80*	*Drewery*	*Noble*	*Duncliffe*	*Iley*	*Wile*	*Wright*	*Moss*	*Conmy*	*Garwood*	*Hall*	*Robson*	
							Ref: D Civil	Jim Iley's Posh are becalmed in Division 4, having been demoted in 1968 for 'financial irregularities'. This is regarded as a bad draw for the Dons, and it takes just 21 seconds for Sanderson to pass direct to Colin Garwood. Soon after he pulled a goal back, Cooke was stretchered off.											

FA Trophy								1	2	3	4	5	6	7	8	9	10	11	12
1	H	DARTFORD	2	D	1-1	1-0	Collins 1	Guy	Law	Martin	Shreeve	McCready	Sanderson	Hodges	Cooke	O'Mara	Collins	O'Rourke	Burton
16/1		1,422	*15*				*Stevens 72p*	*Hawke*	*Read*	*Richardson*	*Morgan*	*Burns*	*Judges*	*Ripley*	*Payne*	*Mitchell*	*Stevens*	*Halliday K*	
							Ref: B Daniels	Wimbledon score in seconds from a twice-taken indirect free-kick, and hang on to the lead for over an hour, until Martin fouls Ripley inside the box. O'Mara could never escape the attentions of Les Burns. The Dons' substitute, Alan Burton, gets his first action in four months.											
1R	A	DARTFORD		W	3-2	0-2	Cooke 53, 75, Bailham 80	Guy	Willis	Shreeve	Davies	McCready	Sanderson	Bailham	Cooke	O'Mara	Collins	O'Rourke	
18/1		*732*					*Burns 21, Mitchell 43*	*Hawke*	*Read*	*Stevens*	*Morgan*	*Burns*	*Richardson*	*Ripley*	*Payne*	*Mitchell*	*McKenna*	*Halliday*	
							Ref: B Daniels	Wimbledon lost here in the same competition last season, and at half-time it seems they are headed for the same fate. The turning point was Cooke's first goal, which hit the bar twice, then bounced down and out. The referee turned to the linesman, who signalled a goal.											

Rd		Opponent	Att	Pos	Res	Score	H-T	Scorers, Times, and Referees	1	2	3	4	5	6	7	8	9	10	11	12
2	H	BROMSGROVE			W	4-0	3-0	O'Mara 30, 33, O'Rourke 38,	Guy	Martin	Willis	Davies	McCready	Shreeve	Hodges	Cooke*	O'Mara	Collins	O'Rourke	Bailham
	6/2		2,238					[Bailham 75]	*Hooper*	*Reynolds*	*Gwynne*	*Stafford*	*Wood*	*Adams*	*Hellawell M*	*Broadbent*	*Craddock*	*Merrick*	*Hellawell J*	
								Ref: K Ridden	West Midland League Bromsgrove field ex-England internationals Peter Broadbent and Mike Hellawell, and bring 14 coaches of supporters, plus a special train. They get little pleasure from this match, turned Wimbledon's way on the half-hour by John O'Mara's volley.											
3	H	YEOVIL		3	D	1-1	0-1	Hodges 69	Guy	Martin	Law	Davies	McCready	Shreeve	Hodges	Bailham	O'Mara	Collins	O'Rourke	
	27/2		3,194	*4*				*Moffatt 3*	*Clarke*	*Bayliss*	*Smith*	*Myers*	*Dixon*	*Hughes*	*Housley*	*Moffatt*	*Weller*	*Thompson*	*Clancy*	
								Ref: A Oliver	Plough Lane's biggest gate of the season turns up hoping that the Dons can get to Wembley. The referee has to halt play after a bottle is thrown on the pitch. The game produced two excellent goals, and Bailham was denied by the crossbar in the final minute.											
3R	A	YEOVIL		3	L	0-4	0-1		Guy	Martin	Law	Davies	McCready	Shreeve*	Hodges	Bailham	O'Mara	Collins	O'Rourke	Willis
	3/3		*5,157*	*5*				*Weller 44, 50, 78, Moffatt 66*	*Clark*	*Herrity*	*Bayliss*	*Myers*	*Dixon*	*Smith*	*Housley*	*Moffatt*	*Weller*	*Thompson*	*Clancy*	*P*
								Ref: M Washer	Afterwards, all the talk is of 'if only'. If only Eddie Bailham had kept his shot down, when faced with just the goalkeeper to beat after 20 minutes, with the game still goalless. Seconds before half-time Chris Weller's close-range header opens up the floodgates.											

		Home						Away					
	P	W	D	L	F	A	W	D	L	F	A	Pts
1 Yeovil	42	17	2	2	42	8	8	5	8	24	23	57
2 Cambridge C	42	12	7	2	39	19	10	4	7	28	19	55
3 Romford	42	13	4	4	35	19	10	5	6	28	23	55
4 Hereford	42	16	2	3	46	22	7	6	8	24	31	54
5 Chelmsford	42	12	4	5	44	17	8	7	6	17	15	51
6 Barnet	42	14	5	2	42	18	4	9	8	27	31	50
7 Bedford	42	13	5	3	37	16	7	5	9	25	30	50
8 WIMBLEDON	42	15	4	2	47	19	5	4	12	25	35	48
9 Worcester	42	12	4	5	39	21	8	4	9	22	25	48
10 Weymouth	42	10	8	3	37	21	4	8	9	27	27	44
11 Dartford	42	8	8	5	22	18	7	4	10	31	33	42
12 Dover	42	11	5	5	41	22	5	4	12	23	41	41
13 Margate	42	10	4	7	34	29	5	6	10	30	40	40
14 Hillingdon B	42	12	4	5	41	22	5	2	14	20	46	40
15 Bath	42	10	6	5	25	19	3	6	12	23	49	38
16 Nuneaton B	42	9	6	6	31	27	3	6	12	12	39	36
17 Telford	42	10	3	8	41	30	3	5	13	23	40	34
18 Poole	42	10	5	6	33	22	4	1	16	24	53	34
19 King's Lynn	42	9	5	7	30	25	2	2	17	14	42	29
20 Ashford	42	6	7	8	31	38	2	6	13	21	48	29
21 Kettering	42	6	6	9	29	38	2	5	14	19	46	27
22 Gloucester	42	5	5	11	19	32	1	5	15	15	49	22
	924	240	109	113	785	502	113	109	240	502	785	924

Odds & ends

Double wins: (3) Nuneaton, Bedford, King's Lynn.
Double losses: (1) Barnet.

Won from behind: (3) Cambridge C (h), King's Lynn (h), Bedford (a).
Lost from in front: (3) Worcester (a), Hereford (a), Barnet (a).

High spots: 5 successive wins up to 9th January.
Finishing the season as the league's highest scorers.
Reaching the semi-final of the Southern League Cup.

Low spots: Sacking Les Henley.
Winning only 3 of the final 11 games.
Humiliating 0-4 defeat at Yeovil in the FA Trophy.
The first season in which the Dons never topped the Premier table.
For the first time, attendances dipped below the league's average.

Ever-presents: (1) Dickie Guy.
Hat-tricks: Ian Cooke (2), Gerry O'Rourke (1).
Leading Scorer: Ian Cooke (27).

	Appearances					Goals				
	Lge	Sub	SLC	FAC	FAT	Lge	SLC	FAC	FAT	Total
Ardrey, Bobby	**2**									
Bailham, Eddie	**22**	(3)	1	2	3/1	**9**	2	2	2	**15**
Burton, Alan	**15**	(2)	2		0/1	**5**				**5**
Collins, Jimmy	**41**		5	2	5	**1**			1	**2**
Cooke, Ian	**37**		3	2	3	**22**	2	1	2	**27**
Davies, Stuart	**27**	(1)	3	0/1	4	**3**				**3**
Guy, Dickie	**42**		5	2	5					
Harney, David		(1)								
Hodges, Paul	**31**	(1)	4	2	4	**4**	2		1	**7**
Law, Roy	**32**		4	2	3	**2**				**2**
McCready,Tom	**40**		5	2	5	**4**	2			**6**
Martin, John	**33**		5	2	4					
O'Mara, John	**21**	(3)	4/1	1	5	**7**			2	**9**
O'Rourke, Gerry	**40**		5	1/1	5	**11**			1	**12**
Sanderson, Keith	**28**		3	2	2					
Shreeve, Peter	**34**		4	2	5	**1**				**1**
Toal, Colin	**4**	(2)				**1**				**1**
Willis, Dave	**13**	(2)	2		2/1					
(own-goals)						**2**	2			**4**
17 players used	**462**	**(15)**	**55/1**	**22/2**	**55/3**	**72**	**10**	**3**	**9**	**94**

/ denotes substitutes

No	Date	Att	Pos	Pts	F-A	H-T	Scorers, Times, and Referees	1	2	3	4	5	6	7	8	9	10	11	12 sub used
1	A HEREFORD			D	1-1	0-0	Cooke 49	Guy	**Marchant**	Shreeve	Law	McCready	**Rice**	Collins	Cooke	O'Rourke	**Everitt**	**Morton**	
	14/8	***5,502***		1			*McLaughlin 65*	*Icke*	*Griffiths*	*Mallender*	*Jones*	*Tucker*	*Rodgerson*	*McLaughlin*	*Tyler*	*Meadows*	*Inglis*	*George*	
								Mike Everitt's philosophy is all too clear. 'We want 0-0 draws away from home,' he says. Hereford are pre-season favourites to lift the title. David Icke, their goalkeeper, will become famous as a New Age thinker. Everitt puts his two new players, Rice and Marchant, into his team.											
2	H WORCESTER			D	1-1	0-0	Cooke 46	Guy	Marchant	Everitt	Law	McCready	Collins	O'Rourke	Cooke	Morton	Rice	Hodges	
	17/8	1,601		2			*Knight 74*	*Knight*	*McEwan*	*Bassett*	*Newton*	*McQuarrie*	*Carson*	*Dyer*	*Aggio*	*Davis*	*Barton*	*Ewis*	
							Ref: D Chainey	Once again Wimbledon fail to hang on to a lead secured early in the second half. Ian Cooke's header was cancelled out by Knight lashing in the equaliser. Selwyn Rice has an outstanding game for the Dons, though he is booked for a foul. The Dons might have won by three or four.											
3	H WEYMOUTH			W	1-0	0-0	McCready 50	Guy	Marchant	Everitt	Rice*	McCready	Shreeve	Bailham	Cooke	Morton	Collins	Hodges	O'Rourke
	21/8	1,594		4				*Clarke*	*Flay*	*Rounsevell*	*Bradbury*	*Hobson*	*Hill*	*Bumpstead*	*Goodfellow*	*Allen*	*Barry*	*Ames**	*Pound*
							Ref: B Chapman	Wimbledon's first win inflicts Weymouth's first defeat. Shreeve plays in place of the injured Law. The goal comes when Eddie Bailham is fouled outside the box. Jimmy Collins' free-kick sets up Tom McCready's volley. There is no sign yet of Wimbledon's traumas to come.											
4	A WORCESTER			L	**1-4**	0-2	Morton 65	Guy	Marchant	Everitt	Shreeve	McCready	Collins	Bailham	Cooke	Morton	Rice	O'Rourke	
	24/8	*1,650*		4			*Davies 23, 40, 84, Dyer 74*	*Knight*	*McEwan*	*Bassett*	*Newton*	*McQuarrie*	*Carson*	*Dyer*	*Aggio*	*Davies*	*Barton*	*Ewis*	
								Wimbledon had 50% of the play, but they did not have 6' 3", 20-year-old centre-forward Roger Davies. He has a sensational debut, scoring three times, and alerting every club in the land. In a few weeks he will be signed by Derby County for £14,000, a Southern League record fee.											
5	A GRAVESEND			W	3-1	0-0	Rice 65, Cooke 72, 75	Guy	Marchant	**Stanley**	Everitt	McCready	Collins	Bailham	Cooke	Morton	Rice	O'Rourke	
	28/8	*800*		6			*Sitford 85p*	*Hawke*	*Challis*	*Crudace*	*Brooks*	*Burrett*	*Thurgood*	*Glover*	*O'Sullivan*	*Sitford*	*Adams*	*Fowler*	
							Ref: Hazell	Newly promoted Gravesend have lost all previous matches and scored just one goal, from the penalty spot. They manage another penalty, after Adams had been fouled. Malcolm Stanley stands in for Law in defence. Ian Cooke hits two goals, one a lob, the other direct from a corner.											
6	A BEDFORD			L	2-3	1-1	Morton 13, Collins 47	Guy	Marchant	Stanley	Everitt	McCready	Collins	Hodges	Cooke	Morton	Rice	O'Rourke	
	30/8	*1,500*		6			*Fry 10, Cleary 55, Figg 89*	*Barron*	*Shinn*	*Dougan*	*Scurr*	*Lawson*	*Cooley*	*Cleary*	*Davies*	*Figg*	*Hawksby*	*Fry*	
								The Dons fall to Roger Figg's 89th minute winner, when he bursts through the middle. Pick of the earlier goals was Jimmy Collins' solo effort, when he ran 50 yards to put the Dons in front after half-time. Bedford's Barry Fry will later manage Barnet, Southend, and Birmingham.											
7	A CAMBRIDGE C		10	W	2-1	1-0	Rice 30, Morton 57	Guy	Marchant	Everitt	Shreeve	McCready	Collins	Bailham	Cooke	Morton	Rice	O'Rourke	
	4/9	*1,437*	*16*	8			*Marshall 62*	*Vasper*	*Way*	*Keenan*	*Knight*	*Stevens*	*Smith*	*Hyde*	*Hunter*	*Slack*	*Marshall*	*Clark*	
							Ref: A Harrington	City finished runners-up last season. This is only their third game of the current campaign. They are set on the path to defeat by Selwyn Rice, signed from Gloucester, whose shot is deflected past Vasper. Wimbledon had begun the game with massed defence, and gradually opened up.											
8	H BEDFORD		9	W	3-1	1-0	Morton 14, 70, O'Rourke 56	Guy	Marchant	Everitt	Shreeve	McCready	Collins	Bailham	Cooke	Morton	Rice	O'Rourke	
	7/9	1,644	*10*	10			*Davies 80*	*Barron*	*Skinn*	*Dougan*	*Scurr*	*Roach*	*Cooley*	*Cleary*	*Davies*	*Figg*	*Hawksby*	*Fry*	
							Ref: K Ridden	Four successive away games have yielded four points, so Everitt is on target. His players look super fit, even Eddie Bailham has shed some pounds. Alan Morton takes his season's tally to five, making him the club's top scorer. Paul Hodges rows with Everitt and storms out.											
9	A MARGATE		6	W	3-2	3-2	Rice 10, McCready 41, Bailham 44	Guy	Marchant	Shreeve	Rice	McCready	Law	Bailham	Cooke	Morton	Collins	O'Rourke	
	11/9	*1,170*	*7*	12			*King 22, Baber 30*	*Brodie*	*Yorath*	*Butterfield*	*Clayton*	*Wickens R*	*Houston*	*Baber*	*King*	*Baker*	*Brown*	*Johnson*	
								Six away games in the first nine is the fixture computer's idea of equity. Everitt has only 12 fit players from which to choose. Rice scores past Chic Brodie – formerly with Brentford – with an 18-yard shot. This sparks a thrilling first half, with great goals flying in at both ends.											
10	H GRAVESEND		7	W	4-0	2-0	Bailham 28, Morton 32, [McCready 60, 75]	Guy	Marchant	Stanley	Rice	McCready	Law	Bailham	Cooke	Morton	Collins	O'Rourke	
	14/9	1,788	*22*	14				*Gunner*	*Dudley*	*Crudace*	*Sitford*	*Burrett*	*Thurgood*	*Reed*	*Adams*	*Brooks*	*Bibby*	*Moss*	
							Ref: J Griffiths	A comfortable double over woeful Gravesend, though Selwyn Rice finds himself booked for the third time this season. Tom McCready's two headers make him second top scorer behind Alan Morton. The Dons have climbed to 7th, their highest position so far.											

No / Date	H/A	Opponent	Att	Pos	Res	Pts	F-A	H-T	Scorers, Times, and Referees	1	2	3	4	5	6	7	8	9	10	11	12
11	H	TELFORD		5	W		2-1	1-0	Cooke 13, Morton 76	Guy	Marchant	Stanley	Rice	McCready	Law	Bailham	Cooke	Morton	Collins	O'Rourke	
18/9			1,734	*18*		16			*Bentley 89*	*Weir*	*Harris*	*Ross*	*Ray*	*Carr*	*Jagger*	*Coton**	*Owen*	*Bentley*	*Gott*	*Fidge*	*Flowers*
									Ref: L Holland	Telford have scored 17 goals in their previous three games, but are swept away. Ron Flowers comes on for Coton, and supplies the cross from which Bentley reduces the arrears. By then it is too late. Wimbledon debate applying to the Football League, three years after their last bid.											
12	A	BATH		2	W		3-2	1-2	Cooke 5, 86, O'Rourke 57	Guy	Marchant	Stanley	Rice	McCready	Law	Bailham	Cooke	Morton	Collins	O'Rourke	
25/9			*1,444*			18			*Mitten 3, Fry 24*	*McAuley*	*Ryan*	*Albin*	*Burt*	*Swift*	*Marsland*	*Mitten*	*Laycock*	*Rose*	*Crowe*	*Fry*	
										Only Chelmsford are above the Dons now, as they end Bath's unbeaten home record. Mind you, Bath had only nine fit players, so they signed two more just before kick-off. Ian Cooke returns to goal-scoring ways, as Worcester's Roger Davies makes history by signing for Derby.											
13	H	HEREFORD		1	W		2-1	1-0	Collins 43, Morton 60	Guy	Marchant	Stanley	Rice	McCready	Law	Everitt	Cooke*	Morton	Collins	O'Rourke	**Davidson**
2/10			2,188	*3*		20			*Tyler 75*	*Potter*	*Griffiths*	*Mallender*	*Jones*	*Tucker*	*Radford*	*Gough*	*Tyler*	*Meadows*	*Owen*	*George*	
									Ref: F Lane	Wimbledon's seventh successive victory takes them to the top of the pile. Hereford have lost on their last four visits to Plough Lane, though most neutrals agreed that Alan Morton's goal was well offside. Alan Davidson substitutes for the injured Ian Cooke.											
14	A	CHELMSFORD		2	L		0-3	0-0		Guy	Marchant	Everitt	Rice	McCready	Law!	Cooke	Shreeve	Morton	Collins	O'Rourke	
9/10			*3,891*	*1*		20			*Delea 58, Price 65, Peterson 69*	*Taylor*	*Lawrence*	*Gomersall*	*Foster*	*Loughton*	*Smith*	*Price*	*Coakley*	*Peterson*	*Dilsworth!*	*Delea*	
									Ref: J Craigie	The Dons crash as Roy Law is dismissed for the third time in his career. At 0-3 Law tugs Dilsworth's beard, and in the ensuing punch-up both are ordered off. The Dons had defended stubbornly, but were sunk by three headers. Their winning run is over, as is their league leadership.											
15	H	FOLKESTONE		3	W		2-1	0-0	Rice 84, Bailham 89	Guy	Marchant	Shreeve	Everitt*	McCready	Law	Bailham	Rice	Morton	Collins	O'Rourke	Shreeve
16/10			1,459	*17*		22			*Lay 60*	*Hills*	*Idle*	*Nash*	*Weston*	*Pearce*	*Bentley*	*Smillie*	*Sharp*	*Terry*	*Archell*	*Lay*	
									Ref: D Drewitt	Lucky, lucky Wimbledon. They looked to be heading for defeat as the match entered the closing stages. Then Rice's cross swirls over the keeper's head and into goal. A linesman flagged before Bailham scored the winner. The ref ignored him, and needed a police escort at the end.											
16	H	POOLE		2	D		2-2	0-1	Thornhill 52 (og), Morton 75	Guy	Stanley	Shreeve	Rice	McCready	Law	**Armstrong**	Bailham	Morton	Collins	O'Rourke	
23/10			1,709	*16*		23			*Brown 45, Bolton 89*	*Buck*	*Stockley*	*Thornhill*	*Ferns*	*Knapp*	*Eyden*	*Pegram*	*Brown J*	*Bolton*	*Taylor*	*McKevitt*	
									Ref: J Hazell	Dave Armstrong makes his debut, and sends over the corner-kick from which Alan Morton hits the bar in the dying minutes. Ron Thornhill's spectacular overhead kick had earlier levelled for the Dons, as he tried to clear Eddie Bailham's corner-kick.											
17	A	NUNEATON B			L		0-1	0-0		Guy	Marchant	Shreeve	Rice	McCready	Law	Armstrong	Cooke	Morton	Collins	O'Rourke	
30/10			*2,995*			23			*Notley 75*	*Robinson*	*Lewis*	*Smith*	*Howshall*	*Gill*	*Shepherd*	*Pleat*	*Baker*	*Notley*	*Goodall*	*Cutler*	
									Ref: W Jones	Law makes the error which costs Wimbledon the goal and the match, permitting Barry Notley time to turn and shoot. Nuneaton had lost only twice in 17 games, and Wimbledon were hanging on as best they could up to the goal.											
18	A	ROMFORD		2	L		1-2	0-2	Armstrong 80	Guy	Marchant	Stanley	Morton	McCready	Law	Armstrong	Cooke	Bailham	O'Rourke	Hodges*	**Smith**
13/11			1,742	*8*		23			*Sorrell 11, Chandler 24*	*Hollins*	*Obeney*	*Tapping*	*Sorrell*	*Bickles*	*Freeman*	*Sanders*	*Chandler*	*King*	*Manning*	*Brabrook*	
									Ref: P Saubergue	Ex-England Peter Brabrook tormented the Dons from first till last. David Armstrong turned up with an injured ankle, but had to play. Another youngster, Graham Smith, an amateur, comes on as sub. Law is to blame for Romford's first goal, and top scorer Chandler smashes the second.											
19	H	MERTHYR TYDFIL		4	W		**6-0**	2-0	Cooke 6, 75, Armstrong 11, [O'Rourke 46, Bailham 60, 85]	Guy	Marchant	Stanley	Rice	**Hurley***	McCready	Armstrong	Cooke	Bailham	O'Rourke	Hodges	Smith
27/11			1,537	*20*		25				*John*	*Murphy*	*Davies*	*Crotty*	*Mapley*	*Hayes*	*Robinson*	*Wilkins*	*Collins*	*Matthews*	*Fitzgerald*	
									Ref: G Keeble	Dover centre-half Chris Hurley has signed for the Dons. He is required to do little defending in this match, against a club so hard up that they travel to away games in a mini-bus. They arrived late too. With Wimbledon leading 1-0, Guy saved Collins' penalty.											
20	A	DOVER			L		2-3	1-1	Bailham 37, Armstrong 90	Guy	Marchant	Stanley	Rice	Hurley	McCready	Armstrong	Cooke	Bailham	O'Rourke	Hodges	
4/12			*1,479*			25			*Cutler 32, Moy 58, 72*	*White*	*Fursdon*	*Reynolds*	*Beesley*	*Carragher*	*O'Connell*	*Johnson*	*Robinson*	*Cutler*	*Moy*	*Harrison*	*Gould*
									Ref: C Cuthbert	Hurley has a quick reunion with his former team. Dover's Paul Cutler scores on his debut after signing from Nuneaton. Bailham equalises from out near the touchline. Tony Moy destroys Wimbledon in the second half. Armstong's reply is too little, too late.											
21	H	DARTFORD		5	L		1-3	0-2	Bailham 79	Guy	McCready	Stanley	Rice	Hurley	**Langford**	Armstrong	Cooke	Bailham	O'Rourke	Hodges	
11/12			1,549	*11*		25			*Halliday K, 4, Light 20, Hales 80*	*Morton*	*Charman*	*Stevens*	*Payne*	*Burns*	*Judges*	*Ripley*	*Light*	*Hales*	*Halliday K*	*Richardson*	
									Ref: Morton	The first home reverse of the season, inflicted on an experimental defence, which partners debut-boy Steve Langford alongside newcomer Chris Hurley. Derek Hales scored the crucial third goal for Dartford, seconds after Bailham had put the Dons back into contention.											

No	Date		Att	Pos	Pts	F-A	H-T	Scorers, Times, and Referees	1	2	3	4	5	6	7	8	9	10	11	12 sub used
22	H	HILLINGDON B		5	W	5-1	2-0	Bailham 20, Moore 25 (og), Hurley 50	Guy	Stanley	Everitt	McCready	Law	**Silkman**	Armstrong	Cooke	Hurley	Bailham	Hodges	
	27/12		**2,200**	*8*	27			*Hipwell 70* [Cooke 54, 56]	*Lowe*	*Ryan*	*Meldrum*	*Moore*	*Newcombe*	*Higginson*	*Vafiadis*	*Bishop*	*Reeve*	*Butler*	*Hipwell*	P
								Ref: J Bellamy	Everitt reshuffles his team, drops Gerry O'Rourke and Selwyn Rice, and gives a debut to Barry Silkman. Eddie Bailham is pulled back into midfield and Chris Hurley asked to play centre-forward. The concoction works, for Hillingdon are truly crushed.											
23	A	HILLINGDON B		5	L	0-1	0-0		Guy	Stanley	Everitt	Silkman	McCready	Law	Armstrong	Cooke	Hurley	Bailham	Hodges	
	1/1		*871*	*8*	27			*Bishop 53*	*Lowe*	*Ryan*	*Butler*	*Hipwell*	*Newcombe*	*Moore*	*Fairchild*	*Bishop*	*Reeve*	*Carter*	*Knox*	P
								Ref: J Christopher	Swift revenge for Hillingdon, as they inflict Wimbledon's fifth consecutive away defeat. The Dons set out their defensive stall and never looked like scoring until Boro did. Having fallen behind, the Dons piled forward and looked twice the team they had looked while defending.											
24	H	BATH		5	W	3-2	0-0	Cooke 58, 61, Silkman 75	Guy	Stanley	Everitt	Silkman	McCready	Law	Armstrong	Cooke	Hurley	Bailham	Hodges	
	8/1		1,326	*17*	29			*Everitt 63 (og), Mitten 80p*	*McAulay*	*Ryan*	*Albin*	*Burt*	*Swift*	*Marsland*	*Mitten*	*Laycock*	*Rose*	*Crowe*	*Fry*	P
								Ref: C Watts	Plough Lane is a sea of mud. Bath have taken only one away point all season, but chase the Dons all the way. Wimbledon's first two goals are identical, both scored by Ian Cooke from flick-ons by Chris Hurley. Bath's penalty was punishment for Bailham's push on Marsland.											
25	H	CAMBRIDGE C		5	D	1-1	0-0	Cooke 65	Guy	Stanley	Everitt	Silkman	McCready	Law	Armstrong	Cooke	Hurley	Bailham	Hodges	
	15/1		1,420	*16*	30			*Hyde 87*	*Peacock*	*Way*	*Keenan*	*Elliott*	*James*	*Stevens*	*Jones*	*Smith*	*Hunter*	*Hyde*	*Marshall*	P
								Ref: D Bone	City drop Stan Marshall for the first time in three years. The Dons force 20 corners to Cambridge's three, and Cooke might have had a hat-trick before he stabbed in Armstrong's cross. Ex-Don David Hyde's corner-kick somehow found its way straight into the net.											
26	A	WEYMOUTH		5	L	**1-4**	1-2	Morton 15p	Guy	Stanley	Everitt	Silkman	McCready	Hurley	Armstrong	Rice	Morton	Smith	O'Rourke	
	29/1		*850*	*14*	30			*Allen 10, 40, 70, Bradbury 72*	*Clarke*	*Flay*	*Glover*	*Miller*	*Rounsevell*	*Bradbury*	*Adams*	*Barry*	*Allen*	*Hill*	*Pound*	
								Ref: G Biddlestone	Yeovil have crushed Wimbledon 5-1 in the FA Trophy. Paul Hodges and Eddie Bailham are the latest players to be dropped, and even Dickie Guy's place is under threat. Despite the score, the Dons played quite well in parts, but have no answer to Trevor Allen's hat-trick.											
27	H	CHELMSFORD		5	L	**1-4**	1-2	Silkman 40	Guy	Marchant	Stanley	Silkman	McCready	Law	Armstrong	Morton	Hurley	Rice	O'Rourke	
	5/2		1,300	*1*	30			*Grant 30, 50, Peterson 42, 72*	*Taylor*	*Lawrence*	*Gommersall*	*Foster*	*Loughton*	*Delea*	*Horrey*	*Price*	*Peterson*	*Grant*	*Thornley*	P
								Ref: J Cook	The Dons' last three results are 1-5, 1-4, 1-4. The club is in disarray. Chelmsford top the table, and all Wimbledon have to offer is Silkman's fine shot on the run. Grant and Peterson torment the Dons' defence. Eddie Bailham has gone to Cambridge City on a free-transfer.											
28	A	POOLE		5	L	1-2		O'Rourke 75	Guy	Marchant	Stanley	Silkman	McCready	Law	Cooke	Rice	Morton	Smith	O'Rourke	
	12/2		***498***	*19*	30			*Taylor (2)*	*Buck*	*Stockley*	*Thornhill*	*Pegram*	*Eyden*	*Bolton*	*McKevitt*	*Keeley*	*Brown J*	*Knapp*	*Taylor*	
								Ref: V Templar	Recent signing Chris Hurley is attracting the boo-boys already, and finds himself dropped. Gerry O'Rourke is the new captain. Poole win their first home match since November, thanks to Tommy Taylor's goals. His first came from a long throw, his second from a free-kick.											
29	H	NUNEATON B		7	W	1-0	0-0	Armstrong 62	Guy	Marchant	Stanley	Silkman	McCready	Law	Armstrong	Cooke	Morton	Rice	O'Rourke	
	19/2		**1,150**	*17*	32				*Robinson*	*Jones*	*Bircumshaw*	*Lewis*	*Howshall*	*Turpie*	*Gill*	*Goodall*	*Notley*	*Shepherd*	*Smith*	
								Ref: M Taylor	For some reason Nuneaton set their sights on a goalless draw, even though Wimbledon's abject recent form might have made them bolder. So frail is the Dons' defence that this is only the fourth time the opposition has failed to score against them this season.											
30	A	GUILDFORD		6	L	0-1	0-1		Guy	Marchant	Law	McCready	Stanley	Silkman	Rice	Armstrong	Shreeve	Morton	O'Rourke	
	26/2		*1,380*	*20*	32			*Burge 44*	*Brooks*	*Watts*	*Sleap*	*More*	*Harris*	*Kerr*	*Smith*	*Malley*	*Burge*	*Burns*	*Tyler*	P
								Ref: B Stockley	Had the league season commenced in the New Year, Wimbledon would now be in desperate straits. Ian Cooke drops out with flu, and Peter Shreeve plays his first game since October. City's Dennis Malley lines up against his old club. The game's first corner brings the goal.											
31	H	ROMFORD		6	W	2-0	1-0	Morton 25, Cooke 56	Guy	Marchant	Stanley	Silkman	Law	McCready	Armstrong	Cooke	Morton	Rice	Collins	
	4/3		1,305	*5*	34				*Smith*	*Howe*	*Tapping*	*Sorrell*	*Bickles*	*Bailey*	*Brabrook*	*Chandler*	*King*	*Tough*	*Manning*	P
								Ref: D Burlingham	High-flying Romford are favourites to overturn struggling Wimbledon, but it is they who are overturned. Morton dallies, but still shoots under the goalkeeper, and Cooke adds a close-range header after his shot had been palmed up in the air by the keeper.											

No	Venue	Opponent / Date	Att	Pos	Res / Pts	FT	HT	Scorers / Ref	1	2	3	4	5	6	7	8	9	10	11	12	
32	A	BARNET			L	0-2	0-1		Guy	Marchant	Stanley	Silkman	McCready	Law	Hurley	Cooke	Morton	Collins	O'Rourke		
		14/3	*1,423*		34			*Powell 5, 80*	*McClelland*	*Lye*	*Jenkins*	*Ward*	*Embery*	*King*	*Powell*	*Ferry*	*Flatt*	*Eason*	*Plume*		
								Ref: K Ridden	This is Wimbledon's ninth away loss on the trot. Barnet are going for the treble, but Wimbledon hit the woodwork twice in sliding to defeat. Powell plays a one-two with Plume to score neatly, then surges past Law and Stanley to add a late second.												
33	A	MERTHYR TYDFIL			W	2-0	2-0	Larkin 5, 38	Guy	Marchant	Stanley	Silkman	Law	McCready	Armstrong	Collins	Cooke	**Larkin**	O'Rourke		
		18/3	*701*		36				*John*	*Bird*	*Harris*	*Williams*	*Madeley*	*Chambers*	*Lloyd*	*Wilkins*	*Fordyce*	*Murphy*	*Derrick*		*P*
									These are Wimbledon's first away points since September, and are secured by two goals by unknown amateur Dave Larkin. With five straight defeats behind them, Merthyr were already relegated. The second half was as excruciatingly bad as anything anyone could remember.												
34	A	FOLKESTONE		5	D	1-1	0-1	Cooke 76	Guy	Marchant	Stanley	Silkman	Law	McCready	Armstrong	Cooke	Larkin	Collins	O'Rourke		
		21/3	*552*	*14*	37			*Cook 17*	*Hughes*	*Idle*	*Bibby*	*Tredwell*	*Pearce*	*Bentley*	*Smillie*	*Cook*	*Sharp*	*Terry*	*Weston*		*P*
								Ref: J Cook	An unchanged side. Andy Larkin runs until he drops. Barry Silkman's wonderful run and shot from 40 yards brought the save of the match from Hughes. The Dons were heading for defeat until Gerry O'Rourke set up Ian Cooke for the equaliser.												
35	H	DOVER		5	W	3-2	1-1	McCready 1, Cooke 63 , Larkin 70	Guy	Marchant	Stanley	Silkman	McCready	Law	Armstrong	Cooke	Larkin	Collins*	O'Rourke	Morton	
		25/3	1,473	*4*	39			*Horsfall 11, Crush 87*	*Prior*	*Reynolds*	*Carragher*	*Beesley*	*Dennis*	*O'Connell*	*Johnson*	*Robinson*	*Moy*	*Izatt*	*Horsfall*	*Crush*	
								Ref: R Rodell	Injury-hit Dons make heavy weather of overcoming Dover, even though they take a first-minute lead after the keeper failed to clear. Morton came on for Collins, who had a bloody nose, and O'Rourke dropped back into midfield. Goal-of-the-match was Larkins'. He celebrated wildly.												
36	H	BARNET		5	W	5-0	3-0	McCready 7, Armstrong 23, Cooke 35, [Law 55, Larkin 70]	Guy	Marchant	Rice	Silkman	McCready	Law	Armstrong	Cooke	Larkin	Collins	O'Rourke		
		28/3	1,250	*3*	41				*McClelland*	*Lye*	*Jenkins*	*Ward*	*Embery*	*King*	*Flatt**	*Powell*	*Plume*	*Eason*	*Adams*	*Fusedale*	
								Ref: R Wood	Barnet's season is crumbling, having been unbeaten since New Year's Day. Keeper McClelland blunders twice. Best of the goals was Larkin's diving header which made it 5-0. Former Dons' hero Eddie Reynolds was a spectator at the match, and even he applauded.												
37	A	DARTFORD		3	L	0-3	0-2		Guy	Marchant	Rice	Law	McCready	Silkman	Armstrong	Cooke	Larkin	Collins	O'Rourke		
		1/4	*1,006*	*15*	41			*Stevens 15p, Read 43, Payne 70*	*Morton*	*Read*	*Stevens*	*Richardson*	*Burns*	*Judges*	*Light*	*Payne*	*Mitchell*	*Ripley*	*Halliday*		*P*
								Ref: D Burlingham	Dartford do the double over the Dons. Marchant fells John Ripley and concedes the penalty. All eyes are on Andy Larkin, who has scored four goals in four games. He saw little of the ball, but did put the ball in the net, only to be given offside.												
38	H	GUILDFORD		3	L	2-3	0-2	Cooke 65, 66	Guy	Marchant	Stanley	Silkman	McCready	Law	Armstrong	Cooke	Larkin	Collins	O'Rourke		
		4/4	1,607	*18*	41			*Burge 35, Smith 38, Dobson 78*	*Brooks*	*Sleap*	*Watts*	*More*	*Harris*	*Kerr*	*Smith*	*Malley*	*Burge*	*Tyler*	*Dobson*		*P*
									A thrilling match. Wimbledon are the league's second top scorers, but have let in more goals than anyone else outside the bottom four. They might have been 2-0 up at the break, but found themselves 0-2 down. Cooke squared the match, but defenders stood off as Dobson clinched it.												
39	H	MARGATE		3	D	1-1	1-0	Larkin 16	Guy	Marchant	Stanley	Silkman	McCready	Law	Armstrong	Cooke	Morton*	Collins	Larkin	O'Rourke	
		8/4	1,266	*8*	42			*Jones 57*	*Simpson*	*Clewlow*	*Butterfield*	*Jones*	*Paton*	*Baker*	*Yorath*	*Clayton*	*Barry*	*Brown*	*Baber*		
								Ref: J Hazell	Andy Larkin scores his fifth goal in seven games, and only the crossbar near the end denies him a sixth. Alan Morton was due to be transferred to Poole, but the deal fell through. He plays, and misses badly and often. The four-pace rule catches out Guy, Jones heading in the free-kick.												
40	A	YEOVIL		4	D	1-1	0-0	Morton 63	Guy	Marchant	Stanley	Langford	**Young**	McCready	Law	Cooke	Larkin	Rice	Morton		
		15/4	*2,004*	*14*	43			*Weller 86*	*Clark*	*Herrity*	*Bayliss*	*Hughes*	*Smith*	*Thompson*	*Housley*	*Myers*	*Cotton*	*Grey*	*Wookey*	*Weller*	*P*
								Ref: B Marchant	Roy Law announces his imminent retirement, and Alan Young from Torquay endures a taxing debut. Chris Weller comes off the bench for Yeovil and scores a late equaliser. Morton's volley seemed to have given the Dons both points. Shreeve and Hodges have joined Stevenage.												
41	H	YEOVIL		4	W	2-0	2-0	O'Rourke 8, 25	Guy	Marchant	Stanley	Rice	McCready	Law	Armstrong	Cooke	Larkin*	Langford	O'Rourke	Silkman	
		22/4	1,165	*15*	45				*Clark*	*Herrity*	*Bayliss*	*Hughes*	*Smith*	*Thompson*	*Housley*	*Myers*	*Cotton*	*Gray*	*Wookey*		*P*
								Ref: Harrington	Belated revenge for the 1-5 FA Trophy hammering. Alan Young had to stand down with a tummy bug. Malcolm Stanley was tormented throughout the match by Stuart Housley on the wing. Two Cooke crosses produced goals for O'Rourke. Collins has also joined Stevenage.												
42	A	TELFORD			L	1-2	1-2	Morton 26	Guy	Marchant	Stanley	Rice	Young	McCready	Law	Cooke	Larkin	Langford*	Morton	Silkman	
		29/4	*1,196*		45			*Hart 3, Bentley 23*	*Weir*	*Harris*	*Croft*	*Ross*	*Flowers*	*Coton*	*Ray*	*Fudge*	*Bentley*	*Owen*	*Hart*		*P*
	Average	Home 1,555	*Away 1680*						This is Roy Law's last match. 33-year-old Gerry O'Rourke also contemplates hanging up his boots. But does not. Alan Larkin has proved to be the discovery of the season. Telford's Brian Hart squeezes between Alan Young and Tom McCready to score within three minutes.												

Southern League Cup

Southern League Cup	F-A	H-T	Scorers, Times, and Referees	1	2	3	4	5	6	7	8	9	10	11	12 sub used
1:1 A WATERLOOVILLE	L 1-2	0-0	Cooke 85	Guy	Marchant	Stanley	Rice	McCready	Everitt	Shreeve	Cooke	Morton	Collins	O'Rourke	
13/10 *1,000*			*Dyer 62, Mitchell 80*	*Damarell*	*Wright*	*MacDonald*	*Phillips*	*Kill*	*Avery*	*Dyer*	*Cheverton*	*Allen*	*Bradwell*	*Mitchell*	*P*
(at Fratton Park)				This is Waterlooville's first season as professionals, having previously competed in the Hampshire League. This tie is played at Fratton Park. Selwyn Rice's sloppy back-pass allows Mitchell to put Waterlooville two up, and leave Wimbledon with a mountain to climb.											
1:2 H WATERLOOVILLE 2	L 1-2	1-2	Morton 3p	Guy	Stanley	Everitt*	Rice	McCready	Law	Bailham	O'Rourke	Morton	Collins	Hodges	Cooke P
26/10 1,500			*Allen 6, Cheverton 42*	*Damarell*	*Wright*	*MacDonald*	*Phillips*	*Kill*	*Avery*	*Dyer*	*Cheverton*	*Allen*	*Bradwell*	*Mitchell*	*P*
			(Dons lose 2-4 on aggregate)	Almost every visiting player stands six feet or more. Though Wimbledon quickly square the aggregate scores with a penalty for handball, they trail once again to a quickly taken free-kick, and are scuppered before half-time by a shot from improbably long range.											

FA Cup

FA Cup	F-A	H-T	Scorers, Times, and Referees	1	2	3	4	5	6	7	8	9	10	11	12 sub used
4Q A MARGATE	L 0-1	0-1		Guy	Marchant	Stanley	Rice	McCready	Law	Bailham	Cooke	Morton	O'Rourke	Hodges	
6/11 *1,365*			*Baber 20*	*Brodie*	*Yorath*	*Butterfield*	*Clayton*	*Wickens*	*Houston*	*Baber*	*King*	*Baker*	*Brown*	*Johnson*	*P*
				Everitt's preference is unashamedly to play for a draw, even though the Dons won here 3-2 in the league. Morton drops back to add weight to the defence. Margate winger John Baber always saves his best for Wimbledon, and smashes the winner from the angle of the penalty box.											

FA Trophy

FA Trophy	F-A	H-T	Scorers, Times, and Referees	1	2	3	4	5	6	7	8	9	10	11	12 sub used
1 H YEOVIL 5	L 1-5	0-3	Hurley 77 *[Cotton 47, 85]*	Guy	Stanley	Everitt	Silkman	McCready	Law*	Hodges	Cooke	Hurley	Bailham	Armstrong	Morton
22/1 1,967 *12*			*Myers 15, 43, Thompson 35,*	*Clark*	*Herrity*	*Bayliss*	*Myers*	*Smith*	*Thompson*	*Housley*	*Jones*	*Cotton*	*Weller*	*Clancy*	
			Ref: J Bent	Crisis. The Dons have toppled at the first hurdle of every cup competition. Dons fans stay behind at the end, baying for Mike Everitt's blood. The players, too, are mocked and jeered as never before. Yeovil also eliminated Wimbledon from this competition last season.											

	Home						Away					
	P	W	D	L	F	A	W	D	L	F	A	Pts
1 Chelmsford	42	16	4	1	65	15	12	2	7	44	31	62
2 Hereford *	42	13	6	2	41	15	11	6	4	27	15	60
3 Dover	42	15	3	3	35	13	5	8	8	32	32	51
4 Barnet	42	13	5	3	51	18	8	2	11	29	39	49
5 Dartford	42	15	4	2	49	16	5	4	12	26	52	48
6 Weymouth	42	14	4	3	44	17	7	1	13	25	26	47
7 Yeovil	42	14	4	3	45	19	4	7	10	22	32	47
8 Hillingdon B	42	15	2	4	46	19	5	4	12	18	39	46
9 Margate	42	12	3	6	42	30	7	5	9	32	38	46
10 WIMBLEDON	42	14	4	3	50	24	5	3	13	25	40	45
11 Romford	42	10	7	4	34	23	6	6	9	20	26	45
12 Guildford	42	15	4	2	50	20	5	1	15	21	45	45
13 Telford	42	14	2	5	60	29	4	5	12	23	39	43
14 Nuneaton B	42	12	6	3	30	12	4	4	13	16	35	42
15 Bedford	42	12	6	3	40	22	4	3	14	19	44	41
16 Worcester	42	14	2	5	32	15	3	5	13	14	42	41
17 Cambridge C	42	9	6	6	45	32	3	8	10	23	39	38
18 Folkestone	42	10	4	7	38	24	4	3	14	20	40	35
19 Poole	42	6	4	11	24	33	3	7	11	17	39	29
20 Bath	42	10	3	8	25	23	1	1	19	20	63	26
21 Merthyr Tyd	42	4	5	12	19	33	3	3	15	10	60	22
22 Gravesend	42	4	3	14	17	44	1	3	17	13	66	16
* *Football Lge*	924	261	91	110	882	496	110	91	261	496	882	924

Odds & ends

Double wins: (3) Gravesend, Bath, Merthyr Tydfil.
Double losses: (3) Dartford, Chelmsford, Guildford.

Won from behind: (3) Folkestone (h), Margate (a), Bath (a).
Lost from in front: (1) Bedford (a).

High spots: 7 consecutive league wins in Sept and Oct to go top.

Low spots: Dreadful run in Jan and Feb that brings three heavy defeats.
Just one win in the last 7, dropping from 3rd to 10th.
64 league goals conceded is the Dons' worst in the Southern League.

Player of the Year: Roy Law.
Ever-presents: (2) Dickie Guy, Tom McCready.
Hat-tricks: (0).
Leading scorer: Ian Cooke (21).

	Appearances					Goals				
	Lge	Sub	SLC	FAC	FAT	Lge	SLC	FAC	FAT	Total
Armstrong, David	**23**				1	**5**				**5**
Bailham, Eddie	**19**		1	1	1	**8**				**8**
Collins, Jimmy	**26**		2			**2**				**2**
Cooke, Ian	**37**		1/1	1	1	**20**	1			**21**
Davidson, Alan		(1)								
Everitt, Mlke	**16**		2		1					
Guy, Dickie	**42**		2	1	1					
Hodges, Paul	**11**		1	1	1					
Hurley, Chris	**10**				1	**1**			1	**2**
Langford, Steve	**4**									
Larkin, Andy	**10**					**5**				**5**
Law, Roy	**32**		1	1	1	**1**				**1**
McCready, Tom	**42**		2	1	1	**6**				**6**
Marchant, Andy	**35**		1	1						
Morton, Alan	**28**	(1)	2	1	0/1	**13**	1			**14**
O'Rourke, Gerry	**33**	(2)	2	1		**6**				**6**
Rice, Selwyn	**31**		2	1		**4**				**4**
Shreeve, Peter	**11**	(1)	1							
Silkman, Barry	**18**	(2)			1	**2**				**2**
Smith, Graham	**2**	(2)								
Stanley, Malcolm	**30**		2	1	1					
Young, Alan	**2**									
(own-goals)						**2**				**2**
22 players used	**462**	**(9)**	**22/1**	**11**	**11/1**	**75**	**2**		**1**	**78**

No	Date	Att	Pos	Pts	F-A	H-T	Scorers, Times, and Referees	1	2	3	4	5	6	7	8	9	10	11	12 sub used
1	A WATERLOOVILLE			D	1-1	0-1	O'Rourke 47	Guy	**Stockley**	**Loughlan**	Everitt	Young	McCready	**Summerhill**	Cooke	Larkin	Silkman	O'Rourke	
	12/8	*950*		1			*Dyer 25*	*Dyke*	*Rice*	*Stones*	*Phillips*	*Kill*	*Avery*	*Dyer*	*Bradwell*	*Allen*	*Cheverton*	*Jack*	
								Newly promoted Waterlooville are Portsmouth FC's nursery club. Mike Everitt leaves Armstrong out to play a defensive 4-4-2 away from home. Waterlooville's Barry Allen blames his new boots for denying him a hat-trick. The Dons put up the shutters in the second half.											
2	A NUNEATON B			D	0-0	0-0		Guy	Marchant	Loughlan	Silkman	McCready	Summerhill	Rice	Cooke	Larkin	Stockley	O'Rourke	
	14/8	***3,843***		2				*Robinson*	*Harris*	*Bridgett*	*Goodfellow*	*Gill*	*Lewis*	*Shepherd*	*Baker*	*Franklin*	*Smith*	*Turpie*	
							Ref: W Jones	Mike Everitt has signed a two-year contract and been told that money is available for new players. David Pleat's Boro are never threatened, for the simple reason that Wimbledon never attacked. Near the end Guy carried the ball outside his area. 21 players came up for the free-kick.											
3	H BARNET			D	1-1	1-0	Larkin 30	Guy	Stockley!	Loughlan	Summerhill	Young	McCready	Rice	Cooke	Larkin	Everitt	Armstrong	
	19/8	**1,850**		3			*Powell 50*	*McClelland*	*Lye*	*Fusedale*	*Ward*	*Embery*	*King*	*Powell*	*Ferry*	*Flatt*	*Thom*	*Adams*	
							Ref: M Taylor	No prisoners taken in a match that produced four bookings and one sending off – Bob Stockley, on the hour – for a blatant foul on Powell. Even with a man more, Barnet – minus strikers Davis and Eason – could not press home their numerical advantage, and drop their first point.											
4	A POOLE			D	0-0	0-0		Guy	Marchant	Loughlan	Stockley	Young	McCready	Summerhill	Cooke	Larkin*	Rice	O'Rourke	Armstrong
	26/8	*608*		4				*Buck*	*Hill*	*Arrowsmith*	*Bazeley*	*Pegram*	*Priscott*	*White*	*Putnam*	*Johnson*	*Manns*	*Ames*	
								Poole lost seven goals to Chelmsford last time out, so Wimbledon's fourth successive draw is hardly cause for celebration. After being sent off against Barnet, Stockley behaves himself against his old club. Best effort for Poole saw Young hook off the line, while Rice hit the Poole bar.											
5	H ROMFORD		11	W	3-1	0-0	McCready 49, Silkman 65, Armstrong 85	Guy	Marchant	Loughlan	Silkman	McCready	Langford	Armstrong	Cooke	Larkin	Summerhill	O'Rourke	Stockley
	2/9	1,088	*4*	6			*Hearn 89*	*Lightfoot*	*Howe*	*Obeney*	*Sorrell*	*Robinson*	*Bickles*	*Sanderson*	*Newton*	*Hearn*	*Manning*	*Hudson*	
							Ref: J Bellamy	Romford hadn't conceded a goal in six and a half matches. Then Tom McCready, up with the attack, stoops to head in Armstrong's free-kick. Best of the goals was Wimbledon's third. A string of passes sent Larkin clear. He rounded Lightfoot in goal and Armstrong tapped it in.											
6	H NUNEATON B		12	D	1-1	1-1	Silkman 25p	Guy	Marchant	Loughlan	Silkman	McCready	Langford	Armstrong	Cooke	Larkin	Summerhill	O'Rourke	
	5/9	1,083	*17*	7			*Franklin 44*	*Robinson*	*Harris*	*Bridgett*	*Harris*	*Gill*	*Swift*	*Baker*	*Shepherd*	*Franklin*	*Lewis*	*Turpie*	
							Ref: J Bellamy	After two minutes skipper Loughlan hits the bar from long range. The penalty was a curious affair, given by a linesman as Robinson cleared off the line for Boro. The ref had seen nothing wrong, but pointed to the spot. Just before the interval Franklin turned Harris's shot past Guy.											
7	A TELFORD			W	2-1	0-0	Armstrong 60, Cooke 65	Guy	Marchant	Loughlan	Rice	Langford	McCready	O'Rourke	Stockley	Larkin*	Summerhill	Armstrong	Cooke
	9/9	*1,150*		9			*Fudge 75p*	*Irvine*	*Harris*	*Croft*	*Ray*	*Ross*	*Carr*	*Fudge*	*Owen*	*Bentley*	*Coaton**	*Jagger*	*Thompson*
								Only goal-average keeps the Dons off the top now, as they become the first team to win on Telford's spacious pitch. Armstrong ghosted past two defenders for the first goal; substitute Ian Cooke heads in the second; and a penalty against Marchant rounds off the scoring.											
8	H DARTFORD		5	D	1-1	0-1	Stockley 60	Guy	Marchant	Loughlan	Rice*	Langford	McCready	Armstrong	Cooke	Stockley	Summerhill	O'Rourke	Silkman
	12/9	1,086	*12*	10			*Burns 8*	*Morton*	*Read*	*Stevens*	*Burns*	*Fogg*	*Judge*	*Light*	*Richardson*	*Mitchell*	*Payne*	*Halliday*	
							Ref: R Ridden	A lucky point for the Dons keeps alive their unbeaten record and extends their best-ever start. Young, Everitt, and Larkin are all out injured. Burns put Dartford in front, blasting back Marchant's clearance from a corner. Stockley levelled, striking a rebound off a defensive wall.											
9	A DARTFORD		6	L	0-3	0-1		Guy	Marchant	Rice	Silkman	Young	McCready	Armstrong	Cooke	**MacHattie**	Summerhill	O'Rourke	
	19/9	*678*	*15*	10			*Smith 8, Richardson 50, Burns 90p*	*Morton*	*Read*	*Stevens*	*Burns*	*Fogg*	*Judges*	*Light*	*Richardson*	*Mitchell*	*Payne*	*Smith*	*P*
							Ref: J Hazell	The first defeat of this season, but the fourth on the trot on Dartford's sloping pitch. With only 11 fit players, Everitt fields Palace triallist Ian MacHattie. Dartford led from the eighth minute, when Brian Smith hammered Read's free-kick past Guy. Young conceded the penalty.											
10	A BEDFORD		9	W	1-0	0-0	McCready 80	Guy	Marchant	Loughlan	Silkman	Young	McCready	Armstrong	Cooke	Everitt	Summerhill	O'Rourke	
	23/9	*1,203*	*5*	12				*Alexander*	*Skinn*	*Foulds*	*Townsend*	*Garvey*	*Scurr*	*Horrey*	*Rodney*	*Sorbie*	*Boyds*	*Silous*	
							Ref: T Hardman	Bedford's second defeat of the season is brought about after O'Rourke cut in from the wing and rounded two defenders. By that time both teams were playing for a shameless goalless draw. In Bedford's case, that was down to starting the match without both their leading scorers.											

No		Opponent	Pos	Res	F-A	H-T	Scorers, Times, and Referees	1	2	3	4	5	6	7	8	9	10	11	12	
11	H	BURTON ALB	7	W	**4-0**	2-0	Silkman 3, Cooke 36, Armstrong 50, 86	Guy	Marchant	Loughlan	Silkman	Young	McCready	Armstrong	Everitt*	Cooke	Summerhill	O'Rourke	Rice	
30/9		1,230	*19*	14				*Allsop*	*Goodwin*	*Norman*	*Hickton*	*Annable*	*Goodall*	*Cowlishaw*	*Brown*	*Naylor*	*Beresford*	*Wright*		*P*
							Ref: C Dixon	Silkman and Armstrong have the crowd in raptures with their ball skills. Albion keeper Mick Allsop appears to let his attention wander – he's getting wed the next day – for he flaps foolishly at Silkman's undemanding early lob. Pick of the goals was Armstrong's, from Cooke's pass.												
12	A	WEYMOUTH	7	L	1-3	1-1	Summerhill 35	Guy	Marchant	Loughlan	Everitt	Young	McCready	Armstrong	Silkman	Cooke	Summerhill	O'Rourke		
14/10		*1,350*	*6*	14			*Skirton 21, 72, Beer 59*	*Clarke*	*Rounsevell*	*Escudier*	*Williams*	*Hobson*	*Miller*	*Adams*	*Bimpson*	*Pound*	*Skirton*	*Beer*		*P*
							Ref: P Ackrill	In earlier times Alan Skirton played 144 league games for Arsenal. A week before this match he played in the South African Cup Final in front of 50,000 spectators. Now he celebrates his Weymouth debut with two goals. The other was scored by promising teenager Micky Beer.												
13	A	MARGATE		W	3-0	0-0	Armstrong 60, 89, Cooke 75	Guy	Marchant	Loughlan	Rice	McCready	Summerhill	Armstrong	Silkman	Cooke	Everitt	O'Rourke		
28/10		*1,316*		16				*Brodie*	*Summers*	*Butterfield*	*Jones*	*Clewlow*	*Houston*	*Baber*	*Clayton*	*Barry*	*Brown*	*Walker*	*Fusco*	
								After two soul-sapping cup defeats, this win was vital. Silkman and Armstrong return to form to inflict Margate's first home reverse. With the wind and slope at their backs after half-time, Armstrong flashes a 30-yard free-kick into the net. But where was this form in the cups?												
14	H	WATERLOOVILLE	9	D	1-1	1-0	Everitt 8	Guy	Marchant	Loughlan	Rice	McCready	Summerhill	Armstrong	Everitt	Cooke	Silkman	O'Rourke		
4/11		1,147	*19*	17			*Phillips 67*	*Dyke*	*Hare*	*Wright*	*Phillips*	*Kill*	*Avery*	*Mitchell*	*Slaymaker**	*Pointer*	*Cheverton*	*Jack*	*Allen*	
							Ref: W Whittington	Everitt needs a striker desperately. Seconds after Waterlooville equalise, John Kill handles on the line but Barry Silkman wastes the penalty. Keeper Dyke had gifted the Dons the lead, when his clearance was charged down, and ex-England Ray Pointer crosses to level the scores.												
15	H	WEYMOUTH	9	D	1-1	0-1	Loughlan 53	Guy	Marchant	Loughlan	Rice	McCready	Summerhill	Armstrong	**White**	Cooke	Silkman	O'Rourke		
11/11		1,324	*4*	18			*Williams 24*	*Clarke*	*Rounsevell*	*Escudier*	*Williams*	*Hobson*	*Miller*	*Skirton*	*Simpson*	*Pound*	*Brown*	*Beer*		*P*
							Ref: I Walton	Teenager Tony White, who is black, plays his first game for Wimbledon. Summerhill and Loughlan get into a tangle to present Weymouth with their goal. Loughlan redeems himself with a shot that appears to be going wide until it hits the back-peddling Williams.												
16	H	DOVER	9	L	0-1	0-0		Guy	Marchant	Loughlan	Stockley	McCready	Summerhill	Armstrong	White	Cooke	Silkman	O'Rourke		
18/11		1,000	*3*	18			*Cutler 89*	*Gadsby*	*Reynolds*	*Hall*	*Tranter*	*Carragher*	*Carter*	*Johnson*	*Robinson*	*MacHattie*	*Stevenson*	*Moy*	*Cutler*	
							Ref: J Birden	Rampant Dover ended Romford's unbeaten home record last week, and Wimbledon's this. Their team includes Ian MacHattie, who played for the Dons two months earlier. Just before substitute Cutler scored the last-minute winner, Wimbledon hit the goal-post at the other end.												
17	A	WORCESTER	10	D	1-1	1-0	Cooke 28	Guy	Marchant	Loughlan	Langford	McCready	Summerhill	Stockley	Cooke	Larkin	Everitt	O'Rourke		
25/11		*1,094*	*8*	19			*Kelchure 89*	*Knight*	*Allen*	*Langford*	*Aggio*	*Hadley*	*Merrick*	*Jones*	*Inglis*	*Kelchure*	*Martin*	*Chester*		
							Ref: B Mullen	With Silkman and Armstrong out with flu, Everitt packs his team with defenders. Andy Larkin returns after fracturing his shin, but has a predictably quiet game. Worcester are unbeaten at home in 19, but rely on Bryan Kelchure's 11th of the season, as Guy mishandles.												
18	A	HILLINGDON B	10	L	1-2	1-1	Silkman 43	Guy	Marchant	Loughlan	Stockley	McCready	Summerhill	Armstrong	Cooke	Larkin	Silkman	O'Rourke		
9/12		*624*	*20*	19			*Neilson 16, Bishop 68*	*Lowe*	*Ryan*	*Archer*	*Higginson*	*Roach*	*Moore*	*Neilson*	*Peachey*	*Reeve*	*Bishop*	*Harris*		*P*
							Ref: P Hough	Three wins out of three has lifted Hillingdon off the bottom, and they are indubitably the better team. Wimbledon's best chance of squaring the match fell to Barry Silkman eight minutes before the end. Dancing past defenders he forces a super save, and sinks to his knees in frustration.												
19	H	YEOVIL	10	L	0-2	0-1		Guy	Stockley	Loughlan	Rice	McCready	Summerhill	Armstrong	Everitt	Larkin*	Cooke	O'Rourke	Silkman	
16/12		906	*3*	19			*Thompson 35, Clancy 76*	*Clark*	*Spencer*	*Smith*	*Bertram*	*Cotton*	*Myers*	*Housley*	*Weller*	*Brown*	*Thompson*	*Clancy*		*P*
							Ref: J Jode	It is now six without a win for dismal Dons, and they appear to offer little resistance against a demoralised side knocked out of two cups in two weeks. For the second half Mike Everitt pushes himself forward into attack, but Wimbledon never get a sniff of a goal.												
20	A	BURTON ALB	10	W	1-0	1-0	Larkin 39	Guy	Stockley	Loughlan	Rice	McCready	Summerhill	Armstrong	Cooke	Larkin	Silkman	O'Rourke		
23/12		*546*	*21*	21				*Allsop*	*Goodwin*	*Norman*	*Stewart*	*Beresford*	*Annable*	*Hickton*	*Mattershead*	*Brown*	*Naylor*	*Wright*		*P*
							Ref: B Marchant	Albion are sent to the bottom by Andy Larkin, who flicked in O'Rourke's free-kick at the near post. Wimbledon did most of the defending, and were indebted to Loughlan's clearance off the goal-line from Burton's leading scorer, Graham Brown.												
21	H	GUILDFORD	10	W	3-0	0-0	Armstrong 62, 70p, Larkin 65	Guy	Stockley	Loughlan	Rice	McCready	Summerhill	Armstrong	Cooke	Larkin	Silkman	O'Rourke		
26/12		961	*15*	23				*Brooks*	*Peters*	*Westburgh*	*Watts*	*Harris*	*More*	*Dobson*	*Tyler*	*Burge*	*Malley*	*Kerr*		*P*
							Ref: D Drewitt	For an hour Guildford had the better of this match, but Guy was at his most defiant. Then Kerr nudges Armstrong's shot wide of Brooks. The penalty came when Larkin was pulled down in the box. Armstrong was entrusted with taking it.												

No	Date	Opponent	Att	Pos	Pts	F-A	H-T	Scorers, Times, and Referees	1	2	3	4	5	6	7	8	9	10	11	12 sub used
22	A	BARNET			L	1-2	0-0	O'Rourke 66	Guy	Stockley	Loughlan	Rice	McCready	Summerhill	Armstrong	Cooke	Larkin	Silkman	O'Rourke	
	30/12		*1,271*		23			*Powell 49, Davies 79*	*Woodend*	*Fusedale**	*Plume*	*Fascione*	*Tom*	*Godfrey*	*Powell*	*Ferry*	*Cogger*	*Davies*	*George*	*Embery*
								Ref: J Roost	O'Rourke's 85th minute header is cleared off the line to prevent a merited Wimbledon equaliser. Woodend makes his debut in the Barnet goal. Barnet went 1-0 up against the run of play when Powell's blistering shot was saved at full stretch by Guy. Davies ran in the loose ball.											
23	H	BEDFORD		10	W	1-0	0-0	McCready 88	Guy	Stockley	Loughlan	Rice	McCready	Summerhill	Armstrong	Cooke	Larkin	Silkman	O'Rourke	
	6/1		906	*7*	25				*Alexander*	*Skinn*	*Cooley*	*Scurr*	*Townsend*	*Boyd*	*Walker*	*Cleary*	*Garvey*	*Folds*	*Adams*	
								Ref: D Jackman	Ultra-defensive Bedford are two minutes from their objective. Player-manager Brian Garvey wears No 9 but plays in the back four. Inspired goalkeeping by Alec Alexander keeps the Dons at bay, but even he is powerless against Tom McCready's late header.											
24	H	FOLKESTONE		8	W	4-1	1-1	Summerhill 18, Cooke 65, Marchant 86,	Guy	Stockley	Loughlan	Rice	McCready	Summerhill	Armstrong	Cooke	White*	Silkman	O'Rourke	Marchant
	13/1		932	*21*	27			*Harfield 32* [McCready 89]	*Bowley*	*Woodridge*	*Crook*	*Dawson*	*Pearce*	*Weston*	*Lazarus*	*Shovellar*	*Whitington*	*Sharp*	*Harfield*	
								Ref: J Tree	Folkestone have signed striker Eric Whitington from Crawley. Mike Everitt had pursued him relentlessly, but the Wimbledon board would not pay the £1,500 fee. Whitington has a good game, but does not score. Wimbledon striker Andy Larkin misses the game with flu.											
25	H	TELFORD		7	W	2-1	1-0	Cooke 15, 90	Guy	Stockley	McCready	Summerhill	Loughlan	Silkman	Rice	Armstrong	Marchant	O'Rourke	Cooke	
	27/1		1,068	*6*	29			*Fudge 80*	*Irvine*	*Harris*	*Croft*	*Ray*	*Fairhurst*	*Ross*	*Fudge*	*Owen*	*Bentley*	*Nicholls*	*Jagger*	
								Ref: W Dance	Wimbledon are enjoying a good spell. This is their fifth win in six in the league, secured in the last seconds when Ross almost puts into his own goal. Irvine keeps the ball out, but Cooke is on hand. Micky Fudge, who scored a hat-trick on his WBA debut, had levelled for Telford.											
26	A	ROMFORD		7	L	**1-4**	1-3	Silkman 29	Guy	Stockley	Loughlan	Rice	Silkman	Marchant	Armstrong	Cooke	O'Rourke	McCready	Summerhill	
	29/1		*1,062*	*13*	29			*Sanders 16, 80, Chandler 20, Tapping 23*	*Lightfoot*	*Obeney*	*Tapping*	*Bailey*	*Robinson*	*Bickles*	*Sanders*	*Amato*	*Chandler*	*Manning*	*Hudson*	
								Ref: J Christopher	Ian Cooke misses at one end and Romford immediately score at the other. Roy Sanders, stocky and bald, volleys the first instalment of his hat-trick. He completes it with a hook while almost on his backside. Romford have averaged barely a goal a match: this is their biggest win.											
27	A	FOLKESTONE		7	L	1-2	1-0	Cooke 14	Guy	Stockley	Loughlan	Rice	McCready	Summerhill	Armstrong	Marchant	Cooke	Silkman	O'Rourke	
	3/2		*1,026*	*20*	29			*Whittington 59, Shovellar 66*	*Bowley*	*Wooldridge*	*Crook*	*Tredwell*	*Pearce*	*Bentley*	*Lazarus*	*Shovellar*	*Whitington*	*Harfield*	*Chambers*	
								Ref: J Cook	Folkestone started so timidly that defensive-minded Dons had no choice but to attack. Ian Cooke puts them ahead at the second attempt. After half-time ex-QPR and Orient winger Mark Lazarus goes on the rampage. Guy struggles with both goals following a collision with Whitington.											
28	A	KETTERING		9	D	1-1	1-0	O'Rourke 28	Guy	Stockley	Marchant	Rice	Langford	Summerhill	Armstrong	Everitt	Cooke	Silkman	O'Rourke	
	17/2		*2,281*	*2*	30			*Pawley 56*	*Dighton*	*Ashby*	*Goodall*	*Atkinson*	*Peck*	*Keirnan*	*Harrington*	*Clayton*	*Webster*	*Jones*	*Pawley*	
								Ref: J Simms	Kettering are unbeaten at home. They trailed for half an hour, though Dighton got a hand to O'Rourke's header. But once Pawley had fired the equaliser, after a short free-kick had been touched to him, only the gods kept the Dons' goal intact. Pawley came nearest, hitting the bar.											
29	H	CAMBRIDGE C		9	W	1-0	1-0	Cooke 43	Guy	Stockley	Loughlan	Rice	Langford	Summerhill	Marchant	Larkin	Cooke	Silkman*	O'Rourke	Everitt
	24/2		1,311	*5*	32				*Barker*	*Murray J*	*Way*	*Murray M*	*James*	*McDonald!*	*Jones*	*Bailham*	*Knight*	*Keenan*	*Marshall*	
								Ref: P Hough	Near half-time Murray whacked Silkman so severely on the ankle that the Dons' midfielder had to hobble off. Substitute Mike Everitt immediately crossed for the only goal. The second premature exit was that of City skipper Alan McDonald, for punching Ian Cooke.											
30	A	RAMSGATE			L	1-3	0-2	Smith 84	Guy	Stockley	Loughlan	Rice	Summerhill	Everitt	Armstrong	Smith	Larkin	Marchant	O'Rourke	
	27/2		***402***		32			*Cassidy 3, Fusco 38, Cutler 66*	*Huddart*	*Taylor*	*Lloyd*	*Burton*	*Priestley*	*Fusco*	*Godfrey*	*Swain*	*Cassidy*	*Cutler*	*Stanley*	
									Bill Cassidy was once so prolific for Chelmsford. He gives struggling Ramsgate an early lead and the Dons never recover. Swain's free-kick was hooked in by Cutler to make it 0-3. Graham Smith scores for Wimbledon on his first appearance of the season.											
31	A	CAMBRIDGE C		8	L	0-2	0-1		Guy	Marchant	Loughlan	Rice	Langford	Summerhill	**Ware**	Everitt	O'Rourke	Smith	White	
	3/3		*1,373*	*11*	32			*Bailham 26, 58*	*Barker*	*Way*	*Keenan*	*Murray M*	*James*	*McDonald*	*Jones*	*Bailham*	*Hunter*	*Marshall*	*Conmy*	
								Ref: K Clark	Former-Don Eddie Bailham proves to be a revelation for Cambridge City. Not only does he score twice against Wimbledon: his 24 goals this season will make him the division's third highest scorer. Everitt's dreadful tackle on ex-Tottenham Cliff Jones almost provokes a riot.											

32	H	KETTERING		11		W	2-1	0-0	Armstrong 52, O'Rourke 69	Guy	Marchant	Loughlan	Rice	Langford	Summerhill	Armstrong	Everitt	O'Rourke	Silkman	Smith	
		10/3	1,002	*3*	34				*Clayton 85*	*Dighton*	*Ashby*	*Goodall*	*Atkinson*	*Peck*	*Kiernan*	*Harrington*	*Clayton*	*Webster*	*Jones*	*Hastie*	
									Ref: D Gent	Kettering field Ron Atkinson and £8,000 signing from Oxford Utd, Roy Clayton, who pulls his new team back near the end. The game is won for Wimbledon by Armstrong's shot from 25 yards, followed by O'Rourke's header. Kettering try to sign Phil Neal from Northampton.											
33	A	CHELMSFORD				L	0-1	0-0		Guy	Marchant	Loughlan	Rice	McCready	Summerhill	Armstrong	Everitt	O'Rourke	Silkman	Larkin	
		16/3	*2,701*		34				*Coakley 57*	*Taylor*	*Coakley*	*Gomershall*	*Delea*	*Loughton*	*Tomkins*	*Dilsworth*	*Barnard*	*Woolcott*	*Grant*	*Lewis*	
										Chelmsford captain Tommy Coakley settles the outcome with a long-range winner. The home crowd were becoming restless when he advanced, shaped to cross, then blasted past Guy from 30 yards. Tom McCready had returned to the Wimbledon team.											
34	H	RAMSGATE		11		D	1-1	1-0	Silkman 44	Guy	Marchant	Loughlan	Rice	McCready	Summerhill	Armstrong	Everitt	O'Rourke	Silkman	Larkin	
		20/3	769	*18*	35				*Flanagan 80*	*Huddart*	*Taylor*	*Lloyd*	*Burton*	*Priestley*	*Fusco*	*Godfrey*	*Swain*	*Cassidy*	*Cutler*	*Flanagan*	
									Ref: J Marshall	England amateur international Tony Bass is the latest striker to turn down a move to Plough Lane. In desperation, Everitt plays Barry Silkman up front, but despite his goal he looks completely lost. Andy Larkin was also asked to play out of position, wide on the left.											
35	H	MARGATE		12		W	1-0	1-0	Larkin 8	Guy	Marchant	McCready	Summerhill	Loughlan	Rice	Silkman	Armstrong	Larkin	Cooke*	O'Rourke	Everitt
		24/3	798	*9*	37					*Brodie*	*Clewlow*	*Summers*	*Sawyer*	*Breach*	*Houston*	*Baber*	*Clayton*	*Barry*	*Brown*	*Walker*	*Smith*
									Ref: B Stockley	A frozen pitch covered with mud contributes to this wretchedly boring spectacle. Chic Brodie presents Larkin with a gift goal. Just before the break Steve Breach thunders into Ian Cooke, and the Wimbledon forward is carried off, to be substituted by the manager.											
36	H	WORCESTER		9		D	0-0	0-0		Guy	Marchant	Loughlan	Rice	McCready	Summerhill	Armstrong	**Tuite**	O'Rourke	Silkman	Larkin	
		31/3	**760**	*6*	38					*Knight*	*Allen*	*Langford*	*Aggio*	*Bache*	*Merrick*	*Hadley*	*Inglis*	*Belcher*	*Martin*	*Jones*	
									Ref: C MacKnight	Alan Summerhill and Andy Marchant have not been retained for next season. Everitt gives a debut to 18-year-old Tommy Tuite. Transfer-listed Gerry O'Rourke heads against a post and twice shoots against keeper Knight's body. A woefully small crowd attends the match.											
37	A	YEOVIL		10		L	0-2	0-1		Guy	Marchant	Loughlan	Rice	McCready	**Bennett**	Armstrong	Summerhill	O'Rourke	Silkman*	Larkin	Smith
		7/4	*3,727*	*3*	38				*Trebilcock 39, Thompson 51*	*Clark*	*Cottle*	*Smith*	*Bertram*	*Cotton*	*Myers*	*Housley*	*Trebilcock*	*Brown*	*Thompson*	*Clancy*	
									Ref: V Templar	This reconstructed Dons side never threatened title-chasing Yeovil. Summerhill was asked to play in attack, and 18-year-old Willie Bennett instructed to mark on-loan Mike Trebilcock, who scored two goals in the 1966 FA Cup Final. Trebilcock wins this unequal battle.											
38	H	CHELMSFORD		9		D	1-1	1-0	Armstrong 4p	Guy	Marchant	Loughlan	Rice	McCready	Bennett	Armstrong	Cooke*	O'Rourke	Smith	Larkin	Silkman
		10/4	989	*2*	39				*Smith 54*	*Taylor*	*Coakley*	*Gomershall*	*Delea*	*Loughton*	*Tomkins*	*Dilsworth*	*Barnard*	*Woolcott*	*Grant*	*Smith*	
									Ref: R East	A quick lead for Wimbledon as Loughton pushes O'Rourke in the box, and Armstrong is equal to the penalty. A set-piece brings Chelmsford level. Coakley's free-kick is parried by Guy and Bobby Smith taps in. Silkman takes the eye when he comes on for the last five minutes.											
39	H	HILLINGDON B		11		D	2-2	1-0	Armstrong 7, McCready 56	Guy	Marchant	Loughlan	Silkman	McCready	Bennett	Armstrong	Cooke	Summerhill	Smith	Larkin	
		17/4	947	*15*	40				*Harris 65p, Bishop 77*	*Lowe*	*Butler*	*Archer*	*Ryan*	*Roach*	*Titterton*	*Neilson*	*Peachey*	*Reeve*	*Bishop*	*Harris*	
									Ref: C Smith	Gerry O'Rourke has signed for Chelmsford. Bennett and Summerhill look ill-equipped to take his place up front. Wimbledon's two-goal lead is halved when Boro's Harris falls over in the area and wins a penalty. Even after Hillingdon equalise, McCready hits a post.											
40	H	POOLE				W	2-1	0-1	Marchant 64, Larkin 77	Guy	Marchant	Loughlan	Silkman	McCready	**Bryant**	Armstrong	Cooke	Tuite*	Smith	Larkin	Stockley
		20/4	870		42				*Priscott 44*	*Buck*	*Bazeley*	*Pegram*	*Carr*	*Eyden*	*Rawlings*	*Walker*	*Priscott*	*Hill*	*Brankin*	*Calloway*	
										Relegation-haunted Poole snatch a half-time lead, and seek to defend it in the second half by any means, with skipper Pegram setting a brutal example. His tactics backfire when Marchant lobs Walker and then goalkeeper Buck to level the scores. Poole win no points and few friends.											
41	A	DOVER				L	0-2	0-0		Guy	Stockley	Loughlan	Silkman	McCready	Bryant	Armstrong	Cooke	Summerhill	Smith	Marchant	
		21/4	*1,069*		42				*Robinson 64, Moy 80*	*Gadsby*	*Reynolds*	*Hamshare*	*Kurila*	*Carragher*	*Stevenson*	*Arnott*	*Robinson*	*Moss*	*Moy*	*Fursdon*	*MacHattie*
										Dover will be pipped for the title by two points, so they cannot hold Wimbledon responsible for their failure. Dover complete a comfortable double, with Moy and Stevenson behind all their better moves. Yet again Armstrong failed to impress against his former team-mates.											
42	A	GUILDFORD		10		L	2-3	1-1	Cooke 16, 60	Guy	Marchant	Loughlan	Silkman	McCready	Bryant	Armstrong	Cooke	Summerhill	Smith	Larkin	
		23/4	*862*	*20*	42				*Malley 40p, Tyler 47, Burge 75*	*Brooks*	*Peters*	*Westburgh*	*Watts*	*Harris*	*Glozier*	*Smith*	*Malley*	*Burge*	*Tyler*	*Dobson*	
	Home	*Away*							Ref: C Smith	Guildford's premier survival is in their own hands. Anything less than two points and Guildford would be relegated. They take advantage of Loughlan's foul to cancel Cooke's opener. Tyler's corner is then cleared off the line, the linesman signals a goal, and Guy goes berserk.											
Average	1,064	*1,468*																			

Southern League Cup	F-A	H-T	Scorers, Times, and Referees	1	2	3	4	5	6	7	8	9	10	11	12 sub used
1:1 H BOGNOR REGIS	W 4-0	3-0	Armstong 26, Marchant 28, Everitt 40,	Guy	Marchant	Loughlan	Summerhill	Young	McCready	Armstrong	Cooke	Larkin	Everitt*	O'Rourke	Rice
22/8 1,241			[Cooke 60]	*Doon*	*Edwards*	*Knight*	*Pearce*	*Hedley*	*Edwards*	*Allport*	*Borlace*	*Woon*	*Wiltshire*	*Fitzjohn*	
			Ref: G Keeble	League newcomers Bognor provide Mike Everitt with his first knock-out victory in any competition. Armstrong paves the way following a mesmerising run at a retreating defence. Marchant then floats over a cross, O'Rourke decoys, and the ball falls beyond keeper Doon.											
1:2 A BOGNOR REGIS	W 1-0	1-0	O'Rourke 29	Guy	Marchant	Loughlan	Silkman	Young*	McCready	Armstrong	Cooke	Larkin	Summerhill	O'Rourke	Stockley
30/8 *575*				*Minto*	*Pearce*	*Hedley*	*Bennett*	*Turnhill*	*Allport*	*Prebble*	*Croney*	*Woon*	*Knight*	*Aylward*	
			Ref: K Guilder (Dons win 5-0 on aggregate)	Bognor have only their reputations to safeguard. In truth, they deserved better than to lose this meaningless second leg, settled by O'Rourke's shot on the run. Bognor don't have any floodlights, and it was dark by the time the referee called a halt.											
2 H STEVENAGE	L 1-3	0-2	Armstrong 84	Guy	Marchant	Rice	Silkman	Young	McCready	Armstrong	Everitt	Cooke	Stockley	O'Rourke	
17/10 1,117			*Parkinson 6, 79, Pitt 44,*	*Gaveux*	*Long*	*Shreeve*	*Parkinson*	*Dingwall*	*Turner*	*Hodges*	*Whishaw*	*Terry*	*Collins*	*Pitt*	
			Ref: J Hazell	Stevenage are low in Division 1, despite four former Dons on their books – Hodges, Shreeve, Collins, and Davies. Shreeve is dropped from the FA Cup defeat 10 days previously. Brian Parkinson looked good then, and even better now. The crowd hoot and slow hand-clap.											

FA Cup	F-A	H-T	Scorers, Times, and Referees	1	2	3	4	5	6	7	8	9	10	11	12 sub used
1Q A CHESHUNT	W 4-0	2-0	Larkin 19, Armstrong 33, O'Rourke 51,	Guy	Marchant	Stockley	Silkman	Young	McCready	Armstrong	Rice	Larkin*	Summerhill	O'Rourke	Cooke
16/9 *400*			[McCready 65]	*Neill*	*Dillon*	*Twidell*	*Picking*	*Lucas*	*Bevans*	*Poole*	*Munn*	*Twigg*	*Cooper*	*Buckle*	
			Ref: K Clarke	The Athenian League amateurs do their best, but this is one of Wimbledon's most one-sided matches of recent years. The only mystery is why Everitt packs his side with defenders. Munn shaved the bar at one end, whereupon Larkin promptly opened the scoring at the other.											
2Q H STEVENAGE	W 3-1	1-1	O'Rourke 18, 70, 75	Guy	Marchant	Loughlan	Silkman	Young	McCready	Armstrong	Everitt*	Cooke	Summerhill	O'Rourke	Rice
7/10 1,568			*Parkinson 35*	*Gaveux*	*Long*	*Shreeve*	*Parkinson*	*Dingwall*	*Turner*	*Hodges*	*Whishaw*	*Terry*	*Collins*	*George*	
			Ref: P Bradbury	The Dons have been paired with Stevenage in two cups in 10 days. Their team includes a sackful of former Dons, plus Ricky George, hero last season of Hereford's FA Cup exploits against Newcastle. O'Rourke's completes his first hat-trick in two years with a rebound from a penalty.											
3Q A SUTTON	L 1-3	0-2	Cooke 50	Guy	Marchant	Rice	Everitt	Young	McCready	Armstrong	Silkman	Cooke	Stockley	O'Rourke	
21/10 *1,300 Isth:8*			*Gonzales 36, 55, Dennis 41*	*Thomas*	*Strong*	*Mears*	*Ray*	*Webb P*	*Peck*	*Webb E*	*Butterfill*	*Jolly*	*Dennis*	*Gonzales*	
				Sutton will forever conjure memories of Wimbledon's greatest moment. Now, four days after Stevenage eliminate the Dons from the FA Cup, Sutton inflict this crushing blow. Roy Law, as true a Don as ever lived, now coaches the amateurs, and he dances with joy at the outcome.											

FA Trophy	F-A	H-T	Scorers, Times, and Referees	1	2	3	4	5	6	7	8	9	10	11	12 sub used
1 H BANBURY 9	D 1-1	1-0	Armstrong 25	Guy	Marchant	Loughlan	Stockley	McCready	Summerhill	Armstrong	Everitt	Larkin	Cooke	O'Rourke	
2/12 764 *1N:7*			*Foster 60*	*Rennie*	*Kearns*	*Butler*	*Moulsdale*	*Baker*	*Svenson*	*Crognale*	*Foster*	*Jacques*	*Lines*	*Hall*	
				A mixture of modest opposition, poor weather, and the All Blacks on TV dragged fewer than 1,000 spectators out of their homes. Larkin returns too soon after injury. The Dons come close to being k.o.'d from a cup by lesser lights three times in one season.											
1R A BANBURY	W 1-0	0-0	Cooke 118	Guy	Marchant	Loughlan	Stockley	McCready	Summerhill	Armstrong	Rice	Larkin	Cooke	O'Rourke	Silkman
5/12 *560 1N:7*	*aet*			*Rennie*	*Kearns*	*Baker*	*Moulsdale*	*Butler*	*Svenson*	*Lines*	*Foster*	*Jacques*	*Duester*	*Crognale*	
			Ref: R Lewis	The 1st Division North side were two minutes away from the end of extra-time when O'Rourke took the corner kick from which Cooke scored from almost on the goal-line. O'Rourke had hit a post in the last seconds of normal time, whereupon Cooke's tap-in stuck in the mud.											
2 A NUNEATON B	W 3-2	2-1	Marchant 15, 40, 70	Guy	Stockley	Loughlan	Rice	McCready	Summerhill	Armstrong	Marchant	Cooke	Silkman	O'Rourke	
20/1 *1,468*			*Franklin 30, Turpie 49*	*Robinson*	*Stephens*	*Bridgett*	*Lewis*	*Swift*	*Jones*	*Starkey*	*Shepherd*	*Franklin*	*Goodfellow*	*Turpie*	
				Full-back Andy Marchant can only get into the side as an inside-forward. Sleet and snow make for a thrill-a-minute match, memorable chiefly for Marchant's unexpected hat-trick. Near the end Guy threw the ball to the feet of Starkey, who was so astonished that Guy had time to block.											

3	A	BEDFORD		L	1-3	0-1	Armstrong 52	Guy	Stockley	Loughlan	Rice	Langford	Summerhill	Armstrong	Marchant	Cooke	Silkman	O'Rourke
	10/2		*2,000*				*Boyd 30, Adams 58, Campbell 88*	*Alexander*	*Skinn*	*Folds*	*Townsend*	*Garvey*	*Scurr*	*Horrey*	*Rodney*	*Sorbie*	*Cooley*	*Silous*

Ref: A Turvey

Once again the Dons fail to get beyond the 3rd Round of this trophy. Their season is effectively over, and it is early February. After four minutes Cooke strikes the underside of the crossbar. Armstrong's free-kick makes it 1-1, but Rice is then dispossessed, with dire consequences. P

		Home						Away					
	P	W	D	L	F	A	W	D	L	F	A	Pts
1 Kettering	42	11	9	1	34	19	9	8	4	40	25	57
2 Yeovil	42	15	3	3	47	13	6	11	4	20	18	56
3 Dover	42	14	5	2	31	11	9	4	8	30	27	55
4 Chelmsford	42	14	3	4	45	17	9	4	8	30	26	53
5 Worcester	42	15	5	1	43	16	5	8	8	25	31	53
6 Weymouth	42	15	5	1	52	23	5	7	9	20	28	52
7 Margate	42	10	7	4	43	24	7	8	6	37	36	49
8 Bedford	42	12	3	6	25	16	4	12	5	18	20	47
9 Nuneaton B	42	8	8	5	25	17	8	6	7	26	24	46
10 Telford	42	10	9	2	39	21	2	11	8	18	26	44
11 Cambridge C	42	10	7	4	40	22	4	8	9	24	31	43
12 WIMBLEDON	42	10	9	2	32	17	4	5	12	18	33	42
13 Barnet	42	12	5	4	37	20	3	6	12	23	39	41
14 Romford	42	14	2	5	35	20	3	3	15	16	45	39
15 Hillingdon B	42	11	3	7	32	25	5	3	13	20	33	38
16 Dartford	42	9	8	4	30	21	3	3	15	19	42	35
17 Folkestone	42	8	6	7	27	27	3	5	13	14	45	33
18 Guildford	42	6	9	6	37	32	4	2	15	22	52	31
19 Ramsgate	42	4	6	11	22	39	5	7	9	13	22	31
20 Poole	42	9	9	3	34	26	1	1	19	16	62	30
21 Burton Alb	42	8	4	9	29	25	1	3	17	14	56	25
22 Waterlooville	42	3	8	10	17	28	1	8	12	16	35	24
	924	228	133	101	756	479	101	133	228	479	756	924

Odds & ends

Double wins: (4) Bedford, Telford, Margate, Burton.
Double losses: (2) Dover, Yeovil.

Won from behind: (1) Poole (h).
Lost from in front: (2) Folkestone (a), Guildford (a).

High spots: 8-game unbeaten start to the season, though 6 were drawn.
5 wins out of 6 in December and January lifted the Dons to 7th.

Low spots: Worst season so far. Fewest wins, fewest goals scored.
6 games without a win in November and December.
Dreadful final three months. 4 wins from the final 17 games.
Defeat by 1st Division Stevenage in the Southern League Cup.
Defeat by the amateurs of Sutton in the FA Cup.

Wimbledon finished the season with a perfectly symmetrical record.
P42, W14, D14, L14, F50, A50, Pts 42.

Player of the Year: Tom McCready.
Ever-presents: (0).
Hat-tricks: Andy Marchant (1).
Leading scorer: David Armstrong (16).

	Appearances					Goals				
	Lge	Sub	SLC	FAC	FAT	Lge	SLC	FAC	FAT	Total
Armstrong, David	**36**	1	3	3	4	**11**	2	1	2	**16**
Bennett, Willie	**3**									
Bryant, Geoff	**3**									
Cooke, Ian	**34**	1	3	2/1	4	**11**	1	1	1	**14**
Everitt, Mike	**15**	2	2	2	1	**1**	1			**2**
Guy, Dickie	**42**		3	3	4					
Langford, Steve	**9**				1					
Larkin, Andy	**25**		2	1	2	**5**		1		**6**
Loughlin, John	**40**		2	1	4	**1**				**1**
McCready, Tom	**37**		3	3	3	**5**		1		**6**
MacHattie, Ian	**1**									
Marchant, Andy	**34**	1	3	3	4	**2**	1		3	**6**
O'Rourke, Gerry	**37**		3	3	4	**4**	1	4		**9**
Rice, Selwyn	**29**	1	1/1	2/1	3					
Silkman, Barry	**33**	3	2	3	2/1	**6**				**6**
Smith, Graham	**8**	1				**1**				**1**
Stockley, Bob	**22**	2	1/1	2	4	**1**				**1**
Summerhill, Alan	**40**		2	2	4	**2**				**2**
Tuite, Tom	**2**									
Ware, John	**1**									
White, Tony	**4**									
Young, Alan	**7**		3	3						
22 players used	**462**	**12**	**33/2**	**33/2**	**44/1**	**50**	**6**	**8**	**6**	**70**

No	Date	Att	Pos	Pts	F-A	H-T	Scorers, Times, and Referees	1	2	3	4	5	6	7	8	9	10	11	12 sub used
1	A MAIDSTONE			L	1-2	1-0	Debnam 5 (og)	Guy	Stockley	Loughlan	**Brown**	McCready	Larkin	Marchant	Cooke	**Smart**	Smith	**Gadston**	
	11/8	*1,666*		–			*Priestley 60, Everest 89*	*Maggs*	*Sheridan*	*Barker*	*Richardson*	*Priestley*	*Evans*	*Debnam*	*Brown*	*McVeigh*	*Tough*	*Watson*	
							Ref: M Dixon	Just as the new season is about to start, Mike Everitt, who had presided over the worst Wimbledon team for a decade, landed the plum job of manager of Brentford. Dick Graham took over, a year after he had left Colchester, whom he guided to a 3-2 win over Leeds in the FA Cup.											
2	H DOVER			W	1-0		Cooke	Guy	Stockley	Loughlan	Brown	McCready	Langford	Marchant	Cooke	Smart	Smith	Gadston	
	14/8	1,035		2				*Gadsby*	*Hamshare*	*Hall*	*Kurila*	*Brooks*	*Stevenson*	*Thornley*	*Moy*	*Wright*	*Down*	*Robinson*	
							Ref: A Harrington	Young Jeff Bryant has been suspended for five months for giving his age falsely when a youngster with Fulham. This is a big blow to the player and the club. With five home fixtures in their first seven, it is imperative that Wimbledon win them to climb the league table.											
3	H WEYMOUTH			W	**5-2**	3-2	Cooke 2, 38, Marchant 39	Guy	Stockley	Loughlan	McCready	Langford	Brown	Smith	Marchant	Gadston	Cooke	Larkin	
	18/8	1,293		4			*Brown 18, 28* [McCready 55, 57]	*Clarke*	*Lawrence*	*Williams*	*Gater*	*Hobson*	*Brown*	*Skirton*	*Howshall*	*Trebilcock*	*Adams*	*Beer*	
							Ref: R Rodell	Goals a-plenty, and most of them going to the Dons. They don't please Joe Gadston, who appears always to be moaning about something. The key moment came at 1-2. Cooke missed twice in rapid succession, but Graham Williams turned Cooke's second shot into his own net.											
4	H CAMBRIDGE C			W	2-0	0-0	Larkin 53, Gadston 63	Guy	Stockley	Marchant	McCready	Loughlan	Brown	**Bloss**	**Crosby**	Smith	Gadston	Larkin	
	25/8	1,043		6				*Barker*	*Way*	*Keenan*	*Murray*	*James*	*MacDonald*	*Conmy*	*Crane*	*Hunter*	*Barnard*	*Moden*	
							Ref: A Bridges	Unbeaten City were on top in the first half, and Guy saves well from Chris Barnard's inswinger. City no longer have prolific Eddie Bailham in their ranks. The Dons secure the points when Gadston pounces on Tom McCready's shot for his fifth goal in three matches.											
5	A ROMFORD		3	L	1-2	1-1	Gadston 30	Guy	Marchant	McCready	Langford	Stockley	Brown	Bloss	Crosby	Larkin	Cooke	Gadston	
	1/9	*1,152*	*16*	6			*Chandler 32, Tapping 83*	*Lightfoot*	*Yorath*	*Tapping*	*Mann*	*Robinson*	*Bickles*	*Fascione*	*Sanders*	*Chandler*	*Hudson*	*Manning*	
							Ref: D Jackson	Captain Loughlan is out with a torn hamstring. Cooke puts Gadston through for his sixth goal in four games, but Chandler immediately heads the equaliser, from a Tapping free-kick. Tapping settles the match with another free-kick, this time after ex-Chelsea Joe Fascione was fouled.											
6	H MARGATE		3	W	1-0	0-0	Cooke 70	Guy	Stockley	Loughlan	Brown	McCready	Langford	Marchant	Cooke	Gadston	Bloss	Smith	
	4/9	1,319	*4*	8				*Bowtell*	*Summers*	*Clewlow*	*Sawyer*	*Breach*	*Houston*	*Walker*	*Clayton*	*Hold*	*Barry*	*Fusco*	*Brown*
								A sensational volley by Ian Cooke, as Loughlan's cross drops behind the Margate defence, decides the outcome of this match. Eddie Clayton – once of Tottenham Hotspur – let fly with a last-minute curler that Dickie Guy just reached with his finger-tips.											
7	H CHELMSFORD		5	L	1-2	0-0	Cooke 89	Guy	Stockley	Loughlan	McCready	Langford	Brown	Bloss	Crosby	Marchant*	Cooke	Gadston	Larkin
	8/9	**1,321**	*15*	8			*O'Rourke 50, Price 65*	*Carrick*	*Coakley*	*Tomkins*	*O'Kane*	*Loughton*	*Delea*	*Hall*	*Grant*	*O'Rourke*	*Thompson*	*Price*	
							Ref: D Bone	The Dons' all-action work-rate is ill-suited to these blisteringly hot conditions. Chelmsford play casual beach football, and it pays. Their wingers tear Wimbledon's defenders apart, and ex-Don Gerry O'Rourke gives McCready a tough time, even scoring with a tame header.											
8	A MARGATE			W	1-0	1-0	Cooke 35	Guy	Stockley	Loughlan	Brown	McCready	Langford	Marchant	Cooke	Gadston	Crosby	Smith	
	17/9	*611*		10				*Bowtell*	*Summers*	*Butterfield*	*Sawyer*	*Breach*	*Houston*	*Baber*	*Stockley*	*Hold*	*Brown*	*Walker*	
								A quick double over Margate for the Dons, both by the same score, both by the same player. Margate win the second half 11-2 on corner-kicks. Their manager, Les Riggs, complains: 'We've outplayed them twice and got nothing to show for it.'											
9	A CAMBRIDGE C		10	D	0-0	0-0		Guy	Stockley	McCready	Langford	Loughlan	Brown	Crosby	Bloss	Smith	Cooke	Gadston	
	29/9	*1,107*	*16*	11				*Barker*	*Way*	*Keenan*	*Murray*	*James*	*MacDonald*	*Conmy*	*Waters*	*Hunter*	*Barnard*	*Knight*	
							Ref: P Stoakley	Wimbledon began at a crawl and ended at a gallop. They are still smarting from their controversial elimination from the London Challenge Cup by Fulham. Dick Graham admits that his team took awhile to get going, but at least this is another clean sheet.											
10	H GUILDFORD		9	D	3-3	0-2	Cooke 49, 53, McCready79	Guy	Stockley	McCready	Langford	Loughlan	Smith	Brown	Marchant*	Bloss	Cooke	Gadston	Larkin
	2/10	1,150	*4*	12			*Peters 14, Loughlan 36 (og), Smith 70*	*Anscombe*	*Peters*	*Watts*	*Goucher*	*Harris*	*Westburgh*	*Malley*	*Smith*	*Burge*	*Moody*	*Summerhill*	
							Ref: D Drewitt	Andy Marchant collides in mid-air with City's debut keeper Anscombe and fractures his leg. His versatility will be missed. It was 2-2 at the time. Guy rolls the ball to Paul Smith for City's third, but is rescued by McCready's header. Home fans used fog horns to drive on their team.											
11	A GRANTHAM			L	0-2	0-1		Guy	Stockley	McCready	Langford	Loughlan*	Bloss	Brown	Crosby	**Lucas**	Cooke	Gadston	Smith
	13/10	*1,369*		12			*Nixon 26, 60*	*Gardiner*	*Down*	*Crawford*	*Thompson*	*Harrison*	*Chambers*	*Horobin*	*Taylor*	*Nixon*	*Norris*	*Benskin*	
								The Gingerbreads, as Grantham are nicknamed, prove to be as tough as nails. John Loughan is caught by a wild boot and has to be substituted at half-time. Prolific Ernie Nixon got behind Langford for the first goal, then capitalised on Malcolm Crosby's poor back-pass for the second.											

No	Venue	Opponent / Date	Att	Pos	Pts	Res	H-T	Scorers, Times, Referees	1	2	3	4	5	6	7	8	9	10	11	12
12	A	BEDFORD		13	D	0-0	0-0		Guy	Brown	**Hall**	Langford	McCready	Lucas	Cooke	**Moss**	Crosby	Gadston	Bloss	
		27/10	*745*	*16*	13				*Alexander*	*Skinn*	*Folds*	*Gould*	*Cooley*	*Earl*	*Hawkins*	*Silous*	*Sergeant*	*Dove*	*Dean*	
									No goals, but both sides battered the woodwork. Five minutes before half-time McCready hit a post, and after the turnaround Norman Dean headed against the underside of the bar. Bedford were camped in the Wimbledon half for much of the second period.											
13	A	WORCESTER			W	2-0	1-0	Moss 25, Brown 80	Guy	Loughlan	Hall	Langford	McCready	Lucas	Bloss	Moss	Cooke	Brown	Smith	
		10/11	*950*		15				*Knight*	*Allen*	*Chester*	*Aggio*	*Bache*	*Merrick*	*Ross*	*Inglis*	*Kelcher*	*Martin*	*Hensman*	
									This match produced a series of 'firsts' – first goals for Wimbledon for Bobby Moss and for Stan Brown, and the first occasion the Dons had scored more than one goal away from home this season.											
14	H	FOLKESTONE		10	L	1-2	1-1	Gadston 18	Guy	Loughlan	Hall	Langford	McCready	Rice	Lucas	Brown	Cooke	Gadston	Bloss	
		17/11	1,069	*15*	15			*Nicholas 9, Whitington 68*	*Bowley*	*Wooldridge*	*Hogg*	*Bentley*	*Pearce*	*Sharp*	*Pearce*	*Pointer*	*Whitington*	*Nicholas*	*Shovellar*	
								Ref: J Jones	Wimbledon have forgotten how to win at home. Joe Gadston's first league goal in 10 weeks cancels out an early deficit, but cannot prevent the Kent side notching a shock win. This is the first time the Dons have failed to beat Folkestone at home, and starts a seven-match winless run.											
15	H	WORCESTER		11	L	1-3	1-2	Crosby 40	Guy	Stockley	Hall	Langford	McCready	Rice	Lucas	Bloss	Cooke	Crosby	Smith	
		1/12	714	*18*	15			*Inglis 26, 31, 79*	*Smith*	*Allen*	*Chester*	*Aggio*	*Bache*	*Merrick*	*Ross*	*Inglis*	*Kelcher*	*Martin*	*Hensman*	
								Ref: J Griffiths	Worcester's first away win of the season is achieved upon a freezing pitch. It does not impede their speedy winger Hensman, or Inglis with his hat-trick. To make matters worse, Loughlan wants a transfer. Dick Graham sells his supermarket business to manage the Dons full-time.											
16	A	TELFORD			L	1-2	0-1	Hall 49	Guy	Hall	Langford	McCready	Loughlan	Bloss	Lucas	Brown*	Cooke	Crosby	Smith	Rice
		8/12	*783*		15			*Fudge 40p, Bentley 79*	*Irvine*	*Harris*	*Croft*	*Ross*	*Ray*	*Bridgwood*	*Hawkins*	*Fudge*	*Bentley*	*Draycott*	*Lang*	
									Telford had not scored against anybody for five matches. They are fortunate to score their first goal now, the ball bouncing awkwardly against McCready's arm. The Dons' goal was equally lucky, a deflected free-kick. Bentley's diving header from a corner deserved to win the match.											
17	A	YEOVIL		14	D	1-1	0-1	Pinkney 69	Guy	Stockley	McCready	Langford	Loughlan	Lucas	Smith	**Pinkney**	Crosby	Cooke	Gadston	
		15/12	*1,739*	*7*	16			*Cottle 20*	*Clark*	*Cottle*	*Harrison*	*Briggs*	*Cotton*	*Impey*	*Slattery*	*Pickett*	*Brown*	*Thompson*	*Clancy*	
								Ref: K Bell	Yeovil's attendance is healthy by Plough Lane standards, but it is their lowest for two years. Centre-forward Alan Pinkney has signed for the Dons on a month's loan. He scores a fine equaliser, taking the ball past two defenders before shooting on the run.											
18	H	NUNEATON B		14	D	1-1	0-0	Lewis 50 (og)	Guy	Stockley	Loughlan	Langford	McCready	Lucas	Bloss	Cooke	Pinkney	Crosby	Smith	
		22/12	643	*20*	17			*Turpie 85*	*Robinson*	*Stephens*	*Newton*	*Baxter*	*Branston*	*Jones*	*Mackay*	*Owen*	*Vincent*	*Lewis*	*Turpie*	
								Ref: J Bellamy	On-loan Malcolm Crosby takes a corner which is headed into his own net by full-back Dave Lewis. When Boro winger Turpie heads a late equaliser, it means that Wimbledon have not won at home since 4 September, three and a half months previously.											
19	A	DARTFORD		13	D	1-1		Pinkney	Guy	Hall	Loughlan	Langford	McCready	Lucas	Bloss	Cooke	Pinkney	Crosby	Smith	
		26/12	*1,500*	*1*	18			*Stevens (p)*	*Morton*	*Read*	*Stevens*	*Carr*	*Burns*	*Binks*	*Payne*	*Light*	*Mitchell*	*Robinson*	*Halliday*	
								Ref: R Rodell	An away draw with the runaway league leaders has to be cause for satisfaction. Dartford begin the match six points ahead of their nearest rivals, and even though they drop a point here, they will go on to win the league by eight points.											
20	A	GUILDFORD		13	L	1-2	0-0	Pinkney 90	Guy	Hall*	Loughlan	Langford	McCready	Bloss	**Mahon**	Cooke	Pinkney	Lucas	Smith	Stockley
		29/12	*1,020*	*11*	18			*Harris 57, Smith 65*	*Brooks*	*Peters*	*Watts*	*Finn*	*Harris*	*Westburgh*	*Dickinson*	*Smith*	*Burge*	*Moody*	*Wright*	
								Ref: R Roberts	Dick Graham has bought winger Mick Mahon from his old club Colchester. Mahon has a quiet debut, well shackled by Gary Peters. The Dons score late on when the keeper fails to hold Lucas's drive. The referee blows for time before the ball can be retrieved from the back of the net.											
21	H	TONBRIDGE		13	W	2-1	0-0	McCready 60, Cooke 66	Guy	Stockley	Loughlan	Rice	McCready	Bloss	Mahon	Cooke	Pinkney	Lucas	Smith	
		1/1	802	*20*	20			*Brown 81*	*White*	*Smith*	*Kinsey*	*Kears*	*Carragher*	*Gilchrist*	*Brown*	*Stonebridge*	*Crush*	*Davies*	*Davie*	
								Ref: B Chapman	Alan Pinkney's missed penalty makes Wimbledon sweat out the last few minutes. They are leading 2-0 when Pinkney is brought down in the box by Carragher. He gets up to take the kick himself, but shoots against the junction of post and bar. Tonbridge score soon afterwards.											
22	H	BARNET		15	L	1-3	1-1	Smith 28	Guy	Loughlan	McCready	Lucas	Stockley	Bloss	Rice	Smith	Pinkney	Cooke	Mahon	
		5/1	777	*2*	20			*George 31, Silkman 59, Ferry 75*	*McClelland*	*Lye*	*Fusedale*	*Tom*	*Embery*	*Court*	*Eason*	*Ferry*	*George*	*Silkman*	*Bibby*	
								Ref: J McCrete	Barnet inflict Wimbledon's fourth home defeat of the season, which is only half completed. All the breaks go Barnet's way. They level when Loughlan's clearance hits Ricky George on the bum and flies in. Pinkney and Rice hit the woodwork. Ex-Don Barry Silkman plays a blinder.											
23	A	CHELMSFORD		14	D	2-2	0-1	Cooke 58, Bryant 90	Guy	Loughlan!	Hall	McCready	Langford	Bryant	Bloss	Lucas	Rice	Mahon	Cooke	
		19/1	*2,019*	*3*	21			*Dunwell 31, Grant 79p*	*Carrick*	*Coakley*	*Gomersall*	*O'Kane*	*Delea*	*Tomkins*	*Lewis*	*Dunwell*	*Peterson*	*Grant*	*Hall*	
								Ref: C Lawchom	Chelmsford are unbeaten in 10 games. At 0-0 John Loughlan is sent off for the first time in his 14-year career. Colin Hall head-butted him, and Loughlan swung his fists and was off. Chelmsford's second goal was a twice-taken penalty, for hand-ball after Langford had chested the ball.											

No	Date		Att	Pos	Pts	F-A	H-T	Scorers, Times, and Referees	1	2	3	4	5	6	7	8	9	10	11	12 sub used
24	A	BARNET		13	W	2-0	0-0	Lucas 81, 83	Guy	Stockley	Rice	McCready	Langford	Bryant	Bloss	Cooke	Lucas	**Bennett**	Mahon	
	26/1		*1,239*	*2*	23				*McClelland*	*Lye*	*Fusedale*	*Tom*	*Embery*	*Plume*	*Eason*	*Ferry**	*George*	*Silkman*	*Bibby*	*Court*
								Ref: J Hazell	Bob Bennett has arrived on loan from Southend United. Selwyn Rice, the 'Tank', softens up ex-Don Barry Silkman with granite tackles, and also injured Gordon Ferry, who had to be subbed. Dave Lucas's far-post header made it 1-0. Andy Larkin's registration is cancelled.											
25	H	YEOVIL		11	W	1-0	1-0	Bennett 26	Guy	Stockley	Langford	McCready	Rice	Bloss	Bryant	Mahon	Cooke	Bennett	Lucas	
	2/2		1,018	*9*	25				*Clark*	*Irwin*	*Impey*	*Verity*	*Cotton*	*Dixon*	*Housley*	*Pickett*	*Plumb*	*Thompson*	*Clancy*	
								Ref: D Chainey	Bennett's inclusion means Cooke has to play wide on the wing.The newcomer is on hand after Lucas heads against the bar. Yeovil miss a sackful, especially in the second half. Off the pitch there is talk about Wimbledon quitting the Southern League and rejoining the Isthmian.											
26	A	NUNEATON B		14	D	0-0	0-0		Guy	Stockley	Langford	Bryant	Rice	Bloss	Mahon	Smith	Cooke	Bennett!	Lucas	
	9/2		*1,262*	*19*	26				*Ball*	*Stephens*	*Bridgett*	*Baxter*	*Branston*	*Jones*	*Mackay*	*Owen*	*Vincent*	*Turpie*	*Lewis*	
								Ref: J Bellamy	An eventful goalless draw. Aston Villa spies run the eye over Dave Lucas. After 54 minutes Bob Bennett is sent off for kicking Branston. Dickie Guy turns in an epic show, making three heroic saves in the final minutes that earns him a standing ovation.											
27	H	ROMFORD		11	D	2-2	0-2	Crosby 70, Cooke 75	Guy	Stockley	Langford	Bryant	Rice	Lucas	Mahon	Smith*	Cooke	Bennett	Crosby	Hall
	16/2		1,008	*13*	27			*Ferry 13, Chandler 26*	*Lightfoot*	*Parmenter*	*Tapping*	*Mann*	*Robinson*	*Bickles*	*Sanders*	*Chandler*	*Ferry*	*Yorath*	*Manning*	
								Ref: L Burden	Mick Mahon has a magical game, tormenting Romford's former-Fulham defender Terry Parmenter. Malcolm Crosby also returns for a third loan period from Aldershot. It is he who reduces arrears, setting up a furious finale, in one of the matches of the season.											
28	H	MAIDSTONE		12	L	**0-3**	0-2		Guy	Stockley	Hall	Bryant	McCready	Lucas	Bloss	Smith	Cooke	Gadston*	Crosby	Loughlan
	2/3		1,225	*2*	27			*Everest 6, Morton 41, 88*	*Maggs*	*Sheridan*	*Baker*	*Richardson*	*Priestley*	*Debnam*	*O'Sullivan*	*McVeigh*	*Tough*	*Everest*	*Morton*	
								Ref: B Baldry	Wimbledon's first defeat in six is so bad that Dick Graham admits: 'No team of mine has ever played as badly as that.' Alan Morton had been rejected by Les Henley. Maidstone bought him from Ashford for £3,000, and he looks worth every penny. Even Guy boobed for goal No 3.											
29	H	HILLINGDON B		12	L	**0-3**	0-2		Guy	**Willingham**	Loughlan	Lucas	Langford	Bryant	Crosby	Bennett	Smith	Bloss	Stockley	Marchant
	9/3		**554**	*21*	27			*Taylor 30, 39, 62*	*Phillips*	*Butler*	*Ryan*	*Titterton*	*Archer*	*Watt*	*Taylor*	*Swain*	*Hatt*	*Reeve*	*Huxley*	
								Ref: G Marshall	Hillingdon arrive bottom of the league, but this win lifts them above Worcester. Dick Graham can hardly field a side. Mahon is out with German measles. David Willingham plays, aged 17. Only Guy and Loughlan are over 23 years old. Marchant returns after breaking his leg.											
30	A	HILLINGDON B		12	L	0-1	0-1		Guy	McCready	Langford	Loughlan	Stockley	Gadston	Bloss	Bryant	Lucas	Smith	Bennett	
	16/3		*656*	*21*	27			*Hatt 12*	*Phillips*	*Butler*	*Ryan*	*Titterton*	*Archer*	*Swain*	*Taylor*	*Bishop*	*Reeve*	*Hatt*	*Huxley*	
								Ref: J Bellamy	Dick Graham has quit, forced to resign say some, having had to revert to part-time management after being appointed full-time. Skipper Loughlan and trainer Danny Keenan pick the team, which present Hillingdon with a priceless double and their first home win of the season.											
31	H	GRANTHAM		15	L	1-3	1-1	Mahon 1p	Guy	Loughlan	Hall	Langford	McCready	Bryant	Smith	Mahon	Lucas	Cooke	Marchant	
	23/3		625	*7*	27			*Horobin 22, 66, Dixon 70*	*Gardiner*	*Down*	*Crawford*	*Thompson*	*Harrison*	*Chambers*	*Horobin*	*Taylor*	*Nixon*	*Norris*	*Benskin*	
								Ref: D Jackson	Luckless Dickie Guy is at fault for Grantham's first goal, and probably their second too. The Dons had got off to the perfect start. Ian Cooke, playing his first game in a month, is held back by Gerry Taylor, but Mick Mahon scores the first of many valuable penalties for the Dons.											
32	A	KETTERING			L	1-2	1-1	Cooke 17	Guy	Loughlan	McCready	Langford	Stockley	Bryant	Smith	Mahon	Lucas	Cooke	Marchant	
	29/3		***2,525***		27			*Clayton 19, Hawksby 82*	*Livesey*	*Ashby*	*Goodall*	*Atkinson*	*Suddards*	*Peck*	*Pawley*	*Clayton*	*Hawksby*	*Cleary*	*Harrington*	
									A fifth straight defeat, against title-chasing Kettering, may be harsh, but it leaves Wimbledon deep in the mire. This is the deepest hole they will ever find themselves in, in the Southern League. Lucas hits the post for the luckless Dons, and Bryant twice comes close at the end.											
33	H	ATHERSTONE		11	W	3-2	0-0	Bryant 71, Mahon 72, 85	Guy	Stockley	Loughlan	Bryant	McCready	Langford	Mahon	Cooke	Lucas	Marchant	Smith	
	6/4		690	*17*	29			*Franklin 46, 78*	*Johnson*	*Kavanagh*	*Russell*	*Smith*	*Preston*	*Kiernan*	*Smith*	*Webster*	*Franklin*	*Quinney*	*Mellor*	
								Ref: C Lawthom	Newcomers Atherstone play their part in a bright, refreshing match, which gives little hint of Wimbledon's desperate plight. The contest swings several ways before being finally settled by Mick Mahon, who capitalises upon an underhit back-pass.											
34	A	DOVER			D	1-1	1-1	Smith 15	Guy	Stockley	Loughlan	Bryant	McCready	Langford	Mahon	Cooke	Lucas	Marchant	Smith!	
	8/4		***253***		30			*Brooks 37*	*Gadsby*	*Reynolds*	*Hall*	*Arnott*	*Wood*	*Fursdon*	*Watson*	*Brooks*	*Simpson*	*Hamshare*	*Thornley*	*Donoghue*
								Ref: I Walton	Three away fixtures may hold the key toWimbledon's future. Graham Smith will remember this match for contradictory reasons. He puts the Dons in front from Lucas's cross, but 15 minutes from time is dismissed for kicking Fursden in the back. Brooks had levelled with a miskick.											

No	Venue	Opponent / Date	Att	Pos	Res	Pts	F-A	H-T	Scorers, Times, and Referees	1	2	3	4	5	6	7	8	9	10	11	12
35	A	TONBRIDGE			W		1-0	0-0	Mahon 51	Guy	Stockley	Loughlan	Bryant	McCready*	Langford	Mahon	Cooke	Lucas	Marchant	Smith	Bloss
		12/4	*920*			32				*Seymour*	*Smith*	*Kinsey*	*Kears*	*Carragher*	*Gilchrist*	*Brown*	*Stonebridge*	*Crush*	*Davies*	*Davie*	
										Goalkeeper Seymour is at the near post as Mahon's angled shot beats him at the far. McCready had to be substituted after 23 minutes with a badly gashed eye. Easter had traditionally been a graveyard to Wimbledon's championship aspirations, but is kinder to them when struggling.											
36	A	FOLKESTONE			W		1-0	0-0	Lucas 64	Guy	Stockley	Loughlan	Bryant	Bloss	Langford	Mahon	Cooke	Lucas	Marchant	Smith	
		13/4	*1,153*			34				*Wardle*	*Bentley*	*Rogers*	*Crowley*	*Pearce*	*Shovellar*	*Howell*	*Pointer*	*Whitington*	*Tredwell*	*Watson*	
									Ref: A Heselgrave	Another four-pointer goes Wimbledon's way. They defended against a strong wind in the first half, during which Whitington shot wide with the goal at his mercy. But Dave Lucas's soaring header earns two more away points in the space of two days.											
37	H	DARTFORD			L		0-2	0-2		Guy	Stockley	Loughlan	Bryant	Bloss	Langford	Mahon	Cooke	Lucas	Marchant	Smith	
		15/4	1,185	*1*		34			*Glozier 30, Hearn 42*	*Morton*	*Read*	*Glozier*	*Carr*	*Burns*	*Binks*	*Payne*	*Light*	*Hearn*	*Cunningham*	*Halliday*	
									Ref: J Roberts	Nottingham Forest are the latest team to express interest in Dave Lucas. Wimbledon lose to two goals scored against the run of play, while accumulating 13 corner-kicks to Dartford's one. Mahon hit a post with just the keeper to beat, and Bryant's leaping header was touched over.											
38	H	TELFORD		15	D		1-1	1-0	Mahon 24p	Guy	Stockley	Loughlan	Bryant	Bloss	Langford	Mahon	Cooke	Lucas	McCready	Smith	
		20/4	757	*16*		35			*Draycott 68*	*Irvine*	*Harris*	*Croft*	*Ross*	*Ray*	*Bridgwood*	*Hawkins*	*Fudge*	*Bentley*	*Draycott*	*Lang*	
									Ref: J Craigie	Telford are one position below Wimbledon. Tom McCready plays up front, and wins a penalty when he is checked in the box. Telford's equaliser stems from a long throw-in. Bentley headed it on and Draycott swept it in. This might prove to be an expensive dropped point.											
39	A	ATHERSTONE			W		1-0	0-0	Lucas 63	Guy	Stockley	Loughlan	Bryant	Bloss	Langford	Mahon	Cooke	Lucas	McCready	Smith	
		23/4	*724*			37				*Johnson*	*Kavanagh*	*Russell*	*Smith*	*Preston*	*Kiernan*	*Smith*	*Webster*	*Franklin*	*Quinney*	*Mellor*	
										A second win over new-boys Atherstone banishes relegation fears completely. Only a freakish combination of results can send Wimbledon down now. When Franklin broke clear, Bryant grabbed him round the waist. The professional foul saved the day. Bryant was not even booked.											
40	H	KETTERING		13	W		3-1	1-0	Mahon 37, 65, 80	Guy	Stockley	Loughlan	Bryant	Bloss	Langford	Smith	Cooke	Lucas	McCready	Mahon	
		27/4	714	*3*		39			*Clayton 70*	*Livesey*	*Ashby*	*Goodall*	*Atkinson*	*Suddards*	*Peck*	*Pawley*	*Clayton*	*Hawksby*	*Cleary*	*Harrington*	
									Ref: D Drewitt	Mick Mahon is not only man-of-the-match, he is almost man-of-the-season. Wimbledon have taken 12 points from their last eight games, in which Mahon has scored seven times. The first of his hat-trick against Kettering flies in straight from a corner-kick.											
41	H	BEDFORD			W		2-1	1-0	Cooke 17, 74	Guy	Stockley	Loughlan	Bryant	Marchant	Langford	Smith	Cooke	Lucas	McCready	Mahon	
		30/4	815			41			*Parrott 82*	*Alexander*	*Skinn*	*Folds*	*Gould*	*Cooley*	*Earl*	*Hawkins*	*Silous*	*Sargeant*	*Dove*	*Parrott*	
									Ref: D Gent	Ian Cooke's two goals condemn Bedford to relegation. One point was all Bedford needed to ensure survival. The Dons' retained list shows a big exodus. Loughlan and Marchant are surplus to requirements, and Steve Langford is emigrating to Australia.											
42	A	WEYMOUTH			L		**0-3**	0-0		Guy	Stockley	Loughlan	Bryant	Marchant	Langford	Smith	Cooke	Lucas	McCready	Rice	
		3/5	*447*			41			*Brown 83, Beer 86, Skirton 89*	*Clarke*	*Lawrence*	*Williams*	*Gater*	*Hobson*	*Brown J*	*Skirton*	*Howshall*	*Trebilcock*	*Adams*	*Beer*	
		Home	*Away*							Dickie Guy plays his 241st consecutive game, his 186th in the league. Wimbledon director Alec Fuce takes over as linesman for the final 10 minutes, in which time Weymouth score three cracking goals. Alan Skirton's was a candidate for goal of the season.											
Average		941	*1,184*																		

Southern League Cup

No	Venue	Opponent / Date	Att	Round	Res	F-A	H-T	Scorers, Times, and Referees	1	2	3	4	5	6	7	8	9	10	11	12
1:1	H	BANBURY			W	3-0	2-0	Gadston 30p, 42, 70	Guy	Stockley	Marchant	McCready	Loughlan	Brown	Bloss	Crosby	Gadston	Larkin	**Bascombe**	
		21/8	1,010	*1N*					*Rennie*	*Matthews*	*Pollard*	*Duester*	*Svenson*	*Archibald*	*Butler*	*Foster*	*Jacques*	*Haynes*	*Hastie*	
								Ref: J Hazell	Dick Graham signs three teenagers in the space of half an hour and throws all three into this cup-tie. Banbury had won their first three in their own division, but can't repeat last season's feat in the FA Trophy of holding the Dons at Plough Lane. Gadston was fouled for the penalty.											
1:2	A	BANBURY			W	2-1	1-0	Cooke 43, Gadston 88	Guy	Loughlan	Stockley	Brown	McCready	Langford	Marchant	Gadston	Cooke*	Bloss	Crosby	Larkin
		28/8	*605*	*1N*				*Foster 70p*	*Rennie*	*Matthews*	*Haynes*	*Moulsdale*	*Butler*	*Archibald*	*Duester*	*Foster*	*Jacques*	*Pollard*	*Hastie*	
								Ref: T Ackerill (Dons win 5-1 on aggregate)	Joe Gadston certainly enjoys playing Banbury. He adds to his hat-trick in the first leg with a late winner in the second. Ian Cooke had put Wimbledon in front with a banana shot, a lead wiped out on the night when Langford felled Foster. Guy got a hand to the penalty.											

Southern League Cup	Att	Pos	F-A	H-T	Scorers, Times, and Referees	1	2	3	4	5	6	7	8	9	10	11	12 sub used
2 A WEALDSTONE			D 1-1	0-0	Crosby 49	Guy	Stockley	Langford	Cooke	Crosby	Brown	Bloss	Lucas	Smith	Larkin	Gadston	
16/10	*814*	*1S:5*			*Duck 47*	*Dyson*	*Presland*	*Watson*	*Kinnear*	*McCormick*	*Burgess*	*Fairclough*	*Dyson*	*Byrne*	*Henderson*	*Duck*	
					Ref: D Hayden	Wimbledon are crippled by injuries and barely muster 11 fit men. Wealdstone beat Barnet 4-1 in the 1st Round, so must be taken seriously. Byrne heads down Fulton's free-kick for Duck to score. Later, Byrne's rocket was headed out by Langford, knocking the defender into goal.											
2R H WEALDSTONE			D 2-2	1-1	Larkin 10, Lucas 83	Guy	Stockley	Langford	McCready	Brown	Bloss	Lucas	Smith	Cooke	Larkin	Moss	
6/11	997	*1S:5*	*aet*		*McCormick 31, Henderson 87*	*MacKenzie*	*Presland*	*Fulton*	*McCormick*	*Burgess*	*Fairclough*	*Dyson*	*Godfrey*	*Duck*	*Watson*	*Brown*	
						The Dons think they can play with Wealdstone like a toy, even though they have Terry Dyson in their ranks, a member of Spurs' double team of the early 60s. Dave Lucas's first goal for the Dons is cancelled three minutes from time when Guy spills the ball from his grasp.											
2R A WEALDSTONE		13	D 3-3		Moss, Rice 85, McCready 89	Guy	Rice	Langford	McCready	Brown	Bloss	Lucas	Smith*	Cooke	Larkin	Moss	Stockley
R 13/11	*824*		*aet*		*Duck, Byrne, Presland*	*MacKenzie*	*Presland*	*Fulton*	*Kinnear*	*McCormick*	*Fairclough*	*Dyson*	*Godfrey*	*Byrne*	*Duck*	*Henderson*	
					Ref: D Bone	Wealdstone look set for a memorable victory, but reckon without Wimbledon's barnstorming finish. Selwyn Rice plays his first game of the season, and marks it with a goal. Tom McCready, foraging upfield as is his habit, takes the tie into extra-time.											
2R H WEALDSTONE			W 3-0	2-0	Crosby 9, Stockley 29, Cooke 87	Guy	Stockley	Langford	McCready	Loughlan	Crosby	Bloss	Rice	Lucas	Cooke	Smith	
RR 28/11	373					*MacKenzie*	*Presland*	*Fulton*	*Kinnear*	*McCormick*	*Fairclough*	*Dyson*	*Godfrey*	*Byrne*	*Duck*	*Henderson*	
						After seven hours of combat, the Dons finally put paid to the Wealdstone challenge. Having been beaten by King's Lynn in the FA Cup, the Dons dare not slip up again. Bobby Moss returns to Barnet after the match, having completed his month's loan.											
3 A GRANTHAM			D 1-1	0-1	Mahon 74	Guy	Stockley	Rice	Langford	McCready	Bryant	Smith	Bloss	Lucas	Cooke	Mahon	
30/1	*1,215*				*Nixon 43*	*Gardiner*	*Down*	*Crawford*	*Thompson*	*Harrison*	*Chambers*	*Horobin*	*Taylor*	*Nixon*	*Norris*	*Benskin*	
						Grantham's only home defeat is by 2nd Division Middlesbrough in the FA Cup. Ernie Nixon is the league's leading scorer, and his header gives Grantham the lead. After Mahon's equalising free-kick, Nixon's shot hits the underside of the bar, then the post.											
3R H GRANTHAM		11	L 0-2	0-1		Guy	Stockley	Langford	Bryant	Rice	Bloss	Smith	Mahon	Cooke	Lucas	Bennett	
10/2	980	*3*			*Norris 15, 74*	*Gardiner*	*Down*	*Crawford*	*Thompson*	*Harrison*	*Chambers*	*Horobin*	*Taylor*	*Nixon*	*Norris*	*Benskin*	
					Ref: R Woolven	Wimbledon play their first ever Sunday match, having played the previous day at Nuneaton in the league. National power cuts prevent evening matches under floodlights. Wind and rain, and Leeds on TV, keep the crowd down. Even without Ernie Nixon, Grantham are too strong.											

FA Cup	Att	Pos	F-A	H-T	Scorers, Times, and Referees	1	2	3	4	5	6	7	8	9	10	11	12 sub used
1Q A EPSOM & EWELL			W 5-1	3-0	Cooke 12, 32, Gadston 40p, 46, 65	Guy	Stockley	McCready	Langford	Loughlan	Smith	Brown	Bloss	Larkin*	Cooke	Gadston	Marchant
15/9	*1,000*				*Wales 55*	*Self*	*Bennett*	*Gunter*	*Kidwell*	*Webb*	*Frewin*	*Wales*	*Smith*	*O'Connell*	*Reeves*	*Tuite*	
					Ref: G Keeble	Three of Wimbledon's five goals stem from the aerial power of Tom McCready every time he goes forward. The first goal comes when Self drops the ball under his challenge. Gadston takes his penalty with a Mohammed Ali shuffle. Tommy Tuite played for the Dons last season.											
2Q H SOUTHALL			W 2-1	0-1	Cooke 80, 83	Guy	Stockley	Langford	McCready	Loughlan	Brown	Bloss	Smith	**Thompson***	Cooke	Gadston	Larkin
6/10	1,066				*Austin 15*	*Revell*	*Secker*	*Woods*	*Pike*	*Williams*	*Donlevy*	*Davies*	*Austin*	*Smith*	*Devis*	*Hill*	
					Ref: W Dance	The Dons nearly lose to an Isthmian League Division 2 side which they beat 4-0 in a pre-season friendly. Hugh Thompson is on loan from Ayr, but is withdrawn at half-time. With time running out two right-wing crosses provide two goals for Ian Cooke, a header and a volley.											
3Q A STAINES			D 1-1	1-0	Cooke 29	Guy	Stockley	Langford	Lucas	Brown	Bloss	Crosby	Smith	Cooke	Gadston	Larkin	
20/10	*867*	*Isth*			*Salkeld 82p*	*Yates*	*Talbot*	*Maclean*	*Barker*	*Butler*	*Goode*	*Salkeld*	*Walsh*	*Souter*	*Proctor*	*Vandenberg*	
					Ref: Gardiner	Ian Cooke's volley looks more than enough to brush aside this challenge from the Isthmian League side. It should have been, too. The Dons were coasting to victory when Langford tackled midfielder Souter. The referee gave a penalty. There was still time for Bloss to hit the bar.											
3Q H STAINES			W 4-3	2-2	Cooke 7, 67, Crosby 10, Gadston 78p	Guy	Stockley	Langford	McCready	Brown	Crosby	Bloss	Lucas	Smith	Cooke	Gadston	
R 23/10	1,300				*Vandenberg 8, 20, Procter 65*	*Yates*	*Talbot*	*Hoard*	*Barker*	*Butler*	*Goode*	*Salkeld*	*Rowlands*	*Souter*	*Proctor*	*Vandenberg*	
					Ref: Gardiner	The moral victory belonged to Staines, of the Isthmian League 2nd Division. Joe Gadston scores his first goal in eight matches, from the spot. The award was for Crosby being sandwiched between Talbot and Hoard. Talbot then knocked the celebrating Gadston to the ground.											

4Q	H	MAIDSTONE	13	W	1-0	0-0	Cooke 61	Guy	Stockley	Langford	McCready	Brown	Bloss	Smith	Lucas	Larkin	Cooke	Gadston
3/11		2,385	8					*Maggs*	*Sheridan*	*Barker*	*Richardson*	*Priestley*	*Evans*	*Debnam*	*McVeigh*	*Tough*	*Watson*	*Everest*
							Ref: D Reeves	One more hurdle before the 1st Round proper. Maidstone have lost just once in the league so far, are unbeaten away from home, and have conceded just seven goals, the lowest in the league. Cooke knocks in Smith's cross-cum-shot before Plough Lane's biggest crowd for 2½ years.										
1	A	KING'S LYNN		L	0-1	0-0		Guy	Stockley	McCready	Langford	Bloss	Lucas	Brown	Gadston*	Moss	Cooke	Hall	Larkin
24/11		*2,033*	*1S*				*Elliott 61*	*Steele*	*Brooks*	*Smith*	*Adams*	*Painter*	*Wright*	*Woolmer*	*Rudd*	*Lindsay*	*Wignall*	*Elliott*
							Ref: A Parsons	A bad draw for Wimbledon, even though they are away to a 1st Division side. King's Lynn win this match by a mile, and might have had four or five after Elliott's low drive from 18 yards beat Guy. Crowd trouble in the first half required the players to leave the pitch for 10 minutes.										

FA Trophy

1	H	WEALDSTONE	15	L	0-1	0-1		Guy	Stockley*	Loughlan	Langford	Bloss	Lucas	Mahon	McCready	Larkin	Cooke	Smith	Bryant
12/1		1,084					*Presland 35*	*MacKenzie*	*Presland*	*Watson*	*Kinnear*	*McCormick*	*Burgess*	*Dyson*	*Fulton*	*Byrne*	*Duck*	*Henderson*	
							Ref: K Underwood	Having played Wealdstone four times in the Southern League Cup, the Dons are asked to play them again. Jeff Bryant returns after his five-month suspension, coming on as a sub with five mintes to play. He then misses a sitter. Better the Dons lose in this competition than any other.											

		Home						Away					
	P	W	D	L	F	A	W	D	L	F	A	Pts
1 Dartford	42	13	7	1	42	18	9	6	6	25	19	57
2 Grantham	42	15	5	1	39	10	3	8	10	31	39	49
3 Chelmsford	42	11	5	5	36	21	8	5	8	26	28	48
4 Kettering	42	13	7	1	44	22	3	9	9	18	29	48
5 Maidstone	42	10	6	5	31	17	6	8	7	23	26	46
6 Yeovil	42	9	11	1	26	13	4	9	8	19	26	46
7 Weymouth	42	14	3	4	37	10	5	4	12	23	31	45
8 Barnet	42	12	5	4	34	19	6	4	11	21	27	45
9 Nuneaton B	42	9	11	1	33	14	4	8	9	21	33	45
10 Cambridge C	42	12	5	4	26	18	3	7	11	19	36	42
11 Atherstone	42	11	4	6	39	24	5	5	11	22	35	41
12 WIMBLEDON	42	9	4	8	32	35	6	7	8	18	21	41
13 Telford	42	12	5	4	33	17	0	11	10	18	40	40
14 Dover	42	7	10	4	23	22	4	7	10	18	24	39
15 Tonbridge	42	9	5	7	24	22	3	10	8	14	23	39
16 Romford	42	9	6	6	23	22	2	11	8	16	30	39
17 Margate	42	10	7	4	35	28	5	1	15	21	35	38
18 Guildford	42	11	6	4	34	18	2	5	14	14	49	37
19 Worcester	42	8	9	4	32	25	3	5	13	21	42	36
20 Bedford	42	6	8	7	21	23	5	6	10	17	28	36
21 Folkestone	42	7	7	7	30	24	4	5	12	26	41	34
22 Hillingdon B	42	4	10	7	22	31	5	5	11	22	34	33
	924	221	146	95	696	453	95	146	221	453	696	924

Odds & ends

Double wins: (3) Margate, Tonbridge, Atherstone.
Double losses: (3) Maidstone, Grantham, Hillingdon.

Won from behind: (2) Weymouth (h), Atherstone (h).
Lost from in front: (5) Barnet (h), Grantham (h), Maidstone (a), Romford (a), Kettering (a).

High spots: 4 wins out of the first 6, taking the Dons to 3rd.
Finishing the season with 6 wins and 2 draws from 10 games.

Low spots: Ending 1973 with 7 games without a win, dropping to 13th.
March 1974 is the worst month in the club's history. Five straight losses drops the Dons to 15th, and into the heart of the relegation struggle.
This is the only season in which Wimbledon lose more than they win.
This season they lose at home 8 times, twice as many as any other.
Losing to Wealdstone in the FA Trophy.
The average home attendance of 947 is Wimbledon's lowest in the Southern League.

Player of the Year: Steve Langford.
Ever-presents: (1) Dickie Guy.
Hat-tricks: Mick Mahon (1), Joe Gadston (2).
Leading scorer: Ian Cooke (24).

	Appearances					Goals				
	Lge	**Sub**	**SLC**	**FAC**	**FAT**	**Lge**	**SLC**	**FAC**	**FAT**	**Total**
Bascombe			1							
Bennett, Bob	**6**		1			**1**				**1**
Bloss, Phil	**29**	(1)	8	6	1					
Brown, Stan	**15**		5	6		**1**				**1**
Bryant, Jeff	**20**		2		0/1	**2**				**2**
Cooke, Ian	**39**		7	6	1	**14**	2	8		**24**
Crosby, Malcolm	**15**		4	2		**2**	2	1		**5**
Gadston, Joe	**16**		3	6		**3**	4	4		**11**
Guy, Dickie	**42**		8	6	1					
Hall, Brian	**10**	(1)		1		**1**				**1**
Langford, Steve	**37**		7	6	1					
Larkin, Andy	**4**	(2)	4/1	3/2	1	**1**	1			**2**
Loughlan, John	**34**	(1)	3	2	1					
Lucas, Dave	**32**		6	4	1	**4**	1			**5**
Mahon, Mick	**19**		2		1	**8**	1			**9**
Marchant, Andy	**18**	(1)	2	0/1		**1**				**1**
McCready, Tom	**37**		6	5	1	**4**	1			**5**
Moss, Bobby	**2**		2	1		**1**	1			**2**
Pinkney, Alan	**6**					**3**				**3**
Rice, Selwyn	**10**	(1)	4				1			
Smart	**2**									**1**
Smith, Graham	**34**	(1)	6	5	1	**2**				**2**
Stockley, Bob	**34**	(1)	7/1	6	1		1			**1**
Thompson, Hugh				1						
Willingham, David	**1**									
(own-goals)						**2**				**2**
25 players used	**462**	**(9)**	**88/2**	**66/3**	**11/1**	**50**	**15**	**13**		**78**

No	Date		Att	Pos	Pts	F-A	H-T	Scorers, Times, and Referees	1	2	3	4	5	6	7	8	9	10	11	12 sub used
1	A	NUNEATON B			L	**0-2**	0-1		Guy	Stockley	Bryant	**Donaldson**	**Edwards**	**Bassett**	Lucas	Rice!	**Connell**	**Somers**	Mahon	
	17/8		*1,576*		–			*Vincent 28p, 70*	*Knight*	*Stephens*	*Bruck*	*Oakes*	*Baxter*	*Goodwin*	*Mackay*	*Turpie*	*Vincent*	*Lewis*	*Briscoe*	
								Ref: D Hutchinson	New boss Allen Batsford has retained just seven players from the old regime, while giving debuts to five players signed from Walton & Hersham. Guy pulls down Boro skipper Lewis, and last season's top scorer Bob Vincent nets. Rice is sent off for aiming a kick at Bob Turpie.											
2	H	YEOVIL			W	1-0	0-0	Edwards 58	Guy	Stockley	Bryant	Donaldson	Edwards	Bassett	Cooke	Rice	Connell	Somers	Mahon	
	20/8		1,260		2				*Clark*	*Thompson*	*Cottle*	*Verity*	*Dixon*	*Harrison*	*Housley*	*Brown*	*Plumb*	*Thompson*	*McMahon!*	
								Ref: R Rodwell	1-0 does scant justice to Wimbledon's domination, for the Yeovil goal endured a rare pounding. Billy Edwards scored the only goal, when Kieron Somers flicked on a long throw. Eight minutes from time Yeovil's Frank McMahon hacked the goal-scorer and was sent off.											
3	H	BARNET			W	3-1	1-1	Connell, 32, 56, Cooke 88	Guy	Stockley	Bryant	Donaldson	Edwards	Bassett	Cooke	Rice	Connell	Somers	Mahon	
	24/8		1,001		4			*Embery 6*	*Christopher*	*Woodend*	*Wingate*	*Fusedale!*	*Tom*	*Ferry*	*Court*	*Bibby*	*Embery*	*Moss*	*Bristow*	
								Ref: J Christopher	Barnet have now lost their opening three games, though the Dons made hard work of this win. Their decisive third goal came when Barnet player-manager Gordon Ferry allowed the ball to bounce over his head. Barnet's Fusedale found himself sent off after the final whistle.											
4	A	TELFORD		5	W	1-0	0-0	Somers 52	Guy	Stockley	Bryant	Donaldson	Edwards	Bassett	Cooke	Rice	Connell	Somers	Mahon*	Lucas
	31/8		*1,318*	*17*	6				*Weir*	*Harris*	*Donaldson*	*Ray*	*Ross*	*Spavin*	*Fudge*	*Draycott*	*Bentley*	*Hawkins*	*Garbett*	
									Allen Batsford gets married before this match. His players give him the perfect wedding present, especially Somers, who fires in Mick Mahon's left-wing cross. Dickie Guy saves thrillingly from Dick Bentley's flying header. For the first time this season, no one was sent off.											
5	H	BURTON ALB		5	W	3-2	1-2	Bassett 15, Connell 53, 90	Guy	Stockley	Bryant	Donaldson	Edwards	Bassett	Cooke	Rice	Connell	Somers	Lucas	
	7/9		1,043	*21*	8			*Ward 4, Bowtell 39*	*Robinson*	*Gregg*	*Hogg*	*Fletcher*	*Fairhurst*	*Thornhill*	*Phillips!*	*Hickton*	*Wignall*	*Ward*	*Bowtell*	
								Ref: P Willett	For punching Cooke in the face after 75 minutes, Brendan Phillips becomes the fourth player sent off in five Wimbledon matches. Burton include ex-England Frank Wignall. Bassett's volley atones for his underhit back-pass. Connell's header wins the game after 93 minutes.											
6	A	GUILDFORD-DORK		5	W	**5-0**	1-0	Mahon 5p, 88p, Cooke 75, 82, 85	Guy	Stockley	Bryant	Bassett	Edwards	**Heath**	Cooke	Rice	Connell	Somers	Mahon	
	18/9		*975*	*19*	10				*Brooks*	*Peters*	*Summerhill*	*Finn*	*Edwards*	*Malley*	*Smith*	*Westburgh*	*Harman*	*Wright*	*Chapple*	
								Ref: G Campbell	This is the Dons's first visit to Meadowbank. Guildford manager Harry Hughes drops ex-QPR keeper Alan Spratley in favour of Brooks, who topples Somers for the first of Mick Mahon's two penalties. This is Wimbledon's eighth successive victory in all competitions.											
7	A	YEOVIL		4	W	1-0	0-0	Somers 83	Guy	Stockley	Bryant	Donaldson	Edwards	Bassett	Cooke	Rice	Connell*	Somers	Mahon	**Cummings**
	21/9		*2,353*	*3*	12				*Clark*	*Thompson*	*Irwin*	*Verity*	*Cotton*	*Harrison*	*Housley*	*Pickett**	*Plumb*	*McMahon*	*Brown*	*Cottle*
								Ref: B Stockley	Wimbledon's second 1-0 victory over Yeovil has the home fans giving their team the bird. Yeovil keeper Tony Clark conceded a needless corner, then missed it when it came across to Somers. Yeovil managed only three shots all match. Connell goes off with hamstring trouble.											
8	H	GRANTHAM		4	W	3-2	1-1	Connell 12, Bassett 66, Cooke 70	Guy	Stockley	Bryant	Donaldson	Edwards	Bassett	Cooke	Heath	Connell	**Swain**	Mahon	
	24/9		1,335	*12*	14			*Harrison 17, Norris 59*	*Gardiner*	*Bloomer*	*Crawford*	*Thompson*	*Harrison*	*Chalmers*	*Horobin*	*Taylor*	*Nixon*	*Norris*	*Benskin*	
								Ref: E Chaffer	At last Wimbledon defeat one of their biggest bogey sides. Grantham manager Terry Bly feels hard done by, for a late equaliser was ruled out for offside. Selwyn Rice missed the game – beginning his suspension – which chalked up a 10th straight win in all competitions.											
9	A	MAIDSTONE		4	W	1-0	1-0	Bryant 27	Guy	Stockley	Edwards	Donaldson	Bryant	Bassett	Rice	Cooke	Connell	Somers	Mahon	
	8/10		*940*	*17*	16				*Maggs*	*Sheridan*	*Barker*	*Priestley*	*Plume*	*O'Sullivan*	*McVeigh*	*Tough*	*Basey*	*Everest*	*Morton*	
								Ref: E Hopper	Ian Cooke weaves the magic; Jeff Bryant scores the goal. Maidstone's smallest crowd of the season witness an all-out attacking display by the Dons. In injury time keeper Maggs hacks down Connell. Both players are laid out, but rather than give a penalty the refereee blows for time.											
10	A	WEYMOUTH		3	W	3-0	0-0	Somers 65, 85, Connell 75	Guy	Stockley	Bryant	Donaldson	Edwards	Bassett	Cooke	Rice	Connell	Somers	Mahon	
	9/11		*1,246*	*5*	18				*Smith*	*Lawrence*	*Miller*	*Hobson*	*Williams*	*Foote*	*Courtney*	*Brown R*	*Brown J*	*Adams*	*Beer*	
								Ref: L Burden	Wimbledon have not played a league match for a month; now they must play three in a week. Weymouth came into this match unbeaten in nine, but they are outplayed on their own paddy-field. Keiron Somers' diving header through the mud sets up this crucial victory.											
11	H	WEYMOUTH		3	W	3-0	1-0	Somers 14, Connell 55, 80	Guy	Stockley	Bryant	Donaldson	Edwards	Bassett	Cooke	**Aitken**	Connell	Somers	Mahon	
	12/11		1,626	*7*	20				*Smith*	*Lawrence*	*Williams*	*Miller*	*Hobson*	*Foote*	*Courtney*	*Brown J*	*Brown R*	*Adams*	*Beer*	
								Ref: D Simmons	The Dons now have six games in hand on the leaders. Weymouth lack punch in attack; otherwise they look a useful side. But they become the Dons' 19th successive victims. Reckless back-passes to Guy could have proved suicidal. A power-cut interrupted play in the second half.											

No	Venue	Opponent	Att	Pos	Res	F-A	H-T	Scorers, Times, Referees	1	2	3	4	5	6	7	8	9	10	11	12
12	H	TONBRIDGE		4	W	4-1		Connell (2), Mahon, own-goal	Guy	Stockley	Bryant	Donaldson	Edwards	Bassett	Cooke	Rice	Connell	Somers	Mahon	
	16/11		1,802	*10*	22			*Bimson*	*Seymour*	*Flood*	*Prince*	*Kinsey*	*Keirs*	*Smith*	*Crush*	*Stonebridge*	*Thorburn*	*Putman*	*Bimson*	
								Ref: D Drewitt	Tonbridge are managed by George Cohen, who won a World Cup-winners medal for England in 1966. He took over as manager of Tonbridge at the end of the previous season, when he staved off relegation. Tonbridge provide Wimbledon with an 11th straight league win.											
13	A	CAMBRIDGE C		3	D	1-1	1-1	Bryant 43	Guy	Stockley	Bryant	Donaldson	Edwards	Bassett	Cooke	Rice	Connell	Somers	Mahon	
	3/12		***475***	*14*	23			*Martin 7*	*Barker*	*Duncliffe*	*Keenan*	*Guild*	*Kitchener*	*MacDonald*	*Newell*	*Heffer*	*Moden*	*Murray*	*Martin*	
								Ref: R Jackson	Modest Cambridge City halt Wimbledon's winning run at 22 in all competitions. In fact, City would have beaten the complacent Dons but for a generous referee, who consulted his linesman and allowed Wimbledon's equaliser to stand, even though Bryant appeared to use his arm.											
14	H	CAMBRIDGE C		3	W	1-0	1-0	Cooke 41	Guy	Stockley	Bryant	Donaldson	Edwards	Bassett	Cooke	Rice	Connell	Somers	Mahon*	Lucas
	17/12		1,415	*9*	25				*Barker*	*Duncliffe*	*Keenan*	*Guild*	*Crane*	*MacDonald*	*Newell*	*Heffer*	*Moden*	*Murray*	*Martin*	
								Ref: J Bellamy	Somers and Connell are still out of touch, but Wimbledon rap City over the knuckles for ending their winning run when substitute Lucas heads Bassett's long ball into the box and Keenan unintentionally sets up Cooke for the only goal of the game.											
15	A	STOURBRIDGE		4	L	1-2	1-1	Somers 35	Guy	Stockley	Bryant	Donaldson	Edwards	Bassett	Cooke	Rice	Connell	Somers	Mahon	
	21/12		*634*	*11*	25			*Allner 44, Davies 57*	*Moore*	*Richards*	*Saint*	*Pridgeon*	*Green*	*Davies*	*Booth*	*Cope*	*Barton*	*Chambers*	*Allner*	
								Ref: V Wood	Here's a shock. Wimbledon's first defeat in 26 games, and it is mediocre Stourbridge – whose team includes Worcestershire fast bowler Paul Pridgeon – who inflict it. Stourbridge had won at home only twice, but two headers put them in front, whereupon the Dons fell apart.											
16	H	DARTFORD		3	D	1-1	1-0	Cooke 33	Guy	Stockley	Bryant	Donaldson	Edwards	Bassett	Cooke	Rice	Connell	Somers	Lucas	
	26/12		1,820	*19*	26			*Jacques 89p*	*Keen*	*Lindsay*	*Shovellar*	*Carr*	*Burns*	*Mitchell*	*Light*	*Henderson*	*Robinson!*	*Jacques*	*Halliday*	
								Ref: J Raymond	Defending champions Dartford are headed for immediate relegation, but are grateful to Donaldson for his late trip on Halliday, which lets Joe Jacques level from the spot. This ends the Don's 100% home record. Robinson, sent off for attacking Bassett, V-signs the crowd as he goes.											
17	A	ROMFORD		4	W	2-0	0-0	Connell 60, Cooke 80	Guy	Stockley	Bryant	Donaldson	Edwards	Bassett	Cooke	Rice	Connell	Somers	Mahon	
	28/12		*882*	*22*	28				*Lightfoot*	*Yorath*	*Tapping*	*Mann*	*Bickles!*	*Ferry*	*Sanders*	*Chandler*	*Burge*	*Lewis J*	*Lewis B*	
								Ref: G Marshall	Yet another match with more punches than shots, and marred by inconsistent refereeing. The game erupted midway through the second half. Cooke appeared to be kicked in the head, and Romford's Bickles was shortly sent off for dissent. The game had hardly any football to report.											
18	A	WEALDSTONE		3	L	0-1	0-0		Guy	Stockley	Bryant	Donaldson	Aitken	Bassett!	Cooke	Lucas	Connell	Somers	Mahon	
	1/1		*3,400*	*7*	28			*Bryant 70 (og)*	*Morton*	*Kinnear*	*Watson!*	*Fairclough*	*McCormick*	*Godfrey*	*Fulton*	*Henderson*	*Moss*	*Duck*	*Eglite*	
								Ref: L Bartels	New Year, and the visit of Wimbledon, brings out Wealdstone's biggest crowd. FA Cup opponents Burnley have spies up in the stand. Sir Stanley Rous also spectates. They witness the expulsion of Dave Bassett and Jim Watson, who retaliated following Bassett's crude foul.											
19	H	ATHERSTONE		3	L	0-1	0-1		Guy	Stockley	Bryant	Aitken*	Edwards	Rice	Cooke	Bassett	Connell	Somers	Mahon	Lucas
	7/1		2,226	*16*	28			*Quinney 41*	*Withers*	*Russell*	*Beard*	*Smith*	*Preston*	*Kiernan*	*Smith*	*Dyer*	*Franklin*	*Hunt*	*Quinney*	
								Ref: B Baldry	Wimbledon humbled Burnley three days previously, and their emotionally drained heroes surrender their unbeaten home record. Donaldson was missing with a throat infection. Steve Quinney returns to the Atherstone team after two months out, and scores the all-important goal.											
20	H	CHELMSFORD		3	W	2-0	1-0	Cooke 30, Lucas 60	Guy	Stockley	Bryant	Donaldson	Edwards	Rice	Cooke	Lucas	Connell	Somers	Mahon	
	14/1		1,893	*11*	30				*Taylor*	*Coakley*	*Gomershall*	*Delea*	*Pittaway*	*Dunnell*	*Campbell*	*Barnard*	*Dilsworth*	*Kellock*	*Price*	
								Ref: J Jode	Cup feats mean that the Dons have won just one out of the last five in the league. Two players have special reason to remember this match – Dave Lucas, who enjoys a storming match, and Chelmsford's Eddie Dilsworth, who achieves the miss of the season from a wobbly back-pass.											
21	A	KETTERING		4	L	**0-2**	0-2		Guy	Stockley	Bryant	Donaldson	Edwards	Bassett	Cooke	Rice	Connell	Somers	Mahon	
	7/2		***3,696***	*3*	30			*Conde 11, Pawley 18*	*Livsey*	*Ashby*	*Loughlan*	*Ferris*	*Suddards*	*Rathbone*	*Large*	*Vowden*	*Conde**	*Clayton*	*Pawley*	*Myton*
									Brian Clough takes in the match. He is reportedly interested in Dickie Guy, but it is Billy Edwards' performance that catches his eye. The Dons are preoccupied with the Leeds replay, and hadn't the stomach to offer much resistance. Bassett was booked for the fourth time this season.											
22	H	KETTERING		5	L	0-1	0-1		Guy	Stockley	Bryant	Edwards	Donaldson	Bassett	Lucas	Cooke	Connell	Somers	Mahon	
	15/2		2,338	*2*	30			*Clayton 3*	*Livsey*	*Ashby*	*Loughlan*	*Myton*	*Suddards*	*Rathbone*	*Large*	*Vowden*	*Jones**	*Clayton*	*Pawley*	*Buckby*
								Ref: R Chaffer	Kettering achieve a rapid league double. Wimbledon have won just twice in eight in the league, and their title aspirations are slipping away. Nuneaton are 12 points clear, though the Dons have nine games in hand. Police have to be called after Batsford is harassed by angry fans.											
23	H	NUNEATON B		6	W	1-0	0-0	Somers 48	Guy	Stockley	Bryant	Edwards*	Donaldson	Bassett	Aitken	Cooke	Connell	Somers	Mahon	Lucas
	1/3		**3,856**	*1*	32				*Knight*	*Stephens*	*Newton*	*Bruck*	*Hayward*	*Baxter*	*Fleet*	*Owen*	*Briscoe*	*Lewis*	*Matthams*	
								Ref: D Bone	The most critical league match of the season brings out Plough Lane's biggest Southern League gate. For all its significance, it is a dull game played in dull weather. The result avenged defeat on the opening day. The priceless goal came after Connell dummied Mahon's cross.											

No	Date		Att	Pos	Pts	F-A	H-T	Scorers, Times, and Referees	1	2	3	4	5	6	7	8	9	10	11	12 sub used
24	A	CHELMSFORD		4	W	1-0	0-0	Lucas 55	Guy	Stockley	Bryant	Donaldson	Smith G'm	Bassett	Lucas	Cooke	Connell	Somers	Mahon	
	3/3		*2,786*	*16*	34				*Taylor*	*Coakley*	*Gomersall*	*Dyson*	*Pittaway*	*Tomkins*	*Dilsworth*	*Lee*	*Key*	*Kellock*	*Price*	
								Ref: D Jacklin	Lanky Lucas has become the boo-boy at Plough Lane, but he cracks home Cooke's short free-kick from 35 yards to delight the Dons travelling support. Dickie Guy had to go off for lengthy treament for a head injury, and returned to play with a white turban wrapped around him.											
25	H	DOVER		5	D	0-0	0-0		Guy	Stockley	Bryant	Donaldson	Edwards!	Bassett	Rice	Cooke	Lucas	Connell	Mahon	
	18/3		**968**	*13*	35				*Gadsby*	*Reynolds*	*Thornley*	*Fursden*	*Hamshare*	*Yorath*	*Wallace*	*Arnold*	*Cooper*	*Glazier*	*Simpson*	
								Ref: M Dixon	Knocked out of two cups, and the crowd dips below 1,000 for the first time. Connell is so angered by the referee that he courts expulsion by applauding him from the pitch. Edwards had already been sent off for ungentlemanly remarks when booked for throwing the ball away.											
26	A	TONBRIDGE		6	W	2-1	2-0	Cooke 13, Mahon 17	Guy	Stockley	Bryant	Donaldson	Edwards	Bassett	Cooke	Rice	Connell	Lucas	Mahon	
	22/3		*1,105*	*19*	37			*Keirs 80*	*Seymour*	*Evans*	*Prince*	*Kinsey*	*Keirs*	*Hancock*	*Flood*	*Smith*	*Crush*	*Stonebridge*	*Burnett**	*Walsh*
								Ref: R Woolven	Dons face two or three matches a week for the rest of the season. Tonbridge's ex-Charlton skipper Brian Kinsey blundered when Cooke out-jumped him to put Wimbledon ahead. Near the end Tonbridge fans among the record crowd ran onto the pitch for a kickabout with the ball.											
27	H	MAIDSTONE		5	W	2-1	2-1	Mahon 20, Donaldson 40	Guy	Stockley	Bryant	Donaldson	Edwards	Bassett	Cooke	Rice	Connell	Lucas	Mahon	
	25/3		1,982	*17*	39			*Woon 22*	*Maggs*	*Barker*	*Richardson*	*Priestley*	*Tough*	*Finch*	*Basey**	*Everest*	*Morton*	*Brown*	*Woon*	*McVeigh*
								Ref: R Banning	A second double over a Kent side in four days. Mahon hit the first, with a 20-yard rocket. Woon quickly levelled with an unchallenged header. Brown hit Dickie Guy's crossbar before Donaldson sealed the points for Wimbledon. All the action came in the first half.											
28	H	MARGATE		5	W	2-0	1-0	Cooke 40, Somers 87	Guy	Stockley	Bryant	Donaldson	Edwards	Bassett	Cooke	Rice	Connell*	Lucas	Mahon	Somers
	29/3		1,998	*6*	41				*Bowtell*	*Summers*	*Butler*	*Fusco*	*Breach*	*Clewlow*	*Clayton*	*Rouse**	*Gilbert*	*Gregory*	*Walker*	*Brown*
								Ref: L Burden	Roger Connell had to limp off after 36 minutes. Shortly afterwards Cooke scored from close range off Bowtell's fingers. In the second half Margate's Rouse was stretchered off following a collision with Lucas. Wimbledon substitute Kieron Somers then tapped into an empty net.											
29	A	DARTFORD		5	W	1-0	1-0	Somers 45	Guy	Stockley	**Smith Gary**	Donaldson	Edwards	Bassett	Cooke	Lucas	Rice	Somers	Mahon	
	31/3		*1,368*	*18*	43				*Vasper*	*Read*	*Stevens*	*Carr*	*Sampson*	*Robinson*	*Reeves*	*Marshall*	*Payne*	*Henderson*	*Halliday*	
								Ref: N Benton	Four wins in 10 days, all against Kent teams, have transformed Wimbledon's title prospects. Batsford gives a debut to Gary Smith, signed from Brentford just hours before the match. Mahon's cross made the goal. The relegation-threatened champs threw everyone forward after half-time.											
30	H	WEALDSTONE		5	L	1-2	1-1	Mahon 23p	Guy	Stockley	Smith Gary	Donaldson	Edwards	Bassett	Cooke	Rice	Somers	Lucas*	Mahon	**George**
	3/4		2,118	*4*	43			*Moss 34, Duck 61*	*Morton*	*Kinnear*	*Kitchener*	*Godfrey*	*Byrne*	*Watson*	*Fulton*	*Henderson*	*Moss*	*Duck*	*Eglite*	
								Ref: D Drewitt	Wealdstone repeat their New Year's Day win, despite Mahon's early penalty when he, himself, was fouled by Byrne. Former Ajax player Adrian Eglite crossed for Bobby Moss to level. George Duck, holder of Wealdstone's post-war record of 64 goals, got the winner.											
31	H	BATH		5	L	0-1	0-0		Guy	Stockley	Bryant	Donaldson	Edwards	Bassett	Cooke	Rice	Somers	Lucas	Heath*	George
	5/4		1,758	*6*	43			*Jones 60*	*Allen*	*Rogers*	*Scarrott*	*Smart*	*Gover*	*Tavener*	*Rogers*	*McInch*	*Jones*	*Edwards*	*Evans*	
								Ref: R Higgins	Two days later, another crippling home setback. Mick Heath returns to the Wimbledon side after a spell at college. This is referee Higgins' last match before retirement. Brian Evans set up the only goal for Dai Jones. The Dons pressed relentlessly, but the Bath defence soaked it all up.											
32	A	GRANTHAM		5	L	**0-2**	0-1		Guy	Stockley	Bryant	Donaldson	Edwards	Rice	Bassett	Cooke	Lucas	Somers	Mahon	
	7/4		*1,216*	*10*	43			Nixon 3, Horobin 74	*Gardiner*	*Clapham*	*Crawford*	*Ball*	*Harrison*	*Chambers*	*Horobin*	*Taylor*	*Nixon*	*Norris*	*Bentley*	
								Ref: S Smith	Once again Easter consumes Wimbledon's title hopes. They have yet to win at London Road in four attempts. Ernie Nixon sends the Dons on their way to a third defeat in five days when shooting through a ruck of players. Horobin poached the rebound when Guy saved from Bentley.											
33	A	BURTON ALB		5	D	0-0	0-0		Guy	Heath	Bryant	Donaldson	Edwards	Rice	Bassett	Cooke	Lucas	Connell	Mahon	
	10/4		*1,105*	*8*	44				*Robinson*	*Gregg*	*Hogg*	*Fletcher*	*Fairhurst*	*Thornhill*	*Phillips*	*Hickton*	*Wignall*	*Bridgewood*	*Storey-Moore*	
									Wimbledon have beaten Leatherhead 2-0 in the Final of the London Senior Cup, but they cannot win in the league. Burton include ex-England Ian Storey-Moore in their side. Guy saves well in the first half, Wimbledon dominate the second. At least the Dons avoid a fourth defeat.											
34	A	BATH			D	0-0	0-0		Guy	Stockley	Bryant	Donaldson	Edwards	Rice	Bassett	Cooke	Lucas	Connell	Somers	
	14/4		*2,908*		45				*Allen*	*Rogers*	*Scarrott*	*Smart*	*Gover*	*Tavener*	*Rogers*	*McInch*	*Jones*	*Edwards*	*Evans*	
								Ref: B Uzzell	Bath's biggest gate of the season endures yet another low-scoring match between these sides. It is five without a win for the Dons now, though they stand seven points behind Nuneaton with seven games in hand. Somers hit a post, but Rogers' header skimmed Guy's post at the death.											

No	Date	Opponent	Att	Pos	Res	FT	HT	Scorers / Referee	1	2	3	4	5	6	7	8	9	10	11	12
35 H	17/4	ROMFORD	2,030	6 *18*	W 47	3-0	2-0	Connell 4, 18, Somers 74 Ref: R Cocup	Guy *Lightfoot*	Stockley *Woodward*	Bryant *Tapping*	Donaldson *Mann*	Edwards *Peck*	Bassett *Bickles*	Cooke *Robinson**	Rice *Chandler*	Connell *Davies*	Somers *Burge*	Mahon *Ferry*	Lucas *Sanders* P
									Wimbledon need to rediscover the winning habit, and they are helped when keeper Lightfoot can only get his fingers to Connell's header. The scorer shortly scores again, another header from another Mahon cross. Somers' effort goes in off the bar. The Dons' first win in six games.											
36 A	19/4	MARGATE	*871*		D 48	3-3	0-1	Connell 49, Cooke 70, Donaldson 88 *Gregory 15, 60, Gilbert 85* Ref: J Hazell	Guy *Bowtell*	Stockley *Summers*	Bryant *Butler*	Donaldson *Fusco*	Edwards *Clewlow*	**Lambert** *Breach*	Cooke *Clayton*	Rice *Rouse*	Connell *Gilbert*	Somers *Gregory*	Mahon *Brown*	P
									Second-half palpitations as three times the Dons come from behind, the last of which through Donaldson just two minutes from time. Dickie Guy is beaten three times, and blunders for Brian Gregory's first goal, but Guy will remember this match for the many shots he saved.											
37 A	21/4	DOVER	*500*		L 48	0-2	0-0	*Wallace 58, Thornley 64p*	Guy *Gadsby*	Stockley *Reynolds*	Bryant *Thornley*	Donaldson *Fursden*	Smith Gary *Hamshare*	Lambert *Yorath*	George* *Wallace*	Rice *Arnold*	Connell *Cooper*	Somers *Simpson*	Lucas *O'Brian*	Cooke P
									Given the situation at the top, Wimbledon wanted a point and set out to get one, with Dave Bassett out injured. Kenny Wallace's left-foot volley is followed by Gary Smith's clumsy challenge on Dave Clay. Guy got a finger to Barry Thornley's spot-kick, but couldn't keep it out.											
38 H	22/4	GUILDFORD-DORK	2,314	2 *22*	W 50	3-1	1-1	Mahon 32, Bryant 55, Cooke 70 *Thorburn 14* Ref: R Rodell	Guy *Spratley*	Stockley *Summerhill*	Bryant *Westburgh*	Donaldson *Harris*	Smith Gary *Wright*	Lambert *Walker*	Cooke *Moody*	Lucas *Oates*	Connell *Harman*	Somers *Chapple*	Mahon* *Thorburn*	George P
									Guildford are bottom and doomed to relegation, yet they fought as though their lives depended on the result. Thorburn's goal is a gem, a solo effort ending with a chip over Guy. Mahon's flashing cross-shot puts the Dons on the road to recovery. Wimbledon are now second.											
39 A	24/4	BARNET	*762*	4 *21*	W 52	3-2	2-1	Cooke 31, Mahon 42p, 64 *Kempton 2, Tom 85* Ref: M Jermey	Guy *Embery*	Stockley *Webb*	Lambert *Williams*	Donaldson* *Tom*	Aitken *Kempton*	Lucas *Oliver*	Cooke *Potrac*	Rice *Blackaller*	Connell *Holmes*	Somers *Selwyn*	Mahon *Bibby*	George P
									Barnet are already relegated. Wimbledon are down to the wire: Bryant is injured, and Bassett and Edwards are suspended. To make matters worse, Donaldson breaks an arm. Barnet use Ben Embery, an outfield player, in goal. The Dons lead 2-1 when Paul Blackaller upends Mahon.											
40 H	29/4	STOURBRIDGE	3,054	2 *15*	W 54	2-0	1-0	Mahon 15p, Somers 65 Ref: C Lawthom	Guy *Moore*	Stockley *Barton*	Smith, Gary *Taylor*	Lambert *Pridgeon*	Edwards *Green*	Bassett *Davies*	Cooke *McGrath*	Rice *Cope*	Connell *Booth*	Somers *Rossi*	Mahon *Allner*	P
									An incident packed match, with three bookings and one penalty. Mahon was elbowed off the ball by Taylor, and takes the spot-kick which all but hands the Dons the title. They now top the table on goal-average and need just one more point. The fans chant 'champions, champions'.											
41 H	1/5	TELFORD	2,860	1 *10*	D 55	1-1	1-1	Somers 41 *Fudge 24* Ref: L Bartels	Guy *Weir*	Stockley *Harris*	Smith, Gary *Croft*	Edwards *Ray*	Aitken *Ross*	Bassett *Mallender*	Lucas *Fudge*	Rice *Watts*	Connell *Bentley*	Somers *Draycott*	Mahon *Garbett*	P
									Ian Cooke misses the celebrations because of an ankle injury. The game itself was disappointing, the Wimbledon players looking drained. The draw was enough for the championship, but three minutes from time Mahon's 25-yard 'winner' is disallowed. Somers was offside.											
42 A	2/5	ATHERSTONE	*710*		W 57	2-0	1-0	Connell 14, 65	Guy *Smith D*	Stockley *King*	Edwards *Beard*	Bassett *Smith*	Aitken *Preston*	Lucas *Kiernan*	Rice *Smith R*	George *Hunt*	Connell *Franklin*	Somers *Webster*	Mahon* *Kurila*	Cooke *Mellor* P
Average	Home 1,938		Away *1,468*						What a finish. Eight games in 16 days have yielded 13 points. Wimbledon sprint to the finishing line with a fifth successive win. Ray Webster misses two chances for the Adders, while Roger Connell accepts two for the Dons. These avenge defeat at Plough Lane back in January.											

Southern League Cup

No	Date	Opponent	Att		Res	FT	HT	Scorers / Referee	1	2	3	4	5	6	7	8	9	10	11	12
1:1 H	27/8	BOGNOR REGIS	1,127		W	4-0	0-0	Somers 52, 77, 80, 82 Ref: B Mullen	Guy *Patterson*	Stockley *Wiltshire*	Bryant *Pearce*	Donaldson *Phillips*	Edwards *Kill*	Bassett *Surrey*	Rice* *Dyer*	Cooke *Game*	Connell *Glue*	Somers *Holmes*	Mahon *Bennett*	Lucas P
									Eddie Reynolds was the last Wimbledon player to head four goals in a match, so Kieron Somers' achievement is another hint that great times are around the corner. The match ends in controversy when Connell's header passes through a hole in the net, and the ref gives a goal-kick.											
1:2 A	4/9	BOGNOR REGIS			W	3-1	1-1	Connell 36, 77, Somers 48 *Bennett 2* Ref: J Raymond (Dons win 7-1 on aggregate)	Guy *Patterson*	Stockley *Pearce*	Bryant *Wiltshire*	Donaldson *Phillips*	Edwards *Kill*	Bassett *Sheppard*	Cooke *Bradwell*	Rice *Watts*	Connell *Glue*	Somers *Holmes*	Lucas *Bennett*	P
									Bognor have no realistic chance of overhauling their four-goal deficit, but they make early inroads. Bryant is beaten by the pace of the ball on a greasy pitch and Bennett capitalises. Roger Connell's two-goal riposte – first a header, then a lob – ends Bognor's interest in the outcome.											
2 H	4/11	ASHFORD	1,158		W	4-0	3-0	Aitken 15, Cooke 31, Bryant 33, [Somers 49] Ref: A Harrington	Guy *Goddon*	Stockley *Bentley*	Bryant *Nash*	Donaldson *Coventry*	Edwards *Hurley*	Bassett* *Street*	Cooke *Pearce*	Aitken *Prager*	Connell *Muir*	Somers *Hold*	Mahon *Coates*	Lucas P
									A match to fill a notebook. The referee pulled a hamstring and had to be replaced by a linesman. A power failure interrupted play in the second half. Aitken – preferred to Rice – blasts the first goal. Cooke and Bryant both score with near-post headers from Mahon's corners.											

Southern League Cup			F-A	H-T	Scorers, Times, and Referees	1	2	3	4	5	6	7	8	9	10	11	12 sub used
3 H BIDEFORD		3 W	4-1	2-0	Somers 27, Cooke 35, 53, Mahon 83	Guy	Stockley	Bryant	Donaldson	Aitken	Lucas	Cooke	Rice	Connell	Somers	Mahon	
26/11	1,550				*Druce 81*	*Stevens*	*Anthony*	*Morris*	*May*	*Berry*	*Mock*	*Rowe*	*Sykes*	*Morris*	*Druce*	*Moxham*	
					Ref: W Druce	This match marks a milestone. It is Wimbledon's 22nd successive victory in all competitions, during which they have scored 66 and conceded just 11 goals. Cambridge City will end the run in their next match. Bideford, from north Devon, bring out Plough Lane's biggest midweek gate.											
QF H STOURBRIDGE		5 W	3-1	2-1	Somers 2, 88, Bryant 8	Guy	Stockley	Bryant	Donaldson	Edwards	Lucas	Cooke	Aitken*	Connell	Somers	Mahon	Rice
17/2	1,903	*11*			*Cope 4*	*Dulleston*	*Saint*	*Richards*	*Pridgeon*	*Green*	*Davies*	*Booth*	*Cope*	*Barton*	*Chambers*	*Allner*	
					Ref: R Smith	Stourbridge had in December ended Wimbledon's 26-match unbeaten run, so the Dons had a score to settle. Three goals in the first eight minutes got the game off to an electric start. Bryant's goal came from Wimbledon's sixth corner, which rebounded to him off a post.											
SF A KETTERING		6 L	0-3	0-3		Guy	Stockley	Bryant	Donaldson	Edwards	Bassett	Cooke	Lucas	Connell	Somers	Mahon	
10/3	*2,700*	*3*			*Pawley 14, Conde 24, 37*	*Livsey*	*Ashby*	*Loughlan*	*Ferris*	*Suddards*	*Rathbone*	*Large!*	*Vowden*	*Conde*	*Clayton*	*Pawley*	
					Ref: D Meredith	There is a private war betwen these two clubs, who now meet for the fifth time. Kettering had won twice in the league but been knocked out of two cups. They now snatch the rubber 3-2, though much-travelled Frank Large was sent off after 89 minutes for knocking out Connell.											

FA Cup			F-A	H-T	Scorers, Times, and Referees	1	2	3	4	5	6	7	8	9	10	11	12 sub used
1Q A BRACKNELL		2 W	3-1	3-1	Cooke 20, Connell 30, 38	Guy	Stockley	Bryant	Donaldson	Edwards	Bassett	Rice	Cooke	Connell	Somers	Mahon	
14/9	*917*	*SpL:4*			*Adams 4*	*Gurney*	*Baker*	*McLurg*	*Swain*	*Jeffries*	*Woodcock*	*Herbert**	*Gunn*	*Adams*	*Rudd*	*Lawrence*	*Hennessey*
						Bracknell are unbeaten in the Spartan League, and the visit of Wimbledon pulls in a bumper gate. The game has an explosive opening. Cooke hits the bar in the opening seconds, but a few minutes later the Dons are trailing. Cooke's header puts them back on course.											
2Q H MAIDENHEAD		W	4-0	1-0	Connell 31, 62, 78, Somers 52	Guy	Stockley	Bryant	Donaldson	Edwards	Bassett	Cooke	Rice	Connell	Somers	Swain	
5/10	1,357	*Isth2*				*Junger*	*Shiell*	*Watt*	*Johnson*	*Faulkes*	*Kent*	*Hutchinson*	*Kiely*	*Kemp*	*Senior*	*Wright*	
						Maidenhead play in Division 2 of the Isthmian League. Wimbledon almost face a crisis when Glenn Aitken – stripped and ready to play – learns that his transfer from Gillingham has not been cleared. Malcolm Swain was summoned from the bar to take his place.											
3Q H WOKINGHAM		W	2-0	1-0	Stockley 44, Cooke 55	Guy	Stockley	Bryant	Donaldson	Edwards	Bassett	Rice	Cooke	Connell	Somers	Mahon	
19/10	1,530					*Dixon*	*Corbin*	*Gale*	*Hartridge*	*Hatt*	*Harris*	*Burbidge*	*Ings*	*Weatherley*	*Wilks*	*McKevitt*	
					Ref: M Richardson	This one-sided match saw Wokingham win their first corner after 80 minutes. Controversy attended Wimbledon's first goal. Keeper Dixon gathered the ball from Stockley, but the linesman signals he had carried it over the line. After 65 minutes Mahon's penalty was easily saved.											
4Q A GUILDFORD-DORK		5 W	3-0	1-0	Connell 9, Donaldson 83, Cooke 89	Guy	Stockley	Bryant	Donaldson	Edwards	Bassett	Rice	Cooke	Connell	Somers	Mahon	
2/11	*1,201*	*21*				*Spratley*	*Peters*	*Summerhill*	*Finn*	*Wright*	*Ledger*	*Newman*	*Westburgh*	*Harman*	*O'Neill*	*Chapple*	
					Ref: A Gunn	Wimbledon won this fixture 5-0 in the league. For most of this cup-tie there is only one goal in it, a bullet header by Connell from Mahon's cross. Harman then hit Guy's post, but the keeper grabbed the rebound. Wright's poor back-pass, to make it 0-2, sends the Dons into Round 1.											
1 H BATH		3 W	1-0	0-0	Mahon 88	Guy	Stockley	Bryant	Donaldson	Edwards	Bassett	Cooke	Rice	Connell	Somers	Mahon	
23/11	5,450	*13*				*Allen*	*Gover*	*Scarrott*	*Smart*	*Goldthorpe*	*Tavener*	*Skirton*	*Edwards*	*Fairbrother*	*Rogers*	*Hall*	
					Ref: A Robinson	This pulsating match was settled in dramatic style. Mahon's 25-yard screamer sent Wimbledon into Round 2, registered their 21st consecutive win, and left Bath manager Bert Head conceding that such a goal deserved to win the tie. Cancellations elsewhere contributed to the large gate.											
2 H KETTERING		3 W	2-0	2-0	Cooke 13, Mahon 37p	Guy	Stockley	Bryant	Donaldson	Edwards	Bassett	Cooke	Rice	Connell	Somers	Mahon	
14/12	5,983	*4*				*Livsey*	*Ashby*	*Loughlan*	*Goodall*	*Rathbone*	*Suddard*	*Large*	*Myton*	*Conde*	*Clayton*	*Pawley*	
					Ref: A Turvie	Kettering had beaten Swansea City 3-1 in Round 1. The prospect of the Dons reaching Round 3 for the first time entices Plough Lane's biggest crowd for 11 years. Cooke's header, and keeper Livsey's trip on Connell, settle the outcome. Stockley is booked for V-signing Kettering fans.											
3 A BURNLEY		W	1-0	0-0	Mahon 49	Guy	Stockley	Bryant	Donaldson	Edwards	Bassett	Cooke	Rice	Connell	Somers	Mahon	
4/1	*19,683*	*Div1:7*				*Stevenson*	*Noble*	*Newton*	*Flynn*	*Waldron*	*Thomson**	*Ingham*	*Hankin*	*Fletcher*	*Collins*	*James*	*Morris*
					Ref: R Lee	The most sensational result in post-war FA Cup history. Yellow-kitted Wimbledon hold their own in the first half, and no sooner is the second under way than Cooke shoots, Stevenson parries, and Mahon scores. Somers might then have made it two. Sadly, no TV cameras were present.											
4 A LEEDS		D	0-0	0-0		Guy	Stockley	Bryant	Donaldson	Edwards	Bassett	Cooke	Rice*	Connell	Somers	Lucas	Aitken
25/1	*46,230*	*Div1:9*				*Harvey*	*Reaney*	*Gray F*	*Bremner*	*McQueen*	*Madeley*	*McKenzie*	*Yorath*	*Lorimer*	*Giles*	*Gray E*	

4R	H	LEEDS		4	L	0-1	0-0		Guy	Stockley	Bryant	Donaldson	Edwards	Bassett	Cooke	Rice	Connell	Somers	Mahon	
	10/2	(Selhurst Park)	45,701					*Bassett 50 (og)* Ref: D Turner	*Harvey*	*Reaney*	*Gray F*	*Bremner*	*Yorath*	*Madeley*	*McKenzie*	*Clarke*	*Jordan*	*Giles*	*Gray E*	

Switching the replay to Selhurst Park does not please everyone. Nor does Batsford's unashamedly defensive tactics. A couple of half-chances early on, then it is backs-to-the-wall stuff. Poor Bassett once again undermines the Wombles' cause, this time deflecting Giles' wayward shot.

FA Trophy

1	H	SUTTON U		4	W	3-1	1-1	Somers 3, 60, Edwards 70	Guy	Stockley	Bryant	Donaldson	Edwards	Bassett*	Rice	Cooke	Somers	Connell	Mahon	Lucas
	11/1		2,947					*Dennis 11* Ref: C White	*Collier*	*Fountain*	*Grose*	*Rains*	*Preston*	*McDonald*	*Ives*	*Pritchard*	*Walker*	*Dennis*	*Kidd*	

Batsford can hardly muster a full team. Once Wimbledon have opened a 3-1 lead, he pulls off the groin-strained Dave Bassett as a precaution. Leeds' spy, George Male, observes the Dons' every move, and could not help note that had Sutton taken their chances they would have won.

2	H	KETTERING		4	W	1-0	0-0	Cooke 75	Guy	Stockley	Bryant	Donaldson	Edwards	Bassett	Cooke	Lucas	Somers	Connell	Mahon
	1/2		3,221	*2*				Ref: C Maskell	*Livsey*	*Ashby*	*Loughlan*	*Goodhall*	*Rathbone*	*Suddard*	*Large*	*Myton*	*Conde*	*Clayton*	*Pawley*

Donaldson's long throw, Somers' flick-on, and Cooke's volley finally ruins Kettering's resistance. The visitors had been grateful to Livsey for his acrobatic save from Connell's header in the third minute. Football League clubs are reportedly enquiring about Guy and Stockley.

3	H	TELFORD		6	W	4-1	1-1	Cooke 18, Connell 68, 88, Aitken 79	Guy	Stockley	Bryant	Donaldson	Edwards	Aitken	Cooke	Lucas	Somers	Connell	Mahon
	22/2		3,490	*4*				*Bentley 1* Ref: J Bent	*Weir*	*Harris*	*Croft*	*Ray*	*Ross*	*Spavin*	*Fudge*	*Head*	*Bentley*	*Garbett*	*Hawkins*

Into the quarter-finals of this competition for the first time. Telford won this trophy in 1971, and knocked out the current holders, Morecombe, in Round 2. Two days before this match Bill Shankly presented the Dons with a Sportsmen's award in recognition of their FA Cup run.

QF	A	SCARBOROUGH			L	0-1	0-0		Guy	Stockley	Bryant	Donaldson	Edwards	Bassett	Cooke	Lucas	Connell	Somers	Mahon
	8/3		*8,015*	*NP:4*				*Aveyard 58* Ref: G Courtenay	*Williams*	*Fountain*	*Pettit*	*Dunn*	*Marshall*	*Todd*	*Houghton*	*Hewitt*	*Davidson*	*Barmby*	*Aveyard*

This result stands as the most disappointing in Wimbledon's tumultuous season. Scarborough won this trophy in 1973, and reach the last four again courtesy of Edwards' terrible back-pass. The Dons hit the woodwork three times. Scarborough will lose the Final 0-4 to Matlock Town.

		Home					Away					
	P	W	D	L	F	A	W	D	L	F	A	Pts
1 WIMBLEDON	42	14	3	4	36	15	11	4	6	27	18	57
2 Nuneaton B	42	16	3	2	40	15	7	5	9	16	22	54
3 Yeovil	42	17	3	1	50	8	4	6	11	14	26	51
4 Kettering	42	13	4	4	49	16	7	6	8	24	24	50
5 Burton Alb	42	11	7	3	30	16	7	6	8	24	32	49
6 Bath	42	12	6	3	40	22	8	2	11	23	28	48
7 Margate	42	11	7	3	38	20	7	4	10	27	44	47
8 Wealdstone	42	11	6	4	34	21	6	5	10	28	40	45
9 Telford	42	10	6	5	30	18	6	7	8	25	38	45
10 Chelmsford	42	10	4	7	40	25	6	8	7	22	26	44
11 Grantham	42	13	7	1	48	16	3	4	14	23	46	43
12 Dover	42	10	4	7	20	15	5	9	7	23	38	43
13 Atherstone	42	11	7	3	34	20	3	7	11	14	33	42
14 Maidstone	42	12	4	5	31	16	3	8	10	21	34	42
15 Weymouth	42	11	5	5	41	24	2	7	12	25	36	38
16 Stourbridge	42	8	9	4	32	25	5	3	13	24	45	38
17 Cambridge C	42	7	7	7	31	25	4	7	10	19	31	36
18 Tonbridge	42	6	7	8	23	25	5	5	11	21	41	34
19 Romford	42	7	8	6	27	24	3	5	13	19	38	33
20 Dartford	42	6	7	8	31	29	3	6	12	21	41	31
21 Barnet	42	8	4	9	28	30	2	5	14	16	46	29
22 Guildford & Dk	42	8	3	10	36	40	2	2	17	9	42	25
	924	232	121	109	769	465	109	121	232	465	769	924

Odds & ends

Double wins: (8) Yeovil, Barnet, Guildford & Dorking, Weymouth, Maidstone, Tonbridge, Romford, Chelmsford.
Double losses: (2) Kettering, Wealdstone.

Won from behind: (5) Barnet (h), Burton (h), Grantham (h), Guildford & Dorking (h), Barnet (a).
Lost from in front: (2) Wealdstone (h), Stourbridge (a).

High spots: 22-match winning sequence from August to December.
A run of 26 unbeaten games, in all competitions, in that period.
First championship, most points, for Wimbledon in the Southern League.
First non-league team to win at a 1st Division ground since 1945.

Low spots: Just 2 league wins out of 8, December to February.
5 games without a win, including three straight defeats, in early April.

Wimbledon had three players score more than 20 goals in one season.
11 players played 35 or more league games. The side picked itself.

Player of the Year: Ian Cooke.
Ever-presents: (1) Dickie Guy.
Hat-tricks: Roger Connell (1), Keiron Somers (1), Ian Cooke (1).
Leading scorer: Roger Connell (26).

	Appearances					Goals				
	Lge	Sub	SLC	FAC	FAT	Lge	SLC	FAC	FAT	Total
Aitken, Glen	**7**		3	0+1	1		1		1	**2**
Bassett, Dave	**37**		4	9	3	**2**				**2**
Bryant, Jeff	**36**		6	9	4	**3**	2			**5**
Connell, Roger	**38**		6	9	4	**16**	2	6	2	**26**
Cooke, Ian	**38**	(2)	6	9	4	**14**	3	4	2	**23**
Cummings		(1)								
Donaldson, Dave	**37**		6	9	4	**2**		1		**3**
Edwards, Billy	**37**		5	9	4	**1**			1	**2**
George, Ricky	**2**	(4)								
Guy, Dickie	**42**		6	9	4					
Heath, Mick	**4**									
Lambert, Chris	**5**									
Lucas, Dave	**22**	(5)	4/2	1	3/1	**2**				**2**
Mahon, Mick	**37**		5	7	4	**10**	1	3		**14**
Rice, Selwyn	**35**		3/1	9	1					
Smith, Gary	**6**									
Smith, Graham	**1**									
Somers, Keiron	**36**	(1)	6	9	4	**12**	9	1	2	**24**
Stockley, Bob	**41**		6	9	4			1		**1**
Swain, Mal	**1**			1						
(own-goals)						**1**				**1**
20 players used	**462**	**(13)**	**66/3**	**100**	**44/1**	**63**	**18**	**16**	**8**	**105**

/ denotes substututes

SOUTHERN LEAGUE PREMIER DIVISION

Manager: Allen Batsford

SEASON 1975-76

No	Date		Att	Pos	Pts	F-A	H-T	Scorers, Times, and Referees	1	2	3	4	5	6	7	8	9	10	11	12 sub used	
1	A	CAMBRIDGE C			D	1-1	1-0	Mahon 43p	Guy	**Falconer**	Bryant	Donaldson	Edwards	Bassett*	Aitken	Cooke	**Holmes**	Somers	Mahon	Connell	P
	16/8		*758*		1			*Moden 83*	*Johnson*	*Rule*	*Elliott*	*Keenan*	*Crane*	*Newell*	*Coe*	*Moden*	*Kettleborough*	*Murray*	*Martin*		
									Wimbledon have beaten Kettering 1-0 in the annual fixture between the Southern League champs and cup-winners. Henry Falconer and Billy Holmes now make their league debuts. Falconer takes the place of Bob Stockley, who is suspended. Bassett goes off with a badly cut eye.												
2	H	BURTON ALB		5	W	4-0	2-0	Mahon 30p, 74p, Cooke 45, Holmes 70	Guy	Falconer	Bryant	Donaldson	Edwards	Bassett	Rice	Cooke	Holmes	Somers	Mahon		P
	23/8		1,662	*22*	3				*Allcock*	*Gregg*	*Mole*	*Shone*	*Annable*	*Sykes*	*Fletcher*	*Phillips*	*Hickton*	*Thompson*	*Lang*		
								Ref: L Bartels	Burton have never won at Plough Lane. This match had its chaotic moments. When Phil Annable inexplicably handled, Mahon fired his spot-kick over the top, only to be invited to try again. This time he scored. Falconer hit a back-pass from the halfway line that flew for a corner.												
3	A	HILLINGDON B		3	W	1-0	1-0	Somers 39	Guy	Falconer	Bryant	Bassett	Edwards	Donaldson	Aitken	Cooke	Holmes	Somers	Connell		P
	30/8		*650*	*19*	5				*Phillips*	*Hawley*	*Gelson*	*Ryan*	*Archer*	*Johnson*	*Wagstaff*	*Brown*	*McGovern*	*Bishop*	*Reeve*		
								Ref: V Wood	Boro are without a manager following Jim Langley's shock resignation. Mahon is dropped to accommodate Somers and Connell in attack. Somers responds with his first goal of the season, heading in Connell's cross. Four days earlier the Dons won 3-0 in the Southern League Cup.												
4	H	MARGATE		5	W	2-1	1-0	Somers 6, 80	Guy	Falconer	Bryant	Donaldson	Edwards	Aitken	Bassett	Cooke	Mahon	Somers	Connell		P
	6/9		1,633	*19*	7			*Gregory 55*	*Bowtell*	*Summers*	*Butler*	*Fusco*	*Dean*	*Clewlow*	*Baber*	*Brown*	*Gilbert*	*Gregory*	*Thornley*		
								Ref: D Bone	Not the most fluid of games. Somers bagged two but missed four equally good chances. Keeper Bowtell is off his line as Somers heads Mahon's cross into an empty net. Somers also grabs the winner from close range after the ball bounces back off the crossbar.												
5	A	MAIDSTONE			W	4-2	3-2	Bryant 3, Cooke 37, Somers 45, Rice 55	Guy	Falconer	Bryant	Donaldson	Aitken	Bassett	Rice	Cooke	Connell	Somers	Mahon		
	9/9		*1,313*		9			*McVeigh 10p, Sparks 40*	*Bellotti*	*McVeigh*	*Glozier*	*Priestley*	*Richardson*	*Sparks*	*Smith**	*Brown*	*Basey*	*Woon*	*Crush*	*O'Sullivan*	
								Ref: D Drewitt	A demonstration of Wimbledon's power game. Maidstone's new keeper, Derek Bellotti, does not know where to hide. Cooke's shot comes back off the post to Bryant. But Maidstone quickly level when Donaldson fells Crush in the box. The rest of the first half rained goals.												
6	A	GRANTHAM		1	W	1-0	0-0	Somers 85	Guy	Falconer	Bryant	Donaldson	Aitken	Bassett	Rice	Cooke	Holmes	Somers	Connell		P
	13/9		*983*	*11*	11				*Gardiner*	*Capewell*	*Clapham*	*Taylor*	*Harrison*	*Chambers**	*Jackson*	*Bower*	*Nixon*	*Norris*	*Benskin*	*Dixon*	
								Ref: B Hill	Wimbledon win at Grantham for the first time, but it is an awful match. Somers, unmarked, heads past Gardiner for the goal that takes the Dons top of the league. Cooke supplied one of the few memorable moments, pulling down a cross with one foot and shooting with the other.												
7	H	GRAVESEND		1	W	2-1	1-0	Norman 26 (og), Holmes 90p	Guy	Falconer	Bryant	Donaldson	Edwards	Bassett	Aitken	Cooke	Connell	Somers	Holmes		P
	16/9		1,506	*12*	13			*Woolfe 60*	*Cowan*	*Weston*	*Hall*	*Embery*	*Pearce*	*Burrett*	*Jeffrey*	*Norman*	*Bostock*	*Thurgood*	*Woolfe*		
								Ref: L Burden	Newly promoted Gravesend are within seconds of maintaining their unbeaten start to the season. In injury-time Ken Pearce needlessly shoves Connell off the ball, though the keeper claimed it anyway. With Mahon out with flu, Holmes takes responsiblity from the penalty spot.												
8	H	KETTERING		1	W	2-0	0-0	Mahon 78, 83	Guy	Falconer	Donaldson	Bryant	Edwards	Rice	Bassett	Cooke	Mahon	Somers	Connell*	Holmes	P
	20/9		1,953	*17*	15				*Livsey*	*Ashby*	*Loughlan*	*Goodall*	*Suddards*	*Ferris*	*Rathbone*	*Myton*	*Conde*	*Clayton*	*Harris*		
								Ref: J Jenkin	The recalled Rice brings added bite to midfield. Time is running out when substitute Holmes, with his first touch, sets up Mahon's first goal. Roy Clayton should have levelled before Mahon made sure. Kettering look less potent now that Frank Large and McVeigh have departed.												
9	H	TELFORD		1	W	3-0	0-0	Falconer 47, Holmes 62, 70	Guy	Falconer	Bryant	Donaldson	Edwards	Rice	Bassett	Cooke	Somers	Holmes	Mahon		P
	27/9			*8*	17				*Weir*	*Harris*	*Croft*	*Mallender*	*Ross*	*Pearce*	*Fudge*	*Davies*	*Bentley*	*Ray*	*Cochrane*		
								Ref: M Hazzard	Telford can barely get out of their own half, but they somehow survive till after half-time. Then Harris heads Falconer's cross into his own net. Falconer claims the goal. Holmes is later denied a hat-trick by the outstretched boot of Ross, which deflects his shot against the post.												
10	A	ATHERSTONE		1	L	1-2	0-1	Mahon 51	Guy	Falconer	Bryant	Donaldson	Edwards	Aitken	Rice	Cooke	Connell	Somers	Mahon		
	4/10		*982*	*5*	17			*Jennings 2, Franklin 59*	*Hall*	*Stockley*	*Beard*	*Smith G*	*Preston*	*Kiernan*	*Smith R*	*Franklin*	*Tearse*	*Vincent*	*Jennings*		
								Ref: J Ball	Bob Stockley makes a dream debut for the Adders. The former Wimbledon full-back keeps a tight grip on Mahon and has a goal disallowed just after half-time. Barry Franklin scores Atherstone's winner off the post, leaving mediocre Wimbledon to sniff defeat for the first time.												
11	A	BEDFORD		1	W	1-0	0-0	Connell 76	Guy	Falconer	Bryant	Donaldson	Edwards	Aitken	Rice	Cooke	Connell	Holmes	Mahon*	**Tilley**	
	11/10		*1,673*	*7*	19				*Peacock*	*Skinn*	*Folds*	*Gould*	*Cooley*	*Earl*	*Hawkins*	*Phillips*	*Sargent*	*Dove*	*Burdett*		
								Ref: T Hardman	An entertaining match that sees the Dons survive a first-half siege. Both Sargent and and Hawkins have goals for Bedford wiped out for offside. When Peacock drops a deep cross, Connell is permitted to walk the ball in. Sargent hits Dickie Guy's crossbar near the end.												

No	Date	Opponent	Att	Pos	Pts	Res	F-A	H-T	Scorers, Times, and Referees	1	2	3	4	5	6	7	8	9	10	11	12
12	H	BATH		1		L	0-2	0-1		Guy	Tilley	Donaldson	Bryant	Edwards	Aitken	Rice	Connell	Cooke	Somers	Holmes	
	18/10		2,011	*19*	19				*McInch 17, Edwards 86 (og)*	*Allen*	*Gover*	*Jones*	*Smart*	*Edwards*	*Tavener*	*Rogers*	*McInch*	*Fairbrother*	*Rogers**	*Evans*	
									Ref: D Holland	Bath are bottom and winless, but they are proving something of a bogey-side. Wimbledon scored just once in three meetings against them last season, and the scorer – Mahon – is injured. Aitken's back-pass sets up the first goal, and 6' 6" keeper Kenny Allen gobbles up high balls.											
13	A	BURTON ALB		1		W	2-1	2-0	Aitken 13, Mahon 18	Guy	Tilley	Bryant	Donaldson	Aitken	Bassett	**Vansittart**	Rice	Connell	Holmes	Mahon	
	8/11		*1,053*	*13*	21				*Wright 46*	*Alcock*	*Thompson*	*Hallsworth*	*Shone*	*Annable*	*Fletcher*	*Sykes*	*Wright*	*Hickton*	*Phillips*	*Lang*	
										Cooke, Somers, and Edwards are all injured, allowing Tommy Vansittart to make his debut. Wimbledon fire two super first-half goals, both from long range. Albion hit back within 35 seconds of the second half, when Wright climbs higher than three Wimbledon defenders.											
14	H	BEDFORD		1		D	0-0	0-0		Guy	Tilley	Bryant	Donaldson	Aitken	Bassett	Rice	Cooke	Connell	Holmes	Mahon	
	15/11		2,157	*12*	22					*Peacock*	*Skinn*	*Cooley*	*Gould*	*Folds*	*Buck*	*Campbell*	*Phillips*	*Sargent*	*Hawkins*	*Markham*	
									Ref: A Harrington	Wimbledon have claimed the non-League Champions' Trophy, defeating Northern Premier champions Wigan 2-1 over two legs and extra-time. Back in the league, Leo Markham lines up for Bedford in this grim battle, which produced no clear-cut chances for either side.											
15	A	DUNSTABLE		1		L	0-1	0-0		Guy	Tilley	Bryant	Donaldson	Aitken	Bassett	Rice*	Cooke	Connell	Holmes	Mahon	Vansittart
	25/11		*962*	*4*	22				*Spillane 48*	*Steel*	*Minton*	*Collard*	*Millett*	*Robinson*	*Davies*	*Adams*	*Woolgar*	*Mortimer*	*Spillane*	*Cleary*	
									Ref: P Willett	Dunstable are going well. Batsford appears to be playing for a draw, but once Dave Spillane's header opens the scoring, keeper Steel is forced to save well from Holmes and Mahon. Bryant heads against the junction. 'We played badly against a terrible team,' declares Allen Bastford.											
16	A	TELFORD		1		D	0-0	0-0		Guy	Tilley	Bryant	Donaldson	Aitken	Bassett	Rice	Cooke	Connell	Holmes	Vansittart	
	29/11		*846*	*10*	23					*Weir*	*Harris*	*Croft*	*Mallender*	*Ross*	*Pearce*	*Fudge*	*Head*	*Bentley*	*Ray*	*Garbett*	
									Ref: A Corr	Three games without a goal for Wimbledon. Injuries and suspensions force Batsford to play a defensive 4-4-2. Mahon is also unable to get time off from his teaching job. On the hour Guy makes the save of the match from Garbett. The Dons still top the table, but only just.											
17	H	DOVER		1		W	3-0	1-0	Vansittart 37, Cooke 65, Holmes 87	Guy	Tilley	Bryant	Donaldson	Aitken	Bassett	Rice	Vansittart	Cooke	Holmes	Mahon	
	20/12		**1,102**	*20*	25					*Raine*	*Reynolds*	*Keely*	*Breach*	*Waite*	*Coupland*	*Hamshare!*	*Coxhill*	*Housden*	*Light*	*Rogers*	
									Ref: B Uzzell	In the FA Cup Brentford have just beaten the Dons 2-0. They get back to goalscoring ways despite the absence through injury of both Connell and Somers. Vansittart gets his first goal. Hamshare then slings a lump of mud at the Dons bench and is sent off, sparking a war of words.											
18	A	WEALDSTONE		2		W	2-0	1-0	McCormick 31 (og), Cooke 51	Guy	Tilley*	Bryant	Donaldson	Aitken	Bassett	Rice	Cooke	Connell	Holmes	Mahon	Vansittart
	26/12		*2,167*	*10*	27					*Morton*	*Kinnear*	*Watson*	*Fairclough*	*McCormick*	*Lewis*	*Moss*	*Fulton*	*Byrne*	*Duck*	*Henderson*	
									Ref: R Telfer	Wimbledon lose to Enfield in the London Senior Cup, then become the first team to win at Lower Mead this season. Wealdstone did the double in 1974-75. Ex-Palace centre-half John McCormick is credited with an own-goal when George Duck's attempted clearance hits him.											
19	A	KETTERING		2		D	3-3	0-2	Bryant 47, Mahon 72p, Bassett 86	Guy	Tilley	Bryant	Donaldson	Edwards	Bassett*	Rice	Cooke	Connell	Holmes	Mahon	Vansittart
	1/1		*2,679*	*15*	28				*Clayton 6, 57, Wardrop 42*	*Livsey*	*Ashby*	*Myton*	*Wardrop*	*Suddards*	*Rathbone*	*Harris*	*Goodall*	*Dougan*	*Clayton*	*Smith*	
									Ref: D Jackson	A pulsating match. Derek Dougan has just become player-manager of Kettering. He 'scores' within a minute, but the effort is disallowed. At 1-3 Connell is fouled in the box. Bassett then equalises with a flying header in off the bar. Bassett and Livsey collide and both are hospitalised.											
20	A	NUNEATON B				L	0-1	0-1		Guy	Tilley!	Bryant	Donaldson	Edwards	Vansittart	Aitken	Cooke	Connell	Holmes*	Mahon	**Leslie**
	3/1		*1,526*		28				*Stephens 31*	*Knight*	*Stephens*	*Newton*	*Lewis*	*Bennett*	*Cross*	*Hawkins*	*Fleet*	*Allan!*	*Thompson*	*Goodwin*	
									Ref: P Willett	John Leslie, signed from Dulwich, comes off the bench for his debut and ends up being stretchered to hospital. Tilley and Allan clash in injury time and are both sent off, leaving the Dons with nine men. Guy had parried Stephens's shot, but the ball had dropped into the goal.											
21	A	MARGATE				L	0-2	0-0		Guy	Falconer	Bryant	Donaldson	Edwards	Bassett	Vansittart	Cooke	Connell	Holmes	Mahon	
	17/1		*626*		28				*Gregory 53, 81*	*Bowtell*	*Byford*	*Thornley*	*Fusco*	*Dean*	*Clewlow*	*Pain*	*Summers*	*Gilbert*	*Gregory*	*Tough*	
									Ref: D Mardle	Four away games on the trot and just one point from the last three. Margate's top scorer Bryan Gregory is the difference between the sides, scoring one in the air and one on the ground. Wimbledon persisted with long-ball tactics though they seldom looked like succeeding.											
22	H	YEOVIL		4		D	0-0	0-0		Guy	Tilley	Donaldson	Bryant	Edwards	Bassett	Vansittart	Cooke	Holmes	Leslie	Mahon	
	24/1		1,734	*6*	29					*Clarke*	*Thompson*	*Cottle*	*Jones*	*Cotton*	*Harrison*	*McMahon*	*Brown*	*Plumb*	*Adams*	*Clancy*	
									Ref: E Chaffer	Four games without a win and the slide continues. Connell is suspended and Somers injured. Yeovil have a poor away record, but they create several chances in the first half. John Leslie plays his first full game, but doesn't enjoy conditions on this snow-swept pitch.											
23	H	GRANTHAM		5		W	2-1	1-1	Mahon 33, Vansittart 90	Guy	Tilley	Bryant	Donaldson	Edwards	Rice	Vansittart	Cooke	Connell	Holmes	Mahon	
	14/2		1,295	*4*	31				*Jackson 23*	*Gardiner*	*Bower*	*Capewell*	*Taylor*	*Harrison*	*Jackson*	*Capewell*	*McMenamin*	*Nixon*	*Carr*	*Platt*	
									Ref: R Banning	The first win in the league for seven weeks, courtesy of an injury-time winner. Grantham borrow Carr and Platt from Leicester hours before kick-off. Keeper Gardiner plays despite a slipped disc, which keeps him rooted to the ground when Mahon's cross floats over his head.											

SOUTHERN LEAGUE PREMIER DIVISION Manager: Allen Batsford SEASON 1975-76

No	Date	Att	Pos	Pts	F-A	H-T	Scorers, Times, and Referees	1	2	3	4	5	6	7	8	9	10	11	12 sub used
24	A BATH		4	W	1-0	1-0	Connell 21	Guy	Tilley	Bryant	Donaldson	Edwards	Bassett	Rice	Cooke	Connell	Holmes	Vansittart*	Leslie
	21/2	*1,037*	*16*	33				*Parry*	*Blackmore*	*Tavener*	*Gover*	*Edwards*	*Rogers M*	*Rogers P*	*Evans*	*Owen*	*Griffin*	*Fairbrother*	
							Ref: James	The Dons avenge a home defeat by Bath. They do so by rolling up their sleeves and softening up the opposition, aided by a lenient referee. At one stage Tilley appeared to punch Martin Rogers in front of the ref, who did nothing. Wimbledon defended Connell's strike at all costs.											
25	A YEOVIL		4	W	2-1	1-1	Cooke 44, Bryant 50	Guy	Tilley	Bryant	Donaldson	Vansittart	Edwards	Rice	Cooke	Connell	Holmes	Mahon	
	25/2	***2,912***	*3*	35			*Clancy 7*	*Clark*	*Thompson*	*Cottle*	*Jones*	*Cotton*	*Harrison*	*McMahon*	*Brown*	*Hickton*	*Harland*	*Clancy*	*Adams*
							Ref: D Hurved	Thick fog rolled over the Huish so that nobody could see what was going on. Once Bryant had put the Dons 2-1 up, the home crowd bayed for the match to be called off. Though the referee could barely see the end of his nose he allowed the match to finish, to Wimbledon's relief.											
26	H TONBRIDGE		2	W	3-0	0-0	Bassett 67, Connell 71, 86	Guy	Tilley	Bryant	Donaldson	Edwards	Bassett*	Vansittart	Cooke	Connell	Leslie	Mahon	Falconer
	28/2	1,878	*17*	37				*Hughes*	*Flood*	*Cooper*	*Hickey*	*Keirs*	*Hancock*	*Debnam*	*Arnold*	*Walsh*	*Smith*	*Stonebridge*	
							Ref: M Dixon	Wimbledon turn on a scorching second half to notch a sixth successive win in all competitions. George Cohen's Tonbridge did well for an hour and were then blown away. The saddest man was Tommy Vansittart. He scores from the halfway line, but the ref says Connell was offside.											
27	H CAMBRIDGE C		2	D	0-0	0-0		Guy	Tilley	Bryant	Donaldson	Edwards	Bassett	Rice	Cooke	Connell	Holmes	Leslie	
	3/3	1,475	*22*	38				*Johnson*	*Rule*	*Elliott*	*Keenan*	*Crane*	*Newell*	*Coe*	*Moden*	*Kettleborough*	*Murray*	*Duguid*	
							Ref: J Jenkins	City are marooned at the bottom but wage a desperate rearguard battle to earn this precious point. It might have been two had Duguid taken either of two rare first-half chances. Mick Mahon is again out injured. The Dons look leg-weary after playing three matches in five days.											
28	A CHELMSFORD			L	**0-3**	0-2		Guy	Tilley	Bryant	Bassett	Edwards	Aitken	Rice	Cooke	Connell	Holmes	Leslie	
	6/3	*1,228*		38			*Lamb 12, 47, Roe 42*	*Taylor*	*Rowell*	*Tomkins*	*Burney*	*Shore*	*Walker*	*Rowe*	*Kellard*	*Lamb*	*Little*	*Price*	
							Ref: D Holland	There is ill-feeling between these sides. Wimbledon have been fined £50 for failing to turn up at Chelmsford in January for a Southern League Cup replay. Dave Donaldson fails to turn up, missing his only match. 21-year-old Steve Lamb, just signed from Southend, has a cracker.											
29	H HILLINGDON B		1	D	2-2	2-0	Leslie 38, Connell 43	Guy	Tilley	Bryant	Donaldson	Edwards	Bassett	Rice	Cooke	Connell	Holmes	Leslie	
	9/3	1,356	*18*	39			*Wagstaffe 75, Huxley 89*	*Phillips*	*Mace*	*Ryan*	*Gelson*	*Hawley*	*McGovern*	*Smith*	*Wagstaffe*	*Reeve*	*Burge*	*Huxley*	
							Ref: R Chaffer	The Dons beat Hillingdon three times early in the season, and this point is enough to take them back to the top. Dickie Guy complains that when Boro equalised near the end he lost the ball briefly in the floodlights. It bounced inside the six yard box and Gary Huxley swept it in.											
30	H WEYMOUTH		1	W	4-0	2-0	Holmes 18, 48, Mahon 35p, Connell 83	Guy	Tilley	Bryant	Donaldson	Edwards	Rice	Cooke	Leslie	Connell	Holmes	Mahon	
	13/3	1,521	*11*	41				*Corbett*	*Lawrence*	*Olsen*	*Miller*	*Hobson*	*Carr*	*Courtney*	*Arnold*	*Astle*	*Owen*	*Verity*	
							Ref: D Bone	Weymouth's Jeff Astle, best remembered for that miss against Brazil in World Cup '70, is the league's top scorer. Yet this is the 11th game without a win for Dietmar Bruck's team. Their goalkeeper, Corbett, was repeatedly beaten to high crosses by Roger Connell.											
31	A GRAVESEND		1	D	0-0	0-0		Guy	Tilley	Bryant	Donaldson	Edwards	Bassett	Aitken	Cooke	Connell	Holmes	Leslie	
	16/3	*1,579*	*6*	42				*Cowan*	*Evans*	*Hall*	*Embery*	*Pearce*	*Binks*	*Brown*	*Burrett*	*Norman*	*Finch*	*Woolfe*	
							Ref: L Smith	A whistle-happy referee does not assist free-flowing football. Gravesend are unbeaten at home for two years. Only in injury time does that record look in danger, but Cooke's header is not quite accurate enough. Colin Norman's 'goal' for the home team after 10 minutes was offside.											
32	H DUNSTABLE		1	W	3-0	1-0	Holmes 37, 55, Mahon 83p	Guy	Tilley	Bryant	Donaldson	Edwards	Bassett	Cooke	Leslie	Holmes*	Connell	Mahon	Somers
	20/3	1,842	*3*	44				*Steel*	*Minton*	*Collard*	*Millett*	*Robinson*	*Davies*	*Adams*	*Woolgar*	*Waters*	*Iannone*	*Spillane*	
							Ref: D Hutchinson	Dunstable boss Barry Fry is totally committed to attack, but top striker Lou Adams is well shackled and the high wind seemed to affect Dunstable more than Wimbledon. Kieron Somers comes off the bench for his first action in five months, but he is on borrowed time.											
33	A WEYMOUTH		1	W	1-0	1-0	Connell 15	Guy	Tilley	Bryant	Donaldson	Edwards	Bassett	Cooke	Leslie	Holmes	Connell	Aitken	
	24/3	*678*	*15*	46				*Corbett*	*Lawrence*	*Bruck*	*Miller*	*Hobson*	*Carr*	*Courtney*	*Astle*	*Durkin*	*Verity*	*Dorrington*	
							Ref: T Atkins	Batsford's no-nonsense philosophy wins more admirers than friends. Three of his players are booked for time-wasting, including Dickie Guy, who stands there juggling the ball behind his back. Earlier Roger Connell had blasted a corner-kick into the net, and that proved decisive.											
34	A STOURBRIDGE		1	W	**6-0**	4-0	Leslie 23, 26, 35, 52, Rice 30, Connell 69	Guy	Tilley	Bryant	Donaldson	Bassett*	Edwards	Rice	Cooke	Connell	Holmes	Leslie	Somers
	27/3	***395***	*21*	48				*Moore M*	*Moore T*	*Rumjahn*	*Taylor*	*Green G*	*Green D*	*McGrath*	*Hogg*	*Cooper*	*Lissman*	*Dyer*	
							Ref: J Beaman	The biggest away win since 7-0 at Deal in 1964-65. The Glassboys looked the better side for 20 minutes. John Leslie's four goals, with just a handful of matches behind him, marks him as one to watch. The Dons are five points clear, with games in hand, almost all of them at home.											

No	Ven/Date	Opponent / Att	Div/Pos	Res/Pts	Score	HT	Scorers / Referee	1	2	3	4	5	6	7	8	9	10	11	12	
35	H	ATHERSTONE	1	D	1-1	0-0	Edwards 60	Guy	Falconer	Bryant	Donaldson	Edwards	Bassett	Rice	Cooke	Connell	Holmes	Mahon		
	29/3	2,057	*5*	49			*Jennings 70*	*Wither*	*Stockley*	*Russell*	*Smith*	*Preston*	*Kiernan*	*Smith*	*Franklin*	*Tearse*	*Hunt*	*Jennings*		
							Ref: W Whittington	John Leslie's reward for his four-goal haul is a place on the bench. Batsford says he cannot leave out Mick Mahon when teams like Atherstone come to defend. Ex-Don Bob Stockley has another good game, all the forwards have stinkers, and the referee looked to favour the home team.												
36	H	CHELMSFORD	1	W	2-0	1-0	Connell 34, Holmes 82p	Guy	Tilley	Bryant	Donaldson	Edwards	Bassett!	Rice	Cooke	Connell	Holmes	Leslie		
	6/4	1,608	*9*	51				*Spink*	*Rowell*	*Tomkins*	*Burney*	*Loughton*	*McCarthy*	*Coakley*	*Price*	*Lamb*	*Gregory*	*Kellard*		*P*
							Ref: R Banning	Matches with Chelmsford are not for the faint-hearted. After seven minutes Bassett throws a punch at Terry Price and is sent off. Price stays. City keeper Nigel Spink will win a European Champions' medal with Aston Villa. Bobby Kellard brings down Donaldson for the penalty.												
37	H	STOURBRIDGE	1	W	4-0	2-0	Holmes 7, 59, Connell 35, Cooke 62	Guy	Tilley	Bryant	Donaldson	Edwards	Aitken	Rice	Cooke	Connell*	Holmes	Leslie	Somers	
	13/4	1,925	*21*	53				*Moore*	*Barton*	*Taylor*	*Runjahn*	*Green G*	*Green D*	*McGrath*	*Hogg*	*Cooper*	*Dyer*	*Booth*		*P*
							Ref: M Hazzard	Wimbledon make it 10 against Stourbridge in a fortnight. The four they add now include the spectacular and the bizarre. Connell scores with an acrobatic bicycle kick. Billy Holmes makes it 3-0 with a corner-kick that touches nobody. Three points from five games will land the title.												
38	H	MAIDSTONE	1	D	1-1	0-1	Edwards 72	Guy	Tilley	Bryant	Donaldson	Edwards	Rice	Aitken	Cooke	Holmes	Leslie	Connell		
	17/4	**2,317**	*4*	54			*Hayes 1*	*Bellotti*	*Fraser*	*Russo*	*Glozier*	*Priestley*	*Fusco*	*Lucas*	*Wallace*	*Hayes*	*McVeigh*	*Dilsworth*		*P*
							Ref: C Lawthom	But for the Dons, Maidstone would be title-chasers themselves. Former-Don Dave Lucas, who had no place in the Batsford set-up, has a quiet game. Gary Hayes, goalkeeper turned striker, scores inside a minute, but Derek Bellotti drops the ball under pressure for Edwards to level.												
39	A	DOVER	1	W	2-1	0-0	Holmes 61, Cooke 62	Guy	Tilley	Bryant	Donaldson	Edwards	Aitken	Rice	Cooke	Connell	Holmes	Leslie		
	19/4	*789*	*18*	56			*Brooks 64*	*Gilchrist*	*Norton*	*Keeley*	*Hamshare*	*Brooks*	*White*	*Clay*	*Coupland*	*Osborne*	*Reynolds*	*Rogers*		*P*
							Ref: G Campbell	An Easter Monday match at the Crabble. Guy looks shaky in goal, so it is as well that Holmes and Cooke smash two in a minute to ease the nerves. Wimbledon are almost home. The only team that can match their points total is Yeovil. That depends on the Dons losing the last three.												
40	H	NUNEATON B	1	W	2-0	2-0	Leslie 24, 37	Guy	Tilley	Bryant	Donaldson	Edwards	Aitken	Rice	Cooke	Connell*	Holmes	Leslie	Somers	
	22/4	2,140	*3*	58				*Knight*	*Stephens*	*Cross*	*Peake*	*Bennett*	*Oakes*	*Goodwin*	*Fleet**	*Hawkins*	*Lewis*	*Smithers*	*Turpie*	
							Ref: G Marshall	The Dons are champions again. Nuneaton, runners-up last season, and in contention this, sportingly applaud them on to the pitch. Boro played well for 20 minutes, but then Leslie heads the first of his two goals. Wimbledon have overtaken last season's total of 57 points.												
41	H	WEALDSTONE	1	W	4-1	1-1	Connell 36, 54, Cooke 56, Holmes 62	Guy	Tilley	Bryant	Donaldson	Edwards	Aitken!	Rice!	Cooke	Connell	Holmes	Leslie!		
	27/4	2,181	*19*	60			*Light 30*	*Bullen*	*Edmondson*	*Watson!*	*Light!*	*McHale*	*Dyson*	*Halliday*	*Moss!*	*Byrne*	*Duck*	*Henderson*		*P*
							Ref: M Taylor	The league trophy is presented before a disgraceful match. Wealdstone need points to avoid the drop. Six players are sent off (a league record), three from Wimbledon (a club record). Aitken and Moss go in the first half; Rice and Watson after 77 minutes; Leslie and Light after 82.												
42	A	TONBRIDGE	1	W	2-1	0-0	Cooke 54, Connell 55	Guy	Tilley	Bryant	Donaldson	Edwards	Rice	Cooke	Leslie	Connell	Somers	Holmes		
	30/4	*752*	*20*	62			*Putman 60*	*Hughes*	*Prince*	*Cooper*	*Smith*	*Keirs*	*Hickey*	*Hancock*	*O'Sullivan*	*Stonebridge*	*Debnam*	*Walsh*	*Putman*	*P*
	Home	*Away*					Ref: K Guilder	Tonbridge went into liquidation some weeks earlier and need to win to stay up. Vansittart and Falconer have not been retained. Somers plays his first full game since October, and he too will soon be gone. The match is of less interest than the aftermath of the Wealdstone battle.												
Average	1,766	*1,242*																		

Southern League Cup																				
1:1	H	HILLINGDON B		W	3-0	0-0	Cooke 47, Connell 56, Holmes 80	Guy	Falconer	Bryant	Donaldson	Edwards	Bassett	Rice	Cooke	Holmes	Somers	Connell		
	26/8	1,813						*Phillips*	*Hawley*	*Gelson*	*Ryan*	*Archer*	*Wagstaffe*	*McGovern*	*Bishop*	*Reeve*	*Smee*	*Johnson*		*P*
							Ref: J Craig	At 2-0 comes the decisive moment. Selwyn Rice barges over Neil Johnson in the box. Phil Archer takes the penalty but Dickie Guy keeps it out. A third goal for Holmes makes it an uphill struggle for Boro in the second leg.												
1:2	A	HILLINGDON B		W	2-0	1-0	Cooke 30, Connell 70	Guy	Falconer	Bryant	Donaldson	Edwards	Bassett	Aitken	Cooke*	Connell	Somers	Mahon	Holmes	
	1/9	*500*						*Phillips*	*Hawley*	*Gelson*	*Ryan*	*Archer*	*Johnson*	*Wagstaff*	*Brown*	*McGovern*	*Bishop*	*Reeve*		*P*
							Ref: M Dixon (Dons win 5-0 on aggregate)	Managerless Hillingdon suffer a third defeat by Wimbledon inside a week. Goalkeeper Gordon Phillips is so distressed by the Dons' second goal on the night, their fifth on aggregate, that he chases the referee and tugs at his sleeve like a terrier. He is lucky to escape punishment.												
2	H	ROMFORD		W	4-1	0-1	Holmes 52p, Cooke 66, 86, Edwards 90	Guy	Tilley	Donaldson	Bryant	Edwards	Vansittart	Bassett	Cooke	Holmes	Connell	Somers		
	21/10	1,479					*Mann 3*	*Lightfoot*	*Parmenter*	*Tapping*	*Woodward*	*Peck*	*Bickles*	*Sanders*	*Chandler*	*Mann*	*Ferry*	*Pettit!*		*P*
							Ref: A Heselgrave	Division 1 side Romford enjoy the perfect start, suffer a nightmare second half, and have three men booked and one sent off. It is their first defeat of the season. Mann scores direct from a corner. Connell is pushed for the penalty, but Ray Pettit is sent off for abusive protests.												

Southern League Cup			F-A	H-T	Scorers, Times, and Referees	1	2	3	4	5	6	7	8	9	10	11	12 sub used
3 H CHELMSFORD	1	D	1-1	1-0	Cooke 9	Guy	Tilley*	Bryant	Donaldson	Edwards	Bassett	Rice	Cooke	Connell	Holmes	Mahon	Vansittart
2/12	1,991	12			*Dyson 75*	*Taylor*	*Coakley*	*Walker*	*Quirke!*	*Loughton*	*Tomkins*	*Lee*	*Dilsworth*	*Kellock*	*Shore*	*Dyson*	
					Ref: J Jenkins	An eventful tie for Chelmsford's Barry Dyson. He misses a penalty, is booked, and then smashes an equaliser. With his Kojak haircut, Dyson becomes an instant celebrity with the crowd. Quirke was sent off seconds before Dyson's strike for creating a rumpus during a bounce-up.											
3R A CHELMSFORD	4	D	2-2	1-2	Connell 29, Bryant 65	Guy	Falconer	Bryant	Donaldson	Edwards	Bassett*	Vansittart	Cooke	Connell	Holmes	Mahon	Aitken
19/1	*1,452*	*9*	*aet*		*Price 37, Shore 45*	*Taylor*	*Coakley*	*Tomkins*	*Dyson*	*Loughton*	*Walker*	*Dillsworth*	*Kellard*	*Shore*	*Kellock*	*Price*	
					Ref: M Hazzard	A blood and thunder match. This is Bobby Kellard's first home appearance since his appointment as Chelmsford's player-manager. Both sides fancy their chances at home to Burton Albion in the quarter-final, and neither gives an inch in this hard-fought replay.											
3 A CHELMSFORD	4	W	2-1	1-0	Holmes 15, Mahon 81	Guy	Tilley	Bryant	Donaldson	Edwards	Aitken	Rice	Cooke	Vansittart	Holmes	Mahon*	Bassett
RR 26/1	*923*	*12*			*Shore 71*	*Taylor*	*Rowell*	*Tomkins*	*Quirke*	*Loughton*	*Shore*	*Rowe*	*Kellard*	*Kellock*	*Gregory*	*Price*	
					Ref: M Taylor	Chelmsford won the toss to decide the venue for this second replay. Snow delays the kick-off, which is delayed further when Chelmsford cannot find an orange ball. Someone is sent round to the local shop to fetch one. Mahon settles the outcome with a flashing free-kick.											
QF H BURTON ALB	4	W	2-0	1-0	Bryant 43, Connell 74	Guy	Tilley	Bryant	Donaldson	Edwards	Rice	Vansittart	Cooke	Holmes	Connell	Mahon	
10/2	1,439	*10*				*Allcock*	*Gregg*	*Mole*	*Shore*	*Annable*	*Fletcher*	*Spinner*	*Sykes*	*Wright**	*Phillips*	*Storey-Moore*	*Harrison*
					Ref: K Guilder	Wimbledon have already completed the double over Albion in the league. Despite the presence of Ian Storey-Moore in their side, Burton's aim is a replay. Jeff Bryant's seventh goal of the season sets up Wimbledon for a place in the semi-final.											
SF1 H DOVER	5	W	3-0	1-0	Cooke 31, Mahon 58p, Holmes 76	Guy	Tilley	Bryant	Donaldson	Edwards	Bassett*	Vansittart	Cooke	Connell	Holmes	Mahon	Leslie
19/2	1,450	*21*				*Gadsby*	*Reynolds*	*Keely*	*Breach*	*Waite*	*Housden*	*Hamshare*	*Coxhill*	*Clay*	*Rogers*	*Light**	*White*
					Ref: D Bone	The luck of the draw favours Wimbledon. The other semi-final pitches Yeovil against Kettering, both of whom look stronger than struggling Dover. Dover also have three key players cup-tied. Dave Clay's mistimed back pass lets in Cooke. Breach fouls Holmes in the box for No. 2.											
SF2 A DOVER	2	W	1-1	1-1	Leslie 30	Guy	Tilley	Bryant	Donaldson	Edwards	Bassett	Vansittart	Cooke	Connell	Holmes	Leslie	
1/3	*1,604*	*20*			*Reynolds 40*	*Gadsby*	*Reynolds*	*Keely*	*Breach*	*Waite*	*Packman*	*Hamshare*	*Coxhill*	*Coupland*	*Housden*	*Rogers*	
(at Plough Lane)					Ref: D Drewitt (Dons win 4-1 on aggregate)	Dover know they are chasing a lost cause. Rather than incur the expense of staging the second leg, before an expected pitifully small crowd, they invite Wimbledon switch the tie. Batsford agrees. The result is a formality long before John Leslie adds salt to Dover's wounds.											
F1 A YEOVIL	1	D	1-1	0-1	Holmes 50p	Guy	Tilley	Bryant	Donaldson	Edwards	Bassett	Rice	Cooke	Connell	Holmes	Leslie	
3/4	*2,441*	*8*			*Cotton 8*	*Franklin*	*Thompson B*	*Cottle*	*McMahon*	*Harland*	*Harrison*	*Adams*	*Brown*	*Cotton*	*Thompson K*	*Clancy*	*Plumb*
					Ref: R Thomas	Yeovil seek a record fifth Southern League Cup triumph. Tommy Cottle upends Cooke, and Holmes sends Franklin the wrong way from the spot. That cancels out Terry Cotton's early goal for Yeovil, and Wimbledon have the upper hand for the rest of the match.											
F2 H YEOVIL	1	W	2-1	1-0	McMahon 17 (og), Cooke 60	Guy	Tilley	Bryant	Donaldson	Edwards	Bassett	Rice	Cooke	Connell	Holmes	Leslie	
10/4	3,350	*7*			*Plumb 90*	*Franklin*	*Thompson B*	*Cottle*	*McMahon**	*Harland*	*Harrison*	*Housley*	*Brown*	*Cotton*	*Thompson K*	*Plumb*	*Adams*
					Ref: R Thomas (Dons win 3-2 on aggregate)	Yeovil boss Stan Harland is confident, pointing out that Yeovil took five points at Wimbledon, Nuneaton, and Dunstable. He reckons without McMahon's misdirected header. Cambridge Utd were the last team to do the league and cup double, and were elected to the Football League.											

FA Cup			F-A	H-T	Scorers, Times, and Referees	1	2	3	4	5	6	7	8	9	10	11	12 sub used
4Q H KINGSTONIAN	1	W	6-1	3-1	Cooke 7, Bryant 22, 55, Mahon 45,	Guy	Tilley	Bryant	Donaldson	Edwards	Bassett	Rice*	Cooke	Connell	Holmes	Mahon	Vansittart
1/11	3,089	*Isth:16*			*Cook 10* [Connell 56, Edwards 88]	*Brooks*	*Mahon*	*Dade*	*Kelsall*	*Procter*	*Roach*	*Waughman*	*Hunn*	*Cook*	*Webb*	*Proctor*	
					Ref: C Downey	Kingstonian provide the Dons with their biggest home win in two years. Goal of the match was Mick Mahon's, Wimbledon's third, on the stroke of half-time. He blasts the ball home from long range to put the tie beyond the amateurs, for whom Joe Fascione failed a fitness test.											
1 A NUNEATON B		W	1-0	0-0	Connell 48	Guy	Tilley	Bryant	Donaldson	Edwards*	Bassett	Rice	Cooke	Connell	Holmes	Mahon	Vansittart
22/11	*4,435*					*Knight*	*Stephens*	*Newton*	*Hawkins*	*Bennett*	*Cross*	*Goodwin*	*Fleet*	*Briscoe*	*Oakes*	*Matthams*	
					Ref: R Capey	Nuneaton are unbeaten this season in 18 games, a club record, yet they lose emphatically at Manor Park in front of the season's biggest crowd. Boro manager George Coleman graciously admitted 'the best side won'. Now Nuneaton can concentrate on the league.											
2 H BRENTFORD	1	L	0-2	0-2		Guy	Tilley	Bryant	Donaldson	Aitken	Bassett	Rice	Cooke	Connell	Holmes	Mahon	
13/12	8,395				*Johnson 15, 34p*	*Priddy*	*Nelmes*	*Allen*	*Bence*	*Lawrence*	*Smith*	*Graham*	*Scales*	*Cross*	*Sweetzer*	*Johnson*	
					Ref: D Nippard	This is a good draw, against a side midway in Divison 4. Brentford's keeper, Paul Priddy, was signed from Wimbledon. Roger Cross began											

FA Trophy						1	2	3	4	5	6	7	8	9	10	11	12 sub used
1 A SUTTON U	3	D	0-0	0-0		Guy	Tilley	Bryant	Donaldson	Edwards	Rice	Vansittart	Cooke	Connell	Holmes	Mahon	
10/1	*2,509 Isth:11*					*Collier*	*Sorensen*	*Grose*	*Rains*	*Preston*	*Steer*	*White*	*Pritchard*	*Kidd*	*Dennis*	*Di Palma*	
					Ref: K Salmon	Sutton had the better of this at Gander Green Lane. Three Dons were booked from a side who clearly hoped to escape with a draw. The match was spoiled by a strong wind. Sutton included Tony White in their side, the black player who cut his teeth with Wimbledon.											
1R H SUTTON U	3	W	3-1	2-0	Mahon 8, 44, Sheer 90 (og)	Guy	Falconer	Bryant	Donaldson	Edwards	Rice	Vansittart	Cooke	Connell	Holmes	Mahon	
13/1	2,531				*Dennis 51*	*Collier*	*Sorensen*	*Grose*	*Rains*	*Preston*	*Steer*	*White*	*Pritchard*	*Kidd*	*Dennis*	*Di Palma*	
					Ref: K Salmon	An ill-tempered replay in which players showed little respect for the referee's eccentric decisions. Mahon fired a free-kick through the gap as Cooke peeled away from the wall. Sutton boss Ted Powell had raised temperatures by criticising the Dons for time-wasting tactics at Sutton.											
2 H DAGENHAM	4	D	0-0	0-0		Guy	Tilley	Donaldson	Edwards	Bryant	Bassett	Rice	Cooke	Holmes	Connell	Mahon	
31/1	1,606 *Isth:3*					*Huttley*	*Currie*	*Lye*	*Welch*	*Dunwell*	*Moore*	*Harkins*	*Borland*	*Fox*	*Gray*	*Holder*	
					Ref: C Lawton	Dagenham have won their last nine games in the Rothmans Isthmian League. They have scored 106 goals already. Dagenham press forward as though they were the home team. Mahon and Holmes cannot get a kick, and Bassett looks so bad that the crowd hoot for him to be taken off.											
2R A DAGENHAM	4	L	0-2	0-2		Guy	Tilley	Donaldson	Bryant	Edwards	Bassett	Vansittart	Cooke	Holmes	Connell	Mahon	
2/2	*900 Isth:3*				*Gray 17, Harkins 20*	*Huttley*	*Lye*	*Currie*	*Dunwell**	*Welch*	*Moore*	*Harkins*	*Borland*	*Fox*	*Gray*	*Holder*	*Springett*
						Wimbledon crumble with hardly a whimper. Their problems in attack are there for all to see – just 15 goals from their last 20 games. They manage just two shots on target. Out of the FA Cup, too, and slipping down the league, Wimbledon's season is in disarray.											

		Home					Away					
	P	W	D	L	F	A	W	D	L	F	A	Pts
1 WIMBLEDON	42	14	6	1	44	10	12	4	5	30	19	62
2 Yeovil	42	15	3	3	45	13	6	9	6	23	22	54
3 Atherstone	42	11	8	2	32	21	7	7	7	24	34	51
4 Maidstone	42	13	5	3	34	20	4	11	6	18	19	50
5 Nuneaton B	42	7	11	3	21	16	9	7	5	20	17	50
6 Gravesend	42	12	9	0	27	10	4	9	8	22	37	50
7 Grantham	42	10	6	5	31	21	5	8	8	25	26	44
8 Dunstable*	42	11	5	5	31	17	6	4	11	21	26	43
9 Bedford	42	10	8	3	31	16	3	9	9	24	35	43
10 Burton Alb	42	13	5	3	37	16	4	4	13	15	37	43
11 Margate	42	10	5	6	35	25	5	7	9	27	35	42
12 Hillingdon B	42	9	8	4	40	24	4	6	11	21	30	40
13 Telford	42	9	6	6	36	24	5	6	10	18	27	40
14 Chelmsford	42	9	7	5	34	23	4	7	10	18	34	40
15 Kettering	42	9	9	3	28	16	2	8	11	20	36	39
16 Bath	42	9	8	4	41	21	2	8	11	21	36	38
17 Weymouth	42	8	6	7	27	26	5	3	13	24	41	35
18 Dover	42	6	8	7	28	22	2	10	9	23	38	34
19 Wealdstone	42	11	4	6	43	31	1	5	15	18	51	33
20 Tonbridge	42	8	5	8	26	26	3	6	12	19	44	33
21 Cambridge C	42	5	10	6	28	30	3	5	13	13	37	31
22 Stourbridge	42	6	5	10	22	32	4	4	13	16	40	29
* *withdrew*	924	215	147	100	721	460	100	147	215	460	721	924

Odds & ends

Double wins: (7) Burton, Grantham, Dover, Wealdstone, Tonbridge, Weymouth, Stourbridge.
Double losses: (0).

Won from behind: (3) Grantham (h), Wealdstone (h), Yeovil (a).
Lost from in front: (0).

High spots: 8 consecutive wins in August and September to top the table.
Finishing the season unbeaten in 14 games.
Winning the Southern League Cup.

Low spots: Losing at home to winless Bath in the league.
4 games without a win in January.
Defeat by Dagenham in the FA Trophy and by Enfield in the London Senior Cup.

Player of the Year: Jeff Bryant.
Ever-presents: (2) Dickie Guy, Jeff Bryant.
Hat-tricks: (1) John Leslie.
Leading scorers: Roger Connell & Billy Holmes (19 each).

	Appearances					Goals				
	Lge	Sub	SLC	FAC	FAT	Lge	SLC	FAC	FAT	Total
Aitken, Glen	**24**		2/1	1		**1**				**1**
Bassett, Dave	**29**		9/1	3	2	**2**				**2**
Bryant, Jeff	**42**		11	3	4	**3**	2	2		**7**
Connell, Roger	**37**	(1)	10	3	4	**13**	4	2		**19**
Cooke, Ian	**41**		11	3	4	**9**	7	1		**17**
Donaldson, Dave	**41**		11	3	4					
Edwards, Billy	**34**		11	2	4	**2**	1	1		**4**
Falconer, Henry	**13**	(1)	3		1	**1**				**1**
Guy, Dickie	**42**		11	3	4					
Holmes, Billy	**37**	(1)	10/1	3	4	**14**	5			**19**
Leslie, John	**17**	(2)	3/1			**7**	1			**8**
Mahon, Mick	**23**		6	3	4	**11**	2	1	2	**16**
Rice, Selwyn	**31**		6	3	3	**2**				**2**
Somers, Keiron	**12**	(4)	3			**5**				**5**
Tilley, Kevin	**29**	(1)	8	3	3					
Vansittart, Tommy	**10**	(3)	6/1	0/2	3	**2**				**2**
(own-goals)						**2**	1		1	**4**
16 players used	**462**	**(13)**	**121/5**	**33/2**	**44**	**74**	**23**	**7**	**3**	**107**

/ denotes substitutes

No	Date	Att	Pos	Pts	F-A	H-T	Scorers, Times, and Referees	1	2	3	4	5	6	7	8	9	10	11	12 sub used
1 H	AP LEAMINGTON			D	0-0	0-0		Guy	Tilley	Bryant	Donaldson	Edwards	Bassett	**Eames**	Cooke	Connell	Holmes	**Marlowe**	
	28/8	1,225		1				*Garratt*	*Jones*	*Kavanagh*	*Griffiths*	*Brown*	*Boot*	*Taylor*	*Lee*	*Keeley*	*Stewart*	*Talbot*	
							Ref: D Jackson	Allen Batsford rushes through the transfer of Ricky Marlowe – a free from Brighton – on the eve of this match with the division's newcomers. Marlowe forces two sharp saves from goalkeeper Garratt. On the hour Garratt saves Billy Holmes' penalty and leaves the pitch a hero.											
2 A	GRAVESEND			L	0-1	0-1		Guy	Tilley	Bryant	Donaldson	Edwards	Bassett	Eames	Cooke	Connell	Marlowe	Leslie	
	31/8	*1,094*		1			*Norman 33*	*Cowan*	*Idle*	*Hall*	*Embery*	*Pearce*	*Burrett*	*Winston*	*Finch*	*Norman*	*Jacks*	*Woolfe*	
							Ref: R Stevenson	Not the start to the season that the two-times champions had hoped for. Gravesend are customarily whipping boys for Wimbledon, taking just one point from 10 previous matches. Defender Len Hall clears three Dons' efforts off the line to protect their first goal of the season.											
3 A	KETTERING			L	0-1	0-0		Guy	Tilley	Bryant	Donaldson	Edwards	Bassett	Aitken*	Cooke	Connell	Marlowe	Leslie	Eames
	4/9	*1,943*		1			*Kellock 81*	*Livsey*	*Lucas*	*Wood*	*Mortimer*	*Suddards*	*Dixey*	*Faulkner*	*Clayton*	*Kellock*	*Ashby*	*Phipps*	
							Ref: B Hill	This is Wimbledon's ninth league visit to Kettering, and still they can't win there. The Dons won 10-4 on corner-kicks, but Derek Dougan's side get the only goal. Time is running out when Billy Kellock's effort is blocked by Dickie Guy, but the ball rebounds for a second attempt.											
4 H	WEALDSTONE		19	W	**5-1**	2-1	Leslie 22, 80, Aitken 37, Connell 46,	Guy	Tilley	Bryant	Donaldson	Edwards	Bassett	Aitken*	Cooke	Connell	Marlowe	Leslie	Eames
	11/9	1,356	*15*	3			*Aitken 40 (og)* [Marlowe 85]	*Morton*	*Kinnear*	*Prince*	*Watson*	*Lawrence*	*Woolgar*	*Arnold*	*Moss*	*Light*	*Duck*	*Halliday*	
							Ref: R Rodell	Just four months previously these teams waged a disgraceful battle. But for Dunstable's withdrawal, Wealdstone would have been relegated. New manager Geoff Coleman promises there will be no vendettas. George Duck was wanted by Batsford recently. The Dons win at last.											
5 H	CHELMSFORD		9	W	2-1	0-1	Edwards 55, Leslie 76	Guy	Tilley	Bryant	Donaldson	Edwards	Bassett	Aitken	Cooke	Connell*	Marlowe	Holmes	Leslie
	18/9	1,591	*7*	5			*Coker 44*	*Penn*	*Rowell*	*Horner*	*Coker*	*Loughlan*	*Burney*	*Foggo*	*Walker!*	*Little**	*Tomkins*	*Martin*	*Quinn*
							Ref: D Drewitt	Only when City were reduced to 10 men did Wimbledon get on top. Just after half-time skipper Clive Walker had clashed with Bassett and been dismissed. Edwards squares the match by volleying in a corner, and Leslie scores with his first touch after coming on as a substitute.											
6 H	BURTON ALB		7	W	2-0	1-0	Marlowe 23, Connell 65	Guy	**Godwin**	Bryant	Donaldson	Edwards	Bassett	Aitken*	Leslie	Connell	Marlowe	Holmes	Cooke
	25/9	1,442	*18*	7				*Allcocks*	*Gregg*	*Hallsworth*	*Shone*	*Rioch*	*Sykes*	*Fearn*	*Spinner*	*Wright*	*Fletcher*	*Storey-Moore*	
							Ref: M Hazzard	Burton's eighth defeat in nine league visits to Plough Lane. Mike Walker's team attack Wimbledon from the off and pay for their enterprise. Holmes misses his second penalty of the season. With Ian Cooke out, the 'worst disciplined player,' Dave Bassett, becomes stand-in captain.											
7 A	WEYMOUTH		5	W	2-1	1-1	Leslie 13, Cooke 85	Guy	Tilley	Bryant	Donaldson	Edwards*	Bassett	Cooke	Leslie	Connell	Marlowe	Holmes	**Markham**
	2/10	*1,137*		9			*Keirs 7p*	*Gadsby*	*Lawrence*	*Carr*	*Keirs*	*Tumbridge*	*Stanton*	*Housley*	*Courtney*	*Astle*	*Iannone*	*Huxley*	
							Ref: B Stockley	On the run of play Weymouth scarcely deserved to lose for a fifth successive time to Wimbledon. Guy was much the busier goalkeeper. John Leslie wiped out Keirs' penalty with a far post header, and Cooke steals in for the winner when Holmes' corner wasn't properly cleared.											
8 H	ATHERSTONE		5	W	3-1	1-1	Leslie 28, Marlowe 75, Connell 83	Guy	Tilley	Bryant	Donaldson	Aitken*	Bassett	**O'Brien**	Leslie	Connell	Marlowe	Holmes	Cooke
	11/10	1,736	*19*	11			*Adams 12*	*Jones*	*Stockley*	*Shotton*	*Preston*	*Brown*	*Riceman**	*Dangerfield*	*Dawkins*	*Franklin*	*Adams*	*Collard*	
							Ref: J Jenkins	Wimbledon have lost to Yeovil, 1-2 after extra time, in the match between league and cup winners. Yeovil took part as runners-up to the Dons in the Southern League Cup. Keeper Jones cost the Adders this match, failing to cut out high balls. Five wins on the trot for Wimbledon.											
9 A	MAIDSTONE		6	L	**0-2**	0-0		Guy	Tilley	Bryant	Donaldson	Aitken	Bassett!	Rice!	Leslie*	Connell	Marlowe	Holmes	**Scullion**
	16/10	*1,252*	*12*	11			*Coupland 67, 89*	*Bellotti*	*Fraser*	*Glozier*	*Priestley*	*Russo*	*Wallace*	*Walsh*	*Street*	*Stonebridge*	*Crush*	*Coupland*	
							Ref: L Bartels	Two Dons are sent off amid ugly scenes on the touchline involving Allen Batsford. Bassett was the first to go, just before half-time, after the linesman drew the referee's attention to Crush's prostrate body. No sooner had Coupland put Maidstone in front than Rice was dismissed too.											
10 H	BATH		6	L	**0-2**	0-0		Guy	Tilley	Bryant	Donaldson	Edwards	Bassett	O'Brien*	Aitken	Connell	Marlowe	Holmes	Cooke
	23/10	1,462	*2*	11			*Griffin 64, 70*	*Allen*	*Ryan*	*Taverner*	*Godfrey*	*Bourne*	*Broom*	*Rogers M*	*McInch*	*Rogers P*	*Griffin*	*Higgins*	
							Ref: D Holland	Bath win at Plough Lane for the third time in three seasons, during which Wimbledon fail to score at all. Bath owe their triumph to keeper Ken Allen, who held everything on a gluey pitch, and to Kevin Griffin, who was booked for dissent, then scored two goals.											

No	Date	Opponent	Att	Pos	Pts	F-A	H-T	Scorers, Times, and Referees	1	2	3	4	5	6	7	8	9	10	11	12
11	H 6/11	MARGATE	**917**	5 *18*	W 13	2-1	1-0	Markham 33, Edwards 86	Guy	**Hawley**	Bryant	Donaldson	Edwards	Aitken	O'Brien	Markham	Connell	Marlowe	Holmes	
								Clewlow 75	*Bowtell*	*Barr*	*Thornley*	*Fusco*	*Summers*	*Clewlow*	*Byford**	*Turner*	*Gilbert*	*Cook*	*Bacon*	*Plumb*
								Ref: P Jackson	The season's lowest ebb. Barnet have just k.o.'d the Dons from the Southern League Cup, and the gate reflects the general disappointment. Wimbledon forced 13 corners to Margate's two. Alan Hawley, signed from Hillingdon, makes his debut. So does Leo Markham.											
12	A 13/11	BATH	*1,761*		L 13	0-1	0-1		Guy	Tilley	Bryant	Donaldson	Edwards	Markham*	Aitken	O'Brien	Connell	Marlowe	Holmes	Bassett
								McInch 12	*Allen*	*Ryan*	*Taverner*	*Godfrey*	*Bourne*	*Broom*	*Rogers*	*McInch*	*Redrobe*	*Griffin*	*Higgins*	
								Ref: T Atkins	Bath complete a quick double, secured when ex-Yeovil Jim McInch fires a cracker from 18 yards. The way Bath are playing, they are determined to bring the championship to Tiverton Park. They show no fear of, or respect for Allen Batsford's double title-holders.											
13	A 27/11	YEOVIL	*2,223*	10 *9*	D 14	1-1	1-0	Connell 44	Guy	Tilley	Bryant	Donaldson	Edwards	Bassett	Aitken	Cooke	Connell	Marlowe	Holmes	
								Brown 71	*Franklin*	*Thompson B Flay*	*Jones*	*Harland*	*Harrison*	*McMahon*	*Brown*	*Plumb*	*Thompson K Leigh*			
								Ref: P Pittaway	Wimbledon have beaten Runcorn 3-2 on aggregate to claim the Non-League Championship Trophy. Back on league duty, three Dons are booked as Wimbledon hang on by hook or by crook. Dick Plumb hits a back-pass past his keeper, then races back to clear off the line.											
14	H 21/12	DARTFORD	1,207	11 *15*	W 16	1-0	1-0	Holmes 43p	Guy	Tilley	Bryant	Donaldson	Edwards	Bassett	Cooke	Aitken	Connell	Marlowe	Holmes	
									Keen	*Robinson*	*Shovelar*	*Jones*	*Linton*	*Gibbs*	*Dennis*	*Payne*	*Dudman*	*Mitchell*	*Greenhalgh*	
								Ref: D Bone	A first league win for six weeks is the reward for Billy Holmes' penalty-kick. Marlowe had intercepted a poor goal-kick, and Linton pulled down Connell as he was about to score. Holmes located the white spot on the muddy pitch, and sent the keeper sprawling the wrong way.											
15	A 27/12	HILLINGDON B	*1,353*		W 18	2-0	0-0	Connell 47, Bryant 75	Guy	Tilley	Bryant	Donaldson	Edwards	Bassett	Leslie	Aitken	Connell*	Marlowe	Holmes	**Friend**
									Phillips	*Millett*	*Ryan*	*Gelson*	*Pearce*	*Smith*	*Adams*	*Metchik*	*Richardson*	*Cleary*	*Basey**	*Griffiths*
									Hillingdon are now managed by Barry Fry and are unbeaten in 10. Bassett is booked yet again. Billy Holmes sets up both goals – a Connell volley from a Holmes cross, and a Bryant header from a Holmes corner. Substitute Barry Friend makes his debut three minutes from time.											
16	H 1/1	BEDFORD	1,446	9 *10*	W 20	3-0		Connell (2), Bryant	Guy	Tilley	Bryant	Donaldson	Edwards	Bassett	Leslie	Aitken	Connell	Marlowe	Holmes	
									Peacock	*Skinn*	*Folds*	*Gould*	*Cooley*	*Earl*	*Hawkins*	*Spillane*	*Sargent*	*Dove*	*Burdett*	
								Ref: P Pittaway	Bedford hate the sight of Plough Lane, having taken just one point in their last eight visits. Wimbledon's victory in this New Year's Day clash is emphatic enough, but minds are distracted by the looming visit of Jack Charlton's 1st Division Middlesbrough in the FA Cup.											
17	A 24/1	NUNEATON B	***2,445***		L 20	0-1	0-1		Guy	Tilley	Bryant	Donaldson	Edwards	Bassett	Leslie	Aitken	Connell	Marlowe	Holmes	
								Lewis 14	*Knight*	*Stephens*	*Smith*	*Briscoe*	*Peake*	*Bennett*	*Phillips*	*Lewis*	*Jones*	*Fleet*	*Smithers*	
								Ref: A Blake	Wimbledon are sunk by the sort of wonder-goal that defences cannot legislate against. Bryant lost out to Timmy Smithers, who centred for Lewis to score with a spectacular airborne header. The rest of the contest paled into insignificance, degenerating into a dour muddy battle.											
18	H 29/1	GRAVESEND	1,667	11 *6*	W 22	2-1	1-1	Holmes 34p, Marlowe 90	Guy	Tilley*	Bryant	Donaldson	Edwards	Bassett	Aitken	Leslie	Connell	Holmes	Friend	Marlowe
								Woolfe 40	*Smelt*	*Kinnear*	*Hall*	*Embery*	*Pearce*	*Walker*	*Brown*	*Finch*	*Woon*	*Jacks*	*Woolfe*	
								Ref: W Whittington	Gravesend are within seconds of securing their first league point at Plough Lane. They are indebted to keeper Lee Smelt for keeping them afloat, but deep into injury time he drops a corner-kick. Chris Kinnear's handball and Bryant's errant back-pass produced the first two goals.											
19	H 8/2	REDDITCH	1,464	10 *3*	W 24	3-0	3-0	Marlowe 33, Bryant 38, Holmes 40	Guy	Tilley	Bryant	Donaldson	Edwards	Bassett	Leslie	Aitken	Marlowe	Holmes	Friend	
									Edwards	*Grice*	*Clements*	*Pugh*	*Chadwick*	*MacMorran*	*Wright*	*Dale*	*Gardiner*	*Lawrence*	*Smart*	
								Ref: J Bellamy	Three headers late in the first half, two of them laid on by tiny Barry Friend, sink third-placed Redditch. They have no chance of pulling the game out of the fire, but thereafter play an extra forward, less in hope of scoring themselves than to prevent the Dons back four piling forward.											
20	H 12/2	NUNEATON B	1,894	2 *6*	W 26	4-0	2-0	Connell 4, Donaldson 10, Edwards 75, [Holmes 88]	Guy	Tilley	Bryant	Donaldson	Edwards	Bassett	Cooke	Aitken	Connell*	Holmes	Friend	Marlowe
									Knight	*Stephens*	*Smith*	*Briscoe*	*Peake*	*Cross*	*Phillips*	*Fleet*	*Jones*	*Vincent*	*Smithers*	
								Ref: J Carter	Nuneaton have been coming to Plough Lane for 12 seasons. They have never won, and all they have managed is three draws. This time they are without three key players, including skipper Dave Lewis. Connell nudges Friend's low cross past Knight for 1-0.											
21	A 15/2	ATHERSTONE	*807*	1 *21*	W 28	2-0	0-0	Holmes 77, Aitken 87	Guy	Tilley	Bryant	Donaldson	Edwards	Bassett	Cooke	Aitken	Connell	Holmes	Friend*	Marlowe
									Withers	*Stockley*	*Shotton*	*Brown*	*Preston*	*Kiernan*	*Smith*	*Tearse*	*Franklin*	*Vincent*	*Minton*	
								Ref: L Robinson	The Adders' previous nine home games have yielded just four goals. Wimbledon enjoy the rub of the green in notching their third win on this ground in four years. They went ahead when an Adders' clearance struck former-Don Bob Stockley and bobbed up to the unmarked Holmes.											

No	Date		Att	Pos	Pts		F-A	H-T	Scorers, Times, and Referees	1	2	3	4	5	6	7	8	9	10	11	12 sub used
22	A	AP LEAMINGTON				W	3-0	2-0	Aitken 5, Holmes 42, 55	Guy	Tilley	Bryant	Donaldson	Edwards	Bassett	Cooke	Aitken	Connell	Holmes	Friend*	Marlowe
	22/2		*826*		30					*Garnell*	*Taylor*	*Kavanagh*	*Jones*	*Brown*	*Boot*	*Dyer*	*Lee*	*Stewart*	*Keeley*	*Turpie**	*Gorman*
									Ref: D Hutchinson	The midfield trio of Cooke, Bassett, and Aitken dominate this match, aided by quicksilver Billy Holmes in attack. He bags two close-range goals. Wimbledon had earlier taken advantage of a non-existent wall, when Bassett touched a free-kick to Glen Aitken, who let fly.											
23	A	BURTON ALB				W	1-0	0-0	Connell 84	Guy	Tilley	Bryant	Donaldson	Edwards	Markham	Marlowe	Aitken	Connell	Holmes	Friend	
	5/3		*891*		32					*Allcock*	*Eaton*	*Hallsworth*	*Harrison*	*Annable*	*Jentas*	*Fearn*	*Sykes*	*Wright*	*Hogan*	*Storey-Moore*	
									Ref: A Blake	Burton's record against Wimbledon is atrocious. They have taken just one point from the last ten matches. They were within six minutes of doubling that tally when Connell's looping shot beats reserve keeper Allcock. The Dons are distracted by their FA Trophy saga with Chorley.											
24	A	DOVER		2		D	1-1	0-1	Aitken 50	Guy	Tilley	Bryant	Donaldson	Edwards	Markham	Marlowe	Aitken	Connell	Holmes	Friend	
	9/3		*623*	*8*	33				*Wilson 23*	*Raine*	*Reynolds*	*Keeley*	*Brown*	*Waite*	*Hamshare*	*Clay*	*Wilson*	*Lloyd*	*Marley*	*Rogers*	
									Ref: K Guilder	Dover's goal upsets Guy. He parries the ball upwards, but clearly thinks it stays out of the net. The linesman does not agree, whereupon the goalkeeper chases the referee all the way to the centre circle. Glen Aitken equalises from a free-kick with the Dover wall in a dither.											
25	H	WEYMOUTH		2		W	1-0	0-0	Markham 88	Guy	Tilley	Bryant	Donaldson	Edwards	Markham	Marlowe	Aitken	Connell	Holmes	Friend	
	12/3		1,805	*22*	35					*Clarke*	*Lawrence*	*Tonbridge*	*Carr**	*Durkin*	*Dyer*	*Iannoni*	*Henderson*	*Courtney*	*Tombs*	*Housley*	*Huxley*
									Ref: J Hazell	Wimbledon beat Weymouth for the sixth time in a row thanks to a farcical late goal. Leo Markham barely makes contact with Holmes' flick, but the ball then bounces off defender Lawrence's toe to crawl over the line with veteran keeper John Clarke committed the other way.											
26	H	DOVER		2		W	2-1	0-1	Markham 66, 72	Guy	Tilley	Bryant	Donaldson	Edwards	Aitken	Markham	Marlowe	Connell	Holmes	Friend	
	14/3		1,358	*8*	37				*Marley 40*	*Raine*	*Reynolds*	*Keeley*	*Brown*	*Waite*	*Brooks*	*Wilson*	*Hamshare*	*Christie*	*Marley*	*Rogers*	
									Ref: R Chaffer	Three goals in three days for Leo Markham, and they have all been crucial. Dover have only won once at Plough Lane in 11 attempts, but they lead till midway through the second half, whereupon the bearded buccaneer heads an equaliser, then plays a one-two with Holmes for No 2.											
27	A	MINEHEAD		2		W	1-0	0-0	Bryant 77	Guy	Tilley	Bryant	Donaldson	Edwards	Bassett	Markham	Aitken	Marlowe	Holmes	Friend	
	22/3		*746*	*3*	39					*Crabtree*	*Brown*	*Clausen*	*Carter*	*Boyd*	*Burns*	*Risdale*	*Bryant*	*Leitch*	*Jenkins*	*Freeman*	
									Ref: S Bates	The Premier League newcomers are having a terrific season. They keep the Dons under constant pressure in the first half, but lose the game – a mite harshly – when Jeff Bryant heads in from a corner. Wimbledon are now one point behind leaders Bath, but have five games in hand.											
28	H	MAIDSTONE		1		W	2-1	1-0	Marlowe 40, 64	Guy	Tilley	Bryant	Donaldson	Edwards	Bassett	Markham	Aitken	Marlowe	Holmes	Friend	
	26/3		1,719	*13*	41				*Wallace 75*	*Bellotti*	*McVeigh*	*Hill*	*Glozier*	*Merrick*	*Irvine*	*Fraser*	*Wallace*	*Coupland*	*Stonebridge*	*O'Mara*	
									Ref: J Raymond	Wimbledon go top for the first time. Maidstone adopt an adventurous policy of attacking the Dons throughout the match, but pay for their abandon when Marlowe beats their offside trap to knee the ball into goal. He adds a second when Markham's header comes off the woodwork.											
29	H	GRANTHAM		2		W	1-0	1-0	Connell 40	Guy	Tilley	Byrant	Donaldson	Edwards	Aitken	Bassett	Marlowe	Connell	Holmes	Friend	
	29/3		1,400	*6*	43					*Gardiner*	*Bower*	*Capewell*	*Norris*	*Harrison*	*Taylor*	*Capewell*	*Jackson*	*Platt*	*Gould*	*Carr*	
									Ref: W Whittington	A niggling match. Grantham seek to avenge defeat in the FA Trophy, and boast the division's highest scoring attack. The goal is controversial. Bassett drags the injured Capewell to his feet. A brawl ensues. Bassett whips over a free-kick and Connell – back from suspension – heads in.											
30	A	MARGATE		2		W	3-0	0-0	Edwards 67, Holmes 80, Markham 84	Guy	Tilley	Bryant	Donaldson	Edwards	Bassett	Marlowe	Markham	Connell	Holmes	Friend	
	1/4		***315***	*20*	45					*Bowtell*	*Byford*	*Thornley*	*Turner B*	*Priestley*	*Clewlow*	*Pain*	*Turner A*	*Summers*	*Fusco*	*Bacon*	
									Ref: L Bartels	Blustery conditions at Hartsdown Road blow Margate nearer relegation. With the gale behind them in the first half, they fail to break through. But when the teams turn round Billy Edwards sprints 20 yards to nod Jeff Bryant's clever free-kick past Bowtell.											
31	A	DARTFORD		1		L	0-1	0-1		Guy	Tilley	Bryant	Donaldson	Edwards	Bassett	Marlowe	Markham	Connell	Holmes	Friend	
	5/4		*1,342*	*17*	45				*Robinson 30*	*Keen*	*Robinson*	*Shovelar*	*Jones*	*Pittaway*	*Akers*	*Craker*	*Light*	*Denny*	*Harrison*	*Dudman*	
										Dartford end the Dons' sequence of six league wins. They have proved a constant nuisance over the years, Wimbledon winning just two of the last 10. Dartford had to do without 26-goal Brian Greenhalgh. Relegation-haunted Dartford have a date with the Southern League Cup Final.											

32	A	BEDFORD	1	W	2-0	2-0	Connell 15, Aitken 30	Guy	Godwin	Bryant	Donaldson	Edwards	Markham	Marlowe	Aitken	Connell	Holmes	Friend*	Eames
9/4		*1,068*	*4*	47				*Peacock*	*Skinn*	*Folds*	*Gould*	*Cooley*	*Earl*	*Goodall*	*Spillane*	*Sargent*	*Dove*	*Burdett*	
							Ref: C Taylor	Allen Batsford's tongue lashing following the defeat at Dartford has sent Kevin Tilley AWOL. When he failed to turn up, Danny Godwin was thrown in for his second game Tilley was eventually discovered at home with dad, complaining of a cold – in his head, not his feet.											
33	H	HILLINGDON B	1	D	1-1	0-0	Holmes 46	Guy	Godwin	Bryant	Donaldson	Edwards	Markham	Marlowe	Aitken	Connell	Holmes	Friend	
11/4		1,968	*12*	48			*Cleary 70p*	*Phillips*	*Davies*	*Pearce*	*Millett*	*Ryan**	*Kirkup*	*Hullett*	*Smith*	*Richardson*	*Burge*	*Cleary*	
							Ref: A Harrington	It is five years since Wimbledon beat Hillingdon at Plough Lane. Cynical Dons grab the lead then hold it at all costs, playing possession football that irritates their own fans. Then Bryant chased Cleary and clipped his heels. Hullett was booked for kicking Aitken in the crutch.											
34	A	CHELMSFORD		W	2-1	1-1	Connell 27, Markham 85	Guy	Godwin	Donaldson	Bryant	Edwards	Markham	Aitken	Marlowe	Connell	Holmes	Friend*	Eames
16/4		*1,172*		50			*Wigley 33*	*Penn*	*Rowell*	*Coker*	*Binks*	*Loughton**	*Norman*	*Coventry*	*Burney*	*Foggo*	*Greaves*	*Wigley*	*Martin*
							Ref: A Rodell	Struggling Chelmsford used to be Wimbledon's bogey, but this is the Dons' fifth win in the last six meetings. City fielded a chubby Jimmy Greaves. He managed one shot, high into the crowd, but was slowed by Aitken's thigh-high tackle. Greaves kept inspecting the stud-marks.											
35	H	TELFORD	1	D	0-0	0-0		Guy	Tilley	Bryant	Donaldson	Edwards	Aitken	Markham	Marlowe	Connell	Holmes	Friend	
18/4		2,244	*15*	51				*Weir*	*Harris*	*Pearce*	*Mallender*	*Ross*	*Macauley*	*Kemp*	*Draycott*	*Hurst*	*Bentley*	*Garbett*	
							Ref: D Jackson	Telford have never won at Plough Lane, and player-manager Geoff Hurst appears resigned to the fact that his team won't do so now. His tubby frame is employed not up front but in defence. Another England international, cricketer Tony Greig, has joined the Dons' board.											
36	H	KETTERING	1	W	2-0	1-0	Leslie 42, Bryant 86	Guy	Tilley	Bryant	Donaldson	Edwards	Bassett	Cooke	Aitken	Connell	Holmes	Leslie	
25/4		**4,108**	*3*	53				*Livsey*	*Lucas*	*Wood*	*Richards**	*Suddards*	*Dixey*	*Mortimer*	*Kellock*	*Clayton*	*Conde*	*Ashby*	*Newson*
							Ref: E Hopper	Crunch time. Derek Dougan's Kettering pose the biggest threat of Wimbledon's title rivals. Had they won, they would have joined the Dons on 51 points from 36 games. John Leslie salutes his header by giving two fingers to the Kettering fans – an accurate prediction of the final score.											
37	A	GRANTHAM		D	0-0	0-0		Guy	Tilley	Bryant	Donaldson	Edwards	Bassett	Cooke	Aitken	Connell	Holmes	Leslie	
29/4		*626*		54				*Gardiner*	*Shaw*	*Capewell*	*Norris*	*Harrison*	*Bower*	*Gulson*	*Carr*	*Platt*	*Gibson*	*Benskin*	
							Ref: M Elding	Grantham are without four regulars, but still carry enough firepower for the league's leading scorer – David Platt – to plant a header that Billy Edwards somehow heads off the line. Wimbledon's best chance came earlier, when Ian Cooke's curler shaved the crossbar.											
38	A	TELFORD		W	3-1	1-1	Bryant 30, Leslie 79, Cooke 85	Guy	Tilley	Bryant	Donaldson	Edwards	Bassett	Cooke	Aitken	Connell	Holmes	Leslie	
2/5		*729*		56			*Hurst 29*	*Weir*	*Harris*	*Daley*	*Bache*	*Ross*	*Devlin*	*Kemp*	*Draycott*	*Bentley*	*Hurst*	*Garbett*	
							Ref: L Robinson	Geoff Hurst lingers back to his England days as he blasts Telford ahead. Thankfully, Wimbledon don't have to live too long with the deficit. Jeff Bryant levels within seconds from Bassett's free-kick. Leslie's far-post header from Holmes' corner puts the Dons in front.											
39	H	MINEHEAD	1	W	1-0	1-0	Clausen 20 (og)	Guy	Tilley	Bryant	Donaldson	Edwards	Bassett	Cooke	Aitken	Connell	Holmes	Leslie	
4/5		2,839	*3*	58				*Macey*	*Brown*	*Clausen*	*Carter*	*Boyd*	*Burns*	*Risdale*	*Bryant*	*Leitch*	*Jenkins*	*Durbin*	
							Ref: D Mardle	No one seems to mention Minehead among the serious title-chasers, though they will eventually finish laudable runners-up. Wimbledon's second win over them is as tight as the first, and is abetted by an own-goal when Tony Clausen miscues his attempted headed clearance.											
40	H	YEOVIL	1	W	1-0	1-0	Cooke 35	Guy	Tilley	Bryant	Donaldson	Edwards	Bassett	Cooke	Aitken*	Connell	Holmes	Leslie	Marlowe
7/5		2,740	*8*	60				*Franklin*	*Thompson*	*Cottle*	*Jones*	*Cotton*	*Harrison*	*Annalls*	*Leigh*	*Hickton*	*Plumb*	*Harland*	
							Ref: A Lisney	The BBC cameras are out to record Wimbledon's success for Bob Wilson's Football Focus. Yeovil play their part by attacking feverishly, but are undone when Leslie flicks the ball over his head and Cooke wriggles free of defenders to score. Only Kettering can still muster 60 points.											
41	A	WEALDSTONE	1	D	0-0	0-0		Guy	Tilley	Bryant	Donaldson	Edwards	Bassett	Cooke	Aitken	Connell	Holmes	Leslie	
12/5		*1,375*	*15*	61				*Lightfoot*	*Thomas*	*Price*	*Downes*	*Parratt*	*Watson*	*O'Kane*	*Griffiths*	*Moss*	*Byrne*	*Brinkman*	
							Ref: Heselgrave	The previous evening Yeovil beat Kettering 5-1. The Dons are champs, and Wealdstone applaud them onto the pitch. Better that, than to risk any repetition of last season's disgraceful scenes. All's well that ends well. Wimbledon stay unbeaten and Wealdstone stay up.											
42	A	REDDITCH		W	3-0	2-0	Connell 8, 23, Clements 80 (og)	Guy	Tilley	Bryant	Donaldson	Edwards	Bassett	Cooke	Aitken	Connell*	Holmes	Leslie	Marlowe
14/5		*742*		63				*Edwards*	*Grice*	*Clements*	*Lawrence*	*Punshen*	*Bruck*	*Smart*	*Dale*	*Tuohe*	*Taylor*	*Pugh*	
Average	Home 1,790	*Away* *1,165*					Ref: B Jackson	Connell's two strikes make him top Dons goal-getter for the third consecutive season. Wimbledon have equalled Merthyr Tydfil's feat in the early 1950s of winning three Southern League titles in a row, and break Portmouth's 1927 record of the meanest defence of any champions.											

Southern League Cup		F-A	H-T	Scorers, Times, and Referees	1	2	3	4	5	6	7	8	9	10	11	12 sub used
1:1 A ROMFORD	L	0-2	0-0		Guy	Tilley	Donaldson	**Teather**	Edwards	Bassett	Eames	**West**	Holmes!	**Watts**	Markham	
21/8 *788 SL1*				*Donaldson 60 (og), Parker 65*	*Halsey*	*Woodward*	*Gilbert*	*Handelaar*	*Peck*	*Pettit*	*Whitehead*	*Parker*	*Ferry*	*Bishop*	*Bailey*	*P*
				Ref: D Holland	Wimbledon have so many players suspended that Batsford sends out five newcomers and has nobody to wear the substitute's shirt. Holmes adds to the problems by being sent off for dissent just before the break. This leaves the Dons without any recognised striker.											
1:2 H ROMFORD	W	2-0	1-0	Holmes 30, Connell 88	Guy	Tilley	Bryant	Donaldson	Edwards	Bassett	Cooke	Eames	Connell	Holmes	West	
24/8 1,457 *SL1*					*Halsey*	*Woodward*	*Bickles*	*Handelaar*	*Peck*	*Pettit*	*Whitehead*	*Parker*	*Hamilton*	*Ferry*	*Bishop*	*P*
				Ref: R Banning (2-2 on aggregate)	Three of Batsford's six suspended players return. In their attempt to pull two goals back Wimbledon strike the woodwork five times and have four efforts cleared off the line. Against that, Romford's Pat Ferry had what looked a good goal annulled for offside. Connell saves their bacon.											
1R A ROMFORD	W	2-0	0-0	Cooke 96, Connell 106	Guy	Tilley	Bryant	Donaldson	Edwards	Bassett	Cooke	Aitken	Connell	Marlowe	Holmes	
21/9 *721 SL1*		*aet*			*Briggs*	*Pettit*	*Gilbert*	*Handelaar*	*Peck*	*Hamilton*	*Barker*	*Bailey*	*Ferry*	*Hanson*	*Hammond*	*P*
				Ref: K Guilder	Romford win the toss to stage this replay. They may be bottom of Division 1 South, but they had the better chances in normal time. In extra-time Cooke's shot is deflected past Briggs. The first action of the second period sees Connell dispossess the goalkeeper to seal the tie.											
2 A BARNET	6 D	1-1	1-0	Connell 11	Guy	Tilley*	Bryant	Donaldson	Edwards	Aitken	O'Brien	Cooke	Connell	Marlowe	Holmes	Markham
26/10 *814 SL1:5*				*Fairbrother 72*	*Woodend*	*Oliver*	*Lees*	*Hinton*	*Tapping**	*McNab*	*Price*	*Brown*	*Fairbrother*	*Aggio*	*Williams*	*George*
				Ref: D Bone	A game of two halves, as they say. Wimbledon had the first, but found themselves defending desperately in the second. They went in front when Woodend dropped the ball under pressure from Marlowe. Barnet rallied when, with both subs on, Fairbrother shot through a packed box.											
2R H BARNET	L	2-3	1-1	Holmes 16p, Edwards 74	Guy	Godwin	Bryant	Donaldson	Edwards	Aitken	O'Brien	Cooke	Connell	Marlowe	Holmes	
2/11 1,212				*Fairbrother 6, 76, Brown 81*	*Woodend*	*Oliver*	*Lees*	*Hinton*	*Tapping*	*McNab*	*Price*	*Brown*	*Fairbrother*	*Aggio*	*Williams*	
				Ref: L Bartels	Wimbledon lose their grip on the Southern League Cup, and in the process suffer their third home defeat in a month. The Dons' disciplinary record is grim. Connell fouls ex-Arsenal Bob McNab and is booked, but refuses to give his name. Holmes scores his first penalty in four tries.											

FA Cup																
1 H WOKING	9 W	1-0	0-0	Bryant 72	Guy	Tilley	Bryant	Donaldson	Edwards	Aitken	O'Brien	Bassett	Leslie*	Connell	Holmes	Marlowe
20/11 2,266 *Isth:9*					*Overton*	*Stratford*	*Cooper*	*Poole*	*Whatford*	*Cottrell**	*Alexander*	*Brown*	*Morton*	*Hill*	*Roberts*	*Godfrey*
				Ref: A Glasson	Dickie Guy celebrates his 500th first-team match by keeping a clean sheet, though Woking's Tony Roberts missed two great chances after half-time. Leslie had damaged ligaments training in the car-park, and had to come off. Bassett's free-kick and Holmes flick-on created the goal.											
2 A LEATHERHEAD	10 W	3-1	1-0	Bryant 36, Marlowe 47, 85	Guy	Tilley	Bryant	Donaldson	Edwards	Bassett	Aitken	Cooke	Connell	Marlowe	Holmes	
14/12 *4,195 Isth:5*				*Reid 65*	*Swannell*	*Sargent*	*Eaton*	*Woffinden*	*Reid*	*Bailey**	*Cooper*	*Baker*	*Kelly*	*Smith*	*Doyle*	*Wells*
				Ref: C White	Middlesbrough's Jack Charlton sits in the stands but leaves with the Dons 2-0 up. He is disappointed at having to play Wimbledon, partly because they are better, and partly because Leatherhead would have switched the tie. A phantom whistler contributes to Bryant's goal.											
3 H MIDDLESBRO	D	0-0	0-0		Guy	Tilley	Bryant	Donaldson	Edwards	Bassett	Cooke	Aitken	Connell	Marlowe	Holmes	
8/1 8,539 *1:6*					*Cuff*	*Craggs*	*Cooper*	*Souness*	*Boam*	*Maddren*	*McAndrew*	*Mills*	*Brine*	*Wood*	*Armstrong*	
				Ref: D Turner	A David and Goliath on paper, but both sides have such well-drilled defences that few are really surprised by the goalless outcome. A dour match. A poor gate, considering the Dons hope to get into the Football League. Boro refused to play under flood-lights. Kick-off was at 2 pm.											
3R A MIDDLESBRO	6 L	0-1	0-0		Guy	Tilley	Bryant	Donaldson	Edwards	Bassett	Cooke	Aitken	Connell	Marlowe	Holmes	
11/1 *22,845 1:6*				*Armstrong 56p*	*Cuff*	*Craggs*	*Cooper*	*Souness*	*Boam*	*Maddren*	*McAndrew*	*Mills*	*Brine*	*Wood*	*Armstrong*	
					The pitch is covered with snow. Wimbledon hold out comfortably enough through the first half. But, as at Leeds, they concede a second-half penalty. David Armstrong, fouled by Tilley, took the kick. The Dons hadn't threatened until then, but fired half a dozen shots afterwards.											

FA Trophy																
1 A GRANTHAM	11 W	1-0	0-0	Leslie 47	Guy	Tilley	Bryant	Donaldson	Edwards	Bassett	Cooke	Aitken	Connell	Marlowe	Leslie	
19/1 *1,755 3*					*Gardiner*	*Taylor*	*Capewell G*	*Norris*	*Harrison*	*Jackson*	*Capewell M*	*Carr*	*Platt*	*Gulson*	*Benskin*	*P*
				Ref: K Baker	Billy Holmes missed the bus, so to speak, so John Leslie wears the No 11 shirt. The biggest London Road gate of the season braves a cold											

2	H	WIGAN		W	3-2	2-1	Edwards 8, Holmes 30, 65	Guy	Tilley	Bryant	Donaldson	Edwards	Bassett	Leslie	Aitken	Connell*	Holmes	Friend	Marlowe
	5/2		2,418				*Worswick 17, Bryant 47 (og)*	*Critchley*	*Gore*	*Bannister*	*Ward*	*Hinnigan*	*Gillibrand*	*Worswick*	*Prescott*	*Makin**	*Wilkie*	*Morris*	
							Ref: P Totney	A brutal match of five goals and five bookings, a repeat of last season's non-league champions' duel. In the second half Bryant chipped an own-goal over Guy's head, Holmes put the Dons back in front, and the game exploded with four bookings to add to Bassett's in the first half.											
3	H	CHORLEY		D	2-2	0-2	Holmes 56, Connell 70	Guy	Tilley	Bryant	Donaldson	Edwards	Bassett	Aitken	Cooke	Connell	Holmes	Friend	
	26/2		3,042 *CL:4*				*Garrett 5, Pearson 30*	*McMahon*	*Barrow*	*Wilkinson*	*Humphries*	*Brown*	*Pickering*	*Galliers*	*Pearson*	*Telfer*	*Dickinson*	*Garrett*	
							Ref: A Gunn	Chorley are 4th in the Cheshire League. They unearthed future England star Paul Mariner, whom they sold to Plymouth Argyle for £15,000. Another player to catch the eye is Steve Galliers. 'We played like a load of fairies in the first half,' (Batsford). Holmes then hits a screamer.											
3R	A	CHORLEY		D	2-2	0-0	Holmes 52, Bryant 89	Guy	Tilley	Bryant	Donaldson	Edwards	Bassett	Cooke*	Aitken	Connell	Holmes	Friend	Marlowe
	1/3		*6,310*		*aet*		*Dickinson 50, Barrow 80*	*McMahon*	*Barrow*	*Birchall*	*Galliers**	*Brown*	*Pickering*	*Lang*	*Pearson*	*Telfer*	*Dickinson*	*Garrett*	*Humphries*
							Ref: J Worrall	A huge crowd and an electric atmosphere. Dickie Guy felt queasy on the bus, and he is out of sorts as he spills Lennie Dickinson's corner. Bryant forces extra-time, during which a Connell score is ruled out after a linesman indicated that the ball had earlier gone out of play.											
3	N	CHORLEY		L	0-2	0-0		Guy	Tilley	Bryant	Donaldson	Edwards	Bassett	Aitken	Marlowe	Connell*	Holmes	Friend	Markham
RR	7/3		*1,568*				*Pearson 56, Dickinson 85p*	*McMahon*	*Barrow*	*Birchall*	*Humphries*	*Brown*	*Pickering*	*Lang*	*Pearson*	*Telfer*	*Dickinson*	*Garrett*	*Galliers*
		(at Walsall)					Ref: R Perkin	The managers could not agree a venue, so Fellows Park, Walsall, stages this neutral decider. Cooke is out injured. There is no Rice to add bite to midfield, and he is transfer-listed at £350. Donaldson boobs twice, and Wimbledon slide limply from a Cup that they continue to fail in.											

		Home					Away					
	P	W	D	L	F	A	W	D	L	F	A	Pts
1 WIMBLEDON	42	17	3	1	38	10	11	4	6	26	12	63
2 Minehead	42	13	4	4	37	16	10	8	3	36	23	58
3 Kettering	42	13	6	2	38	20	7	10	4	28	26	56
4 Bath	42	12	6	3	27	10	8	9	4	24	20	55
5 Nuneaton B	42	13	4	4	31	12	7	7	7	21	23	51
6 Bedford	42	10	5	6	30	21	7	9	5	24	26	48
7 Yeovil	42	12	7	2	42	17	3	9	9	12	25	46
8 Dover	42	10	11	0	31	13	3	5	13	15	30	42
9 Grantham	42	11	6	4	38	17	3	6	12	17	33	40
10 Maidstone	42	10	8	3	30	18	3	6	12	16	32	40
11 Gravesend	42	9	8	4	19	13	4	5	12	19	30	39
12 AP Leamington	42	9	7	5	23	16	3	8	10	21	37	39
13 Redditch	42	7	6	8	26	30	5	8	8	19	24	38
14 Wealdstone	42	8	7	6	36	34	5	5	11	18	32	38
15 Hillingdon B	42	7	5	9	27	30	7	5	9	18	29	38
16 Atherstone	42	8	7	6	22	18	6	2	13	19	31	37
17 Weymouth	42	11	2	8	29	21	5	3	13	24	52	37
18 Dartford	42	10	4	7	32	22	3	6	12	20	35	36
19 Telford	42	9	4	8	26	25	2	8	11	10	25	34
20 Chelmsford	42	5	10	6	34	32	4	3	14	22	36	31
21 Burton Alb	42	8	6	7	27	20	2	4	15	14	32	30
22 Margate	42	4	7	10	21	34	5	3	13	26	51	28
	924	216	133	113	664	449	113	133	216	449	664	924

Odds & ends

Double wins: (8) Chelmsford, Burton, Weymouth, Atherstone, Margate, Bedford, Redditch, Minehead.
Double losses: (1) Bath.

Won from behind: (5) Chelmsford (h), Atherstone (h), Dover (h), Weymouth (a), Telford (a).
Lost from in front: (0).

High spots: 2 runs of 6 wins in a row (January to March; March to April)
Just 1 defeat in final 25 league games.
Taking Middlesbrough to an FA Cup replay.

Low spots: Bad start, just 1 point from first 3 games.
1 win in 5 games between mid-October and November.
Defeats by Barnet and Chorley in various cups.

No other team in Wimbledon's era have won the title with 63 points.
The Dons increased their title-winning points total each season.
Only 1 player managed double figures in league scoring charts.
Dickie Guy kept 22 clean sheets in the league.

Player of the Year: Billy Edwards.
Ever-presents (3) Dickie Guy, Dave Donaldson, Jeff Bryant (league only).
Hat-tricks: (0).
Leading scorer: Roger Connell (18).

	Appearances					Goals				
	Lge	Sub	SLC	FAC	FAT	Lge	SLC	FAC	FAT	Total
Aitken, Glen	37		3	4	5	5				5
Bassett, Dave	32	(1)	3	4	5					
Bryant, Jeff	42		4	4	5	6		2	1	9
Connell, Roger	39		4	4	5	14	3		1	18
Cooke, Ian	18	(3)	4	3	3	3	1			4
Donaldson, Dave	42		5	4	5	1				1
Eames, Terry	2	(4)	2							
Edwards, Billy	40		5	4	5	4	1		1	6
Friend, Barry	18	(1)			4					
Godwin, Danny	4		1							
Guy, Dickie	42		5	4	5					
Hawley, Alan	1									
Holmes, Billy	39		5	4	4	9	2		4	15
Leslie, John	19	(1)		1	2	7			1	8
Markham, Leo	14	(1)	1/1		0/1	6				6
Marlowe, Ricky	31	(6)	3	3/1	2/2	7		2		9
O'Brien, Neil	4		2	1						
Rice, Selwyn	1									
Scullion		(1)								
Teather, Chris			1							
Tilley, Kevin	37		4	4	5					
Watts			1							
West			2							
(own-goals)						2				2
23 players used	**462**	**(18)**	**55/1**	**44/1**	**55/3**	**64**	**7**	**4**	**8**	**83**

LEAGUE DIVISION 4

Manager: Allen Batsford / Dario Gradi

SEASON 1977-78

No	Date		Att	Pos	Pts	F-A	H-T	Scorers, Times, and Referees	1	2	3	4	5	6	7	8	9	10	11	12 sub used
1	H	HALIFAX			D	3-3	0-1	Bryant 51, Leslie 70, Connell 86	Guy	Bryant	**Galvin**	Donaldson	Aitken	**Davies**	**Galliers**	**Smith**	Connell	Holmes	Leslie	
	20/8		4,616		1			*Carroll 40, 55, Bell 87*	*Gennoe*	*Flavell*	*Loska*	*Smith*	*Dunleavy*	*Bradley*	*Carroll*	*Johnston*	*Bullock*	*Bell*	*Horsfall*	
								Ref: D Smith	Dons stalwart Ian Cooke, at Plough Lane for over 14 years, announces his retirement on the eve of the new season, which sparks into life with a six-goal thriller. The Dons go in front for the first time with four minutes to play, only to concede a quick equaliser. 'Disgraceful' – Batsford.											
2	A	BRENTFORD			L	**1-4**	1-2	Bryant 10 *[Lloyd 78]*	Guy	Tilley	Bryant	Donaldson	Aitken	Davies	Galliers	Smith	Connell	Holmes	Leslie	
	22/8		*11,001*		1			*McCulloch 6, Phillips 30, Sweetzer 60,*	*Bond*	*Fraser*	*Allen**	*Lloyd*	*Kruse*	*Shrubb*	*Walker*	*Graham J*	*Sweetzer*	*McCulloch*	*Phillips*	*Smith*
								Ref: B Hill	London rivals Brentford inflict Wimbledon's heaviest defeat for over three years. Two weeks later the Bees score six at Crewe, which shows their qualities. They will win promotion. Only three Bees played in the FA Cup-tie of 1975-76. Phillips will often be a thorn in the Dons' side.											
3	A	TORQUAY		18	D	1-1	0-1	Connell 90	**Teale**	Tilley	Bryant	Donaldson	Edwards	Bassett	Galliers*	Davies	Connell	Holmes	Aitken	Leslie
	27/8		*4,162*	*8*	2			*Brown 30*	*Lee T*	*Twitchin*	*Parsons*	*Vassallo*	*Green*	*Boulton*	*Rudge*	*Lee C*	*Lawrence*	*Brown*	*Raper*	
								Ref: K Cooper	Goalkeeper Dickie Guy, hero of Wimbledon's recent Cup exploits, had been ever-present for seven seasons. But he is axed after the thumping by Brentford. He had a poor game against them in the FA Cup, too. After Brown's bullet header, both Galliers and Leslie hit the crossbar.											
4	H	SOUTHPORT		16	D	2-2	1-1	Connell 25, Harrison 59 (og)	Teale	Tilley	Bryant	Donaldson	Edwards	Bassett	Leslie	Davies	Connell	Holmes	Aitken	
	3/9		3,609	*13*	3			*Ashworth 35, O'Neil 70*	*Harrison*	*Kisby*	*Snookes*	*O'Neil*	*Brooks*	*Fisher*	*Cooper*	*Ashworth*	*Jones*	*Suddick*	*Wilson*	
								Ref: J Martin	Dons fail to beat perennial strugglers Southport. They might have done so had Billy Holmes not squandered an early penalty. The Dons lead when Geoff Davies bundles keeper Harrison into the net. When Southport player-manager Hugh Fisher fouls Holmes again, no penalty results.											
5	A	HARTLEPOOL		19	L	0-2	0-1		Teale	Bryant	Galvin	Donaldson	Edwards	Bassett	**Denny**	Davies	Connell	Holmes	Aitken	
	10/9		*2,709*	*11*	3			*McMordie 41, Poskett 59*	*Edgar*	*Malone*	*Wiggett*	*Gibb*	*Ayre*	*Simpkin*	*McMordie*	*Downing*	*Newton*	*Poskett*	*Bielby*	
								Ref: T Morris	Ex-Northern Ireland international Eric McMordie leads the Dons a merry dance as the Dons fail to score for the first time in their short league career. 'Workington would have put up a better show than the Dons,' insist Hartlepool supporters. Wimbledon hover outside the bottom four.											
6	H	ALDERSHOT		22	L	1-2	0-1	Edwards 50	Teale	Bryant	Galvin	Donaldson	Edwards	Bassett	Aitken	Galliers	Davies	Leslie	Holmes	
	13/9		4,446	*3*	3			*Needham 43, Dungworth 83*	*Johnson*	*Earls*	*Butler*	*Dixon*	*Youlden*	*Jopling*	*Crosby*	*Brodie*	*Needham*	*Dungworth*	*McGregor*	
								Ref: R Challis	Penalty misses are proving crucial. The Dons would have preserved their unbeaten home record had not Geoff Davies – in for the injured Connell – seen his last-minute kick saved by Glen Johnson. Yet in truth Wimbledon deserved nothing from this feeble performance.											
7	A	SCUNTHORPE		23	L	0-3	0-0		Teale	Bryant	Galvin	Donaldson*	Edwards	Bassett	Galliers	Leslie	Davies	Holmes	Aitken	Connell
	17/9		*2,618*	*15*	3			*Oates 57, 66, Lumby 62*	*Crawford*	*Czuczman*	*Peacock*	*Kavanagh*	*Money*	*Bridges*	*Oates*	*Kilmore**	*Keeley*	*Lumby*	*Heron*	*Pilling*
								Ref: J Sewell	At least Dave Donaldson cannot be blamed for this latest defeat. Within 10 minutes of him limping off Scunthorpe scored all three of their goals. The Dons have now failed to win any of their first seven league games. To make matters worse, Scunthorpe had lost their last four.											
8	H	NORTHAMPTON		23	W	2-0	2-0	Holmes 35, Summerill 38	Teale	Tilley	Galvin	Bryant	Edwards	Bassett	Galliers	Davies	**Summerill**	Holmes	Leslie	
	24/9		3,326	*10*	5				*Garnham*	*Tucker*	*Mead*	*Liddle*	*Litt*	*Bryant*	*Farrington*	*Williams**	*Reilly*	*Martin*	*McGowan*	*Best*
								Ref: A Turvey	Northampton will always be remembered as Wimbledon's first league scalp. Billy Holmes' header bobbled in off a post. Phil Summerill, a free transfer from Millwall, then scores an angled volley on his debut. Bryant later headed against a post. Northampton will lose often to the Dons.											
9	H	NEWPORT		16	W	3-0	2-0	Galvin 19, Davies 32, Holmes 60	Teale	Tilley	Galvin	Bryant	Edwards	Bassett	Galliers	Davies	Summerill	Holmes	Leslie	
	27/9		3,941	*9*	7				*Plumley*	*Derrett*	*Byrne*	*Emanuel*	*Walker R*	*Jones*	*Preece*	*Woods*	*Goddard**	*Relish*	*Williams*	*Clark*
								Ref: A Robinson	'We were thoroughly, comprehensively, systematically taken apart,' moaned Newport manager Ron Addison, whose club lay 7th at the start of play. Batsford had retained the winning formula which lined up against Northampton. The Dons are looking up, and climb to 16th.											
10	A	READING		18	D	2-2	1-1	Summerill 35, Holmes 75	Teale	Tilley	Galvin	Bryant	Edwards	Bassett	Galliers	Davies	Summerill	Holmes	Leslie	
	1/10		*4,369*	*23*	8			*Earles 23, Cumming 61*	*Death*	*Peters*	*Lewis*	*Cumming*	*Hetzke*	*Moreline*	*Earles*	*Nelson*	*Williams*	*Sanchez*	*Bowman*	
								Ref: A Glasson	Reading, just relegated, have made a dreadful start to life in Division 4, but they should have won this match. They twice took the lead, twice hit the woodwork, but had to settle for a point. Wearing Reading's No 10 on a wet and windy day is schoolboy debutant Lawrie Sanchez.											
11	A	GRIMSBY		20	L	1-3	0-2	Summerill 55	Teale	Tilley	Galvin	Bryant	Edwards	Bassett	Galliers*	Davies	Summerill	Holmes	Aitken	Connell
	4/10		*4,048*	*8*	8			*Drinkell 35, 82, Liddell 43*	*Wainman*	*Mawer*	*Moore*	*Waters*	*Barker*	*Partridge*	*Ford*	*Liddell*	*Drinkell*	*Cumming*	*Brolly*	
								Ref: H Robinson	Phil Summerill sparks a second-half revival until Kevin Drinkell – later to play for a host of top clubs – seals the Dons' fate with his second goal of the game. It was Kevin Tilley's mistake that invited it, mistiming a back-pass to Richard Teale. Dario Gradi joins the Dons from Derby.											

No	Venue / Date	Opponent	Att	Pos	Res / Pts	F-A	H-T	Scorers, Times, Referees	1	2	3	4	5	6	7	8	9	10	11	12 sub used
12	H	CREWE		19	D	0-0	0-0		Teale	Tilley	Galvin	Bryant	Edwards	Bassett	Galliers	Davies	Summerill	Holmes	Leslie	
	8/10		2,634	*7*	9				*Crudgington*	*Collier*	*Cheetham*	*Rimmer*	*Bowles*	*Bevan*	*Davies D**	*McGinley*	*Purdie*	*Coyne*	*Tully*	*Spence*
								Ref: W Bombroff	New assistant manager Dario Gradi, and the smallest crowd to date, watch the Dons struggle against a team which has won five of its previous six matches. Long-haired Peter Coyne made the game's best chances for Crewe, but McGinley and Purdie missed them.											
13	A	BOURNEMOUTH		17	W	2-1	1-0	Holmes 21, Leslie 72	Teale	Tilley	Galvin	Bryant	Edwards	Bassett	Galliers	Davies	Summerill	Holmes	Leslie	
	15/10		*4,272*	*20*	11			*Barton 87*	*Baker*	*Cunningham*	*Butler*	*Miller*	*Impey*	*Barton*	*Johnson*	*Showers*	*Shanahan*	*Lennard*	*Riley**	*Paterson*
								Ref: C Gardner	Two headed goals bring about Wimbledon's first away victory. It is no great triumph, for Bournemouth have now lost three times at Dean Court already. Billy Holmes headed in the first goal from Edwards' cross. Brillo-haired John Leslie then added a second, made by Holmes.											
14	H	SOUTHEND		18	L	1-3	1-1	Galvin 13	Teale	Tilley	Galvin	Bryant	Edwards	Bassett	Galliers	Davies	Summerill	Holmes	Leslie	
	22/10		4,448	*2*	11			*Clark 2, Morris 60, Goodwin 86*	*Freeman*	*Young*	*Banks*	*Laverick*	*Moody*	*Clark*	*Morris*	*Goodwin*	*Parker*	*Polycarpou**	*Foggon*	*Hadley*
								Ref: A Lees	This is Southend's fifth away victory in seven games. Wimbledon's best patch came at the start of the second half, but highly rated Colin Morris scuppers their hopes. Southend had scored after just 70 seconds, tubby Alan Foggon chipping a free-kick onto Paul Clark's head.											
15	A	DARLINGTON		21	L	1-3	1-1	Holmes 44p	Teale	Bryant	Edwards	Donaldson	Galvin	Bassett	Galliers	Davies	Summerill	Holmes	Leslie	
	29/10		*2,710*	*11*	11			*Hague 30, Nattrass 65, Wann 81p*	*Owers*	*Cochrane*	*Stone*	*Hague*	*Craig*	*Nattrass*	*Lyons*	*Rowles*	*Ferguson*	*Seal*	*Wann*	
								Ref: M Peck	The Dons were in with a chance until Ron Ferguson appeared to be tripped, and won a controversial late penalty. It gave the Quakers their three-goal haul of the season. They would achieve this feat just once more. This is their 7th unbeaten game on the trot.											
16	H	SWANSEA		21	D	1-1	0-1	Summerill 73	Teale	Bryant	Galvin	Donaldson	Edwards	Bassett	Aitken*	Davies	Summerill	Connell	Leslie	Galliers
	5/11		2,701	*10*	12			*Lally 16*	*Potter*	*Evans*	*Bartley*	*Bruton*	*May*	*Morrissey*	*Lally*	*James R*	*Curtis*	*Griffiths**	*Chappell*	*Charles*
									Atrocious weather, puddles all over the ground, prompted up-and-under football more suited to Welsh rugby. Swansea failed to take advantage. The Dons miss Billy Holmes, transferred to Hereford United for £8,000. Phil Summerill equalises with a 30-yard drive.											
17	H	DARLINGTON			D	1-1	1-0	Aitken 39	Teale	Bryant	Galvin	Donaldson	Edwards!	Bassett	Aitken	Davies	Summerill	Connell	Leslie	
	7/11		2,028		13			*Hague 82*	*Owers*	*Nattrass*	*Cochrane*	*Hague*	*Craig!*	*Stone*	*Lyons*	*Rowles*	*Ferguson!*	*Seal*	*Wann*	
								Ref: P Reeves	Maybe there was a hangover from these teams' recent clash, for this was a stormy match both on the pitch and off. Three players were sent off and Quakers' boss Peter Madden described the Dons as the 'worst side I have ever seen for conning the ref'. He happened to be a FIFA ref.											
18	H	YORK		19	W	2-1	1-0	Leslie 44, 50	Guy	Bryant	Eames	Galvin	Donaldson	Bassett	Summerill	Aitken	Connell*	Davies	Leslie	Galliers
	19/11		2,056	*20*	15			*Topping 82*	*Brown*	*Clements*	*Hunt*	*Topping*	*James*	*Scott*	*Young*	*McDonald*	*Hope**	*Randall*	*Staniforth*	*Hunter*
								Ref: D Nippard	The Dons fizzled out in the second half once striker Roger Connell had limped off at half-time. York have now gone eight away games since their last away win – at champions-elect Watford. Dickie Guy returns to the Wimbledon goal, by public demand it seems. He won't last long.											
19	A	STOCKPORT		18	D	2-2	0-1	Leslie 64, 77	Guy	Tilley	Galvin	Donaldson	Eames	Bassett	Galliers	Davies	Summerill	Denny	Leslie	
	2/12		*5,008*	*10*	16			*Rutter 15, Prudham 60*	*Rogan*	*Lawler*	*Rutter*	*Thompson*	*Loadwick*	*Fogarty*	*Summerbee*	*Halford*	*Park*	*Prudham**	*Massey*	*Fletcher*
								Ref: M Baker	Stockport, who scored six against Hartlepool in their last home match, fielded two former England internationals – Chris Lawler and Mike Summerbee. Two John Leslie headers ensure that the Dons will not go the way of Hartlepool. Stockport play home matches on Fridays.											
20	H	BARNSLEY		19	D	0-0	0-0		Guy	Bryant	Eames	Galvin	Donaldson	Bassett	Galliers	Davies	Summerill	Connell	Leslie	
	10/12		2,406	*5*	17				*Springett*	*Murphy*	*Collins*	*Brown*	*Saunders*	*McCarthy*	*Warnock*	*Joicey*	*Peachey*	*Little*	*Collier*	
								Ref: D Hedges	Evergreen Barnsley keeper Peter Springett holds his breath as Roger Connell blasts over the top from point-blank range with just five minutes to play. Much admired defender Mick McCarthy also looks solid, though Geoff Davies missed two chances. How are Barnsley as high as 5th?											
21	A	HUDDERSFIELD		20	L	0-3	0-1		Guy	Bryant	Galvin	Donaldson	Edwards	Bassett	Galliers	Davies	Summerill	Connell	Leslie*	Denny
	17/12		***3,544***	*15*	17			*Holmes 25, Baines 56, Butler 86*	*Starling*	*Brown*	*Sandercock*	*Holmes*	*Baines*	*Sidebottam*	*Gray*	*Branagan*	*Mountford*	*Johnson*	*Butler*	
								Ref: K McNally	Huddersfield have notched 13 goals from their previous five home matches. They bag another three against the Dons, but in the first-half much of the play was in the other direction. Ian Holmes drove back a half-cleared corner-kick to make it 1-0 to Huddersfield.											
22	A	ROCHDALE		21	L	0-3	0-1		Guy	Bryant	Galvin	Donaldson	Edwards	Bassett	**Bithell**	Davies*	Summerill	**Parsons**	Leslie	Denny
	26/12		***1,283***	*24*	17			*Scaife 45, 54, O'Loughlin 75*	*Poole*	*Hallows*	*Green*	*O'Loughlin*	*Boslem*	*Bannon*	*Owen*	*Scaife*	*Melledew*	*Morrin*	*Esser*	
								Ref: J Ashley	This result takes the cake. Rochdale are rooted in bottom place. They have not won in nine games, and promptly chalk up what will stand as their biggest win of the season. Bobby Scaife scored on the blind side just before the break. The smallest crowd to see the Dons in 1977-78.											
23	H	DONCASTER			D	3-3	2-2	Galliers 11, Leslie 37, Parsons 58p	Guy	Bryant	Galvin	Donaldson	Edwards	Bassett	Galliers	Denny	Summerill	Parsons	Leslie	
	28/12		2,032		18			*O'Callaghan 16, Snodin 18, Laidlaw 53p*	*Peacock*	*Robinson!*	*Reed*	*Laidlaw*	*Owen*	*Taylor*	*Miller*	*Habbin*	*O'Callaghan*	*Snodin**	*Bentley*	*Jones C*
								Ref: A Gunn	Enough action to satisfy any sceptic. The Dons score first and last, equalising Doncaster's penalty with one of their own. In the closing minutes Fred Robertson wallops John Leslie and is shown the red card. There were also four bookings, all of which came with the score 3-3.											

No	Date		Att	Pos	Pts	F-A	H-T	Scorers, Times, and Referees	1	2	3	4	5	6	7	8	9	10	11	12 sub used
24	H	WATFORD		21	L	1-3	0-1	Edwards 80	Guy	Bryant	Galvin	Donaldson	Edwards	Bassett	Galliers	Denny	Summerill	Parsons	Leslie	
	31/12		**7,324**	*1*	18			*Mayes, 24 Jenkins, 49 Downes 51*	*Rankin*	*Geidmintis*	*Bolton*	*Booth*	*Ellis*	*Garner*	*Downes*	*Joslyn**	*Jenkins*	*Mayes*	*Pollard*	*Blissett*
								Ref: D Hutchinson	Plough Lane's biggest gate of the season is a fitting tribute to Graham Taylor's Watford, who are running away with the 4th Division and who will soon grace the 1st – where these clubs will next meet. Alan Mayes and towering Ross Jenkins torment the Dons' defence.											
25	A	SWANSEA			L	0-3	0-1		Guy	Bryant	Davies	Donaldson	Edwards	Bassett	Galliers	Denny	Summerill	Parsons	Leslie	
	2/1		*9,700*		18			*Bassett 15 (og), R James 60p, Charles 87*	*Barber*	*Evans*	*Morris*	*Lally*	*May*	*Bartley*	*Chappell*	*James R*	*Curtis*	*Moore G**	*Moore K*	*Charles*
								Ref: S Bates	It is seven games now without a win. Poor Dickie Guy has a nightmare match, conceding a penalty and failing to cut out a cross for Swansea's third. Bassett also plays badly, passing into his own net and contributing to the penalty. Manager Allen Batsford can take no more and resigns.											
26	H	BRENTFORD		21	D	1-1	0-1	Galvin 68	Guy	Bryant	Galvin	Donaldson	Bithell	Bassett	Galliers	Denny	Summerill	Parsons	Leslie	
	7/1		5,411	*8*	19			*Sweetzer 29*	*Bond*	*Shrubb*	*Fraser*	*Salman*	*Sweetzer*	*Aylott*	*Graham W*	*Sweetzer*	*Allder*	*McCulloch*	*Phillips*	
								Ref: T Bune	Caretaker manager Dario Gradi takes charge and gives a second game to Brian Bithell, signed from Stoke City. It is five games without a win now for the Bees, and they slip to 8th, though they will eventually claim the fourth promotion spot. They killed this game with the offside trap.											
27	A	HALIFAX		21	W	2-1	0-1	Bryant 56, Denny 80	Guy	Bryant	Galvin	Donaldson	Edwards	Bassett	Galliers	Bithell*	Summerill	Parsons	Denny	Tilley
	14/1		*2,774*	*20*	21			*Bullock 11*	*Gennoe*	*Flavell*	*Loska*	*Smith*	*Trainer*	*Dunleavy*	*Horsfall**	*Carroll*	*Bullock*	*Lawson*	*Bell*	*Bradley*
								Ref: M Scott	Halifax are improving under new boss Jimmy Lawson. Paul Denny's late effort brings about their first defeat in nine outings, and Wimbledon's first win in nine. Something of an upset, really. Dario Gradi has now been confirmed as Wimbledon's new manager.											
28	H	TORQUAY		21	L	0-1	0-0		Guy	Bithell	Eames	Donaldson	Bryant	Bassett	Galliers*	Denny	Summerill	Parsons	Leslie	Tilley
	21/1		2,300	*11*	21			*Green 64*	*Lee T*	*Twitchin*	*Parsons*	*Darke*	*Dunne*	*Green*	*Tomlin*	*Boulton*	*Coffill*	*Brown*	*Raper*	
								Ref: R Challis	Torquay create no chances at all with foot or head. Skipper Mike Green has to chest the ball over the line to earn this away victory – Torquay's first since the opening day of the season. Previously, they had managed just five goals on their travels.											
29	H	SCUNTHORPE		21	D	0-0	0-0		**Goddard**	Bithell	Eames	Galvin	Donaldson	Bassett	Leslie*	Denny	Connell	Parsons	**Cork**	Galliers
	11/2		1,603	*17*	22				*Crawford*	*Davy*	*Holyoak**	*Oates*	*Czuczman*	*Pilling*	*O'Donnell*	*Kavanagh*	*Keeley*	*Grimes*	*Lumby*	*Wigg*
								Ref: H Richardson	Dickie Guy reports late at the ground and is dropped. His place in goal is taken by Ray Goddard, a £4,000 signing from Millwall. Goddard is one of two fresh faces. The other belongs to 18-year-old Alan Cork, who impressed Dario Gradi when at Derby County.											
30	H	HARTLEPOOL		18	W	3-0	1-0	Connell 16, Galvin 59, 82	Goddard	Bryant	Eames	Denny	Galvin	Donaldson	Leslie	Bassett	Connell	Cork	Parsons	
	20/2		**1,440**	*23*	24				*Edgar*	*Malone*	*Downing*	*Gibb*	*Ayre*	*Smith G*	*Creamer*	*McMordie*	*Newton*	*Foggon*	*Bielby**	*Smith T*
								Ref: T Bune	Hartlepool had been saving their best for the FA Cup, knocking out Crystal Palace, before bowing out to eventual winners Ipswich Town. Their team, including several ex-1st Division players, invites the Dons' lowest attendance of the season. Bassett is now assistant manager.											
31	H	READING		20	D	1-1	0-1	Connell 58	Goddard	Bryant	Eames	Denny	Galvin	Donaldson	Leslie	Bassett*	Connell	Cork	Parsons	Summerill
	24/2		2,567	*11*	25			*Earles 10*	*Death*	*Peters*	*White*	*Bowman*	*Hicks*	*Bennett*	*Earles*	*Kearney*	*Kearns*	*Cumming*	*Davies*	
								Ref: D Smith	The second draw between these sides this season. Roger Connell heads Wimbledon's leveller through the legs of Reading keeper Steve Death. Death redeems himself with thrilling saves later on. Wimbledon experiment with a Friday night fixture in the hope of luring bigger crowds.											
32	A	NORTHAMPTON			W	3-0	3-0	Connell 23, 44, Parsons 30	Goddard	Bryant	Bithell	Bassett	Galvin	Donaldson	Leslie	Denny	Connell	Cork	Parsons	
	28/2		*2,643*		27				*Jayes*	*Geidmintis*	*Liddle*	*Best*	*Lyon**	*Poppy*	*Farrington*	*Hall*	*Reilly*	*McGowan*	*Christie*	*Martin*
								Ref: A McDonald	Wimbledon are proving to be Northampton's bogey team. Having provided the Dons with their first league win, they now provide them with their first league double. Wimbledon score three away goals for the first time, and inflict on the Cobblers their heaviest home defeat.											
33	A	CREWE		19	D	0-0	0-0		Goddard	Bryant	Eames	Denny	Galvin	Donaldson	Leslie*	Bassett	Connell	Cork	Parsons	**Briley**
	4/3		*1,871*	*17*	28				*Crudgington*	*Bevan*	*Roberts*	*Lugg*	*Bowles*	*Rimmer*	*Davies D*	*Cheetham**	*Purdie*	*Davies W*	*Tully*	*McGinley*
								Ref: R Toseland	Les Briley makes his first appearance for the Dons, replacing Leslie for the last eight minutes. Crewe fans are becoming desperate for a home goal: they haven't seen one now for 270 minutes. Ray Goddard prevented one several times in a backs-to-the-wall second half.											
34	A	ALDERSHOT		18	L	1-3	0-2	Wooler 89 (og)	Goddard	Bryant	Eames*	Briley	Galvin	**Bradley**	Leslie	Bassett	Connell	Summerill	Parsons	Denny
	8/3		*4,632*	*7*	28			*Dungworth 17, Bell 40, Brodie 77*	*Johnson*	*Earls*	*Wooler*	*Dixon*	*Youlden*	*Jopling*	*Crosby*	*Brodie*	*Bell*	*Dungworth*	*McGregor**	*Needham*
								Ref: M Taylor	Aldershot are unbeaten at home, and prevail over Wimbledon's five-match unbeaten run. Dave Bradley and Les Briley have their first full games. Bradley is on loan from Manchester U; Briley a £16,000 record signing from Hereford. A late own-goal gives dignity to the score.											

35	H	BOURNEMOUTH	18	W	3-1	1-0	Connell 45, Cork 48, Leslie 56	Goddard	Bryant	Bradley	Briley	Galvin	Donaldson	Leslie	Denny	Connell	Cork	Parsons	
11/3		2,834	*13*	30			*Miller 80*	*Baker*	*Cunningham*	*Miller*	*Impey*	*Brown*	*Finnigan**	*Paterson*	*Showers*	*Shanahan*	*Lennard*	*Riley*	*Borthwick*
							Ref: J Bent	Bournemouth provide the Dons with their second 'double' of the season. The Cherries had been climbing the table: this was only their second defeat in 11 games. Wimbledon are assisted by Alan Cork's first ever goal, but hindered by Steve Parsons' wasted penalty.											
36	A	SOUTHEND	21	L	0-1	0-1		Goddard	Bryant*	Bradley	Briley	Galvin	Donaldson	Leslie	Denny	Connell	Cork	Parsons	Summerill
17/3		*7,120*	*2*	30			*Parker 1*	*Freeman*	*Young*	*Yates*	*Laverick*	*Townsend*	*Moody*	*Morris*	*Pountney*	*Parker*	*Abbott*	*Polycarpou*	
							Ref: A Grey	Derrick Parker chips Goddard in the first minute, but thereafter Southend keeper Neil Freeman – newly back after a broken wrist – thwarts Wimbledon's spirited recovery, saving from Cork, Connell, and former Southend player Paul Denny.											
37	A	DONCASTER	19	W	2-0	0-0	Bryant 61, Cork 75	Goddard	Bryant	Bradley	Briley*	Galvin	Donaldson	Leslie	Denny	Connell	Cork	Parsons	Eames
25/3		*2,484*	*18*	32				*Peacock*	*Robinson*	*Hemsley*	*Laidlaw*	*Cannell*	*Taylor*	*Olney*	*Jones M**	*Owen*	*Bailey*	*Habbin*	*Snodin*
							Ref: J Hunting	Doncaster end a sequence of four successive league draws with this defeat, sparked by Jeff Bryant ghosting in to score from a free-kick after the break. Substitute Terry Eames robbed Laidlaw to send Alan Cork sprinting 40 yards to score the second goal.											
38	H	ROCHDALE	17	W	5-1	2-0	Cork 11, 85, Leslie 45, Bryant 62, [Parsons 90]	Goddard	Bryant	Bradley	Briley	Galvin	Donaldson	Leslie	Denny	Connell	Cork	Parsons	
27/3		2,737	*24*	34			*Scaife 47*	*Slack*	*Hallows*	*Oliver*	*Morrin*	*Scott*	*Bannon*	*Seddon*	*Scaife*	*Shaw**	*Esser*	*O'Loughlin*	*Owen*
								Rochdale remain adrift at the bottom, and suffer due revenge for the pasting they handed Wimbledon at Spotland. Alan Cork's double helps the Dons to their biggest home win of the season. Many neutrals thought the final score rather harsh on Rochdale.											
39	A	WATFORD	19	L	0-2	0-0		Goddard	Bryant	Eames	Briley	Galvin	Donaldson	Denny*	Bassett	Connell	Cork	Parsons	Galliers
1/4		***11,212***	*1*	34			*Mayes 64, Pritchett 79p*	*Rankin*	*How*	*Pritchett*	*Booth**	*Bolton*	*Garner*	*Downes*	*Mayes*	*Jenkins*	*Joslyn*	*Pollard*	*Blissett*
							Ref: C Thomas	Watford provide the largest audience to watch the Dons both at home and away. They are on course to win the title by a massive 11 points. They have not conceded a home goal since December. It was deep into the second half when Mayes' volley shattered Wimbledon's hopes.											
40	H	GRIMSBY		D	2-2	1-0	Leslie 37, Parsons 66p	Goddard	Bryant	Eames	Briley	Galvin	Donaldson	Leslie	Denny	Connell	Cork	Parsons	
4/4		2,380		35			*Partridge 84, Lester 89*	*Wainman*	*Mawer*	*Booth*	*Waters*	*Moore*	*Hanvey*	*Ford*	*Lester*	*Donovan**	*Cumming*	*Brolly*	*Partridge*
							Ref: C Maskell	Grimsby have left their promotion surge too late. But they were on course for only their fourth defeat in 17 games when they popped in two late, point-saving goals in this breathtaking match. Grimsby hit a post, had a goal disallowed, and Waters shot wastefully wide in injury time.											
41	H	HUDDERSFIELD	18	W	2-0	2-0	Bryant 10, Leslie 24	Goddard	Bryant	Eames	Briley	Galvin	Donaldson	Leslie	Denny	Connell	Cork	Parsons	
8/4		2,602	*8*	37				*Starling*	*Brown*	*Sandercock*	*Holmes*	*Sutton*	*Branagan*	*Butler*	*Hart*	*Howey*	*Johnson*	*Gray*	
							Ref: T Spencer	Huddersfield have blown their promotion hopes, and this is the third of five straight defeats. Wimbledon appear safe from the threat of having to apply for re-election and can start to build for next season. Both Les Briley and Alan Cork enjoy super matches.											
42	A	YORK	20	D	1-1	0-0	Connell 72	Goddard	Bryant	Eames	Galvin	Donaldson	Briley	Leslie	Denny*	Connell	Cork	Parsons	Galliers
15/4		*1,617*	*21*	38			*Staniforth 81p*	*Brown*	*Clements*	*Hunt*	*Scott**	*Topping*	*Bainbridge*	*Novacki*	*Hunter*	*Randall*	*McDonald*	*Staniforth*	*Hope*
							Ref: N Ashley	York's misery seems never ending. Relegated from the 2nd to the 4th Division in successive seasons, they are now doomed to seek re-election. In injury-time Hunt heads Leslie's glancing header off the line. The Dons twice hit the woodwork. Parsons fouled Hope for the penalty.											
43	A	SOUTHPORT	16	W	**5-0**	2-0	Connell 41, 43, Parsons 46, Leslie 75, [Bryant 85]	Goddard	Bryant	Eames	Briley	Galvin	Donaldson	Leslie	Bassett	Connell	Cork	Parsons	
17/4		*1,604*	*23*	40				*Cumbes*	*Kisby*	*Snookes*	*O'Neil*	*Brooks*	*Fisher*	*Hilton*	*Wilson*	*Jones*	*Gay*	*Birchall**	*Brookfield*
								5-0 is a rare enough victory at home: away from home it is astonishing. Dispirited Southport must now apply for re-election for the third successive season. They will be replaced by Wigan. The Dons, meanwhile, are able to bask in their record league win.											
44	H	STOCKPORT	15	W	2-0	0-0	Briley 57, Leslie 65	Goddard	Bryant	Eames	Briley	Galvin	Donaldson	Leslie	Bassett	Connell	Cork	Parsons	
22/4		2,763	*19*	42				*Rogan*	*Lawler*	*Rutter*	*Fletcher*	*Smith*	*Park*	*Summerbee*	*Halford**	*Massey*	*Prudham*	*McBeth*	*Howard*
							Ref: R Challis	This midfield stalemate was ended by Alan Cork. He didn't score, but he engineered both goals. This marks Stockport's 10th defeat in 13 games. Les Briley scores his first goal, having made many for others. This win finally ends the Dons' lingering re-election worries.											
45	A	NEWPORT	10	W	1-0	1-0	Connell 43	Goddard	Bryant	Eames	Briley	Bradley	Donaldson	**Cowley**	Denny	Connell	Cork	Parsons	
25/4		*2,112*	*15*	44				*Plumley*	*Byrne*	*Relish*	*Emanuel*	*Walker R*	*Jones*	*Vaughan*	*Goddard*	*Clark*	*Sinclair*	*Williams*	
							Ref: L Shapter	Newport were third in early March, but have since gone to pieces. This is their 11th winless game, and Roger Connell's 13th goal of the season permits Wimbledon to leapfrog above them. Parsons almost scored in the first minute, but thereafter Newport missed a sackful.											
46	A	BARNSLEY	13	L	2-3	0-2	Connell 46, 88	Goddard	Bradley	Eames	Briley	Galvin	Donaldson	Leslie	Denny	Connell	Cork	Cowley	
29/4		*2,479*	*7*	44			*Millar 13, 65p, Riley 25*	*Springett*	*Pugh*	*Chambers*	*Collier*	*Saunders*	*McCarthy*	*Riley*	*Peachey*	*Millar*	*Little*	*Brown*	
	Home	*Away*					Ref: G Nolan	Wimbledon sign off with only their second defeat in ten matches. Had they drawn they would have finished in the top half of the table. Barnsley's promotion hopes blew up in the home straight, and this match is watched by their lowest gate. Leslie fouled Brown for the penalty.											
Average	3,139	*4,063*																	

League Cup	Att		F-A	H-T	Scorers, Times, and Referees	1	2	3	4	5	6	7	8	9	10	11	12 sub used
1:1 A GILLINGHAM		D	1-1	0-1	Holmes 85	Guy	Tilley	Bryant	Donaldson	Edwards	Bassett	Galliers	Smith	Connell	Holmes	Leslie	
13/8	*4,782 3:7*				*Westwood 40*	*Hillyard*	*Williams*	*Armstrong*	*Overton*	*Shipperley*	*Hughes*	*Nicholl*	*Crabbe*	*Price*	*Westwood*	*Richardson*	
					Ref: R Toseland	Gillingham may be a division above the Dons, but there is little in the play to suggest any gap in standards. Yet it takes a late leveller for the Dons to avoid a home defeat. Danny Westwood had latched onto Smith's error to open the scoring. Holmes levelled with a glancing header.											
1:2 H GILLINGHAM		W	3-1	1-0	Bassett 35, Connell 68, Holmes 72	Guy	Tilley	Bryant	Donaldson	Edwards	Bassett	Galliers	Smith	Connell*	Holmes	Leslie	Davies
16/8	3,868 *3:7*				*Price 54*	*Hillyard*	*Williams*	*Armstrong*	*Overton*	*Shipperley*	*Hughes*	*Nicholl*	*Crabbe*	*Price*	*Westwood*	*Richardson*	
					Ref: A Gunn (Dons win 4-2 on aggregate)	Six months hence, Gillingham will top the 3rd Division table, before slipping away in the final weeks of the season. The league campaign has yet to begin, however, and two goals in four minutes sends the Gills spinning out of the League Cup. Guy kept the Gills at bay in the first half.											
2 A TOTTENHAM		L	0-4	0-2		Teale	Tilley	Bryant	Donaldson	Edwards	Bassett	Galliers*	Davies	Connell	Holmes	Aitken	Leslie
31/8	*22,807 2:3*				*Duncan 24, 30, 82 Osgood 83p*	*Daines*	*Naylor*	*Holmes*	*Hoddle*	*Osgood*	*Perryman*	*Pratt*	*McNab*	*Duncan*	*Jones*	*Taylor*	
					Ref: A Grey	Spurs are in the 2nd Division, though their side is graced by stars such as Glenn Hoddle and Steve Perryman. Wimbledon are never in the hunt and are dumped by a hat-trick of headers from John Duncan. The Dons' two best chances fall to Billy Holmes, but he fails to capitalise.											

FA Cup																	
1 A ENFIELD		L	0-3	0-1		Guy	Bryant	Galvin	Donaldson	Eames	Aitken	Davies	Bassett	Summerill	Denny*	Leslie	Galliers
26/11	*2,849 Isth:1*				*Knapman 38, Bass 71, O'Sullivan 85*	*Moore*	*Wright*	*Tone*	*Jennings*	*Elley*	*Howell*	*O'Sullivan*	*Knapman*	*Bass*	*Searle*	*Bishop*	
					Ref: M Porter	It used to be Wimbledon who were the giant killers. Enfield, destined once again for the Isthmian League championship, record their first ever triumph over league opposition in the FA Cup. The score is an embarrassment to the Dons. The renowned Tony Bass scores with a header.											

	P	W	D	L	F	A	W	D	L	F	A	Pts
				Home					Away			
1 Watford	46	18	4	1	44	14	12	7	4	41	24	71
2 Southend	46	15	5	3	46	18	10	5	8	20	21	60
3 Swansea	46	16	5	2	54	17	7	5	11	33	30	56
4 Brentford	46	15	6	2	50	17	6	8	9	36	37	56
5 Aldershot	46	15	8	0	45	16	4	8	11	22	31	54
6 Grimsby	46	14	6	3	30	15	7	5	11	27	36	53
7 Barnsley	46	15	4	4	44	20	3	10	10	17	29	50
8 Reading	46	12	7	4	33	23	6	7	10	22	29	50
9 Torquay	46	12	6	5	43	25	4	9	10	14	31	47
10 Northampton	46	9	8	6	32	30	8	5	10	31	38	47
11 Huddersfield	46	13	5	5	41	21	2	10	11	22	34	45
12 Doncaster	46	11	8	4	37	26	3	9	11	15	39	45
13 WIMBLEDON	46	8	11	4	39	26	6	5	12	27	41	44
14 Scunthorpe	46	12	6	5	31	14	2	10	11	19	41	44
15 Crewe	46	11	8	4	34	25	4	6	13	16	44	44
16 Newport	46	14	6	3	43	22	2	5	16	22	51	43
17 Bournemouth	46	12	6	5	28	20	2	9	12	13	31	43
18 Stockport	46	14	4	5	41	19	2	6	15	15	37	42
19 Darlington	46	10	8	5	31	22	4	5	14	21	37	41
20 Halifax	46	7	10	6	28	23	3	11	9	24	39	41
21 Hartlepool	46	12	4	7	34	29	3	3	17	17	55	37
22 York	46	8	7	8	27	31	4	5	14	23	38	36
23 Southport	46	5	13	5	30	32	1	6	16	22	44	31
24 Rochdale	46	8	6	9	29	28	0	2	21	14	57	24
	1104	286	161	105	894	533	105	161	286	533	894	1104

Odds & ends

Double wins (3): Northampton, Newport, Bournemouth.
Double losses (3): Aldershot, Southend, Watford.

Won from behind (1): Halifax (a).
Lost from in front: (0).

High spots: 6 unbeaten games in April to end re-election fears.

Low spots: Failing to win any of opening 7 league games.
Losing 0-3 at bottom-placed Rochdale, and to Enfield in FA Cup.

Wimbledon failed to beat any of the top 9 sides in the league.

Player of the Year: Dave Donaldson.
Ever-presents: (0).
Hat-tricks: (0).
Leading scorer: Roger Connell (15).

	Appearances						Goals			
	Lge	Sub	LC	Sub	FAC	Sub	**Lge**	LC	FAC	**Total**
Aitken, Glen	**11**		1		1		**1**			**1**
Bassett, Dave	**35**		3		1			1		**1**
Bithell, Brian	**6**									
Bradley, Dave	**7**									
Briley, Les	**13**	(1)					**1**			**1**
Bryant, Jeff	**43**		3		1		**7**			**7**
Connell, Roger	**28**	(2)	3				**14**	1		**15**
Cork, Alan	**17**						**4**			**4**
Cowley, Fran	**2**									
Davies, Geoff	**23**		1	(1)	1		**1**			**1**
Denny, Paul	**23**	(3)			1		**1**			**1**
Donaldson, Dave	**38**		3		1					
Eames, Terry	**17**	(1)			1					
Edwards, Billy	**21**		3				**2**			**2**
Galliers, Steve	**22**	(5)	3			(1)	**1**			**1**
Galvin, Dave	**40**				1		**5**			**5**
Goddard, Ray	**18**									
Guy, Dickie	**13**		2		1					
Holmes, Billy	**15**		3				**5**	2		**7**
Leslie, John	**40**	(1)	2	(1)	1		**13**			**13**
Parsons, Steve	**24**						**5**			**5**
Smith, Willie	**2**		2							
Summerill, Phil	**22**	(2)			1		**4**			**4**
Teale, Richard	**15**		1							
Tilley, Kevin	**11**	(2)	3							
(own-goals)							**2**			**2**
25 players used	**506**	**(17)**	**33**	**(2)**	**11**	**(1)**	**66**	**4**		**70**

No	Date		Att	Pos	Pts	F-A	H-T	Scorers, Times, and Referees	1	2	3	4	5	6	7	8	9	10	11	12 sub used
1	A	ALDERSHOT			D	1-1	1-1	Bryant 11	Goddard	Bryant	Galvin	Donaldson	Eames	Galliers	Leslie	Briley	Cork	Summerill	Parsons	
	19/8		*3,510*		1			*Wooler 32*	*Johnson*	*Edwards**	*Wooler*	*Dixon*	*Youlden*	*Earle*	*Longhorn*	*Brodie*	*McGregor*	*Dungworth*	*Tomlin*	*Howitt*
								Ref: S Bates	Aldershot remained unbeaten at home throughout last season, and are in no mood to throw away their proud record this time. Both teams appear to wilt in blazing second-half sunshine, when Murray Brodie and John Leslie missed sitters at either end. A useful start for the Dons.											
2	H	PORT VALE			W	1-0	1-0	Cork 11	Goddard	Bryant	Galvin	Galliers	Eames	Donaldson	Leslie	Briley	Connell	Cork	Parsons	
	22/8		2,638		3				*Connaughton*	*Wilkinson*	*Griffiths*	*Bentley*	*Sproson*	*Hawkins*	*Bromage*	*Todd**	*Wright*	*Froggatt*	*Stenson*	*Bloor*
								Ref: W Bromroff	Port Vale were relegated on the last day of last season, and they will need to pick their spirits up quickly. They were beaten by an exquisite curling shot from Alan Cork that beat Connaughton from 25 yards. Skipper Les Briley is the Dons' man of the match.											
3	H	NORTHAMPTON		3	W	4-1	3-1	Cork 11, 40, 43, Leslie 71	Goddard	Bryant	Eames	Galliers	Galvin	Donaldson	Briley	Leslie	Connell	Cork	Parsons*	Denny
	26/8		2,644	*13*	5			*Reilly 38*	*Jayes*	*Walker*	*Mead*	*Woollett*	*Robertson*	*Bryant*	*Farrington*	*Williams*	*Reilly*	*Liddle**	*Christie*	*Bowen*
								Ref: A Grey	The Dons enjoy playing the Cobblers. That's three wins out of three since Wimbledon joined the league, and Alan Cork's hat-trick is likewise a Dons' league first. Ironically, the visitors looked the better team until late in the first half, when Cork's second and third goals sealed the win.											
4	A	STOCKPORT		3	W	1-0	0-0	Cork 65	Goddard	Bryant	Eames	Galliers	Galvin	Donaldson	Leslie*	Briley	Denny	Cork	Parsons	**Knowles**
	1/9		*5,604*	*10*	7				*Rogan*	*Thorpe*	*Rutter*	*Thompson*	*Park*	*Edwards*	*Summerbee**	*Halford*	*Bradd*	*Loadwick*	*Lee*	*Prudham*
								Ref: T Morris	For the first time this season Wimbledon fail to score in the 11th minute. Alan Cork's fifth goal of the new campaign erases the gloom instilled by the eight-goal midweek thrashing by Everton. Scouts from top clubs are eyeing him. This Friday night win sends the Dons top overnight.											
5	H	WIGAN		3	W	2-1	0-1	Denny 68, Eames 71p	Goddard	Bryant	Eames	Galliers	Galvin	Donaldson	Leslie	**Ketteridge**	Denny	Cork*	Parsons	Knowles
	9/9		3,217	*24*	9			*Corrigan 1*	*Brown*	*Smart*	*Hinnigan*	*Gore*	*Ward*	*Gillibrand*	*Corrigan*	*Wright*	*Moore*	*Crompton*	*Purdie*	
								Ref: B Hill	Wimbledon are no longer the league's new boys. They were followed one year later by Wigan, who have taken just one point from their first five matches. Wigan's first-minute lead was wiped out by a deflected goal and a harsh-looking penalty. Life can be tough at the bottom.											
6	A	GRIMSBY		2	D	2-2	0-0	Bryant 55, Cork 60	Goddard	Bryant	Eames	Galliers	Galvin	Donaldson	Leslie	Knowles	Denny	Cork	Summerill	
	12/9		*6,794*	*4*	10			*Waters 65p, Bryant 70 (og)*	*Batch*	*Mawer*	*Moore K*	*Waters*	*Barker*	*Crombie*	*Ford**	*Liddell*	*Lester*	*Young*	*Brolly*	*Partridge*
								Ref: D Webb	Both clubs have started the season brightly. Had the Dons hung on to their lead they would have gone top, but – as happened the previous April – the Mariners claw their way back from a two-goal deficit, helped by Bryant's 20-yard lobbed own-goal and Terry Eames' handball.											
7	A	NEWPORT		3	W	3-1	0-0	Leslie 78, 81, Cork 87	Goddard	Bryant	Eames	Galliers	Galvin	Donaldson	Leslie	Denny	Cork	Knowles	Summerill	
	16/9		*2,903*	*22*	12			*Clark 76*	*Plumley*	*Walden*	*Relish**	*Thompson*	*Oakes*	*Jones!*	*Bailey*	*Goddard*	*Lowndes*	*Woods*	*Armstrong*	*Clark*
								Ref: L Shapter	Newport have now lost six out of seven, as they continue the sequence of defeats that began the previous spring. Despite having Rod Jones sent off in the first half, the Welsh team take the lead in the second. Newport keeper Plumley then gifts the Dons their win.											
8	H	READING		1	W	1-0	0-0	Cork 72	Goddard	Bryant	Eames	Galliers	Galvin	Donaldson	Leslie	Denny	Knowles*	Cork	Summerill	Parsons
	23/9		5,001	*3*	14				*Death*	*Peters*	*White*	*Bowman*	*Hicks*	*Bennett*	*Earles*	*Hetzke*	*Kearns**	*Sanchez*	*Lewis*	*Kearney*
								Ref: J Hunting	The clash of two unbeaten teams swells the gate at Plough Lane. Alan Cork's ninth goal of the new campaign – holding off two challenges and shooting from 20 yards – sinks Reading and sends Wimbledon clear at the top. Les Briley is still out with an injured foot.											
9	A	ROCHDALE		1	D	0-0	0-0		Goddard	Bryant	Eames	Galliers	Galvin	Donaldson	Leslie	Denny	Knowles	Cork	Summerill	
	25/9		*1,263*	*23*	15				*Shyne*	*Hallows*	*O'Loughlin*	*Hart*	*Scott*	*Scaife*	*Owen*	*Hoy*	*Ashworth*	*Esser*	*Mullington*	
								Ref: G Tyson	From the top to the bottom. The entire division stands between Wimbledon and Rochdale, who have managed just four goals all season. With minutes to play Galliers pulls down Owen, Rochdale are awarded a penalty, and O'Loughlin shoots criminally wide.											
10	H	BRADFORD C		1	W	2-1	0-1	Denny 57, Parsons 80	Goddard	Bryant	Eames	Donaldson	Galvin	Galliers	Leslie*	Denny	Knowles	Cork	Parsons	Ketteridge
	30/9		2,819	*15*	17			*Baines 4*	*Downsborough*	*Podd*	*Watson*	*Bates*	*Baines*	*Middleton*	*Johnson*	*Jackson D*	*Cooke*	*Szabo*	*Martinez*	*McNiven*
								Ref: T Bune	Bradford City are another relegated team finding life difficult in the 4th Division, having recently lost six goals at Aldershot. Once again the Dons show their mettle by coming from behind to win. Birthday-boy Ray Knowles' long throw brings about Paul Denny's equaliser.											
11	A	YORK		1	W	4-1	2-0	Parsons 33, Knowles 44, Leslie 49, [Cork 82]	Goddard	Bryant	Eames	Galliers	Galvin	Donaldson	Leslie	Denny	Knowles	Cork	Parsons	
	7/10		*3,329*	*11*	19			*Loggie 48*	*Neenan*	*Kay*	*Walsh*	*Collier*	*Faulkner*	*Clements*	*Young*	*Stronach**	*Randall*	*Loggie*	*Staniforth*	*Wellings*
								Ref: P Richardson	The game turned when Cork's boot made contact with keeper Neenan's head as the keeper dives at his feet. The ball ran loose for Knowles to score. The referee might have blown for a foul, but he did not. That goal made it 2-0 to the Dons, and put the game beyond York's recall.											

No	Venue / Date	Opponent / Att	Pos	Res	F-A	H-T	Scorers, Times, Referees	1	2	3	4	5	6	7	8	9	10	11	12
12	H	SCUNTHORPE	1	W	3-1	2-0	Leslie 33, 55, Cork 37	Goddard	Bryant	Eames	Galliers	Galvin	Donaldson	Leslie*	Denny	Knowles	Cork	Parsons	Cowley
	14/10	3,808	*14*	21			*Wigg 70*	*Crawford*	*O'Donnell*	*Peacock*	*Oates*	*Deere*	*Czuczman*	*Grimes*	*Pilling*	*Wigg*	*Kilmore*	*Kavanagh*	
							Ref: P Reeves	John Leslie celebrates his 100th first team appearance for Wimbledon by scoring the two goals that send his club three points clear at the top. Scunthorpe began the match with intimidatory tackles, and their manager – Ron Ashman – was later booked for gestures to the referee.											
13	H	CREWE	1	D	1-1	0-0	Cork 80	Goddard	Bryant	Eames	Galliers	Galvin	Donaldson	Leslie	Denny*	Knowles	Cork	Parsons	Cowley
	17/10	3,555	*18*	22			*Coyne 52*	*Caswell*	*Bevan*	*Cheetham*	*Wilshaw*	*Bowles*	*Wilkinson**	*Davies*	*Purdie*	*Coyne*	*Nelson*	*Robertson*	*Rimmer*
							Ref: H Richardson	Alan Cork's late header preserved Wimbledon's unbeaten record, but they were fortunate to do so against struggling Crewe, who will finish bottom. Crewe have ex-Spurs and Arsenal winger Jimmy Robertson spraying the ball about to good effect. 13 unbeaten games for the Dons.											
14	A	HUDDERSFIELD	1	L	**0-3**	0-1		Goddard	Bryant	Eames	Galliers	Galvin	Donaldson	Leslie	Cowley	Knowles*	Cork	Parsons	Summerill
	21/10	*3,374*	*18*	22			*Robins 35, 50, Bielby 70*	*Starling*	*Brown*	*Sandercock*	*Lillis*	*Sutton*	*Topping*	*Gray*	*Hart*	*Cowling*	*Robins*	*Bielby*	
							Ref: R Bridges	For the second year running, Wimbledon are thumped 0-3 at Leeds Road. Gradi's team may be badly hit by injuries, but that hardly excusees such a result against a team three from bottom at start of play. The Dons were run ragged throughout the game.											
15	H	DONCASTER	1	W	3-2	3-1	Leslie 9, 45, Cork 36	Goddard	**Perkins**	Eames	Galliers	Donaldson	Bryant	Leslie*	**Haverson**	Knowles	Cork	Parsons	Summerill
	28/10	3,252	*22*	24			*Jones 15, 75*	*Peacock*	*Owen*	*Bentley*	*Cork*	*Bradley*	*Olney*	*Habbin*	*Lewis*	*Jones*	*French*	*Laidlaw*	
							Ref: D Hutchinson	Steve Perkins and Paul Haverson – both signed from QPR –pull on a Wimbledon shirt for the first time as the Dons revert to winning ways against lowly Rovers. The win was achieved despite Eames' fluffed penalty. Rovers' scorer, Chris Jones, plays his first game of the season.											
16	A	BARNSLEY	2	L	1-3	0-1	Galvin 75	Goddard	Bryant!	Perkins	Galliers	Galvin	Donaldson	Leslie*	Haverson	Knowles	Cork	Parsons	Cowley
	4/11	*11,761*	*3*	24			*Bell 20, 65, Riley 87*	*Springett*	*Collins*	*Chambers*	*Pugh*	*Saunders*	*McCarthy*	*Bell**	*Clarke*	*Riley*	*Joicey*	*Millar*	*Speedie*
							Ref: D Shaw	Barnsley have lost their way: this is their first win in six games, and it knocks the Dons off the top. New signing Derek Bell strikes twice for the home side before being substituted by David Speedie. Jeff Bryant is sent off for dissent. Barnsley are player-managed by Allan Clarke.											
17	H	STOCKPORT	1	W	2-0	1-0	Denny 7, 80	Goddard	Perkins	Eames	Galliers	Galvin	Donaldson	Leslie	Haverson	Denny	Cork	Parsons	
	11/11	3,177	*10*	26				*Rogan*	*Thorpe*	*Rutter*	*Fogarty*	*Park*	*Edwards*	*Henson*	*Armstrong**	*Bradd*	*Summerbee*	*Lee*	*Halford*
							Ref: A Seville	Paul Denny returns from injury to grab the headlines in this flattering victory over a side including ex-Arsenal star George Armstrong and player-manager Mike Summerbee, the ex-Manchester City favourite. This win takes Wimbledon back to the top again.											
18	A	NORTHAMPTON	1	D	1-1	1-0	Leslie 10	Goddard	Perkins	Eames*	Galliers	Galvin	Donaldson	Leslie	Haverson	Denny	Cork	Parsons	Knowles
	18/11	*3,623*	*13*	27			*Geidmintis 66p*	*Poole*	*Geidmintis*	*Mead*	*Woollett*	*Robertson*	*Bryant*	*Farrington*	*Williams*	*Froggatt*	*Cordice*	*Wassall*	
							Ref: C Maskell	Tony Geidmintis's penalty can't topple Wimbledon off the top of the table, but it does end their 100% record against the Cobblers. The Dons force seven corners in the first nine minutes and score from the eighth. Unable to get into the Dons side, Phil Summerill is transfer-listed.											
19	H	HALIFAX	1	W	2-1	1-0	Cork (2)	Goddard	Perkins	Haverson	Galliers	Galvin	Donaldson	Leslie	Briley	Denny	Cork	Parsons	
	2/12	**2,374**	*24*	29			*Campbell*	*Leonard*	*Hutt*	*Loska*	*Smith*	*Burke**	*Dunleavy*	*Nixon*	*Mountford*	*Campbell*	*Sidebottom*	*Johnson*	*Kennedy*
								Here is an oddity. A team top of the league in December registers its lowest gate of the season. Mind you, the opposition are bottom, and as it happens Halifax might well have won. Alan Cork's second goal brings Wimbledon's tally of league goals to 100 in one and a half seasons.											
20	A	HARTLEPOOL	1	D	1-1	1-0	Denny 15	Goddard	Perkins*	Galliers	Haverson	Galvin	Donaldson	Leslie	Briley	Denny	Cork	Parsons	Knowles
	9/12	*3,098*	*13*	30			*Ayre 52*	*Richardson*	*Smith D*	*Gorry*	*Lawrence*	*Brooks*	*Ayre*	*Linacre*	*Goldthorpe*	*Crumplin*	*Houchen*	*Loadwick*	
							Ref: K Walmsley	This rough-house of a match ended 1-1 in goals and 4-4 in bookings. Paul Denny's goal looked suspiciously offside, but Hartlepool are happy to avoid a third defeat in four matches.											
21	A	BOURNEMOUTH	1	W	2-1	2-1	Galliers 20, Briley 32	Goddard	Bryant	Haverson	Galliers	Galvin	Eames	Leslie*	Briley	Denny	Cork	Cowley	Knowles
	23/12	*3,922*	*8*	32			*Lennard 34*	*Allen*	*Cunningham*	*Miller*	*Impey*	*Brown R*	*Barton*	*Borthwick*	*McDougall*	*Butler M*	*Showers*	*Lennard*	
								What with two FA Cup ties, these teams meet for a third time in quick succession. Again the Dons are triumphant, but Bournemouth are frustrated by the hobbling heroics of goalkeeper Ray Goddard, who defies them in the second half.											
22	H	PORTSMOUTH		L	2-4	2-1	Knowles 5, 41	Goddard	Bryant	Haverson	Galliers	Galvin	Eames	Leslie*	Briley	Knowles	Cork	Cowley	Driver
	26/12	**7,862**		32			*Barnard 10, Davey 50, Wilson 70, [Hemmerman 85]*	*Mellor*	*Ellis*	*Viney*	*Denyer*	*Foster*	*Davey*	*Hemmerman*	*Lathan*	*Wilson*	*Barnard*	*Pullar*	
								Once-proud Pompey find themselves in the soccer basement for the first time in their history. This, their fifth straight victory, keeps them in second place, though they will fade in the spring. Boxing Day brings the largest gate to Plough Lane. They witness a second-half collapse.											
23	H	ROCHDALE	2	W	3-2	1-2	Parsons 17, Galvin 50, Denny 70	Goddard	Bryant	Haverson	Ketteridge	Galvin	Perkins	**Driver***	Briley	Leslie	Denny	Parsons	Knowles
	3/2	3,166	*23*	34			*Jones 12, Hoy 20*	*Felgate*	*Creamer*	*Taylor*	*Scaife*	*Scott*	*Snookes*	*Hoy*	*Owen*	*Jones*	*O'Loughlin*	*Esser*	*Bannon*
							Ref: H Robinson	Lowly Rochdale twice take the lead against a Wimbledon side missing Alan Cork (tonsilitis) for the only time this season. Parsons is booed by the crowd, then scores a super volley. Dario Gradi predicts the Dons will be in the 1st Division within 10 years. He will be several years out.											

No	Date		Att	Pos	Pts	F-A	H-T	Scorers, Times, and Referees	1	2	3	4	5	6	7	8	9	10	11	12 sub used
24	A	WIGAN		1	W	2-1	2-0	Leslie 9, 21	Goddard	Bryant	Eames	Haverson	Galvin	Perkins	Leslie	Ketteridge	Denny	Cork	Parsons	
	14/2		*6,704*		36			Purdie 53p	*Brown*	*Gore*	*Smart*	*Brownhill*	*Ward*	*Fretwell*	*Corrigan*	*Wright*	*Houghton*	*Crompton*	*Purdie*	
								Ref: M Baker	New boys Wigan, bottom of the league in September, have surged up to 7th, thanks to eight home wins on the trot. They saw more of the ball in this game too. Only a feeble run-in will deny them promotion at the first attempt. Their average home gate is double that of Wimbledon.											
25	A	TORQUAY		2	W	**6-1**	2-0	Cork 7, 35, 87, 88, Haverson 57, [Leslie 89]	**Priddy**	Bryant	Ketteridge	Haverson	Galvin	Perkins	Leslie	Galliers*	Denny	Cork	Parsons	Driver
	28/2		*2,739*	*9*	38			*Murphy 82*	*Turner*	*Twitchin*	*Darke*	*Raper**	*Johnson*	*Green*	*Wilson*	*Lawrence*	*Cooper*	*Murphy*	*Davies*	
								Ref: E Hughes	Goddard has flu, so Paul Priddy plays his first game, despite having a broken finger. Galliers returns after suspension and Alan Cork smashes four goals. Torquay sit comfortably in the top half of the table. Three goals in the last three minutes gives the result a freakish air.											
26	H	HUDDERSFIELD		2	W	2-1	0-1	Leslie 50, Driver 85	Goddard	Bryant	Haverson	Ketteridge	Galvin	Perkins	Leslie	Galliers	Denny*	Cork	Parsons	Driver
	3/3		3,265	*18*	40			*Holmes 40*	*Starling*	*Brown*	*Sandercock*	*Hart*	*Haverty*	*Sutton*	*Holmes*	*Cowling*	*Fletcher*	*Robins*	*Howey*	
									Substitute Phil Driver scores his first league goal – a stinging volley – as Wimbledon come from behind to beat a Huddersfield side heading for its fifth reverse in six outings. The Dons looked jaded after the Torquay bonanza. 'Play football!' yelled Dario Gradi from the touchline.											
27	H	NEWPORT		2	D	0-0	0-0		Goddard	Bryant	Haverson	Ketteridge	Galvin	Perkins	Leslie	Galliers	Denny	Cork	Parsons*	Driver
	6/3		2,980	*8*	41				*Plumley*	*Warriner*	*Byrne**	*Davies*	*Oakes*	*Bruton*	*Moore*	*Lowndes*	*Goddard*	*Tynan*	*Bailey*	*Relish*
								Ref: R Challis	'Newport were one of the best sides to play here,' says Dario Gradi after the match. This is the first of four matches in which Wimbledon will fail to score. Five minutes from time Alan Cork swung at a loose ball, but missed it.											
28	A	DONCASTER		3	L	0-1	0-1		Goddard	Bryant	Eames	Ketteridge	Galvin	Perkins	Leslie*	Galliers	Denny	Cork	Parsons	Driver
	9/3		*1,927*	*14*	41			*Cox 31*	*Peacock*	*Olney*	*Snodin*	*Meagen*	*Bradley*	*Flanagan*	*Laidlaw*	*French*	*Cox*	*Cannell*	*Pugh*	
								Ref: D Richardson	A snowstorm interrupted the second half by 16 minutes. The Dons were by then trailing to a goal from Mark Cox, enjoying only his second full appearance for the Rovers, who have seven players out injured. A cross from the right was headed down by Micky French to Cox.											
29	H	GRIMSBY		5	L	0-1	0-1		Goddard	Briley	Eames	Ketteridge	Galvin	Perkins	Leslie	Galliers	Denny	Cork	Driver*	Parsons
	20/3		2,392	*3*	41			*Waters 4*	*Batch*	*Moore D*	*Moore K*	*Waters*	*Wiggington*	*Crombie*	*Ford*	*Liddell*	*Cumming*	*Mitchell*	*Brolly*	
								Ref: R Toseland	This top of the table clash was settled by the Mariners' Irish international Joe Waters in the fourth minute. Wimbledon drop to 5th place, but they have five games in hand over leaders Reading and several over the others above them. Gradi experiments with 4-2-4 but it does not work.											
30	A	PORT VALE		5	L	0-1	0-1		Goddard	Briley	Eames	Driver*	Galvin	Bryant	Leslie	Galliers	Denny	Cork	Parsons	Haverson
	24/3		*2,906*	*12*	41			*Beech 44*	*Dance*	*Keenan*	*Griffiths*	*Beech*	*Delgado*	*Bentley*	*Sinclair*	*Farrell*	*Wright*	*Todd*	*Healy*	
								Ref: B Stevens	Wimbledon's third straight 0-1 setback was settled by the only goal Port Vale could manage in what is their second win in nine games. It is now over six hours since the Dons last scored. Kenny Beech headed in at the far post from Ken Todd's cross. Vale also hit the crossbar.											
31	H	ALDERSHOT		4	W	3-1	1-0	Haverson 8p, Knowles 54, Parsons 89	Goddard	Bryant*	Haverson	Briley	Galvin	Perkins	Leslie	Galliers	Knowles	Cork	Parsons	Denny
	27/3		5,382	*3*	43			*Longhorn 73*	*Johnson*	*Howitt*	*Edwards**	*Dixon*	*Youlden*	*Jopling*	*Crosby*	*Longhorn*	*Needham*	*Dungworth*	*McGregor*	*Hooper*
								Ref: G Napthine	Wimbledon dare not lose this match to 3rd placed Aldershot, who have lost just once in 1979. The strategy for success was to shackle 28-goal Shots' striker John Dungworth and for Steve Galliers to run riot in midfield. Paul Haverson's penalty ended the Dons' 373-minute goal drought.											
32	H	HEREFORD		4	W	2-0	1-0	Cork 36, Leslie 80	Goddard	Perkins	Haverson	Briley	Galvin	Cunningham	Leslie	Galliers	Knowles	Cork	Parsons*	Denny
	31/3		2,636	*11*	45				*Hughes*	*Price**	*Burrows*	*Strong*	*Layton*	*Emery*	*Stephens*	*Hendry*	*White*	*Powell*	*Gould*	*Thomas*
								Ref: L Burden	Wimbledon parade their record signing, £45,000 Tommy Cunningham from QPR. Les Briley enjoys this victory over his former club, which is sparked by Alan Cork's first home goal of 1979. Bobby Gould plays in Mike Bailey's Hereford side. The Plough Lane pitch looks dreadful.											
33	A	BRADFORD C		6	L	0-1	0-0		Goddard	Perkins	Haverson	Galliers	Galvin	Cunningham	Leslie*	Briley	Knowles	Cork	Ketteridge	Denny
	4/4		*2,701*	*14*	45			*Dolan 82p*	*Smith*	*Podd*	*Watson*	*Reaney**	*Baines*	*Wood*	*Robertson*	*Dolan*	*Bates*	*McNiven*	*Hutchins*	*Jackson D*
								Ref: G Flint	Tommy Cunningham's tackle from behind on David McNiven was punished by a penalty. Cunningham had already been booked, so he was lucky not to be sent off. Leslie fell awkwardly in the first half and was stretchered off. Paul Reaney, ex-Leeds and England, plays for City.											
34	A	HALIFAX		6	L	1-2	1-2	Ketteridge 41	Goddard	Perkins!	Haverson	Briley	Galvin	Cunningham	Galliers	Denny*	Knowles	Cork	Ketteridge	Parsons
	7/4		*1,576*	*24*	45			*Trainer 20, Johnson 25*	*Kilner*	*Hutt*	*Dunleavy*	*Smith*	*Trainer*	*Sidebottom*	*Firth*	*Kennedy*	*Mountford*	*Johnson**	*Loska*	*Nixon*
								Ref: A Porter	Promotion seems to be slipping away after this, the Dons' fifth defeat in seven games, and against the club propping up the division. Near the end Steve Perkins punches Mick Kennedy and is shown the red card. Both Perkins and Galliers (booked for dissent) will be fined by Grady.											

No	H/A	Opponent / Date	Att	Pos	Pts	Res	F-A	H-T	Scorers, Times, and Referees	1	2	3	4	5	6	7	8	9	10	11	subs used
35	H	BOURNEMOUTH		6		W	4-0	3-0	Leslie 11, Cork 19, 35, Parsons 51	Goddard	Haverson	Donaldson	Galliers	**Bowgett**	Cunningham	Leslie	Briley*	Knowles	Cork	Parsons	Driver
		10/4	3,205	*15*	47					*Allen*	*Miller*	*Ferns*	*Impey*	*Brown R*	*Holder*	*Borthwick*	*McDougall*	*Butler M**	*Lennard*	*Massey*	*Brown K*
									Ref: R Reeves	Paul Bowgett, signed from Spurs for £1,000, helps rejuvenated Wimbledon to this handsome win. Poor Bournemouth – k.o'd from the FA Cup by the Dons and now beaten twice by them in the league – tumble to their fourth successive defeat. Galvin and Ketteridge have been dropped.											
36	A	PORTSMOUTH		6		D	0-0	0-0		Goddard	Perkins	Haverson	Galliers	Bowgett	Cunningham	Leslie	Briley	Knowles*	Cork	Parsons	Driver
		14/4	*11,453*	*7*	48					*Mellor*	*Ellis*	*Viney*	*Barnard*	*Foster**	*Davey*	*Hemmerman*	*Lathan*	*Garwood*	*Showers*	*Bryant*	*Pullar*
									Ref: B Hill	On paper this looks like a famous draw for the Dons, but Pompey have won just once in eight games and their promotion bubble is bursting. Steve Foster will play for England. Goddard saves Hemmerman's header at the death. 'We were bad but they were worse,' (Gradi).											
37	H	TORQUAY		6		W	5-0	4-0	Knowles 2, Galliers 23, Leslie 29, [Cunningham 41, Parsons 51]	Goddard	Perkins	Haverson	Galliers	Bowgett	Cunningham	Leslie	Briley	Knowles	Cork	Parsons	
		16/4	4,171	*11*	50					*Turner*	*Twitchin*	*Clarke*	*Green*	*Payne*	*Dunne*	*Davies*	*Murphy*	*Cooper*	*Cox**	*Coffill*	*Lawrence*
									Ref: D Hutchinson	Wimbledon follow up their 6-1 triumph at Plainmoor with another five at Plough Lane. The glut commences when Ray Knowles intercepts player-manager Mike Green's back-pass. Knowles had come off with double vision against Pompey. Torquay are still in mid-table.											
38	A	DARLINGTON		5		D	1-1	0-0	Leslie 68	Goddard	Perkins	Haverson	Briley	Bowgett	Cunningham*	Leslie	Galliers	Knowles	Cork	Parsons	Bryant
		21/4	*1,674*	*21*	51				*Ferguson 65*	*Burleigh*	*Nattrass*	*Cochrane*	*Hedley*	*Craig*	*Stone!*	*Lyons*	*Wann*	*Ferguson*	*Peachey**	*Walsh*	*Seal*
										Darlington skipper John Stone is sent off for the second time this season, clattering Les Briley in the final minutes. Both sides needed two points in the battles at opposite ends of the division. Galliers breaks from midfield to set up Leslie for the equaliser in this niggly match.											
39	A	CREWE		5		W	2-1	2-0	Leslie 19, Parsons 44	Goddard	Haverson	Perkins*	Galliers	Bowgett	Cunningham	Leslie	Briley	Knowles	Cork	Parsons	Bryant
		25/4	***1,254***	*23*	53				*Coyne 78*	*Rafferty*	*Wilkinson*	*Dulson*	*Nicholls*	*Bowles*	*Bevan*	*Robertson*	*Cheetham*	*Spence*	*Coyne*	*Roberts!*	
									Ref: G Owen	Once again a Dons opponent is dismissed. This time it is Ian Roberts for persistent dissent, two minutes after he had been booked. Steve Perkins is hospitalised with concussion. This is Crewe's fourth straight defeat. They will lose the next four too, creating a record eight losses.											
40	H	HARTLEPOOL		3		W	3-1	0-0	Cunningham 72, T Smith 74 (og), [Galliers 86]	Goddard	Haverson	Ketteridge	Galliers	Bowgett	Cunningham	Leslie	Briley	Knowles	Cork	Parsons*	Bryant
		28/4	3,546	*20*	55				*Houchen 82*	*Watson*	*Smith T*	*Gorry*	*Smith G*	*Goldthorpe*	*Ayre*	*Linacre*	*Hogan*	*Houchen*	*Harding*	*Loadwick*	*Lawrence*
									Ref: J Martin	Wimbledon leave it late in their quest for both points. All three goals come from set pieces. Gradi was upset by Pool's ale-house tactics in the game. This defeat concludes Hartlepool's 16-match winless sequence. They will win five of their next six.											
41	A	READING		4		L	0-1	0-1		Goddard	Bryant	Donaldson	Galliers	Bowgett	Cunningham	Leslie	Briley	Knowles*	Cork	Parsons	Ketteridge
		2/5	***13,131***	*1*	55				*Alexander 24*	*Death*	*Peters*	*White*	*Bowman*	*Hicks*	*Bennett*	*Earles*	*Alexander*	*Hetzke*	*Shipley*	*Sanchez*	
									Ref: M Taylor	The largest crowd to watch the Dons this season, as Reading head relentlessly for the title. It was not a bright game, but Reading were without question the brighter side. It is their 10th match without conceding a goal. Gradi recalled Bryant and Donaldson to the side.											
42	A	HEREFORD		4		D	0-0	0-0		Goddard	Perkins	Donaldson	Galliers	Bowgett	Cunningham	Leslie	Briley	Ketteridge	Cork	Haverson	
		5/5	*3,809*	*11*	56					*Hughes*	*Emery*	*Thomas*	*Cornes*	*Layton*	*Holmes K*	*Spiring*	*Feeley*	*McGrellis*	*Gould*	*White*	
									Ref: T Spencer	Hereford have dropped two divisions since Les Briley left them to join Wimbledon. Both sets of defences were well on top in this unenterprising game, played on a bone-hard pitch. Hereford led 10-0 on corner-kicks before Wimbledon won their first, in the 74th minute.											
43	A	SCUNTHORPE				L	0-2	0-1		Goddard	Perkins	Eames	Galliers	Bowgett	Cunningham	Leslie	Briley	Ketteridge	Cork	Haverson*	**Dziadul'wicz**
		8/5	*1,777*		56				*Kilmore 36p, Earl 76*	*Crawford*	*Davy*	*Peacock*	*Oates*	*Deere*	*Keeley*	*Grimes*	*Kilmore*	*Earl*	*Kavanagh*	*Couch*	
									Ref: J Worrall	This defeat means the Dons can no longer finish as champions, but they are left with three home games with which to clinch promotion. The game presents a commentator's nightmare, Mark Dziadulewicz, signed from Chelmsford for £3,000. Bowgett fouled Kavanagh for the penalty.											
44	H	YORK				W	2-1	0-1	Leslie 62, Cork 85	Goddard	Perkins	Eames	Galliers	Bowgett	Cunningham	Leslie	Ketteridge	**Downes***	Cork	Parsons	Knowles
		11/5	3,897		58				*Ford 34*	*Brown*	*Kay*	*Walsh*	*Pugh*	*Faulkner*	*Clements*	*Ford*	*Stronach*	*Wellings**	*McDonald*	*Staniforth*	*Randall*
									Ref: A Grey	Amid celebratory scenes, Wimbledon clinch promotion five minutes from time, with a hooked goal from Alan Cork. Young Wally Downes, nephew of boxer Terry Downes, led the front line in a tactical reshuffle. Briley was suspended. Gary Ford put York in front from 20 yards.											
45	H	BARNSLEY				D	1-1	1-0	Downes 12	Goddard	Perkins	Eames*	Galliers	Bowgett	Cunningham	Leslie	Briley	Downes	Cork	Parsons	Knowles
		14/5	5,794		59				*Chambers 53*	*Springett*	*Collins*	*Chambers*	*Speedie*	*Saunders*	*McCarthy*	*Little*	*Riley*	*Graham*	*Millar*	*Bell*	
									Ref: B Daniels	Allan Clarke's Barnsley clinch promotion at the expense of luckless Aldershot, who miss out by one place for the second year running. Barnsley brought down 16 coachloads of supporters. Mick McCarthy was booked. The Dons, too, are mathematically sure of going up.											
46	H	DARLINGTON				W	2-0	1-0	Stone 12 (og), Cunningham 74	Goddard	Perkins	Haverson	Galliers	**Harwood***	Cunningham	Ketteridge	Briley	Dziadulewic	Cork	Downes	Leslie
		17/5	3,638		61					*Owers*	*Crosson*	*Cochrane*	*Nattrass*	*Craig*	*Stone*	*Hedley*	*Wann*	*Hague**	*Peachey*	*Seal*	*Walsh*
		Home	*Away*						Ref: A Gunn	Dario Gradi releases Dave Galvin, Jeff Bryant, Dave Donaldson and Roger Connell as he sets about strengthening his squad for the 3rd Division. They have given priceless service. Downes' late booking takes the Dons over 150 disciplinary points, and a big fine looms.											
Average		3,670	*4,384*																		

League Cup	Att		F-A	H-T	Scorers, Times, and Referees	1	2	3	4	5	6	7	8	9	10	11	12 sub used
1:1 A SOUTHEND		L	0-1	0-0		Goddard	Bryant	Eames	Denny	Galvin	Donaldson	Leslie	Briley	Connell	Cork	Summerill	
12/8	*4,845*	*3:13*			*Donaldson 55 (og)*	*Horn*	*Goodwin*	*Yates*	*Laverick*	*Hadley*	*Moody*	*Fell*	*Pountney*	*Parker*	*Abbott*	*Morris*	
					Ref: M Taylor	A second successive 0-1 defeat at Roots Hall due to inspired home goalkeeping. Last season's magician, Neil Freeman, has been sold to Birmingham, but Graham Horn looks no less gifted. Dave Donaldson stoops to head an own-goal. It was carnival day on Southend's sea-front..											
1:2 H SOUTHEND		W	4-1	3-1	Galvin 32, Galliers 36, Cork 39,	Goddard	Bryant	Eames	Galliers	Galvin	Donaldson	Leslie*	Briley	Denny	Cork	Summerill	Ketteridge
15/8	2,687	*3:13*			*Donaldson 43 (og)* [Townsend 61 (og)]	*Horn*	*Hadley*	*Yates*	*Laverick*	*Townsend*	*Moody*	*Fell*	*Morris*	*Parker*	*Abbott**	*Pountney*	*Dudley*
					Ref: H Robinson (Dons win 4-2 on aggregate)	Wimbledon record their first victory over Southend in four attempts. Two own-goals, one apiece, disfigure the scoreline after the Dons had swiftly erased the first-leg deficit. Donaldson's headed own-goal gave Southend hope, until their stopper, Neil Townsend, repeated the favour.											
2 A EVERTON		L	0-8		*[Dobson (3)]*	Goddard	Bryant	Eames	Galliers	Galvin	Donaldson	Leslie	Denny	Connell	Cork	Parsons	
29/8	*23,137*	*1:4*			*Latchford 8, 18, 63, 82, 85,*	*Wood*	*Robinson*	*Pejic*	*Lyons*	*Wright*	*Nulty*	*King*	*Dobson*	*Latchford*	*Walsh**	*Thomas*	*Ross*
					Ref: K Hackett	Referee Keith Hackett's pencil is worn away keeping tab of the goals. Bob Latchford bags five, and Martin Dobson three, as Everton run riot. Donaldson has a nightmare match. The biggest defeat in Wimbledon's 89-year history. How will this humiliation affect their promotion push?											
FA Cup																	
1 A GRAVESEND		D	0-0	0-0		Goddard	Perkins	Haverson	Galliers	Galvin	Donaldson	Leslie	Denny	Connell	Cork	Parsons	
25/11	*3,758*	*SL:12*				*Smelt*	*Idle*	*Sargent*	*Glozier*	*Osborne*	*Jacks*	*Brown*	*Hunt*	*Woon*	*Dudman*	*Woolfe**	*Stonebridge*
					Ref: A Gunn	Gravesend & Northfleet goalkeeper Lee Smelt keeps his Southern League team in the FA Cup by saving a twice-taken penalty by Steve Parsons. Gravesend have reached the 1st Round for the first time since 1965. Roger Connell had not played since the Everton debacle.											
1R H GRAVESEND		W	1-0	0-0	Cork 117	Goddard	Perkins	Haverson	Galliers	Galvin	Donaldson	Leslie	Denny	Connell*	Cork	Parsons	Briley
28/11	3,369	*SL:12*	*aet*			*Smelt*	*Idle*	*Sargent*	*Glozier*	*Osborne*	*Jacks*	*Brown*	*Hunt*	*Woon*	*Dudman*	*Woolfe**	*Stonebridge*
					Ref: A Gunn	No team changes are made to either side in this replay. At the end of the day it was only the greater fitness of the Wimbledon players that saw them through to the next round. Three minutes from the end of extra-time Sargent heads off the line from Denny, but Cork pops the ball in.											
2 H BOURNEMOUTH		D	1-1	0-1	Denny 58	Goddard	Bryant	Haverson	Galliers	Galvin	Donaldson	Leslie	Briley	Denny	Cork	Parsons	
16/12	3,308				*McDougall 10*	*Allen*	*Cunningham*	*Miller*	*Impey*	*Brown R*	*Barton*	*Borthwick*	*McDougall*	*Butler*	*Showers*	*Lennard*	
						Fading superstar Ted McDougall dearly wants to win this one, so he can face his previous club Southampton in the next round. Alan Cork and John Leslie hit bar and post at the death, after Paul Denny had cancelled out McDougall's effort.											
2R A BOURNEMOUTH		W	2-1	0-0	Cork 88, Parsons	Goddard	Perkins	Eames	Ketteridge	Galvin	Donaldson*	Parsons	Briley	Knowles	Cork	Haverson	Denny
19/12	*7,192*		*aet*		*McDougall*	*Allen*	*Cunningham*	*Miller*	*Impey*	*Brown R*	*Barton*	*Borthwick*	*McDougall*	*Butler M*	*Showers**	*Lennard*	*Massey*
						Drama at Dean Court. The teams know that the winners will play Southampton in Round 3. That will be a local derby for Bournemouth, and they are desperate to win. They lead with two minutes to play. Cork sends the tie into extra-time, and Parsons' corner-kick flies straight in.											
3 H SOUTHAMPTON		H	0-2	0-0		Goddard	Perkins	Eames	Ketteridge	Galvin	Denny	Parsons	Briley	Knowles*	Cork	Haverson	Leslie
9/1	9,254	*1:14*			*Boyer 49, 89*	*Gennoe*	*Golac*	*Peach*	*Williams*	*Nicholl*	*Waldron*	*Ball*	*Boyer*	*Hebberd*	*Holmes*	*Curran*	
						The highest attendance in Plough Lane's history sees Wimbledon bow out to their 1st Division opponents. Southampton leave out new signing Charlie George. Phil Boyer's two goals divide the teams. At least the Saints cannot emulate Everton and score eight.											

		Home					Away					
	P	W	D	L	F	A	W	D	L	F	A	Pts
1 Reading	46	19	3	1	49	8	7	10	6	27	27	65
2 Grimsby	46	15	5	3	51	23	11	4	8	31	26	61
3 WIMBLEDON	46	18	3	2	50	20	7	8	8	28	26	61
4 Barnsley	46	15	5	3	47	23	9	8	6	26	19	61
5 Aldershot	46	16	5	2	38	14	4	12	7	25	33	57
6 Wigan	46	14	5	4	40	24	7	8	8	23	24	55
7 Portsmouth	46	13	7	3	35	12	7	5	11	27	36	52
8 Newport	46	12	5	6	39	28	9	5	9	27	27	52
9 Huddersfield	46	13	8	2	32	15	5	3	15	25	38	47
10 York	46	11	6	6	33	24	7	5	11	18	31	47
11 Torquay	46	14	4	5	38	24	5	4	14	20	41	46
12 Scunthorpe	46	12	3	8	33	30	5	8	10	21	30	45
13 Hartlepool	46	7	12	4	35	28	6	6	11	22	38	44
14 Hereford	46	12	8	3	35	18	3	5	15	18	35	43
15 Bradford City	46	11	5	7	38	26	6	4	13	24	42	43
16 Port Vale	46	8	10	5	29	28	6	4	13	28	42	42
17 Stockport	46	11	5	7	33	21	3	7	13	25	39	40
18 Bournemouth	46	11	6	6	34	19	3	5	15	13	29	39
19 Northampton	46	12	4	7	40	30	3	5	15	24	46	39
20 Rochdale	46	11	4	8	25	26	4	5	14	22	38	39
21 Darlington	46	8	8	7	25	21	3	7	13	24	45	37
22 Doncaster	46	8	8	7	25	22	5	3	15	25	51	37
23 Halifax	46	7	5	11	24	32	2	3	18	15	40	26
24 Crewe	46	3	7	13	24	41	3	7	13	19	49	26
	1104	281	141	130	852	557	130	141	281	557	852	1104

Odds & ends

Double wins: (5) Stockport, Wigan, York, Bournemouth, Torquay.
Double losses: (0).

Won from behind: (6) Wigan (h), Bradford C (h), Rochdale (h), Huddersfield (h), York (h), Newport (a).
Lost from in front: (1) Portsmouth (h).

High spots: 13 unbeaten games at start of season.
Scoring 6 goals at Torquay.
Coming from behind 5 times to win matches at Plough Lane.
Low spots: 3 consecutive defeats in March.
An 8-goal massacre by Everton in the League Cup.

Wimbledon scored 11 goals against Torquay over 2 games.

For the first time in 5 seasons, Roger Connell is not top scorer.

Wimbledon played no league games in January, but 8 in April.

Player of the Year: Steve Galliers.
Ever-presents: (0).
Hat-tricks: Alan Cork (2).
Leading scorer: Alan Cork (25).

	Appearances						Goals			
	Lge	Sub	LC	Sub	FAC	Sub	**Lge**	LC	FAC	**Total**
Bowgett, Paul	**11**									
Briley, Les	**26**		2		3	(1)	**1**			**1**
Bryant, Jeff	**27**	(3)	3		1		**2**			**2**
Connell, Roger	**2**		2		2					
Cork, Alan	**45**		3		5		**22**	1	2	**25**
Cowley, Fran	**3**	(3)								
Cunningham, Tom	**15**						**3**			**3**
Denny, Paul	**24**	(4)	3		4	(1)	**6**		1	**7**
Donaldson, Dave	**23**		3		4					
Downes, Wally	**3**						**1**			**1**
Driver, Phil	**3**	(7)					**1**			**1**
Dziadulewicz, Mark	**1**	(1)								
Eames, Terry	**26**		3		2		**1**			**1**
Galliers, Steve	**44**		2		3		**3**	1		**4**
Galvin, Dave	**33**		3		5		**2**	1		**3**
Goddard, Ray	**45**		3		5					
Harwood, Lee	**1**									
Haverson, Paul	**26**	(1)			5		**2**			**2**
Ketteridge, Steve	**15**	(2)		(1)	2		**1**			**1**
Knowles, Ray	**23**	(8)			2		**5**			**5**
Leslie, John	**44**	(1)	3		3	(1)	**19**			**19**
Parsons, Steve	**34**	(3)	1		5		**7**		1	**8**
Perkins, Steve	**26**				4					
Priddy, Paul	**1**									
Summerill, Phil	**5**	(2)	2							
(own-goals)							**2**	1		**3**
25 players used	**506**	**(35)**	**33**	**(1)**	**55**	**(3)**	**78**	**4**	**4**	**86**

No	Date	Att	Pos	Pts	F-A	H-T	Scorers, Times, and Referees	1	2	3	4	5	6	7	8	9	10	11	12 sub used
1	H CHESTER			L	2-3	1-2	Leslie 40, Cork 85	Goddard	Perkins	**Jones***	Briley	Bowgett	Cunningham	Ketteridge	Parsons	Leslie	Cork	Knowles	Galliers
	18/8	3,549		–			*Ruggiero 34, Henderson 35, Edwards 55*	*Lloyd*	*Raynor*	*Walker*	*Storton*	*Cottam*	*Oakes*	*Jeffries*	*Ruggiero*	*Edwards*	*Henderson*	*Phillips R*	
							Ref: A Grey	36-year-old Alan Oakes, once a hero at Manchester City, masterminded this win, setting up both Chester's first-half goals. Wimbledon still cannot win their opening match of the league season. They had chances to do so, but were undone by two goals in a minute for Chester.											
2	A EXETER			W	2-0	0-0	Parsons 74, Leslie 81	Goddard	Perkins	Jones	Briley	Bowgett	Cunningham	Ketteridge	Parsons	Leslie	Cork	Knowles	
	22/8	*4,051*		2				*O'Keefe*	*Roberts P*	*Rogers M*	*Hore*	*Giles*	*Hatch*	*Neville*	*Pearson*	*Rogers P**	*Delve*	*Pullar*	*Sims*
							Ref: L Burden	Exeter, thrashed 1-4 at Grimsby in their opening match, hand Wimbledon their first win in Division 3. Steve Parsons puts the Dons on their way by lobbing O'Keefe from 20 yards. Both teams might have scored in the first two minutes of the match.											
3	H SOUTHEND		14	L	0-1	0-0		Goddard	Perkins	Jones	Galliers	Bowgett	Cunningham	Ketteridge	Parsons	Leslie	Cork*	Knowles	Briley
	25/8	4,173	*5*	2			*Morris 80*	*Cawston*	*Dudley*	*Moody*	*Cusack*	*Yates*	*Stead*	*Otulakowski*	*Morris*	*Tuohy**	*Parker*	*Hadley*	*Fell*
							Ref: A Glasson	Wimbledon still have to take their first league point off Southend. The best player on the pitch, Colin Morris, left it late before sealing the Dons' fate. Leslie and Cork accomplished so little that Dario Gradi had to take Cork off. Only in midfield did the Dons match the visitors.											
4	A BLACKPOOL		20	L	0-3	0-1		Goddard	Perkins	Jones	Galliers	Bowgett	Cunningham	Ketteridge	Parsons	Leslie	Downes	Knowles	
	1/9	*4,556*	*12*	2			*Wilson 40, Kerr 50, Weston 72*	*McAlister*	*Thompson*	*Pashley*	*Doyle*	*Suddaby*	*McEwan*	*Kerr*	*Wilson*	*Kellow*	*Smith B*	*Weston*	
							Ref: C Seal	Three league defeats out of four leave the Dons hovering just outside the relegation zone. Dario Gradi was not downhearted after this result, feeling that each of Blackpool's goals came out of the blue. The result, he insisted, flattered the seasiders.											
5	H BLACKBURN		17	W	1-0	0-0	Knowles 74	Goddard	Perkins	Jones	Galliers	Bowgett	Cunningham!	Briley*	Parsons	Leslie	Downes	Knowles	Denny
	8/9	3,671	*9*	4				*Butcher*	*Morley*	*Round*	*Kendall*	*Keeley*	*Fazackerley*	*Garner**	*Coughlin*	*Parker*	*McKenzie*	*Parkes*	*Craig*
							Ref: B Hill	Blackburn's first defeat of the season. Wimbledon's first home win. Five minutes from time Cunningham was sent off for head-butting Stuart Parker. Knowles scores with a 15-yard header. Howard Kendall is Rovers' player-manager. Goddard saves Duncan McKenzie's fine free-kick.											
6	A PLYMOUTH		20	L	0-3	0-1		Goddard	Perkins	Jones	Galliers	Bowgett	Haverson	Leslie*	Parsons	Denny	Cork	Knowles	Downes
	15/9	*5,744*	*19*	4			*Kemp 44, 47, Trusson 75*	*Brown*	*Hodges*	*Harrison*	*Phill-Masters*	*Foster*	*Bason*	*Megson*	*Kemp*	*Trusson*	*Randall*	*Johnson*	
							Ref: T Spencer	Plymouth have lost four on the trot before today. Alan Cork returns to the Dons' side after injury, but is upstaged by the Pilgrims' record signing, David Kemp (£75,000 from Carlisle), who scores twice on his debut. Goalkeeper David Brown also makes his debut for Plymouth.											
7	A GILLINGHAM		24	L	0-1	0-0		Goddard	Perkins	Jones	Galliers	Bowgett	Cunningham	**Richards**	Parsons	Downes	Cork	Knowles	
	18/9	*8,074*	*5*	4			*Cunningham 73 (og)*	*Hillyard*	*Sharpe*	*Barker*	*Overton*	*Weatherly*	*Crabbe*	*Nicholl*	*Bruce*	*Price*	*Funnell*	*Richardson*	
							Ref: D Vickers	Gillingham have Cunningham's own-goal to thank for their first home win of the season. Goddard had earlier saved Mick Barker's penalty-kick, after Cunningham had fouled Steve Bruce. 19-year-old Craig Richards plays his first game for the Dons, who are now rock-bottom.											
8	H BRENTFORD		24	D	0-0	0-0		Goddard	Perkins	Jones!	Galliers	Bowgett	Cunningham	Richards	Parsons	Downes	Cork	Knowles*	Leslie
	22/9	5,524	*13*	5				*Bond*	*Salman*	*Tucker*	*McNichol*	*Kruse*	*Shrubb*	*Carlton*	*Graham J*	*Smith**	*Holmes W*	*Phillips*	*Allder*
							Ref: T Bune	Steve Jones is sent off for toppling Doug Allder of Brentford, who include ex-Don Billy Holmes in their side. Dario Gradi rages at his players at half-time. Off the pitch, all the talk is of the Dons' imminent signing of Ray Lewington from Vancouver Whitecaps.											
9	A BURY		19	W	2-1	1-1	Leslie 20, Ketteridge 79	Goddard	Perkins	Jones	Galliers	Bowgett	Cunningham	Ketteridge	Parsons	Leslie	Cork	**Lewington**	
	29/9	*2,790*	*23*	7			*Beamish 43p*	*Forrest*	*Constantine*	*Kennedy*	*Waldron*	*Waddington*	*Howard*	*Wilson*	*Halford*	*Beamish*	*Gregory*	*Mullen*	
							Ref: J Lovatt	This desperate basement struggle turns Wimbledon's way thanks to a spirited debut by Ray Lewington. Yet it was Lewington who handled to permit Ken Beamish to equalise from the penalty spot. The Dons had been under the cosh for the first 20 minutes, until Leslie headed his goal.											
10	A CARLISLE		21	D	1-1	1-1	Cunningham 9	Goddard	Perkins	Jones	Galliers	Bowgett	Cunningham	Ketteridge	Parsons	Leslie*	Cork	Lewington	Dziadulewicz
	6/10	*4,476*	*19*	8			*Bonnyman 32*	*Swinburne*	*Hoolickin*	*Winstanley*	*MacDonald*	*Beardsley*	*Parker*	*McVitie*	*Bonnyman*	*Bannon*	*Hamilton*	*Staniforth*	
								Carlisle were in the 1st Division five years earlier, and are now threatened with dropping to the 4th. The home team would have won this clash, but for Ray Goddard's defiance in the second half. Peter Beardsley is playing his first season of league football, and wears No 5.											
11	H EXETER		21	D	2-2	0-1	Dziadulewicz 55, Leslie 90	Goddard	Perkins	Jones	Galliers*	Bowgett	Cunningham	Ketteridge	Parsons	Leslie	Cork	Lewington	Dziadulewicz
	9/10	2,999	*17*	9			*Bowker 35, Neville 46p*	*O'Keefe*	*Mitchell*	*Hatch*	*Hore*	*Giles*	*Forbes*	*Neville*	*Rogers P*	*Bowker*	*Delve*	*Pullar*	
							Ref: D Letts	The Dons are now unbeaten in six league and cup games, and are looking for their first double of the season. Instead they are seconds away from defeat, in front of their smallest home crowd so far. 19-year-old sub Dziadulewicz sparks the Dons' revival, capped by Leslie's header.											

No	Date	Venue	Opponent	Att	Pos	Pts	Res	FT	HT	Scorers, Times, Referees	1	2	3	4	5	6	7	8	9	10	11	subs used
12		H	SWINDON		18		W	2-0	1-0	Cork 10, 52	Goddard	Perkins	Jones	Ketteridge	Bowgett	Cunningham	Lewington	Parsons	Leslie	Cork	Dziadulewicz	
	13/10			4,206	*10*	11					*Allan*	*Templeman*	*Lewis*	*McHale*	*Tucker*	*Stroud*	*Miller**	*Carter*	*Rowland*	*Mayes*	*Williams*	*Kamara*
										Ref: R Challis	Wimbledon continue their revival, thanks to Alan Cork's first goals since the opening match of the season. He had spent the whole week practising his finishing in training, especially his heading, and the effort pays off. He missed a hat-trick with a header that hit the crossbar.											
13		A	CHESTERFIELD		16		D	0-0	0-0		Goddard	Perkins	Jones	Downes	Bowgett	Cunningham	Ketteridge	Parsons	Dziadulewicz	Cork	Lewington	
	20/10			*5,122*	*9*	12					*Tingay*	*Tartt*	*O'Neill*	*Ridley*	*Green*	*Hunter*	*Birch*	*Moss*	*Walker*	*Salmons*	*Crawford*	
										Ref: J Warner	12 points from 13 games has hoisted the Dons clear of danger. This games produced few chances, other than for two headers by Chesterfield's towering Ernie Moss, both of which flew wide. 'We had all the play,' moans Chesterfield manager Arthur Cox. Now the Dons' slide begins.											
14		A	COLCHESTER				L	**0-4**	0-2		Goddard	Perkins	Jones	Eames	Bowgett	Cunningham	Dziadulewicz	Parsons*	Leslie	Cork	Lewington	Ketteridge
	23/10			*4,396*		12				*Hodge 17p, Lee 19, Gough 77, [Wignall 86]*	*Walker*	*Cook*	*Packer*	*Leslie*	*Wignall*	*Dowman*	*Hodge*	*Gough*	*Foley*	*Lee*	*Allinson*	
										Ref: A Gunn	High-flying Colchester inflict upon Wimbledon the biggest defeat in their short league history. Goalkeeper Mike Walker made good saves early on. The deluge commenced after Steve Jones brought down Ian Allinson in the box. Colchester have now gone 10 games without defeat.											
15		H	SHEFFIELD WED		21		L	3-4	1-2	Leslie 13, Parsons 60, Cork 88	Goddard	Perkins	Jones	Galliers	Bowgett	Cunningham	Ketteridge*	Parsons	Leslie	Cork	Lewington	Dziadulewicz
	27/10			**6,009**	*4*	12				*Lowey 6, Curran 31, 74, Smith 68p*	*Cox*	*Johnson*	*Grant*	*Mullen*	*Smith*	*Leman*	*Wylde*	*Porterfield*	*Lowey*	*King*	*Curran*	
										Ref: J Sewell	The Owls – managed by Jack Charlton – have fallen on hard times. This cracking match was played before Plough Lane's best league crowd of the season. At 2-2, a Dziadulewicz free-kick struck the bar. Then Goddard felled Jeff King for Mark Smith's penalty-kick.											
16		A	CHESTER		21		L	1-3	1-0	Walker 4 (og)	Goddard	Eames	Jones	Galliers	Bowgett	Cunningham	Lewington	Parsons	Leslie*	Cork	Dziadulewicz	Denny
	3/11			*2,891*	*8*	12				*Rush 50, Walker 52, Storton 75*	*Millington*	*Raynor*	*Walker*	*Storton*	*Cottam*	*Oakes*	*Sutcliffe*	*Jeffries*	*Rush*	*Phillips R*	*Henderson*	
											Three straight defeats, 11 goals conceded, and the Dons are accelerating downwards. Chester do the double, cancelling out Jim Walker's early own-goal with a strike from 18-year-old Ian Rush, playing instead of Ian Edwards. Chester had the wind behind them in the second half.											
17		H	COLCHESTER		21		D	3-3	2-0	Parsons 12, 18p, Leslie 70	Goddard	Eames	Jones	Galliers	Bowgett	Downes	Dziadulewicz	Parsons	Leslie	Cork	Lewington	
	6/11			2,465	*3*	13				*Wignall 57, Lee 64, Gough 80*	*Walker*	*Cook*	*Wright**	*Leslie*	*Wignall*	*Dowman*	*Hodge*	*Gough*	*Foley*	*Lee*	*Packer*	*Rowles*
										Ref: J Bray	The Dons owe Colchester for their recent good hiding. Steve Parsons is an expert with the dead ball, and a free-kick and a penalty put his side two up by half-time, but Wimbledon cannot hold on. United's tactical switch turns the tide. The Dons have now leaked 16 goals in five games.											
18		H	ROTHERHAM		24		L	0-1	0-0		Goddard	Briley	Jones	Galliers	Bowgett	Downes	Lewington	Parsons	Leslie	Cork	Dziadulewicz	
	10/11			2,798	*10*	13				*Fern 74*	*Mountford*	*Tiler*	*Breckin*	*Rhodes*	*Stancliffe*	*Green*	*Nix*	*McEwan*	*Gwyther*	*Fern*	*Finney*	
										Ref: B Daniels	Rotherham led the table in September, but go into this match with just one win in their last eight. They send the Dons to the bottom of the league after John Breckin handles, but Parsons misses the penalty and is booked for the 4th time this season. Rotherham won 11-2 on corners.											
19		A	GRIMSBY		24		L	0-1	0-1		Goddard	Briley*	Jones	Galliers	Bowgett	Downes	Lewington	Parsons	Leslie	Cork	Dziadulewicz	Ketteridge
	17/11			*6,716*	*11*	13				*Waters 22p*	*Batch*	*Stone*	*Moore K*	*Waters*	*Wiggington*	*Crombie*	*Brolly*	*Ford*	*Liddell*	*Kilmore*	*Mitchell*	
											Grimsby were promoted with Wimbledon, but after a shaky start are storming up the table. Dziadulewicz was the guilty Don, tripping Mike Brolly to concede the crucial penalty. With time running out, skipper Lewington races clear, but keeper Nigel Batch saves at his feet.											
20		A	HULL		24		D	1-1	0-0	Cork 87	Goddard	Briley	Jones	Galliers	Bowgett	Downes	Dziadulewicz	Parsons	Leslie	Cork	Lewington	
	1/12			*3,750*	*17*	14				*Hawker 76*	*Blackburn*	*Nisbet*	*Devries*	*Haigh*	*Dobson*	*Hawker*	*Roberts G*	*Moss*	*Edwards*	*Bannister*	*Farley*	
										Ref: L Robinson	Hull are in the midst of a desperate sequence of 13 games without a win. Ray Goddard's 100th appearance for the Dons is rewarded with a valuable point after Cork's late glancing header from Steve Parsons' cross. After the match Hull supporters stay behind to demonstrate.											
21		H	SHEFFIELD UTD		24		D	1-1	1-1	Cork 26	Goddard	Briley	Jones	Galliers	Bowgett	Downes	Dziadulewicz	Parsons	Leslie	Cork	Lewington	
	8/12			4,740	*1*	15				*Butlin 3*	*Ramsbottom*	*Cutbush*	*Garner*	*Kenworthy*	*McPhail*	*Matthews*	*de Goey*	*Flood*	*Butlin*	*Speight*	*Sabella*	
										Ref: C Maskell	Sheff Utd have sunk to Division 3 for the first time in their history, joining Wednesday. United are top of the table, striving to escape at the first attempt. Argentine Alex Sabella is man of the match, but he could not swing it United's way. Both goals in this thriller were headers.											
22		A	SOUTHEND		24		W	**3-1**	0-1	Denny 50, 73, Cork 58	Goddard	Briley	Jones	Galliers	Bowgett	Downes	Dziadulewicz*	Parsons	Denny	Cork	Lewington	Leslie
	29/12			*3,952*	*23*	17				*Polycarpou 17*	*Cawston*	*Cusack*	*Yates*	*Pountney*	*Moody*	*Hadley*	*Otulakowski*	*Polycarpou*	*Parker*	*Gray*	*Nelson*	
										Ref: M Taylor	Wimbledon come out on top of these Relegation Stakes. Paul Denny, now 22, was signed from Southend on a free transfer three years earlier. The match turns when Galliers snaps up Dave Cusack's wretched back-pass and squares for Denny. This is the Dons biggest win of the season.											
23		H	BLACKPOOL		24		L	1-2	1-1	Galliers 17	**Beasant**	Briley	Jones	Galliers	Bowgett	Cunningham	Lewington	Parsons	Leslie	Cork	Dziadulewicz	
	12/1			2,688	*18*	17				*Jones 30, Morris 67*	*Hesford*	*Gardener*	*Pashley*	*Malone*	*Ashurst*	*Thompson*	*Morris*	*Doyle*	*Jones*	*Kellow*	*Harrison*	
											Wimbledon have three games in hand. With one win in their last 13 Blackpool look to be heading down. Galliers' first goal of the season is cancelled out by Lewington's bad back-pass. Dave Beasant's debut is marred by fumbling Colin Morris's shot. Cork hit a post in injury time.											

No	Date	Att	Pos	Pts	F-A	H-T	Scorers, Times, and Referees	1	2	3	4	5	6	7	8	9	10	11	12 sub used
24	A BLACKBURN		24	L	0-3	0-1	*[Rathbone 68]*	Goddard	Briley	Jones	Galliers	**Smith**	Cunningham	Dziadulewicz	Parsons	Leslie	Denny	Lewington	
	19/1	*8,037*	*11*	17			*Crawford 26, McKenzie 53,*	*Arnold*	*Rathbone*	*Branagan*	*Metcalfe*	*Keeley*	*Fazackerly**	*Brotherston*	*McKenzie*	*Garner*	*Crawford*	*Kendall*	*Round*
								Bowgett is dropped to make way for Mike Smith (£12,500 from Lincoln) to make his league debut. Star of the match was Duncan McKenzie. Blackburn are on their way to winning 14 games out of 15 and to storm to promotion. This match was played on a frozen pitch.											
25	A MANSFIELD		24	D	1-1	1-0	Cunningham 30	Goddard!	Briley	Jones	Galliers	Smith	Cunningham	Ketteridge	Parsons	Leslie	Denny	Lewington	
	26/1	*3,895*	*21*	18			*Bird 83*	*Arnold*	*Thompson**	*Wood*	*Curtis*	*Bird*	*McClelland*	*Pollard*	*Taylor*	*Austin*	*Mann*	*Allen*	*Hamilton*
							Ref: K Walmsley	This is Mansfield's 9th game without a win. The match might have yielded the Dons both points, until Kevin Bird bundled Ray Goddard and the ball over the line. The goal stood, and Goddard was 'sent off' after the final whistle for continuing to protest.											
26	A BRENTFORD		24	W	1-0	1-0	Parsons 28	Goddard	Briley	Jones	Galliers	Smith*	Cunningham	Ketteridge	Parsons	Leslie	Denny	Lewington	Cork
	9/2	*7,380*	*12*	20				*Bond*	*Salman*	*Tucker*	*Harding*	*Kruse*	*Fraser*	*Carlton**	*Shrubb*	*Allder*	*Holmes L*	*Phillips*	*Smith*
								Brentford's 9th match without a win gives Wimbledon a precious victory, their fourth away from home. Mike Smith was taken off with a nasty head injury. Cork harassed Pat Kruse, won the ball and slipped the perfect pass to Steve Parsons. John Leslie was expected to join Exeter City.											
27	H GILLINGHAM		22	W	1-0	0-0	Leslie 65	Goddard	Briley	Jones	Galliers	Smith	Cunningham	Ketteridge	Parsons	Leslie	Cork	Lewington	
	12/2	3,697	*14*	22				*Hillyard*	*Sharpe**	*Barker*	*Bruce*	*Weatherly*	*Crabbe*	*Nicholl*	*Hughes!*	*Price*	*Duncan*	*Richardson*	*Funnell*
							Ref: A Robinson	The Dons' first home win since October is an eventful affair. Smith keeps his place despite his head injury, and has a fine match. Gillingham's Billy Hughes is sent off for kicking Leslie, and three minutes later Leslie heads in from Briley's corner-kick. Gillingham want to sign him.											
28	H PLYMOUTH		22	W	**3-1**	2-0	Leslie 14, Parsons 15, Cork 48	Beasant	Briley	Jones	Galliers	Smith	Cunningham	Ketteridge	Parsons	Leslie	Cork	Lewington	
	19/2	3,488	*12*	24			*Kemp 84p*	*Crudgington*	*James*	*Harrison*	*Randall*	*Foster*	*Phill-Masters*	*Hodges*	*Cooper*	*Sims*	*Bason*	*Kemp*	
								Plymouth are on the up, riding on a 10-game unbeaten sequence. So are Wimbledon, with their third straight win, deflating the Pilgrims as they had in the League Cup earlier in the season. Two goals in 30 seconds does the damage. Beasant plays as Goddard is suspended.											
29	A SWINDON		23	L	1-2	0-0	Denny 81	Goddard	Briley	Bowgett	Denny	Smith	Cunningham	Ketteridge	Parsons	Leslie	Cork	Lewington	
	23/2	*10,743*	*7*	24			*Stroud 50, McHale 78*	*Allan*	*Lewis*	*Stroud*	*McHale*	*Tucker*	*Carter*	*Miller*	*Kamara*	*Rowland*	*Mayes*	*Williams*	
								High-riding Swindon needed this win to get back on track. They were helped by Ray Goddard giving a fragile performance in goal. Helped by Denny's strike – converting Briley's corner – the Dons found their second wind, but it came too late to save them. Stroud's goal was deflected.											
30	H BURY		23	L	0-1	0-0		Goddard	Briley	Bowgett*	Galliers	Smith	Cunningham	Ketteridge	Parsons	Leslie	Cork	Lewington	Denny
	26/2	3,030	*24*	24			*Madden 62*	*Forrest*	*Constantine*	*Graham*	*McIlwraith*	*Waddington*	*Howard*	*Halford*	*Wilson*	*Johnson*	*Hilton*	*Madden*	
							Ref: S Bates	Bury are bottom; Wimbledon next to bottom. The visitors travel to Plough Lane having lost their last four in the league, and in the wake of a 0-2 defeat at Liverpool in the FA Cup Round 5. A 20-yard shot by Craig Madden beats Goddard at his near post. A terrible result for the Dons.											
31	H CHESTERFIELD		23	D	1-1	1-1	Parsons 22	Goddard	Briley	Bowgett	Galliers	Smith	Cunningham	Ketteridge	Parsons	Leslie	Cork	Lewington	
	1/3	3,609	*4*	25			*Crawford 25*	*Turner*	*Tartt*	*O'Neill*	*Ridley*	*Green*	*Rowland*	*Birch*	*Salmons*	*Walker*	*Simpson*	*Crawford*	
							Ref: T Spencer	This was a good point against fancied Chesterfield who had lost just one of their last eight. This is also Ray Lewington's last match before signing for Fulham. Colin Tartt clears off the line from Ketteridge. Keeper John Turner makes his debut after signing from Torquay.											
32	A READING		23	L	0-3	0-1		Goddard	Briley	Bowgett	Galliers	Smith	Cunningham	Denny	Parsons	Leslie	Cork	Ketteridge	
	5/3	*5,246*	*11*	25			*Kearns 36, 46, Bowman 80*	*Death*	*Joslyn*	*White*	*Bowman*	*Hetzke*	*Moreline*	*Earles*	*Kearns*	*Heale*	*Sanchez*	*Wanklyn*	
							Ref: D Lloyd	Reading were promoted with Wimbledon, but are racked by injury, with seven first-teamers out of contention. Lawrie Sanchez was the inspiration behind this win, which was sparked by Ollie Kearns' 20-yard volley. Kearns' second goal was a downward header.											
33	A SHEFFIELD WED		24	L	1-3	0-2	Cunningham 65	Goddard	Briley!	Jones	Galliers	Smith	Cunningham	Denny*	Parsons	Leslie	Cork	Ketteridge	Downes
	8/3	***20,803***	*1*	25			*McCulloch 23, Curran 29, 69*	*Bolder*	*Blackhall*	*Grant*	*Smith*	*Pickering*	*Curran*	*Taylor*	*Johnson*	*Mellor*	*McCulloch*	*Curran*	
								This match sends Wednesday top and Wimbledon bottom, watched by the largest crowd to watch the Dons since they entered the Football League. Briley is sent off after the final whistle for foul and abusive language. Andy McCulloch put the Owls ahead with a near-post header.											
34	H BARNSLEY		24	L	1-2	0-1	Ketteridge 56	Goddard	Briley	Jones	Galliers	Smith	Cunningham	Ketteridge	Dziadulewicz	Leslie	Cork	Downes	
	11/3	2,753	*17*	25			*Glavin 22, Cooper 89*	*Pierce*	*Cooper*	*Chambers*	*Glavin*	*Hunter**	*McCarthy*	*Evans*	*Parker*	*Aylott*	*Lester*	*Downes*	*Banks*
							Ref: A Seville	Steve Parsons has signed for Orient for £42,000. Barnsley have drawn their last four, and were one minute from a fifth when Neil Cooper's screaming volley broke the stalemate. Internationals Norman Hunter (England) and Ronnie Glavin (Scotland) caught the eye.											

No	Venue	Opponents / Date	Att	Pos	Pts	Res	F-A	H-T	Scorers, Times, and Referees	1	2	3	4	5	6	7	8	9	10	11	12
35	H	CARLISLE		24	D		0-0	0-0		Goddard	Denny	Jones	Galliers	Smith	Cunningham	Ketteridge	Dziadulewicz	Leslie	Cork	Downes	
		14/3	2,093	*10*	26					*Swinburne*	*Hoolickin*	*Collins*	*MacDonald*	*Ludlam*	*Winstanley*	*McVitie*	*Houghton*	*Beardsley*	*Hamilton*	*Staniforth*	
										Les Briley signs for Aldershot before the transfer deadline. This was a nothing match, played on a Friday night, with mid-table Carlisle failing to exert themselves. Wimbledon could not afford this further dropped point. Peter Beardsley's shot spins out of Goddard's hands.											
36	A	OXFORD			L		1-4	0-1	Ketteridge 54 *[McGrogan 82]*	Goddard	Jones	**Armstrong**	**Klug***	Smith	Cunningham	Ketteridge	Dziadulewicz	Leslie	Cork	Downes	Denny
		19/3	***2,603***		26				*Jeffrey 43, O'Dowd 65, Taylor 80,*	*Burton*	*Taylor*	*Fogg*	*Briggs*	*Cooke*	*Jeffrey*	*McGrogan*	*Brook*	*Berry*	*O'Dowd*	*Hodgson*	
									Ref: A Glasson	No wins in their last five, but Oxford are far too strong for sorry Wimbledon, who entice Oxford's lowest gate in 18 years of league football. New signings Gary Armstrong and Bryan Klug won't have enjoyed their baptism. Gradi experimented by playing Alan Cork in midfield.											
37	A	ROTHERHAM		24	D		0-0	0-0		Goddard	Downes	Armstrong	Klug	Smith	Cunningham	Ketteridge	Dziadulewicz	Leslie	Cork	Denny	
		22/3	*3,810*	*17*	27					*Brown*	*Forrest*	*Taylor*	*Henson*	*Stancliffe*	*Green*	*Tiler*	*Rhodes*	*Fern**	*Owen*	*Halom*	*Carr*
										One win in nine for Rotherham, so this was not such a famous draw for the Dons. Even though Galliers and Jones are out injured, one point is hardly good enough to stir thoughts of survival. This awful match presents just one chance to the Dons, spurned by Cork.											
38	H	GRIMSBY		24	L		3-6	1-1	Ketteridge 22, Leslie 70, Cunningham	Goddard	Downes	Armstrong	Klug	Smith	Cunningham	Ketteridge	Dziadulewicz	Leslie	Cork	Denny*	Driver
		29/3	2,485	*1*	27				*Kilmore (3) Cumming, Drinkell, Mitchell*	*Batch*	*Moore D*	*Cumming*	*Waters*	*Wiggington*	*Crombie*	*Brolly*	*Kilmore*	*Drinkell*	*Mitchell**	*Ford*	*Crosby*
										Grimsby were 17th at the end of September. They go top with this stunning victory. The Dons led 1-0, but were trailing 1-6 before two late strikes eased the complexion of the score. Dario Gradi rated Goddard the best player in his team, which says it all. The pitch resembled a bog.											
39	A	MILLWALL			D		2-2	1-1	Ketteridge 29, Cork 80	Goddard	Downes	Jones	Klug	Smith	Cunningham	Ketteridge	Dziadulewicz*	Leslie	Cork	Denny	**Belfield**
		5/4	*5,354*		28				*Lyons 39, Towner 53*	*Jackson*	*Roberts*	*Gregory*	*Chatterton*	*Blyth*	*Kitchener*	*Towner*	*Mehmet*	*Guthrie*	*Lyons*	*Martin*	
										This is the first ever meeting between these south London neighbours. The Lions manager, George Petchey, blamed his keeper, John Jackson, for both Wimbledon goals. Surely nothing can save the Dons now. Once again the Dons score first, but cannot hold on.											
40	H	READING			D		1-1	0-0	Ketteridge 70	Goddard	Downes	Bowgett!	Klug	Smith	Cunningham	Ketteridge	Dziadulewicz	Leslie	Cork	Denny	
		7/4	4,198		29				*Wanklyn 72*	*Death*	*Joslyn*	*White*	*Bowman*	*Hetzke*	*Moreline*	*Earles*	*Kearney*	*Williams**	*Sanchez*	*Wanklyn*	*Heale*
									Ref: L Shapter	10 minutes from time Bowgett is expelled for head-butting Reading's Pat Earles. Gary Heale thought he had won it at the death for Reading, but Cunningham clears his shot off the line. Wimbledon are still glued to the bottom of the league.											
41	A	BARNSLEY		24	L		**0-4**	0-3		Goddard	Downes	Armstrong	Klug	Jones	Cunningham	Ketteridge	Dziadulewicz*	Leslie	Cork	Denny	Galliers
		11/4	*10,032*	*14*	29				*Glavin 2, Lester 28, Banks 38, 76*	*Pierce*	*Cooper*	*Chambers*	*Glavin*	*Banks*	*McCarthy*	*Evans*	*Parker*	*Riley*	*Lester*	*Downes*	
									Ref: D Clarke	Barnsley, no wins in their last five, inflict on the Dons their heaviest defeat of the season. Barnsley did not miss the injured Norman Hunter, and with most of the other lowly clubs winning, the Dons find themselves five points adrift. Ronnie Glavin headed his 21st goal of the season.											
42	H	OXFORD		24	L		1-3	1-1	Cork 25	Goddard	Downes	Jones	Galliers	Bowgett	Cunningham	Ketteridge	Klug	Leslie	Cork	Denny	
		15/4	2,256	*13*	29				*Taylor 33, Cooke 46, McGrogan 74*	*Burton*	*Kingston*	*Fogg*	*Briggs*	*Cooke*	*Jeffrey*	*McGrogan*	*Taylor*	*Berry*	*Foley**	*Hodgson*	*O'Dowd*
									Ref: R Toseland	Alan Cork's first home goal in six months puts Wimbledon in front, but Oxford quickly fashion a farcical equaliser, and long before the end the match has slipped away from the Dons. Gradi acknowledges relegation as a fact, even though mathematically they are still alive.											
43	H	HULL		24	W		3-2	1-1	Downes 10p, Leslie 47, 75	Goddard	Downes	Jones	Galliers	Smith	Cunningham	Ketteridge	Klug*	Leslie	Cork	Denny	Dziadulewicz
		19/4	**2,046**	*21*	31				*Norrie 13, Roberts D 60*	*Norman*	*Nisbet*	*Devries*	*Croft*	*Roberts D*	*Moss*	*Roberts G*	*Tait*	*Edwards**	*Deacy*	*Norrie*	*Horswill*
										Too little, too late. That is the verdict of Plough Lane's smallest attendance of the season to the Dons' first win in 16 games. It was no idle kickabout – Hull were desperate for points themselves. Afterwards, Gradi put the entire Wimbledon squad up for sale.											
44	H	MILLWALL			D		2-2	0-1	Downes 55, Cork 79	Goddard	Downes	Jones	Galliers	Smith	Cunningham	Ketteridge	Klug	Leslie	Cork	Denny	
		22/4	4,085		32				*Chatterton 17, 65*	*Jackson*	*Shinton*	*Gregory*	*Chatterton*	*Kitchener*	*Tagg*	*Towner*	*Mehmet*	*Mitchell*	*Lyons*	*Coleman*	
										This was Millwall's 8th game without a win. Alan Cork denied them a win bonus, but one point is not enough for the Dons. They are now definitely down. The 4th Division beckons just one season after Wimbledon had left											
45	A	SHEFFIELD UTD		24	L		1-2	0-1	Downes 81p	Goddard	Downes	Jones	Galliers	Smith	Cunningham	Ketteridge	Klug*	Leslie	Cork	Denny	Dziadulewicz
		26/4	*8,675*	*12*	32				*Flood 1, Verde 86*	*Poole*	*Cutbush*	*Tibbott*	*Kenworthy*	*McPhail*	*Keeley*	*Flood*	*Speight*	*Verde*	*Charles**	*Sabella*	*Steane*
										Sheffield United's plunge has been spectacular. Top of the table in early February, they win just one of the next 13, and Bramall Lane is seething with discontent. United will eventually finish 12th, helped by Pedro Verde's shot after 15 seconds which squeezes over the line.											
46	H	MANSFIELD		24	W		3-2	2-0	Galliers, Cunningham, Cork	Goddard	Armstrong	Jones	Galliers	Bowgett	Cunningham	Ketteridge	Downes	Dziadulewicz*	Cork	Denny	Klug
		3/5	2,149	*23*	34				Taylor, Pollard	*Arnold*	*McJanett*	*Foster*	*Bird*	*McClelland*	*Burrows*	*Taylor*	*Pollard*	*Austin*	*Mann*	*Hamilton**	*Allen*
		Home	*Away*							Like Wimbledon, Mansfield are also doomed. In the circumstances, both teams serve up enterprising fare, though as the Dons went into the match four points behind the visitors, the result cannot spare Wimbledon the wooden spoon. This is the only time the Dons ever finish last.											
Average		3,390	*6,222*																		

League Cup	Att		F-A	H-T	Scorers, Times, and Referees	1	2	3	4	5	6	7	8	9	10	11	12 sub used
1:1 H ALDERSHOT		W	4-1	3-1	Parsons 10, Cork 38, Leslie 43,	Goddard	Perkins	Jones	Briley	Bowgett	Cunningham	Leslie	Ketteridge	Knowles*	Cork	Parsons	Galliers
11/8	3,463 *4:10*				*Wooller 15* [Knowles 59]	*Johnson*	*Edwards*	*Wooller*	*Crosby*	*Youlden*	*Jopling*	*Green**	*Brodie*	*Needham*	*French*	*McGregor*	*Longhorn*
					Ref: D Hedges	Paul Bowgett has signed for Wimbledon from Spurs for £1,000. Aldershot have missed promotion by one place for two seasons running, but on this showing don't belong in the same league as the Dons. Malcolm Crosby once played for Wimbledon. Parsons' thunderbolt makes it 1-0.											
1:2 A ALDERSHOT		W	2-1	1-1	Leslie 41, Knowles 68	Goddard	Perkins	Jones	Briley	Bowgett	Cunningham	Ketteridge	Parsons	Leslie	Cork	Knowles	
14/8	*3,280* *4:10*				*French 20p*	*Johnson*	*Edwards*	*Wooler*	*Longhorn*	*Youlden*	*Jopling**	*Crosby*	*Brodie*	*Needham*	*French*	*McGregor*	*Tomlin*
					Ref: C Maskell (Dons win 6-2 on aggregate)	A first-half penalty raises Aldershot's hopes, but only briefly. The tie is over long before the end, leaving Aldershot to reflect on their endemic failure in this competition. It is now eight seasons since they got beyond the first round. Leslie dives amongst the boots to make it 1-1.											
2:1 A ORIENT		D	2-2	1-0	Parsons 1, Leslie 50	Goddard	Perkins	Jones	Galliers	Bowgett	Cunningham	Ketteridge	Parsons	Leslie	Downes	Knowles*	Briley
29/8	*4,964* *2:14*				*Chiedozie 69, Hughton 70*	*Day*	*Fisher*	*Roffey*	*Margerrison*	*Hamberger**	*Taylor*	*Chiedozie*	*Jennings*	*Mayo*	*Hughton*	*Coates*	*Whittle*
					Ref: M Taylor	Mervyn Day, John Chiedozie, Alan Whittle, and Ralph Coates (ex-England) are among the big names in Orient's team. With the Dons leading 1-0 from the first minute, the 'O's twice hit the wood, only for the Dons to extend their lead – until they are rocked by two goals in seconds.											
2:2 H ORIENT		D	2-2	1-0	Downes 14, Parsons 115	Goddard	Perkins	Jones	Galliers	Bowgett	Cunningham	Ketteridge	Parsons	Leslie	Downes	Knowles	
4/9	3,510 *2:14*		*aet*		*Mayo 62, Margerrison 116*	*Day*	*Fisher*	*Roffey*	*Margerrison*	*Taylor*	*Banjo*	*Chiedozie**	*Jennings*	*Mayo*	*Hughton*	*Coates*	*Whittle*
					Ref: R Baker (Dons win 5-4 on penalties)	1-1 after 90 minutes; 2-2 after 120. It is all down to penalty kicks. At 4-4 Goddard saves from Joe Mayo off a post. Goddard, the ex-Orient goalkeeper, steps up to take the kick that sends the Dons into Round 3. England manager Ron Greenwood spectates, but leaves before the fun.											
3 A PLYMOUTH		D	0-0	0-0		Goddard	Perkins	Downes	Galliers	Bowgett	Cunningham	Richards	Parsons	Leslie	Cork	Knowles	
25/9	*6,090*					*Brown*	*Hodges*	*McNeill*	*James*	*Foster*	*Bason*	*Megson*	*Trusson*	*Binney*	*Randall*	*Harrison*	
					Ref: S Bates	Plymouth have just beaten Wimbledon 3-0 in the league. David Kemp, scourge of the Dons on that occasion, is cup-tied, and without his potential goal-supply Plymouth's attack looks emaciated. Fred Binney returns to lead their attack, but gets little support.											
3R H PLYMOUTH		W	1-0	0-0	Leslie 112	Goddard	Perkins	Jones	Galliers*	Bowgett	Cunningham	Ketteridge	Parsons	Leslie	Cork	Lewington	Dziadulewicz
2/10	5,042		*aet*			*Brown*	*Hodges*	*McNeill*	*James*	*Foster*	*Bason*	*Harrison*	*Trusson*	*Binney*	*Randall*	*Johnson**	*Forde*
					Ref: D Johnson	More extra-time tensions. Once again the Dons emerge victorious, but Dario Gradi does not appear as happy as one might expect. He knows the Dons' cup run is distracting from the business of gathering league points. In extra-time John Leslie shoots on the turn inside the near post.											
4 H SWINDON		L	1-2	0-0	Perkins 68	Goddard	Perkins	Jones*	Galliers	Bowgett	Cunningham	Dziadulewicz	Parsons	Leslie	Cork	Lewington	Denny
30/10	7,478				*Rowland 53, Bates 84*	*Allan*	*Templeman*	*Lewis*	*McHale*	*Tucker*	*Stroud*	*Miller**	*Carter*	*Rowland*	*Mayes*	*Williams*	*Bates*
					Ref: J Martin	Wimbledon might have hoped for a giant in the 4th Round. Instead they get Swindon Town, whom they beat 2-0 a few weeks earlier. A packed Plough Lane sees Steve Perkins' first senior goal wiped out by Swindon sub Chic Bates' hooked winner. Swindon march to the semis.											

FA Cup																	
1 A GILLINGHAM		D	0-0	0-0		Goddard	Briley	Jones	Galliers	Bowgett	Cunningham	Dziadulewicz	Parsons	Leslie*	Cork	Lewington	Downes
24/11	*7,027*					*Hillyard*	*Young*	*Barker*	*Overton*	*Weatherley*	*Crabbe*	*Nicholl*	*White*	*Price*	*Westwood*	*Richardson**	*Funnell*
					Ref: A Grey	Wimbledon lost 0-1 at Priestfield in the league, but hang on for a replay, despite losing transfer-listed John Leslie after 17 minutes with a dislocated shoulder. Les Briley wins a surprise recall. Danny Westwood missed good chances for Gillingham.											
1R H GILLINGHAM		W	4-2	2-1	Leslie 13, 84, Parsons 25, Dziad'icz 64	Goddard	Briley	Jones	Galliers	Bowgett	Downes	Dziadulewicz	Parsons	Leslie*	Cork	Lewington	Denny
28/11	4,612				*Price 14, 87*	*Hillyard*	*Young**	*Barker*	*Overton*	*Weatherley*	*Crabbe*	*Nicholl*	*White*	*Price*	*Westwood*	*Richardson*	*Funnell*
					Ref: A Grey	Striker John Leslie is unsettled at Plough Lane. But he scores twice and is the club's leading scorer this season. Despite his double, all the talk after the match is of Dziadulewicz's stunning curling goal, one of the goals of the season. Tom Cunningham missed this thriller with tonsilitis.											

Rd	Venue	Opponent	Res	F-A	H-T	Scorers, Times, and Referees	1	2	3	4	5	6	7	8	9	10	11	12
2	H	PORTSMOUTH	D	0-0	0-0		Goddard	Briley	Jones	Galliers	Bowgett	Downes	Dziadulewicz	Parsons	Denny	Cork	Lewington	
18/12		10,850 *4:4*					*Knight*	*Ellis*	*Viney*	*Brisley*	*Aizlewood*	*Davey*	*Garwood**	*Laidlaw*	*Hemmerman*	*Bryant*	*Rogers*	*Perrin*
						Ref: C Thomas	Up against the 4th Division leaders, on a quagmire of a pitch, the Dons looked to have lost it in the final minute, but Steve Perrin – signed from Plymouth Argyle – fluffed his shot. This did not quell the sound of Pompey chimes ringing in the air. Middlesbrough await the winners.											
2R	A	PORTSMOUTH	D	3-3	2-2	Lewington 35, Denny 45, 75	Goddard	Briley	Jones	Galliers	Bowgett	Downes	Dziadulewicz	Parsons	Denny	Cork	Lewington	
24/12		*17,265 4:4*		*aet*		*Gregory 6, Laidlaw 25, Bryant 54*	*Knight*	*Ellis*	*Viney*	*Brisley*	*Aizlewood*	*Davey*	*Gregory*	*Laidlaw*	*Hemmerman*	*Bryant*	*Rogers*	
						Ref: R Charles	Transfer-listed John Leslie is left out. Paul Denny comes in for his third game of the season and scores twice. The winners know that 1st Division Middlesbrough await them in the 3rd Round. After this pulsating tie, the Dons win the toss for choice of venue for the second replay.											
2	H	PORTSMOUTH	L	0-1	0-1		Goddard	Briley	Jones	Galliers	Bowgett	Cunningham	Perkins	Parsons	Denny	Cork	Lewington*	Leslie
RR 5/1		7,848 *4:4*				*Hemmerman 12*	*Mellor*	*McLoughlan*	*Viney*	*Brisley*	*Perrin*	*Ellis*	*Gregory*	*Laidlaw*	*Hemmerman*	*Bryant*	*Rogers*	
						Ref: B Hill	Jeff Hemmerman decides this protracted tie, catching out Paul Bowgett's attempted offside trap. The much-hyped arrival of Ray Lewington has not produced the goods. He now wants to leave. Downes and Dziadulewicz were dropped. This ends a seven-game unbeaten run.											

		Home						Away					
	P	W	D	L	F	A	W	D	L	F	A	Pts
1 Grimsby	46	18	2	3	46	16	8	8	7	27	26	62
2 Blackburn	46	13	5	5	34	17	12	4	7	24	19	59
3 Sheffield Wed	46	12	6	5	44	20	9	10	4	37	27	58
4 Chesterfield	46	16	5	2	46	16	7	6	10	25	30	57
5 Colchester	46	10	10	3	39	20	10	2	11	25	36	52
6 Carlisle	46	13	6	4	45	26	5	6	12	21	30	48
7 Reading	46	14	6	3	43	19	2	10	11	23	46	48
8 Exeter	46	14	5	4	38	22	5	5	13	22	46	48
9 Chester	46	14	6	3	29	18	3	7	13	20	39	47
10 Swindon	46	15	4	4	50	20	4	4	15	21	43	46
11 Barnsley	46	10	7	6	29	20	6	7	10	24	36	46
12 Sheffield Utd	46	13	5	5	35	21	5	5	13	25	45	46
13 Rotherham	46	13	4	6	38	24	5	6	12	20	42	46
14 Millwall	46	14	6	3	49	23	2	7	14	16	36	45
15 Plymouth	46	13	7	3	39	17	3	5	15	20	38	44
16 Gillingham	46	8	9	6	26	18	6	5	12	23	33	42
17 Oxford	46	10	4	9	34	24	4	9	10	23	38	41
18 Blackpool	46	10	7	6	39	34	5	4	14	23	40	41
19 Brentford	46	10	6	7	33	26	5	5	13	26	47	41
20 Hull	46	11	7	5	29	21	1	9	13	22	48	40
21 Bury	46	10	4	9	30	23	6	3	14	15	36	39
22 Southend	46	11	6	6	33	23	3	4	16	14	35	38
23 Mansfield	46	9	9	5	31	24	1	7	15	16	34	36
24 WIMBLEDON	46	6	8	9	34	38	4	6	13	18	43	34
	1104	287	144	121	893	530	121	144	287	530	893	1104

Odds & ends

Double wins: (0).
Double losses: (6) Chester, Blackpool, Sheff W, Grimsby, Barnsley, Oxford.

Won from behind: (1) Southend (a).
Lost from in front: (4) Blackpool (h), Grimsby (h), Oxford (h), Chester (a).

High spots: 6 unbeaten games in September and October, up to 16th.
3 consecutive wins in February.
Beating Blackburn Rovers, who gained promotion.
Reaching the 4th Round of the League Cup.

Low spots: 9 games without a win from October, dropping to 24th.
14 league games without a win from February.
Losing to 4th Division Portsmouth after 2 replays in FA Cup.

Player of the Year: Steve Galliers
Ever-presents: (0).
Hat-tricks: (0).
Leading scorer: John Leslie (17).

	Appearances					Goals				
	Lge	Sub	LC	Sub	FAC	Sub	**Lge**	LC	FAC	**Total**
Armstrong, Gary	**5**									
Beasant, Dave	**2**									
Belfield, Mick		(1)								
Bowgett, Paul	**30**		7		5					
Briley, Les	**20**	(1)	2	(1)	5					
Cork, Alan	**41**	(1)	5		5		**12**	1		**13**
Cunningham, Tom	**39**		7		2		**5**			**5**
Denny, Paul	**19**	(4)		(1)	3	(1)	**3**		2	**5**
Driver, Phil		(1)								
Downes, Wally	**24**	(2)	3		3	(1)	**3**	1		**4**
Dziadulewicz, Mark	**21**	(5)	1	(1)	4		**1**		1	**2**
Eames, Terry	**3**									
Galliers, Steve	**34**	(2)	5	(1)	5		**2**			**2**
Goddard, Ray	**44**		7		5					
Haverson, Paul	**1**									
Jones, Steve	**39**		6		5					
Ketteridge, Steve	**32**	(2)	5				**6**			**6**
Klug, Bryan	**10**	(1)								
Knowles, Ray	**8**		5				**1**	2		**3**
Leslie, John	**41**	(2)	7		2	(1)	**11**	4	2	**17**
Lewington, Ray	**23**		2		5				1	**1**
Parsons, Steve	**33**		7		5		**7**	3	1	**11**
Perkins, Steve	**15**		7		1			1		**1**
Richards, Craig	**2**		1							
Smith, Mick	**20**									
(own-goals)							**1**			**1**
25 players used	**506**	**(22)**	**77**	**(4)**	**(55)**	**(3)**	**52**	**12**	**7**	**71**

No	Date	Att	Pos	Pts	F-A	H-T	Scorers, Times, and Referees	1	2	3	4	5	6	7	8	9	10	11	12 sub used
1	H BRADFORD C			D	2-2	1-1	Cork 25, Downes 89	Goddard	Jones	Armstrong*	Galliers	Smith	Cunningham	Ketteridge	Downes	Leslie	Cork	Denny	Davies
	16/8	2,161		1			*Dolan 28p, Gallagher 46*	*Smith*	*Podd*	*Watson*	*Dolan*	*Jackson*	*Wood**	*Gallagher*	*Staniforth*	*Campbell*	*Ingham*	*Chapman*	*Cooper*
							Ref: H Taylor	Wimbledon, still unable to win their first league game of the season, are within seconds of defeat. Wally Downes' 89th minute penalty is saved, but he is quickest to the rebound. Steve Jones and Gary Armstrong picked up serious injuries, leaving the Dons with just 10 men.											
2	A ALDERSHOT			L	0-2	0-1		Goddard	**Brown**	Perkins	Galliers	Smith	Cunningham	Ketteridge	Downes	Leslie	Cork	Denny	
	19/8	*2,922*		1			*Brodie 22, 55*	*Johnson*	*Edwards*	*Wooler*	*Briley*	*Bennett*	*Jopling*	*McGregor*	*Brodie*	*Garwood*	*Crosby*	*Robinson*	
							Ref: D Hedges	The Dons lost by the same score on the same pitch a few days earlier in the League Cup. 19-year-old full-back Peter Brown makes his first appearance, but he, like his colleagues, cannot prevent that scourge of 4th Division defences – Murray Brodie – capitalising.											
3	H PORT VALE			W	1-0	1-0	Cork 22	Goddard	Brown	Perkins	Galliers	Smith	Cunningham	Ketteridge*	Downes	Leslie	Cork	Driver	Davies
	23/8	**1,775**		3				*Harrison*	*Keenan*	*Griffiths*	*Beech*	*Bowles*	*Sproson*	*Jones**	*Farrell*	*Allen*	*Chamberlain*	*Bromage*	*Brissett*
							Ref: D Hutchinson	Vale are still reeling from a 1-5 crushing by Southend in midweek. They are keen to register a clean sheet this time, but a pitifully small Plough Lane crowd sees Alan Cork give the Dons their first win of the season, heading in Ketteridge's cross. Cork later hit the crossbar.											
4	A SCUNTHORPE		14	W	2-1	0-0	Driver 53, 78	Goddard	Brown	Perkins	Galliers	Smith	Cunningham	Davies	Downes	Leslie	Cork	Driver	
	30/8	*1,624*	*19*	5			*O'Berg 83*	*Gordon*	*Dall*	*Pilling*	*Grimes*	*Boxall*	*Oates*	*Pugh*	*Cammack*	*Lambert*	*Partridge**	*Stewart*	*O'Berg*
							Ref: D Webb	Back to the bread and butter of the league after the drama of Hillsborough. Scunthorpe are still looking for their first win. They are undone by Phil Driver, who is asked to play wide, and who responds by scoring both Wimbledon goals. Both were angled drives.											
5	H STOCKPORT		9	L	1-2	0-0	Leslie 54	Goddard	Brown	Perkins	Galliers	Smith	Cunningham	Davies*	Downes	Leslie	Cork	Driver	Denny
	6/9	2,018	*12*	5			*Rutter 76, Bradd 89*	*Lawson*	*Rutter*	*Sherlock*	*Fowler*	*Sword*	*Uzelac*	*Williams*	*Sunley*	*Bradd*	*Galvin*	*Coyle*	
							Ref: H King	Les Bradd has been knocking them in in the lower divisions for as long as anyone can remember. He bungles to present John Leslie with the opener, but then pounces for a late winner after Ray Goddard drops the ball. County had drawn all their previous matches this season.											
6	A CREWE		12	W	3-0	2-0	Cork (3)	Beasant	Brown	Perkins	Galliers	Smith*	Cunningham	Denny	Downes	Leslie	Cork	Armstrong	Driver
	13/9	*1,881*	*22*	7				*Mulhearn*	*McMahon*	*Lewis*	*Hunter*	*Scott*	*Prophett*	*Davies**	*Guy*	*Conroy*	*Palios*	*Bowers*	*Wilkinson*
							Ref: D Lloyd	Goddard finds himself dropped for his late blunder against Stockport. He had previously missed just two matches (both for injury) in two seasons. Cork helps himself to a hat-trick against struggling Crewe, for whom Eire international Terry Conroy makes little impact.											
7	A MANSFIELD		8	L	0-1	0-1		Beasant	Brown	Armstrong	Galliers	Perkins	Cunningham	Denny	Downes*	Leslie	Cork	Driver	Smith
	15/9	*2,903*	*7*	7			*McClelland*	*Arnold*	*Dawkins*	*Mann*	*Hamilton*	*McClelland*	*Bird*	*Allen*	*Phillips*	*Austin*	*Parkinson*	*Pollard*	
							Ref: M Robinson	Mansfield were relegated with the Dons, but are making strides to get back up again quickly. Northern Ireland centre-half John McClelland, soon to sign for Glasgow Rangers, pops up to score the decisive goal. McClelland will go on to win 53 caps for his country.											
8	H LINCOLN		9	L	0-1	0-1		Beasant	Perkins	Armstrong*	Galliers	Smith	Cunningham	Denny	Downes	Leslie	Cork	Brown	Davies
	20/9	2,320	*1*	7			*Hobson*	*Felgate*	*Thompson T*	*Keeley*	*Hughes*	*Peake*	*Carr*	*Neale*	*Harford*	*Hobson*	*Cunningham*	*Shipley*	
							Ref: R Challis	High-flying Lincoln have conceded just three goals all season. Phil Neale plays cricket for Worcestershire. Trevor Peake and Ray Harford are just two Imps destined for better things, in Harford's case an Indian summer with the Dons. Gordon Hobson nets his sixth goal of the season.											
9	A HALIFAX		13	W	1-0	0-0	Leslie 72	Beasant	Brown	Perkins	Galliers	Smith	Cunningham	Davies	Downes	Leslie	Cork	**Hubbick***	**Hodges**
	27/9	***1,407***	*19*	9				*Kilner*	*Nattrass*	*Burton*	*Ward*	*Harris*	*Dunleavy*	*Firth*	*Hendrie*	*Allatt*	*Johnson*	*O'Neil*	
							Ref: R Bridges	Halifax are struggling once again, and lose their third home match of the season. Dave Hubbick, displaced at Ipswich by the arrival of Kevin O'Callaghan, has signed for the Dons, and his cross is converted by John Leslie, whom Halifax Town had been courting.											
10	H MANSFIELD			W	2-1	1-1	Hubbick 37, Leslie 84	Beasant	Brown	Perkins	Galliers	Smith	Downes	Ketteridge	Davies	Leslie	Cork	Hubbick	
	30/9	2,052		11			*Austin 38*	*Arnold*	*Dawkins*	*Mann*	*Hamilton*	*McClelland*	*Bird*	*Allen*	*Phillips*	*Austin*	*Parkinson*	*Pollard*	
							Ref: B Hill	The fixture list has thrown up a quick return with Mansfield. Wimbledon's revenge is joyously exacted. Hubbick scores his first goal for his new club, and John Leslie celebrates coming off the transfer list by stealing a late winner and signing a new three-year contract.											
11	A TRANMERE		9	L	0-3	0-2		Beasant	Brown	Perkins	Galliers	Smith	Cunningham	Davies	Downes*	Leslie	Cork	Hubbick	Ketteridge
	3/10	*2,507*	*17*	11			*Evans 16, Beamish 42p, Lumby 65*	*Johnson*	*Mathias*	*Flood*	*Williams*	*Parry*	*Evans*	*Peplow*	*Mungall*	*Lumby*	*Beamish*	*Kelly**	*Hamilton*
							Ref: K Hackett	Tranmere are picking up after a shaky start, and this win follows 3-0 and 5-0 victories. This match proves to be a personal nightmare for Wally Downes, who presents Rovers with their first two goals. Clive Evans stuck out a boot to claim Tranmere's opener.											

No	Venue	Date	Opponents	Att	Pos	Pts	Res	H-T	Scorers, Times, Referees	1	2	3	4	5	6	7	8	9	10	11	Sub
		7/10		2,117	*3*	11			*Spence 18*	*Cawston*	*Dudley*	*Yates*	*Hadley*	*Moody*	*Cusack*	*Gray**	*Pountney*	*Spence*	*Mercer*	*Otulakowski*	*Nelson*
									Ref: T Spencer	Southend are streaking away with the division, and will never be caught. Dario Gradi tipped them pre-season, but in the end only a toe-poke from Northern Ireland international Derek Spence separates the sides. During the match the kitchen under the main stand caught fire.											
13	H		HARTLEPOOL		10	W	**5-0**	3-0	Galliers 10, Leslie 13, 85, Cork 30, [Ketteridge 54]	Beasant	Brown	Armstrong	Galliers	Smith	Cunningham	Ketteridge	Hodges	Leslie	Cork	Hubbick	
		11/10		1,971	*8*	13				*Richardson*	*Sweeney*	*Brown*	*Hodges*	*Bird*	*Linacre J*	*Kerr*	*Lawrence*	*Newton*	*Houchen*	*Forster*	
									Ref: P Reeves	Hartlepool are not having the worst of seasons, so they are unlikely candidates to present Wimbledon with their biggest win. Pick of the five goals, according to Gradi, was the last, Leslie's second. Ketteridge's goal flew in straight from a corner. Glyn Hodges plays his first full game.											
14	A		HEREFORD		10	D	1-1	0-1	Hubbick 62	Beasant	Brown	Armstrong	Galliers	Smith	Cunningham	Hodges	Leslie	Hubbick	Cork	Ketteridge	
		18/10		*2,369*	*22*	14			*Jones 15*	*Brand*	*Spiring*	*Bartley*	*Hicks*	*Dobson*	*Price*	*Lane*	*Strong**	*Ames*	*Jones G*	*White*	*Harvey*
									Ref: P Tyldesley	Hereford are having a desperate time. Doncaster and Crewe have already hit them for five, and Mansfield for four. They haven't scored themselves for four matches. Garry Jones' early strike is an achievement, until cancelled by Hubbick's second goal for the Dons.											
15	A		ROCHDALE			L	0-2	0-2		Beasant	Brown	Armstrong	Galliers	Smith	Cunningham	Ketteridge	Hodges	Leslie	Cork	Hubbick	
		21/10		*2,391*		14			*O'Loughlin 12, Wellings 29*	*Crawford*	*Jones*	*Snookes**	*Essex*	*Burke*	*Taylor*	*Hoy*	*O'Loughlin*	*Hilditch*	*Wellings*	*Martinez*	*Seal*
									Ref: P Richardson	Rochdale maintain their unbeaten home record with two quick goals. Strangely, it was Wimbledon who had looked most threatening, forcing four corners before midfielder Nigel O'Loughlin scores the first goal. Hubbick misses a similar chance to that which he took against Hereford.											
16	H		YORK		9	W	3-0	2-0	Hodges 38, Cork 43, Kay 55 (og)	Beasant	Brown	Armstrong	Galliers	Smith	Cunningham	Ketteridge	Hodges	Leslie*	Cork	Hubbick	Jones
		25/10		2,082	*16*	16				*Blackburn*	*Hood*	*Kay*	*Smith*	*Clements*	*Craig*	*Walsh*	*Byrne*	*Eccles*	*Millar*	*McDonald*	
									Ref: M Taylor	York were unbeaten in their first four matches, but will finally end up bottom. They belied their position with some sprightly play before 17-year-old Glyn Hodges scores his first goal for his club. John Leslie made the first two goals, then came off with a temperature of 104 degrees.											
17	H		PETERBOROUGH		9	W	2-1	0-0	Leslie 88, Cork 89	Beasant	Brown	Armstrong	Galliers	Smith	Cunningham	Ketteridge	Hodges	Leslie	Cork	Hubbick	
		28/10		1,901	*3*	18			*Quow 73*	*Waugh*	*Winters*	*Robson*	*Hodgson*	*Slough*	*Foster*	*Quow*	*Kellock*	*Cooke*	*Syrett*	*Gallagher**	*Guy*
									Ref: D Letts	Posh are slipping after a fine start. This is their third defeat on the trot, as Wimbledon snatch two goals and two points in the last two minutes. Roy of the Rovers stuff. Peter Brown hit an early penalty against a post. Off the field, Ron Noades is trying to find a new ground for the club.											
18	A		DONCASTER		12	L	1-2	0-0	Cork 57p	Beasant	Brown	Armstrong	Galliers	Smith	Cunningham	Ketteridge	Hodges	Leslie	Cork	Hubbick	
		1/11		*3,245*	*6*	18			*Brown 55 (og), Mell 89*	*Boyd*	*Russell*	*Lally*	*Lister*	*Dowie*	*Dowd*	*Mell*	*Nimmo*	*Warboys**	*Snodin G*	*Little*	*Pugh*
									Ref: D Shaw	Billy Bremner's Doncaster have won only one of the last seven, but they will finish the season strongly. Phil Brown's own-goal puts their noses in front. This time it is Stuart Mell who inflicts a last-minute heart-breaker. Rovers violently protested the penalty award for Ketteridge.											
19	A		SOUTHEND		12	L	0-1	0-0		Beasant	Brown	Armstrong	Galliers	Smith	Cunningham	Ketteridge	Hodges	Leslie	Cork	Hubbick*	Jones
		3/11		*4,935*	*1*	18			*Spence 66*	*Cawston*	*Dudley*	*Stead*	*Hadley*	*Moody**	*Cusack*	*Gray*	*Pountney*	*Spence*	*Mercer*	*Otulakowski*	*Nelson*
									Ref: R Toseland	Derek Spence once again settles the game in Southend's favour. This is their 19th straight win at Roots Hall, almost entirely due to the heroics of keeper Mervyn Cawston. The following day Wimbledon host Crystal Palace in a friendly to inaugurate Plough Lane's new floodlights.											
20	H		NORTHAMPTON		12	W	1-0	1-0	Cork 18	Beasant	Jones	Armstrong	Downes	Smith	Cunningham	Ketteridge	Hodges	Leslie	Cork	Hubbick*	Brown
		8/11		2,029	*11*	20				*Poole*	*Saxby*	*Sandercock*	*Waldock*	*Byatt*	*Sandy*	*Carlton*	*Denyer*	*Phillips*	*Williams*	*Bowen*	
									Ref: D Vickers	West Ham scouts are watching Dave Beasant, who brings off a wonderful save to foil danger-man Steve Phillips, who found the net so often for Brentford. Steve Galliers misses the match through suspension, and Dario Gradi is off scouting somewhere.											
21	H		ALDERSHOT		8	W	4-0	1-0	Leslie 23, Cork 62p, Cunningham 65, 75	Beasant	Jones	Armstrong	Denny	Smith	Cunningham	Ketteridge	Hodges	Leslie	Cork	Hubbick	
		11/11		2,538	*5*	22				*Johnson*	*Scott*	*Wooler*	*Briley*	*Youlden*	*Bennett*	*Lucas*	*French*	*Garwood*	*Crosby*	*Brodie*	
									Ref: D Vickers	Poor Aldershot are destined to narrowly miss out on promotion for the third season running. Not that they look much of a threat on this showing. Briley and Crosby are ex-Dons. Young Hodges has a hand in all four goals. Tommy Cunningham bags his first goals for the club.											
22	A		BRADFORD C		9	L	0-2	0-1		Beasant	Jones	Armstrong	Denny	Smith	Cunningham	Ketteridge	Hodges	Leslie	Cork	Hubbick*	Brown
		15/11		*3,327*	*7*	22			*Watson 36, 76*	*Smith*	*Thompson*	*Watson*	*Ingham*	*Jackson*	*Wood*	*Chapman*	*Staniforth*	*Campbell*	*Dolan*	*Hutchins*	
									Ref: D Allison	City's fifth successive league win is down to two goals from full-back Garry Watson. The damage to the Dons would have been worse but for Beasant's 56th minute penalty save from Terry Dolan. It was Dolan's first miss in five years, having scored 19 times from the spot.											
23	A		BURY		9	L	0-1	0-1		Beasant	Jones	Armstrong*	Galliers	Smith	Cunningham	Ketteridge	Hodges	Leslie	Cork	Hubbick	Denny
		29/11		*2,292*	*22*	22			*Hilton 23*	*Southall*	*Phillips*	*Kennedy*	*Gore*	*Hilton*	*Howard*	*Mullen*	*Butler*	*Johnson*	*Jakob*	*Farley*	
									Ref: D Civil	Lowly Bury inflict a fifth successive away defeat on Wimbledon. Paul Hilton's goal is well-protected by veteran defender Pat Howard (once of Newcastle) and young keeper Neville Southall. Ketteridge plays stopper, and Cork misses at the end. The Dons' last defeat for a long time.											

No	Date	Att	Pos	Pts	F-A	H-T	Scorers, Times, and Referees	1	2	3	4	5	6	7	8	9	10	11	12 sub used
24	H DARLINGTON		9	D	1-1	0-1	Joseph 77	Beasant	Brown	Jones	Galliers	Smith	Cunningham	Ketteridge*	Denny	Leslie	Cork	Hubbick	**Joseph**
	6/12	1,811	*14*	23			*Hawker 30*	*Cuff*	*Kamara*	*Wilson*	*Smith*	*Skipper*	*Speedie*	*Hawker*	*McLean*	*Stalker**	*Hamilton*	*Walsh*	*Ball*
							Ref: J Deakin	Darlington end the Dons' run of five home wins. Francis Joseph, Wimbledon's first black player in the league, signed for £3,000 from Hillingdon, makes his debut as substitute. He takes 10 minutes for his first touch and scores with his second. Phil Driver has gone to Chelsea.											
25	A TORQUAY			W	3-2	2-1	Leslie 16, Hubbick 23, Cork 72	Beasant	Jones	Armstrong	Galliers	Smith	Cunningham	Ketteridge	Denny	Leslie!	Cork	Hubbick	
	26/12	*3,191*		25			*Lawrence 19, Fell 47p*	*O'Keefe*	*Jones*	*Pethard*	*Coffill*	*Bourne**	*Rioch*	*Fell*	*Lawrence*	*Cooper!*	*Twichin*	*Weston*	*Sermanni*
							Ref: C Thomas	Bruce Rioch of Scotland is playing out his days in the west country. Three times Wimbledon take the lead in this eventful match, which finishes with 10 men apiece. John Leslie is sent off for a threatening gesture, Torquay's Steve Cooper for persistent fouling.											
26	H BOURNEMOUTH			W	2-0	1-0	Cork 16, Hubbick 54	Beasant	Jones	Armstrong	Galliers	Smith	Cunningham	Ketteridge	Denny	Cork	Downes	Hubbick	
	27/12	2,681		27				*Allen*	*Cunningham*	*Moore*	*Impey*	*Compton*	*Hefferman*	*Spackman*	*Mooney*	*Morgan*	*Massey*	*Butler**	*McGrath*
							Ref: A Grey	After a 14-hour round trip to Torquay on Boxing Day, the Dons turn out 24 hours later to clinch two more points. Cork and Hubbick are again in goalscoring form. This is just as well, for Leslie is out, suspended. All of a sudden Wimbledon are within sight of the promotion pack.											
27	H SCUNTHORPE		12	D	2-2	0-1	Cork 60p, Galliers 90	Beasant	Jones	Armstrong	Galliers	Smith	Brown*	Ketteridge	Hodges	Denny	Cork	Downes	Hubbick
	19/1	2,112	*20*	28			*Green 39, O'Berg 75*	*Neenan*	*Davy*	*Jarvis*	*Grimes*	*Dall*	*Oates*	*O'Berg*	*Cammack*	*Green*	*Pugh*	*Stewart**	*Partridge*
							Ref: B Daniels	FA Cup business has occupied the Dons for the past weeks. This is Scunthorpe's sixth draw in eight matches, though Wimbledon were rescued by Galliers shooting through a forest of legs in injury time. Smith and Ketteridge had earlier hit the post. Dario Gradi is set to join Palace.											
28	A PORT VALE		11	W	3-2	1-1	Cork 35, Hodges 50, Smith 77	Beasant	Jones	Armstrong	Galliers	Smith	Cunningham	Ketteridge	Hodges	Leslie*	Cork	Downes	Denny
	31/1	*2,372*	*24*	30			*Miller 20, 65p*	*Harrison*	*Brissett*	*Bromage*	*Beech*	*Bowles*	*Sproson*	*Miller*	*Farrell*	*Chamberl'n N*	*Chamberl'n M*	*Jones*	
							Ref: A Dobson	This is a fifth straight defeat for bottom club Port Vale, though they put up a fight. Now that Gradi has decamped to Selhurst Park, his 36-year-old deputy, Dave Bassett, takes control. Mick Smith's super volley gives Bassett his first win. Mark Chamberlain will play for England.											
29	H CREWE		10	W	2-0	2-0	Cork 40, 45	Beasant	Jones	Armstrong	Galliers	Smith	Cunningham	Ketteridge	Hodges*	Leslie	Cork	Downes	Joseph
	7/2	2,782	*18*	32				*Mulhearn*	*McMahon*	*Lewis*	*Hunter*	*Scott*	*Prophett*	*Bowers*	*Guy**	*Palios*	*Greenhoff*	*Nelson*	*Davies*
							Ref: A Robinson	Ex-Manchester United star Jimmy Greenhoff does his best to inject life into struggling Crewe, who have won just one of their last 13. But the Dons had created nothing before the goals. A post-match terrace sit-in protests against any move away from Plough Lane.											
30	A STOCKPORT		9	D	0-0	0-0		Beasant	Jones	Armstrong	Galliers	Smith	Cunningham	Ketteridge	Hodges	Leslie*	Cork	Downes	Joseph
	13/2	*1,772*	*18*	33				*Lawson*	*Rutter*	*Sherlock*	*Fowler*	*Thorpe*	*Sword*	*Williams*	*Sunley*	*Bradd*	*Galvin*	*Coyle*	
							Ref: K Redfern	Stockport had lost nine of their previous 10, so something is evidently preying on Wimbledon's minds. Mind you, the Dons dominated in everything but goals, forcing 17 corners. Downes hit the post and Steve Jones the bar. Wimbledon are up to 9th. Friday the 13th is the date.											
31	H HALIFAX		9	W	3-0	2-0	Galliers 18, Downes 30, Cork 80	Beasant	Jones	Armstrong	Galliers	Smith	Cunningham	Ketteridge*	Hodges	Leslie	Cork	Downes	Joseph
	21/2	2,501	23	35				*Kilner*	*Ward*	*Burton*	*Evans*	*Flavell*	*Hendrie*	*Firth*	*Graham*	*Allatt**	*McIlwraith*	*Nattrass*	*Goodman*
							Ref: J Martin	One win in 13, and Halifax will struggle to finish above 24th place. They look a bad-tempered team, and well they might. Once again the rich and famous take in Beasant's every move. The ref favours the Dons on key decisions, like over-ruling a flagging linesman for Galliers' goal.											
32	A LINCOLN		8	D	0-0	0-0		Beasant	Jones	Armstrong	Galliers	Smith	Cunningham	Ketteridge	Hodges*	Leslie	Cork	Downes	Denny
	28/2	*3,988*	*2*	36				*Felgate*	*ThompsonT*	*Keeley*	*Hughes*	*Peake*	*Carr*	*Neale*	*Turner*	*Hobson*	*Cunningham*	*Shipley*	
							Ref: D Richardson	A major triumph for Wimbledon, preventing tearaway Lincoln from scoring at home for the first time this season. This time the Dons keep a padlock around Gordon Hobson, but offer no penetration up front themselves. The club decide not to move to Selhurst Park after all.											
33	A PETERBOROUGH		8	D	1-1	0-0	Cork 86	Beasant	Jones	Armstrong	Galliers	Smith	Cunningham	Ketteridge	Hodges	Leslie	Cork	Downes	
	4/3	*3,201*	*9*	37			*Cooke 83*	*Waugh*	*Winters*	*Robson*	*Gynn*	*Slack*	*Smith*	*Quow*	*Kellock**	*Cooke*	*Hodgson*	*Gallagher*	*Cliss*
							Ref: M Heath	Peterborough are one of those teams Wimbledon must brush aside if they hope to claim a promotion spot. Robbie Cooke's 23rd goal of the season is cancelled out by Alan Cork's 22nd, a header on the run over the keeper's head. A win would have carried the Dons to 5th place.											
34	H TRANMERE		6	W	2-1	0-0	Leslie 56, Hodges 82	Beasant	Jones	Armstrong	Galliers	Smith	Cunningham	Ketteridge	Hodges	Leslie	Cork*	Downes	Hubbick
	7/3	2,394	19	39			*Evans 66*	*Johnson*	*Mathias*	*Edwards*	*Bramhall*	*Parry*	*Evans*	*Powell*	*Hamilton*	*Kelly*	*Kerr*	*Griffiths*	
							Ref: A Glasson	Floundering Tranmere come within eight minutes of holding the Dons. Bassett proclaims this to be his team's best performance since he took charge. Glyn Hodges, who only turned professional the previous month, prods the winner. John Leslie scores his first goal of 1981.											

No / Date	Venue	Opponent / Att	Pos	Res / Pts	F-A	H-T	Scorers, Times, Referees	1	2	3	4	5	6	7	8	9	10	11	12
35	A	HARTLEPOOL	[illegible]	W	[illegible]	[illegible]	Cork 27, 53, Downes 55	Beasant	Jones	Armstrong	Galliers	Smith	Cunningham	Ketteridge	Hodges	Leslie	Cork	Downes	Denny
14/3		*2,329*	*8*	*41*			*Houchen 72, Newton 82*	*Richardson*	*Linacre J*	*Sweeney*	*Harding**	*Bird*	*Brown*	*Kerr*	*Fagan*	*Newton*	*Houchen*	*Johnson*	*Hogan*
							Ref: T Morris	Hartlepool were once riding high, but this marks a fifth straight loss. Influenza kept Bassett away from the match. He would not have enjoyed the sight of his players almost squandering a three-goal lead. Keith Houchen would later go on to trouble other defences in higher divisions.											
36	A	DARLINGTON		L	**1-4**	1-2	Smith 30 *[Walsh 80]*	Beasant	Jones	Armstrong	Galliers!	Smith	Cunningham!	Ketteridge	Hodges	Leslie	Cork	Downes	
17/3		*2,091*		41			*Speedie 2, Hamilton 35, Charlton 70,*	*Cuff*	*Kamara*	*McLean*	*Smith*	*Skipper*	*Speedie*	*Charlton*	*Wicks*	*Stalker**	*Hamilton*	*Walsh*	*Wilson*
							Ref: K Walmsley	Disaster. Wimbledon's first defeat in 13 games, and two players sent off by referee Ken Walmsley, who in recent seasons booked four Dons at Hartlepool and sent off Ray Goddard at Mansfield. David Speedie scored for the Quakers, whose third goal, insisted the Dons, was out of play.											
37	H	HEREFORD	7	D	0-0	0-0		Goddard	Jones	Armstrong	Denny	Smith	Downes	Ketteridge	Hodges	Leslie	Cork	Hubbick*	Joseph
22/3		**3,898**	24	42				*Cashley*	*Price*	*Pejic*	*Hicks*	*Cornes*	*Bartley*	*Harvey*	*Laidlaw*	*Showers*	*McGrellis*	*White*	
							Ref: D Hedges	Sunday brings out Plough Lane's biggest gate of the season to witness this dreadful spectacle. Beasant broke a finger in training and was replaced by Goddard. Wally Downes, just 19, was made captain for the day. Hereford are heading for re-election; on this form the Dons, too.											
38	A	YORK	5	W	1-0	1-0	Cork 8	Goddard	Jones	Armstrong	Denny	Smith	Cunningham	Ketteridge	Hodges	Leslie	Cork	Downes	
28/3		*2,026*	*23*	*44*				*Blackburn*	*Hood*	*Walsh*	*Stanley*	*Clements*	*Craig*	*Ford*	*Byrne*	*Randall*	*McDonald*	*Pugh*	
							Ref: G Flint	This is York's ninth defeat in 10 games, but the Dons made heavy weather of it. Alan Cork notched his 25th goal of the season, and John Leslie later hit a post. York keeper Edwin Blackburn made save after save to keep his team in the hunt.											
39	H	WIGAN	4	W	1-0	1-0	Hodges 20	Goddard	Jones	Armstrong	Denny	Smith	Cunningham	Ketteridge	Hodges*	Leslie	Cork	Downes	Joseph
31/3		2,638	*11*	*46*				*Ward*	*Curtis*	*McAdam*	*Cribley*	*Methven*	*Lloyd*	*Urquhart G*	*Wright*	*Quinn M*	*Houghton*	*Corrigan*	
							Ref: A Gunn	Wigan's new player-manager, Larry Lloyd, formerly of Liverpool and England, felt his team deserved a point. It was denied by a rare header by Glyn Hodges, which takes Wimbledon into the top four for the first time. When Mick Quinn punched Cunningham he was only lectured.											
40	H	DONCASTER	3	W	1-0	1-0	Cork 30	Goddard	Brown	Armstrong	Denny	Smith	Cunningham	Ketteridge	Hodges	Leslie	Cork	Downes	
4/4		3,595	*4*	*48*				*Boyd*	*Russell*	*Bremner*	*Snodin I*	*Swan*	*Lister*	*Pugh*	*Nimmo**	*Warboys*	*Snodin*	*Harle*	*Dawson*
							Ref: L Burden	This game is so important to both sides that Doncaster manager Billy Bremner picks himself for his first match of the season. For the third time in a row the Dons hang on to a first-half lead. Four shut-outs for Goddard. Bassett is relieved that Alan Cork has signed a new contract.											
41	A	NORTHAMPTON	4	D	1-1	0-1	Cunningham 75	Goddard	Brown	Armstrong	Denny	Smith	Cunningham	Ketteridge	Belfield	Leslie	Cork*	Downes	Joseph
11/4		*2,121*	*13*	*49*			*Bowen 42*	*Poole*	*Saxby*	*Gage*	*Farmer*	*Saunders*	*Denyer*	*Carlton*	*Williams*	*Phillips!*	*Bowen*	*Heeley*	
							Ref: D Shaw	Mick Belfield is hauled out of the reserves, a late replacement for Hodges, and lays on Wimbledon's equaliser. The Cobblers' captain, Steve Phillips is sent off four minutes from time. Northampton scorer Keith Bowen is the son of manager Dave Bowen.											
42	A	BOURNEMOUTH	3	W	1-0	1-0	Downes 41	Goddard	Brown	Armstrong	Galliers	Smith	Cunningham	Ketteridge	Denny	Leslie	Joseph	Downes	
18/4		***5,048***	*10*	*51*				*Allen*	*Impey*	*Butler*	*Smith*	*Compton*	*Hefferman*	*Dawtry*	*Morgan*	*Mooney*	*Spackman**	*Sulley*	*Pugh*
							Ref: B Stevens	Easter brings out the largest crowd to watch Wimbledon this season. Bournemouth's first defeat in 15 games is brought about by a low shot by Wally Downes. With Alan Cork injured, Francis Joseph stakes his place. It is six league wins out of six over Bournemouth now.											
43	H	TORQUAY	3	W	1-0	1-0	Cunningham 23	Beasant	Jones	Armstrong	Galliers	Smith	Cunningham	Ketteridge	Denny	Leslie	Joseph	Downes	
20/4		3,190	*16*	*53*				*O'Keefe*	*Jones*	*Pethard*	*Coffill**	*Bourne*	*Larmour*	*Fell*	*Cox*	*Cooper*	*Twichin*	*Wilson*	*Bowker*
							Ref: J Warner	This is Wimbledon's fifth 1-0 win in six games, and each time they successfully defended a half-time lead. Gerry Fell's 25-yard volley that smacked against restored keeper, Beasant's crossbar nearly wiped the smile from the Dons' faces. Tom Cunningham had scored with a header.											
44	A	WIGAN	3	L	0-1	0-0		Beasant	Brown	Armstrong*	Galliers	Smith	Cunningham	Ketteridge	Denny	Leslie	Joseph	Downes	Hodges
25/4		*3,381*	*11*	*53*			*Methven 50*	*Ward*	*Fretwell*	*McAdam**	*Cribley*	*Methven*	*Lloyd*	*Hutchinson*	*Wignall*	*Quinn M*	*Houghton*	*Wright*	*Quinn T*
							Ref: C Seel	The Dons need two more points. Wigan spoil the party and keep Wimbledon on tenterhooks awhile longer. Skipper Colin Methven outjumped Paul Denny to head the decisive goal. Armstrong broke a bone in his foot. The Dons now have the chance to clinch promotion at Plough Lane.											
45	H	ROCHDALE		W	4-1	2-1	Leslie 4, 10, Hodges 75, Galliers 78	Beasant	Jones	Brown	Galliers	Smith	Cunningham	Ketteridge	Denny	Leslie	Hodges	Downes	
28/4		3,884		*55*			*Wann 40*	*Crawford*	*Jones*	*Snookes*	*Weir*	*Burke*	*Taylor*	*Wann*	*O'Loughlin*	*Hilditch*	*Wellings*	*Martinez*	
							Ref: L Shapter	Any nerves were swept away when Wimbledon sprinted to a two-goal lead inside 10 minutes. Beasant blundered to give Dennis Wann his goal. Steve Galliers, who lost the captaincy to Cunningham, celebrated with the fourth and clinching goal. Two defeats from 18 for Bassett.											
46	H	BURY	3	L	2-4	0-1	Goddard 63p, Denny 72 *[Jakob 70]*	Goddard	Brown	Downes	**Gage**	Jones	Cunningham	Ketteridge	Denny	Hodges	Joseph	Hubbick*	Leslie
2/5		*2,293*	*13*	*55*			*Johnson 31p, Whitehead 50, Madden 55,*	*Southall*	*Howard*	*Kennedy*	*Gore*	*Whitehead*	*Hilton*	*Johnson*	*Butler*	*Madden*	*Jakob*	*Cruickshank*	
Average	Home 2,367	*Away 2,853*					Ref: R Toseland	This defeat damaged the Dons' pride, not their promotion, happily secured against Rochdale. A week after his 17th birthday, Kevin Gage makes his debut. Ray Goddard bows out of football with his first league goal, a penalty against Neville Southall with the Dons losing 0-3.											

League Cup	Att		F-A	H-T	Scorers, Times, and Referees	1	2	3	4	5	6	7	8	9	10	11	12 sub used
1:1 A ALDERSHOT		L	0-2	0-1		Goddard	Jones	Armstrong	Galliers	Smith	Cunningham	Ketteridge*	Downes	Leslie	Cork	Davies	Denny
9/8	*3,023*				*Garwood 6, 48*	*Johnson*	*Edwards*	*Wooler*	*Briley*	*Bennett*	*Jopling*	*Lucas*	*Sanford*	*Garwood*	*Scott*	*Robinson**	*Tomlin*
					Ref: B Stevens	Les Briley turns out for Aldershot; Roy Davies, signed from Torquay, turns out for Wimbledon. At the same stage last season, Wimbledon ran out 6-2 winners overall. Colin Garwood has been scoring goals regularly for six league clubs. Downes blunders for No 1, Smith for No 2,											
1:2 H ALDERSHOT		W	4-1	3-0	Leslie 20, 25, Denny 37, Downes 84	Goddard	Jones	Armstrong	Galliers	Smith	Cunningham	Ketteridge	Downes	Leslie	Cork	Denny	
12/8	2,444				*Brodie 55*	*Johnson*	*Edwards*	*Wooler*	*Briley*	*Bennett*	*Jopling*	*Lucas*	*Brodie*	*Garwood*	*Crosby*	*Sanford*	
					Ref: J Bray (Dons win 4-3 on aggregate)	The deficit is overturned by half-time. John Leslie is still on the transfer list, but it is he who brings Wimbledon level on aggregate. Poor Aldershot must feel they will never get the better of Wimbledon. Leslie's two headers restore parity. Goddard boobs for the Shots' goal.											
2:1 H SHEFFIELD WED		W	2-1	2-1	Cunningham 43, Leslie 45	Goddard	Brown	Perkins	Galliers	Smith	Cunningham	Davies	Downes	Leslie	Cork	Driver	
26/8	3,549	*2:10*			*Owen 29*	*Bolder*	*Blackhall*	*Grant*	*Smith*	*Pickering*	*King*	*Owen*	*Johnson*	*Lowey*	*McCulloch*	*Curran*	
					Ref: J Martin	Jack Charlton's Wednesday, newly promoted to the 2nd Division, find themselves victims of an explosive end to the first half. Cunningham hit the woodwork, then dived to head in the rebound. Seconds later John Leslie hoisted the ball up, and in it went. Was it a lob or a fluke?											
2:2 A SHEFFIELD WED		L	1-3	1-1	Cork 5	Goddard	Brown	Perkins	Galliers	Smith	Cunningham	Davies	Downes	Leslie	Cork	Driver	
2/9	*15,131*	*2:10*			*Owen 10, Grant 65, Curran 89*	*Cox*	*Blackhall*	*Grant*	*Smith*	*Pickering*	*King*	*Taylor*	*Johnson*	*Owen*	*McCulloch*	*Curran*	
					Ref: P Willis (Dons lose 3-4 on aggregate)	A night of passion at Hillsborough, sparked by Alan Cork's early header from a corner, the first goal Wednesday have conceded at home this season. Gordon Owen's equaliser bounced down and over Goddard. Extra time was only seconds away when Terry Curran scored the winner.											

FA Cup	Att		F-A	H-T	Scorers, Times, and Referees	1	2	3	4	5	6	7	8	9	10	11	12 sub used
1 H WINDSOR & ETON		9 W	7-2	2-1	Smith 19,31, Hubbick 51,59,67, Cunn'm 71,	Beasant	Jones	Armstrong	Galliers	Smith	Cunningham	Ketteridge	Hodges	Leslie	Cork	Hubbick	
22/11	3,087	*Ath:1*			*McCulloch 21, Hill 85* [Cork 81]	*Mitchell K*	*Mitchell J*	*Edwards**	*Richardson*	*Smith*	*King*	*Hill*	*Harris*	*McCulloch*	*Cadogan*	*Yates*	*Beckett*
					Ref: D Hedges	Windsor & Eton of the Athenian League won two quick corners, then lost seven goals. Hubbick scored a hat-trick while concussed. Hill's 85th minute effort allowed overwhelmed Windsor the distinction of being only the third team to score twice at Plough Lane this season.											
2 H SWINDON		9 W	2-0	2-0	Denny 3, Leslie 18	Beasant	Brown	Jones	Galliers	Smith	Cunningham	Ketteridge*	Hodges	Leslie	Cork	Denny	Hubbick
13/12	3,470	*3:17*				*Allan*	*Walsh**	*Peach*	*Kamara*	*Lewis*	*Stroud*	*Miller*	*Carter*	*Greenwood*	*Mayes*	*Williams*	*Hughes*
					Ref: B Daniels	Wimbledon exact revenge for their League Cup defeat by Swindon last season. Dave Beasant was pleased with his performance, having recently made howlers. 'The season could hinge on this win,' said Dario Gradi, though he would not be around to see it.											
3 H OLDHAM		12 D	0-0	0-0		Beasant	Jones	Armstrong	Galliers	Smith	Cunningham*	Ketteridge	Denny	Leslie	Cork	Hubbick	Downes
3/1	4,693	*2:15*				*Platt*	*Edwards*	*Blair*	*Keegan*	*Clements*	*Hurst*	*Wylde*	*Futcher!*	*Steel*	*Palmer*	*Kowenicki*	
					Ref: M Baker	Oldham have Paul Futcher sent off after 27 minutes after he struck Tommy Cunningham. The nearest to a goal was when Steve Ketteridge hit the bar. John Leslie played in midfield, but still fired in three shots at John Platt. The Dons won the territorial battle with ease.											
3R A OLDHAM		W	1-0	0-0	Cork 86	Beasant	Jones	Armstrong	Galliers	Smith	Brown	Ketteridge	Denny	Leslie	Cork	Hubbick*	Hodges
6/1	*6,789*	*2:15*				*Platt*	*Edwards*	*Blair*	*Keegan*	*Clements*	*Hurst*	*Wylde*	*Atkinson**	*Steel*	*Palmer*	*Kowenicki*	*Hilton*
					Ref: M Baker	Four minutes from extra-time, transfer-listed Alan Cork sinks Oldham, who forced 11 corners to Wimbledon's two. Earlier, John Platt had touched Hubbick's header onto a post. Oldham had won just twice in 20 games in Division 2. Gradi gets his manager of the month award.											
4 A WREXHAM		L	1-2	0-1	Denny 68	Beasant	Jones	Armstrong	Galliers	Smith	Cunningham	Ketteridge	Hodges*	Denny	Cork	Downes	Hubbick
24/1	*12,267*	*2:16*			*Fox 36, McNeil 58*	*Davies*	*Hill*	*Kenworthy*	*Jones J*	*Cegielski*	*Arkwright*	*Fox*	*Sutton*	*Edwards*	*McNeil*	*Cartwright*	
					Ref: J Hunting	2nd Division Wrexham have just put out FA Cup-holders West Ham. The timeless Dixie McNeil has been the scourge of opposing defences for many years. He heads Wrexham's second, killer goal, but sets up a storming finish from the Dons. Sub Hubbick misses the best chance.											

	Home						Away					
	P	W	D	L	F	A	W	D	L	F	A	Pts
1 Southend	46	19	4	0	47	6	11	3	9	32	25	67
2 Lincoln	46	15	7	1	44	11	10	8	5	22	14	65
3 Doncaster	46	15	4	4	36	20	7	8	8	23	29	56
4 WIMBLEDON	46	15	4	4	42	17	8	5	10	22	29	55
5 Peterborough	46	11	8	4	37	21	6	10	7	31	33	52
6 Aldershot	46	12	9	2	28	11	6	5	12	15	30	50
7 Mansfield	46	13	5	5	36	15	7	4	12	22	29	49
8 Darlington	46	13	6	4	43	23	6	5	12	22	36	49
9 Hartlepool	46	14	3	6	42	22	6	6	11	22	39	49
10 Northampton	46	11	7	5	42	26	7	6	10	23	41	49
11 Wigan	46	13	4	6	29	16	5	7	11	22	39	47
12 Bury	46	10	8	5	38	21	7	3	13	32	41	45
13 Bournemouth	46	9	8	6	30	21	7	5	11	17	27	45
14 Bradford City	46	9	9	5	30	24	5	7	11	23	36	44
15 Rochdale	46	11	6	6	33	25	3	9	11	27	45	43
16 Scunthorpe	46	8	12	3	40	31	3	8	12	20	38	42
17 Torquay	46	13	2	8	38	26	5	3	15	17	37	41
18 Crewe	46	10	7	6	28	20	3	7	13	20	41	40
19 Port Vale	46	10	8	5	40	23	2	7	14	17	47	39
20 Stockport	46	10	5	8	29	25	6	2	15	15	32	39
21 Tranmere	46	12	5	6	41	24	1	5	17	18	49	36
22 Hereford	46	8	8	7	29	20	3	5	15	9	42	35
23 Halifax	46	9	3	11	28	32	2	9	12	16	39	34
24 York	46	10	2	11	31	23	2	7	14	16	43	33
	1104	280	144	128	861	503	128	144	280	503	861	1104

Odds & ends

Double wins: (7) Port Vale, Crewe, Halifax, Hartlepool, York, Torquay, Bournemouth.

Double losses: (2) Southend, Bury.

Won from behind: (2) Peterborough (h), Port Vale (a).

Lost from in front: (1) Stockport (h).

High spots: 12-match unbeaten league run from December to March.

Reaching Round 4 of the FA Cup.

Low spots: 1 win in 5 games between 3rd October and 21st October.

In a full season, 55 points is the lowest ever to be rewarded with promotion from Division 4.

Player of the Year: Dave Beasant.

Ever-presents: (0).

Hat-tricks: Alan Cork (1), Dave Hubbick (1).

Leading scorer: Alan Cork (26).

	Appearances						Goals			
	Lge	Sub	LC	Sub	FAC	Sub	Lge	LC	FAC	Total
Armstrong, Gary	**35**		2		4					
Beasant, Dave	**34**				5					
Belfield, Mick	**1**									
Brown, Peter	**26**	(2)	2		2					
Cork, Alan	**41**		4		5		23	1	2	**26**
Cunningham, Tom	**43**		4		4		4	1	1	**6**
Davies, Roy	**6**	(3)	3							
Denny, Paul	**21**	(5)	1	(1)	4		1	1	2	**4**
Downes, Wally	**34**		4		1	(1)	4	1		**5**
Driver, Phil	**4**	(1)	2				2			**2**
Gage, Kevin	**1**									
Galliers, Steve	**37**		4		5		4			**4**
Goddard, Ray	**12**		4				1			**1**
Hodges, Glyn	**27**	(3)			3	(1)	5			**5**
Hubbick, Dave	**20**	(2)			3	(2)	4		3	**7**
Jones, Steve	**24**	(2)	2		5					
Joseph, Francis	**4**	(7)					1			**1**
Ketteridge, Steve	**38**	(1)	2		5		1			**1**
Leslie, John	**43**	(1)	4		4		11	3	1	**15**
Perkins, Steve	**11**		2							
Smith, Mick	**44**	(1)	4		5		2		2	**4**
(own-goals)							1			**1**
21 players used	**506**	**(28)**	**44**	**(1)**	**55**	**(4)**	**64**	**7**	**11**	**82**

No	Date		Att	Pos	Pts	F-A	H-T	Scorers, Times, and Referees	1	2	3	4	5	6	7	8	9	10	11	12 sub used
1	A	SWINDON			L	1-4	0-1	Ketteridge 74 *[Greenwood 77]*	Beasant	Brown	Armstrong	Galliers	Smith	Jones	Ketteridge	Joseph	Leslie	Cork	Hodges*	Gage
	29/8		*5,632*		–			*Carter 14, Graham 53, Hughes 62*	*Allan*	*Henry*	*Williams*	*Hughes*	*Lewis*	*Graham*	*Carter R*	*Emmanuel*	*Rowland*	*Greenwood*	*Moores*	
								Ref: J Bray	Wimbledon have enjoyed good pre-season performances in the Group Cup. Swindon missed relegation by one point last season, so the Dons must be hopeful of some reward. They force 14 corners to Swindon's five, and hit the post twice, but the Dons' defence looks woeful.											
2	H	MILLWALL			L	1-3	0-1	Joseph 78	Beasant	Jones	Armstrong	Galliers	Smith	Cunningham	Ketteridge	Joseph	Leslie	Cork	Downes	
	5/9		5,102		–			*Anderson 16, Dibble 79, 90*	*Gleasure*	*Roberts*	*Warman*	*Chatterton*	*Tagg*	*Martin*	*Dibble*	*Anderson*	*Horrix*	*Hayes**	*West*	*Massey*
								Ref: B Stevens	The Lions' player-manager, Peter Anderson, opens the scoring and also makes another goal. Once again the Dons only come to life once the game has slipped away. Millwall's Chris Dibble will only score one more goal all season. Chelsea's Bobby Gould joins the Dons non-contract.											
3	A	HUDDERSFIELD			D	1-1	0-0	Leslie 55	Beasant	Jones	Armstrong	Galliers	Smith	Cunningham	Ketteridge	Joseph	Leslie	Cork	Downes	
	12/9		*7,326*		1			*Fletcher 63*	*Rankin*	*Brown*	*Burke*	*Stanton**	*Sutton*	*Purdie*	*Lillis*	*Kennedy*	*Fletcher*	*Kindon*	*Wilson*	*Robins*
								Ref: R Nixon	Neither side has yet managed a win. Huddersfield missed promotion by one place last season, but it is Wimbledon who appear to be panicking. Strikers Alan Cork and John Leslie have been threatened with the sack, and Tommy Cunningham has signed for Orient for £40,000.											
4	H	DONCASTER		23	L	0-1	0-0		Beasant	Jones	Armstrong	Galliers	Smith	Downes	Ketteridge*	Gage	Leslie	Cork!	Hodges	Hubbick
	19/9		2,364	*9*	1			*Warboys 82p*	*Boyd*	*Russell*	*Dawson*	*Snodin I*	*Lally**	*Dowd*	*Pugh*	*Harle*	*Warboys*	*Lister*	*Douglas*	*Nimmo!*
								Ref: M Taylor	This match was decided by penalty kicks and sendings off. Alan Cork missed his kick – Willie Boyd saving after 30 minutes. Later on, Cork was sent off, followed by Doncaster sub Ian Nimmo. Beasant drops the ball for Alan Warboys. Tempers flared again after the final whistle.											
5	H	FULHAM		23	L	1-3	0-1	Leslie 48	Beasant	Jones	Armstrong	Galliers	Smith	Downes	Ketteridge	Gage*	Leslie	Cork	Hodges	Hubbick
	22/9		**5,554**	*12*	1			*Coney 2, 60, Davies 88*	*Peyton*	*Hopkins*	*Strong*	*O'Driscoll*	*Brown*	*Gale*	*Davies*	*Wilson*	*Coney*	*O'Sullivan*	*Lewington*	
								Ref: T Spencer	This south-west London derby attracts Plough Lane's biggest gate of the season. Fulham's Dean Coney is only 18, but he scores twice to extend Wimbledon's early season agony. Highly rated Gordon Davies gets Fulham's third. Ex-Don Ray Lewington lines up for Fulham.											
6	A	WALSALL			L	0-1	0-0		Beasant	Brown	Jones	Galliers	Smith	Downes	Ketteridge	Hodges	Leslie	Cork*	Joseph	Gage
	26/9		*3,027*		1			*Penn 75*	*Green*	*Macken*	*Mower*	*Beech*	*Serella*	*Hart*	*Rees*	*WaddingtonS*	*Penn*	*Buckley**	*Caswell*	*Round*
								Ref: T Fitzharris	Walsall's survival in Division 3, through two late penalties at Bramall Lane, is the stuff of legend. Fellows Park now brings personal misery to Alan Cork, who misses a penalty, then collides with keeper Ron Green and breaks a leg. Don Penn scores, then misses from the penalty spot.											
7	A	BRISTOL ROV			D	2-2	0-0	Hubbick 47, 66	Beasant	Brown	**Thomas**	Galliers	Smith	Jones	Ketteridge	Armstrong	Hubbick*	Downes	Hodges	Joseph
	29/9		*5,364*		2			*Mabbutt 46, 65*	*Kite*	*Gillies*	*Slatter*	*McCaffery*	*Parkin*	*Hughes*	*Barrett*	*Williams D*	*Mabbutt*	*Randall*	*Williams G*	
								Ref: A Glasson	Bristol Rovers propped up Division 2 last season. The Dons are depleted by the loss of Cork (broken shin-bone), Leslie (flu), and Gage (playing in Australia in the World Youth Championships). Two goals by young Gary Mabbutt are quickly erased by two from Dave Hubbick.											
8	H	GILLINGHAM		24	L	0-2	0-1		Beasant	Jones	Thomas*	Galliers	Smith	Boyle	Ketteridge!	Hodges	Hubbick	Downes	Armstrong	**Lazarus**
	3/10		2,510	*13*	2			*Bowman 24, 83p*	*Hillyard*	*Sitton*	*Ford*	*Bruce*	*Weatherly*	*Bowman*	*White*	*Duncan*	*Tydeman*	*Lee*	*Price*	
								Ref: D Letts	The Gills' team includes Steve Bruce, the future Manchester United captain. This match offers five bookings, two penalties, and a sending off (Ketteridge for dissent). Hodges' penalty was saved by Ron Hillyard. Gills' Richie Bowman was more accurate with his spot-kick.											
9	A	LINCOLN		24	L	1-5	1-2	Leslie 37 *[Cammack 64, Hobson 67]*	Beasant	Jones	Thomas	Galliers	Smith	Boyle	Ketteridge	Hodges	Leslie	Downes	Lazarus	
	10/10		*3,168*	*11*	2			*Cockerill 15, 77, Cunningham 25,*	*Felgate*	*Thompson T*	*McVay*	*Cockerill*	*Peake*	*Carr*	*Cammack*	*Shipley*	*Hobson*	*Cunningham*	*Neale**	*Bell*
								Ref: A Robinson	The Dons are spiked by 4th Division runners-up Lincoln City, who have made a quiet start to life in Division 3, but will soon step on the accelerator. Last season Wimbledon managed a 0-0 draw at Sincil Bank. This will be Lincoln's best win; it won't be the Dons' worst loss.											
10	H	CHESTER			W	1-0	1-0	Lazarus 15	Beasant	Brown	Jones	Galliers	Smith	Boyle	Leslie	Hodges	Lazarus	Downes	**Suddaby**	
	17/10		1,659		5				*Millington*	*Needham*	*Raynor*	*Storton*	*Cottam*	*Oakes*	*Jones**	*Simpson*	*Ludlam*	*Phillips*	*Sutcliffe*	*Burns*
								Ref: E Read	The Dons had managed just two points from nine games. With three points for a win, they are adrift of the pack. Chester have only lost once so far, though they will finish bottom. Paul Lazarus, over from Finland, has two goals disallowed in front of the smallest gate for three seasons.											
11	H	PLYMOUTH		23	W	2-1	0-0	Joseph 80, Boyle 90	Beasant	Brown	Jones*	Galliers	Smith	Suddaby	**Boyle**	Leslie	Lazarus	Downes	Hodges	Joseph
	20/10		2,114	*24*	8			*Randall 85*	*Crudgington*	*Nisbet*	*McCartney*	*Phill-Masters*	*Foster*	*Cooper*	*Hodges*	*Cook*	*Sims*	*Randell*	*Rogers*	
								Ref: D Axcell	Six points in four days. That's more like it. All the action is saved for the end. Plymouth are winless at the foot of the table. It is Galliers' last match before transferring to Palace for £70,000. Terry Boyle, on loan from Palace, scores with the last kick. Steve Jones is out for the season.											

No	Venue	Opponent / Date	Att	Pos	Pt	F-A	H-T	Scorers, Times, and Referees	1	2	3	4	5	6	7	8	9	10	11	12
		24/10	3,732	9	8			Webb 40p, Hicks 43	Fearon	Williams	Lewis	Hicks	Wood	Dixon	Heale	Kearney	Beavon	Webb	Sanchez*	Earles
								Ref: L Robinson	After a runaway start to the season, this is Reading's first win in six games. Future England international Neil Webb scores with a disputed penalty. A Sanchez free-kick sets up No 2. Peter Brown replies from the spot, his first goal for the Dons, after Jerry Williams felled Joseph.											
13	H	EXETER		24	D	1-1	1-0	Lazarus 23	Beasant	**Clement**	Brown	Gage	Smith	**Morris**	Leslie*	Ketteridge	Lazarus	Downes	Joseph	Hodges
		31/10	2,152	15	9			Lester 68	Bond	Rogers M	Sparrow	Lester	Roberts P	Davey	Cooke*	Rogers P	Kellow	Delve	Pullar	Pratt
								Ref: J Hunting	Wimbledon have two new boys. One is ex-QPR, ex-England full-back Dave Clement. He had been with Rangers for 17 years. In the second half, Exeter lost their keeper, Len Bond, with a rib injury. Having used their sub, they are down to 10 men. Then Mick Smith is stretchered off.											
14	A	PORTSMOUTH		24	L	0-1	0-0		Beasant	Clement	Brown	Gage	Morris	**Geddes**	Leslie*	Ketteridge	Lazarus	Downes	Joseph	**Fishenden**
		3/11	9,063	16	9			Cropley 73	Knight	Ellis	Viney	Doyle	Garner	Rollings	Hemmerman	Tait	Rafferty*	Cropley	Crown	Gregory
								Ref: D Lloyd	With seven players incapacitated by injury, Wimbledon wanted to postpone this match. The Football League refused, so debuts were given to Paul Geddes and Paul Fishenden, on the bench. Alex Cropley (ex-Hibernian) steals the winner for cash-strapped Pompey.											
15	A	BURNLEY		24	D	2-2	0-1	Lazarus 55, Clement 81	Beasant	Clement	Brown	Gage	Morris	Geddes	Leslie	Ketteridge	Lazarus	Downes	Joseph	
		7/11	4,231	20	10			Hamilton 28, Overson 82	Stevenson	Laws	Wharton	Cassidy	Overson	Phelan	Potts	Steven	Hamilton	McGee	Young	
								Ref: A Saunders	Burnley will overturn a dreadful start to the season to win the title. They are now seven games into a 20-match unbeaten run. They missed chances galore in this match, yet came within nine minutes of losing it, when Dave Clement rifled in a free-kick. Burnley hit back at once.											
16	H	PRESTON		24	W	3-2	1-2	Leslie 16, 63, Belfield 78	Beasant	Clement	Brown	Gage	Morris	Suddaby	Leslie	Ketteridge!	Lazarus	Downes	Joseph*	Belfield
		14/11	2,428	22	13			Dunn 8, Bruce 23	Litchfield	Coleman*	McAteer	Clark	Anderson	O'Riordan	Buckley!	Elliott	Bruce	Doyle	Dunn	Naughton
								Ref: D Hedges	Tommy Docherty's Preston can't get going. Clement captains the Dons to this important win, in a match having two expulsions, five goals and a missed penalty – by Preston stalwart Alex Bruce – whose kick hits the post. Ketteridge and Buckley were sent off for fisticuffs.											
17	A	CHESTERFIELD		24	L	0-2	0-1		Beasant	Clement	Armstrong	Gage*	Morris	Suddaby	Brown	Leslie	Hodges	Downes	Joseph	Belfield
		28/11	4,604	1	13			Henderson 18, Walker 55	Turner	Stirk	O'Neill	Wilson	Green	Pollard	Windridge	Henderson	Bonnyman	Kowalski	Walker	
								Ref: D Owen	This match provided one of those 'was it' or 'wasn't it' moments. Wimbledon were two goals down to the league leaders when, on the hour, Wally Downes' shot came back off a stanchion and the referee ruled play on. Downes was booked for protesting the matter too vehemently.											
18	H	NEWPORT		24	L	2-3	0-2	Clement 65, Lazarus 73	Beasant	Clement	Armstrong	Fishenden	Morris	Suddaby	Brown	Leslie	Lazarus	Downes	Joseph	
		5/12	2,056	16	13			Tynan 4, Elsey 8, Waddle 57	Kendall	Walden	Relish	Davies	Oakes	Bailey	Vaughan	Lowndes	Waddle	Tynan	Elsey	Bishop
								Ref: I Borrett	Newport have the soon-to-be-famous John Aldridge missing. Even without him, and having won just twice in 14 games, County have too much firepower, despite the Dons' late fight-back. Dave Beasant is blamed for some of the goals, and his star appears to be fading.											
19	A	BRISTOL CITY		23	W	3-1	1-1	Ketteridge 40, Lazarus 64, 77	Beasant	Clement	Thomas	Smith	Morris	Downes	Ketteridge	Leslie	Lazarus	Hodges	Joseph	
		2/1	4,660	21	16			Stevens 43	Moller	Stevens	Williams	Aitken	Boyle	Nicholas	Tainton	Mann	Chandler	Harford	Devine*	Sweeney
								Ref: K Barratt	Bristol City, just down from Division 2, are heading for a second successive relegation. Manager Bob Houghton resigns before the match, replaced as caretaker by Roy Hodgson (who will lead Switzerland in USA '94). Wimbledon climb off the bottom with their first away win.											
20	H	SWINDON		24	D	1-1	1-0	Ketteridge 18	Beasant	Clement	Thomas	Smith	Morris	Downes	Ketteridge	Leslie	**Blochel**	Hodges	Joseph	
		23/1	2,084	20	17			Rideout 86	Allan	Henry	Baddeley	Williams	Lewis	Stroud	Emmanuel	Carter R	Rideout	Greenwood	Pritchard	
								Ref: J Deakin	This makes it 11 without a win for struggling Swindon. Paul Rideout, former England schoolboy international, deprives the Dons of two valuable points with his late leveller. Wimbledon give a run out to Joe Blochel, a 19-year-old striker on loan from Southampton.											
21	A	DONCASTER		24	W	3-1	2-1	Blochel 18, Leslie 36, 70	Beasant	Clement	Thomas	Smith	Morris	Downes	Ketteridge*	Leslie	Blochel	Hodges	Joseph	Gage
		29/1	5,849	15	20			Dawson 4	Humphries S	Lally	Cooper	Snodin I	Parkinson	Dowd	Pugh*	Dawson	Douglas	Snodin G	Lister	Russell
								Ref: J Haugh	Doncaster haven't won since October, not even with their defence shored up by ex-England star Terry Cooper. Wimbledon take the lead when Cooper's pass is charged down by Blochel. 10 minutes from time Dave Clement breaks a leg, but the Dons hold out with 10 men.											
22	H	HUDDERSFIELD		24	W	2-0	1-0	Ketteridge 8, 81	Beasant	Brown	Thomas	Smith	Morris	Downes	Ketteridge	Leslie	Blochel	Armstrong	Joseph	
		6/2	2,499	16	23				Taylor	Brown	Burke	Stanton	Sutton	Hanvey	Lillis	Kennedy	Hotte*	Austin	Cowling	Wilson
								Ref: A Seville	10 points from four games has not been enough to lift the Dons off the basement. Ketteridge's double takes his seasons tally to six. Huddersfield's problem is there for all to see; their top scorer this season won't exceed eight goals. The Dons' first clean sheet for four months.											
23	A	FULHAM		24	L	1-4	0-1	Ketteridge 55 [Wilson 85]	Beasant	Brown	Thomas	Smith	Morris	Downes	Ketteridge	Lazarus	Blochel	Armstrong	Joseph	
		9/2	7,802	1	23			Coney 12, 89, Downes 75 (og),	Peyton	Lock	Strong	O'Driscoll	Brown	Gale	Davies	Wilson	Coney	O'Sullivan	Lewington	
								Ref: K Baker	Fulham are unbeaten in 10 games, and are embarked on a successful promotion push. They complete a double over the Dons, inspired by ex-Don Ray Lewington. Downes' own-goal gives Wimbledon a mountain to climb. Wimbledon's first visit to Craven Cottage for half a century.											

No	Date		Att	Pos	Pts	F-A	H-T	Scorers, Times, and Referees	1	2	3	4	5	6	7	8	9	10	11	12 sub used
24	A	GILLINGHAM		24	L	**1-6**	1-3	Ketteridge 40p *[Bruce 80, Cascarino 86]*	Beasant	Brown	Thomas*	Smith	Morris	Downes	Ketteridge	Lazarus	Blochel	Armstrong	Joseph	Hodges
	13/2		*4,214*	*12*	23			*White 4p, Price 30, 34, Brown 70 (og),*	*Hillyard*	*Sharpe*	*Adams*	*Bruce*	*Sitton*	*Duncan*	*Powell*	*Tydeman*	*White**	*Kemp*	*Price*	*Cascarino*
								Ref: D Civil	Tony Cascarino joins Steve Bruce in this demolition. Gillingham went into this match without a win in eight, during which they had scored just three goals. For the second successive match a Ketteridge goal is undone by a cruel own-goal. Cascarino's is his first ever goal.											
25	H	BRISTOL ROV		24	W	1-0	0-0	Smith 73	Beasant	Gage	Armstrong	Smith	Morris	Downes	Ketteridge	Lazarus	Blochel	Hodges	Joseph	
	20/2		2,408	8	26				*Kite*	*Hughes*	*Parkin*	*Mabbutt*	*Bailey*	*Williams D*	*Parkin*	*Holloway*	*Barrett**	*Randall*	*Kelly*	*Curle*
								Ref: C Maskell	This is Mick Smith's 100th first-team game for the Dons. He is made captain for the day, and celebrates by scoring the only goal of the game. Having conceded 10 goals in two games, a defensive clean sheet is highly welcome. Rovers' new-boy Kelly saw his effort headed off the line.											
26	A	MILLWALL		24	L	1-2	0-0	Fishenden 64	Beasant	Gage	Armstrong	Smith	Morris	Brown	Ketteridge	Lazarus	Fishenden	Hodges	Joseph	
	24/2		*4,072*	*10*	26			*Shinton 73, Chatterton 88p*	*Gleasure*	*Roberts*	*Warman*	*Chatterton*	*Allardyce*	*Tagg*	*Shinton*	*Massey*	*Horrix*	*Neal*	*West*	
								Ref: B Hill	The Dons play seven at the back in an attempt to squeeze a point out of the Den. They might have had three points had they clung on to Paul Fishenden's first goal for the club. They are denied any by a late disputed penalty, for which Armstrong was booked for protesting.											
27	H	LINCOLN		24	D	1-1	1-0	Gage 10	Beasant	Gage	Armstrong	Smith	Brown	Downes	Ketteridge	Lazarus	Fishenden*	Hodges	Joseph	Leslie
	27/2		2,094	11	27			*Cockerill 54*	*Felgate*	*Carr*	*Turner P*	*Cockerill*	*Peake*	*Thompson S*	*Shipley*	*Turner W*	*Hobson*	*Cunningham*	*Hibberd**	*Gilbert*
								Ref: A Robinson	Wimbledon are not in the habit of beating Lincoln, but for much of this dreadful game they lead by Kevin Gage's first league goal – a 20-yard volley. Midfielder Glenn Cockerill scored twice against the Dons at Sincil Bank, and it is he who punctures their spirits this time.											
28	H	READING		24	D	0-0	0-0		Beasant	Brown	Armstrong	Smith	Morris	Downes	Ketteridge	Lazarus	Leslie*	Hodges	Joseph	**Elliott**
	13/3		2,551	4	28				*Fearon*	*Williams*	*Lewis*	*Webb*	*Hicks*	*Hetzke*	*Beavon*	*Kearney*	*Dixon*	*Sanchez*	*Donnellan**	*Cullen*
								Ref: B Stevens	This match threw up an intriguing duel between two players making a name for themselves, Dave Beasant versus Kerry Dixon. Beasant won, though Dixon hit a post and the ball flew across the goal-line. The Reading side also included Neil Webb and Lawrie Sanchez.											
29	A	EXETER		24	L	1-2	1-2	Joseph 30	Beasant	Brown	Armstrong	Smith*	Morris	Downes	Ketteridge	Joseph	**Evans**	Hodges	Elliott	Leslie
	20/3		*3,002*	*15*	28			*Pratt 14, Kellow 40*	*Main*	*Kirkup*	*Sparrow*	*Rogers M*	*Foster*	*Roberts P*	*Pratt*	*Rogers P*	*Kellow**	*Pullar*	*Delve*	*Marker*
								Ref: L Burden	Wimbledon introduce lofty Stewart Evans, on loan from Sheffield United. He doesn't get a look in as Exeter dominate. The closeness of the score is entirely down to Dave Beasant. Glyn Hodges almost caught Exeter goalkeeper Ian Main off his line in the closing seconds.											
30	H	SOUTHEND		23	W	**3-0**	2-0	Smith 15, Evans 30, Joseph 65	Beasant	Brown	Armstrong	Smith	Morris	Downes	Ketteridge	Joseph	Evans	Hodges*	Elliott	Leslie
	23/3		2,051	*11*	31				*Keeley*	*Dudley*	*Yates*	*Pennyfather**	*Moody*	*Cusack*	*Pountney*	*Phillips*	*Nelson*	*Mercer*	*Otulakowski*	*Greaves*
								Ref: A Grey	Southend, one win in 12, present the Dons with their biggest win of the season, and takes them off the bottom. New boys Mark Elliott and Stewart Evans both catch the eye. Smith and Evans score with headers. Dave Beasant is booked before kick-off for marking out his goal.											
31	H	BURNLEY		23	D	0-0	0-0		Beasant	Brown	Armstrong	Smith	Morris	Downes	Ketteridge	Joseph	Evans	Leslie*	Elliott	Belfield
	27/3		2,641	*6*	32				*Stevenson*	*Laws*	*Anderson*	*Scott*	*Overson*	*Phelan**	*Dobson*	*Steven*	*Hamilton*	*McGee*	*Young*	*Potts*
								Ref: A Glasson	Burnley arrive having lost just once in 24 league games. In the circumstances, this is a creditable point for the Dons, though Ketteridge's 34th-minute penalty was kept out by Alan Stevenson. The ref permitted seven minutes' injury time, mostly for Mike Phelan's fractured cheekbone.											
32	A	CHESTER		23	D	1-1	0-0	Joseph 82	Beasant	Brown!	Armstrong	Smith	Morris	Downes!	Ketteridge	Joseph	Evans	Leslie	Elliott*	Belfield
	31/3		***1,359***	*24*	33			*Simpson 70*	*Millington*	*Raynor*	*Burns*	*Cottam*	*Zelem*	*Blackwell*	*Sutcliffe*	*Jones*	*Simpson*	*Ludlam*	*Henderson*	
								Ref: J Key	Wimbledon FC is stunned by the suicide of Dave Clement. It was intended to keep the news from the players until after the final whistle, but news leaked out. Alan Oakes had just been sacked as Chester manager. Brown and Downes are sent off, but the Dons still salvage a point.											
33	A	PRESTON		23	L	2-3	0-1	Leslie 60, Brown 89	Beasant	Brown	Armstrong	Smith	Morris	Downes	Ketteridge	Joseph	Evans	Hodges	Belfield*	Leslie
	3/4		*4,964*	*18*	33			*Bruce 10, 87, O'Riordan 50*	*Hodge*	*Anderson*	*McAteer*	*Naughton*	*Booth*	*O'Riordan*	*Kelly*	*Doyle*	*Elliott*	*Buckley*	*Bruce*	
								Ref: C Newsome	Wimbleon have collected just 33 league points, but over 250 disciplinary points. Bassett's team is also stricken with injuries. The manager does not like scoring two away goals with no return. John Leslie had looped an overhead kick into goal from a near impossible angle.											
34	A	SOUTHEND		23	L	0-2	0-2		Beasant	Brown	Armstrong	Smith	Morris	Downes	Gage	Joseph	Evans	Hodges	Lazarus*	Elliott
	9/4		*4,779*	*11*	33			*Cusack p, Mercer*	*Cawston*	*Stead*	*Yates*	*Pountney*	*Moody*	*Cusack*	*Greaves*	*Phillips*	*Spence*	*Mercer*	*Otulakowski*	
								Ref: V Callow	Southend are making a late charge for promotion, and easily avenge their heavy defeat of a fortnight earlier. Danny Greaves hasn't the eye for goal of his famous dad. Following Hodges' clumsy challenge, Cusack scores from the spot. He and Otulakowski later sign for Millwall.											

No	Date	Opponent	Att	Pos	Pts	Res	F-A	H-T	Scorers, Times, and Referees												
	12/4		4,513	*10*	33				*Hurlock 60, Roberts 75*	*McKellar*	*McNichol*	*Tucker*	*Salman*	*Whitehead**	*Hurlock*	*Booker*	*Johnson G*	*Bowen*	*Bowles*	*Roberts*	*Harris*
									Ref: M Dimblebee	Brentford's player-coach is Ron 'Chopper' Harris of Chelsea fame. Brentford looked to be heading for defeat until he came on to stiffen his team. Other notable Bees include the much-travelled Stan Bowles, and Terry Hurlock, later to sign for Glasgow Rangers.											
36	A	PLYMOUTH		23		L	0-2	0-0		Beasant	Thomas	Armstrong	Smith	Morris	Belfield	Elliott	**Hughes***	Leslie	Evans	Joseph	Gage
	14/4		*4,748*	*6*	33				*Nisbet 68, Sims 84*	*Crudgington*	*Nisbet*	*Uzzell*	*Harrison*	*Phill-Masters*	*Cooper*	*Hodges*	*Cook*	*Sims*	*McCartney**	*Rogers*	*Rowe*
									Ref: T Spencer	This is Plymouth's seventh win in nine games. The Dons give a baptism to Billy Hughes, a free transfer from Crystal Palace. The result might have been more favourable to the Dons had Francis Joseph's shot which hit the bar at 0-0 gone in. Joseph missed two other chances as well.											
37	A	NEWPORT		23		D	0-0	0-0		Beasant	Thomas	Armstrong	Smith	Morris	Belfield	Hughes*	Leslie	Evans	Fishenden	Elliott	Ketteridge
	17/4		*3,900*	*20*	34					*Kendall*	*Walden*	*Relish*	*Davies*	*Oakes*	*Johnson*	*Elsey*	*Lowndes*	*Tynan*	*Aldridge**	*Moore*	*Gwyther*
									Ref: R Bridges	Struggling Newport have won their last three. John Aldridge is playing this time, and he hits the bar with a header. In injury time Paul Fishenden heads over the top when he should have scored. This tedious match was not helped by a strong wind that blew passes astray.											
38	H	OXFORD		23		L	2-3	2-1	Evans 5, Joseph 39	Beasant	Leslie	Armstrong	Smith	Morris	Downes	Ketteridge	Joseph	Hodges	Evans	Belfield	
	20/4		2,903	*4*	34				*Hebberd 30, Lawrence 63, Leslie 79 (og)*	*Burton*	*Fogg*	*Smithers*	*Train*	*Briggs*	*Shotton*	*Lawrence*	*Foley**	*Hebberd*	*Brock*	*Thomas*	*Kearns*
									Ref: J Bodenham	Oxford are battling for promotion. Wimbledon's longest-serving player – John Leslie – playing full-back, spoils a fighting Dons performance with a messy own-goal, sticking out a leg to try to push it back to Dave Beasant. Wimbledon had twice been in front, so this is a cruel defeat.											
39	H	CHESTERFIELD		22		W	3-1	1-0	Belfield 28, 52, Hodges 57	Beasant	Leslie	Armstrong	Smith	Morris	Downes	Ketteridge	Joseph	Hodges	Evans	Belfield	
	24/4		2,138	*8*	37				*Walker 86*	*Turner*	*Bellamy*	*O'Neill*	*Wilson*	*Green*	*Hunter*	*Henson**	*Henderson*	*Bonnyman*	*Kowalski*	*Crawford*	*Walker*
									Ref: R Milford	There are just eight matches to go. The Dons look doomed, but they now turn on promotion form. Mick Belfield takes the honours, but his first goal was against the run of play. Leslie becomes the first Don to play 200 league games, while Ketteridge leaves the ground on crutches.											
40	A	BRENTFORD		22		W	3-2	0-2	Joseph 52, 67, Belfield 61	Beasant	Leslie	Armstrong	Smith	Morris	Downes*	Thomas	Joseph	Hodges	Evans	Belfield	Gage
	26/4		*6,612*	*7*	40				*Bowles 11, Johnson 36*	*McKellar*	*McNichol*	*Tucker*	*Salmon*	*Whitehead*	*Hurlock*	*Kamara*	*Johnson G*	*Bowen**	*Bowles*	*Roberts*	*Booker*
									Ref: B Daniels	Brentford's wretched home record will cost them promotion. Stan Bowles' stunning free-kick might have demoralised the Dons, especially when Gary Johnson doubles the lead. But in-form Mick Belfield and Francis Joseph (seven goals in 12 games) turn the game around.											
41	A	CARLISLE		22		L	1-2	1-0	Hodges 15	Beasant	Leslie	Armstrong	Smith	Morris	Downes	Thomas	Joseph	Hodges	Evans	Belfield	
	1/5		*4,466*	*1*	40				*Staniforth 57p, Leslie 79 (og)*	*Swinburne*	*Parker*	*Rushbury*	*Larkin*	*Ashurst*	*Craig*	*Ritchie*	*Coughlin*	*Robson*	*Lee*	*Staniforth*	
									Ref: P Tyldesley	Carlisle are on the winning run that will take them up. But they need a mysterious penalty and yet another Leslie own-goal to overtake Glyn Hodges' 25-yard shot that he appeared to scuff. Bob Lee was bundled over for the penalty. Barring improbable results, Wimbledon are down.											
42	H	WALSALL		22		W	2-0	1-0	Serella 26 (og), Evans 72	Beasant	Leslie	Armstrong	Smith	Morris	Downes	Thomas	Joseph	Hodges	Evans	Belfield	
	4/5		**1,503**	*20*	43					*Green*	*Macken*	*Mower*	*Baines*	*Serella*	*Hart*	*Rees*	*Caswell*	*Round**	*Buckley*	*WaddingtonS*	*O'Kelly*
									Ref: J Martin	Walsall will escape relegation by a coat of paint for the second season running. Wimbledon fans stay away in droves, presuming their team is down. This young, makeshift Dons side is inspired by the outstanding player on the field, Glyn Hodges. Pity so few were there to watch him.											
43	H	BRISTOL CITY		22		D	0-0	0-0		Beasant	Leslie	Armstrong	Smith	Morris	Downes	Thomas	Hodges	Joseph	Evans	Belfield*	Ketteridge
	8/5		2,114	*23*	44					*Shaw*	*Stevens*	*Hay*	*Musker*	*Nicholls*	*Williams*	*Bray*	*Devine*	*Chandler*	*Newman*	*Economou*	
									Ref: D Axcell	Bristol City, one win in 14, are already down. With hindsight, had Francis Joseph's header gone in, instead of coming back off a post, Wimbledon would have escaped relegation. The players trooped off afterwards stony-faced, and were dragged back for Sunday training.											
44	H	CARLISLE		22		W	3-1	1-0	Evans 36, Joseph 71, 75	Beasant	Leslie	Gage	Smith	Morris	Downes	Thomas	Joseph	Hodges	Evans	Ketteridge	
	11/5		2,022	*2*	47				*Coughlin 64*	*Swinburne*	*Parker*	*Rushbury*	*Houghton*	*Ashurst*	*Craig*	*Ritchie*	*Coughlin*	*Robson*	*Lee**	*Bannon*	*Staniforth*
									Ref: S Bates	Carlisle's sprint to the finishing line is stalled by Wimbledon's never-say-die approach. Francis Joseph scores his 10th and 11th goals of the season. It is little consolation for Carlisle that Russell Coughlin's 25-yard scorcher is the goal of the match. Stewart Evans kneed his goal.											
45	A	OXFORD		22		W	**3-0**	0-0	Elliott 74, Joseph 81, Brown 89	Beasant	Leslie	Thomas	Brown	Morris	Downes	Ketteridge	Joseph	Hodges*	Evans	Gage	Elliott
	15/5		*4,319*	*5*	50					*Burton*	*Doyle*	*Smithers*	*Train*	*Briggs*	*Shotton*	*Lawrence**	*Foley*	*Hebberd*	*Brock*	*Thomas*	*Fogg*
									Ref: M Heath	Oxford have faded at the death, losing their last four of the season. Wimbledon's biggest winning margin came about in the last minute. Peter Brown's penalty was saved by Roy Burton, but Brown reacted fastest to the rebound. Sub Mark Elliott earlier sent the Dons on their way.											
46	H	PORTSMOUTH		21		W	3-2	1-1	Morris 28, Joseph 71, Leslie 86	Beasant	Leslie	Thomas	Brown	Morris	Downes	Ketteridge	Joseph	Hodges*	Evans	Gage	Elliott
	18/5		2,642	*13*	53				*Hemmerman 34, Doyle 80p*	*Knight*	*McLoughlin*	*Sullivan*	*Doyle*	*Ellis*	*Viney*	*Hemmerman*	*Crown*	*Rafferty*	*Berry*	*Rogers*	
		Home	*Away*						Ref: L Shapter	Wimbledon need to win by 11-0 to stay up and send Walsall down. Though that kind of score is beyond them, victory is not. It is secured by Leslie's late winner. The Dons won six of their last eight. This match marked Dave Beasant's 50th consecutive appearance for the Dons.											
Average		2,613	*4,482*																		

League Cup	Att	F-A	H-T	Scorers, Times, and Referees	1	2	3	4	5	6	7	8	9	10	11	12 sub used
1:1 A ALDERSHOT		D 0-0	0-0		Beasant	Jones	Armstrong	Galliers	Smith	Downes	Ketteridge	Joseph	Leslie	Cork	Hodges	
1/9	*2,098 4:16*				*Johnson*	*Edwards*	*Wooler*	*Briley*	*Bennett*	*Jopling*	*McGregor*	*Sanford*	*Garwood*	*Crosby*	*Robinson*	
				Ref: L Shapter	For the third successive season, Wimbledon and Aldershot are thrown together in the first round. Wimbledon won on both previous occasions, and having had almost all the play at the Recreation Ground, they must fancy their chances again. Glen Johnson distinguishes himself in goal.											
1:2 H ALDERSHOT		L 1-3	0-1	Cork 84p	Beasant	Brown*	Armstrong	Galliers	Smith	Downes	Ketteridge	Josph	Leslie	Cork	Hodges	Gage
15/9	2,181 *4:16*			*Garwood 19, 50, Crosby 89*	*Johnson*	*Edwards*	*Wooler*	*Briley*	*Bennett*	*Jopling*	*Wanklyn*	*Sanford*	*Garwood*	*Crosby*	*Brodie*	
				Ref: A Gunn (Dons lose 1-3 on aggregate)	Wimbledon rue their missed chances in the first leg. They strike the crossbar before Colin Garwood hits the first of his two goals. The second of these is a delicate chip. Malcolm Crosby had noted Beasant's discomfort, and in the last minute lobs him almost from the halfway line.											

FA Cup	Att	F-A	H-T	Scorers, Times, and Referees	1	2	3	4	5	6	7	8	9	10	11	12 sub used
1 A BEDFORD		W 2-0	1-0	Suddaby 6, Ketteridge 47	Beasant	Clement	Brown	Gage	Morris	Suddaby	Ketteridge	Leslie	Lazarus*	Downes	Belfield	Hodges
21/11	*3,900 SL*				*Luff*	*Platnauer*	*James*	*Gould**	*Goodeve*	*Best*	*Kurila*	*McGowan*	*Robinson*	*Campbell*	*Felton*	*Grant*
				Ref: A Hamil	Dons' Peter Suddaby played over 300 games for Blackpool. He is given a free header after six minutes. Injuries to Bedford players reduce their team to 10 men for the final 15 minutes, but by then the damage had been done. Just one more hurdle for the Dons to clear before Round 3.											
2 A ENFIELD		L 1-4	1-0	Brown 8p *[Waite 88]*	Beasant	Clement	Brown	Fishenden	Morris	Suddaby	Ketteridge	Leslie	Lazarus	Downes	Joseph	
15/12	*2,730 APL*			*Turner 59, Ironton 72, Oliver 86,*	*Jacobs*	*Barrett*	*Tone*	*Jennings*	*Waite*	*Ironton*	*Ashford*	*Taylor*	*Turner*	*Oliver*	*King*	
				Ref: B Daniels	Wimbledon had lost to these same opponents, at the same stage, and by the same huge margin, four seasons earlier. This time they try to sit on their lead, secured from the penalty spot, after Fishenden was fouled. Turner equalised direct from a corner kick. Enfield now play Palace.											

	P	W	D	L	F	A	W	D	L	F	A	Pts
		Home					Away					
1 Burnley	46	13	7	3	37	20	8	10	5	29	25	80
2 Carlisle	46	17	4	2	44	21	6	7	10	21	29	80
3 Fulham	46	12	9	2	44	22	9	6	8	33	29	78
4 Lincoln	46	13	7	3	40	16	8	7	8	26	24	77
5 Oxford	46	10	8	5	28	18	9	6	8	35	31	71
6 Gillingham	46	14	5	4	44	26	6	6	11	20	30	71
7 Southend	46	11	7	5	35	23	7	8	8	28	28	69
8 Brentford	46	8	6	9	28	22	11	5	7	28	25	68
9 Millwall	46	12	4	7	36	28	6	9	8	26	34	67
10 Plymouth	46	12	5	6	37	24	6	6	11	27	32	65
11 Chesterfield	46	12	4	7	33	27	6	6	11	24	31	64
12 Reading	46	11	6	6	43	35	6	5	12	24	40	62
13 Portsmouth	46	11	10	2	33	14	3	9	11	23	37	61
14 Preston	46	10	7	6	25	22	6	6	11	25	34	61
15 Bristol Rov*	46	12	4	7	35	28	6	5	12	23	37	61
16 Newport	46	9	10	4	28	21	5	6	12	26	33	58
17 Huddersfield	46	10	5	8	38	25	5	7	11	26	34	57
18 Exeter	46	14	4	5	46	33	2	5	16	25	51	57
19 Doncaster	46	9	9	5	31	24	4	8	11	24	44	56
20 Walsall	46	10	7	6	32	23	3	7	13	19	32	53
21 WIMBLEDON	46	10	6	7	33	27	4	5	14	28	48	53
22 Swindon	46	9	5	9	37	36	4	8	11	18	35	52
23 Bristol City	46	7	6	10	24	29	4	7	12	16	36	46
24 Chester	46	2	10	11	16	30	5	1	17	20	48	32
	1104	258	155	139	827	594	139	155	258	594	827	1499

* *2 points deducted*

Odds & ends

Double wins: (0).
Double losses (3): Millwall, Fulham, Gillingham.

Won from behind: (3) Preston (h), Doncaster (a), Brentford (a).
Lost from in front: (4) Brentford (h), Oxford (h), Millwall (a), Carlisle (a).

High spots: Winning 6 of the last 8 games.

Low spots: Failing to win any of the first 11 games in league and League Cup.
Winning just 2 of 16 matches between 9th February and 20th April.
Losing 1-6 at Gillingham, a record defeat at that time.
Losing at Enfield in the FA Cup.

17 different players scored league goals for Wimbledon.

Player of the Year: Francis Joseph.
Ever-presents: (1) Dave Beasant.
Hat-tricks: (0).
Leading scorer: Francis Joseph (13).

	Appearances						Goals			
	Lge	Sub	LC	Sub	FAC	Sub	**Lge**	LC	FAC	**Total**
Armstrong, Gary	**31**		2							
Beasant, Dave	**46**		2		2					
Belfield, Mick	**9**	(5)			1		**4**			**4**
Blochel, Joe	**6**						**1**			**1**
Boyle, Terry	**5**						**1**			**1**
Brown, Peter	**27**		1		2		**3**		1	**4**
Clement, Dave	**9**				2		**2**			**2**
Cork, Alan	**6**		2					1		**1**
Cunningham, Tom	**2**									
Downes, Wally	**42**		2		2					
Elliott, Mark	**7**	(4)					**1**			**1**
Evans, Stewart	**18**						**4**			**4**
Fishenden,Paul	**4**	(1)			1		**1**			**1**
Gage, Kevin	**15**	(6)		(1)	1		**1**			**1**
Galliers, Steve	**11**		2							
Geddes, Paul	**2**									
Hodges, Glyn	**32**	(2)	2			(1)	**2**			**2**
Hubbick, Dave	**2**	(2)					**2**			**2**
Hughes, Billy	**2**									
Jones, Steve	**11**		1							
Joseph, Francis	**38**	(2)	2		1		**13**			**13**
Ketteridge, Steve	**34**	(2)	2		2		**7**		1	**8**
Lazarus, Paul	**17**	(1)			2		**6**			**6**
Leslie, John	**34**	(4)	2		2		**9**			**9**
Morris, Mark	**33**				2		**1**			**1**
Smith, Mick	**39**		2				**2**			**2**
Suddaby, Peter	**6**				2				1	**1**
Thomas, Dean	**18**									
(own-goals)							**1**			**1**
28 players used	**506**	**(29)**	**22**	**(1)**	**22**	**(1)**	**61**	**1**	**3**	**65**

No	Date	Att	Pos	Pts	F-A	H-T	Scorers, Times, and Referees	1	2	3	4	5	6	7	8	9	10	11	12 sub used
1	H NORTHAMPTON			D	1-1	1-1	Ketteridge 44	Beasant	Peters	Thomas	Galliers	Tagg	Morris	Evans	Ketteridge	Leslie	Downes	Dibble	
	28/8	1,703		1			Syrett 7	Freeman	Brady	Phillips	Gage	Burrows*	Heeley	Coffill	Denyer	Saunders	Syrett	Perrin	Saxby
							Ref: A Robinson	Northampton had to apply for re-election in the summer. England youth international Dave Syrett gives the Cobblers an early lead, and although this is wiped out by Steve Ketteridge before half-time, Wimbledon still cannot win their opening league fixture.											
2	A HULL		13	D	1-1	1-1	Thomas 35	Beasant	Peters	Thomas	Galliers	Tagg	Morris	Evans*	Ketteridge	Leslie	Downes	Dibble	Gage
	4/9	3,674	17	2			Flounders 40	Norman	McNeil	Thompson	Roberts	Skipper	Booth	Marwood	McClaren	Flounders*	Mutrie	Roberts	Whitehurst
							Ref: M Scott	Hull are pre-season favourites for promotion. They dominated this game from start to finish, and would have taken all three points but for full-back Dean Thomas's 25-yard thunderbolt that flew in off a post. It is Dave Bassett's 38th birthday, and he is happy with the draw.											
3	A PETERBOROUGH			W	3-0	1-0	Evans 29, Ketteridge 59, Thomas 89p	Beasant	Peters	Thomas	Galliers	Tagg	Morris	Evans	Ketteridge	Leslie	Downes	Dibble	
	8/9	3,458		5				Seaman	Rayment*	Collins	Gynn	Firm	Rodaway	Slack	Linton	Cooke	Benjamin	Chard	Imlach
							Ref: D Hedges	Peterborough missed promotion by one place for the last two seasons. Teenage goalkeeper David Seaman cannot prevent Posh sliding to their first defeat of the new campaign. Robbie Cooke, in particular, carries the can for lamentable finishing. The Dons are full value for the points.											
4	H SCUNTHORPE		7	D	2-2	1-0	Peters 12, Evans 59	Beasant	Peters	Thomas	Galliers	Tagg	Morris	Evans	Ketteridge	Leslie	Downes	Dibble*	Entwhistle
	11/9	1,611	8	6			O'Berg 61, 63	Neenan	Keeley	Pointon	Fowler	Boxall	Hunter	O'Berg	Parkinson	Duncan*	Telfer	Leman	Baines
							Ref: A Glasson	Scunthorpe were 23rd last season, but have begun strongly this. Full-back Neil Pointon would graduate to the big time with Everton and Manchester City. Fine attacking football by Wimbledon should have sealed the points, but Paul O'Berg punishes their unprofessionalism.											
5	A BLACKPOOL		7	D	1-1	0-0	Leslie 84	Beasant	Peters*	Thomas	Galliers	Tagg	Morris	Evans	Ketteridge	Leslie	Downes	Hodges	Gage
	18/9	3,929	14	7			Hockaday 62	Hesford	Simmonite	Brockbank	Deary!	Hetzke	Serella	Noble	Stewart	Bamber	Pashley	Hockaday	
							Ref: T Jones	Blackpool are leading 1-0 but losing on players, having had John Deary sent off after 66 minutes for clobbering Ketteridge. John Leslie's first goal of the season, sweeping in a low cross with just six minutes left, means that both sides have just one win to show so far.											
6	H TORQUAY		5	W	4-1	3-0	Evans 4, 14, 38, Ketteridge 65	Beasant	Peters	Tagg	Morris	Thomas	Galliers	Ketteridge	Downes	Evans	Leslie	Hodges*	Gage
	25/9	2,047	4	10			Doyle 85	Horn	Doyle	Wilson	Wigginton	Smith	Grapes	Anderson	Rioch	Steeples	Cooper*	Gallagher	Sermanni
							Ref: M Taylor	Unbeaten Torquay lead the table at the start of play, shored up by their player-manager, ex-Scotland skipper Bruce Rioch. He cannot prevent Stewart Evans snatching a first-half hat-trick (the Dons' first for two years). The Dons climb to within one point of Torquay, who drop to 4th.											
7	H HEREFORD		4	W	1-0	0-0	Morris 58	Beasant	Peters	Thomas	Galliers	Jones*	Morris	Evans	Ketteridge	Leslie	Downes	Hodges	Gage
	28/9	**1,604**	24	13				Plumley	Bray	Bartley	Hicks	Pejic	Spiring	Crabbe	Harvey	Phillips	Showers	White	
							Ref: T Spencer	With just one point, managerless Hereford are rooted to the bottom, and have just been crushed 0-5 by Chester. Hereford draw the season's smallest gate to Plough Lane. Mark Morris has just celebrated his 20th birthday, and his header takes Wimbledon up to 4th.											
8	A TRANMERE		2	W	2-0	1-0	Leslie 24, Gage 70	Beasant	Peters	Thomas	Galliers	Jones	Morris	Evans*	Ketteridge	Leslie	Downes	Hodges	Gage
	2/10	1,231	22	16				Endersby	Burgess	Mooney*	Ferguson	Hamilton	Williams J	Powell	Prosser	Kerr	Aspinall	Griffiths	McGuire
							Ref: D Hutchinson	Tranmere are in the bottom four, and look to ex-Northern Ireland veteran (and future manager) Bryan Hamilton, to lead them to safety. The game's chief talking point was Galliers' header that hit the post and went in just as the referee blew for half-time. The 'goal' did not stand.											
9	H ALDERSHOT		1	W	6-1	2-1	Hodges 22, 70, Ketteridge 27, Leslie 77, [Gage 64, 88]	Beasant	Peters	Thomas	Gage	Tagg	Morris	Evans	Ketteridge	Leslie	Downes	Hodges	
	9/10	2,440	14	19			Banton 21	Johnson	Andru'zewski	Gillard	Shrubb	Scott	Fielder	Sanford	Banton	Goddard	McDonald	Brodie	
							Ref: M Robinson	It is fitting that the season's biggest win should lift the Dons to the top. The match was missed by Dave Bassett, who was away spying on next opponents York at Bristol City. Aldershot take a shock lead. The Dons equalised at once, otherwise they might not have found goals so easy.											
10	A YORK		1	W	4-1	0-0	Leslie 61,77, Hood 70(og), Entwhistle 85	Beasant	Peters	Thomas	Gage	Tagg	Morris	Evans*	Ketteridge	Leslie	Downes	Hodges	Entwhistle
	16/10	2,064	15	22			Pollard 84	Jones	Evans	Dawson*	Sbragia	Crosby	Hood	Pollard	Ford	Walwyn	Byrne	Laverick	Busby
							Ref: G Courtney	York's biggest gate of the season, so far, witness Wimbledon's fifth straight win, which leaves the Dons as the only unbeaten team in the country. All the goals came in the second half, after York had looked stronger in the first. Wayne Entwhistle gets his first goal for the Dons.											
11	H ROCHDALE		1	W	3-0	1-0	Peters 5, 64, Leslie 90	Beasant	Peters	Thomas	Gage	Tagg	Morris	Evans*	Ketteridge	Leslie	Downes	Hodges	Fishenden
	19/10	2,294	20	25				Pearce	Keenan	Snookes	Farrell	Taylor*	Williams	Thompson D	Comstive	French	Wellings	Hilditch	Martinez
							Ref: L Burden	Rochdale had to apply for re-election – yet again – last season, and are struggling again now. As this was the only match in London, the sparse crowd seemed to be outnumbered by scouts. Luton's David Pleat was eyeing up Glyn Hodges. Tony Tagg was hospitalised with concussion.											

No	Venue	Opponent	Pos/Att	Res	Pts	F-A	H-T	Scorers, Times, Referees	1	2	3	4	5	6	7	8	9	10	11	12
		23/10	*4,723*	22	25			*Nicholls 31, Riley 34, 44, 69*	*Shaw*	*Newman*	*Johnson L*	*Nicholls*	*Boyle*	*Riley*	*Economou*	*Ritchie*	*Chandler*	*Cooper*	*Crawford*	
								Ref: D Civil	City were relegated with the Dons, but have not won since the opening match, 11 games ago. The Bristol match is over by half-time, when City lead 3-0. Terry Cooper pulls the strings as Glyn Riley scores his first league hat-trick. Sub Steve Galliers was sent off after 70 mins.											
13	H	STOCKPORT	2	W		2-1	1-0	Leslie 38, Thomas 85	Beasant	Peters	Thomas	Galliers	Tagg	Morris	Evans	Ketteridge	Leslie	Downes	Hodges	
		30/10	2,294	*18*	28			*Quinn 75*	*Lloyd*	*Rutter**	*Sherlock*	*Emerson*	*Bowles*	*Thorpe*	*Williams*	*Phillips*	*Quinn*	*Park*	*Wardrobe*	*Smith*
								Ref: I Borrett	A home banker, one would think, despite the threat of Mick Quinn's scoring potential. Yet with five minutes to go Stockport are holding on to a point. It is then that Dean Thomas steps up for another blaster. His 30-yarder flies in after hitting both the crossbar and a goalpost.											
14	A	COLCHESTER	3	L		**0-3**	0-1		Beasant	Peters	Thomas	Galliers	Tagg	Morris*	Entwhistle	Ketteridge	Leslie	Downes	Hodges	Gage
		2/11	*2,219*	*10*	28			*Allinson 31, McDonough 52, 70*	*Walker*	*Cook*	*Coleman*	*Longhorn*	*Wignall*	*Hunter*	*Allinson*	*Osborne*	*Lyons*	*McDonough*	*Leslie*	
								Ref: H Taylor	Wimbledon's heaviest setback of the season is put down to a combination of fog and much-travelled striker Roy McDonough. Colchester led the table early on, but haven't won in six games. Mike Walker is their goalkeeper. As visibility deteriorated, an orange ball was introduced.											
15	A	HARTLEPOOL	4	L		0-1	0-0		Beasant	Peters	Thomas	Dibble	Tagg	Morris	Belfield	Fishenden	Leslie	Downes	Hodges	
		6/11	***1,081***	*13*	28			*Linacre 86*	*Wright*	*Brown*	*Stimpson*	*Hogan*	*Bird*	*Linighan*	*Lowe*	*Staff*	*Lawrence**	*Linacre*	*Barker*	*Dobson*
								Ref: N Midgley	Hartlepool have just lost five goals to York and four to Mansfield, so this is a real upset. Barely 1,000 fans turned up. Dean Thomas had two efforts cleared off the line and Leslie wasted chances galore, but Pool's midfielder Phil Linacre has the last laugh with an 18-yard low drive.											
16	H	HALIFAX	6	L		2-4	0-1	Entwhistle 56, Thomas 79p	Beasant	Peters	Thomas	Dibble	Tagg	Morris	Belfield	Entwhistle	Leslie*	Downes	Hodges	Gage
		13/11	2,104	*20*	28			*Davison 42, 52, 68, Allatt 53*	*Smelt*	*Nobbs*	*Wood*	*Evans*	*Smith*	*Hendrie*	*Staniforth*	*Davison*	*Allatt*	*Spooner*	*Goodman*	
								Ref: K Barratt	Crisis at Plough Lane. Lowly Halifax hadn't won for 11 games, but once Bobby Davison puts them ahead shortly before half-time, he is on to a memorable away hat-trick, and the Dons to a crushing home defeat. Three straight losses invites Dave Bassett to swing the axe.											
17	A	DARLINGTON	8	W		2-0	2-0	Leslie 1, 36	Beasant	Peters	**Ferns**	Galliers	Smith	**Hatter**	Evans	Ketteridge	Leslie*	Downes	Gage	Hodges
		4/12	*1,117*	*15*	31				*Cuff*	*Liddle*	*Wilson H*	*Smith*	*Rhodes*	*Kamara*	*Gilbert*	*McLean*	*Honour*	*Walsh*	*Dunn**	*McDermott*
								Ref: D Allison	Following defeats by Halifax and Northampton (in the FA Cup), Bassett does not just tinker with the team, he dismembers it, bringing in six fresh faces. Debuts await on-loan Phil Ferns and Steve Hatter, from Charlton and Fulham. Leslie's far-post header comes inside a minute.											
18	A	ROCHDALE	5	W		2-0	1-0	Evans 12, Entwhistle 75	Beasant	Peters	Jones	Galliers	Smith	Hatter	Evans	Ketteridge	Entwhistle*	Downes	Gage	Hodges
		11/12	*1,096*	*20*	34				*Pearce*	*Keenan*	*Nicholson*	*McElhinney*	*Wiilliams*	*Thompson D*	*Farrell*	*Snookes*	*Greaves*	*Hilditch*	*Wellings**	*Thompson S*
								Ref: T Holbrook	Wimbledon's first double of the season. Wayne Entwhistle had eaten a huge lunch at a funeral, but was drafted in when John Leslie failed a late fitness test. Entwhistle scored the second vital goal. It was as well that he did; Mark Hilditch then volleyed against Beasant's crossbar.											
19	A	PORT VALE	7	L		0-1	0-1		Beasant	Peters	Ferns	Galliers	Smith	Hatter	Evans	Ketteridge	Entwhistle	Downes*	Gage	Hodges
		18/12	*2,761*	*5*	*34*			*Moss 15*	*Siddall*	*Tartt*	*Bromage*	*Hunter*	*Sproson*	*Cegielski*	*Fox*	*Moss*	*Newton*	*Greenhoff*	*Armstrong*	
								Ref: F Roberts	Vale are going well, so this match on a snowy pitch is tantamount to a six-pointer. Ernie Moss has scored frequently in the lower divisions for many years, and he beats Beasant with a rising drive. Jimmy Greenhoff will be released in May. Three Dons miss chances in the second-half.											
20	H	MANSFIELD	6	D		1-1	0-0	Galliers 56	Beasant	Peters	Ferns	Galliers	Smith	Hatter	Evans	Ketteridge	Leslie	Downes*	Gage	Hodges
		27/12	2,517	*11*	*35*			*Nicholson 89*	*Arnold*	*Bird*	*Kearney*	*Bell*	*Ayre*	*Calderwood*	*Matthews*	*Hutchinson*	*Dungworth!*	*Caldwell*	*Nicholson*	
								Ref: R Milford	Steve Galliers scores his first goal since returning from Crystal Palace. Mansfield's John Dungworth, who seems to have played for half the teams in the league, is sent off, but 10-man Mansfield still snatch a late draw.											
21	A	SWINDON	6	W		1-0	0-0	Leslie 74	Beasant	Peters	Ferns!	Galliers	Smith	Hatter	Evans	Ketteridge	Leslie	Downes	Gage	
		28/12	***8,164***	*2*	*38*				*Allan*	*Bailie*	*Baverstock*	*Emmanuel*	*Lewis*	*Graham*	*Pritchard*	*Batty*	*Quinn*	*Rowland*	*Barnard*	
								Ref: J Bray	Relegated Swindon are determined to get up at the first attempt. They pack them in for this holiday fixture, only to slump to their second defeat in 17 games. Ferns was sent off for toppling Pritchard from behind, a professional foul, and the Dons live on their nerves till the end.											
22	H	BURY	6	W		2-1	0-0	Brown 52 (og), Leslie 62	Beasant	Peters	Ferns	Galliers	Smith	Hatter	Evans	Ketteridge	Leslie	Downes	Gage*	Hodges
		1/1	2,467	*2*	*41*			*Parker 86*	*Brown*	*Gardner*	*Davies*	*Gore*	*Bramhall*	*Halliday*	*Firth*	*Madden*	*Parker*	*Jakub*	*Potts**	*Cutler*
								Ref: A Robinson	Bury are knocked off their proud perch following this second critical, top-of-the-table match for Wimbledon in four days. The key to the result was David Brown's fragility in the Bury goal. His errors decide the match. Bury boss Wilf McGuinness, ex-Man U, calls them 'a bloody joke'.											
23	A	CHESTER	4	W		2-1	0-0	Evans 50, Smith 75	Beasant	Peters	Ferns	Galliers	Smith	Hatter	Evans	Ketteridge	Leslie	Downes	Gage	
		4/1	*1,549*	*13*	*44*			*Thomas 74*	*Salmon*	*Dean*	*Wilson*	*Moffatt*	*Bradley*	*Needham**	*Sloan*	*Lane*	*Thomas*	*Ludlam*	*Bulmer*	*Cooke*
								Ref: N Glover	The traffic was so one-way in this one-sided match that Dave Beasant did not touch the ball for the first 15 minutes. Wimbledon frittered away chance after chance, but in the end are grateful to Mark Smith's instant header after John Thomas's shock equaliser – a free header.											

No	Date			Att	Pos	Pts	F-A	H-T	Scorers, Times, and Referees	1	2	3	4	5	6	7	8	9	10	11	12 sub used
24		H	HULL		4	L	1-2	0-1	Evans 54	Beasant	Peters	Ferns	Galliers	Smith	Hatter	Evans	Ketteridge	Leslie	Downes	Gage	
	8/1			2,766	1	44			Roberts 3, Whitehurst 89	Davies	Swann	Askew*	Roberts	Skipper	Booth	Marwood	McClaren	Whitehurst	Mutrie	Roberts	McNeil
									Ref: A Grey	Hull are the new league leaders. Bassett springs a surprise tactical change, and switches from zonal marking to man-for-man. A fantastic match is all square until the last minute. Beasant pushes away Marwood's stinging shot, but Marwood's corner-kick reaches Billy Whitehurst.											
25		A	NORTHAMPTON		4	D	2-2	2-1	Leslie 18, 44	Beasant	Peters	Morris	Galliers	Smith	Hatter	Evans	Ketteridge	Leslie*	Downes	Gage	Entwhistle
	15/1			2,290	17	45			Brady 17, Saunders 57	Freeman	Tucker	Phillips	Gage	Brady	Coffill	Saunders	Muir	Syrett	Massey	Saxby	
									Ref: V Callow	Northampton used to be the Dons' whipping boys in their early league career. Cobblers' defenders Brady and Saunders score rare goals in the third draw between the sides this season. At 2-2, goalkeeper Freeman tips Kevin Gage's shot against a post and smothers the rebound.											
26		H	PETERBOROUGH		4	W	2-1	1-1	Evans 42, Leslie 86	Beasant	Peters	**Sparrow**	Galliers	Smith	Hatter	Evans	Ketteridge	Leslie	Downes	Gage*	Entwhistle
	22/1			2,119	10	48			Quow 33	Seaman	Winters	Collins	Gynn	Rodaway	Slack	Clarke	Chard	Cooke	Benjamin	Quow	
									Ref: M Bodenham	Another double for the Dons. John Leslie is Wimbledon's last link with their Southern league days. He is now the top scorer in Division 4. For his 17th goal he beats David Seaman off a post. Posh had looked good, and Brian Sparrow, on loan from Arsenal, had an uncomfortable debut.											
27		A	SCUNTHORPE		4	D	0-0	0-0		Beasant	Peters	Sparrow	Galliers	Smith	Morris	Evans	Ketteridge	Leslie	Dibble*	Hodges	Entwhistle
	29/1			3,846	5	49				Neenan	Oates	Pointon	Boxall	Baines	Hunter	O'Berg	Cammack	Cowling	Parkinson	Leman	
									Ref: D Shaw	Scunthorpe are still up there with the leaders. The match was not helped by a swirling wind that assisted Wimbledon in the first half, their opponents, Scunthorpe's in the second. Chris Dibble, playing instead of the injured Downes, tore knee ligaments and had to go off.											
28		A	TORQUAY		4	W	1-0	0-0	Hatter 82	Beasant	Peters	Sparrow	Galliers	Smith	Hatter	Evans	Ketteridge	Leslie	Hodges*	Gage	Belfield
	5/2			2,316	10	52				Horn	Doyle*	Wilson	Sheridan	Little	Hughes	Bishop	O'Donnell	Cooper	Anderson	Gallagher	Thompson
									Ref: E Read	Torquay were having a good season, but this is their fourth defeat on the trot. They are beaten by Steve Hatter's first goal for Wimbledon – a soaring header at the far post. He had just returned to the side after suspension. Brian Sparrow twice cleared off the line in the second half.											
29		H	COLCHESTER			W	2-1	0-1	Smith 70, Hodges 72	Beasant	Peters	Sparrow	Galliers	Smith	Hatter	Evans	Ketteridge	Leslie	Hodges	Fishenden	
	15/2			1,753		55			Adcock 20	Walker	Cook	Packer	McDonough	Wignall	Coleman	Allinson	Osborne*	Linford	Adcock	Hull	
									Ref: L Shapter	Mike Walker, future manager of Norwich and Everton, keeps goal for Colchester, but the Dons come from behind to win. Explained Bassett: 'We started the season using a sweeper, but have now switched to getting the ball up to the front men as quickly as possible.'											
30		A	ALDERSHOT		4	D	1-1	1-0	Fishenden 18p	Beasant	Peters	Sparrow	Galliers!	Smith	Hatter	Evans	Ketteridge	Leslie*	Hodges	Fishenden	Belfield
	19/2			2,720	13	56			Banton 48p	Johnson	Andru'zewski	Scott	Briley	Wooler	Jopling	Shrubb	Banton	Goddard	McDonald	Brodie	
									Ref: L Burden	Aldershot extend their unbeaten sequence to seven, courtesy of Dale Banton's penalty equalising that of Paul Fishenden. This ill-tempered encounter saw the previously booked Steve Galliers sent off after 70 minutes, and three players from each side booked. The ref upset everyone.											
31		H	YORK		3	W	4-3	2-0	Evans 6, 16, Leslie 68, Barnett 80	Beasant	Peters	Sparrow	Galliers	Smith	Hatter	Evans	Ketteridge	Leslie*	Hodges	**Barnett**	Fishenden
	26/2			2,168	8	59			Smith 57 (og), Walwyn 75, Hay 85	Jones!	Evans	Hay	Sbragia	Smith	Hood	Ford	Crosby	Walwyn	Byrne	McPhail*	Pollard
									Ref: A Crickmore	Wimbledon scored four against York in October, too. In the 51st minute, with the Dons leading 2-0, York's Roger Jones handles outside his area and becomes the 13th keeper sent off this season, under an FA crackdown. Malcolm Crosby deputises. Gary Barnett scores on his debut.											
32		H	BRISTOL CITY		3	W	2-1	2-0	Newman 25 (og), Leslie 30	Beasant	Peters	Sparrow	Barnett	Smith	Hatter*	Evans	Belfield	Leslie	Hodges	Gage	Fishenden
	5/3			2,541	20	62			Kelly 47	Shaw	Newman	Williams G	Nicholls	Phill-Masters	Riley	Ritchie	Economou	Kelly	Musker	Crawford	
									Ref: M Dimblebee	Bristol City are improving. Bottom of the table in December, this will be their last defeat for nine games. Once Steve Hatter had withdrawn with a head injury, the Dons had to hang on desperately after Errington Kelly's goal. Brian Sparrow cleared off the line in the closing seconds.											
33		A	STOCKPORT		2	W	3-1	2-0	Morris 16, Hodges 19, Leslie 77	Beasant	Peters	Sparrow	Galliers	Smith	Morris	Evans	Belfield	Leslie*	Hodges	Barnett	Downes
	11/3			2,260		65			Coyle 58	Lloyd	Rutter	Sherlock	Emerson	Sword	Thorpe	Phillips	Wardrobe*	Quinn	Power	Coyle	Smith
									Ref: D Richardson	Another double for the Dons, inflicting upon Stockport their first home defeat since November. Wimbledon had to weather a second-half storm after Tony Coyle had sidefooted County back into the match. But then John Leslie scored for the third match in a row.											
34		H	TRANMERE			W	4-0	2-0	Peters 20, Leslie 39, 46, Galliers 67	Beasant	Peters	Sparrow	Galliers	Smith	Hatter*	Evans	Ketteridge	Leslie	Hodges	Barnett	Downes
	15/3			2,113		68				Adkins	Williams G	Burgess	Oliver	Palios*	Williams J	Ferguson!	Aspinall	Wellings	Brown	Griffiths	Warriner
									Ref: T Spencer	Tranmere have eased themselves out of the bottom four. In addition to the four goals, Smith and Evans both headed against the woodwork. Pick of the goals was Peters' long-range blaster. Tranmere's Mark Ferguson becomes the League's 200th player to be sent off this season.											

No	Venue / Date	Opponent	Att	Pos	Pts	Res	F-A	H-T	Scorers, Times, and Referees	1	2	3	4	5	6	7	8	9	10	11	12 sub used
35	H	HARTLEPOOL		1		W	2-0	0-0	Leslie 65, Hodges 82	Beasant	Peters	Sparrow	Belfield	Smith	Hatter	Evans	Ketteridge	Leslie	Hodges	Barnett	
	19/3		2,324	*19*	*71*					*Blackburn*	*Brown*	*Barker*	*Robinson*	*Linighan D*	*Linighan A*	*Lowe*	*Smith*	*Linacre*	*Dobson**	*Staff*	*McNamee*
									Ref: B Stevens	Sliding Hartlepool field both Andy and David Linighan, and provide dour opposition. John Leslie, the division's leading scorer, helps send the Dons back to the top, for the first time in five months. Glyn Hodges scores the vital second goal, but otherwise has a disappointing match.											
36	H	SWINDON				D	0-0	0-0		Beasant	Peters	Sparrow	Galliers	Morris	Hatter	Evans	Ketteridge	Belfield	Hodges*	Downes	Dibble
	1/4		3,400		*72*					*Allan*	*Bailie*	*Baddeley*	*Batty*	*Lewis*	*Graham*	*Baverstock*	*Barnard*	*Rideout*	*Rowland*	*Blackler*	
									Ref: M Taylor	This is Swindon's ninth game without a win, and their promotion hopes are receding. The Dons are without Leslie – a flu victim – and fail to score at home for the first time this season. Few chances were created, though Belfield had the ball in the net. He was given offside.											
37	A	MANSFIELD				D	2-2	1-1	Bird 40 (og), Evans 60	Beasant	Peters	Sparrow	Galliers	Morris	Hatter	Evans	Ketteridge	Cork	Hodges	Downes	
	5/4		*3,519*		*73*				*Dungworth 35, 47p*	*Arnold*	*Woodhead*	*Kearney*	*Matthews*	*Bird**	*Ayre*	*Bell*	*Hutchinson*	*Dungworth*	*Caldwell*	*Nicholson*	*Sindall*
									Ref: D Scott	Mansfield have lost just one in 10, but have left their surge too late. The match marks the return of Alan Cork, out for a season and a half with a broken leg. He hit a post. Mansfield's penalty came when Brian Sparrow thought he heard the ref's whistle and picked up the ball.											
38	H	DARLINGTON		2		W	3-1	2-0	Evans 17, Ketteridge 43, Morris 47	Beasant	Peters	Thomas	Galliers	Morris	Hatter	Evans	Ketteridge	Cork	Hodges*	Downes	Leslie
	9/4		1,970	*17*	*76*				*Walsh 59*	*Barber*	*Kamara*	*Young**	*Smith*	*Barton*	*Cartwright*	*Gilbert*	*McLean*	*Todd*	*Walsh*	*McFadden*	*Honour*
									Ref: D Axcell / D King	Five undefeated matches have lifted the Quakers out of the re-election zone. They are managed by ex-Spurs star Cyril Knowles, later to die prematurely. The Dons win in a canter. Evans headed the opener. The Dons then pepper 19-year-old keeper Fred Barber, who plays a blinder.											
39	A	HEREFORD		3		W	4-1	2-0	Cork 8, Ketteridge 13, Hodges 77, 82	Beasant	Peters	Thomas	Galliers	Morris	Hatter	Evans	Ketteridge	Cork*	Hodges	Downes	Leslie
	16/4		*2,637*	*24*	*79*				*Phillips 59*	*Wilmot*	*Price*	*Spiring*	*Hicks*	*Larkin*	*Maddy*	*Spiring*	*Lane*	*Phillips*	*Carter*	*Showers*	
									Ref: J Hunting	Hereford have been bottom since January and will stay bottom. Despite his goals, Leslie is dropped to make way for Cork. The Dons force five corners in the first eight minutes, when Cork scores his first goal since his return. Hereford were pressing hard when Hodges bagged No 3.											
40	H	CREWE		2		W	3-2	1-1	Hodges 8, Cork 74, Leslie 88	Beasant	Peters	Thomas	Galliers	Morris	Hatter	Evans*	Ketteridge	Cork	Hodges	Leslie	Gage
	19/4		2,505	*22*	*82*				*Morris 24 (og), Scott 89*	*Smith*	*Brady*	*Bowers*	*Edwards**	*Scott*	*Hart*	*Haselgrave*	*Bancroft*	*Waller*	*Walker*	*Cliss*	*Chapman*
									Ref: K Baker	Nothing can save Dario Gradi's Crewe from re-election, but they give Wimbledon a run for their money. Alan Cork scores the Dons' 400th league goal. The club win £25,000 for being the first in London to reach 80 goals, and pay £100,000 for the freehold of Plough Lane stadium.											
41	H	PORT VALE		2		W	1-0	0-0	Ketteridge 85	Beasant	Peters	Sparrow	Galliers	Smith	Hatter	Leslie	Ketteridge	Cork	Hodges	Downes	
	23/4		**4,061**	*3*	*85*					*Siddall*	*Tartt*	*Bromage*	*Hunter*	*Sproson*	*Cegielski*	*Fox*	*Steel*	*Newton*	*Ridley**	*Armstrong*	*Lawrence M*
									Ref: B Hill	This stirring top-of-the-table clash lures the season's record crowd to Plough Lane. The Dons force 17 corners, but have to wait till the 85th minute to break through. Promotion is now all but guaranteed, and struggling Chelsea could even be facing the Dons in Division 3.											
42	A	CREWE		1		W	2-0	0-0	Downes 49, Smith 89	Beasant	Peters	Sparrow	Thomas	Smith	Hatter	Leslie	Ketteridge	Cork*	Hodges	Downes	Evans
	30/4		*2,552*	*23*	*88*					*Smith*	*Brady*	*Bowers*	*Edwards*	*Scott*	*Hart*	*Haselgrave*	*Bancroft**	*Waller*	*Walker*	*Cliss*	*Chapman*
									Ref: D Civil	It is Easter Saturday and these teams meet for the second time in 12 days. Wally Downes' first goal in two years lightens the Dons' frustration. The final whistle takes Wimbledon back to the top of the table. This time they will stay there. Visiting Port Vale fans attack Dons supporters.											
43	H	CHESTER		1		W	4-0	1-0	Cork 1, 73, 89, Smith 60	Beasant	Peters	Sparrow	Thomas	Smith	Hatter	Leslie	Ketteridge*	Cork	Hodges	Downes	Evans
	2/5		2,576	*14*	*91*					*Harrington*	*Moffatt*	*Lane**	*Storton*	*Zelem*	*Blackwell*	*Sloan*	*Allen*	*Thomas*	*Manns*	*Bulmer*	*Bradley*
									Ref: S Bates	Alan Cork signals his return to goalscoring ways with a super hat-trick, his first in three years. The rout began in the first minute, when Cork headed in Hodges' corner. After the match, Cork flew out to play close-season football in Sweden.											
44	H	BLACKPOOL		1		W	5-0	3-0	Leslie 13, Sparrow 18, Hodges 38, [Fishenden 81, Gage 89]	Beasant	Peters	Sparrow	Thomas	Smith	Hatter	Evans	Downes	Leslie	Hodges*	Gage	Fishenden
	7/5		2,717	*18*	*94*					*Hesford*	*Bardsley*	*Pritchett*	*Deany*	*Serella*	*Greenall*	*Bamber*	*McNiven*	*Stewart*	*Downes*	*Pashley*	*Bramhall*
									Ref: B Daniels	John Leslie is voted Player of the Year. He responds by scoring his 100th Wimbledon goal. The club's target now is 100 points (they already have 94) and 100 league goals (currently 92). Strange to say, this result slightly flattered them. Blackpool twice hit the inside of the same post.											
45	A	HALIFAX				D	1-1	0-1	Fishenden 88	Beasant	Peters	Sparrow	Thomas	Morris	Hatter	Evans	Fishenden	Leslie	Downes	Gage*	Hodges
	10/5		*1,233*		*95*				*Spooner 9*	*Smelt*	*Nobbs*	*Wood*	*Evans*	*Smith*	*Hendrie*	*Gallagher*	*Spooner*	*Kendall*	*Ward*	*Staniforth*	
									Ref: K Redfern	Halifax, fresh from a 1-6 thrashing by Aldershot three days earlier, spoil the Dons' party. Though their unbeaten run now stands at 21 games, they are carrying too many injuries and semi-fit players. Paul Fishenden returns from loan to Wokingham to hook the late equaliser.											
46	A	BURY		1		W	3-1	2-0	Evans 9, Downes 39, Fishenden 89	Beasant	Peters	Smith	Hatter	Thomas	Fishenden	Downes	Morris	Evans	Leslie	Hodges	
	14/5		*6,760*	*5*	*98*				*Parker 80*	*Brown*	*Gardner*	*Halliday*	*Bramhall*	*Breckin*	*Gore*	*Hilton*	*Jakub*	*Potts*	*Johnson*	*Madden*	*Parker*
		Home	*Away*						Ref: A Saunders	Joy for Wimbledon; tears for Bury, who would have also have been promoted had they won. At 0-2 Bury have a penalty. Ever-present Dave Beasant has seen a picture in the Bury programme of Tommy Gore taking a penalty. Beasant dives the same way, and saves.											
Average		2,352	*2,922*																		

LEAGUE DIVISION 4 (CUP-TIES)

Manager: Dave Bassett

SEASON 1982-83

Milk Cup	Att		F-A	H-T	Scorers, Times, and Referees	1	2	3	4	5	6	7	8	9	10	11	12 sub used
1:1 H BRENTFORD		D	1-1	0-1	Leslie 61	Beasant	Peters	Thomas	Galliers	Tagg	Morris	Evans	Ketteridge	Leslie	Downes	Dibble	
30/8	3,926 *3:9*				*Roberts 30*	*Roche*	*Tucker*	*Spencer*	*Booker*	*Whitehead*	*Hurlock*	*Kamara*	*Joseph*	*Mahoney*	*Bowles*	*Roberts*	
					Ref: T Bune	Wimbledon line up against Francis Joseph, whom they sold to Brentford, ex-England Stan Bowles, and ex-Manchester United goalkeeper Paddy Roche. Having hit the woodwork twice, the Dons must feel they are up against it against 3rd Division opponents in the second leg.											
1:2 A BRENTFORD		L	0-2	0-1		Beasant	Peters	Thomas	Hodges*	Morris	Jones	Ketteridge	Downes	Leslie	Galliers	Evans	Gage
14/9	*5,747 3:9*				*Mahoney 45, 70*	*Roche*	*Rowe*	*Tucker*	*McNicholl*	*Whitehead*	*Hurlock*	*Kamara*	*Joseph*	*Mahoney*	*Bowles*	*Roberts*	
					Ref: D Axcell (Dons lose 1-3 on aggregate)	Brentford look far superior to Wimbledon on this showing. They force 16 corners and create 14 good scoring chances. The Dons' best player was undoubtedly Dave Beasant, who kept the score respectable, long after the tie had slipped away. Stewart Evans missed a gaping goal.											

FA Cup	Att		F-A	H-T	Scorers, Times, and Referees	1	2	3	4	5	6	7	8	9	10	11	12 sub used
1 A NORTHAMPTON		D	2-2	0-1	Leslie 68, Entwhistle 73	Beasant	Leslie	Jones!	Galliers	Smith	Morris	Entwhistle	Ketteridge	Fishenden*	Downes	Dibble	Gage
20/11	*2,832 12*				*Burrows 27, Denyer 50*	*Freeman*	*Brady*	*Phillips*	*Gage*	*Burrows*	*Heeley!*	*Saxby*	*Buchanan**	*Saunders*	*Denyer*	*Massey*	*Coffill*
					Ref: D Axcell	Wimbledon's ex-Millwall player, Chris Dibble, fluffs a great chance in the 89th minute, heading wide from four yards. With Mark Heeley sent off, and Paul Saunders off with a torn hamstring, the Cobblers are down to nine players. This encourages Wimbledon's fight-back.											
1R H NORTHAMPTON		L	0-2	0-1		Beasant	Leslie	Jones	Galliers	Smith	Morris	Dibble	Ketteridge	Entwhistle*	Downes	Evans	Gage
23/11	2,097 *12*				*Coffill 19, 89*	*Freeman*	*Brady*	*Phillips*	*Gage*	*Burrows*	*Heeley*	*Saxby*	*Buchanan*	*Coffill*	*Denyer*	*Massey*	
					Ref: D Axcell	Glyn Hodges has been dropped, apparently for lack of effort. Two Steve Massey crosses and two Peter Coffill goals knock out the Dons, and end their unbeaten run. Bassett decided to play John Leslie at full-back, once again. The match was played in torrential rain.											

	Home						Away					
	P	W	D	L	F	A	W	D	L	F	A	Pts
1 WIMBLEDON	46	17	4	2	57	23	12	7	4	39	22	98
2 Hull	46	14	8	1	48	14	11	7	5	27	20	90
3 Port Vale	46	15	4	4	37	16	11	6	6	30	18	88
4 Scunthorpe	46	13	7	3	41	17	10	7	6	30	25	83
5 Bury	46	15	4	4	43	20	8	8	7	31	26	81
6 Colchester	46	17	5	1	51	19	7	4	12	24	36	81
7 York	46	18	4	1	59	19	4	9	10	29	39	79
8 Swindon	46	14	3	6	45	27	5	8	10	16	27	68
9 Peterborough	46	13	6	4	38	23	4	7	12	20	29	64
10 Mansfield	46	11	6	6	32	26	5	7	11	29	44	61
11 Halifax	46	9	8	6	31	23	7	4	12	28	43	60
12 Torquay	46	12	3	8	38	30	5	4	14	18	35	58
13 Chester	46	8	6	9	28	24	7	5	11	27	36	56
14 Bristol City	46	10	8	5	32	25	3	9	11	27	45	56
15 Northampton	46	10	8	5	43	29	4	4	15	22	46	54
16 Stockport	46	11	8	4	41	31	3	4	16	19	48	54
17 Darlington	46	8	5	10	27	30	5	8	10	34	41	52
18 Aldershot	46	11	5	7	40	35	1	10	12	21	47	51
19 Tranmere	46	8	8	7	30	29	5	3	15	19	42	50
20 Rochdale	46	11	8	4	38	25	0	8	15	17	48	49
21 Blackpool*	46	10	8	5	32	23	3	4	16	23	51	49
22 Hartlepool	46	11	5	7	30	24	2	4	17	16	52	48
23 Crewe	46	9	5	9	35	32	2	3	18	18	39	41
24 Hereford	46	8	6	9	19	23	3	2	18	23	56	41
	1104	283	142	127	915	587	127	142	283	587	915	1512

* *2 points deducted*

Odds & ends

Double wins: (11) Peterborough, Torquay, Hereford, Tranmere, York, Rochdale, Stockport, Darlington, Bury, Chester, Crewe.
Double losses: (0).

Won from behind: (3) Peterborough (h), Colchester (h), Aldershot (a).
Lost from in front: (0).

High spots: 11-game unbeaten start to the season.
22-game unbeaten finish to the season.

Low spots: 3 straight defeats in November, plus elimination from the FA Cup at home to Northampton.
Losing badly at home to lowly Halifax.

17 different Wimbledon players scored in the league.
Wimbledon's 98 goals was the highest total in the Football League.

Player of the Year: John Leslie.
Ever-presents: (2) Dave Beasant, Gary Peters (league only).
Hat-tricks: Stewart Evans (1), Alan Cork (1).
Leading scorer: John Leslie (25).

	Appearances						Goals			
	Lge	Sub	MC	Sub	FAC	Sub	**Lge**	MC	FAC	**Total**
Beasant, Dave	**46**		2		2					
Barnett, Gary	**5**						**1**			**1**
Belfield, Mick	**6**	(2)								
Cork, Alan	**7**						**5**			**5**
Dibble, Chris	**7**	(1)	1		2					
Downes, Wally	**36**	(2)	2		2		**2**			**2**
Entwhistle, Wayne	**4**	(5)			2		**3**		1	**4**
Evans, Stewart	**40**	(2)	2		1		**14**			**14**
Ferns, Phil	**7**									
Fishenden, Paul	**5**	(4)			1		**4**			**4**
Gage, Kevin	**18**	(8)		(1)		(2)	**4**			**4**
Galliers, Steve	**33**	(1)	2		2		**2**			**2**
Hatter, Steve	**28**						**1**			**1**
Hodges, Glyn	**31**	(6)	1				**9**			**9**
Jones, Steve	**3**		1		2					
Ketteridge, Steve	**39**		2		2		**7**			**7**
Leslie, John	**40**	(2)	2		2		**23**	1	1	**25**
Morris, Mark	**26**		2		2		**3**			**3**
Peters, Gary	**46**		2				**4**			**4**
Smith, Mick	**24**				2		**4**			**4**
Sparrow, Brian	**17**						**1**			**1**
Tagg, Tony	**14**		1							
Thomas, Dean	**24**		2				**5**			**5**
(own-goals)							**4**			**4**
23 players used	**506**	**(33)**	**22**	**(1)**	**22**	**(2)**	**96**	**1**	**2**	**99**

No	Date	Att	Pos	Pts		F-A	H-T	Scorers, Times, and Referees	1	2	3	4	5	6	7	8	9	10	11	12 sub used
1	A BOLTON				L	0-2	0-0		Beasant	Peters	**Winterburn**	Galliers	Morris	Hatter	Evans	Ketteridge	Sayer*	Hodges	Fishenden	Gage
	27/8	*3,992*		–				*Rudge 50, Chandler 75p*	*Farnworth*	*Borrows*	*Deakin*	*Joyce*	*McElhinney*	*Valentine*	*Saunders*	*Chandler*	*Rudge*	*Caldwell*	*Redfearn*	
								Ref: T Mills	Just three months earlier these two teams were two divisions apart. It is only three years since Bolton were in the top flight. For the 7th season the Dons fail to start the league season with a win. 19-year old keeper Simon Farnworth defies them. This ends the 22-match unbeaten run.											
2	H NEWPORT		10		W	**6-0**	2-0	Cork 17, 65, 85p, Evans 30, 76, [Ketteridge 61]	Beasant	Peters	Winterburn	Galliers	Morris	Hatter	Evans	Ketteridge	Cork	Downes	Hodges	
	3/9	**2,007**	*14*	3					*Kendall*	*Jones V*	*Vaughan*	*Bailey*	*Boyle*	*Stroud*	*Elsey*	*Aldridge*	*Woodruff**	*Reid*	*Williams*	*Relish*
								Ref: J Bray	Alan Cork returns from Swedish club Orebro to take up where he left off against Chester, with another hat-trick. Never previously had the Dons scored more than three goals in a 3rd Division game. Ironically, this record score was witnessed by the season's smallest crowd.											
3	H BOURNEMOUTH				W	3-2	2-0	Cork 6, Hodges 24, Downes 49	Beasant	Peters	Winterburn	Galliers	Morris	Hatter	Evans*	Ketteridge	Cork	Downes	Hodges	Driver
	6/9	2,345		6				*Graham 65, Morgan 68p*	*Ramsbottom*	*Nightingale*	*Morrell**	*Duffield*	*ThompsonM!*	*Beck*	*Williams*	*Sulley*	*Morgan*	*Thompson I*	*Graham*	*Lee*
								Ref: D Axcell	Fresh from losing 1-5 at Burnley, Bournemouth crash again. Dave Beasant's booming punts downfield provide Wimbledon's most potent weapon. Nigel Winterburn, on loan from Oxford, stars again. Late in the game he is crunched by Max Thompson, who is summarily expelled.											
4	A SOUTHEND		8		D	1-1	1-1	Cork 43	Beasant	Peters	Winterburn	Galliers	Morris	Hatter	Evans	Ketteridge	Cork	Downes	Hodges*	Driver
	10/9	*3,106*	*21*	7				*Shepherd 45*	*Cawston*	*Stead*	*Collins*	*Phillips*	*Yates*	*Clark*	*Pountney*	*Kellock*	*McDonagh*	*Shepherd*	*Cartwright*	
								Ref: I Borrett	Struggling Southend beat Wimbledon 1-0 at Roots Hall in the first leg of the Milk Cup. Southend parade three new signings, among them former England international Tony Currie. But he limps off in the pre-match warm-up and plays no part. 'Our worst performance,' Bassett.											
5	H PORT VALE		4		W	4-2	1-1	Evans 37, Ketteridge 46, Morris 59,	Beasant	Peters	Winterburn	Galliers	Morris	Hatter	Evans*	Ketteridge	Cork	Downes	Hodges	Gage
	17/9	2,690	*18*	10				*Newton 16, 54* [Hodges 64]	*Siddall*	*Tartt*	*Bromage*	*Hunter*	*Sproson*	*Pollard*	*Steel*	*Gore*	*Newton*	*O'Keefe*	*Fox*	
								Ref: M Dimblebee	Vale came up with the Dons, but are finding it harder to adjust. Wimbledon take their home tally for the new season to 19 from four games, the best in the country. Alan Cork's penalty was saved at 0-1. Glyn Hodges flies off after the match to play for Wales Under-21s in Norway.											
6	A EXETER		3		W	3-0	1-0	Fishenden 36, 88, Gage 90	Beasant	Peters	Winterburn	Galliers	Morris	Hatter	Evans	Ketteridge	Fishenden	Downes	Hodges*	Gage
	24/9	*3,046*	*24*	13					*Bond*	*Howarth*	*Viney*	*Marker**	*Hicks*	*McEwan*	*Neville*	*Harle*	*Kellow*	*Taylor*	*Ling*	*Auguste*
								Ref: J Deakin	Exeter escaped relegation by a point, and are faring worse this time. Player-manager Gerry Francis sits out this match, which is only tied up by Wimbledon in the dying minutes. Two-goal Paul Fishenden only played because Cork failed a late fitness test. There were seven bookings.											
7	A HULL				L	0-1	0-0		Beasant	Peters	Winterburn	Galliers	Morris	Hatter	Evans	Ketteridge	Cork	Downes	Hodges*	Gage
	27/9	*9,633*		13				*Whitehurst 50*	*Norman*	*McNeil*	*Hollifield*	*Roberts D*	*Skipper*	*Askew*	*Marwood*	*McClaren*	*Whitehurst*	*Mutrie*	*Swann*	
								Ref: N Midgley	Hull's titanic battles with Wimbledon last season look set to be resumed. They stay top by inflicting a first defeat on Bassett's team. Billy Whitehurst shrugs off Mark Morris's feeble tackle to score with a low shot. Wimbledon would have gone top of the table had they won.											
8	H ORIENT		5		D	2-2	0-0	Corbett 57 (og), Peters 71	Beasant	Peters	Winterburn*	Galliers	Morris	Hatter	Evans	Ketteridge	Cork	Downes	Hodges	Gage
	1/10	3,323	*7*	14				*McNeil 54, Houchen 74*	*Key*	*Cornwell*	*Corbett*	*Hales*	*Cunningham*	*Roffey*	*Godfrey*	*Silkman*	*Houchen*	*Sussex*	*McNeil*	
								Ref: C Thomas	Only by winning their final match did Orient survive in the 3rd Division. Frank Clark's team look better this time, and topped the table after five games. Wimbledon's direct style is attracting goals and criticism. Goal of the match was Keith Houchen's brave header for the 'O's.											
9	H BRISTOL ROV		5		D	1-1	0-1	Hatter 85	Beasant	Peters	Winterburn	Galliers	Morris	Hatter	Evans	Ketteridge	Cork	Downes*	Hodges	Gage
	8/10	3,462	*3*	15				*Barrett 9*	*Kite*	*Slatter*	*Williams B*	*Bater*	*Parkin*	*McCaffery*	*Holloway*	*Pulis*	*White**	*Randall*	*Barrett*	*Stephens*
								Ref: M Taylor	The Dons are on Cloud 9 for beating Nott'm Forest at home in the Milk Cup, but Rovers come to Plough Lane with the confidence of four straight wins under their belts. Steve Hatter steams to the rescue with a twice-taken deflected free-kick. Comedian Terry Scott is in the crowd.											
10	A WALSALL		8		L	0-4	0-1		Beasant	Peters*	Winterburn	Galliers	Morris	Hatter	Evans	Ketteridge	Cork	Downes	Hodges	Gage
	15/10	*2,546*	*7*	15				*O'Kelly 14, 76, Rees 46, 75*	*Godden*	*Caswell*	*Mower*	*Shakespeare*	*Brazier*	*Hart*	*Rees*	*Brown*	*O'Kelly*	*Preece*	*Childs*	
								Ref: P Tyldesley	Walsall are recovering nicely atter a wretched start, and inflict a crushing defeat on Bassett's boys. At 0-2, Dave Beasant tries to show outfield players how it should be done, by embarking on a mazy 40-yard dribble upfield. Nothing comes of it. Bassett's face turned blue with rage.											
11	A PRESTON				W	3-2	2-2	Smith 5, Downes 20, Ketteridge 55	Beasant	Peters	Winterburn	Morris	Smith*	Hatter	Evans	Ketteridge	Fishenden	Downes	Hodges	Gage
	18/10	*3,515*		18				*Elliot 30, 43*	*Litchfield*	*Farrelly*	*McAteer*	*Twentyman*	*Booth*	*Lodge*	*Houston*	*Walsh**	*Elliott*	*Clark*	*Houghton*	*Naughton*
								Ref: M Heath	Preston are midway through an eight-game losing streak. Mick Smith, restored to the Dons team after injury, heads them into an early lead, but he has to limp off in the second half. Five players were booked as Wimbledon squander a two-goal advantage before striking the winning goal.											

No Date	H/A	Opponent Att	Pos	Res Pts	FT	HT	Scorers, Times, and Referees	1	2	3	4	5	6	7	8	9	10	11	12
12	H	ROTHERHAM	4	W	3-1	1-0	Morris 27, Fishenden 72, Cork 77	Beasant	Peters	Winterburn	Gage*	Morris	Hatter	Evans	Ketteridge	Fishenden	Downes	Hodges	Cork
22/10		2,579	*14*	21			*Kilmore 63*	*Stevenson*	*Forrest*	*Crosby*	*McEwan*	*Johnson*	*Stone*	*Gooding*	*Kilmore*	*Walker*	*Mitchell*	*Rhodes**	*Durham*
							Ref: T Bune	Rotherham have been relegated from Division 2. Dave Beasant is attracting comment for his pioneering tactic of taking his team's free-kicks up to the halfway line. Dave Bassett has also invited controversy by insisting that 'energy accomplishes more than genius'. Cork was dropped.											
13	A	SCUNTHORPE	9	L	**1-5**	1-2	Cork 10 *[Cammack 54, 74]*	Beasant	Peters*	Winterburn	Thomas	Morris	Hatter	Evans	Ketteridge	Cork	Downes	Hodges	Fishenden
29/10		*2,347*	*17*	21			*Peters 24 (og), Wilson 32p, 49,*	*Neenan*	*Longden*	*Pointon*	*Wilson*	*Green*	*Cowling*	*Brolly*	*Cammack*	*Broddle*	*Lester*	*O'Berg*	
							Ref: L Bilkes	Promoted Scunthope are struggling, losing 1-6 at home to Southend and 1-4 at Bristol Rovers. This result is therefore a shock, though the Dons were distracted by dumping Forest from the Milk Cup. Dean Thomas returned after a spell in Finland. Bassett drags the players in on Sunday.											
14	H	OXFORD	7	W	3-1	2-0	Hodges 11, Cork 24, 49	Beasant	Peters	Winterburn	Galliers	Morris	Hatter	Evans*	Ketteridge	Cork	Downes	Hodges	Thompson
1/11		3,821	*2*	24			*Thomas 89*	*Hardwick*	*Hinshelwood*	*McDonald*	*Thomas*	*Briggs*	*Shotton*	*Lawrence*	*Barnett*	*Whatmore**	*Hebberd*	*Brock*	*Jones*
							Ref: A Gunn	Oxford led the table, but are dethroned following an emphatic Wimbledon win. Glyn Hodges scored one goal and made the others – both Alan Cork headers. Plough Lane is swamped with scouts, among them Oldham's Joe Royle. But who is the intended target?											
15	H	BRADFORD C	5	W	4-1	1-0	Cork 17, 46, Evans 58, Hodges 85	Beasant	Peters	Winterburn	Galliers	Morris	Hatter	Evans	Ketteridge	Cork	Downes*	Hodges	Thompson
5/11		2,408	*23*	27			*Ellis 65*	*McManus*	*Abbot*	*Withe*	*McCall*	*Pickering*	*Cherry*	*Haire**	*Gray*	*Campbell*	*Yorath*	*Ellis*	*Lampkin*
							Ref: T Spencer	Bradford City were on the brink of folding during the summer. Ex-Leeds stalwarts Terry Yorath and Trevor Cherry are in their side, as is the future Rangers and Scotland midfielder Stuart McCall. City's coach conked out and they arrived in taxis. The Dons are England's top scorers.											
16	A	WIGAN	7	L	2-3	0-0	Fishenden 78, Cork 90	Beasant	Peters	Thomas	Galliers	Morris	Smith	Evans	Fishenden	Cork	Downes	Hodges*	Thompson
12/11		*3,470*	*15*	27			*Bruce 52, Barrow 56, Langley 74*	*Tunks*	*Cribley*	*Comstive*	*Bailey*	*Walsh*	*Methven*	*Langley*	*Barrow*	*Butler*	*Taylor*	*Bruce*	
							Ref: V Callow	Wigan have lost their last four. Ordinarily they appear to be no match for the Dons, who once again are hung-over after Milk Cup success (beating Oldham). Wimbledon's much-changed team is torn apart after half-time, and Alan Cork's header after 97 minutes is hard on Wigan.											
17	H	LINCOLN	7	W	3-1	1-0	Ketteridge 29, Hodges 47p, 81	Beasant	Peters	Winterburn	Galliers	Morris	Hatter	Evans	Ketteridge	Cork	Downes*	Hodges	Fishenden
3/12		2,434	*13*	30			*Shipley 53*	*Felgate*	*Simmonite*	*Neale*	*Cockerill*	*Walker*	*Saxby**	*Houghton*	*Turner*	*Fashanu*	*Jack*	*Shipley*	*Hobson*
							Ref: E Crickmore	Commitments in Milk and FA Cups necessitate three weeks between league fixtures. Lincoln's No 9 is John Fashanu, in his first full season of league football. He scored a hat-trick in his previous match (against Bristol Rovers). Now Fashanu sets up a goal for George Shipley.											
18	H	BURNLEY	9	L	1-4	1-3	Cork 24	Beasant	Morris	Winterburn	Galliers	Smith	Hatter	Evans	Ketteridge	Cork	Fishenden	Hodges	
17/12		2,883	*7*	30			*Reeves 22, Hamilton 25, Scott 44, 63*	*Hansbury*	*Scott*	*Donachie*	*Phelan*	*Overson*	*Waldron*	*Hutchison*	*Reeves*	*Hamilton*	*Daley*	*Dobson*	
							Ref: J Ashworth	In a few short weeks Wimbledon have been knocked out of both cups, and now lose their 26-match unbeaten home record. Burnley register their first away victory, and manager John Bond enjoys his 51st birthday. Beasant saved a Derek Scott penalty six minutes from time.											
19	A	BRENTFORD	8	W	4-3	1-2	Evans 33, 65, Morris 51, Cork 86	Beasant	Morris	Winterburn	Thomas	Smith	Hatter	Evans	Ketteridge	Cork	Downes	Hodges	
24/12		*6,689*	*23*	33			*Kamara 32, McNichol 43, Hurlock*	*Swinburne*	*McNicholl*	*Roberts P*	*Bolton*	*Whitehead*	*Hurlock*	*Kamara**	*Joseph*	*Mahoney*	*Bowles*	*Roberts G*	*Cassells*
							Ref: J Moules	Brentford recently knocked Wimbledon out of the FA Cup, but lose out in this seven-goal thriller. Brentford lie 23rd in the table and have not won in the league since October. Chris Kamara's 20-yarder was quickly cancelled out by Evans. Better to win in the league than the cup.											
20	H	MILLWALL	7	W	4-3	2-1	Smith 26, Cork 29, 87, Evans 71	Beasant	Morris	Winterburn	Thomas	Smith	Hatter	Evans	Ketteridge	Cork	Downes	Hodges	
27/12		5,613	*13*	36			*Otula' 32, Bremner 80, Downes 90 (og)*	*Wells*	*Lovell*	*Sparrow*	*McLeary*	*Nutton*	*Cusack*	*Chatterton*	*Bremner*	*Martin**	*Otulakowski*	*White*	*Massey*
							Ref: J Martin	Back-to-back 4-3 wins are statistically extremely rare. Millwall also won 4-3 on Boxing Day, and manager George Graham is livid at losing seven goals in 24 hours. The ref booked eight, played eight minutes' injury time, and allowed Downes' free-kick over Beasant's head to stand.											
21	A	GILLINGHAM	4	W	1-0	1-0	Cork 10	Beasant	Morris	Winterburn	Galliers	Smith	Hatter	Evans*	Ketteridge	Cork	Downes	Thomas	Fishenden
31/12		*5,024*	*11*	39				*Fry*	*Sitton*	*Armstrong**	*Bruce*	*Weatherly*	*Shaw*	*Cochrane*	*Johnson*	*Leslie*	*Mehmet*	*Musker*	*Cascarino*
							Ref: D Hedges	The Gills' attack is led by former Wimbledon favourite John Leslie; their defence shored up by Steve Bruce and ex-Don Gary Armstrong. Sub is Tony Cascarino, who blazes over an empty net three minutes from time. After conceding 10 in three games, this clean sheet delights Bassett.											
22	H	SHEFFIELD UTD	4	W	3-1	0-0	Smith 70, Cork 81, 84	Beasant	Morris	Winterburn	Galliers	Smith	Hatter	Evans	Ketteridge	Cork	Downes	Thomas	
2/1		5,020	*3*	42			*Edwards 65*	*Tomlinson*	*Hefferman*	*Bolton*	*West*	*Stancliffe*	*Henderson*	*Morris*	*Arnott*	*Edwards*	*McHale*	*Philiskirk*	
							Ref: M James	Ian Porterfield's prolific goalscorer Keith Edwards does his bit in this promotion humdinger, but he is outshone by two more Alan Cork headers. Edwards now has 24 goals, Cork 23. Four wins over the holiday period. The Dons join United on 42 points, but have a game in hand.											
23	A	BRADFORD C	5	L	2-5	2-3	Cork 3, Downes 33	Beasant	Morris!	Winterburn	Galliers*	Smith	Hatter	Evans	Ketteridge	Cork	Downes	Thomas	Hodges
7/1		*4,563*	*14*	42			*Haire 21, Hawley 32, 43p, 63, 86*	*McManus*	*Podd*	*Withe*	*McCall*	*Jackson*	*Cherry*	*Haire*	*Hawley*	*Campbell*	*Gray*	*Ellis*	
							Ref: T Fitzharris	A shock result at first sight, but this is City's eighth successive win, and two more will follow, establishing a club record. Wimbledon's cause was not helped by Morris's dismissal after 58 minutes. Bassett insists three of City's goals were illegal. John Hawley scores four times.											

No	Date		Att	Pos	Pts	F-A	H-T	Scorers, Times, and Referees	1	2	3	4	5	6	7	8	9	10	11	12 sub used
24	H	BOLTON		4	W	4-0	1-0	Cork 5, Downes 54, Hodges 56, Evans 70	Beasant	Peters	Winterburn	Galliers	Smith	Morris	Evans	Ketteridge	Cork	Downes	Hodges	
	14/1		2,955	*8*	45				*Farnworth*	*Berry*	*Snookes*	*Joyce*	*McElhinney*	*Deakin*	*Thompson*	*Chandler*	*Foster**	*Rudge*	*Redfearn*	*Oghani*
								Ref: K Barratt	Wimbledon enjoy handsome revenge for their opening day defeat in this, their 300th league fixture. Coincidentally, five home teams in Division 3 scored four on the same day, detracting from the Dons' achievement. They might have scored eight. Gary Peters is recalled.											
25	A	PORT VALE		5	L	0-2	0-1		Beasant	Peters	Winterburn	Galliers	Smith	**Shanks***	Evans	Ketteridge	Cork	Downes	Hodges	Gage
	21/1		*3,627*	*24*	45			*O'Keefe 30, Bright 86*	*Siddall*	*Sproson*	*Bromage*	*Hunter*	*Ridley*	*Cegielski*	*Gore*	*Young**	*Henderson*	*O'Keefe*	*Fox*	*Bright*
								Ref: R Nixon	Vale have recently emerged from a dreadful sequence of 13 defeats and two draws in 15 matches. Wimbledon would have gone top had they won, but they are finally sunk by substitute Mark Bright lobbing Dave Beasant to score with his first touch. Both teams hit the woodwork.											
26	H	SOUTHEND		2	W	3-2	2-2	Evans 17, Peters 43, Hodges 62	Beasant	Peters	Winterburn	Galliers	Smith	Hatter	Evans	Ketteridge	Cork	Downes	Hodges	
	28/1		2,752	*18*	48			*Pennyfather 32, Phillips 37*	*Keeley*	*Stead*	*Collins*	*Pennyfather*	*Turner*	*Whymark*	*Pountney*	*Shepherd*	*Ferguson*	*Fuccillo**	*Phillips*	*May*
								Ref: B Hill	The last match between these sides was in the Milk Cup, Wimbledon winning 6-4. This time Southend include ex-Ipswich and England Trevor Whymark. Best player on the field was Glyn Hodges, who tormented Southend down the left and scored the winner with a brave header.											
27	A	ORIENT		2	W	6-2	3-1	Thomas 14, 33, Gage 32, Cork 54, 83, [Hodges 70]	Beasant	Peters	Winterburn	Thomas	Smith	Hatter	Evans	Ketteridge	Cork	Gage	Hodges	
	4/2		*3,377*	*9*	51			*Kitchen 26, Corbett 78*	*Key*	*Cornwell*	*Corbett*	*Roffey*	*Cunningham*	*Hales*	*Silkman*	*Brooks**	*Houchen*	*Kitchen*	*Roffey*	*Godfrey*
								Ref: J Hunting	This remarkable result destroys what is left of Orient's season. In addition to their six goals, Wimbledon hit the woodwork twice, had two efforts cleared off the line, and three others well saved by Key. Alan Cork scores his 100th goal for Wimbledon in his 218th first-team game.											
28	H	EXETER		2	W	2-1	0-1	Gage 73, Hodges 78	Beasant	Peters	Winterburn	Thomas	Smith	Hatter	Evans	Ketteridge	Cork	Gage	Hodges	
	11/2		3,013	*22*	54			*Smith 6 (og)*	*Bond*	*Kirkup*	*Viney*	*O'Connor*	*Webster**	*McEwan*	*Neville*	*Atkinson*	*Marker*	*McDonough!*	*Ling*	*Pratt*
								Ref: D Brazier	Exeter's fourth straight defeat is a strange affair. Gerry Francis is missing again, and they play with five men in defence. Four Dons were booked in frustration. The game turned when Roy McDonough was dismissed for kicking Gary Peters. Hodges scored one and made one.											
29	A	OXFORD			L	0-2	0-2		Beasant	Peters	Winterburn	Thomas	Morris	Hatter	Evans	Ketteridge	Cork	Downes!	Hodges*	Fishenden
	15/2		*7,640*		54			*McDonald 8p, Morris 43 (og)*	*Hardwick*	*Hinshelwood*	*McDonald*	*Trewick*	*Briggs*	*Shotton*	*Lawrence*	*Hebberd*	*Vinter**	*Brock*	*Biggins*	*Rhoades-Br'n*
								Ref: A Seville	Three recent defeats have knocked Jim Smith's Oxford off the top, though they will reclaim top spot before long. In thick mist Oxford won comfortably. The Dons had no corner-kicks and just a couple of feeble shots. Wally Downes was sent off in his first match after suspension.											
30	H	SCUNTHORPE		2	D	1-1	0-0	Ketteridge 78	Beasant	Peters	Winterburn	Galliers	Smith	Hatter	Evans	Ketteridge	Cork	Downes	Hodges*	Fishenden
	18/2		3,117	*22*	55			*Cammack 55p*	*Neenan*	*Longden*	*Pointon*	*Matthews*	*Green*	*Webster*	*Brolly*	*Cammack*	*Bell*	*Lester*	*Dey*	
								Ref: B Stevens	Scunthorpe have won only once since they slaughtered Wimbledon 5-1 in October. This match might have been more interesting had Ian Botham appeared for the Irons. Hodges wastes a first-half penalty. Steve Cammack scores from the spot for Scunthorpe after Smith handles.											
31	A	ROTHERHAM		1	W	2-1	1-0	Fishenden 8, Cork 82	Beasant	Peters	Winterburn	Galliers	Smith	Hatter	Evans*	Ketteridge	Cork	Downes	Fishenden	Hodges
	25/2		*3,141*	*20*	58			*Dungworth 86*	*Stevenson*	*Forrest*	*Crosby*	*Trusson*	*Johnson*	*Pickering*	*McEwan*	*Kilmore*	*Dungworth*	*Mitchell*	*Raynes**	*O'Dell*
								Ref: R Guy	Rotherham have won just one match in 14, so do not put up the stiffest resistance. A combination of leaders Walsall's defeat at home to Bradford City, and Dave Beasant's 89th minute penalty save from Kevin Kilmore, sends Wimbledon to the top of Division 3 for the first time.											
32	H	PRESTON		2	D	2-2	1-1	Cork 17, Fishenden 62	Beasant	Peters	Winterburn	Galliers	Smith	Hatter	Fishenden	Ketteridge	Cork	Gage*	Hodges	Evans
	3/3		2,524	*16*	59			*Booth 45, Hinnigan 72*	*Litchfield*	*Hinnigan*	*McAteer*	*Booth**	*Twentyman*	*Clark*	*Farrelly*	*Kelly*	*Elliott*	*Naughton*	*Houghton*	*Houston*
								Ref: T Bune	Last season, Preston lost only one of their last 13, and against all the odds hauled themselves to safety. Although Wimbledon are the league's top scorers, they are conceding goals by the sackful. Joe Hinnigan's header from a corner knocks the Dons off the top after just one week.											
33	A	NEWPORT			D	1-1	1-1	Cork 19	Beasant	Morris	Winterburn	Galliers	Smith	Hatter	Evans	Ketteridge	Cork	Gage	Fishenden*	Hodges
	6/3		*2,538*		60			*Pratt 35*	*Kendall*	*Jones L*	*Matthewson*	*Reid*	*Oakes*	*Boyle*	*Williams*	*Woodruff**	*Jones V*	*Randell*	*Lewis*	*Pratt*
								Ref: K Baker	Newport are missing John Aldridge, thank goodness. The Dons' own goal-grabber, Alan Cork, bags his 30th of the season. Previously he had always found goals hard to come by in the 3rd Division, as opposed to the 4th. Newport substitute Mike Pratt heads the equaliser.											
34	H	WIGAN		2	D	2-2	0-1	Fishenden 88, Evans 90	Beasant	Morris	Winterburn	Galliers	Smith*	Hatter	Evans	Ketteridge	Cork	Downes	Hodges	Fishenden
	10/3		2,565	*16*	61			*Johnson 12, Lowe 86*	*Tunks*	*Cribley*	*Comstive*	*Kelly*	*Walsh*	*Methven*	*Langley*	*Barrow*	*Johnson*	*Lowe*	*Bruce**	*Newell*
								Ref: L Shapter	A game of two subs. Young Mike Newell – later to play for Everton and Blackburn – crosses for David Lowe to put the Latics two up in the 86th minute. Wimbledon's super-sub, Paul Fishenden, helps rescue a point in a furious finale, heading inside Roy Tunks' near post.											

No	Date	H/A	Opponent	Att	Pos	Pts	Res	F-A	H-T	Scorers, Times, and Referees	1	2	3	4	5	6	7	8	9	10	11	12
35		A	BRISTOL ROV		2		D	1-1	0-0	Thomas 70	Beasant	Peters	Winterburn	Thomas	Smith	Hatter*	Evans	Morris	Cork	Downes	Hodges	Gage
	17/3			*5,383*	*5*	62				*White 65*	*Cashley*	*Hughes*	*Bater*	*Pulis*	*Parkin*	*McCaffery*	*Williams G**	*Williams D*	*White*	*Stephens*	*Williams B*	*Barrett*
										Ref: M Robinson	Rovers are just off the promotion pace. These two sides draw 1-1 for the second time this season. Rovers take the lead when Beasant races out of his box but fails to clear. After Thomas has levelled, Rovers sub Mike Barrett hits the bar, and the ball flies into Dave Beasant's arms.											
36		H	WALSALL		2		W	2-0	1-0	Cork 31, Downes 55	Beasant	Peters	Winterburn	Thomas	Smith	Morris	Evans	Gage	Cork*	Downes	Hodges	Fishenden
	24/3			4,057	*4*	65					*Godden*	*O'Kelly*	*Mower*	*Shakespeare*	*Brazier*	*Hart*	*Handysides*	*Summerfield*	*Bamber*	*Preece*	*Childs**	*Buckley*
										Ref: M Bodenham	Wimbledon end their sequence of draws, before a TV audience, by defeating the recent league leaders. Walsall have been badly distracted by reaching the semi-final of the Milk Cup, losing to Liverpool after a replay. Wally Downes' goal is a freak cross that sails over Goddard's head.											
37		A	BOURNEMOUTH		3		W	3-2	2-2	Hodges 13, Galliers 14, Ketteridge 62	Beasant	Peters	Thomas	Galliers	Smith	Morris	Evans	Ketteridge	Cork*	Downes	Hodges	Fishenden
	31/3			*3,538*	*18*	68				*/ Thompson 5, 26*	*Leigh*	*Nightingale*	*Sulley*	*Williams**	*Brown*	*Brignull*	*O'Driscoll*	*Savage*	*Rafferty*	*Beck*	*Thompson I*	*Graham*
										Ref: A Robinson	Bournemouth's season is memorable only for beating Manchester United in the FA Cup. A swirling wind does not prevent Wimbledon scoring their 100th goal of the season. The 99th had been Galliers' first of the season. The Dons have beaten Bournemouth eight times out of eight.											
38		H	HULL		3		L	1-4	0-2	Hodges 85 *[McEwan 62p]*	Beasant	Peters	Winterburn	Galliers	Smith	Morris	Evans	Ketteridge	Cork	Downes*	Hodges	Fishenden
	7/4			4,495	*4*	68				*Marwood 15, Flounders 42, G Roberts 49,*	*Norman*	*McNeil*	*Hollifield*	*McEwan*	*Skipper*	*Swann*	*Marwood**	*McClaren*	*Flounders*	*Askew*	*Roberts G*	*Roberts D*
										Ref: D Axcell	High-flying Hull hand out a thrashing. Wimbledon never recovered from losing an early goal and losing Wally Downes with an ankle injury. Hull's third straight win over the Dons was set up when Dave Beasant allowed Brian Marwood's shot to squirm under his body.											
39		A	PLYMOUTH		2		W	2-1	0-1	Hatter 67p, Cork 81	Beasant	Peters	Winterburn	Galliers	Morris	Hatter	Evans	Ketteridge	Cork	Gage*	Hodges	Fishenden
	10/4			*6,471*	*18*	71				*Tynan 43p*	*Crudgington*	*Nisbet*	*Rowe*	*Harrison*	*Smith L*	*Cooper*	*Hodges*	*Phillips*	*Tynan*	*Staniforth**	*Rogers*	*Swiggs*
										Ref: K Cooper	Sad Plymouth are in the midst of an 11-game run without a victory. Both sides scored from the spot, Plymouth when Hatter fouled Leigh Cooper, and Hatter, himself, equalising when Cork was bundled over. Four days later Plymouth lose an FA Cup semi-final to Watford.											
40		A	LINCOLN		2		W	2-1	0-1	Evans 52, Hodges 89	Beasant	Peters	Winterburn	Galliers	Morris	Hatter	Evans	Ketteridge	Cork	Gage	Hodges	
	14/4			***1,986***	*15*	74				*Redfearn 23*	*Felgate*	*Strodder*	*Neale*	*Burke*	*Walker*	*Webb*	*Redfearn*	*Turner*	*Thomas*	*Jack*	*Shipley**	*Fashanu*
										Ref: D Richardson	Less than 2,000 are enticed to view the league's top scorers. John Fashanu is on the bench for Lincoln, who take the lead with a goal which Wimbledon insist is offside. The Dons force nine first-half corners. Hodges beats two defenders to score off the post for the late winner.											
41		H	BRENTFORD		2		W	2-1	1-0	Ketteridge 1, Hodges 47	Beasant	Peters	Winterburn	Galliers	Morris	Hatter	Fishenden	Ketteridge	Cork	Gage	Hodges*	Dibble
	21/4			5,487	*17*	77				*Joseph 72*	*Roche*	*Fisher*	*Roffey*	*Roberts P*	*Gray*	*Hurlock*	*Kamara*	*Rowe*	*Joseph*	*Booker*	*Cassells**	*Roberts G*
										Ref: R Milford	Easter Saturday brings Wimbledon's first ever home win over Brentford. Ex-Don Francis Joseph scores his 17th league goal of the season, but Beasant shoulders the blame. He is having a mediocre season in goal. Ketteridge scores Wimbledon's first and sets up the second for Hodges.											
42		A	MILLWALL				D	1-1	1-0	Peters 12	Beasant	Peters	Winterburn	Galliers	Morris	Hatter	Evans	Ketteridge	Cork	Gage	Hodges	
	23/4			*5,153*		78				*Lovell 81*	*Sansome*	*Stevens*	*Robinson**	*Lovell*	*Nutton*	*Martin*	*McLeary*	*Bremner*	*Neal D*	*Otulakowski*	*White*	*Sheringham*
										Ref: C Thomas	Two days earlier Millwall had fallen 3-5 at Orient. Millwall are down to 10 men – Dave Martin receiving treatment for a head injury – when Gary Peters scores. Millwall showed little enterprise until Steve Lovell headed in from a corner-kick with Beasant stranded off his line.											
43		H	PLYMOUTH		2		W	1-0	1-0	Winterburn 3	Beasant	Peters	Winterburn	Galliers	Morris	Hatter	Evans	Ketteridge	Cork	Gage	Thomas	
	28/4			3,706	*20*	81					*Crudgington*	*Nisbet*	*Uzzell*	*Harrison*	*Smith L*	*Cooper*	*Rowe*	*Phillips*	*Chamberlain*	*Staniforth*	*Rogers**	*Hodges*
										Ref: A Gunn	Plymouth have just lost an FA Cup semi-final to Watford, but now resume their desperate fight against relegation. Nigel Winterburn scores his first goal for Wimbledon, and the same evening is voted Player of the Year. The Dons win Capital Radio's prize for London's top-scorers.											
44		A	SHEFFIELD UTD		2		W	2-1	1-0	Evans 41, Cork 70	Beasant	Peters	Winterburn	Galliers	Morris	Hatter	Evans	Ketteridge	Cork	Gage	Fishenden*	Smith
	5/5			***22,850***	*3*	84				*Morris 80*	*Tomlinson*	*Hefferman*	*Bolton*	*Arnott*	*Stancliffe**	*West*	*Morris*	*Cockerill*	*Edwards*	*McHale*	*Garner*	*Atkins*
										Ref: G Courtney	This is not only the largest crowd to watch the Dons this season, it is also Bramall Lane's largest. The Blades have won their last four, but are sunk by a header from Stewart Evans, who had twice been released by United manager Ian Porterfield. The Dons have one foot in Division 2.											
45		H	GILLINGHAM		2		L	1-3	1-0	Gage 1	Beasant	Peters	Winterburn*	Galliers	Morris	Hatter	Evans	Ketteridge	Cork	Gage	Hodges	Fishenden
	7/5			**6,009**	*8*	84				*Bruce 50, Cascarino 51, Sitton 60*	*Fry*	*Sitton*	*Sage*	*Bruce*	*Handford*	*Shaw*	*Weatherly*	*Johnson*	*Leslie*	*Mehmet**	*Cascarino*	*Cavener*
										Ref: E Read	Plough Lane is almost packed. Latecomers miss a 10-second goal by Kevin Gage, set up by Hodges. But future stars Steve Bruce and Tony Cascarino turn the game around for the Gills after half-time. Sheffield United's defeat at Bolton sends the Dons up into Division 2.											
46		A	BURNLEY		2		W	2-0	2-0	Fishenden 21, Hodges 27	Beasant	Gage	Thomas	Galliers	Smith	Morris	Evans	Ketteridge	Sayer*	Fishenden	Hodges	Hatter
	12/5			*3,340*	*12*	87					*Hansbury*	*Scott*	*Donachie*	*Phelan*	*Overson*	*Flynn*	*Daley*	*Miller*	*Hamilton*	*Biggins*	*Hutchinson*	
		Home		*Away*						Ref: T Mills	Wimbledon need to score five to reach 100 league goals. When Hodges rounds keeper Roger Hansbury to score from a sharp angle, the Dons need three more with almost an hour to play. As runners-up Wimbledon receive £8,000 from Canon, plus £3,500 as the division's top scorers.											
Average		3,443		*5,086*																		

Milk Cup	Att			F-A	H-T	Scorers, Times, and Referees	1	2	3	4	5	6	7	8	9	10	11	12 sub used
1:1 A SOUTHEND			L	0-1	0-0		Beasant	Peters	Winterburn	Galliers	Morris	Hatter	Evans	Ketteridge	Gage	Hodges	Fishenden	
29/8	*2,572*					*Shepherd 84*	*Cawston*	*Stead*	*Collins*	*Ferguson*	*Yates*	*Clark**	*Pountney*	*Skivington*	*McDonough*	*Shepherd*	*Phillips*	*Pennyfather*
						Ref: G Napthine	Three seasons ago, against the same opponents at the same stage, the Dons also lost 0-1, but pulled it round in the second leg. This time it is Greg Shepherd who beats Beasant with a powerful header. The closest the Dons came was when Ketteridge's header clipped the crossbar.											
1:2 H SOUTHEND			W	6-4	2-1	Cork 4, Ket 13,101, Gal 80, Ev 106, Hod 113	Beasant	Peters	Winterburn	Galliers	Morris	Hatter	Evans	Ketteridge	Cork	Downes	Driver*	Hodges
13/9	1,962			*aet*		*Shepherd 45, 85, Kellock 100, Phillips 116*	*Cawston*	*Angus*	*Collins*	*Pennyfather*	*Clark*	*May*	*Pountney**	*Kellock*	*McDonough*	*Shepherd*	*Cartwright*	*Phillips*
						Ref: A Robinson (Dons win 6-5 on aggregate)	What a thriller! Too bad so few saw it. Phil Driver returns to the team, collides with Southend keeper Mervyn Cawston and breaks his leg. Greg Shepherd's third goal of the tie necessitates extra time, after the Dons have twice hit the post. Extra time serves up five more goals.											
2:1 H NOTTINGHAM F			W	2-0	1-0	Galliers 28, Hodges 87	Beasant	Peters	Winterburn	Galliers	Morris	Hatter	Evans	Ketteridge	Cork	Downes	Hodges	
4/10	7,554	*1:3*					*V Breukelen*	*Anderson*	*Swain*	*Todd*	*Hart*	*Bowyer*	*Wigley*	*Davenport*	*Birtles*	*Hodge*	*Walsh*	
						Ref: M Bodenham	Brian Clough's team include the future Dutch World Cup hero, goalkeeper Hans Van Breukelen. This amazing result for Wimbledon was achieved against a Forest side that did not appear to relish a physical battle. Glyn Hodges missed a sitter, then curled a wonder goal.											
2:2 A NOTTINGHAM F			D	1-1	0-0	Evans 71	Beasant	Peters	Winterburn	Galliers*	Morris	Hatter	Evans	Ketteridge	Cork	Downes	Hodges	Fishenden
26/10	*13,718*	*1:3*				*Wallace 87*	*Sutton*	*Anderson*	*Swain*	*Todd*	*Hart*	*Bowyer*	*Wigley*	*Wallace*	*Davenport*	*Thijssen**	*Hodge*	*Walsh*
						Ref: D Scott (Dons win 3-1 on aggregate)	Wimbledon have lived on their nerves for three weeks since the first leg. Cork and Evans unsettled Colin Todd and Paul Hart all evening. £1 million striker Ian Wallace spared Forest's blushes with a late leveller. Afterwards, Clough congratulated the Dons in their changing room.											
3 H OLDHAM			W	3-1	1-1	Hodges 27, Cork 70, Fishenden 83	Beasant	Peters	Winterburn	Galliers	Morris	Hatter*	Evans	Ketteridge	Cork	Downes	Hodges	Fishenden
8/11	4,624	*2:19*				*Cross 4*	*Grew*	*Sinclair*	*Hoolickin*	*Bowden**	*Clements*	*McDonough*	*Ward*	*Henry*	*Cross*	*Parker*	*Palmer*	*Anderson*
						Ref: R Milford	2nd Division strugglers Oldham were swept aside. After former Hammer, Roger Cross, gave Oldham the lead, manager Joe Royle admitted 'we were lucky not to be beaten by five or six'. Hodges levelled with a header off the post, and sub Paul Fishenden scored with his first touch.											
4 A ROTHERHAM		7	L	0-1	0-1		Beasant	Peters	Morris	Galliers	Smith*	Hatter	Evans	Ketteridge	Cork	Hodges	Winterburn	Downes
29/11	*6,946*	*16*				*Kilmore 30*	*Stevenson*	*Forrest*	*Mitchell*	*Rhodes*	*Johnson*	*Stone*	*Seasman**	*Kilmore*	*Walker*	*Gooding*	*Raynes*	*O'Dell*
						Ref: A Saunders	Wimbledon defeat modest Rotherham twice in the league, but lose this one. Bassett opted to play five at the back, rather than his usual formation. Near the end, Glyn Hodges lobbed keeper Alan Stevenson. The ball struck a post and rebounded into the goalie's arms.											

FA Cup																		
1 H ORIENT		7	W	2-1	1-1	Cork 20, 60	Beasant	Peters	Winterburn	Galliers	Smith	Hatter	Evans	Morris	Cork	Downes	Hodges	
19/11	4,330	*5*				*Smith 32 (og)*	*Key*	*Cornwell*	*Corbett*	*Silkman*	*Cunningham*	*Hales*	*Godfrey*	*Brooks*	*Houchen*	*Kitchen*	*Roffey*	
						Ref: D Reeves	The league encounter between these sides at Plough Lane ended 2-2. Wimbledon shade this one, Cork scoring for the 7th successive game. Ex-Don Tom Cunningham was at fault. Smith then deflected Godfrey's cross. The winner was a header at the far post from Hodges' free-kick.											
2 A BRENTFORD		7	L	2-3	1-1	Peters 3, Downes 70	Beasant	Peters	Winterburn	Galliers	Morris	Hatter	Evans*	Ketteridge	Cork	Downes	Hodges	Fishenden
10/12	*5,666*	*23*				*Kamara 37, Roberts 48, Joseph 54*	*Swinburne*	*Rowe*	*Roberts P*	*McNichol*	*Whitehead*	*Hurlock*	*Kamara*	*Joseph*	*Mahoney*	*Bowles*	*Roberts G*	
						Ref: R Bridges	Francis Joseph scores a rasping goal to put this thrilling cup-tie beyond his former team. The match had 50 fouls, 31 committed by Wimbledon, 19 by Brentford. Bassett does not shed too many tears afterwads. The Dons can now concentrate on the league, as they say.											

	Home						Away					
	P	W	D	L	F	A	W	D	L	F	A	Pts
1 Oxford	46	17	5	1	58	22	11	6	6	33	28	95
2 WIMBLEDON	46	15	5	3	58	35	11	4	8	39	41	87
3 Sheffield Utd	46	14	7	2	56	18	10	4	9	30	35	83
4 Hull	46	16	5	2	42	11	7	9	7	29	27	83
5 Bristol Rov	46	16	5	2	47	21	6	8	9	21	33	79
6 Walsall	46	14	4	5	44	22	8	5	10	24	39	75
7 Bradford City	46	11	9	3	46	30	9	2	12	27	35	71
8 Gillingham	46	13	4	6	50	29	7	6	10	24	40	70
9 Millwall	46	16	4	3	42	18	2	9	12	29	47	67
10 Bolton	46	13	4	6	36	17	5	6	12	20	43	64
11 Orient	46	13	5	5	40	27	5	4	14	31	54	63
12 Burnley	46	12	5	6	52	25	4	9	10	24	36	62
13 Newport	46	11	9	3	35	27	5	5	13	23	48	62
14 Lincoln	46	11	4	8	42	29	6	6	11	17	33	61
15 Wigan	46	11	5	7	26	18	5	8	10	20	38	61
16 Preston	46	12	5	6	42	27	3	6	14	24	39	56
17 Bournemouth	46	11	5	7	38	27	5	2	16	25	46	55
18 Rotherham	46	10	5	8	29	17	5	4	14	28	47	54
19 Plymouth	46	11	8	4	38	17	2	4	17	18	45	51
20 Brentford	46	8	9	6	41	30	3	7	13	28	49	49
21 Scunthorpe	46	9	9	5	40	31	0	10	13	14	42	46
22 Southend	46	8	9	6	34	24	2	5	16	21	52	44
23 Port Vale	46	10	4	9	33	29	1	6	16	18	54	43
24 Exeter	46	4	8	11	27	39	2	7	14	23	45	33
	1104	286	142	124	996	590	124	142	286	590	996	1514

Odds & ends

Double wins: (7) Bournemouth, Exeter, Rotherham, Lincoln, Brentford, Sheffield Utd, Plymouth.
Double losses: (1) Hull.

Won from behind: (8) Port Vale (h), Sheff U (h), Southend (h), Exeter (h), Brentford (a), Bournemouth (a), Plymouth (a), Lincoln (a).
Lost from in front: (3) Gillingham (h), Scunthorpe (a), Bradford C (a).

High spots: Winning 8 out of 10 matches from late December.
Reaching top position on 25 February.
Reaching Round 4 of the Milk Cup.

Low spots: Losing 1-4 at home to Burnley on 17 December, dropping to 9th.

11 Dons played more than 30 league games, confirming a settled side.
Wimbledon's 3 home defeats were all heavy – 1-4, 1-4, 1-3.
The Dons conceded 4 or 5 goals five times, but scored 6 twice.
Wimbledon lost at Scunthorpe and Port Vale, who were both relegated.
Scunthorpe conceded fewer goals than the Dons, but were relegated.
Hull missed promotion despite having an identical record to Sheffield Utd.

Player of the Year: Nigel Winterburn.
Ever-presents: (1) Dave Beasant.
Hat-tricks: Alan Cork (1).
Leading scorer: Alan Cork (33).

	Appearances						Goals			
	Lge	Sub	MC	Sub	FAC	Sub	**Lge**	MC	FAC	**Total**
Beasant, Dave	**46**		6		2					
Cork, Alan	**41**	(1)	5		2		**29**	2	2	**33**
Dibble, Chris		(1)								
Downes, Wally	**32**		4	(1)	2		**5**		1	**6**
Driver, Phil		(2)	1							
Evans, Stewart	**44**	(1)	6		2		**12**	2		**14**
Fishenden, Paul	**12**	(11)	1	(2)		(1)	**8**	1		**9**
Gage, Kevin	**14**	(10)	1				**4**			**4**
Galliers, Steve	**36**		6		2		**1**	2		**3**
Hatter, Steve	**39**	(1)	6		2		**2**			**2**
Hodges, Glyn	**39**	(3)	5	(1)	2		**15**	3		**18**
Ketteridge, Steve	**43**		6		1		**7**	2		**9**
Morris, Mark	**39**		6		2		**3**			**3**
Peters, Gary	**37**		6		2		**3**		1	**4**
Sayer, Andy	**2**									
Shanks, Don	**1**									
Smith, Mick	**23**	(1)	1		1		**3**			**3**
Thomas, Dean	**15**						**3**			**3**
Thompson, Keith		(3)								
Winterburn, Nigel	**43**		6		2		**1**			**1**
(own-goals)							**1**			**1**
20 players used	**506**	**(34)**	**66**	**(4)**	**22**	**(1)**	**97**	**12**	**4**	**113**

No	Date		Att	Pos	Pts		F-A	H-T	Scorers, Times, and Referees	1	2	3	4	5	6	7	8	9	10	11	12 sub used
1	H	MANCHESTER C				D	2-2	2-1	Evans 5, Hodges 14	Beasant	**Kay**	Winterburn	Galliers*	Smith M	Morris	Evans	Ketteridge	Cork	**O'Berg**	Hodges	Gage
	25/8		**8,365**		1				*Cunningham 41, Parlane 50*	*Williams*	*Phillips*	*Power*	*Bond*	*McCarthy*	*Wilson*	*McNab*	*Baker*	*Cunningham*	*Smith**	*Parlane*	*Tolmie*
									Ref: I Borrett	City missed promotion by one place but by 10 points last season. No bigger crowd will watch 2nd Division football at Plough Lane this season. 'It was like a boxing match' said City boss Billy McNeill. The Dons were hanging on desperately at the end, when Parlane hit a post.											
2	A	BIRMINGHAM				L	2-4	0-1	Cork 61, 85	Beasant	Kay	Winterburn	Galliers*	Smith M	Hatter	Evans	Ketteridge	Cork	O'Berg	Hodges	Gage
	1/9		*10,445*		1				*Ferguson 19, Hopkins 58, Clarke 76, 88*	*Coton*	*Roberts*	*V d Hauwe*	*Wright*	*Hagen*	*Daly*	*Stevenson**	*Gorman*	*Ferguson*	*Clarke*	*Hopkins*	*Kuhl*
									Ref: R Dilkes	Ron Saunders' Birmingham – with the worst disciplinary record – were relegated from the top flight on the last day of last season. Alan Cork salutes his return with two goals, but City's new signing (from Wolves), Wayne Clarke, also gets two. Gerry Daly played 46 times for Ireland.											
3	H	OXFORD		19		L	1-3	0-0	Cork 89	Beasant	Kay	Winterburn	**Handford***	Morris	Hatter	Evans	Ketteridge	Cork	Gage	Hodges	O'Berg
	8/9		4,408	*6*	1				*McDonald 62, Aldridge 74, Brock 75*	*Hardwick*	*Langan*	*McDonald*	*Trewick*	*Briggs*	*Shotton*	*Rh-Brown**	*Aldridge*	*Hamilton*	*Hebberd*	*Brock*	*Biggins*
									Ref: M Bodenham	Last season's Division 3 champions have made a good start and are unbeaten in 16 games. Cork misses two chances in the first five minutes and also heads against a post. John Aldridge was more accurate. Bobby McDonald's free-kick flew past Dave Beasant from nearly 40 yards.											
4	A	SHREWSBURY				W	2-1	1-0	Hodges 10, Gage 65	Beasant	Kay	Winterburn	Handford	Morris	Hatter	Evans	Ketteridge	Cork	Gage	Hodges	
	15/9		*4,094*		4				*Robinson 60*	*Green*	*Williams*	*Johnson*	*MacLaren*	*Griffith*	*Cross*	*McNally*	*Bates C*	*Stevens*	*Robinson*	*Hackett*	
									Ref: J Worrall	Shrewsbury had been unbeaten at home since January 1984. Wimbledon survived a late onslaught and Beasant's uncertain handling to register their first win in this division. Hodges might have claimed a second goal, but Cork was offside. Ketteridge and Cork were both booked.											
5	A	MIDDLESBRO				W	4-2	1-1	Evans 33, Ketteridge 57,80, Hatter 59p	Beasant	Kay	Winterburn	Handford	Morris	Hatter	Evans	Ketteridge	Cork	Gage	Hodges	
	18/9		*4,275*		7				*Mills 13, Currie 53*	*O'Hanlon*	*Woods*	*Ward*	*Buckley*	*Mowbray*	*Gill*	*Roberts*	*Mills*	*Otto*	*Currie**	*Bell*	*Sugrue*
									Ref: A Robinson	Two away wins in four days has settled the Dons. Five of the six goals were down to defensive errors. At 1-0 David Currie mis-hits a pass back, allowing Stewart Evans to equalise. Boro still seek a first win, having lost 18 goals in 7 matches. This is their lowest ever attendance.											
6	H	CHARLTON		15		L	1-3	1-2	Evans 45	Beasant	Kay	Winterburn	Handford	Morris	Hatter*	Evans	Ketteridge	Cork	Gage	Hodges	**Martin**
	22/9		6,018	*6*	7				*Hales 3, Flanagan 31, Moore 58*	*Johns*	*Friar*	*Dickinson*	*Gritt*	*Moore*	*Berry*	*Towner*	*Hales**	*Lee*	*Aizlewood*	*Flanagan*	*Robinson*
									Ref: H King	Lennie Lawrence's team have made a fair start. Wimbledon seemed to huff and puff, while Charlton expended less effort to greater effect. Derek Hales toe-poked his goal. Stewart Evans, despite his thundering header, looked at sixes and sevens throughout the match.											
7	A	BLACKBURN		17		L	0-2	0-1		Beasant	Gage	Winterburn	Galliers	Morris	Martin	Evans	Ketteridge	Cork	Driver*	Hodges	Hatter
	29/9		*5,906*	*4*	7				*Thompson 11, Garner 63*	*Gennoe*	*Branagan*	*Rathbone*	*Barker**	*Keeley*	*Fazackerley*	*Hamilton*	*Randall*	*Thompson*	*Garner*	*Brotherston*	*Quinn*
									Ref: J Key	Four straight wins for Bobby Saxton's Blackburn lift them into the top four. The result might have been different had the referee awarded a penalty for a foul on Galliers in the fourth minute. New-boy Dave Martin has a miserable time, contributing to both Blackburn goals.											
8	H	BRIGHTON		13		W	1-0	0-0	Cork 67	Beasant	Gage	Winterburn	Galliers	Morris	Hatter	Martin	Ketteridge	Cork	Driver*	Hodges	Evans
	2/10		6,531	*7*	10					*Moseley*	*Hutchings*	*Gatting*	*Jacobs*	*Young E*	*O'Reilly*	*Wilson*	*Case*	*Worthington**	*Connor*	*Ryan*	*Penney*
									Ref: D Hedges	Wimbledon's first home win in the 2nd Division is secured by Alan Cork's 99th league goal. Phil Driver returns after a year out with a broken leg. Brighton only threatened at the end, when Hatter acrobatically cleared off the line. Ex-England Frank Worthington plays for Brighton.											
9	H	CARLISLE		12		W	3-0	1-0	Martin 44, Sayer 64, 66	Beasant	Gage	Winterburn	Galliers	Morris	Hatter	Martin	Ketteridge	Cork*	**Sayer**	Hodges	Evans
	6/10		2,876	*17*	13					*McKellar*	*McCartney*	*Rushbury*	*Ashurst*	*O'Riordan*	*Haigh*	*Hill**	*Craig*	*Poskett*	*Robson*	*Shoulder*	*MacDonald*
									Ref: R Milford	Bob Stokoe's Carlisle lost four goals at Oxford, and now three at Plough Lane. Dave Martin and Andy Sayer – only 18, and in for the rested Driver – score their first goals for the Dons. Sayer's first was from six inches out. Once they were in front, the Dons never looked in trouble.											
10	A	HUDDERSFIELD		14		L	1-2	0-0	Ketteridge 64	Beasant	Gage	Winterburn	Galliers	Morris	Hatter	Martin	Ketteridge	Cork	Sayer*	Hodges	Evans
	13/10		*5,001*	*18*	13				*Tempest 50, Doyle 66*	*Cox*	*Laws*	*Burke*	*Doyle*	*Jones*	*Allardyce*	*Lillis*	*Cooper*	*Tempest*	*Wilson*	*Pugh*	
									Ref: K Walmsley	Wimbledon hand Mick Buxton's 'Terriers' their second win of the season. Five Dons defenders hung around aimlessly for the first home goal. Steve Ketteridge equalised from eighteen yards. Ex-Fulham forward Dale Tempest plays a one-two with Steve Doyle for the winner.											

No	Venue	Opponent / Date	Pos / Att		Pts	Res	H-T	Scorers, Times, and Referees	1	2	3	4	5	6	7	8	9	10	11	12
11	H	PORTSMOUTH	12	W		3-2	2-0	Cork 44, 67, Blake 45 (og)	Beasant	Gage	Winterburn	Galliers	Morris	Hatter	Martin	Ketteridge	Cork	Sayer	Hodges	
		20/10	8,212	3	16			Doyle 50, Biley 79	Knight	Stanley*	Tait	Doyle	Blake	Gilbert	Webb	Kennedy	Morgan	McGarvey	Dillon	Biley
								Ref: D Axcell	High-flying Pompey, managed by Alan Ball, were the last unbeaten team in the Football League. Beasant pulls off two wonder saves, in addition to keeping out Kevin Dillon's late penalty. Pompey's Noel Blake passes into his own net, past bemused Alan Knight, from 30 yards.											
12	A	SHEFFIELD UTD	14	L		0-3	0-0		Beasant	Gage	Winterburn	Galliers	Morris	Hatter	Martin	Ketteridge	Cork	Sayer*	Hodges	Evans
		27/10	9,279	18	16			Arnott 60, Edwards 63, Cockerill 86	Burridge	Heffernan	Bolton	Arnott	Stancliffe	West	Morris	Cockerill	Edwards	McHale	Henderson	
								Ref: N Glover	Ian Porterfield's promoted team haven't won in seven. Much-travelled keeper John Burridge frustrated the Dons in this, his debut for the Blades, denying Alan Cork on at least three occasions. A hint of offside accompanied United's first goal.											
13	H	CRYS PALACE	13	W		3-2	0-1	Sayer 67, Winterburn 69, Cork 72	Beasant	Kay	Winterburn	Galliers*	Martin	Hatter	Evans	Ketteridge	Cork	Gage	Hodges	Sayer
		4/11	7,674	20	19			Nicholas 8p, Mahoney 85	Wood	Hughton	Lindsay	Barber	Whyte	Cannon	Irvine*	Murphy	Aylott	Nicholas	Mahoney	Stebbing
								Ref: A Gunn	Steve Coppell's team are losing week after week. Six players were booked in this no-nonsense Sunday derby. Wimbledon are indebted to a purple patch midway through the second half. Cork's seventh of the season is followed by substitute Andy Sayer scoring with his first touch.											
14	A	FULHAM	13	L		1-3	1-1	Kay 33	Beasant	Kay	Winterburn	Galliers	Morris	Hatter	Evans	Ketteridge	Cork*	Gage	Hodges	Sayer
		10/11	8,834	8	19			Davies 44, Carr 88, Coney 90	Peyton	Parker	Carr	Marshall	Hopkins	Lock	Davies	Wilson	Coney	Houghton	Lewington	
								Ref: L Shapter	Fulham boss Ray Harford will later join up with the Dons. His bright team are spurred on by two Rays – Houghton and Lewington. Gordon Davies scores in his last match before transferring to Chelsea. Cork tweaks a hamstring, and Stewart Evans hits the bar after 87 minutes.											
15	A	WOLVES	13	D		3-3	1-2	Cork 31, Winterburn 73, Morris 84	Beasant	Kay	Winterburn	Galliers	Morris	Hatter	Evans	Ketteridge	Cork	Gage*	Martin	Sayer
		17/11	7,134	16	20			Barnes 14, Ainscow 37, Butler 48	Flowers	Humphrey	Barnes	Cartwright	Pender	Dodd	Ryan	Langley	Ainscow	Buckland	Butler	
								Ref: J Ball	Poor Wolves, bottom of the 1st Division last season, and headed for bottom of the 2nd this. Beasant collides with a post and looks groggy. Winterburn races 50 yards and rounds keeper Tim Flowers to score. Hatter hits a post. Morris's late header ends a run of four away defeats.											
16	H	GRIMSBY	14	D		1-1	1-0	Evans 29	Beasant	Gage	Winterburn	Galliers	Morris	Hatter	Evans	Ketteridge	Cork	Sayer	Martin	
		24/11	3,314	7	21			K Moore 74	Batch	Seagraves	Crombie	Foley	Nicholl	Moore K	Ford	Wilkinson	Drinkell	Bonnyman	Emson	
								Ref: B Hill	Grimsby have won at Everton in the 4th round of the Milk Cup. They are also the top scorers in the 2nd Division. Keeper Nigel Batch says 'With Wimbledon it's like schoolboys all chasing the ball at the same time.' Dave Bassett attends the press conference in his birthday suit.											
17	A	LEEDS	13	L		2-5	1-2	Ketteridge 5, Cork 82 [Sellars 76]	Beasant	Gage	Winterburn	Galliers	Morris	Hatter	Evans	Ketteridge	Cork	Sayer	Martin*	**Welch**
		1/12	10,899	6	21			Wright 13, Ritchie 42, 62, 78,	Harvey	Irwin	Hamson	Sellars	Linighan	Aspen	Wright	Sheridan	Ritchie	Lorimer*	Gray	Eli
								Ref: G Napthine	It was 10 years past that these teams met famously in the FA Cup. Now they find themselves in the same division, with the match on TV. Dave Martin blunders for Leeds' first. Ketteridge fires a 25-yard screamer. But the goal-of-the-match was surely Scott Sellars' exquisite chip.											
18	H	BARNSLEY	13	D		3-3	2-0	Evans 32, 43, Fishenden 67	Beasant	Kay	Winterburn	Galliers	Morris	Smith M	Evans	Ketteridge	Cork	Gage*	Fishenden	Welch
		8/12	2,871	4	22			Geddis 51p, 66, Owen 55	Baker	Joyce	Law	Ronson	Jeffels	Futcher P	Owen	Thomas	Wylde	Geddis	Campbell	
								Ref: M Dimblebee	Barnsley lost their first three, but none of their next 15. The Dons salvaged a point when Fishenden met Cork's centre with a free header. Beasant fouled Owen for the penalty. Barnsley protest at Wimbledon's style of football. Hatter and Kay rock the boat by demanding transfers.											
19	A	CARDIFF	12	W		3-1	1-0	Evans 29, 61, Gage 66	Beasant	Kay	Winterburn	Galliers*	Morris	Smith M	Evans	Ketteridge	Welch	Gage	Fishenden	Martin
		15/12	2,976	22	25			Dwyer 49	Felgate	Smith	Mullen	Dwyer	Martin	Gibbins	Flynn	Meacock	Vaughan*	Summerfield	Elsey	McLoughlin
								Ref: R Groves	This defeat takes Alan Durban's Welsh side back to the bottom. Dons new-boy Mickey Welch, from the Isthmian League, replaces Alan Cork. Evans' 7th and 8th goals of the season are upstaged by Kevin Gage, who broke from the halfway line. This is Cardiff's lowest gate in 51 years.											
20	H	BIRMINGHAM	13	L		1-2	0-2	Fishenden 83	Beasant	Kay	Winterburn	**Sanchez**	Morris	Smith M	Evans	Ketteridge	Welch	Gage*	Fishenden	Cork
		22/12	3,674	4	25			Geddis 13, 23	Seaman	Ranson	Roberts	Wright	Armstrong	Daly	Platnauer	Clarke	Bremner	Geddis	Hopkins	
								Ref: E Read	Lawrie Sanchez has signed from Reading for £30,000. Birmingham do the double over Wimbledon. The Dons are tormented by debut-boy David Geddes, who scored twice at Plough Lane for Barnsley two weeks previously. Bassett blasted his players for lacking professionalism.											
21	H	NOTTS CO	13	W		3-2	2-2	Evans 2, Cork 26, Fishenden 66	Beasant	Kay	Winterburn	Sanchez*	Morris	Smith M	Evans	Ketteridge	Cork	Gage	Fishenden	Martin
		26/12	2,992	21	28			Harkouk 36, 38	McDonagh	Benjamin*	Clarke	Richards	Watson	Sims	O'Neill	Goodwin	Harkouk	Waitt	Hunt	Young
								Ref: A Robinson	Like Wolves, Notts Co are heading from the 1st to the 3rd Divisions in two seasons. Not even the wiles of Martin O'Neill can save them. He does his best, hitting the Dons' woodwork in both halves. Since his return from Sweden, Paul Fishenden has scored three goals in four games.											

No	Date		Att	Pos	Pts	F-A	H-T	Scorers, Times, and Referees	1	2	3	4	5	6	7	8	9	10	11	12 sub used
22	A	BRIGHTON		13	L	1-2	1-0	Evans 13	Beasant	Gage	Winterburn	Sanchez	Morris	Smith M	Evans	Ketteridge	Cork	**Fairweather**	Fishenden	Martin
	29/12		*11,106*	*10*	28			*Wilson 54, Worthington 85*	*Moseley*	*Hutchings*	*Pearce*	*Case*	*Young E*	*O'Reilly*	*Penney*	*Wilson*	*Ryan*	*Worthington*	*O'Regan**	*Smillie*
								Ref: T Spencer	Ex-England entertainer Frank Worthington, now 36, is still turning it on. His 25-yard rocket goes in off the bar and Beasant to seal Brighton's first win in six. Just five minutes' play remained. Earlier Stewart Evans had scored his sixth goal in seven matches for the Dons.											
23	A	OLDHAM		13	W	1-0	1-0	Fairweather 35	Beasant	Gage	Winterburn	Galliers	Martin	Smith M	Evans	Sanchez	Cork	Fairweather	Fishenden	
	1/1		*3,512*	*18*	31				*Goram*	*Henry*	*Barlow*	*McDonough*	*Clements*	*Hoolickin*	*Ward*	*Palmer*	*Quinn*	*Harrison*	*Bowden**	*Colville*
								Ref: P Vanes	Joe Royle's Latics are little improved this season, having barely survived last. On a bitterly cold morning, Carlton Fairweather, a £3,000 buy from Tooting, scores his first goal. Future Scotland keeper Andy Goram performs heroics. In added time, Mike Quinn shot over the bar.											
24	A	MANCHESTER C		13	L	0-3	0-1		Beasant	Gage	Winterburn	Ketteridge	Morris	Smith M	Evans*	Fishenden	Cork	Sanchez	Hodges	Fairweather
	19/1		***23,303***	*3*	31			*Smith 44, Phillips 49, Baker 78*	*Williams*	*May*	*Power*	*McNaught*	*McCarthy*	*Phillips*	*Smith*	*Baker*	*Melrose**	*Wilson*	*Kinsey*	*Cunningham*
								Ref: T Holbrook	One defeat in 14 now for City. This is one of the few matches to survive the weather, and is BBC's Match of the Day. The Dons continue to be camera-shy: only Cardiff, bottom of the table, have conceded more goals. At the other end, neither Evans nor Cork had a sniff of a chance.											
25	H	BLACKBURN		13	D	1-1	0-0	Cork 71	Beasant	Gage*	Winterburn	Handford	Morris	Smith M	Evans	Fishenden	Cork	Sanchez	Hodges	Downes
	2/2		3,953	*2*	32			*Quinn 65*	*Gennoe*	*Glenn*	*Rathbone*	*Barker*	*Keeley*	*Fazackerley*	*Miller*	*Randall*	*Thompson*	*Quinn*	*Brotherston*	
								Ref: A Seville	Three 1-1 draws on the trot for front-runners Rovers. The Dons are still feeling the effects of the cup-tie with Forest. Fishenden neatly sets up Corks' leveller. Wimbledon end the match with ten fit players. Gage had been replaced by Downes, and Evans was limping badly.											
26	A	CRYS PALACE		13	W	**5-0**	1-0	Fishenden 39p, 49, 72, Evans 59, 70	Beasant	Gage	Winterburn	Galliers	Morris	Smith M	Evans	Fishenden	Cork	Sanchez	Hodges*	Downes
	24/2		*8,005*	*18*	35				*Wood*	*Locke*	*Sparrow*	*Barber*	*Nebberling*	*Cannon*	*Irvine**	*Murphy*	*Aylott*	*Gray*	*Hughton*	*Mabbutt*
								Ref: H Taylor	It's one win in six for struggling Palace, after this Sunday fixture served up their heaviest home defeat in many years. Wimbledon clearly enjoyed their three-week rest between matches, and Fishenden enjoyed his first hat-trick. Ron Noades is coming under increasing pressure.											
27	H	SHEFFIELD UTD		13	W	**5-0**	2-0	Fairweather 14, Galliers 27, Evans 47, [Fishenden 64, Sanchez 82]	Beasant	Gage	Winterburn	Galliers	Morris	Smith M	Evans	Fishenden	Cork*	Sanchez	Fairweather	Downes
	2/3		3,396	*14*	38				*Burridge*	*Heffernan*	*Kenworthy*	*Arnott*	*Stancliffe*	*Thompson**	*Morris*	*Cockerill*	*Edwards*	*Eves*	*Bolton*	*Philliskirk*
								Ref: D Axcell	United went into this match buoyed by three straight wins but find themselves humiliated by another 5-star Dons performance. Wimbledon took the lead with a super header from Fairweather – on his home debut – from Evans's cross. Sanchez scores his first goal for his new club.											
28	A	PORTSMOUTH		13	L	0-1	0-1		Beasant	Gage	Winterburn	Galliers	Morris	Martin	Evans	Fishenden	Cork*	Sanchez	Fairweather	Downes
	8/3		*11,444*	*5*	38			*Webb 6*	*Knight*	*Golac*	*Hardyman*	*Dillon*	*Blake*	*Gilbert*	*O'Callaghan*	*Kennedy*	*Bamber*	*Webb*	*Hilaire*	
								Ref: R Milford	Pompey have been up there all season. Wimbledon play their fourth match in eight days and look punch-drunk. A looping back-header from highly rated Neil Webb over the stranded Beasant settles the outcome. Cork's header was nodded out by Paul Hardyman from under the bar.											
29	A	OXFORD		13	L	0-4	0-2	*[McDermott 87]*	Beasant	Gage	Winterburn	Galliers	Morris	Martin*	Evans	Fishenden	Sanchez	Downes	Fairweather	Cork
	13/3		*8,592*	*1*	38			*Aldridge 5, 56, Shotton 13,*	*Hardwick*	*Langan*	*Spearing*	*Trewick**	*Briggs*	*Shotton*	*Rh-Brown*	*Aldridge*	*Jones*	*Hebberd*	*Brock*	*McDermott*
								Ref: K Barratt	Five games without a win had knocked Oxford off the top for the first time. They return to winning ways thanks to John Aldridge's brace – to add to the goal he scored against the Dons at Plough Lane. Wally Downes played instead of the out-of-sorts Alan Cork.											
30	A	CARLISLE		13	L	**1-6**	0-4	Sayer 49 *[Poskett 43, 76]*	Beasant	Kay	Winterburn	Handford	Morris	Smith M	Evans*	Fishenden	Fairweather	Sayer	Ketteridge	Gage
	23/3		***2,779***	*16*	38			*McCartney 3p, Hill 11, 40, 55,*	*McKellar*	*Haigh*	*McCartney*	*Ashurst*	*O'Riordan*	*Carney*	*Shoulder*	*Halsall*	*Poskett*	*Hill*	*Halpin*	
								Ref: A Saunders	Modest Carlisle serve up this expected thrashing, as Wimbledon – weakened by suspensions and influenza – continue their unpredictable ways. Bassett objected to the early penalty that put Carlisle ahead, en route to Andy Hill's hat-trick and Carlisle's biggest win for 15 years.											
31	H	SHREWSBURY		13	W	4-1	2-0	Sanchez 20, 62, Evans 34, Sayer 52	Beasant	Kay	Winterburn	Galliers*	**Gayle**	Smith M	Evans	Fishenden	Sayer	Downes	Sanchez	Ketteridge
	27/3		2,337	*11*	41			*Robinson 68*	*Perks*	*Williams*	*Johnson*	*MacLaren*	*Griffith*	*Petts*	*McNally*	*Hackett**	*Stevens*	*Robinson*	*Tester*	*Kerr*
								Ref: J Moules	Shrewsbury are proving as schizophrenic as the Dons. Their three previous scores were 5-1, 0-4, 3-0. Now a 1-4 thumping. Wimbledon notch their second double, with Winterburn shrugging off a stomach virus, Downes playing at sweeper, and Brian Gayle his first match.											

32	H	MIDDLESBRO	13	D	1-1	1-0	Sayer 21	Beasant	Kay	Winterburn	Galliers	Gayle	Smith M	Evans	Fishenden	Sayer	Downes	Sanchez	Gage
30/3		2,338	*19*	42			*Stephens 49*	*O'Hanlon*	*Laws*	*Strong*	*McAndrew*	*Mowbray*	*Nattrass*	*Hamilton*	*Mills*	*Otto*	*Stephens*	*Currie*	
							Ref: K Baker	Boro manager Willie Maddren is grateful for this point on an otherwise miserable afternoon, which saw Wally Downes limp out of the fray with an ankle fracture. Shot-shy Dons are badly missing the injured Alan Cork. John Kay had earlier been on loan to Middlesbrough.											
33	A	NOTTS CO	13	W	3-2	2-1	Fishenden 5, Sanchez 44, Winterburn 65	Beasant	Gage	Winterburn	Galliers	Gayle	Smith M	Evans	Ketteridge	Fishenden*	Sanchez	**Thorn**	Fairweather
6/4		*4,800*	*20*	45			*Fashanu 13, Harkouk 55*	*Leonard*	*Yates*	*Richards*	*Goodwin*	*Watson*	*Sims*	*Harkouk*	*Fashanu*	*Robinson*	*Waitt**	*Hunt*	*Daws*
							Ref: J McAuley	County's goals are scored by ex-Palace forward Rachid Harkouk and Justin Fashanu, at that time the more famous brother. Nigel Winterburn heads Wimbledon's late winner. Ex-England Dave Watson plays at the heart of County's defence. Andy Thorn makes his debut for the Dons.											
34	H	OLDHAM	13	W	1-0	0-0	Sayer 84	Beasant	Gage	Winterburn	Galliers	Gayle	Smith M	Evans	Ketteridge	Fishenden*	Sanchez	Thorn	Sayer
9/4		2,649	*15*	48				*Goram*	*Barlow*	*Donachie*	*McDonough*	*O'Callagh'n**	*McGuire*	*Ward*	*Henry*	*Quinn*	*Parker*	*Palmer*	*Bowden*
							Ref: J Deakin	Andy Thorn plays his second match for the Dons as sweeper, instead of the injured Downes. Substitute Andy Sayer's far-post header earns the Dons their fourth double of the season. Oldham manager Joe Royle protests that the corner that led to the goal was awarded in error.											
35	A	CHARLTON	13	W	1-0	1-0	Fishenden 27	Beasant	Gage	Winterburn	Galliers	Smith M	Gayle	Evans	Ketteridge	Fishenden	Sanchez	Thorn	
13/4		*4,521*	*17*	51				*Vaughan*	*Curtis*	*Friar*	*Gritt*	*Dowman*	*Aizlewood*	*Towner**	*Curbishley*	*Stuart*	*Moore*	*Flanagan*	*Lee*
							Ref: M Bodenham	Fishenden's sizzling 25-yard goal was almost cancelled out in the dying seconds by Steve Dowman's header which flies over the crossbar. Fishenden was lucky to be playing at all, having to shrug off a pelvic strain. Charlton are in serious relegation trouble after this defeat.											
36	H	FULHAM	13	D	1-1	1-0	Fishenden 2p	Beasant	Gage	Winterburn	**McClure**	Gayle	Smith M	Sayer	Ketteridge*	Fishenden	Sanchez	Thorn	Fairweather
16/4		5,811	*11*	52			*Wilson 67*	*Peyton*	*Parker*	*Carr*	*Elkins*	*Hopkins*	*Achampong*	*Sealy*	*Wilson*	*Rosenior*	*Houghton*	*Lewington*	
							Ref: D Hedges	Bassett's injury list allows a debut for 19-year-old Doug McClure, a free-transfer from QPR. Galliers was down with a virus, and Ketteridge's torn ankle ligaments will keep him out for the season. Rosenior felled Sanchez for the penalty. Gary Elkins' free-kick led to Fulham's goal.											
37	H	WOLVES	13	D	1-1	1-0	Sayer 37	Beasant	Gage	Winterburn	Galliers	Gayle	Smith M	Evans*	Sayer	Fishenden	Sanchez	Thorn	Fairweather
20/4		3,277	*21*	53			*Ainscow 51*	*Flowers*	*Humphrey*	*Heywood*	*Pender*	*Zelem*	*Herbert*	*Ainscow*	*Chapman C*	*Buckland*	*Evans**	*Crainie*	*Blackwell*
							Ref: I Borrett	Tommy Docherty's abject Wolves lose to everybody else, but have now drawn twice with Wimbledon. Wolves dominated the second half, protected at the back by the promising Tim Flowers. Sayer volleys the Dons' goal, but Alan Ainscow levels from Danny Crainie's cross.											
38	A	GRIMSBY	13	L	1-2	0-2	Hodges 55p	Beasant	Kay	Gage*	Galliers	Gayle	Smith M	Evans	Sayer	Hodges	Sanchez	Thorn	Martin
27/4		*4,283*	*9*	53			*Cumming 13, Lund 33p*	*Felgate*	*Robinson*	*Agnew*	*Hine*	*Moore A*	*Moore K*	*Ford*	*Lund*	*Drinkell**	*Bonnyman*	*Cumming*	*Emson*
							Ref: J Bray	Once Bob Cumming had put Grimsby two up from a corner, the Dons were always chasing this match. Their second-half rally sees Glyn Hodges – back after two months – score from the spot after Galliers was tripped. The Dons haven't beaten Grimsby in eight attempts.											
39	H	HUDDERSFIELD	13	L	0-1	0-1		Beasant	Kay	Winterburn	Handford	Gayle	Smith M*	Evans	Sayer	Hodges	Sanchez	Thorn	Fairweather
30/4		**2,335**	*11*	53			*Webster 40*	*Cox*	*Measham*	*Cooper*	*Doyle*	*Webster*	*Allardyce*	*Lillis*	*Pugh*	*Tempest*	*Wilson*	*Cowling*	
							Ref: M James	Huddersfield arrive at Plough Lane in a trough after four defeats. They would have lost this one, too, had Wimbledon taken a quarter of their chances. Simon Webster, a free transfer from Spurs, scores with a 30-yard deflected free-kick. The Dons fail to score at home for the first time.											
40	H	LEEDS	13	D	2-2	0-1	Sanchez 63, Winterburn 73	Beasant	Kay	Winterburn	Galliers	Gayle	Smith M*	Evans	Sayer	Hodges	Sanchez	Thorn	Fairweather
4/5		6,638	*6*	54			*Baird 16, 78*	*Day*	*Irwin*	*Hamson*	*Sellars*	*Linighan*	*Aspin*	*Wright*	*Sheridan*	*Baird*	*Lorimer**	*Gray*	*Ritchie*
							Ref: B Stevens	Leeds will miss out on promotion, but they contribute fully to this thriller. Ex-Southampton striker Ian Baird gives them two goals, but the Dons feel they should have won. The referee blew for a penalty just as Sayer 'scored', but Glyn Hodges promptly misses from the spot.											
41	A	BARNSLEY	13	D	0-0	0-0		Beasant	Kay	Winterburn!	Galliers	Gayle	Morris	Evans	Sayer*	Fairweather	Martin	Thorn	Hodges
6/5		*3,053*	*11*	55				*Baker*	*Joyce*	*Gray*	*Ronson*	*Law**	*Jeffers*	*Owen!*	*Thomas*	*Futcher R*	*Plummer*	*Campbell*	*Goodison*
							Ref: I Hendrick	Barnsley are losing regularly as the season winds up, but they bring some aggro to this match. A first-half flare-up between Winterburn and Gordon Owen sees both sent off. The crowd is Barnsley's smallest since 1978, when the Dons last visited Oakwell. Evans struck a post.											
42	H	CARDIFF	12	W	2-1	0-0	Martin 74, Gayle 83	Beasant	Kay	Winterburn	McClure*	Gayle	Morris	Evans	Sayer	Hodges	Martin	Thorn	**Wise**
11/5		3,252	*21*	58			*Micallef 59*	*Plumley*	*Flynn*	*Mullen*	*Gibbins*	*Ford M*	*Tong*	*Elsey*	*Micallef*	*Withey*	*Vaughan*	*Hamilton*	
	Home	*Away*					Ref: T Bune	Brian Gayle's first goal for Wimbledon dooms Cardiff to the 3rd Division, after they had taken the lead through Tarki Micallef. Beasant could not hold his shot. Martin levelled the scores with a lob that Gary Plumley might have saved. Dennis Wise took the eye with some neat touches.											
Average	4,424	7,344																	

Milk Cup	Att	Pos	Res	F-A	H-T	Scorers, Times, and Referees	1	2	3	4	5	6	7	8	9	10	11	12 sub used
1:1 A PORTSMOUTH			L	0-3	0-2		Beasant	Kay	Winterburn	Galliers	Smith M!	Morris	Evans	Ketteridge	O'Berg	Gage	Hodges	
28/8	*8,999*					*Webb 32, 41, Dillon 87p*	*Knight*	*Stanley*	*Waldron**	*Doyle*	*Blake*	*Gilbert*	*Webb*	*Tait*	*McGarvey*	*Biley*	*Dillon*	*Wood*
						Ref: B Stevens	Alan Cork missed this match through concussion. Mick Smith was sent off after 65 minutes, and three other Dons were cautioned. Portsmouth's Neil Webb scores twice – a low drive and a cheeky lob. Beasant knocked over Alan Biley for the critical late penalty.											
1:2 H PORTSMOUTH			W	1-0	1-0	Gage 37	Beasant	Kay	Winterburn	Handford*	Morris	Hatter	Evans	Ketteridge	Cork	Gage	Hodges	**Kemp**
4/9	4,670						*Knight*	*Stanley*	*Tait*	*Doyle*	*Blake*	*Gilbert*	*Webb*	*Kennedy*	*McGarvey*	*Biley*	*Dillon*	
						Ref: T Bune (Dons lose 1-3 on aggregate)	1,500 Portsmouth fans swell the crowd, and set up a cascading version of the Pompey Chimes. The hushed Wimbledon supporters did little to raise the spirits of the team, who have too much to do. David Kemp makes his one appearance for the Dons, ironically against his former team.											

FA Cup	Att	Pos	Res	F-A	H-T	Scorers, Times, and Referees	1	2	3	4	5	6	7	8	9	10	11	12 sub used
3 H BURNLEY		13	W	3-1	1-0	Evans 27, Fishenden 77, 85p	Beasant	Gage	Winterburn	Galliers	Martin	Smith	Evans	Sanchez	Cork	Sayer	Fishenden	
5/1	3,381	*3:20*				*Devine 89*	*Hansbury*	*Palmer*	*Hampton*	*Phelan*	*Kennedy*	*Hird*	*Grewcock*	*Overson*	*Devine*	*Biggins*	*Hutchison*	
						Ref: H Taylor	It is 10 years to the day since the Dons' cup triumph at Turf Moor. Burnley are now destined for Division 4, despite the efforts of veteran Tommy Hutchison, who scored in the 1981 Final. Roger Hansbury assisted the Dons by palming Gage's free-kick under his own crossbar.											
4 A NOTTINGHAM F		13	D	0-0	0-0		Beasant	Gage	Winterburn	Galliers	Morris	Smith	Evans	Fishenden	Cork	Sanchez	Hodges*	Downes
26/1	*17,178*	*1:7*					*Segers*	*McInally*	*Swain*	*Fairclough*	*Hart*	*Bowyer*	*Wigley*	*Metgod*	*Birtles*	*Davenport*	*Hodge*	
						Ref: N Midgley	Brian Clough took his players off for a pre-match holiday in Tenerife, wary of last season's results in the Milk Cup. Beasant plays out of his skin, Kevin Gage twice kicks off the line, and Peter Davenport hits the post. Gary Birtles returned to the Forest side after a 10-month lay-off.											
4R H NOTTINGHAM F		13	W	1-0	1-0	Fishenden 12	Beasant	Gage	Winterburn	Galliers	Morris	Smith	Evans	Fishenden	Cork	Sanchez	Hodges	
30/1	10,348	*1:7*					*Segers*	*McInally*	*Swain*	*Fairclough*	*Hart*	*Bowyer**	*Wigley*	*Metgod*	*Birtles*	*Davenport*	*Hodge*	*Walsh*
						Ref: N Midgley	The FA Cup is Brian Clough's only missing trophy. Paul Fishenden's goal went in off the foot of Kenny Swain. When Galliers crash-tackled Steve Hodge, Clough had to be restrained on the touchline. The Dons are in the 5th round for the first time. Gate receipts are £27,000, a record.											
5 H WEST HAM			D	1-1	0-0	Evans 82	Beasant	Gage	Winterburn	Galliers	Morris	Smith	Evans	Fishenden	Cork	Sanchez	Hodges*	Downes
4/3	13,500	*1:16*				*Cottee 72*	*McAlister*	*Stewart*	*Brush*	*Walford*	*Martin*	*Devonshire*	*Allen*	*Orr*	*Goddard*	*Cottee*	*Pike*	
						Ref: K Hackett	The Hammers are struggling, as usual, and have yet to win in the league in 1985. Plough Lane is packed, with the quarter-finals beckoning. Hodges hits the post at 0-0. Ray Stewart's shot is deflected to Tony Cottee, who scores. Sub Downes crosses for Evans' headed equaliser.											
5R A WEST HAM			L	1-5	1-2	Fishenden 18	Beasant	Gage	Winterburn	Galliers	Morris	Smith	Evans	Fishenden	Cork	Sanchez	Downes*	Martin
6/3	*20,258*	*1:16*				*Cottee 5, 42, 85, Dickens 56, Allen 80*	*McAlister*	*Stewart*	*Brush*	*Hilton*	*Martin*	*Devonshire*	*Allen*	*Orr*	*Goddard**	*Cottee*	*Dickens*	*Swindlehurst*
						Ref: R Lewis	The Dons are sunk. England Under-21 striker Paul Goddard was a constant threat, Alan Devonshire was back to England form, and Tony Cottee bags his first FA Cup hat-trick. Wimbledon's long-ball tactics played into West Ham's hands. 'We lost our discipline,' moans Bassett.											

	P	W	D	L	Home F	Home A	W	D	L	Away F	Away A	Pts
1 Oxford	42	18	2	1	62	15	7	7	7	22	21	84
2 Birmingham	42	12	6	3	30	15	13	1	7	29	18	82
3 Manchester C	42	14	4	3	42	16	7	7	7	24	24	74
4 Portsmouth	42	11	6	4	39	25	9	8	4	30	25	74
5 Blackburn	42	14	3	4	38	15	7	7	7	28	26	73
6 Brighton	42	13	6	2	31	11	7	6	8	23	23	72
7 Leeds	42	12	7	2	37	11	7	5	9	29	32	69
8 Shrewsbury	42	12	6	3	45	22	6	5	10	21	31	65
9 Fulham	42	13	3	5	35	26	6	5	10	33	38	65
10 Grimsby	42	13	1	7	47	32	5	7	9	25	32	62
11 Barnsley	42	11	7	3	27	12	3	9	9	15	30	58
12 WIMBLEDON	42	9	8	4	40	29	7	2	12	31	46	58
13 Huddersfield	42	9	5	7	28	29	6	5	10	24	35	55
14 Oldham	42	10	4	7	27	23	5	4	12	22	44	53
15 Crys Palace	42	8	7	6	25	27	4	5	12	21	38	48
16 Carlisle	42	8	5	8	27	23	5	3	13	23	44	47
17 Charlton	42	8	7	6	34	30	3	5	13	17	33	45
18 Sheffield Utd	42	7	6	8	31	28	3	8	10	23	38	44
19 Middlesbro	42	6	8	7	22	26	4	2	15	19	31	40
20 Notts Co	42	6	5	10	25	32	4	2	15	20	41	37
21 Cardiff	42	5	3	13	24	42	4	5	12	23	37	35
22 Wolves	42	5	4	12	18	32	3	5	13	19	47	33
	924	224	113	125	734	521	125	113	224	521	734	1273

Odds & ends

Double wins: (5) Shrewsbury, Crystal Palace, Cardiff, Notts Co, Oldham.
Double losses: (3) Birmingham, Oxford, Huddersfield.

Won from behind: (3) Crystal Palace (h), Cardiff (h), Middlesbrough (a).
Lost from in front: (3) Fulham (a), Leeds (a), Brighton (a).

High spots: 3 consecutive wins in April.
Back-to-back 5-0 wins in February and March.
Beating Nottingham Forest in FA Cup, reaching Round 5 for the first time.

Low spots: 1 point from first 3 league games.
5 games without a win in November and December.
3 consecutive league defeats in March, including 0-4 and 1-6 thrashings.
6 games without a win in April and May.

From November to May, the Dons were almost permanently locked in 13th position.

Player of the Year: Nigel Winterburn.
Ever-presents: (1) Dave Beasant.
Hat-tricks: Paul Fishenden (1).
Leading scorer: Stewart Evans (16).

	Appearances Lge	Sub	MC	Sub	FAC	Sub	Goals Lge	MC	FAC	Total
Beasant, Dave	**42**		2		5					
Cork, Alan	**26**	(2)	1		5		**11**			**11**
Downes, Wally	**3**	(4)			1	(2)				
Driver, Phil	**2**									
Evans, Stewart	**36**	(4)	2		5		**14**		2	**16**
Fairweather, Carlton	**7**	(6)					**2**			**2**
Fishenden, Paul	**20**				5		**10**		4	**14**
Gage, Kevin	**33**	(4)	2		5		**2**	1		**3**
Galliers, Steve	**29**		1		5		**1**			**1**
Gayle, Brian	**12**						**1**			**1**
Handford,Phil	**7**		1							
Hatter, Steve	**15**	(1)	1				**1**			**1**
Hodges, Glyn	**21**	(1)	2		3		**3**			**3**
Kay, John	**21**		2				**1**			**1**
Kemp, David				(1)						
Ketteridge, Steve	**28**	(1)	2				**4**			**4**
Martin, Dave	**15**	(5)			1	(1)	**2**			**2**
McClure, Doug	**2**									
Morris, Mark	**29**		2		4		**1**			**1**
O'Berg, Paul	**2**	(1)	1							
Sanchez, Lawrie	**20**				5		**5**			**5**
Sayer, Andy	**16**	(4)			1		**8**			**8**
Smith, Mick	**23**		1		5					
Thorn, Andrew	**10**									
Welch, Mick	**2**	(2)								
Winterburn, Nigel	**41**		2		5		**4**			**4**
Wise, Dennis		(1)								
(own-goal)							**1**			**1**
27 players used	**462**	**(36)**	**22**	**(1)**	**55**	**(3)**	**71**	**1**	**6**	**78**

No	Date	Att	Pos	Pts	F-A	H-T	Scorers, Times, and Referees	1	2	3	4	5	6	7	8	9	10	11	12 sub used
1 H	MIDDLESBRO			W	3-0	2-0	Evans 5, Gage 40p, Sanchez 64	Beasant	Kay	Gage	Galliers	Gayle	Smith	Evans*	**Holloway**	Cork	Sanchez	Thorn	Hodges
	17/8	2,844		3				*Pears*	*Laws*	*Corden**	*Pallister*	*Mowbray*	*Nattrass*	*Roberts*	*O'Riordan*	*Stephens*	*McAndrew*	*Powell*	*Currie*
							Ref: K Barratt	The tragedies of Heysel and Valley Parade means soccer kicks off the new season in sombre mood. Alcohol is banned at Plough Lane, as at other grounds. Boro's Steve Corden breaks a leg on his debut and never plays again. The Dons win the opening league match for the first time.											
2 A	LEEDS			D	0-0	0-0		Beasant	Kay	Gage	Galliers	Gayle	Smith	Evans	Sayer	Cork*	Sanchez	Thorn	Hodges
	21/8	*12,426*		4				*Day*	*Irwin*	*Harrison*	*Snodin*	*Linighan*	*Aspin*	*McCluskey*	*Sheridan*	*Baird*	*Lorimer*	*Sellars*	
							Ref: K Walmsley	Within 20 seconds of the start Andy Sayer forces Mervyn Day to save with his legs. The Dons never come so close again, and owe their point to two athletic saves by Dave Beasant, one from George McCluskey, the other to prevent a Brian Gayle own-goal. Eddie Gray is Leeds' boss.											
3 A	SHEFFIELD UTD		10	L	**0-4**	0-3	*[McNaught 29]*	Beasant	Kay	Gage	Galliers	Gayle	Morris*	Evans!	Sayer	Cork	Sanchez	Thorn	Winterburn
	24/8	*11,914*	*3*	4			*Gayle 2 (og), Morris 12p, 51p,*	*Burridge*	*Eckhardt*	*Kenworthy*	*Thompson*	*Stancliffe*	*McNaught*	*Morris*	*Cockerill*	*Withe*	*Lewington*	*Bolton*	
							Ref: M Heath	United retain their 100% start. The match brings a hammering for the Dons and an early bath for Stewart Evans. Afterwards Dave Bassett defends the player, insisting he was only sent off because United players chased the referee up the field to demand his expulsion.											
4 H	BRADFORD C			W	1-0	0-0	Evans 77	Beasant	Kay	Winterburn	Gage	Gayle	Martin	Evans	Holloway	Fishenden*	Sanchez	Thorn	Hodges
	26/8	3,205		7				*Litchfield*	*Abbott*	*Withe*	*McCall*	*Jackson*	*Evans*	*Hendrie*	*Thorpe*	*Campbell*	*Singleton*	*Graham*	
							Ref: D Axcell	Division 3 champions Bradford City, stunned by the fire at their stadium, will take time to settle in their new environment. Evans' header from Andy Thorn's free-kick secures the points in this Bank Holiday fixture. Thorn and Gayle subdued City's prolific striker Bobby Campbell.											
5 A	GRIMSBY		5	W	1-0	0-0	Evans 85	Beasant	Kay	Winterburn	Gage	Gayle	Martin	Evans	Cork	Fishenden	Sanchez	Thorn	
	31/8	*3,476*	*16*	10				*Felgate*	*Barratt*	*Crombie*	*Peake*	*Moore A*	*Moore K*	*Ford*	*Lund*	*Gilligan*	*Bonnyman*	*Hobson*	
							Ref: T Jones	Grimsby are still searching for their first win after Stewart Evans nods a late goal. The Dons' first win over Grimsby in nine attempts comes about when David Felgate, the goalkeeper Bassett tried to sign in the close season, palms Kevin Gage's cross straight out to the lurking Evans.											
6 H	BARNSLEY			W	1-0	1-0	Fishenden 15	Beasant	Kay	Winterburn	Gage	Gayle	Martin	Evans*	Sayer	Fishenden	Sanchez	Thorn	Cork
	3/9	**2,351**		13				*Baker*	*Joyce*	*Goodison*	*Glavin*	*Burns*	*Futcher*	*Owen*	*Jeffels*	*Walsh*	*Gray*	*Campbell*	
							Ref: B Hill	Barnsley match Wimbledon with ale-house tactics of their own. Wimbledon had never beaten them before, but take the points when Kay's low cross to the far post is laid back by Winterburn into the path of Paul Fishenden. This result takes the Dons up to 2nd place.											
7 H	OLDHAM		2	D	0-0	0-0		Beasant	Kay	Winterburn	Gage	Gayle	Martin	Cork	Sayer	Fishenden	Sanchez*	Thorn	Hodges
	7/9	2,749	*6*	14				*Goram*	*Donachie*	*Ryan*	*McDonough*	*Hoolickin*	*McGuire*	*Palmer*	*Henry*	*Quinn*	*Futcher*	*Atkinson*	
							Ref: M Dimblebee	Oldham haven't lost since the opening day of the season. Unsettled Dave Beasant has just signed a new two-year contract. He keeps his sixth clean sheet in seven matches thanks to the protection afforded by a sweeper and a five-man defence. Goram saved well from Gayle.											
8 A	BLACKBURN		5	L	0-2	0-1		Beasant	Kay	Winterburn	Gage	Smith	Martin	Cork	Fishenden*	Sayer	Sanchez	Thorn	Hodges
	14/9	*5,006*	*2*	14			*Patterson 31, 47*	*Gennoe*	*Hamilton*	*Rathbone*	*Barker*	*Keeley*	*Fazackerley*	*Brotherston*	*Lowey*	*Quinn*	*Garner*	*Patterson*	
							Ref: T Holbrook	All the talk is of ground-sharing, perhaps with Millwall, now that Charlton are leaving the Valley. Wimbledon have neither scored nor taken any points from Ewood Park. Mark Patterson's header is somewhat against the run of play, but when he makes it 2-0 the Dons fade badly.											
9 A	BRIGHTON		8	L	0-2	0-1		Beasant	Kay*	Winterburn	Galliers	Gayle	Martin	Evans	Cork	Gage	Sanchez	Thorn	Hodges
	21/9	*9,973*	*4*	14			*Wilson 2, Ferguson 47*	*Digweed*	*O'Reilly*	*Pearce*	*Wilson*	*Young*	*Oliver*	*Jacobs*	*Saunders*	*Ferguson*	*Biley*	*Mortimer*	
							Ref: D Hedges	Wimbledon have scored just three goals in eight matches, and Alan Cork hasn't managed any. Mick Ferguson's close-range header ended the Dons' resistance in a match whose main talking point was when a ball-boy ran on to the pitch and picked up the ball before it went out of play.											
10 H	CHARLTON		5	W	3-1	2-1	Evans 2, 51, Holloway 27	Beasant	Thorn	Winterburn*	Galliers	Gayle	Martin	Evans	Cork	Holloway	Sanchez	Gage	Hodges
	28/9	4,527	*6*	17			*Humphrey 19*	*Johns*	*Humphrey*	*Reid*	*Gritt**	*Thompson*	*Berry*	*Shipley*	*Lee*	*Pearson*	*Curbishley*	*Stuart*	*Towner*
							Ref: L Shapter	Charlton are riding high, but Wimbledon leap-frog over them. Fighting had broken out between opposing fans when Stewart Evans got a touch to Andy Thorn's corner for the first goal. Charlton keeper Nicky Johns was at fault for the Dons' second and third goals.											

No	Venue	Opponent	Pos	Res	F-A	H-T	Scorers, Times, Referees	1	2	3	4	5	6	7	8	9	10	11	12
5/10		12,707	9	20			Drinkell 5	Woods	Haylock	Spearing*	Bruce	Phelan	Watson	Barham	Drinkell	Rosario	Mendham	Van Wyk	Brooke
							Ref: H Taylor	Yo-yo club Norwich were relegated on the last day of last season. They haven't yet found their feet in the 2nd Division. Kevin Drinkell heads the opener. Steve Bruce handles Cork's shot and Martin levels from the spot. Beasant saves Bruce's penalty after Brian Gayle pushed Bruce.											
12	H	FULHAM	4	W	1-0	0-0	Cork 55	Beasant	Gage	Winterburn	Galliers	Gayle	Martin	Evans	Cork*	Holloway	Sanchez	Thorn	Hodges
12/10		5,953	14	23				Peyton	Cottington	Carr	Scott	Hopkins	Parker	Marshall	Hicks*	Coney	Pike	Barnett	Achampong
							Ref: J Moules	Wimbledon's first win over Fulham comes about when Alan Cork intercepts Cliff Carr's weak header. All eyes, however, are on Nigel Winterburn, who has another superb match. Fulham boss Ray Harford describes him as the best player on the pitch. The biggest gate so far.											
13	H	MILLWALL	5	D	1-1	1-1	Winterburn 37	Beasant	Gage	Winterburn	Galliers	Gayle	Martin	Evans	Cork	Holloway	Sanchez	Hodges	
19/10		4,644	17	24			Lovell 21	Sansome	Stevens	Hinshelwood	Briley	Walker	Nutton	Lowndes	Chatterton*	Fashanu	Lovell	Kinsella	Leslie
							Ref: A Gunn	George Graham's Millwall are back up in the 2nd Division. This splendid match was marked by an eye-catching duel between the Dons' ex-Lion Dave Martin and future Don John Fashanu. Winterburn heads his first goal of the season to cancel out Steve Lovell's chip.											
14	A	STOKE	4	D	0-0	0-0		Beasant	Gage	Winterburn	Galliers	Smith	Martin	Evans	Holloway	Cork	Sanchez	Thorn	
25/10		6,708	19	25				Fox	Bould	Mills	Hemming*	Dyson	Berry	Adams	Maskery	Bertschin	Saunders	Heath	Williams
							Ref: K Cooper	Stoke were relegated from Division 1 with just 17 points, and Mick Mills' team are struggling again. This Friday night game saw the Dons jeered by the home fans for their safety-first tactics. Ian Holloway missed the Dons' two best chances and Galliers and Thorn were booked.											
15	H	CARLISLE	2	W	4-1	0-1	Smith 50, 82, Cork 54, 70	Beasant	Kay	Winterburn	Galliers	Smith	Martin	Evans	Cork	Holloway	Sanchez	Thorn*	Hodges
3/11		3,882	22	28			Hill 15	Carr	Baker	McCartney	Ashurst	Saunders	Halsall	Wakenshaw	Cooke	Hill	Bishop	Halpin	
							Ref: J Ball	Bob Stokoe's labouring side have won only once all season. This Sunday evening match allows Wimbledon to jump from 7th to 2nd. Yet Andy Hill lobbed Carlisle in front. Bassett roared with rage, and transfer-listed Mick Smith responded with two goals. Martin was carried off.											
16	A	SUNDERLAND	4	L	1-2	0-1	Fairweather 82	Beasant	Kay	Winterburn	Galliers	Smith	Thorn	Holloway*	Cork!	Fishenden	Sanchez	Hodges	Fairweather
9/11		15,518	12	28			Swindlehurst 44, 74	Bolder	Burley	Kennedy	Venison	Bennett	Elliott	Gray	Pickering	Swindlehurst	Gates	Gayle	
							Ref: D Hutchinson	Lawrie McMenemy has taken control of relegated Sunderland. This is their fourth win in five. The manager fields a future England man in Barry Venison. Dave Swindlehurst sinks the Dons. Cork is sent off for striking Shaun Elliott, but is cheered by the birth of a daughter.											
17	H	SHREWSBURY	2	W	2-1	1-1	Sanchez 31, Galliers 71	Beasant	Kay	Winterburn	Galliers	Smith	Thorn	Holloway	Cork	Fishenden	Sanchez	Hodges	
16/11		2,584	21	31			Daly 23	Perks	Kerr	Gunn	Cross	Pearson	Griffin	McNally	Hackett	Nardiello	Robinson	Daly	
							Ref: I Borrett	Ireland's Gerry Daly puts lowly Shrewsbury ahead with a 25-yard curler. A first of the season for Lawrie Sanchez levels, and before Galliers fired the winner Colin Robertson clipped Beasant's bar with an overhead kick. The match welcomed the return of Glyn Hodges.											
18	A	HULL	3	D	1-1	1-0	Sanchez 18	Beasant	Kay	Winterburn	Galliers	Smith	Thorn	Morris	Fairweather	Fishenden	Sanchez	Hodges*	Evans
23/11		6,576	10	32			McEwan 59p	Norman	Brentano	Swann	Doyle	Skipper	McEwan	Williams	Bunn	Whitehurst	Askew	Roberts	
							Ref: R Banks	Brian Horton, later to manage Oxford and Manchester City, has taken Hull from the 3rd Division into the top half of the 2nd. Four Dons are booked. Winterburn gave away the penalty for pushing Neil Williams. Dave Beasant stands defiant in the second half.											
19	H	HUDDERSFIELD	5	D	2-2	0-2	Morris 50, Fishenden 61	Beasant	Kay	Winterburn	Galliers	Smith*	Thorn	Evans	Fishenden	Morris	Sanchez	Hodges	Fairweather
30/11		2,805	18	33			Cork 26, Raynor 42	Cox	Brown	Bray	Doyle	Webster	Jones P	Wilson Phil	Cork	Tempest*	Raynor	Cowling	Winter
							Ref: I Hemley	Huddersfield arrive at Plough Lane on the back of seven defeats and one draw. Their tactics are the offside trap and the long ball. For some reason Bassett plays a five-man defence. Mick Smith makes a hash of a back-pass, but after the break substitute Carlton Fairweather runs riot.											
20	H	LEEDS	6	L	0-3	0-2		Beasant	Kay	Winterburn	Galliers*	Morris	Thorn	Evans	Fishenden	Fairweather	Sanchez	Hodges	Cork
7/12		3,492	12	33			Snodin 38, Baird 41, Dickinson 48	Day	Caswell	Robinson	Snodin	Aspin	Linighan	Ritchie	Stiles	Baird!	Harrison	Dickinson	
							Ref: J Ashworth	Bremner's Leeds are in the wrong half of the table, but their muscular approach brings about Wimbledon's first home defeat, in front of Sports Minister Dick Treacy. Leeds' Ian Baird was sent off for spitting at Andy Thorn. Mervyn Day saved Fishenden's 27th minute penalty.											
21	A	MIDDLESBRO	7	L	0-1	0-0		Beasant	Kay	Winterburn	Galliers	Smith!	Thorn	Evans*	Cork	Holloway	Sanchez	Downes	Hodges
14/12		4,693	19	33			Mowbray 72	Pears	Laws	McAndrew	Mowbray	O'Riordan	Pallister	Hamilton	Heard	Slaven	Stephens	Rowell	
							Ref: D Phillips	Boro just staved off relegation, but won't be so lucky this time. The club will be wound up by the High Court. But this is their third successive win at home. Just before the goal Mick Smith was sent off for retaliating, after Tony McAndrew threw the ball at him.											

No	Date		Att	Pos	Pts	F-A	H-T	Scorers, Times, and Referees	1	2	3	4	5	6	7	8	9	10	11	12 sub used
22	H	SHEFFIELD UTD		5	W	**5-0**	3-0	Kay 20, Hodges 22, 88, Sanchez 27,	Beasant	Kay	Winterburn	Galliers	Smith	Thorn	**Wise**	Cork	Holloway	Sanchez	Hodges	
	21/12		3,756	*6*	36			[Stancliffe 77 (og)]	*Burridge*	*Eckhardt*	*Kenworthy*	*Thompson*	*Stancliffe*	*McNaught!*	*Wigley*	*Edwards*	*Withe!*	*Lewington*	*Foley*	
								Ref: M Bodenham	An ageing United side are swept contemptuously away. Dennis Wise marks his debut with a penalty high and wide. Glyn Hodges claimed the own-goal as his own, and went off with the match ball. Ex-Villa players Peter Withe and Ken McNaught are sent off at 3-0. Eight are booked.											
23	A	CRYS PALACE		4	W	3-1	2-0	Cork 3, 43, Sanchez 72	Beasant	Kay	Winterburn	Galliers	Smith	Thorn	Evans	Cork	Holloway	Sanchez*	Hodges	Wise
	26/12		*7,929*	*6*	39			*Droy 64*	*Wood*	*O'Doherty*	*Brush**	*Taylor*	*Droy*	*Cannon*	*Irvine*	*Wright*	*Aylott*	*Barber*	*Ketteridge*	*Hughton*
								Ref: M James	Millwall manager George Graham takes in this match, for his side face the Dons in the FA Cup. He is highly impressed at what he sees, describing Wimbledon as 'absolutely brilliant'. Ian Wright, in his first full season with Palace, is kept tightly in check.											
24	A	BARNSLEY		3	W	1-0	1-0	Sanchez 21	Beasant	Kay	Winterburn	Downes	Martin	Thorn	Evans	Cork	Holloway	Sanchez	Hodges	
	28/12		*8,949*	*6*	42				*Baker*	*Joyce*	*Gray*	*Goodison*	*May*	*Futcher*	*Owen*	*Thomas*	*Campbell*	*Hirst*	*Plummer**	*Burns*
								Ref: K Breen	Hard and slippery conditions do not make for a good match. Nor do Wimbledon in this mood, for they are accused of inciting the home crowd. Downes takes a free-kick and Cork heads it into the path of Sanchez. That goal heralds Wimbledon's first win at Oakwell.											
25	H	PORTSMOUTH		3	L	1-3	0-2	Cork 50	Beasant	Kay	Winterburn	Downes	Martin	Thorn	Evans	Cork	Holloway*	Sanchez	Hodges	Wise
	1/1		**9,025**	*2*	42			*Channon 29, 49, Hilaire 34*	*Knight*	*Tait*	*Swain*	*Dillon*	*Blake*	*Gilbert*	*O'Callaghan*	*Kennedy*	*Channon*	*Wood*	*Hilaire*	
								Ref: M Reed	37-year-old Mike Channon scores the 266th and 267th goals of his long career, in front of Plough Lane's biggest gate. Channon's first – a volley – curled over Beasant from 25 yards. Wimbledon were left to rue their early missed chances. Cork had hit the bar in the second minute.											
26	A	OLDHAM		3	L	1-2	0-1	Holloway 51	Beasant	Kay	Gage	Galliers	Smith	Martin*	Holloway	Cork	Fairweather	Sanchez	Downes	Hodges
	11/1		***3,035***	*17*	42			*Futcher 9, Palmer 81*	*Goram*	*Donachie**	*Barlow*	*Hoolickin*	*Jones*	*Smith*	*Palmer*	*McGuire*	*Colville*	*Futcher*	*Atkinson*	*Williams*
								Ref: G Courtney	Pompey, Millwall in the Cup, and now Oldham. Three defeats to kick off the New Year. Of Oldham's previous 11 league games, they had lost nine and drawn two. The defeat might have been worse, for Beasant saved a first-half penalty. Roger Palmer scored his 12th of the season.											
27	H	GRIMSBY		3	W	3-0	0-0	Sanchez 51, Hodges 67, Cork 82	Beasant	Kay	Winterburn	Gage	Gayle	Morris*	Evans	Cork	Holloway	Sanchez	Hodges	Sayer
	18/1		2,770	*16*	45				*Batch*	*Barratt*	*Agnew*	*Peake*	*Lyons*	*Crombie*	*Ford**	*Lund*	*Hobson*	*Bonnyman*	*Emson*	*Gilligan*
								Ref: A Robinson	Brian Gayle returns to the side with his right knee heavily strapped after a cartilage operation, and in the first minute he is outpaced by Gordon Hobson for the only time. Once Sanchez headed in Gage's free-kick, Grimsby were out of it. Evans had three headers cleared off the line.											
28	H	BRIGHTON		4	D	0-0	0-0		Beasant	Gage	Winterburn	Galliers	Morris	Smith	Evans	Cork	Holloway*	Sanchez	Fairweather	Wise
	22/2		5,797	*6*	46				*Digweed*	*Hutchings*	*Gatting*	*Wilson*	*Young*	*O'Reilly*	*Saunders*	*Penney*	*Biley*	*Connor*	*Jacobs*	
								Ref: D Axcell	More than a month has been lost to the weather, and this match was touch and go, too. It went ahead, on a bone-hard-pitch, despite Brighton manager Chris Cattlin's protests. The nearest either side came to a goal was when Alan Cork hit the Brighton post with a second-half volley.											
29	H	NORWICH		4	W	2-1	0-1	Evans 61, Cork 64	Beasant	Gage	Winterburn	Galliers	Morris	Smith	Evans	Cork	Fishenden	Sanchez	Fairweather	
	8/3		5,827	*1*	49			*Barham 22*	*Woods*	*Culverhouse*	*Deehan*	*Bruce*	*Phelan*	*Watson*	*Barham*	*Drinkell*	*Biggins*	*Mendham*	*Williams*	
								Ref: G Ashby	Leaders Norwich lose for the first time in 18 matches, when they had been beaten by Wimbledon! The Dons achieve a famous double, helped by playing four up front, which means no place in midfield for Galliers. The aerial bombardment brings Evans' first goal since September.											
30	A	MILLWALL		3	W	1-0	0-0	Fairweather 74	Beasant	Gage	Winterburn	Galliers	Morris	Smith	Evans	Cork	Fishenden*	Sanchez	Fairweather	Downes
	11/3		*4,643*	*17*	52				*Sansome*	*Stevens*	*Hinshelwood*	*Briley*	*Walker*	*McLeary*	*Lowndes*	*Wilson*	*Fashanu*	*Lovell*	*Otulakowski*	
								Ref: E Scales	The latest speculation concerns Wimbledon's possible move to an indoor stadium. The team gain revenge for their Cup defeat, but provoke chants of 'boring' from the home crowd. 'One of the worst games I have ever seen,' moans George Graham. The Dons twice hit the bar.											
31	A	FULHAM		3	W	2-0	2-0	Sanchez 36, Cork 42	Beasant	Gage	Winterburn	Galliers	Morris	Smith	Evans	Cork	Fishenden*	Sanchez	Fairweather	Downes
	15/3		*6,209*	*22*	55				*Peyton*	*Cottington*	*Carr*	*Scott*	*Gore**	*Parker*	*Marshall*	*Donnellan*	*Coney*	*Pike*	*Barnett*	*Achampong*
								Ref: K Barratt	Bassett is in his sick-bed, but he is cheered by this defeat that sends luckless Fulham to the bottom. Gary Barnett blasts a 77th minute Fulham penalty against the crossbar. Steve Galliers had set up Lawrie Sanchez's goal; Carlton Fairweather's cross set up Alan Cork's back-header.											

No	Venue	Opponent	Att	Pos	Pt	F-A	H-T	Scorers, Times, and Referees	1	2	3	4	5	6	7	8	9	10	11	12 sub used
32	H	BLACKBURN		3	D	1-1	1-1	Fairweather 29	Beasant	Gage	Winterburn	Galliers	Morris	Smith	Evans*	Cork	Fishenden	Sanchez	Fairweather	Downes
22/3			3,261	15	56			*Miller 11*	*O'Keefe*	*Branagan*	*Rathbone*	*Barker*	*Keeley*	*Mail*	*Miller*	*Hamilton*	*Quinn*	*Patterson*	*Brotherston*	
								Ref: J Bray												
Beasant fumbles Ian Miller's early flick over the line, but Rovers' stand-in keeper, Vince O'Keefe, then allows Fairweather's free-kick to float over his head to equalise. Wimbledon had beaten Rovers 5-0 in the Milk Cup, but despite leading 15-1 on corners, cannot force the winner.																				
33	A	PORTSMOUTH		3	D	1-1	0-0	Smith 60	Beasant	Gage	Winterburn	Galliers	Morris	Smith	Evans	Cork	Fishenden*	Sanchez	Fairweather	**Fashanu**
29/3			***18,809***	2	57			*Blake 53*	*Knight*	*Swain*	*Hardyman*	*Tait**	*Blake*	*Gilbert*	*O'Callaghan*	*Kennedy*	*Quinn*	*Channon*	*Hilaire*	*Dillon*
								Ref: R Groves												
Pompey led the table but are wobbling. They are the first team to meet John Fashanu in a Wimbledon shirt. He had played at Fratton Park four days earlier for Millwall. He appears as a 54th minute sub, and Alan Ball accuses him of elbowing. Beasant saved O'Callaghan's penalty.																				
34	H	CRYS PALACE		4	D	1-1	1-0	Fashanu 34	Beasant	Gage	Winterburn	Galliers	Morris	Smith	Downes*	Cork	Fashanu	Sanchez	Fairweather	Evans
1/4			8,429	6	58			*Wright 62*	*Wood*	*Finnigan*	*Brush*	*Taylor*	*Nebbeling*	*Cannon*	*Irvine*	*Ketteridge*	*Gray*	*Barber*	*Wright*	
								Ref: A Gunn												
Evans and Fishenden are the players under threat from new signing John Fashanu, who strikes a new partnership with Alan Cork. Fash is accused by Bassett of being unfit, but he heads his first goal for the club. Ian Wright, fresh from the Spartan League, scores for Crystal Palace.																				
35	A	CARLISLE		4	W	3-2	1-1	Fashanu 35, Fairweather 61, 64	Beasant	Kay	Winterburn	Galliers	Morris	Smith	Gage	Cork	Fashanu	Sanchez	Fairweather	
6/4			*5,593*	*21*	61			*Cooke 42, McGarvey 80p*	*Endersby*	*Haigh*	*McCartney*	*Ashurst*	*Saunders*	*Halsall*	*Hill*	*Cooke*	*McGarvey*	*Bishop*	*Tolmie*	
								Ref: J Key												
Carlisle's four-match winning run is ended by Fairweather's bum, which diverts Winterburn's miscued shot over the line for his second goal. Wind and hard pitch hamper this match but Scott McGarvey's twice-taken penalty sets up a furious climax. The Dons lost 1-6 here last season.																				
36	H	SUNDERLAND		3	W	3-0	0-0	Hodges 63, 67, 86p	Beasant	Kay	Winterburn	Gage	Morris	Smith	Hodges	Cork	Fashanu	Sanchez	Fairweather	
12/4			6,051	*20*	64				*Dibble*	*Venison*	*Kennedy**	*Armstrong*	*Hetzke*	*Bennett*	*Ford*	*White*	*Wallace*	*Gray*	*Proctor*	*Gayle*
								Ref: I Borrett												
This was billed as a grudge match, Cork having been sent off controversially at Roker. This was the Sunderland's first visit to Plough Lane. Glyn Hodges had been out of favour for months. His second-half hat-trick was completed from the spot after Gary Bennett handled from Cork.																				
37	A	SHREWSBURY		3	D	1-1	1-0	Fairweather 43	Beasant	Gage	Winterburn	Galliers	Morris	Smith	Hodges	Cork	Fashanu	Sanchez	Fairweather	
19/4			*3,948*	*16*	65			*Hackett 50*	*Perks*	*Williams*	*Johnson*	*Cross*	*Pearson*	*Griffin*	*McNally*	*Hackett*	*Stevens!*	*Robinson*	*Daly*	
								Ref: D Scott												
Shrewsbury boss Chic Bates employs a similar direct style to the Dons. Fashanu and stopper Colin Griffin engage in a battle royal, and Shrewsbury's Gary Stevens was sent off after 56 minutes. Keeper Steven Perks' 23rd birthday was spoiled by Fairweather's scoring header.																				
38	H	HULL		4	W	3-1	2-1	Fashanu 36, 60, Fairweather 37	Beasant	Gage	Winterburn	Galliers	Smith*	Morris	Hodges	Cork	Fashanu	Sanchez	Fairweather	Sayer
26/4			5,155	*7*	68			*Flounders 34*	*Norman*	*Jobson*	*Swann*	*Doyle*	*Skipper*	*McEwan*	*Parker*	*Bunn*	*Flounders*	*Heard*	*Askew**	*Williams*
								Ref: G Napthine												
Hull boss Brian Horton confessed 'We couldn't cope with Fashanu and Cork.' Fashanu's sizzling half-volley from Cork's near-post header was followed 30 seconds later by Carlton Fairweather smashing a second. Fashanu's record transfer fee – £125,000 – is already looking cheap.																				
39	H	STOKE		3	W	1-0	0-0	Cork 48	Beasant	Gage	Winterburn	Galliers	Morris	Thorn	Hodges*	Cork	Fashanu	Sanchez	Fairweather	Downes
29/4			5,959	*9*	71				*Fox*	*Curtis*	*Hemming*	*Mills*	*Bould*	*Berry*	*Adams*	*Saunders*	*Bertschin*	*Devine*	*Heath*	
								Ref: B Stevens												
This is Wimbledon's last home match of the season, and it is spoiled by lashing rain. Cork's head beat the outstretched arm of Stoke keeper Peter Fox, from Kevin Gage's free-kick, for the only goal. A below-par performance, for whom Fairweather was the Dons' best player.																				
40	A	HUDDERSFIELD		3	W	1-0	0-0	Sanchez 61	Beasant	Gage	Winterburn	Galliers	Morris	Thorn	Hodges	Cork	Fashanu	Sanchez	Fairweather*	Fishenden
3/5			*6,083*	*16*	74				*Cox*	*Brown*	*Bray*	*Doyle*	*Webster*	*Jones J*	*Curran!*	*Cork*	*Shearer*	*Wilson Phil*	*Raynor!*	
								Ref: G Courtney												
Three away matches to come, and Wimbledon need to win one of them to secure promotion. 300 bedraggled fans braved thunder, lightning, and rain to cheer on their team. Terry Curran and Paul Raynor of Huddersfield were sent off, but Sanchez drove in Gage's short free-kick.																				
41	A	CHARLTON		3	D	0-0	0-0		Beasant	Kay	Winterburn	Galliers*	Morris	Thorn	Hodges	Cork	Fashanu	Sanchez	Fairweather	Fishenden
6/5			*13,214*	*2*	75				*Johns*	*Humphrey*	*Reid*	*Lee*	*Thompson*	*Pender*	*Shipley*	*Melrose**	*Pearson*	*Aizlewood*	*Stuart*	*Flanagan*
								Ref: M James												
Both teams are already promoted, otherwise this might have turned into a south London war. As it was, it was the mildest of friendlies. Fash and Charlton stopper Steve Thompson were team-mates at Lincoln. Thompson won this duel, limiting Fash to hitting the bar in the last minute.																				
42	A	BRADFORD C		3	D	1-1	1-1	Gannon 25	Beasant	Kay	Winterburn	Gannon	Morris	Thorn	Holloway*	Evans	Fishenden	Sanchez	Fairweather	Hodges
8/5			*4,316*	*13*	76			*Hendrie 34*	*Litchfield*	*Oliver*	*Evans*	*McCall*	*Jackson*	*Clegg*	*Hendrie*	*Goodman*	*Campbell*	*Singleton**	*Ormondroyd*	*Ellis*
Average	Home 4,578		*Away* *8,1¯¯*					Ref: K Lupton												
Three Dons were booked, together with assistant manager Alan Gillett, and Winterburn was stretchered off with ligament damage. The Dons miss the chance to finish second and the extra prize money from the Canon League. The Dons' 37 goals conceded is the division's lowest.																				

Milk Cup	Att			F-A	H-T	Scorers, Times, and Referees	1	2	3	4	5	6	7	8	9	10	11	12 sub used
2:1 H BLACKBURN		8	W	5-0	3-0	Cork 10, 29, 84, Gayle 34, Evans 57	Beasant	Gage	Winterburn	Galliers	Gayle	Martin	Evans	Cork	Holloway*	Sanchez	Hodges	Fishenden
24/9	2,072	*2*					*Gennoe*	*Hamilton*	*Rathbone*	*Barker!*	*Keeley*	*Fazackerley*	*Lowey*	*Patterson*	*Quinn*	*Garner*	*Brotherston*	
						Ref: R Milford	Wimbledon have just been beaten 0-2 at Ewood Park in the league. Bassett employs two wide players in Ian Holloway and Glyn Hodges, and Alan Cork reaps the benefit. Rovers' Simon Barker is sent off for throwing a punch at Steve Galliers. Bassett abandons the sweeper system.											
2:2 A BLACKBURN		6	L	1-2	1-1	Cork 24	Beasant	Thorn	Winterburn	Galliers	Gayle	Martin	Evans	Cork	Holloway	Hodges*	Gage	Downes
8/10	*2,160*	*3*				*Patterson 30, Quinn 65*	*O'Keefe*	*Branagan*	*Rathbone*	*Hamilton*	*Keeley*	*Fazackerley*	*Miller*	*Lowey*	*Quinn*	*Garner*	*Patterson**	*Mail*
						Ref: A Saunders (Dons win 6-2 on aggregate)	On a rain-lashed pitch Mark Patterson bags a freak equaliser, his angled shot flying in off Beasant's boot and the crossbar. Blackburn won the match, but not the tie, when Gayle upended Miller. Beasant saved Quinn's spot-kick, but not the rebound. Cork bags his fourth goal of the tie.											
3 A TOTTENHAM		2	L	0-2	0-0		Beasant	Kay	Winterburn	Galliers	Smith	Thorn	Evans*	Cork	Holloway	Sanchez	Hodges	Downes
6/11	*16,919*	*1:12*				*Mabbutt 56, Leworthy 74*	*Clemence*	*Stevens G*	*Hughton*	*Roberts*	*Miller*	*Perryman*	*Cooke**	*Falco*	*Mabbutt*	*Hoddle*	*Waddle*	*Leworthy*
						Ref: G Napthine	This match was postponed several times in the aftermath of the Tottenham riots. Galliers is the sole survivor of the Dons team that lost 0-4 in the same competition eight years earlier. Mabbutt heads in Hoddle's free-kick, and Roberts and Perriman are unruffled throughout.											

FA Cup	Att			F-A	H-T	Scorers, Times, and Referees	1	2	3	4	5	6	7	8	9	10	11	12 sub used
3 A MILLWALL		3	L	1-3	0-2	Gage 89	Beasant	Kay	Winterburn	Galliers	Smith	Martin	Evans	Cork	Holloway	Downes*	Hodges	Gage
4/1	*5,840*	*18*				*Lovell 11, Fashanu 35, Walker 77*	*Sansome*	*Stevens*	*Hinshelwood*	*Briley*	*Walker*	*Button*	*Lowndes*	*Wilson*	*Fashanu*	*Lovell*	*Otulakowski**	*Chatterton*
						Ref: H King	John Fashanu returns for Millwall after a five-match suspension, and his speed shreds the Wimbledon defence. The Dons try to push up and employ the offside trap, but Fashanu and Steve Lovell start their runs from deep and cause havoc. Thorn was injured and Sanchez suspended.											

		Home					Away					
	P	W	D	L	F	A	W	D	L	F	A	Pts
1 Norwich	42	16	4	1	51	15	9	5	7	33	22	84
2 Charlton	42	14	5	2	44	15	8	6	7	34	30	77
3 WIMBLEDON	42	13	6	2	38	16	8	7	6	20	21	76
4 Portsmouth	42	13	4	4	43	17	9	3	9	26	24	73
5 Crys Palace	42	12	3	6	29	22	7	6	8	28	30	66
6 Hull	42	11	7	3	39	19	6	6	9	26	36	64
7 Sheffield Utd	42	10	7	4	36	24	7	4	10	28	39	62
8 Oldham	42	13	4	4	40	28	4	5	12	22	33	60
9 Millwall	42	12	3	6	39	24	5	5	11	25	41	59
10 Stoke	42	8	11	2	29	16	6	4	11	19	34	57
11 Brighton	42	10	5	6	42	30	6	3	12	22	34	56
12 Barnsley	42	9	6	6	29	26	5	8	8	18	24	56
13 Bradford City	42	14	1	6	36	24	2	5	14	15	39	54
14 Leeds	42	9	7	5	30	22	6	1	14	26	50	53
15 Grimsby	42	11	4	6	35	24	3	6	12	23	38	52
16 Huddersfield	42	10	6	5	30	23	4	4	13	21	44	52
17 Shrewsbury	42	11	5	5	29	20	3	4	14	23	44	51
18 Sunderland	42	10	5	6	33	29	3	6	12	14	32	50
19 Blackburn	42	10	4	7	30	20	2	9	10	23	42	49
20 Carlisle	42	10	2	9	30	28	3	5	13	17	43	46
21 Middlesbro	42	8	6	7	26	23	4	3	14	18	30	45
22 Fulham	42	8	3	10	29	32	2	3	16	16	37	36
	924	242	108	112	767	497	112	108	242	497	767	1278

Odds & ends

Double wins: (5) Grimsby, Barnsley, Norwich, Fulham, Carlisle.
Double losses: (0).

Won from behind: (5) Carlisle (h), Shrewsbury (h), Norwich (h), Hull (h), Norwich (a).
Lost from in front: (0).

High spots: Ending the season unbeaten in 16 games.
Conceding just 37 goals, the best in the division.

Low spots: 4 games without a win in late November and early December.
Being outplayed by Millwall in the FA Cup.

John Fashanu played against the Dons three times before signing for them, even scoring against the Dons in the 3rd round of the FA Cup.

Wimbledon's best and worst results were both against Sheffield United, losing 0-4 at Bramall Lane and winning 5-0 at Plough Lane.

Player of the Year: Nigel Winterburn.
Ever-presents: (2) Dave Beasant, Lawrie Sanchez (league only).
Hat-tricks: Glyn Hodges (1), Alan Cork (1).
Leading scorer: Alan Cork (15).

	Appearances						Goals			
	Lge	Sub	MC	Sub	FAC	Sub	**Lge**	MC	FAC	**Total**
Beasant, Dave	**42**		3		1					
Cork, Alan	**36**	(2)	3		1		**11**	4		**15**
Downes, Wally	**5**	(4)		(2)	1					
Evans. Stewart	**27**	(3)	3		1		**6**	1		**7**
Fairweather, Carlton	**18**	(2)					**7**			**7**
Fashanu, John	**8**	(1)					**4**			**4**
Fishendon, Paul	**16**	(2)		(1)			**2**			**2**
Gage, Kevin	**29**		2			(1)	**1**		1	**2**
Galliers, Steve	**32**		3		1		**1**			**1**
Gannon, John	**1**						**1**			**1**
Gayle, Brian	**13**		2					1		**1**
Holloway, Ian	**19**		3		1		**2**			**2**
Hodges, Glyn	**18**	(12)	3		1		**6**			**6**
Kay, John	**26**		1		1		**1**			**1**
Martin, Dave	**15**		2		1		**1**			**1**
Morris, Mark	**20**						**1**			**1**
Sanchez, Lawrie	**42**		2				**9**			**9**
Sayer, Andy	**5**	(2)								
Smith, Mick	**24**		1		1		**3**			**3**
Thorn, Andy	**27**	(1)	2							
Winterburn, Nigel	**38**	(1)	3		1		**1**			**1**
Wise, Dennis	**1**	(3)								
(own-goals)							**1**			**1**
22 players used	**462**	**(33)**	**33**	**(3)**	**11**	**(1)**	**58**	**6**	**1**	**65**

No	Date	Att	Pos	Pts	F-A	H-T	Scorers, Times, and Referees	1	2	3	4	5	6	7	8	9	10	11	12 sub used
1	A MANCHESTER C			L	1-3	0-0	Thorn 54	Beasant	Kay	Winterburn	Galliers	Morris	Thorn*	Wise	Cork	Fashanu	Sanchez	Hodges	Gage
	23/8	*20,756*		–			*Baker 58, 63, Christie 64*	*Suckling*	*May*	*Wilson*	*Clements*	*McCarthy*	*Redmond*	*Davies*	*McNab*	*Christie*	*Baker*	*Brightwell**	*Simpson*
							Ref: K Hackett	With Liverpool's Grobbelaar injured, Beasant has the longest run of any goalkeeper – 226 matches dating back to May 1981. City were also the Dons' first opponents in Division 2. Thorn's first ever goal is wiped out by two made by Paul Simpson. City won't win again for 17 games.											
2	H ASTON VILLA	6,366		W	3-2	2-1	Hodges 10, Fashanu 45, Gage 87p	Beasant	Gage	Winterburn	Galliers	Morris	Smith	Wise	Cork	Fashanu*	Sanchez	Hodges	**Gordon**
	26/8			3			*Evans 22p, Thompson 88*	*Poole*	*Williams!*	*Dorigo*	*Evans*	*Elliott*	*Blair*	*Hunt*	*Stainrod*	*Thompson*	*Hodge*	*Daley*	*Keown*
							Ref: J Martin	Back in February, Millwall's John Fashanu had bundled Villa from the FA Cup. Now, his header two minutes into first-half injury time floors Graham Turner's team. Winterburn had dumped Hodge for Villa's penalty, and Gary Williams was sent off in the first half for belting Hodges.											
3	H LEICESTER		4	W	1-0	1-0	Cork 31	Beasant	Gage	Winterburn	Galliers	Morris	Smith	Wise	Cork	Fashanu	Sanchez	Hodges	
	30/8	5,987	*20*	6				*Andrews*	*Ramsey*	*Venus*	*Osman*	*Walsh*	*McAllister*	*Kelly*	*Bright*	*Smith*	*Morgan*	*Banks**	*Sealy*
							Ref: R Milford	Wimbledon's star is Dennis Wise; Leicester's dunce is Mark Bright, who misses two sitters. Leicester played a sweeper to try to counter Wimbledon's long ball game. The Dons' goal stems from Fashanu's leap, which unsettles Steve Walsh, allowing Cork to poach his 134th goal.											
4	A CHARLTON			W	1-0	0-0	Wise 87	Beasant	Gage	Winterburn	Galliers	Morris	Smith	Wise	Cork	Fashanu	Sanchez	Hodges	
	2/9	***6,531***		9				*Jones*	*Humphrey*	*Reid*	*Shipley**	*Thompson*	*Shirtliff*	*Lee*	*Gritt*	*Pearson*	*Aizlewood*	*Stuart*	*Melrose*
							Ref: D Hutchinson	Charlton – promoted with Wimbledon – have just won at Old Trafford. This is Dennis Wise's fifth 1st team game since signing from Saints, and his goal, seizing on Sanchez's flick into the area, takes the Dons top on Bassett's 42nd birthday. Robert Lee's shot was cleared off the line.											
5	A WATFORD		1	W	1-0	0-0	Hodges 89	Beasant	Thorn	Winterburn	Galliers	Morris	Smith	Wise	Gage	Fashanu	Sanchez	Hodges	
	6/9	*14,822*	*17*	12				*Coton*	*Franklin*	*Rostron*	*Richardson*	*Terry*	*McClelland*	*Bardsley*	*Blissett*	*Barnes*	*Jackett*	*Sterling*	
							Ref: V Callow	Another, even later away winner, gives Wimbledon their best league position in history. Bassett has won Bells Whisky Manager of the Month award. He plays three centre-backs against Graham Taylor's team. Hodges scores through McClelland's legs. Hodges is in the Welsh squad.											
6	H EVERTON		4	L	1-2	1-1	Cork 34	Beasant	Gage	Winterburn	Galliers	Morris	Smith	Wise	Cork	Fashanu	Sanchez	Hodges	Fairweather
	13/9	11,708	*3*	12			*Sheedy 4, Sharp 57*	*Mimms*	*Harper*	*Power*	*Ratcliffe*	*Watson*	*Langley*	*Steven*	*Heath**	*Sharp*	*Mountfield*	*Sheedy*	*Wilkinson*
							Ref: K Barratt	Runners-up Everton are unbeaten so far. Wimbledon enjoyed 11 days as Division 1 leaders. Howard Kendall is without five internationals, and plays a sweeper against the Dons. This live TV game featured a streaker. Cork and Galliers played in the 0-8 drubbing at Goodison in 1978.											
7	A NEWCASTLE		8	L	0-1	0-0		Beasant	Gage	Winterburn	Galliers	Morris	Smith	Wise*	Cork	Fashanu	Sanchez	Hodges	Gayle
	20/9	*21,545*	*20*	12			*Gascoigne 54*	*Kelly*	*Anderson*	*Bailey*	*McCreery*	*Clarke*	*Roeder*	*McDonald*	*Gascoigne*	*Whitehurst*	*Thomas A*	*Stewart*	
							Ref: K Walmsley	Newcastle were propping up the table, winless until Paul Gascoigne's lob, after Sanchez had misjudged Neil McDonald's through ball. Fash had earlier missed a great chance, and has scored just once so far this season. Tony Kelly was making his debut in goal for the Magpies.											
8	H SOUTHAMPTON		9	D	2-2	1-1	Fashanu 26, 89	Beasant	Gage	Winterburn	Galliers*	Morris	Gayle	Wise	Cork	Fashanu	Sanchez	Hodges	Fairweather
	27/9	7,147	*13*	13			*Winterburn 25 (og), Cockerill 73*	*Shilton*	*Forrest**	*Dennis*	*Case*	*Gittens*	*Bond*	*Lawrence*	*Cockerill*	*Clarke*	*Armstrong*	*Jordan*	*Baker*
							Ref: B Stevens	Southampton's matches are awash with goals at both ends. Fashanu was dropped for the Littlewoods Cup, but is recalled and responds with two goals. He lobs the first over Shilton – who provoked him throughout – and might have had a hat-trick but for a header that hit a post.											
9	H LIVERPOOL		11	L	1-3	0-0	Fairweather 82	Beasant	Gage	Winterburn	Galliers	Morris	Gayle	Wise	Cork*	Fashanu	Sanchez	Hodges	Fairweather
	4/10	**15,978**	*3*	13			*Molby 51, Rush 57, 89*	*Grobbelaar*	*Gillespie*	*Beglin*	*Lawrenson*	*Whelan*	*Hansen*	*Wark*	*Nicol*	*Rush*	*Molby*	*McMahon*	
							Ref: J Deakin	Marvellous Rush goals, his 115th and 116th for Liverpool, show why Juventus will pay £3 million for his services. His strikes take him past Kenny Dalglish's scoring record for Liverpool. The Dons threatened early, but Liverpool had never lost a game in which Rush has scored.											
10	A QP RANGERS		14	L	1-2	0-1	Gage 62p	Beasant	Gage	Winterburn	Galliers*	Morris	Thorn	**Gannon**	Cork	Gordon	Downes	Hodges	Wise
	11/10	*14,112*	*12*	13			*Bannister 1, McDonald 76*	*Seaman*	*Fereday*	*Dawes*	*Allen**	*McDonald*	*Chivers*	*Lee*	*James*	*Bannister*	*Byrne*	*Walker*	*Robinson*
							Ref: R Lewis	Clive Walker's cross after just 16 seconds set up Rangers' opener. Two penalties lay in store. Rangers', just before half-time, saw Beasant save Bannister's attempt; the Dons', also for handball, was driven in by Gage. Man of the match was QPR's Sammy Lee, once of Liverpool.											

No	Date	Venue	Opponent	Att	Pos	Pt	Res	F-A	H-T	Scorers, Times, and Referees	1	2	3	4	5	6	7	8	9	10	11	12
	19/10			*11,099*	*8*	13				*Bennett 59*	*Ogrizovic*	*Borrows*	*Downs*	*Painter*	*Kilcline**	*Peake*	*Bennett*	*Phillips*	*Regis*	*Pickering*	*Houchen*	*Williams*
										Ref: N Midgley	Five defeats in six games have seen the Dons slump from 4th to 16th. This Sunday fixture saw their offside trap catch Coventry's forwards 27 times. Cyrille Regis's cross set up ex-Man City's Dave Bennett. Fashanu damaged a kidney after colliding with a photographer at Anfield.											
12		H	NORWICH		14		W	2-0	2-0	Fashanu 13, Gayle 38	Beasant	Kay	Winterburn	Galliers	Gayle	Thorn	Cork	Fairweather	Fashanu	Sanchez	Hodges*	Downes
	25/10			6,172	*2*	16					*Benstead*	*Culverhouse*	*Spearing*	*Bruce*	*Phelan*	*Elliott*	*Crook*	*Drinkell*	*Biggins**	*Barham*	*Gordon*	*Putney*
										Ref: P Vanes	Ken Brown's 2nd Division champions have sold keeper Chris Woods to Rangers and defender Dave Watson to Everton. Norwich arrive at Plough Lane unbeaten on their travels, but having lost twice to the Dons last year, do so again. Graham Benstead couldn't handle high balls.											
13		A	TOTTENHAM		10		W	2-1	1-0	Cork 14, Fashanu 55	Beasant	Kay	Winterburn	Galliers	Gayle	Thorn	**Clement***	Cork	Fashanu	Sanchez!	Fairweather	Gage
	1/11			*21,820*	*9*	19				*M Thomas 80*	*Clemence*	*Stevens**	*Thomas*	*Roberts!*	*Gough*	*Mabbutt*	*Allen C*	*Claesen*	*Waddle*	*Hoddle*	*Allen P*	*Ardiles*
										Ref: D Axcell	Four players were booked, as well as Sanchez and Graham Roberts sent off following Mitchell Thomas's goal. Gary Stevens breaks a collar-bone. Fashanu is widely accused of being too physical. The first goal resulted from a free-kick, awarded when Richard Gough fouled Fashanu.											
14		H	LUTON		12		L	0-1	0-0		Beasant	Kay	Winterburn	Galliers	Gayle	Thorn	Downes	Cork	Fashanu	Sanchez*	Fairweather	Gage
	8/11			5,928	*5*	19				*M Stein 58*	*Sealey*	*Braecker*	*Johnson*	*Nicholas*	*Foster*	*Donaghy*	*Hill*	*Stein B**	*Newell*	*Stein M*	*McDonough*	*Wilson*
										Ref: L Shapter	Luton are the better of two awful sides. Cork, among others, has a stinker. Ricky Hill's curling centre is knocked down by Mike Newell for Mark Stein to score. Beasant admits he should have cut out the cross. Galliers' pile-driver, touched over, is the Dons' only attempt on goal.											
15		H	WEST HAM		13		L	0-1	0-0		Beasant	Kay	Winterburn	Galliers*	Gayle	Thorn	Clement	Cork	Fashanu	Downes	Fairweather	Gage
	15/11			10,342	*5*	19				*Cottee 48*	*Parkes*	*Stewart*	*Parris*	*Gale*	*Hilton*	*Devonshire**	*Ward*	*McAvennie*	*Dickens*	*Cottee*	*Orr*	*Walford*
										Ref: J Moules	High-flying Hammers come out to score goals. They only manage one, a simple far-post effort by Tony Cottee that Wimbledon suggest is offside. The Dons have the chances to win, but Cork and Fashanu have left their shooting boots at home. Bassett blames the pair of them.											
16		A	NOTTINGHAM F		14		L	2-3	1-2	Fairweather 2, Hodges 47	Beasant	Kay	Winterburn	**Jones**	Gayle	Thorn	Clement*	Wise	Fashanu	Downes	Fairweather	Hodges
	22/11			*15,481*	*2*	19				*Clough 17p, Thorn 30 (og), Metgod 59*	*Segers*	*Butterworth*	*Williams*	*Walker*	*Metgod*	*Bowyer*	*Carr*	*Webb*	*Clough*	*Birtles*	*Mills*	
										Ref: P Tyldesley (D Wragg)	A terrific match, settled by Johnnie Metgod's 25-yard free-kick. Wimbledon have twice faced Forest in recent League Cup clashes, and never before today lost to a Brian Clough side. Vince Jones, signed from Wealdstone, makes his debut, and punches the ball away for a penalty.											
17		H	MANCHESTER U		13		W	1-0	1-0	Jones 42	Beasant	Kay	Winterburn	Jones	Gayle	Thorn	Wise	Hodges*	Fashanu	Downes	Fairweather	Cork
	29/11			12,112	17	22					Turner	Sivebaek	Duxbury	Moses	McGrath	Moran	Olsen	Blackmore	Stapleton	Davenport	Barnes*	Robson
										Ref: T Holbrook	This is Alex Ferguson's third game in charge of United and his team are a shambles. In only his second game for the Dons, Vince Jones hits a post, and then heads in Hodges' corner. The scorer is so ecstatic he rushes over to salute his parents and dozens of friends in the main stand.											
18		A	CHELSEA		12		W	**4-0**	3-0	Fashanu 1, Fairweather 11, Cork 38, [Jones 75]	Beasant	Kay	Winterburn	Jones	Gayle	Thorn	Cork	Fairweather*	Fashanu	Downes	Hodges	Wise
	6/12			*15,446*	*21*	25					*Niedzwiecki*	*Rougvie!*	*Dublin*	*Isaac**	*Wicks*	*Bumstead*	*Nevin*	*Spackman*	*Dixon*	*Speedie*	*Hazard*	*Wood*
										Ref: H King	Wimbledon's biggest win in the 1st Division is achieved against a team boasting internationals David Speedie and 200-goal Kerry Dixon in attack. Vince Jones nets his second goal in three games, and former Aberdeen defender Doug Rougvie gets his marching orders.											
19		H	SHEFFIELD WED		11		W	3-0	2-0	Jones 21, Fashanu 36, Wise 61	Beasant	Kay	Winterburn	Jones	Gayle	Thorn	Wise	Cork	Fashanu	Downes	Fairweather*	Hodges
	13/12			6,010	*8*	28					*Hodge*	*Sterland*	*Worthington*	*Hart*	*Madden*	*Snodin*	*Morris*	*Megson*	*Chapman*	*Bradshaw*	*Shelton*	
										Ref: A Seville	Vince Jones is on the scoresheet yet again, for the third consecutive match. He is setting Plough Lane alight, in more ways than one. Howard Wilkinson's Wednesday lost just one of their first 10 fixtures, and are still near the top of the table, but will win just once in their next 11.											
20		A	EVERTON		11		L	**0-3**	0-2		Beasant	Kay	Winterburn	Jones	Gayle	Thorn	Wise	Fairweather	Fashanu	Downes	Cork*	Hodges
	20/12			*25,553*	*4*	28				*Steven 25, Sheedy 31, Heath 60*	*Southall*	*Stevens*	*Aspinall**	*Ratcliffe*	*Watson*	*Power*	*Steven*	*Heath*	*Sharp*	*Harper*	*Sheedy*	*Reid*
										Ref: K Redfern	This is Wimbledon's first return to Goodison since their shattering 0-8 crushing in the League Cup in 1978. At least the result is kinder this time, though Everton give the Dons the runaround. England World Cup hero Peter Reid, injured all season, comes on for the last 20 minutes.											
21		H	OXFORD				D	1-1	1-0	Hodges 39p	Beasant	Kay	Winterburn	Jones*	Gayle	Thorn	Wise	Cork	Fashanu	Downes	Hodges	Fairweather
	26/12			6,491		29				*Aldridge 84*	*Hardwick*	*Langan*	*Trewick*	*Phillips*	*Briggs*	*Dreyer*	*Houghton*	*Aldridge*	*Whitehurst**	*Hebberd*	*Brock*	*McDonald*
										Ref: M Cotton	Wimbledon and Oxford have now faced each other in Divisions 1, 2, and 3, Oxford having also climbed from 4th to 1st. Although they have won just once in seven, John Aldridge pops up six minutes from time to earn a valuable point. He and Ray Houghton keep Oxford afloat.											

No	Date	Att	Pos	Pts	F-A	H-T	Scorers, Times, and Referees	1	2	3	4	5	6	7	8	9	10	11	12 sub used
22	A WEST HAM		10	W	3-2	2-2	Fashanu 12, Sayer 37, Fairweather 64	Beasant	Kay	Winterburn	Sanchez	Gayle	Thorn	Fairweather	Sayer	Fashanu	Downes	Hodges	
	27/12	*19,122*	*12*	32			*Cottee 3, Hilton 35*	*Parkes*	*Potts*	*Parris*	*Hilton*	*Martin*	*Ince*	*Ward*	*McAvennie*	*Kean**	*Cottee*	*Pike*	*Dickens*
							Ref: B Hill	The Dons' last visit to Upton Park saw Tony Cottee smash an FA Cup hat-trick in a 1-5 mauling two years earlier. The Dons partnership of Fashanu and the restored Sayer has only been tested once before, but both score in this cracker, settled after a slip by Alvin Martin.											
23	A ARSENAL		10	L	1-3	0-1	Fairweather 81	Beasant	Kay	Winterburn	Sanchez	Gayle	Thorn	Fairweather	Sayer	Fashanu	Downes*	Hodges	Gage
	1/1	*36,144*	*1*	32			*Nicholas 22, 68, Hayes 54p*	*Lukic*	*Anderson*	*Sansom*	*Williams*	*O'Leary*	*Adams*	*Rocastle**	*Davis*	*Quinn*	*Nicholas*	*Hayes*	*Allinson*
							Ref: A Gunn	Arsenal are in the midst of a daunting 22-game unbeaten run in all competitions. Charlie Nicholas will only score four league goals this season, half of them in this match. He also earns a penalty after Beasant's dubious challenge. Beasant half-saves, but the ball dribbles past him.											
24	H WATFORD		9	W	2-1	0-1	Jones 52, Sayer 75	Beasant	Kay	Winterburn	Jones*	Gayle	Thorn	Wise	Sayer	Fashanu	Sanchez	Fairweather	Hodges
	3/1	8,063	*11*	35			*Porter 27*	*Coton*	*Bardsley*	*Rostron*	*Richardson*	*Sims*	*McClelland*	*Blissett*	*Barnes*	*Falco*	*Jackett*	*Porter*	
							Ref: R Groves	Watford rejected Vinnie Jones as a youngster. Jones now takes a throw-in, Fairweather back-heads it, and Andy Sayer – playing instead of the injured Cork – scores with a diving header. The win lifts Wimbledon up to 9th. John Barnes' brilliance cannot prevent the Dons' first double.											
25	H MANCHESTER C		11	D	0-0	0-0		Beasant	Kay	Winterburn	Jones	Gayle	Thorn	Wise*	Sayer	Fashanu	Sanchez	Fairweather	Hodges
	24/1	5,667	*16*	36				*Suckling*	*May*	*Wilson*	*Clements*	*McCarthy*	*Redmond*	*Lake*	*McNab*	*Varadi*	*Beckford**	*Barnes*	*Simpson*
							Ref: R Milford	City are slipping inexorably towards relegation, have not won away from home all season, and recently lost 0-5 at Charlton. The Dons miss a sackful, and England Under-21 keeper Perry Suckling – rejected by the Dons as a schoolboy – plays a blinder. Shots on goal 21-2 to the Dons.											
26	A LEICESTER		11	L	1-3	1-2	Fairweather 31	Beasant	Kay*	Winterburn	Jones	Gayle	Thorn!	Hodges	Sayer	Cork	Sanchez	Fairweather	Wise
	7/2	*8,369*	*18*	36			*Smith 17, Ramsey 43, 58*	*Andrews*	*Mauchlen*	*Morgan*	*O'Neil*	*Walsh*	*McAllister*	*Lynex*	*Moran*	*Smith*	*Ramsey*	*Venus**	*Wilson*
							Ref: A Allison	The last visitors to Filbert Street were Sheffield Wednesday, who lost 1-6. Fashanu misses this match with a stomach bug. Future Arsenal striker Alan Smith opens the scoring. Thorn is sent off for the first time – on 82 minutes – for fouling future Scotland skipper Gary McAllister.											
27	H CHARLTON		9	W	2-0	1-0	Gage 29p, Winterburn 81	Beasant	Gage	Winterburn	Jones	Gayle	Thorn	Hodges*	Sayer	Fashanu	Sanchez	Fairweather	Cork
	15/2	6,608	*20*	39				*Bolder*	*Humphrey*	*Reid*	*Pender**	*Thompson*	*Shirtliff*	*Peake*	*Lee*	*Melrose*	*Curbishley*	*Walsh*	*Stuart*
							Ref: A Buksh	Six games without a win for lowly Charlton after this 11.30 Sunday game. The Dons won a rare penalty when John Pender fouls Fashanu. Gage has never missed from the spot. It was Pender's debut. He was injured in the collison and is out for the season. Both full-backs scored.											
28	H NEWCASTLE		9	W	3-1	1-0	Sayer 15, 52, 68	Beasant	Gage	Winterburn	Jones	Gayle	Morris	Downes*	Sayer	Cork	Sanchez	Hodges	Clement
	28/2	6,779	*22*	42			*Beardsley 51*	*Thomas M*	*McDonald*	*Wharton*	*Scott*	*Jackson P*	*Clarke*	*Thomas A**	*Cunningham*	*Goddard*	*Beardsley*	*Craig*	*Wrighton*
							Ref: B Stevens	Fashanu is sidelined with flu, but stand-in Sayer – who almost left the club – hits a hat-trick, his first. His second goal comes seconds after World Cup star Peter Beardsley slots a splendid equaliser. Newcastle are bottom of the league, but they pick up in the weeks to come.											
29	A ASTON VILLA		9	D	0-0	0-0		Beasant	Gage	Winterburn	Jones	Gayle	Thorn	Wise*	Sayer	Fashanu	Sanchez	Hodges	Joseph
	4/3	*12,484*	*20*	43				*Spink*	*Norton*	*Williams*	*Keown*	*Elliott*	*Cooper*	*Daley*	*Aspinall*	*Thompson*	*Hunt*	*Dorigo*	*Stainrod*
							Ref: P Harrison	Wimbledon win their first point outside London, but Billy McNeill's men deserved better. Paul Elliott snuffed out the threat posed by Fashanu, and neither Sayer nor on-loan Francis Joseph get a kick. Beasant tipped over a blockbuster from ex-Aberdeen Neale Cooper.											
30	A NORWICH		9	D	0-0	0-0		Beasant	Gage	Winterburn	Jones	Gayle	Thorn	Wise	Sayer	Fashanu	Downes	Hodges	
	7/3	*14,293*	*7*	44				*Gunn*	*Brown*	*Spearing*	*Bruce*	*Phelan*	*Butterworth*	*Crook*	*Drinkell*	*Rosario*	*Putney*	*Gordon**	*Biggins*
							Ref: K Hackett	Norwich haven't lost since November, but Wimbledon have beaten them on their last three meetings. In a biting wind, Norwich have the better of things. Kevin Drinkell fires wide, and Beasant saves well. These are the Dons' first back-to-back 0-0s since entering the League.											
31	H QP RANGERS		10	D	1-1	1-0	Sayer 31	Beasant	Gage	Winterburn	Jones	Gayle	Thorn	Wise	Sayer	Fashanu!	Sanchez*	Hodges	Cork
	21/3	6,038	*12*	45			*Rosenior 70*	*Seaman*	*Neill*	*James*	*Lee*	*McDonald*	*Fenwick*	*Allen*	*Fillery*	*Bannister*	*Byrne*	*Walker**	*Rosenior*
							Ref: H Taylor	A fiery match that saw Fashanu sent off after 72 minutes, having earlier been booked for dissent. When Fenwick fouled Cork, David Seaman saved Gage's penalty – his first ever miss. Sayer's glancing header was cancelled out when Leroy Rosenior skipped round Gayle to equalise.											

No	Date	Opponent	Pos	Res	F-A	H-T	Scorers, Times, and Referees	1	2	3	4	5	6	7	8	9	10	11	12
32	H	COVENTRY		W	2-1	2-1	Fashanu 27, Fairweather 40	Beasant	Gage	Winterburn	Jones	Gayle	Thorn	Fairweather	Sayer	Fashanu	Downes	Hodges	Cork
	24/3	**4,370**	*8*	48			*Gynn 5*	*Ogrizovic*	*Borrows*	*Downs*	*Gynn*	*Sedgley*	*Peake*	*Bennett*	*Phillips*	*Regis*	*Houchen*	*Pickering*	
							Ref: K Cooper	A puny crowd enjoys a thrilling match. Coventry had won their last six in league and cup and are headed for Wembley. Fashanu shrugs off Steve Sedgley to cancel out Micky Gynn's early goal. Beasant's booming downfield punt sets up the winner. Wally Downes breaks an ankle.											
33	A	LIVERPOOL	8	W	2-1	1-0	Winterburn 39, Cork 78	Beasant	Gage	Winterburn	Jones	Gayle	Thorn	Fairweather	Sayer*	Fashanu	Morris	Hodges	Cork
	28/3	***36,409***	*1*	51			*Dalglish 48*	*Grobbelaar*	*Spackman*	*Venison*	*Lawrenson**	*Whelan*	*Hansen*	*Dalglish*	*Johnson*	*Rush*	*Gillespie*	*McMahon*	*Aldridge*
							Ref: G Courtney	Liverpool are hanging on to top spot, but won't hang on for long. Juventus-bound Ian Rush is wrapped up by Gayle and Thorn. Dalglish is 36, but his curler wipes out Winterburn's opener. Substitute Cork had only been on for three minutes when he heads in from Hodges' corner.											
34	A	LUTON	8	D	0-0	0-0		Beasant	Gage	Winterburn	Jones	Morris	Thorn	Fairweather	Sayer	Cork	Sanchez*	Hodges	Joseph
	4/4	*9,729*	*3*	52				*Sealey*	*Braecker*	*Harvey*	*Nicholas*	*North S*	*Donaghy*	*Hill*	*Stein B*	*Newell*	*Harford*	*McDonough*	
							Ref: J Key	John Moore's team climb to third following this grim draw. Wimbledon are jeered as they depart the plastic pitch, having been cheered from Anfield a week earlier. Luton play an offside-game to stifle opponents. Dave Beasant blocked Mick Harford's shot with his legs.											
35	A	SOUTHAMPTON	8	D	2-2	0-1	Fairweather 55, Joseph 77	Beasant	Gage	Winterburn	Jones	Gayle	Thorn	Wise	Joseph	Cork*	Morris	Fairweather	Sayer
	7/4	*12,811*	*15*	53			*Gayle 2(og), Lawrence 82*	*Shilton*	*Forrest**	*Armstrong*	*Case*	*Wright*	*Bond*	*Le Tissier*	*Cockerill*	*Lawrence*	*Hobson*	*Wallace*	*Townsend*
							Ref: K Baker	Saints will end the season with nine unbeaten games, beginning today. Hodges and Fashanu are missing, suspended. Wimbledon get off to a dreadful start when Gayle heads past Beasant. Francis Joseph's wayward pass is snapped up for Danny Wallace to cross for George Lawrence.											
36	H	ARSENAL	9	L	1-2	1-1	Thorn 36	Beasant	Gage	Winterburn	Jones!	Gayle	Thorn	Fairweather	Joseph*	Fashanu	Sanchez	Hodges	Sayer
	18/4	8,515	*5*	53			*Merson 32, Davis 58*	*Lukic*	*Anderson*	*Caesar*	*Williams*	*O'Leary*	*Adams*	*Rocastle**	*Davis*	*Merson*	*Nicholas*	*Rix*	*Allinson*
							Ref: J Martin	Vinnie Jones blows a fuse, and having been kicked from behind by Graham Rix elbows him in the head and is expelled. 'Quite right, too!' rages Bassett afterwards, blaming his player. Man of the match was 19-year-old Paul Merson. Another Paul – Davis – heads Arsenal's winner.											
37	A	OXFORD	10	L	1-3	0-2	Hodges 49	Beasant	Gage	Winterburn	Jones	Morris	Thorn	Fairweather*	Sayer	Fashanu	Sanchez	Hodges	Joseph
	20/4	*8,616*	*18*	53			*Saunders 19, 77, Whitehurst 34*	*Hucker*	*Langan*	*Dreyer*	*Phillips*	*Briggs*	*Caton*	*Houghton*	*Saunders*	*Whitehurst*	*Hebberd*	*Brock*	
							Ref: M James	Oxford have only won once in 11 games, and Bassett is so ashamed of his team of 'poseurs' that he keeps them out on the pitch at half-time. 'They thought they were on holiday, so I sent them out to continue sunbathing,' he ranted. Whitehurst's goal went in off Beasant's shoulder.											
38	H	TOTTENHAM		D	2-2	0-1	Hodges 71p, 80p	Beasant	Gage	Winterburn	Jones	Gayle!	Thorn	Wise	Cork*	Fashanu	**Ryan**	Hodges	Morris
	22/4	7,887	*3*	54			*Claesen 36p, Bowen 67*	*Clemence*	*Polston*	*Thomas M*	*Ardiles*	*Gough*	*Ruddock*	*O'Shea*	*Allen P*	*Claesen**	*Bowen*	*Galvin*	*Allen C*
							Ref: J Moules	Spurs won at Plough Lane last month in the FA Cup. Brian Gayle now clashes with Nico Claesen and is sent off for spitting. Seven other players are booked and the FA are poised to clamp down. Spurs went in front from the penalty spot after Gage fouled Ossie Ardiles.											
39	H	NOTTINGHAM F	9	W	2-1	1-1	Hodges 28p, Fashanu 78	Beasant	Gage	Winterburn	Morris	Gayle	Thorn	Wise	Gordon*	Fashanu	Sanchez	Hodges	Cork
	25/4	5,012	*8*	57			*Pearce 19p*	*Sutton*	*Fleming*	*Pearce*	*Walker*	*Foster*	*Fairclough*	*Mills*	*Metgod*	*Clough*	*Wilkinson**	*Osvold*	*Starbuck*
							Ref: D Hedges	Goalkeeper Steve Sutton saves Forest in a game of two penalties. Beasant brought down Paul Wilkinson for Forest's; Colin Foster then handled Fashanu's near-post header for Wimbledon's riposte. Fashanu has a storming match, heading the winner from Andy Thorn's corner.											
40	A	MANCHESTER U	10	W	1-0	0-0	Wise 89	Beasant	Gage	Winterburn	Morris	Gayle!	Thorn	Wise	Sayer*	Fashanu	Sanchez	Hodges	Cork
	2/5	*31,686*	*11*	60				*Walsh*	*Duxbury*	*Albiston*	*Moses**	*McGrath*	*Moran*	*Robson*	*Strachan*	*Davenport*	*Olsen*	*Gibson C*	*Stapleton*
							Ref: R Bridges	Gayle is sent off (70 mins) for the second time in three games. Booked in the first half, he was then dismissed for fouling Peter Davenport. In wet and windy conditions, Dennis Wise chests a last-gasp winner after Fashanu had held off Jesper Olsen to cut the ball back.											
41	H	CHELSEA	7	W	2-1	0-0	Fashanu 47, Wise 87	Beasant	Gage	Winterburn	Morris	Gayle	Thorn	Wise	Sayer	Fashanu	Sanchez	Hodges	
	5/5	9,582		63			*Wegerle 73*	*Freestone*	*Rougvie*	*Dublin*	*Wicks*	*McLaughlin*	*Bumstead*	*Wegerle*	*Wood*	*Dixon*	*Speedie*	*Coady*	
							Ref: R Lewis	For the second time in four days Wise claims a late Wimbledon winner. He is keeping Fairweather out of the side, and with three minutes to play sweeps home Gage's cross. Wise was earlier booked for fouling Speedie. Roy Wegerle scored soon after Beasant had saved his penalty.											
42	A	SHEFFIELD WED	6	W	2-0	0-0	Sayer 65, Hodges 89	Beasant	Gage	Winterburn	Jones	Morris	Thorn	Wise	Sayer	Fashanu*	Sanchez	Hodges	Gayle
	9/5	*18,823*	*13*	66				*Hodge*	*Morris*	*Smith**	*May*	*Madden*	*Worthington*	*Marwood*	*Megson*	*Chapman*	*Hirst*	*Shelton*	*Chamberlain*
	Home	*Away*					Ref: A Allinson	This match marks the end of Dave Bassett's 13-year association with Wimbledon. Glyn Hodges describes his stunning solo goal as the best he has ever scored. It secures Wimbledon's 6th place. But for the ban following the Heysel tragedy, they might have qualified for Europe.											
Average	7,810	*17,888*																	

Littlewoods Cup			Att			F-A	H-T	Scorers, Times, and Referees	1	2	3	4	5	6	7	8	9	10	11	subs used
2:1	A	CAMBRIDGE		8	D	1-1	1-0	Gordon 24	Beasant	Gage	Winterburn	Galliers	Morris	Gayle	Wise*	Thorn	Gordon	Sanchez	Fairweath'^	Fashanu/Hodges
23/9			*5,290*	*4:5*				*Beattie 87*	*Branagan*	*Measham*	*Dowman*	*Beattie*	*Smith*	*Beck**	*Tong*	*Spriggs*	*Cooper*	*Crown*	*Flanagan*	*Rayment*
								Ref: D Hedges	Fashanu has been dropped for not scoring enough goals, and Colin Gordon makes his debut in his place. Cambridge's young centre-half, Andy Beattie, outjumps everyone around him to head an equaliser from a cross by Steve Spriggs. Fashanu had replaced Wise after 55 minutes.											
2:2	H	CAMBRIDGE		11	D	2-2	2-1	Cork 3, 40	Beasant	Gage	Winterburn	Galliers	Morris	Gayle	Wise	Cork	Gordon*	Sanchez^	Hodges	Sayer/Fairweather
7/10			3,359	*4:5*				*Cooper 5, Rigby 48*	*Branagan*	*Measham*	*Dowman*	*Beattie*	*Smith*	*Beck**	*Littlejohns*	*Spriggs*	*Cooper*	*Crown*	*Flanagan*	*Rigby*
								Ref: A Gunn (Dons lose on away goals rule)	Wimbledon showed too much respect for Liverpool in the league and too little to Cambridge now. Twice the Dons were ahead, and twice Cambridge quickly pegged them back. Just before Jon Rigby's decisive second leveller, Beasant had saved Lindsay Smith's penalty kick.											
FA Cup																				
3	H	SUNDERLAND		9	W	2-1	0-1	Sanchez 87, Hodges 90	Beasant	Kay	Winterburn	Sanchez	Gayle	Thorn	Fairweather	Sayer	Fashanu*	Downes^	Hodges	Cork/Jones
10/1			6,231	*2:14*				*Gates 43*	*Hesford*	*Burley*	*Kennedy*	*Armstrong*	*Saddington*	*Bennett*	*Doyle*	*Gates*	*Swindlehurst*	*Proctor*	*Gray**	*Corner*
								Ref: M Bodenham	What an escape for Wimbledon. Beasant was rooted to his line as Eric Gates enjoyed space and time to put Lawrie McMenemy's 2nd Division side ahead. With time running out Lawrie Sanchez converts Glyn Hodges' corner; then Hodges himself darts through to win the tie.											
4	H	PORTSMOUTH		11	W	4-0	3-0	Fashanu 13, 61, Blake 20 (og), Sayer 45	Beasant	Kay	Winterburn	Jones*	Gayle	Thorn	Hodges	Sayer	Fashanu^	Sanchez	Fairweather	Cork/Downes
31/1			11,379	*2:1*					*Knight*	*Swain*	*Hardyman*	*Dillon*	*Blake*	*Gilbert*	*O'Callaghan*	*Tait**	*Mariner^*	*Ball*	*Hilaire*	*Collins/Russell*
								Ref: I Hemley	Division 2 leaders Portsmouth are soundly thrashed and allowed to concentrate thereafter on their promotion quest. Manager Alan Ball had told his players beforehand that the FA Cup was second only to the World Cup. Keeper Alan Knight failed to clear a cross, and Fash made it 1-0.											
5	H	EVERTON		9	W	3-1	1-1	Hodges 44, Fashanu 60, Sayer 75	Beasant	Gage	Winterburn	Jones	Gayle	Morris	Hodges	Sayer	Fashanu	Sanchez	Fairweather	
22/2			9,924	*1*				*Wilkinson 4*	*Southall*	*Stevens*	*VdHauwe**	*Ratcliffe*	*Watson*	*Reid^*	*Steven*	*Heath*	*Wilkinson*	*Snodin*	*Power*	*Pointon/Harper*
								Ref: L Shapter	Champions-elect Everton are swept away in dramatic fashion. John Fashanu steals the live TV show, scoring once, winning a penalty (saved from Gage, Hodges netting the rebound) and setting up Sayer for No 3. Fash blots his copy-book, striking Kevin Ratcliffe and an Everton fan.											
QF	H	TOTTENHAM		9	L	0-2	0-0		Beasant	Gage	Winterburn	Jones	Gayle	Thorn	Wise*	Sayer	Fashanu	Sanchez	Hodges^	Fairweather/Cork
15/3			15,686	*4*				*Waddle 84, Hoddle 88*	*Clemence*	*Stevens**	*Thomas M*	*Hodge*	*Gough*	*Mabbutt*	*Allen C*	*Allen P*	*Waddle*	*Hoddle*	*Ardiles^*	*Claeson/Ruddock*
								Ref: N Midgley	David Pleat's terrible twins Hoddle and Waddle break the Dons' hearts with their double-burst late in the game. Winterburn was beaten for pace down the flank, allowing Waddle to squeeze his shot inside the near post. Hoddle rubbed in salt with an explosive 30-yard free-kick.											

	P	Home W	D	L	F	A	Away W	D	L	F	A	Pts
1 Everton	42	16	4	1	49	11	10	4	7	27	20	86
2 Liverpool	42	15	3	3	43	16	8	5	8	29	26	77
3 Tottenham	42	14	3	4	40	14	7	5	9	28	29	71
4 Arsenal	42	12	5	4	31	12	8	5	8	27	23	70
5 Norwich	42	9	10	2	27	20	8	7	6	26	31	68
6 WIMBLEDON	42	11	5	5	32	22	8	4	9	25	28	66
7 Luton	42	14	5	2	29	13	4	7	10	18	32	66
8 Nottingham F	42	12	8	1	36	14	6	3	12	28	37	65
9 Watford	42	12	5	4	38	20	6	4	11	29	34	63
10 Coventry	42	14	4	3	35	17	3	8	10	15	28	63
11 Manchester U	42	13	3	5	38	18	1	11	9	14	27	56
12 Southampton	42	11	5	5	44	24	3	5	13	25	44	52
13 Sheffeld Wed	42	9	7	5	39	24	4	6	11	19	35	52
14 Chelsea	42	8	6	7	30	30	5	7	9	23	34	52
15 West Ham	42	10	4	7	33	28	4	6	11	19	39	52
16 QP Rangers	42	9	7	5	31	27	4	4	13	17	37	50
17 Newcastle	42	10	4	7	33	29	2	7	12	14	36	47
18 Oxford	42	8	8	5	30	25	3	5	13	14	44	46
19 Charlton*	42	7	7	7	26	22	4	4	13	19	33	44
20 Leicester	42	9	7	5	39	24	2	2	17	15	52	42
21 Manchester C	42	8	6	7	28	24	0	9	12	8	33	39
22 Aston Villa	42	7	7	7	25	25	1	5	15	20	54	36
* *avoid relegation after play-offs*	924	238	123	101	756	459	101	123	238	459	756	1263

Odds & ends

Double wins: (5) Man U, Charlton, Watford, Chelsea, Sheffield Wed.
Double losses: (2) Everton, Arsenal.

Won from behind: (4) Watford (h), Coventry (h), Nott'm F (h), West Ham (a).
Lost from in front: (2) Manchester C (a), Nott'm F (a).

High spots: Winning 4 of the first 5 games to go top of Division1.
Unbeaten run of 9 league games, February to April.
Reaching the quarter-final of the FA Cup for the first time.

Low spots: Losing 5 out of 6 in September and October, dropping to 16th.
Elimination from the Littlewoods Cup by 4th Division Cambridge.

Player of the Year: Nigel Winterburn.
Ever-presents: (2) Dave Beasant, Nigel Winterburn.
Hat-tricks: Andy Sayer (1).
Leading scorer: John Fashanu (14).

	Appearances Lge	Sub	LC	Sub	FAC	Sub	Goals Lge	LC	FAC	Total
Beasant, Dave	**42**		2		4					
Clement, Andrew	**3**	(1)								
Cork, Alan	**22**	(8)	1			(3)	**5**	2		**7**
Downes, Wally	**15**	(1)			1	(1)				
Fairweather, Carlton	**22**	(4)	1	(1)	3	(1)	**8**			**8**
Fashanu, John	**37**			(1)	4		**11**		3	**14**
Gage, Kevin	**25**	(5)	2		2		**3**			**3**
Galliers, Steve	**14**		2							
Gannon, John	**2**									
Gayle, Brian	**31**	(2)	2		4		**1**			**1**
Gordon, Colin	**2**	(1)	2					1		**1**
Hodges, Glyn	**32**	(5)	1	(1)	4		**9**		2	**11**
Jones, Vinnie	**22**				3	(1)	**4**			**4**
Joseph, Francis	**2**	(3)					**1**			**1**
Kay, John	**16**				2					
Morris, Mark	**20**	(1)	2		1					
Ryan, Vaughan	**1**									
Sanchez, Lawrie	**29**		2		4				1	**1**
Sayer, Andy	**18**	(2)		(1)	4		**7**		2	**9**
Smith, Mark	**6**									
Thorn, Andy	**34**		1		3		**2**			**2**
Winterburn, Nigel	**42**		2		4		**2**			**2**
Wise, Dennis	**25**	(3)	2		1		**4**			**4**
(own-goals)									1	**1**
23 players used	**462**	**(36)**	**22**	**(4)**	**44**	**(6)**	**57**	**3**	**9**	**69**

No	Date		Att	Pos	Pts	F-A	H-T	Scorers, Times, and Referees	1	2	3	4	5	6	7	8	9	10	11	subs used
1	A	WATFORD			L	0-1	0-1		Beasant	**Scales**	**Phelan**	Cork	**Young**	Thorn	Galliers*	Sayer^	Fashanu	Sanchez	Fairweather	**Miller**/Ryan
	15/8		*15,344*		–			*Blissett 40*	*Coton*	*Gibbs*	*Rostron*	*Jackett*	*Morris*	*McClelland*	*Bardsley*	*Blissett**	*Senior*	*Porter*	*Agana*	*Roberts*
								Ref: K Hackett	Watford have lost Graham Taylor to Villa and John Barnes to Liverpool. In their place they have recruited Dave Bassett and Mark Morris from Wimbledon. Dons' new boss, Bobby Gould, refused to sell Beasant. Luther Blissett escaped from Sanchez to head the only goal.											
2	H	EVERTON			D	1-1	1-0	Cork 23	Beasant	Scales	Phelan	Ryan	Young	Thorn	Cork	Sayer	Fashanu	Sanchez	Fairweather*	Gannon
	18/8		7,763		1			*Sharp 83*	*Mimms*	*V d Hauwe*	*Pointon*	*Ratcliffe*	*Watson*	*Harper*	*Adams*	*Clarke*	*Sharp*	*Marshall**	*Power*	*Mountfield*
								Ref: K Cooper	Colin Harvey's Everton champions contribute to a crude match. Alan Cork outjumps Neil Pointon to put Wimbledon ahead, then had a scare as Andy Thorn heads against his own goalpost. Graeme Sharp preserves Everton's unbeaten start to the new season. Eric Young has a fine match.											
3	H	OXFORD		15	D	1-1	0-1	Cork 90	Beasant	Scales	Phelan	Ryan	Young	Thorn	Wise*	Sayer	Fashanu	Sanchez	Cork	Gannon
	22/8		4,229	*6*	2			*Foyle 16*	*Hucker*	*Slatter*	*Dreyer*	*Shetton*	*Briggs*	*Caton*	*Houghton*	*Foyle*	*Whitehurst*	*Hebberd**	*Trewick*	*Shotton*
								Ref: M Reed	Wimbledon are ten seconds from defeat when Alan Cork spares his own, and his team's blushes. After four minutes Cork had seen his penalty saved, after Neil Slatter had sent Fashanu flying. Martin Foyle's goal was adjudged offside by Dons' players, but the referee disagrees.											
4	A	DERBY		11	W	1-0	0-0	Fashanu 71	Beasant	Gayle*	Phelan	Ryan	Young	Thorn	Wise	**Gibson**^	Fashanu	Sanchez	Cork	**Fairweather/Goodyear**
	29/8		*15,165*	*13*	5				*Shilton*	*Sage*	*Forsyth*	*Williams*	*Hindmarch**	*Wright*	*Micklewhite*	*Gee*	*Davison*^	*Gregory*	*Callaghan*	*Blades/Lillis*
								Ref: R Nixon	Promoted Derby lose for the first time this season. Wimbledon give a debut to Terry Gibson, a £200,000 buy from Manchester United. He and Fash are immediately dubbed Little and Large. Yet the breakthrough only comes after Gibson limps off – Fash latching onto Sanchez's pass.											
5	H	CHARLTON			W	4-1	1-1	Ryan 45, Cork 70, Fashanu 74, 75	Beasant	Scales	Phelan	Ryan	Young	Thorn	Wise	Gibson*	Fashanu	Sanchez	Cork	Fairweather
	1/9		5,184	*21*	8			*Stuart 29*	*Bolder*	*Humphrey*	*Reid!*	*Miller*	*Thompson*	*Pender*	*Peake*	*Stuart*	*Melrose*	*Mackenzie*	*Crooks**	*Williams*
								Ref: A Seville	Charlton owe their survival in the top flight to the palpitations of the play-offs. They looked the stronger team in the first half, but Ryan's header on the stroke of half-time changed the destiny of the match. After 52 minutes Mark Reid was expelled for a feeble foul on Fashanu.											
6	A	NEWCASTLE		5	W	2-1	2-0	Thomas 9 (og), Cork 10	Beasant	Scales	Phelan*	Ryan	Young	Thorn	Wise	Sayer	Fashanu	Sanchez	Cork^	Clement/Gayle
	5/9		*22,684*		11			*McDonald 76p*	*Thomas*	*McDonald*	*Wharton*	*McCreery*	*Jackson P*	*Roeder*	*Anderson*	*Gascoigne*	*Goddard*	*Mirandinha*	*Hodges*	
								Ref: M Peck	The Geordies are excited by the Brazilian, Mirandinha's debut, but are silenced by two Wimbledon goals inside a minute. The first of these was a Fash shot that flew in off keeper Martin Thomas. Sanchez fouls Gazza for the penalty. Glyn Hodges had an awful game for the Magpies.											
7	H	WEST HAM		4	D	1-1	1-0	Wise 20	Beasant	Scales	Phelan	Ryan	Young*	Thorn	Wise	Sayer^	Fashanu	Sanchez	Cork	Gibson/Gayle
	12/9		8,507	*16*	12			*Cottee 62*	*McAllister*	*Stewart*	*Parris*	*Strodder*	*Martin*	*Brady*	*Ward!*	*McAvennie*	*Ince*	*Cottee*	*Robson*	
								Ref: A Buksh	England-capped Tony Cottee is restricted to just one chance for lowly Hammers, but he takes it. Wimbledon might have been two up by that time, Cork having struck wood before Dennis Wise volleyed in. Wise also accounted for the dismissal of Mark Ward, who had thumped him.											
8	A	ARSENAL		8	L	**0-3**	0-3		Beasant	Gayle	Phelan	Ryan	Young	Thorn	Wise	Gibson	Fashanu	Sanchez	Fairweather*	Clement
	19/9		*27,752*	*9*	12			*Thomas 2p, Smith 20, Rocastle 43*	*Lukic*	*Thomas*	*Sansom*	*Williams**	*O'Leary*	*Adams*	*Rocastle*	*Davis*	*Smith*	*Groves*^	*Rix*	*Richardson/Merson*
								Ref: T Holbrook	Arsenal are embarked on a run of 14 straight victories in league and Littlewoods Cup. They continue to have the Indian sign over the Dons, who were on the slippery slope once Dennis Wise toppled Perry Groves inside the box. Rocastle's goal went in off Andy Thorn's heel.											
9	A	PORTSMOUTH		10	L	1-2	1-1	Sanchez 26	Beasant	Scales	Phelan	Jones*	Young	Gayle	Wise	Gibson	Fashanu	Sanchez	Fairweather	Ryan
	26/9		*13,088*	*12*	12			*Quinn 39, Sandford 85*	*Knight*	*Swain*	*Sandford*	*Fillery**	*Shotton*	*Gilbert*	*Horne*	*Kennedy*	*Mariner*	*Quinn*	*Hilaire*	*Whitehead*
								Ref: R Milford	After a batch of near misses, Alan Ball's Pompey are back in Division 1, where they think they belong. Sanchez puts the Dons in front, his first goal for nine months, and then hits the post when they are 1-2 down. In the closing seconds Carlton Fairweather fluffs an easy header.											
10	H	QP RANGERS		11	L	1-2	0-0	Fashanu 87	Beasant	Scales	Phelan	Jones	Young	Thorn	Cork	Gibson	Fashanu	Sanchez*	Fairweather^	Ryan/Miller
	3/10		8,552	*1*	12			*Bannister 68, Fenwick 77p*	*Seaman*	*Neil*	*Dawes*	*Parker*	*McDonald*	*Fenwick*	*Allen*	*Coney*	*Bannister*	*Byrne*	*Brock*	*Kerslake*
								Ref: P Don	Jim Smith's Rangers top the league after a blistering start. They collect another three points from a match Wimbledon thought they had controlled. Vinnie Jones plays his first full match after knee surgery in the summer, but gave away the penalty on QPR's lively Kevin Brock.											

No Date	Venue	Opponent Att	Pos	Pts	Res	F-A	H-T	Scorers, Times, and Referees	1	2	3	4	5	6	7	8	9	10	11	subs used
11	A	LUTON	13		L	0-2	0-1		Beasant	Ryan	Phelan	Jones	Gayle	Thorn	Gannon	Cork	Fashanu	Sanchez	Fairweather*	Clement
17/10		*7,018*	*16*	12				*B Stein 20, D Wilson 58*	*Sealey*	*Braecker*	*Grimes*	*McDonough*	*Foster*	*Donaghy*	*Wilson D*	*Stein B*	*Harford*	*Black**	*Weir*	*Allinson*
								Ref: B Hill	Lowly Luton become the fourth side to defeat Wimbledon in succession. Yet had the Dons taken just a fraction of the chances they created, the result could so easily have been different. Lawrie Sanchez hit the bar, John Fashanu the post, and John Gannon's 40-yarder hit the junction.											
12	A	TOTTENHAM	13		W	3-0	1-0	Fashanu 22, Gibson 50, Gannon 66	Beasant	Goodyear	**Bedford**	Ryan	Gayle	Thorn	Gannon	Gibson*	Fashanu	Sanchez	Fairweather	Cork
31/10		*22,282*	*8*	15					*Parks*	*Hughton*	*Thomas**	*Samways^*	*Fairclough*	*Mabbutt*	*Allen C*	*Allen P*	*Ardiles*	*Stevens*	*Claesen*	*Close/Ruddock*
								Ref: G Ashby	The Dons return to winning ways. Fashanu leaps like a salmon for the first; then Beasant's downfield punt sets up Gibson. The icing on the cake was John Gannon's screamer from 20 yards. England manager Bobby Robson voted this the Barclays performance of the week.											
13	H	LIVERPOOL			D	1-1	0-0	Fairweather 76	Beasant	Goodyear	Bedford	Ryan	Gayle	Thorn	Fairweather	Gibson*	Fashanu	Sanchez	Gannon^	Cork/**Hazel**
4/11		13,454	*1*	16				*Houghton 62*	*Grobbelaar*	*Gillespie*	*Lawrenson*	*Nicol*	*Whelan*	*Hansen*	*Beardsley*	*Aldridge*	*Johnson**	*Barnes*	*McMahon*	*Houghton*
								Ref: B Hill	Liverpool have topped the table from the off and have still to taste defeat. But Fairweather diverted a wayward shot from Vaughan Ryan past Grobbelaar. Liverpool had steamrollered forward in the second half, and taken the lead seconds after sub Ray Houghton had stripped off.											
14	H	SOUTHAMPTON	10		W	2-0	1-0	Fairweather 27, Cork 86	Beasant	Goodyear	Bedford	Ryan	Gayle	Thorn	Fairweather*	Wise^	Fashanu	Sanchez	Gannon	Cork/Hazel
7/11		5,014	*11*	19					*Burridge*	*Forrest*	*Statham*	*Case*	*Moore*	*Bond*	*Townsend*	*Cockerill*	*Clarke*	*Baker G**	*Wallace D*	*Wallace R*
								Ref: G Courtney	Southampton, managed by Chris Nicholl, created almost nothing in this match, despite the promptings of Jimmy Case in midfield. He was outshone by Lawrie Sanchez and Vaughan Ryan. Saints have much-travelled John Burridge in goal, not the future England man, Tim Flowers.											
15	A	COVENTRY	9		D	3-3	0-1	Fashanu 61, 72, Wise 65	Beasant	Goodyear	Bedford*	Hazel	Gayle	Thorn	Fairweather	Wise	Fashanu	Sanchez	Gannon^	Cork/Scales
14/11		*13,966*	*14*	20				*Kilcline 39p, Speedie 84, Gynn 89*	*Ogrizovic*	*Borrows*	*Downs*	*Emerson*	*Kilcline*	*Smith K*	*Bennett*	*McGrath**	*Regis^*	*Speedie*	*Pickering*	*Phillips/Gynn*
								Ref: G Tyson	John Sillett's Coventry, proud holders of the FA Cup, have lost six on the trot. It would have been seven but for Speedie and Gynn's late riposte. Speedie got in his header despite being surrounded by defenders. Four more bookings takes the Dons' total to 25 for the season.											
16	H	MANCHESTER U	8		W	2-1	0-0	Fairweather 72, Scales 88	Beasant	Goodyear	Scales	Jones	Gayle	Thorn	Fairweather	Cork	Fashanu	Sanchez	Wise	
21/11		11,532	*6*	23				*Blackmore 66*	*Walsh*	*Anderson*	*Duxbury**	*Moses*	*Blackmore*	*Moran*	*Robson*	*Graham^*	*McClair*	*Whiteside*	*Olsen*	*Albiston/O'Brien*
								Ref: I Borrett	A first defeat in 12 for Alex Ferguson, in his first full season at Old Trafford. The match was scarred by friction between Fashanu and Viv Anderson, a long-running feud. At 1-1, Beasant saved from first Olsen, then Moran. Then Scales drove the ball in through a forest of legs.											
17	A	CHELSEA	8		D	1-1	0-0	Wise 57	Beasant	Young	Scales	Jones	Gayle!	Thorn	Fairweather!	Cork	Fashanu	Sanchez	Wise	
28/11		*15,608*	*7*	24				*Durie 65p*	*Freestone*	*Clarke**	*Dorigo*	*Pates*	*McLaughlin*	*Wood*	*Nevin*	*Murphy*	*Dixon*	*Durie*	*Wilson C*	*Hall*
								Ref: R Lewis	Two sendings off for disgraced Wimbledon – Brian Gayle for abusing a linesman, and Carlton Fairweather for toppling Clive Wilson. All this drama came in the wake of Chelsea's penalty, awarded when Beasant felled Tony Dorigo. The Dons claimed Durie had been offside.											
18	H	NOTTINGHAM F	8		D	1-1	0-1	Wise 55	Beasant	Goodyear*	Scales	Jones	Gayle	Thorn	Fairweather	Cork^	Fashanu	Sanchez	Wise	Sayer/Young
5/12		5,170	*4*	25				*Clough 25*	*Sutton*	*Chettle*	*Pearce*	*Walker*	*Foster*	*Wilson*	*Plummer*	*Webb*	*Clough*	*Gaynor*	*Rice*	
								Ref: H Taylor	Vinnie Jones accomplishes two achievements, controlling both Neil Webb and his own temper. Tommy Gaynor makes his debut for Forest and manufactures a goal for Nigel Clough. Wimbledon equalise when Wise controls Jones' throw on his chest and uncorks a special.											
19	A	SHEFFIELD WED	8		L	0-1	0-0		Beasant	Goodyear	Scales	Jones	Young	Thorn	Gannon*	Hazel^	Fashanu	Sanchez	Wise	Phelan/Cork
12/12		*14,289*	*16*	25				*Chapman 72*	*Hodge*	*Sterland*	*Worthington*	*Madden*	*Pearson*	*Proctor*	*Marwood**	*Owen*	*Chapman*	*West^*	*Chamberlain*	*Bradshaw/Fee*
								Ref: K Breen	Howard Wilkinson's Owls are recovering from a bad start, but they despatch lacklustre Dons, who contribute little except a wearisome offside-trap. Lee Chapman heads in an inswinging corner. Bobby Gould wins the 'Golden Bull' award for his long-winded programme notes.											
20	H	NORWICH			W	1-0	1-0	Fashanu 14	Beasant	Goodyear	Scales	Jones	Young	Thorn	Fairweather	Cork	Fashanu*	Sanchez	Wise	**Turner**
18/12		**4,026**	*20*	28					*Gunn*	*Culverhouse*	*Elliott**	*O'Neill^*	*Phelan*	*Butterworth*	*Crook*	*Drinkell*	*Fleck*	*Putney*	*Gordon*	*Rosario/Goss*
								Ref: A Seville	This Friday match was settled by John Fashanu's header, his 12th goal of the season. But for two thrilling saves by Beasant from Kevin Drinkell, wobbly Norwich would have earned a point. Fashanu was later substituted by 6' 3" Robbie Turner, signed from Bristol Rovers.											

No	Date	Att	Pos	Pts	F-A	H-T	Scorers, Times, and Referees	1	2	3	4	5	6	7	8	9	10	11	subs used
21	A WEST HAM 26/12	 *18,605*	7 *10*	W 31	2-1	2-0	Sanchez 15, Fashanu 45 *Stewart 58p* Ref: A Gunn	Beasant *McAllister*	Goodyear *Bonds*	Scales *Parris**	Jones *Strodder*	Young *Stewart*	Thorn *Keen*	Fairweather *Ward*	Cork* *Dickens^*	Fashanu *Ince*	Sanchez *Cottee*	Wise *Robson*	Turner *Hilton/Brady*
								A beautiful move climaxes with Wise's cross and Sanchez scoring from close in. Fashanu increases the lead with a spectacular bicycle kick. West Ham pull one back when Stewart Robson is fouled by Dennis Wise inside the penalty box. The Dons did not like the decision.											
22	H ARSENAL 28/12	 12,473	7 *3*	W 34	3-1	0-1	Cork 46, Wise 48, Jones 90 *Quinn 23* Ref: J Moules	Beasant *Lukic*	Goodyear *Thomas*	Scales *Sansom*	Jones *Williams*	Young *Caesar*	Thorn *Adams*	Fairweather *Rocastle*	Cork *Hayes**	Fashanu *Quinn*	Sanchez *Groves*	Wise *Richardson*	 *Smith*
								Arsenal have won just once in seven now, and their title dreams are fading. Wimbledon's first ever win over the Gunners is secured despite Niall Quinn's first goal of the season. Man of the match Dennis Wise crosses for Cork to head level; then Cork repays the favour to Wise.											
23	H DERBY 1/1	 5,479	7 *16*	W 37	2-1	1-1	Cork 41, Fashanu 61 *Callaghan 35* Ref: K Morton	Beasant *Shilton*	Goodyear *MacLaren*	Scales *Forsyth*	Jones *Williams*	Young *Wright*	Thorn* *Blades*	Fairweather *Callaghan*	Cork *Penney*	Fashanu *Gee*	Sanchez *Gregory*	Wise *McCord*	Phelan
								Derby are mired in a 10-game losing streak, but Nigel Callaghan gives them the lead with a 25-yard free-kick. Alan Cork heads an equaliser against the club who let him go all those years ago, and John Fashanu heads an unstoppable winner. Andy Thorn tears a hamstring.											
24	A OXFORD 2/1	 *6,926*	5 *18*	W 40	**5-2**	3-0	Fairweather 4, Sanchez 15, Fashanu 27 *Saunders 55p, Foyle 65* [Cork 60, 75] Ref: P Durkin	Beasant *Hucker*	Goodyear *Bardsley*	Phelan* *Dreyer*	Jones *Shetton*	Young *Whitehurst*	Gayle *Caton*	Fairweather *Hebberd*	Cork *Foyle*	Fashanu *Saunders*	Sanchez *Phillips*	Wise *Rhodes-Brown*	Ryan
								Mid-table in November, Oxford have now lost their last six. They hand the Dons their fifth win in a row and their biggest of the season. Cork's 150th goal puts him in sight of Bobby Gould's 160. Fash's bum scored. Beasant saves Saunders' second penalty, both conceded by Young.											
25	H WATFORD 16/1	 6,848	6 *20*	L 40	1-2	0-0	Young 61 *Sterling 49, Allen 74p* Ref: T Mills	Beasant *Coton*	Goodyear *Chivers*	Phelan *Rostron*	Jones *Sherwood*	Young *Morris*	Gayle *McClelland*	Fairweather* *Sterling*	Cork *Allen*	Fashanu *Blissett*	Sanchez *Porter*	Gannon^ *Hodges*	Turner/Ryan
								It all went wrong for Watford and for Dave Bassett, who has decamped to Bramall Lane. Hornets' boss Steve Harrison enjoys a fine baptism, and the double over the Dons. But the referee gave Watford a crucial penalty when Eric Young rugby-tackled Luther Blissett outside the box.											
26	H NEWCASTLE 6/2	 10,505	7 *10*	D 41	0-0	0-0	 Ref: M Dimblebee	Beasant *Kelly*	Goodyear *Anderson*	Phelan *Wharton*	Jones *Jackson D*	Gayle *Jackson P*	Thorn *Roeder*	Gibson *McDonald*	Cork* *Gascoigne*	Fashanu *Goddard*	Sanchez *Mirandinha*	Wise *O'Neill*	Clement
								One of the more eventful goalless draws. Terry Gibson returns after three months out with a groin strain, and twice comes close. Beasant makes a super save from Paul Goddard's header. Vinnie Jones subdues Paul Gascoigne with the aid of a well-publicised grab at his manhood.											
27	A CHARLTON 13/2	 ***5,520***	7 *21*	D 42	1-1	0-1	Gibson 70 *Reid 32p* Ref: R Wiseman	Beasant *Bolder*	Goodyear *Humphrey*	Phelan *Reid*	Jones *Mackenzie*	Gayle *Shirtliff*	Thorn *Thompson*	Gibson *Stuart*	Cork *Campbell*	Fashanu *Jones*	Sanchez *Lee**	Wise* *Mortimer^*	Clement *Williams/Crooks*
								Yawn, yawn. Charlton haven't won in seven and it shows. Phelan fells Robert Lee for the penalty. Gibson levels by turning in Jones' cross to the far post. Wise's overhead kick thuds against the bar. Ex-Lincoln duo Fashanu and Steve Thompson enjoy another physical tussle.											
28	A QP RANGERS 27/2	 *9,080*	7 *6*	L 42	0-1	0-0	 *Byrne 81* Ref: N Midgley	Beasant *Seaman*	Goodyear *Dawes*	Phelan *Neil*	Jones *Parker*	Gayle *Maddix*	Thorn *Maguire*	Gibson *Allen**	Clement* *Falco*	Fashanu *Byrne*	Sanchez *Fereday*	**Cunningh'm** *Kerslake*	Cork *Fleming*
								Wimbledon suffer from 'plastophobia', a hatred of plastic pitches. They might have felt differently but for David Kerslake's corner which wasn't properly cleared, allowing transfer-seeking John Byrne the chance to score. Paul Parker marked John Fashanu out of the game.											
29	H LUTON 5/3	 5,058	7 *9*	W 45	2-0	1-0	Fashanu 12, Gibson 49 Ref: R Gifford	Beasant *Sealey*	Goodyear *Braecker*	Phelan *Grimes*	Jones *Johnson R*	Gayle *Johnson M*	Thorn *Donaghy*	Gibson *Wilson D*	Cork* *Stein B*	Fashanu *Harford*	Sanchez *Stein M*	Scales *Allinson*	Clement
								Luton like to play one-touch football, but it got them nowhere. Dons' John Fashanu and Luton's Ray Harford both now stand on 18 goals. Fashanu's 18th was set up by Jones, after hesitancy from Luton debutant Martyn Johnson. Harford was denied a 19th by Beasant's save.											
30	H TOTTENHAM 19/3	 8,616	7 *8*	W 48	3-0	0-0	Jones 63, Fashanu 82, Wise 90 Ref: A Ward	Beasant *Mimms*	Goodyear* *Statham*	Phelan *Thomas*	Jones *Fenwick*	Young *Fairclough*	Thorn *Mabbutt*	Gibson *Allen C*	Cork *Allen P*	Fashanu *Ardiles**	Sanchez *Samways*	Wise *Walsh*	Scales *Hodge*
								Tottenham lost manager David Pleat earlier in the season, and his replacement, Terry Venables, can work no instant magic. Spurs looked good at the start of this match, but when Thorn floats over a free-kick, Cork knocks it on, and Vinnie Jones volleys past Bobby Mimms.											

No	Venue	Date	Opponent	Att	Pos	Pts	F-A	H-T	Scorers, Times, and Referees	1	2	3	4	5	6	7	8	9	10	11	subs used
31	A	26/3	LIVERPOOL	**36,464**	7 1	L 48	1-2	0-1	Young 89	Beasant	Scales	Phelan	Ryan	Young	Thorn	Cunningham	Cork*	Fashanu	Sanchez	Wise	Sayer
									Aldridge 33, Barnes 79	*Grobbelaar*	*Gillespie*	*Ablett*	*Nicol*	*Spackman*	*Hansen*	*Beardsley*	*Aldridge**	*Johnson*	*Barnes*	*McMahon^*	*Dalglish/Molby*
									Ref: G Courtney	No bigger league crowd will watch Wimbledon this season, as Liverpool march inexorably – they hope – towards a league and cup double. Aldridge's glancing header brings his 22nd goal of the season. Young, booked early on, then drags back Beardsley without getting a red card.											
32	A	29/3	EVERTON	20,351	4	D 49	2-2	2-2	Cunningham 2, Wise 23	Beasant	Ryan	Phelan	Jones!	Young	Thorn*	Cunningham	Cork	Fashanu	Sanchez	Wise	Clement
									Steven 11p, Pointon 19	*Southall*	*Stevens*	*Pointon*	*Harper*	*Mountfield*	*Reid*	*Steven*	*Clarke*	*Heath*	*Power*	*Sheedy*	
									Ref: J Rushton	Everton's crown is slipping. Vinnie Jones celebrates his first game back after suspension by kicking Peter Reid in the face as he lay on the ground. Ex-England international Lawrie Cunningham had startled the hosts with a 2nd minute goal. All the goals came in a 21-minute spell.											
33	A	2/4	SOUTHAMPTON	13,036	7 14	D 50	2-2	1-0	Cunningham 38, Gayle 88	Beasant	Scales	Phelan	Ryan	Young	Thorn	Cunningham	Cork*	Fashanu	Sanchez^	Wise	Gayle/Clement
									Baker 70, Cockerill 82	*Burridge*	*Forrest*	*Statham*	*Case*	*Blake*	*Bond*	*Baker G*	*Cockerll*	*Clarke*	*Townsend*	*Wallace D*	
									Ref: G Ashby	Lawrie Cunningham's fine header puts Wimbledon one up. Vaughan Ryan mishits a clearance to allow Graham Baker to equalise. The Saints go ahead when Andy Townsend crosses for Glen Cockerill. Sub Gayle stoops to head in to make it 2-2 after Andy Clement pulls the ball back.											
34	H	5/4	COVENTRY	5,920	9	L 50	1-2	1-2	Young 39	Beasant	Scales	Phelan	Jones	Young	Thorn	Clement*	Ryan	Fashanu^	**Miller**	Wise	Sayer/Gayle
									Kilcline 27p, Houchen 28	*Ogrizovic*	*Borrows*	*Pickering*	*Sedgley*	*Kilcline*	*Peake*	*Emerson*	*Phillips*	*Houchen*	*Speedie*	*Smith*	
									Ref: R Groves	Mediocre Coventry send the Dons into their FA Cup semi-final in low spirits. Fashanu has to limp off after just five minutes. Debut-boy Paul Miller had a shot cleared off the line by Trevor Peake. Coventry went ahead from the spot when Terry Phelan handled David Phillips' shot.											
35	H	19/4	PORTSMOUTH	9,009	19	D 51	2-2	1-0	Wise 17, 84	Beasant	Scales	Phelan	Ryan	Young	Gayle	Gibson	Cork*	Fashanu	Hazel	Wise	Gannon
									Mariner 62, Dillon 73	*Knight**	*Swain*	*Sandford*	*Gilbert*	*Blake*	*Ball*	*Horne*	*Whitehead*	*Mariner*	*Quinn*	*Hilaire*	*Dillon*
									Ref: A Gunn	Pompey cannot arrest their slide, but must have thought they'd earned a rare win in this stormy match. They lost keeper Alan Knight in the second minute when Young's elbow breaks his nose. Lee Sandford deputised, but could not prevent Wise pouncing from Phelan's pass.											
36	H	23/4	CHELSEA	**15,128**	7 16	D 52	2-2	1-0	Sanchez 30, Wise 70	Beasant	Scales	Phelan	Ryan*	Young	Thorn	Gannon^	Miller	**Swind'hurst**	Sanchez	Wise	Clement/Gayle
									Durie 73p, 81	*Hitchcock*	*Hall*	*Dorigo*	*Wicks*	*McLaughlin*	*Clarke*	*Nevin*	*Hazard*	*Dixon*	*Durie*	*Bumstead*	
									Ref: D Vickers	Just before half-time Chelsea keeper Kevin Hitchock saved Wise's penalty. Wise had insisted on taking it and wrestled the ball away from Phelan. Gordon Durie scores from the spot after being fouled by Young. Chelsea pull level after Dave Beasant loses a high ball in the sun.											
37	A	30/4	NOTTINGHAM F	14,341	7 5	D 53	0-0	0-0		Beasant	Scales*	Phelan	Jones	Young	Thorn	Gannon	Miller	Swind'hurst^	Sanchez	Wise	Turner/Gayle
										Sutton	*Fleming*	*Williams*	*Chettle*	*Foster*	*Wilson*	*Carr*	*Webb*	*Gaynor*	*Parker*	*Rice*	
									Ref: R Nixon	Reserve striker Robbie Turner comes on for Dave Swindlehurst and finds himself one on one with Steve Sutton, but the keeper kicks away. Forest debutant Gary Parker also wastes a good chance. Near the end Thorn handles Andy Rice's cross, but Dave Beasant saves Rice's penalty.											
38	H	3/5	SHEFFIELD WED	7,854	9	D 54	1-1	1-0	Gibson 3	Beasant	Goodyear	Phelan	Jones	Young	Thorn	Gibson	Cork*	Fashanu	Sanchez	Cunningham	Wise
									Chapman 66	*Pressman*	*Sterland*	*Fee*	*Madden*	*May*	*Proctor*	*West*	*Megson*	*Chapman*	*Hirst*	*Jonsson*	
									Ref: R Hamer	It is eight league games now without a win for Wembley-bound Dons, eight without defeat for rampant Wednesday. Terry Gibson gives Wimbledon hope early on, but Lee Chapman's 19th goal of the season restores parity. He had also scored the winner at Hillsborough.											
39	A	7/5	NORWICH	11,782	7 14	W 57	1-0	0-0	Gibson 82	Beasant	Goodyear	Phelan	Jones	Gayle	Thorn	Gibson	Cork	Fashanu	Sanchez	Wise	
										Gunn	*Culverhouse*	*Spearing*	*Linighan*	*Phelan*	*Butterworth*	*Fox*	*Drinkell*	*Biggins*	*Goss**	*Putney*	*Gordon*
									Ref: J Martin	Norwich's season dribbles away and they put up little fight. Bobby Gould and Don Howe, by contrast, intensify their players' training to prevent them going soft. Tom Spearing's inattentive back-pass gives the Dons a gift goal, as Terry Gibson steals in. A first league win in nine.											
40	A	9/5	MANCHESTER U	28,040	2	L 57	1-2	1-0	Gibson 32	Beasant	Goodyear	Phelan	Jones	Young	Gayle	Gibson*	Gannon^	Fashanu	Sanchez	Cunningham	Hazel/Sayer
									McClair, 51, 76p	*Turner*	*Anderson*	*Blackmore*	*Bruce*	*McGrath*	*Moses**	*Robson*	*Strachan*	*McClair*	*Davenport*	*Gibson*	*Martin*
Average			Home 7,994	Away 16,56-					Ref: J Watson	United sprint for the finishing line, but Liverpool have long ago crossed it. Terry Gibson scores against the club where he endured an unhappy spell. Brian McClair takes his season's goal-tally to 32, heading in at the far post and converting a penalty when Phelan handled.											

Littlewoods Cup	Att			F-A	H-T	Scorers, Times, and Referees	1	2	3	4	5	6	7	8	9	10	11	subs used
2:1 A ROCHDALE		8	D	1-1	1-1	Fashanu 26p	Beasant	Gayle	Phelan	Ryan*	Young	Thorn	Wise	Gibson	Fashanu	Sanchez	Fairweather	Jones
22/9	*2,801*	*4:22*				*Simmonds 42p*	*Welch*	*Lomax*	*Hampton*	*Reid*	*Bramhall*	*Smart*	*Seasman*	*Simmonds*	*Hunt**	*Coyle^*	*Gavin*	*Stanton/Thompson*
						Ref: K Redfern	Basement-club Rochdale employ former Millwall striker John Seasman as sweeper. Fashanu scores from the spot after keeper Keith Welch upended Dennis Wise. Rochdale's Lyndon Simmonds reciprocates with a twice-taken kick after he was toppled by Eric Young.											
2:2 H ROCHDALE		11	W	2-1	0-0	Fashanu 67, Cork 72	Beasant	Ryan	Phelan	Jones	Young!	Thorn	Fairweather	Gibson	Fashanu	Sanchez	Cork	
6/10	*2,600*	*4:21*				*Parker 52*	*Welch*	*Lomax*	*Hampton*	*Holden*	*Bramhall*	*Smart*	*Seasman*	*Simmonds**	*Parlane*	*Coyle*	*Parker*	*Stanton*
						Ref: I Borrett (Dons win 3-2 on aggregate)	Just after half-time Eric Young is expelled for elbowing Ronnie Coyle. Debutant Derrick Parker promptly heads Rochdale into the lead, only for Keith Welch to drop the ball for the lurking Fashanu. Alan Cork ruins Rochdale's dreams and saves Wimbledon's bacon.											
3 H NEWCASTLE		13	W	2-1	1-1	Fashanu 34, Gibson 90	Beasant	Goodyear	Bedford	Ryan	Gayle	Thorn	Fairweather	Gibson	Fashanu	Sanchez	Cork*	Gannon
28/10	6,443	*12*				*McDonald 43p*	*Kelly*	*Anderson*	*Wharton*	*McCreery*	*Jackson P*	*Roeder*	*McDonald*	*Gascoigne*	*Goddard*	*Mirandinha*	*Jackson D**	*O'Neill*
						Ref: D Axcell	By the end of the season the Magpies will hate the sight of Wimbledon, who have already won at St James's in the league. Not even the magic of Paul Gascoigne can save Newcastle. Terry Gibson's first goal for the Dons is an injury-time header. Beasant fouled Jackson for the penalty.											
4 A OXFORD		9	L	1-2	0-1	Cork 65	Beasant	Goodyear	Scales	Hazel	Gayle	Thorn	Fairweather	Wise*	Fashanu	Sanchez	Gannon^	Jones/Cork
18/11	*5,516*	*11*				*Saunders 4, Phillips 75*	*Hucker*	*Bardsley*	*Dreyer*	*Shetton*	*Slatter*	*Caton*	*Hebberd*	*Whitehurst*	*Saunders*	*Phillips*	*Rhodes-Brown*	
						Ref: J Key	Oxford are something of a jinx team for Wimbledon: this is their 8th win in 12 meetings. Two howlers by Brian Gayle give the game away. Dean Saunders beats him for pace; Gayle later presents the ball to Les Phillips. It is only November, but Oxford won't win again in the league.											

FA Cup																		
3 H WEST BROM		5	W	4-1	1-0	Fashanu 44, Wise 54, Turner 71	Beasant	Goodyear	Phelan	Jones	Gayle	Thorn	Fairweather	Cork	Fashanu	Sanchez	Wise*	Turner
9/1	7,252	*2:19*				*Thorn 87 (og)* [Fairweather 90]	*Powell*	*Dickenson*	*Cowdrill*	*Palmer*	*North*	*Kelly*	*Hopkins*	*Goodman*	*Reilly*	*Burrows*	*Williamson*	
						Ref: M Bodenham	Ron Atkinson's strugglers have just ended a 10-match run without a win. Fashanu's header just before half-time turns the tide against them. Wise scores from 30 yards, then limps off allowing Turner his first goal. The players celebrate with Fash's ghetto-blaster in the changing room.											
4 A MANSFIELD		6	W	2-1	1-0	Cork 43, Phelan 60	Beasant	Goodyear	Phelan	Jones	Gayle	Thorn	Wise	Cork	Fashanu	Sanchez	Scales	
30/1	*10,462*	*3:17*				*Kent 67*	*Hitchcock*	*Graham*	*Garner*	*Lowery*	*Foster*	*Coleman*	*McKernon**	*Ryan*	*Kent*	*Cassells*	*Charles*	*Stringfellow*
						Ref: H Taylor	This could have been a tricky one, but Cork's header settles the nerves. Fairweather is out with a broken leg, but Terry Phelan pushes forward and scores his first Wimbledon goal, a sweet volley. At 1-2 Beasant smothers Steve Charles' penalty, after Sanchez had fouled Tony Lowery.											
5 A NEWCASTLE		7	W	3-1	1-0	Gibson 6, Gayle 56, Fashanu 85	Beasant	Goodyear	Phelan	Jones	Gayle	Thorn	Gibson	Cunningh'm*	Fashanu	Sanchez	Wise	Cork
20/2	*28,769*	*12*				*McDonald 57*	*Kelly*	*Anderson*	*Wharton*	*McCreery*	*Jackson P*	*Roeder*	*McDonald*	*Gascoigne*	*Goddard*	*Mirandinha*	*Jackson D**	*O'Neill*
						Ref: J Worrall	The St James's faithful boo the Dons onto the pitch. When Brian Gayle put the visitors two up, they must have thought they were through, but within seconds Neil McDonald's header from Gascoigne's corner flew in off Alan Cork's head. Fash's volley sets up the celebrations.											
QF H WATFORD		7	W	2-1	0-1	Young 49, Fashanu 73	Beasant	Goodyear	Phelan	Jones	Gayle!	Thorn	Gibson	Cork*	Fashanu	Sanchez	Wise	Young
12/3	12,228	*21*				*Allen 18*	*Coton*	*Gibbs*	*Rostron*	*Jackett*	*Morris*	*McClelland*	*Sterling**	*Allen*	*Blisssett*	*Porter*	*Hodges*	*Roberts*
						Ref: N Midgley	Watford have beaten the Dons twice in the league, and for a while things looked black again. At half-time Wimbledon are a goal down and reduced to 10 men, when Gayle thumped goalscorer Malcolm Allen. Sub Eric Young heads a leveller, and Fashanu smashes a glorious winner.											
SF N LUTON		7	W	2-1	0-0	Fashanu 56p, Wise 80	Beasant	Scales	Phelan	Jones	Young	Thorn	Gibson*	Cork	Fashanu	Sanchez	Wise	Cunningham
9/4 (White Hart Lane)	*25,963*	*13*				*Harford 48*	*McEvoy*	*Braecker*	*McDonough**	*Black*	*Stein M*	*Donaghy*	*Wilson*	*Stein B*	*Harford*	*Allinson*	*Johnson R*	*Foster*
						Ref: K Hackett	Spurs is the venue for this nerve-racking semi-final. Luton are without keeper Les Sealey, but Andy Dibble stands tall. Ray Harford's 21st goal stems from Mark Stein's flick-on; Fashanu's 21st comes from the spot after Dibble took Gibson's legs. Beasant's son was born the day before.											

F	N	LIVERPOOL	7	W	1-0	1-0	Sanchez 36	Beasant	Goodyear	Phelan	Jones	Young	Thorn	Gibson*	Cork^	Fashanu	Sanchez	Wise	Scales/Cunningham
14/5		*98,203*	*1*					*Grobbelaar*	*Gillespie*	*Ablett*	*Nicol*	*Spackman**	*Whelan*	*Beardsley*	*Aldridge^*	*Houghton*	*Barnes*	*McMahon*	*Molby/Johnston*

(Wembley) Ref: B Hill

A day to remember. Dennis Wise's free-kick from near the corner flag is glanced in by Sanchez. Goodyear's challenge on Aldridge on the hour looked innocuous, but a penalty ensued. Aldridge had scored 10 times from the spot this season, but Beasant thrillingly saves to his left.

		Home					Away					
	P	W	D	L	F	A	W	D	L	F	A	Pts
1 Liverpool	40	15	5	0	49	9	11	7	2	38	15	90
2 Manchester U	40	14	5	1	41	17	9	7	4	30	21	81
3 Nott'm Forest	40	11	7	2	40	17	9	6	5	27	22	73
4 Everton	40	14	4	2	34	11	5	9	6	19	16	70
5 QP Rangers	40	12	4	4	30	14	7	6	7	18	24	67
6 Arsenal	40	11	4	5	35	16	7	8	5	23	23	66
7 WIMBLEDON	40	8	9	3	32	20	6	6	8	26	27	57
8 Newcastle	40	9	6	5	32	23	5	8	7	23	30	56
9 Luton	40	11	6	3	40	21	3	5	12	17	37	53
10 Coventry	40	6	8	6	23	25	7	6	7	23	28	53
11 Sheffield Wed	40	10	2	8	27	30	5	6	9	25	36	53
12 Southampton	40	6	8	6	27	26	6	6	8	22	27	50
13 Tottenham	40	9	5	6	26	23	3	6	11	12	25	47
14 Norwich	40	7	5	8	26	26	5	4	11	14	26	45
15 Derby	40	6	7	7	18	17	4	6	10	17	28	43
16 West Ham	40	6	9	5	23	21	3	6	11	17	31	42
17 Charlton	40	7	7	6	23	21	2	8	10	15	31	42
18 Chelsea*	40	7	11	2	24	17	2	4	14	26	51	42
19 Portsmouth	40	4	8	8	21	27	3	6	11	15	39	35
20 Watford	40	4	5	11	15	24	3	6	11	12	27	32
21 Oxford	40	5	7	8	24	34	1	6	13	20	46	31
	840	182	132	106	610	439	106	132	182	439	610	1128

* *relegated after play-offs*

Odds & ends

Double wins: (3) Derby, Tottenham, Norwich.
Double losses: (2) Watford, QPR.

Won from behind: (4) Charlton (h), Manchester U (h), Arsenal (h), Derby (h).
Lost from in front: (2) Portsmouth (a), Manchester U (a).

High spots: Winning the FA Cup.
6 unbeaten games in August and September lifted the Dons to 4th.
6 consecutive wins in league and FA Cup in December and January.

Low spots: Losing 4 matches on the trot to 17th October, down to 13th.

The Dons had a bad record against the relegated teams, winning 1 of 8.

The Dons lost twice to relegated Watford, but beat them in the FA Cup.

Wimbledon ruined Newcastle's season, knocking them out of both cups, and winning and drawing in the league.

Player of the Year: Dennis Wise.
Ever-presents: (1) Dave Beasant.
Hat-tricks: (0).
Leading scorer: John Fashanu (20).

	Appearances						Goals			
	Lge	Sub	LC	Sub	FAC	Sub	Lge	LC	FAC	Total
Beasant, Dave	**40**		4		6					
Bedford, Kevin	**4**		1							
Clement, Andy	**2**	(9)								
Cork, Alan	**28**	(6)	2	(1)	5	(1)	**9**	2	1	**12**
Cunningham, Lawrie	**6**				1	(2)	**2**			**2**
Downes, Wally										
Fairweather, Carlton	**19**	(2)	4		1		**4**		1	**5**
Fashanu, John	**38**		4		6		**13**	3	4	**20**
Galliers, Steve	**1**									
Gannon, John	**10**	(3)	1	(1)			**1**			**1**
Gayle, Brian	**20**	(6)	3		4		**1**		1	**2**
Gibson, Terry	**16**	(1)	3		4		**6**	1	1	**8**
Goodyear, Clive	**21**	(1)	2		5					
Hazel, Ian	**3**	(3)	1							
Jones, Vinnie	**24**		1	(2)	6		**2**			**2**
Miller, Paul	**3**	(2)								
Phelan, Terry	**28**	(2)	2		6				1	**1**
Ryan, Vaughan	**17**	(5)	3				**1**			**1**
Sanchez, Lawrie	**38**		4		6		**4**		1	**5**
Sayer, Andy	**5**	(4)								
Scales, John	**23**	(2)	1		2	(1)	**1**			**1**
Swindlehurst, Dave	**2**									
Thorn, Andy	**35**		4		6					
Turner, Robert		(4)				(1)			1	**1**
Wise, Dennis	**29**	(1)	2		6		**10**		2	**12**
Young, Eric	**28**	(1)	2		2	(1)	**3**		1	**4**
(own-goals)							**1**			**1**
26 players used	**440**	**(52)**	**44**	**(4)**	**66**	**(6)**	**58**	**6**	**14**	**78**

BARCLAYS LEAGUE DIVISION 1 — Manager: Bobby Gould — SEASON 1988-89

No	Date	Att	Pos	Pts	F-A	H-T	Scorers, Times, and Referees	1	2	3	4	5	6	7	8	9	10	11	subs used
1	H ARSENAL			L	**1-5**	1-3	Fashanu 8 *[Merson 85]*	**Tracey**	**Joseph**	Phelan	Ryan	Young	**Cawley***	Gibson	Fairweather	Fashanu^	Sanchez	Wise	Scales/Cork
	27/8	**15,710**		–			*Marwood 16, Smith 24, 27, 58,*	*Lukic*	*Dixon*	*Winterburn*	*Thomas*	*Bould*	*Adams*	*Rocastle*	*Davis*	*Smith*	*Merson*	*Marwood*	
							Ref: J Martin	The FA Cup winners suffer a mighty hangover. Wimbledon have lost Beasant and Thorn to Newcastle, and – with three defenders making their league debuts – are bowled over. Fash climbs above Bould to score, but Simon Tracey then drops Brian Marwood's cross over the line.											
2	A LUTON		16	D	2-2	1-1	Fashanu 41p, Fairweather 73	**Green**	Joseph	Phelan	Ryan	Young	Scales	Gibson*	Fairweather	Fashanu	Sanchez^	Wise	**Brooke**/Turner
	3/9	*8,067*		1			*Ryan 44 (og), Black 56*	*Sealey*	*Johnson R*	*Grimes*	*Williams*	*Foster*	*Donaghy*	*Wilson*	*Preece*	*Harford*	*Oldfield*	*Black*	
							Ref: B Stevens	The Littlewoods Cup winners versus the FA Cup winners. Bobby Gould axes Tracey and Cawley and brings in veteran Ron Green in goal. Fashanu scores from the spot after ex-England man Steve Foster upended Wise, but Ryan then turns Mick Harford's cross into his own goal.											
3	H WEST HAM		18	L	0-1	0-1		Green	Joseph	Phelan	Ryan*	Young	Scales	Gibson	Fairweather	Fashanu	Cork	Wise	Brooke
	10/9	7,730	*13*	1			*Ward 20*	*McKnight*	*Parris*	*Dicks*	*Hilton*	*Martin*	*Ince*	*Ward*	*Kelly**	*Rosenior*	*Dickens*	*Robson*	*Devonshire*
							Ref: R Lewis	John Lyall's Hammers escaped the play-offs on goal difference and have lost their first two matches this time. They are thankful to Paul Ince clearing off the line from Wise and Fashanu within seconds, and for Mark Ward, who shot home after Green had handled outside the area.											
4	A MIDDLESBRO		19	L	0-1	0-1		Green	Joseph	Phelan	Hazel	Young	Scales	Gibson	Fairweather	Fashanu	Sanchez	Brooke*	Cork
	17/9	*17,709*	*15*	1			*Hamilton 7*	*Pears*	*Parkinson*	*Cooper*	*Mowbray*	*Hamilton*	*Pallister*	*Slaven*	*Brennan*	*Senior*	*Kerr**	*Ripley*	*Kernaghan*
							Ref: S Lodge	Bruce Rioch's Boro came up through the play-offs, but have lost all three league openers. Like West Ham, they derive their first points from an obliging Wimbledon. The only goal comes from a cross that floats over Phelan to the unmarked Gary Hamilton. Fashanu is the new skipper.											
5	H COVENTRY		20	L	0-1	0-1		Green	Joseph	Clement	Jones	Young	Scales	Gibson*	Fairweath'r^	Fashanu	Sanchez	Wise	Cork/Turner
	24/9	4,474	*6*	1			*Bannister 38*	*Ogrizovic*	*Borrows*	*Downs*	*Sedgley*	*Kilcline*	*Peake*	*Gynn*	*Speedie*	*Regis*	*Bannister*	*Smith*	
							Ref: G Ashby	John Sillett's Coventry have made an impressive start, and inflict upon Wimbledon their third 0-1 defeat in a row. David Speedie outjumps defenders and nods a free-kick down to Gary Bannister. Brian Kilcline polices Fashanu with ease. Jones returns after injury to a fine reception.											
6	H EVERTON		19	W	2-1	2-0	Fashanu 13, Cork 31	**Segers**	Joseph	Clement	Jones	Young	Scales	Brooke	Cork	Fashanu	Sanchez	Wise	
	1/10	6,367	*10*	4			*Heath 57*	*Southall*	*McDonald*	*Pointon*	*Snodin*	*V d Hauwe*	*Reid*	*Heath*	*McCall*	*Sharp*	*Cottee*	*Sheedy*	
							Ref: P Foakes	Debuts for Hans Segers, and for Tony Cottee of Everton, whose third league defeat on the trot allows Wimbledon win at last. Alan Cork – in for injured Gibson – and Fashanu give Pat van den Hauwe and Ian Snodin a wretched time. Segers' huge downfield punt brings the first goal.											
7	A ASTON VILLA		18	W	1-0	0-0	Scales 86	Segers	Joseph	Clement	Jones	Young	Scales	Brooke	Cork	Fashanu*	Sanchez	Wise	Turner
	8/10	*15,416*	*16*	7				*Spink*	*Price*	*Mountfield*	*Gray A*	*Gage*	*Keown*	*Daley*	*Platt*	*Thompson**	*Cowans*	*Gray S*	*Evans*
							Ref: N Midgley	Graham Taylor has brought Villa back to Division 1 at the first attempt. This is only their second defeat, brought about four minutes from time by man of the match John Scales – nicknamed 'Son of Bobby'. (Gould brought him from Bristol Rovers.) Scales scores from six inches out.											
8	H MANCHESTER U		17	D	1-1	0-1	Wise 76	Segers	Joseph	Clement	Jones	Young	Scales	Brooke*	Cork	Turner^	Sanchez	Wise	Fairweather/**Curle**
	22/10	12,143	*7*	8			*Hughes 23*	*Leighton*	*Blackmore*	*Sharpe*	*Bruce*	*Garton*	*Duxbury*	*Robson*	*Strachan**	*McClair*	*Hughes*	*Davenport^*	*Beardsmore/Robins*
							Ref: A Seville	A game of two halves, as they say. United were rampant in the first half, but Dons superior in the second. Vinnie Jones was all set to score from Cork's cross when Wise leaps in front of him. Lawrie Sanchez celebrates his birthday by knocking out one of Jim Leighton's teeth.											
9	A DERBY		17	L	1-4	1-1	Jones 39 *[Micklewhite 85]*	Segers	Joseph	Clement	Jones	Young	Scales	Fairweather	Cork*	Fashanu	Sanchez	Wise	Brooke
	29/10	*15,050*	*13*	8			*Saunders 35, 67, Sage 62,*	*Shilton*	*Sage*	*Forsyth*	*Williams*	*Hindmarch*	*Blades*	*McMinn*	*Saunders*	*Goddard*	*Hebberd*	*Callaghan**	*Micklewhite*
							Ref: L Shapter	Arthur Cox's Derby only just managed to stave off the drop last time, and had only scored four times this. They double that tally by going bananas in the second half, building on £1 million signing Dean Saunders' horizontal header. Segers' huge punt brought Jones' leveller.											
10	H NORWICH		17	L	0-2	0-1		Segers	Joseph	Phelan	Jones	Young	Scales	Wise*	Gibson	Fashanu	Sanchez	Fairweath'r^	Cork/Curle
	5/11	5,853	*1*	8			*Linighan 36, Allen 72*	*Gunn*	*Culverhouse*	*Bowen*	*Butterworth*	*Linighan*	*Townsend*	*Gordon*	*Fleck**	*Rosario*	*Phelan*	*Putney*	*Allen*
							Ref: J Rushton	Dave Stringer's Norwich are the surprise leaders of Division 1. They only created three good chances in this match, but they took two of them. Their football is calm and relaxed, unlike Wimbledon's. Mike Phelan and Andy Townsend eclipse Jones and Sanchez in midfield.											

No	Date	H/A	Opponent	Att	Pos	Pts	Res	F-A	H-T	Scorers, Times, and Referees	1	2	3	4	5	6	7	8	9	10	11	subs used
11		A	TOTTENHAM		19		L	2-3	1-1	Gibson 21, 82	Segers	Joseph	Phelan	Jones	Young	Scales	Curle	Gibson	Fashanu*	Sanchez	Wise^	Fairweather/Cork
	12/11			*23,589*	*18*	8				*Fenwick 18p, Butters 61, Samways 62*	*Mimms*	*Stevens**	*Thomas*	*Fenwick*	*Fairclough*	*Mabbutt*	*Moran*	*Gascoigne*	*Waddle*	*Stewart*	*Samways*	*Butters*
										Ref: H King	Spurs have lost their last four in the league, so both sides lack confidence. It is also the match in which Vinnie Jones ends Gary Stevens' career with a touchline lunge. Wise impeded Fenwick for the penalty. In the second half Paul Gascoigne and Chris Waddle overran the Dons.											
12		H	CHARLTON		17		D	1-1	0-0	Fashanu 72	Segers	Joseph*	Phelan	Jones	Young	Curle	Fairweather	Cork^	Fashanu	Sanchez	Wise	Scales/Brooke
	19/11			5,631	*15*	9				*R Lee 46*	*Bolder*	*Humphrey*	*Reid*	*MacKenzie*	*Caton*	*Gritt*	*Bennett*	*Williams**	*Peake*	*Leaburn*	*Mortimer*	*Lee R*
										Ref: D Elleray	Lennie Lawrence again kept his Charlton side up by a thread. They end their losing streak, despite having top scorer Paul Williams carried off after half an hour. Curle's intended back header to Segers fell to Robert Lee. New signing Tommy Caton did a manful job containing Fashanu.											
13		A	LIVERPOOL		18		D	1-1	0-0	Nicol 87 (og)	Segers	Joseph	Scales	Jones	Young	Curle	Fairweather*	Gibson^	Fashanu	Sanchez	Wise	Clement/Cork
	26/11			*36,188*		10				*Houghton 63*	*Hooper*	*Ablett*	*Venison*	*Nicol*	*Whelan*	*Spackman*	*Beardsley*	*Staunton*	*Rush**	*Houghton*	*McMahon*	*Aldridge*
										Ref: J Key	Wimbledon's spoiling tactics brought howls of protest from the Kop. Once Ray Houghton had put Liverpool in front, following a bout of sustained passing, only goalkeeper Mike Hooper kept Wimbledon at bay. Jones' huge throw was bundled into his own net by Steve Nicol.											
14		H	SOUTHAMPTON		18		W	2-1	1-1	Gibson 31, Fairweather 82	Segers	Joseph*	Scales	Jones	Young	Curle	Fairweather	Gibson	Turner^	Ryan	Wise	Cork/Phelan
	3/12			6,040	*7*	13				*Maddison 37*	*Burridge*	*WallaceRay*	*Staunton*	*Case*	*Moore*	*Osman*	*WallaceRod*	*Cockerill*	*Le Tissier*	*Maddison*	*Wallace D*	
										Ref: D Hedges	Saints' Chris Nicholl becomes the latest manager to launch a verbal tirade against Wimbledon's tactics. His neat-running side are bludgeoned into submission. Not that Southampton are angels. Jimmy Case succeeded in breaking Vaughan Ryan's jaw in three places.											
15		A	NEWCASTLE		18		L	1-2	0-1	Gibson 50	Segers	Phelan	Scales	Jones*	Young	Curle	Fairweather	Gibson	Miller	Sanchez	Wise	Ryan
	10/12			*20,146*	*20*	13				*Hendrie 41, 80*	*Beasant*	*Anderson*	*Tinnion*	*McCreary*	*Cornwell*	*Thorn*	*Hendrie*	*O'Brien*	*Jackson**	*Mirandinha^*	*Brock*	*McDonald/Wharton*
										Ref: R Nixon	Newcastle, with Dave Beasant and Andy Thorn, had gone 588 minutes without a goal. Three points from this dour battle pleased Jim Smith, who has replaced Willie McFaul. John Hendrie got goal-side of Young for No 1, then robs Jones to curl the winner. Dons miss Cork and Fash.											
16		A	NOTTINGHAM F				W	1-0	0-0	Sanchez 78	Segers	Phelan	Scales	Jones	Young	Curle	Fairweather	Gibson*	Fashanu	Sanchez	Wise	Cork
	18/12			*16,427*		16					*Sutton*	*Chettle**	*Williams*	*Walker*	*Foster*	*Parker^*	*Carr*	*Webb*	*Clough*	*Chapman*	*Rice*	*Laws/Hodge*
										Ref: L Dilkes	Forest had won only one league game in six, so this is not so much of an upset. They are hussled and harried throughout. Sanchez fires into the net after a long ball had been headed out. Lee Chapman hits a post for Forest and the ball bounces straight to Segers. Sanchez missed a sitter.											
17		H	MILLWALL		21		W	1-0	0-0	Fairweather 53	Segers	Scales	Phelan	Jones	Young	Curle	Fairweather	Gibson	Fashanu	Sanchez	Wise	
	26/12			11,398	*4*	19					*Horne*	*Stevens*	*Dawes*	*Hurlock*	*Wood*	*McLeary*	*Stephenson**	*Briley*	*Sheringham*	*Cascarino*	*O'Callaghan*	*Horrix*
										Ref: D Vickers	John Docherty's Division 2 champions have carried on their winnng ways, but they look dreadful here, and Wimbledon not much better. Jones and Sanchez get the better of Terry Hurlock and Les Briley in midfield. Channel 4 shows the match, rather than the usual American Football.											
18		H	LUTON		14		W	**4-0**	2-0	Jones 15, Gibson 29, Scales 46, [Fashanu 84]	Segers	Scales	Phelan	Jones	Young	Curle	Fairweather	Gibson	Fashanu	Sanchez	Wise	
	31/12			4,899	*16*	22					*Sealey*	*Johnson R*	*Harvey*	*Preece*	*Foster*	*Johnson M*	*Wilson*	*Wegerle**	*Harford*	*Hill*	*Oldfield*	*Black*
										Ref: T Holbrook	Wimbledon look quite elegant as they dispose of Luton, helped on their way by a thumping shot by Vinnie Jones. John Scales makes it 3-0 from a corner, heading home from Jones' near-post flick-on. Luton exact their revenge on Southampton two days later, winning 6-1.											
19		A	WEST HAM		12		W	2-1	1-1	Wise 14, 84	Segers	Scales	Phelan	Jones	Young	Curle	Fairweather	Gibson*	Fashanu	Sanchez	Wise^	Cork/**Kruszynski**
	2/1			*18,346*	*20*	25				*Rosenior 39*	*McKnight*	*Potts*	*Dicks*	*Gale*	*Martin*	*Stewart*	*Brady*	*Kelly*	*Rosenior*	*Dickens*	*Keen*	
										Ref: R Milford	The Dons repeat last season's example and continue their Christmas rampage. Leroy Rosenior was West Ham's hero and villain. He had equalised from Kevin Keen's through ball – though looking offside – but then deflected Dennis Wise's free-kick into the net off his knee.											
20		H	QP RANGERS		10		W	1-0	1-0	Scales 32	Segers	Scales	Phelan	Jones	Young*	Curle	Fairweath'r^	Gibson	Cork	Sanchez	Wise	Joseph/Turner
	14/1			7,118	*15*	28					*Seaman*	*Ardiles*	*Pisanti*	*Parker*	*Law!*	*Maddix*	*Stein*	*Barker*	*Fereday*	*Coney*	*Kerslake**	*Herrera*
										Ref: J Martin	Five wins out of five takes Wimbledon up to 10th. Wise's two-footed lunge at Dean Coney provokes the fracas that ends with Brian Law sent off before half-time. QPR boss Trevor Francis fires up his men after half-time. Even Ossie Ardiles gets booked in this niggling, nasty match.											

No	Date		Att	Pos	Pts	F-A	H-T	Scorers, Times, and Referees	1	2	3	4	5	6	7	8	9	10	11	12 subs used
21	A	COVENTRY		11	L	1-2	1-1	Scales 28	Segers	Scales	Phelan	Jones	Young	Curle	Fairweather	Gibson	Miller	Sanchez	Wise	
	21/1		*12,472*	*3*	28			*Kilcline 25, Speedie 66*	*Ogrizovic*	*Borrows*	*Phillips*	*Sedgley*	*Kilcline*	*Peake*	*Emerson*	*Speedie*	*Regis*	*McGrath*	*Smith*	*Clark*
								Ref: J Worrall	Improbably, Coventry find themselves 3rd in the league, and they put a stop to Wimbledon's winning ways. Bobby Gould is full of praise for David Speedie's winner, a volley after Segers had repulsed Kilcline's effort. 'The best goal I have seen scored against my team!' says Gould.											
22	A	EVERTON		12	D	1-1	1-1	Sanchez 11	Segers	Scales	Phelan	Jones!	Young	Curle	Fairweather	Gibson*	Fashanu	Sanchez	Wise	Kruszynski
	4/2		*23,365*	*9*	29			*Sharp 44p*	*Southall*	*McDonald*	*V d Hauwe*	*Ratcliffe*	*Watson*	*Steven*	*Nevin*	*McCall*	*Sharp*	*Cottee*	*Wilson**	*Ebbrell*
								Ref: M Peck	Everton have lost their last three in the league, as cup commitments take their toll. Vinnie Jones is shown a red card after his inexplicable foul on Graeme Sharp. Gould is under pressure to sell him. Curle's foul on Ian Wilson results in a third penalty against the Dons in as many games.											
23	H	ASTON VILLA		10	W	1-0	1-0	Fashanu 44	Segers	Scales	Phelan	Jones	Joseph	Curle	Fairweather	Miller*	Fashanu	Sanchez	Wise	Cork
	11/2		6,201	*12*	32				*Spink*	*Price*	*Gray S*	*Gage*	*Mountfield*	*Evans*	*Callaghan*	*Platt*	*McInally*	*Cowans**	*Ormondroyd*	*Birch*
								Ref: L Shapter	John Fashanu needed two attempts to put away Wise's cross, but it brought Wimbledon's third 1-0 win over Villa this season. Fairweather might have had a bagful as the Dons press their advantage. Villa's Scottish international, Allan Evans, spent the match fouling Paul Miller.											
24	H	SHEFFIELD WED		9	W	1-0	1-0	Fashanu 24	Segers	Scales	Phelan	Kruszynski	Joseph	Curle	Fairweather*	Miller^	Fashanu	Sanchez	Wise	Clement/Cork
	25/2		4,384	*18*	35				*Turner*	*Sterland*	*Madden*	*Palmer*	*Pearson*	*Cranson*	*Proctor*	*Wood*	*Varardi**	*Hirst*	*Galvin*	*Reeves*
								Ref: M Reed	Ron Atkinson opts for wearing sunglasses throughout the match, even though it is played in torrential rain and ankle-deep mud. Maybe he can't bear to watch: this is Wednesday's 12th winless match. The crowd endure the tedium, enlivened by Fash's header from Wise's free-kick.											
25	H	DERBY			W	**4-0**	3-0	Fashanu 6, Miller 41, 45, 70p	Segers	Scales	Phelan	Kruszynski	Joseph	Curle	Fairweather	Miller	Fashanu	Sanchez*	Wise	Young
	1/3		**4,207**	*8*	38				*Shilton*	*Blades*	*Forsyth*	*Williams*	*Wright*	*Hindmarch*	*Micklewhite**	*Saunders*	*Goddard*	*Hebberd^*	*Pickering*	*Penney/Cross*
								Ref: V Callow	Derby's heaviest defeat of the season obliterates their biggest win, also against Wimbledon. Paul Miller had never before scored a senior goal for the Dons, but now he enjoys a hat-trick. Fashanu began the rout, heading past Peter Shilton after just six minutes. Derby managed one shot.											
26	A	NORWICH		9	L	0-1	0-0		Segers	Scales	Phelan	Kruszynski	Joseph	Curle*	Fairweather	Miller	Fashanu	Sanchez	Wise	Young
	11/3		*15,159*	*2*	38			*Putney 52*	*Gunn*	*Culverhouse*	*Bowen*	*Butterworth*	*Linighan*	*Townsend*	*Gordon*	*Rosario*	*Allen*	*Phelan*	*Putney*	
								Ref: D Hedges	Norwich keep up their winning habit, but Gould is infuriated by his players' – back from a break in Tenerife – inability to break through after half-time. The match is lost when Roger Joseph dithers and is dispossessed by Trevor Putney. Gould doesn't attend the press conference.											
27	H	MIDDLESBRO		10	D	1-1	1-1	Scales 26	Segers	Scales	Phelan	Jones	Joseph	Young	Kruszynski	Miller	Fashanu	Sanchez	Wise	
	25/3		5,276		39			*Slaven 13*	*Pears*	*Parkinson*	*Cooper*	*Mowbray*	*Proctor*	*Pallister*	*Slaven*	*Gill*	*Ripley*	*Davenport*	*Barham*	
								Ref: K Cooper	Eight league games without a win, and Boro are heading back whence they came. The Dons have just surrendered the FA Cup. They would have beaten Boro but for Stephen Pears' goalkeeping, and the woodwork, which denied them three times. Scales scrambled the equaliser.											
28	A	MILLWALL		9	W	1-0	0-0	Fashanu 55p	Segers	Scales	Phelan	Jones	Joseph	Young	Kruszynski	Miller*	Fashanu	Sanchez	Wise	Cork
	27/3		*13,679*	*4*	42				*Horne*	*McLeary*	*Sparham*	*Hurlock*	*Thompson*	*Wood*	*Carter**	*Briley*	*Sheringham!*	*Cascarino*	*O'Callaghn^*	*Horrix/Salman*
								Ref: P Don	Millwall start this match in 3rd place, but will fail to win any of their final 10 games. Wimbledon become the first team to do the double over them. Teddy Sheringham is dismissed for a high kick at Phelan. Fashanu fooled David Thompson into conceding a penalty in this fierce match.											
29	H	NOTTINGHAM F		8	W	4-1	2-1	Sanchez 10, 86, Miller 14, Fashanu 79	Segers	Scales	Clement	Jones	Joseph	Young	Kruszynski	Miller	Fashanu	Sanchez	Wise	
	1/4		7,867	*5*	45			*Clough 31*	*Sutton*	*Chettle*	*Walker*	*Wilson*	*Pearce*	*Hodge*	*Gaynor*	*Webb*	*Parker*	*Clough*	*Chapman*	
								Ref: J Moules	Forest collapse in their heaviest defeat of the season. Brian Clough is incensed by Wise's tackle that puts his son Nigel out of the game. More constructively, Wise sets up three of the Dons' goals. All five goals are scrambled inside the six-yard box. Is Brian Clough about to quit Forest?											
30	A	SHEFFIELD WED			D	1-1	0-0	Fashanu 77p	Segers	Scales	Clement	Jones	Young*	Joseph	Kruszynski	Miller	Fashanu	Sanchez	Wise	Cork
	5/4		*15,777*	*14*	46			*Hirst 54*	*Turner*	*Harper*	*Worthington*	*Palmer*	*Pearson*	*Johnson*	*Bennett*	*Fee*	*Whitton*	*Hirst*	*Barrick*	
								Ref: R Hart	Wednesday have started winning again. Big Ron Atkinson rages about Nigel Pearson's supposed handball that hands Wimbledon a lifeline from the penalty spot. David Hirst had put Wednesday ahead when he seized upon a deflected clearance and raced clear. A rain-swept match.											

31	A	QP RANGERS	8	L	3-4	1-3	Fashanu 4p, Sanchez 55, Wise 90	Segers	Scales	Clement	Jones	Young	Joseph*	Kruszynski^	Miller	Fashanu	Sanchez	Wise	Brooke/Phelan
8/4		*9,056*	*12*	46			*Clarke 9, Spackman 13, Falco 37, Reid 49*	*Seaman*	*Channing**	*Dennis*	*Parker*	*McDonald*	*Spackman*	*Allen M*	*Falco^*	*Clarke*	*Reid*	*Sinton*	*Fereday/Stein*
							Ref: I Hemley	This was not quite the evenly-balanced humdinger it might appear. At one stage Rangers led 4-1, and were so much on top after the break that the Dons were hanging on. Things had started well, with a twice-taken penalty awarded after Alan McDonald had pulled down Fashanu.											
32	H	TOTTENHAM	9	L	1-2	0-1	Young 71	Segers	Joseph	Phelan	Jones	Young	Scales	Brooke*	Miller	Fashanu	Sanchez	Wise	Fairweather
15/4		12,366	*5*	46			*Stewart 33, Waddle 61*	*Thorstvedt*	*Butters*	*Hughton*	*Fenwick*	*Howells*	*Mabbutt*	*Walsh*	*Gascoigne*	*Waddle*	*Stewart*	*Allen*	
							Ref: A Buksh	On this same day 95 Liverpool fans were crushed to death at Hillsborough. Wimbledon were lackadaisical, Gascoigne was magical. The Dons didn't manage a shot for over half an hour, while Terry Venables' Spurs scored with a typical Wimbledon tactic – long throw and flick-on.											
33	A	SOUTHAMPTON	9	D	0-0	0-0		Segers	Joseph	Phelan	Jones	Young	Scales	Kruszynski	Miller*	Fashanu	Sanchez	Wise	**Cotterill**
22/4		*13,805*	*15*	47				*Burridge*	*Wallace Ray*	*Adams*	*Case*	*Ruddock*	*Osman*	*Wallace Rod*	*Cockerill*	*Rideout*	*Horne*	*Le Tissier*	
							Ref: M Bodenham	Saints have recently ended a run of 17 league games without a win, and will narrowly keep their place in the top flight. Hans Segers saves Neil Ruddock's 61st-minute penalty – after Terry Phelan handled. It is Segers' sixth penalty save of the season, and prevents a third league defeat.											
34	H	NEWCASTLE	9	W	**4-0**	1-0	Wise 25p, Miller 72, Jones 80, [Cotterill 83]	Segers	Joseph	Phelan	Jones	**Fiore***	Scales	Kruszynski	Miller	**Gayle^**	Sanchez	Wise	Cork/Cotterill
29/4		5,206	*19*	50				*Kelly*	*Kristensen**	*Sansom*	*McCreary*	*Scott*	*Roeder*	*Pingel^*	*Sweeney*	*Thorn*	*O'Neill*	*Brock*	*Ranson/McDonald*
							Ref: L Shapter	By the season's end Newcastle will prop up the table, and on this abject performance it is easy to see why. Former-Don Andy Thorn clattered Jones for the penalty, whereupon Newcastle fell apart. Steve Cotterill, signed from Burton Albion, bags the Dons' fourth with a flying header.											
35	A	MANCHESTER U		L	0-1	0-0		Segers	Joseph	Clement	Jones	Young	Scales	Kruszynski	Miller*	Gayle^	Sanchez	Wise	Cork/Cotterill
2/5		*23,386*		50			*McClair 89*	*Leighton*	*Duxbury*	*Donaghy*	*Bruce*	*McGrath*	*Whiteside**	*Robson*	*Beardsmore*	*McClair*	*Hughes*	*Martin*	*Maiorana*
							Ref: K Hackett	Had they won, Wimbledon would have climbed to 6th. A game of few chances and little excitement was turned United's way in the final minute. From a quickly-taken free-kick Paul McGrath heads goalwards, Hans Segers saves, but Brian McClair pounces.											
36	A	CHARLTON	9	L	0-1	0-1		Segers	Joseph	Phelan	Jones	Young	Scales	Miller	Fairweather*	Cork	Sanchez^	Wise	Kruszynski/Cotterill
6/5		***7,230***	*15*	50			*Leaburn 12*	*Bolder*	*Humphrey*	*Reid*	*Shirtliff*	*Pates*	*Gritt*	*Lee R*	*Williams*	*MacKenzie*	*Mortimer**	*Leaburn^*	*Walsh/Jones*
							Ref: R Nixon	Charlton will escape the drop once again, even though they have to play their home matches at Selhurst Park, and even though Wimbledon missed so many chances as to beggar belief. Wise's 75th minute penalty is saved by Bob Boulder. Miller hit the angle at the death.											
37	H	LIVERPOOL	12	L	1-2	1-0	Hansen 18 (og)	Segers	Joseph*	Phelan	Jones	Young	Scales	Kruszynski	Miller	Fashanu	**Quamina^**	Wise	Cork/Sanchez
13/5		14,730	*2*	50			*Aldridge 59, Barnes 73*	*Grobbelaar*	*Ablett*	*Staunton*	*Nicol*	*Whelan*	*Hansen*	*Watson**	*Aldridge*	*Houghton*	*Barnes*	*McMahon*	*Rush*
							Ref: G Courtney	In their last 14 matches Liverpool have won 13 and drawn one, as they set up their high-noon showdown with Arsenal. On this, the anniversary of their FA Cup triumph, the Dons are outplayed in the second half. Debut-boy Mark Quamina is caught out by John Barnes for the winner.											
38	A	ARSENAL		D	2-2	1-1	Cork 31, McGee 55	Segers	Joseph	Phelan*	Jones	Young	Scales	Kruszynski	Cork^	Fashanu	**McGee**	Wise	Miller/Sanchez
17/5		***39,132***	*1*	51			*Winterburn 14, Merson 50*	*Lukic*	*Dixon*	*Winterburn*	*Thomas*	*O'Leary*	*Adams*	*Rocastle*	*Richardson*	*Smith*	*Hayes**	*Merson^*	*Groves/Bould*
	Home	*Away*					Ref: R Groves	Wimbledon's fate is to meet the two title challengers back to back. They do Liverpool a mighty favour by twice pegging Arsenal back.											
Average	7,824	*18,105*						Gould gives a debut to Paul McGee, signed from Colchester, and he celebrates his 20-yard scissors-kick equaliser as if it had won the FA Cup.											

FA Charity Shield

	N	LIVERPOOL		L	1-2	1-1	Fashanu 17	Tracey	Scales*	Phelan	Ryan	Young	Cawley	Gibson	Fairweather	Fashanu^	Sanchez	Wise	Clement/Turner
20/8		*54,000*					*Aldridge 23, 69*	*Grobbelaar*	*Gillespie*	*Venison*	*Ablett*	*Whelan*	*Watson*	*Beardsley*	*Aldridge*	*Houghton*	*Barnes*	*McMahon*	
		(Wembley)					Ref: J Martin	This is the annual showpiece between the league champions and the FA Cup winners. Liverpool's revenge comes a few months too late. John Aldridge missed a penalty last time. Now he cancels out Fashanu's header by side-footing an equaliser, and juggles the ball for the winner.											

Littlewoods Cup	Att			F-A	H-T	Scorers, Times, and Referees	1	2	3	4	5	6	7	8	9	10	11	subs used
2:1 A BARNSLEY		20	W	2-0	1-0	Fashanu 26, 51	Green	Joseph	Clement	Jones	Young	Scales	Brooke	Cork*	Fashanu	Sanchez	Wise	Turner
27/9	*5,194*	*2:16*					*Baker*	*Joyce*	*Beresford*	*Thomas*	*McGugan*	*Futcher*	*Lowndes*	*Agnew*	*Rees*	*Currie*	*Broddle*	
						Ref: I Hendrick	Alan Clarke's Barnsley beat West Ham over two legs in this competition last year, so they cannot be taken lightly. Indeed, strikers Tony Rees and David Currie are a handful throughout. The first goal of John Fashanu's double is a header from Andy Clement's deep free-kick.											
2:2 H BARNSLEY		18	L	0-1	0-1		Segers	Joseph	Clement	Jones	Young	Scales	Brooke*	Cork	Turner	Sanchez	Wise	Phelan
12/10	2,259	*2:5*				*Currie 16*	*Baker*	*Joyce*	*Beresford*	*Thomas*	*McGugan*	*Futcher*	*Lowndes*	*Dobbin*	*Rees*	*Currie*	*Broddle*	
						Ref: K Cooper (Dons win 2-1 on aggregate)	Barnsley have won three out of three since the first leg and have climbed from 16th to 5th in their division. David Currie outmanoeuvres John Scales and Eric Young to pull a goal back, but thereafter Barnsley keeper Clive Baker keeps the tie alive with a string of fine saves.											
3 H MANCHESTER U		17	W	2-1	1-1	Gibson 31, 59	Segers	Joseph	Phelan	Jones	Young	Scales	Wise	Gibson*	Fashanu	Sanchez	Fairweather	Cork
2/11	10,864	*12*				*Robson 30*	*Leighton*	*Blackmore*	*Gibson*	*Bruce*	*Garton*	*Duxbury**	*Robson*	*O'Brien*	*McClair*	*Hughes*	*Olsen^*	*Strachan/Anderson*
						Ref: B Hill	11 days after these teams fought a 1-1 league draw at Plough Lane, Manchester United return, only to be deflated by Terry Gibson. He finishes off Fairweather's lob for a quick equaliser, then stoops to head in John Scales' flick. Three times McClair was through on goal, missing the lot.											
4 A QP RANGERS		17	D	0-0	0-0		Segers	Joseph	Clement	Jones	Young	Scales	Fairweather	Gibson*	Fashanu	Sanchez^	Wise	Cork/Phelan
30/11	*10,504*	*14*					*Seaman*	*Coney*	*Allen M*	*Parker*	*Ardiles**	*Maddix*	*Falco*	*Francis*	*Fereday*	*Pisanti*	*Brock*	*Maguire*
						Ref: J Deakin	With the final whistle, the Dons were still in the Cup, but that was the best that could be said of them. Dennis Wise was made captain for the day. Terry Gibson wasted the Dons' best chance. At the other end, Trevor Francis's deflected shot was touched over by Hans Segers.											
4R H QP RANGERS		18	L	0-1	0-0		Segers	Joseph*	Phelan	Jones	Young	Scales	Fairweath'r^	Gibson	Fashanu	Sanchez	Wise	Miller/Kruszynski
14/12	6,585	*13*				*Falco 65*	*Seaman*	*McDonald*	*Allen M*	*Parker*	*Dennis*	*Maddix*	*Falco*	*Francis*	*Fereday*	*Coney*	*Kerslake**	*Pisanti*
						Ref: A Gunn	QPR player-manager Trevor Francis, 34, is the oldest man on the field, and the best. His reward was to be hacked down repeatedly by Dons' acting captain Vinnie Jones. Francis's corner breaks the deadlock, being headed in by Falco. Seaman touches Wise's free-kick onto the bar.											

FA Cup	Att			F-A	H-T	Scorers, Times, and Referees	1	2	3	4	5	6	7	8	9	10	11	subs used
3 A BIRMINGHAM		17	W	1-0	1-0	Gibson 28	Segers	Scales	Phelan	Jones	Young	Curle	Fairweather	Gibson	Fashanu	Sanchez	Cork	
7/1	*10,431*	*2:23*					*Thomas*	*Ashley*	*Trewick*	*Roberts*	*Overson*	*Langley*	*Bremner*	*Tait*	*Whitton*	*Robinson**	*Wigley*	*Yates*
						Ref: J Worrall	Birmingham have lost their last five, scoring just one goal, yet the Cup is a great leveller. Birmingham play neat football in midfield, but lack punch up front. Vinnie Jones' contribution was to set up Gibson's goal and to treat John Trewick to a forearm smash that went unpunished.											
4 A ASTON VILLA		11	W	1-0	0-0	Jones 60	Segers	Scales	Phelan	Jones	Young!	Curle	Fairweather	Gibson	Fashanu	Sanchez	Wise	
28/1	*25,043*	*14*					*Spink*	*Gage*	*Gray S*	*Evans*	*Mountfield*	*Keown*	*Gray A*	*Platt*	*McInally*	*Cowans*	*Daley*	
						Ref: N Midgley	Wimbledon head back up the M1 again to Brum. Graham Taylor's side are left battered and bewildered. John Scales dominates the division's leading scorer, Alan McInally. Eric Young is sent off for fouling McInally, and Segers saves a penalty. Vinnie Jones toe-pokes the winner.											
5 H GRIMSBY		10	W	3-1	0-1	Fashanu 57, Phelan 60, Wise 90	Segers	Scales	Phelan	Kruszynski	Joseph	Curle	Fairweather	Miller	Fashanu	Sanchez	Wise	
18/2	12,517	*4:17*				*Alexander 14*	*Sherwood*	*North*	*Agnew*	*Tillson*	*Lever*	*Cunnington*	*Jobling*	*Saunders*	*O'Kelly*	*Cockerill*	*Alexander*	*Dixon*
						Ref: G Tyson	Alan Buckley's Division 4 strugglers descend on Plough Lane, cheered on by 7,000 fans waving inflatable haddocks. They rejoice when Keith Alexander out-jumps Segers and Scales, but Dennis Wise masterminds Wimbledon's recovery, snatching the third goal, in injury-time, himself.											
QF A EVERTON		9	L	0-1	0-0		Segers	Scales	Phelan	Kruszynski*	Young	Joseph	Fairweather	Miller^	Fashanu	Sanchez	Wise	Jones/Cork
19/3	*24,562*	*11*				*McCall 59*	*Southall*	*McDonald*	*Pointon*	*Ratcliffe*	*Watson*	*Bracewell*	*Steven*	*McCall*	*Sharp*	*Cottee*	*Sheedy*	
						Ref: K Hackett	Everton put the Dons out of the Simod Cup, and now – infinitely more painfully – out of the FA Cup too. Before a huge Sunday TV audience, Segers saves Graeme Sharp's weak penalty. Despite this reprieve, Stuart McCall is unmarked to score. Sub Jones receives hysterical abuse.											

		Home					Away					
	P	W	D	L	F	A	W	D	L	F	A	Pts
1 Arsenal	38	10	6	3	35	19	12	4	3	38	17	76
2 Liverpool	38	11	5	3	33	11	11	5	3	32	17	76
3 Nottingham F	38	8	7	4	31	16	9	6	4	33	27	64
4 Norwich	38	8	7	4	23	20	9	4	6	25	25	62
5 Derby	38	9	3	7	23	18	8	4	7	17	20	58
6 Tottenham	38	8	6	5	31	24	7	6	6	29	22	57
7 Coventry	38	9	4	6	28	23	5	9	5	19	19	55
8 Everton	38	10	7	2	33	18	4	5	10	17	27	54
9 QP Rangers	38	9	5	5	23	16	5	6	8	20	21	53
10 Millwall	38	10	3	6	27	21	4	8	7	20	31	53
11 Manchester U	38	10	5	4	27	13	3	7	9	18	22	51
12 WIMBLEDON	38	10	3	6	30	19	4	6	9	20	27	51
13 Southampton	38	6	7	6	25	26	4	8	7	27	40	45
14 Charlton	38	6	7	6	25	24	4	5	10	19	34	42
15 Sheffield Wed	38	6	6	7	21	25	4	6	9	13	26	42
16 Luton	38	8	6	5	32	21	2	5	12	10	31	41
17 Aston Villa	38	7	6	6	25	22	2	7	10	20	34	40
18 Middlesbro	38	6	7	6	28	30	3	5	11	16	31	39
19 West Ham	38	3	6	10	19	30	7	2	10	18	32	38
20 Newcastle	38	3	6	10	19	28	4	4	11	13	35	31
	760	157	112	111	538	424	111	112	157	424	538	1028

Odds & ends

Double wins: (3) Aston Villa, Nottingham F, Millwall.
Double losses: (3) Coventry, Norwich, Tottenham.

Won from behind: (0) – but did so against Man U and Grimsby in cups.
Lost from in front: (3) Arsenal (h), Liverpool (h), QPR (a).
The Dons also lost to Liverpool in the Charity Shield after taking the lead.

High spots: 7 straight wins in December and January. This includes a penalty shoot-out victory in the Simod Cup, and an FA Cup-tie win.
Inflicting the heaviest defeat on Nott'm F (who finished 3rd) to go to 8th.

Low spots: Opening the season with 4 defeats and a draw.
Closing the season with just 1 win in 9 games.

Wimbledon enjoyed 2 own-goals, both against Liverpool.

Player of the Year: John Scales.
Ever-presents: (0).
Hat-tricks: Paul Miller (1).
Leading scorer: John Fashanu (15) + 1 in Charity Shield.

	Appearances						Goals			
	Lge	Sub	LC	Sub	FAC	Sub	**Lge**	LC	FAC	**Total**
Brooke, Gary	**5**	(5)	2							
Cawley, Peter	**1**									
Clement, Andrew	**9**	(2)	3							
Cork, Alan	**9**	(16)	2	(2)	1	(1)	**2**			**2**
Cotterill, Steve		(4)					**1**			**1**
Curle, Keith	**16**	(2)			3					
Fairweather, Carlton	**23**	(3)	3		4		**3**			**3**
Fashanu, John	**30**		4		4		**12**	2	1	**15**
Fiore, Mark	**1**									
Gayle, John	**2**									
Gibson, Terry	**17**		3		2		**5**	2	1	**8**
Green, Ron	**4**		1							
Hazel, Ian	**1**									
Jones, Vinnie	**31**		5		2	(1)	**3**		1	**4**
Joseph, Roger	**30**	(1)	5		2					
Kruszynski, Zbigniew	**13**	(3)		(1)	2					
McGee, Paul	**1**						**1**			**1**
Miller, Paul	**17**	(1)		(1)	2		**5**			**5**
Phelan, Terry	**27**	(2)	2	(2)	4				1	**1**
Quamina, Mark	**1**									
Ryan, Vaughan	**4**	(1)								
Sanchez, Lawrie	**34**	(2)	5		4		**5**			**5**
Scales, John	**36**	(2)	5		4		**5**			**6**
Segers, Hans	**33**		4		4					
Tracey, Simon	**1**									
Turner, Robbie	**2**	(4)	1	(1)						
Wise, Dennis	**37**		5		3		**5**		1	**6**
Young, Eric	**33**	(2)	5		3		**1**			**1**
(own-goals)							**2**			**2**
28 players used	**418**	**(50)**	**55**	**(7)**	**45**	**(2)**	**50**	**4**	**5**	**59**

BARCLAYS LEAGUE DIVISION 1 — Manager: Bobby Gould — SEASON 1989-90

No	Date	Att	Pos	Pts	F-A	H-T	Scorers, Times, and Referees	1	2	3	4	5	6	7	8	9	10	11	subs used
1	H CHELSEA			L	0-1	0-0		Segers	Curle	Phelan	Kruszynski	Young	Scales	Joseph*	Cork	Gayle	Sanchez	Wise	Brooke
	19/8	**14,625**		–			*K Wilson 81*	*Beasant*	*Clarke*	*Dorigo*	*Roberts*	*Lee*	*Monkou*	*Dickens*	*Nicholas*	*Dixon*	*Durie*	*McAllister^*	*Bumstead/Wilson K*
							Ref: G Courtney	Coach Don Howe and midfielder Vinnie Jones have departed for pastures new. Chelsea are back in the top flight with 99 points and 96 goals. 'A travesty of justice,' moans Bobby Gould after this match. Chelsea sub Kevin Wilson played a one-two with Dixon for a breakaway goal.											
2	A DERBY			D	1-1	1-0	Cork 28	Segers	Curle	Phelan	Kruszynski	Young	Scales	McGee*	Cork	Fashanu	Sanchez	Wise^	Fairweather/Joseph
	23/8	*13,874*		1			*Hebberd 84*	*Shilton*	*Sage*	*Forsyth*	*Williams*	*Wright*	*Hindmarch*	*McMinn*	*Saunders*	*Goddard**	*Pickering^*	*Micklewhite*	*Hebberd/Gee*
							Ref: R Milford	With Fashanu unfit, Cork backs himself at 8-1 to score the first goal. He wins his bet, glancing in McGee's free-kick. Derby are then let off the hook. Late in the game Nick Pickering takes a corner, Phil Gee heads it down, and Trevor Hebberd swings a boot to equalise for Derby.											
3	A ARSENAL			D	0-0	0-0		Segers	Curle	Phelan	Kruszynski	Young	Scales	Fairweather	Cork	Fashanu	Sanchez	Wise	
	26/8	*32,279*	*12*	2				*Lukic*	*Dixon*	*Winterburn*	*Thomas*	*O'Leary*	*Adams*	*Rocastle*	*Richardson*	*Smith*	*Merson**	*Marwood*	*Groves*
							Ref: N Midgley	Arsenal are still agog after their injury-time championship win at Anfield. This was an unexceptional match, the first half being littered with offside decisions. Only in the closing minutes did the champions turn the screw, but Wimbledon held out comfortably enough.											
4	H MILLWALL			D	2-2	1-1	Fairweather 8, Cork 55	Segers	Curle	Phelan	Kruszynski	Young!	Scales	Fairweather	Cork	Fashanu*	Sanchez	Wise	Gibson
	29/8	8,865	*1*	3			*Anthrobus 41, Cascarino 85*	*Horne*	*Stevens*	*Dawes*	*Hurlock*	*Thompson*	*Wood*	*Carter*	*Briley*	*Sheringham*	*Cascarino*	*Anthrobus**	*Torpey*
							Ref: J Martin	Millwall go top after Tony Cascarino adds a second to Steve Anthrobus's first league goal. This nasty, niggling match saw four Lions booked and Wimbledon's Eric Young sent off after 26 minutes for hauling back Teddy Sheringham. It was Young's second bookable offence.											
5	A CRYS PALACE		19	L	0-2	0-1		Segers	Curle	Phelan	Kruszynski	Young	Scales	Fairweather*	Cork^	Fashanu	Sanchez	Wise	Gibson/Joseph
	9/9	*12,116*	*15*	3			*Thomas 19, Wright 75*	*Suckling*	*Pemberton*	*Burke*	*Gray*	*Hopkins*	*O'Reilly*	*McGoldrick*	*Thomas*	*Bright*	*Wright*	*Pardew*	
							Ref: A Gunn	Palace were promoted through the play-offs, and provide Wimbledon with their fourth London derby in five fixtures. The critical first goal of this – Palace's first win of the season – came when Geoff Thomas's low shot squirmed under Segers' body. The Dons showed few ideas.											
6	H MANCHESTER C		16	W	1-0	1-0	Fashanu 35	Segers	Curle	Phelan	Kruszynski	Joseph*	Scales	Fairweather	Ryan	Fashanu	Gibson^	Wise	Blackwell/Miller
	16/9	6,815	*18*	6				*Cooper*	*Fleming*	*Hinchcliffe*	*Bishop*	*Gayle*	*Redmond*	*White*	*Morley*	*Oldfield*	*McNab**	*Lake*	*Brightwell*
							Ref: R Groves	Wimbledon have quickly faced all three promoted sides. Mel Machin's youthful team have got off to a shaky start, and provide the Dons with a belated first win. Fashanu's header was only the second goal from open play so far. Gibson returned after breaking his ankle five months ago.											
7	A LUTON		15	D	1-1	1-1	Kruszynski 28	Segers	Curle	Phelan	Kruszynski*	Young	Scales	Fairweather	Ryan	Fashanu^	Gibson	Wise	Sanchez/Gayle
	23/9	*8,449*	*10*	7			*Wegerle 35p*	*Chamberlain*	*Braecker*	*Dreyer*	*Wilson*	*McDonough**	*Beaumont*	*Kennedy!*	*Wegerle*	*Elstrup^*	*Preece*	*Black*	*Harvey/Cooke*
							Ref: K Hackett	Ray Harford's Luton just hung on last season. Fashanu fouls Roy Wegerle, Segers saves Kingsley Black's penalty, but the referee orders a retake. Darron McDonough dislocates a shoulder after a clash with Fashanu. Fash then elbows Mick Kennedy, who retaliates and is sent off.											
8	A SOUTHAMPTON		15	D	2-2	1-0	Young 23, Wise 73	Segers	Curle	Phelan	Kruszynski	Young	Scales	Fairweather	Ryan	Fashanu	Sanchez*	Wise	Cork
	30/9	*12,904*	*8*	8			*Le Tissier 52, 75p*	*Flowers*	*Wallace Ray*	*Forrest**	*Case*	*Ruddock*	*Osman*	*Le Tissier*	*Cockerill*	*Shearer^*	*Rideout*	*Wallace Rod*	*Benali/Moore*
							Ref: K Morton	Chris Nicholl's Saints will have a good season. With Terry Gibson out and Cork semi-fit, Gould abandons his bludgeoning tactics for more subtle weapons. No sooner has Wise's crisp volley put the Dons ahead for a second time than Eric Young pushes Paul Rideout in the box.											
9	H LIVERPOOL		18	L	1-2	0-1	Wise 48	Segers	Curle	Phelan	Kruszynski*	Young	Scales	Fairweather	Ryan	Fashanu^	Gibson	Wise	Sanchez/Cork
	14/10	13,510	*1*	8			*Beardsley 3, Whelan 56*	*Grobbelaar*	*Hysen*	*Burrows*	*Nicol*	*Whelan*	*Hansen*	*Beardsley*	*Venison*	*Staunton*	*Barnes*	*McMahon*	
							Ref: L Shapter	Liverpool have responded to last season's heartbreak in typical fashion. They are unbeaten so far. John Barnes and Peter Beardsley are at their scintillating best. Beardsley throws a dummy before scoring the first goal. Bruce Grobbelaar drops a cross for Wise to head in to make it 1-2.											
10	H NOTTINGHAM F		19	L	**1-3**	1-2	Young 10	Segers	Curle	Phelan	Gibson	Young	Scales	Fairweather	Ryan*	Fashanu^	Sanchez	Wise	Cork/Gayle
	21/10	5,184	*8*	8			*Hodge 24, Parker 42, Pearce 88p*	*Sutton*	*Laws*	*Pearce*	*Walker*	*Wilson*	*Hodge*	*Crosby*	*Parker*	*Clough**	*Chapman*	*Chettle*	*Starbuck*
							Ref: A Seville	Forest were 3rd last season, when Wimbledon beat them twice. Brian Clough's team are rampant for most of this match, gaining sweet revenge. But it all started so brightly, with Eric Young driving Fairweather's free-kick past Steve Sutton. Steve Hodge levelled from 18 yards.											

No	Date	Venue	Opponent	Att	Pos	Res	Pts	F-A	H-T	Scorers, Times, and Referees	1	2	3	4	5	6	7	8	9	10	11	subs used
11		A	SHEFFIELD WED		17	W		1-0	0-0	Gibson 67	Segers	Joseph	Phelan	McGee*	Young	Curle	Fairweather	Gayle^	Gibson	Sanchez	Wise	Ryan/Miller
	28/10			*13,728*	*20*		11			Ref: R Nixon	*Turner*	*Newsome*	*Harper*	*Palmer*	*Shirtliff*	*Madden*	*Taylor**	*Pearson*	*Hirst*	*Atkinson*	*Barrick^*	*Whitton/Shakespear*
											Ron Atkinson's Wednesday have just one win to their name, and at the start of play both sides prop up the table. This apology of a football match on a windswept afternoon was settled in the Dons' favour when from Wise's corner Terry Gibson swivelled and shot high into the net.											
12		H	QP RANGERS		18	D		0-0	0-0		Segers	Joseph	Phelan	McGee	Young	Curle	Fairweather	Gayle*	Gibson!	Sanchez	Wise	Miller
	4/11			5,912	*19*		12			Ref: P Don	*Seaman*	*Channing*	*Sansom*	*Parker*	*McDonald*	*Spackman*	*Bardsley*	*Reid*	*Clarke*	*Maddix*	*Sinton**	*Ferdinand*
											QPR are in the throes of revolution, as manager Trevor Francis upsets everyone around him. This is yet another appalling match in which Wimbledon have participated recently. After 55 minutes Terry Gibson races 50 yards to up-end Andy Sinton, and off he goes.											
13		A	TOTTENHAM		13	W		1-0	0-0	Sanchez 62	Segers	Joseph	Phelan	Ryan	Young	Curle	Fairweather	Miller	Gibson*	Sanchez	Wise	Cork
	11/11			*26,876*	*9*		15			Ref: J Key	*Thorstvedt*	*Thomas*	*V d Hauwe*	*Bergsson*	*Howells*	*Mabbutt*	*Walsh**	*Gascoigne*	*Samways^*	*Lineker*	*Sedgley*	*Stewart/Allan P*
											This is a vital win for Wimbledon, secured by a fortuitous deflected goal by Lawrie Sanchez. Dennis Wise is man of the match, while Vaughan Ryan snuffs out the threat posed by Paul Gascoigne. Gary Lineker enjoys few opportunities to make his mark. Another priceless away win.											
14		A	EVERTON		14	D		1-1	0-0	Cotterill 89	Segers	Joseph	Phelan	Ryan	Young	Curle	Fairweather	Miller*	Cotterill	Sanchez^	Wise	Cork/McGee
	18/11			*21,561*	*7*		16			*Sheedy 50p* Ref: F Roberts	*Southall*	*Ebbrell*	*Pointon*	*Keown*	*McDonald*	*Beagrie*	*Snodin*	*McCall*	*Sharp*	*Newell*	*Sheedy*	
											Everton topped the league in October, but have lost their last two, including a 2-6 drubbing by Villa. Wimbledon create most of the chances, but trail to a penalty won by Graeme Sharp's theatrical dive. With seconds remaining, Southall fails to hold Fairweather's overhead kick.											
15		H	ASTON VILLA		14	L		0-2	0-1		Segers	Joseph*	Phelan	McGee^	Young	Curle	Fairweather	Cotterill	Fashanu	Ryan	Wise	Scales/Cork
	25/11			5,888	*2*		16			*Platt 23, Daley 82* Ref: B Hill	*Spink*	*Price*	*Gray*	*McGrath*	*Mountfield*	*Nielsen*	*Daley*	*Platt*	*Olney*	*Cowans*	*Ormondroyd*	
											Villa survived by one point last season, but Graham Taylor's team will do much better this time. Wimbledon's dreadful home form continues. Fashanu returns after missing seven games with injury, but the key to the match is Tony Daley's pace, which Terry Phelan cannot equal.											
16		A	CHELSEA		13	W		**5-2**	3-2	Gibson 2, 33, Wise 21, 55, Cork 60	Segers	Joseph	Phelan	Scales	Young	Curle	Fairweather*	Cork	Gibson	Ryan	Wise	Kruszynski
	2/12			*19,976*	*4*		19			*Dixon 1, Roberts 40p* Ref: K Cooper	*Beasant*	*Bumstead*	*Dorigo*	*Roberts*	*Lee*	*Monkou**	*Dickens*	*Nicholas^*	*Dixon*	*Wilson K*	*Hazard*	*WilsonC/McAllister*
											The opening day's fixtures reversed. Chelsea have been in the leading pack all season. 'We gift-wrapped victory,' moans Bobby Campbell. Fashanu is dropped, and the speeed of Wise and Gibson shreds Chelsea. For No 5, Dave Beasant drops the ball onto Cork's head one yard out.											
17		H	DERBY		14	D		1-1	0-1	Scales 86	Segers	Joseph	Phelan	Scales	Young	Curle	Fairweather	Cork	Gibson*	Ryan	Wise	Miller
	9/12			5,024	*7*		20			*Goddard 37* Ref: M Bodenham	*Shilton*	*Sage*	*Forsyth*	*Williams*	*Wright*	*Hindmarch*	*Pickering*	*Saunders*	*Goddard*	*Hebberd*	*Micklewhite*	
											Earlier in the week John Scales hit his first hole-in-one at golf. Now – playing in his new midfield role – he drills his first goal of the season. The Dons are grateful to Arthur Cox's team for falling back to try to protect their lead. Earlier in the game Scales had twice shot over the bar.											
18		A	COVENTRY		16	L		1-2	1-1	Young 45	Segers	Joseph	Phelan	Scales	Young	Curle	Fairweath'r*	Cork	Gibson	Ryan	Wise	Brooke
	16/12			*8,308*	*8*		20			*Borrows 18p, Curle 90 (og)* Ref: N Midgley	*Ogrizovic*	*Borrows*	*Downs*	*McDonald*	*McGrath*	*Dobson*	*Gynn*	*Emerson*	*Regis*	*Drinkell*	*Smith*	
											Never mind the injury-time bombshell, when David Smith's looping cross is turned over Segers by Keith Curle's shin. Wimbledon deserved no reward from this match. It was not Curle's finest hour: he had previously flattened Kevin Drinkell to concede a first-half penalty.											
19		H	CHARLTON		12	W		3-1	2-0	Curle 6p, Kruszynski 29, Gayle 69	Segers	Kruszynski	Phelan	Scales	Young	Curle	Fairweather	Cork*	Gibson	Ryan	Wise^	Gayle/Joseph
	26/12			5,988	*20*		23			*Bennett 80* Ref: J Moules	*Bolder*	*Humphrey*	*Reid*	*MacKenzie*	*McLaughlin*	*Mortimer**	*Lee R*	*Williams*	*Leaburn*	*Walsh*	*Minto^*	*Caton/Bennett*
											After years of escapology, woeful Charlton won't pull it off this time. There is a chasm in ability between these sides. Paul Mortimer knocked over Gibson for the penalty, and John Gayle later fired in from one yard for his first senior goal. The Dons then took their foot off the gas.											
20		H	MANCHESTER U		14	D		2-2	1-0	Young 21, Cork 88	Segers	Kruszynski	Phelan	Scales	Young	Curle	Fairweather	Fashanu	Gibson	Ryan	Wise*	Cork
	30/12			9,622	*15*		24			*Anderson 74, Robins 75* Ref: D Axcell	*Leighton*	*Anderson*	*Martin*	*Bruce*	*Phelan*	*Pallister*	*Blackmore*	*Ince**	*McClair*	*Hughes*	*Robins*	*Sharpe*
											Struggling United are two minutes away from their first win in seven. Alan Cork has just come on for Wise, and it is he who curls a dramatic equaliser. According to the United programme, Cork is the Dons' player of the decade. Mark Hughes was involved in both United goals.											

No	Date		Att	Pos	Pts	F-A	H-T	Scorers, Times, and Referees	1	2	3	4	5	6	7	8	9	10	11	subs used
21	A	NORWICH			W	1-0	0-0	Gibson 90	Segers	Kruszynski	Phelan	Scales	Young	Curle	Fairweather	Fashanu	Gibson	Ryan	Wise*	Cork
	1/1		*16,680*	*6*	27				*Gunn*	*Culverhouse*	*Bowen*	*Butterworth*	*Linighan*	*Townsend*	*Gordon*	*Fleck*	*Rosario*	*Crook*	*Phillips*	
								Ref: D Phillips	Three 0-1 defeats in a row knocks Norwich off the pace. They outplay the Dons for long stretches and Hans Segers makes three thrilling saves. In injury time Keith Curle disobeys instructions to stay back, and his upfield presence helps Terry Gibson snatch another late goal.											
22	H	ARSENAL		12	W	1-0	0-0	Bennett 88	Segers	Kruszynski	**McAllister**	Scales	Young	Curle	**Bennett**	Joseph	Gayle	Sanchez	McGee	
	13/1		13,793	*3*	30				*Lukic*	*Dixon*	*Winterburn*	*Davis*	*O'Leary**	*Adams*	*Groves*	*Richardson*	*Smith^*	*Bould*	*Merson*	*Caesar/Rocastle*
								Ref: R Lewis	Gould makes six changes after the FA Cup defeat by WBA, among them league debuts for Brian McAllister and Mickey Bennett. Wise, Gibson, and Fairweather are dropped. Tactically, the Dons return to basics. In an abject match, Tony Adams boobs and Bennett pounces.											
23	A	MILLWALL		11	D	0-0	0-0		Segers	Joseph	Phelan	Scales	Ryan	Curle	Bennett*	Kruszynski	Gayle	Sanchez	McGee	Cork
	20/1		*7,780*	*18*	31				*Branagan*	*Salman*	*Dawes*	*Waddock*	*Wood*	*McLeary*	*Sheringham*	*Hurlock*	*Goddard**	*Cascarino*	*Stephenson*	*Carter*
								Ref: K Redfern	Millwall have won only once in the league since September. This forgettable bore aroused the crowd's excitement only to the extent of booing Wimbledon's safety-first tactics. The Dons' one chance was squandered by McGee shooting over. Sheringham and Cascarino got nowhere.											
24	A	MANCHESTER C		12	D	1-1	0-0	Cork 78	Segers	Joseph*	Phelan!	Kruszynski	Scales	Curle	Wise	Bennett^	Gayle	Sanchez	McGee	Ryan/Cork
	10/2		*24,126*	*16*	32			*Hendry 74*	*Dibble*	*Harper*	*Hinchcliffe*	*Brightwell*	*Hendry*	*Redmond*	*White*	*Ward*	*Clarke*	*Megson*	*Lake**	*Allen*
								Ref: R Hart	City's season is slipping into nothingness. Dons' Terry Phelan is sent off after 39 minutes following a nasty lunge at Mark Ward. The 10 men hold out for while, but when Colin Hendry scores Alan Cork strips off and immediately fastens onto Lawrie Sanchez's long ball.											
25	H	LUTON		12	L	1-2	0-0	Wise 72	Segers	Curle	Phelan	Kruszynski	Scales	Young	Bennett*	Gayle^	Cork	Sanchez	Wise	McGee/Ryan
	14/2		**3,496**	*18*	32			*Nogan 51, Dowie 89*	*Chamberlain*	*Braecker*	*Harvey*	*Kennedy*	*James*	*Dreyer*	*Wilson*	*Nogan*	*Dowie*	*Preece*	*Black**	*Wegerle*
								Ref: K Barratt	Luton end their 11-match sequence without a win in front of Plough Lane's lowest crowd of the season. 'They were off on their St Valentine Day's dates,' suggested Gould. With a minute to play, David Preece crosses unhindered for Iain Dowie to head the winner.											
26	A	ASTON VILLA		11	W	3-0	0-0	Fashanu 57p, 69, Miller 84	Segers	Scales	McGee	Ryan	Young	Curle	**Anthrobus**	Miller	Fashanu	Sanchez*	Wise	Cork
	24/2		*29,325*	*1*	35				*Spink*	*Price*	*Gage*	*McGrath*	*Mountfield*	*Nielson*	*Daley*	*Platt*	*Olney**	*Cowans*	*Ormondroyd*	*Birch/Gray*
								Ref: M James	Villa have just gone top of the table for the first time, but Wimbledon inflict upon them their heaviest defeat of the season. Segers keeps out David Platt's penalty (as he did Evans' last season), while at the other end Fashanu scores from the spot after Mountfield brought him down.											
27	H	EVERTON		9	W	3-1	1-1	Fashanu 25, 79p, Wise 77	Segers	Scales	McGee	Ryan	Young	Curle	Anthrobus	Miller	Fashanu	Fairweather	Wise	
	3/3		6,512	*10*	38			*Sheedy 13*	*Southall*	*Snodin*	*McDonald**	*Ratcliffe*	*Watson*	*Atteveld*	*Keown*	*McCall*	*Sharp*	*Cottee^*	*Sheedy*	*Whiteside/Newell*
								Ref: T Holbrook	Everton were swept aside in a match free from physical excess, apart from Everton sub Norman Whiteside's thigh-high tackle on Fashanu. Sheedy's exquisite free-kick suggested a good afternoon for the visitors, but fortunes changed once Kevin Ratcliffe had felled Wise in the box.											
28	H	SOUTHAMPTON		11	D	3-3	2-1	Young 28, Scales 35, Fashanu 53	Segers	Scales	McGee*	Ryan	Young	Curle	Anthrobus	Miller	Fashanu	Cork	Wise	McAllister
	17/3		5,382	*7*	39			*Le Tissier 18, 63, 66*	*Andrews*	*Dodd*	*Benali!*	*Davis*	*Moore*	*Osman**	*Wallace Rod*	*Cockerill*	*Shearer*	*Horne*	*Le Tissier*	*Ruddock*
								Ref: P Tyldesley	Thrills a minute, but this is a match – in front of a TV audience – that Wimbledon feel they should have won. Saints' Francis Benali was sent off for hacking Fashanu, but the Dons somehow throw away a two-goal lead. This is Matthew Le Tissier's second hat-trick in a month.											
29	H	SHEFFIELD WED		12	D	1-1	0-0	Fashanu 63p	Segers	Scales	Phelan	Ryan	Young	Curle	Anthrobus	Kruszynski	Fashanu	Gayle*	Wise	Cork
	24/3		5,034	*13*	40			*Shirtliff 51*	*Turner*	*Nilsson*	*King*	*Palmer*	*Shirtliff*	*Pearson*	*Francis**	*Sheridan*	*Hirst*	*Atkinson*	*Palmer^*	*Bennett/Madden*
								Ref: A Gunn	Four wins and a draw from their last five makes Wednesday tough opponents. Three times in the opening minutes the Dons forwards waste clear chances. Peter Shirtliff's diving header is cancelled out when his tackle on Fashanu brings a theatrical dive. The referee says penalty.											
30	A	NOTTINGHAM F		10	W	1-0	1-0	Wise 15	Segers	Scales	Phelan	Ryan	Young	Curle	Anthrobus*	Kruszynski	Fashanu	Gibson^	Wise	McAllister/Cork
	31/3		*16,821*	*7*	43				*Sutton*	*Laws*	*Pearce*	*Walker*	*Wilson*	*Rice*	*Crosby*	*Parker*	*Clough*	*Currie*	*Carr*	
								Ref: V Callow	Forest are on a losing run, so this result is no surprise. Despite Des Walker's faultless defending, Wimbledon take all three points when Eric Young's knock back falls to Dennis Wise, who volleys spectacularly past Steve Sutton. Skipper Keith Curle plays a blinder.											

No	Venue / Date	Opponent / Att	Pos	Res / Pts	F-A	H-T	Scorers, Times, and Referees	1	2	3	4	5	6	7	8	9	10	11	subs used
31	A	LIVERPOOL		L	1-2	0-2	Hansen 72 (og)	Segers	Scales	Phelan	Ryan	Young	Curle	Anthrobus*	Kruszynski	Fashanu	Gibson	Wise	Cork
	3/4	***33,319***	*1*	43			*Rush 10, Gillespie 44*	*Grobbelaar*	*Hysen*	*Burrows*	*Gillespie*	*Whelan*	*Hansen*	*Staunton*	*Houghton*	*Rush*	*Barnes*	*McMahon*	
							Ref: K Redfern	Wimbledon put up a good show against champions-elect Liverpool, but are undone by two well-crafted goals. John Barnes sets up Rush's opener, and just before half-time Steve McMahon picks out Gary Gillespie with an astute lob. Alan Hansen's outstretched leg brings hope.											
32	H	NORWICH	12	D	1-1	0-1	Fashanu 55	Segers	Scales	Phelan	Ryan	Young	Curle	Anthrobus*	Kruszynski	Fashanu	Gibson	Wise	Cork
	14/4	4,638	*8*	44			*Bowen 42*	*Gunn*	*Culverhouse*	*Bowen*	*Sherwood*	*Linighan*	*Fox**	*Townsend*	*Mortensen*	*Rosario*	*Crook*	*Phillips*	*Goss*
							Ref: K Burge	Dismal fare, end of season rubbish. The main entertainment came from Hans Segers, who several times attempted to score from his own half. Gibson's chip forward and Fashanu's header rescues a point. It's his 11th goal of the season. Earlier, Ian Crook had put Mark Bowen in on goal.											
33	A	CHARLTON	11	W	2-1	2-0	Wise 2, Fashanu 9p	Segers	Goodyear	Phelan	Ryan	Young	Curle	Bennett*	Miller	Fashanu	Kruszynski	Wise	**Newhouse**
	17/4	***5,679***	*19*	47			*Young 70 (og)*	*Bolder*	*Humphrey*	*Reid*	*Peake*	*McLaughlin*	*Caton*	*Lee R*	*Williams*	*Jones*	*Minto*	*Mortimer*	
							Ref: K Cooper	Wimbledon and Charlton came up together in 1986. It is the Dons who send their neighbours back to Division 2 with this result. Ex-Charlton player Mickey Bennett sets up Wise's 2nd-minute stunner. Clive Goodyear returns to the side, having last played in the FA Cup Final.											
34	H	COVENTRY	11	D	0-0	0-0		Segers	Goodyear	Phelan	Ryan	Young	Curle	Bennett*	Miller	Fashanu^	Kruszynski	Wise	Joseph/Cork
	21/4	4,086	*10*	48				*Ogrizovic*	*Borrows*	*Edwards*	*Clark*	*Dobson*	*Peake*	*Gallagher*	*McDonald*	*Regis*	*Drinkell*	*Smith*	
							Ref: S Lodge	This match was so bad it was punishment for spectators and players alike. The only consolation was that Coventry were even worse than the Dons. Coventry boss John Sillett sent coach Dixie McNeill along to the post-match press-conference. McNeill said Coventry had played well.											
35	H	TOTTENHAM	9	W	1-0	0-0	Fashanu 7	Segers	Goodyear	Phelan	Ryan	Young	Curle	Anthrobus*	Miller	Fashanu	Kruszynski	Wise^	Cork/**Fitzgerald**
	28/4	12,800	*3*	51				*Thorstvedt*	*Bergsson**	*Vd Hauwe^*	*Sedgley*	*Howells*	*Polston*	*Stewart*	*Gascoigne*	*Nayim*	*Lineker*	*Allan P*	*Samways/Thomas*
							Ref: C Trussell	Terry Venables' expensive team have won their last six, but they appear not to want to make a fight of it. Gascoigne alone poses problems for Wimbledon. Fashanu's overhead kick comes back off the post after two minutes, but he soon shrugs off Bergsson and cuts inside to score.											
36	A	MANCHESTER U		D	0-0	0-0		Segers	Joseph	Phelan	Ryan	Young	Curle	Cork*	Miller	Newhouse^	Kruszynski	Anthrobus	Bennett/Blackwell
	30/4	*29,281*	*14*	52				*Bosnich*	*Anderson*	*Martin*	*Bruce*	*Phelan*	*Pallister*	*Beardsmore*	*Ince*	*Robins**	*Hughes*	*Gibson^*	*Wallace/Blackmore*
							Ref: J Key	United are not quite safe from the nightmare of relegation. Hans Segers – Dons' player of the year – defies them, and his performance inspires Bobby Gould into sending a video of the match to Dutch coach Leo Beenhaaker, who has yet to finalise Holland's 1990 World Cup squad.											
37	H	CRYS PALACE		L	0-1	0-0		Segers	Goodyear	Phelan	Ryan	Young	Curle	McGee*	Miller	Fashanu	Kruszynski	Wise	Cork
	2/5	8,209	*14*	52			*Bright 62*	*Martyn*	*Pemberton*	*Shaw*	*Madden*	*Hedman*	*Thorn*	*Barber*	*Thomas*	*Bright*	*Thompson*	*Salako**	*Pardew*
							Ref: M Peck	Palace are bound for Wembley in 10 days' time, so this victory keeps their spirits up. Mark Bright's bullet header, his 17th goal of the season, enables Palace to do the double over the Dons. But this is a testy encounter with several unseemly flare-ups. The Dons pressed for long spells.											
38	A	QP RANGERS	8	W	3-2	1-1	Fashanu 31, Miller 59, Curle 89	Segers	Joseph	Phelan	Ryan	Young	Curle	Anthrobus*	Miller	Fashanu^	Kruszynski	Wise	Cork/Blackwell
	5/5	*9,676*	*11*	55			*Wegerle 43p, Channing 64*	*Seaman*	*Bardsley*	*Sansom*	*Law*	*McDonald*	*Maddix*	*Wilkins*	*Channing*	*Clarke**	*Wegerle*	*Sinton*	*Ferdinand*
	Home	*Away*					Ref: D Vickers	Including this match, Rangers have only won one of their last seven. It is a sign of Wimbledon's unquenchable spirit that at Wise's corner, with the score standing at 2-2, they pile men forward and Keith Curle drives in a late, late winner. Afterwards the Dons toss shirts to their fans.											
Average	7,756	*18,040*																	

Littlewoods Cup	Att		F-A	H-T	Scorers, Times, and Referees	1	2	3	4	5	6	7	8	9	10	11	subs used
2:1 A PORT VALE		16 W	2-1	1-1	Fairweather 29, Fashanu 66	Segers	Curle	Phelan	Kruszynski	Young	Scales	Fairweather	Ryan	Fashanu	Gibson	Wise	
18/9	*5,827*	*2:19*			*Futcher 5*	*Grew*	*Webb*	*Hughes*	*Walker*	*Aspin*	*Glover*	*Cross*	*Earle*	*Futcher*	*Beckford*	*Mills^*	*Miller I*
					Ref: D Scott	Rain sweeps across Vale Park, but there is only sunshine for Vaughan Ryan. He was subject to terrace taunts at home matches as he attempted to fill Vinnie Jones' shoes. Here, he sets up both goals and does a creditable marking job on Vale's talented Robbie Earle, soon to be a Don.											
2:2 H PORT VALE		15 W	3-0	0-0	Fashanu 55p, Gibson 65, 76	Segers	Curle	Phelan	Kruszynski	Young	Scales	Fairweather	Ryan	Fashanu	Gibson	Wise	
4/10	2,757	*2:20*				*Grew*	*Webb*	*Hughes*	*Walker*	*Aspin*	*Glover**	*Porter^*	*Mills*	*Futcher*	*Beckford*	*Miller I*	*Earle/Finney*
					Ref: J Ashworth (Dons win 5-1 on aggregate)	Dennis Wise's unstoppable sorties down both flanks make him the key player in this match. The crucial penalty was the result of Phelan being dragged down by Neil Aspin. The referee hesitates before pointing to the spot. Terry Gibson's goals are his first for nine months.											
3 A MIDDLESBRO		19 D	1-1	1-0	Gibson 2	Segers	Joseph	Phelan	McGee*	Young	Curle	Fairweather	Gayle^	Gibson	Sanchez	Wise	Fiore/Miller
25/10	*12,933*	*2:20*			*Slaven 48*	*Poole*	*Parkinson*	*Cooper*	*Mowbray*	*Kernaghan*	*Putney*	*Slaven*	*Proctor*	*Ripley*	*Brennan*	*Comfort*	
					Ref: T Simpson	Bruce Rioch's Boro are struggling. Even without Scales and Fashanu, Wimbledon look comfortably in control. Boro's equaliser comes out of the blue. Stuart Ripley shakes off Eric Young to set up the goal for Bernie Slaven. Windy conditions curtail goalmouth action at both ends.											
3R H MIDDLESBRO		18 W	1-0	1-0	McGee 4	Segers	Joseph	Phelan	McGee	Young	Curle	Fairweather	Miller	Gibson	Sanchez	Wise	
8/11	3,554	*2:20*				*Poole*	*Parkinson*	*Cooper*	*Mowbray*	*Kernaghan*	*Putney*	*Slaven*	*Proctor*	*Davenport*	*Brennan*	*Burke*	
					Ref: R Milford	Despite the score, this was a clear-cut victory. Boro goalkeeper Kevin Poole denied Wimbledon on countless occasions, while at the other end Hans Segers was allowed to slumber. This win sends the Dons into the last 16, where they are due to face 2nd Division West Ham.											
4 A WEST HAM		14 L	0-1	0-0		Segers	Joseph	Phelan	Ryan	Young	Curle	Fairweather	Miller*	Cotterill	Sanchez^	Wise	Cork/Scales
22/11	*24,756*	*2:5*			*Allen 81*	*Parkes*	*Potts*	*Dicks!*	*Strodder*	*Martin*	*Keen**	*Brady*	*Slater*	*Allen*	*Ward*	*Parris*	*Devonshire*
					Ref: A Buksh	Having seen off two 2nd Division strugglers, Wimbledon must now overcome Lou Macari's promotion-chasing Hammers. Alas, the Dons prove no match for their opponents, who are reduced to 10 men when Julian Dicks' assault on Dennis Wise provokes an ale-house brawl.											

FA Cup																	
3 A WEST BROM		14 L	0-2	0-1		Segers	Kruszynski	Phelan	Scales	Young	Curle	Fairweather	Fashanu*	Gibson	Ryan^	Wise	Cork/Joseph
5/1	*12,988*	*2:16*			*Robson 37, Bartlett 47*	*Naylor*	*Dobbins*	*Harbey*	*Robson*	*North*	*Whyte*	*Ford*	*Goodman*	*West*	*McNally*	*Bartlett*	
					Ref: H King	Wimbledon's favourite competition sees them collapse limply. The midfield disappears, Fashanu can't get going. Albion attacked venomously down both flanks. Don Goodman crossed for Gary Robson's goal; Eric Young is then left floundering in the wake of Kevin Bartlett.											

		Home					Away					
	P	W	D	L	F	A	W	D	L	F	A	Pts
1 Liverpool	38	13	5	1	38	15	10	5	4	40	22	79
2 Aston Villa	38	13	3	3	36	20	8	4	7	21	18	70
3 Tottenham	38	12	1	6	35	24	7	5	7	24	23	63
4 Arsenal	38	14	3	2	38	11	4	5	10	16	27	62
5 Chelsea	38	8	7	4	31	24	8	5	6	27	26	60
6 Everton	38	14	3	2	40	16	3	5	11	17	30	59
7 Southampton	38	10	5	4	40	27	5	5	9	31	36	55
8 WIMBLEDON	38	5	8	6	22	23	8	8	3	25	17	55
9 Nottingham F	38	9	4	6	31	21	6	5	8	24	26	54
10 Norwich	38	7	10	2	24	14	6	4	9	20	28	53
11 QP Rangers	38	9	4	6	27	22	4	7	8	18	22	50
12 Coventry	38	11	2	6	24	25	3	5	11	15	34	49
13 Manchester U	38	8	6	5	26	14	5	3	11	20	33	48
14 Manchester C	38	9	4	6	26	21	3	8	8	17	31	48
15 Crys Palace	38	8	7	4	27	23	5	2	12	15	43	48
16 Derby	38	9	1	9	29	21	4	6	9	14	19	46
17 Luton	38	8	8	3	24	18	2	5	12	19	39	43
18 Sheffield Wed	38	8	6	5	21	17	3	4	12	14	34	43
19 Charlton	38	4	6	9	18	25	3	3	13	13	32	30
20 Millwall	38	4	6	9	23	25	1	5	13	16	40	26
	760	183	99	98	580	406	98	99	183	406	580	1041

Odds & ends

Double wins: (2) Tottenham, Charlton.
Double losses: (2) C Palace, Liverpool.

Won from behind: (2) Everton (h), Chelsea (a).
Lost from in front: (1) Nottingham F (h).

High spots: 2 defeats in final 13 games, climbing to 8th.

Low spots: opening the season with 5 games without a win.
Losing to 2nd Division teams in Littlewoods, Zenith-Data, and FA Cup.

Only Charlton and Millwall had worse home records.
Only Liverpool had a better away record, and no team lost fewer away games than Wimbledon.

Just 9 league defeats is Wimbledon's fewest in the top division.

Player of the Year: Hans Segers.
Ever-presents: (2) Hans Segers, Keith Curle.
Hat-tricks: (0).
Leading scorer: John Fashanu (13) + 1 in Zenith-Data Cup.

	Appearances						Goals			
	Lge	Sub	LC	Sub	FAC	Sub	**Lge**	LC	FAC	**Total**
Anthrobus, Steve	**10**									
Bennett, Michael	**6**	(1)					**1**			**1**
Blackwell, Dean		(3)								
Brooke, Gary		(2)								
Cotterill, Steve	**2**		1				**1**			**1**
Cork, Alan	**12**	(19)		(1)		(1)	**5**			**5**
Curle, Keith	**38**		5		1		**2**			**2**
Fairweather, Carlton	**20**	(1)	5		1		**1**	1		**2**
Fashanu, John	**24**		2		1		**11**	2		**13**
Fiore, Mark				(1)						
Fitzgerald, Scott		(1)								
Gayle, John	**8**	(3)	1				**1**			**1**
Gibson, Terry	**16**	(2)	4		1		**4**	3		**7**
Goodyear, Clive	**4**									
Joseph, Roger	**15**	(4)	3			(1)				
Kruszynski, Zbigniew	**26**	(1)	2		1		**2**			**2**
McAllister, Brian	**1**	(2)								
McGee, Paul	**11**	(2)	2					1		**1**
Miller, Paul	**11**	(4)	2	(1)			**2**			**2**
Newhouse, Aiden	**1**	(1)								
Phelan, Terry	**34**		5		1					
Ryan, Vaughan	**28**	(3)	3		1					
Sanchez, Lawrie	**16**	(2)	3				**1**			**1**
Scales, John	**27**	(1)	2	(1)	1		**2**			**2**
Segers, Hans	**38**		5		1					
Wise, Dennis	**35**		5		1		**8**			**8**
Young, Eric	**35**		5		1		**5**			**5**
(own-goals)							**1**			**1**
27 players used	**418**	**(52)**	55	**(4)**	**11**	**(2)**	**47**	**7**		**54**

No	Date		Att	Pos	Pts	F-A	H-T	Scorers, Times, and Referees	1	2	3	4	5	6	7	8	9	10	11	subs used
1	H	ARSENAL			L	**0-3**	0-0		Segers	Joseph	Phelan	**Barton***	Scales	Curle	Cork	Miller^	Fashanu	Sanchez	Fairweather	Blackwell/Kruszynski
	25/8		**13,733**		–			*Merson 57, Smith 59, Groves 90*	*Seaman*	*Dixon*	*Winterburn*	*Thomas*	*Bould*	*Adams*	*Rocastle*	*Davis*	*Smith*	*Merson*	*Limpar**	*Groves*
								Ref: L Shapter	Ray Harford leads the Dons into the new season, with several big name players departed. Scales hit the post in the first half, but an injury to Paul Miller forced a reorganisation. David Seaman's quick goal-kick ignited the touchpaper. Anders Limpar crossed and Merson headed in.											
2	A	QP RANGERS			W	1-0	0-0	Fashanu 79	Segers	Joseph	Phelan	Barton	Scales	Curle	Gayle*	Kruszynski	Fashanu	Sanchez	McGee	Blackwell
	29/8		*9,762*		3				*Roberts*	*Bardsley*	*Sansom*	*Channing**	*McDonald*	*Maddix*	*Wilkins*	*Wilson*	*Falco*	*Wegerle^*	*Sinton*	*Barker/Ferdinand*
								Ref: A Ward	Filthy weather appropriate to an awful match. Rangers fans booed the Dons from the pitch after a game in which Hans Segers proved to be Wimbledon's best defender and best attacker. It was from one of the keeper's downfield punts that John Fashanu back-headed the winning goal.											
3	A	DERBY		12	D	1-1	1-0	Cotterill 4	Segers	Joseph	Phelan	Barton	Scales	Curle	Gayle*	Kruszynski^	Fashanu	Sanchez	Cotterill	Cork/Blackwell
	1/9		*12,469*	*16*	4			*Saunders 72p*	*Shilton*	*Sage*	*Forsyth*	*Williams G*	*Wright*	*Watson*	*Mickl'white**	*Saunders*	*Harford*	*Ramage^*	*Williams P*	*Hebberd/Francis*
								Ref: R Gifford	Arthur Cox kept his side up last season. They won't be so lucky this time, even though they are graced by Peter Shilton, Mark Wright, and Dean Saunders. This bore draw was marked by Scales' tame back header, which led to Segers pulling down Paul Williams for the penalty.											
4	H	LIVERPOOL		16	L	1-2	0-2	Cork 75	Segers	Joseph	Phelan	Barton	Scales	Curle	Gayle	Kruszynski*	Fashanu	Sanchez	Cotterill^	Blackwell/Cork
	8/9		12,364	*1*	4			*Barnes 26, Whelan 31*	*Grobbelaar*	*Hysen*	*Burrows*	*Nicol*	*Whelan*	*Gillespie*	*Ablett*	*Molby*	*Rush*	*Barnes*	*McMahon*	
								Ref: R Groves	Kenny Dalglish's team are en route to winning their first eight league games. Ray Harford has switched from 4-4-2 to 4-3-3, which makes the Dons even more reliant on Route 1 football. John Barnes' wonder chip puts Liverpool in front; Whelan's weaving run doubles their advantage.											
5	A	COVENTRY		16	D	0-0	0-0		Segers	Joseph	Phelan	Barton	Scales!	Curle	Gayle	Kruszynski	Fashanu*	Sanchez	Cotterill	Cork
	15/9		*8,925*	*15*	5				*Ogrizovic*	*Borrows*	*Edwards*	*Perdomo**	*Kilcline*	*Peake*	*Gallacher*	*Gynn*	*Speedie*	*Drinkell*	*Smith^*	*McDonald/Livingst'n'*
								Ref: I Borrett	Matches between these sides tend to be wretched, and this was no exception. Scales was sent off after 10 minutes for hacking David Speedie. Thereafter the Dons defended in depth. John Sillett tells the press afterwards that Wimbledon are killing football. He will shortly quit City.											
6	H	SUNDERLAND		15	D	2-2	0-1	Kruszynski 76, Scales 88	Segers	Joseph	Phelan	Barton	Scales	Curle	Gayle	Kruszynski	Fashanu*	Sanchez	Fairweath'r^	Bennett/Cork
	22/9		6,143	*13*	6			*Armstrong 39, Davenport 72*	*Norman*	*Kay*	*Ord*	*Bennett*	*Ball*	*Owers*	*Bracewell*	*Armstrong*	*Davenport*	*Gabbiadini**	*Hardyman*	*Hauser*
								Ref: M Reed	Denis Smith's mediocre Sunderland only find themselves in the top flight after Swindon had been demoted. They would have won this match, though, but for Scales' late equaliser from yet another set piece. The Dons had forced 14 corners but had rarely threatened keeper Norman.											
7	H	MANCHESTER C		14	D	1-1	0-0	Gayle 89	Segers	Joseph	Phelan	Barton	Blackwell	Curle	Gayle	Kruszynski	Cork	Sanchez	Cotterill*	McGee
	29/9		6,158	*7*	7			*Allen 78*	*Coton*	*Brightwell*	*Pointon*	*Harper*	*Hendry*	*Redmond*	*White**	*Heath^*	*Quinn*	*Brennan*	*Ward M*	*Beckford/Allen*
								Ref: I Hemley	Howard Kendall will soon depart Maine Road for Goodison. City sub Clive Allen pounces after the ball reaches him from a corner. Terry Phelan is playing in Dons' midfield. He wins a penalty that is missed by Keith Curle. John Gayle's turn and shot from 16 yards earns a point.											
8	A	SHEFFIELD UTD		10	W	2-1	1-1	Fairweather 26, Fashanu 71	Segers	Joseph	Phelan	Barton	Blackwell	Curle	Gayle!	Kruszynski	Cork	Sanchez*	Fairweather	Fashanu
	6/10		*17,650*	*19*	10			*Barnes 11*	*Kite*	*Pemberton*	*Barnes*	*Jones*	*Morris*	*Booker**	*Hoyland*	*Beesley*	*Agana^*	*Deane*	*Marwood*	*Wood/Whitehurst*
								Ref: T Lunt	Sheffield United are back in Division 1, but after a shaky start manager Dave Bassett has lured Vinnie Jones from Leeds. After half-time John Gayle tangles with Jones, is red-carded, and never plays for the Dons again. Fashanu strips off to fire the low winner from 25 yards.											
9	H	ASTON VILLA		12	D	0-0	0-0		Segers	Joseph*	Phelan	Barton	Blackwell	Curle	McGee	Kruszynski	Fashanu	Scales	Cork^	Fairweath'r/Newhouse
	20/10		6,646	*9*	11				*Spink*	*Price*	*Gray*	*Comyn*	*Mountfield*	*Nielson*	*Daley*	*Pratt*	*Ormondr'yd**	*Cowans*	*Cascarino*	*Birch*
								Ref: R Nixon	John Gayle has paid the ultimate price for his many indiscretions. Villa, last year's runners-up under Graham Taylor, are now under Dr Josef Venglos. They await a UEFA Cup-tie with Inter Milan. Despite forcing 18 corners, the Dons couldn't score, and lost their shape and discipline.											
10	A	CRYS PALACE		13	L	3-4	1-1	McGee 9, 86, Fashanu 82 *[Bright 83]*	Segers	Joseph	Phelan*	Barton	Blackwell	Curle	McGee	Kruszynski	Fashanu	Scales	Cork^	Fairweather/Sanchez
	27/10		*17,220*	*4*	11			*Thomas 13, Humphey 49, Gray 77,*	*Martyn*	*Humphrey*	*Shaw*	*Gray*	*Young*	*Thorn*	*Salako*	*Thomas*	*Bright*	*Wright*	*Hodges**	*Barber*
								Ref: G Pooley	Unbeaten Palace are embarked on a fine season. Wimbledon lose their unbeaten away record after this corker. Palace full-back John Humphrey scores his first goal. Dons' Paul McGee bags two and hits the post. Fashanu hits a beauty and Lawrie Sanchez heads wide in injury time.											

No	Venue	Opponent / Att	Pos	Res / Pts	F-A	H-T	Scorers, Times, Referees	1	2	3	4	5	6	7	8	9	10	11	subs used
11	H	SOUTHAMPTON	14	D	1-1	0-0	Flowers 61 (og)	Segers	Joseph	Phelan	Barton	Blackwell	Curle	McGee	Kruszynski	Fashanu	Scales	Newhouse*	Gibson
3/11		5,485	*15*	12			*Le Tissier 80p*	*Flowers*	*Dodd*	*Adams*	*Case*	*Ruddock*	*Moore*	*Le Tissier*	*Horne*	*Shearer*	*Rideout*	*WallaceRod*	
							Ref: J Moules	This game heralded the freakiest of goals for the Dons. Saints' keeper Tim Flowers dived in as Micky Adams cleared. The ball could have gone anywhere, but it bobbled over the line. Roger Joseph's wild tackle on Alan Shearer brought the penalty from which Le Tissier levelled.											
12	A	TOTTENHAM	16	L	2-4	2-2	Cork 26, McGee 42 *[Lineker 89p]*	Segers	Joseph	Phelan*	Barton^	Blackwell	Curle	McGee	Kruszynski	Gibson	Scales	Cork	Sanchez/Newhouse
10/11		*-28,769*	*3*	12			*Stewart 9, Mabbutt 45, Walsh 85,*	*Thorstvedt*	*Thomas*	*V d Hauwe**	*Sedgley^*	*Howells*	*Mabbutt*	*Stewart*	*Gascoigne*	*Nayim*	*Lineker*	*Allen*	*Edinburgh/Walsh*
							Ref: A Gunn	High-flying Spurs have just lost for the first time – to Liverpool. This absorbing match featured Gascoigne's terrible back-pass, which set up Cork, and two late Spurs goals which won the points. Blackwell felled Nayim for Lineker's penalty. Gibson missed with the keeper to beat.											
13	H	CHELSEA	10	W	2-1	1-0	Nicholas 1 (og), Gibson 58	Segers	Joseph	**Elkins**	Barton	Blackwell	Curle	McGee*	Kruszynski	Gibson^	Scales	Cork	Sanchez/Newhouse
17/11		10,773	*14*	15			*Durie 80*	*Hitchcock*	*Hall*	*Dorigo*	*Townsend*	*Cundy*	*Lee*	*Wise*	*Nicholas**	*Dixon*	*Durie*	*Wilson*	*Le Saux*
							Ref: T Simpson	The acquisition of Andy Townsend and ex-Don Dennis Wise cost Chelsea more than the entire Dons team. Peter Nicholas's headed own-goal gives Wimbledon an instant lead. Gary Elkins celebrates his Wimbledon debut by snuffing Wise out of the game. Durie scores and hits the bar.											
14	H	EVERTON	8	W	2-1	1-0	Barton 21, Gibson 55	Segers	Joseph	Phelan*	Barton	Blackwell	Curle	McGee	Kruszynski	Fashanu	Scales	Gibson^	Sanchez/Cork
24/11		6,411	*18*	18			*Sheedy 78p*	*Southall*	*McDonald*	*Ebbrell*	*Ratcliffe*	*Keown*	*Whiteside**	*Attevelt*	*McCall*	*Sharp^*	*Newell*	*Sheedy*	*Nevin/Cottee*
							Ref: K Morton	Howard Kendall's team are beaten by two crisp goals, one scored, the other created by Terry Gibson. Warren Barton's header is his first goal for the club. Roger Joseph pulled down Everton's Ray Attevelt for the penalty. This defeat intensifies Everton's flirtation with relegation.											
15	A	NORWICH	8	W	4-0	4-0	Fashanu 1, 28, Barton 19, Scales 21	Segers	Joseph	Phelan	Barton	Blackwell	Curle	McGee	Kruszynski*	Fashanu	Scales	Gibson	Sanchez
1/12		*12,324*	*13*	21				*Gunn*	*Culverhouse*	*Bowen*	*Butterworth*	*Blades*	*Crook**	*Gordon*	*Power^*	*Sherwood*	*Fox*	*Phillips*	*Goss/Fleck*
							Ref: J Ashworth	This results earns Wimbledon the Barclays' performance of the week award. After just 26 seconds Fashanu burst past three defenders to fire an unstoppable shot. Ray Harford is still officially the Dons' caretaker manager, but his position will be made permanent during the week.											
16	H	QP RANGERS	6	W	3-0	1-0	McGee 25, Fashanu 61, 67	Segers	Joseph	Phelan	Barton	Blackwell	Curle	McGee	Kruszynski	Fashanu	Scales	Gibson	
8/12		5,358	*19*	24				*Roberts*	*Bardsley*	*Sansom*	*Herrera**	*Caesar*	*Wilson*	*Wilkins*	*Barker*	*Falco*	*Wegerle*	*Sinton*	*McCarthy*
							Ref: R Pawley	This is Rangers' sixth defeat on the run, Wimbledon's fourth victory. A woeful back-pass by Clive Wilson sets up McGee for the first goal. Thereafter, two more goals from Fashanu, a sweet volley and a header, finish the job. Terry Gibson also hit a post, so QPR got off lightly.											
17	A	ARSENAL	8	D	2-2	1-2	Kruszynski 44, Fashanu 90	Segers	Joseph	Phelan	Barton	Blackwell	Curle	McGee*	Kruszynski	Fashanu	Scales	Gibson	Cork
15/12		*30,163*	*2*	25			*Merson 30, Adams 34*	*Seaman*	*Dixon*	*Winterburn**	*Thomas*	*Bould*	*Adams*	*Groves*	*Davis*	*Smith*	*Merson*	*Limpar*	*O'Leary*
							Ref: M Bodenham	Arsenal are still unbeaten (and will lose just once in the league all season). Their four nimble forwards manufacture two goals and exert heavy pressure. The game is in injury time when, from Curle's 50-yard free-kick, Fashanu jumps all over Seaman to equalise. Arsenal are furious.											
18	H	MANCHESTER U	10	L	1-3	1-0	Fashanu 22	Segers	Joseph	Phelan	Barton	Blackwell*	Curle!	McGee	Kruszynski	Fashanu	Scales	Gibson	Sanchez
22/12		9,744	*7*	25			*Bruce 69p, 88p, Hughes 80*	*Sealey*	*Blackmore**	*Donaghy*	*Bruce*	*Phelan*	*Pallister*	*Robson*	*Ince*	*McClair*	*Hughes*	*Webb*	*Wallace*
							Ref: J Rushton	Keith Curle had a fine match, but was sent off two minutes from time for tripping Mark Hughes. The Dons' skipper will now be suspended for three matches. Curle was understandably frustrated as Wimbledon failed to protect their first-half advantage. Two penalties turned the tide.											
19	A	NOTTINGHAM F	10	L	1-2	1-2	Fashanu 44	Segers	Joseph	Phelan	Barton	Blackwell	Curle	McGee	Kruszynski	Fashanu	Scales	Gibson*	Cork
26/12		*16,221*	*11*	25			*Pearce 12, Keane 45*	*Crossley*	*Laws*	*Pearce*	*Walker*	*Chettle*	*Hodge**	*Carr*	*Keane*	*Clough*	*Jemson^*	*Parker*	*Wilson/Starbuck*
							Ref: J Key	Segers drives the ball against Stuart Pearce's chest for the first goal. No sooner does Fashanu head his 10th goal of the season than Roy Keane restores Forest's advantage. In the second half both Scales and McGee hit Crossley's post, and two more Dons efforts are cleared off the line.											
20	A	LEEDS	10	L	0-3	0-3		Segers	Joseph	Phelan	Barton	Blackwell	Curle	McGee	Sanchez*	Fashanu	Scales	Elkins^	Kruszynski/Cork
29/12		*29,292*	*3*	25			*Chapman 10, Speed 15, Sterland 45*	*Lukic*	*Sterland*	*Snodin**	*Batty*	*Fairclough*	*Whyte*	*Strachan*	*Shutt^*	*Chapman*	*McAllister*	*Speed*	*Whitlow/Pearson*
							Ref: K Lupton	Wimbledon usually prosper over the festive season, but not this year. Howard Wilkinson has brought Leeds back to Division 1, and this win takes them 3rd, their highest placing. The Dons looked lightweight. Chapman turned Blackwell for No 1; the Dons stand around ball-watching.											

BARCLAYS LEAGUE DIVISION 1 — Manager: Ray Harford — SEASON 1990-91

No	Date		Att	Pos	Pts	F-A	H-T	Scorers, Times, and Referees	1	2	3	4	5	6	7	8	9	10	11	subs used
21	H	LUTON		9	W	2-0	1-0	Fashanu 44, Cork 83	Segers	Joseph	Phelan	Barton	Blackwell	Curle	McGee	Kruszynski	Fashanu*	Scales	Gibson	Cork
	1/1		4,521	*14*	28				*Chamberlain*	*Johnson**	*Harvey*	*Pembridge*	*McDonough*	*Dreyer*	*Elstrup*	*Preece*	*Farrell*	*Rees^*	*Black*	*James/Dowie*
								Ref: K Barratt	A win at last for Wimbledon, as Ray Harford schemes victory over his former team. A lifeless game draws the smallest 1st Division crowd so far this season. Luton's only real chance came with Kingsley Black's early header, saved by Segers. Fashanu heads in Warren Barton's corner.											
22	H	DERBY		8	W	3-1	0-0	Gibson 61, Fashanu 68, 90p	Segers	Joseph	Phelan	Barton	Blackwell	Scales	McGee	Kruszynski	Fashanu	Sanchez	Gibson^	Cork
	12/1		4,724	*18*	31			*Harford 76*	*Shilton*	*Sage*	*Pickering**	*Patterson*	*Wright*	*Kavanagh*	*Cross*	*Saunders*	*Harford*	*Hebberd*	*Briscoe*	*Davidson*
								Ref: P Foakes	A sign of the times. Peter Shilton protested that the referee had not protected him fromWimbledon's buffeting, though he was clearly at fault with two goals. Admitted Fashanu: 'We planned to hit him with high crosses because he just can't take a bombardment any more.'											
23	A	LIVERPOOL		7	D	1-1	0-1	Barton 81	Segers	Joseph	Phelan	Barton	Blackwell	Curle	McGee	Kruszynski	Fashanu*	Scales	Gibson	Cork
	19/1		*35,030*	*2*	32			*Barnes 32*	*Grobbelaar*	*Ablett*	*Burrows*	*Nicol*	*Staunton*	*Gillespie*	*Carter*	*Molby**	*Rush*	*Barnes*	*McMahon*	*Rosenthal*
								Ref: H King	This is the result that knocks Liverpool off the top for the first time this season. Kenny Dalglish, soon to depart, is scathing about the Dons' approach. Liverpool could have been three up when Barton drove in a free-kick. Barton said: 'the lads told me not to let Detzi have a shot.'											
24	H	COVENTRY		7	W	1-0	0-0	Gibson 66	Segers	Joseph	Phelan	Barton	Blackwell	Curle	McGee	Kruszynski	Fashanu	Scales	Gibson	
	2/2		**4,061**	*15*	35				*Sutton*	*Borrows*	*Hurst*	*Emerson*	*Kilcline*	*Billing*	*McDonald**	*Gynn*	*Regis*	*Smith*	*Drinkell*	*Fleming*
								Ref: A Gunn	Heads are low after Wimbledon's KO from the FA Cup. Terry Butcher is the new Coventry helmsman, but this is yet another dire match between these sides. Cyrille Regis collided with team-mate David Smith, Roger Joseph broke away, and Gibson scored against his former club.											
25	A	CHELSEA		8	D	0-0	0-0		Segers	Joseph	Phelan	Barton	Blackwell	Curle	McGee	Kruszynski*	Fashanu	Scales	Gibson	Sanchez
	16/2		*13,378*	*9*	36				*Beasant*	*Clarke*	*Dorigo*	*Dickens*	*Cundy*	*Moncou*	*Le Saux*	*Bumstead**	*Dixon*	*Mitchell*	*Wise*	*Matthew*
								Ref: J Martin	Bobby Campbell is in his final weeks as Chelsea manager. He says to the press after the match: 'Well, you try describing that God-awful game.' Ray Harford, for his part, described Chelsea's forwards as 'brain-dead for getting caught offside so many times'. Hardly a classic.											
26	H	TOTTENHAM		6	W	**5-1**	1-0	McGee 9, Curle 60, Gibson 79,	Segers	Joseph	Phelan	Barton	Blackwell	Curle	McGee*	Kruszynski^	Fashanu	Scales	Gibson	Cork/Sanchez
	23/2		10,303	*8*	39			*Bergsson 71* [Fashanu 82, Cork 87]	*Thorstvedt*	*Bergsson*	*Edinburgh*	*Sedgley*	*Nayim**	*Mabbutt*	*Samways*	*Thomas*	*Moncur*	*Lineker*	*Allen*	*Gray*
								Ref: K Breen	Spurs' worst, Wimbledon's best result of the season. Five separate Dons get on the scoresheet. Four of the goals stem from crosses, Curle's from a free-kick. Psychologically, the signing of Barnet winger Andy Clarke (who did not play) seems to have given the other players a jolt.											
27	H	NORWICH		6	D	0-0	0-0		Segers	Joseph	Elkins	Barton	Sanchez	Curle	McGee*	Kruszynski	Fashanu	Scales	Gibson^	Cork/**Clarke**
	2/3		4,541	*10*	40				*Gunn*	*Culverhouse*	*Bowen*	*Blades*	*Polston*	*Smith*	*Gordon*	*Fleck*	*Sherwood*	*Goss*	*Phillips*	
								Ref: R Dilkes	Dave Stringer's humdrum Norwich are not a side to set pulses racing. There was no atmosphere either on or off the pitch. Andy Clarke shows his worth when he comes on for Terry Gibson. But not even he can lift the game out of the realms of tedium. Very few chances were created.											
28	A	MANCHESTER C		7	D	1-1	1-1	Fashanu 43	Segers	Joseph	Elkins	Barton*	Blackwell	Curle	McGee	Sanchez	Fashanu	Scales	Gibson^	Cork/Clarke
	16/3		*21,089*	*6*	41			*Ward 45p*	*Coton*	*Brightwell*	*Hill*	*Reid*	*Hendry*	*Redmond*	*White*	*Allen**	*Quinn*	*Harper*	*Ward M*	*Heath*
								Ref: K Burge	Peter Reid took over the reins at Maine Road in mid-season. This sterile match was entirely forgettable, apart from the two minutes that preceded half-time. Fashanu stooped to head in Wimbledon's one and only chance; then Mark Ward's cross struck Sanchez's hand. Penalty!											
29	H	SHEFFIELD UTD		6	D	1-1	1-0	Cork 21	Segers	Joseph	Elkins	Barton	Blackwell	Curle	Bennett*	Sanchez	Fashanu	Scales	Cork	Clarke
	23/3		7,031	*13*	42			*Deane 70p*	*Tracey*	*Wilder*	*Barnes*	*Jones*	*Beesley*	*Hill*	*Bradshaw*	*Booker*	*Hodges*	*Deane*	*Bryson*	
								Ref: P Durkin	Having not won a match till December, United have now won their last seven. Yet this is a match of mind-numbing tedium. Not for 75 minutes did either side manage three consecutive passes. Vinnie Jones treated Barton to a forearm smash. John Fashanu handled to concede the penalty.											
30	H	NOTTINGHAM F		6	W	3-1	1-1	Fashanu 22, McGee 53, Clarke 66	Segers	Joseph	Elkins	Barton	Blackwell	Curle	McGee*	Sanchez	Fashanu	Scales	Cork^	Bennett/Clarke
	30/3		6,392	*14*	45			*Loughlan 1*	*Crossley*	*Charles*	*Pearce**	*Walker*	*Chettle*	*Wassall*	*Loughlan*	*Keane^*	*Clough*	*Glover*	*Parker*	*Woan/Gemmill*
								Ref: R Groves	Forest have not won in the league for nine games. Brian Clough experiments with a sweeper system based around his son Nigel. After 36 seconds Sanchez's back-pass was snapped up by Tony Loughlan, but thereafter Forest's central defence crumbles under Fashanu's weight.											

No	Venue/Date	Opponent	Att	Pos	Pts	Res	F-A	H-T	Scorers, Times, and Referees	1	2	3	4	5	6	7	8	9	10	11	12
	2/4		**36,660**	*5*	45				*Bruce 54, McClair 88*	*Walsh*	*Irwin*	*Donaghy*	*Bruce**	*Phelan*	*Pallister*	*Blackmore*	*Ince*	*McClair*	*Webb*	*Sharpe^*	*Wratten/Robins*
									Ref: D Phillips	Alex Ferguson was another top manager who had considered buying Andy Clarke, for whom Ray Harford smashed the non-league transfer record when paying Barnet £350,000 for his services. Brian McClair's late goal heralds Wimbledon's first league defeat of 1991.											
32	H	LEEDS		7		L	0-1	0-1		Segers	Joseph	Elkins	Barton	Blackwell*	Curle	Clarke	Sanchez	Fashanu^	Scales	Anthrobus	Bennett/Cork
	6/4		6,805	*4*	45				*Chapman 13*	*Lukic*	*Sterland*	*Whitlow*	*Batty*	*McClelland*	*Whyte*	*Strachan*	*Shutt**	*Chapman*	*McAllister*	*Speed*	*Williams*
									Ref: M Reed	Leeds have just smashed Sunderland for five, and the visitors set off in the same vein, with Gordan Strachan in scintillating form. He nutmegs Gary Elkins, and crosses for Lee Chapman to head in at the far post. Thereafter the match deteriorates into a physical battle and offside traps.											
33	A	EVERTON				W	2-1	1-1	Fashanu 29, Clarke 71	Segers	Joseph	Elkins*	Barton	Blackwell	Curle	Clarke	Sanchez^	Fashanu	Scales	McGee	Newhouse/Ryan
	10/4		*14,590*	*9*	48				*Cottee 12*	*Southall*	*McDonald**	*Hinchcliffe*	*Ratcliffe*	*Watson*	*Milligan^*	*Warzycha*	*McCall*	*Nevin*	*Cottee*	*Beagrie*	*Youds/Barlow*
									Ref: V Callow	Wimbledon win at Goodison for the first time, as Kendall's Everton are beaten for pace and power. Andy Clarke gives Neil McDonald a three-yard handicap but sprints past him to score the winner. Harford's experiment of partnering Clarke and Fashanu up front seems to profit.											
34	A	LUTON		7		W	1-0	0-0	Fashanu 79	Segers	Joseph	Elkins	Barton	Blackwell	Curle	Clarke	Sanchez	Fashanu	Gibson*	Scales	Newhouse
	13/4		***8,219***	*18*	51					*Chamberlain*	*Johnson*	*Harvey*	*Beaumont**	*Rodger*	*Dreyer*	*Elstrup*	*Preece*	*Farrell*	*Pembridge*	*Black*	*Rees*
									Ref: J Moules	A travesty. Luton's seventh game without a win is directing them to the drop, but they outplayed Wimbledon in everything but goals. A first-half brouhaha sees Fash lunge at Dave Beaumont and Luton physio Dave Galley then stamp upon Fashanu. Concussed Segers does wonders.											
35	A	ASTON VILLA		7		W	2-1	1-1	Fashanu 42, Newhouse 81	**Sullivan**	Joseph	Phelan	Ryan	Blackwell	Curle	Clarke	**Ardley***	Fashanu	McGee	Scales	Newhouse
	20/4		*17,001*	*17*	54				*Olney 35*	*Spink*	*Price*	*Gage*	*Comyn**	*Mountfield*	*Nielsen*	*Olney*	*Platt*	*Cascarino*	*Cowans*	*Ormondr'yd^*	*Penrice/Daley*
									Ref: P Wright	Josef Venglos's Villa are tumbling towards the danger zone. Harford sends out the youngest Dons side in years, with debuts for Neil Ardley and keeper Neil Sullivan, and youngsters Ryan and Newhouse also returning. Wimbledon win with ease, with Fashanu heading his 19th goal.											
36	A	SUNDERLAND				D	0-0	0-0		Segers	Joseph	Phelan	Barton	Blackwell	Curle	Clarke	Sanchez	Fashanu	Scales	McGee*	Newhouse
	23/4		*24,036*	*19*	55					*Norman*	*Owers*	*Hardyman*	*Bennett*	*Ball!*	*Pascoe*	*Bracewell*	*Armstrong*	*Hauser*	*Gabbiadini**	*Davenport^*	*Brady/Ord*
									Ref: P Harrison	Sunderland look doomed to a swift return to Division 2. Kevin Ball delivers a forearm smash to Keith Curle and is red-carded. 'The referee was conned,' insists manager Denis Smith. Wimbledon's offside-trap infuriates the Roker faithful. Barton strikes the Sunderland crossbar.											
37	H	CRYS PALACE		7		L	0-3	0-0		Segers	Joseph	Phelan	Barton*	Blackwell	Curle	McGee	Clarke	Fashanu	Sanchez	Scales	Bennett
	4/5		10,092	*3*	55				*Wright 54, 60, 72*	*Martyn*	*Humphrey*	*Bodin*	*Pardew*	*Shaw*	*Thorn*	*Salako*	*Thomas*	*Thompson**	*Wright*	*McGoldrick*	*Collymore*
									Ref: D Elleray	Wimbledon were wresting the initiative when Ian Wright demonstrated his explosive talents. He was perhaps miffed at being overlooked by England a week earlier. His second goal was best, beating Blackwell on halfway and scoring from 40 yards. Stan Collymore comes on as sub.											
38	A	SOUTHAMPTON		7		D	1-1	0-1	Fashanu 48	Segers	Joseph	Phelan	Barton	Blackwell	Curle	Scales	Gibson	Fashanu	Sanchez	Anthrobus*	Clarke
	11/5		*17,052*	*14*	56				*Case 43*	*Flowers*	*Kenna*	*Adams*	*Case*	*Ruddock**	*Gittens*	*LeTissier^*	*Horne*	*Shearer*	*McLoughlin*	*WallaceRod*	*Hall/Banger*
		Home	*Away*						Ref: A Seville	Saints are reeling from conceding six goals to basement-club Derby. They must have hoped that Jimmy Case's goal would be enough, but after the break Wimbledon swarm all over them. John Fashanu sticks out a long leg to prod home Lawrie Sanchez's cross to equalise.											
Average		7,631	*19,466*																		

BARCLAYS LEAGUE DIV 1 (CUP-TIES) Manager: Ray Harford SEASON 1990-91

Rumbelows Cup	Att		F-A	H-T	Scorers, Times, and Referees	1	2	3	4	5	6	7	8	9	10	11	subs used
2:1 A PLYMOUTH		15	0-1	0-0		Segers	Joseph	Phelan	Barton	Scales	Curle	Fairweather	Kruszynski	Gayle*	Sanchez	Cotterill	Cork
25/9	*4,506*	*2:17*			*Thomas 67*	*Wilmot*	*Brown*	*Morgan*	*Marker*	*Burrows*	*Hodges*	*Byrne*	*Fiore**	*Turner*	*Thomas*	*Salman*	*King*
					Ref: K Cooper	David Kemp's gutsy Plymouth make the Dons – lacking Fashanu – look insipid. Roger Joseph commits the error which leads to Andy Thomas's goal. Poor Steve Cotterill and John Gayle play so poorly that they look like the non-league players they once were.											
2:2 H PLYMOUTH		10	0-2	0-1		Segers	Joseph	Phelan	Barton	Blackwell	Curle	Gayle*	Kruszynski	Fashanu	Cork	Fairweath'r^	Newhouse/McGee
10/10	3,473	*2:15*			*Thomas 1, Fiore 63*	*Wilmot!*	*Brown*	*Morgan*	*Marker*	*Burrows*	*Hodges*	*Byrne**	*Fiore*	*Turner*	*Thomas*	*Salman*	*Morrison*
					Ref: M Pierce (Dons lose 0-3 on aggregate)	Wimbledon force 18 corners and unleash eight shots, whereas Plymouth create just three chances throughout, one of them converted in the first minute. Seven minutes from time keeper Rees Wilmot is sent off for a professional foul on Kruszynksi. Nicky Marker took his jersey.											

FA Cup																	
3 A ASTON VILLA		9	1-1	1-0	McGee 40	Segers	Joseph	Phelan	Barton	Blackwell	Kruszynski	McGee	Sanchez	Fashanu	Scales	Gibson	
5/1	*19,305*	*13*			*Gray 58*	*Spink*	*Price*	*Gray*	*McGrath*	*Comyn**	*Nielsen*	*Yorke*	*Platt*	*Cascarino*	*Cowans*	*Ormondr'yd^*	*Birch/Callaghan*
					Ref: A Gunn	Curle is missing, suspended. Scales is acting captain. McGee's super goal – an angled shot across Nigel Spink – puts Wimbledon ahead. Villa Park hoots with derision at Villa's puny efforts. Wimbledon would have won but for Fashanu's deflected goal wrongly disallowed for offside.											
3R H ASTON VILLA		9	1-0	0-0	Cork 119	Segers	Joseph	Phelan	Barton	Blackwell	Scales	McGee*	Kruszynski	Fashanu	Sanchez	Gibson	Cork
9/1	7,358	*13*	*aet*			*Spink*	*Price*	*Gray**	*McGrath*	*Comyn*	*Nielsen*	*Yorke*	*Platt*	*Cascarino*	*Cowans*	*Callaghan*	*Birch*
					Ref: A Gunn	Arctic win and rain suits Villa more than Wimbledon, for they are the better team second time round. Alas for them, Tony Cascarino cannot shoot straight. In the last seconds of extra time substitute Cork dives at Warren Barton's cross and the ball goes in off Paul Birch's knee.											
4 A SHREWSBURY		7	0-1	0-1		Segers	Joseph	Phelan	Barton	Blackwell	Curle	McGee*	Kruszynski^	Cork	Scales	Gibson	Bennett/Sanchez
27/1	*8,269*	*3:22*			*Shaw 38*	*Hughes*	*Summerfield*	*Lynch*	*Kelly*	*Clements*	*Blake*	*Brown*	*Askew*	*Spink*	*Shaw*	*Heathcote*	
					Ref: D Allison	3rd Div Shrewsbury lost their previous home match 2-6 against 4th Div Torquay in the Leyland-Daf Cup. Asa Hartford was promptly sacked and replaced by John Bond. Minus Fashanu, the Dons are disgraced. This is the 6th cup-tie in two years they have lost to a lower division side.											

	P	W	D	L	F	A	W	D	L	F	A	Pts
1 Arsenal**	38	15	4	0	51	10	9	9	1	23	8	83
2 Liverpool	38	14	3	2	42	13	9	4	6	35	27	76
3 Crys Palace	38	11	6	2	26	17	9	3	7	24	24	69
4 Leeds	38	12	2	5	46	23	7	5	7	19	24	64
5 Manchester C	38	12	3	4	35	25	5	8	6	29	28	62
6 Manchester U*	38	11	4	4	34	17	5	8	6	24	28	59
7 WIMBLEDON	38	8	6	5	28	22	6	8	5	25	24	56
8 Nottingham F	38	11	4	4	42	21	3	8	8	23	29	54
9 Everton	38	9	5	5	26	15	4	7	8	24	31	51
10 Tottenham	38	8	9	2	35	22	3	7	9	16	28	49
11 Chelsea	38	10	6	3	33	25	3	4	12	25	44	49
12 QP Rangers	38	8	5	6	27	22	4	5	10	17	31	46
13 Sheffield Utd	38	9	3	7	23	23	4	4	11	13	32	46
14 Southampton	38	9	6	4	33	22	3	3	13	25	47	45
15 Norwich	38	9	3	7	27	32	4	3	12	14	32	45
16 Coventry	38	10	6	3	30	16	1	5	13	12	33	44
17 Aston Villa	38	7	9	3	29	25	2	5	12	17	33	41
18 Luton	38	7	5	7	22	18	3	2	14	20	43	37
19 Sunderland	38	6	6	7	15	16	2	4	13	23	44	34
20 Derby	38	3	8	8	25	36	2	1	16	12	39	24
	760	189	103	88	629	420	88	103	189	420	629	1034

** 1 pt deducted*
*** 2 pts deducted*

Double wins: (3) QPR, Everton, Luton.
Double losses: (3: C Palace, Manchester U, Leeds.

Won from behind: (4) Nott'm F (h), Sheff U (a), Everton (a), Aston Villa (a).
Lost from in front: (4) Manchester U (h & a), C Palace (a), Spurs (a).

High spots: 4 straight wins in November and December, up to 6th place.
Unbeaten in the first 10 league games of 1991, back up to 6th.

Low spots: Failing to win any of the first 7 at home in league and cup.
Losing at Spurs2-4 in November and dropping to 16th place.
Defeat by 2nd Division teams in Rumbelows Cup and Zenith-Data Cup (the latter by Ipswich for the second season running).
Defeat by 3rd Division Shrewsbury in FA Cup.

Only the bottom 3 plus QPR won fewer home points than Wimbledon.
Only the top 3 won more away points than Wimbledon.

Player of the Year: Warren Barton.
Ever-presents: (1) Roger Joseph.
Hat-tricks: (0).
Leading scorer: John Fashanu (20).

	Lge	Sub	RC	Sub	FAC	Sub	**Lge**	RC	FAC	**Total**
Anthrobus, Steve	**3**									
Ardley, Neal	**1**									
Barton, Warren	**37**		2		3		**3**			**3**
Bennett, Michael	**1**	(5)				(1)				
Blackwell, Dean	**31**	(4)	1		3					
Clarke, Andy	**7**	(5)					**3**			**3**
Cotterill, Steve	**4**		1				**1**			**1**
Cork, Alan	**9**	(16)	1	(1)	1	(1)	**5**		1	**6**
Curle, Keith	**37**		2		1		**1**			**1**
Elkins, Gary	**10**									
Fairweather, Carlton	**3**	(2)	2				**1**			**1**
Fashanu, John	**34**	(1)	1		2		**20**			**20**
Gayle, John	**7**		2				**1**			**1**
Gibson, Terry	**18**	(1)			3		**5**			**5**
Joseph, Roger	**38**		2		3					
Kruszynski, Zbigniew	**25**	(2)	2		3		**2**			**2**
McGee, Paul	**26**	(1)		(1)	3		**6**		1	**7**
Miller, Paul	**1**									
Newhouse, Aiden	**1**	(7)		(1)			**1**			**1**
Phelan, Terry	**29**	(2)	2		3					
Ryan, Vaughan	**1**	(1)								
Sanchez, Lawrie	**21**	(8)	1		2	(1)				
Scales, John	**36**		1		3		**2**			**2**
Segers, Hans	**37**		2		3					
Sullivan, Neil	**1**									
(own-goals)							**2**			**2**
25 players used	**418**	**(55)**	**22**	**(3)**	**33**	**(3)**	**53**		**2**	**55**

BARCLAYS LEAGUE DIVISION 1 — Manager: Harford / Withe / Kinnear — SEASON 1991-92

No	Date	Opponent	Att	Pos	Pts	F-A	H-T	Scorers, Times, and Referees	1	2	3	4	5	6	7	8	9	10	11	subs used
1	A	CHELSEA			D	2-2	1-1	Fashanu 23, Earle 56	Segers	Joseph	Phelan	Barton	Scales	Fitzgerald*	Clarke	**Earle**	Fashanu	Ryan	Fairweather	Cork
	17/8		*22,574*		1			*Elliott 36, Allon 86*	*Beasant*	*Clarke*	*Boyd*	*Townsend*	*Elliott*	*Monkou*	*Le Saux*	*Hall**	*Dixon*	*Wilson^*	*Wise*	*Dickens/Allon*
								Ref : T Ward	Earle makes his debut, Fitzgerald plays central defence, and Fashanu is made captain for the day instead of Scales. Earle puts Wimbledon 2-1 up by diving to head in Carlton Fairweather's free-kick. Chelsea substitute Joe Allon, also making his debut, equalises with a first-time shot.											
2	H	WEST HAM		8	W	2-0	1-0	Earle 31, Fashanu 70	Segers	Joseph	Phelan	Barton	Scales	Fitzgerald	Clarke*	Earle	Fashanu!	Ryan	Fairweather^	Cork/Elkins
	24/8		10,081		4				*Miklosko*	*Brown*	*Thomas*	*Braecker*	*Foster*	*Parris*	*Bishop*	*Slater**	*Small*	*Rosenior*	*Allen^*	*Rush/Morley*
								Ref: R Wiseman	Promoted Hammers are the first visitors to Selhurst Park. John Fashanu holds the key to this result, booked for an ugly foul on Colin Foster, heading over Ludo Miklosko to put the Dons 2-0 up, and then being sent off for a two-footed lunge at the keeper. Earle scored from 18 yards.											
3	A	CRYS PALACE			L	2-3	1-2	Fashanu 10, Earle 87	Segers	Joseph	Phelan!	Barton	Scales	Fitzgerald*	Cork	Earle	Fashanu^	Ryan!	Fairweather	Elkins/Clarke
	27/8		*16,736*	*13*	4			*Bright 41, Gray 44p, Wright 63*	*Martyn!*	*Humphrey*	*Shaw**	*Gray*	*Sinnott*	*Thorn*	*Salako*	*Thomas*	*Bright*	*Wright*	*McGoldrick*	*Bodin*
								Ref: D Elleray	A Selhurst Park derby. Palace finished 3rd last season, but minus Ian Wright will struggle. This match saw three players expelled and Fashanu carried off with a dead-leg. Martyn was sent off for fouling Earle outside the box (Salako going into goal), and Phelan for handling on the line.											
4	A	COVENTRY		10	W	1-0	1-0	Cork 31	Segers	Joseph	Phelan	Barton*	Scales	Fitzgerald	Cork	Earle	Fashanu^	Ryan	Fairweather	Clarke/Newhouse
	31/8		*9,469*	*8*	7				*Ogrizovic*	*Borrows*	*Billing*	*Robson*	*Pearce*	*Atherton*	*McGrath*	*Furlong*	*Rosario**	*Gallacher*	*Smith*	*Ndlovu*
								Ref: R Dilkes	Terry Butcher seems ill-equipped for management, though Coventry have hit five past Luton and three past Sheffield Utd at Highfield Road. Hans Segers dashed madly up to the halfway line to topple Stewart Robson, but escaped with a caution. Cork headed in Fairweather's cross.											
5	H	MANCHESTER U			L	1-2	0-2	Fashanu 82	Segers	Joseph	Phelan	Barton	Scales	Fitzgerald*	Elkins	Cork^	Fashanu	Ryan	Fairweather	Ardley/Clarke
	3/9		13,824	*1*	7			*Blackmore 25, Pallister 43*	*Schmeichel*	*Parker*	*Donaghy*	*Bruce*	*Phelan**	*Pallister*	*Robson*	*Webb*	*McClair*	*Hughes*	*Blackmore*	*Irwin*
								Ref: M James	Armed with the European Cup-Winners' Cup United have started the new season with a bang. When Fash's header halves United's lead eight minutes from time, the Dons press strongly for an equaliser. Segers then pulls down Irwin in the box, but Bruce hits the penalty against the bar.											
6	H	LUTON		7	W	**3-0**	1-0	Clarke 25, Ryan 62, 75	Segers	Joseph	Phelan	Barton	Scales	Fitzgerald	Clarke	Elkins	Cork*	Ryan	Fairweath'r^	Newhouse/McGee
	7/9		3,231	*20*	10				*Chamberlain*	*Jackson*	*Harvey**	*McDonagh*	*Dreyer*	*Peake*	*Gray*	*Preece*	*Nogan*	*Pembridge*	*Holsgrove^*	*Telfer/Ridger*
								Ref: A Bennett	Only two teams were relegated in May, so Luton survived again. A pitifully small crowd watches this comfortable Dons victory. Vaughan Ryan – injured for most of last season – was 23 earlier in the week. He celebrates with two goals, but the atmosphere is like a reserve match.											
7	A	NOTTINGHAM F		11	L	2-4	1-2	McGee 2, Fashanu 75p	Segers	Joseph	Elkins	Barton	Scales	Fitzgerald	Gibson*	Earle	Fashanu	Kruszynski^	McGee	Cork/Clarke
	14/9		*19,707*	*10*	10			*Keane 11, 47, Black 45, Elkins 62 (og)*	*Crossley*	*Charles*	*Williams*	*Chettle*	*Tiler*	*Keane*	*Crosby*	*Gemmill*	*Clough*	*Sheringham*	*Black*	
								Ref: T Lunt	Despite taking an early lead, when Paul McGee stabbed home Fashanu's flick, Wimbledon are swept aside by Clough's rampant Forest. To concede four goals is bad enough, but three times in the last 10 minutes Hans Segers pulls off wonder saves to prevent a complete rout.											
8	A	SOUTHAMPTON			L	0-1	0-0		Segers	Joseph	Elkins*	Barton	Scales	Fitzgerald	Clarke	Earle	Fashanu	Ryan	McGee^	Cork/Newhouse
	18/9		*11,280*	*19*	10			*Cockerill 50*	*Flowers*	*Dodd*	*Adams*	*Horne**	*Gittens*	*Ruddock*	*Le Tissier^*	*Cockerill*	*Shearer*	*Dowie*	*Lee*	*Hurlock/Benali*
								Ref: M Bodenham	New boss Ian Branfoot is having a tough baptism, this being the Saints' second win of the season and their first at home. The Dons show little fight. Ruddock shackles Fashanu, Andy Clarke is always offside, Barton and McGee don't cross the ball, and Flowers has just one shot to save.											
9	H	TOTTENHAM		16	L	3-5	1-3	Fashanu 5p, Cork 60, Bennett 77	Segers	Joseph	Phelan	Barton	Scales	Fitzgerald*	Bennett	Earle	Fashanu	Ryan	McGee^	Cork/Clarke
	21/9		11,927	*3*	10			*Lineker 11, 32p, 46, 55, Samways 39*	*Walker*	*Bergsson*	*V d Hauwe*	*Nayim*	*Sedgley*	*Mabbutt*	*Stewart*	*Durie*	*Samways*	*Lineker*	*Allen**	*Hendon*
								Ref: P Vanes	Gary Lineker – in his final season in English football – scores four goals, the first Spurs player to post such a feat in the league for 14 years. No 1 was a flashing volley; No 2 a penalty after Earle tripped Nayim; No 3 a header; and No 4 a swerving shot inside the near post.											
10	A	SHEFFIELD UTD		17	D	0-0	0-0		Segers	Joseph	Phelan	Barton*	Scales	Fitzgerald	Bennett^	Earle	Fashanu	Ryan	Cork	Blackwell/Clarke
	28/9		*16,062*	*22*	11				*Kite*	*Pemberton*	*Cowan*	*Gannon*	*Gayle*	*Hill*	*Bryson*	*Hoyland**	*Agana*	*Mendonca^*	*Hodges*	*Lake/Booker*
								Ref: K Breen	Wimbledon end their run of four defeats (including Peterborough in the Rumbelows Cup) with this wretched draw against the basement club. Former Dons favourite Glyn Hodges tried to leave his mark on every Wimbledon player to come within fouling distance. A game to forget.											

No	Venue	Opponent	Pos	Res	FT	HT	Scorers, Times, and Referees	1	2	3	4	5	6	7	8	9	10	11	12
11	H	SHEFFIELD WED		W	2-1	0-0	Blackwell 50, Newhouse 70	Segers	Joseph	Phelan	Barton	Scales	Fitzgerald	Bennett*	Earle	Newhouse	Ryan^	Cork	Clarke/Blackwell
2/10		**3,121**	*5*	14			*Pearson 79*	*Woods*	*Nilsson*	*King**	*Palmer*	*Warhurst*	*Pearson*	*Wilson*	*Harkes*	*Jemson^*	*Williams*	*Worthington*	*Anderson/Francis*
							Ref: I Borrett	Wednesday's new manager, Trevor Francis, has supervised an encouraging start. The Dons' sterling display is watched by the smallest post-1945 1st Division crowd. Two headers won the match. Ryan was booked for a two-footed challenge on Danny Wilson and was swiftly subbed.											
12	H	NORWICH	7	W	3-1	1-0	Fitzgerald 3, Fashanu 73, Clarke 75	Segers	Joseph	Phelan	Barton	Scales	Fitzgerald	Bennett*	Earle	Fashanu	Newhouse^	Elkins	Clarke/Blackwell
5/10		3,531	*15*	17			*Beckford 69*	*Gunn*	*Phillips*	*Bowen*	*Butterworth*	*Blades*	*Crook**	*Gordon*	*Beckford*	*Newman*	*Fox*	*Ullathorne*	*Goss*
							Ref: R Groves	A game of two firsts. Scott Fitzgerald, playing as sweeper, scores his first goal for Wimbledon, heading home after Barton's cross was flicked on. Norwich's Darren Beckford follows suit with his first goal for the Canaries. This is Ray Harford's last game before joining Blackburn.											
13	H	QP RANGERS	11	L	0-1	0-0		Segers	Joseph*	Phelan	Barton	Blackwell	Fitzgerald	Bennett	Earle	Fashanu	Scales	Clarke	Cork
19/10		4,630	*19*	17			*Bailey 81*	*Stejskal*	*Bardsley*	*Wilson*	*Tillson*	*Peacock*	*Maddix*	*Holloway*	*Barker*	*Thompson*	*Bailey*	*Sinton*	
							Ref: J Worrall	New boss Gerry Francis enjoys this, QPR's second win under him. The Dons have fallen to Posh in the Rumbelows Cup. Dennis Bailey is unmarked. 'What a load of rubbish' burns new manager Withe's ears. After the match Fash and Phelan announce that they will quit the Dons.											
14	A	ASTON VILLA	12	L	1-2	0-2	Fashanu 78	Segers	Ardley	Phelan	Barton	Elkins	Ryan	Gibson*	Earle	Fashanu	Scales	McGee	Cork
26/10		*16,928*	*6*	17			*Olney 10, Yorke 29*	*Sealey*	*Kubicki*	*Staunton*	*Teale*	*McGrath*	*Richardson*	*Daley*	*Regis*	*Olney*	*Blake*	*Yorke*	
							Ref: R Nixon	Ron Atkinson walked out on Hillsborough for Villa Park, but is settling into winning ways. Peter Withe returns to Villa, just three weeks after leaving. Near the end Steve Staunton clears off the line and Neil Ardley blazes over the bar, but the Dons deserved nothing over 90 minutes.											
15	H	LEEDS	13	D	0-0	0-0		Segers	Elkins	Phelan	Barton	Scales	Fitzgerald	Ardley	Earle	Fashanu	Gibson	Anthrobus	
2/11		7,025	*2*	18				*Lukic*	*Sterland*	*Dorigo*	*Shutt*	*Fairclough*	*Whyte*	*Strachan*	*Wallace R**	*Chapman*	*McAllister*	*Speed*	*Newsome*
							Ref: A Gunn	Leeds were top at the start of play, but slip down a place after Withe's team earn their first league point with a backs-to-the-wall display, surrendering the midfield. Steve Anthrobus returned after a year out with a knee injury. John Scales completely dominated Lee Chapman.											
16	A	EVERTON	15	L	0-2	0-1		Segers	Elkins	Phelan	Barton	Scales	Fitzgerald	Ardley*	Earle	Fashanu	Gibson	Anthrobus^	Joseph/Clarke
16/11		*18,762*	*9*	18			*Cottee 42p, Watson 57*	*Southall*	*Jackson*	*Hinchcliffe*	*Ebbrell*	*Watson*	*Keown*	*Ward*	*Beardsley*	*Cottee*	*Harper*	*Beagrie*	
							Ref: R Shepherd	A season of fluctuating form for Everton. Dispirited Dons seemed to lose heart following Everton's first – doubtful – goal. The ball looked outside the box when Fitzgerald felled Mark Ward. Segers saved Tony Cottee's first attempt from the spot, but the referee ordered a retake.											
17	H	LIVERPOOL	16	D	0-0	0-0		Segers	Joseph	Phelan	Barton	Scales	Fitzgerald	Ardley	Earle	Cork*	Gibson	Anthrobus	Clarke
23/11		13,373	*11*	19				*Grobbelaar*	*Jones*	*Burrows*	*Nicol*	*Molby*	*Tanner*	*Saunders*	*Marsh*	*Rosenthal**	*Ablett*	*McManaman*	*Hysen*
							Ref: R Pawley	Liverpool are eight months into Graeme Souness's destructive reign. They look a drab, incohesive outfit on this showing, but they still created more chances than Wimbledon, who, despite Fashanu's absence through injury, offered little more than a stream of high balls into the box.											
18	A	MANCHESTER C	16	D	0-0	0-0		Segers	Joseph	Phelan	Barton	Scales	Fitzgerald	Ardley*	Earle	Fashanu	Gibson	Anthrobus	Elkins
30/11		*22,429*	*3*	20				*Coton*	*Hill**	*Pointon*	*Megson^*	*Curle*	*Redmond*	*White*	*Heath*	*Quinn*	*Brightwell I*	*Hughes*	*Allen/Sheron*
							Ref: K Lupton	Peter Reid is doing a sterling job at Maine Road. Peter Withe is having a wretched time, six league games without a win and knocked out of the Rumbelows, and Zenith-Data Cup by Brighton. Gibson has the Dons' only shot on target. Segers' saves from Niall Quinn earn a point.											
19	H	OLDHAM	14	W	2-1	1-0	Earle 43, 60	Segers	Joseph	Phelan	Barton	Scales	Fitzgerald	Elkins	Earle	Fashanu	Gibson	Anthrobus	
7/12		4,011	*16*	23			*Marshall 70p*	*Hallworth*	*Fleming*	*Barlow**	*Henry*	*Barrett*	*Jobson*	*Palmer*	*Marshall*	*Sharp*	*Milligan*	*Holden*	*Ritchie*
							Ref: G Ashby	Promoted Oldham are holding their own, but are sunk by Robbie Earle. His first goal, lobbing John Hallworth, was the Dons' first in over 700 minutes. But Wimbledon were fortunate. Scales fouled Sharp, who wasted a third-minute penalty, and Ian Marshall shot against both posts.											
20	A	SHEFFIELD WED	16	L	0-2	0-0		Segers	Joseph	Phelan	Barton	Scales	Fitzgerald	Elkins	Earle	Fashanu	Miller	Anthrobus*	Newhouse
21/12		*20,574*	*3*	23			*Sheridan 49p, 60*	*Woods*	*Nilsson*	*King*	*Palmer*	*Pearson*	*Warhurst*	*Bart-W'ms*	*Sheridan*	*Hirst**	*Jemson*	*Harkes*	*Williams*
							Ref: K Barratt	Paul Miller returns after a 16-month absence and spurns two inviting chances. In squally conditions, Phelan handles to give the Owls their penalty. Segers palmed out for John Sheridan's second. Scott Fitzgerald thumped a 40-yard free-kick against Chris Woods' crossbar.											
21	H	CRYS PALACE	16	D	1-1	0-0	Barton 67	Segers	Joseph	Phelan	Barton	Scales	Fitzgerald	Elkins	Earle	Fashanu	Miller*	Anthrobus	Newhouse
26/12		**15,009**	*10*	24			*Gabbiadini 51*	*Martyn*	*Southgate*	*Sinnott*	*Gray*	*Mortimer**	*Humphrey*	*Rodger*	*Osborn*	*Bright*	*Gabbiadini*	*McGoldrick*	*Whyte*
							Ref: P Don	Wimbledon inflict Boxing Day misery on their long-suffering fans, against an injury-wrecked Palace who field a crop of youngsters. Marco Gabbiadini, a £1.8 million misfit replacement for Ian Wright, scores his first league goal at Selhurst Park. Dons' best player, Barton, levels.											

No	Date		Att	Pos	Pts	F-A	H-T	Scorers, Times, and Referees	1	2	3	4	5	6	7	8	9	10	11	subs used
22	H	COVENTRY		17	D	1-1	0-1	Earle 50	Segers	Joseph	Phelan	Barton	Scales	Fitzgerald	Elkins	Earle	Fashanu	Miller*	Anthrobus	Newhouse
	28/12		3,270	*13*	25			*Robson 38*	*Ogrizovic*	*Borrows*	*Sansom*	*Robson*	*Billing*	*Atherton*	*McGrath*	*Flynn*	*Rosario*	*Gallacher*	*Smith*	*Furlong*
								Ref: B Hill	Crisis is looming. The Dons are outfought by a nondescript Coventry side who are losing to everybody else. Coventry muster half a dozen goal attempts to Wimbledon's one. Chants of 'Withe out' echo around Selhurst Park, for the Dons look destined for the drop.											
23	A	ARSENAL		17	D	1-1	1-0	Miller 19	Segers	Joseph*	Phelan	Barton	Scales	Fitzgerald	Elkins^	Earle	Fashanu	Miller	Anthrobus	Ryan/Clarke
	1/1		*26,839*	*7*	26			*Merson 46*	*Seaman*	*Dixon*	*Winterburn*	*Hillier*	*Linighan*	*Adams*	*Rocastle*	*Wright**	*Smith*	*Merson*	*Carter*	*Campbell*
								Ref: D Axcell	This New Year's match was anything but festive. It snarled from start to finish. It was against Arsenal that Paul Miller was injured 18 months earlier, so his was a joyous moment, tapping in after Nigel Winterburn rolled a back-pass to him. Paul Merson always scores against the Dons.											
24	A	WEST HAM		17	D	1-1	0-0	Sanchez 52	Segers	McGee	Phelan	Barton	Scales	Fitzgerald	Newhouse*	Earle	Fashanu	Sanchez	Anthrobus	Clarke
	11/1		*18,485*	*21*	27			*Morley 89*	*Miklosko*	*Braecker*	*Dicks*	*Gale*	*Foster*	*Thomas**	*Bishop*	*McAvennie*	*Brown*	*Kean^*	*Slater*	*Morley/Small*
								Ref: R Gifford	Wimbledon's fifth successive 1-1 draw in league and cup. They lead through Sanchez's header when, with a minute to go, Barton gets caught in possession and hacks down Ian Bishop. Julian Dicks' penalty is saved by Segers, but Trevor Morley heads in. The Hammers will finish last.											
25	H	CHELSEA		17	L	1-2	0-1	Earle 76	Segers	Ryan	**McAllister**	Barton	Scales	Fitzgerald	Miller	Earle	Fashanu	Sanchez	Clarke	
	18/1		8,413	*8*	27			*Townsend 41, Allen 72*	*Hitchcock*	*Hall*	*Boyd*	*Jones*	*Elliott*	*Cundy*	*Stuart*	*Townsend*	*Dixon*	*Allen*	*Wise*	
								Ref: C Wilkes	The Dons were dumped from the FA Cup in midweek and Peter Withe faces the axe after 104 days in charge. Ian Porterfield's Chelsea score first when Segers punches out to Townsend. The board meet on Monday morning, when new boss Joe Kinnear declares 'it's back to basics'.											
26	A	QP RANGERS		18	D	1-1	0-1	Fashanu 48p	Segers	Cork	Phelan	Barton	Scales	Ryan	Miller*	Earle	Fashanu	Sanchez	McAllister	Clarke
	1/2		*9,149*	*13*	28			*Penrice 18*	*Stejskal*	*Ready*	*Wilson*	*Wilkins*	*Peacock*	*Tillson*	*Holloway*	*Barker**	*Bailey*	*Penrice*	*Sinton*	*Wegerle*
								Ref: D Elleray	The new regime of Kinnear and Burton means business. Crunching tackles – especially from Ryan and Fashanu on Ray Wilkins – enrage QPR fans. Segers' clearance from Ryan's back-pass hit Gary Penrice and flew into goal. Fash levelled from the spot after Miller had been fouled.											
27	H	ASTON VILLA		18	W	2-0	1-0	Fashanu 24, Phelan 87	Segers	Cork	Phelan	Barton	Scales	McAllister	Miller	Earle	Fashanu	Sanchez*	McGee^	Ryan/Clarke
	8/2		5,534	*8*	31				*Sealey*	*Ehiogu*	*Small**	*Teale*	*McGrath*	*Richardson*	*Daley*	*Carruthers*	*Regis*	*Parker*	*Staunton*	*Froggatt*
								Ref: R Bigger	Joe Kinnear receives a rapturous reception as he takes his place in the dugout, and at the final whistle Sam Hammam sends him out to milk the applause. John Fashanu's 12th goal of the season was capped by Terry Phelan's first ever league strike.Warren Barton snuffed out Tony Daley.											
28	H	MANCHESTER C		16	W	2-1	2-0	Fashanu 2, Earle 41	Segers	Cork	Phelan	Barton	Scales	McAllister	Miller	Earle	Fashanu	Ryan	McGee	
	22/2		5,802	*3*	34			*Sheron 56*	*Coton*	*Hill*	*Pointon*	*Reid*	*Curle*	*Redmond**	*White*	*Brightwell I^*	*Quinn*	*McMahon*	*Heath*	*Brightwell D/Sheron*
								Ref: G Courtney	Peter Reid's City are aiming for a UEFA Cup place, but they are gunned down by a Dons outfit that could have been four goals up at the break. Alan Cork, shunned by Withe, is immediately restored by Kinnear – in the No 2 shirt! Fashanu pole-axes Neil Pointon, but escapes dismissal.											
29	A	NOTTS CO			D	1-1	0-1	Fashanu 74p	Segers	Joseph*	Phelan	Barton	Scales	McAllister^	Miller	Earle	Fashanu	Ardley	McGee	Ryan/Clarke
	25/2		***6,198***		35			*Craig Short 20*	*Cherry*	*Palmer*	*Dryden*	*Short Craig*	*Short Chris*	*Harding*	*Thomas*	*Williams*	*Slawson*	*Bartlett*	*Johnson**	*Agana*
								Ref: S Lodge	John Fashanu has signed a new 2½ year contract and celebrates with a leveller from the spot after Neil Ardley was fouled by Andy Williams. Fash later clashed heads with Craig Short. Notts keeper Steve Cherry urgently summoned the physio, for Fashanu had swallowed his tongue.											
30	A	OLDHAM		12	W	1-0	1-0	McGee 35	Segers	Cork	Phelan	Barton	Scales	Fitzgerald	Miller	Earle	Fashanu*	Sanchez	McGee^	Clarke/Ryan
	29/2		*12,166*	*13*	38				*Hallworth*	*Fleming*	*Barlow*	*Henry*	*Jobson*	*Marshall*	*Milligan*	*Bernard*	*Sharp*	*McDonald*	*Holden**	*Adams*
								Ref: J Lloyd	For the second time this season Wimbledon 'steal' victory over Oldham. Paul McGee scores after an interchange with Cork, and thereafter the Dons shut up shop and permit Hans Segers to make a hero of himself. Five unbeaten games under Joe Kinnear takes Wimbledon up to 12th.											
31	H	NOTTS CO		11	W	2-0	1-0	Fashanu 40, Earle 80	Segers	Cork*	Phelan	Barton	Scales	Fitzgerald	Miller	Earle	Fashanu	Sanchez	McGee	Clarke
	7/3		4,196		41				*Cherry*	*Palmer*	*Dryden*	*McClelland*	*Short Chris*	*Draper*	*Williams*	*Harding*	*Slawson**	*Thomas^*	*Johnson*	*Lund/Bartlett*
								Ref: M Bodenham	Neil Warnock's County are sliding back into Division 2, and are in the midst of a 15-game sequence without a win. Fashanu's chipped opener was either genius or fluke. Either way, it extends the Dons' good run. Earle's goal was set up by Sanchez. Wimbledon are now in the top half.											

No	Venue / Date	Opponent / Att	Pos	Pts	Res	F-A	H-T	Scorers, Times, and Referees	1	2	3	4	5	6	7	8	9	10	11	12 sub used
32	H	EVERTON	11		D	0-0	0-0		Segers	Clarke	Phelan	Barton	Scales	Fitzgerald	Miller	Earle	Fashanu	Sanchez	McGee	**Hayes**
	10/3	3,569	*7*	42					*Southall*	*Jackson*	*Ablett*	*Ebbrell*	*Ratcliffe*	*Keown*	*Ward*	*Beardsley*	*Johnston**	*Warzycha^*	*Hinchcliffe*	*Beagrie/Harper*
								Ref: D Gallagher	Seven games without defeat for both Wimbledon and Everton, so this draw was always on the cards. Howard Kendall had such respect for Joe Kinnear's record that he shamelessly packed his defence. What action there was came early. For the last hour no chances fell to either team.											
33	A	LEEDS	12		L	**1-5**	0-3	Miller 51 *[Cantona 74]*	Segers	Hayes	Phelan	Barton	Scales	Fitzgerald	Miller	Earle	Fashanu*	Sanchez	McGee	Clarke
	14/3	*26,760*	*1*	42				*Chapman 23, 27, 80, Wallace 31,*	*Lukic*	*Newsome*	*Cantona*	*Batty*	*Fairclough*	*Whyte*	*Strachan**	*Wallace*	*Chapman*	*McAllister*	*Speed*	*Shutt*
								Ref: D Gallagher	Leeds will snatch the title from Manchester United, but first they must recover from a 1-4 midweek mauling by QPR. They truly stuffed the Dons. Lee Chapman scored a simple hat-trick, each of his goals poked from inside the six-yard box. Eric Cantona wears No 3 and scores No 5.											
34	A	MANCHESTER U	14		D	0-0	0-0		Segers	Ardley	Phelan	Barton	Scales	Fitzgerald	Miller	Earle	Newhouse*	Sanchez	McGee	Clarke
	21/3	***45,428***	*2*	43					*Schmeichel*	*Blackmore*	*Irwin*	*Bruce*	*Webb**	*Pallister*	*Kanchelskis*	*Ince*	*McClair*	*Hughes*	*Giggs*	*Sharpe*
								Ref: M Peck	The Dons do Leeds a mighty favour, in this second table-topping tussle. This is only the second occasion United have failed to score at Old Trafford all season, though Wimbledon rode their luck in a howling gale. Kanchelskis fluffed a good chance, striking an upright.											
35	H	ARSENAL	16		L	1-3	0-2	Earle 60	Segers	Newhouse*	Phelan	Barton	Scales	Fitzgerald	Miller	Earle	Fashanu	Sanchez	Clarke	Ryan
	28/3	11,299	*5*	43				*Parlour 1, Wright 7, Campbell 64*	*Seaman*	*Dixon*	*Winterburn*	*Hillier*	*Bould*	*O'Leary*	*Parlour*	*Wright*	*Campbell*	*Merson**	*Groves^*	*Lydersen/Limpar*
								Ref: R Lewis	Arsenal are in the midst of a 17-game unbeaten run which will extend to the end of the season. Wimbledon were outclassed, though Kinnear – in public – insisted that Arsenal's double-quick openers were both offside. In the first minute the Dons back four had rushed out at a free-kick.											
36	H	NOTTINGHAM F			W	**3-0**	2-0	Earle 30, Fashanu 35, 71	Segers	Ryan	Phelan*	Barton	Scales	Fitzgerald	Miller	Earle	Fashanu	Sanchez	**Dobbs^**	McAllister/Clarke
	2/4	3,542	*12*	46					*Marriot*	*Charles*	*Chettle*	*Walker*	*Wassal*	*Keane*	*Black*	*Gemmill*	*Clough*	*Glover*	*Woan*	*Laws*
								Ref: M Bailey	Joe Kinnear got it right, free-flowing football stretching Forest to breaking point. Robbie Earle had four good chances before he scored. John Fashanu added a header and a volley. Gerald Dobbs made his happy debut in this, Wimbledon's biggest and most handsome win of the season.											
37	A	LUTON	14		L	1-2	1-1	Fashanu 6	Segers	Ryan	Phelan	Barton	Scales	Fitzgerald	Miller	Earle	Fashanu	Sanchez*	Dobbs	Clarke
	4/4	*7,754*	*20*	46				*Varadi 27, Preece 64*	*Chamberlain*	*James*	*Harvey*	*Kamara*	*Dreyer*	*Peake*	*Varadi*	*Stein*	*Harford*	*Pembridge*	*Preece*	
								Ref: B Hill	Wimbledon were turning the screw when Barton let a loose ball bounce over his head for Preece to snatch the winner. Anarchy ruled at times in this fierce contest. John Fashanu deprived his marker – John Dreyer – of two teeth. This win will not save Luton from the drop.											
38	A	LIVERPOOL			W	3-2	1-2	Sanchez 35, Clarke 65, Fashanu 72p	Segers	Clarke	Phelan	Barton	Scales	McAllister*	Miller	Earle	Fashanu	Sanchez	McGee	Fitzgerald
	8/4	*26,134*	*5*	49				*Thomas 6, Rosenthal 44*	*Grobbelaar*	*Jones*	*Venison*	*Tanner*	*Whelan*	*Rosenthal**	*Saunders*	*Houghton*	*Walters*	*Molby*	*Thomas*	*Marsh*
								Ref: J Key	Graeme Souness has had a heart by-pass and Ronnie Moran takes charge. This result could have done neither of them any good, as the Dons come from behind. With a coming FA Cup semi-final replay Pool left out seven regulars. Rob Jones trips Fash for a fiercely contested penalty.											
39	A	TOTTENHAM	14		L	2-3	1-2	Sanchez 1, Earle 83	Segers	Clarke*	Phelan	Barton	Scales	Joseph	Miller	Earle	Fashanu	Sanchez	McGee^	Fitzgerald/Dobbs
	18/4	*23,934*	*12*	49				*Lineker 5, 11, Hendry 76*	*Walker*	*V d Hauwe*	*Gray*	*Gray**	*Cundy*	*Mabbutt*	*Stewart*	*Walsh^*	*Nayim*	*Lineker*	*Allen*	*Hendry/Sedgley*
								Ref: T Fitzharris	For the sixth time this season Wimbledon take the lead but lose. This was a tale of two strikers. Gary Lineker signs off from English football with two instinctive headers – six goals against the Dons this season. Andy Clarke spurns five chances, forcing Hans Segers to join the attack.											
40	H	SOUTHAMPTON	16		L	0-1	0-1		Sullivan	Clarke	Phelan	Barton	Scales	McAllister	Miller*	Earle	Fashanu	Sanchez	Joseph	Newhouse
	20/4	4,025	*17*	49				*Hall 24*	*Flowers*	*Kenna*	*Rideout*	*Horne*	*Hall*	*Moore*	*Le Tissier**	*Cockerill*	*Shearer*	*Hurlock*	*Benali*	*Dowie*
								Ref: J Rushton	The Dons' worst performance under Kinnear guarantees the Saints top-flight football next season. The only goal was scored when Moore flicked on to Le Tissier, who found Richard Hall in space. Wimbledon looked drained by the end, unable to lay siege to Tim Flowers' goal.											
41	A	NORWICH	17		D	1-1	0-1	Elkins 52	Segers	Joseph	Elkins	Barton	Scales*	McAllister	Miller	Earle	Fashanu	Fitzgerald	Clarke	**Castledine**
	25/4	*11,061*	*18*	50				*Fleck 20*	*Walton*	*Culverhouse*	*Bowen*	*Blades*	*Polston*	*Goss*	*Fox*	*Fleck*	*Newman*	*Beckford**	*Phillips*	*Woodthorpe*
								Ref: I Hemley	Gary Elkins' first goal for Wimbledon – receiving a short free-kick and shooting – gives him something to remember from this tedious game. The lads had told him to 'have a go', despite his record in practice games. Segers had saved Rob Newman's header, but Robert Fleck pounced.											
42	H	SHEFFIELD UTD	13		W	**3-0**	3-0	Fashanu 18, Earle 21, 36	Segers	Joseph	Elkins	Barton	Fitzgerald	McAllister	Miller	Earle	Fashanu	Sanchez*	Clarke^	Castledine/Dobbs
	2/5	8,768	*9*	53					*Day*	*Pemberton*	*Cowan*	*Gannon*	*Gayle*	*Beesley*	*Whitehouse*	*Rogers*	*Davison**	*Deane*	*Bradshaw^*	*Bryson/Reed*
	Home	*Away*						Ref: K Redfearn	Robbie Earle's wonderful first season is capped by two more headers, though he is sad to hear that his former club – Port Vale – have been relegated. In August Ray Harford had set him a target of 15 goals. Earle would have had 16 and a hat-trick, but Day saved and Fash swooped.											
Average	6,905	*18,497*																		

Rumbelows Cup	Att	F-A	H-T	Scorers, Times, and Referees	1	2	3	4	5	6	7	8	9	10	11	subs used
2:1 H PETERBOROUGH	16 L	1-2	1-2	McGee 24	Segers	Joseph	Phelan	Barton	Scales	Fitzgerald*	Bennett	Earle	Fashanu	Ryan	McGee^	Cork/Clarke
24/9	2,081 *3:16*			*Charlery 28, Sterling 32*	*Barber*	*Luke*	*Butterworth*	*Halsall*	*Robinson*	*Welsh*	*Sterling*	*Cooper*	*Gavin*	*Charlery**	*Kimble*	*Riley*
				Ref: P Foakes	Despite Paul McGee's half-volley which made it 1-0, Chris Turner's Peterborough are not in the slightest overawed. They should be: they have not won in six games in Division 3. The deficit is turned around before half-time. 'The worst I have seen us play,' complains Ray Harford.											
2:2 A PETERBOROUGH	7 D	2-2	0-1	Clark 57, Fashanu 71p	Segers	Joseph	Phelan	Barton*	Scales	Fitzgerald	Elkins^	Earle	Fashanu	Blackwell	Clarke	Cork/Bennett
8/10	*5,939 3:19*			*Kimble 35, Riley 46*	*Barber*	*Luke*	*Butterworth*	*Halsall*	*Robinson*	*Welsh*	*Sterling*	*Cooper*	*Riley*	*Charlery**	*Kimble^*	*Ebdon/Gavin*
				Ref: K Morton (Dons lose 3-4 on aggregate)	Peter Withe's first game in charge is not a happy one. He abandons the sweeper system for 4-4-2. Worrell Sterling's pace tormented the Dons. Future Don Alan Kimble hit the post before he scored. Andy Clarke was bundled down by Mick Halsall for Fashanu's penalty.											

FA Cup																
3 A BRISTOL CITY	17 D	1-1	1-0	Fashanu 38	Segers	McGee	Phelan	Barton	Scales	Fitzgerald	Newhouse	Earle	Fashanu	Sanchez	Anthrobus	
4/1	*12,679 2:13*			*Barton 88 (og)*	*Leaning*	*Llewellyn**	*Scott*	*May*	*Bryant*	*Aizlewood*	*Osman*	*Rennie*	*Allison*	*Taylor*	*Gavin*	*Bent*
				Ref: K Cooper	The Dons are coasting. Fashanu has toe-poked a goal, and it looks like the two free headers that Steve Anthrobus directed straight at the keeper won't be costly. Then City win three quick corners. From the third Segers punches out and Warren Barton somehow heads back in.											
3R H BRISTOL CITY	17 L	0-1	0-1		Segers	McGee	Phelan	Barton	Scales	Fitzgerald	Newhouse	Earle	Fashanu	Sanchez	Anthrobus*	Clarke
14/1	3,747 *2:14*			*May 10*	*Leaning*	*Caesar*	*Scott*	*Osman*	*Bryant*	*Aizlewood*	*Bent**	*May*	*Morgan*	*Edwards*	*Gavin*	*Taylor*
				Ref: K Cooper	Oh dear. With Brighton eliminating the Dons from the Zenith-Data Cup, the Dons are once again out of all the cups. Lower division clubs do the damage. Andy May's 25-yard shot creeps past Segers. All the Dons could offer was high balls. It is one win in 16 under Peter Withe.											

		Home					Away					
	P	W	D	L	F	A	W	D	L	F	A	Pts
1 Leeds	42	13	8	0	38	13	9	8	4	36	24	82
2 Manchester U	42	12	7	2	34	13	9	8	4	29	20	78
3 Sheffield Wed	42	13	5	3	39	24	8	7	6	23	25	75
4 Arsenal	42	12	7	2	51	22	7	8	6	30	24	72
5 Manchester C	42	13	4	4	32	14	7	6	8	29	34	70
6 Liverpool	42	13	5	3	34	17	3	11	7	13	23	64
7 Aston Villa	42	13	3	5	31	16	4	6	11	17	28	60
8 Nottingam F	42	10	7	4	36	27	6	4	11	24	31	59
9 Sheffield Utd	42	9	6	6	29	23	7	3	11	36	40	57
10 Crys Palace	42	7	8	6	24	25	7	7	7	29	36	57
11 QP Rangers	42	6	10	5	25	21	6	8	7	23	26	54
12 Everton	42	8	8	5	28	19	5	6	10	24	32	53
13 WIMBLEDON	42	10	5	6	32	20	3	9	9	21	33	53
14 Chelsea	42	7	8	6	31	30	6	6	9	19	30	53
15 Tottenham	42	7	3	11	33	35	8	4	9	25	28	52
16 Southampton	42	7	5	9	17	28	7	5	9	22	27	52
17 Oldham	42	11	5	5	46	36	3	4	14	17	31	51
18 Norwich	42	8	6	7	29	28	3	6	12	18	35	45
19 Coventry	42	6	7	8	18	15	5	4	12	17	29	44
20 Luton	42	10	7	4	25	17	0	5	16	13	54	42
21 Notts Co	42	7	5	9	24	29	3	5	13	16	33	40
22 West Ham	42	6	6	9	22	24	3	5	13	15	35	38
	924	208	135	119	678	496	119	135	208	496	678	1251

Odds & ends

Double wins: (1) Oldham.

Double losses: (2) Southampton, Tottenham.

Won from behind: (1) Liverpool (a).

Lost from in front: (5) Spurs (h & a), Palace (a), Nott'm F (a), Luton (a).

High spots: 7 unbeaten games when Joe Kinnear took charge, up to 11th.

Low spots: 1 win in 17 games under Peter Withe, down from 7th to 17th in the league and knocked out of all three cups at the first stage by lower division sides.

Wimbledon failed to score more than 3 goals in any match.

5 times the Dons lost matches in which they led. Untypical Wimbledon.

The Dons played 5 consecutive 1-1 draws over Christmas and New Year.

The Dons enjoyed no own-goals this season in any competition.

Player of the Year: Robbie Earle.

Ever-presents: (1) Warren Barton.

Hat-tricks: (0).

Leading scorer: John Fashanu (20).

	Appearances						Goals			
	Lge	Sub	RC	Sub	FAC	Sub	**Lge**	RC	FAC	**Total**
Anthrobus, Steve	**10**				2					
Ardley, Neal	**7**	(1)								
Barton, Warren	**42**		2		2		**1**			**1**
Bennett, Michael	**5**		1	(1)			**1**			**1**
Blackwell, Dean	**1**	(3)	1				**1**			**1**
Castledine, Stewart		(2)								
Clarke, Andy	**13**	(21)	1	(1)		(1)	**3**	1		**4**
Cork, Alan	**12**	(7)		(2)			**2**			**2**
Dobbs, Gerald	**2**	(2)								
Earle, Robbie	**40**		2		2		**14**			**14**
Elkins, Gary	**15**	(3)	1				**1**			**1**
Fairweather, Carlton	**6**									
Fashanu, John	**38**		2		2		**18**	1	1	**20**
Fitzgerald, Scott	**34**	(2)	2		2		**1**			**1**
Gibson, Terry	**7**									
Hayes, Martin	**1**	(1)								
Joseph, Roger	**25**	(1)	2							
Kruszynski, Zbigniew	**1**									
McAllister, Brian	**9**	(1)								
McGee, Paul	**15**	(1)	1		2		**2**	1		**3**
Miller, Paul	**22**						**2**			**2**
Newhouse, Aiden	**5**	(7)			2		**1**			**1**
Phelan, Terry	**37**		2		2		**1**			**1**
Ryan, Vaughan	**16**	(5)	1				**2**			**2**
Sanchez, Lawrie	**16**				2		**3**			**3**
Scales, John	**41**		2		2					
Segers, Hans	**41**		2		2					
Sullivan, Neil	**1**									
28 players used	**462**	**57**	**22**	**(4)**	**22**	**(1)**	**53**	**3**	**1**	**57**

No	Date	Att	Pos	Pts	F-A	H-T	Scorers, Times, and Referees	1	2	3	4	5	6	7	8	9	10	11	subs used
1	A LEEDS			L	1-2	0-1	Barton 76	Segers	Joseph	Elkins	Barton	Scales*	Fitzgerald	Miller	Earle	**Holdsworth**	Sanchez	Clarke^	Blackwell/Dobbs
	15/8	25,795		–			Chapman 14, 86	Lukic	Newsome*	Dorigo	Batty^	Fairclough	Whyte	Cantona	Wallace	Chapman	McAllister	Speed	Strachan/Hodge
							Ref: G Ashby	A date with the champs, but Fashanu is out with a torn hamstring and Scales limps off after half-time. Leeds' first goal is the result of the new back-pass rule. Joseph dithers in possession and Chapman swoops. Barton's 35-yarder loops over John Lukic. Then Chapman strikes again.											
2	H IPSWICH			L	0-1	0-1		Segers	Joseph*	Elkins	Barton	Blackwell	Fitzgerald	Miller	Earle	Holdsworth	Sanchez	**Berry^**	Dobbs/Clarke
	18/8	4,964		–			Johnson 38	Forrest	Whelan	Thompson	Stockwell	Wark	Linighan	Williams	Goddard	Johnson	Dozzell	Kiwomya*	Milton
							Ref: R Hart	Promoted Ipswich settle quickly in the top flight. Mick Stockwell's low cross was swept home by Gavin Johnson. The Dons had almost all the play after half-time, but without Fashanu, Holdsworth had to forage alone. Ipswich boss Mick McGiven thought the Dons unlucky.											
3	H COVENTRY		22	L	1-2	0-1	Holdsworth 73	Segers	Joseph	Elkins	Barton	Blackwell	Fitzgerald*	Dobbs^	Earle	Holdsworth	Sanchez	Anthrobus	Clarke/Miller
	22/8	3,759	1	–			Gynn 13, Rosario 46	Ogrizovic	Fleming	Sansom	Robson	Pearce	Atherton	Gynn*	Hurst	Rosario	Williams^	Smith	McGrath/Ndlovu
							Ref: I Borrett	Coventry missed the drop by one place, but go top after winning their first three. The killer-blow for Wimbledon comes 25 seconds into the second half when Segers lets Rosario's half-hit shot through his legs. Holdsworth's far-post shot brings his first Premier goal.											
4	A SHEFFIELD UTD			D	2-2	1-0	Barton 34, Holdsworth 74	Segers	Miller	McAllister	Barton	Blackwell	Fitzgerald	Dobbs*	Earle	Holdsworth^	Sanchez	Anthrobus	Clarke/Elkins
	25/8	15,463	12	1			Beesley 48, Hodges 68	Tracey	Gage	Cowan	Hartfield	Gayle	Beesley	Bryson*	Lake	Cork	Deane	Hodges	Bradshaw
							Ref: K Barrett	At last Lady Fortune smiles on Wimbledon, as Holdsworth's floater flies over Simon Tracey's head. Barton had earlier hit a free-kick through the wall after Mike Lake had fouled Anthrobus. Alan Cork played for United. Earlier in the week Terry Phelan signed for Manchester City.											
5	A EVERTON		21	D	0-0	0-0		Segers	Miller	McAllister	Barton	Blackwell	Fitzgerald	Dobbs*	Earle	Holdsworth	Sanchez	Anthrobus	Clarke
	29/8	18,118	4	2				Southall	Harper	Hinchcliffe	Ebbrell	Watson	Ablett	Warzycha	Beardsley	Rideout*	Horne	Ward^	Johnston/Beagrie
							Ref: H King	Everton have yet to lose, and are twice denied by the woodwork. First, Robert Warzycka finds himself with only Segers to beat, but hits the underside of the bar. Second, substitute Peter Beagrie's inswinging corner strikes the base of the near post. The Dons seldom threaten Southall.											
6	H MANCHESTER C			L	0-1	0-0		Segers	Anthrobus	McAllister	Barton	Blackwell	Fitzgerald	Miller*	Earle	Fashanu	Sanchez	Holdsworth	Clarke
	1/9	4,714	11	2			White 49	Coton	Brightwell	Phelan	Reid*	Curle	Vonk	White	Flitcroft	Quinn	Simpson	Holden	McMahon
							Ref: M Reed	Three home fixtures; three home defeats. That is Wimbledon's sorry record. The only ray of light in this sad game was City player-manager Peter Reid. It was Reid who sent David White in for the only goal. Fashanu returned to the Dons side, but was well shackled by Curle.											
7	H ARSENAL		19	W	3-2	1-1	Sanchez 39, Fashanu 80, Earle 86	Segers	Gibson	McAllister*	Barton	Blackwell	Fitzgerald	Holdsworth	Earle	Fashanu	Sanchez	Clarke^	Ardley/Anthrobus
	5/9	12,906	7	5			Wright 34, 82	Seaman	Dixon	Winterburn	Pates	Bould	Adams*	Jensen^	Wright	Campbell	Merson	Parlour	Smith/O'Leary
							Ref: K Burge	Three goals in the last 10 minutes capped this stirring match, which was marred by a second-half flare up among players. Star of the show was Earle, who set up Fashanu with a 30-yard pass, then fired the winner. In between, Segers spilled Winterburn's cross onto Ian Wright's head.											
8	A IPSWICH		20	L	1-2	1-1	Holdsworth 27	Segers	Barton	Joseph*	Jones	Blackwell	Scales	Gibson^	Earle	Fashanu	Holdsworth	Clarke	Fitzgerald/Miller
	12/9	13,333	7	5			Stockwell 15, 49	Forrest	Whelan	Thompson	Stockwell	Wark	Linighan	Williams	Pennyfather	Johnson	Dozzell	Yallop	
							Ref: S Lodge	The computer pairs these sides twice in eight games. Ipswich are still undefeated, beating the Dons twice but drawing with everyone else. Fash missed three sitters, Clarke hit the bar, and Jones – back from Chelsea – set about Jason Dozzell. Hans Segers joined the attack at a corner.											
9	H BLACKBURN		21	D	1-1	1-1	Ardley 24	Segers	Barton	Elkins	Jones!	Scales	Blackwell*	Ardley	Earle	Fashanu	Holdsworth	Clarke	Fitzgerald
	19/9	6,117	2	6			Shearer 33	Mimms	May	Dobson!	Sherwood	Henrdy	Moran	Ripley*	Atkins	Shearer	Newell!	Wright	Hill
							Ref: M Bodenham	Newly-promoted Blackburn had just lost for the first time. Both managers agree that the ref has a stinker and should not have expelled Jones (for verbal abuse of Moran) or Tony Dobson (for his first tackle). Newell's crime was handball. Shearer swivelled and shot for his ninth goal.											
10	A LIVERPOOL			W	3-2	2-2	Fashanu 12, Earle 27, 76	Segers	Barton	**Skinner**	Jones	Scales	Fitzgerald	Ardley	Earle	Fashanu	Holdsworth*	Clarke	Miller/Sanchez
	26/9	29,574	19	9			Molby 35p, McManaman 39	Grobbelaar	Marsh	Burrows	Piechnik	Redknapp	Wright	Rosenthal	McManaman	Hutchinson	Molby	Walters*	Kozma
							Ref: R Milford	The season is not two months old, but Liverpool have already lost six times, and find themselves 19th in the league. Magnificent Robbie Earle scores two and sets up one for Fash. Rosenthal's swan-dive won the penalty. Then Rosenthal's scoop hits the bar for McManaman to level.											

No	H/A, Date	Opponent, Att	Pos	Res, Pts	F-A	H-T	Scorers, Times, Referees	1	2	3	4	5	6	7	8	9	10	11	subs used
11	H	ASTON VILLA	21	L	2-3	1-2	Miller 34, Clarke 90	Segers	Barton	Elkins	Miller	Scales	Fitzgerald	Ardley	Earle	Fashanu	Sanchez	Clarke	Newhouse
	3/10	6,849	5	9			*Saunders 5, 29, Atkinson 77*	*Spink*	*Barton*	*Staunton*	*Teale*	*McGrath*	*Richardson*	*Houghton*	*Parker*	*Saunders*	*Atkinson*	*Froggatt**	*Yorke*
							Ref: S Lodge	Andy Clarke is nicknamed 'jigsaw', because every time he gets into the box he goes to pieces. He and Newhouse miss chances in this match, best remembered for Dalian Atkinson's remarkable goal, when he jinked from his own half, skirted three challenges, and chipped Hans Segers.											
12	A	SOUTHAMPTON	20	D	2-2	0-0	Cotterill 50, 67	Sullivan	Barton	Joseph	Jones	**McLeary**	Fitzgerald	Miller	Earle	Fashanu	Cotterill	Clarke	
	17/10	***11,221***	*18*	10			*Dowie 58, Groves 85*	*Flowers*	*Dodd*	*Benali**	*Hurlock*	*Monkou*	*Wood*	*Groves*	*Cockerill*	*Moody^*	*Dowie*	*Adams*	*Maddison/Powell*
							Ref: K Barratt	Two poor sides produce a dreadful first half, a sprightly second. On-loan players decide the match. Steve Cotterill returns from Brighton, for whom he scored four times, and bags two. Dons' on-loan defender Alan McLeary was blamed for Saints' goals, deflecting Groves' equaliser.											
13	H	TOTTENHAM		D	1-1	1-0	Gibson 38	Segers	Barton	Joseph	Jones	McLeary	Fitzgerald	Gibson*	Earle	Fashanu	Cotterill	Clarke^	Holdsw'th/McAllister
	25/10	8,615	*18*	11			*Barmby 47*	*Walker**	*Edinburgh*	*Austin*	*Samways*	*Mabbutt*	*Ruddock*	*Sedgley*	*Durie^*	*Nayim*	*Sheringham*	*Allen*	*Thorstvedt/Barmby*
							Ref: A Gunn	Ailing Spurs have won just twice. This Sunday match, shown live on Sky, saw the Dons dominate after half-time. Controversy attended the Dons' goal. In the build-up Fashanu collided with keeper Ian Walker, who had to go off. Teddy Sheringham crossed for Nick Barmby's header.											
14	A	MANCHESTER U	18	W	1-0	0-0	Sanchez 79	Segers	Barton	Joseph	Jones	McLeary	McAllister	Gibson	Earle	Holdsworth	Sanchez	Dobbs*	Clarke
	31/10	*32,622*	*7*	14				*Schmeichel*	*Parker*	*Blackmore*	*Bruce*	*Ferguson*	*Pallister*	*Kanchelskis**	*Ince*	*McClair*	*Hughes*	*Giggs*	*Robson*
							Ref: K Morton	Out of the UEFA Cup and Coca-Cola Cup, United have drawn their last five in the league. This is Sanchez's 500th league match, and he turns in Gibson's free-kick at the near post. Sanchez played in the last win at Old Trafford. The Dons have beaten Arsenal, Liverpool and Man U.											
15	H	QP RANGERS	20	L	0-2	0-2		Segers	Barton	Joseph	Jones	McLeary	McAllister	Gibson*	Earle	Holdsworth	Sanchez^	Dobbs	Clarke/Cotterill
	7/11	6,671	*5*	14			*Allen 23, Wilkins 41*	*Roberts*	*Bardsley*	*Wilson*	*Wilkins*	*Peacock*	*McDonald*	*Impey*	*Holloway*	*Ferdinand*	*Allen*	*Sinton*	
							Ref: P Don	Gerry Francis has got Rangers buzzing. Kinnear offers no excuses after this defeat, though QPR's first goal saw Bradley Allen's effort flick off McAllister and over Segers. No 2 saw Segers miscue his clearance, whereupon Ray Wilkins chipped the ball over the stranded goalkeeper.											
16	A	MIDDLESBRO	20	L	0-2	0-0		Segers	Barton	Joseph	Jones	Scales	McAllister	Gibson	Earle	Holdsworth	Dobbs*	McGee^	Cotterill/Miller
	21/11	*14,524*	*11*	14			*Hendrie 49, Morris 56*	*Pears*	*Fleming*	*Phillips**	*Gittens*	*Whyte*	*Mustoe*	*Falconer*	*Pollock^*	*Wilkinson*	*Hendrie*	*Morris*	*Proctor/Kavanagh*
							Ref: J Worrall	Promoted Boro have started the season better than they will end it. The Dons are out of the Coca-Cola Cup, and suffer further misfortune. John Hendrie's goal was disallowed for offside, but the Boro bench protested that the injured Joseph was on the pitch, not off it, and the ref agreed.											
17	H	SHEFFIELD WED	20	D	1-1	0-1	Jones 89p	Segers	Barton	Joseph	Jones	Scales	McAllister	Blackwell	Earle	Holdsworth	Sanchez	Miller*	Gibson
	28/11	5,740	*15*	15			*Bart-Williams 14*	*Woods*	*Nilsson*	*Worthington*	*Anderson*	*Bart-Williams*	*Warhurst*	*Wilson**	*Waddle*	*Hirst*	*Bright*	*Sheridan*	*Harkes*
							Ref: R Milford	3rd last season, the Owls are struggling. This is their fifth successive draw. With a minute left John Sheridan handles Sanchez's header. Jones almost snatches the ball from a ballboy and belts the penalty past Chris Woods. Earle played up front to add firepower to the dismal Dons.											
18	A	NORWICH	20	L	1-2	0-0	Sanchez 53	Segers	**Talboys**	Joseph	Jones*	Scales	McAllister	Blackwell	Earle	Holdsworth^	Sanchez	Miller	Fashanu/Gibson
	5/12	*14,161*	*1*	15			*Robins 77, Phillips 88*	*Gunn*	*Culverhouse*	*Bowen*	*Butterworth*	*Polston*	*Sutch**	*Crook*	*Beckford^*	*Robins*	*Fox*	*Phillips*	*Megson/Sutton*
							Ref: R Groves	Norwich barely survived last season, but under Mike Walker appear unstoppable. They outplay the Dons and outfight them in a late onslaught. Ruel Fox set up the winner for Dave Phillips at the far post, Sanchez having headed in McAllister's corner. Strugglers Palace and Forest won.											
19	H	OLDHAM	19	W	5-2	3-0	Ardley 17, 25, Holdsworth 22, 52,	Segers	Ardley	Joseph	Jones	Scales	McAllister	Blackwell	Earle	Holdsworth	Sanchez	Clarke	
	12/12	3,386	*20*	18			*Brennan 46, Milligan 63* [Clarke 51]	*Gerrard*	*Halle*	*Pointon*	*Henry*	*Jobson*	*Redmond**	*Adams*	*Olney*	*Sharp*	*Milligan*	*Brennan^*	*Fleming/Palmer*
							Ref: K Hackett	Tough times for Joe Royle's Oldham as their defence again falls apart. Vinnie Jones was the architect of this thrashing, controlling midfield. Two of his long throws were hammered past Paul Gerrard by Neal Ardley. These points briefly take the Dons out of the relegation places.											
20	A	NOTTINGHAM F		D	1-1	1-1	Clarke 13	Segers	Ardley*	Joseph	Jones	Scales	McAllister	Blackwell	Earle	Holdsworth	Talboys	Clarke^	Fashanu/Miller
	20/12	*19,326*	*22*	19			*Clough 5*	*Crossley*	*Laws*	*Pearce*	*Chettle*	*Tiler*	*Keane*	*Crosby*	*Gemmill*	*Clough*	*Webb*	*Black*	
							Ref: R Hart	Brian Clough's valedictory season sees Forest rooted to the bottom. This Sunday game saw the Dons cancel Forest's quick opener when keeper Mark Crossley fumbled Jones's long pass. Steve Talboys, signed from non-league Gloucester for £10,000, subdued highly rated Roy Keane.											
21	A	CRYS PALACE	21	L	0-2	0-2		Segers	Holdsworth	Joseph	Jones	Scales	McAllister!	Blackwell*	Earle	Fashanu	Sanchez	Clarke^	Talboys/Ardley
	26/12	*16,825*	*17*	19			*Coleman 3, Thomas 30*	*Martyn*	*Humphrey*	*Shaw*	*Southgate**	*Young*	*Thorn*	*Coleman*	*Thomas*	*Armstrong*	*Rodger*	*McGoldrick*	*Osborn*
							Ref: R Lewis	Wobbly Palace secure their fourth straight win, thanks to errors by Joseph and Segers. Palace's Gareth Southgate breaks a bone in his foot and misses 10 matches. McAllister was sent off after 85 minutes. Kinnear said the first half was 'the worst display by a Dons team since I came'.											

No	Date	Att	Pos	Pts	F-A	H-T	Scorers, Times, and Referees	1	2	3	4	5	6	7	8	9	10	11	subs used
22 H	CHELSEA		21	D	0-0	0-0		Segers	Joseph	McAllister	Jones	Scales	Blackwell	Ardley*	Earle	Fashanu	Sanchez	Clarke^	Talboys/Miller
	28/12	14,687	*6*	20				*Hitchcock*	*Hall*	*Sinclair*	*Townsend*	*Lee*	*Donaghy*	*Stuart*	*Fleck*	*Myers*	*Newton*	*Wise*	
							Ref: D Elleray	Chelsea are unbeaten in 10 in league and cups, but are also embarked on a run of 13 without a win. This dull match offered little excitement to the spectators, with both sets of strikers out of touch. Nevertheless, Wimbledon felt aggrieved that two precious points had slipped away.											
23 A	BLACKBURN		21	D	0-0	0-0		Segers	Joseph	Elkins	Jones	Scales	Blackwell	Berry	Earle	Fashanu	Sanchez	Clarke	
	9/1	*14,504*	*4*	21				*Mimms*	*May*	*Wright*	*Sherwood*	*Hendry*	*Moran**	*Ripley*	*Marker*	*Wegerle*	*Newell*	*Wilcox*	*Andersson*
							Ref: R Hart	Wimbledon's third consecutive 0-0 in league and cup, but this time they make no apologies for their negativity. Rovers have lost Shearer for the season. Out of sorts Fash is joined in attack by Jones, who is booked for mickey-taking a linesman. He faces his third ban of the season..											
24 H	LIVERPOOL		20	W	2-0	1-0	Fashanu 36p, Cotterill 62	Segers	Joseph	Elkins	Cotterill	Scales	Blackwell	Ardley	Earle	Fashanu*	Sanchez	Clarke^	Talboys/Holdsworth
	16/1	11,294	*12*	24				*James*	*Marsh*	*Jones*	*Stewart*	*Piechnik**	*Wright*	*Walters^*	*Redknapp*	*Hutchinson*	*Barnes*	*Bjornbye*	*Harkness/Rosenthal*
							Ref: R Dilkes	This is Liverpool's seventh game without a win in various competitions. They have just been dumped from the FA Cup by Bolton. Steve Cotterill plays instead of Holdsworth. He is felled for the penalty and later scores himself. Wimbledon complete the double over Liverpool.											
25 H	EVERTON			L	1-3	0-0	Fashanu 75	Segers	Joseph	Elkins	Jones	Scales	Blackwell	Ardley	Earle	Fashanu	Sanchez*	Holdsworth	Clarke
	26/1	**3,039**	*12*	24			*Cottee 60, 71, Snodin 72*	*Southall*	*Jackson*	*Ablett*	*Snodin*	*Watson*	*Keown*	*Harper*	*Beardsley*	*Cottee*	*Horne*	*Radosav'ic**	*Barrow*
							Ref: K Hackett	This is the sixth meeting of these sides this season and the third in a month. The wretched earlier matches, not to mention being fed up with the sight of Everton, pulls a record low crowd. The Dons are said to be losing £5,000 a day. Blunders by Dean Blackwell contribute to two goals.											
26 A	COVENTRY		18	W	2-0	1-0	Holdsworth 4, Clarke 55	Segers	Joseph	McAllister	Jones	Scales	Blackwell	Ardley	Earle	Fashanu	Holdsworth	Clarke*	Dobbs
	30/1	*11,774*	*8*	27				*Ogrizovic*	*Borrows*	*Babb*	*Atherton*	*Busst*	*Williams*	*Billing**	*Gynn*	*Rosario*	*Quinn*	*Hurst*	*Flynn*
							Ref: R Gifford	The Dons win this one surprisingly comfortably. Once Bobby Gould's Coventry have fallen behind early on – John Fashanu flicking on for Holdsworth – the Dons appear to be comfortably in charge. Jones displays touches of elegance in setting up the second goal, for Andy Clarke.											
27 H	LEEDS		17	W	1-0	0-0	Holdsworth 60	Segers	Joseph	McAllister	Sanchez	Scales	Elkins	Ardley	Earle*	Fashanu	Holdsworth	Dobbs^	Talboys/Clarke
	6/2	6,704	*16*	30				*Lukic*	*Sellars*	*Dorigo*	*Batty*	*Newsome*	*Whyte*	*Rocastle*	*Strandli**	*Chapman^*	*McAllister*	*Speed*	*Shutt/Bowman*
							Ref: V Callow	Deposed champions Leeds have been bundled from the FA Cup by Arsenal, and Howard Wilkinson can do little to stop the rot. For their part, the Dons turned down an Everton bid for John Scales. Wimbledon take all three points thanks to Segers' injury-time save from Gary Speed.											
28 A	ARSENAL		16	W	1-0	1-0	Holdsworth 19	Segers	Joseph	Elkins	Talboys*	Scales	Fitzgerald	Ardley	Earle	Fashanu	Holdsworth	Dobbs	**Fear**
	10/2	*18,253*	*12*	33				*Seaman*	*Keown*	*Winterburn*	*Hillier*	*Linighan*	*Adams*	*Selley*	*Wright*	*Smith**	*Merson^*	*Campbell*	*Morrow/Carter*
							Ref: P Don	Preoccupied with various cups, Arsenal have slipped into the bottom half. This match is remembered for a scrambled goal for Wimbledon; Ian Wright being kept on a tight leash; a fracas when Ian Selley lashed out at Dobbs; and a Dons debut for Peter Fear, replacing injured Talboys.											
29 H	SHEFFIELD UTD		13	W	2-0	2-0	Fashanu 1, Dobbs 44	Segers	Joseph	Elkins	Jones	Scales	McAllister	Ardley	Earle	Fashanu	Holdsworth	Dobbs	
	20/2	3,979	*21*	36				*Kelly*	*Ward*	*Cowan*	*Gannon*	*Gayle*	*Beesley**	*Carr^*	*Rogers*	*Hoyland*	*Deane*	*Littlejohn*	*Cork/Hodges*
							Ref: R Hart	The Blades will shortly start their annual uprising against relegation, and are buoyed by dumping Man Utd from the FA Cup. Wimbledon's fourth consecutive win stems from Fashanu's 25-yarder into the top corner inside a minute. Dobbs scores after Kelly blocked Ardley's shot.											
30 A	ASTON VILLA		16	L	0-1	0-0		Segers	Joseph	Elkins	Jones	Scales	McAllister	Ardley	Earle	Fashanu	Dobbs	Cotterill	Clarke
	27/2	***34,496***	*1*	36			*Yorke 79*	*Bosnich*	*Barrett*	*Staunton*	*Teale*	*McGrath*	*Richardson*	*Houghton*	*Cox*	*Saunders*	*Yorke*	*Regis*	
							Ref: S Lodge	Dumped by the Dons from the FA Cup, Villa stay top of the league in front of a large crowd boosted by slashing admission prices to many parts of the ground. The longer the match went on, the more the Dons retreated. They were beaten when Regis flicked on to Dwight Yorke.											
31 H	SOUTHAMPTON		16	L	1-2	1-1	Holdsworth 16	Segers	Joseph	Elkins	Jones	Scales	McAllister	Ardley	Earle	Fashanu	Holdsworth	Clarke	
	6/3	4,534	*11*	36			*Le Tissier 34, Moore 71*	*Flowers*	*Kenna*	*Adams*	*Widdrington*	*Moore*	*Monkou*	*Le Tissier**	*Cockerill*	*Dowie*	*Maddison*	*Dodd*	*Banger*
							Ref: A Gunn	Ian Branfoot has temporarily silenced Saints' critics with some good results. This match provided the goal of the month, that never was. Andy Clarke's volley has everyone on their feet, until they notice a linesman's raised flag. Le Tissier scores off McAllister, then crosses for Moore.											

No	Venue / Date	Opponent / Att	Pos	Res / Pts	F-A	H-T	Scorers, Times, and Referees	1	2	3	4	5	6	7	8	9	10	11	subs used
32	H	MIDDLESBRO		W	2-0	1-0	Scales 33, Holdsworth 78	Segers	Joseph	Elkins	Jones	Scales	McAllister	Ardley	Earle	Fashanu	Holdsworth	Clarke	Berry
	9/3	5,821	*20*	39				*Pears*	*Morris*	*Phillips*	*Kernaghan*	*Peake*	*Whyte*	*Hendrie*	*Mustoe*	*Wilkinson*	*Falconer*	*Wright**	*Slaven*
							Ref: M Reed	This is Lennie Lawrence's Boro's sixth defeat in seven, and they are going down. Kinnear sent his players out to the training pitch before the match to gee them up. Stephen Pears fumbles Earle's header and Scales pounces. McAllister sets ups the second goal, a flick by Holdsworth.											
33	A	QP RANGERS	15	W	2-1	1-1	Fashanu 8, Earle 79	Segers	Joseph	Elkins	Jones*	Scales	McAllister	Ardley	Earle	Fashanu	Holdsworth	Dobbs	Sanchez
	13/3	*12,270*	*5*	42			*Ferdinand 4*	*Roberts**	*Bardsley*	*Brevett*	*Doyle*	*Peacock*	*McDonald*	*Impey*	*Wilson*	*Ferdinand^*	*Allen*	*Meaker*	*Stejskal/White*
							Ref: P Don	Four defeats in five for QPR. This result offers sweet revenge for the Dons, outclassed earlier in the season. Injuries took their toll during the match. QPR keeper Tony Roberts went off with an eye injury, and Ferdinand also hobbled off. Jones also departed with a gaping head wound.											
34	H	NORWICH	12	W	3-0	2-0	Holdsworth 16, 82, Ardley 29	Segers	Joseph	Elkins	Jones	Scales	McAllister	Ardley	Earle	Fashanu	Holdsworth	Dobbs	
	20/3	10,875	*3*	45				*Gunn*	*Culverhouse*	*Bowen*	*Sutton*	*Polston*	*Smith*	*Crook*	*Woodth'rpe**	*Robins*	*Fox*	*Phillips*	*Power*
							Ref: K Cooper	Wimbledon knock Norwich off the top with this win. 1-0, when Fashanu crosses for Holdsworth to head in on the run; 2-0, when Scales flicks on for Ardley to score at the second attempt; 3-0, when Jones centres for Holdsworth. Norwich's title hopes never recover from this setback.											
35	A	SHEFFIELD WED	11	D	1-1	0-0	Holdsworth 90	Segers	Joseph	Elkins	Jones*	Scales	McAllister	Ardley	Earle	Fashanu!	Holdsworth	Dobbs^	Blackwell/Sanchez
	24/3	*20,918*	*5*	46			*Bright 76*	*Woods*	*Nilsson**	*Worthington*	*Palmer*	*Jones*	*Anderson*	*Wilson*	*Waddle*	*Bart-Will'ms^*	*Bright*	*Sheridan*	*Watts/Jemson*
							Ref: J Lloyd	17th in December, the Owls have climbed to 4th. They are denied two more points deep into injury-time, when Holdsworth meets Ardley's cross. The crowd were seething from Fashanu's dismissal after an off-the-ball clash with Viv Anderson. Fashanu was red-carded on a stretcher.											
36	A	OLDHAM	12	L	**2-6**	0-3	Holdsworth 61, 68 *[Beckford 87]*	Segers	Joseph	Fear	Sanchez	Scales	Blackwell	Ardley	Earle	Fashanu*	Holdsworth	Dobbs!	Cotterill
	3/4	*11,606*	*19*	46			*Fashanu 5 (og), Bernard 13, Olney 42,69,*	*Gerrard*	*Halle*	*Pointon*	*Henry*	*Jobson*	*Fleming*	*Adams*	*Ritchie**	*Olney*	*Milligan*	*Bernard*	*Beckford*
							Ref: J Martin	Oldham avenge their 5-2 hiding at Selhurst Park with their biggest win. The Dons concede six goals, two bookings, and have Dobbs sent off for handball – the fourth Don to be sent off so far. Jones, Elkins and McAllister are already suspended. Fash's headed own-goal sets the scene.											
37	H	CRYS PALACE	12	W	**4-0**	2-0	Earle 19, 52, Holdsworth 24, 46	Segers	Joseph	Barton	Sanchez	Scales	Fitzgerald	Ardley	Earle	Dobbs	Holdsworth*	Clarke^	Miller/Blackwell
	7/4	12,275	*19*	49				*Martyn*	*Shaw*	*Southgate*	*Coleman*	*Gordon*	*Thorn**	*Osborn^*	*Thomas*	*Williams*	*Rodger*	*McGoldrick*	*Watts/Humphrey*
							Ref: V Callow	Four days separate the Dons' heaviest defeat from their biggest win. This is Palace's first league defeat in seven. The first goal was an Earle header; the second came from a blunder from Nigel Martyn, flapping at Ardley's cross. Despite gaining 49 points, Palace will be relegated.											
38	A	CHELSEA	11	L	2-4	0-1	Holdsworth 55, Sanchez 88	Segers	Joseph^	Barton	Sanchez	Scales	Fitzgerald	Ardley	Earle	Dobbs	Holdsworth	Clarke*	Miller/Blackwell
	12/4	*13,138*	*7*	49			*Wise 45p, Hall 50, Spencer 81, Ship'ley 85*	*Kharin*	*Clarke*	*Sinclair*	*Matthew**	*Johnsen*	*Donaghy*	*Stuart^*	*Spencer*	*Shipperley*	*Hall*	*Wise*	*Hopkin/Barnard*
							Ref: D Elleray	David Webb is caretaker manager at Stamford Bridge. His side have just lost their first match in eight. The first half is four minutes over-long when John Spencer tumbles over Warren Barton's foot. Wise converts the penalty. Later, with the Dons 1-2 down, Holdsworth hits a post.											
39	H	NOTTINGHAM F	11	W	1-0	1-0	Clarke 33	Segers	Barton	McAllister	Sanchez*	Scales	Fitzgerald	Ardley^	Earle	Miller	Holdsworth	Clarke	Blackwell/Fear
	17/4	9,358	*21*	52				*Marriott*	*Laws*	*Williams*	*Stone*	*Tiler*	*Keane*	*Black**	*Bannister*	*Clough*	*Rosario*	*Woan*	*Glover*
							Ref: K Barratt	Forest look beyond redemption. Even without five first-teamers, Wimbledon look better. That the score was tight was due to Andrew Marriott in the Forest goal. He was beaten by Clarke, who burst past Nigel Clough into the clear. Rosario missed badly for Forest after the break.											
40	A	MANCHESTER C	10	D	1-1	0-0	Miller 50	Segers	Barton	McAllister	Jones	Scales	Fitzgerald	Miller*	Earle	Fashanu	Fear	Clarke	McGee
	21/4	*19,524*	*9*	53			*Holden 84*	*Coton*	*Ranson**	*Phelan*	*Reid^*	*Curle*	*Vonk*	*White*	*Sheron*	*Quinn*	*Flitcroft*	*Simpson*	*Holden/Brightwell*
							Ref: H King	City fans bay for chairman Peter Swales's blood. Paul Miller's second-half equaliser sends Wimbledon up to the dizzy heights of 10th place for the only time. Earle's chip is turned in under the bar by Miller. Holden equalises when he mis-controls the ball and steers it into the corner.											
41	A	TOTTENHAM	11	D	1-1	0-1	Earle 63	Segers	Barton	McAllister!	Jones	Scales	Fitzgerald	Ardley	Earle	Fashanu	Holdsworth*	Clarke^	McGee/Sanchez
	1/5	*24,473*	*9*	54			*Anderton 39*	*Walker*	*Nethercott**	*V d Hauwe*	*Samways*	*Mabbutt*	*Ruddock*	*Sedgley*	*Turner*	*Anderton*	*Sheringham*	*Allen^*	*Hodges/Gray*
							Ref: R Lewis	All is volcanic beneath the surface at White Hart Lane, which soon erupts with the Sugar-Venables saga. McAllister is sent off for elbowing Paul Allen in the face. Allen retired for stitches. Down to 10 men, the Dons found the resources to equalise, when Ardley crossed for Earle.											
42	H	MANCHESTER U	12	L	1-2	0-0	Holdsworth 82	Segers	Barton	McAllister	Jones	Scales	Fitzgerald	Ardley	Earle	Fashanu	Holdsworth	Clarke	
	9/5	**30,115**	*1*	54			*Ince 63, Robson 72*	*Schmeichel*	*Parker*	*Irwin**	*Bruce*	*Sharpe*	*Pallister*	*Robson*	*Ince*	*McClair*	*Hughes*	*Cantona*	*Giggs*
	Home	*Away*					Ref: J Worrall	For the first time in 25 years United are champions, and Selhurst Park is packed for this Sunday fixture to see them crowned. This is their seventh straight win. Bryan Robson starts his first match of the year, scoring United's second. Holdsworth's header cannot break their grip.											
Average	8,405	*18,662*																	

F.A. PREMIER LEAGUE (CUP-TIES) Manager: Joe Kinnear SEASON 1992-93

Coca-Cola Cup	Att			F-A	H-T	Scorers, Times, and Referees	1	2	3	4	5	6	7	8	9	10	11	subs used
2:1 A BOLTON		21	W	3-1	2-0	Fashanu 26, Ardley 33, Jones 74	Segers	Barton	Elkins*	Jones	Scales	Fitzgerald	Ardley	Earle	Fashanu	Holdsworth	Clarke	Miller
22/9	*5,049*	*2:11*				*Stubbs 46*	*Branagan*	*Brown*	*Burke*	*Kelly*	*Carne*	*Winstanley*	*Green*	*Stubbs*	*Walker*	*Philliskirk*	*Patterson*	
						Ref: J Rushton	Bruce Rioch's Bolton seldom threatened Wimbledon, apart from when Alan Stubbs, just after the turnaround, glanced a corner over Segers' head. Overall, the Dons created more chances than their hosts. More importantly, they took more. Rioch and Stubbbs will know better times.											
2:2 H BOLTON		21	L	0-1	0-0		Segers	Barton	Elkins	Miller	Scales	Fitzgerald	Ardley*	Earle	Newhouse^	Sanchez	Clarke	Talboys/Joseph
6/10	1,987	*2:11*				*Philliskirk 47*	*Branagan*	*Spooner*	*Oliver*	*Darby*	*Lydiate*	*Winstanley*	*Green*	*Fisher*	*Philliskirk*	*Stubbs*	*Patterson*	
						Ref: J Martin (Dons win 3-2 on aggregate)	Bolton came close to causing a mighty upset, on a night when Elkins, Clarke and Newhouse cannot get their acts together. Minus Fashanu and Holdsworth, the Dons carry little threat. Seconds after Tony Philliskirk pulled one back for Bolton, he shoots straight at Segers.											
3 A EVERTON		20	D	0-0	0-0		Segers	Barton	Joseph	Jones	McLeary	McAllister	Gibson	Earle	Fashanu*	Dobbs	Anthrobus	Holdsworth
28/10	*9,541*	*16*					*Southall*	*Jackson*	*Ablett*	*Kenny*	*Watson*	*Keown*	*Warzycha**	*Beardsley^*	*Rideout*	*Horne*	*Beagrie*	*Hinchcliffe/Barlow*
						Ref: W Flood	For the second time this season Goodison yawns through a goalless draw between these sides. Segers is outstanding in a match that witnessed a brawl when Martin Keown and Dons sub Holdsworth clash. Everton saved their best chance till late, when Paul Rideout's header flew wide.											
3R H EVERTON		20	L	0-1	0-0		Segers	Barton	Joseph	Jones	McLeary	McAllister	Gibson	Earle	Holdsworth	Dobbs*	Clarke	Fashanu
10/11	3,686	*17*				*Beardsley 86*	*Southall*	*Jackson**	*Ablett*	*Snodin*	*Watson*	*Keown*	*Harper*	*Beardsley*	*Rideout*	*Horne*	*Ebbrell^*	*Hinchcliffe/Warzycha*
						Ref: D Axcell	Holdsworth has one of those games in which no matter how many chances fall his way he fails to find the net. Fashanu comes on as a sub, but hardly has a kick. Earle comes nearest to scoring with a bicycle kick which hits Southall's bar. Everton created little before Beardsley struck.											

FA Cup	Att			F-A	H-T	Scorers, Times, and Referees	1	2	3	4	5	6	7	8	9	10	11	subs used
3 H EVERTON		21	D	0-0	0-0		Segers	Joseph	McAllister	Jones	Scales	Blackwell	Miller*	Earle	Fashanu	Sanchez	Clarke	Berry
2/1	7,818	*18*					*Southall*	*Jackson*	*Ablett*	*Snodin**	*Watson*	*Keown*	*Harper^*	*Beardsley*	*Rideout*	*Kenny*	*Ebbrell*	*Horne/Barlow*
						Ref: P Durkin	Four matches between these sides so far have produced just one goal. This cup-tie was one of few to survive the weather, but it was so dire that few would have mourned its postponement. Fash was shackled by Keown. Beardsley had one good shot, but Segers pushed it onto the bar.											
3R A EVERTON		21	W	2-1	1-0	Fashanu 35, Earle 50	Segers	Joseph	Elkins	Cotterill	Scales	Blackwell	Ardley	Earle	Fashanu	Sanchez	Clarke*	Talboys
12/1	*15,293*	*17*				*Watson 67*	*Kearton*	*Jackson*	*Ablett*	*Snodin**	*Watson*	*Keown*	*Radosavijevi*	*Beardsley*	*Barlow*	*Kenny^*	*Ebbrell*	*Warzycha/Harper*
						Ref: P Durkin	Fashanu had not scored since September, but now he sprints past Martin Keown and Dave Watson and squeezes the ball in off the post. Neville Southall is missing, suspended. After the break Preki's free-kick hits the angle of post and bar. In a trice the Dons sweep upfield to lead 2-0.											
4 A ASTON VILLA		20	D	1-1	1-1	Elkins 35	Segers	Joseph	Elkins	Jones	Scales	Blackwell	Ardley	Earle	Fashanu	Sanchez	Cotterill*	Holdsworth
23/1	*21,088*	*1*				*Yorke 3*	*Spink*	*Barrett*	*Staunton*	*Teale*	*McGrath*	*Richardson*	*Houghton*	*Parker*	*Saunders*	*Yorke*	*Froggatt*	
						Ref: K Redfern	A tough draw for the Dons, away to Ron Atkinson's league leaders. Villa were one, and should have been two goals up in three minutes. Steve Cotterill is hospitalised after colliding with keeper Nigel Spink. Elkins levels from a free-kick that goes in via a post and Spink's shoulder.											
4R H ASTON VILLA		18	D	0-0	0-0		Segers	Joseph	McAllister	Jones	Scales	Blackwell	Ardley	Earle	Fashanu	Holdsworth	Clarke*	Dobbs
3/2	8,048	*3*		*aet*			*Bosnich*	*Barrett*	*Staunton*	*Teale*	*McGrath*	*Richardson*	*Houghton*	*Parker*	*Saunders*	*Yorke*	*Cox*	
						Ref: K Redfern (Dons win 6-5 on penalties)	Two hours, no goals – though Ardley missed an extra-time sitter – and so to a penalty shoot-out. This has to be interrupted halfway through when keeper Mark Bosnich collapses with cramp. At 6-5, Neil Cox and Holdsworth having missed, Kevin Richardson blazes over the crossbar.											
5 A TOTTENHAM		16	L	2-3	0-3	Dobbs 63, Cotterill 90	Segers	Joseph*	Elkins	Jones	Scales	McAllister	Ardley	Earle	Fashanu	Holdsworth	Dobbs	Cotterill
14/2	*26,529*	*10*				*Anderton 25, Sher'm 43, Barmby 45*	*Thorstvedt*	*Austin*	*Edinburgh*	*Samways*	*Mabbutt*	*Ruddock*	*Howells*	*Barmby*	*Anderton*	*Sheringham*	*Allen*	
						Ref: M Bodenham	Live on Sky! Ex-Spur Gary Lineker has incensed the Dons by saying he would rather watch Ceefax. Alas, Tottenham run all over Wimbledon and the tie is over by half-time. Neil Ruddock snuffs out Fashanu and finds time to get forward. Two of his headers set up two Spurs goals.											

	Home						Away					
	P	W	D	L	F	A	W	D	L	F	A	Pts
1 Manchester U	42	14	5	2	39	14	10	7	4	28	17	84
2 Aston Villa	42	13	5	3	36	16	8	6	7	21	24	74
3 Norwich	42	13	6	2	31	19	8	3	10	30	46	72
4 Blackburn	42	13	4	4	38	18	7	7	7	30	28	71
5 QP Rangers	42	11	5	5	41	32	6	7	8	22	23	63
6 Liverpool	42	13	4	4	41	18	3	7	11	21	37	59
7 Sheffield Wed	42	9	8	4	34	26	6	6	9	21	25	59
8 Tottenham	42	11	5	5	40	25	5	8	10	20	41	59
9 Manchester C	42	7	8	6	30	25	8	4	9	26	26	57
10 Arsenal	42	8	8	7	25	20	7	5	9	15	18	56
11 Chelsea	42	9	7	5	29	22	5	7	9	22	32	56
12 WIMBLEDON	42	9	4	8	32	23	5	8	8	24	32	54
13 Everton	42	7	6	8	26	27	8	2	11	27	28	53
14 Sheffield Utd	42	10	6	5	33	19	4	4	13	21	34	52
15 Coventry	42	7	4	10	29	28	6	9	6	23	29	52
16 Ipswich	42	8	9	4	29	22	4	7	10	21	33	52
17 Leeds	42	12	8	1	40	17	0	7	14	17	45	51
18 Southampton	42	10	6	5	30	21	3	5	13	24	40	50
19 Oldham	42	10	6	5	43	30	3	4	14	20	44	49
20 Crys Palace	42	6	9	6	27	25	5	7	9	21	36	49
21 Middlesbro	42	8	5	8	33	27	3	6	12	21	48	44
22 Nottingham F	42	6	4	11	17	25	4	6	11	24	37	40
	924	214	132	118	723	499	118	132	214	499	723	1256

Odds & ends

Double wins: (2) Arsenal, Liverpool.
Double losses: (2) Ipswich, Aston Villa.

Won from behind: (2) Arsenal (h), QPR (a).
Lost from in front: (2) Southampton (h), Norwich (a).

High spots: 4 straight wins from end of January.
Being one of only two sides to win at champions-elect Manchester U.
Enjoying the best season in cup competitions since 1988-89.

Low spots: Starting the season with just 2 points from 6 games.
Next to bottom going into New Year.

The Dons faced Everton twice in the league, twice in the Coca-Cola Cup, twice in the FA Cup. Wimbledon won just once.

Though the Dons won only 3 of their first 18 league games, their victims were Arsenal, Liverpool, and Manchester United.

The highest home attendance (v Man U) was more than double that of the second highest (v Chelsea).

Norwich finished 3rd, but they conceded more goals than they scored.

Player of the Year: John Scales.
Ever-presents: (1) Robbie Earle.
Hat-tricks: (0).
Leading scorer: Dean Holdsworth (19).

	Appearances						Goals			
	Lge	Sub	CCC	Sub	FAC	Sub	**Lge**	CCC	FAC	**Total**
Anthrobus, Steve	**4**	(1)	1							
Ardley, Neal	**24**	(2)	2		4		**4**	1		**5**
Barton, Warren	**23**		4				**2**			**2**
Berry, Greg	**2**	(1)				(1)				
Blackwell, Dean	**19**	(5)			4					
Clarke, Andy	**23**	(10)	3		3		**5**			**5**
Cotterill, Stephen	**4**	(3)			2	(1)	**3**		1	**4**
Dobbs, Gerald	**16**	(3)	2		1	(1)	**1**		1	**2**
Earle, Robbie	**42**		4		5		**7**		1	**8**
Elkins, Gary	**17**	(1)	2		3				1	**1**
Fashanu, John	**27**	(2)	2	(1)	5		**6**	1	1	**8**
Fear, Peter	**2**	(2)								
Fitzgerald, Scott	**18**	(2)	2							
Gibson, Terry	**6**	(2)	2				**1**			**1**
Holdsworth, Dean	**34**	(2)	2	(1)	2	(1)	**19**			**19**
Jones, Vinnie	**27**		3		4		**1**	1		**2**
Joseph, Roger	**31**	(1)	2	(1)	5					
McAllister, Brian	**26**	(1)	2		3					
McGee, Paul	**1**	(2)								
McLeary, Alan	**4**		2							
Miller, Paul	**11**	(8)	1	(1)	1		**2**			**2**
Newhouse, Aiden		(1)	1							
Sanchez, Lawrie	**23**	(4)	1		3		**4**			**4**
Segers, Hans	**41**		4		5					
Scales, John	**32**		2		5		**1**			**1**
Skinner, Justin	**1**									
Sullivan, Neil	**1**									
Talboys, Steven	**3**	(4)		(1)		(1)				
28 players used	**462**	**(57)**	**44**	**(5)**	**55**	**5**	**56**	**3**	**5**	**64**

F.A. CARLING PREMIERSHIP

Manager: Joe Kinnear

SEASON 1993-94

No	Date		Att	Pos	Pts	F-A	H-T	Scorers, Times, and Referees	SQUAD	NUMBERS	IN	USE								subs used
1	A	WEST HAM			W	2-0	0-0	Fashanu 63, Sanchez 72	Segers	Joseph	Fitzgerald	Scales	**Kimble**	Fear*	Earle	Sanchez	Clarke^	Fashanu	Holdsworth	Blackwell/Barton
	14/8		*20,363*		3				*Miklosko*	*Braecker*	*Gale*	*Potts*	*Dicks*	*Allen M*	*Butler*	*Gordon*	*Holmes**	*Allen C*	*Morley*	*Rowland*
								Ref: K Burge	Squad numbers are the new fashion, with Alan Kimble wearing shirt No 35. Upton Park resembles a building site for this, promotion-winning Hammers' first match in the Premiership. They are all at sea as the new, navy-blue kitted Wimbledon cruise to a second-half victory.											
2	H	CHELSEA			D	1-1	0-0	Fashanu 81	Segers	Joseph	Blackwell	Scales	Kimble	Talboys	Earle	Sanchez	Clarke	Fashanu	Holdsworth	
	17/8		11,263		4			*Wise 78*	*Kharin*	*Clarke*	*Sinclair*	*Hoddle*	*Kjeldberg*	*Myers*	*Wise*	*Donaghy*	*Peacock*	*Fleck**	*Cascarino*	*Spencer*
								Ref: M Reed	John Scales was involved in goals at either end. It is his mistake that enabled former Dons star Dennis Wise to score from close range. Only 12 minutes were left to play, but that was time enough for Scales to flick on Kimble's corner-kick for Fashanu to duck among the flying boots.											
3	H	ASTON VILLA		11	D	2-2	1-1	Holdsworth 38, Fashanu 85	Segers	Joseph	Blackwell	Scales	Kimble	Barton	Earle	Sanchez	Clarke*	Fashanu	Holdsworth	Dobbs
	21/8		7,564	*10*	5			*Richardson 17, McGrath 82*	*Spink*	*Barrett*	*McGrath*	*Teale*	*Staunton*	*Froggatt*	*Houghton*	*Richardson*	*Cowans*	*Atkinson*	*Saunders*	
								Ref: J Borrett	Ron Atkinson refuses to attend the post-match press-conference. Eight minutes from time Paul McGrath gets a faint touch to Staunton's corner. 'On the 18-yard box I'm paid to be hurt; on the 6-yard line I'm paid to die,' says John Fashanu, after he scores his third goal in as many games.											
4	A	SHEFFIELD UTD		12	L	1-2	0-1	Clarke 59	Segers	Joseph	Blackwell*	Scales	Kimble	Barton	Earle	Sanchez	Dobbs	Fashanu	Holdsworth	Clarke
	24/8		*15,555*	*10*	5			*Flo 43, Falconer 58*	*Kelly*	*Gage*	*Wirmola*	*Pemberton*	*Beesley*	*Bradshaw*	*Kamara*	*Falconer*	*Whitehouse*	*Flo*	*Cork*	
								Ref: A Wilkie	Kinnear brings in Gerald Dobbs for Andy Clarke, but Dobbs concedes the free-kick, taken by former-Don Kevin Gage, from which towering newcomer Jostein Flo heads the Blades in front. This is the Dons' first defeat of the season, and their first by United in seven attempts.											
5	A	OLDHAM		12	D	1-1	0-1	Jones 49	Segers	Joseph	Fitzgerald	Scales	Kimble	Barton*	Earle	Sanchez	Jones	Fashanu	Holdsworth	Dobbs
	28/8		***9,633***	*15*	6			*Bernard 7*	*Gerrard*	*Fleming*	*Jobson*	*Redmond*	*Pointon*	*Henry*	*Halle*	*Milligan*	*Bernard*	*Olney**	*Ritchie*	*Beckford*
								Ref: P Durkin	There is a score to settle at Boundary Park, namely the 6-2 thrashing inflicted by Joe Royle's team just four months previously. Paul Bernard's goal looks like bringing Oldham their first home win of the season, but Vinnie Jones – playing in his first game back after injury – denies them.											
6	H	SOUTHAMPTON		9	W	1-0	1-0	Barton 34	Segers	Joseph	Fitzgerald	Scales	Kimble	Barton	Earle	Sanchez*	Jones	Fashanu	Holdsworth	Clarke
	31/8		6,035	*19*	9				*Flowers*	*Kenna*	*Moore*	*Monkou*	*Benali*	*Cockerill*	*Maddison*	*Bartlett**	*Adams^*	*Le Tissier*	*Dowie*	*Charlton/Banger*
								Ref: K Hackett	Warren Barton had not scored in over a year when he connected with a sweet half-volley. The ball had been cleared from Kimble's corner-kick, but was now blasted past Tim Flowers, who two months later signs for Blackburn Rovers. The Saints seldom threaten to get back in the game.											
7	A	NORWICH		7	W	1-0	0-0	Sanchez 57	Segers	Joseph	Fitzgerald	Scales	Kimble	Barton	Earle	Sanchez	Jones	Fashanu	Holdsworth	
	11/9		*14,851*	*9*	12				*Gunn*	*Culverhouse*	*Polston*	*Prior**	*Bowen*	*Fox*	*Crook*	*Goss*	*Newman*	*Ekoku*	*Sutton*	*Robins*
								Ref: G Ashby	Mike Walker's Norwich have scored just one goal at home this season, in which they will shortly beat Bayern Munich in the UEFA Cup. Their play is pretty, but Spencer Prior kicks air on his home debut, allowing Warren Barton to despatch the cross that is swept in by Sanchez.											
8	H	MANCHESTER C			W	1-0	0-0	Earle 54	Segers	Joseph	Fitzgerald	Scales	Kimble	Barton*	Earle	Sanchez	Jones	Fashanu	Holdsworth	Clarke
	20/9		8,533		15				*Coton*	*Edghill*	*Kernaghan*	*Curle*	*Brightwell*	*Flitcroft*	*McMahon*	*Groen'dijk**	*Simpson*	*Sheron*	*Quinn*	*Mike*
								Ref: K Barrett	City's new boss, Brian Horton, has enjoyed a 100% record up to now, but City were second best in every department in this contest. Richard Edghill will remember his debut in sky blue for all the wrong reasons, as Robbie Earle scores at the far post – his first goal of the season.											
9	H	QP RANGERS		4	D	1-1	1-1	Ferdinand 42 (og)	Segers	Barton*	Fitzgerald	Scales	Kimble	Clarke^	Earle	Sanchez	Jones	Fashanu	Holdsworth	Ardley/**Blissett**
	27/9		9,478		16			*McDonald 19*	*Stejskal*	*Bardsley*	*Peacock*	*McDonald*	*Wilson*	*Impey*	*Wilkins*	*Barker*	*Sinclair*	*Ferdinand**	*Penrice^*	*Ready/White*
								Ref: P Don	QPR's England striker Les Ferdinand has a miserable match. He heads a spectacular own-goal past keeper Jan Stejskal, and then limps off with a torn hamstring. QPR skipper, Alan McDonald's, goal was his first in 2½ seasons, and the first Wimbledon had conceded in 463 minutes.											
10	A	LEEDS		9	L	**0-4**	0-2		Segers	Blackwell*	Fitzgerald	Scales	Kimble	Ardley	Earle	Sanchez	Jones	Fashanu^	Holdsworth	Dobbs/Blissett
	2/10		*30,020*	*3*	16			*Speed 2, 90, McAllister 18, 81*	*Beeney*	*Kelly*	*Fairclough*	*Newsome*	*Wetherall*	*Dorigo*	*Strachan*	*McAllister*	*Speed*	*Wallace**	*Deane*	*Strandli*
								Ref: J Worrall	The Dons' second defeat in 10 games is predictable, for they customarily get stuffed at Elland Road. Kinnear has won the Bells Manager of the Month award. Howard Wilkinson celebrates five years with Leeds, who win their fifth straight game with bullets from Speed and McAllister.											

11		A	SHEFFIELD WED		9		D	2-2	0-1	Blissett 46, Jones 89	Segers	Fear	Fitzgerald	McAllister	Kimble	Ardley*	Earle	Sanchez	Jones	Blissett	Holdsworth	Clarke
	16/10			*21,572*	*19*	17				*Waddle 9, Jones 84*	*Pressman*	*Williams*	*Pearce*	*Walker*	*Sinton*	*Bart-Will'ms**	*Palmer*	*Hyde*	*Jones*	*Bright*	*Waddle*	*Poric*
										Ref: R Gifford	This is the third successive match between the sides in which the Dons snatch a last-minute equaliser. The habit is wearing a bit thin on Trevor Francis. Wednesday looked slick for so long, but Gary Blissett scores his first goal for Wimbledon and Vinnie Jones is on hand at the death.											
12		H	IPSWICH				L	0-2	0-0		Segers	Fear	Fitzgerald	McAllister	Kimble	Ardley*	Earle	Sanchez	Jones	Blissett^	Holdsworth	Barton/Fashanu
	25/10			7,756		17				*Mason 71, Stockwell 81*	*Forrest*	*Stockwell*	*Linighan*	*Whelan*	*Thompson*	*Mason*	*Wark*	*Williams**	*Slater*	*Marshall*	*Kiwomya^*	*Palmer/Milton*
										Ref: A Gunn	The Dons' first home defeat had to happen sometime, but not to Ipswich, who had gone eight games without winning. But Ipswich do have the Indian sign on Wimbledon. Paul Mason's 20-yard effort is a fitting prelude to Mick Stockwell's head-down sprint from the halfway line.											
13		A	NEWCASTLE		12		L	**0-4**	0-1		Segers	Barton	Fitzgerald	McAllister	Kimble	Fear	Earle	Clarke*	Jones	Fashanu	Holdsworth	Dobbs
	30/10			*33,392*	*9*	17				*Beardsley 36p, 63, 71, Cole 60*	*Hooper*	*Watson*	*Beresford*	*Venison*	*Scott*	*Bracewell*	*Lee*	*Beardsley*	*Cole*	*Clarke*	*Sellars*	
										Ref: V Callow	Three days earlier a Cole-less Newcastle lost at Selhurst in the Coca-Cola Cup. Revenge is swift and emphatic. Bad boys Cole and Lee Clark are back in harness, but all eyes are on Peter Beardsley, recently recovered from a fractured cheek-bone, who scores three and orchestrates all.											
14		H	SWINDON		9		W	3-0	1-0	Fashanu 29, Blissett 67, Holdsworth 70	Segers	Barton	Fitzgerald	McAllister	Kimble*	Blissett	Earle	Talboys	Jones	Fashanu	Holdsworth	Ardley
	6/11			7,758	*22*	20					*Digby*	*Summerbee*	*Bodin*	*Ling*	*Taylor*	*Moncur*	*MacLaren*	*Fjortoft**	*Whitbread^*	*Horlock*	*Mutch*	*White/Maskell*
										Ref: S Lodge	Wooden-spoonists Swindon are haemorrhaging goals. Kinnear chooses this moment to give Garry Blissett his first full game and to play with three strikers. They score one apiece. Fashanu ends his own drought with a swivelling shot off the post, but Martin Ling should have equalised.											
15		A	MANCHESTER U		12		L	1-3	0-0	Fashanu 64	Segers	Barton	Fitzgerald	Scales	Joseph	McAllister	Earle	Talboys	Jones	Fashanu	Holdsworth*	Clarke
	20/11			***44,748***	*1*	20				*Pallister 53, Hughes 66, Kanchelskis 79*	*Schmeichel*	*Parker*	*Irwin*	*Bruce*	*Sharpe*	*Pallister*	*Cantona*	*Ince*	*Robson**	*Hughes*	*Kanchelskis*	*Phelan*
										Ref: J Lloyd	Wimbledon were the last team to win at Old Trafford, 13 months earlier, but now begins a series of emphatic defeats there. When Fashanu equalised, it looked like Alex Ferguson would be frustrated again, but Mark Hughes' instant volley and Kanchelskis' flashing drive win the day.											
16		A	TOTTENHAM		11		D	1-1	0-1	Holdsworth 72	Segers	Barton	Berry	Scales	Joseph	Ardley	Earle	Talboys	Jones	Fashanu	Holdsworth	
	24/11			*17,744*	*10*	21				*Barmby 6*	*Thorstvedt*	*Campbell*	*Edinburgh*	*Samways*	*Calderwood*	*Mabbutt**	*Sedgley*	*Barmby*	*Anderton*	*Howells*	*Hazard*	*Caskey*
										Ref: K Hackett	Fashanu's elbow makes dreadful contact with Gary Mabbutt's face. The game was only seven minutes old, with much bad feeling in the air. Spurs had just gone ahead through Nick Barmby's first goal of the season, but are pegged back by Dean Holdsworth's close-range header.											
17		H	EVERTON		11		D	1-1	0-1	Berry 48	Segers	Barton	Berry*	Scales	Joseph	Ardley	Earle	Talboys^	Jones	Fashanu	Holdsworth	Clarke/Fitzgerald
	27/11			6,934	*12*	22				*Barlow 33*	*Southall*	*Jackson*	*Hinchcliffe*	*Snodin*	*Watson*	*Ablett*	*Ward*	*Cottee*	*Horne**	*Ebbrell*	*Barlow^*	*Preki/Stuart*
										Ref: M Reed	Not the brightest of games. Stuart Barlow has been missing them for Everton all season, but now he buries a far-post header. Greg Berry does not get many games for Wimbledon, and fewer goals, but he is on the spot when Neville Southall spills Holdsworth's powerful shot.											
18		H	WEST HAM		15		L	1-2	0-1	Holdsworth 82	Segers	Barton	Fitzgerald	Scales	McAllister	Ardley	Earle	Clarke	Jones	Berry*	Holdsworth	Talboys
	4/12			10,903	*10*	22				*Chapman 45, 79*	*Miklosko*	*Braecker*	*Potts*	*Allen*	*Butler*	*Morley*	*Gale*	*Bishop*	*Holmes*	*Chapman*	*Burrows*	
										Ref: D Gallagher	West Ham profess to loathe the long ball, but that is how they win this game. Miklosko punts the ball downfield, Scales misreads the bounce, and Lee Chapman nabs his second goal. John Fashanu is mysteriously omitted. Hamstring, says Kinnear. Or maybe the fall-out from Mabbutt?											
19		A	ASTON VILLA		14		W	1-0	0-0	Holdsworth 77	Segers	Barton	Fitzgerald	Scales	McAllister	Ardley	Earle	Fear	Jones	Fashanu	Holdsworth	
	11/12			*17,940*	*7*	25					*Bosnich*	*Barrett*	*Cox*	*Teale*	*McGrath*	*Cowans*	*Houghton**	*Parker*	*Saunders*	*Atkinson^*	*Beinlich*	*Ehiogu/Whittingham*
										Ref: A Gunn	Villa's fourth home defeat of the season, as the Dons return to winning ways. Though the goal was scrappy, Peter Fear and Vinnie Jones both had goals chalked off, as did Villa's Guy Whittingham. Hail, sleet and driving wind did its best to disrupt any entertainment for the spectators.											
20		H	SHEFFIELD UTD		12		W	2-0	0-0	Barton 49, Holdsworth 67	Segers	Barton	Fitzgerald	Scales	McAllister	Ardley	Earle	Talboys*	Jones	Fashanu	Holdsworth	Dobbs
	18/12			6,728	19	28					*Kelly*	*Gage*	*Flo*	*Tuttle*	*Beesley*	*Bradshaw*	*Whitehouse*	*Falconer**	*Cork*	*Kamara*	*Wirmola*	*Hodges*
										Ref: P Durkin	Matches against Dave Bassett's teams always carry an extra edge to them. The Dons avenge defeat at Bramall Lane thanks to a deflected free-kick by Warren Barton and a low swoop from Dean Holdsworth. Steve Talboys had earlier fluffed a double chance to put the Dons ahead.											
21		H	COVENTRY		12		L	1-2	1-1	Holdsworth 38	Segers	Barton	Fitzgerald*	Scales	McAllister	Ardley	Earle	Fear^	Jones	Fashanu	Holdsworth	Clarke/Dobbs
	26/12			**4,739**	15	28				*Ndlovu 26, J Williams 71*	*Ogrizovic*	*Borrows*	*Atherton*	*Babb*	*Morgan*	*Flynn*	*Darby*	*Marsden*	*Ndlovu*	*Williams J*	*Wegerle*	
										Ref: M Bodenham	This is the lowest crowd in the history of the Premiership. On Boxing Day, too. John Scales is caught in possession by John Williams, who snaps the winner. John Fashanu appears so tamed and preoccupied by the Gary Mabbutt affair that he does not concede a single free-kick.											

No	Date	Att	Pos	Pts	F-A	H-T	Scorers, Times, and Referees	SQUAD	NUMBERS	IN	USE								subs used
22	A LIVERPOOL		14	D	1-1	1-1	Fashanu 40	Segers	Barton	Fitzgerald	Scales	McAllister*	Ardley	Earle	Fear	Jones	Fashanu	Holdsworth	Clarke
	28/12	_32,232_	_8_	_29_			_Scales 29 (og)_	_Grobbelaar_	_Jones_	_Wright_	_Ruddock_	_Nicol*_	_McManaman_	_Clough_	_Redknapp_	_Matteo_	_Fowler_	_Rush_	_Walters_
							Ref: K Cooper	Graeme Souness has been manager at Anfield for three years now, but has still to register his first win over the Crazy Gang in seven attempts. Not even the gift of Scales' own-goal can turn the tables. Fashanu's first goal since the Mabbutt affair is the least the Dons deserve on the day.											
23	H ARSENAL		15	L	0-3	0-2		Segers	Barton	Fitzgerald	Blackwell	Elkins	Ardley	Earle	Fear*	Jones	Fashanu	Holdsworth	Clarke
	1/1	16,584	_3_	_29_			_Campbell 18, Parlour 23, Wright 55_	_Seaman_	_Dixon*_	_Winterburn_	_Adams_	_Campbell_	_Wright_	_McGoldrick_	_Bould_	_Jensen^_	_Hillier_	_Parlour_	_Keown/Merson_
							Ref: G Ashby	Arsenal always seem to be the most troublesome London opponents, and this win – the Gunners' third over the holiday – lifts them to 3rd. Only for the first 10 minutes did the Dons really threaten, but once Kevin Campbell scored his seventh goal in four games, the tide turned abruptly.											
24	H SHEFFIELD WED		12	W	2-1	2-0	Ardley, 12, Fashanu 42	Segers	Barton	Fitzgerald	Scales	Elkins	Ardley	Earle	Sanchez	Jones	Fashanu*	Holdsworth	Blissett
	15/1	5,536	_8_	_32_			_Pearce 67_	_Pressman_	_Palmer_	_Bright_	_Pearce_	_Sinton_	_Hyde_	_Walker_	_Watson_	_Jones_	_Linighan*_	_Coleman_	_Bart-Williams_
							Ref: M Bodenham	Four days previously Wednesday had k.o.'d the Dons from the Coca-Cola Cup. Trevor Francis's team now lose for only the second time in 22 matches. Fashanu's glancing header wins the day. But he is booked for fouling Sinton and promptly subbed. Fash then squares up to Francis.											
25	A IPSWICH		12	D	0-0	0-0		Segers	Barton	Fitzgerald	Scales	Elkins	Ardley	Earle	Sanchez	Joseph	Fashanu	Holdsworth*	Blissett
	22/1	_12,372_	_13_	33				_Forrest_	_Stockwell_	_Wark_	_Linighan_	_Thompson_	_Youds*_	_Williams_	_Johnson_	_Slater^_	_Marshall_	_Guentchev_	_Mason/Kiwomya_
							Ref: B Hill	The first half was as bad as can be; the second only slightly better. The only consolation was that Ipswich were even worse than the Dons. It was the visitors who had the more and better chances. Holdsworth is pulled off injured. Manchester United are said to want him for £3 million.											
26	A BLACKBURN		13	L	0-3	0-3		Segers	Barton	Fitzgerald	Scales	Elkins	Ardley*	Earle	Sanchez	Joseph	Fashanu	Holdsworth	Blissett
	5/2	_16,215_	_2_	33			_Shearer 7p, Wilcox 30, Ripley 39_	_Flowers_	_Marker_	_Berg_	_Sherwood*_	_Moran_	_Le Saux_	_Ripley_	_Gallacher_	_Shearer^_	_Batty_	_Wilcox_	_Morrison/Pearce_
							Ref: A Wilkie	The Dons are three goals down before they know what has hit them. Alan Shearer's 27th of the season comes from the penalty spot after Barton lunges at Le Saux. Jason Wilcox's explosive second suggested a rout, but thankfully the Rovers tornado extinguished itself after the break.											
27	H NEWCASTLE		11	W	4-2	2-0	Earle 9, Blissett 26, Fashanu 55,	Segers	Barton	Fitzgerald	Scales	Elkins	Fear	Earle	Blissett	Jones	Fashanu*	Holdsworth	Clarke
	12/2	13,358	_2_	36			_Beardsley 50p, 90p_ [Holdsworth 63]	_Hooper_	_Venison_	_Beresford_	_Fox_	_Howey_	_Lee*_	_Beardsley_	_Clark_	_Sellars_	_Watson_	_Elliott_	_Mathie_
							Ref: J Lloyd	This is the third free-scoring match between these sides this season. By rights, Wimbledon should have equalled the 4-0 whitewash inflicted upon them at St James's. But referee Lloyd sees fit to award the Magpies two ludicrous penalties. Pick of the Dons' goals was Blissett's header.											
28	A SOUTHAMPTON		14	L	0-1	0-0		Segers	Barton	Fitzgerald	Scales	Elkins*	McAllister	Earle	Blackwell	Jones	Clarke^	Holdsworth	Blissett/Dobbs
	26/2	_14,790_	_17_	36			_Le Tissier 74_	_Beasant_	_Kenna_	_Wood_	_Monkou_	_Charlton_	_Benali_	_Magilton_	_Dowie_	_Le Tissier_	_Maddison_	_Maskell*_	_Allen_
							Ref: D Gallagher	Southampton have recently appointed Alan Ball as manager, and their fortunes have picked up. This otherwise dreadful game was illuminated by Le Tissier's sixth goal in four matches. He tees up Magilton's free-kick and volleys into the top corner. Fashanu was mysteriously left out.											
29	H NORWICH		11	W	3-1	1-1	Earle 37, 65, Holdsworth 75	Segers	Barton	Fitzgerald	Scales	McAllister	Fear	Earle	Blissett	Jones	Fashanu	Holdsworth	
	5/3	7,206	_9_	39			_Ekoku 6_	_Gunn_	_Bowen_	_Newman_	_Crook_	_Culverhouse_	_Adams_	_Ekoku_	_Goss_	_Butterworth_	_Ullathorne_	_Sutton_	
							Ref: A Gunn	The Canaries have drawn their last seven, and now lose for the first time since John Deehan succeeded Mike Walker. Barton's underhit back-pass gives Norwich an early lead. Two Earle goals set up the Dons' first double of the season. They will beat Norwich twice next season too.											
30	A MANCHESTER C		11	W	1-0	1-0	Earle 31	Segers	Barton	Fitzgerald	Scales	McAllister*	Fear	Earle	Dobbs	Jones	Fashanu	Holdsworth^	Clarke/Blissett
	12/3	_23,891_	_19_	42				_Coton_	_Edghill_	_Phelan_	_Kernigan_	_Vonk_	_Rocastle_	_McMahon_	_Walsh_	_Simpson*_	_Hill^_	_Rosler_	_Mike/Karl_
							Ref: D Frampton	Another double for the Dons. City succumb without a whimper, and their fans are outraged. Wimbledon had the game by the scruff of the neck long before Earle's goal. Vinnie Jones' long throw into the penalty box caused pandemonium, leaving Earle with the goal at his mercy.											
31	A CHELSEA		11	L	0-2	0-1		Segers	Barton	Fitzgerald	Scales	Elkins*	Fear	Earle	Dobbs	Jones	Fashanu^	Holdsworth	Blackwell/Blissett
	16/3	_11,903_	_16_	42			_Hopkin 21, Burley 73_	_Kharin_	_Clarke_	_Kjeldbjerg_	_Johnsen_	_Sinclair_	_Burley_	_Newton_	_Peacock_	_Wise_	_Hopkin*_	_Shipperley_	_Hoddle_
							Ref: K Morton	Chelsea have reached the semi-final of the FA Cup, and have lost just two of the last 16. Wimbledon did not surrender easily, and until Craig Burley's 20 yarder Chelsea were living on their nerves. Fashanu's earlier own-goal was re-assigned to David Hopkin, his first goal for Chelsea.											

No	H/A	Opponent	Pos	Res	F-A	H-T	Scorers, Times, and Referees	1	2	3	4	5	6	7	8	9	10	11	subs used
32	A	QP RANGERS	11	L	0-1	0-0		Segers	Barton	Fitzgerald	Scales	Elkins	Fear*	Earle	Berry	Jones	Blissett	Holdsworth	Clarke
19/3		*11,368*	*8*	42			*Peacock 70*	*Stejskal*	*Ready*	*Wilson*	*Wilkins*	*Peacock*	*Yates*	*Holloway*	*Meaker*	*White*	*Ferdinand*	*Sinclair*	
							Ref: M Reed	Rangers are distracted by the row between chairman Richard Thompson and manager Gerry Francis. Darren Peacock's third goal of the season – a strike from the edge of the box – gives QPR their first win of 1994. Both sides miss many chances. Jones' booking is his eighth this season.											
33	H	LEEDS	11	W	1-0	1-0	Fear 3	Segers	Barton	Blackwell	Scales	Elkins	Fear	Earle	**Gayle**	Jones	Fashanu	Holdsworth	
26/3		9,036	*5*	45				*Lukic*	*Dorigo*	*Fairclough*	*Strachan*	*Wallace*	*Deane*	*McAllister*	*Speed*	*Newsome**	*Wetherall*	*Kelly*	*White*
							Ref: K Burge	All eyes are on Marcus Gayle, making his debut. He has scored eight times for Brentford this season, but the nearest he comes here is to shoot into the side-netting. The match was decided by Peter Fear's sliced shot, after Fashanu had bulldozed his way into the enemy nerve centre.											
34	H	BLACKBURN	9	W	**4-1**	0-1	Earle 50,82, Berg 75 (og), Holdsworth 79	Segers	Barton	Blackwell	Scales	Elkins	Fear	Earle	Gayle	Jones	Fashanu	Holdsworth	
29/3		10,537	*2*	48			*Wilcox 15*	*Flowers*	*Berg*	*May*	*Moran**	*Le Saux*	*Ripley*	*Batty*	*Sherwood*	*Wilcox*	*Newell*	*Shearer*	*Warhurst*
							Ref: J Lloyd	This amazing turnaround destroys Blackburn's championship challenge. Kinnear tells his players at half-time to up the tempo. Most of the game's five goals were gems – Wilcox bamboozling Barton for the first; Fear's run for the fourth; Holdsworth setting up Earle for the fifth.											
35	A	COVENTRY	8	W	2-1	2-0	Castledine 32, Holdsworth 40	Segers	Barton	Blackwell	Scales	Elkins	Fear	Earle	Gayle	Castledine	Fashanu*	Holdsworth	Blissett
2/4		*11,290*	*13*	51			*Ndlovu 64*	*Ogrizovic*	*Borrows*	*Morgan*	*Atherton*	*Babb*	*Rennie*	*Flynn*	*Darby*	*Quinn*	*Williams**	*Ndlovu*	*Jenkinson*
							Ref: M Bodenham	Coventry's fifth defeat in six games brings a smile to Wimbledon, though Peter Ndlovu enhanced his growing reputation with a spectacular strike. A glancing header by Stewart Castledine – playing his first full match, and in for the suspended Jones – had put the Dons in control.											
36	H	LIVERPOOL	8	D	1-1	0-0	Elkins 90	Segers	Barton*	Blackwell	Scales	Elkins	Fear	Earle	Gayle	Castledine^	Fashanu	Holdsworth	Perry/Blissett
4/4		13,819	*7*	52			*Redknapp 65*	*James*	*Jones*	*Nicol*	*Ruddock*	*Dicks*	*Redknapp*	*Whelan*	*Barnes*	*McManaman*	*Fowler*	*Rush*	
							Ref: J Borrett	This is the fourth draw in four games between these sides this season. Late in the game it looked like Liverpool would bury their Wimbledon hoodoo. Fowler hit the post, Redknapp scored off it, and the game was in added time when Gary Elkins' free-kick was deflected past James.											
37	H	MANCHESTER U	8	W	1-0	1-0	Fashanu 22	Segers	Barton	Blackwell	Scales	Elkins	Fear	Earle	Gayle	Jones	Fashanu	Holdsworth	
16/4		**28,553**	*1*	55				*Schmeichel*	*Parker**	*Irwin*	*Bruce*	*Pallister*	*Ince*	*McClair*	*Hughes*	*Giggs*	*Robson^*	*Kanchelskis*	*Dublin/Sharpe*
							Ref: T Holbrook	The Wimbledon tornado gathers momentum. Both leaders – Blackburn and Man U – lose at Selhurst in quick succession. Kinnear schemes to avoid a repetition of United's cup win by playing Holdsworth and Gayle wide to clamp down on the full-backs. Schmeichel drops Elkins' cross.											
38	A	ARSENAL	8	D	1-1	1-0	Earle 37	Segers	Barton	Blackwell	Scales	Elkins	Fear	Earle	Gayle	Castledine	Fashanu	Holdsworth	
19/4		*21,292*	*4*	56			*Bould 51*	*Seaman*	*Dixon*	*Adams*	*Bould*	*Keown*	*Parlour*	*Davis**	*Selley*	*Wright*	*Smith*	*Campbell*	*Flatts*
							Ref: R Gifford	Arsenal are unbeaten in the league for 17 games and have a date with Parma in the Cup-Winners' Cup Final. The Dons have beaten four of the top five recently, and aim for the fifth. Seaman mishandles Elkins' corner and Earle heads in. Bould volleys his first league goal in 20 months.											
39	A	SWINDON	8	W	4-2	1-0	Fashanu 13, Earle 71, 75, Holdsworth 81	Segers*	Barton	Blackwell	Scales	Elkins	Fear	Earle	Gayle	Jones	Fashanu^	Holdsworth	Sullivan/Clarke
23/4		*12,237*	*22*	59			*Summerbee 67, Barton 80 (og)*	*Hammond*	*Summerbee*	*Bodin*	*Nijholt*	*Taylor*	*Fjortoft*	*Horlock*	*Fenwick*	*Scott*	*Kilcline*	*Sanchez**	*Mutch*
							Ref: G Poll	This defeat condemns Swindon to a swift return to the second grade. Goal of the match was the first, a 30-yard curler by Fashanu. Both Fash and Segers were substituted at half-time. Peter Fear engineered two goals for Robbie Earle after Swindon had equalised through Fjortoft.											
40	H	OLDHAM	6	W	3-0	1-0	Holdsworth 32, 47, 55	Sullivan	Barton	Blackwell	Scales	Elkins	Fear	Earle	Gayle	Jones	Fashanu*	Holdsworth	Clarke
26/4		6,766	*21*	62				*Gerrard*	*Fleming*	*Jobson**	*Redmond*	*Malkin*	*Henry*	*Milligan*	*Brennan^*	*Holden*	*Sharp*	*McCarthy*	*Beckford/Halle*
							Ref: R Milford	The Dons are striving for their highest league position, and in so doing condemn Oldham to a fourth successive defeat. Dean Holdsworth's hat-trick is his first in the league. Both teams field reserve goalkeepers, but it is Paul Gerrard of Oldham who appeared the more indecisive.											
41	H	TOTTENHAM	6	W	2-1	0-0	Holdsworth 58, Clarke 63	Segers	Barton	Blackwell	Scales	Elkins	Fear	Earle	Gayle	Jones*	Clarke^	Holdsworth	Perry/Blissett
30/4		20,875		65			*Sheringham 72p*	*Thorstvedt*	*Austin*	*Edinburgh*	*Samways*	*Mabbutt*	*Barmby*	*Anderton**	*Sheringham*	*Sedgley^*	*Howells*	*Nethercott*	*Hazard/Rosenthal*
							Ref: D Allison	The Dons are the curse of sprinters and dawdlers alike. They have now inflicted successive defeats on three strugglers. Andy Clarke, in for the back-strained Fashanu, might have had five, but has to settle for one, putting the final touch to a sweeping move from one end to the other.											
42	A	EVERTON	6	L	2-3	2-1	Holdsworth 4p, Ablett 20 (og)	Segers	Barton	Blackwell	Scales	Elkins	Fear*	Earle	Gayle	Jones	Clarke	Holdsworth	Blissett
7/5		*31,297*	*17*	65			*Stuart 24p, 81, Horne 67*	*Southall*	*Snodin*	*Ablett*	*Unsworth*	*Watson*	*Stuart*	*Horne*	*Ebbrell**	*Cottee*	*Rideout*	*Limpar*	*Barlow*
	Home	*Away*					Ref: R Hart	Wimbledon have it in their power to condemn mighty Everton to relegation for the first time ever. A penalty, followed by an own-goal, break Goodison's heart, but the referee gives Everton a phoney penalty and Segers gets the jitters. Questions are asked about the Dons' capitulation.											
Average	10,474	*20,224*																	

Coca-Cola Cup		Att	Pos	Res	F-A	H-T	Scorers, Times, and References	SQUAD NUMBERS IN USE											subs used
2:1	A HEREFORD		6	W	1-0	1-0	Clarke 37	Segers	Barton	Fitzgerald	Scales	Kimble	Joseph*	Earle	Sanchez	Jones	Fashanu	Holdsworth	Clarke
22/9		4,872	*3:20*					*Judge*	*Clark**	*Downs*	*Davies*	*Smith*	*Morris*	*Hall*	*Fry*	*May*	*Pickard*	*Nicholson*	*Abraham*
							Ref: H King	Roger Joseph is injured after half an hour. Andy Clarke takes his place, and shortly cracks Warren Barton's free-kick past Alan Judge. Hereford look more likely to fall further behind than to equalise. These teams met regularly in the lower divisions; Hereford have now won 5 out of 22.											
2:2	H HEREFORD		8	W	4-1	3-0	Ardley 6, Jones 32, Holdsworth 43,	Segers	Blackwell*	Fitzgerald	Scales	Kimble	Ardley	Earle	Clarke	Jones	Fashanu	Holdsworth	Blissett
5/10		2,151	*3:18*				*Hall 69* [Earle 89]	*Thomas*	*Clark*	*Downs*	*Davies*	*Smith*	*Morris**	*Hall*	*Anderson*	*May^*	*Fry*	*Nicholson*	*Pickard/Brain*
							Ref: G Poll (Dons win 5-1 on aggregate)	The tie was put beyond Hereford after just six minutes, when Holdsworth's shot comes back off a post to Neal Ardley. Holdsworth could have done with the goal himself – he had not scored in eight games – though he later capitalised on Alan Judge's illegal handling of a back-pass.											
3	H NEWCASTLE		8	W	2-1	1-1	Barton 23, Holdsworth 68	Segers	Barton	Fitzgerald	McAllister	Kimble	Fear	Earle	Clarke*	Jones	Fashanu	Holdsworth	Ardley
27/10		11,602	*11*				*Sellars 28*	*Hooper*	*Watson*	*Venison*	*Scott*	*Beresford*	*Lee*	*Beardsley*	*Bracewell*	*Sellars*	*Allen**	*Mathie*	*Kilcline*
							Ref: I Hemley	Andy Cole goes a.w.o.l. before kick-off, and Kevin Keegan storms out of the press conference when questioned about it. Peter Beardsley is caught napping in his own penalty area for the first goal. Fashanu and Holdsworth combine for the winner with typically brave headers.											
4	A LIVERPOOL		11	D	1-1	0-1	Earle 84	Segers	Barton	Fitzgerald	Scales	McAllister	Joseph	Earle	Ardley	Jones	Fashanu*	Holdsworth	Clarke
1/12		*19,290*	*9*				*Molby 15p*	*Grobbelaar*	*Jones*	*Wright*	*Ruddock*	*Harkness*	*Redknapp*	*Molby*	*Matteo*	*Barnes**	*Fowler*	*Rush*	*Walters*
							Ref: R Dilkes	Sensational performance by the Dons, who create numerous chances after the recalled Molby put Liverpool ahead from the spot. Scales had up-ended Rush. Fashanu has a goal inexplicably annulled. Having wasted one header, Earle sends another flashing into the bottom corner.											
4R	H LIVERPOOL		14	W	2-2	1-1	Holdsworth 18, Earle 70	Segers	Barton	Fitzgerald	Scales	McAllister	Fear*	Earle	Ardley	Jones	Fashanu	Holdsworth	Clarke
14/12		11,343	*8*		*aet*		*Ruddock 38, Segers 90 (og)*	*Grobbelaar*	*Jones R*	*Wright**	*Ruddock*	*Nicol*	*McManaman*	*Redknapp*	*Molby**	*Barnes*	*Rush*	*Fowler*	*Harkness/Walters*
							Ref: H King (Dons win 4-3 on penalties)	Excitement by the bucketful. Jones and Fear set up Holdsworth. Ruddock's free-kick and Earle's tap in follow. In injury-time Segers punches the ball into his own net, then saves Barnes' extra-time penalty. In the shoot-out, Redknapp, Jones, and Walters miss, and Neal Ardley seals it.											
QF	H SHEFFIELD WED		15	L	1-2	0-0	Holdsworth 77	Segers	Barton	Fitzgerald	Scales	Elkins	Clarke*	Earle	Ardley	Jones	Fashanu	Holdsworth	Blissett
11/1		8,919	*6*				*Watson 46, Bright 82*	*Pressman*	*Linighan*	*Walker*	*Pearce*	*Coleman*	*Palmer*	*Hyde*	*Jones*	*Sinton*	*Watson*	*Bright*	
							Ref: P Alcock	Wimbledon have not come so close to Wembley since 1988, and they are sunk by a goal few teams could have prevented. It had beforehand been a tepid cup-tie, but then Mark Bright beat Scales in the air, swivelled, and from 25 yards struck a thunderous half-volley past Segers.											

FA Cup		Att	Pos	Res	F-A	H-T	Scorers, Times, and References	SQUAD NUMBERS IN USE											subs used
3	H SCUNTHORPE		15	W	3-0	2-0	Holdsworth 11, 45, 71	Segers	Barton	Fitzgerald	Scales	Elkins	Clarke*	Earle	Ardley	Jones	Fashanu^	Holdsworth	Blackwell/Blissett
8/1		4,944	*3:7*					*Samways*	*Alexander*	*Mudd*	*Hope*	*Knill*	*Bradley*	*Trebble**	*Martin*	*Carmichael*	*Bullimore*	*Smith*	*Watson*
							Ref: G Poll	Upsets away from home in the cup usually rely on avoiding a bad start. Scunthorpe had only beaten the Dons twice in 10 attempts in their soccer basement years, and never came close to improving on that tally. Dean Holdsworth's first hat-trick for Wimbledon is their undoing.											
4	H SUNDERLAND		12	W	2-1	1-1	Scales 3, Fashanu 59	Segers	Barton	Fitzgerald	Scales	Elkins	Joseph	Earle	Ardley	Sanchez	Fashanu	Holdsworth	
29/1		10,447	*1:13*				*Smith 45*	*Chamberlain*	*Ord**	*Bennett*	*Ferguson*	*Ball*	*Owers*	*Goodman*	*Gray*	*Atkinson^*	*Melville*	*Smith*	*Howey/Russell*
							Ref: J Worrall	Scales puts the skids under Sunderland, heading in Elkins' free-kick. Martin Smith sets up an enthralling second half with an equaliser late in the first. Fashanu restores the lead from Segers' downfield punt, but then Joseph brings down Smith in the box. 'No penalty,' says Joe Worrall.											
5	H MANCHESTER U		11	L	0-3	0-1		Segers	Barton	Fitzgerald	Scales	Elkins	Fear	Earle	Blissett	Jones	Fashanu	Holdsworth	
20/2		27,511	*1*				*Cantona 42, Ince 63, Irwin 71*	*Schmeichel*	*Parker*	*Bruce*	*Pallister*	*Irwin*	*Kanchelskis*	*Ince*	*Keane*	*Giggs*	*Cantona**	*Hughes^*	*McClair/Dublin*
							Ref: D Elleray	A third home tie for the Dons, but that is all they enjoy from this humiliating footballing lesson. United are still on course for a domestic treble, and are unbeaten in 32 games. Two of their goals are classics – Cantona's control and volley; and Denis Irwin's final touch to a 15-man move.											

		Home					Away					
	P	W	D	L	F	A	W	D	L	F	A	Pts
1 Manchester U	42	14	6	1	39	13	13	5	3	41	25	92
2 Blackburn	42	14	5	2	31	11	11	4	6	32	25	84
3 Newcastle	42	14	4	3	51	14	9	4	8	31	27	77
4 Arsenal	42	10	8	3	25	15	8	9	4	28	13	71
5 Leeds	42	13	6	2	37	18	5	10	6	28	21	70
6 WIMBLEDON	42	12	5	4	35	21	6	6	9	21	32	65
7 Sheffield Wed	42	10	7	4	48	24	6	9	6	28	30	64
8 Liverpool	42	12	4	5	33	23	5	5	11	26	32	60
9 QP Rangers	42	8	7	6	32	29	8	5	8	30	32	60
10 Aston Villa	42	8	5	8	23	18	7	7	7	23	32	57
11 Coventry	42	9	7	5	23	17	5	7	9	20	28	56
12 Norwich	42	4	9	8	26	29	8	8	5	39	32	53
13 West Ham	42	6	7	8	26	31	7	6	8	21	27	52
14 Chelsea	42	11	5	5	31	20	2	7	12	18	33	51
15 Tottenham	42	4	8	9	29	33	7	4	10	25	26	45
16 Manchester C	42	6	10	5	24	22	3	8	10	14	27	45
17 Everton	42	8	4	9	26	30	4	4	13	16	33	44
18 Southampton	42	9	2	10	30	31	3	5	13	19	35	43
19 Ipswich	42	5	8	8	21	32	4	8	9	14	26	43
20 Sheffield Utd	42	6	10	5	24	23	2	8	11	18	37	42
21 Oldham	42	5	8	8	24	33	4	5	12	18	35	40
22 Swindon	42	4	7	10	25	45	1	8	12	22	55	30
	924	192	142	128	663	532	128	142	192	532	663	1244

Odds & ends

Double wins: (3) Norwich, Manchester C, Swindon.
Double losses: (0).

Won from behind: (2) Norwich (h), Blackburn (h).
Lost from in front: (1) Everton (a).

High spots: 1 defeat in first 9 games, up to 4th.
Taking 23 points from undefeated 9 games in March and April, up to 6th.
Beating the top 3 (Man U, Blackburn and Newcastle) in quick succession.
Reaching quarter-finals of the Coca-Cola Cup.

Low spots: Winning 3 of 15 games from late September, down to 15th.
Losing at Everton after leading 2-0. The first time the Dons have ever squandered such a lead.

Wimbledon finish above Liverpool for the first time.

Player of the Year: John Scales.
Ever-presents: (2) Dean Holdsworth, Robbie Earle.
Hat-tricks: Dean Holdsworth (2).
Leading Scorer: Dean Holdsworth (24).

	Appearances						Goals			
	Lge	Sub	CCC	Sub	FAC	Sub	Lge	CCC	FAC	Total
Ardley, Neal	**14**	(2)	4	(1)	2		**1**	1		**2**
Barton, Warren	**37**	(2)	5		3		**2**	1		**3**
Berry, Greg	**4**						**1**			**1**
Blackwell, Dean	**16**	(2)	1			(1)				
Blissett, Gary	**6**	(12)		(2)	1	(1)	**3**			**3**
Castledine, Stewart	**3**						**1**			**1**
Clarke, Andy	**9**	(14)	3	(3)	1		**2**	1		**3**
Dobbs, Gerald	**3**	(7)								
Earle, Robbie	**42**		6		3		**9**	3		**12**
Elkins, Gary	**18**		1		3		**1**			**1**
Fashanu, John	**35**	(1)	6		3		**11**		1	**12**
Fear, Peter	**23**		2		1		**1**			**1**
Fitzgerald, Scott	**27**	(1)	6		3					
Gayle, Marcus	**10**									
Holdsworth, Dean	**42**		6		3		**17**	4	3	**24**
Jones, Vinnie	**33**		6		2		**2**	1		**3**
Joseph, Roger	**13**		2		1					
Kimble, Alan	**14**		3							
McAllister, Brian	**13**		3							
Perry, Chris		(2)								
Sanchez, Lawrie	**15**		1		1		**2**			**2**
Scales, John	**37**		5		3				1	**1**
Segers, Hans	**41**		6		3					
Sullivan, Neil	**1**	(1)								
Talboys, Steve	**6**	(1)								
(own-goals)							**3**			**3**
25 players used	**462**	**(45)**	**66**	**(6)**	**33**	**(2)**	**56**	**11**	**5**	**72**

No	Date		Att	Pos	Pts	F-A	H-T	Scorers, Times, and Referees	SQUAD	NUMBERS	IN	USE								subs used
1	A	COVENTRY			D	1-1	0-0	Castledine 55	Segers	Barton	Fitzgerald	Scales	Elkins	Talboys*	Jones	Castledine	Gayle	**Harford^**	Holdsworth	Ardley/Blissett
	20/8		**10,952**		1			*Busst 70*	*Ogrizovic*	*Borrows*	*Morgan*	*Babb*	*Busst*	*Darby*	*Rennie*	*Boland**	*Flynn*	*Quinn*	*Jenkinson^*	*Wegerle/Cook*
								Ref: R Gifford	Fashanu has been sold to Villa, and Mick Harford snapped up from Coventry for £50,000. Jones refuses the captaincy, which passes to Dean Holdsworth. Stewart Castledine's deflected shot wrong-foots Ogrizovic. Holdsworth misses a sitter, and David Busst levels with a fine header.											
2	H	IPSWICH			D	1-1	1-0	Holdsworth 19	Segers	Barton	Fitzgerald	Scales	Elkins	Ardley	Jones	Castledine	Gayle	Blissett*	Holdsworth	Clarke
	23/8		6,341		2			*Milton 61*	*Forrest*	*Stockwell*	*Wark*	*Linighan*	*Yallop*	*Mason*	*Williams*	*Milton*	*Slater*	*Marshall*	*Kiwomya*	
								Ref: J Worrall	Holdsworth's 25-yard bullet into the top corner deserves to win any match, but Deano misses other chances to seal the points, and when Scott Fitzgerald miscontrols the ball near the penalty spot Simon Milton levels. Ipswich won at Selhurst the two previous seasons. A bogey team.											
3	H	SHEFFIELD WED		16	L	0-1	0-0		Segers	Barton	Fitzgerald	Scales	Elkins	Ardley	Jones	Castledine	Gayle	Blissett*	Harford	Clarke
	27/8		7,453	*14*	2			*Watson 76*	*Pressman*	*Atherton*	*Nolan*	*Taylor*	*Petrescu**	*Hirst*	*Sheridan*	*Pearce*	*Bart-Will'ms^*	*Walker*	*Jones*	*Hyde/Watson*
								Ref: R Hart	Trevor Francis's Wednesday have lost their first two, and would have lost this, too, but for astonishing saves from Kevin Pressman, who has displaced England keeper Chris Woods. Gordon Watson netted at the second attempt in one of Wednesday's few attacking sorties.											
4	A	MANCHESTER U		16	L	0-3	0-1		Segers	Barton	Fitzgerald	Elkins	Kimble	Ardley	Jones	Castledine*	Gayle	Talboys	Harford	Clarke
	31/8		***43,440***	*2*	2			*Cantona 40, McClair 81, Giggs 84*	*Schmeichel*	*May*	*Bruce*	*Pallister*	*Irwin*	*Kanchelskis*	*McClair*	*Sharpe*	*Giggs*	*Cantona*	*Hughes*	
								Ref: T Holbrook	Champions United have set off like a train. Cantona returns to action after suspension, and his wonderful header puts United in front. It took United till the 81st minute to make sure of the points, when Jones lost possession to McClair. Segers was captain in Holdsworth's absence.											
5	H	LEICESTER		14	W	2-1	2-1	Harford 29, Willis 45 (og)	Segers	Barton	Fitzgerald	**Reeves**	Kimble	Ardley	Jones!	Elkins*	Gayle	Harford	Holdsworth^	Fear/Clarke
	10/9		7,683	*21*	5			*Lowe 25*	*Poole*	*Grayson*	*Willis*	*Blake*	*Roberts*	*Draper*	*Carey!*	*Philpott*	*Carr**	*Lewis^*	*Lowe!*	*Joachim/Agnew*
								Ref: G Poll	Neither side has won so far, so this is a critical match. Lowe blasts Leicester in front, but Harford quickly levels after Jones' throw-in was headed on by Marcus Gayle. Harford also set up the own-goal with his cut-back. Jones and Lowe are sent off for fisticuffs, and Carey too.											
6	A	CRYS PALACE		13	D	0-0	0-0		Segers	Barton	Fitzgerald	Reeves	Kimble	Ardley	Jones	Elkins	Gayle	Harford	Holdsworth	
	17/9		*12,100*	*21*	6				*Martyn*	*Gordon*	*Southgate*	*Coleman*	*Armstrong*	*Dyer*	*Salako*	*Matthew**	*Shaw*	*Pitcher*	*Newman*	*Ndah*
								Ref: K Cooper	Palace are winless, and this is nominally a home game for them. It drops them down to 21st place. To the neutral, this was a terrible match, devoid of goals and any other entertainment. What few chances there were fell to Palace. These were missed, or else saved by Hans Segers.											
7	A	QP RANGERS		10	W	1-0	0-0	Reeves 48	Segers	Barton	Fitzgerald	Reeves	Kimble	Fear*	Talboys	Elkins	Gayle^	Harford	Clarke!	Perry/Blissett
	24/9		*11,059*	*15*	9				*Roberts*	*Bardsley*	*Brevett*	*McDonald*	*Yates*	*Barker*	*Impey*	*Wilson**	*Ferdinand*	*Penrice*	*Meaker*	*Gallen*
								Ref: K Burge	Alan Reeves signed from Rochdale some weeks ago, replacing the Anfield-bound John Scales. Without Fashanu and Scales, unrest has set in, and other big names want to decamp. Flu strickens the squad, but Reeves pops in a fine header. Clarke gets sent off but the Dons are now 10th.											
8	H	TOTTENHAM		13	L	1-2	1-1	Talboys 29	Segers	Barton	Fitzgerald	Reeves*	Kimble	Fear	Talboys	Elkins	Ardley^	Harford	Holdsworth	Perry/Clarke
	1/10		16,802	*10*	9			*Sheringham 27, Popescu 63*	*Walker*	*Austin*	*Popescu*	*Mabbutt*	*Dumitrescu**	*Anderton*	*Sheringham*	*Dozzell*	*Klinsmann*	*Scott*	*Kerslake*	*Hazard*
								Ref: M Reed	They came in their thousands to see Jurgen Klinsmann. Manager Ossie Ardiles is under fire, but two super goals give him breathing space. No love is lost between these clubs, after last season's Fashnau/Mabbutt incident. But Fash has moved on, and combative Jones is suspended.											
9	H	ARSENAL		15	L	1-3	0-1	Jones 82	Segers	Barton	Fitzgerald	Reeves	Kimble	Fear	Jones	Elkins	Gayle*	Harford^	Holdsworth	Ardley/Thorn
	8/10		10,842	*12*	9			*Wright 11, Smith 58, Campbell 65*	*Seaman*	*Dixon*	*Adams*	*Bould*	*Winterburn*	*Parlour*	*Schwarz**	*Jensen*	*Smith*	*Wright*	*Campbell*	*Hillier*
								Ref: G Ashby	A second home defeat by a North London side in eight days is hard to take. Jones returns, but Arsenal win pretty much as they please. Kinnear knows he must strengthen his side. Ian Wright looked as sharp as ever and Segers denied him a hat-trick. Andy Thorn makes his second debut.											
10	A	NOTTINGHAM F		17	L	1-3	0-1	Gayle 81	Segers	Barton	Fitzgerald	Reeves	Thorn	Fear*	Jones	Elkins	Gayle	Castledine	**Ekoku**	Ardley
	17/10		*20,287*	*2*	9			*Bohinen 40, Collymore 66, Woan 74*	*Crossley*	*Haaland*	*Cooper*	*Chettle*	*Pearce*	*Stone*	*Phillips*	*Bohinen*	*Woan*	*Collymore*	*Roy*	
								Ref: R Hart	Unbeaten Forest climb to 2nd, thanks to a sweet strike by Lars Bohinen and a sensational goal from Stan Collymore. Efan Ekoku makes his debut for Wimbledon, but has little chance to shine. Early on, Kinnear had sought to contain Collymore and Roy with man-to-man marking.											

No	Venue	Opponent	Pos	Res	F-A	H-T	Scorers, Times, and Referees												
11	A	LIVERPOOL	19	L	0-3	0-2		Segers	Barton	Fitzgerald	Reeves	Perry*	Fear	Joseph	Elkins	Gayle	Ardley	Ekoku	Blissett/Castledine
22/10		*31,139*	*4*	9			*McManaman 20, Fowler 35, Barnes 63*	*James*	*Jones R*	*Scales*	*Ruddock*	*Babb*	*McManaman*	*Bjornebye*	*Barnes*	*Redknapp*	*Fowler**	*Rush^*	*Jones P/Clough*
							Ref: P Jones	John Scales is reacquainted with his former team-mates. Joe Kinnear can hardly put a team together, what with injuries. Despite monsoonal conditions, his makeshift team offers little resistance to Roy Evans's outfit. But this is Liverpool's first victory over the Dons in 10 attempts.											
12	H	NORWICH	17	W	1-0	0-0	Ekoku 63	Segers	Barton	Thorn	Reeves	Joseph	Talboys	Jones	Elkins	Gayle*	Blissett	Ekoku	Clarke
30/10		8,242	*8*	12				*Gunn*	*Sutch*	*Polston*	*Prior*	*Bowen*	*Ullathorne**	*Mulligan*	*Goss*	*Sheron*	*Newman*	*Akinbiyi^*	*Crook/Adams*
							Ref: D Gallagher	Four defeats by four big names have left the Dons in the bottom four. From here things can only get better. This Sunday match was played in heavy rain. Efan Ekoku burst through to score from a tight angle, to inflict upon his former club a sixth straight defeat away to Wimbledon.											
13	A	LEEDS	18	L	1-3	1-3	Ekoku 25	Segers	Barton	Thorn	Reeves	Joseph	Talboys	Jones	Elkins	Gayle	Blissett	Ekoku*	Clarke
5/11		*27,284*	*6*	12			*Wetherall 13, Speed 38, White 45*	*Lukic*	*Kelly*	*Palmer*	*Wetherall*	*Worthington*	*White**	*McAllister*	*Speed*	*Wallace*	*Deane^*	*Whelan*	*Radebe/Masinga*
							Ref: B Hill	Vinnie Jones was cheered, not jeered, on his return to Elland Road. The Dons had never won there, and blistering shots from Gary Speed and David White ensured they would not win now. Ekoku scored his second goal in successive matches, but in truth the Dons looked overawed.											
14	H	ASTON VILLA	16	W	4-3	1-2	Barton 8p, Ardley 65, Jones 83, Leon' 90	Segers	Barton	Thorn	Reeves	Elkins	Talboys*	Jones	**Leonhardsen**	Ardley	Clarke^	Ekoku	Harford/Fitzgerald
9/11		6,221	*18*	15			*Parker 19, Saunders 38, 50*	*Bosnich*	*Barrett*	*McGrath*	*Ehiogu*	*King*	*Houghton**	*Parker*	*Townsend!*	*Atkinson*	*Saunders^*	*Yorke*	*Richardson/Fenton*
							Ref: D Elleray	A sensational match. A life-saver to the Dons, a tragedy to Villa, and in particular to Ron Atkinson, sacked by Doug Ellis the next day. Villa's eighth defeat in nine games. Villa led 2-1 when skipper Andy Townsend was ordered off. 'Leo' celebrates his debut with a last-gasp winner.											
15	H	NEWCASTLE	14	W	3-2	3-2	Clarke 2, Ekoku 27, Harford 36	Segers	**Cunningham**	Thorn	Reeves	Elkins	Barton*	Jones!	Leonhardsen	Clarke	**Goodman^**	Ekoku	Fitzgerald/Harford
19/11		14,203	*3*	18			*Beardsley 30, Kitson 32*	*Srnicek*	*Venison*	*Beresford*	*Fox*	*Howey*	*Lee*	*Beardsley*	*Hottiger*	*Peacock**	*Albert*	*Kitson^*	*Clark/Watson*
							Ref: P Don	Another wonderful match. Two new stars join the Crazy Gang – from Millwall – and play their part in a roller-coaster game, in which six Dons were booked, Jones sent off, and Barton missed a second-half penalty. Andy Cole was injured. Newcastle have never won away to the Dons.											
16	A	MANCHESTER C	15	L	0-2	0-1		Segers	Cunningham	Thorn	Reeves!	Elkins	Barton	Jones	Leonhardsen	Clarke	Ekoku	Holdsworth*	Fitzgerald
26/11		*21,131*	*7*	18			*Flitcroft 7, Rosler 89*	*Dibble*	*Hill**	*Curle*	*Brightwelll*	*Summerbee*	*Flitcroft*	*Lomas*	*Beagrie*	*Quinn^*	*Walsh*	*BrightwellD*	*Kernaghan/Rosler*
							Ref: A Wilkie	Another red card, this time for Reeves for elbowing Paul Walsh. City interrupt the Dons' winning run, but scarcely deserve to do so. City were left hanging on desperately. Holdsworth hit the bar, and had another shot hooked out of goal. Then Reeves saw red and City scored again.											
17	H	BLACKBURN	16	L	0-3	0-0		Segers	Cunningham	Fitzgerald	Thorn	Elkins	Barton	Fear*	Leonhardsen	Clarke	Ekoku	Holdsworth	Harford
3/12		12,341	*1*	18			*Atkins 52, Wilcox 72, Shearer 74*	*Flowers*	*Sherwood*	*Hendry*	*Le Saux*	*Ripley*	*Shearer*	*Wilcox*	*Sutton*	*Berg*	*Atkins*	*Warhurst*	
							Ref: P Jones	Rovers have taken over from Newcastle at the top. Their title hopes were shattered by the Dons last season. Kenny Dalglish ensures there is no repetition, but this is a dour showing from the coming champions. But once in front, they never looked likely to slip up this time.											
18	H	COVENTRY	15	W	**2-0**	0-0	Leonhardsen 4, Harford 17	Segers	Cunningham	Fitzgerald	Thorn	Kimble	Barton	Elkins	Leonhardsen	Harford*	Ekoku	Holdsworth^	Clarke/Goodman
10/12		7,349	*11*	21				*Ogrizovic*	*Borrows*	*Morgan*	*Darby*	*Pressley*	*Flynn*	*Wegerle**	*Ndlovu*	*Cook*	*Busst*	*Jones*	*Williams*
							Ref: R Dilkes	Phil Neal's Coventry are unbeaten in four and are comfortably placed, though Dion Dublin is injured. They are sunk by the player they let go, Mick Harford, who flicks the ball on for Leo's opener, then adds a second from Barton's pass. Segers saves Paul Cook's 37th minute penalty.											
19	A	IPSWICH		D	2-2	1-1	Holdsworth 2, Goodman 62	Segers	Cunningham	Fitzgerald	Thorn	Kimble	Barton	Jones	Leonhardsen*	Goodman	Ekoku	Holdsworth^	Elkins/Harford
16/12		*11,367*		22			*Milton 7, Sedgley 83*	*Forrest*	*Yallop*	*Whelan*	*Sedgley*	*Vaughan*	*Mason*	*Williams*	*Milton*	*Thomsen*	*Kiwomya*	*Gregory**	*Paz*
							Ref: D Elleray	Ipswich have slumped to bottom and lose regularly at home, so this is two points lost for the Dons, who led twice. Holdsworth, struggling against injury, out of goals, and the subject of transfer talk, nets after 97 seconds with a crisp volley. It is his first league goal since August.											
20	A	SOUTHAMPTON	13	W	3-2	2-2	Holdsworth 20p, 72, Harford 38	Segers	Cunningham	Perry	Thorn!	Kimble	Barton	Earle	Elkins	Harford	Ekoku	Holdsworth*	Ardley
26/12		*14,603*	*14*	25			*Dodd 11, Le Tissier 43*	*Grobbelaar*	*Kenna*	*Hall*	*Widdrington*	*Monkou*	*Dodd*	*Magilton*	*Hughes**	*Heaney^*	*Dowie*	*Le Tissier*	*Maskell/McDonald*
							Ref: G Poll	This would have been a minor classic but for referee Graham Poll, who flourished 12 yellow cards, two of them to dismiss Andy Thorn. Best goal was Le Tissier's magic juggle and volley; worst was Dodd's mishit that crept through Segers' legs. The Dons were given an iffy penalty.											
21	H	WEST HAM	12	W	1-0	0-0	Fear 55	Segers	Cunningham	Perry	Thorn	Kimble	Barton	Jones*	Elkins^	Harford	Ekoku	Holdsworth	Fear/Clarke
28/12		11,212	*18*	28				*Miklosko*	*Breacker*	*Martin*	*Potts*	*Rieper**	*Dicks*	*Bishop*	*Holmes*	*Hughes*	*Cottee*	*Boere*	*Rush*
							Ref: P Don	Struggling Hammers won this match on possession but lost it on goals. Kimble's cross from the left threaded through to the far post where Peter Fear – a half-time substitute – shot diagonally past Miklosko. Tony Cottee then somehow contrived to hit the bar from two yards.											

No	Date		Att	Pos	Pts	F-A	H-T	Scorers, Times, and Referees	SQUAD	NUMBERS	IN	USE								subs used
22	A	CHELSEA		12	D	1-1	0-0	Ekoku 68	Segers	Cunningham	Perry	Thorn	Kimble	Barton	Jones	Earle	Harford	Ekoku	Holdsworth*	Clarke
	31/1		*16,105*	*10*	29			*Furlong 57*	*Kharin*	*Clarke*	*Kjeldbjerg*	*Johnsen*	*Sinclair*	*Spencer*	*Furlong*	*Stein*	*Peacock*	*Spackman**	*Newton*	*Hoddle*
								Ref: K Morton	Efan Ekoku shines at Stamford Bridge, and is rewarded with a fine header from Robbie Earle's right-wing cross. Glenn Hoddle's team are outplayed for long stretches and barely deserved a draw, but had gone in front through Paul Furlong's equally fine goal from a tight angle.											
23	H	EVERTON		9	W	2-1	2-1	Harford 4, 8	Segers	Cunningham	Perry	Reeves	Kimble	Barton	Jones	Earle	Clarke	Ekoku*	Harford	Fear
	2/1		9,506	*20*	32			*Rideout 17*	*Southall*	*Jackson*	*Watson*	*Unsworth*	*Burrows**	*Horne*	*Ebrell*	*Parkinson*	*Hinchcliffe*	*Ferguson*	*Rideout*	*Barlow*
								Ref: K Burge	Wimbledon's winning momentum gathers pace. Joe Royle has replaced Mike Walker as Everton manager and begun their revival. This is only Royle's second defeat since he took over. The Dons might have had six in their opening cascade but were hanging on anxiously after half-time.											
24	A	NORWICH		7	W	2-1	1-1	Reeves 44, Ekoku 49	Segers	Cunningham	Perry	Reeves	Kimble	Barton	Jones	Earle	Goodman*	Ekoko	Holdsworth^	Elkins/Clarke
	14/1		*18,261*	*9*	35			*Goss 22*	*Marshall*	*Sutch*	*Brown*	*Polston*	*Newsome*	*Adams**	*Crook^*	*Goss*	*Ullathorne*	*Sheron*	*Ward*	*Prior/Akinbiyi*
								Ref: M Bodenham	Seven league games without defeat, five won, sees Wimbledon soar to 7th. Alan Reeves and Efan Ekoku head the decisive goals. Reeves was rejected by Norwich as a youngster. Ekoku has twice scored the winner against his former team. The Dons' first double of the season.											
25	A	NEWCASTLE		8	L	1-2	0-1	Ekoku 78	Segers	Cunningham	Perry	Thorn	Kimble*	Barton	Jones	Earle	Clarke^	Ekoku	Goodman	Elkins/Blissett
	25/1		*34,374*	*4*	35			*Fox 34, Kitson 51*	*Srnicek*	*Hottiger*	*Peacock*	*Howey*	*Elliott*	*Gillespie*	*Bracewell*	*Venison*	*Fox*	*Kitson*	*Beardsley*	
								Ref: M Reed	Newcastle have not won for six weeks and Geordies are becoming restless. They should have been more agitated after this match, for having seen their team lead 2-0, they are stunned by the Dons' fight-back. Goodman levels at the death, but the ref says no. Kinnear is hopping mad.											
26	H	LEEDS		9	D	0-0	0-0		Segers	Cunningham	Thorn	Reeves	Elkins	Barton	Jones	Earle	Leonhardsen	Ekoku*	Harford^	Blissett/Goodman
	4/2		10,211	*6*	36				*Lukic*	*Kelly*	*Dorigo*	*Palmer*	*Deane*	*McAllister*	*Pemberton*	*White*	*Worthington*	*Massinga*	*Radebe*	
								Ref: G Ashby	Wimbledon have that 1-3 defeat at Elland Road to avenge, but they seldom look like doing so. Ekoku's clean header from eight yards, which sails over the crossbar, is the nearest they come. If the Dons wish to qualify for Europe, teams just above them – like Leeds – must be beaten.											
27	A	ASTON VILLA		9	L	**1-7**	1-4	Barton 11 */Saunders 48, 67p, Yorke 83/*	Segers	Cunningham	Thorn	Reeves	Elkins	Barton	Jones	Leonhardsen	Harford*	Ekoku	Holdsworth^	Perry/Goodman
	11/2		*23,982*	*11*	36			*Reeves 12 (og), Johnson 22, 36, 38,*	*Bosnich*	*Charles*	*Staunton*	*Teale*	*McGrath*	*Small*	*Taylor*	*Yorke*	*Saunders*	*Johnson*	*Townsend*	
								Ref: B Hill	Wimbledon's bubble bursts in spectacular fashion, as Villa's revival continues. Warren Barton even puts the Dons in front, but within seconds Reeves puts into his own net, and then the sluice gates open. Villa's goals are a mix of the comical, tragic, and superb – such as Saunders' first.											
28	A	BLACKBURN		11	L	1-2	1-2	Ekoku 39	Segers	Cunningham	Perry	Reeves	Kimble	Barton	Earle	Leonhardsen	Ardley	Ekoku*	Clarke^	Harford/Holdsworth
	21/2		*20,586*	*1*	36			*Shearer 3, Atkins 25*	*Mimms*	*Berg*	*Hendry*	*Pearce*	*Le Saux*	*Slater**	*Sherwood*	*Atkins*	*Warhurst*	*Shearer*	*Newell*	*Ripley*
								Ref: S Lodge	Rovers become the first side to complete the double over the Dons, but are even less convincing than they had been at Selhurst Park. Rovers go two up on a pudding pitch, but from the moment Barton shoots, Mimms saves, and Ekoku heads in, the home team back-pedal till the end.											
29	A	TOTTENHAM		10	W	2-1	1-0	Ekoku 39, 64	Segers	Cunningham	Perry	Reeves	Kimble	Barton	Earle	Thorn	Fear	Ekoku	Gayle	
	25/2		*27,258*	*7*	39			*Klinsmann 49*	*Walker*	*Edinburgh*	*Popescu**	*Calderwood*	*Mabbutt*	*Barmby*	*Anderton*	*Sheringham*	*Howells*	*Klinsmann*	*Campbell^*	*Rosenthal/Austin*
								Ref: D Gallagher	Spurs have their minds on Wembley, and are beaten by two virtuoso goals from Efan Ekoku. The first, a sweetly struck drive from 22 yards, was eclipsed by the second, begun by Ekoku on the halfway line and finished in style. Kinnear afterwards adjudges it his goal of the season.											
30	H	QP RANGERS		10	L	1-3	1-1	Holdsworth 12	Segers	Cunningham	Perry	Reeves	Kimble	Barton	Earle*	Jones	Leonhardsen^	Harford	Holdsworth	Clarke/Goodman
	4/3		9,176	*16*	39			*Ferdinand 24, 58, Holloway 48*	*Roberts*	*Wilson*	*Ready*	*McDonald*	*Impey*	*Holloway*	*Ferdinand**	*Barker*	*Brevett*	*Maddix*	*Gallen*	*Penrice*
								Ref: G Willard	QPR will end the season with a late charge in which they overhaul the Dons. The match belongs to Les Ferdinand. Holdsworth's early goal is cancelled out by a 25-yard belter. Ferdinand's second was reminiscent of Ekoku's at Spurs, leaving a trail of defenders scattered on the grass.											
31	H	MANCHESTER U		12	L	0-1	0-0		Segers	Cunningham	Perry	Reeves	Kimble!	Barton	Elkins	Jones	Gayle*	Goodman	Holdsworth	Ardley
	7/3		**18,224**	*1*	39			Bruce 84	*Schmeichel*	*Neville G*	*Pallister*	*Bruce*	*Irwin*	*Giggs*	*McClair*	*Ince*	*Sharpe*	*Cole*	*Hughes*	
								Ref: R Hart	Wimbledon's biggest gate of the season witnessed a match that only just survived a pre-match monsoon. Title-chasing United have heaps of possession but don't look like scoring. Then Alan Kimble is sent off for encroaching at a corner, Segers mishandles, and Kinnear blows his top.											

No / Date	Venue	Opponent / Att	Pos	Res / Pts	F-A	H-T	Scorers, Times, Referees	1	2	3	4	5	6	7	8	9	10	11	subs used
32	A	SHEFFIELD WED	9	W	1-0	0-0	Reeves 63	Sullivan	Cunningham	Perry	Reeves	Kimble	Barton	Elkins	Jones	Gayle	Goodman	Holdsworth	Harford/Leonhardsen
11/3		*20,395*	*8*	42				*Pressman*	*Atherton*	*Nolan*	*Petrescu**	*Waddle*	*Bright*	*Pearce*	*Sinton*	*Hyde^*	*Walker*	*Williams*	*Poric/Whittingham*
							Ref: J Worrall	The Dons return to winning ways against a Wednesday team enjoying their best sequence of the season. Joe Kinnear watches from the stand as Alan Reeves, venturing upfield, controls a weak clearance with his first touch and with his second slots the ball inside the near post.											
33	H	CRYS PALACE	8	W	**2-0**	1-0	Jones 36, Gayle 60	Sullivan	Cunningham	Perry	Reeves	Kimble	Barton	Elkins	Jones*	Gayle^	Goodman	Holdsworth	Harford/Leonhardsen
18/3		8,835	*19*	45				*Martyn*	*Southgate*	*Young*	*Coleman*	*Dowie*	*Armstrong*	*Salako*	*Shaw*	*Pitcher*	*Preece**	*Newman^*	*Gordon/Humphrey*
							Ref: D Gallagher	Two cup semi-finals and a desperate fight to stay in the Premiership. That sums up Palace's season. The tenants beat the landlords for the first time in three attempts. The game's highlight is the run and pass with which Warren Barton sets up the Dons' second goal, for Marcus Gayle.											
34	H	MANCHESTER C	8	W	**2-0**	0-0	Thorn 59, Elkins 76	Sullivan	Cunningham	Perry	Reeves	Thorn	Leonhardsen	Elkins	Jones	Gayle*	Goodman^	Holdsworth	Fear/Harford
21/3		**5,268**	*13*	48				*Coton*	*Foster*	*Vonk*	*Curle*	*Phelan*	*Walsh*	*Gaudino**	*Flitcroft*	*Simpson^*	*Beagrie*	*Rosler*	*Quinn/Summerbee*
							Ref: R Gifford	Brian Horton's City have been struggling since the autumn. They attract Wimbledon's smallest home gate of the season, and head back north smarting from Andy Thorn's scrambled strike – his first since rejoining the club – which sends them slithering towards another defeat.											
35	A	LEICESTER	8	W	4-3	0-1	Goodman 63, 90, Leonhardsen 65, 85	Sullivan	Cunningham	Thorn	Reeves	Kimble	Barton*	Elkins	Leonhardsen	Gayle^	Goodman	Holdsworth	Perry/Harford
1/4		*15,489*	*22*	51			*Robins 13, Willis 79, Lawrence 84*	*Poole*	*Grayson*	*Hill**	*Mohan^*	*Willis*	*Parker*	*Lowe*	*Ormandroyd*	*Carey*	*Whitlow*	*Robins*	*Lawrence/McMahon*
							Ref: D Elleray	With three straight wins under their belt, this should have been an away banker at doomed Leicester. In fact, the Dons trail 0-1 and 2-3. Two close range headers seem to have won it for City, before the Dons strike. Both Goodman and Leonhardsen notch their first doubles for the club.											
36	H	CHELSEA	8	D	1-1	0-1	Goodman 57	Sullivan	Cunningham	Thorn	Reeves	Kimble*	Barton	Elkins	Jones	Leonhardsen	Goodman^	Holdsworth	Harford/Gayle
10/4		7,002	*16*	52			*Sinclair 37*	*Hitchcock*	*Hall*	*Kjeldberg*	*Sinclair*	*Minto*	*Burley*	*Peacock*	*Spackman*	*Hopkin*	*Stein**	*Furlong*	*Spencer*
							Ref: K Cooper	For the second time this season Chelsea escape with a 1-1 draw, thereby halting Wimbledon's four-game winning streak. Chelsea have just lost 0-3 away to Real Zaragoza in the Cup-Winners Cup. A similar defeat now would not have flattered them. The Dons have two goals disallowed.											
37	A	WEST HAM	9	L	0-3	0-1		Sullivan	Cunningham	Thorn	Reeves	Elkins	Barton	Leonhardsen	Jones	Gayle*	Harford	Holdsworth	Clarke
13/4		*21,804*	*17*	52			*Dicks 40p, Boere 76, Cottee 77*	*Mikosko*	*Braecker*	*Rieper*	*Potts*	*Dicks*	*Hughes*	*Allen*	*Bishop*	*Holmes*	*Boere*	*Cottee*	
							Ref: M Reed	In the end there is no arguing with the result, but Wimbledon were pressing forward strongly when Jerome Boere extended the Hammers' lead with a firm header. Earlier, Sullivan had come so close to saving Dicks' penalty. The Dons' first loss in six, but their fifth defeat by three goals.											
38	H	SOUTHAMPTON	9	L	0-2	0-2		Sullivan	Cunningham	Thorn	Reeves	Goodman*	Barton	Leonhardsen	Jones	Gayle	Ekoku	Holdsworth	Clarke
17/4		10,521	*11*	52			*Le Tissier 9, Magilton 32*	*Beasant*	*Charlton*	*Hall*	*Benali*	*Dodd*	*Magilton*	*Le Tissier*	*Heaney**	*Widdrington*	*Shipperley*	*Watson*	*Tisdale*
							Ref: G Ashby	Qualification for the UEFA Cup seems far-fetched after this result. Wimbledon's downfall was executed by Matthew Le Tissier. His goal was his 27th of the season, and his 10th against the Dons in 12 games. The Saints are pulling steadily clear of the drop.											
39	A	EVERTON	9	D	0-0	0-0		Sullivan	Cunningham	Thorn*	Reeves	Kimble	Fear	Leonhardsen	Jones	Elkins	Ekoku^	Holdsworth	Perry/Goodman
29/4		*33,063*	*16*	53				*Southall*	*Barrett*	*Watson*	*Unsworth*	*Ablett*	*Limpar**	*Horne*	*Parkinson*	*Hinchcliffe*	*Stuart*	*Amokachi*	*Rideout*
							Ref: P Danson	All the talk is of last season, when Everton famously came from behind in the final match to secure their Premiership survival. This match has none of that drama, even though Everton are hovering on the brink. They came nearest when Gary Ablett's lob was clutched under the crossbar.											
40	H	LIVERPOOL	9	D	0-0	0-0		Sullivan	Cunningham	Perry	Reeves	Kimble	Barton	Elkins	Jones	Gayle*	Ekoku^	Goodman	Fear/Clarke
2/5		12,041	*4*	54				*James*	*Thomas*	*Scales*	*Ruddock**	*Harkness*	*McManaman*	*Redknapp*	*Barnes*	*Walters*	*Rush*	*Fowler*	*Matteo*
							Ref: T Holbrook	Wimbledon have forgotten how to score. Their season is meandering to a close. Liverpool's too, now that they appear to have sewn up their European qualification for next season. The game barely flickered into life, but Neil Ruddock's torn hamstring ends his season prematurely.											
41	A	ARSENAL	8	D	0-0	0-0		Sullivan	Cunningham	Perry	Reeves	Kimble	Barton	Leonhardsen*	Jones	Elkins	Goodman	Holdsworth^	Fear/Clarke
4/5		*32,822*	*11*	55				*Seaman*	*Dixon*	*Linighan*	*Adams*	*Winterburn*	*Merson*	*Jensen*	*Parlour*	*Helder*	*Wright*	*Hartson**	*Kiwomya*
							Ref: R Gifford	Wimbledon win plaudits across the football spectrum for agreeing to advance this fixture by two days to give Arsenal more time to prepare for the Cup-Winners Cup Final with Real Zaragoza in Paris. The match itself bore the goalless stamp from the first minute to the last.											
42	H	NOTTINGHAM F	9	D	2-2	2-1	Holdsworth 35, 40p	Sullivan*	Cunningham	Perry	Reeves	Kimble	Elkins	Leonhardsen	Jones	Gayle^	Ekoku	Holdsworth	Segers/Clarke
13/5		15,341	*3*	56			*Phillips 14, Stone 73*	*Crossley*	*Lyttle*	*Cooper*	*Chettle*	*Pearce*	*Stone*	*Gemmill*	*Phillips*	*Woan*	*Collymore*	*Lee*	
Average	Home 10,229	*Away 22,262*					Ref: S Lodge	Wimbledon's goal-drought has extended to eight and a half hours by the time Holdsworth's angled shot squeezed under Mark Crossley's body. The season ends anti-climactically for the Dons – failing to win in seven – and sadly for Neil Sullivan, who, challenged by Lee, breaks a leg.											

Coca-Cola Cup	Att		F-A	H-T	Scorers, Times, and Referees	SQUAD	NUMBERS	IN	USE								subs used
2:1 H TORQUAY	13		2-0	2-0	Gayle 35, Harford 43	Segers	Barton	Fitzgerald	Perry	Kimble	Ardley*	Jones	Elkins	Gayle	Harford^	Holdsworth	Fear/Clarke
20/9	2,451 *3:4*					*Davis*	*Barrow*	*Kelly*	*Burton*	*Moore*	*Curran*	*Trollope*	*Buckle*	*Hancox*	*Okorie*	*Goodridge*	
					Ref: P Foakes	Torquay are the only Football League team who cost nothing, being composed entirely of free-transfers, cast-offs and rejects. Holdsworth's point-blank header was kept out by Kelvin Davis, but Marcus Gayle knocked in the loose ball. Harford's second brings breathing space.											
2:2 A TORQUAY	13		1-0	1-0	Holdsworth 38	Segers	Barton	Fitzgerald	Perry	Kimble	Fear	Talboys*	Elkins	Clarke^	Harford	Holdsworth	Ardley/Joseph
5/10	*4,244* *3:10*					*Bayes*	*Burton*	*Kelly*	*Hathaway*	*Moore*	*Curran*	*Trollope*	*Buckle*	*Hancox*	*Okorie*	*Goodridge*	
					Ref: M Bodenham (Dons win 3-0 on aggregate)	Torquay have to strike quickly if they are to cause an upset. This they seldom look like doing. And once Dean Holdsworth has extended Wimbledon's aggregate lead to three, there is little doubt the Dons will take their place in Round 3. There they will entertain Palace.											
3 H CRYS PALACE	19		0-1	0-0		Segers	Barton	Fitzgerald*	Thorn	Joseph	Ardley	Jones	Elkins	Gayle^	Clarke	Blissett	Harford/Fear
26/10	9,394 *17*				*Armstrong 72*	*Martyn*	*Humphrey*	*Shaw*	*Coleman*	*Gordon*	*Bowry*	*Southgate*	*Newman*	*Salako*	*Armstrong*	*Preece*	
					Ref: R Gifford	This is Wimbledon's fifth straight defeat in league and cup. They look the worst of two bad sides, and are beaten by Chris Armstrong's far-post effort from Gareth Southgate's right-wing cross. The Dons never look like saving the tie, and Kinnear rushes off to borrow Leonhardsen.											

FA Cup																	
3 H COLCHESTER	9	W	1-0	1-0	Harford 8	Segers	Cunningham	Thorn	Reeves	Kimble	Fear	Jones	Earle	Clarke	Harford	Holdsworth	
7/1	6,903 *3:7*					*Cheesewright*	*Betts*	*English*	*Cawley*	*Caesar*	*Locke*	*Putney*	*Brown*	*Whitton*	*Kinsella*	*Abrahams**	*Dennis*
					Ref: P Danson	Managerless Colchester lost their Football League status a few seasons back, but regained it at the first attempt. This is a huge match for them, but a test of nerve for the Dons. Harford settles them early on. Colchester win a lot of the ball, but are forced to shoot from long range.											
4 A TRANMERE	9	W	2-0	1-0	Leonhardsen 31, Earle 51	Segers	Cunningham	Thorn	Perry	Elkins	Barton	Jones	Earle	Leonhardsen	Harford*	Ekoku^	Goodman/Blissett
28/1	*11,637* *1:4*					*Nixon*	*Thomas*	*Garnett*	*McGreal*	*Stevens*	*Morrisey*	*O'Brien**	*Irons*	*Nevin*	*Malkin*	*Muir^*	*Brannan/Aldridge*
					Ref: P Durkin	Tranmere are once again chasing promotion to the Premiership. The prolific John Aldridge has been out injured for six weeks, but is named as substitute. Rovers had faced top division sides at Prenton Park 10 times in recent years, and only lost once before today. Barton runs the show.											
5 A LIVERPOOL	9	D	1-1	1-1	Clarke 2	Segers	Cunningham	Perry	Reeves	Kimble	Barton	Leonhardsen	Earle	Ardley	Clarke*	Ekoku^	Holdsworth/Harford
19/2	*25,124* *4*				*Fowler 33*	*James*	*Jones R*	*Scales*	*Ruddock*	*Bjornebye*	*McManaman*	*Redknapp*	*Barnes*	*Walters*	*Rush*	*Fowler*	
					Ref: A Wilkie	Vinnie Jones has been dropped for a prank in Dublin. Andy Clarke scores the goal of the month in the second minute, and sets up a Dons performance that draws praise from all quarters. Robbie Fowler's first FA Cup goal was almost wiped out by Ekoku's late shot which hit a post.											
5R H LIVERPOOL	10	L	0-2	0-2		Segers	Cunningham	Perry	Thorn*	Kimble	Barton	Leonhardsen	Earle	Ardley	Clarke	Ekoku^	Harford/Holdsworth
28/2	12,553 *4*				*Barnes 10, Rush 38*	*James*	*Jones*	*Scales*	*Ruddock*	*Babb*	*Bjornebye*	*McManaman*	*Redknapp*	*Barnes*	*Fowler**	*Rush*	*Walters*
						All the omens favoured Wimbledon, who Liverpool had beaten just once in 11 attempts. But the Dons look strangely limp, and are beaten from the moment Ian Rush equals Denis Law's all-time FA Cup scoring record of 41. The Dons lost Ekoku and Thorn injured and rarely threatened.											

	Home						Away					
	P	W	D	L	F	A	W	D	L	F	A	Pts
1 Blackburn	42	17	2	2	54	21	10	6	5	26	18	89
2 Manchester U	42	16	4	1	42	4	10	6	5	35	24	88
3 Nottingham F	42	12	6	3	36	18	10	5	6	36	25	77
4 Liverpool	42	13	5	3	38	13	8	6	7	27	24	74
5 Leeds	42	13	5	3	35	15	7	8	6	24	23	73
6 Newcastle	42	14	6	1	46	20	6	6	9	21	27	72
7 Tottenham	42	10	5	6	32	25	6	9	6	34	33	62
8 QP Rangers	42	11	3	7	36	26	6	6	9	25	33	60
9 WIMBLEDON	42	9	5	7	26	26	6	6	9	22	39	56
10 Southampton	42	8	9	4	33	27	4	9	8	28	36	54
11 Chelsea	42	7	7	7	25	22	6	8	7	25	33	54
12 Arsenal	42	6	9	6	27	21	7	3	11	25	28	51
13 Sheffield Wed	42	7	7	7	26	26	6	5	10	23	31	51
14 West Ham	42	9	6	6	28	19	4	5	12	16	29	50
15 Everton	42	8	9	4	31	23	3	8	10	13	28	50
16 Coventry	42	7	7	7	23	25	5	7	9	21	37	50
17 Manchester C	42	8	7	6	37	28	4	6	11	16	36	49
18 Aston Villa	42	6	9	6	27	24	5	6	10	24	32	48
19 Crys Palace	42	6	6	9	16	23	5	6	10	18	26	45
20 Norwich	42	8	8	5	27	21	2	5	14	10	33	43
21 Leicester	42	5	6	10	28	37	1	5	15	17	43	29
22 Ipswich	42	5	3	13	24	34	2	3	16	12	59	27
	924	205	134	123	697	498	123	134	205	498	697	1252

Odds & ends

Double wins: (2) Leicester, Norwich.
Double losses: (2) Manchester U, Blackburn.

Won from behind: (5) Leicester (h & a), Villa (h), Southampton (a), Norwich (a).
Lost from in front: (2) QPR (h), Villa (a).

High spots: 8 undefeated games from 10th December, up to 7th.
4 straight wins from 11th March, up to 8th.

Low spots: Bad start, 2 points from first 4 games.
Dreadful finish: 7 games without a win, in which 5 goalless games in a row.
Being crushed 1-7 at Aston Villa.

Wimbledon finish above Arsenal for the first time, but have a worse goal-difference than relegated Palace.

The Dons did not win any match by more than 2 goals, but lost by more than 2 goals 5 times.

Never before has the Dons' leading scorer failed to make double figures.

Player of the Year: Warren Barton.
Ever-presents: (0).
Hat-tricks: (0).
Leading Scorer: Efan Ekoku (9).

	Appearances						Goals			
	Lge	Sub	CCC	Sub	FAC	Sub	**Lge**	CCC	FAC	**Total**
Ardley, Neil	**9**	(5)	2	(1)	2		**1**			**1**
Barton, Warren	**39**		3		3		**2**			**2**
Blissett, Gary	**4**	(4)	1			(1)				
Castledine, Stewart	**5**	(1)					**1**			**1**
Clarke, Andy	**8**	(17)	2	(1)	3		**1**		1	**2**
Cunningham, Kenny	**28**				4					
Earle, Steve	**9**				4				1	**2**
Ekoku, Efan	**24**				3		**9**			**9**
Elkins, Gary	**33**	(3)	3		1		**1**			**1**
Fear, Peter	**8**	(6)	1	(2)	1		**1**			**1**
Fitzgerald, Scott	**14**	(3)	3							
Gayle, Brian	**22**	(1)	2				**2**	1		**3**
Goodman, Don	**13**	(5)				(1)	**4**			**4**
Harford, Mick	**17**	(10)	2	(1)	2	(2)	**6**	1	1	**8**
Holdsworth, Dean	**27**	(1)	2		1	(2)	**7**	1		**8**
Jones, Vinnie	**33**		2		2		**3**			**3**
Joseph, Roger	**3**		1	(1)						
Kimble, Alan	**26**		2		3					
Leonhardsen, Oyvind	**18**	(2)			3		**4**		1	**4**
Perry, Chris	**17**	(5)	2		3					
Reeves, Alan	**31**				2		**3**			**3**
Scales, John	**3**									
Segers, Hans	**31**	(1)	3		4					
Sullivan, Neil	**11**									
Talboys, Steve	**7**		1				**1**			**1**
Thorn, Andy	**22**	(1)	1		3		**1**			**1**
(own goals)							**1**			**1**
26 players used	**462**	**(65)**	**33**	**(6)**	**44**	**(6)**	**48**	**3**	**4**	**55**

No		Date	Att	Pos	Pts	F-A	H-T	Scorers, Times, and Referees	SQUAD	NUMBERS	IN USE									subs used
1	H	BOLTON			W	3-2	2-2	Ekoku 5, Earle 25, Holdsworth 55	Heald	Perry	Reeves	Thorn	Kimble*	Fear	Jones	Earle	Leonhardsen	Ekoku	Holdsworth^	Elkins/Blissett
		19/8	9,317		3			*Thompson 27p, De Freitas 40*	*Branagan*	*Green*	*Bergsson**	*Stubbs*	*Phillips*	*McAteer*	*Patterson*	*Fairclough*	*De Freitas*	*Paatelainen^*	*Thompson*	*Lee/Coyle*
								Ref: K Cooper	Paul Heald has signed from Leyton Orient for £125,000. The blazing summer encourages almost the whole Wimbledon team to shear off their hair. Holdsworth is the exception. Roy McFarland's promoted Bolton look enterprising in attack, fragile in defence. Hairy Holdsworth wins it.											
2	A	QP RANGERS		2	W	3-0	1-0	Leo 29, Holdsworth 56, Goodman 83	Heald	Perry	Reeves	Thorn	Kimble	Fear*	Jones	Earle	Leonhardsen	Ekoku^	Holdsworth!	Elkins/Goodman
		23/8	*11,837*	*20*	6				*Roberts*	*Bardsley*	*McDonald**	*Maddix*	*Brevitt*	*Sinclair*	*Holloway*	*Barker^*	*Impey*	*Gallen*	*Dichio*	*Zelic/Wilkins*
								Ref: G Poll	The Dons have a good record at Loftus Road. Both clubs were punished in the close season for their poor disciplinary records. Seven players are booked and Holdsworth is sent off for a clash with Maddix. Rufus Brevitt's stumble permits Leo to score the first. Roberts boobs for No 3.											
3	A	MANCHESTER U		3	L	1-3	0-1	Earle 65	Heald	Perry	Reeves	Thorn	Kinble	Elkins*	Jones	Earle	Leonhardsn^	Ekoku"	Holdsworth	Goodm/Talboys/Bliss
		26/8	*32,226*	*5*	6			*Keane 27, 80, Cole 60*	*Schmeichel*	*Irwin*	*Bruce*	*Sharpe*	*Pallister*	*Keane*	*Cole**	*Butt*	*Neville*	*Scholes^*	*Beckham*	*Giggs/Davies*
								Ref: P Durkin	Wimbledon have never before won the first two, never mind the first three. United's reshaped team, minus Ince, Hughes, and Kanchelskis, begin patiently but win in style. Earle's goal had threatened a typical Dons fight-back, until Heald spills Sharpe's shot into Roy Keane's path.											
4	H	SHEFFIELD WED		6	D	2-2	1-1	Goodman 17, Holdsworth 84p	Heald	Perry	Reeves	Thorn*	Kimble	Leonhardsn^	Jones	Earle	Goodman	Ekoku"	Holdsworth	Gayle/Elkins/Blissett
		30/8	6,352	*12*	7			*Degryse 10, Hirst 46*	*Pressman*	*Atherton*	*Watts*	*Walker*	*Nolan*	*Petrescu*	*Degryse*	*Sheridan*	*Pembridge*	*Hirst**	*Bright*	*Ingesson*
								Ref: A Wilkie	With six minutes to play the Dons are losing and look to have thrown away their fine start to the season. Belgium's World Cup captain, Marc Degryse, wrong-foots Jones for No 1, and David Hirst, in his first match for nearly a year, sweeps a second. Watts fells Blissett for the penalty.											
5	H	LIVERPOOL		3	W	1-0	1-0	Babb 30 (og)	Heald	Cunningham	Reeves	Thorn*	Kimble	Leonhardsen	Jones!	Earle	Gayle^	Ekoku	Harford	Perry/Clarke
		9/9	19,530	*6*	10				*James*	*Jones*	*Wright*	*Ruddock*	*Babb*	*Harkness**	*Barnes*	*Redknapp*	*McManaman*	*Fowler*	*Collymore*	*Thomas*
								Ref: K Burge	An extraordinary match. Liverpool look terrific. Then a flare-up between Thorn and Collymore results in Jones being sent off for an alleged head-butt (later annulled), and Thorn thinking he had been expelled as well. Thorn's free-kick prompts Babb's own goal. Then it's a siege.											
6	A	ASTON VILLA		6	L	0-2	0-1		Heald	Cunningham	Reeves	Perry	Kimble	Leonhardsen	Jones	Earle*	Gayle^	Ekoku	Harford"	Goodman/Fitzg/Holds
		16/9	*26,928*	*3*	10			*Draper 7, Taylor 47*	*Bosnich*	*Charles*	*Wright*	*Southgate*	*McGrath*	*Ehiogu*	*Taylor*	*Draper*	*Milosevic*	*Yorke*	*Townsend*	
								Ref: D Elleray	In the old days Villa were whipping boys for the Dons, but no longer. This was an improvement on last season's 1-7 crushing, but Villa were no less superior. Alan Wright's pass, Yorke's knock-down, Mark Draper's calm finish – 1-0. The Dons created nothing. Jones coaches at Eton.											
7	H	LEEDS		9	L	2-4	1-3	Holdsworth 43, Reeves 58	Heald	Cunningham	Reeves	Perry	Elkins	Fear*	Jones	Earle	Gayle^	Clarke	Holdsworth	Goodman/Ekoku
		23/9	13,307	*6*	10			*Palmer 32, Yeboah 42, 45, 73*	*Lukic*	*Kelly*	*Palmer*	*Wetherall*	*Beesley*	*McAllister*	*Pemberton*	*Speed*	*Masinga**	*Yeboah*	*Deane*	*Tinkley*
								Ref: R Dilkes	Having lost 4-5 to Charlton in midweek, the Dons contribute to another corker. Kinnear warns that his team are in danger of becoming entertainers. Star of the match is Tony Yeboah, whose second goal will live in the mind. Kinnear knows in his heart that Leeds might have had 10.											
8	A	TOTTENHAM		11	L	1-3	1-2	Earle 40	Heald	Cunningham	Thorn	Perry	Elkins	Fear*	Jones	Earle	Leonhardsn^	Gayle	Holdsworth	Goodman/Clarke
		30/9	*25,321*	*9*	10			*Sheringham 8, 33, Elkins 63 (og)*	*Walker*	*Austin*	*Howells**	*Calderwood*	*Mabbutt*	*McMahon*	*Wilson*	*Campbell*	*Rosenthal*	*Armstrong*	*Sheringham*	*Dozell*
								Ref: G Ashby	Five wins in a row for Gerry Francis's Spurs, and four defeats for Wimbledon, whose defence is haemorrhaging. The match starts 15 minutes late because Jason Dozzell is stuck in traffic. Spurs change their team-sheet! Elkins' own-goal denies Chris Armstong his first goal for Spurs.											
9	H	WEST HAM			L	0-1	0-1		Heald	Cunningham	Thorn*	Perry	McAllister	Skinner^	Jones	Earle	Leonhardsn"	Goodman	Holdsworth	Fitzger/Gayle/Clarke
		16/10	9,411		10			*Cottee 18*	*Miklosko*	*Potts*	*Martin*	*Rieper*	*Dicks*	*Slater*	*Bishop*	*Moncur*	*Hughes*	*Dowie*	*Cottee*	
								Ref: D Gallagher	It is six months since Tony Cottee last scored – against Wimbledon in April – and he breaks his bad run with a neat chip after Heald had saved from Robbie Slater. Cottee might have had more, as the Hammers counter-attacked at speed. Robbie Earle's hook hit the crossbar.											
10	A	NEWCASTLE		13	L	1-6	0-3	Gayle 60 *[Clark 59, Albert 84]*	Heald	Cunningham	Reeves	Perry*	McAllister^	Fitzgerald	Jones	Earle	Gayle	Harford	Holdsworth	Goodman/Talboys
		21/10	*36,434*	*1*	10			*Howey 31, Ferdinand 35, 41, 63*	*Hislop*	*Barton*	*Beresford*	*Peacock*	*Howey**	*Lee^*	*Clark"*	*Ginola*	*Gillespie*	*Beardsley*	*Ferdinand*	*Albert/Hottiger/Sellars*
								Ref: G Poll	Five straight wins for super Newcastle; five straight league defeats for demoralised Dons. Les Ferdinand scores for the 7th successive match. The Dons hold out for half an hour, then capsize under a torrent of crosses. At 3-0 Heald is sent off for fouling Ferdinand. Jones goes in goal.											

Coca-Cola Cup		F-A	H-T	Scorers, Times, and Referees	SQUAD	NUMBERS	IN	USE								subs used
2:1 H CHARLTON	6	L	4-5	1-2 Holdsworth 10, 69, Earle 71, Clarke 87	Heald	Cunningham	Reeves	Perry	Kimble	Jones	Leonhards'n*	Earle	Gayle	Ekoku^	Holdsworth	Clarke/Goodman
19/9	3,717	*1:6*		*Garland 24, Bowyer 41,76,78, Grant 84*	*Salmon*	*Humphrey*	*Rufus*	*Balmer*	*Stuart*	*Newton*	*Garland*	*Bowyer*	*Robinson**	*Leaburn*	*Nelson*	*Grant*
				Ref: M Reed	Wimbledon have never before scored four goals and lost. They led 1-0 and 3-2, but are finally sunk by Lee Bowyer's hat-trick. Only 18, and having served a drug ban, midfielder Bowyer is hot property. Almost as hot as Kinnear's temper. Kimble and Leo are dropped for Leeds.											
2:2 A CHARLTON	11	D	3-3	1-2 Holdsworth 31, 81p, Earle 46	Heald	Cunningh'm*	Thorn	Perry	Elkins	Jones	Talboys	Earle^	Ardley	Gayle"	Holdsworth	Clarke/Leo/Harford
3/10	*9,823*	*1:4*	*aet*	*Newton 21, Leaburn 79, Robinson 97*	*Salmon*	*Humphrey*	*Chapple*	*Balmer*	*Stuart*	*Newton*	*Garland**	*Bowyer*	*Robinson*	*Grant*	*Leaburn*	*Robson*
				Ref: P Durkin (Dons lose 7-8 on aggregate)	15 goals all-told in this epic. Away goals counted after extra-time, so the Dons never quite got back on terms, and needed two more by the close. Seven were booked, including Jones for the fifth time this season. 17 goals conceded in 5 games, and Kinnear is determined to buy.											

POINTS EARNED IN THE ENGLISH TOP DIVISION – 1986-87 to 1994-95

	The number of seasons the Dons finished higher – lower.	*86-87*	*87-88*	*88-89*	*89-90*	*90-91*	*91-92*	*92-93*	*93-94*	*94-95*	*Total*
Liverpool	*1-8*	77	90	76	79	76	64	59	60	74	655
Manchester Utd	*2-7*	56	81	51	48	59	78	84	92	88	637
Arsenal	*1-8*	70	66	76	62	83	72	56	71	51	607
Everton	*4-5*	86	70	54	59	51	53	53	44	50	520
WIMBLEDON		**66**	**57**	**51**	**55**	**56**	**53**	**54**	**65**	**56**	**513**
Tottenham	*4-5*	71	47	57	63	49	52	59	45	62	505
QP Rangers	*4-5*	50	67	53	50	46	54	63	60	60	503
Nottingham For	*4-4*	65	73	64	54	54	59	40		77	486
Norwich	*6-3*	68	45	62	53	45	45	72	53	43	486
Coventry	*8-1*	63	53	55	49	44	44	52	56	50	466
Southampton	*8-1*	52	50	45	55	45	52	50	43	54	446
Sheffield Wed	*6-2*	52	53	42	43		75	59	64	51	439
Aston Villa	*5-3*	36		40	70	41	60	74	57	48	426
Chelsea	*6-2*	52	42		60	49	53	56	51	54	417
Manchester City	*4-3*	39			48	62	70	57	45	49	370
Leeds	*1-4*					64	82	51	70	73	340
Newcastle	*3-2*	47	56	31					77	72	283
Luton	*6-0*	66	53	41	43	37	42				282
West Ham	*6-0*	52	42	38			38		52	50	272
Crystal Palace	*3-2*				48	69	57	49		45	268
Blackburn	*0-3*							71	84	89	244
Sheffield Utd	*3-1*					46	57	52	42		197
Derby	*3-1*		43	58	46	24					171
Charlton	*4-0*	44	42	42	30						158
Oldham	*3-0*						51	49	40		140
Ipswich	*3-0*							52	43	27	122

VOTES FOR THE MOST POPULAR WIMBLEDON PLAYER SINCE 1964

Subscriber	Vote
David John Adams	Alan Cork
Colin Adkins	All of them
Peter Agar	Alan Cork
Fazal Ahmad	Alan Cork
Rob Aitkenhead	Lawrie Sanchez
M Allen	Vinnie Jones
Daniel Allwright	Alan Cork
Mark Andrews	Vinnie Jones
Nathan Andrews	John Scales
Mr W W Andrews	Glyn Hodges
Patrick Anger	Alan Cork
Ray Armfield	Dickie Guy
Simon Babar	Lawrie Sanchez
P J Bailey	Warren Barton
Peter Bailey	John Fashanu
Gary Baker	John Leslie
Michael Adrian Baker	John Leslie
Ron Balch	Alan Cork
John-David Balchin	Alan Cork
Steve Bale	Alan Cork
Gary Barnes	Steve Galliers
Richard C C Barry	Dave Beasant
Jason Baskaran	Efan Ekoku
Rupert Bayfield	Alan Cork
Dennis J Beckett	Alan Cork
Monica Bedford	Warren Barton
Robin Bedford	Warren Barton
Simon Bedford	Vinnie Jones
Mr J A Beech	Vinnie Jones
Mr Kevin Berry	Wally Downes

Subscriber	Vote
Frank Blackmore	John Scales
Nick Blanchard	Vinnie Jones
John R Bliss	Dave Beasant
Peter Bond	Alan Cork
Alan Bone	Alan Cork
Mark Bonnett	Dennis Wise
W B Bonnor	
Richard D Bottomley	Alan Cork
Mr S P Brewer	Dennis Wise
William Brewster	Dean Holdsworth
Jim Brittain	Carlton Fairweather
James Brittin	Alan Cork
Helen Brown	Neil Sullivan
Nick Budgen	Alan Cork
Ronald Bugg	Roger Connell
Frank Burch	
Steve Burt	Ian Cooke
John Butcher	Dickie Guy
Warren Butler	Alan Cork
Philip Carlon	Alan Cork
Simon Carr	Dickie Guy
Phil Castle	Warren Barton
Rob Ceccarelli	John Scales
Malcolm Challis	Dave Bassett
David John Chivers	Roy Law
Michael Churchman	
R J Clapshoe	Alan Cork
Dennis John Clark	Dean Holdsworth
Greg Clarke	Vinnie Jones
Garry Cole	Robbie Earle

Subscriber	Vote
Malcolm Collignon	John Fashanu
Jack Colvin	Dean Holdsworth
S Comper	Mick Harford
Eamon Connolly	Alan Cork
Steve Connolly	Wally Downes
Andy Connor	Vinnie Jones
Howard G Cooper	Peter Fear
Jonathan Coppin	Dennis Wise
Mr Richard Coyte	
Stephen Crabtree	John Leslie
Steve Crocker	Lawrie Sanchez
Mick Croggon	John Fashanu
John Culf	Lawrie Sanchez
Martin & Michelle Cullip	Alan Cork
Jerzy Dabrowski	Alan Cork
Peter Davey	Dave Beasant
Tony & Paul Davies	Dave Beasant
Alan Dearman	Alan Cork
Suzanne Denné	Vinnie Jones
Rob Dickinson	Dennis Wise
Caroline DiFranco	Alan Cork
Danny Donovan	Alan Cork
James P Doris	Alan Cork
Peter Douglass	Dave Bassett
Paul Dowell	Alan Cork
David Dowse	Dave Beasant
Stephen Dowse	John Fashanu
Mr John Dryland	Vinnie Jones
Nick Dukes	Steve Galliers

Subscriber	Vote
Robert E P Dunford	Nigel Winterburn
Russell A Earl	Glyn Hodges
Mrs Wendy Edwards	Warren Barton
Peter Elliott	Dave Beasant
Steve Elson	Roger Connell
E Elstub	Robbie Earle
Mr D J Everett	Dave Bassett
Neal Exall	Alan Cork
Alan & Aaron Fayers	Hans Segers
Nick Fernyhough	Vinnie Jones
Bob Ferrier	John Leslie
Kevin Field	Alan Cork
Michael Field	Alan Cork
Sandra Finch	Dickie Guy
Mr C W Finlay	Vinnie Jones
Kevin Fitzpatrick	Billy Holmes
Stephen Barry T Fletcher	Alan Cork
Steven Flynn	Warren Barton
Mike Folkes	Alan Cork
Christopher Frame	
Rod Fraser	John Fashanu
Mr G E Gibbs	Eddie Reynolds
T T Gilbert	Glyn Hodges
Miss Tina Gilbert	Dennis Wise
Adrian Gill	Lawrie Sanchez
Alastair Glass	John Fashanu
Barry Glover	Dave Beasant
Scott Goddard	
Adrian Goodchild	Dave Beasant

Subscriber	Player
Alan Goodridge	Eddie Bailham
Dean Gould	Alan Cork
Colin Graham	Eddie Reynolds
Mr Gary Stewart Grant	Alan Cork
Harry James Greed	Roy Law
John Greig	Alan Cork
Mr Liam Grigg	Dennis Wise
Paul Grigson	Vinnie Jones
Alex Gunn	Alan Cork
Mark Halls	Vinnie Jones
Vanessa Harby	Alan Cork
Andy Harrison	Alan Cork
Kevin Gerard Harrison	John Leslie
Scott Harrison	Dean Holdsworth
Mrs Jane Hart	
Phil Hawkins	Dave Beasant
Chris Hayes	Eddie Reynolds
Eamonn Hayes	Alan Cork
Paul R Hayes	Alan Cork
Mr A R Helliar	Alan Cork
Leonard Hersey	Alan Cork
Adam Hillman	Vinnie Jones
John Hillsley	Vinnie Jones
Kevin Hillyer	Dickie Guy
Mark Hillyer	Roger Connell
Tim Hillyer	Ian Cooke
Gary Hodge	Alan Cork
Graeme Hodge	Alan Cork
Mr J Holland	Alan Cork
Nigel Holley	Dennis Wise
Paul Holloway	Dennis Wise
Ivor G Holmes	Dennis Wise
Kyle Hough	Efan Ekoku
John C Howard	Stewart Evans
Marc Howson	John Fashanu
Mark Hubble	Alan Cork
Nicki Hubble	Robbie Earle
John Hudnott	Nigel Winterburn
Frank Hung	Lawrie Sanchez
Kevin D Hunt	Alan Cork
Stuart C Hunter	Dennis Wise
Chris Hutchinson	Dave Beasant
Peter T Jackson	
Mark Jacob	Alan Cork
Dave James	Alan Cork
Gavin Jamieson	Alan Cork
Mike Jay	Roy Law
Paul Jeater	Roy Law
Paul Jerome	Vinnie Jones
Alex Jones	Dean Holdsworth
Mr David Jones	John Fashanu
Gary Jordan	Dennis Wise
Mr J T Kavanagh	John Scales
John Keat	Steve Galliers
David Kennett	Warren Barton
Stewart Kevill-Davies	Dave Donaldson
Clayton Patrict	Mick Mahon
Kilcoyne	
Terry Kilroy	Nigel Winterburn
Mr R Kimber	Vinnie Jones
Bob King	Gerry O'Rourke
Philip King	Alan Cork
Stefan King	John Scales
Sue & Terry Knight	Vinnie Jones
James Lamont	Alan Cork
Paul Lapraik	Dave Donaldson
Adrian Larkins	John Gayle
Malcolm Lawther	Nigel Winterburn
Simon Lawther	Glyn Hodges
Steve Leadon	Dickie Guy
Paul Le-Faye	Vinnie Jones
Jim Leake	John Leslie
Edward Leek	Dave Beasant
Pasi Lehtonen	Vinnie Jones
Ian Lemon	Alan Cork
Mark Lewis	Alan Cork
Kevin D Leyden	Roy Law
Ian Lightwood	Vinnie Jones
John Lloyd	Vinnie Jones
Michael Lloyd	John Scales
Mike Lloyd	Warren Barton
Mark Lobel	Vinnie Jones
Michael Lonergan	Dave Beasant
James Longhurst	Warren Barton
Mr I Lowe	Alan Cork
Laurence Lowne	John Leslie
Mr Jack Lyons	John Scales
Bruce McCarthy	John Fashanu
Alan McIlmoyle	Vinnie Jones
David McKnight	Vinnie Jones
Roy Maggs	John O'Mara
Mr Daniele Mandelli	Dennis Wise
Victor Barry Marley	Dennis Wise
Derek Mason	John Scales
David May	Brian Gayle
Jimmie Meldrum	
Paul Merritt	Alan Cork
Mr R P Milkins	Alan Cork
B Moir	Warren Barton
P Moir	Ian Cooke
John Moody	Mick Mahon
Mr Glen Moore	Alan Cork
Mr Peter Morey	Alan Cork
David Mortimer	Dave Beasant
Tracy Morton	Warren Barton
J Motson	
David Mullaney	Stewart Evans
John Mulligan	Steve Galliers
P W Mumford	Dennis Wise
Paul Munday	John Fashanu
Mr D Munsey	John Fashanu
Danny Nicholas	Vinnie Jones
Mark Noble	Alan Cork
Steve Nuttall	Alan Cork
John Nye	Alan Cork
Matt O'Brien	Alan Cork
Susan Oliver	Alan Cork
Alan Painter	Ian Cooke
Nick Palmowski	Vinnie Jones

VOTES FOR THE MOST POPULAR WIMBLEDON PLAYER SINCE 1964

Subscriber	Vote
Stephen Pannell	Warren Barton
Fess Parker	Dickie Guy
Greg Parker	Alan Cork
Alan Partleton	Roy Law
Richard Paul	Ian Cooke
Kenneth James Peacock	Roy Law
Mrs A Penfold	
Mark Penfold	Dickie Guy
Matthew D T Penfold	Lawrie Sanchez
Nick Pittman	Alan Cork
Don Porteous	Lawrie Sanchez
Alistair Powell	Alan Cork
Keith Prothero	Vinnie Jones
Mick Pugh	Dickie Guy
Alastair Rabagliati	Dennis Wise
Robin Rance	Dennis Wise
Imogen Rao	Steve Galliers
T W E Rees	Warren Barton
Charlotte Reynolds	Hans Segers
Paul Ricôt	Alan Cork
Mark Ridout	Lawrie Sanchez
Barry Edward Ringsell	Alan Cork
Laurence Ringsell	Dennis Wise
Jeff Roberts	Roger Connell
Keith Roberts	Warren Barton
Michael Ross	Vinnie Jones
Kevin P Rowe	Dean Holdsworth
Stuart Rush	Vinnie Jones
Gavin Saddington	Alan Cork
Mr Y Saito	Warren Barton
Bill, Dick, Alan, David, Andrew, Saker	Dave Beasant
Mark Satchell	Vinnie Jones
Richard Sawyer	Roger Connell
John K Sayers	John Fashanu
Steve Scarr	Robbie Earle
Jonathan Sewell	Vinnie Jones
Robert Seymour	Roger Connell
Barrie Shapland	Dickie Guy
Keith Slatter	John Fashanu
Kevin Smith	Lawrie Sanchez
Lawrence Smith	Alan Cork
Peter Edward Smith	Vinnie Jones
Robert Smith	
Robert T Smith	Alan Cork
David Sore	Vinnie Jones
Paul Sparks	Steve Galliers
Mark K Swaden	Robbie Earle
David James Tate	Vinnie Jones
Ian Taylor	Alan Cork
Mr M S Taylor	John Scales
Chris Teasdale	John Scales
Sam Tebboth	Lawrie Sanchez
Peter Tillbrook	Lawrie Sanchez
Graham Timms	Dave Beasant
Ed Tisdale	Robbie Earle
Satesh Tolat	Steve Galliers
Suresh Tolat	Alan Cork
Paul Townley	Warren Barton
Ron Trayhorn	Vinnie Jones
Michael Trollope	Alan Cork
Mark Trowbridge	Dennis Wise
D W Trunks	Roger Connell
Grant Tryon	Lawrie Sanchez
Darren Alex Turner	Warren Barton
Andy Vanstan	Steve Galliers
John Vesey	Alan Cork
Geoffrey K Wakefield	Roy Law
Lee Walker	Vinnie Jones
Stuart Wallace	Alan Cork
Richard Ward	Dean Holdsworth
Mervyn Richard Waring	Alan Cork
John Waters	Vinnie Jones
Lawrence S Watkins	John Fashanu
Andy Watson	Alan Cork
Gray Weedon	Lawrie Sanchez
Tony Wellby	Dennis Wise
Tim Westbey	John Scales
Shaun Whiteside	Vinnie Jones
Mr N J Whitley	Dickie Guy
Jon Wigg	Nigel Winterburn
Juliette Wilkes	Vinnie Jones
John Wilkins	Steve Galliers
Paul J Wilkins	Dickie Guy
Lee Willett	
Brian Williams	Dennis Wise
George & Hazel Williams	Alan Cork
R L Williams	John Leslie
Mark Willson	Steve Galliers
Denise Mary Kathleen Wingrove	Dean Holdsworth
M C Woods	Steve Galliers
Michael John Woods	Billy Edwards
Mark Worledge	Dave Bassett
Gordon Wright	Warren Barton
John Young	Eddie Bailham
Peter & Harry Young	Selwyn Rice
Stuart Young	Hans Segers

MOST POPULAR DONS PLAYERS
(38 different players received votes)

1st	Alan Cork
2nd	Vinnie Jones
3rd	Dennis Wise
4th	Warren Barton
5th	Dave Beasant
6th	Lawrie Sanchez
7th	John Fashanu
8th	Steve Galliers
9th	Dickie Guy
10th	John Scales
11th	Dean Holdsworth
12th	John Leslie
13th	Roy Law
14th	Roger Connell
15th	Robbie Earle